Isil Dillig · Serdar Tasiran (Eds.)

Computer Aided Verification

31st International Conference, CAV 2019
New York City, NY, USA, July 15–18, 2019
Proceedings, Part II

Editors
Isil Dillig
University of Texas
Austin, TX, USA

Serdar Tasiran
Amazon Web Services
New York, NY, USA

https://doi.org/10.1007/978-3-030-25543-5

LNCS Sublibrary: SL1 – Theoretical Computer Science and General Issues

Preface

It was our privilege to serve as the program chairs for CAV 2019, the 31st International Conference on Computer-Aided Verification. CAV 2019 was held in New York, USA, during July 15–18, 2019. The tutorial day was on July 14, 2019, and the pre-conference workshops were held during July 13–14, 2019. All events took place in The New School in New York City.

CAV is an annual conference dedicated to the advancement of the theory and practice of computer-aided formal analysis methods for hardware and software systems. The primary focus of CAV is to extend the frontiers of verification techniques by expanding to new domains such as security, quantum computing, and machine learning. This put CAV at the cutting edge of formal methods research, and this year's program is a reflection of this commitment.

CAV 2019 received a very high number of submissions (258). We accepted 13 tool papers, two case studies, and 52 regular papers, which amounts to an acceptance rate of roughly 26%. The accepted papers cover a wide spectrum of topics, from theoretical results to applications of formal methods. These papers apply or extend formal methods to a wide range of domains such as concurrency, learning, and industrially deployed systems. The program featured invited talks by Dawn Song (UC Berkeley), Swarat Chaudhuri (Rice University), and Ken McMillan (Microsoft Research) as well as invited tutorials by Emina Torlak (University of Washington) and Ranjit Jhala (UC San Diego). Furthermore, we continued the tradition of Logic Lounge, a series of discussions on computer science topics targeting a general audience.

In addition to the main conference, CAV 2019 hosted the following workshops: The Best of Model Checking (BeMC) in honor of Orna Grumberg, Design and Analysis of Robust Systems (DARS), Verification Mentoring Workshop (VMW), Numerical Software Verification (NSV), Verified Software: Theories, Tools, and Experiments (VSTTE), Democratizing Software Verification, Formal Methods for ML-Enabled Autonomous Systems (FoMLAS), and Synthesis (SYNT).

Organizing a top conference like CAV requires a great deal of effort from the community. The Program Committee for CAV 2019 consisted of 79 members, a committee of this size ensures that each member has to review a reasonable number of papers in the allotted time. In all, the committee members wrote over 770 reviews while investing significant effort to maintain and ensure the high quality of the conference program. We are grateful to the CAV 2019 Program Committee for their outstanding efforts in evaluating the submissions and making sure that each paper got a fair chance.

Like last year's CAV, we made artifact evaluation mandatory for tool submissions and optional but encouraged for the rest of the accepted papers. The Artifact Evaluation Committee consisted of 27 reviewers who put in significant effort to evaluate each artifact. The goal of this process was to provide constructive feedback to tool developers and help make the research published in CAV more reproducible. The Artifact Evaluation Committee was generally quite impressed by the quality of the artifacts, and, in fact, all accepted tools passed the artifact evaluation. Among regular papers, 65% of the authors submitted an artifact, and 76% of these artifacts passed the evaluation. We are also very grateful to the Artifact Evaluation Committee for their hard work and dedication in evaluating the submitted artifacts.

CAV 2019 would not have been possible without the tremendous help we received from several individuals, and we would like to thank everyone who helped make CAV 2019 a success. First, we would like to thank Yu Feng and Ruben Martins for chairing the Artifact Evaluation Committee and Zvonimir Rakamaric for maintaining the CAV website and social media presence. We also thank Oksana Tkachuk for chairing the workshop organization process, Peter O'Hearn for managing sponsorship, and Thomas Wies for arranging student fellowships. We also thank Loris D'Antoni, Rayna Dimitrova, Cezara Dragoi, and Anthony W. Lin for organizing the Verification Mentoring Workshop and working closely with us. Last but not least, we would like to thank Kostas Ferles, Navid Yaghmazadeh, and members of the CAV Steering Committee (Ken McMillan, Aarti Gupta, Orna Grumberg, and Daniel Kroening) for helping us with several important aspects of organizing CAV 2019.

We hope that you will find the proceedings of CAV 2019 scientifically interesting and thought-provoking!

June 2019

Isil Dillig
Serdar Tasiran

Organization

Program Chairs

Isil Dillig	The University of Texas at Austin, USA
Serdar Tasiran	Amazon, USA

Workshop Chair

Oksana Tkachuk	Amazon, USA

Publicity Chair

Zvonimir Rakamaric	University of Utah, USA

Sponsorship Chair

Peter O'Hearn	Facebook, USA

Fellowship Chair

Thomas Wies	NYU, USA

CAV Award Committee

Natarajan Shankar	SRI International, USA
Pierre Wolper	Liege University, Belgium
Somesh Jha	University of Wisconsin, USA
Parosh Abdulla	Uppsala University, Sweden

Program Committee

Aws Albarghouthi	University of Wisconsin-Madison, USA
Jade Alglave	University College London, UK
Rajeev Alur	University of Pennsylvania, USA
Christel Baier	TU Dresden, Germany
Gilles Barthe	Max Planck Institute for Security and Privacy, Germany; IMDEA Software Institute, Spain
Osbert Bastani	University of Pennsylvania, USA
Josh Berdine	Facebook, USA
Per Bjesse	Synopsys Inc., USA
Nikolaj Bjorner	Microsoft, USA
Roderick Bloem	Graz University of Technology, Austria

Marc Brockschmidt	Microsoft, UK
Pavol Cerny	University of Colorado Boulder, USA
Swarat Chaudhuri	Rice University, USA
Wei-Ngan Chin	National University of Singapore
Adam Chlipala	Massachusetts Institute of Technology, USA
Hana Chockler	King's College London, UK
Eva Darulova	Max Planck Institute for Software Systems, Germany
Cristina David	University of Cambridge, UK
Dana Drachsler Cohen	ETH Zurich, Switzerland
Cezara Dragoi	Inria Paris, ENS, France
Constantin Enea	IRIF, University of Paris Diderot, France
Azadeh Farzan	University of Toronto, Canada
Grigory Fedyukovich	Princeton University, USA
Yu Feng	University of California, Santa Barbara, USA
Dana Fisman	Ben-Gurion University, Israel
Milos Gligoric	The University of Texas at Austin, USA
Patrice Godefroid	Microsoft, USA
Laure Gonnord	University of Lyon/Laboratoire d'Informatique du Parallélisme, France
Aarti Gupta	Princeton University, USA
Arie Gurfinkel	University of Waterloo, Canada
Klaus Havelund	Jet Propulsion Laboratory, USA
Chris Hawblitzel	Microsoft, USA
Alan J. Hu	The University of British Columbia, Canada
Shachar Itzhaky	Technion, Israel
Franjo Ivancic	Google, USA
Ranjit Jhala	University of California San Diego, USA
Rajeev Joshi	Automated Reasoning Group, Amazon Web Services, USA
Dejan Jovanović	SRI International, USA
Laura Kovacs	Vienna University of Technology, Austria
Burcu Kulahcioglu Ozkan	MPI-SWS, Germany
Marta Kwiatkowska	University of Oxford, UK
Shuvendu Lahiri	Microsoft, USA
Akash Lal	Microsoft, India
Stephen Magill	Galois, Inc., USA
Joao Marques-Silva	Universidade de Lisboa, Portugal
Ruben Martins	Carnegie Mellon University, USA
Ken McMillan	Microsoft, USA
Vijay Murali	Facebook, USA
Peter Müller	ETH Zurich, Switzerland
Mayur Naik	Intel, USA
Hakjoo Oh	Korea University, South Korea
Oded Padon	Stanford University, USA
Corina Pasareanu	CMU/NASA Ames Research Center, USA
Ruzica Piskac	Yale University, USA

Nir Piterman	University of Gothenburg, Sweden
Pavithra Prabhakar	Kansas State University, USA
Sylvie Putot	LIX, Ecole Polytechnique, France
Grigore Rosu	University of Illinois at Urbana-Champaign, USA
Dorsa Sadigh	Stanford University, USA
Roopsha Samanta	Purdue University, USA
Sriram Sankaranarayanan	University of Colorado, Boulder, USA
Koushik Sen	University of California, Berkeley, USA
Sanjit A. Seshia	University of California, Berkeley, USA
Natarajan Shankar	SRI International, USA
Rahul Sharma	Microsoft, USA
Natasha Sharygina	Università della Svizzera italiana (USI Lugano), Switzerland
Sharon Shoham	Tel Aviv University, Israel
Alexandra Silva	University College London, UK
Rishabh Singh	Google, USA
Anna Slobodova	Centaur Technology, USA
Marcelo Sousa	University of Oxford, UK
Cesare Tinelli	The University of Iowa, USA
Ufuk Topcu	University of Texas at Austin, USA
Caterina Urban	Inria, France
Margus Veanes	Microsoft, USA
Yakir Vizel	The Technion, Israel
Chao Wang	USC, USA
Georg Weissenbacher	Vienna University of Technology, Austria
Eran Yahav	Technion, Israel
Hongseok Yang	KAIST, South Korea

Artifact Evaluation Committee

Uri Alon	Technion, Israel
Yaniv David	Technion, Israel
Yufei Ding	University of California, Santa Barbara, USA
Yu Feng (Co-chair)	University of California, Santa Barbara, USA
Radu Grigore	University of Kent, UK
Saurabh Joshi	IIIT Hyderabad, India
William Hallahan	Yale University, USA
Travis Hance	Carnegie Mellon University, USA
Marijn Heule	The University of Texas at Austin, USA
Antti Hyvärinen	University of Lugano, Switzerland
Alexey Ignatiev	Universidade de Lisboa, Portugal
Tianhan Lu	University of Colorado Boulder, USA
Ruben Martins (Co-chair)	Carnegie Mellon University, USA
Aina Niemetz	Stanford University, USA
Filip Nikšić	University of Pennsylvania, USA
Lauren Pick	Princeton University, USA

Sorawee Porncharoenwase	University of Washington, USA
Mathias Preiner	Stanford University, USA
Talia Ringer	University of Washington, USA
John Sarracino	University of California San Diego, USA
Xujie Si	University of Pennsylvania, USA
Calvin Smith	University of Wisconsin-Madison, USA
Caleb Stanford	University of Pennsylvania, USA
Miguel Terra-Neves	INESC-ID/IST, Universidade de Lisboa, Portugal
Jacob Van Geffen	University of Washington, USA
Xinyu Wang	The University of Texas at Austin, USA
Wei Yang	The University of Texas at Dallas, USA

Mentoring Workshop Organizing Committee

Loris D'Antoni (Chair)	University of Wisconsin, USA
Anthony Lin	Oxford University, UK
Cezara Dragoi	Inria, France
Rayna Dimitrova	University of Leicester, UK

Steering Committee

Ken McMillan	Microsoft, USA
Aarti Gupta	Princeton, USA
Orna Grunberg	Technion, Israel
Daniel Kroening	University of Oxford, UK

Additional Reviewers

Sepideh Asadi
Lucas Asadi
Haniel Barbosa
Ezio Bartocci
Sam Bartocci
Suda Bharadwaj
Erdem Biyik
Martin Biyik
Timothy Bourke
Julien Braine
Steven Braine
Benjamin Caulfield
Eti Chaudhary
Xiaohong Chaudhary
Yinfang Chen
Andreea Costea
Murat Costea
Emanuele D'Osualdo
Nicolas Dilley
Marko Dilley
Bruno Dutertre
Marco Eilers
Cindy Eilers
Yotam Feldman
Jerome Feret
Daniel Feret
Mahsa Ghasemi
Shromona Ghosh
Anthony Ghosh
Bernhard Gleiss
Shilpi Goel
William Goel
Mirazul Haque
Ludovic Henrio

Andreas Henrio
Antti Hyvärinen
Duligur Ibeling
Rinat Ibeling
Nouraldin Jaber
Swen Jacobs
Maximilian Jacobs
Susmit Jha
Anja Karl
Jens Karl
Sean Kauffman
Ayrat Khalimov
Bettina Khalimov
Hillel Kugler
Daniel Larraz
Christopher Larraz
Wonyeol Lee
Matt Lewis
Wenchao Lewis
Kaushik Mallik
Matteo Marescotti
David Marescotti
Dmitry Mordvinov
Matthieu Moy
Thanh Toan Moy
Victor Nicolet
Andres Noetzli
Abraham Noetzli
Saswat Padhi
Karl Palmskog
Rong Palmskog
Daejun Park
Brandon Paulsen
Lucas Paulsen
Adi Yoga Prabawa
Dhananjay Raju
Andrew Raju
Heinz Riener
Sriram Sankaranarayanan
Mark Sankaranarayanan
Yagiz Savas
Traian Florin Serbanuta
Fu Serbanuta
Yahui Song
Pramod Subramanyan
Rob Subramanyan
Sol Swords
Martin Tappler
Ta Quang Tappler
Anthony Vandikas
Marcell Vazquex-Chanlatte
Yuke Vazquex-Chanlatte
Min Wen
Josef Widder
Bo Widder
Haoze Wu
Zhe Xu
May Xu
Yi Zhang
Zhizhou Zhang

Contents – Part II

Verification

Distributed Systems and Networks

Verification and Invariants

Contents – Part I

Synthesis

Model Checking

Cyber-Physical Systems and Machine Learning

Probabilistic Systems, Runtime Techniques

Dynamical, Hybrid, and Reactive Systems

Logics, Decision Procedures, and Solvers

Satisfiability Checking for Mission-Time LTL

Jianwen Li[1(✉)], Moshe Y. Vardi[2], and Kristin Y. Rozier[1(✉)]

[1] Iowa State University, Ames, IA, USA
lijwen2748@gmail.com, kyrozier@iastate.edu
[2] Rice University, Houston, TX, USA

Abstract. Mission-time LTL (MLTL) is a bounded variant of MTL over naturals designed to generically specify requirements for mission-based system operation common to aircraft, spacecraft, vehicles, and robots. Despite the utility of MLTL as a specification logic, major gaps remain in analyzing MLTL, e.g., for specification debugging or model checking, centering on the absence of any complete MLTL satisfiability checker. We prove that the MLTL satisfiability checking problem is NEXPTIME-complete and that satisfiability checking MLTL_0, the variant of MLTL where all intervals start at 0, is PSPACE-complete. We introduce translations for MLTL-to-LTL, MLTL-to-LTL_f, MLTL-to-SMV, and MLTL-to-SMT, creating four options for MLTL satisfiability checking. Our extensive experimental evaluation shows that the MLTL-to-SMT transition with the Z3 SMT solver offers the most scalable performance.

1 Introduction

Mission-time LTL (MLTL) [34] has the syntax of Linear Temporal Logic with the option of integer bounds on the temporal operators. It was created as a generalization of the variations [3, 14, 25] on finitely-bounded linear temporal logic, ideal for specification of missions carried out by aircraft, spacecraft, rovers, and other vehicular or robotic systems. MLTL provides the readability of LTL [32], while assuming, when a different duration is not specified, that all requirements must be upheld during the (a priori known) length of a given mission, such as during the half-hour battery life of an Unmanned Aerial System (UAS). Using integer bounds instead of real-number or real-time bounds leads to more generic specifications that are adaptable to model checking at different levels of abstraction, or runtime monitoring on different platforms (e.g., in software vs in hardware). Integer bounds should be read as generic time units, referring to the basic temporal resolution of the system, which can generically be resolved to units such as clock ticks or seconds depending on the mission. Integer bounds also allow generic specification with respect to different granularities of time, e.g., to allow easy updates to model-checking models, and re-usable specifications for the same requirements on different embedded systems that may have different resource limits for storing runtime monitors. MLTL has been used in many industrial case studies [18, 28, 34, 37, 42–44], and was the official logic of the 2018 Runtime Verification Benchmark Competition [1]. Many specifications from other case studies, in logics such as MTL [3] and STL [25], can be represented in MLTL. We intuitively relate MLTL to LTL and MTL-over-naturals as follows: (1) MLTL formulas are LTL formulas with bounded intervals over temporal operators, and interpreted over

I. Dillig and S. Tasiran (Eds.): CAV 2019, LNCS 11562, pp. 3–22, 2019.
https://doi.org/10.1007/978-3-030-25543-5_1

finite traces. (2) MLTL formulas are MTL-over-naturals formulas without any unbounded intervals, and interpreted over finite traces.

Despite the practical utility of MLTL, no model checker currently accepts this logic as a specification language. The model checker nuXmv encodes a related logic for use in symbolic model checking, where the $\Box$ and $\Diamond$ operators of an `LTLSPEC` can have integer bounds [21], though bounds cannot be placed on the $\mathcal{U}$ or $\mathcal{V}$ (the Release operator of nuXmv) operators.

We also critically need an MLTL satisfiability checker to enable specification debugging. Specification is a major bottleneck to the formal verification of mission-based, especially autonomous, systems [35], with a key part of the problem being the availability of good tools for *specification debugging*. Satisfiability checking is an integral tool for specification debugging: [38,39] argued that for every requirement φ we need to check φ and $\neg\varphi$ for satisfiability; we also need to check the conjunction of all requirements to ensure that they can all be true of the same system at the same time. Specification debugging is essential to model checking [39–41] because a positive answer may not mean there is no bug and a negative answer may not mean there is a bug if the specification is valid/unsatisfiable, respectively. Specification debugging is critical for synthesis and runtime verification (RV) since in these cases there is no model; synthesis and RV are both entirely dependent on the specification. For synthesis, satisfiability checking is the best-available specification-debugging technique, since other techniques, such as vacuity checking (cf. [6,10]) reference a model in addition to the specification. While there are artifacts one can use in RV, specification debugging is still limited outside of satisfiability checking yet central to correct analysis. A false positive due to RV of an incorrect specification can have disastrous consequences, such as triggering an abort of an (otherwise successful) mission to Mars. Arguably, the biggest challenge to creating an RV algorithm or tool is the dearth of benchmarks for checking correctness or comparatively analyzing these [36], where a benchmark consists of some runtime trace, a temporal logic formula reasoning about that trace, and some verdict designating whether the trace at a given time satisfies the requirement formula. A MLTL satisfiability solver is useful for RV benchmark generation [22].

Despite the critical need for an MLTL satisfiability solver, no such tool currently exists. To the best of our knowledge, there is only one available solver (*zot* [8]) for checking the satisfiability of MTL-over-naturals formulas, interpreted over infinite traces. Since MLTL formulas are interpreted over finite traces and there is no trivial reduction from one to another, *zot* cannot be directly applied to MLTL satisfiability checking.

Our approach is inspired by satisfiability-checking algorithms from other logics. For LTL satisfiability solving, we observe that there are multiple efficient translations from LTL satisfiability to model checking, using nuXmv [40]; we therefore consider here translations to nuXmv model checking, both indirectly (as a translation to LTL), and directly using the new KLIVE [13] back-end and the BMC back-end, taking advantage of the bounded nature of MLTL. The bounded nature of MLTL enables us to also consider a direct encoding at the word-level, suitable as input to an SMT solver. Our contribution is both theoretic and experimental. We first consider the complexity of such translations. We prove that the MLTL satisfiability checking problem is NEXPTIME-complete and that satisfiability checking MLTL_0, the variant of MLTL where all intervals start at 0, is PSPACE-complete. Secondly, we introduce translation algorithms for MLTL-to-LTL_f (LTL over finite traces [14]), MLTL-to-LTL, MLTL-to-SMV, and

MLTL-to-SMT, thus creating four options for MLTL satisfiability checking. Our results show that the MLTL-to-SMT transition with the Z3 SMT solver offers the most scalable performance, though the MLTL-to-SMV translation with an SMV model checker can offer the best performance when the intervals in the MLTL formulas are restricted to small ranges less than 100.

2 Preliminaries

A (closed) interval over naturals $I = [a, b]$ ($0 \leq a \leq b$ are natural numbers) is a set of naturals $\{i \mid a \leq i \leq b\}$. I is called *bounded* iff $b < +\infty$; otherwise I is *unbounded*. MLTL is defined using bounded intervals. Unlike Metric Temporal Logic (MTL) [4], it is not necessary to introduce open or half-open intervals over the natural domain, as every open or half-open bounded interval is reducible to an equivalent closed bounded interval, e.g., (1,2) = $\emptyset$, (1,3) = [2,2], (1,3] = [2,3], etc. Let $\mathcal{AP}$ be a set of atomic propositions, then the syntax of a formula in MLTL is

$$\varphi ::= \mathsf{true} \mid \mathsf{false} \mid p \mid \neg\varphi \mid \varphi \wedge \psi \mid \varphi \vee \psi \mid \Box\varphi \mid \Diamond\varphi \mid \varphi\, \mathcal{U}_I\, \psi \mid \varphi \mathcal{R}_I \psi$$

where I is a bounded interval, $p \in \mathcal{AP}$ is an *atom*, and φ and ψ are subformulas.

Given two MLTL formulas φ, ψ, we denote $\varphi = \psi$ iff they are *syntactically equivalent*, and $\varphi \equiv \psi$ iff they are *semantically equivalent*, i.e., $\pi \models \varphi$ iff $\pi \models \psi$ for a finite trace π. In MLTL semantics, we define $\mathsf{false} \equiv \neg\mathsf{true}$, $\varphi \vee \psi \equiv \neg(\neg\varphi \wedge \neg\psi)$, $\neg(\varphi\, \mathcal{U}_I\, \psi) \equiv (\neg\varphi \mathcal{R}_I \neg\psi)$ and $\neg\Diamond_I\varphi \equiv \Box_I\neg\varphi$. MLTL keeps the standard operator equivalences from LTL, including $(\Diamond_I\varphi) \equiv (true\, \mathcal{U}_I \varphi)$, $(\Box_I\varphi) \equiv (false\, \mathcal{R}_I\, \varphi)$, and $(\varphi\, \mathcal{R}_I\, \psi) \equiv (\neg(\neg\varphi\, \mathcal{U}_I\, \neg\psi))$. Notably, MLTL discards the neXt ($\mathcal{X}$) operator, which is essential in LTL [32], since $\mathcal{X}\varphi$ is semantically equivalent to $\Box_{[1,1]}\varphi$.

The semantics of MLTL formulas is interpreted over finite traces bounded by base-10 (decimal) intervals. Let π be a finite trace in which every position $\pi[i]$ ($i \geq 0$) is over $2^{\mathcal{AP}}$, and $|\pi|$ denotes the length of π ($|\pi| < +\infty$ when π is a finite trace). We use π_i ($|\pi| > i \geq 0$) to represent the suffix of π starting from position i (including i). Let $a, b \in \mathbb{I}$, $a \leq b$; we define that π models (satisfies) an MLTL formula φ, denoted as $\pi \models \varphi$, as follows:

- $\pi \models p$ iff $p \in \pi[0]$;
- $\pi \models \neg\varphi$ iff $\pi \not\models \varphi$;
- $\pi \models \varphi \wedge \psi$ iff $\pi \models \varphi$ and $\pi \models \psi$;
- $\pi \models \varphi\, \mathcal{U}_{[a,b]}\, \psi$ iff $|\pi| > a$ and, there exists $i \in [a, b]$, $i < |\pi|$ such that $\pi_i \models \psi$ and for every $j \in [a, b], j < i$ it holds that $\pi_j \models \varphi$;

Compared to the traditional MTL-over-naturals[1] [16], the Until formula in MLTL is interpreted in a slightly different way. In MTL-over-naturals, the satisfaction of $\varphi\, \mathcal{U}_I\, \psi$ requires φ to hold from position 0 to the position where ψ holds (in I), while in MLTL φ is only required to hold within the interval I, before the time ψ holds. From the perspective of writing specifications, cf. [34,37], this adjustment is more user-friendly.

[1] In this paper, MTL-over-naturals is interpreted over finite traces.

It is not hard to see that MLTL is as expressive as the standard MTL-over-naturals: the formula $\varphi\, \mathcal{U}_{[a,b]}\, \psi$ in MTL-over-naturals can be represented as $(\Box_{[0,a-1]}\varphi) \wedge (\varphi\, \mathcal{U}_{[a,b]}\, \psi)$ in MLTL; $\varphi\, \mathcal{U}_{[a,b]}\, \psi$ in MLTL can be represented as $\Diamond_{[a,a]}(\varphi\, \mathcal{U}_{[0,b-a]}\, \psi)$ in MTL-over-naturals.

We say an MLTL formula is in *BNF* if the formula contains only $\neg$, $\wedge$ and $\mathcal{U}_I$ operators. It is trivial to see that every MLTL formula can be converted to its (semantically) equivalent BNF with a linear cost. Consider $\varphi = (\neg a) \vee ((\neg b)\mathcal{R}_I(\neg c))$ as an example. Its BNF form is $\neg(a \wedge (b\, \mathcal{U}_I\, c))$. Without explicit clarification, this paper assumes that every MLTL formula is in BNF.

The closure of an MLTL formula φ, denoted as $cl(\varphi)$, is a set of formulas such that: (1) $\varphi \in cl(\varphi)$; (2) $\varphi \in cl(\varphi)$ if $\neg\varphi \in cl(\varphi)$; (3) $\varphi, \psi \in cl(\varphi)$ if $\varphi\ op\ \psi \in cl(\varphi)$, where *op* can be $\wedge$ or $\mathcal{U}_I$. Let $|cl(\varphi)|$ be the size of $cl(\varphi)$. Since the definition of $cl(\varphi)$ ignores the intervals in φ, $|cl(\varphi)|$ is linear in the number of operators in φ. We also define the closure(*) of an MLTL formula φ, denoted $cl^*(\varphi)$, as the set of formulas such that: (1) $cl(\varphi) \subseteq cl^*(\varphi)$; (2) if $\varphi\, \mathcal{U}_{[a,b]}\, \psi \in cl^*(\varphi)$ for $0 < a \leq b$, then $\varphi\, \mathcal{U}_{[a-1,b-1]}\, \psi$ is in $cl^*(\varphi)$; (3) if $\varphi\, \mathcal{U}_{[0,b]}\, \psi \in cl^*(\varphi)$ for $0 < b$, then $\varphi\, \mathcal{U}_{[0,b-1]}\, \psi$ is in $cl^*(\varphi)$. Let $|cl^*(\varphi)|$ be the size of $cl^*(\varphi)$ and K be the maximal natural number in the intervals of φ. It is not hard to see that $|cl^*(\varphi)|$ is at most $K \cdot |cl(\varphi)|$.

We also consider a fragment of MLTL, namely MLTL_0, which is more frequently used in practice, cf. [18,34]. Informally speaking, MLTL_0 formulas are MLTL formulas in which all intervals start from 0. For example, $\Diamond_{[0,4]}a \wedge (a\, \mathcal{U}_{[0,1]}\, b)$ is a MLTL_0 formula, while $\Diamond_{[2,4]}a$ is not.

Given an MLTL formula φ, the *satisfiability problem* asks whether there is a finite trace π such that $\pi \models \varphi$ holds. To solve this problem, we can reduce it to the satisfiability problem of the related logics LTL and LTL_f (LTL over finite traces [14]), and leverage the off-the-shelf satisfiability checking solvers for these well-explored logics. We abbreviate MLTL, LTL, and LTL_f satisfiability checking as MLTL-SAT, LTL-SAT, and LTL_f-SAT respectively.

LTL_f: Linear Temporal Logic over Finite Traces [14]**.** We assume readers are familiar with LTL (over infinite traces). LTL_f is a variant of LTL that has the same syntax, except that for LTL_f, the dual operator of $\mathcal{X}$ is $\mathcal{N}$ (weak Next), which differs $\mathcal{X}$ in the last state of the finite trace. In the last state of a finite trace, $\mathcal{X}\psi$ can never be satisfied, while $\mathcal{N}\psi$ is satisfiable. Given an LTL_f formula φ, there is an LTL formula ψ such that φ is satisfiable iff ψ is satisfiable. In detail, $\psi = \Diamond Tail \wedge t(\varphi)$ where $Tail$ is a new atom identifying the end of the satisfying trace and $t(\varphi)$ is constructed as follows:

- $t(p) = p$ where p is an atom;
- $t(\neg\psi) = \neg t(\psi)$;
- $t(\mathcal{X}\psi) = \neg Tail \wedge \mathcal{X}t(\psi)$;
- $t(\psi_1 \wedge \psi_2) = t(\psi_1) \wedge t(\psi_2)$;
- $t(\psi_1 U \psi_2) = t(\neg Tail \wedge \psi_1) U t(\psi_2)$.

In the above reduction, φ is in BNF. Since the reduction is linear in the size of the original LTL_f formula and LTL-SAT is PSPACE-complete [45], LTL_f-SAT is also a PSPACE-complete problem [14].

3 Complexity of MLTL-SAT

It is known that the complexity of MITL (Metric Interval Temporal Logic) satisfiability is EXPSPACE-complete, and the satisfiability complexity of the fragment of MITL named $\mathsf{MITL}_{0,\infty}$ is PSPACE-complete [2]. MLTL (resp. MLTL_0) can be viewed as a variant of MITL (resp. $\mathsf{MITL}_{0,\infty}$) that is interpreted over the naturals. We show that MLTL satisfiability checking is NEXPTIME-complete, via a reduction from MLTL to LTL_f.

Lemma 1. *Let φ be an MLTL formula, and K be the maximal natural appearing in the intervals of φ (K is set to 1 if there are no intervals in φ). There is an LTL_f formula θ that recognizes the same language as φ. Moreover, the size of θ is in $O(K \cdot |cl(\varphi)|)$.*

Proof (Sketch). For an MLTL formula φ, we define the LTL_f formula $f(\varphi)$ recursively as follows:

- If $\varphi = \mathsf{true}, \mathsf{false}$, or an atom p, $f(\varphi) = \varphi$;
- If $\varphi = \neg\psi$, $f(\varphi) = \neg f(\psi)$;
- If $\varphi = \xi \wedge \psi$, $f(\varphi) = f(\xi) \wedge f(\psi)$;
- If $\varphi = \xi\, \mathcal{U}_{[a,b]}\, \psi$,

$$f(\varphi) = \begin{cases} \mathcal{X}(f(\xi\, \mathcal{U}_{[a-1,b-1]}\, \psi)), & \text{if } 0 < a \leq b; \\ f(\psi) \vee (f(\xi) \wedge \mathcal{X}(f(\xi U_{[a,b-1]}\psi))), & \text{if } a = 0 \text{ and } 0 < b; \\ f(\psi), & \text{if } a = 0 \text{ and } b = 0; \end{cases}$$

$\mathcal{X}$ represents the neXt operator in LTL_f. Let $\theta = f(\varphi)$; we can prove by induction that φ and θ accept the same language. Moreover, the size of θ is at most linear to $K \cdot |cl(\varphi)|$, i.e., in $O(K \cdot |cl(\varphi)|)$, based on the aforementioned construction. □

We use the construction shown in Lemma 1 to explore several useful properties of MLTL. For instance, the LTL_f formula translated from an MLTL formula contains only the $\mathcal{X}$ temporal operator or its dual $\mathcal{N}$, which represents weak Next [19,23], and the number of these operators is strictly smaller than $K \cdot |cl(\varphi)|$. Every $\mathcal{X}$ or $\mathcal{N}$ subformula in the LTL_f formula corresponds to some temporal formula in $cl^*(\varphi)$. Notably, because the natural-number intervals in φ are written in base 10 (decimal) notation, the blow-up in the translation of Lemma 1 is exponential.

The next lower bound is reminiscent of the NEXPTIME-lower bound shown in [31] for a fragment of Metric Interval Temporal Logic (MITL), but is different in the details of the proof as the two logics are quite different.

Theorem 1. *The complexity of MLTL satisfiability checking is NEXPTIME-complete.*

Proof (Sketch). By Lemma 1, there is an LTL_f formula θ that accepts the same traces as MLTL formula φ, and the size of θ is in $O(K \cdot |cl(\varphi)|)$. The only temporal connectives used in θ are $\mathcal{X}$ and $\mathcal{N}$, since the translation to LTL_f reduces all MLTL temporal connectives in φ to nested $\mathcal{X}$'s or $\mathcal{N}$'s (produced by simplifying $\neg\mathcal{X}$). Thus, if θ is satisfiable, then it is satisfiable by a trace whose length is bounded by the length of θ.

Thus, we can just guess a trace π of exponential length of θ and check that it satisfies φ. As a result, the upper bound for MLTL-SAT is NEXPTIME.

Before proving the NEXPTIME lower bound, recall the PSPACE-lower bound proof in [45] for LTL satisfiability. The proof reduces the acceptance problem for a linear-space bounded Turing machine M to LTL satisfiability. Given a Turing machine M and an integer k, we construct a formula φ_M such that φ_M is satisfiable iff M accepts the empty tape using k tape cells. The argument is that we can encode such a space-bounded computation of M by a trace π of length c^k for some constant c, and then use φ_M to force π to encode an accepting computation of M. The formula φ_M has to match corresponding points in successive configurations of M, which can be expressed using a $O(k)$-nested $\mathcal{X}$'s, since such points are $O(k)$ points apart.

To prove a NEXPTIME-lower bound for MLTL, we reduce the acceptance problem for exponentially bounded non-deterministic Turing machines to MLTL satisfiability. Given a non-deterministic Turing machine M and an integer k, we construct an MLTL formula φ_M of length $O(k)$ such that φ_M is satisfiable iff M accepts the empty tape in time 2^k. Note that such a computation of a 2^k-time bounded Turing machines consists of 2^k many configurations of length 2^k each, so the whole computation is of exponential length – 4^k, and can be encoded by a trace π of length 4^k, where every point of π encodes one cell in the computation of M. Unlike the reduction in [45], in the encoding here corresponding points in successive configurations are exponentially far (2^k) from each other, because each configuration has 2^k cells, so the relationship between such successive points cannot be expressed in LTL. Because, however, the constants in the intervals of MLTL are written in base-10 (decimal) notation, we can write formulas of size $O(k)$, e.g., formulas of the form $p\,\mathcal{U}_{[0,2^k]}\,q$, that relate points that are 2^k apart.

The key is to express the fact that one Turing machine configuration is a proper successor of another configuration using a formula of size $O(k)$. In the PSPACE-lower-bound proof of [45], LTL formulas of size $O(k)$ relate successive configurations of k-space-bounded machines. Here MLTL formulas of size $O(k)$ relate successive configurations of 2^k-time-bounded machines. Thus, we can write a formula φ_M of length $O(k)$ that forces trace π to encode a computation of M of length 2^k. □

Now we consider MLTL_0 formulas, and prove that the complexity of checking the satisfiability of MLTL_0 formulas is PSPACE-complete. We first introduce the following lemma to show an inherent feature of MLTL_0 formulas.

Lemma 2. *The conjunction of identical* MLTL_0 *$\mathcal{U}$-rooted formulas is equivalent to the conjunct with the smallest interval range:* $(\xi\,\mathcal{U}_{[0,a]}\,\psi) \wedge (\xi\,\mathcal{U}_{[0,b]}\,\psi) \equiv (\xi\,\mathcal{U}_{[0,a]}\,\psi)$*, where* $b > a$*.*

Proof. We first prove that for $i \geq 0$, the equation $(\xi\,\mathcal{U}_{[0,i]}\,\psi) \wedge (\xi\,\mathcal{U}_{[0,i+1]}\,\psi) \equiv (\xi\,\mathcal{U}_{[0,i]}\,\psi)$ holds. When $i = 0$, we have $(\xi\,\mathcal{U}_{[0,0]}\,\psi) \equiv f(\psi)$ and $(\xi\,\mathcal{U}_{[0,1]}\,\psi) \equiv (f(\psi) \vee f(\xi) \wedge \mathcal{X}(f(\psi)))$. So $(\xi\,\mathcal{U}_{[0,0]}\,\psi) \wedge (\xi\,\mathcal{U}_{[0,1]}\,\psi) \equiv f(\psi) \equiv (\xi\,\mathcal{U}_{[0,0]}\,\psi)$ is true. Inductively, assume that $(\xi\,\mathcal{U}_{[0,k]}\,\psi) \wedge (\xi\,\mathcal{U}_{[0,k+1]}\,\psi) \equiv (\xi\,\mathcal{U}_{[0,k]}\,\psi)$ is true for $k \geq 0$. When $i = k+1$, we have $(\xi\,\mathcal{U}_{[0,k+1]}\,\psi) \equiv (f(\psi) \vee f(\xi) \wedge \mathcal{X}(\xi\,\mathcal{U}_{[0,k]}\,\psi))$ and $(\xi\,\mathcal{U}_{[0,k+2]}\,\psi) \equiv (f(\psi) \vee f(\xi) \wedge \mathcal{X}(\xi\,\mathcal{U}_{[0,k+1]}\,\psi))$. By hypothesis assumption,

$(\xi\,\mathcal{U}_{[0,k]}\,\psi) \wedge (\xi\,\mathcal{U}_{[0,k+1]}\,\psi) \equiv (\xi\,\mathcal{U}_{[0,k]}\,\psi)$ implies that the following equivalence is true:

$$
\begin{aligned}
&(\xi\,\mathcal{U}_{[0,k+1]}\,\psi) \wedge (\xi\,\mathcal{U}_{[0,k+2]}\,\psi)\\
\equiv\;& (f(\psi) \vee (f(\xi) \wedge \mathcal{X}(\xi\,\mathcal{U}_{[0,k]}\,\psi))) \wedge (f(\psi) \vee (f(\xi) \wedge \mathcal{X}(\xi\,\mathcal{U}_{[0,k+1]}\,\psi)))\\
\equiv\;& f(\psi) \vee (f(\xi) \wedge \mathcal{X}(\xi\,\mathcal{U}_{[0,k]}\,\psi \wedge \xi\,\mathcal{U}_{[0,k+1]}\,\psi))\\
\equiv\;& f(\psi) \vee (f(\xi) \wedge \mathcal{X}(\xi\,\mathcal{U}_{[0,k]}\,\psi))\\
\equiv\;& (\xi\,\mathcal{U}_{[0,k+1]}\,\psi).
\end{aligned}
$$

Since $(\xi\,\mathcal{U}_{[0,i]}\,\psi) \wedge (\xi\,\mathcal{U}_{[0,i+1]}\,\psi) \equiv (\xi\,\mathcal{U}_{[0,i]}\,\psi)$ is true, we can prove by induction that $(\xi\,\mathcal{U}_{[0,i]}\,\psi) \wedge (\xi\,\mathcal{U}_{[0,j]}\,\psi) \equiv (\xi\,\mathcal{U}_{[0,i]}\,\psi)$ is true, where $j > i$. Because $b > a$ is true, it directly implies that $(\xi\,\mathcal{U}_{[0,a]}\,\psi) \wedge (\xi\,\mathcal{U}_{[0,b]}\,\psi) \equiv (\xi\,\mathcal{U}_{[0,a]}\,\psi)$ is true. □

Lemma 3. *$\mathcal{X}$-free* LTL_f-SAT *is reducible to* MLTL_0-SAT *at a linear cost.*

Proof. According to [45], the satisfiability checking of $\mathcal{X}$-free LTL formulas is still PSPACE-complete. This also applies to the satisfiability checking of $\mathcal{X}$-free LTL_f formulas. Given an $\mathcal{X}$-free LTL_f formula φ, we construct the corresponding MLTL formula $m(\varphi)$ recursively as follows:

- $m(p) = p$ where p is an atom;
- $m(\neg\xi) = \neg m(\xi)$;
- $m(\xi \wedge \psi) = m(\xi) \wedge m(\psi)$;
- $m(\xi\,\mathcal{U}\,\psi) = m(\xi)\,\mathcal{U}_{[0,2^{|\varphi|}]}\,m(\psi)$.

Notably for the Until LTL_f formula, we bound it with the interval $[0, 2^{|\varphi|}]$, where φ is the original $\mathcal{X}$-free LTL_f formula, in the corresponding MLTL formula, which is motivated by the fact that every satisfiable LTL_f formula has a finite model whose length is less than $2^{|\varphi|}$ [14]. The above translation has linear blow-up, because the integers in intervals use the decimal notation. Now we prove by induction over the type of φ that φ is satisfiable iff $m(\varphi)$ is satisfiable. That is, we prove that ($\Rightarrow$) $\pi \models \varphi$ implies $\pi \models m(\varphi)$ and ($\Leftarrow$) $\pi \models m(\varphi)$ implies $\pi \models \varphi$, for some finite trace π.

We consider the Until formula $\eta = \xi\,\mathcal{U}\,\psi$ (noting that φ is fixed to the original LTL_f formula), and the proofs are trivial for other types. ($\Rightarrow$) η is satisfiable implies there is a finite trace π such that $\pi \models \eta$ and $|\pi| \leq 2^{|\varphi|}$ [14]. Moreover, $\pi \models \eta$ holds iff there is $0 \leq i$ such that $\pi_i \models \psi$ and for every $0 \leq j < i$, $\pi_j \models \xi$ is true (from LTL_f semantics). By the induction hypothesis, $\pi_i \models \psi$ implies $\pi_i \models m(\psi)$ and $\pi_j \models \xi$ implies $\pi_j \models m(\xi)$. Also, $i \leq 2^{|\varphi|}$ is true because of $|\pi| \leq 2^{|\varphi|}$. As a result, $\pi \models \eta$ implies that there is $0 \leq i \leq 2^{|\varphi|}$ such that $\pi_i \models m(\psi)$ and for every $0 \leq j < i$, $\pi_j \models m(\xi)$ is true. According to the MLTL semantics, $\pi \models m(\eta)$ is true. ($\Leftarrow$) $m(\eta)$ is satisfiable implies there is a finite trace π such that $\pi \models m(\eta)$. According to MLTL semantics, there is $0 \leq i \leq 2^{|\varphi|}$ such that $\pi_i \models m(\psi)$ and for every $0 \leq j < i$ it holds that $\pi_j \models m(\xi)$. By hypothesis assumption, $\pi_i \models m(\psi)$ implies $\pi_i \models \psi$ and $\pi_j \models m(\xi)$ implies $\pi_j \models \xi$. Also, $0 \leq i \leq 2^{|\varphi|}$ implies $0 \leq i$. As a result, $\pi \models m(\eta)$ implies that there is $0 \leq i$ such that $\pi_i \models \psi$ and for every $0 \leq j < i$ it holds that $\pi_j \models \xi$. From LTL_f semantics, it is true that $\pi \models \eta$. □

Theorem 2. *The complexity of checking the satisfiability of* MLTL$_0$ *is PSPACE-complete.*

Proof. Since Lemma 3 shows a linear reduction from $\mathcal{X}$-free LTL$_f$-SAT to MLTL$_0$-SAT and $\mathcal{X}$-free LTL$_f$-SAT is PSPACE-complete [14], it directly implies that the lower bound of MLTL$_0$-SAT is PSPACE-hard.

For the upper bound, recall from the proof of Theorem 1 that an MLTL formula φ is translated to an LTL$_f$ formula θ of length $K \cdot |cl(\varphi)|$, which, as we commented, involved an exponential blow-up in the notation for K. Following the automata-theoretic approach for satisfiability, one would translate θ to an NFA and check its non-emptiness [14]. Normally, such a translation would involve another exponential blow-up. We show that this is not the case for MLTL$_0$. Recalling from the automaton construction in [14] that every state of the automaton is a set of subformulas of θ, the size of a state is at most $K \cdot |cl(\varphi)|$. In the general case, if ψ_1, ψ_2 are two subformulas of θ corresponding to the MLTL formulas $\xi\ \mathcal{U}_{I_1}\ \psi$ and $\xi\ \mathcal{U}_{I_2}\ \psi$, ψ_1 and ψ_2 can be in the same state of the automaton, which implies that the size of the state can be at most $K \cdot |cl(\varphi)|$. When the formula φ is restricted to MLTL$_0$, we show that the exponential blow-up can be avoided. Lemma 2 shows that either ψ_1 or ψ_2 in the state is enough, since assuming $I_1 \subseteq I_2$, then $(\psi_1 \wedge \psi_2) \equiv \psi_1$, by Lemma 2. So the size of the state in the automaton for a MLTL$_0$ formula φ is at most $|cl(\varphi)|$. For each subformula in the state, there can be K possible values (e.g., for $\Diamond_I \xi$ in the state, we can have $\Diamond_{[0,1]}\xi$, $\Diamond_{[0,2]}\xi$, etc.). Therefore the size of the automaton is in $O(2^{|cl(\varphi)|} \cdot K^{|cl(\varphi)|}) \approx 2^{O(|cl(\varphi)|)}$. Therefore, MLTL$_0$ satisfiability checking is a PSPACE-complete problem. □

4 Implementation of MLTL-SAT

We first show how to reduce MLTL-SAT to the well-explored LTL$_f$-SAT and LTL-SAT. Then we introduce two new satisfiability-checking strategies based on the inherent properties of MLTL formulas, which are able to leverage the state-of-art model-checking and SMT-solving techniques.

4.1 MLTL-SAT via Logic Translation

For a formula φ from one logic, and ψ from another logic, we say φ and ψ are *equi-satisfiable* when φ is satisfiable under its semantics iff ψ is satisfiable under its semantics. Based on Lemma 1 and Theorem 1, we have the following corollary,

Corollary 1 (MLTL-SAT to LTL$_f$-SAT). MLTL-SAT *can be reduced to* LTL$_f$-SAT *with an exponential blow-up.*

From Corollary 1, MLTL-SAT is reducible to LTL$_f$-SAT, enabling use of the off-the-shelf LTL$_f$ satisfiability solvers, cf. aaltaf [23]. It is also straightforward to consider MLTL-SAT via LTL-SAT; LTL-SAT has been studied for more than a decade, and there many off-the-shelf LTL solvers are available, cf. [24,38,40].

Theorem 3 (**MLTL to LTL**). *For an* MLTL *formula φ, there is an* LTL *formula θ such that φ and θ are equi-satisfiable, and the size of θ is in $O(K \cdot |cl(\varphi)|)$, where K is the maximal integer in φ.*

Proof. Lemma 1 provides a translation from the MLTL formula φ to the equivalent LTL_f formula φ', with a blow-up of $O(K \cdot |cl(\varphi)|)$. As shown in Sect. 2, there is a linear translation from the LTL_f formula φ' to its equi-satisfiable LTL formula θ [14]. Therefore, the blow-up from φ to θ is in $O(K \cdot |cl(\varphi)|)$. □

Corollary 2 (**MLTL-SAT to LTL-SAT**). MLTL-SAT *can be reduced to* LTL-SAT *with an exponential blow-up.*

Since MLTL-SAT is reducible to LTL-SAT, MLTL-SAT can also benefit from the power of LTL satisfiability solvers. Moreover, the reduction from MLTL-SAT to LTL-SAT enables leveraging modern model-checking techniques to solve the MLTL-SAT problem, due to the fact that LTL-SAT has been shown to be reducible to model checking with a linear blow-up [38,39].

Corollary 3 (**MLTL-SAT to LTL-Model-checking**). MLTL-SAT *can be reduced to* LTL *model checking with an exponential blow-up.*

In our implementation, we choose the model checker nuXmv [12] for LTL satisfiability checking, as it allows an LTL formula to be directly input as the temporal specification together with a universal model as described in [38,39].

4.2 Model Generation

Using the LTL formula as the temporal specification in nuXmv has been shown, however, to not be the most efficient way to use model checking for satisfiability checking [40]. Consider the MLTL formula $\Diamond_{[0,10]}a \wedge \Diamond_{[1,11]}a$. The translated LTL_f formula is $f(\Diamond_{[0,10]}a) \wedge \mathcal{X}(f(\Diamond_{[0,10]}a))$, where $f(\Diamond_{[0,10]}a)$ has to be constructed twice. To avoid such redundant construction, we follow [40] and encode directly the input MLTL formula as an SMV model (the input model of nuXmv) rather than treating the LTL formula, which is obtained from the input MLTL formula, as a specification.

An SMV [27] model consists of a Boolean transition system $Sys = (V, I, T)$, where V is a set of Boolean variables, I is a Boolean formula representing the initial states of Sys, and T is the Boolean transition formula. Moreover, a specification to be verified against the system is also contained in the SMV model (here we focus on the LTL specification). Given the input MLTL formula φ, we construct the corresponding SMV model M_φ as follows.

- Introduce a Boolean variable for each atom in φ as well as for "$Tail$" (new variable identifying the end of a finite trace).
- Introduce a Boolean variable $\mathcal{X}\_\psi$ for each $\mathcal{U}$ formula ψ in $cl^*(\varphi)$, which represents the intermediate temporal formula $\mathcal{X}\psi$.
- Introduce a temporary Boolean variable[2] T_ψ for each $\mathcal{U}$ formula in $cl^*(\varphi)$.

[2] A temporary variable is introduced in the DEFINE statement rather than the VAR statement of the SMV model, as it will be automatically replaced with those in VAR statements.

- A Boolean formula $e(\psi)$ is used to represent the formula ψ in $cl^*(\varphi)$ in the SMV model, which is defined recursively as follows.
  1. $e(\psi) = \psi$, if ψ is an Boolean atom;
  2. $e(\psi) = \neg e(\psi_1)$, if $\psi = \neg\psi_1$;
  3. $e(\psi) = e(\psi_1) \wedge e(\psi_2)$, if $\psi = \psi_1 \wedge \psi_2$;
  4. $e(\psi) = T\_\psi$, if ψ is an $\mathcal{U}$ formula.
- Let the initial Boolean formula of the system Sys be $e(\varphi)$.
- For each temporary variable T_ψ, create a DEFINE statement according to the type and interval of ψ, as follows.

$$T_{\psi_1\mathcal{U}_{[a,b]}\psi_2} = \begin{cases} \mathcal{X}\_(\psi_1\mathcal{U}_{[a-1,b-1]}\psi_2), & \text{if } 0 < a \leq b; \\ e(\psi_2) \vee (e(\psi_1) \wedge \mathcal{X}\_(\psi_1\mathcal{U}_{[0,b-1]}\psi_2)), & \text{if } a = 0 \text{ and } 0 < b; \\ e(\psi_2), & \text{if } a = 0 \text{ and } b = 0. \end{cases}$$

- Create the Boolean formula $(\mathcal{X}\_\psi \leftrightarrow (\neg Tail \wedge next(e(\psi))))$ for each $\mathcal{X}\_\psi$ in the VAR list (the set V in Sys) of the SMV model.
- Finally, designate the LTL formula $\Box\neg Tail$ as the temporal specification of the SMV model M_φ (which implies that a counterexample trace satisfies $\Diamond Tail$).

Encoding Heuristics for MLTL$_0$ Formulas. We also encode the rules shown in Lemma 2 to prune the state space for checking the satisfiability of MLTL$_0$ formulas. These rules are encoded using the INVAR constraint in the SMV model. Taking the $\mathcal{U}$ formula as an example, we encode $T\_(\psi_1\mathcal{U}_{[0,a]}\psi_2) \wedge T\_(\psi_1\mathcal{U}_{[0,a-1]}\psi_2) \leftrightarrow T\_(\psi_1\mathcal{U}_{[0,a-1]}\psi_2)$ $(a > 0)$ for each $\psi_1\mathcal{U}_{[0,a]}\psi_2$ in $cl^*(\varphi)$. Similar encodings also apply to the $\mathcal{R}$ formulas in $cl^*(\varphi)$. Theorem 4 below guarantees the correctness of the translation, and it can be proved by induction over the type of φ and the construction of the SMV model.

Theorem 4. *The* MLTL *formula φ is satisfiable iff the corresponding* SMV *model M_φ violates the* LTL *property $\Box\neg Tail$.*

There are different techniques that can be used for LTL model checking. Based on the latest evaluation of LTL satisfiability checking [24], the KLIVE [13] back-end implemented in the SMV model checker nuXmv [12] produces the best performance. We thus choose KLIVE as our model-checking technique for MLTL-SAT.

Bounded MLTL-SAT**.** Although MLTL-SAT is reducible to the satisfiability problem of other well-explored logics, with established off-the-shelf satisfiability solvers, a dedicated solution based on inherent properties of MLTL may be superior. One intuition is, since all intervals in MLTL formulas are bounded, the satisfiability of the formula can be reduced to Bounded Model Checking (BMC) [9].

Theorem 5. *Given an* MLTL *formula φ with K as the largest natural in the intervals of φ, φ is satisfiable iff there is a finite trace π with $|\pi| \leq K \cdot |cl(\varphi)|$ such that $\pi \models \varphi$.*

Theorem 5 states that the satisfiability of a given MLTL formula can be reduced to checking for the existence of a satisfying trace. To apply the BMC technique in nuXmv, we compute and set the maximal depth of BMC to be the value of $K \cdot |cl(\varphi)|$ for a given MLTL formula φ. The input SMV model for BMC is still M_φ, as described in Sect. 4.2.

However to ensure correct BMC checking in nuXmv, the constraint "FAIRNESS TRUE" has to be added into the SMV model.[3] The LTLSPEC remains $\Box\neg Tail$. According to Theorem 5, φ is satisfiable iff the model checker returns a counterexample by using the BMC technique within the maximal depth of $K \cdot |cl(\varphi)|$.

4.3 MLTL-SAT via SMT Solving

Another approach to solve MLTL-SAT is via SMT solving, considering that using SMT solvers to handle intervals in MLTL formulas is straightforward. Since the input logic of SMT solvers is First-Order Logic, we must first translate the MLTL formula to its equi-satisfiable formula in First-Order Logic over the natural domain N. We assume that readers are familiar with First-Order Logic and only focus on the translation. Given an MLTL formula φ and the alphabet Σ, we construct the corresponding formula in First-Order Logic over N in the following way.

1. For each $p \in \Sigma$, define a corresponding function $f_p : Int \rightarrow Bool$ such that $f_p(k)$ is true ($k \in N$) iff there is a satisfying (finite) trace π of φ and p is in $\pi[k]$.
2. The First-Order Logic formula $\mathsf{fol}(\varphi, k, len)$ for φ ($k, len \in N$) is constructed recursively as below:
   - $\mathsf{fol}(\mathsf{true}, k, len) = (len > k)$ and $\mathsf{fol}(\mathsf{false}, k, len) = false$;
   - $\mathsf{fol}(p, k, len) = (len > k) \wedge f_p(k)$ for $p \in \Sigma$;
   - $\mathsf{fol}(\neg\xi, k, len) = (len > k) \wedge \neg\mathsf{fol}(\xi, k, len)$;
   - $\mathsf{fol}(\xi \wedge \psi, k, len) = (len > k) \wedge \mathsf{fol}(\xi, k, len) \wedge \mathsf{fol}(\psi, k, len)$;
   - $\mathsf{fol}(\xi\, \mathcal{U}_{[a,b]}\, \psi, k, len) = (len > a+k) \wedge \exists i.(\, (a+k \leq i \leq b+k) \wedge \mathsf{fol}(\psi, i, len-i) \wedge \forall j.(\, (a+k \leq j < i) \rightarrow \mathsf{fol}(\xi, j, len-j)))$;

In the formula $\mathsf{fol}(\varphi, k, len)$, k represents the index of the (finite) trace from which φ is evaluated, and len indicates the length of the suffix of the trace starting from the index k. Since the formula is constructed recursively, we need to introduce k to record the index. Meanwhile, len is necessary because the MLTL semantics, which is interpreted over finite traces, constrains the lengths of the satisfying traces of the Until formulas. The following theorem guarantees that MLTL-SAT is reducible to the satisfiability of First-Order Logic.

Theorem 6. *For an* MLTL *formula φ, φ is satisfiable iff the corresponding First-Order Logic formula $\exists len.\mathsf{fol}(\varphi, 0, len)$ is satisfiable.*

Proof. Let the alphabet of φ be Σ, and $\pi \in (2^{\Sigma})^*$ be a finite trace. For each $p \in \Sigma$, we define the function $f_p : Int \rightarrow Bool$ as follows: $f_p(k) = \mathsf{true}$ iff $p \in \pi[k]$ if $0 \leq k < |\pi|$. We now prove by induction over the type of φ and the construction of $\mathsf{fol}(\varphi, k, len)$ with respect to φ that $\pi_k \models \varphi$ holds iff $\{f_p | p \in \Sigma\}$ is a model of $\mathsf{fol}(\varphi, k, |\pi|)$: here $|\pi|$ is the length of π. The cases when φ is true or false are trivial.

- If $\varphi = p$ is an atom, $\pi_k \models \varphi$ holds iff $p \in \pi[k]$ (i.e., $\pi_k[0]$) is true, which means $f_p(k) = \mathsf{true}$. As a result, $\{f_p\}$ is a model of $\mathsf{fol}(\varphi, k, |\pi|)$, which implies that $\pi_k \models \varphi$ holds iff $\{f_p | p \in \Sigma\}$ is a model of $\mathsf{fol}(\varphi, k, |\pi|)$.

[3] Based on comments in emails from the nuXmv developers.

- If $\varphi = \neg\xi$, $\pi_k \models \varphi$ holds iff $\pi_k \not\models \xi$ holds. By hypothesis assumption, $\pi_k \models \xi$ holds iff $\{f_p | p \in \Sigma\}$ is a model of $\mathsf{fol}(\xi, k, |\pi|)$, which is equivalent to saying $\pi_k \not\models \xi$ holds iff $\{f_p | p \in \Sigma\}$ is not a model of $\mathsf{fol}(\xi, k, |\pi|)$. As a result, $\pi_k \models \neg\xi$ holds iff $\{f_p | p \in \Sigma\}$ is a model of $\neg\mathsf{fol}(\xi, k, |\pi|)$.
- If $\varphi = \xi \wedge \psi$, $\pi_k \models \varphi$ holds iff $\pi_k \models \xi$ and $\pi_k \models \psi$. By hypothesis assumption, $\pi_k \models \xi$ (resp. $\pi_k \models \psi$) holds iff $\{f_p | p \in \Sigma\}$ is a model of $\mathsf{fol}(\xi, k, |\pi|)$ (resp. $\mathsf{fol}(\psi, k, |\pi|)$). According to the construction of the fol function, $\{f_p | p \in \Sigma\}$ is a model of $\mathsf{fol}(\xi \wedge \psi, k, |\pi|)$. As a result, $\pi_k \models \xi \wedge \psi$ holds iff $\{f_p | p \in \Sigma\}$ is a model of $\mathsf{fol}(\xi \wedge \psi, k, |\pi|)$.
- If $\varphi = \xi\, \mathcal{U}_{[a,b]}\, \psi$, $\pi_k \models \varphi$ holds iff there is $a + k \leq i \leq b + k$ such that $\pi_i \models \psi$ and $\pi_j \models \xi$ holds for every $a + k \leq j < i$. By hypothesis assumption, $\pi_i \models \psi$ holds iff $\{f_p | p \in \Sigma\}$ is a model of $\mathsf{fol}(\psi, i, len - i)$ (the length of π_i is $len - i$), and $\pi, j \models \xi$ holds iff $\{f_p | p \in \Sigma\}$ is a model of $\mathsf{fol}(\xi, j, |\pi| - j)$ (the length of π_j is $|\pi| - j$). Moreover, $|\pi| > a + k$ must be true according to the MLTL semantics. As a result, $\{f_p | p \in \Sigma\}$ is a model of $\mathsf{fol}(\varphi, k, |\pi|)$, which implies that $\pi_k \models \xi\, \mathcal{U}_{[a,b]} \psi$ holds iff $\{f_p | p \in \Sigma\}$ is a model of $\mathsf{fol}(\xi\, \mathcal{U}_{[a,b]}\, \psi, k, |\pi|)$.

This proof holds for all values of k, including the special case where $k = 0$. □

We then encode $\exists len.\mathsf{fol}(\varphi, 0, len)$ into the SMT-LIB v2 format [7], which is the input of most modern SMT solvers; we call the full SMT-LIB v2 encoding $\mathsf{SMT}(\varphi)$. We first use the "declare-fun" command to declare a function $f_a : Int \rightarrow Bool$ for each $p \in \Sigma$. We also define the function $f_\varphi : Int \times Int \rightarrow Bool$ for the First-Order Logic formula $\mathsf{fol}(\varphi, k, len)$. The corresponding SMT-LIB v2 command is "define-fun f_φ $((k\ Int)\ (len\ Int))\ Bool\ S(\mathsf{fol}(\varphi, k, len))$", where $S(\mathsf{fol}(\varphi, k, len))$ is the SMT-LIB v2 implementation of $\mathsf{fol}(\varphi, k, len)$. In detail, $S(\mathsf{fol}(\varphi, k, len))$ is acquired recursively as follows.

- $S(\mathsf{fol}(p, k, len)) \longrightarrow$ (and ($>$ len k) (f_p k))
- $S(\neg\mathsf{fol}(\varphi, k, len)) \longrightarrow$ (and ($>$ len k) (not $S(\mathsf{fol}(\varphi, k))$)))
- $S(\mathsf{fol}(\varphi_1 \wedge \psi, k, len) \longrightarrow$ (and ($>$ len k) (and $S(\mathsf{fol}(\varphi_1, k, len))$ $S(\mathsf{fol}(\psi, k, len))$)))
- $S(\mathsf{fol}(\varphi_1\, \mathcal{U}_{[a,b]}\, \psi, k, len)) \longrightarrow$ (and ($>$ len $a{+}k$) (exists (i Int) (and ($\leq$ ($+$ a k) i) ($\geq$ i ($+$ b k)) $S(\mathsf{fol}(\psi, i, len - i))$ (forall (j Int) ($\Rightarrow$ (and ($\leq$ ($-$ a k) j) ($<$ j i)) $S(\mathsf{fol}(\varphi_1, j, len - j))$))))))

Finally, we use the "assert" command "(assert (exists ((len Int)) (f_φ 0 len)))" together with the "(check-sat)" command to request SMT solvers for the satisfiability of $\exists len.\mathsf{fol}(\varphi, 0, len)$. In a nutshell, the general framework of the SMT-LIB v2 format for $\mathsf{SMT}(\varphi)$ (i.e., $\exists len.\mathsf{fol}(\varphi, 0, len)$) is shown in Table 1, and the correctness is guaranteed by Theorem 7 below.

Table 1. The SMT-LIB v2 template for $\mathsf{SMT}(\varphi)$.

(declare-fun f_a (Int) Bool) //declare corresponding function for $a \in \Sigma$
...
//define function for $\mathsf{fol}(\varphi, k, len)$
(define-fun f_φ ((k Int) (len Int)) Bool $S(\mathsf{fol}(\varphi, k, len))$)
(assert (exists ((len Int)) (f_φ 0)))
(check-sat)

Theorem 7. *The First-Order Logic formula* $\exists len.fol(\varphi, 0, len)$ *is satisfiable iff the* SMT *solver returns SAT with the input* $\mathsf{SMT}(\varphi)$.

An inductive proof for the theorem can be conducted according to the construction of $\mathsf{SMT}(\varphi)$. Notably, there is no difference between the SMT encoding for MLTL formulas and that for MLTL_0 formulas, as the SMT-based encoding does not require unrolling the temporal operators in the formula.

5 Experimental Evaluations

Tools and Platform. We implemented the translator MLTLconverter in C++, including encodings for an MLTL formula as equi-satisfiable LTL and LTL_f formulas, and corresponding SMV and SMT-LIB v2 models. We leverage the extant LTL solver aalta [24], LTL_f solver aaltaf [23], SMV model checker nuXmv [12], and the SMT solver Z3 [29] to check the satisfiability of the input MLTL formula in their respective encodings from MLTLconverter. The solvers, including the runtime flags we used, are summarized in Table 2. We evaluated both BMC and KLIVE [13] model-checking back-ends in nuXmv, and the corresponding commands are shown in Fig. 1. Notably in the figure, the maximal length "*MAX*" to run BMC is computed dynamically for each MLTL formula, based on Theorem 5.

Table 2. List of solvers and their runtime flags.

Encoding	MLTLconverter flag	Solver	Solver flag
LTL	-ltl	aalta	default
LTL_f	-ltlf	aaltaf	default
SMV	-smv	nuXmv	-source bmc.cmd (BMC)
			-source klive.cmd (KLIVE)
SMT-LIB v2	-smtlib	Z3	-smt2

```
read_model                          read_model
flatten_hierarchy                   flatten_hierarchy
encode_variables                    encode_variables
build_boolean_model                 build_boolean_model
bmc_setup                           check_ltlspec_klive -d
go_bmc                              quit
check_ltlspec_bmc -k MAX
quit
```

Fig. 1. nuXmv commands for BMC (left) and KLIVE (right).

All experiments were executed on Rice University's NOTS cluster,[4] running RedHat 5, with 226 dual socket compute blades housed within HPE s6500, HPE Apollo 2000, and Dell PowerEdge C6400 chassis. All the nodes are interconnected with 10 GigE network. Each satisfiability check over one MLTL formula and one solver was executed with exclusive access to one CPU and 8 GB RAM with a timeout of one hour, as measured by the Linux `time` command. We assigned a time penalty of one hour to benchmarks that segmentation fault or timeout.

Experimental Goals. We evaluate performance along three metrics. (1) Each satisfiability check has two parts: the encoding time (consumed by MLTLconverter) and the solving time (consumed by solvers). We evaluate how each encoding affects the performance of both stages of MLTL-SAT. (2) We comparatively analyze the performance and scalability of end-to-end MLTL-SAT via LTL-SAT, LTL_f-SAT, LTL model checking, and our new SMT-based approach. (3) We evaluate the performance and scalability for $MLTL_0$ satisfiability checking using $MLTL_0$-SAT encoding heuristics (Lemma 2).

Benchmarks. There are few MLTL (or even MTL-over-naturals) benchmarks available for evaluation. Previous works on MTL-over-naturals [2–4] mainly focus on the theoretic exploration of the logic. To enable rigorous experimental evaluation, we develop three types of benchmarks, motivated by the generation of LTL benchmarks [38].[5]

(1) *Random* MLTL *Formulas (*R*)*: We generated 10,000 R formulas, varying the formula length L (20, 40, 60, 80, 100), the number of variables N (1, 2, 3, 4, 5), and the probability of the appearance of the $\mathcal{U}$ operator P (0.33, 0,5, 0.7, 0.95); for each (L, N, P) we generated 100 formulas. For every $\mathcal{U}$ operator, we randomly chose an interval $[i, j]$ where $i \geq 0$ and $j \leq 100$.

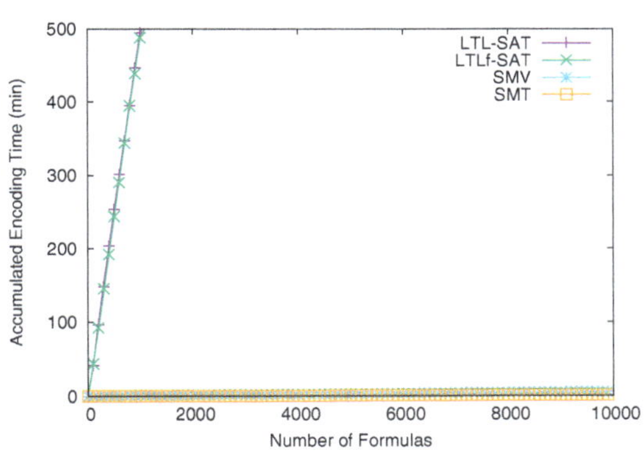

Fig. 2. Cactus plot for different MLTL encodings on R formulas: LTL-SAT and LTL_f-SAT lines overlap; SMV and SMT lines overlap.

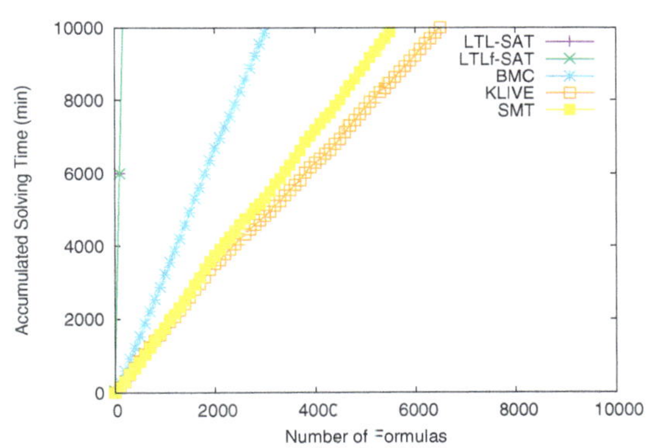

Fig. 3. Cactus plot for different MLTL solving approaches on R formulas: LTL-SAT and LTL_f-SAT lines overlap.

[4] https://docs.rice.edu/confluence/display/CD/NOTS+Overview.

[5] All experimental materials are at http://temporallogic.org/research/CAV19/. The plots are best viewed online.

(2) *NASA-Boeing* MLTL *Formulas (*NB*)*: We use challenging benchmarks [15] created from projects at NASA [17,26] and Boeing [11]. We extract 63 real-life LTL requirements from the SMV models of the benchmarks, and then randomly generate an interval for each temporal operator. (We replace each $\mathcal{X}$ with $\Box_{[1,1]}$.) We create 3 groups of such formulas (63 in each) to test the scalability of different approaches, by restricting the maximal number of the intervals to be 1,000, 10,000, and 100,000 respectively.

(3) *Random* MLTL_0 *Formulas (*R0*)*: We generated 500 R0 formulas in the same way as the R formulas, except that every generated interval was restricted to start from 0; we generated sets of five for each (L, N, P). This small set of R benchmarks serve to compare the performance on MLTL_0 formulas whose SMV encodings were created with/without heuristics.

Correctness Checking. We compared the verdicts from all solvers for every test instance and found no inconsistencies, excluding segmentation faults. This exercise aided with verification of our implementations of the translators, including diagnosing the need for including FAIRNESS TRUE in BMC models.

Experimental Results. Figure 2 compares encoding times for the R benchmark formulas. We find that (1) Encoding MLTL as either LTL and LTL_f is not scalable even when the intervals in the formula are small; (2) The cost of MLTL-to-SMV encoding is comparable to that from MLTL to SMT-LIB v2. Although the cost of encoding MLTL as LTL/LTL_f and SMV are in $O(K \cdot |cl(\varphi)|)$, where K is the maximal interval length in φ, the practical gap between the LTL/LTL_f encodings and SMV encoding affirms our conjecture that the SMV model is more compact in general than the corresponding LTL/LTL_f formulas. Also because K is kept small in the R formulas, the encoding cost between SMV and SMT-LIB v2 becomes comparable.

Figure 3 shows total satisfiability checking times for R benchmarks. Recall that the inputs of both BMC and KLIVE approaches are SMV models. The MLTL-SAT via KLIVE is the fastest solving strategy for MLTL formulas with interval ranges of less than 100. The portion of satisfiable/unsatisfiable formulas of this benchmark is approximate 4/1. Although BMC is known to be good at detecting counterexamples with short lengths, it does not perform as well as the KLIVE and SMT approaches on checking satisfiable formulas since only longer counterexamples (with length greater than 1000) exist for most of these formulas. While nuXmv successfully checked all such models, Fig. 4 shows that increasing the interval range constraint results in segmentation faults; more than half of our benchmarks produced this outcome for formulas with allowed interval ranges of up to 600. Meanwhile, the solving solutions via LTL-SAT/LTL_f-SAT are definitely not competitive for any interval range.

The SMT-based approach dominates the model-checking-approaches when considering scalable NB benchmarks, as shown in Fig. 5. Here, e.g., "BMC-1000" means using BMC to check the group of benchmarks with a maximal interval range of 1,000. Due to segmentation faults, "BMC-1000" and "KLIVE-1000" have almost the same performance because the SMV models generated from our translator MLTLconverter are too large for nuXmv to handle. The performance of the model-checking approaches is constrained by the scalability of the model checker (nuXmv). However, the SMT encoding does not face such a bottleneck; see "Z3-1000," "Z3-10000," and "Z3-100000" in Fig. 5. We conclude that the SMT approach is the best available strategy for MLTL satisfiability checking.

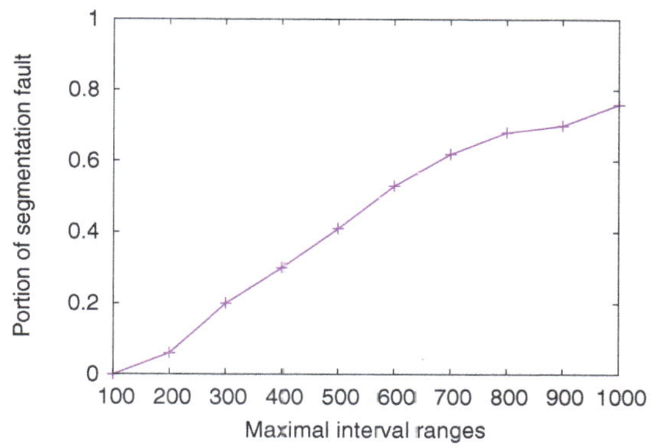

Fig. 4. Proportion of segmentation faults for sets of 200 R formulas with maximal interval ranges varying from 100 to 1000.

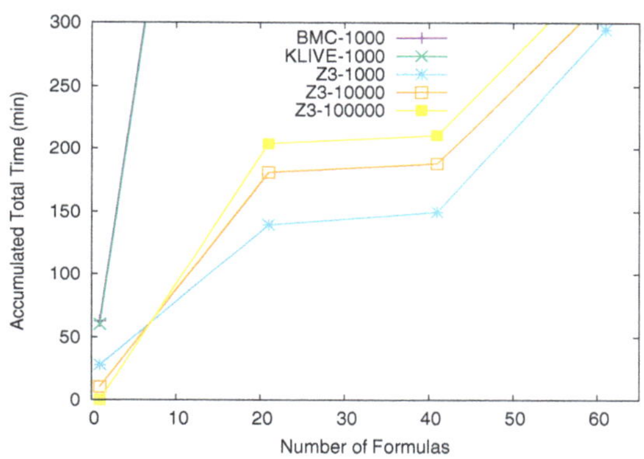

Fig. 5. Cactus plot for BMC,KLIVE and SMT-solving approaches on the NB benchmarks; BMC and KLIVE overlap.

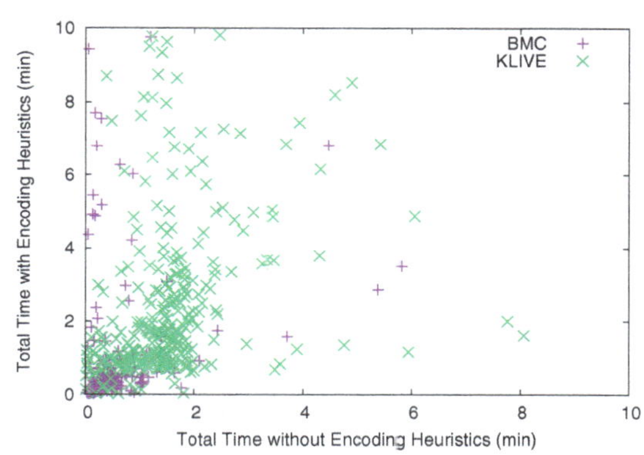

Fig. 6. Scatter plot for both the BMC and KLIVE approaches to checking $MLTL_0$ formulas ith/without encoding heuristics.

Finally, we evaluated the performance of model-checking-based approaches on the R0 formulas, observing that there is an exponential complexity gap between MLTL-SAT and $MLTL_0$-SAT. Figure 6 compares the performance of satisfiability solving via the BMC and KLIVE approaches. There is no significant improvement when the SMV encoding heuristics for $MLTL_0$ are applied. For the BMC solving approach, performance is largely unaffected by encoding heuristics. For the KLIVE solving approach, encoding heuristics decrease solving performance. The results support the well-known phenomenon that the theoretic analysis and the practical evaluations do not always match.

We summarize with three conclusions. (1) For satisfiability checking of MLTL formulas, the new SMT-based approach is best. (2) For satisfiability checking of MLTL formulas with interval ranges less than 100, the MLTL-SAT via KLIVE approach is fastest. (3) The dedicated encoding heuristics for MLTL_0 do not significantly improve the satisfiability checking time of MLTL_0-SAT over MLTL-SAT. They do not solve the nuXmv scalability problem.

6 Discussion and Conclusion

Metric Temporal Logic (MTL) was first introduced in [3], for describing continuous behaviors interpreted over infinite real-time traces. The later variants Metric Interval Temporal Logic (MITL) [5], and Bounded Metric Temporal Logic (BMTL) [30] are also interpreted over infinite traces. Intuitively, MLTL is a combination of MITL and BMTL that allows only bounded, discrete (over natural domain) intervals that are interpreted over finite traces. There are several previous works on the satisfiability of MITL, though their tools only support the infinite semantics. Bounded satisfiability checking for MITL formulas is proposed in [33], and the reduction from MITL to LTL is presented in [20]. Since previous works focus on MITL over infinite traces and there is no trivial way to reduce MLTL over finite traces to MITL over infinite traces, the previous methodologies are not comparable to those presented in this paper. This includes the SMT-based solution of reducing MITL formulas to equi-satisfiable Constraint LTL formulas [8]. Compared to that, our new SMT-based approach more directly encodes MLTL formulas into the SMT language without translation through an intermediate language.

The contribution of a complete, correct, and open-source MLTL satisfiability checking algorithm and tool opens up avenues for a myriad of future directions, as we have now made possible specification debugging MLTL formulas in design-time verification and benchmark generation for runtime verification. We plan to explore alternative encodings for improving the performance of MLTL satisfiability checking and work toward developing an optimized multi-encoding approach, following the style of the previous study for LTL [40]; the current SMT model generated from the MLTL formula uses a relatively simple theory (uninterpreted functions). We also plan to explore lazy encodings from MLTL formulas to SMT models. For example, instead of encoding the whole MLTL formula into a monolithic SMT model, we may be able to decrease overall satisfiability-solving time by encoding the MLTL formula in parts with dynamic ordering similar to [15]. To make the output of SMT-based MLTL satisfiability checking more usable, we plan to investigate translations from the functions returned from Z3 for satisfiable instances into more easily parsable satisfying assignments.

Acknowledgment. We thank anonymous reviewers for their helpful comments. This work is supported by NASA ECF NNX16AR57G, NSF CAREER Award CNS-1552934, NSF grants IIS-1527668, IIS-1830549, and by NSF Expeditions in Computing project "ExCAPE: Expeditions in Computer Augmented Program Engineering."

References

1. Runtime Verification Benchmark Competition (2018). https://www.rv-competition.org/2018-2/
2. Alur, R., Feder, T., Henzinger, T.A.: The benefits of relaxing punctuality. J. ACM **43**(1), 116–146 (1996)
3. Alur, R., Henzinger, T.A.: Real-time logics: complexity and expressiveness. In: LICS, pp. 390–401. IEEE (1990)
4. Alur, R., Henzinger, T.A.: A really temporal logic. J. ACM **41**(1), 181–204 (1994)
5. Alur, R., Henzinger, T.A.: Reactive modules. In: Proceedings of the 11th IEEE Symposium on Logic in Computer Science, pp. 207–218 (1996)
6. Armoni, R., Fix, L., Flaisher, A., Grumberg, O., Piterman, N., Vardi, M.Y.: Enhanced vacuity detection in linear temporal logic. In: Hunt, W.A., Somenzi, F. (eds.) CAV 2003. LNCS, vol. 2725, pp. 368–380. Springer, Heidelberg (2003). https://doi.org/10.1007/978-3-540-45069-6_35
7. Barrett, C., Stump, A., Tinelli, C.: The SMT-LIB standard: version 2.0. In: Workshop on Satisfiability Modulo Theories (2010)
8. Bersani, M., Rossi, M., San Pietro, P.: An SMT-based approach to satisfiability checking of MITL. Inf. Comput. **245**(C), 72–97 (2015)
9. Biere, A., Cimatti, A., Clarke, E., Zhu, Y.: Symbolic model checking without BDDs. In: Cleaveland, W.R. (ed.) TACAS 1999. LNCS, vol. 1579, pp. 193–207. Springer, Heidelberg (1999). https://doi.org/10.1007/3-540-49059-0_14
10. Bloem, R., Chockler, H., Ebrahimi, M., Strichman, O.: Synthesizing non-vacuous systems. In: Bouajjani, A., Monniaux, D. (eds.) VMCAI 2017. LNCS, vol. 10145, pp. 55–72. Springer, Cham (2017). https://doi.org/10.1007/978-3-319-52234-0_4
11. Bozzano, M., et al.: Formal design and safety analysis of AIR6110 wheel brake system. In: Kroening, D., Păsăreanu, C.S. (eds.) CAV 2015, Part I. LNCS, vol. 9206, pp. 518–535. Springer, Cham (2015). https://doi.org/10.1007/978-3-319-21690-4_36
12. Cavada, R., et al.: The NUXMV symbolic model checker. In: Biere, A., Bloem, R. (eds.) CAV 2014. LNCS, vol. 8559, pp. 334–342. Springer, Cham (2014). https://doi.org/10.1007/978-3-319-08867-9_22
13. Claessen, K., Sörensson, N.: A liveness checking algorithm that counts. In: FMCAD, pp. 52–59. IEEE (2012)
14. De Giacomo, G., Vardi, M.: Linear temporal logic and linear dynamic logic on finite traces. In: IJCAI, pp. 2000–2007. AAAI Press (2013)
15. Dureja, R., Rozier, K.Y.: More scalable LTL model checking via discovering design-space dependencies (D^3). In: Beyer, D., Huisman, M. (eds.) TACAS 2018, Part I. LNCS, vol. 10805, pp. 309–327. Springer, Cham (2018). https://doi.org/10.1007/978-3-319-89960-2_17
16. Furia, C.A., Spoletini, P.: Tomorrow and all our yesterdays: MTL satisfiability over the integers. In: Fitzgerald, J.S., Haxthausen, A.E., Yenigun, H. (eds.) ICTAC 2008. LNCS, vol. 5160, pp. 126–140. Springer, Heidelberg (2008). https://doi.org/10.1007/978-3-540-85762-4_9
17. Gario, M., Cimatti, A., Mattarei, C., Tonetta, S., Rozier, K.Y.: Model checking at scale: automated air traffic control design space exploration. In: Chaudhuri, S., Farzan, A. (eds.) CAV 2016, Part II. LNCS, vol. 9780, pp. 3–22. Springer, Cham (2016). https://doi.org/10.1007/978-3-319-41540-6_1
18. Geist, J., Rozier, K.Y., Schumann, J.: Runtime observer pairs and bayesian network reasoners on-board FPGAs: flight-certifiable system health management for embedded systems. In: Bonakdarpour, B., Smolka, S.A. (eds.) RV 2014. LNCS, vol. 8734, pp. 215–230. Springer, Cham (2014). https://doi.org/10.1007/978-3-319-11164-3_18

19. De Giacomo, G., Vardi, M.: Synthesis for LTL and LDL on finite traces. In: IJCAI, pp. 1558–1564 (2015)
20. Hustadt, U., Ozaki, A., Dixon, C.: Theorem proving for metric temporal logic over the naturals. In: de Moura, L. (ed.) CADE 2017. LNCS (LNAI), vol. 10395, pp. 326–343. Springer, Cham (2017). https://doi.org/10.1007/978-3-319-63046-5_20
21. Kessler, F.B.: nuXmv 1.1.0 (2016-05-10) Release Notes (2016). https://es-static.fbk.eu/tools/nuxmv/downloads/NEWS.txt
22. Li, J., Rozier, K.Y.: MLTL benchmark generation via formula progression. In: Colombo, C., Leucker, M. (eds.) RV 2018. LNCS, vol. 11237, pp. 426–433. Springer, Cham (2018). https://doi.org/10.1007/978-3-030-03769-7_25
23. Li, J., Zhang, L., Pu, G., Vardi, M.Y., He, J.: LTL_f satisfibility checking. In: ECAI, pp. 91–98 (2014)
24. Li, J., Zhu, S., Pu, G., Vardi, M.Y.: SAT-based explicit LTL reasoning. In: Piterman, N. (ed.) HVC 2015. LNCS, vol. 9434, pp. 209–224. Springer, Cham (2015). https://doi.org/10.1007/978-3-319-26287-1_13
25. Maler, O., Nickovic, D.: Monitoring temporal properties of continuous signals. In: Lakhnech, Y., Yovine, S. (eds.) FORMATS/FTRTFT 2004. LNCS, vol. 3253, pp. 152–166. Springer, Heidelberg (2004). https://doi.org/10.1007/978-3-540-30206-3_12
26. Mattarei, C., Cimatti, A., Gario, M., Tonetta, S., Rozier, K.Y.: Comparing different functional allocations in automated air traffic control design. In: Proceedings of Formal Methods in Computer-Aided Design (FMCAD 2015), Austin, Texas, USA. IEEE/ACM, September 2015
27. McMillan, K.: Symbolic model checking: an approach to the state explosion problem. Ph.D. thesis, Carnegie Mellon University, Pittsburgh, PA, USA (1992). UMI Order No. GAX92-24209
28. Moosbrugger, P., Rozier, K.Y., Schumann, J.: R2U2: monitoring and diagnosis of security threats for unmanned aerial systems. In: FMSD, pp. 1–31, April 2017
29. de Moura, L., Bjørner, N.: Z3: an efficient SMT solver. In: Ramakrishnan, C.R., Rehof, J. (eds.) TACAS 2008. LNCS, vol. 4963, pp. 337–340. Springer, Heidelberg (2008). https://doi.org/10.1007/978-3-540-78800-3_24
30. Ouaknine, J., Worrell, J.: Some recent results in metric temporal logic. In: Cassez, F., Jard, C. (eds.) FORMATS 2008. LNCS, vol. 5215, pp. 1–13. Springer, Heidelberg (2008). https://doi.org/10.1007/978-3-540-85778-5_1
31. Pandya, P.K., Shah, S.S.: The unary fragments of metric interval temporal logic: bounded versus lower bound constraints. In: Chakraborty, S., Mukund, M. (eds.) ATVA 2012. LNCS, pp. 77–91. Springer, Heidelberg (2012). https://doi.org/10.1007/978-3-642-33386-6_8
32. Pnueli, A.: The temporal logic of programs. In: IEEE FOCS, pp. 46–57 (1977)
33. Pradella, M., Morzenti, A., Pietro, P.: Bounded satisfiability checking of metric temporal logic specifications. ACM Trans. Softw. Eng. Methodol. **22**(3), 20:1–20:54 (2013)
34. Reinbacher, T., Rozier, K.Y., Schumann, J.: Temporal-logic based runtime observer pairs for system health management of real-time systems. In: Ábrahám, E., Havelund, K. (eds.) TACAS 2014. LNCS, vol. 8413, pp. 357–372. Springer, Heidelberg (2014). https://doi.org/10.1007/978-3-642-54862-8_24
35. Rozier, K.Y.: Specification: the biggest bottleneck in formal methods and autonomy. In: Blazy, S., Chechik, M. (eds.) VSTTE 2016. LNCS, vol. 9971, pp. 8–26. Springer, Cham (2016). https://doi.org/10.1007/978-3-319-48869-1_2
36. Rozier, K.Y.: On the evaluation and comparison of runtime verification tools for hardware and cyber-physical systems. In: RV-CUBES, vol. 3, pp. 123–137. Kalpa Publications (2017)
37. Rozier, K.Y., Schumann, J., Ippolito, C.: Intelligent hardware-enabled sensor and software safety and health management for autonomous UAS. Technical Memorandum NASA/TM-2015-218817, NASA Ames Research Center, Moffett Field, CA 94035, May 2015

38. Rozier, K.Y., Vardi, M.Y.: LTL satisfiability checking. In: Bošnački, D., Edelkamp, S. (eds.) SPIN 2007. LNCS, vol. 4595, pp. 149–167. Springer, Heidelberg (2007). https://doi.org/10.1007/978-3-540-73370-6_11
39. Rozier, K.Y., Vardi, M.Y.: LTL satisfiability checking. Int. J. Softw. Tools Technol. Transf. **12**(2), 123–137 (2010)
40. Rozier, K.Y., Vardi, M.Y.: A multi-encoding approach for LTL symbolic satisfiability checking. In: Butler, M., Schulte, W. (eds.) FM 2011. LNCS, vol. 6664, pp. 417–431. Springer, Heidelberg (2011). https://doi.org/10.1007/978-3-642-21437-0_31
41. Rozier, K.Y., Vardi, M.Y.: Deterministic compilation of temporal safety properties in explicit state model checking. In: Biere, A., Nahir, A., Vos, T. (eds.) HVC 2012. LNCS, vol. 7857, pp. 243–259. Springer, Heidelberg (2013). https://doi.org/10.1007/978-3-642-39611-3_23
42. Schumann, J., Moosbrugger, P., Rozier, K.Y.: R2U2: monitoring and diagnosis of security threats for unmanned aerial systems. In: Bartocci, E., Majumdar, R. (eds.) RV 2015. LNCS, vol. 9333, pp. 233–249. Springer, Cham (2015). https://doi.org/10.1007/978-3-319-23820-3_15
43. Schumann, J., Moosbrugger, P., Rozier, K.Y.: Runtime analysis with R2U2: a tool exhibition report. In: Falcone, Y., Sánchez, C. (eds.) RV 2016. LNCS, vol. 10012, pp. 504–509. Springer, Cham (2016). https://doi.org/10.1007/978-3-319-46982-9_35
44. Schumann, J., Rozier, K.Y., Reinbacher, T., Mengshoel, O.J., Mbaya, T., Ippolito, C.: Towards real-time, on-board, hardware-supported sensor and software health management for unmanned aerial systems. IJPHM **6**(1), 1–27 (2015)
45. Sistla, A.P., Clarke, E.M.: The complexity of propositional linear temporal logic. J. ACM **32**, 733–749 (1985)

High-Level Abstractions for Simplifying Extended String Constraints in SMT

Andrew Reynolds[1], Andres Nötzli[2(✉)], Clark Barrett[2], and Cesare Tinelli[1]

[1] Department of Computer Science, The University of Iowa, Iowa City, USA
[2] Department of Computer Science, Stanford University, Stanford, USA
noetzli@cs.stanford.edu

Abstract. Satisfiability Modulo Theories (SMT) solvers with support for the theory of strings have recently emerged as powerful tools for reasoning about string-manipulating programs. However, due to the complex semantics of *extended string functions*, it is challenging to develop scalable solvers for the string constraints produced by program analysis tools. We identify several classes of simplification techniques that are critical for the efficient processing of string constraints in SMT solvers. These techniques can reduce the size and complexity of input constraints by reasoning about arithmetic entailment, multisets, and string containment relationships over input terms. We provide experimental evidence that implementing them results in significant improvements over the performance of state-of-the-art SMT solvers for extended string constraints.

1 Introduction

Most programming languages support strings natively and a considerable number of programs perform some form of string manipulation. Automated reasoning about string-manipulating programs for verification and test case generation purposes is then highly relevant for these languages and programs. Applications to security, such as finding SQL injection and XSS vulnerabilities in web applications [16,18,23] or proving their absence, are of critical importance. String constraints have also been used to generate relational database tables from SQL queries for unit testing purposes [21]. These applications require modeling all of the string operations that appear in real programs. This is challenging since some of those operations are complex and often realized by iterative applications of simpler operations. Additionally, since strings in many programming languages have variable length, reasoning accurately about them cannot be done by a reduction to bounded types such as bit-vectors, and requires instead the development of solvers for *unbounded* strings. To make this type of reasoning more scalable, the use of dedicated theory solvers natively supporting common string operations has been proposed [5,9]. Some string solvers are fully integrated within

I. Dillig and S. Tasiran (Eds.): CAV 2019, LNCS 11562, pp. 23–42, 2019.
https://doi.org/10.1007/978-3-030-25543-5_2

Satisfiability Modulo Theories (SMT) solvers [4,12]; some are built (externally) on top of such solvers [9,16,19]; and others are independent of SMT solvers [23].

A major challenge in developing solvers for unbounded string constraints is the complex semantics of *extended string functions* beyond the basic operations of string concatenation and equality. Extended functions include replace, which replaces a string in another string, and indexof, which returns the position of a string in another string. Another challenge is that constraints using extended functions are often combined with constraints over other theories, e.g. integer constraints over string lengths or applications of indexof, which requires the involvement of solvers for those theories. Current string solvers address these challenges by reducing constraints with extended string functions to typically more verbose constraints over basic functions. As with every reduction, some of the higher level structure of the problem may be lost, with negative repercussions on the performance and scalability.

To address this issue, we have developed new techniques that reason about constraints with extended string operators before they are reduced to simpler ones. This analysis of complex terms can often eliminate the need for expensive reductions. The techniques are based on reasoning about relationships over strings with high-level abstractions, such as their arithmetic relationships (e.g., reasoning about their length), their string containment relationships, and their relationships as multisets of characters. We have implemented these techniques in CVC4, an SMT solver with native support for string reasoning. An experimental evaluation with benchmarks from various applications shows that our new techniques allows CVC4 to significantly outperform other state-of-the-art solvers that target extended string constraints.

Our main contributions are:

- A novel procedure for proving entailments over arithmetic predicates built from the theory of strings and linear integer arithmetic.
- Extensions of this technique for showing containment relationships between strings.
- A novel simplification technique based on abstracting strings as multisets.
- Experimental evidence that the simplification techniques provide significant performance improvements over current state-of-the-art solvers.

In the remainder of this section, we discuss related work. In Sect. 2, we provide some background on the theory of strings and how solvers reduce extended functions. In Sects. 3, 4 and 5, we describe, respectively, our arithmetic-based, containment-based, and multiset-based simplification techniques. Section 6 describes our implementation of those techniques, and Sect. 7 presents our evaluation.

Related Work. Various approaches to solving constraints over extended string functions have been proposed. Saxena et al. [16] showed that constraints from the symbolic execution of JavaScript code contain a significant number of extended string functions, which underlines their importance. Their approach translates string constraints to bit-vector constraints, similar to other approaches based on bounded strings such as HAMPI [9]. Bjørner et al. [5] proposed native support for extended string operators in string solvers for scaling symbolic execution of .NET code. They reduce extended string functions to basic ones after getting bounds for string lengths from an integer solver. They also showed that constraints involving unbounded strings and replace are undecidable. PASS [11] reduces string constraints over extended functions to arrays. Z3-str and its successors [4,24,25] reduce extended string functions to basic functions eagerly during preprocessing. S3 [18] reduces recursive functions such as replace incrementally by splitting and unfolding. Its successor S3P [19] refines this reduction by pruning the resulting subproblems for better performance. CVC4 [3] reduces constraints with extended functions lazily and leverages context-dependent simplifications to simplify the reductions [15]. TRAU [1] reduces certain extended functions, such as replace, to context-free membership constraints. OSTRICH [7] implements a decision procedure for a subset of constraints that include extended string functions. The simplification techniques presented in this paper are agnostic to the underlying solving procedure, so they can be combined with all of these approaches.

2 Preliminaries

We work in the context of many-sorted first-order logic with equality and assume the reader is familiar with the notions of signature, term, literal, formula, and formal interpretation of formulas. We review a few relevant definitions in the following. A *theory* is a pair $T = (\Sigma, \mathbf{I})$ where Σ is a signature and $\mathbf{I}$ is a class of Σ-interpretations, the *models* of T. We assume Σ contains the equality predicate $\approx$, interpreted as the identity relation, and the predicates $\top$ (for true) and $\bot$ (for false). A Σ-formula φ is *satisfiable* (resp., *unsatisfiable*) *in* T if it is satisfied by some (resp., no) interpretation in $\mathbf{I}$. We write $\models_T \varphi$ to denote that the Σ-formula φ is T-*valid*, i.e., is satisfied in every model of T. Two Σ-terms t_1 and t_2 are *equivalent in* T if $\models_T t_1 \approx t_2$.

We consider an extended theory T_{S} of strings and length equations, whose signature Σ_{S} is given in Fig. 1 and whose models differ only on how they interpret variables.[1] We assume a fixed finite alphabet $\mathcal{A}$ of characters which includes the digits $\{0, \ldots, 9\}$. The signature includes the sorts Bool, Int, and Str denoting the Booleans, the integers ($\mathbb{Z}$), and Kleene closure of $\mathcal{A}$ ($\mathcal{A}^*$), respectively. The top half of Fig. 1 includes the usual symbols of *linear* integer arithmetic, interpreted as expected, a *string literal* l for each word/string of $\mathcal{A}^*$, a variadic function symbol con, interpreted as word concatenation, and a function symbol len, interpreted as the word length function. We write ϵ for the empty word and abbreviate $\mathsf{len}(s)$ as $|s|$. We use words over the characters a, b, and c, as in abca, as concrete examples of string literals.

We refer to the function symbols in the bottom half of the figure as *extended functions* and refer to terms containing them as *extended terms*. A *position* in

[1] Our implementation supports a larger set of symbols, but for brevity, we only show the subset of the symbols used throughout this paper.

n : Int for all $n \in \mathbb{N}$	$+$: Int × Int → Int	$-$: Int → Int	$\geqslant$: Int × Int → Bool
l : Str for all $l \in \mathcal{A}^*$	con : Str × ⋯ × Str → Str		len : Str → Int

substr :	Str × Int × Int → Str	contains :	Str × Str → Bool
indexof :	Str × Str × Int → Int	replace :	Str × Str × Str → Str
str.to.int :	Str → Int	int.to.str :	Int → Str

Fig. 1. Functions in signature Σ_{S}. Str and Int denote strings and integers respectively.

a string $l \in \mathcal{A}^*$ is a non-negative integer n smaller than the length of l that identifies the $(n+1)^{th}$ character of l—with 0 identifying the first character, 1 the second, and so on. For all models $\mathcal{I}$ of T_{S}, all $l, l_1, l_2 \in \mathcal{A}^*$, and $n, m \in \mathbb{Z}$, $\mathsf{substr}^{\mathcal{I}}(l, n, m)$ (the interpretation of substr in $\mathcal{I}$ applied to l, n, m) is the longest substring of l starting at position n with length at most m, or ϵ if n is an invalid position or m is not positive; $\mathsf{contains}^{\mathcal{I}}(l_1, l_2)$ is true if and only if l_2 is a substring of l_1, with ϵ being a substring of every string; $\mathsf{indexof}^{\mathcal{I}}(l_1, l_2, n)$ is the position of the first occurrence of l_2 in l_1 at or after position n, n if l_2 is empty and $0 \leqslant n \leqslant |l_1|$, and -1 if n is an invalid position, or if no such occurrence exists; $\mathsf{replace}^{\mathcal{I}}(l, l_1, l_2)$ is the result of replacing the first occurrence of l_1 in l by l_2, l if l does not contain l_1, or the result of prepending l_2 to l if l_1 is empty; $\mathsf{str.to.int}^{\mathcal{I}}(l)$ is the non-negative integer represented by l in decimal notation or -1 if the string contains non-digit characters; $\mathsf{int.to.str}^{\mathcal{I}}(n)$ is the result of converting n to the corresponding string in decimal notation if n is non-negative, or ϵ otherwise. We write $\mathsf{substr}(t, u)$ as shorthand for the term $\mathsf{substr}(t, u, |t|)$, i.e. the suffix of t starting at position u.

Note that the semantics for replace and indexof correspond to the semantics in the current draft of the SMT-LIB standard for the theory of strings [17]; they are slightly different from the ones described in previous work [4,15,20].

2.1 Solving Extended String Constraints (with Simplification)

Various efficient solvers have been designed for the satisfiability problem for quantifier-free T_{S}-constraints, including CVC4 [3], S3# [20] and Z3STR3 [4]. In this section, we give an overview of how these solvers process extended functions in practice.

Generally speaking, constraints involving extended functions are converted to basic ones through a series of reductions performed in an incremental fashion by the solver. Operators whose reduction requires universal quantification are dealt with by guessing upper bounds on the lengths of input strings or by lazily adding constraints that block models that do not satisfy extended string constraints.

Example 1. To determine the satisfiability of $\neg\mathsf{contains}(t, s)$, the application of contains is reduced to constraints that ensure that s is not a substring of t at any position. Assuming we have a fixed upper bound n on the length of t, the above constraint is equivalent to the finite conjunction $\mathsf{substr}(t, 0, |s|) \not\approx s \wedge \cdots \wedge \mathsf{substr}(t, n, |s|) \not\approx s$. Each application of substr is then eliminated by introducing an equality that constrains a fresh variable x_i to have the semantics of that substring. Thus, reducing the formula above results in

$$\bigwedge_{i=0}^{n} |t| \geqslant i + |s| \Rightarrow (x_i \not\approx s \wedge t \approx \mathsf{con}(x_i^{pre}, x_i, x_i^{post}) \wedge |x_i^{pre}| \approx i \wedge |x_i| \approx |s|\ )$$

where $x_i, x_i^{pre}, x_i^{post}$ are fresh string variables.[2] The above conjunction involves only string concatenation, string length, and equality, and thus can be handled by a string solver with support for word equations with length constraints.

The reduction in Example 1 introduces $5 \cdot n$ theory literals over basic string functions and $3 \cdot n$ string variables. A full reduction accounting for all corner cases of substr is even more complex and thus more expensive to process, even for small values of n. These performance challenges can be addressed by aggressive simplifications that *eliminate* extended functions using high-level reasoning, as shown in the next example.

Example 2. Consider an instance of the previous example where $s = \mathsf{con}(\mathsf{a}, x)$ and $t = \mathsf{con}(\mathsf{b}, \mathsf{substr}(x, 0, n))$. A full reduction of $\neg\mathsf{contains}(t, s)$ that eliminates all applications of substr, including those in t, introduces $5 \cdot n + 5$ new theory literals and $3 \cdot n + 3$ string variables. However, based on the semantics of contains it is easy to see that $\neg\mathsf{contains}(t, s)$ is T_S-valid: if t were to contain s, then s would have to occur in the portion of t after its first character b, since the first character of s is a. However, $\mathsf{con}(\mathsf{a}, x)$ cannot be contained in $\mathsf{substr}(x, 0, n)$, since the length of the former is at least $|x| + 1$, while the length of the latter is at most $|x|$. A solver which recognizes that $\neg\mathsf{contains}(t, s)$ can be simplified to $\top$ in this case can avoid the reduction altogether.

We advocate for aggressive simplification techniques to improve the performance of string solvers for extended functions. In the next sections, we describe several classes of such techniques that can be applied to inputs as a preprocessing step or during solving as part of a context-dependent solving strategy [15]. We present them as sets R of rewrite rules of the form $t \rightarrow_R s$, where s is a (simplified) term equivalent to t in T_S. We assume a deterministic application strategy for these rules, such that each term t rewrites to a unique *simplified form*, denoted by $t\!\downarrow$, which is irreducible by the rules. We split our simplifications into four categories, presented in Figs. 4, 6, 7 and 8.[3]

3 Arithmetic-Based String Simplification

To simplify string terms, it is useful to establish relationships between quantities such as the lengths of strings. For example, $\mathsf{contains}(t, s)$ can be simplified to $\bot$

[2] This formula is a simplified form of the general reduction. The general reduction also expresses that i is a valid position in t and that the third argument of substr is non-negative [15].

[3] Some specialized rules have been omitted for space reasons.

for a particular s and t if it can be inferred that $|s|$ is strictly greater than $|t|$. This section defines an inference system for such arithmetic relationships and the simplifications that it enables.

We are interested in proving the T_S-validity of formulas of the form $u \geqslant 0$, where u is a Σ_S-term of integer type. We describe an inference system as a set of rules for deriving judgments of the form $\vdash u \geqslant 0$ and a specific rule application strategy we have implemented. The inference system is *sound* in the sense that $\models_{T_\mathsf{S}} u \geqslant 0$ whenever $\vdash u \geqslant 0$ is derivable in it. It is, however, *incomplete* as it may fail to derive $\vdash u \geqslant 0$ in some cases when $\models_{T_\mathsf{S}} u \geqslant 0$. This incompleteness is by design, since proving the T_S-validity of inequalities is generally expensive due to the NP-hardness of linear integer arithmetic. Without loss of generality, we require that the term u be in a simplified form, where terms of the form $|l|$ with l a string literal of n characters are rewritten to n, terms of the form $|\mathsf{con}(t_1, \ldots, t_n)|$ are rewritten to $|t_1| + \cdots + |t_n|$, and like monomials in arithmetic terms are combined in the usual way (e.g., $2 \cdot |x| + |x|$ is rewritten to $3 \cdot |x|$).

Definition 1 (Polynomial Form). *An arithmetic term u is in polynomial form if $u = m_1 \cdot u_1 + \ldots m_n \cdot u_n + m$, where $m_1, \ldots, m_n$ are non-zero integer constants, m is an integer constant, and each $u_1, \ldots, u_n$ is a unique term and one of the following:*

1. *an integer variable,*
2. *an application of length to a string variable, e.g. $|x|$,*
3. *an application of length to an extended function, e.g. $|\mathsf{substr}(t, v, w)|$, or*
4. *an application of an extended function of integer type, e.g. $\mathsf{indexof}(t, s, v)$.*

Given u in polynomial form, our inference system uses a set of over- and under-approximations for showing that $u \geqslant 0$ holds in all models of T_S. We define two auxiliary rewrite systems, denoted $\rightarrow_O$ and $\rightarrow_U$. If u rewrites to v (in zero or more steps) in $\rightarrow_O$, written $u \rightarrow_O^* v$, we say that v is *an over-approximation* of u. We can prove in that case that $\models_{T_\mathsf{S}} v \geqslant u$. Dually, if u rewrites to v in $\rightarrow_U$, written $u \rightarrow_U^* v$, we say that v is *an under-approximation* of u and can prove that $\models_{T_\mathsf{S}} u \geqslant v$. Based on these definitions, the core of our inference system can be summarized by the single inference rule schema provided in Fig. 2 together with the conditional rewrite systems $\rightarrow_O$ and $\rightarrow_U$ which are defined inductively in terms of the inference system and each other.

A majority of the rewrite rules have side conditions requiring the derivability of certain judgments in the same inference system. To improve their readability we take some liberties with the notation and write $\vdash u_1 \geqslant u_2$, say, instead of $\vdash u_1 - u_2 \geqslant 0$. For example, $|\mathsf{substr}(t, v, w)|$ is under-approximated by w if it can be inferred that the interval from v to $v + w$ is a valid range of positions in string t, which is expressed by the side conditions $\vdash v \geqslant 0$ and $\vdash |t| \geqslant v + w$. Note that some arithmetic terms, such as $|\mathsf{substr}(t, v, w)|$, can be approximated in *multiple* ways—hence the need for a strategy for choosing the best approximation for arithmetic string terms, described later. The rules for polynomials are written modulo associativity of + and state that a monomial $m \cdot v$ in them can be over- or under-approximated based on the sign of the coefficient m. For simplicity,

$$\frac{u \rightarrow_U^* n \quad n \geqslant 0}{\vdash u \geqslant 0} \quad \text{where}$$

$$\begin{array}{rll}
|t| \rightarrow_U & 0 & \\
|\mathsf{substr}(t, v, w)| \rightarrow_U & \begin{cases} w & \text{if } \vdash v \geqslant 0 \text{ and } \vdash |t| \geqslant v + w \\ |t| - v & \text{if } \vdash v \geqslant 0 \text{ and } \vdash v + w \geqslant |t| \end{cases} & \\
|\mathsf{replace}(t, s, r)| \rightarrow_U & \begin{cases} |t| & \text{if } \vdash |r| \geqslant |s| \text{ or } \vdash |r| \geqslant |t| \\ |t| - |s| & \end{cases} & \\
|\mathsf{int.to.str}(v)| \rightarrow_U & 1 \quad \text{if } \vdash v \geqslant 0 & \\
\mathsf{indexof}(t, s, v) \rightarrow_U & -1 & \\
\mathsf{str.to.int}(t) \rightarrow_U & -1 & \\
m \cdot v + u' \rightarrow_U & m \cdot w + u' \text{ if } v \rightarrow_U w \text{ and } m > 0 \text{ or } v \rightarrow_O w \text{ and } m < 0 & \\
\\
|\mathsf{substr}(t, v, w)| \rightarrow_O & w \quad \text{if } \vdash w \geqslant 0 & \\
|\mathsf{substr}(t, v, w)| \rightarrow_O & \begin{cases} |t| - v & \text{if } \vdash |t| \geqslant v \\ |t| & \end{cases} & \\
|\mathsf{replace}(t, s, r)| \rightarrow_O & \begin{cases} |t| & \text{if } \vdash |s| \geqslant |r| \\ |t| + |r| & \end{cases} & \\
|\mathsf{int.to.str}(v)| \rightarrow_O & \begin{cases} v & \text{if } \vdash v > 0 \\ v + 1 & \text{if } \vdash v \geqslant 0 \end{cases} & \\
\mathsf{indexof}(t, s, v) \rightarrow_O & \begin{cases} |t| - |s| & \text{if } \vdash |t| \geqslant |s| \\ |t| & \end{cases} & \\
m \cdot v + u' \rightarrow_O & m \cdot w + u' \text{ if } v \rightarrow_O w \text{ and } m > 0 \text{ or } v \rightarrow_U w \text{ and } m < 0 &
\end{array}$$

Fig. 2. Rules for arithmetic entailment based on under- and over-approximations computed for arithmetic terms containing extended string operators. We write t, s, r to denote string terms, u, u', v, w to denote integer terms and m, n to denote integer constants.

we silently assume in the figure that basic arithmetic simplifications are applied after each rewrite step to put the right-hand side in polynomial form.

Example 3. Let u be $|\mathsf{replace}(x, \mathsf{aa}, \mathsf{b})|$. Because $\vdash |\mathsf{aa}| \geqslant |\mathsf{b}|$, the first case of the over-approximation rule for replace applies, and we get that $u \rightarrow_O |x|$. This reflects that the result of replacing the first occurrence, if any, of aa in x with b is no longer than x.

Example 4. Let u be the same as in the previous example and let v be $-1 \cdot u + 2 \cdot |x|$. Since $u \rightarrow_O |x|$ and the coefficient of u in v is negative, we have that $v \rightarrow_U -1 \cdot |x| + 2 \cdot |x|$, which simplifies to $|x|$; moreover, $|x| \rightarrow_U 0$. Thus, $v \rightarrow_U^* 0$ and so $\vdash v \geqslant 0$. In other words, we can use the approximations to show that u is at most $2 \cdot |x|$.

3.1 A Strategy for Approximation

The rewrite systems $\rightarrow_O$ and $\rightarrow_U$ allow for many possible derivations. Thus, it is important to devise a strategy that is efficient and succeeds often in practice. We use a greedy rule application strategy that favors rule applications leading to the cancellation of monomials. For example, consider the term $|x| - |\mathsf{substr}(y, 0, |x|)|$, and observe that the subtrahend can be over-approximated either by $|y|$ or by $|x|$. However, proving the T_S-validity of $|x| - |\mathsf{substr}(y, 0, |x|)| \geqslant 0$ with the former over-approximation is impossible since $|x| - |y| \geqslant 0$ does not hold in all models of T_S. In contrast, the latter approximation produces $|x| - |x| \geqslant 0$ which is trivially T_S-valid.

STR-ARITH-APPROX(u), where $u = u_x + u_\ell + u_s + m$ and:
- $u_x = m^y_1 \cdot y_1 + \ldots + m^y_n \cdot y_n$,
- $u_\ell = m^\ell_1 \cdot |x_1| + \ldots + m^\ell_p \cdot |x_p|$,
- $u_s = m^v_1 \cdot v_1 + \ldots + m^v_q \cdot v_q$.

for variables $x_1, \ldots, x_p, y_1, \ldots, y_n$ and extended terms $v_1, \ldots v_q$:
1. If $q > 0$, choose a v_i and v^a_i that maximize the following criteria (in descending order), where $u' = (u[m^v_i \cdot v_i \mapsto m^v_i \cdot v^a_i])\downarrow$:
   (a) (Soundness) $v_i \rightarrow_U v^a_i$ if $m^v_i > 0$ and $v_i \rightarrow_O v^a_i$ if $m^v_i < 0$;
   (b) (Avoids new terms) Minimizes the size of $\mathsf{negcoeff}(u') \backslash \mathsf{negcoeff}(u)$;
   (c) (Cancels existing terms) Maximizes the size of $\mathsf{negcoeff}(u) \backslash \mathsf{negcoeff}(u')$.
   Return $u \rightarrow_U u'$.
2. If $p > 0$ and $m^\ell_j > 0$ for some j, return $u \rightarrow_U (u[m^\ell_j \cdot |x_j| \mapsto 0])\downarrow$.

Fig. 3. A greedy strategy for showing arithmetic entailments in the theory T_S. We write $\mathsf{negcoeff}(u)$ to denote the set of terms whose coefficient is negative in u.

Recall that, given an arithmetic inequality $u \geqslant 0$, our goal is to find a reduction $u \rightarrow^*_U n$ where n is a non-negative constant. Our strategy for choosing which rule of $\rightarrow_U$ to apply to u is given in Fig. 3. We decompose u into three parts: the portion u_x consisting of a sum of integer variables, the portion u_ℓ consisting of a sum of lengths of string variables, and the remaining portion u_s which is a sum of monomials involving extended terms $v_1, \ldots, v_q$ as defined in Definition 1.

Since there are multiple choices for how terms in u_s are approximated, the strategy focuses primarily on this portion. In particular, we apply an approximation for one of the terms v_i, under-approximating or over-approximating depending on the sign of its coefficient, and replace the monomial in t by its corresponding approximation. The choice of v_i and v^a_i is based on maximizing the likelihood that the overall derivation will produce a non-negative constant.

For a term u in polynomial form, let $\mathsf{negcoeff}(u)$ be a set of integer terms whose coefficient is negative in u, e.g. $\mathsf{negcoeff}(y_1 + -1 \cdot y_2) = \{y_2\}$. Terms in this set can be seen as *obligations* for proving entailments in our derivations since if $y_2 \in \mathsf{negcoeff}(u)$, it must be the case that our derivation applies a rule that introduces a term with a positive coefficient for y_2. In Fig. 3, we say that our choice of $v_i \rightarrow_U v^a_i$ *avoids new terms* if it does not have the effect of adding any new terms to $\mathsf{negcoeff}(u)$, and *cancels existing terms* if it has the effect of removing terms from this set. If the portion u_s is empty, we apply the rule $|x_j| \rightarrow_U 0$ if there exists a monomial $m^\ell_j \cdot |x_j|$ where m^ℓ_j is positive. This rule is applied with lowest priority because these monomials may help to cancel negative terms introduced by the other steps.

Step 1 depends on knowing the set of possible one-step approximations $v_i \to_U v_i^a$ and $v_i \to_O v_i^a$ for terms from u. These are determined using the rules of Fig. 2. Whenever applicable, we break ties between rewrites in Step 1 by considering a fixed arbitrary ordering over extended terms.

Example 5. Let u be $1 + |t_1| + |t_2| - |x_1|$, where t_1 is $\mathsf{substr}(x_2, 1, |x_2| + |x_4|)$ and t_2 is $\mathsf{replace}(x_1, x_2, x_3)$. Step 1 of STR-ARITH-APPROX considers the possible approximations $|t_1| \to_U |x_2| - 1$ and $|t_2| \to_U |x_1| - |x_2|$. Note that under-approximations are needed because the coefficients of $|t_1|$ and $|t_2|$ are positive. The first approximation is an instance of the third rule in Fig. 2, noting that both $\vdash 1 \geqslant 0$ and $\vdash 1 + |x_2| + |x_4| \geqslant |x_2|$ are derivable by a *basic* strategy that, wherever applicable, under-approximates string length terms as zero. Our strategy chooses the first approximation since it introduces no new negative coefficient terms, thus obtaining: $u \to_U |x_2| + |t_2| - |x_1|$. We now choose the approximation $|t_2| \to_U |x_1| - |x_2|$, noting that it introduces no new negative coefficient terms and cancels an existing one, $|x_1|$. After arithmetic simplification, we have derived $u \to_U^* 0$, and hence $\vdash u \geqslant 0$.

One can show that our strategy is sound, terminating, and deterministic. This means that applying STR-ARITH-APPROX to completion produces a unique rewrite chain of the form $t \to_U u_1 \to_U \dots \to_U u_n$ for a finite n, where each step is an application of one of the rewrite rules from Fig. 2.

3.2 Simplification Rules with Arithmetic Side Conditions

We use the inference system from the previous section for simplifications of string terms with arithmetic side conditions. Figure 4 summarizes those simplifications.

The first rule rewrites a string equality to $\bot$ if one of the two sides can be inferred to be strictly longer than the other. In the second rule, if one side of an equality, $\mathsf{con}(s, r, q)$, is such that the sum of lengths of s and q alone can be shown to be greater than or equal to the length of the other side, then r must be empty. The third rule recognizes that string containment reduces to string

$$
\begin{array}{rll}
t \approx s \to & \bot & \text{if } \vdash |t| \geqslant |s| + 1 \\
t \approx \mathsf{con}(s, r, q) \to & t \approx \mathsf{con}(s, q) \wedge r \approx \epsilon & \text{if } \vdash |s| + |q| \geqslant |t| \\
\mathsf{contains}(t, s) \to & t \approx s & \text{if } \vdash |s| \geqslant |t| \\
\mathsf{substr}(t, v, w) \to & \epsilon & \text{if } \vdash 0 > v \vee v \geqslant |t| \vee 0 \geqslant w \\
\mathsf{substr}(\mathsf{con}(t, s), v, w) \to & \mathsf{substr}(s, v - |t|, w) & \text{if } \vdash v \geqslant |t| \\
\mathsf{substr}(\mathsf{con}(s, t), v, w) \to & \mathsf{substr}(s, v, w) & \text{if } \vdash |s| \geqslant v + w \\
\mathsf{substr}(\mathsf{con}(t, s), 0, w) \to & \mathsf{con}(t, \mathsf{substr}(s, 0, w - |t|)) & \text{if } \vdash w \geqslant |t| \\
\mathsf{indexof}(t, s, v) \to & \mathsf{ite}(\mathsf{substr}(t, v) \approx s, v, -1) & \text{if } \vdash v + |s| \geqslant |t|
\end{array}
$$

Fig. 4. String simplification rules. Letters t, s, r, q denote string terms; v, w denote integer terms.

equality when it can be inferred that string s is at least as long as the string t that must contain it. The next rule captures the fact that substring simplifies to the empty string if it can be inferred that its position v is not within bounds, or its length w is not positive. In the figure, we write that rule with a disjunctive side condition; this is a shorthand to denote that we can pick any disjunct and show that it holds assuming the negation of the other disjuncts. We can use those assumptions to perform substitutions to simplify the derivation. Concretely, to show $\vdash u_1 \geqslant u_2 \vee \ldots \vee u \not\approx u'$ it is sufficient to infer $\vdash (u_1 \geqslant u_2)[u \mapsto u']$. We demonstrate this with an example.

Example 6. Consider the term $\mathsf{substr}(t, |t| + w, w)$. Our rules may simplify this term to ϵ by inferring that its start position $(|t| + w)$ is not within the bounds of t if we assume that its size (w) is positive. In detail, assume that $w > 0$ (the negation of the last disjunct in the side condition of the fourth rule), which is equivalent to $w \approx |x| + 1$ where x is a fresh string variable and $|x|$ denotes an unknown non-negative quantity. It is sufficient to derive the formula obtained by replacing all occurrences of w by $|x| + 1$ in the disjunct $|t| + w \geqslant |t|$ to show that the start position of our term is out of bounds. After simplification, we obtain $|x| + 1 \geqslant 0$, which is trivial to derive.

The next two rules in Fig. 4 apply if we can infer respectively that the start position of the substring comes strictly after a prefix t or that the end position of the substring comes strictly before a suffix t of the first argument string. In either case, t can be dropped.

Example 7. Let t be $\mathsf{substr}(\mathsf{con}(x_1, \mathsf{replace}(x_2, x_3, x_4)), 0, w)$, where w is $|x_1| - |x_2|$. We have that $t \rightarrow \mathsf{substr}(x_1, 0, w)$, noting that $\vdash |x_1| \geqslant 0 + |x_1| - |x_2|$. In other words, only the first component x_1 of the string concatenation is relevant to the substring since its end point must occur before the end of x_1.

The final rule for substr shows that a prefix of a substring can be pulled upwards if the start position is zero and we can infer that the substring is guaranteed to include at least a prefix string t. Finally, if we can infer that the last position of s in t starting from position v is at or beyond the end of t, then the indexof term can be rewritten as an if-then-else (ite) term that checks whether s is a suffix of t.

4 Containment-Based String Simplification

This section provides an overview of simplifications that are based on reasoning about the containment relationship between strings. We describe an inference system for deriving when one string is definitely contained or not contained in another. Following the notation from the last section, we write $\vdash t \ni s$ to denote the judgment of our inference system, denoting that string t contains string s in all models of T_{S}. Conversely, we write $\vdash t \not\ni s$ to denote string t does not contain string s. We write $\vdash t \ni^p s$ (resp., $\vdash t \ni^s s$) to denote the judgment indicating that s must be a prefix (resp., suffix) of t.

$$\frac{l_1 \text{ contains } l_2}{\vdash \mathsf{con}(l_1, t) \ni l_2} \qquad \frac{\vdash s \ni r}{\vdash \mathsf{con}(t, s) \ni r} \qquad \frac{\vdash t \ni^s r \quad \vdash s \ni^p q}{\vdash \mathsf{con}(t, s) \ni \mathsf{con}(r, q)} \qquad \frac{}{\vdash t \ni \mathsf{substr}(t, v, w)}$$

$$\frac{l_1 \text{ does not contain } l_2}{\vdash l_1 \not\ni \mathsf{con}(l_2, t)} \qquad \frac{\vdash r \not\ni t}{\vdash r \not\ni \mathsf{con}(s, t)} \qquad \frac{\vdash l_1 \setminus l_2 \not\ni t}{\vdash l_1 \not\ni \mathsf{con}(l_2, t)}$$

$$\frac{l_2 \text{ is a prefix of } l_1}{\vdash \mathsf{con}(l_1, t) \ni^p l_2} \qquad \frac{\vdash s \ni^p r}{\vdash \mathsf{con}(t, s) \ni^p \mathsf{con}(t, r)} \qquad \frac{}{\vdash t \ni^p t} \qquad \frac{\vdash v \leqslant 0}{\vdash t \ni^p \mathsf{substr}(t, v, w)}$$

$$\frac{l_2 \text{ is a suffix of } l_1}{\vdash \mathsf{con}(t, l_1) \ni^s l_2} \qquad \frac{\vdash s \ni^s r}{\vdash \mathsf{con}(s, t) \ni^s \mathsf{con}(r, t)} \qquad \frac{}{\vdash t \ni^s t} \qquad \frac{\vdash v + w \geqslant |t|}{\vdash t \ni^s \mathsf{substr}(t, v, w)}$$

Fig. 5. Inferences for string containment $\ni$, is-prefix $\ni^p$ and is-suffix $\ni^s$.

Rules for inferring judgments of these forms are given in Fig. 5. Like our rules for arithmetic, these rules are solely based on the syntactic structure of terms, so inferences in this system can be computed statically. Both the assumptions and conclusions of the rules assume associativity of string concatenation with identity element ϵ, that is, $\mathsf{con}(t, s)$ may refer to a term of the form $\mathsf{con}(\mathsf{con}(t_1, t_2), s) = \mathsf{con}(t_1, t_2, s)$ or alternatively to $\mathsf{con}(\epsilon, s) = s$. Most of the rules are straightforward. The inference system has special rules for substring terms $\mathsf{substr}(t, v, w)$, using arithmetic entailments from Sect. 3 to show prefix and suffix relationships with the base string t. For negative containment, the rules of the inference system together can show a (possibly non-constant) string cannot occur in a constant string by reasoning that its characters cannot appear in order in that string. We write $l_1 \setminus l_2$ to denote the empty string if l_1 does not contain l_2, or the result of removing the smallest prefix of l_1 that contains l_2 from l_1 otherwise.

Example 8. Let t be abcab and let s be $\mathsf{con}(\mathsf{b}, x, \mathsf{a}, y, \mathsf{c})$. String s is not contained in t for any value of x, y. We derive $\vdash t \not\ni s$ using two applications of the rightmost rule for negative containment in Fig. 5, noting abcab $\setminus$ b = cab, cab $\setminus$ a = b, and b does not contain c. In other words, the containment does not hold since the characters b, a and c cannot be found in order in the constant abcad.

4.1 Simplification Rules Based on String Containment

Figure 6 gives rules for simplifying extended function terms based on the aforementioned judgments pertaining to string containment. First, equalities can be rewritten to false and applications of contains can be rewritten to a constant based on the appropriate judgment of our inference system. Applications of indexof can be simplified to -1 if it can be shown that the second argument does not appear in the suffix of the first argument starting at the position given by the third argument. The next two rules reason about cases where the second argument s definitely occurs in the first argument starting from position v. In this case, if we additionally know that s occurs within (beyond) a prefix t of

$$
\begin{array}{rll}
t \approx s \rightarrow & \bot & \text{if } \vdash t \not\ni s \\
\mathsf{contains}(t, s) \rightarrow & \bot & \text{if } \vdash t \not\ni s \\
\mathsf{contains}(t, s) \rightarrow & \top & \text{if } \vdash t \ni s \\
\mathsf{indexof}(t, s, v) \rightarrow & -1 & \text{if } \vdash \mathsf{substr}(t, v) \not\ni s \\
\mathsf{indexof}(\mathsf{con}(t, r), s, v) \rightarrow & \mathsf{indexof}(t, s, v) & \text{if } \vdash \mathsf{substr}(t, v) \ni s \\
\mathsf{indexof}(\mathsf{con}(t, r), s, v) \rightarrow & \mathsf{indexof}(r, s, v - |t|) + |t| & \text{if } \vdash \mathsf{substr}(\mathsf{con}(t, r), v) \ni s \text{ and} \\
 & & \vdash v \geqslant |t| \\
\mathsf{indexof}(t, s, v) \rightarrow & v & \text{if } \vdash \mathsf{substr}(t, v) \ni^p s \text{ and } \vdash v < |t| \\
\mathsf{replace}(t, s, r) \rightarrow & t & \text{if } \vdash t \not\ni s \\
\mathsf{replace}(\mathsf{con}(t, q), s, r) \rightarrow & \mathsf{con}(\mathsf{replace}(t, s, r), q) & \text{if } \vdash t \ni s \\
\mathsf{replace}(t, s, r) \rightarrow & \mathsf{con}(r, \mathsf{substr}(t, |s|)) & \text{if } \vdash t \ni^p s
\end{array}
$$

Fig. 6. Simplification rules based on string containment.

the first argument, then the suffix r (prefix t) can be dropped, where the start position and the return value of the result are modified accordingly. If we know s is a prefix of the first argument at position v, then the result is v if indeed v is in the bounds of t. Notice that the latter condition is necessary to handle the case where s is the empty string. The three rules for replace are analogous. First, the replace rewrites to the first argument if we know it does not contain the second argument s. If we know s is definitely contained in a prefix of the first argument, then we can pull the remainder of that string upwards. Finally, if we know s is a prefix of the first argument, then we can replace that prefix with r while concatenating the remainder. We use the term $\mathsf{substr}(t, |s|)$ to denote the remainder after the replacement for the sake of brevity, although this term typically does not involve extended functions after simplification, e.g. $\mathsf{replace}(\mathsf{con}(x, y), x, z) \rightarrow \mathsf{con}(z, y)$ noting that $(\mathsf{substr}(\mathsf{con}(x, y), |x|))\downarrow = y$, or $\mathsf{replace}(\mathsf{ab}, \mathsf{a}, x) \rightarrow \mathsf{con}(x, \mathsf{b})$ noting that $(\mathsf{substr}(\mathsf{ab}, |\mathsf{a}|))\downarrow = \mathsf{b}$.

4.2 Simplifications Based on Equivalence of String Containment

We further refine our approach based on inferring when one containment is *equivalent* to another one. For example, $\mathsf{con}(\mathsf{a}, x)$ is contained in $\mathsf{con}(\mathsf{b}, y)$ if and only if $\mathsf{con}(\mathsf{a}, x)$ is contained in y alone. We introduce simplifications for such equivalences by reasoning about the maximal overlap between two strings.

We adapt and extend the notation given in previous work [15]. Given string literals l_1 and l_2, the *sufficient left overlap* of l_1 and l_2, written $l_1 \sqcup_l l_2$, is the largest suffix of l_1 that is a prefix of l_2 or has l_2 as a prefix. For example, we have $\mathsf{abc} \sqcup_l \mathsf{cd} = \mathsf{c}$, $\mathsf{abc} \sqcup_l \mathsf{b} = \mathsf{bc}$, and $\mathsf{abc} \sqcup_l \mathsf{ba} = \epsilon$. We extend this definition to arbitrary strings s such that $l_1 \sqcup_l s$ is equivalent to $l_1 \sqcup_l l_2$ for the largest constant prefix l_2 of s, where notice that l_2 is the empty string if s does not have a constant prefix. For example, we have $\mathsf{abc} \sqcup_l \mathsf{con}(\mathsf{cde}, y) = \mathsf{c}$, $\mathsf{abc} \sqcup_l \mathsf{con}(\mathsf{b}, y) = \mathsf{bc}$, and $\mathsf{abc} \sqcup_l \mathsf{con}(\mathsf{a}, y) = \mathsf{abc}$. We define the dual operator *sufficient right overlap*, written $l_1 \sqcup_r l_2$, which is the largest prefix of l_1 that is a suffix of l_2 or has l_2 as a suffix, e.g. $\mathsf{abc} \sqcup_r \mathsf{b} = \mathsf{ab}$, and extend this to arbitrary strings in an analogous way. The sufficient left (resp., right) overlap operator can be used to determine how much of a constant string prefix l_1 (resp., suffix) can be safely removed from a string without impacting whether it contains another string.

$$
\begin{array}{rlr}
\mathsf{contains}(\mathsf{con}(t, l), s) \rightarrow & \mathsf{contains}(\mathsf{con}(t, l \sqcup_r s), s) & \\
\mathsf{contains}(\mathsf{con}(l, t), s) \rightarrow & \mathsf{contains}(\mathsf{con}(l \sqcup_l s, t), s) & \\
\mathsf{indexof}(\mathsf{con}(t, l), s, v) \rightarrow & \mathsf{indexof}(\mathsf{con}(t, l \sqcup_r s), s, v) & \\
\mathsf{indexof}(\mathsf{con}(l, t), s, v) \rightarrow & \mathsf{indexof}(\mathsf{con}(l_2, t), s, v - |l_1|) & \text{if } l = l_1 \cdot l_2 \text{ and } l_2 = l \sqcup_l s \\
 & +|l_1| & \vdash \mathsf{substr}(\mathsf{con}(l, t), v) \ni s \\
\mathsf{replace}(\mathsf{con}(t, l), s, r) \rightarrow & \mathsf{con}(\mathsf{replace}(\mathsf{con}(t, l_1), s, r), l_2) & \text{if } l = l_1 \cdot l_2 \text{ and } l_1 = l \sqcup_r s \\
\mathsf{replace}(\mathsf{con}(l, t), s, r) \rightarrow & \mathsf{con}(l_1, \mathsf{replace}(\mathsf{con}(l_2, t), s, r)) & \text{if } l = l_1 \cdot l_2 \text{ and } l_2 = l \sqcup_l s
\end{array}
$$

Fig. 7. Simplification rules based on equivalence of string containment. We write l, l_1, l_2 to denote string literals, v, w to denote integer terms and t, s to denote string terms.

The rules in Fig. 7 simplify extended terms by considering string overlaps. The first two rules drop parts of string literals from the suffix or prefix of their first arguments. The two rules for indexof are similar: a suffix of the first argument can be dropped if it does not contribute to whether it contains the second argument. A prefix of an indexof term can be dropped if it does not contribute to containment, but only in the case where we know the second argument is definitely contained in the first argument. This is to guard against the case where the entire indexof term returns -1. The rules for replace are similar to those for contains, except that the suffix (resp., prefix) of the first argument is pulled upwards instead of being dropped.

5 Multiset-Based String Simplification

Next, we introduce simplifications based on reasoning about strings as multisets, i.e. collections of unordered characters. Such reasoning is sufficient for showing that equalities like $\mathsf{con}(\mathsf{a}, x) \approx \mathsf{con}(x, \mathsf{b})$ are equivalent to $\bot$, since the left side of the equality contains exactly one more occurrence of character a than the right-hand side. Similar to arithmetic reasoning from Sect. 3, we use approximations when reasoning about strings as multisets. We define the *multiset abstraction* of t, written $\mathcal{M}_t$, as the multiset $\{t_1, \dots, t_n\}$ where t is equivalent to $\mathsf{con}(t_1, \dots, t_n)$ and all constants in this set are characters. For example, $\mathcal{M}_{\mathsf{con}(\mathsf{aba}, x)} = \{\mathsf{a}, \mathsf{a}, \mathsf{b}, x\}$. We define a rewrite system $\rightarrow_O^{\mathcal{M}}$ over strings where a rewritten string over-approximates the original string in the following sense: if $t \rightarrow_O^{\mathcal{M}} s$, then for all models of T_S and any character c, the number of occurrences of c in the strings in $\mathcal{M}_s$ is greater than or equal to the number of occurrences in the strings in $\mathcal{M}_t$.

Figure 8 lists the rules for the rewrite system $\rightarrow_O^{\mathcal{M}}$ and the simplifications based on multiset reasoning. Given a predicate $\mathsf{contains}(t, s)$, if over-approximating t with respect to the rules of $\rightarrow_O^{\mathcal{M}}$ results in a string r, and it can be determined that s contains strictly more occurrences of some character

c than r, then it cannot be the case that s is contained in t. To establish this, we check whether the multiset difference of $\mathcal{M}_s$ and $\mathcal{M}_r$ contains c, and conversely the difference of $\mathcal{M}_r$ and $\mathcal{M}_s$ contains only character constants which are distinct from c. In the second rule, if one side of an equality can be determined to contain *only* a character c, then one occurrence of that character can be dropped from both sides of the equality, since the relative position of that character does not matter. The three rules for $\rightarrow_O^{\mathcal{M}}$ state that the multiset abstraction of a term of the form $\mathsf{substr}(t, v, w)$ can be over-approximated as the entire string t; a term $\mathsf{replace}(t, s, r)$ can be over-approximated as a string having both t and r; and over-approximation can be applied to the children of con terms.

$$\begin{array}{lll} \mathsf{contains}(t, s) \rightarrow \bot & & \text{if } t \rightarrow_O^{\mathcal{M}} {}^* r, \\ & & \mathcal{M}_s \backslash \mathcal{M}_r = \{c, s_1, \dots, s_n\} \text{ and} \\ & & \mathcal{M}_r \backslash \mathcal{M}_s = \{c_1, \dots, c_m\} \\ \mathsf{con}(t, c, s) \approx \mathsf{con}(q, c, r) \rightarrow \mathsf{con}(t, s) \approx \mathsf{con}(q, r) & & \text{if } \mathcal{M}_{\mathsf{con}(t,c,s)} \rightarrow_O^{\mathcal{M}} {}^* p \text{ and} \\ & & \mathcal{M}_p = \{c, \dots, c\} \end{array}$$

$$\begin{array}{rl} \mathsf{substr}(t, v, w) & \rightarrow_O^{\mathcal{M}} t \\ \text{where } \mathsf{replace}(t, s, r) & \rightarrow_O^{\mathcal{M}} \mathsf{con}(t, r) \\ \mathsf{con}(t, s, r) & \rightarrow_O^{\mathcal{M}} \mathsf{con}(t, q, r) \text{ if } s \rightarrow_O^{\mathcal{M}} q \end{array}$$

Fig. 8. Simplification rules based on multiset reasoning. We write $c, c_1, \dots$ to denote characters, v, w to denote integer terms, and t, s, r, q, p to denote string terms.

Example 9. We have that $\mathsf{con}(\mathsf{aaa}, \mathsf{substr}(x, y_1, y_2)) \approx \mathsf{con}(x, \mathsf{b}) \rightarrow \bot$ by noting that $\mathsf{con}(\mathsf{aaa}, \mathsf{substr}(x, y_1, y_2)) \rightarrow_O^{\mathcal{M}} {}^*\mathsf{con}(\mathsf{aaa}, x)$, $\mathcal{M}_{\mathsf{con}(\mathsf{aaa},x)} = \{\mathsf{a}, \mathsf{a}, \mathsf{a}, x\}$ and $\mathcal{M}_{\mathsf{con}(x,\mathsf{b})} = \{\mathsf{b}, x\}$. The difference of the latter with the former is $\{\mathsf{b}\}$, and the former with the latter is $\{\mathsf{a}, \mathsf{a}, \mathsf{a}\}$. Thus, the right side of the equality contains at least one more occurrence of b than the left side; hence, the equality is equivalent to false.

6 Implementation

We implemented the above simplification rules and others in the DPLL-based SMT solver CVC4, which implements a theory solver for a basic fragment of word equations with length, several other theory solvers, and reduction techniques for extended string functions as described in Sect. 2.1. Our simplification rules are run in a *preprocessing* pass as well as an *inprocessing* pass during solving. For the latter, we use a context-dependent simplification strategy that infers when an extended string constraint, e.g., $\neg\mathsf{contains}(t, s)$, simplifies to $\bot$ based on other assertions, e.g., $s \approx \epsilon$. Our simplification techniques do not affect the core procedure for the theory of strings, nor the compatibility of the string solver with other theories. In total, our implementation is about 3,500 lines of C++ code. We cache the results of the simplifications and the approximation-based arithmetic entailments to amortize their costs.

Additional Simplification Rules. The simplification rules in this paper are a subset of the rules in the implementation. We omit other uncategorized rules for lack of space. Many of these apply to specific term patterns, such as cases where two nested applications of substr can be combined; cases where an application of replace can be eliminated by case splitting; and other cases like $\mathsf{con}(t,t) \approx \mathsf{a} \rightarrow \bot$. An example of such rules is $\mathsf{contains}(\mathsf{replace}(t, w_1, w_2), w_3) \rightarrow \mathsf{contains}(t, w_3)$ if w_3 does not overlap with either w_1 or w_2, because the replace does not change whether t contains w_3 or not. Another class of rules only applies to strings of length one because they cannot span multiple components of a concatenations, e.g. $\mathsf{contains}(\mathsf{con}(t,s),c) \rightarrow \mathsf{contains}(t,c) \vee \mathsf{contains}(s,c)$ where c is a character. Finally, there are rewrites that benefit from multiple techniques presented in this paper. For example, we have a rewrite that splits string equations into multiple smaller equations if it can determine that prefixes must have the same length: $\mathsf{con}(\mathsf{a},t,s) \approx \mathsf{con}(t,\mathsf{b},r) \rightarrow \mathsf{con}(\mathsf{a},t) \approx \mathsf{con}(t,\mathsf{b}) \wedge s \approx r \rightarrow \bot$.

Validating Simplification Rules. The correctness of our simplification techniques is critical to the soundness of the overall solver. Due to the sophistication and breadth of those techniques, it is challenging to formally verify our implementation. As a pragmatic alternative, we periodically test our implementation using a testing infrastructure we developed for this purpose. We found this to be critical in our development process. Our testing infrastructure allows the developer to specify a context-free grammar in the syntax-guided synthesis format [2]. We generate all terms t in this grammar up to a fixed size and test the equivalence of t and its simplified form $t{\downarrow}$ on a set of randomly generated points. The most recent run of this system on two grammars (one for extended string terms and another for string predicates) up to a term size of three, validated 319,867 simplifications of string terms and 188,428 simplifications of string predicates on 1,000 sample points. This run took 924 s for string terms and 971 s for the string predicates using the same hardware as in Sect. 7.

7 Evaluation

We evaluate the impact of each simplification technique as implemented in CVC4 on three benchmark sets that use extended string operators: CMU, a dataset obtained from symbolic execution of Python code [15]; TermEq, a benchmark set consisting of the verification of term equivalences over strings [14]; and Slog, a benchmark set extracted from vulnerability testing of web applications [22]. The Slog set uses the replace function extensively but does not contain other extended functions. We also evaluate the impact on Aplas, a set of handcrafted benchmarks involving looping word equations [10] (string equalities whose left and right sides have variables in common).

We compare CVC4 with Z3 commit `9cb1a0f` [8],[4] a state-of-the-art string solver. Additionally, we compare against Ostrich on the Slog benchmarks but not other sets because it does not support some functions such as contains and

[4] `9cb1a0f` is newer than the current release 4.8.4 and includes several fixes for critical issues.

indexof. We omit a comparison with Z3STR3 4.8.4 because we found multiple issues in its latest release including wrong answers, which we have reported to the authors. We also omit a comparison with S3# due to differing semantics. We compare four configurations of CVC4: **all**, which enables all optimizations; **-arith**, which disables arithmetic-based simplification techniques (discussed in Sect. 3); **-contain**, which disables containment-based simplification techniques (discussed in Sect. 4); and **-msets**, which disables multiset-based simplification techniques (discussed in Sect. 5). Additionally, to test the applicability of our techniques to other solvers, we test the effect of our simplifications on Z3 by using CVC4 to generate simplified benchmarks and then running Z3 on those benchmarks. We generate a set of simplified benchmarks that are simplified with CVC4 with ($Z3_f$) and without ($Z3_b$) the simplification techniques presented in this paper.

Table 1. Number of solved problems per benchmark set. Best results are in **bold**. Gray cells indicate benchmark sets not supported by a solver. "R%" indicates the reduction of extended string functions during preprocessing. All benchmarks ran with a timeout of 600 s.

Set		all	-arith	-contain	-msets	Z3	$Z3_b$	$Z3_f$	OSTRICH	R%
	sat	**5703**	5535	**5703**	**5703**	2343	3923	3943		
CMU	unsat	**65**	29	**65**	**65**	50	58	61		32%
	×	154	358	154	154	3529	1941	1918		
	sat	**10**	**10**	**10**	**10**	4	5	5		
TERMEQ	unsat	51	37	28	51	35	40	**60**		68%
	×	19	33	42	19	41	35	15		
	sat	1302	1302	1302	1302	1133	1225	1225	**1304**	
SLOG	unsat	**2082**	**2082**	**2082**	**2082**	2080	2080	2080	**2082**	27%
	×	7	7	7	7	178	86	86	5	
	sat	**135**	**135**	**135**	**135**	9	51	46		
APLAS	unsat	**292**	**292**	171	171	94	129	**292**		n/a
	×	159	159	280	280	483	406	248		
	sat	**7150**	6982	**7150**	**7150**	3489	5204	5219	1304	
Total	unsat	2490	2440	2346	2369	2259	2307	**2493**	2082	
	×	339	557	483	460	4231	2468	2267	5	

We ran all benchmarks on a cluster equipped with Intel E5-2637 v4 CPUs running Ubuntu 16.04 and dedicated one core, 8 GB RAM, and 600 s for each job. Table 1 summarizes the number of solved instances for each configuration and the baseline solvers grouped by benchmark sets. We remark that the average reduction of extended string functions (with all simplification techniques enabled) shown in column "R%" is significant on all benchmark sets. The scatter plots in Fig. 9 detail the effects of disabling each family of simplifications. They distinguish between satisfiable and unsatisfiable instances. To emphasize

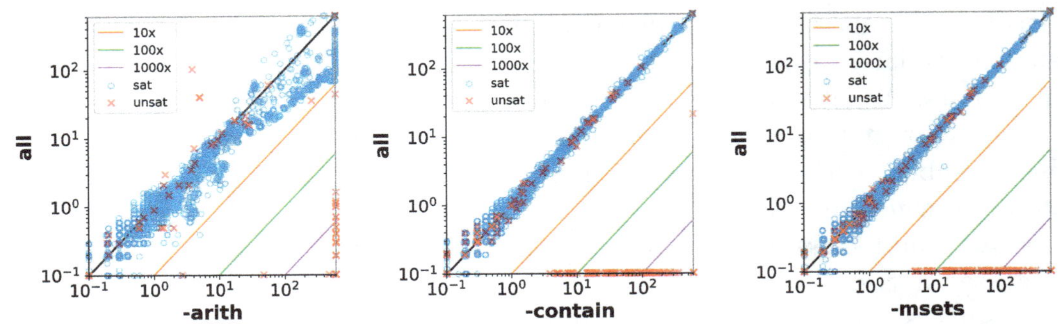

Fig. 9. Scatter plots showing the impact of disabling simplification techniques in CVC4 on both satisfiable and unsatisfiable benchmarks. All benchmarks ran with a timeout of 600 s.

non-trivial benchmarks, we omit the benchmarks that are solved in less than a second by all solvers.

The arithmetic-based simplification techniques have the most significant performance impact on the symbolic execution benchmarks CMU. The number of solved benchmarks is significantly lower when disabling those techniques. The scatter plot shows that for longer running satisfiable queries there is a large portion of the benchmarks that are solved up to an order of magnitude faster with the simplifications. These improvements in runtime on the CMU set are particularly compelling because they come from a symbolic execution application, which involves a large number of queries with a short timeout. The improvements are more pronounced for unsatisfiable benchmarks, where our results show that simplifications often give the solver the ability to derive a refutation in a matter of seconds, something that is infeasible with configurations without these techniques. The APLAS set contains no extended string operators and hence our arithmetic-based simplification techniques have little impact on this set.

In contrast, both containment and multiset-based rewrites have a high impact on the APLAS set, as **-contain** and **-msets** both solve 121 fewer benchmarks. Additionally, **-contain** has a high impact on the TERMEQ set, where the simplifications enable the best configuration to solve 61 out of 80 benchmarks. Since these techniques apply most frequently to looping word equations, they are less important for the CMU set, which does not have such equations. The containment-based and multiset-based techniques primarily help on unsatisfiable benchmarks, as shown in the scatter plots. On TERMEQ benchmarks, it tends to be easier to find counterexamples, i.e. to solve the satisfiable ones, so there is more to gain on unsatisfiable benchmarks.

On SLOG, OSTRICH solves two more instances than CVC4 but CVC4 is over 50 times faster on commonly solved instances while supporting a richer set of string operators. On all benchmark sets, CVC4 solves at least as many benchmarks as Z3 and CVC4 has $12\times$ fewer timeouts than Z3. On the simplified benchmarks, Z3 performs significantly better. On the CMU and the APLAS benchmarks, Z3_b outperforms Z3 by a large margin. Additionally simplifying the benchmarks with the techniques presented in this paper improves performance further on most benchmark sets and allows Z3$_f$ to solve the most unsatisfiable benchmarks overall. These results indicate that Z3 could benefit from additional simplifications, and they underscore the importance of curating and publishing simplification techniques in order to improve the state-of-the-art.

8 Conclusion

We have presented a set of aggressive simplification techniques for reasoning about extended string constraints. Our results suggest that such techniques are key to advancing the state of the art in SMT string solving. Arithmetic-based simplifications lead to significant speedups in benchmarks from a symbolic execution application, while containment and multiset-based simplifications improve the performance on problems consisting of difficult term equivalences and looping word equations. Our approach is not limited to CVC4 and can be adapted to other solvers.

Given the encouraging results for each of the simplification techniques in our evaluation, we plan to extend them to other types of abstraction and make them context-aware. The latter extension involves taking into account other assertions when checking whether a side condition of a rule is fulfilled.

Acknowledgements. This work was partially supported by the National Science Foundation under award 1656926, the Defense Advanced Research Projects Agency under award FA8650-18-2-7854, and Amazon Web Services.

References

1. Abdulla, P.A., et al.: TRAU: SMT solver for string constraints. In: Bjørner, N., Gurfinkel, A. (eds.) 2018 Formal Methods in Computer Aided Design, FMCAD 2018, Austin, TX, USA, 30 October–2 November 2018, pp. 1–5. IEEE (2018)
2. Alur, R., et al.: Syntax-guided synthesis. In: Irlbeck, M., Peled, D.A., Pretschner, A. (eds.) Dependable Software Systems Engineering. NATO Sciencefor Peace and Security Series, D: Information and Communication Security, vol. 40, pp. 1–25. IOS Press (2015)
3. Barrett, C., et al.: CVC4. In: Gopalakrishnan, G., Qadeer, S. (eds.) CAV 2011. LNCS, vol. 6806, pp. 171–177. Springer, Heidelberg (2011). https://doi.org/10.1007/978-3-642-22110-1_14
4. Berzish, M., Ganesh, V., Zheng, Y.: Z3str3: a string solver with theory-aware heuristics. In: Stewart, D., Weissenbacher, G. (eds.) 2017 Formal Methods in Computer Aided Design, FMCAD 2017, Vienna, Austria, 2–6 October 2017, pp. 55–59. IEEE (2017)
5. Bjørner, N., Tillmann, N., Voronkov, A.: Path feasibility analysis for string-manipulating programs. In: Kowalewski, S., Philippou, A. (eds.) TACAS 2009. LNCS, vol. 5505, pp. 307–321. Springer, Heidelberg (2009). https://doi.org/10.1007/978-3-642-00768-2_27

6. Chaudhuri, S., Farzan, A. (eds.): Computer Aided Verification - 28th International Conference, CAV 2016, Toronto, ON, Canada, July 17-23, 2016, Proceedings, Part I. Lecture Notes in Computer Science, vol. 9779. Springer, Switzerland (2016). https://doi.org/10.1007/978-3-319-41528-4
7. Chen, T., Hague, M., Lin, A.W., Rümmer, P., Wu, Z.: Decision procedures for path feasibility of string-manipulating programs with complex operations. PACMPL **3**(POPL), 49:1–49:30 (2019)
8. de Moura, L., Bjørner, N.: Z3: an efficient SMT solver. In: Ramakrishnan, C.R., Rehof, J. (eds.) TACAS 2008. LNCS, vol. 4963, pp. 337–340. Springer, Heidelberg (2008). https://doi.org/10.1007/978-3-540-78800-3_24
9. Kiezun, A., Ganesh, V., Artzi, S., Guo, P.J., Hooimeijer, P., Ernst, M.D.: HAMPI: a solver for word equations over strings, regular expressions, and context-free grammars. ACM Trans. Softw. Eng. Methodol. **21**(4), 25:1–25:28 (2012)
10. Le, Q.L., He, M.: A decision procedure for string logic with quadratic equations, regular expressions and length constraints. In: Ryu, S. (ed.) APLAS 2018. LNCS, vol. 11275, pp. 350–372. Springer, Cham (2018). https://doi.org/10.1007/978-3-030-02768-1_19
11. Li, G., Ghosh, I.: PASS: string solving with parameterized array and interval automaton. In: Bertacco, V., Legay, A. (eds.) HVC 2013. LNCS, vol. 8244, pp. 15–31. Springer, Cham (2013). https://doi.org/10.1007/978-3-319-03077-7_2
12. Liang, T., Reynolds, A., Tinelli, C., Barrett, C., Deters, M.: A DPLL(T) theory solver for a theory of strings and regular expressions. In: Biere, A., Bloem, R. (eds.) CAV 2014. LNCS, vol. 8559, pp. 646–662. Springer, Cham (2014). https://doi.org/10.1007/978-3-319-08867-9_43
13. Majumdar, R., Kuncak, V. (eds.): Computer Aided Verification - 29th International Conference, CAV 2017, Heidelberg, Germany, July 24-28, 2017, Proceedings, Part II. Lecture Notes in Computer Science, vol. 10427. Springer, Heidelberg (2017). https://doi.org/10.1007/978-3-319-63387-9
14. Reynolds, A., et al.: Rewrites for SMT solvers using syntax-guided enumeration. SMT (2018)
15. Reynolds, A., Woo, M., Barrett, C., Brumley, D., Liang, T., Tinelli, C.: Scaling up DPLL(T) string solvers using context-dependent simplification. In: Majumdar and Kuncak [13], pp. 453–474
16. Saxena, P., Akhawe, D., Hanna, S., Mao, F., McCamant, S., Song, D.: A symbolic execution framework for Javascript. In: 31st IEEE Symposium on Security and Privacy, S&P 2010, 16–19 May 2010, Berleley/Oakland, California, USA, pp. 513–528. IEEE Computer Society (2010)
17. Tinelli, C., Barrett, C., Fontaine, P.: Unicode Strings (Draft 1.0) (2018). http://smtlib.cs.uiowa.edu/theories-UnicodeStrings.shtml
18. Trinh, M.T., Chu, D.H., Jaffar, J.: S3: a symbolic string solver for vulnerability detection in webapplications. In: Ahn, G., Yung, M., Li, N. (eds.) Proceedings of the 2014 ACM SIGSAC Conference on Computer and Communications Security, Scottsdale, AZ, USA, 3–7 November 2014, pp. 1232–1243. ACM (2014)
19. Trinh, M.T., Chu, D.H., Jaffar, J.: Progressive reasoning over recursively-defined strings. In: Chaudhuri and Farzan [6], pp. 218–240
20. Trinh, M.T., Chu, D.H., Jaffar, J.: Model counting for recursively-defined strings. In: Majumdar and Kuncak [13], pp. 399–418
21. Veanes, M., Tillmann, N., de Halleux, J.: Qex: symbolic SQL query explorer. In: Clarke, E.M., Voronkov, A. (eds.) LPAR 2010. LNCS (LNAI), vol. 6355, pp. 425–446. Springer, Heidelberg (2010). https://doi.org/10.1007/978-3-642-17511-4_24

22. Wang, H.E., Tsai, T.L., Lin, C.H., Yu, F., Jiang, J.H.R.: String analysis via automata manipulation with logic circuit representation. In: Chaudhuri and Farzan [6], pp. 241–260
23. Yu, F., Alkhalaf, M., Bultan, T.: STRANGER: an automata-based string analysis tool for PHP. In: Esparza, J., Majumdar, R. (eds.) TACAS 2010. LNCS, vol. 6015, pp. 154–157. Springer, Heidelberg (2010). https://doi.org/10.1007/978-3-642-12002-2_13
24. Zheng, Y.: Z3str2: an efficient solver for strings, regular expressions, and length constraints. Form. Methods Syst. Des. **50**(2–3), 249–288 (2017)
25. Zheng, Y., Zhang, X., Ganesh, V.: Z3-str: a z3-based string solver for web application analysis. In: Meyer, B., Baresi, L., Mezini, M. (eds.) Joint Meeting of the European Software Engineering Conference and the ACM SIGSOFT Symposium on the Foundations of Software Engineering, ESEC/FSE 2013, Saint Petersburg, Russian Federation, 18–26 August 2013, pp. 114–124. ACM (2013)

Alternating Automata Modulo First Order Theories

Radu Iosif(✉) and Xiao Xu

CNRS, Verimag, Université de Grenoble Alpes, Grenoble, France
Radu.Iosif@univ-grenoble-alpes.fr, Xiao.Xu@univ-grenoble-alpes.fr

Abstract. We introduce first-order alternating automata, a generalization of boolean alternating automata, in which transition rules are described by multisorted first-order formulae, with states and internal variables given by uninterpreted predicate terms. The model is closed under union, intersection and complement, and its emptiness problem is undecidable, even for the simplest data theory of equality. To cope with the undecidability problem, we develop an abstraction refinement semi-algorithm based on lazy annotation of the symbolic execution paths with interpolants, obtained by applying (i) quantifier elimination with witness term generation and (ii) Lyndon interpolation in the quantifier-free theory of the data domain, with uninterpreted predicate symbols. This provides a method for checking inclusion of timed and finite-memory register automata, and emptiness of quantified predicate automata, previously used in the verification of parameterized concurrent programs, composed of replicated threads, with shared memory.

1 Introduction

Many results in automata theory rely on the finite alphabet hypothesis, which guarantees, in some cases, the existence of determinization, complementation and inclusion checking methods. However, this hypothesis prevents the use of automata as models of real-time systems or even simple programs, whose input and output are data values ranging over very large domains, typically viewed as infinite mathematical abstractions.

Traditional attempts to generalize classical Rabin-Scott automata to infinite alphabets, such as timed automata [1] and finite-memory automata [16] face the *complement closure* problem: there exist automata for which the complement language cannot be recognized by an automaton in the same class. This makes it impossible to encode a language inclusion problem $\mathcal{L}(A) \subseteq \mathcal{L}(B)$ as the emptiness of an automaton recognizing the language $\mathcal{L}(A) \cap \mathcal{L}^c(B)$, where $\mathcal{L}^c(B)$ denotes the complement of $\mathcal{L}(B)$.

Even for finite alphabets, complementation of finite-state automata faces inherent exponential blowup, due to nondeterminism. However, if we allow universal nondeterminism, in addition to the classical existential nondeterminism, complementation is possible is linear time. Having both existential and universal nondeterminism defines the *alternating automata* model [4]. A finite-alphabet

I. Dillig and S. Tasiran (Eds.): CAV 2019, LNCS 11562, pp. 43–63, 2019.
https://doi.org/10.1007/978-3-030-25543-5_3

alternating automaton is described by a set of transition rules $q \xrightarrow{a} \phi$, where q is a state, a is an input symbol and ϕ is a boolean formula, whose propositional variables denote successor states.

Our Contribution. We extend alternating automata to infinite data alphabets, by defining a model of computation in which all boolean operations, including complementation, can be done in linear time. The control states are given by k-ary predicate symbols $q(y_1, \ldots, y_k)$, the input consists of an event a from a finite alphabet and a tuple of data variables $x_1, \ldots, x_n$, ranging over an infinite domain, and transitions are of the form $q(y_1, \ldots, y_k) \xrightarrow{a(x_1,\ldots,x_n)} \phi(x_1, \ldots, x_n, y_1, \ldots, y_k)$, where ϕ is a formula in the first-order theory of the data domain. In this model, the arguments of a predicate atom $q(y_1, \ldots, y_k)$ represent the values of the *internal variables* associated with the state. Together with the input values $x_1, \ldots, x_n$, these values define the next configurations, but remain invisible in the input sequence.

The tight coupling of internal values and control states, by means of uninterpreted predicate symbols, allows for linear-time complementation just as in the case of classical propositional alternating automata. Complementation is, moreover, possible when the transition formulae contain first-order quantifiers, generating infinitely-branching execution trees. The price to be paid for this expressivity is that emptiness of first-order alternating automata is undecidable, even for the simplest data theory of equality [6].

The main contribution of this paper is an effective emptiness checking semi-algorithm for first-order alternating automata, in the spirit of the IMPACT lazy annotation procedure, originally developed for checking safety of nondeterministic integer programs [20,21]. In a nutshell, a lazy annotation procedure unfolds an automaton A trying to find an execution that recognizes a word from $\mathcal{L}(A)$. If a path that reaches a final state does not correspond to a concrete run of the automaton, the positions on the path are labeled with interpolants from the proof of infeasibility, thus marking this path and all continuations as infeasible for future searches. Termination of lazy annotation procedures is not guaranteed, but having a suitable coverage relation between the nodes of the search tree may ensure convergence of many real-life examples. However, applying lazy annotation to first-order alternating automata faces two nontrivial problems:

1. Quantified transition rules make it hard, if not impossible, in general, to decide if a path is infeasible. This is mainly because adding uninterpreted predicate symbols to decidable first-order theories, such as Presburger arithmetic, results in undecidability [10]. To deal with this problem, we assume that the first-order data theory, without uninterpreted predicate symbols, has a quantifier elimination procedure, that instantiates quantifiers with effectively computable *witness terms*.
2. The interpolants that prove the infeasibility of a path are not *local*, as they may refer to input values encountered in the past. However, the future executions are oblivious to *when* these values have been seen in the past and depend only on the relation between the past and current values. We use this fact to define a labeling of nodes, visited by the lazy annotation procedure,

with conjunctions of existentially quantified interpolants combining predicate atoms with data constraints.

We use first-order alternating automata to develop practical semi-algorithms for a number of known undecidable problems, such as: inclusion of regular timed languages [1], inclusion of quasi-regular languages recognized by finite-memory automata [16] and emptiness of predicate automata, a subclass of first-order alternating automata used to verify parameterized concurrent programs [6,7].

Related Work. Recognizers for languages over infinite alphabets have found various applications, ranging from Unicode text recognition [5] to runtime program monitoring [2]. Extending finite automata to infinite alphabets has been considered in the context of *symbolic alternating finite automata* (s-AFA), whose transitions are labeled with guards taken from a decidable theory of the data domain [5]. As in our model, s-AFA are closed under union, intersection and complement and emptiness is decidable, due to the lack of registers. However, s-AFA are strictly less expressive than our model, because comparing data at different positions in the input word is not possible.

Constrained Horn clauses (CHC) are a branching computation model widespread in program verification [9]. The main difference between alternating and bottom-up branching computations is that, in an alternating model, all branches of the computation must synchronize on the same input word. With this in mind, it is possible to express emptiness of first-order alternating automata as the existence of solutions of a CHC over a higher-order theory of data, extended with algebraic data types (lists). The effectiveness of such an encoding depends on the effectiveness of interpolation and witness term generation for theories of algebraic data types [11].

The alternating automata model presented in this paper extends the alternating automata with variables ranging over infinite data considered in [14]. There all variables were required to be observable in the input. We overcome this restriction by allowing internal (invisible) variables. Another closely related work [13] considers an inclusion between an asynchronous product of automata $A_1 \times \ldots \times A_n$, extended with data variables, and a monitor automaton B. The semi-algorithm defined there was based on the assumption that all variables of the observer B must be declared in the automata $A_1, \ldots, A_n$ under check. This limitation can now be bypassed, since the inclusion problem can be encoded as emptiness of a first-order alternating automaton and, moreover, the emptiness checking semi-algorithm can handle invisible variables.

The work probably closest to ours concerns the model of *predicate automata* (PA) [6,7,17], used in the verification of parameterized concurrent programs with shared memory. In this model, the alphabet consists of pairs of program statements and thread identifiers and is considered infinite because the number of threads is unbounded. Since thread identifiers can only be compared for equality, the data theory in PA is the theory of equality. Even with this simplification, the emptiness problem is undecidable when either the predicates have arity greater than one [6] or use quantified transition rules [17]. Checking emptiness of quantifier-free PA is possible semi-algorithmically, by explicitly enumerating reachable configurations and checking coverage by looking for permutations of argument values. However, no semi-algorithm has been given for quantified PA. Dealing with quantified transition rules is one of our contributions.

1.1 Preliminaries

For two integers $0 \leq i \leq j$, we define $[i,j] \stackrel{\text{def}}{=} \{i,\ldots,j\}$ and $[i] \stackrel{\text{def}}{=} [0,i]$. We consider two disjoint sorts $\mathbb{D}$ and $\mathbb{B}$, where $\mathbb{D}$ is an infinite domain and $\mathbb{B} = \{\top,\bot\}$ is the set of boolean values true ($\top$) and false ($\bot$), respectively. The $\mathbb{D}$ sort is equipped with countably many function symbols $f : \mathbb{D}^{\#(f)} \rightarrow \mathbb{D} \cup \mathbb{B}$, where $\#(f) \geq 0$ denotes the number of arguments (arity) of f. A *predicate* is a function symbol $p : \mathbb{D}^{\#(p)} \rightarrow \mathbb{B}$ that is, a $\#(p)$-ary relation.

We consider the interpretation of all function symbols $f : \mathbb{D}^{\#(f)} \rightarrow \mathbb{D}$ to be fixed by the interpretation of the $\mathbb{D}$ sort, for instance if $\mathbb{D}$ is the set of integers $\mathbb{Z}$, these are zero, the successor function and the arithmetic operations of addition and multiplication. We extend this convention to several predicates over $\mathbb{D}$, such as the inequality relation over $\mathbb{Z}$, and write Pred for the set of remaining *uninterpreted predicates*.

Let $\mathsf{Var} = \{x,y,z,\ldots\}$ be a countably infinite set of variables, ranging over $\mathbb{D}$. Terms are either constants of sort $\mathbb{D}$, variables or function applications $f(t_1,\ldots,t_{\#(f)})$, where $t_1,\ldots,t_{\#(f)}$ are terms. The set of first-order formulae is defined by the syntax below:

$$\phi := t = s \mid p(t_1,\ldots,t_{\#(p)}) \mid \neg\phi_1 \mid \phi_1 \wedge \phi_2 \mid \exists x \,.\, \phi_1$$

where $t,s,t_1,\ldots,t_{\#(p)}$ denote terms and p is a predicate symbol. We write $\phi_1 \vee \phi_2$, $\phi_1 \rightarrow \phi_2$ and $\forall x \,.\, \phi_1$ for $\neg(\neg\phi_1 \wedge \neg\phi_2)$, $\neg\phi_1 \vee \phi_2$ and $\neg\exists x \,.\, \neg\phi_1$, respectively. $\mathrm{FV}(\phi)$ is the set of free variables in ϕ and the size $|\phi|$ of a formula ϕ is the number of symbols needed to write it down. A *sentence* is a formula ϕ with no free variables. A formula is *positive* if each uninterpreted predicate symbol occurs under an even number of negations and we denote by $\mathsf{Form}^+(Q,X)$ the set of positive formulae with predicates from the set $Q \subseteq \mathsf{Pred}$ and free variables from the set $X \subseteq \mathsf{Var}$. A formula is in *prenex form* if it is of the form $\varphi = Q_1x_1 \ldots Q_nx_n \,.\, \phi$, where ϕ has no quantifiers. In this case we call ϕ the *matrix* of φ. Every first-order formula can be written in prenex form, by renaming each quantified variable to a unique name and moving the quantifiers upfront.

An *interpretation* $\mathcal{I}$ maps each predicate symbol p into a set $p^{\mathcal{I}} \subseteq \mathbb{D}^{\#(p)}$, if $\#(p) > 0$, or into an element of $\mathbb{B}$ if $\#(p) = 0$. A *valuation* ν maps each variable x into an element of $\mathbb{D}$. Given a term t, we denote by t^{ν} the value obtained by replacing each variable x by the value $\nu(x)$ and evaluating each function application. For a formula ϕ, we define the forcing relation $\mathcal{I},\nu \models \phi$ recursively on the structure of ϕ, as usual. For a formula ϕ and a valuation ν, we define $[\![\phi]\!]_{\nu} \stackrel{\text{def}}{=} \{\mathcal{I} \mid \mathcal{I},\nu \models \phi\}$ and drop the ν subscript for sentences. A sentence ϕ is *satisfiable* if $[\![\phi]\!] \neq \emptyset$. An element of $[\![\phi]\!]$ is called a *model* of ϕ. A formula ϕ is *valid* if $\mathcal{I},\nu \models \phi$ for every interpretation $\mathcal{I}$ and every valuation ν. We say that ϕ *entails* ψ, written $\phi \models \psi$ if and only if $[\![\phi]\!] \subseteq [\![\psi]\!]$.

Interpretations are partially ordered by the pointwise subset order, defined as $\mathcal{I}_1 \subseteq \mathcal{I}_2$ if and only if $p^{\mathcal{I}_1} \subseteq p^{\mathcal{I}_2}$ for each predicate symbol $p \in \mathsf{Pred}$. Given a formula ϕ and a valuation ν, we define $[\![\phi]\!]^{\mu}_{\nu} \stackrel{\mathsf{def}}{=} \{\mathcal{I} \mid \mathcal{I}, \nu \models \phi,\ \forall \mathcal{I}' \subseteq \mathcal{I} \,.\, \mathcal{I}', \nu \not\models \phi\}$ the set of minimal interpretations that, together with ν, form models of ϕ.

2 First Order Alternating Automata

Let Σ be a finite alphabet Σ of *input events*. Given a finite set of variables $X \subseteq \mathsf{Var}$, we denote by $X \mapsto \mathbb{D}$ the set of valuations of the variables X and $\Sigma[X] = \Sigma \times (X \mapsto \mathbb{D})$ be the possibly infinite set of *data symbols* (a, ν), where a is an input symbol and ν is a valuation. A *data word* (simply called word in the following) is a finite sequence $w = (a_1, \nu_1)(a_2, \nu_2) \ldots (a_n, \nu_n)$ of data symbols. Given a word w, we denote by $w_\Sigma \stackrel{\mathsf{def}}{=} a_1 \ldots a_n$ its sequence of input events and by $w_\mathbb{D}$ the valuation associating each time-stamped variable $x^{(i)}$, where $x \in \mathsf{Var}$, the value $\nu_i(x)$, for all $i \in [1, n]$. We denote by ε the empty sequence, by Σ^* the set of finite input sequences and by $\Sigma[X]^*$ the set of finite data words over the variables X.

A *first-order alternating automaton* is a tuple $\mathcal{A} = \langle \Sigma, X, Q, \iota, F, \Delta \rangle$, where Σ is a finite set of input events, X is a finite set of input variables, Q is a finite set of predicates denoting control states, $\iota \in \mathsf{Form}^+(Q, \emptyset)$ is a sentence defining initial configurations, $F \subseteq Q$ is the set of predicates denoting final states and Δ is a set of *transition rules*. A transition rule is of the form $q(y_1, \ldots, y_{\#(q)}) \xrightarrow{a(X)} \psi$, where $q \in Q$ is a predicate, $a \in \Sigma$ is an input event and $\psi \in \mathsf{Form}^+(Q, X \cup \{y_1, \ldots, y_{\#(q)}\})$ is a positive formula, where $X \cap \{y_1, \ldots, y_{\#(q)}\} = \emptyset$. Without loss of generality, we consider, for each predicate $q \in Q$ and each input event $a \in \Sigma$, at most one such rule, as two or more rules can be joined using disjunction. The quantifiers occurring in the right-hand side formula of a transition rule are called *transition quantifiers*. The *size* of $\mathcal{A}$ is $|\mathcal{A}| \stackrel{\mathsf{def}}{=} |\iota| + \sum\{|\psi| \mid q(\mathbf{y}) \xrightarrow{a(X)} \psi \in \Delta\}$.

The semantics of first-order alternating automata is analogous to the semantics of propositional alternating automata, with rules of the form $q \xrightarrow{a} \phi$, where q is a propositional variable and ϕ a positive boolean combination of propositional variables. For instance, $q_0 \xrightarrow{a} (q_1 \wedge q_2) \vee q_3$ means that the automaton can choose to transition in either both q_1 and q_2 or in q_3 alone. This leads to defining transitions as the *minimal models* of the right hand side of a rule[1]. The original definition of alternating automata [4] works around this problem and considers boolean valuations instead of formulae. In contrast, a finite description of a first-order alternating automaton cannot be given in terms of interpretations, as a first-order formula may have infinitely many models, corresponding to infinitely many initial or successor states occurring within an execution step.

Given an uninterpreted predicate symbol $q \in Q$ and data values $d_1, \ldots, d_{\#(q)} \in \mathbb{D}$, the tuple $(q, d_1, \ldots, d_{\#(q)})$ is called a *configuration*, sometimes written $q(d_1, \ldots, d_{\#(q)})$, when no confusion arises. A configuration is

[1] Both $\{q_1 \leftarrow \top, q_2 \leftarrow \top, q_3 \leftarrow \bot\}$ and $\{q_1 \leftarrow \bot, q_2 \leftarrow \bot, q_3 \leftarrow \top\}$ are minimal models, however $\{q_1 \leftarrow \top, q_2 \leftarrow \top, q_3 \leftarrow \top\}$ is a model but is not minimal.

final if $q \in F$. An interpretation $\mathcal{I}$ corresponds to a set of configurations $\mathsf{c}(\mathcal{I}) \stackrel{\text{def}}{=} \{(q, d_1, \ldots, d_{\#(q)}) \mid q \in Q,\ (d_1, \ldots, d_{\#(q)}) \in q^{\mathcal{I}}\}$, called a *cube*. This notation is lifted to sets of configurations in the usual way.

Definition 1. *Given a word $w = (a_1, \nu_1) \ldots (a_n, \nu_n) \in \Sigma[X]^*$ and a cube c, an* execution *of $\mathcal{A} = \langle \Sigma, X, Q, \iota, F, \Delta \rangle$ over w, starting with c, is a forest $\mathcal{T} = \{T_1, T_2, \ldots\}$, where each T_i is a tree labeled with configurations, such that:*

1. *$c = \{T(\epsilon) \mid T \in \mathcal{T}\}$ is the set of configurations labeling the roots of $T_1, T_2, \ldots$ and*
2. *if $(q, d_1, \ldots, d_{\#(q)})$ labels a node on the level $j \in [n-1]$ in T_i, then the labels of its children form a cube from $\mathsf{c}([\![\psi]\!]^{\mu}_{\eta})$, where $\eta = \nu_{j+1}[y_1 \leftarrow d_1, \ldots, y_{\#(q)} \leftarrow d_{\#(q)}]$ and $q(y_1, \ldots, y_{\#(q)}) \xrightarrow{a_{j+1}(X)} \psi \in \Delta$ is a transition rule of $\mathcal{A}$.*

An execution $\mathcal{T}$ over w, starting with c, is *accepting* if and only if all paths in $\mathcal{T}$ have the same length and the frontier of each tree $T \in \mathcal{T}$ is labeled with final configurations. If $\mathcal{A}$ has an accepting execution over w starting with a cube $c \in \mathsf{c}([\![\iota]\!]^{\mu})$, then $\mathcal{A}$ *accepts* w and let $\mathcal{L}(\mathcal{A})$ be the set of words accepted by $\mathcal{A}$. For example, consider the automaton $\mathcal{A} = \langle \{a\}, \{x\}, \{q_0, q_1, q_2, q_f\}, q_0(0), \{q_f\}, \Delta \rangle$, where Δ is the set: $q_0(y) \xrightarrow{a(x)} q_1(y + x) \wedge q_2(y - x)$, $q_1(y) \xrightarrow{a(x)} q_1(y + x) \vee (y > 0 \wedge q_f)$ and $q_2(y) \xrightarrow{a(x)} q_2(y - x) \vee (y > 0 \wedge q_f)$. A possible execution tree of this automaton is the following:

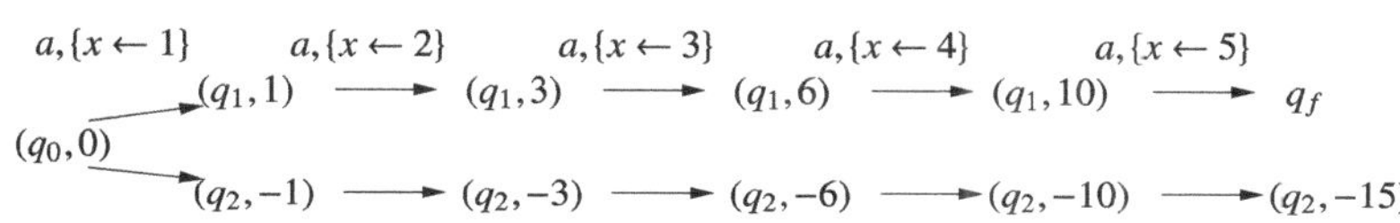

The execution tree is not accepting, since its frontier is not labeled with final configurations everywhere. Incidentally, here we have $\mathcal{L}(\mathcal{A}) = \emptyset$, which is proved by our tool in $\sim$0.5 s on an average machine.
In the rest of this paper, we are concerned with the following problems:

1. *boolean closure*: given automata $\mathcal{A}_i = \langle \Sigma, X, Q_i, \iota_i, F_i, \Delta_i \rangle$, for $i = 1, 2$, do there exist automata $\mathcal{A}_\cap$, $\mathcal{A}_\cup$ and $\overline{\mathcal{A}}_1$ such that $L(\mathcal{A}_\cap) = L(\mathcal{A}_1) \cap L(\mathcal{A}_2)$, $L(\mathcal{A}_\cup) = L(\mathcal{A}_1) \cup L(\mathcal{A}_2)$ and $L(\overline{\mathcal{A}}_1) = \Sigma[X]^* \setminus L(\mathcal{A}_1)$?
2. *emptiness*: given an automaton $\mathcal{A}$, is $L(\mathcal{A}) = \emptyset$?

For technical reasons, we address the following problem next: given an automaton $\mathcal{A}$ and an input sequence $\alpha \in \Sigma^*$, does there exists a word $w \in \mathcal{L}(\mathcal{A})$ such that $w_\Sigma = \alpha$? By solving this problem first, we develop the machinery required to prove that first-order alternating automata are closed under complement and, further, set up the ground for developping a practical semi-algorithm for the emptiness problem.

2.1 Path Formulae

In the upcoming developments it is sometimes more convenient to work with logical formulae defining executions of automata, than with low-level execution forests. For this reason, we first introduce *path formulae* $\Theta(\alpha)$, which are formulae defining the executions of an automaton, over words that share a given sequence α of input events. Second, we restrict a path formula $\Theta(\alpha)$ to an *acceptance formula* $\Upsilon(\alpha)$, which defines only those executions that are accepting among $\Theta(\alpha)$. Consequently, the automaton accepts a word w such that $w_\Sigma = \alpha$ if and only if $\Upsilon(\alpha)$ is satisfiable.

Let $\mathcal{A} = \langle \Sigma, X, Q, \iota, F, \Delta \rangle$ be an automaton for the rest of this section. For any $i \in \mathbb{N}$, we denote by $Q^{(i)} = \{q^{(i)} \mid q \in Q\}$ and $X^{(i)} = \{x^{(i)} \mid x \in X\}$ the sets of time-stamped predicate symbols and variables, respectively. We also define $Q^{(\leq n)} \stackrel{\text{def}}{=} \{q^{(i)} \mid q \in Q, i \in [n]\}$ and $X^{(\leq n)} \stackrel{\text{def}}{=} \{x^{(i)} \mid x \in X, i \in [n]\}$. For a formula ψ and $i \in \mathbb{N}$, we define $\psi^{(i)} \stackrel{\text{def}}{=} \psi[X^{(i)}/X, Q^{(i)}/Q]$ the formula in which all input variables and state predicates (and only those symbols) are replaced by their time-stamped counterparts. Moreover, we write $q(\mathbf{y})$ for $q(y_1, \ldots, y_{\#(q)})$, when no confusion arises.

Given a sequence of input events $\alpha = a_1 \ldots a_n \in \Sigma^*$, the *path formula* of α is:

$$\Theta(\alpha) \stackrel{\text{def}}{=} \iota^{(0)} \wedge \bigwedge_{i=1}^{n} \bigwedge_{q(\mathbf{y}) \xrightarrow{a_i(X)} \psi \in \Delta} \forall y_1 \ldots \forall y_{\#(q)} \,.\, q^{(i-1)}(\mathbf{y}) \rightarrow \psi^{(i)} \tag{1}$$

The automaton $\mathcal{A}$, to which $\Theta(\alpha)$ refers, will always be clear from the context. To formalize the relation between the low-level configuration-based execution semantics and path formulae, consider a word $w = (a_1, \nu_1) \ldots (a_n, \nu_n) \in \Sigma[X]^*$. Any execution $\mathcal{T}$ of $\mathcal{A}$ over w has an associated interpretation $\mathcal{I}_\mathcal{T}$ of time-stamped predicates $Q^{(\leq n)}$:

$$\mathcal{I}_\mathcal{T}(q^{(i)}) \stackrel{\text{def}}{=} \{(d_1, \ldots, d_{\#(q)}) \mid (q, d_1, \ldots, d_{\#(q)}) \text{ labels a node on level } i \text{ in } \mathcal{T}\},\ \forall q \in Q\ \forall i \in [n]$$

Lemma 1. *Given an automaton $\mathcal{A} = \langle \Sigma, X, Q, \iota, F, \Delta \rangle$, for any word $w = (a_1, \nu_1) \ldots (a_n, \nu_n)$, we have $[\![\Theta(w_\Sigma)]\!]^\mu_{w_\mathbb{D}} = \{\mathcal{I}_\mathcal{T} \mid \mathcal{T}$ is an execution of $\mathcal{A}$ over $w\}$.*

Next, we give a logical characterization of acceptance, relative to a given sequence of input events $\alpha \in \Sigma^*$. To this end, we constrain the path formula $\Theta(\alpha)$ by requiring that only final states of $\mathcal{A}$ occur on the last level of the execution. The result is the *acceptance formula* for α:

$$\Upsilon(\alpha) \stackrel{\text{def}}{=} \Theta(\alpha) \wedge \bigwedge_{q \in Q \setminus F} \forall y_1 \ldots \forall y_{\#(q)} \,.\, q^{(n)}(\mathbf{y}) \rightarrow \bot \tag{2}$$

The top-level universal quantifiers from a subformula $\forall y_1 \ldots \forall y_{\#(q)} \,.\, q^{(i)}(\mathbf{y}) \rightarrow \psi$ of $\Upsilon(\alpha)$ will be referred to as *path quantifiers*, in the following. Notice that path quantifiers are distinct from the transition quantifiers that occur within a formula ψ of a transition rule $q(y_1, \ldots, y_{\#(q)}) \xrightarrow{a(X)} \psi$ of $\mathcal{A}$. The relation between the words accepted by $\mathcal{A}$ and the acceptance formula above, is formally captured by the following lemma:

Lemma 2. *Given an automaton $\mathcal{A} = \langle \Sigma, X, Q, \iota, F, \Delta \rangle$, for every word $w \in \Sigma[X]^*$, the following are equivalent: (1) there exists an interpretation $\mathcal{I}$ such that $\mathcal{I}, w_\mathbb{D} \models \Upsilon(w_\Sigma)$ and (2) $w \in \mathcal{L}(\mathcal{A})$.*

As an immediate consequence, one can decide whether $\mathcal{A}$ accepts some word w with a given input sequence $w_\Sigma = \alpha$, by checking whether $\Upsilon(\alpha)$ is satisfiable. However, unlike non-alternating infinite-state models of computation, such as counter automata (nondeterministic programs with integer variables), the satisfiability query for an acceptance (path) formula falls outside of known decidable theories, supported by standard SMT solvers. There are basically two reasons for this, namely (i) the presence of predicate symbols, and (ii) the non-trivial alternation of quantifiers. To understand this point, consider for example, the decidable theory of Presburger arithmetic [24]. Adding even only one monadic predicate symbol to it yields undecidability in the presence of non-trivial quantifier alternation [10]. On the other hand, the quantifier-free fragment of Presburger arithmetic extended with uninterpreted function symbols is decidable, by a Nelson-Oppen style congruence closure argument [22].

To tackle the problem of deciding satisfiability of $\Upsilon(\alpha)$ formulae, we start from the observation that their form is rather particular, which allows the elimination of path quantifiers and uninterpreted predicate symbols, by a couple of satisfiability-preserving transformations. The result of applying these transformations is a formula with no predicate symbols, whose only quantifiers are those introduced by the transition rules of the automaton. Next, in Sect. 3 we shall assume moreover that the first-order theory of the data sort $\mathbb{D}$ (without uninterpreted predicate symbols) has quantifier elimination, providing thus an effective decision procedure.

For the time being, let us formally define the elimination of transition quantifiers and predicate symbols. Let $\alpha = a_1 \ldots a_n$ be a given sequence of input events and let α_i be the prefix $a_1 \ldots a_i$ of α, for $i \in [n]$, where $\alpha_0 = \epsilon$. We consider the sequence of formulae $\widehat{\Theta}(\alpha_0), \ldots, \widehat{\Theta}(\alpha_n)$ defined as $\widehat{\Theta}(\alpha_0) \stackrel{\text{def}}{=} \iota^{(0)}$ and, for all $i \in [1,n]$, let $\widehat{\Theta}(\alpha_i)$ be the conjunction of $\widehat{\Theta}(\alpha_{i-1})$ with all formulae $q^{(i-1)}(t_1, \ldots, t_{\#(q)}) \rightarrow \psi^{(i)}[t_1/y_1, \ldots, t_{\#(q)}/y_{\#(q)}]$, such that $q^{(i-1)}(t_1, \ldots, t_{\#(q)})$ occurs in $\widehat{\Theta}(\alpha_{i-1})$, for some terms $t_1, \ldots, t_{\#(q)}$. Next, we write $\widehat{\Upsilon}(\alpha)$ for the conjunction of $\widehat{\Theta}(\alpha_n)$ with all $q^{(n)}(t_1, \ldots, t_{\#(q)}) \rightarrow \bot$, such that $q^{(n)}(t_1, \ldots, t_{\#(q)})$ occurs in $\widehat{\Theta}(\alpha_n)$, for some $q \in Q \setminus F$. Note that $\widehat{\Upsilon}(\alpha)$ contains no path quantifiers, as required. On the other hand, the scope of the transition quantifiers in $\widehat{\Upsilon}(\alpha)$ exceeds the right-hand side formulae from the transition rules, as shown by the following example.

Example 1. Consider the automaton $\mathcal{A} = \langle \{a_1, a_2\}, \{x\}, \{q, q_f\}, \iota, \{q_f\}, \Delta \rangle$, where:

$$\begin{aligned}
\iota &= \exists z \,.\, z \geq 0 \wedge q(z) \\
\Delta &= \{q(y) \xrightarrow{a_1(x)} x \geq 0 \wedge \forall z \,.\, z \leq y \rightarrow q(x+z),\ q(y) \xrightarrow{a_2(x)} y < 0 \wedge q_f(x+y)\}
\end{aligned}$$

For the input event sequence $\alpha = a_1 a_2$, the acceptance formula is:

$$\begin{aligned}
\Upsilon(\alpha) = \exists z_1 \,.\, & z_1 \geq 0 \wedge q^{(0)}(z_1) \wedge \\
& \forall y \,.\, q^{(0)}(y) \rightarrow [x^{(1)} \geq 0 \wedge \forall z_2 \,.\, z_2 \geq y \rightarrow q^{(1)}(x^{(1)} + z_2)] \wedge \\
& \forall y \,.\, q^{(1)}(y) \rightarrow [y < 0 \wedge {q_f}^{(2)}(x^{(2)} + y)]
\end{aligned}$$

The result of eliminating the path quantifiers, in prenex normal form, is shown below:

$$\begin{aligned}\widehat{\Upsilon}(\alpha) = \exists z_1 \forall z_2 \,.\, & z_1 \geq 0 \wedge q^{(0)}(z_1) \wedge \\ & [q^{(0)}(z_1) \rightarrow x^{(1)} \geq 0 \wedge (z_2 \geq z_1 \rightarrow q^{(1)}(x^{(1)} + z_2))] \wedge \\ & [q^{(1)}(x^{(1)} + z_2) \rightarrow x^{(1)} + z_2 < 0 \wedge q_f{}^{(2)}(x^{(2)} + x^{(1)} + z_2)]\end{aligned}$$

Notice that the transition quantifiers $\exists z_1$ and $\forall z_2$ from $\Upsilon(\alpha)$ range now over $\widehat{\Upsilon}(\alpha)$. ■

Lemma 3. *For any input event sequence* $\alpha = a_1 \ldots a_n$ *and each valuation* $\nu : X^{(\leq n)} \rightarrow \mathbb{D}$*, the following hold, for every interpretation* $\mathcal{I}$*: (1) if* $\mathcal{I}, \nu \models \Upsilon(\alpha)$ *then* $\mathcal{I}, \nu \models \widehat{\Upsilon}(\alpha)$*, and (2) if* $\mathcal{I}, \nu \models \widehat{\Upsilon}(\alpha)$ *there exists an interpretation* $\mathcal{J} \subseteq \mathcal{I}$ *such that* $\mathcal{J}, \nu \models \Upsilon(\alpha)$*.*

Further, we eliminate the predicate atoms from $\widehat{\Upsilon}(\alpha)$, by considering the sequence of formulae $\overline{\Theta}(\alpha_0) \stackrel{\text{def}}{=} \iota^{(0)}$ and $\overline{\Theta}(\alpha_i)$ is obtained by substituting each predicate atom $q^{(i-1)}(t_1, \ldots, t_{\#(q)})$ in $\overline{\Theta}(\alpha_{i-1})$ by $\psi^{(i)}[t_1/y_1, \ldots, t_{\#(q)}/y_{\#(q)}]$, where $q(\mathbf{y}) \xrightarrow{a_i(X)} \psi \in \Delta$, for all $i \in [1, n]$. We write $\overline{\Upsilon}(\alpha)$ for the formula obtained by replacing, in $\overline{\Theta}(\alpha)$, each occurrence of a predicate $q^{(n)}$, such that $q \in Q \setminus F$ (resp. $q \in F$), by $\bot$ (resp. $\top$).

Example 2 (Contd. from Example 1). The result of the elimination of predicate atoms from the acceptance formula in Example 1 is shown below:

$$\overline{\Upsilon}(\alpha) = \exists z_1 \forall z_2 \,.\, z_1 \geq 0 \wedge [x^{(1)} \geq 0 \wedge (z_2 \geq z_1 \rightarrow x^{(1)} + z_2 < 0)]$$

Since this formula is unsatisfiable, by Lemma 5 below, no word w with input event sequence $w_\Sigma = a_1 a_2$ is accepted by the automaton $\mathcal{A}$ from Example 1. ■

At this point, we prove the formal relation between the satisfiability of the formulae $\widehat{\Upsilon}(\alpha)$ and $\overline{\Upsilon}(\alpha)$. Since there are no occurrences of predicates in $\overline{\Upsilon}(\alpha)$, for each valuation $\nu : X^{(\leq n)} \rightarrow \mathbb{D}$, there exists an interpretation $\mathcal{I}$ such that $\mathcal{I}, \nu \models \overline{\Upsilon}(\alpha)$ if and only if $\mathcal{J}, \nu \models \overline{\Upsilon}(\alpha)$, for every interpretation $\mathcal{J}$. In this case we omit $\mathcal{I}$ and simply write $\nu \models \overline{\Upsilon}(\alpha)$.

Lemma 4. *For any input event sequence* $\alpha = a_1 \ldots a_n$ *and each valuation* $\nu : X^{(\leq n)} \rightarrow \mathbb{D}$*, there exists a valuation* $\mathcal{I}$ *such that* $\mathcal{I}, \nu \models \widehat{\Upsilon}(\alpha)$ *if and only if* $\nu \models \overline{\Upsilon}(\alpha)$*.*

Finally, we define the acceptance of a word with a given input event sequence by means of a quantifier-free formula in which no predicate atom occurs.

Lemma 5. *Given an automaton* $\mathcal{A} = \langle \Sigma, X, Q, \iota, F, \Delta \rangle$*, for every word* $w \in \Sigma[X]^*$*, we have* $w_\mathbb{D} \models \overline{\Upsilon}(w_\Sigma)$ *if and only if* $w \in \mathcal{L}(\mathcal{A})$*.*

2.2 Boolean Closure of First Order Alternating Automata

Given a positive formula ϕ, we define the *dual* formula $\phi^\sim$ recursively as follows:

$$(\phi_1 \vee \phi_2)^\sim \stackrel{\text{def}}{=} {\phi_1}^\sim \wedge {\phi_2}^\sim \qquad (\phi_1 \wedge \phi_2)^\sim \stackrel{\text{def}}{=} {\phi_1}^\sim \vee {\phi_2}^\sim \qquad (t = s)^\sim \stackrel{\text{def}}{=} t \neq s$$
$$(\exists x \,.\, \phi_1)^\sim \stackrel{\text{def}}{=} \forall x \,.\, {\phi_1}^\sim \qquad (\forall x \,.\, \phi_1)^\sim \stackrel{\text{def}}{=} \exists x \,.\, {\phi_1}^\sim \qquad (t \neq s)^\sim \stackrel{\text{def}}{=} t = s$$
$$q(x_1, \ldots, x_{\#(q)})^\sim \stackrel{\text{def}}{=} q(x_1, \ldots, x_{\#(q)})$$

The following theorem shows closure of automata under all boolean operations. Note that it is sufficient to show closure under intersection and negation because $\mathcal{L}(\mathcal{A}_1) \cup \mathcal{L}(\mathcal{A}_2)$ is the complement of the language $\mathcal{L}^c(\mathcal{A}_1) \cap \mathcal{L}^c(\mathcal{A}_2)$, for any two automata $\mathcal{A}_1$ and $\mathcal{A}_2$ with the same input event alphabet and set of input variables.

Theorem 1. *Given automata $\mathcal{A}_i = \langle \Sigma, X, Q_i, \iota_i, F_i, \Delta_i \rangle$, for $i = 1, 2$, such that $Q_1 \cap Q_2 = \emptyset$, the following hold:*

1. *$\mathcal{L}(\mathcal{A}_\cap) = \mathcal{L}(\mathcal{A}_1) \cap \mathcal{L}(\mathcal{A}_2)$, where $\mathcal{A}_\cap = \langle \Sigma, X, Q_1 \cup Q_2, \iota_1 \wedge \iota_2, F_1 \cup F_2, \Delta_1 \cup \Delta_2 \rangle$,*
2. *$\mathcal{L}(\overline{\mathcal{A}_i}) = \Sigma[X]^* \setminus \mathcal{L}(\mathcal{A}_i)$, where $\overline{\mathcal{A}_i} = \langle \Sigma, X, Q_i, \iota^\sim, Q_i \setminus F_i, \Delta_i^\sim \rangle$ and $\Delta_i^\sim = \{q(\mathbf{y}) \xrightarrow{a(X)} \psi^\sim \mid q(\mathbf{y}) \xrightarrow{a(X)} \psi \in \Delta_i\}$, for $i = 1, 2$.*

Moreover, $|\mathcal{A}_\cap| = \mathcal{O}(|\mathcal{A}_1| + |\mathcal{A}_2|)$ and $|\overline{\mathcal{A}_i}| = \mathcal{O}(|\mathcal{A}_i|)$, for $i = 1, 2$.

3 The Emptiness Problem

The emptiness problem is undecidable even for automata with predicates of arity two, whose transition rules use only equalities and disequalities, having no transition quantifiers [6]. Since even such simple classes of alternating automata have no general decision procedure for emptiness, we use an abstraction-refinement semi-algorithm based on *lazy annotation* [20,21]. In a nutshell, a lazy annotation procedure systematically explores the set of finite input event sequences searching for an accepting execution. For an input sequence, if the path formula is satisfiable, we compute a word in the language of the automaton, from the model of the path formula. Otherwise, i.e. the sequence is *spurious*, the search backtracks and each position in the sequence is annotated with an interpolant, thus marking the sequence as infeasible. The semi-algorithm uses moreover a coverage relation between sequences, ensuring that the continuations of already covered sequences are never explored. Sometimes this coverage relation provides a sound termination argument, in case when the automaton is empty.

For two input event sequences $\alpha, \beta \in \Sigma^*$, we say that α is a prefix of β, written $\alpha \preceq \beta$, if $\alpha = \beta\gamma$ for some sequence $\gamma \in \Sigma^*$. A set S of sequences is *prefix-closed* if for each $\alpha \in S$, if $\beta \preceq \alpha$ then $\beta \in S$, and *complete* if for each $\alpha \in S$, there exists $a \in \Sigma$ such that $\alpha a \in S$ if and only if $\alpha b \in S$ for all $b \in \Sigma$. A prefix-closed set is the backbone of a tree whose edges are labeled with input events. If the set is, moreover, complete, then every node of the tree has either zero successors, in which case it is called a *leaf*, or it has a successor edge labeled with a for each input event $a \in \Sigma$.

Definition 2. *An* unfolding *of an automaton* $\mathcal{A} = \langle \Sigma, X, Q, \iota, F, \Delta \rangle$ *is a finite partial mapping* $U : \Sigma^* \rightharpoonup_{fin} \mathsf{Form}^+(Q, \emptyset)$*, whose domain* $\mathrm{dom}(U)$ *is a finite prefix-closed complete set, such that* $U(\epsilon) = \iota$*, and for each sequence* $\alpha a \in \mathrm{dom}(U)$*, such that* $\alpha \in \Sigma^*$ *and* $a \in \Sigma$*:*

$$U(\alpha)^{(0)} \wedge \bigwedge_{q(\mathbf{y}) \xrightarrow{a(X)} \psi} \forall y_1 \ldots \forall y_{\#q} \ . \ q^{(0)}(\mathbf{y}) \rightarrow \psi^{(1)} \models U(\alpha a)^{(1)}$$

A path α *is* safe *in* U *if and only if* $U(\alpha) \wedge \bigwedge_{q \in Q \setminus F} \forall y_1 \ldots \forall_{y_{\#(q)}} \ . \ q(\mathbf{y}) \rightarrow \bot$ *is unsatisfiable. The unfolding* U *is safe if and only if every path in* $\mathrm{dom}(U)$ *is safe in* U*.*

Lazy annotation semi-algorithms [20,21] build unfoldings of automata trying to discover counterexamples for emptiness. If the automaton $\mathcal{A}$ in question is non-empty, a systematic enumeration of the input event sequences[2] from Σ^* will suffice to discover a word $w \in \mathcal{L}(\mathcal{A})$, provided that the first-order theory of the data domain $\mathbb{D}$ is decidable (Lemma 2). However, if $\mathcal{L}(\mathcal{A}) = \emptyset$, the enumeration of input event sequences may, in principle, run forever. The typical way of fighting this divergence problem is to define a *coverage* relation between the nodes of the unfolding tree.

Definition 3. *Given an unfolding* U *of an automaton* $\mathcal{A} = \langle \Sigma, X, Q, \iota, F, \Delta \rangle$ *a node* $\alpha \in \mathrm{dom}(U)$ *is* covered *by another node* $\beta \in \mathrm{dom}(U)$*, denoted* $\alpha \sqsubseteq \beta$*, if and only if there exists a node* $\alpha' \preceq \alpha$ *such that* $U(\alpha') \models U(\beta)$*. Moreover,* U *is* closed *if and only if every leaf from* $\mathrm{dom}(U)$ *is covered by an uncovered node.*

A lazy annotation semi-algorithm will stop and report emptiness provided that it succeeds in building a closed and safe unfolding of the automaton. Notice that, by Definition 3, for any three nodes of an unfolding U, say $\alpha, \beta, \gamma \in \mathrm{dom}(U)$, if $\alpha \prec \beta$ and $\alpha \sqsubseteq \gamma$, then $\beta \sqsubseteq \gamma$ as well. As we show next (Theorem 2), there is no need to expand covered nodes, because, intuitively, there exists a word $w \in \mathcal{L}(\mathcal{A})$ such that $\alpha \preceq w_\Sigma$ and $\alpha \sqsubseteq \gamma$ only if there exists another word $u \in \mathcal{L}(\mathcal{A})$ such that $\gamma \preceq u_\Sigma$. Hence, exploring only those input event sequences that are continuations of γ (and ignoring those of α) suffices in order to find a counterexample for emptiness, if one exists.

An unfolding node $\alpha \in \mathrm{dom}(U)$ is said to be *spurious* if and only if $\Upsilon(\alpha)$ is unsatisfiable. In this case, we change (refine) the labels of (some of the) prefixes of α (and that of α), such that $U(\alpha)$ becomes $\bot$, thus indicating that there is no real execution of the automaton along that input event sequence. As a result of the change of labels, if a node $\gamma \preceq \alpha$ used to cover another node from $\mathrm{dom}(U)$, it might not cover it with the new label. Therefore, the coverage relation has to be recomputed after each refinement of the labeling. The semi-algorithm stops when (and if) a safe complete unfolding has been found.

Theorem 2. *If an automaton* $\mathcal{A}$ *has a nonempty safe closed unfolding then* $\mathcal{L}(A) = \emptyset$*.*

[2] For instance, using breadth-first search.

Algorithm 1. IMPACT-based Semi-algorithm for First Order Alternating Automata

input: a first order alternating automaton $\mathcal{A} = \langle \Sigma, X, Q, \iota, F, \Delta \rangle$
output: $\top$ if $L(\mathcal{A}) = \emptyset$, or word $w \in L(\mathcal{A})$, otherwise
data structures: `WorkList` and unfolding tree $\mathcal{U} = \langle N, E, \mathbf{r}, U, \lhd \rangle$, where:

- N is a set of nodes,
- $E \subseteq N \times \Sigma \times N$ is a set of edges labeled by input events,
- $U : N \rightarrow \mathsf{Form}^+(Q, \emptyset)$ is a labeling of nodes with positive sentences
- $\lhd \subseteq N \times N$ is a coverage relation,

initially `WorkList` $= \{\mathbf{r}\}$ and $N = E = U = \lhd = \emptyset$.

1: **while** `WorkList` $\neq \emptyset$ **do**
2: dequeue n from `WorkList`
3: $N \leftarrow N \cup \{n\}$
4: let $\alpha(n)$ be $a_1, \ldots, a_k$
5: **if** $\overline{\Upsilon}(\alpha)(X^{(1)}, \ldots, X^{(k)})$ is satisfiable **then** ▷ counterexample is feasible
6: get model ν of $\overline{\Upsilon}(\alpha)(X^{(1)}, \ldots, X^{(k)})$
7: **return** $w = (a_1, \nu(X^{(1)})) \ldots (a_k, \nu(X^{(k)}))$ ▷ $w \in L(\mathcal{A})$ by construction
8: **else** ▷ spurious counterexample
9: let $(I_0, \ldots, I_k)$ be a GLI for α
10: $b \leftarrow \bot$
11: **for** $i = 0, \ldots, k$ **do**
12: **if** $U(n_i) \not\models I_i$ **then**
13: $Uncover \leftarrow \{m \in N \mid (m, n_i) \in \lhd\}$
14: $\lhd \leftarrow \lhd \setminus \{(m, n_i) \mid m \in Uncover\}$ ▷ uncover the nodes covered by n_i
15: **for** $m \in Uncover$ such that m is a leaf of $\mathcal{U}$ **do**
16: enqueue m into `WorkList` ▷ reactivate uncovered leaves
17: $U(n_i) \leftarrow U(n_i) \wedge J_i$ ▷ strenghten the label of n_i (Lemma 7)
18: **if** $\neg b$ **then**
19: $b \leftarrow$ CLOSE(n_i)
20: **if** n is not covered **then**
21: **for** $a \in \Sigma$ **do** ▷ expand n
22: let s be a fresh node and $e = (n, a, s)$ be a new edge
23: $E \leftarrow E \cup \{e\}$
24: $U \leftarrow U \cup \{(s, \top)\}$
25: enqueue s into `WorkList`
26: **return** $\top$
27: **function** CLOSE(x) **returns** $\mathbb{B}$
28: **for** $y \in N$ such that $\alpha(y) \prec^* \alpha(x)$ **do**
29: **if** $U(x) \models U(y)$ **then**
30: $\lhd \leftarrow [\lhd \setminus \{(p, q) \in \lhd \mid q$ is x or a successor of $x\}] \cup \{(x, y)\}$
31: **return** $\top$
32: **return** $\bot$

We describe the semi-algorithm used to check emptiness of first-order alternating automata. The execution of Algorithm 1 consists of three phases, corresponding to the CLOSE, REFINE and EXPAND of the original IMPACT procedure [20]. Let n be a node removed from the worklist at line 2 and let $\alpha(n)$ be the input sequence labeling the path from the root node to n. If $\overline{\Upsilon}(\alpha(n))$ is satisfiable, the sequence $\alpha(n)$ is feasible, in which case a model of $\overline{\Upsilon}(\alpha(n))$ is obtained and a word $w \in L(\mathcal{A})$ is returned. Otherwise, $\alpha(n)$ is an infeasible input sequence and the procedure enters the refinement phase (lines 9–19). The GLI for $\alpha(n)$ is used to strenghten the labels of all the ancestors of n, by conjoining the formulae of the interpolant, changed according to Lemma 7, to the existing labels.

In this process, the nodes on the path between $\mathbf{r}$ and n, including n, might become eligible for coverage, therefore we attempt to close each ancestor of n that is impacted by the refinement (line 19). Observe that, in this case the call to Close must uncover each node which is covered by a successor of n (line 30 of the Close function). This is required because, due to the over-approximation of the sets of reachable configurations, the covering relation is not transitive, as explained in [20]. If Close adds a covering edge (n_i, m) to $\lhd$, it does not have to be called for the successors of n_i on this path, which is handled via the boolean flag b. Finally, if n is still uncovered (it has not been previously covered during the refinement phase) we expand n (lines 21–25) by creating a new node for each successor s via the input event $a \in \Sigma$ and inserting it into the worklist.

4 Interpolant Generation

Typically, when checking the unreachability of a set of program configurations, the interpolants used to annotate the unfolded control structure are assertions about the values of the program variables in a given control state, at a certain step of an execution [20]. Because we consider alternating computation trees (forests), we must distinguish between (i) locality of interpolants w.r.t. a given control state (control locality) and (ii) locality w.r.t. a given time stamp (time locality). In logical terms, *control-local* interpolants are formulae involving a single predicate symbol, whereas *time-local* interpolants involve only predicates $q^{(i)}$ and variables $x^{(i)}$, for a single $i \geq 0$. When considering alternating executions, control-local interpolants are not always enough to prove emptiness, because of the synchronization of several branches of the computation on the same input word. For this reason, the interpolants considered in this paper will never be control-local and we shall use the term *local* to denote time-local interpolants, with no free variables.

First, let us give the formal definition of the class of interpolants we shall work with. Given a formula ϕ, the *vocabulary* of ϕ, denoted $\mathrm{V}(\phi)$ is the set of predicate symbols $q \in Q^{(i)}$ and variables $x \in X^{(i)}$, occurring in ϕ, for some $i \geq 0$. For a term t, its vocabulary $\mathrm{V}(t)$ is the set of variables that occur in t. Observe that quantified variables and the interpreted function symbols of the data theory[3] do not belong to the vocabulary of a formula. By $\mathrm{P}^+(\phi)$ $[\mathrm{P}^-(\phi)]$ we denote the set of predicate symbols that occur in ϕ under an even [odd] number of negations.

[3] E.g., the arithmetic operators of addition and multiplication, when $\mathbb{D}$ is the set of integers.

Definition 4 ([19]). *Given formulae ϕ and ψ such that $\phi \wedge \psi$ is unsatisfiable, a* Lyndon interpolant *is a formula I such that $\phi \models I$, the formula $I \wedge \psi$ is unsatisfiable,* $\mathrm{V}(I) \subseteq \mathrm{V}(\phi) \cap \mathrm{V}(\psi)$, $\mathrm{P}^+(I) \subseteq \mathrm{P}^+(\phi) \cap \mathrm{P}^+(\psi)$ *and* $\mathrm{P}^-(I) \subseteq \mathrm{P}^-(\phi) \cap \mathrm{P}^-(\psi)$.

In the rest of this section, fix an automaton $\mathcal{A} = \langle \Sigma, X, Q, \iota, F, \Delta \rangle$. The following definition generalizes interpolants from unsatisfiable conjunctions to input sequences:

Definition 5. *Given a sequence of input events $\alpha = a_1 \ldots a_n \in \Sigma^*$, a* generalized Lyndon interpolant (GLI) *is a sequence $(I_0, \ldots, I_n)$ of formulae such that, for all $k \in [n-1]$, the following hold: (1) $\mathrm{P}^-(I_k) = \emptyset$, (2) $\iota^{(0)} \models I_0$, $I_k \wedge \left(\bigwedge_{q(\mathbf{y}) \xrightarrow{a_i(X)} \psi \in \Delta} \forall y_1 \ldots \forall y_{\#(q)} \,.\, q^{(k)}(\mathbf{y}) \rightarrow \psi^{(k+1)} \right) \models I_{k+1}$ and (3) $I_n \wedge \bigwedge_{q \in Q \setminus F} \forall y_1 \ldots \forall y_{\#(q)} \,.\, q(\mathbf{y}) \rightarrow \bot$ is unsatisfiable. Moreover, the GLI is* local *if and only if $\mathrm{V}(I_k) \subseteq Q^{(k)}$, for all $k \in [n]$.*

The following proposition states the existence of local GLI for the theories in which Lyndon's Interpolation Theorem holds.

Proposition 1. *If there exists a Lyndon interpolant for any two formulae ϕ and ψ, in the first-order theory of data with uninterpreted predicate symbols, such that $\phi \wedge \psi$ is unsatisfiable, then any sequence of input events $\alpha = a_1 \ldots a_n \in \Sigma^*$, such that $\Upsilon(\alpha)$ is unsatisfiable, has a local GLI $(I_0, \ldots, I_n)$.*

A problematic point of the above proposition is that the existence of Lyndon interpolants (Definition 4) is proved in principle, but the proof is non-constructive. In other words, the proof of Proposition 1 does not yield an algorithm for computing GLIs, for the following reason. Building an interpolant for an unsatisfiable conjunction of formulae $\phi \wedge \psi$ is typically the job of the decision procedure that proves the unsatisfiability and, in general, there is no such procedure, when ϕ and ψ contain predicates and have non-trivial quantifier alternation. In this case, some provers use instantiation heuristics for the universal quantifiers that are sufficient for proving unsatisfiability, however these heuristics are not always suitable for interpolant generation. Consequently, from now on, we assume the existence of an effective Lyndon interpolation procedure only for decidable theories, such as the quantifier-free linear (integer) arithmetic with uninterpreted functions (UFLIA, UFLRA, etc.) [26].

This is where the predicate-free path formulae (defined in Sect. 2.1) come into play. Recall that, for a given event sequence α, the automaton $\mathcal{A}$ accepts a word w such that $w_\Sigma = \alpha$ if and only if $\overline{\Upsilon}(\alpha)$ is satisfiable (Lemma 5). Assuming further that the equality and interpreted predicates (e.g. inequalities for integers) atoms from the transition rules of $\mathcal{A}$ belong to a decidable first-order theory, such as Presburger arithmetic, Lemma 5 gives us an effective way of checking emptiness of $\mathcal{A}$, relative to a given event sequence. However, this method does not cope well with lazy annotation, because there is no way to extract, from the unsatisfiability proof of $\overline{\Upsilon}(\alpha)$, the interpolants needed to annotate α. This is because (I) the formula $\overline{\Upsilon}(\alpha)$, obtained by repeated substitutions loses track of the steps of the execution, and (II) quantifiers that occur nested in $\overline{\Upsilon}(\alpha)$ make it difficult to write $\overline{\Upsilon}(\alpha)$ as an unsatisfiable quantifier-free conjunction of formulae from which interpolants are extracted (Definition 4).

The solution we adopt for the first issue (I) consists in partially recovering the time-stamped structure of the acceptance formula $\Upsilon(\alpha)$ using the formula $\widehat{\Upsilon}(\alpha)$, in which only transition quantifiers occur. The second issue (II) is solved under the additional assuption that the theory of the data domain $\mathbb{D}$ has *witness-producing quantifier elimination.* More precisely, we assume that, for each formula $\exists x \,.\, \phi(x)$, there exists an effectively computable term τ, in which x does not occur, such that $\exists x \,.\, \phi$ and $\phi[\tau/x]$ are equisatisfiable. These terms, called *witness terms* in the following, are actual definitions of the Skolem function symbols from the following folklore theorem:

Theorem 3 ([3]). *Given $Q_1x_1 \ldots Q_nx_n \,.\, \phi$ a first-order sentence, where $Q_1, \ldots, Q_n \in \{\exists, \forall\}$ and ϕ is quantifier-free, let $\eta_i \stackrel{\text{def}}{=} f_i(y_1, \ldots, y_{k_i})$ if $Q_i = \forall$ and $\eta_i \stackrel{\text{def}}{=} x_i$ if $Q_i = \exists$, where f_i is a fresh function symbol and $\{y_1, \ldots, y_{k_i}\} = \{x_j \mid j < i,\ Q_j = \exists\}$. Then the entailment $Q_1x_1 \ldots Q_nx_n \,.\, \phi \models \phi[\eta_1/x_1, \ldots, \eta_n/x_n]$ holds.*

Examples of witness-producing quantifier elimination procedures can be found in the literature for e.g. linear integer (real) arithmetic (LIA,LRA), Presburger arithmetic and boolean algebra of sets and Presburger cardinality constraints (BAPA) [18].

Under the assumption that witness terms can be effectively built, we describe the generation of a non-local GLI for a given input event sequence $\alpha = a_1 \ldots a_n$. First, we generate successively the acceptance formula $\Upsilon(\alpha)$ and its equisatisfiable forms $\widehat{\Upsilon}(\alpha) = Q_1x_1 \ldots Q_mx_m \,.\, \widehat{\Phi}$ and $\overline{\Upsilon}(\alpha) = Q_1x_1 \ldots Q_mx_m \,.\, \overline{\Phi}$, both written in prenex form, with matrices $\widehat{\Phi}$ and $\overline{\Phi}$, respectively. Because we assumed that the first order theory of $\mathbb{D}$ has quantifier elimination, the satisfiability problem for $\overline{\Upsilon}(\alpha)$ is decidable. If $\overline{\Upsilon}(\alpha)$ is satisfiable, we build a counterexample for emptiness w such that $w_\Sigma = \alpha$ and $w_\mathbb{D}$ is a satisfying assignment for $\overline{\Upsilon}(\alpha)$. Otherwise, $\overline{\Upsilon}(\alpha)$ is unsatisfiable and there exist witness terms $\tau_{i_1} \ldots \tau_{i_\ell}$, where $\{i_1, \ldots, i_\ell\} = \{j \in [1,m] \mid Q_j = \forall\}$, such that $\overline{\Phi}[\tau_{i_1}/x_{i_1}, \ldots, \tau_{i_\ell}/x_{i_\ell}]$ is unsatisfiable (Theorem 3). Then it turns out that the formula $\widehat{\Phi}[\tau_{i_1}/x_{i_1}, \ldots, \tau_{i_\ell}/x_{i_\ell}]$, obtained analogously from the matrix of $\widehat{\Upsilon}(\alpha)$, is unsatisfiable as well (Lemma 6 below). Because this latter formula is structured as a conjunction of formulae $\iota^{(0)} \wedge \phi_1 \ldots \wedge \phi_n \wedge \psi$, where $\mathrm{V}(\phi_k) \cap Q^{(\leq n)} \subseteq Q^{(k-1)} \cup Q^{(k)}$ and $\mathrm{V}(\psi) \cap Q^{(\leq n)} \subseteq Q^{(n)}$, it is now possible to use an existing interpolation procedure for the quantifier-free theory of $\mathbb{D}$, extended with uninterpreted function symbols, to compute a (not necessarily local) GLI $(I_0, \ldots, I_n)$ such that $\mathrm{V}(I_k) \cap Q^{(\leq n)} \subseteq Q^{(k)}$, for all $k \in [n]$.

Example 3 (Contd. from Examples 1 and 2). The formula $\overline{\Upsilon}(\alpha)$ (Example 2) is unsatisfiable and let $\tau_2 \stackrel{\text{def}}{=} z_1$ be the witness term for the universally quantified variable z_2. Replacing z_2 with $\tau_2\ (z_1)$ in the matrix of $\widehat{\Upsilon}(\alpha)$ (Example 1) yields the unsatisfiable conjunction below, obtained after trivial simplifications:

$$[z_1 \geq 0 \wedge q^{(0)}(z_1)] \wedge [q^{(0)}(z_1) \rightarrow x^{(1)} \geq 0 \wedge q^{(1)}(x^{(1)} + z_1)] \wedge \\ [q^{(1)}(x^{(1)} + z_1) \rightarrow x^{(1)} + z_1 < 0 \wedge q_f{}^{(2)}(x^{(2)} + x^{(1)} + z_1)]$$

A non-local GLI for the above conjunction is the sequence of formulae:

$$(q^{(0)}(z_1) \wedge z_1 \geq 0,\ x^{(1)} \geq 0 \wedge q^{(1)}(x^{(1)} + z_1) \wedge z_1 \geq 0,\ \bot)$$ ■

We formalize and prove the correctness for the above construction of non-local GLI. A function $\xi : \mathbb{N} \rightarrow \mathbb{N}$ is *monotonic* iff for each $n < m$ we have $\xi(n) \leq \xi(m)$ and *finite-range* iff for each $n \in \mathbb{N}$ the set $\{m \mid \xi(m) = n\}$ is finite. If ξ is finite-range, we denote by $\xi^{-1}_{\max}(n) \in \mathbb{N}$ the maximal value m such that $\xi(m) = n$.

Lemma 6. *Given a non-empty input event sequence $\alpha = a_1 \ldots a_n \in \Sigma^*$, such that $\Upsilon(\alpha)$ is unsatisfiable, let $Q_1 x_1 \ldots Q_m x_m\ .\ \widehat{\Phi}$ be a prenex form of $\widehat{\Upsilon}(\alpha)$ and let $\xi : [1, m] \rightarrow [n]$ be a monotonic finite-range function mapping each transition quantifier to the minimal index from the sequence $\widehat{\Theta}(\alpha_0), \ldots, \widehat{\Theta}(\alpha_n)$ where it occurs. Then one can effectively build:*

1. *witness terms $\tau_{i_1}, \ldots, \tau_{i_\ell}$, where $\{i_1, \ldots, i_\ell\} = \{j \in [1, m] \mid Q_j = \forall\}$ and $\mathrm{V}(\tau_{i_j}) \subseteq X^{(\leq \xi(i_j))} \cup \{x_k \mid k < i_j, Q_k = \exists\}$, $\forall j \in [1, \ell]$ such that $\widehat{\Phi}[\tau_{i_1}/x_{i_1}, \ldots, \tau_{i_\ell}/x_{i_\ell}]$ is unsatisfiable, and*
2. *a GLI $(I_0, \ldots, I_n)$ for α, such that $\mathrm{V}(I_k) \subseteq Q^{(k)} \cup X^{(\leq k)} \cup \{x_j \mid j < \xi^{-1}_{\max}(k),\ Q_j = \exists\}$, for all $k \in [n]$.*

Consequently, under two assumptions about the first-order theory of the data domain, namely (i) witness-producing quantifier elimination, and (ii) Lyndon interpolation for the quantifier-free fragment with uninterpreted functions, we developed a generic method that produces GLIs for unfeasible input event sequences. Moreover, each formula in the interpolant refers only to the current predicate symbols, the current and past input variables and the existentially quantified transition variables introduced at the previous steps. The remaining questions are how to use these GLIs to label the sequences in the unfolding of an automaton (Definition 2) and compute coverage (Definition 3) between nodes of the unfolding.

4.1 Unfolding with Non-local Interpolants

As required by Definition 2, the unfolding U of an automaton $\mathcal{A} = \langle \Sigma, X, Q, \iota, F, \Delta \rangle$ is labeled by formulae $U(\alpha) \in \mathsf{Form}^+(Q, \emptyset)$, with no free symbols, other than predicate symbols, such that the labeling is compatible with the transition relation of the automaton. Each newly expanded input sequence of $\mathcal{A}$ is initially labeled with $\top$ and the labels are refined using GLIs computed from proofs of spuriousness. The following lemma describes the refinement of the labeling of an input sequence by a non-local GLI:

Lemma 7. *Let U be an unfolding of an automaton $\mathcal{A} = \langle \Sigma, X, Q, \iota, F, \Delta \rangle$ such that $\alpha = a_1 \ldots a_n \in \mathrm{dom}(U)$ and $(I_0, \ldots, I_n)$ is a GLI for α. Then the mapping $U' : \mathrm{dom}(U) \rightarrow \mathsf{Form}^+(Q, \emptyset)$ is an unfolding of $\mathcal{A}$, where:*

- *$U'(\alpha_k) = U(\alpha_k) \wedge J_k$, for all $k \in [n]$, where J_k is the formula obtained from I_k by removing the time stamp of each predicate symbol $q^{(k)}$ and existentially quantifying each free variable, and*
- *$U'(\beta) = U(\beta)$ if $\beta \in \mathrm{dom}(U)$ and $\beta \not\preceq \alpha$,*

Moreover, α is safe in U'.

Observe that, by Lemma 6(2), the set of free variables of a GLI formula I_k consists of (i) variables $X^{(\leq k)}$ keeping track of data values seen in the input at some earlier moment in time, and (ii) variables that track past choices made within the transition rules. Basically, it is not important when exactly in the past a certain input has been read or when a choice has been made, because only the relation between the values of these and the current variables determines the future behavior of the automaton. Quantifying these variables existentially does the job of ignoring when exactly in the past these values have been seen. Moreover, the last point of Lemma 7 ensures that the refined path is safe in the new unfolding and will stay safe in all future refinements of this unfolding.

The last ingredient of the lazy annotation semi-algorithm based on unfoldings consist in the implementation of the coverage check, when the unfolding of an automaton is labeled with conjunctions of existentially quantified formulae with predicate symbols, obtained from interpolation. By Definition 3, checking whether a given node $\alpha \in \mathrm{dom}(U)$ is covered amounts to finding a prefix $\alpha' \preceq \alpha$ and a node $\beta \in \mathrm{dom}(U)$ such that $U(\alpha') \models U(\beta)$, or equivalently, the formula $U(\alpha') \wedge \neg U(\beta)$ is unsatisfiable. However, the latter formula, in prenex form, has quantifier prefix in the language $\exists^*\forall^*$ and, as previously mentioned, the satisfiability problem for such formulae becomes undecidable when the data theory subsumes Presburger arithmetic [10].

Nevertheless, if we require just a yes/no answer (i.e. not an interpolant) recently developed quantifier instantiation heuristics [25] perform rather well in answering a large number of queries in this class. Observe, moreover, that coverage does not need to rely on a complete decision procedure. If the prover fails in answering the above satisfiability query, then the semi-algorithm assumes that the node is not covered and continues exploring its successors. Failure to compute complete coverage may lead to divergence (non-termination) and ultimately, to failure to prove emptiness, but does not affect the soundness of the semi-algorithm (real counterexamples will still be found).

5 Experimental Results

We have implemented a version of the IMPACT semi-algorithm [20] in a prototype tool, avaliable online [8]. The tool is written in Java and uses the Z3 SMT solver [27], via the JavaSMT interface [15], for spuriousness and coverage

Table 1. Experiments with First Order Alternating Automata

Example	$\vert\mathcal{A}\vert$ (bytes)	Predicates	Variables	Transitions	$L(\mathcal{A}) = \emptyset$?	Nodes expanded	Nodes visited	Time (msec)
incdec.pa	499	3	1	12	No	21	17	779
localdec.pa	678	4	1	16	No	49	35	1814
ticket.pa	4250	13	1	73	No	229	91	9543
count_thread0.pa	9767	14	1	126	No	154	128	8553
count_thread1.pa	10925	15	1	135	No	766	692	76771
local0.pa	10595	13	1	117	No	73	27	1431
local1.pa	11385	14	1	126	No	1135	858	101042
array_rotation.ada	1834	8	7	7	Yes	9	8	1543
array_simple.ada	3440	9	5	8	Yes	11	10	6787
array_shift.ada	874	6	5	5	Yes	6	5	413
abp.ada	6909	16	14	28	No	52	47	4788
train.ada	1823	10	4	26	Yes	68	67	7319
hw1.ada	322	3	2	5	Solver error	/	/	/
hw2.ada	674	7	2	8	Yes	20	22	4974
rr-crossing.foada	1780	10	1	16	Yes	67	67	7574
train-simple1.foada	5421	13	1	61	Yes	43	44	2893
train-simple2.foada	10177	16	1	118	Yes	111	113	8386
train-simple3.foada	15961	19	1	193	Yes	196	200	15041
fischer-mutex2.foada	3000	11	2	23	Yes	23	23	808
fischer-mutex3.foada	4452	16	2	34	Yes	33	33	1154

queries and also for interpolant generation. Table 1 reports the size of the input automaton in bytes, the numbers of Predicates, Variables and Transitions, the result of emptiness check, the number of Expanded and Visited Nodes during the unfolding and the Time in miliseconds. The experiments were carried out on a MacOS x64 - 1.3 GHz Intel Core i5 - 8 GB 1867 MHz LPDDR3 machine.

The test cases shown in Table 1, come from several sources, namely predicate automata models (*.pa) [6,7] available online [23], timed automata inclusion problems (`abp.ada`, `train.ada`, `rr-crossing.foada`), array logic entailments (`array_rotation.ada`, `array_simple.ada`, `array_shift.ada`) and hardware circuit verification (`hw1.ada`, `hw2.ada`), initially considered in [13], with the restriction that local variables are made visible in the input. The `train-simpleN. foada` and `fischer-mutexN. foada` examples are parametric verification problems in which one checks inclusions of the form $\bigcap_{i=1}^{N} \mathcal{L}(A_i) \subseteq \mathcal{L}(B)$, where A_i is the i-th copy of the template automaton.

The advantage of using FOADA over the INCLUDER [12] tool from [13] is the possibility of having automata over infinite alphabets with local variables, whose values are not visible in the input. In particular, this is essential for checking inclusion of timed automata that use internal clocks to control the computation.

6 Conclusions

We present first-order alternating automata, a model of computation that generalizes classical boolean alternating automata to first-order theories. Due to their expressivity, first-order alternating automata are closed under union, intersection and complement. However the emptiness problem is undecidable even in the most simple case, of the quantifier-free theory of equality with uninterpreted predicate symbols. We deal with the emptiness problem by developping a practical semi-algorithm that always terminates, when the automaton is not empty. In case of emptiness, termination of the semi-algorithm occurs in most practical test cases, as shown by a number of experiments.

References

1. Alur, R., Dill, D.L.: A theory of timed automata. Theor. Comput. Sci. **126**(2), 183–235 (1994)
2. Barringer, H., Rydeheard, D., Havelund, K.: Rule systems for run-time monitoring: from EAGLE to RULER. In: Sokolsky, O., Taşıran, S. (eds.) RV 2007. LNCS, vol. 4839, pp. 111–125. Springer, Heidelberg (2007). https://doi.org/10.1007/978-3-540-77395-5_10
3. Börger, E., Grädel, E., Gurevich, Y.: The Classical Decision Problem: Perspectives in Mathematical Logic. Springer, Heidelberg (1997)
4. Chandra, A.K., Kozen, D.C., Stockmeyer, L.J.: Alternation. J. ACM **28**(1), 114–133 (1981)
5. D'Antoni, L., Kincaid, Z., Wang, F.: A symbolic decision procedure for symbolic alternating finite automata. Electron. Notes Theor. Comput. Sci. **336**, 79–99 (2018). The Thirty-third Conference on the Mathematical Foundations of Programming Semantics (MFPS XXXIII)

6. Farzan, A., Kincaid, Z., Podelski, A.: Proof spaces for unbounded parallelism. SIGPLAN Not. **50**(1), 407–420 (2015)
7. Farzan, A., Kincaid, Z., Podelski, A.: Proving liveness of parameterized programs. In: Proceedings of the 31st Annual ACM/IEEE Symposium on Logic in Computer Science, LICS 2016, pp. 185–196. ACM (2016)
8. First Order Alternating Data Automata (FOADA). https://github.com/cathiec/FOADA
9. Grebenshchikov, S., Lopes, N.P., Popeea, C., Rybalchenko, A.: Synthesizing software verifiers from proof rules. SIGPLAN Not. **47**(6), 405–416 (2012)
10. Halpern, J.Y.: Presburger arithmetic with unary predicates is π_1^1 complete. J. Symb. Log. **56**(2), 637–642 (1991)
11. Hojjat, H., Rümmer, P.: Deciding and interpolating algebraic data types by reduction. Technical report. CoRR abs/1801.02367 (2018). http://arxiv.org/abs/1801.02367
12. Includer. http://www.fit.vutbr.cz/research/groups/verifit/tools/includer/
13. Iosif, R., Rogalewicz, A., Vojnar, T.: Abstraction refinement and antichains for trace inclusion of infinite state systems. In: Chechik, M., Raskin, J.-F. (eds.) TACAS 2016. LNCS, vol. 9636, pp. 71–89. Springer, Heidelberg (2016). https://doi.org/10.1007/978-3-662-49674-9_5
14. Iosif, R., Xu, X.: Abstraction refinement for emptiness checking of alternating data automata. In: Beyer, D., Huisman, M. (eds.) TACAS 2018. LNCS, vol. 10806, pp. 93–111. Springer, Cham (2018). https://doi.org/10.1007/978-3-319-89963-3_6
15. JavaSMT. https://github.com/sosy-lab/java-smt
16. Kaminski, M., Francez, N.: Finite-memory automata. Theor. Comput. Sci. **134**(2), 329–363 (1994)
17. Kincaid, Z.: Parallel proofs for parallel programs. Ph.D. thesis, University of Toronto (2016)
18. Kuncak, V., Mayer, M., Piskac, R., Suter, P.: Software synthesis procedures. Commun. ACM **55**(2), 103–111 (2012)
19. Lyndon, R.C.: An interpolation theorem in the predicate calculus. Pacific J. Math. **9**(1), 129–142 (1959)
20. McMillan, K.L.: Lazy abstraction with interpolants. In: Ball, T., Jones, R.B. (eds.) CAV 2006. LNCS, vol. 4144, pp. 123–136. Springer, Heidelberg (2006). https://doi.org/10.1007/11817963_14
21. McMillan, K.L.: Lazy annotation revisited. In: Biere, A., Bloem, R. (eds.) CAV 2014. LNCS, vol. 8559, pp. 243–259. Springer, Cham (2014). https://doi.org/10.1007/978-3-319-08867-9_16
22. Nelson, G., Oppen, D.C.: Fast decision procedures based on congruence closure. J. ACM **27**(2), 356–364 (1980)
23. Predicate Automata. https://github.com/zkincaid/duet/tree/ark2/regression/predicateAutomata
24. Presburger, M.: Über die Vollstandigkeit eines gewissen Systems der Arithmetik. Comptes rendus du I Congrés des Pays Slaves, Warsaw (1929)
25. Reynolds, A., King, T., Kuncak, V.: Solving quantified linear arithmetic by counterexample-guided instantiation. Form. Methods Syst. Des. **51**(3), 500–532 (2017)
26. Rybalchenko, A., Sofronie-Stokkermans, V.: Constraint solving for interpolation. J. Symb. Comput. **45**(11), 1212–1233 (2010)
27. Z3 SMT Solver. https://rise4fun.com/z3

Q3B: An Efficient BDD-based SMT Solver for Quantified Bit-Vectors

Martin Jonáš(✉) and Jan Strejček

Masaryk University, Brno, Czech Republic
{xjonas,strejcek}@fi.muni.cz

Abstract. We present the first stable release of our tool Q3B for deciding satisfiability of quantified bit-vector formulas. Unlike other state-of-the-art solvers for this problem, Q3B is based on translation of a formula to a BDD that represents models of the formula. The tool also employs advanced formula simplifications and approximations by effective bit-width reduction and by abstraction of bit-vector operations. The paper focuses on the architecture and implementation aspects of the tool, and provides a brief experimental comparison with its competitors.

1 Introduction

Advances in solving formula *satisfiability modulo theories* (SMT) achieved during the last few decades enabled significant progress and practical applications in the area of automated analysis, testing, and verification of various systems. In the case of software and hardware systems, the most relevant theory is the *theory of fixed-sized bit-vectors*, as these systems work with inputs expressed as bit-vectors (i.e., sequences of bits) and perform bitwise and arithmetic operations on bit-vectors. The quantifier-free fragment of this theory is supported by many general-purpose SMT solvers, such as CVC4 [1], MathSAT [7], Yices [10], or Z3 [9] and also by several dedicated solvers, such as Boolector [21] or STP [12]. However, there are some use-cases where quantifier-free formulas are not natural or expressive enough. For example, formulas containing quantifiers arise naturally when expressing loop invariants, ranking functions, loop summaries, or when checking equivalence of two symbolically described sets of states [8,13,17,18,24]. In the following, we focus on SMT solvers for *quantified* bit-vector formulas. In particular, this paper describes the state-of-the-art SMT solver Q3B including its implementation and the inner workings.

Solving of quantified bit-vector formulas was first supported by Z3 in 2013 [25] and for a limited set of *exists/forall* formulas with only a single quantifier alternation by Yices in 2015 [11]. Both of these solvers decide quantified formulas by *quantifier instantiation*, in which universally quantified variables in the Skolemized formula are repeatedly instantiated by ground terms until the resulting quantifier-free formula is unsatisfiable or a model of the original formula is found.

This work has been supported by Czech Science Foundation, grant GA18-02177S.

I. Dillig and S. Tasiran (Eds.): CAV 2019, LNCS 11562, pp. 64–73, 2019.
https://doi.org/10.1007/978-3-030-25543-5_4

In 2016, we proposed a different approach for solving quantified bit-vector formulas: by using binary decision diagrams (BDDs) and approximations [14]. For evaluation of this approach, we implemented an experimental SMT solver called Q3B, which outperformed both Z3 and Yices. Next solver that was able to solve quantified bit-vector formulas was Boolector in 2017, using also an approach based on quantifier instantiation [22]. Unlike Z3, in which the universally quantified variables are instantiated only by constants or subterms of the original formula, Boolector uses a counterexample-guided synthesis approach, in which a suitable ground term for instantiation is synthesized based on the defined grammar. Thanks to this, Boolector was able to outperform Q3B and Z3 on certain classes of formulas. More recently, in 2018, support of quantified bit-vector formulas has also been implemented into CVC4 [20]. The approach of CVC4 is also based on quantifier instantiation, but instead of synthesizing terms given by the grammar as Boolector, CVC4 uses predetermined rules based on invertibility conditions, which directly give terms that can prune many spurious models without using potentially expensive counterexample-guided synthesis. The authors of CVC4 have shown that this approach outperforms Z3, CVC4, and the original Q3B. However, Q3B has been substantially improved since the original experimental version. In 2017, we extended it with simplifications of quantified bit-vector formulas using unconstrained variables [15]. Further, in 2018, we added the experimental implementation of abstractions of bit-vector operations [16]. With these techniques, Q3B is able to decide more formulas than Z3, Boolector, and CVC4. Besides the theoretical improvements, Q3B was also improved in terms of stability, ease of use, technical parts of the implementation, and compliance with the SMT-LIB standard. This tool paper presents the result of these improvements: Q3B 1.0, the first stable version of Q3B.

We briefly summarize the SMT solving approach of Q3B. As in most of modern SMT solvers, the input formula is first simplified using satisfiability-preserving transformations that may reduce the size and complexity of the formula. The simplified formula is then converted to a binary decision diagram (BDD) that represents all assignments satisfying the formula, i.e., the *models* of the formula. If the BDD represents at least one model, we say that the BDD is *satisfiable* and it implies satisfiability of the formula. If the BDD represents the empty set of models, we say that it is *unsatisfiable* and so is the formula. Unfortunately, there are formulas for which the corresponding BDD (or some of the intermediate BDDs that appear during its computation) is necessarily exponential in the number of bits in the formula. For example, this is the case for formulas that contain multiplication of two bit-vector variables [5]. To be able to deal with such formulas, Q3B computes in parallel also BDDs underapproximating and overapproximating the original set of models, i.e., BDDs representing subsets and supersets of the original set of models, respectively. The approximating BDDs may be much smaller in size than the precise BDD, especially if the approximation is very rough. Still, they can be used to decide satisfiability of the original formula. If an overapproximating BDD is unsatisfiable, the original formula is also unsatisfiable. If the overapproximating BDD is satisfiable, we take one of its models, i.e., an assignment to the top-level existential variables of the formula, and check whether it is a model of the original formula. If the answer is positive, the original formula is satisfiable. In the other case, we build a more precise overapproximating BDD. Underapproximating BDDs are utilized analogously. The only difference is that for unsatisfiable underapproximating BDD, we check the validity of a countermodel, i.e., an assignment to the top-level universal variables that makes the formula unsatisfiable. The approach is depicted in Fig. 1.

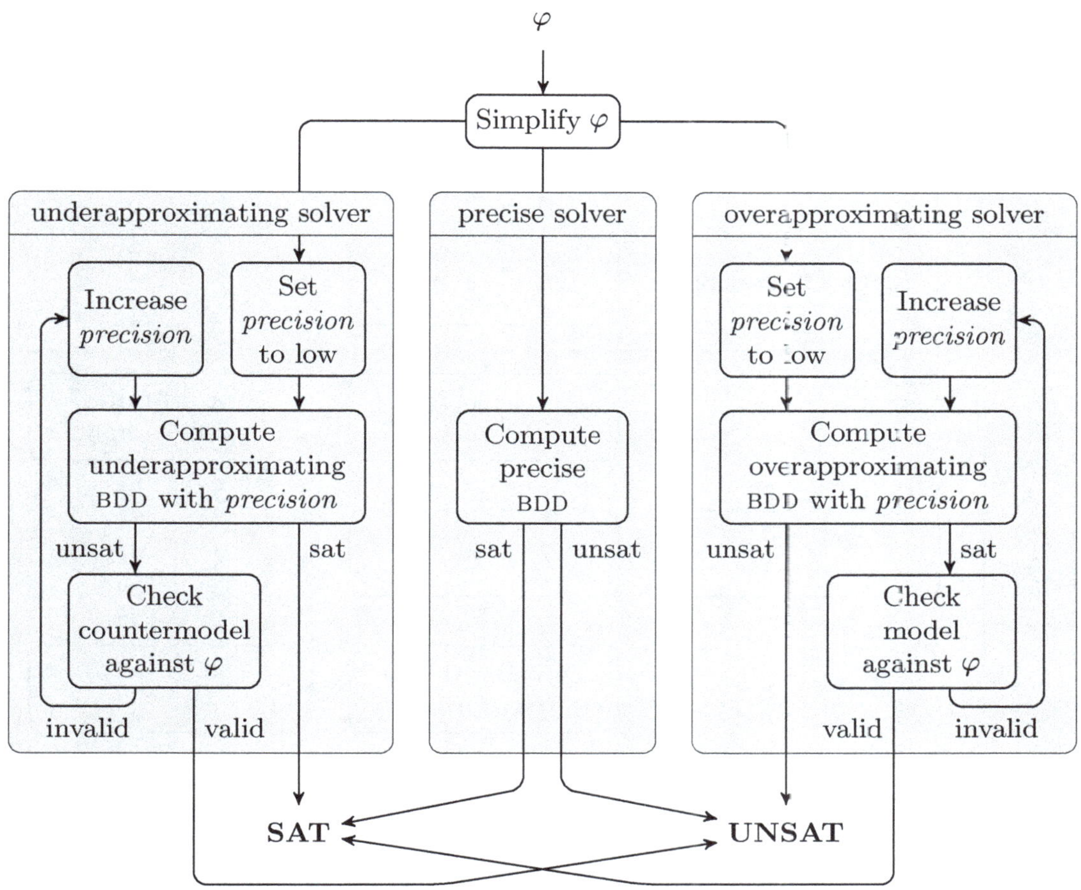

Fig. 1. High-level overview of the SMT solving approach used by Q3B. The three shaded areas are executed in parallel and the first result is returned.

Q3B currently supports two ways of computing the approximating BDDs from the input formula. First of these are *variable bit-width approximations* in which the *effective bit-width* of some variables is reduced. In other words, some of the variables are represented by fewer bits and the rest of the bits is set to zero bits, one bits, or the sign bit of the reduced variable. This approach was originally used by the SMT solvers UCLID [6] and Boolector [21]. Q3B extends this approach to quantified formulas: if bit-widths of only existentially quantified variables are reduced, the resulting BDD is underapproximating; if bit-widths of only universally quantified variables are reduced, the resulting BDD is overapproximating. The second way to obtain an approximation is *bit-vector operation abstraction* [16], during which the individual bit-vector operations may not compute all bits of the result, but produce some *do-not-know bits* if the resulting BDDs would exceed a given number of nodes. An underapproximating BDD then represents assignments that satisfy the formula for all possible values of these do-not-know bits. Analogously, an overapproximating BDD represents all assignments that satisfy the formula for some value of the do-not-know bits. Q3B also supports a combination of these two methods, in which both the effective bit-with of variables is reduced and the limit on the size of BDDs is imposed. During an approximation refinement, either the effective bit-width or the size limit is increased, based on the detected cause of the imprecision.

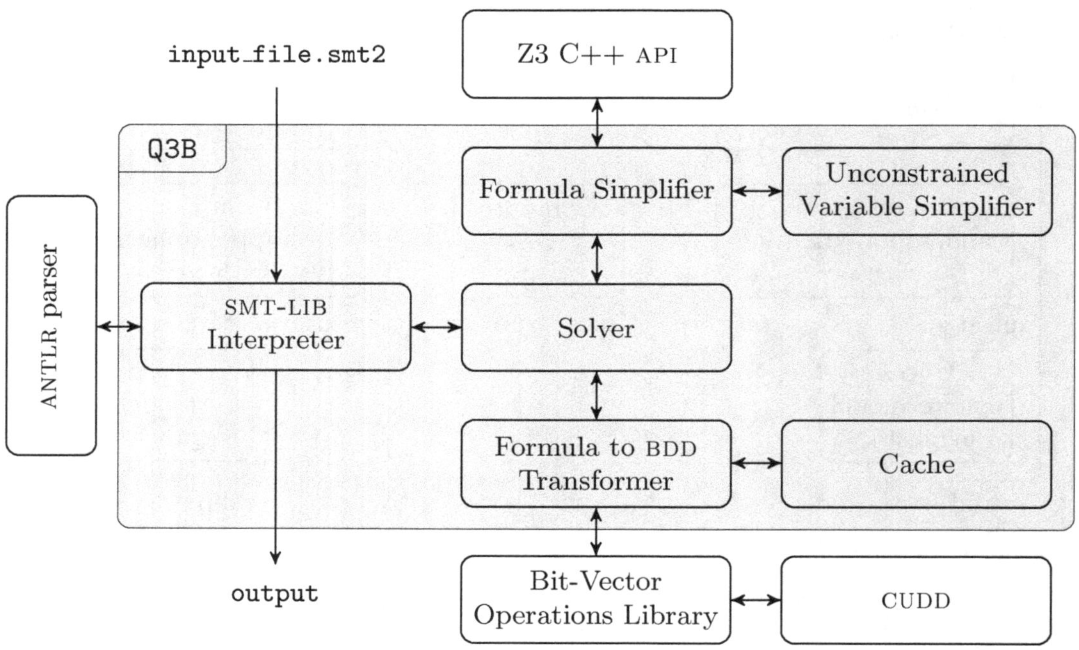

Fig. 2. Architecture of Q3B. Components in the shaded box are parts of Q3B, the other components are external.

2 Architecture

This section describes the internal architecture of Q3B. The overall structure including internal and external components and the interactions between them is depicted in Fig. 2. We explain the purpose of the internal components:

SMT-LIB Interpreter (implemented in `SMTLIBInterpreter.cpp`) reads the input file in the SMT-LIB format [3], which is the standard input format for SMT solvers. The interpreter executes all the commands from the file. In particular, it maintains the assertion stack and the options set by the user, calls solver when `check-sat` command is issued, and queries `Solver` if the user requires the model with the command `get-model`.

Formula Simplifier (implemented in `FormulaSimplifier.cpp`) provides interface for all applied formula simplifications, in particular miniscoping, conversion to negation normal form, pure literal elimination, equality propagation, constructive equality resolution (CER) [14], destructive equality resolution (DER) [25], simple theory-related rewriting, and simplifications using unconstrained variables. Most of these simplifications are implemented directly in this component; only CER, DER, and majority of the theory-related rewritings are performed by calling Z3 API and simplifications using unconstrained variables are implemented in a separate component of Q3B. The simplifier also converts top-level existential variables to uninterpreted constants, so their values are also included in a model. Some simplifications that could change models of the formula are disabled if the user enables model generation, i.e., sets `:produce-models` to `true`.

Unconstrained Variable Simplifier (implemented in `UnconstrainedVariableSimplifier.cpp`) provides simplifications of formulas that contain unconstrained variables, i.e., variables that occur only once in the formula. Besides previously published unconstrained variable simplifications [15], which were present in the previous versions of Q3B, this component now also provides new *goal-directed* simplifications of formulas with unconstrained variables. In these simplifications, we aim to determine whether a subterm containing an unconstrained variable should be minimized, maximized, sign minimized, or sign maximized in order to satisfy the formula. If the subterm should be minimized and contains an unconstrained variable, the term is replaced by a simpler term that gives the minimal result that can be achieved by any value of the unconstrained variable. Similarly for maximization, sign minimization, and sign maximization.

Solver (implemented in `Solver.cpp`) is the central component of our tool. It calls formula simplifier and then creates three threads for the precise solver, the underapproximating solver, and the overapproximating solver. It also controls the approximation refinement loops of the approximating solvers. Finally, it returns the result of the fastest thread and stores the respective model, if the result was `sat`.

Formula to BDD Transformer (implemented in the file `ExprToBDDTransformer.cpp`) performs the actual conversion of a formula to a BDD. Each subterm of the input formula is converted to a vector of BDDs (if the subterm's sort is a bit-vector of width n then the constructed vector contains n BDDs, each BDD represents one bit of the subterm). Further, each subformula of the input formula is converted to a BDD. These conversions proceed by a straightforward bottom-up recursion on the formula syntax tree. The transformer component calls an external library to compute the effect of logical and bit-vector operations on BDDs and vectors of BDDs, respectively. Besides the precise conversion, the transformer can also construct overapproximating and underapproximating BDDs. Precision of approximations depends on parameters set by the solver component.

Cache (implemented as a part of `ExprToBDDTransformer.cpp`) maintains for each converted subformula and subterm the corresponding BDD or a vector of BDDs, respectively. Each of the three solvers has its own cache. When an approximating solver increases precision of the approximation, entries of its cache that can be affected by the precision change are invalidated. All the caches are internally implemented by hash-tables.

3 Implementation

Q3B is implemented in C++17, is open-source and available under MIT license on GitHub: https://github.com/martinjonas/Q3B. The project development process includes continuous integration and automatic regression tests.

Q3B relies on several external libraries and tools. For representation and manipulation with BDDs, Q3B uses the open-source library CUDD 3.0 [23]. Since CUDD does not support bit-vector operations, we use the library by Peter Navrátil [19] that implements bit-vector operations on top of CUDD. The algorithms in this library are inspired by the ones in the BDD library BuDDy[1] and they provide a decent performance. Nevertheless, we have further improved its performance by several modifications. In particular, we added a specific code for handling expensive operations like bit-vector multiplication and division when arguments contain constant BDDs. This for example considerably speeds up multiplication whenever one argument contains many constant zero bits, which is a frequent case when we use the variable bit-width approximation fixing some bits to zero. Further, we have fixed few incorrectly implemented bit-vector operations in the original library. Finally, we have extended the library with the support for do-not-know bits in inputs of the bit-vector operations and we have implemented abstract versions of arithmetic operations that can produce do-not-know bits when the result exceeds a given number of BDD nodes.

For parsing the input formulas in SMT-LIB format, Q3B uses ANTLR parser generated from the grammar[2] for SMT-LIB 2.6 [2]. We have modified the grammar to correctly handle bit-vector numerals and to support `push` and `pop` commands without numerical argument. The parser allows Q3B to support all bit-vector operations and almost all SMT-LIB commands except `get-assertions`, `get-assignment`, `get-proof`, `get-unsat-assumptions`, `get-unsat-core`, and all the commands that work with algebraic data-types. This is in sharp contrast with the previous experimental versions of Q3B, which only collected all the assertions from the input file and performed the satisfiability check regardless of the rest of the commands and of the presence of the `check-sat` command. The reason for this was that the older versions parsed the input file using the Z3 C++ API, which can provide only the list of assertions, not the rest of the SMT-LIB script. Thanks to the new parser, Q3B 1.0 can also provide the user

[1] https://sourceforge.net/projects/buddy/.

[2] https://github.com/julianthome/smtlibv2-grammar.

with a model of a satisfiable formula after calling `get-model`; this important aspect of other SMT solvers was completely missing in the previous versions.

On the other hand, C++ API of the solver Z3 is still used for internal representation of parsed formulas. The Z3 C++ API is also used to perform manipulations with formulas, such as substitution of values for variables, and some of the formula simplifications. Note that these are the only uses of Z3 API in Q3B during solving the formula; no actual SMT- or SAT-solving capabilities of Z3 are used during the solving process.

Some classes of Q3B, in particular `Solver`, `FormulaSimplifier`, and `UnconstrainedVariableSimplifier`, expose a public C++ API that can be used by external tools for SMT solving or just performing formula simplifications. For example, `Solver` exposes method `Solve(formula, approximationType)`, which can be used to decide satisfiability by the precise solver, the underapproximating solver, or the overapproximating solver. `Solver` also exposes the method `SolveParallel(formula)`, which simplifies the input formula and runs all three of these solvers in parallel and returns the first result as depicted in Fig. 1.

4 Experimental Evaluation

We have evaluated the performance of QB3 1.0 and compared it to the latest versions of SMT solvers Boolector (v3.0), CVC4 (v1.6), and Z3 (v4.8.4). All tools were used with their default settings except for CVC4, where we used the same settings as in the paper that introduces quantified bit-vector solving in CVC4 [20], since they give better results than the default CVC4 settings. As the benchmark set, we have used all 5751 quantified bit-vector formulas from the SMT-LIB repository. The benchmarks are divided into 8 distinct families of formulas. We have executed each solver on each benchmark with CPU time limit 20 min and RAM limit of 8 GiB. All the experiments were performed in a Ubuntu 16.04 virtual machine within a computer equipped with Intel(R) Core(TM) i7-8700 CPU @ 3.20 GHz CPU and 32 GiB of RAM. For reliable benchmarking we employed BenchExec [4], a tool that allocates specified resources for a program execution and precisely measures their usage. All scripts used for running benchmarks and processing their results, together with detailed descriptions and some additional results not presented in the paper, are available online[3].

Table 1 shows the numbers of benchmarks in each benchmark family solved by the individual solvers. Q3B is able to solve the most benchmarks in benchmark families *2017-Preiner-scholl-smt08*, *2017-Preiner-tptp*, *2017-Preiner-UltimateAutomizer*, *2018-Preiner-cav18*, and *wintersteiger*, and it is competitive in the remaining families. In total, Q3B also solves more formulas than each of the other solvers: 116 more than Boolector, 83 more than CVC4, and 139 more than Z3. Although the numbers of solved formulas for the solvers seem fairly similar, the cross-comparison in Table 2 shows that the differences among the individual solvers are actually larger. For each other solver, there are at least

[3] https://github.com/martinjonas/q3b-artifact.

Table 1. For each solver and benchmark family, the table shows the number of benchmarks from the given family solved by the given solver. The column *Total* shows the total number of benchmarks in the given family. The last line provides the total CPU times for the benchmarks solved by all four solvers.

Family	Total	Boolector	CVC4	Q3B	Z3
2017-Preiner-keymaera	4035	4022	3998	4009	**4031**
2017-Preiner-psyco	194	193	190	182	**194**
2017-Preiner-scholl-smt08	374	312	248	**319**	272
2017-Preiner-tptp	73	69	**73**	**73**	**73**
2017-Preiner-UltimateAutomizer	153	152	151	**153**	**153**
20170501-Heizmann-UltimateAutomizer	131	30	**128**	124	32
2018-Preiner-cav18	600	553	**565**	**565**	553
wintersteiger	191	163	174	**185**	163
Total	5751	5494	5527	**5610**	5471
CPU time [s]		7794	5877	19853	**4055**

Table 2. For all pairs of the solvers, the table shows the number of benchmarks that were solved by the solver in the corresponding row, but not by the solver in the corresponding column. The column *Uniquely solved* shows the number of benchmarks that were solved only by the given solver.

	Boolector	CVC4	Q3B	Z3	Uniquely solved
Boolector	0	123	69	78	8
CVC4	156	0	60	171	6
Q3B	185	143	0	208	25
Z3	55	115	69	0	6

143 benchmarks that can be solved by Q3B but not by the other solver. We think this shows the importance of developing an SMT solver based on BDDs and approximations besides the solvers based on quantifier instantiation.

5 Conclusions and Future Work

We have described the architecture and inner workings of the first stable version of the state-of-the-art SMT solver Q3B. Experimental evaluation on all quantified bit-vector formulas from SMT-LIB repository shows that this solver slightly outperforms other state-of-the-art solvers for such formulas.

As future work, we would like to drop the dependency on the Z3 API: namely to implement our own representation of formulas and reimplement all the simplifications currently outsourced to Z3 API directly in Q3B. We also plan to extend some simplifications with an additional bookkeeping needed to construct a model of the original formula. With these extensions, all simplifications could be used even if the user wants to get a model of the formula. We would also like to implement production of unsatisfiable cores since they are also valuable for software verification.

References

1. Barrett, C., et al.: CVC4. In: Gopalakrishnan, G., Qadeer, S. (eds.) CAV 2011. LNCS, vol. 6806, pp. 171–177. Springer, Heidelberg (2011). https://doi.org/10.1007/978-3-642-22110-1_14
2. Barrett, C., Stump, A., Tinelli, C.: The SMT-LIB Standard: Version 2.6. Technical report, Department of Computer Science, The University of Iowa (2017). www.SMT-LIB.org
3. CBarrett, C., Stump, A., Tinelli, C.: The SMT-LIB standard: version 2.0. In: Gupta, A., Kroening, D. (eds.) Proceedings of the 8th International Workshop on Satisfiability Modulo Theories, Edinburgh, UK (2010)
4. Beyer, D., Löwe, S., Wendler, P.: Benchmarking and resource measurement. In: Fischer, B., Geldenhuys, J. (eds.) SPIN 2015. LNCS, vol. 9232, pp. 160–178. Springer, Cham (2015). https://doi.org/10.1007/978-3-319-23404-5_12
5. Bryant, R.E.: On the complexity of VLSI implementations and graph representations of boolean functions with application to integer multiplication. IEEE Trans. Comput. **40**(2), 205–213 (1991)
6. Bryant, R.E., Kroening, D., Ouaknine, J., Seshia, S.A., Strichman, O., Brady, B.A.: An abstraction-based decision procedure for bit-vector arithmetic. STTT **11**(2), 95–104 (2009)
7. Cimatti, A., Griggio, A., Schaafsma, B.J., Sebastiani, R.: The MathSAT5 SMT solver. In: Piterman, N., Smolka, S.A. (eds.) TACAS 2013. LNCS, vol. 7795, pp. 93–107. Springer, Heidelberg (2013). https://doi.org/10.1007/978-3-642-36742-7_7
8. Cook, B., Kroening, D., Rümmer, P., Wintersteiger, C.M.: Ranking function synthesis for bit-vector relations. Form. Methods Syst. Des. **43**(1), 93–120 (2013)
9. de Moura, L., Bjørner, N.: Z3: an efficient SMT solver. In: Ramakrishnan, C.R., Rehof, J. (eds.) TACAS 2008. LNCS, vol. 4963, pp. 337–340. Springer, Heidelberg (2008). https://doi.org/10.1007/978-3-540-78800-3_24
10. Dutertre, B.: Yices 2.2. In: Biere, A., Bloem, R. (eds.) CAV 2014. LNCS, vol. 8559, pp. 737–744. Springer, Cham (2014). https://doi.org/10.1007/978-3-319-08867-9_49
11. Dutertre, B.: Solving exists/forall problems with Yices. In: Workshop on satisfiability Modulo Theories (2015)
12. Ganesh, V., Dill, D.L.: A decision procedure for bit-vectors and arrays. In: Damm, W., Hermanns, H. (eds.) CAV 2007. LNCS, vol. 4590, pp. 519–531. Springer, Heidelberg (2007). https://doi.org/10.1007/978-3-540-73368-3_52
13. Gulwani, S., Srivastava, S., Venkatesan, R.: Constraint-based invariant inference over predicate abstraction. In: Jones, N.D., Müller-Olm, M. (eds.) VMCAI 2009. LNCS, vol. 5403, pp. 120–135. Springer, Heidelberg (2008). https://doi.org/10.1007/978-3-540-93900-9_13
14. Jonáš, M., Strejček, J.: Solving quantified bit-vector formulas using binary decision diagrams. In: Creignou, N., Le Berre, D. (eds.) SAT 2016. LNCS, vol. 9710, pp. 267–283. Springer, Cham (2016). https://doi.org/10.1007/978-3-319-40970-2_17
15. Jonáš, M., Strejček, J.: On simplification of formulas with unconstrained variables and quantifiers. In: Gaspers, S., Walsh, T. (eds.) SAT 2017. LNCS, vol. 10491, pp. 364–379. Springer, Cham (2017). https://doi.org/10.1007/978-3-319-66263-3_23

16. Jonáš, M., Strejček, J.: Abstraction of bit-vector operations for BDD-based SMT solvers. In: Fischer, B., Uustalu, T. (eds.) ICTAC 2018. LNCS, vol. 11187, pp. 273–291. Springer, Cham (2018). https://doi.org/10.1007/978-3-030-02508-3_15
17. Kroening, D., Lewis, M., Weissenbacher, G.: Under-approximating loops in C programs for fast counterexample detection. In: Sharygina, N., Veith, H. (eds.) CAV 2013. LNCS, vol. 8044, pp. 381–396. Springer, Heidelberg (2013). https://doi.org/10.1007/978-3-642-39799-8_26
18. Mrázek, J., Bauch, P., Lauko, H., Barnat, J.: SymDIVINE: tool for control-explicit data-symbolic state space exploration. In: Bošnački, D., Wijs, A. (eds.) SPIN 2016. LNCS, vol. 9641, pp. 208–213. Springer, Cham (2016). https://doi.org/10.1007/978-3-319-32582-8_14
19. Navrátil, P.: Adding support for bit-vectors to BDD libraries CUDD and Sylvan. Bachelor's thesis, Masaryk University, Faculty of Informatics, Brno (2018)
20. Niemetz, A., Preiner, M., Reynolds, A., Barrett, C., Tinelli, C.: Solving quantified bit-vectors using invertibility conditions. In: Chockler, H., Weissenbacher, G. (eds.) CAV 2018. LNCS, vol. 10982, pp. 236–255. Springer, Cham (2018). https://doi.org/10.1007/978-3-319-96142-2_16
21. Niemetz, A., Preiner, M., Wolf, C., Biere, A.: Btor2, BtorMC and Boolector 3.0. In: Chockler, H., Weissenbacher, G. (eds.) CAV 2018. LNCS, vol. 10981, pp. 587–595. Springer, Cham (2018). https://doi.org/10.1007/978-3-319-96145-3_32
22. Preiner, M., Niemetz, A., Biere, A.: Counterexample-guided model synthesis. In: Legay, A., Margaria, T. (eds.) TACAS 2017. LNCS, vol. 10205, pp. 264–280. Springer, Heidelberg (2017). https://doi.org/10.1007/978-3-662-54577-5_15
23. Somenzi, F.: CUDD: CU Decision Diagram Package Release 3.0.0. University of Colorado at Boulder (2015)
24. Srivastava, S., Gulwani, S., Foster, J.S.: From program verification to program synthesis. In: Proceedings of the 37th ACM SIGPLAN-SIGACT Symposium on Principles of Programming Languages, POPL 2010, Madrid, Spain, 17–23 January 2010, pp. 313–326 (2010)
25. Wintersteiger, C.M., Hamadi, Y., de Moura, L.M.: Efficiently solving quantified bit-vector formulas. Form. Methods Syst. Des. **42**(1), 3–23 (2013)

CVC4SY: Smart and Fast Term Enumeration for Syntax-Guided Synthesis

Andrew Reynolds[1], Haniel Barbosa[1], Andres Nötzli[2(✉)], Clark Barrett[2], and Cesare Tinelli[1]

[1] The University of Iowa, Iowa City, USA
[2] Stanford University, Stanford, USA
noetzli@cs.stanford.edu

Abstract. We present CVC4SY, a syntax-guided synthesis (SyGuS) solver based on three bounded term enumeration strategies. The first encodes term enumeration as an extension of the quantifier-free theory of algebraic datatypes. The second is based on a highly optimized brute-force algorithm. The third combines elements of the others. Our implementation of the strategies within the satisfiability modulo theories (SMT) solver CVC4 and a heuristic to choose between them leads to significant improvements over state-of-the-art SyGuS solvers.

1 Introduction

Syntax-guided synthesis (SyGuS) [3] is a recent paradigm for program synthesis, successfully used for applications in formal verification and programming languages. Most SyGuS solvers perform counterexample-guided inductive synthesis (CEGIS) [16]: a refinement loop in which a learner proposes solutions, and a verifier, generally a satisfiability modulo theories (SMT) solver [8,9], checks them and provides counterexamples for failures. Generally, the learner enumerates some set of terms, while pruning spurious ones [17]. The simplicity and efficacy of enumerative SyGuS have made it the de facto approach for SyGuS, although alternatives exist for restricted fragments [4,14].

In previous work [14], we have shown how the SMT solver CVC4 [5] can itself act as an efficient synthesizer. This tool paper focuses on recent advances in the enumerative subsolver of CVC4, culminating in the current SyGuS solver CVC4SY. Figure 1 shows its main components. The term enumerator is parameterized by an enumeration strategy chosen before solving: CVC4SY_S, whose constraint-based (smart) enumeration allows for numerous optimizations (Sect. 2); CVC4SY_F, based on a new approach for (fast) enumerative synthesis (Sect. 3), which has significant advantages with respect to the enumerative solver CVC4SY_S and other state-of-the-art approaches; and CVC4SY_H, based on a hybrid approach combining smart and fast enumeration (Sect. 4). All strategies are fully integrated in CVC4, meaning they support inputs in many background theories, including arithmetic, bit-vectors, strings, and floating point. We evaluate these approaches on a large set of benchmarks (Sect. 5).

I. Dillig and S. Tasiran (Eds.): CAV 2019, LNCS 11562, pp. 74–83, 2019.
https://doi.org/10.1007/978-3-030-25543-5_5

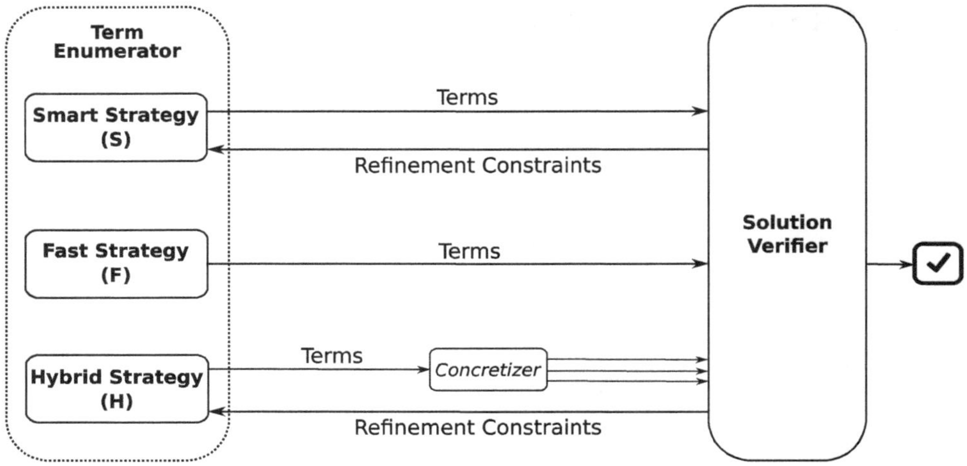

Fig. 1. Architecture of CVC4SY.

The Problem. A syntax-guided synthesis problem for a function f in a background theory T consists of a set of semantic restrictions, or specification, for f given by a (second-order) T-formula of the form $\exists f.\, \varphi[f]$, and a set of syntactic restrictions on the solutions for f, typically expressed as a context-free grammar. An *enumerative* approach to this problem combines a *term enumerator* and a *solution verifier* for solving synthesis conjectures. The role of the term enumerator is to output a stream of terms $t_1, t_2, \ldots$ over some tuple $\bar{x}$ of variables representing the inputs of f, where each $t_i[\bar{x}]$ is a candidate solution. The role of the solution verifier is to check for each t_i whether it is a solution for f by determining if the negated conjecture $\neg\varphi[\lambda\bar{x}.t_i]$ is unsatisfiable.

Bounded term generation considers terms based on an ordering such as term size (the number of non-nullary symbols in a term). For each $k = 0, 1, 2, \ldots$, the term enumerator outputs a *finite* set S_k of terms, each of size at most k. Bounded term generation in CVC4SY is *complete* in the sense that, for any k, if f has a solution of size at most k, then at least one of the terms in S_k is a solution for f. The effectiveness of an approach for (complete) bounded term generation can be evaluated based on two criteria: (i) the number of terms it generates and (ii) the rate at which it generates them.

We follow two approaches for enumerative SyGuS in CVC4SY, each optimized for one of the criteria above: a *smart* approach and a *fast* one. The first aims to generate reasonably quickly the smallest set of terms while maintaining completeness, while the second aims to generate terms as quickly as possible.

Technical Preliminaries. As we showed in previous work [14], syntactic restrictions can be conveniently represented as a set of *(algebraic) datatypes*, for which some SMT solvers have dedicated decision procedures [7, 13]. For instance, given a function $f : (x : \mathsf{Int}) \times (y : \mathsf{Int}) \to \mathsf{Int}$ and the context-free grammar R below specifying what integer (I) and Boolean (B) terms can appear in candidate solutions for f:

$$I ::= 0 \mid 1 \mid x \mid y \mid I + I \mid I - I \mid \mathsf{ite}(B, I, I) \tag{1}$$

$$B ::= B \geqslant B \mid I \approx I \mid \neg B \mid B \wedge B \tag{2}$$

our SyGuS solver generates the following mutually recursive datatypes:

$$\mathcal{I} = 0 \mid 1 \mid \mathsf{x} \mid \mathsf{y} \mid \mathsf{plus}(\mathcal{I},\mathcal{I}) \mid \mathsf{minus}(\mathcal{I},\mathcal{I}) \quad \mathsf{ite}(\mathcal{B},\mathcal{I},\mathcal{I}) \tag{3}$$

$$\mathcal{B} = \mathsf{geq}(\mathcal{I},\mathcal{I}) \mid \mathsf{eq}(\mathcal{I},\mathcal{I}) \mid \mathsf{not}(\mathcal{B}) \mid \mathsf{and}(\mathcal{B},\mathcal{B}) \tag{4}$$

Each datatype constructor corresponds to a production rule of R, e.g. plus corresponds to the rule $I ::= I+I$. A datatype term such as $\mathsf{plus}(\mathsf{x},\mathsf{y})$ represents the arithmetic term $x+y$. We will use these datatypes as a running example.

For a datatype term t, we write $\mathsf{is}_{\mathsf{C}}(t)$ to denote the *discriminator* predicate that is satisfied exactly when t is interpreted as a datatype whose top constructor is C. We write $\mathsf{sel}_n^{\tau}(t)$ to denote a *shared selector* [15] applied to t, interpreted as the nth child of t with type τ if one exists, and interpreted as an arbitrary element of τ otherwise. A term consisting of zero or more consecutive nested applications of shared selectors applied to a term t is a *shared selector chain (for t)*.

2 Smart Enumerative SyGuS

Our *smart enumerative SyGuS* approach CVC4SY_S, is based on finding solutions for an evolving set of constraints in an extension of the quantifier-free fragment of algebraic datatypes. These constraints are constructed to rule out many redundant solutions while not overconstraining the problem, potentially missing actual solutions.

In detail, candidate solutions for the function $f : \tau_1 \rightarrow \tau_2$ to be synthesized are constructed by maintaining a set of constraints F, initially empty, for a first-order variable d ranging over the datatype representing τ_2. For example, consider again the function f with the syntactic restrictions expressed by the datatypes in Eqs. 3 and 4. If the term generator finds a model for F, it provides to the solution verifier the integer term which corresponds to the value of d in the model; for example, it provides $x+1$ when d is interpreted as $\mathsf{plus}(\mathsf{x},1)$. In turn, if the solution verifier finds that $x+1$ is not a solution, it provides the *blocking constraint* $\neg\mathsf{is}_{\mathsf{plus}}(d) \vee \neg\mathsf{is}_{\mathsf{x}}(\mathsf{sel}_1^{\mathcal{I}}(d)) \vee \neg\mathsf{is}_1(\mathsf{sel}_2^{\mathcal{I}}(d))$, i.e., the datatype constraint that rules out the current value for d, which is then added to F. This is a *syntactic* constraint on future candidate solutions from the term generator. Its atoms are discriminators applied to shared selector chains.

CVC4SY_S uses a number of optimization techniques in addition to the basic loop above, which we describe in the remainder of this section. These techniques produce blocking constraints via the lemmas-on-demand paradigm [6] that eagerly rule out spurious candidates, *prior* to the solution verification step. Additionally, whenever possible, it *strengthens* blocking constraints via novel generalization techniques, with the effect of ruling out larger classes of candidates.

Blocking via Theory Rewriting with Structural Generalization. As we describe in previous work [14], the enumerative solver of CVC4 uses its rewriter as an oracle for discovering when candidate solutions are redundant. The motivation is that for any two equivalent terms t and s, only one of them needs to be checked with the solution verifier, since either both t and s are solutions to the synthesis conjecture or neither is. Given a term t, we write $t{\downarrow}$ to denote its *rewritten form*. Note that it is possible for equivalent terms not to have the same rewritten form. This is a consequence of the trade-offs in the implementation of CVC4's rewriter, which must balance efficiency and completeness.

As an example, suppose that the term enumerator previously generated $x{+}y$ and that d's current value is the datatype term representing $y + x$, where, however, $(x + y){\downarrow} = (y + x){\downarrow}$. We first generate a blocking constraint template $R[z]$ of the form $\neg \mathsf{is}_{\mathsf{plus}}(z) \vee \neg \mathsf{is}_{\mathsf{y}}(\mathsf{sel}_1^{\mathcal{I}}(z)) \vee \neg \mathsf{is}_{\mathsf{x}}(\mathsf{sel}_2^{\mathcal{I}}(z))$, where z is a fresh variable. This template is subsequently instantiated with $z \mapsto u$ for any shared selector chain u of type $\mathcal{I}$ that currently (or later) appears in F, starting with d itself. This has the effect of ruling out all candidate solutions that have $y + x$ as a subterm, which is justified by the fact that each such term is equivalent to one in which all occurrences of $y + x$ are replaced by $x + y$.

We employ a refinement of this technique, which we call *theory rewriting with structural generalization*, which searches for and then blocks only the minimal skeleton of the term under test that is sufficient for determining its rewritten form. For example, consider the if-then-else term $t = \mathsf{ite}(x \approx 0 \wedge y \geqslant 0,\ 0,\ x)$, This term is equivalent to x, regardless of the value of predicate $y \geqslant 0$. This can be confirmed by the rewriter by computing that $\mathsf{ite}(x \approx 0 \wedge w,\ 0,\ x){\downarrow} = x$ where w is a fresh Boolean variable. Then, instead of generating a constraint that blocks only (the datatype value corresponding to) t, we generate a stronger constraint that does not depend on the subterm $y \geqslant 0$. In other words, this blocking constraint rules out all candidate solutions that contain the subterm $\mathsf{ite}(x \approx 0 \wedge w,\ 0,\ x)$, for *any* term w. We compute these generalizations using a recursive algorithm that iteratively replaces *each* subterm of the current candidate with a fresh variable, and checks whether its rewritten form remains the same.

Blocking via CEGIS with Structural Generalization. Synthesis solvers based on CEGIS maintain a list of *refinement points* that witness the infeasibility of previous candidate solutions. That is, given a synthesis conjecture $\exists f.\, \forall \bar{x}.\, \varphi[f,\ \bar{x}]$, the solver maintains a growing list $\bar{p}_1, \ldots, \bar{p}_n$ of values for $\bar{x}$ that witness the infeasibility of previous candidates $u_1, \ldots, u_n$ for f. Then, when a new candidate u is generated, we first check whether $\varphi[u,\ \bar{p}_i]$ is false for some $i \leqslant n$. When a candidate u fails to satisfy $\varphi[u, \bar{p}_i]$, CVC4SY_S further applies a form of generalization analogous to the structural generalization described above. We call this *CEGIS with structural generalization*, where the goal is to find the minimal skeleton of u that also fails to satisfy some refinement point.

For example, suppose f is the function to synthesize, φ includes the constraint $f(x, y) \leqslant x - 1$, and $p_1 = (3, 3)$ is a refinement point. Then, the candidate term $u[x, y] = \mathsf{ite}(x \geqslant 0,\ x,\ y + 1)$ will be discarded, because $\mathsf{ite}(3 \geqslant 0,\ 3,\ 4) \nleqslant 2$. Notice, however, that *any* candidate $u' = \mathsf{ite}(x \geqslant 0,\ x,\ w)$ is falsified by p_1, regardless of what w is, since $u'[3, 3] \leqslant 2$ is equivalent to $3 \leqslant 2$. This indicates that we can block *all* ite candidate terms with condition $x \geqslant 0$ and true branch x. We can express this constraint in CVC4SY_S by dropping the disjuncts that relate to the false branch of the ite term. This form of blocking is particularly useful when synthesizing multiple functions (f_1, $\ldots$, f_n), since it is often the case that a candidate for a single f_i is already sufficient to falsify the specification, regardless of what the candidates for the other functions are.

Evaluation Unfolding. This technique uses *evaluation functions* to encode the relationship between the datatype terms assigned to d and their analogs in the theory T. For example, the evaluation function for the datatype $\mathcal{I}$ defined in (3) is a function $\mathsf{E}_{\mathcal{I}} : \mathcal{I} \times \mathsf{Int} \times \mathsf{Int} \mapsto \mathsf{Int}$ defined axiomatically so that $\mathsf{E}_{\mathcal{I}}(d, m, n)$ denotes the result of evaluating d by interpreting any occurrences of x and y in d respectively as m and n and interpreting the other constructors as the corresponding arithmetic/Boolean operators, e.g. $\mathsf{E}_{\mathcal{I}}(\mathsf{minus}(\mathsf{x},\mathsf{y}), 5, 3)$ is interpreted as 2. When a refinement point $\bar{c}$ is generated, we add a constraint requiring that the evaluation of d at $\bar{c}$ must satisfy the specification. For example, for conjecture $\exists f. \forall x. f(x+1, x) \leqslant 0$, and refinement point $x \mapsto 1$, we add the constraint $\mathsf{E}_{\mathcal{I}}(d, 2, 1) \leqslant 0$. Then, when a literal $\mathsf{is}_{\mathsf{C}}(t)$ is asserted for a term t of type $\mathcal{I}$, we can add a constraint corresponding to the one-step unfolding of the evaluation of t. Specifically, when $\mathsf{is}_{\mathsf{ite}}(d)$ is asserted, we generate the constraint

$$\mathsf{is}_{\mathsf{ite}}(d) \Rightarrow \mathsf{E}_{\mathcal{I}}(d, 2, 1) \approx \mathsf{ite}(\mathsf{E}_{\mathcal{B}}(\mathsf{sel}_1^{\mathcal{B}}(d), 2, 1), \mathsf{E}_{\mathcal{I}}(\mathsf{sel}_1^{\mathcal{I}}(d), 2, 1), \mathsf{E}_{\mathcal{I}}(\mathsf{sel}_2^{\mathcal{I}}(d), 2, 1))$$

indicating that the evaluation of d on point $(2, 1)$ indeed behaves like an ite term when d has top symbol ite. Our implementation adds these constraints for all terms t whose top symbols correspond to ite or Boolean connectives. For terms t whose top symbol is any of the other operators, we add constraints corresponding to their total evaluation of t when the value of t is fully determined, for example, $t \approx \mathsf{plus}(\mathsf{x},\mathsf{y}) \Rightarrow \mathsf{E}_{\mathcal{I}}(t, 2, 1) \approx 3$. Notice this constraint with $t = d$ along with the refinement constraint $\mathsf{E}_{\mathcal{I}}(d, 2, 1) \leqslant 0$ suffices to show that d cannot be $\mathsf{plus}(\mathsf{x},\mathsf{y})$.

3 Fast Enumerative SyGuS

The techniques in the previous section prune the search space so that often, only a small subset of the entire possible set of terms is considered for a given term size bound. The main bottleneck, however, is managing the large number of blocking constraints generated. Moreover, the benefits of this approach are limited when the grammar or specification does not admit opportunities for generalization.

For this reason, we have also developed CVC4SY_F, which, in the spirit of other SyGuS solvers (notably ESOLVER [17]), relies on a principled brute-force approach for term generation. In contrast to other solvers, however, which are built as layers on top of the core SMT reasoner, CVC4SY_F is fully integrated as a subsolver of CVC4, so communication with other components has almost no overhead. This technique, *fast enumerative synthesis*, does not use constraint solving to generate new terms. As a result, the majority of optimizations from Sect. 2 are incompatible with it.

Algorithm. To generate terms up to a given size k, we maintain a set S_τ^k of terms of type τ and size k for each datatype τ corresponding to a non-terminal symbol of our input grammar R. First, we compute for each such τ the set $\mathcal{C}_\tau$ of its *constructor classes*, an equivalence relation over the constructors of τ that groups them by their type. For example, the constructor classes for $\mathcal{I}$ are $\{\mathsf{x},\mathsf{y},0,1\}$, $\{\mathsf{plus},\mathsf{minus}\}$ and $\{\mathsf{ite}\}$. Then, we use the following procedure for generating all terms of size k for type τ:

FASTENUM(τ, k):
For all:
- Constructor classes $C \in \mathcal{C}_\tau$, whose elements have type $\tau_1 \times \ldots \times \tau_n \to \tau$,
- Tuple of naturals $(k_1, \ldots k_n)$ such that $k_1 + \ldots + k_n + \mathsf{ite}(n > 0, 1, 0) = k$,

(a) Run FASTENUM(τ_i, k_i) for each $i = 1, \ldots, n$,
(b) Add $\mathsf{C}(t_1, \ldots, t_n)$ to S_τ^k for all tuples $(t_1, \ldots, t_n)$ with $t_i \in S_{\tau_i}^{k_i}$ and all constructors $\mathsf{C} \in C$.

The recursive procedure FASTENUM(τ, k) populates the set S^k_τ of all terms of type τ with size k. These sets are cached globally. We incorporate an optimization that only adds terms $\mathsf{C}(t_1, \ldots, t_n)$ to S^k_τ whose corresponding terms in the theory T are unique up to rewriting. This mimics the effect of blocking via theory rewriting as described in Sect. 2. For example, $\mathsf{plus}(\mathsf{y}, \mathsf{x})$ is not added to $S^1_\mathcal{I}$ if that set already contains $\mathsf{plus}(\mathsf{x}, \mathsf{y})$, noting that $(x + y)\downarrow = (y + x)\downarrow$. By construction of S^k_τ for $k \geqslant 1$, this has the cascading effect of excluding all terms having $y + x$ as a subterm.

We observe that theory rewriting with structural generalization cannot be easily incorporated into this scheme since it requires the use of a constraint solver, something that the above algorithm seeks to avoid.

4 Hybrid Approach: Variable-Agnostic Enumerative SyGuS

We follow a third approach, in solver CVC4SY_H, that combines elements of the previous approaches. The idea is to use the (smart) approach from Sect. 2 to generate terms, but then generate *multiple* candidate solutions from each term using a fast subprocedure we call a *concretizer*. We implement an instance of this scheme, which we call *variable-agnostic* term generation, that produces only terms that are unique modulo alpha-equivalence. In our running example, when a term t such as $x + 1$ is produced, the concretizer produces all terms generated by the grammar R that are alpha-equivalent to t, namely, $\{x + 1, y + 1\}$ in this case. The advantage of this approach is that CVC4SY_H can block any term whose variables are not canonically ordered; that is, assuming for instance that $x < y$, it may block terms like $1 - y$ and $y + y$, noting they are alpha-equivalent to $1 - x$ and $x + x$, respectively. To implement this blocking scheme, we introduce unary Boolean predicates pre_x and $post_x$ for each variable x in our grammar, where pre_x (resp., $post_x$) holds for t if and only if variable x occurs in a depth-first left-to-right traversal of our candidate term before (resp., after) traversing to the position indicated by the selector chain t. We encode the semantics of these predicates based on the arguments of constructors in our signature, e.g. $\mathsf{is}_{\mathsf{plus}}(z) \Rightarrow (pre_x(z) \approx pre_x(\mathsf{sel}^\mathcal{I}_1(z)) \wedge post_x(\mathsf{sel}^\mathcal{I}_2(z)) \approx post_x(z))$. We then assert that pre_x and pre_y are false for our top-level variable d, and require $\mathsf{is}_\mathsf{y}(z) \Rightarrow pre_x(z)$ for all z, stating that x must come before y in the traversal of any generated term.

This technique is useful for grammars with many variables, such as grammars in invariant synthesis problems, where the number of terms of small size is prohibitively large. Blocking based on theory rewriting (with generalization) from Sect. 2 is compatible with this technique and is used in CVC4SY_H. However, the other optimizations are disabled, since they prune solutions in a way that is not agnostic to variables.

5 Evaluation

We evaluated the above techniques in CVC4SY on four benchmark sets: invariant synthesis benchmarks from the verification of Lustre [11] models; a set from work on synthesizing invertibility conditions for bit-vector operators [12] (IC-BV); a set of bit-vector invariant synthesis problems [2] (CegisT); and the SyGuS-COMP 2018 [1] benchmarks from five tracks: assorted problems (General), conditional linear arithmetic

Table 1. Summary of number of problems solved per benchmark set. Best results are in **bold**.

Set	#	a+si	a	s	s-cg	s-eu	s-rg	s-r	f	f-r	h	h-rg	h-r	EUS
General	413	**293**	237	228	229	232	230	220	237	226	221	225	213	290
Gen-CrCi	214	**159**	**159**	**159**	**159**	143	**159**	**159**	155	132	130	137	125	152
CLIA	88	**86**	20	20	19	19	19	18	20	16	16	16	16	85
INV	127	109	109	109	109	109	109	109	**110**	109	109	109	109	68
PBE-BV	753	**751**	**751**	721	721	721	721	628	**751**	717	721	721	628	745
PBE-Str	109	**105**	**105**	104	104	104	87	75	**105**	103	102	87	75	74
Subtotal	1704	**1503**	1381	1341	1341	1328	1325	1209	1378	1303	1299	1295	1166	1414
IC-BV	160	135	135	135	132	130	130	133	**138**	132	128	126	127	
CegisT	79	**56**	43	43	43	43	42	41	42	42	42	42	41	
Lustre	485	**255**	**255**	**255**	**255**	218	211	221	231	213	248	244	234	
Total	2428	**1949**	1814	1774	1771	1719	1708	1604	1789	1690	1717	1707	1568	

problems (CLIA), invariant synthesis problems (INV), and programming-by-examples problems [10] with a set over bit-vectors (PBE-BV) and another over strings (PBE-Str). We also considered separately the CrCi subset from General, which corresponds to cryptographic circuit synthesis. We ran our experiments on a cluster equipped with Intel E5-2637 v4 CPUs running Ubuntu 16.04, providing one core, 1800 s, and 8 GB RAM for each job. Results are summarized in Table 1 and Fig. 2. We denote the strategies from Sects. 2, 3, and 4 by **s**, **f** and **h**, respectively (smart, fast, and hybrid); disabling the optimizations from Sect. 2 is marked by "-" and the suffixes **r** (rewriting), **rg** (rewriting with structural generalization), **cg** (CEGIS with structural generalization), and **eu** (evaluation unfolding). We also evaluated two meta-strategies of CVC4SY: **a** and **a+si**. The auto strategy **a** picks a strategy based on the properties of the problem: **f** for PBE problems and for problems without the Boolean type or the ite operator in their grammar and **s** otherwise. Strategy **a+si** uses the single-invocation solver [14] on problems that are amenable to quantifier elimination and **a** otherwise. We use the state-of-the-art SyGuS solver EUSOLVER [4] (**EUS**) as a baseline, but only for SyGuS-COMP benchmarks due to limitations in its parser.

Overall, strategy **s** excels on more challenging benchmark sets such as Lustre and Gen-Crci, while strategy **f** excels on the majority of the others. The gains for **f** are especially significant on PBE problems, where it outperforms both **s** and **EUS** by several orders of magnitude. Such gains are significant given that CVC4 won this track at SyGuS-COMP 2018 by employing **s** alone, and a variant of **EUS** won it in 2017. This result can be explained as a consequence of two factors. First, the string and bit-vector grammars contain many operators with the same type, making the constructor class optimization of the **f** algorithm very effective. Second, although not described in this paper, all solvers in our evaluation use divide-and-conquer algorithms for PBE problems [4], which are not compatible with the optimizations **cg** and **eu**. The most important optimization for all CVC4SY strategies and with all benchmark sets is **r**. The optimization **eu** is especially effective when grammars contain ite and Boolean connectives, such as those in the Lustre set and in some subsets of General, on which we can

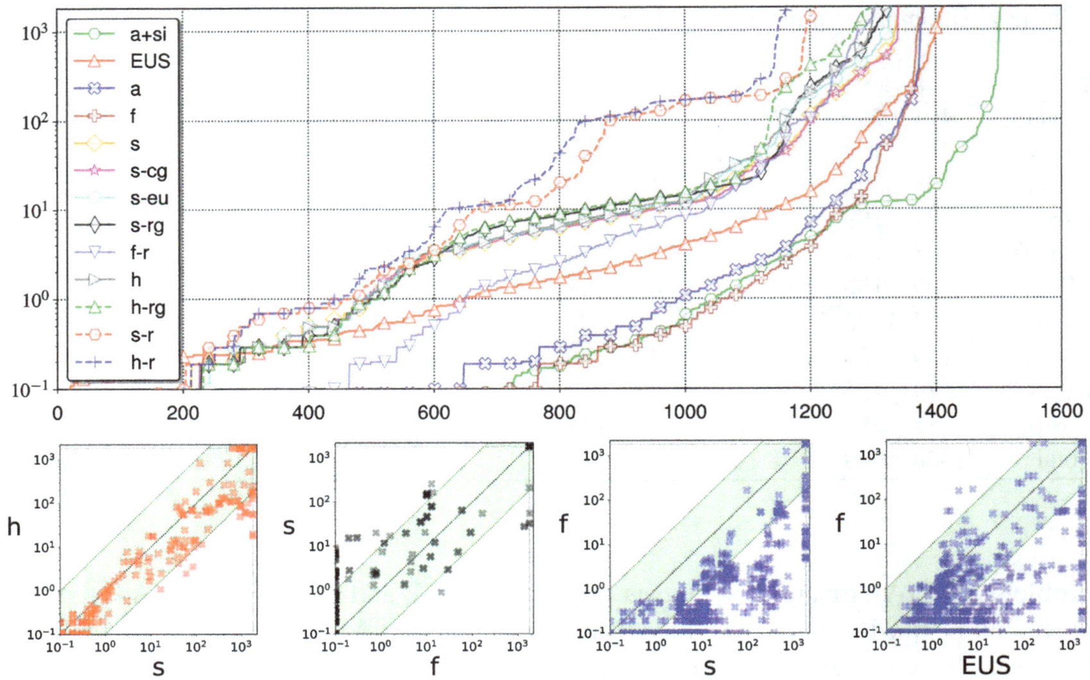

Fig. 2. Cactus plot on commonly supported benchmark sets. The first scatter plot is for the Lustre set, the second for the Gen-Crci set, and the latter two for the 862 benchmarks from the PBE sets.

see the biggest gains of **s** with respect to **s-eu**; **cg** is more helpful for IC-BV, with a few harder benchmarks only solved due to this technique.

The first scatter plot in Fig. 2 shows the advantage of **h** over **s** on Lustre, a benchmark set containing invariant synthesis problems with dozens of variables. We remark this configuration excels at quickly finding small solutions for problems with many variables, although solves fewer problems overall. The second scatter plot shows that while **s** takes significantly longer on easy problems, it outperforms **f** in the long run. The last two plots show that **f** significantly outperforms the state of the art on PBE benchmarks.

For all benchmark sets, the auto strategy **a** chooses the best enumerative strategy of CVC4SY with only a few exceptions, and hence it is the default configuration of CVC4SY. Due to specialized synthesis techniques [4, 14], both **a+si** and **EUS** outperform the purely enumerative strategies of CVC4. This is reflected in the cactus plot on the commonly supported benchmark sets, where **a** and **f** solve more benchmarks than **EUS** for lower times but then **EUS** solves more benchmarks in the end. For **a+si**, the cactus plot shows that it outperforms **EUS** significantly. Nevertheless, we remark that **a+si** is able to solve only 393 (16%) of the overall benchmarks using only single invocation techniques. Hence, we conclude that both smart and fast enumerative strategies are critical subcomponents in our approach to syntax-guided synthesis.

Acknowledgments. This work was partially supported by the National Science Foundation under award 1656926 and by the Defense Advanced Research Projects Agency under award FA8650-18-2-7854.

References

1. SyGuS-COMP 2018 (2018). http://sygus.seas.upenn.edu/SyGuS-COMP2018.html
2. Abate, A., David, C., Kesseli, P., Kroening, D., Polgreen, E.: Counterexample guided inductive synthesis modulo theories. In: Chockler, H., Weissenbacher, G. (eds.) CAV 2018. LNCS, vol. 10981, pp. 270–288. Springer, Cham (2018). https://doi.org/10.1007/978-3-319-96145-3_15
3. Alur, R., et al.: Syntax-guided synthesis. In: Irlbeck, M., Peled, D.A., Pretschner, A., (eds.) Dependable Software Systems Engineering. NATO Science for Peace and Security Series, D: Information and Communication Security, vol. 40, pp. 1–25. IOS Press (2015)
4. Alur, R., Radhakrishna, A., Udupa, A.: Scaling enumerative program synthesis via divide and conquer. In: Legay, A., Margaria, T. (eds.) TACAS 2017. LNCS, vol. 10205, pp. 319–336. Springer, Heidelberg (2017). https://doi.org/10.1007/978-3-662-54577-5_18
5. Barrett, C., et al.: CVC4. In: Gopalakrishnan, G., Qadeer, S. (eds.) CAV 2011. LNCS, vol. 6806, pp. 171–177. Springer, Heidelberg (2011). https://doi.org/10.1007/978-3-642-22110-1_14
6. Barrett, C., Nieuwenhuis, R., Oliveras, A., Tinelli, C.: Splitting on demand in SAT modulo theories. In: Hermann, M., Voronkov, A. (eds.) LPAR 2006. LNCS (LNAI), vol. 4246, pp. 512–526. Springer, Heidelberg (2006). https://doi.org/10.1007/11916277_35
7. Barrett, C., Shikanian, I., Tinelli, C.: An abstract decision procedure for satisfiability in the theory of recursive data types. Electr. Notes Theor. Comput. Sci. **174**(8), 23–37 (2007)
8. Barrett, C., Tinelli, C.: Satisfiability Modulo Theories. Handbook of Model Checking, pp. 305–343. Springer, Cham (2018). https://doi.org/10.1007/978-3-319-10575-8_11
9. Barrett, C.W., Sebastiani, R., Seshia, S.A., Tinelli, C.: Satisfiability modulo theories. In: Biere, A., Heule, M., van Maaren, H., Walsh, T. (eds.) Handbook of Satisfiability. Frontiers in Artificial Intelligence and Applications, vol. 185, pp. 825–885. IOS Press (2009)
10. Gulwani, S.: Programming by examples: applications, algorithms, and ambiguity resolution. In: Olivetti, N., Tiwari, A. (eds.) IJCAR 2016. LNCS (LNAI), vol. 9706, pp. 9–14. Springer, Cham (2016). https://doi.org/10.1007/978-3-319-40229-1_2
11. Halbwachs, N., Caspi, P., Raymond, P., Pilaud, D.: The synchronous data flow programming language LUSTRE. Proc. IEEE **79**(9), 1305–1320 (1991)
12. Niemetz, A., Preiner, M., Reynolds, A., Barrett, C., Tinelli, C.: Solving quantified bit-vectors using invertibility conditions. In: Chockler, H., Weissenbacher, G. (eds.) CAV 2018, Part II. LNCS, vol. 10982, pp. 236–255. Springer, Cham (2018). https://doi.org/10.1007/978-3-319-96142-2_16
13. Reynolds, A., Blanchette, J.C.: A decision procedure for (co)datatypes in SMT solvers. In: Felty, A.P., Middeldorp, A. (eds.) CADE 2015. LNCS (LNAI), vol. 9195, pp. 197–213. Springer, Cham (2015). https://doi.org/10.1007/978-3-319-21401-6_13
14. Reynolds, A., Deters, M., Kuncak, V., Tinelli, C., Barrett, C.: Counterexample-guided quantifier instantiation for synthesis in SMT. In: Kroening, D., Păsăreanu, C.S. (eds.) CAV 2015, Part II. LNCS, vol. 9207, pp. 198–216. Springer, Cham (2015). https://doi.org/10.1007/978-3-319-21668-3_12

15. Reynolds, A., Viswanathan, A., Barbosa, H., Tinelli, C., Barrett, C.: Datatypes with shared selectors. In: Galmiche, D., Schulz, S., Sebastiani, R. (eds.) IJCAR 2018. LNCS (LNAI), vol. 10900, pp. 591–608. Springer, Cham (2018). https://doi.org/10.1007/978-3-319-94205-6_39
16. Solar-Lezama, A., Tancau, L., Bodík, R., Seshia, S.A., Saraswat, V.A.: Combinatorial sketching for finite programs, pp. 404–415. ACM (2006)
17. Udupa, A., Raghavan, A., Deshmukh, J.V., Mador-Haim, S., Martin, M.M.K., Alur, R.: TRANSIT: specifying protocols with concolic snippets. In: ACM SIGPLAN Conference on Programming Language Design and Implementation, PLDI 2013, Seattle, 16–19 June 2013, pp. 287–296 (2013)

Incremental Determinization for Quantifier Elimination and Functional Synthesis

Markus N. Rabe(✉)

Google, Mountain View, CA, USA
mrabe@google.com

Abstract. Quantifier elimination and its cousin functional synthesis are fundamental problems in automated reasoning that could be used in many applications of formal methods. But, effective algorithms are still elusive. In this paper, we suggest a simple modification to a QBF algorithm to adapt it for quantifier elimination and functional synthesis. We demonstrate that the approach significantly outperforms previous algorithms for functional synthesis.

1 Introduction

Given a Boolean formula $\exists Y.\, \varphi$ with free variables X, *quantifier elimination* (also called *projection*) is the problem to find a formula $\psi \equiv \exists Y.\, \varphi$ that only contains variables X. Closely related, the *functional synthesis* problem is to find a function $f_y : 2^X \rightarrow \mathbb{B}$ for all $y \in Y$, such that $\varphi[Y \mapsto f_y(X)] \equiv \exists Y.\, \varphi$.

Quantifier elimination and functional synthesis are fundamental operations in automated reasoning, computer-aided design, and verification. Hence, progress in algorithms for these problems benefits a broad range of applications of formal methods. For example, typical algorithms for reactive synthesis reduce to computing the safe region of a safety game through repeated quantifier eliminations [1–3] or directly employ functional synthesis [4]. Until today, algorithms for quantifier elimination often involve (reduced ordered) Binary Decision Diagrams (BDDs) [5]. However, BDDs often grow exponentially for applications in verification, and extracting formulas (or strategies, etc.) from BDDs typically results in huge expressions. The search for alternatives resulted in CEGAR-style algorithms [6–10].

In this work, we take look at the closely related field of QBF solving. There pure CEGAR solving [11–13] on the CNF representation is not competitive anymore [14], and it has been augmented by preprocessing [15,16], circuit representations [17–21], and Incremental Determinization (ID) [22]. It may hence be fruitful to leverage some of the recent developments of QBF.

The contribution of this work is a simple modification of ID to enable quantifier elimination and functional synthesis. Incremental Determinization (ID) is an algorithm for solving quantified Boolean formulas of the shape $\forall X.\, \exists Y.\, \varphi$, where

M.N. Rabe–Work partially done at University of California at Berkeley.

I. Dillig and S. Tasiran (Eds.): CAV 2019, LNCS 11562, pp. 84–94, 2019.
https://doi.org/10.1007/978-3-030-25543-5_6

φ is a propositional formula in conjunctive normal form (CNF), i.e. 2QBF. It follows a proof-theoretic approach, very similar to a SAT solver, alternating between building a model (i.e. Skolem functions for the existential variables Y) and a refutation proof [23]. This allows ID to provide a model (i.e. a Skolem function) when it determines that a formula is true, which sets it apart from other QBF algorithms.

The modification of ID to enable quantifier elimination for a given formula $\exists Y.\, \varphi$ is very simple: We run ID on the formula as if it was a quantified Boolean formula $\forall X.\, \exists Y.\, \varphi$, where X are the free variables, but add φ to the conflict check within ID. This suppresses the UNSAT result in the ID algorithm and it is hence forced to terminate with a model (that is, a function), which is guaranteed to satisfy the functional synthesis requirements. Quantifier elimination is then only a substitution away.

Our experimental evaluation shows that ID significantly outperforms previous algorithms for functional synthesis and quantifier elimination.

This paper is structured as follows: We review related work in Sect. 2 and introduce standard notation in Sect. 3. In Sect. 4 we first review the Incremental Determinization algorithm before introducing the change necessary to lift it to functional synthesis. The experimental evaluation is in Sect. 5. We summarize the current state of the tool CADET in Sect. 6 and conclude the paper in Sect. 7.

2 Related Work

Functional Synthesis. Early works on functional synthesis tried to exploit Craig interpolation, but did not scale well enough [24]. This was followed by first attempts to use CEGAR [6], which failed, however, to surpass the performance of BDDs [7]. More recent works revisited the use of BDDs, e.g. the tools SSyft [25] and RSynth [26,27]. This motivated the search for alternatives to BDDs [8–10]. At their core, these new algorithms all rely on counter-example guided abstraction refinement (CEGAR) [28], but they apply it in clever, compositional ways. However, they still inherit the well-known weaknesses of CEGAR (as, for example, discussed in the QBF literature): For the simple formula $\varphi = \bigwedge_{i<n} x_i \leftrightarrow y_i$, where $n = |X| = |Y|$ and $x_i \in X$ and $y_i \in Y$, CEGAR needs to browse through 2^n satisfying assignments just to recover that the function we were looking for is $f(x) = x$.

The Back-and-Forth algorithm explores stronger abstraction using MaxSAT solvers as a means to reduce the number of assignments that CEGAR needs to explore [8]. ParSyn attempts to combat the problem with parallel compute power and a compositional approach [9]. This compositional approach has later been refined using a wDNNF decomposition [10].

QBF Certification. Some solvers and preprocessors for QBF have the ability to not only provide a yes/no answer, but also produce a certificate (i.e. Skolem functions) for their result [13,22,29,30]. While most QBF approaches suffer heavy performance penalties when asked to provide a certificate, Incremental Determinization naturally computes Skolem functions that can be extracted easily from the final state [22].

3 Preliminaries

Boolean formulas over a finite set of variables $x \in X$ with domain $\mathbb{B} = \{\mathbf{0}, \mathbf{1}\}$ are generated by the following grammar:

$$\varphi := \mathbf{0} \mid \mathbf{1} \mid x \mid \neg\varphi \mid (\varphi) \mid \varphi \vee \varphi \mid \varphi \wedge \varphi$$

Other logical operations, such as implication, XOR, and equality, are considered syntactic sugar with the usual definitions.

An *assignment* $\boldsymbol{x}$ to a set of variables X is a function $\boldsymbol{x} : X \to \mathbb{B}$ that maps each variable $x \in X$ to either $\mathbf{1}$ or $\mathbf{0}$. We denote the space of assignments to some set of variables X with 2^X.

Given formulas φ and φ', and a variable x, we denote the substitution of x by φ' in φ as $\varphi[x \to \varphi']$. We lift substitutions to sets of variables $\varphi[X \mapsto t_x]$ when t_x maps each $x \in X$ to a formula φ'.

A *literal* l is either a variable $x \in X$, or its negation $\neg x$. We use $\bar{l}$ to denote the literal that is the logical negation of l. A disjunction of literals $(l_1 \vee \ldots \vee l_n)$ is called a *clause* and their conjunction $(l_1 \wedge \ldots \wedge l_n)$ is called a *cube*. We denote the variable of a literal by $var(l)$ and lift the notion to clauses $var(l_1 \vee \cdots \vee l_n) = \{var(l_1), \ldots, var(l_n)\}$.

A formula is in *conjunctive normal form* (CNF), if it is a conjunction of clauses. Throughout this exposition, we assume that the input formula is given in CNF. (The output, however, can be a non-CNF formula.) It is trivial to lift the approach to general Boolean formulas: Given a Boolean formula φ over variables X, the Tseitin transformation provides us a formula ψ with $\varphi \equiv \exists Z.\psi$, where Z are fresh variables [31]. Note that eliminating a group of variables $X' \subseteq X$ in φ is then the same as eliminating $X' \cup Z$ in ψ.

Resolution is a well-known proof rule that allows us to merge two clauses as follows. Given two clauses $C_1 \vee v$ and $C_2 \vee \neg v$, we call $C_1 \otimes_v C_2 = C_1 \vee C_2$ their *resolvent* with pivot v. The resolution rule states that $C_1 \vee v$ and $C_2 \vee \neg v$ imply their resolvent. Resolution is *refutationally complete* for Boolean formulas in CNF, i.e. given a formula in CNF that is equivalent to false, we can derive the empty clause using only resolution.

4 Lifting Incremental Determinization

In the sequel, we formally define functional synthesis, review the working principle of Incremental Determinization for 2QBF, discuss how the solver state corresponds to functions, and then introduce the modification to Incremental Determinization to turn it into an algorithm for functional synthesis. The *functional synthesis* problem is to find a function $f_y : 2^X \to \mathbb{B}$ for all $y \in Y$, such that $\varphi[Y \mapsto f_y(X)] \equiv \exists Y.\,\varphi$. Functional synthesis is closely related to solving 2QBF: Given a true 2QBF problem $\forall X.\,\exists Y.\,\varphi$, any Skolem function that is a model for the formula is also a solution to the functional synthesis problem for variable sets X and Y. Only for false 2QBF there is a difference between the problems: if there is an assignment $\boldsymbol{x}$ to X for which there is no assignment to Y, the 2QBF cannot be proven with a Skolem function, but the functional synthesis problem still requires us to produce a function f. It is clear that for input $\boldsymbol{x}$ the f can produce any output. We will exploit this similarity between 2QBF and functional synthesis in the following to lift the Incremental Determinization algorithm to functional synthesis.

4.1 Working Principle of Incremental Determinization for 2QBF

ID was originally introduced as an algorithm for 2QBF, the fragment of quantified Boolean formulas with at most one quantifier alternation. Given a formula $\forall X.\,\exists Y.\,\varphi$, ID alternates between constructing a model (i.e. a Skolem function) to prove the formula correct, and constructing a Q-resolution proof to refute the formula [32]. During model construction, ID identifies which variables in Y have unique Skolem functions considering the current set of clauses. When all variables with unique Skolem functions are identified, ID greedily introduces additional clauses to reduce the space of possible Skolem functions, such that the remaining variables may get unique Skolem functions, too. Whenever the model construction ends up in a dead-end (=conflict), ID switches to constructing a refutation proof [32] and derives clauses using resolution. As soon as ID found a clause that prevents the model construction from trying the same partial model again, it switches back to the model search. Since there are only finitely many clauses and models, either the model construction or the refutation proof must eventually finish [22,23].

Example 1. We will use the following formula as a running example:

$$\begin{aligned}\forall x_1, x_2.\,\exists y_1, y_2, y_3.\ &(x_1 \vee \neg y_1) \wedge (\neg x_1 \vee y_1) \wedge \\ &(y_1 \vee \neg y_2) \wedge (\neg y_1 \vee \neg x_2 \vee y_2) \wedge \\ &(\neg y_1 \vee y_3) \wedge (y_2 \vee \neg y_3) \wedge (x_2 \vee \neg y_3)\end{aligned}$$

Looking at the first two clauses it is clear that y_1 is uniquely determined by x_1 and y_1's Skolem function must be $f_{y_1}(X) = x_1$. For this step, we intentionally ignore all clauses of y_1 that contain y_2 and y_3, as they do not yet have a Skolem function and we have to consider them as undefined. The other clauses containing y_1 will only become relevant when looking for Skolem functions for y_2 and y_3.

Variables y_2 and y_3 do not have *unique* Skolem functions in the formula above. ID would now greedily add a *decision clause*, such as $(x_2 \vee \neg y_2)$, to also make the Skolem function for y_2 unique. The added clause, plus clauses 3 and 4 in the formula define: $f_{y_2}(X) = f_{y_1}(X) \wedge x_2$.

This results in the situation that there is no Skolem function for y_3: For the assignment $x_1 \mapsto \mathbf{1},\ x_2 \mapsto \mathbf{0}$, the functions for y_1 and y_2 assign $y_1 \mapsto \mathbf{1},\ y_2 \mapsto \mathbf{0}$.

Then clauses 4 and 5 cannot be satisfied both by y_3, which means there is a conflict for this assignment to the universals. During conflict analysis, ID would now resolve clauses 5 and 6 to obtain clause $(\neg y_1 \vee y_2)$, and then backtrack to the point before introducing the decision clause. $\triangleleft$

4.2 Representation of Functions

What is particularly interesting about ID is its ability to produce Skolem functions when it has proven a formula correct. Other than previous QBF algorithms, these Skolem functions are produced without any overhead.

ID avoids costly representations of Skolem functions: It maintains a set $D \subseteq Y$ of variables that have a unique Skolem function, and its state includes a formula δ characterizing the input-output behavior of the Skolem functions for variables D. Formula δ satisfies $\forall X. \exists! D. \delta$, where $\exists! D$ means that there exists exactly one assignment to D. We can thus think of δ also as a function f_δ mapping X assignments to D assignments.

Example 2. Back to our running example. After identifying a unique Skolem function for y_1, formula δ consists exactly of the first two clauses of the formula, $(x_1 \vee \neg y_1) \wedge (\neg x_1 \vee y_1)$. After adding the decision clause and identifying a unique Skolem function for y_2, δ consists exactly of the first four clauses and the decision clause. $\triangleleft$

4.3 Conflict Checks in ID

The formulas representing functions have primarily one purpose: to check for the existence of *conflicts*. Whenever we attempt to grow the set D by a variable v, we need to check whether v has a unique Skolem function. This check consists of two parts; given an arbitrary universal assignment $\boldsymbol{x} \in 2^X$,

(1) is there *at most* one legal assignment to v, and
(2) is there *at least* one legal assignment to v?

To formally define this, let us consider the clauses $(d_1 \vee \cdots \vee d_n \vee l)$ in φ that contain a literal l of variable v and otherwise only contain literals d_i of variables in D and X. We call these the clauses with *unique consequence*, as they can be read as implications $(\neg d_1 \wedge \cdots \wedge \neg d_n \Rightarrow l)$, and we call $\neg d_1 \wedge \cdots \wedge \neg d_n$ the antecedent of that clause. Further, we define $\mathcal{A}_l$ as the disjunction over all antecedents of literal l. (Note that $\mathcal{A}_l$ depends on D and therefore changes as the state of the solver progresses.)

The two checks from above can now be defined as follows:

(1) $\exists X. \delta \wedge \neg\mathcal{A}_v \wedge \neg\mathcal{A}_{\neg v}$
(2) $\exists X. \delta \wedge \quad \mathcal{A}_v \wedge \quad \mathcal{A}_{\neg v}$

Checking for case (1) can be efficiently approximated [22], but checking for case (2) cannot easily be avoided. We thus query a SAT solver with $\delta \wedge \mathcal{A}_v \wedge \mathcal{A}_{\neg v}$ to perform a conflict check.

Example 3. We revisit the conflict described in Example 1. The starting point is the situation when $D = \{y_1, y_2\}$ and δ consists of the first four clauses of the formula as well as the decision clause $(x_2 \vee \neg y_2)$. The antecedents of y_3 are $\mathcal{A}_{y_3} = y_1$ and $\mathcal{A}_{\neg y_3} = \neg y_2 \vee \neg x_2$. It is easy to verify that the universal assignment $x_1 \mapsto \mathbf{1},\ x_2 \mapsto \mathbf{0}, y_1 \mapsto \mathbf{1},\ y_2 \mapsto \mathbf{0}$ satisfies the conflict criterion $\delta \wedge \mathcal{A}_v \wedge \mathcal{A}_{\neg v}$. $\triangleleft$

4.4 Functional Synthesis

Remember that in the case of functional synthesis for φ over sets of variables X and Y, we search for a function $f : 2^X \rightarrow 2^Y$ such that f produces a satisfying assignment whenever it can, but can produce anything when there is no assignment to Y satisfying the formula. In case there are satisfying assignments to Y for all X, we can simply run ID as if it was a QBF $\forall X. \exists. \varphi$ to obtain a Skolem function that also satisfies the functional synthesis criterion. In the other case, that there is an X for which there is no assignment to Y satisfying φ, ID for 2QBF would eventually detect a conflict that did not depend on a decision and return with UNSAT.

In order to lift ID to functional synthesis, we want to ignore universal assignments that have no satisfying assignment to Y. A simple way to suppress these conflicts is to add φ to the conflict check. In order for an assignment to X to remain a conflict, we must now additionally find an assignment to Y that demonstrates that the conflict could be prevented by a different decision.

All other parts of ID, including the extraction of functions, remain untouched. In particular, termination is still guaranteed, as the greedy model construction either results in a function for all variables in Y or in a conflict, upon which at least one model is excluded through resolution.

Example 4. For the conflict in our running example, the universal assignment $x_1 \mapsto \mathbf{1},\ x_2 \mapsto \mathbf{0}$ is excluded in the modified conflict check. Consider the UNSAT core consisting of clauses 2, 5, and 7 for that universal assignment: propagate $y_1 \mapsto \mathbf{1}$ using clause 2; propagate $y_3 \mapsto \mathbf{1}$ using clause 5; and finally propagate $y_3 \mapsto \mathbf{0}$ using clause 7. So, instead of going into conflict analysis and backtracking, ID for functional synthesis concludes that it has found a function for all existential variables and terminates.

4.5 Quantifier Elimination

Given a formula $\exists Y. \varphi$ with free variables X, *quantifier elimination* is the problem to find a formula $\psi \equiv \exists Y. \varphi$ over variables X only. Hence, given a solution f to the functional synthesis problem for φ, we only have to substitute Y by f in φ to obtain the projected formula.

5 Experimental Evaluation

We implemented the modifications to ID in CADET,[1] a competitive 2QBF solver [22]. In this section, we compare CADET experimentally with existing

[1] CADET is available at https://github.com/MarkusRabe/cadet.

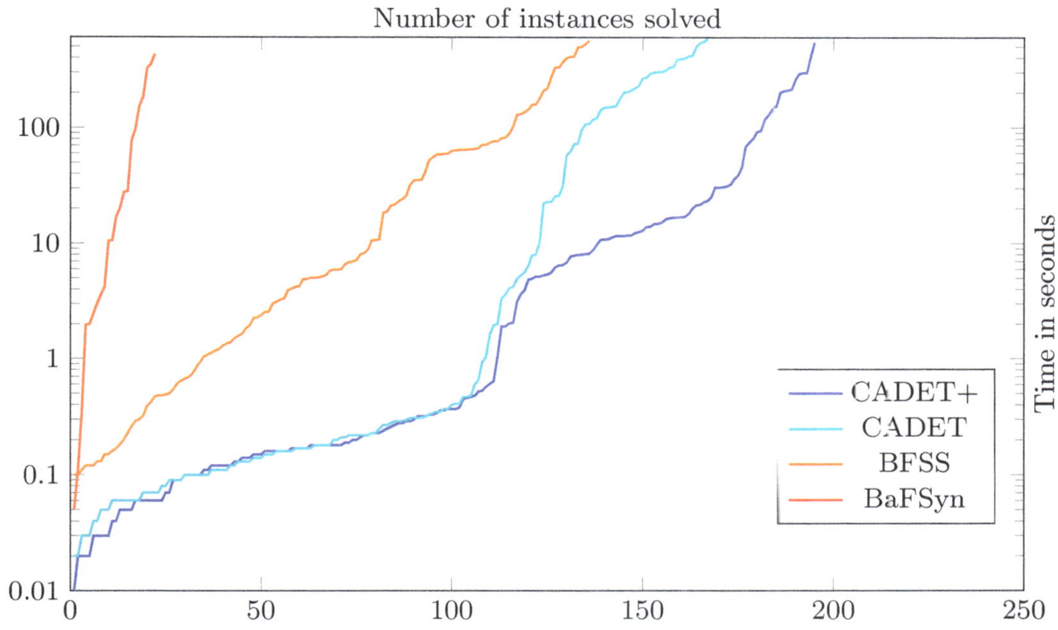

Fig. 1. Log-scale cactus plot comparing the performance over all instances.

algorithms for functional synthesis. Additionally, we implemented a certificate checker for functional synthesis and for quantifier elimination, to make sure that the computed functions are correct. The certificate checker only shares the code for AIGER circuits and the SAT solver (of which we have tried several), but is completely independent otherwise to reduce the chance of correlated bugs. The results of CADET have been checked with the proof checker; running times reported below are excluding the time to check the certificates.

So far, there is no standard benchmark for functional synthesis or quantifier elimination. Like previous works on functional synthesis, we resort to using the 2QBF benchmark from QBFEVAL'17 [14], and re-interpret them as functional synthesis problems. The 2QBF benchmark from QBFEVAL'17 is a collection of 384 formulas from various domains, mostly from software verification, program synthesis, and logical equivalences [33–36].

We compare CADET to the most recent tools on functional synthesis, BaFSyn [8] and BFSS [10], the latter of which has been shown to consistently outperform the earlier, BDD-based tools SSyft [25] and RSynth [26,27]. We ran CADET in two configurations: with (CADET+) and without (CADET) its CEGAR module [23]. We present the results as a cactus plot, which is obtained by running each tool on all formulas, sorting the running times for each tool separately. A point x, y in this plot means that x formulas were solved in less than time y. Note that the time axis is in log-scale (Fig. 1).

CADET shows a clear edge in performance: it is one to two orders of magnitude faster than its strongest competitor, BFSS, and can solve significantly more formulas. But despite the clear performance advantage in this aggregate view, BaFSyn and BFSS can be faster for individual formulas or subfamilies of QBFEval, as shown in previous works [8,10].

6 The Current State of CADET

Originally designed as an experimentation platform, CADET has grown to become a performant and versatile tool for the synthesis of Boolean functions. It consistently wins awards at the annual QBFEVAL competitions, and is the only such tool able to prove all its results [14].

CADET reads specifications in the QDIMACS and the QAIGER formats, and now supports the synthesis of Boolean functions for 2QBF, functional synthesis, and quantifier elimination with the command line options `-c [file]`, `-f [file]`, and `-e [file]`. The functions computed by CADET are much smaller compared to those found by CEGAR-based algorithms [22], and in its default configuration, CADET double-checks its results before reporting them. This can be deactivated by the flag `--dontverify`.

It has also been integrated in py-aiger [37], a Python package for the convenient handling of circuits due to Marcell Vazquez-Chanlatte, which enables us to easily model and prototype new approaches. For example, we can write:

```
import aiger_analysis as aa
import aigerbv as bv
x = bv.atom(32, 'x')  # Create a 32 bit variable
y = bv.atom(32, 'y')
expr = (x != y)
result = aa.eliminate(expr, ['y'])
assert aa.is_equal(x, result)
```

CADET also has an experimental reinforcement learning interface that allows us to automatically learn decision heuristics with the help of graph neural networks. A recent effort shows that there is huge potential in learning better branching heuristics from scratch [38].

7 Conclusions

In this work, we extended ID with the ability to solve functional synthesis and quantifier elimination problems. The extension is very simple—we only need to add the clauses of the original formula to its conflict check. The resulting algorithm significantly outperforms previous algorithms for functional synthesis.

Acknowledgements. The author wants to thank to Shubham Goel, Shetal Shah, and Lucas Tabajara for insightful discussions and for their assistance with running their functional synthesis tools. In particular, I want to express my gratitude to Supratik Chakraborty for inspiring me to work on the topic in a discussion in the summer of 2016.

References

1. Ehlers, R.: Symbolic bounded synthesis. In: Touili, T., Cook, B., Jackson, P. (eds.) CAV 2010. LNCS, vol. 6174, pp. 365–379. Springer, Heidelberg (2010). https://doi.org/10.1007/978-3-642-14295-6_33
2. Brenguier, R., Pérez, G.A., Raskin, J., Sankur, O.: AbsSynthe: abstract synthesis from succinct safety specifications. In: Proceedings of SYNT, pp. 100–116 (2014)
3. Jacobs, S., et al.: The 4th reactive synthesis competition (syntcomp 2017): benchmarks, participants & results. arXiv preprint arXiv:1711.11439 (2017)
4. Zhu, S., Tabajara, L.M., Li, J., Pu, G., Vardi, M.Y.: Symbolic LTLf synthesis. In: Proceedings of IJCAI, IJCAI 2017, pp. 1362–1369. AAAI Press (2017)
5. Bryant, R.E.: Symbolic Boolean manipulation with ordered binary-decision diagrams. ACM Comput. Surv. **24**(3), 293–318 (1992)
6. Goldberg, E., Manolios, P.: Quantifier elimination by dependency sequents. Formal Methods Syst. Des. **45**(2), 111–143 (2014). https://doi.org/10.1007/s10703-014-0214-z
7. Goldberg, E., Manolios, P.: Quantifier elimination via clause redundancy. In: Formal Methods in Computer-Aided Design, pp. 85–92, October 2013
8. Chakraborty, S., Fried, D., Tabajara, L.M., Vardi, M.Y.: Functional synthesis via input-output separation. In: Proceedings of FMCAD, pp. 1–9. IEEE (2018)
9. Akshay, S., Chakraborty, S., John, A.K., Shah, S.: Towards parallel Boolean functional synthesis. In: Legay, A., Margaria, T. (eds.) TACAS 2017. LNCS, vol. 10205, pp. 337–353. Springer, Heidelberg (2017). https://doi.org/10.1007/978-3-662-54577-5_19
10. Akshay, S., Chakraborty, S., Goel, S., Kulal, S., Shah, S.: What's hard about boolean functional synthesis? In: Chockler, H., Weissenbacher, G. (eds.) CAV 2018. LNCS, vol. 10981, pp. 251–269. Springer, Cham (2018). https://doi.org/10.1007/978-3-319-96145-3_14
11. Janota, M., Klieber, W., Marques-Silva, J., Clarke, E.: Solving QBF with counterexample guided refinement. In: Cimatti, A., Sebastiani, R. (eds.) SAT 2012. LNCS, vol. 7317, pp. 114–128. Springer, Heidelberg (2012). https://doi.org/10.1007/978-3-642-31612-8_10
12. Janota, M., Marques-Silva, J.: Solving QBF by clause selection. In: Proceedings of IJCAI, pp. 325–331. AAAI Press (2015)
13. Rabe, M.N., Tentrup, L.: CAQE: a certifying QBF solver. In: Proceedings of FMCAD, pp. 136–143 (2015)
14. QBFEVAL: QBF solver evaluation portal. http://www.qbflib.org/index_eval.php. Accessed Jan 2018
15. Biere, A., Lonsing, F., Seidl, M.: Blocked clause elimination for QBF. In: Bjørner, N., Sofronie-Stokkermans, V. (eds.) CADE 2011. LNCS (LNAI), vol. 6803, pp. 101–115. Springer, Heidelberg (2011). https://doi.org/10.1007/978-3-642-22438-6_10
16. Wimmer, R., Reimer, S., Marin, P., Becker, B.: HQSpre – an effective preprocessor for QBF and DQBF. In: Legay, A., Margaria, T. (eds.) TACAS 2017. LNCS, vol. 10205, pp. 373–390. Springer, Heidelberg (2017). https://doi.org/10.1007/978-3-662-54577-5_21
17. Klieber, W., Sapra, S., Gao, S., Clarke, E.: A non-prenex, non-clausal QBF solver with game-state learning. In: Strichman, O., Szeider, S. (eds.) SAT 2010. LNCS, vol. 6175, pp. 128–142. Springer, Heidelberg (2010). https://doi.org/10.1007/978-3-642-14186-7_12

18. Jordan, C., Klieber, W., Seidl, M.: Non-CNF QBF solving with QCIR. In: AAAI Workshop: Beyond NP (2016)
19. Balabanov, V., Jiang, J.-H.R., Scholl, C., Mishchenko, A., Brayton, R.K.: 2QBF: challenges and solutions. In: Creignou, N., Le Berre, D. (eds.) SAT 2016. LNCS, vol. 9710, pp. 453–469. Springer, Cham (2016). https://doi.org/10.1007/978-3-319-40970-2_28
20. Tentrup, L.: Non-prenex QBF solving using abstraction. In: Creignou, N., Le Berre, D. (eds.) SAT 2016. LNCS, vol. 9710, pp. 393–401. Springer, Cham (2016). https://doi.org/10.1007/978-3-319-40970-2_24
21. Janota, M.: Circuit-based search space pruning in QBF. In: Beyersdorff, O., Wintersteiger, C.M. (eds.) SAT 2018. LNCS, vol. 10929, pp. 187–198. Springer, Cham (2018). https://doi.org/10.1007/978-3-319-94144-8_12
22. Rabe, M.N., Seshia, S.A.: Incremental determinization. In: Creignou, N., Le Berre, D. (eds.) SAT 2016. LNCS, vol. 9710, pp. 375–392. Springer, Cham (2016). https://doi.org/10.1007/978-3-319-40970-2_23
23. Rabe, M.N., Tentrup, L., Rasmussen, C., Seshia, S.A.: Understanding and extending incremental determinization for 2QBF. In: Chockler, H., Weissenbacher, G. (eds.) CAV 2018. LNCS, vol. 10982, pp. 256–274. Springer, Cham (2018). https://doi.org/10.1007/978-3-319-96142-2_17
24. Jiang, J.-H.R.: Quantifier elimination via functional composition. In: Bouajjani, A., Maler, O. (eds.) CAV 2009. LNCS, vol. 5643, pp. 383–397. Springer, Heidelberg (2009). https://doi.org/10.1007/978-3-642-02658-4_30
25. Zhu, S., Tabajara, L.M., Li, J., Pu, G., Vardi, M.Y.: A symbolic approach to safety LTL synthesis. In: Strichman, O., Tzoref-Brill, R. (eds.) Hardware and Software: Verification and Testing. LNCS, vol. 10629, pp. 147–162. Springer, Cham (2017). https://doi.org/10.1007/978-3-319-70389-3_10
26. Tabajara, L.M., Vardi, M.Y.: Factored Boolean functional synthesis. In: Proceedings of FMCAD, pp. 124–131. IEEE (2017)
27. Fried, D., Tabajara, L.M., Vardi, M.Y.: BDD-based Boolean functional synthesis. In: Chaudhuri, S., Farzan, A. (eds.) CAV 2016. LNCS, vol. 9780, pp. 402–421. Springer, Cham (2016). https://doi.org/10.1007/978-3-319-41540-6_22
28. Clarke, E., Grumberg, O., Jha, S., Lu, Y., Veith, H.: Counterexample-guided abstraction refinement. In: Emerson, E.A., Sistla, A.P. (eds.) CAV 2000. LNCS, vol. 1855, pp. 154–169. Springer, Heidelberg (2000). https://doi.org/10.1007/10722167_15
29. Lonsing, F., Biere, A.: DepQBF: a dependency-aware QBF solver. JSAT **7**(2–3), 71–76 (2010)
30. Heule, M.J.H., Seidl, M., Biere, A.: A unified proof system for QBF preprocessing. In: Demri, S., Kapur, D., Weidenbach, C. (eds.) IJCAR 2014. LNCS (LNAI), vol. 8562, pp. 91–106. Springer, Cham (2014). https://doi.org/10.1007/978-3-319-08587-6_7
31. Tseitin, G.S.: On the complexity of derivation in propositional calculus. Stud. Constructive Math. Math. Log. **2**(115–125), 10–13 (1968)
32. Buning, H., Karpinski, M., Flogel, A.: Resolution for quantified Boolean formulas. Inf. Comput. **117**(1), 12–18 (1995)
33. Solar-Lezama, A., Rabbah, R.M., Bodík, R., Ebcioglu, K.: Programming by sketching for bit-streaming programs. In: Proceedings of PLDI, pp. 281–294 (2005)
34. Cook, B., Kroening, D., Rümmer, P., Wintersteiger, C.M.: Ranking function synthesis for bit-vector relations. In: Esparza, J., Majumdar, R. (eds.) TACAS 2010. LNCS, vol. 6015, pp. 236–250. Springer, Heidelberg (2010). https://doi.org/10.1007/978-3-642-12002-2_19

35. Wintersteiger, C.M., Hamadi, Y., De Moura, L.: Efficiently solving quantified bit-vector formulas. Proc. FMSD **42**(1), 3–23 (2013)
36. Jordan, C., Kaiser, Ł.: Experiments with reduction finding. In: Järvisalo, M., Van Gelder, A. (eds.) SAT 2013. LNCS, vol. 7962, pp. 192–207. Springer, Heidelberg (2013). https://doi.org/10.1007/978-3-642-39071-5_15
37. Vazquez-Chanlatte, M.: mvcisback/py-aiger, August 2018. https://doi.org/10.5281/zenodo.1326224
38. Lederman, G., Rabe, M.N., Lee, E.A., Seshia, S.A.: Learning heuristics for automated reasoning through deep reinforcement learning. arXiv preprint arXiv:1807.08058 (2018)

Numerical Programs

Loop Summarization with Rational Vector Addition Systems

Jake Silverman(✉) and Zachary Kincaid

Princeton University, Princeton, USA
{Jakers,ZKincaid}@CS.Princeton.edu

Abstract. This paper presents a technique for computing numerical loop summaries. The method synthesizes a rational vector addition system with resets ($\mathbb{Q}$-VASR) that simulates the action of an input loop, and then uses the reachability relation of that $\mathbb{Q}$-VASR to over-approximate the behavior of the loop. The key technical problem solved in this paper is to automatically synthesize a $\mathbb{Q}$-VASR that is a *best abstraction* of a given loop in the sense that (1) it simulates the loop and (2) it is simulated by any other $\mathbb{Q}$-VASR that simulates the loop. Since our loop summarization scheme is based on computing the *exact* reachability relation of a *best* abstraction of a loop, we can make theoretical guarantees about its behavior. Moreover, we show experimentally that the technique is precise and performant in practice.

1 Introduction

Modern software verification techniques employ a number of heuristics for reasoning about loops. While these heuristics are often effective, they are unpredictable. For example, an abstract interpreter may fail to find the most precise invariant expressible in the language of its abstract domain due to imprecise widening, or a software-model checker might fail to terminate because it generates interpolants that are insufficiently general. This paper presents a loop summarization technique that is capable of generating loop invariants in an expressive and decidable language and provides theoretical guarantees about invariant quality.

The key idea behind our technique is to leverage reachability results of vector addition systems (VAS) for invariant generation. Vector addition systems are a class of infinite-state transition systems with decidable reachability, classically used as a model of parallel systems [12]. We consider a variation of VAS, *rational VAS with resets (*$\mathbb{Q}$-VASR*)*, wherein there is a finite number of rational-typed variables and a finite set of transitions that simultaneously update each variable in the system by either adding a constant value or (re)setting the variable to a constant value. Our interest in $\mathbb{Q}$-VASRs stems from the fact that there is (polytime) procedure to compute a linear arithmetic formula that represents a $\mathbb{Q}$-VASR's reachability relation [8].

Since the reachability relation of a $\mathbb{Q}$-VASR is computable, the dynamics of $\mathbb{Q}$-VASR can be analyzed without relying on heuristic techniques. However,

I. Dillig and S. Tasiran (Eds.): CAV 2019, LNCS 11562, pp. 97–115, 2019.
https://doi.org/10.1007/978-3-030-25543-5_7

there is a gap between $\mathbb{Q}$-VASR and the loops that we are interested in summarizing. The latter typically use a rich set of operations (memory manipulation, conditionals, non-constant increments, non-linear arithmetic, etc) and cannot be analyzed precisely. We bridge the gap with a procedure that, for any loop, synthesizes a $\mathbb{Q}$-VASR that simulates it. The reachability relation of the $\mathbb{Q}$-VASR can then be used to over-approximate the behavior of the loop. Moreover, we prove that if a loop is expressed in linear rational arithmetic (LRA), then our procedure synthesizes a *best* $\mathbb{Q}$-VASR abstraction, in the sense that it simulates any other $\mathbb{Q}$-VASR that simulates the loop. That is, imprecision in the analysis is due to inherent limitations of the $\mathbb{Q}$-VASR model, rather heuristic algorithmic choices.

One limitation of the model is that $\mathbb{Q}$-VASRs over-approximate multi-path loops by treating the choice between paths as non-deterministic. We show that $\mathbb{Q}$-VASRS, $\mathbb{Q}$-VASR extended with control states, can be used to improve our invariant generation scheme by encoding control flow information and inter-path control dependencies that are lost in the $\mathbb{Q}$-VASR abstraction. We give an algorithm for synthesizing a $\mathbb{Q}$-VASRS abstraction of a given loop, which (like our $\mathbb{Q}$-VASR abstraction algorithm) synthesizes *best* abstractions under certain assumptions.

Finally, we note that our analysis techniques extend to complex control structures (such as nested loops) by employing summarization compositionally (i.e., "bottom-up"). For example, our analysis summarizes a nested loop by first summarizing its inner loops, and then uses the summaries to analyze the outer loop. As a result of compositionality, our analysis can be applied to partial programs, is easy to parallelize, and has the potential to scale to large code bases.

The main contributions of the paper are as follows:

- We present a procedure to synthesize $\mathbb{Q}$-VASR abstractions of transition formulas. For transition formulas in linear rational arithmetic, the synthesized $\mathbb{Q}$-VASR abstraction is a *best* abstraction.
- We present a technique for improving the precision of our analysis by using $\mathbb{Q}$-VASR with states to capture loop control structure.
- We implement the proposed loop summarization techniques and show that their ability to verify user assertions is comparable to software model checkers, while at the same time providing theoretical guarantees of termination and invariant quality.

1.1 Outline

This section illustrates the high-level structure of our invariant generation scheme. The goal is to compute a *transition formula* that summarizes the behavior of a given program. A transition formula is a formula over a set of program variables Var along with primed copies Var', representing the state of the program

```
procedure enqueue(elt):
  back := cons(elt,back)
  size := size + 1

procedure dequeue():
  if (front == nil) then
    // Reverse back, append to front
    while (back != nil) do
      front := cons(head(back),front)
      back := tail(back)
  result := head(front)
  front := tail(front)
  size := size - 1
  return result
```

(a) Persistent queue

```
procedure enqueue():
  back_len := back_len + 1
  mem_ops := mem_ops + 1
  size := size + 1
procedure dequeue():
  if (front_len == 0) then
    while (back_len != 0) do
      front_len := front_len + 1
      back_len := back_len - 1
      mem_ops := mem_ops + 3
  size := size - 1
  front_len := front_len - 1
  mem_ops := mem_ops + 2
procedure harness():
  nb_ops := 0
  while nondet() do
    nb_ops := nb_ops + 1
    if (size > 0 && nondet())
      enqueue()
    else
      dequeue()
```

(b) Integer model & harness

Fig. 1. A persistent queue and integer model. `back_len` and `front_len` models the lengths of the lists `front` and `back`; `mem_ops` counts the number of memory operations in the computation.

before and after executing a computation (respectively). For any given program P, a transition formula $\mathbf{TF}[\![P]\!]$ can be computed by recursion on syntax:[1]

$$\mathbf{TF}[\![\texttt{x := } e]\!] \triangleq \mathsf{x}' = e \wedge \bigwedge_{\mathsf{y} \neq \mathsf{x} \in \mathsf{Var}} \mathsf{y}' = \mathsf{y}$$

$$\mathbf{TF}[\![\textbf{if } c \textbf{ then } P_1 \textbf{ else } P_2]\!] \triangleq (c \wedge \mathbf{TF}[\![P_1]\!]) \vee (\neg c \wedge \mathbf{TF}[\![P_2]\!])$$

$$\mathbf{TF}[\![P_1 \, ; P_2]\!] \triangleq \exists X \in \mathbb{Z}.\mathbf{TF}[\![P_1]\!][\mathsf{Var}' \mapsto X] \wedge \mathbf{TF}[\![P_2]\!][\mathsf{Var} \mapsto X]$$

$$\mathbf{TF}[\![\textbf{while } c \textbf{ do } P]\!] \triangleq (c \wedge \mathbf{TF}[\![P]\!])^\star \wedge (\neg c[\mathsf{Var} \mapsto \mathsf{Var}'])$$

where $(-)^\star$ is a function that computes an over-approximation of the transitive closure of a transition formula. The contribution of this paper is a method for computing this $(-)^\star$ operation, which is based on first over-approximating the input transition formula by a $\mathbb{Q}$-VASR, and then computing the (exact) reachability relation of the $\mathbb{Q}$-VASR.

[1] This style of analysis can be extended from a simple block-structured language to one with control flow and recursive procedures using the framework of algebraic program analysis [13, 23].

We illustrate the analysis on an integer model of a persistent queue data structure, pictured in Fig. 1. The example consists of two operations (`enqueue` and `dequeue`), as well as a test harness (`harness`) that non-deterministically executes `enqueue` and `dequeue` operations. The queue achieves $O(1)$ amortized memory operations (`mem_ops`) in `enqueue` and `queue` by implementing the queue as two lists, `front` and `back` (whose lengths are modeled as `front_len` and `back_len`, respectively): the sequence of elements in the queue is the `front` list followed by the reverse of the `back` list. We will show that the queue functions use $O(1)$ amortized memory operations by finding a summary for `harness` that implies a linear bound on `mem_ops` (the number of memory operations in the computation) in terms of `nb_ops` (the total number of `enqueue`/`dequeue` operations executed in some sequence of operations).

We analyze the queue compositionally, in "bottom-up" fashion (i.e., starting from deeply-nested code and working our way back up to a summary for `harness`). There are two loops of interest, one in `dequeue` and one in `harness`. Since the `dequeue` loop is nested inside the `harness` loop, `dequeue` is analyzed first. We start by computing a transition formula that represents one execution of the body of the `dequeue` loop:

$$\mathit{Body}_{\texttt{deq}} = \texttt{back\_len} > 0 \land \begin{pmatrix} \texttt{front\_len}' = \texttt{front\_len} + 1 \\ \land \texttt{back\_len}' = \texttt{back\_len} - 1 \\ \land \texttt{mem\_ops}' = \texttt{mem\_ops} + 3 \\ \land \texttt{size}' = \texttt{size} \end{pmatrix}$$

Observe that each variable in the loop is incremented by a constant value. As a result, the loop update can be captured faithfully by a vector addition system. In particular, we see that this loop body formula is simulated by the $\mathbb{Q}$-VASR $V_{\texttt{deq}}$ (below), where the correspondence between the state-space of $\mathit{Body}_{\texttt{deq}}$ and $V_{\texttt{deq}}$ is given by the identity transformation (i.e., each dimension of $V_{\texttt{deq}}$ simply represents one of the variables of $\mathit{Body}_{\texttt{deq}}$).

$$\begin{bmatrix} w \\ x \\ y \\ z \end{bmatrix} = \begin{bmatrix} 1\,0\,0\,0 \\ 0\,1\,0\,0 \\ 0\,0\,1\,0 \\ 0\,0\,0\,1 \end{bmatrix} \begin{bmatrix} \texttt{front\_len} \\ \texttt{back\_len} \\ \texttt{mem\_ops} \\ \texttt{size} \end{bmatrix}; \quad V_{\texttt{deq}} = \left\{ \begin{bmatrix} w \\ x \\ y \\ z \end{bmatrix} \to \begin{bmatrix} w+1 \\ x-1 \\ y+3 \\ z \end{bmatrix} \right\}.$$

A formula representing the reachability relation of a vector addition system can be computed in polytime. For the case of $V_{\texttt{deq}}$, a formula representing k steps of the $\mathbb{Q}$-VASR is simply

$$w' = w + k \land x' = x - k \land y' = y + 3k \land z' = z. \qquad (\dagger)$$

To capture information about the pre-condition of the loop, we can project the primed variables to obtain $\texttt{back\_len} > 0$; similarly, for the post-condition, we can project the unprimed variables to obtain $\texttt{back\_len}' \geq 0$. Finally, combining (†)

(translated back into the vocabulary of the program) and the pre/post-condition, we form the following approximation of the dequeue loop's behavior:

$$\exists k. k \geq 0 \wedge \begin{pmatrix} \texttt{front\_len}' = \texttt{front\_len} + k \\ \wedge \texttt{back\_len}' = \texttt{back\_len} - k \\ \wedge \texttt{mem\_ops}' = \texttt{mem\_ops} + 3k \\ \wedge \texttt{size}' = \texttt{size} \end{pmatrix} \wedge \left(k > 0 \Rightarrow \begin{pmatrix} \texttt{back\_len} > 0 \\ \wedge \texttt{back\_len}' \geq 0 \end{pmatrix} \right).$$

Using this summary for the dequeue loop, we proceed to compute a transition formula for the body of the harness loop (omitted for brevity). Just as with the dequeue loop, we analyze the harness loop by synthesizing a $\mathbb{Q}$-VASR that simulates it, $V_{\texttt{har}}$ (below), where the correspondence between the state space of the harness loop and $V_{\texttt{har}}$ is given by the transformation $S_{\texttt{har}}$:

$$\begin{bmatrix} v \\ w \\ x \\ y \\ z \end{bmatrix} = \underbrace{\begin{bmatrix} 0&0&0&1&0 \\ 0&1&0&0&0 \\ 0&3&1&0&0 \\ 1&1&0&0&0 \\ 0&0&0&0&1 \end{bmatrix}}_{S_{\texttt{har}}} \begin{bmatrix} \texttt{front\_len} \\ \texttt{back\_len} \\ \texttt{mem\_ops} \\ \texttt{size} \\ \texttt{nb\_ops} \end{bmatrix} ; i.e., \begin{pmatrix} \texttt{size} = v \\ \wedge\ \texttt{back\_len} = w \\ \wedge\ \texttt{mem\_ops} + 3\texttt{back\_len} = x \\ \wedge\ \texttt{back\_len} + \texttt{front\_len} = y \\ \wedge\ \texttt{nb\_ops} = z \end{pmatrix}.$$

$$V_{\texttt{har}} = \left\{ \underbrace{\begin{bmatrix} v \\ w \\ x \\ y \\ z \end{bmatrix} \rightarrow \begin{bmatrix} v+1 \\ w+1 \\ x+4 \\ y+1 \\ z+1 \end{bmatrix}}_{\texttt{enqueue}}, \underbrace{\begin{bmatrix} v \\ w \\ x \\ y \\ z \end{bmatrix} \rightarrow \begin{bmatrix} v-1 \\ w \\ x+2 \\ y-1 \\ z+1 \end{bmatrix}}_{\texttt{dequeue fast}}, \underbrace{\begin{bmatrix} v \\ w \\ x \\ y \\ z \end{bmatrix} \rightarrow \begin{bmatrix} v-1 \\ 0 \\ x+2 \\ y-1 \\ z+1 \end{bmatrix}}_{\texttt{dequeue slow}} \right\}$$

Unlike the dequeue loop, we do not get an exact characterization of the dynamics of each changed variable. In particular, in the slow dequeue path through the loop, the value of front_len, back_len, and mem_ops change by a variable amount. Since back_len is set to 0, its behavior can be captured by a reset. The dynamics of front_len and mem_ops cannot be captured by a $\mathbb{Q}$-VASR, but (using our dequeue summary) we can observe that the sum of front_len + back_len is decremented by 1, and the sum of mem_ops + 3back_len is incremented by 2.

We compute the following formula that captures the reachability relation of $V_{\texttt{har}}$ (taking k_1 steps of enqueue, k_2 steps of dequeue fast, and k_3 steps of dequeue slow) under the inverse image of the state correspondence $S_{\texttt{har}}$:

$$\begin{pmatrix} \texttt{size}' = \texttt{size} + k_1 - k_2 - k_3 \\ \wedge((k_3 = 0 \wedge \texttt{back\_len}' = \texttt{back\_len} + k_1) \vee (k_3 > 0 \wedge 0 \leq \texttt{back\_len}' \leq k_1)) \\ \wedge \texttt{mem\_ops}' + 3\texttt{back\_len}' = \texttt{mem\_ops} + 3\texttt{back\_len} + 4k_1 + 2k_2 + 2k_3 \\ \wedge \texttt{front\_len}' + \texttt{back\_len}' = \texttt{front\_len} + \texttt{back\_len} + k_1 - k_2 - k_3 \\ \wedge \texttt{nb\_ops}' = \texttt{nb\_ops} + k_1 + k_2 + k_3 \end{pmatrix}$$

From the above formula (along with pre/post-condition formulas), we obtain a summary for the harness loop (omitted for brevity). Using this summary we can prove (supposing that we start in a state where all variables are zero) that `mem_ops` is at most 4 times `nb_ops` (i.e., `enqueue` and `dequeue` use O(1) amortized memory operations).

2 Background

The syntax of ∃LIRA, the existential fragment of linear integer/rational arithmetic, is given by the following grammar:

$$s, t \in \mathsf{Term} ::= c \mid x \mid s + t \mid c \cdot t$$
$$F, G \in \mathsf{Formula} ::= s < t \mid s = t \mid F \land G \mid F \lor G \mid \exists x \in \mathbb{Q}.F \mid \exists x \in \mathbb{Z}.F$$

where x is a (rational sorted) variable symbol and c is a rational constant. Observe that (without loss of generality) formulas are free of negation. ∃LRA (linear rational arithmetic) refers to the fragment of ∃LIRA that omits quantification over the integer sort.

A **transition system** is a pair $(S, \rightarrow)$ where S is a (potentially infinite) set of states and $\rightarrow \subseteq S \times S$ is a transition relation. For a transition relation $\rightarrow$, we use $\rightarrow^*$ to denote its reflexive, transitive closure.

A **transition formula** is a formula $F(\mathbf{x}, \mathbf{x}')$ whose free variables range over $\mathbf{x} = x_1, ..., x_n$ and $\mathbf{x}' = x'_1, ..., x'_n$ (we refer to the number n as the *dimension* of F); these variables designate the state before and after a transition. In the following, we assume that transition formulas are defined over ∃LIRA. For a transition formula $F(\mathbf{x}, \mathbf{x}')$ and vectors of terms $\mathbf{s}$ and $\mathbf{t}$, we use $F(\mathbf{s}, \mathbf{t})$ to denote the formula F with each x_i replaced by s_i and each x'_i replaced by t_i. A transition formula $F(\mathbf{x}, \mathbf{x}')$ defines a transition system $(S_F, \rightarrow_F)$, where the state space S_F is $\mathbb{Q}^n$ and which can transition $\mathbf{u} \rightarrow_F \mathbf{v}$ iff $F(\mathbf{u}, \mathbf{v})$ is valid.

For two rational vectors $\mathbf{a}$ and $\mathbf{b}$ of the same dimension d, we use $\mathbf{a} \cdot \mathbf{b}$ to denote the inner product $\mathbf{a} \cdot \mathbf{b} = \sum_{i=1}^{d} a_i b_i$ and $\mathbf{a} * \mathbf{b}$ to denote the pointwise (aka Hadamard) product $(\mathbf{a} * \mathbf{b})_i = a_i b_i$. For any natural number i, we use $\mathbf{e}_i$ to denote the standard basis vector in the ith direction (i.e., the vector consisting of all zeros except the ith entry, which is 1), where the dimension of $\mathbf{e}_i$ is understood from context. We use I_n to denote the $n \times n$ identity matrix.

Definition 1. *A **rational vector addition system with resets** ($\mathbb{Q}$-**VASR**) of dimension d is a finite set $V \subseteq \{0,1\}^d \times \mathbb{Q}^d$ of transformers. Each transformer $(\mathbf{r}, \mathbf{a}) \in V$ consists of a binary reset vector $\mathbf{r}$, and a rational addition vector $\mathbf{a}$, both of dimension d. V defines a transition system $(S_V, \rightarrow_V)$, where the state space S_V is $\mathbb{Q}^d$ and which can transition $\mathbf{u} \rightarrow_V \mathbf{v}$ iff $\mathbf{v} = \mathbf{r} * \mathbf{u} + \mathbf{a}$ for some $(\mathbf{r}, \mathbf{a}) \in V$.*

Definition 2. *A **rational vector addition system with resets and states** ($\mathbb{Q}$-VASRS) of dimension d is a pair $\mathcal{V} = (Q, E)$, where Q is a finite set of control states, and $E \subseteq Q \times \{0,1\}^d \times \mathbb{Q}^d \times Q$ is a finite set of edges labeled by (d-dimensional) transformers. $\mathcal{V}$ defines a transition system $(S_\mathcal{V}, \rightarrow_\mathcal{V})$, where the state space $S_\mathcal{V}$ is $Q \times \mathbb{Q}^n$ and which can transition $(q_1, \mathbf{u}) \rightarrow_\mathcal{V} (q_2, \mathbf{v})$ iff there is some edge $(q_1, (\mathbf{r}, \mathbf{a}), q_2) \in E$ such that $\mathbf{v} = \mathbf{r} * \mathbf{u} + \mathbf{a}$.*

Our invariant generation scheme is based on the following result, which is a simple consequence of the work of Haase and Halfon:

Theorem 1 ([8]). *There is a polytime algorithm which, given a d-dimensional $\mathbb{Q}$-VASRS $\mathcal{V} = (Q, E)$, computes an $\exists$LIRA transition formula reach($\mathcal{V}$) such that for all $\mathbf{u}, \mathbf{v} \in \mathbb{Q}^d$, we have $(p, \mathbf{u}) \to_{\mathcal{V}}^{*} (q, \mathbf{v})$ for some control states $p, q \in Q$ if and only if $\mathbf{u} \to_{reach(\mathcal{V})} \mathbf{v}$.*

Note that $\mathbb{Q}$-VASR can be realized as $\mathbb{Q}$-VASRS with a single control state, so this theorem also applies to $\mathbb{Q}$-VASR.

3 Approximating Loops with Vector Addition Systems

In this section, we describe a method for over-approximating the transitive closure of a transition formula using a $\mathbb{Q}$-VASR. This procedure immediately extends to computing summaries for programs (including programs with nested loops) using the method outlined in Sect. 1.1.

The core algorithmic problem that we answer in this section is: *given a transition formula, how can we synthesize a (best) abstraction of that formula's dynamics as a $\mathbb{Q}$-VASR?* We begin by formalizing the problem: in particular, we define what it means for a $\mathbb{Q}$-VASR to simulate a transition formula and what it means for an abstraction to be "best."

Definition 3. *Let $A = (\mathbb{Q}^n, \to_A)$ and $B = (\mathbb{Q}^m, \to_B)$ be transition systems operating over rational vector spaces. A* **linear simulation** *from A to B is a linear transformation $S : \mathbb{Q}^{m \times n}$ such that for all $\mathbf{u}, \mathbf{v} \in \mathbb{Q}^n$ for which $\mathbf{u} \to_A \mathbf{v}$, we have $S\mathbf{u} \to_B S\mathbf{v}$. We use $A \Vdash_S B$ to denote that S is a linear simulation from A to B.*

Suppose that $F(\mathbf{x}, \mathbf{x}')$ is an n-dimensional transition formula, V is a d-dimensional $\mathbb{Q}$-VASR, and $S : \mathbb{Q}^{d \times n}$ is linear transformation. The key property of simulations that underlies our loop summarization scheme is that if $F \Vdash_S V$, then $reach(V)(S\mathbf{x}, S\mathbf{x}')$ (i.e., the reachability relation of V under the inverse image of S) over-approximates the transitive closure of F. Finally, we observe that simulation $F \Vdash_S V$ can equivalently be defined by the validity of the entailment $F \models \gamma(S, V)$, where

$$\gamma(S, V) \triangleq \bigvee_{(\mathbf{r}, \mathbf{a}) \in V} S\mathbf{x}' = \mathbf{r} * S\mathbf{x} + \mathbf{a}$$

is a transition formula that represents the transitions that V simulates under transformation S.

Our task is to synthesize a linear transformation S and a $\mathbb{Q}$-VASR V such that $F \Vdash_S V$. We call a pair (S, V), consisting of a rational matrix $S \in \mathbb{Q}^{d \times n}$ and a d-dimensional $\mathbb{Q}$-VASR V, a $\mathbb{Q}$-**VASR abstraction**. We say that n is the *concrete dimension* of (S, V) and d is the *abstract dimension*. If $F \Vdash_S V$, then we say that (S, V) is a $\mathbb{Q}$-**VASR abstraction of** F. A transition formula may have many $\mathbb{Q}$-VASR abstractions; we are interested in computing a $\mathbb{Q}$-VASR abstraction (S, V) that results in the most precise over-approximation of the transitive closure of F. Towards this end, we define a preorder $\preceq$ on $\mathbb{Q}$-VASR abstractions, where $(S^1, V^1) \preceq (S^2, V^2)$ iff there exists a linear transformation $T \in \mathbb{Q}^{e \times d}$ such that $V^1 \Vdash_T V^2$ and $TS^1 = S^2$ (where d and e are the abstract dimensions of (S^1, V^1) and (S^2, V^2), respectively). Observe that if $(S^1, V^1) \preceq (S^2, V^2)$, then $\mathit{reach}(V^1)(S^1\mathbf{x}, S^1\mathbf{x}') \models \mathit{reach}(V^2)(S^2\mathbf{x}, S^2\mathbf{x}')$.

Thus, our problem can be stated as follows: given a transition formula F, synthesize a $\mathbb{Q}$-VASR abstraction (S, V) of F such that (S, V) is *best* in the sense that we have $(S, V) \preceq (\widetilde{S}, \widetilde{V})$ for any $\mathbb{Q}$-VASR abstraction $(\widetilde{S}, \widetilde{V})$ of F. A solution to this problem is given in Algorithm 1.

Algorithm 1. `abstract-VASR`(F)

input : Transition formula F of dimension n
output: $\mathbb{Q}$-VASR abstraction of F; Best $\mathbb{Q}$-VASR abstraction if F in $\exists$LRA

1 Skolemize existentials of F;
2 $(S, V) \leftarrow (I_n, \emptyset)$; `//` $(I_n, \emptyset)$ `is least in` $\preceq$ `order`
3 $\Gamma \leftarrow F$;
4 **while** Γ *is satisfiable* **do**
5   Let M be a model of Γ;
6     $C \leftarrow$ cube of the DNF of F with $M \models C$;
7     $(S, V) \leftarrow (S, V) \sqcup \hat{\alpha}(C)$;
8     $\Gamma \leftarrow \Gamma \wedge \neg\gamma(S, V)$
9 **return** (S, V)

Algorithm 1 follows the familiar pattern of an AllSat-style loop. The algorithm takes as input a transition formula F. It maintains a $\mathbb{Q}$-VASR abstraction (S, V) and a formula Γ, whose models correspond to the transitions of F that are *not* simulated by (S, V). The idea is to build (S, V) iteratively by sampling transitions from Γ, augmenting (S, V) to simulate the sample transition, and then updating Γ accordingly. We initialize (S, V) to be $(I_n, \emptyset)$, the canonical least $\mathbb{Q}$-VASR abstraction in $\preceq$ order, and Γ to be F (i.e., $(I_n, \emptyset)$ does not simulate any transitions of F). Each loop iteration proceeds as follows. First, we sample a model M of Γ (i.e., a transition that is allowed by F but not simulated by (S, V)). We then generalize that transition to a set of transitions by using M to select a cube C of the DNF of F that contains M. Next, we use the procedure described in Sect. 3.1 to compute a $\mathbb{Q}$-VASR abstraction $\hat{\alpha}(C)$ that simulates the transitions of C. We then update the $\mathbb{Q}$-VASR abstraction (S, V) to be the least upper bound of (S, V) and $\hat{\alpha}(C)$ (w.r.t. $\preceq$ order) using the procedure described in Sect. 3.2 (line 7). Finally, we block any transition simulated by the least upper bound (including every transition in C) from being sampled again by conjoining $\neg\gamma(S, V)$ to Γ. The loop terminates when Γ is unsatisfiable, in which case we have that $F \Vdash_S V$. Theorem 2 gives the correctness statement for this algorithm.

Theorem 2. *Given a transition formula F, Algorithm 1 computes a simulation S and $\mathbb{Q}$-VASR V such that $F \Vdash_S V$. Moreover, if F is in ∃LRA, Algorithm 1 computes a* best *$\mathbb{Q}$-VASR abstraction of F.*

The proof of this theorem as well as the proofs to all subsequent theorems, lemmas, and propositions are in the extended version of this paper [20].

3.1 Abstracting Conjunctive Transition Formulas

This section shows how to compute a $\mathbb{Q}$-VASR abstraction for a consistent *conjunctive* formula. When the input formula is in ∃LRA, the computed $\mathbb{Q}$-VASR abstraction will be a best $\mathbb{Q}$-VASR abstraction of the input formula. The intuition is that, since ∃LRA is a convex theory, a best $\mathbb{Q}$-VASR abstraction consists of a single transition. For ∃LIRA formulas, our procedure produces a $\mathbb{Q}$-VASR abstract that is not guaranteed to be best, precisely because ∃LIRA is not convex.

Let C be consistent, conjunctive transition formula. Observe that the set $Res_C \triangleq \{\langle \mathbf{s}, a\rangle : C \models \mathbf{s} \cdot \mathbf{x}' = a\}$, which represents linear combinations of variables that are *reset* across C, forms a vector space. Similarly, the set $Inc_C = \{\langle \mathbf{s}, a\rangle : C \models \mathbf{s} \cdot \mathbf{x}' = \mathbf{s} \cdot \mathbf{x} + a\}$, which represents linear combinations of variables that are *incremented* across C, forms a vector space. We compute bases for both Res_C and Inc_C, say $\{\langle \mathbf{s}_1, a_1\rangle, ..., \langle \mathbf{s}_m, a_m\rangle\}$ and $\{\langle \mathbf{s}_{m+1}, a_{m+1}\rangle, ..., \langle \mathbf{s}_d, a_d\rangle\}$, respectively. We define $\hat{\alpha}(C)$ to be the $\mathbb{Q}$-VASR abstraction $\hat{\alpha}(C) \triangleq (S, \{(\mathbf{r}, \mathbf{a})\})$, where

$$S \triangleq \begin{bmatrix} \mathbf{s}_1 \\ \vdots \\ \mathbf{s}_d \end{bmatrix} \quad \mathbf{r} \triangleq [\underbrace{0 \cdots 0}_{m \text{ times}} \; \overbrace{1 \cdots 1}^{(d-m) \text{ times}}] \quad \mathbf{a} \triangleq \begin{bmatrix} a_1 \\ \vdots \\ a_d \end{bmatrix}.$$

Example 1. Let C be the formula $x' = x + y \wedge y' = 2y \wedge w' = w \wedge w = w + 1 \wedge z' = w$. The vector space of resets has basis $\{\langle [0 \; 0 \; -1 \; 1], 0\rangle\}$ (representing that $z - w$ is reset to 0). The vector space of increments has basis $\{\langle [1 \; -1 \; 0 \; 0], 0\rangle, \langle [0 \; 0 \; 1 \; 0], 0\rangle, \langle [0 \; 0 \; -1 \; 1], 1\rangle\}$ (representing that the difference $x - y$ does not change, the difference $z - w$ increases by 1, and the variable w does not change). A best abstraction of C is thus the four-dimensional $\mathbb{Q}$-VASR

$$V = \left\{ \left(\begin{bmatrix} 0 \\ 1 \\ 1 \\ 1 \end{bmatrix}, \begin{bmatrix} 0 \\ 0 \\ 0 \\ 1 \end{bmatrix} \right) \right\}, S = \begin{bmatrix} 0 & 0 & -1 & 1 \\ 1 & -1 & 0 & 0 \\ 0 & 0 & 1 & 0 \\ 0 & 0 & -1 & 1 \end{bmatrix}.$$

In particular, notice that since the term $z - w$ is both incremented and reset, it is represented by two different dimensions in $\hat{\alpha}(C)$.

Proposition 1. *For any consistent, conjunctive transition formula C, $\hat{\alpha}(C)$ is a $\mathbb{Q}$-VASR abstraction of C. If C is expressed in ∃LRA, then $\hat{\alpha}(C)$ is best.*

3.2 Computing Least Upper Bounds

This section shows how to compute least upper bounds w.r.t. the $\preceq$ order.

By definition of the $\preceq$ order, if (S, V) is an upper bound of (S^1, V^1) and (S^2, V^2), then there must exist matrices T^1 and T^2 such that $T^1S^1 = S = T^2S^2$, $V^1 \Vdash_{T^1} V$, and $V^2 \Vdash_{T^2} V$. As we shall see, if (S, V) is a *least* upper bound, then it is completely determined by the matrices T^1 and T^2. Thus, we shift our attention to computing simulation matrices T^1 and T^2 that induce a least upper bound.

In view of the desired equation $T^1S^1 = S = T^2S^2$, let us consider the constraint $T^1S^1 = T^2S^2$ on two *unknown* matrices T^1 and T^2. Clearly, we have $T^1S^1 = T^2S^2$ iff each (T_i^1, T_i^2) belongs to the set $\mathcal{T} \triangleq \{(\mathbf{t}^1, \mathbf{t}^2) : \mathbf{t}^1S^1 = \mathbf{t}^2S^2\}$. Observe that $\mathcal{T}$ is a vector space, so there is a *best* solution to the constraint $T^1S^1 = T^2S^2$: choose T^1 and T^2 so that the set of all row pairs (T_i^1, T_i^2) forms a basis for $\mathcal{T}$. In the following, we use *pushout*(S^1, S^2) to denote a function that computes such a *best* (T^1, T^2).

While *pushout* gives a *best* solution to the equation $T^1S^1 = T^2S^2$, it is not sufficient for the purpose of computing least upper bounds for $\mathbb{Q}$-VASR abstractions, because T^1 and T^2 may not respect the structure of the $\mathbb{Q}$-VASR V^1 and V^2 (i.e., there may be no $\mathbb{Q}$-VASR V such that $V^1 \Vdash_{T^1} V$ and $V^2 \Vdash_{T^2} V$). Thus, we must further constrain our problem by requiring that T^1 and T^2 are *coherent* with respect to V^1 and V^2 (respectively).

Definition 4. *Let V be a d-dimensional $\mathbb{Q}$-VASR. We say that $i, j \in \{1, ..., d\}$ are* ***coherent dimensions*** *of V if for all transitions $(\mathbf{r}, \mathbf{a}) \in V$ we have $r_i = r_j$ (i.e., every transition of V that resets i also resets j and vice versa). We denote that i and j are coherent dimensions of V by writing $i \equiv_V j$, and observe that $\equiv_V$ forms an equivalence relation on $\{1, ..., d\}$. We refer to the equivalence classes of $\equiv_V$ as the* ***coherence classes*** *of V.*

A matrix $T \in \mathbb{Q}^{e \times d}$ ***is coherent with respect to*** *V if and only if each of its rows have non-zero values only in the dimensions corresponding to a single coherence class of V.*

For any d-dimensional $\mathbb{Q}$-VASR V and coherence class $C = \{c_1, ..., c_k\}$ of V, define Π_C to be the $k \times d$ dimensional matrix whose rows are $\mathbf{e}_{c_1}, ..., \mathbf{e}_{c_k}$. Intuitively, Π_C is a projection onto the set of dimensions in C.

Coherence is a necessary and sufficient condition for linear simulations between $\mathbb{Q}$-VASR in a sense described in Lemmas 1 and 2.

Lemma 1. *Let V^1 and V^2 be $\mathbb{Q}$-VASR (of dimension d and e, respectively), and let $T \in \mathbb{Q}^{e \times d}$ be a matrix such that $V^1 \Vdash_T V^2$. Then T must be coherent with respect to V^1.*

Let V be a d-dimensional $\mathbb{Q}$-VASR and let $T \in \mathbb{Q}^{e \times d}$ be a matrix that is coherent with respect to V and has no zero rows. Then there is a (unique) e-dimensional $\mathbb{Q}$-VASR *image*(V, T) such that its transition relation $\rightarrow_{image(V,T)}$

Algorithm 2. $(S^1, V^1) \sqcup (S^2, V^2)$

input : Normal $\mathbb{Q}$-VASR abstractions (S^1, V^1) and (S^2, V^2) of equal concrete dimension

output: Least upper bound (w.r.t. $\preceq$) of (S^1, V^2) and (S^1, V^2)

$S, T^1, T^2 \leftarrow$ empty matrices;

foreach *coherence class* C^1 *of* V^1 **do**

  foreach *coherence class* C^2 *of* V^2 **do**

    $(U^1, U^2) \leftarrow pushout(\Pi_{C^1} S^1, \Pi_{C^2} S^2)$;

    $S \leftarrow \begin{bmatrix} S \\ U^1 \Pi_{C^1} S^1 \end{bmatrix}; T^1 \leftarrow \begin{bmatrix} T^1 \\ U^1 \Pi_{C^1} \end{bmatrix}; T^2 \leftarrow \begin{bmatrix} T^2 \\ U^2 \Pi_{C^2} \end{bmatrix};$

$V \leftarrow image(V^1, T^1) \cup image(V^2, T^2)$;

return (S, V)

is equal to $\{(T\mathbf{u}, T\mathbf{v}) : \mathbf{u} \rightarrow_V \mathbf{v}\}$ (the image of V's transition relation under T). This $\mathbb{Q}$-VASR can be defined by:

$$image(V, T) \triangleq \{(T \boxtimes \mathbf{r}, T\mathbf{a}) : (\mathbf{r}, \mathbf{a}) \in V\}$$

where $T \boxtimes \mathbf{r}$ is the reset vector $\mathbf{r}$ translated along T (i.e., $(T \boxtimes \mathbf{r})_i = r_j$ where j is an arbitrary choice among dimensions for which T_{ij} is non-zero—at least one such j exists because the row T_i is non-zero by assumption, and the choice of j is arbitrary because all such j belong to the same coherence class by the assumption that T is coherent with respect to V).

Lemma 2. *Let V be a d-dimensional $\mathbb{Q}$-VASR and let $T \in \mathbb{Q}^{e \times d}$ be a matrix that is coherent with respect to V and has no zero rows. Then the transition relation of image(V, T) is the image of V's transition relation under T (i.e., $\rightarrow_{image(V,T)}$ is equal to $\{(T\mathbf{u}, T\mathbf{v}) : \mathbf{u} \rightarrow_V \mathbf{v}\}$).*

Finally, prior to describing our least upper bound algorithm, we must define a technical condition that is both assumed and preserved by the procedure:

Definition 5. *A $\mathbb{Q}$-VASR abstraction (S, V) is **normal** if there is no non-zero vector $\mathbf{z}$ that is coherent with respect to V such that $\mathbf{z}S = 0$ (i.e., the rows of S that correspond to any coherence class of V are linearly independent).*

Intuitively, a $\mathbb{Q}$-VASR abstraction that is *not* normal contains information that is either inconsistent or redundant.

We now present a strategy for computing least upper bounds of $\mathbb{Q}$-VASR abstractions. Fix (normal) $\mathbb{Q}$-VASR abstractions (S^1, V^1) and (S^2, V^2). Lemmas 1 and 2 together show that a pair of matrices $\widetilde{T}^1$ and $\widetilde{T}^2$ induce an upper bound (not necessarily *least*) on (S^1, V^1) and (S^2, V^2) exactly when the following conditions hold: (1) $\widetilde{T}^1 S^1 = \widetilde{T}^2 S^2$, (2) $\widetilde{T}^1$ is coherent w.r.t. V^1, (3) $\widetilde{T}^2$ is coherent w.r.t. V^2, and (4) neither $\widetilde{T}^1$ nor $\widetilde{T}^2$ contain zero rows. The upper bound induced by $\widetilde{T}^1$ and $\widetilde{T}^2$ is given by

$$ub(\widetilde{T}^1, \widetilde{T}^2) \triangleq (\widetilde{T}^1 S^1, image(V^1, \widetilde{T}^1) \cup image(V^2, T^2)).$$

We now consider how to compute a *best* such $\widetilde{T}^1$ and $\widetilde{T}^2$. Observe that conditions (1), (2), and (3) hold exactly when for each row i, $(\widetilde{T}^1_i, \widetilde{T}^2_i)$ belongs to the set

$$\mathcal{T} \triangleq \{(\mathbf{t}^1, \mathbf{t}^2) : \mathbf{t}^1 S^1 = \mathbf{t}^2 S^2 \wedge \mathbf{t}^1 \textit{coherent w.r.t. } V^1 \wedge \mathbf{t}^1 \textit{coherent w.r.t. } V^2\}.$$

Since a row vector $\mathbf{t}^i$ is coherent w.r.t. V^i iff its non-zero positions belong to the same coherence class of V^i (equivalently, $\mathbf{t}^i = \mathbf{u}\Pi_{C^i}$ for some coherence class C^i and vector $\mathbf{u}$), we have $\mathcal{T} = \bigcup_{C^1,C^2} \mathcal{T}(C^1, C^2)$, where the union is over all coherence classes C^1 of V^1 and C^2 of V^2, and

$$\mathcal{T}(C^1, C^2) \triangleq \{(\mathbf{u}^1 \Pi_{C^1}, \mathbf{u}^2 \Pi_{C^2}) : \mathbf{u}^1 \Pi_{C^1} S^1 = \mathbf{u}^2 \Pi_{C^2} S^2\}.$$

Observe that each $\mathcal{T}(C^1, C^2)$ is a vector space, so we can compute a pair of matrices T^1 and T^2 such that the rows (T^1_i, T^2_i) collectively form a basis for each $\mathcal{T}(C^1, C^2)$. Since (S^1, V^1) and (S^2, V^2) are normal (by assumption), neither T^1 nor T^2 may contain zero rows (condition (4) is satisfied). Finally, we have that $ub(T^1, T^2)$ is the *least* upper bound of (S^1, V^1) and (S^2, V^2). Algorithm 2 is a straightforward realization of this strategy.

Proposition 2. *Let (S^1, V^1) and (S^2, V^2) be normal $\mathbb{Q}$-VASR abstractions of equal concrete dimension. Then the $\mathbb{Q}$-VASR abstraction (S, V) computed by Algorithm 2 is normal and is a least upper bound of (S^1, V^2) and (S^2, V^2).*

4 Control Flow and $\mathbb{Q}$-VASRS

In this section, we give a method for improving the precision of our loop summarization technique by using $\mathbb{Q}$-VASRS; that is, $\mathbb{Q}$-VASR extended with control states. While $\mathbb{Q}$-VASRs over-approximate control flow using non-determinism, $\mathbb{Q}$-VASRSs allow us to analyze phenomena such as oscillating and multi-phase loops.

We begin with an example that demonstrates the precision gained by $\mathbb{Q}$-VASRS. The loop in Fig. 2a oscillates between (1) incrementing variable i by 1 and (2) incrementing both variables i and x by 1. Suppose that we wish to prove

```
int x = 0; i = 1
while (*) do
  if i%2 == 0 then
    i := i + 1
  else
    i := i + 1
    x := x + 1
```

(a) Oscillating loop

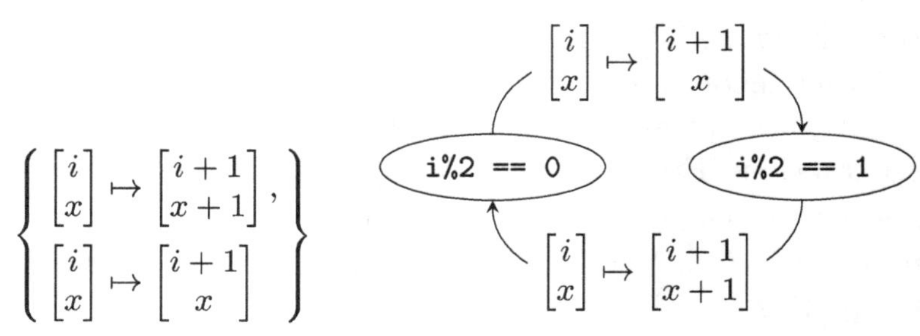

(b) $\mathbb{Q}$-VASR abstraction. (c) $\mathbb{Q}$-VASRS abstraction.

Fig. 2. An oscillating loop and its representation as a $\mathbb{Q}$-VASR and $\mathbb{Q}$-VASRS.

that, starting with the configuration $x = 0 \wedge i = 1$, the loop maintains the invariant that $2x \leq i$. The (best) $\mathbb{Q}$-VASR abstraction of the loop, pictured in Fig. 2b, over-approximates the control flow of the loop by treating the conditional branch in the loop as a non-deterministic branch. This over-approximation may violate the invariant $2x \leq i$ by repeatedly executing the path where both variables are incremented. On the other hand, the $\mathbb{Q}$-VASRS abstraction of the loop pictured in Fig. 2c captures the understanding that the loop must oscillate between the two paths. The loop summary obtained from the reachability relation of this $\mathbb{Q}$-VASRS is powerful enough to prove the invariant $2x \leq i$ holds (under the precondition $x = 0 \wedge i = 1$).

4.1 Technical Details

In the following, we give a method for over-approximating the transitive closure of a transition formula $F(\mathbf{x}, \mathbf{x}')$ using a $\mathbb{Q}$-VASRS. We start by defining *predicate* $\mathbb{Q}$-VASRS, a variation of $\mathbb{Q}$-VASRS with control states that correspond to disjoint state predicates (where the states intuitively belong to the transition formula F rather than the $\mathbb{Q}$-VASRS itself). We extend linear simulations and best abstractions to predicate $\mathbb{Q}$-VASRS, and give an algorithm for synthesizing best predicate $\mathbb{Q}$-VASRS abstractions (for a given set of predicates). Finally, we give an end-to-end algorithm for over-approximating the transitive closure of a transition formula.

Definition 6. *A* ***predicate*** $\mathbb{Q}$***-VASRS*** *over* $\mathbf{x}$ *is a* $\mathbb{Q}$*-VASRS* $\mathcal{V} = (P, E)$*, such that each control state is a predicate over the variables* $\mathbf{x}$ *and the predicates in* P *are pairwise inconsistent (for all* $p \neq q \in P$*,* $p \wedge q$ *is unsatisfiable).*

We extend linear simulations to predicate $\mathbb{Q}$-VASRS as follows:

- Let $F(\mathbf{x}, \mathbf{x}')$ be an n-dimensional transition formula and let $\mathcal{V} = (P, E)$ be an m-dimensional $\mathbb{Q}$-VASRS over $\mathbf{x}$. We say that a linear transformation $S : \mathbb{Q}^{m \times n}$ is a linear simulation from F to $\mathcal{V}$ if for all $\mathbf{u}, \mathbf{v} \in \mathbb{Q}^n$ such that $\mathbf{u} \to_F \mathbf{v}$, (1) there is a (unique) $p \in P$ such that $p(\mathbf{u})$ is valid (2) there is a (unique) $q \in P$ such that $q(\mathbf{v})$ is valid, and (3) $(p, S\mathbf{u}) \to_{\mathcal{V}} (q, S\mathbf{v})$.
- Let $\mathcal{V}^1 = (P^1, E^1)$ and $\mathcal{V}^2 = (P^2, E^2)$ be predicate $\mathbb{Q}$-VASRSs over $\mathbf{x}$ (for some $\mathbf{x}$) of dimensions d and e, respectively. We say that a linear transformation $S : \mathbb{Q}^{e \times d}$ is a linear simulation from $\mathcal{V}^1$ to $\mathcal{V}^2$ if for all $p^1, q^1 \in P^1$ and for all $\mathbf{u}, \mathbf{v} \in \mathbb{Q}^d$ such that $(p^1, \mathbf{u}) \to_{\mathcal{V}^1} (q^1, \mathbf{v})$, there exists (unique) $p^2, q^2 \in P^2$ such that (1) $(p^2, S\mathbf{u}) \to_{\mathcal{V}^2} (q^2, S\mathbf{v})$, (2) $p^1 \models p^2$, and (3) $q^1 \models q^2$.

We define a $\mathbb{Q}$-VASRS abstraction over $\mathbf{x} = x_1, ..., x_n$ to be a pair $(S, \mathcal{V})$ consisting of a rational matrix $S \in \mathbb{Q}^{d \times n}$ and a predicate $\mathbb{Q}$-VASRS of dimension d over $\mathbf{x}$. We extend the simulation preorder $\preceq$ to $\mathbb{Q}$-VASRS abstractions in the natural way. Extending the definition of "best" abstractions requires more care, since we can always find a "better" $\mathbb{Q}$-VASRS abstraction (strictly smaller in $\preceq$ order) by using a finer set of predicates. However, if we consider only predicate

Algorithm 3. `abstract-VASRS`(F, P)

input : Transition formula $F(\mathbf{x}, \mathbf{x}')$, set of pairwise-disjoint predicates P over $\mathbf{x}$ such that for all $\mathbf{u}, \mathbf{v}$ with $\mathbf{u} \rightarrow_F \mathbf{v}$, there exists $p, q \in P$ with $p(\mathbf{u})$ and $q(\mathbf{v})$ both valid

output: Best $\mathbb{Q}$-VASRS abstraction of F with control states P

For all $p, q \in P$, let $(S_{p,q}, V_{p,q}) \leftarrow$ `abstract-VASR`$(p(\mathbf{x}) \wedge F(\mathbf{x}, \mathbf{x}') \wedge q(\mathbf{x}'))$;
$(S, V) \leftarrow$ least upper bound of all $(S_{p,q}, V_{p,q})$;
For all $p, q \in P$, let $T_{p,q} \leftarrow$ the simulation matrix from $(S_{p,q}, V_{p,q})$ to (S, V);
$E = \{(p, \mathbf{r}, \mathbf{a}, q) : p, q \in P, (\mathbf{r}, \mathbf{a}) \in \mathit{image}(V_{p,q}, T_{p,q})\}$;
return $(S, (P, E))$

$\mathbb{Q}$-VASRS that share the same set of control states, then best abstractions do exist and can be computed using Algorithm 3.

Algorithm 3 works as follows: first, for each pair of formulas $p, q \in P$, compute a best $\mathbb{Q}$-VASR abstraction of the formula $p(\mathbf{x}) \wedge F(\mathbf{x}, \mathbf{x}') \wedge q(\mathbf{x}')$ and call it $(S_{p,q}, V_{p,q})$. $(S_{p,q}, V_{p,q})$ over-approximates the transitions of F that begin in a program state satisfying p and end in a program state satisfying q. Second, we compute the least upper bound of all $\mathbb{Q}$-VASR abstractions $(S_{p,q}, V_{p,q})$ to get a $\mathbb{Q}$-VASR abstraction (S, V) for F. As a side-effect of the least upper bound computation, we obtain a linear simulation $T_{p,q}$ from $(S_{p,q}, V_{p,q})$ to (S, V) for each p, q. A best $\mathbb{Q}$-VASRS abstraction of $F(\mathbf{x}, \mathbf{x}')$ with control states P has S as its simulation matrix and has the image of $V_{p,q}$ under $T_{p,q}$ as the edges from p to q.

Proposition 3. *Given an transition formula $F(\mathbf{x}, \mathbf{x}')$ and control states P over $\mathbf{x}$, Algorithm 3 computes the best predicate $\mathbb{Q}$-VASRS abstraction of F with control states P.*

We now describe `iter-VASRS` (Algorithm 4), which uses $\mathbb{Q}$-VASRS to over-approximate the transitive closure of transition formulas. Towards our goal of *predictable* program analysis, we desire the analysis to be *monotone* in the sense that if F and G are transition formulas such that F entails G, then `iter-VASRS`(F) entails `iter-VASRS`(G). A sufficient condition to guarantee monotonicity of the overall analysis is to require that the set of control states that we compute for F is at least as fine as the set of control states we compute for G. We can achieve this by making the set of control states P of input transition formula $F(\mathbf{x}, \mathbf{x}')$ equal to the set of connected regions of the topological closure of $\exists \mathbf{x}'.F$ (lines 1–4). Note that this set of predicates may fail the contract of `abstract-VASRS`: there may exist a transition $\mathbf{u} \rightarrow_F \mathbf{v}$ such that $\mathbf{v} \not\models \bigvee P$ (this occurs when there is a state of F with no outgoing transitions). As a result, $(S, \mathcal{V}) =$ `abstract-VASRS`(F, P) does not necessarily approximate F; however, it *does* over-approximate $F \wedge \bigvee P(\mathbf{x}')$. An over-approximation of the transitive closure of F can easily be obtained from $\mathit{reach}(\mathcal{V})(S\mathbf{x}, S\mathbf{x}')$ (the over-approximation of the transitive closure of $F \wedge \bigvee P(\mathbf{x}')$ obtained from the

$\mathbb{Q}$-VASRS abstraction $(S, \mathcal{V})$) by sequentially composing with the disjunction of F and the identity relation (line 6).

Algorithm 4. `iter-VASRS`(F)

input : Transition formula $F(\mathbf{x}, \mathbf{x}')$
output: Over-approximation of the transitive closure of F
1 $P \leftarrow$ topological closure of DNF of $\exists \mathbf{x}'.F$ (see [17]);
2 `/* Compute connected regions */`
3 **while** $\exists p_1, p_2 \in P$ *with* $p_1 \wedge p_2$ *satisfiable* **do**
4     $P \leftarrow (P \setminus \{p_1, p_2\}) \cup \{p_1 \vee p_2\}$
5 $(S, \mathcal{V}) \leftarrow$ `abstract-VASRS`(F, P);
6 **return** $\mathit{reach}(\mathcal{V})(S\mathbf{x}, S\mathbf{x}') \circ (\mathbf{x}' = \mathbf{x} \vee F)$

Precision Improvement. The `abstract-VASRS` algorithm uses predicates to infer the control structure of a $\mathbb{Q}$-VASRS, but after computing the $\mathbb{Q}$-VASRS abstraction, `iter-VASRS` makes no further use of the predicates (i.e., the predicates are irrelevant in the computation of $\mathit{reach}(\mathcal{V})$). Predicates can be used to improve `iter-VASRS` as follows: the reachability relation of a $\mathbb{Q}$-VASRS is expressed by a formula that uses auxiliary variables to represent the state at which the computation begins and ends [8]. These variables can be used to encode that the pre-state of the transitive closure must satisfy the predicate corresponding to the begin state and the post-state must satisfy the predicate corresponding to the end state. As an example, consider the Fig. 2 and suppose that we wish to prove the invariant $x \leq 2i$ under the pre-condition $i = 0 \wedge x = 0$. While this invariant holds, we cannot prove it because there is counter example if the computation begins at $i\%2 == 1$. By applying the above improvement, we can prove that the computation must begin at $i\%2 == 0$, and the invariant is verified.

5 Evaluation

The goals of our evaluation is the answer the following questions:

- Are $\mathbb{Q}$-VASR sufficiently expressive to be able to generate accurate loop summaries?
- Does the $\mathbb{Q}$-VASRS technique improve upon the precision of $\mathbb{Q}$-VASR?
- Are the $\mathbb{Q}$-VASR/$\mathbb{Q}$-VASRS loop summarization algorithms performant?

We implemented our loop summarization procedure and the compositional whole-program summarization technique described in Sect. 1.1. We ran on a suite of 165 benchmarks, drawn from the C4B [2] and HOLA [4] suites, as well as the safe, integer-only benchmarks in the loops category of SV-Comp 2019 [22]. We ran each benchmark with a time-out of 5 min, and recorded how many benchmarks were proved safe by our $\mathbb{Q}$-VASR-based technique and our $\mathbb{Q}$-VASRS-based technique. For context, we also compare with CRA [14] (a related loop summarization technique), as well as SeaHorn [7] and UltimateAutomizer [9] (state-of-the-art software model checkers). The results are shown in Fig. 3.

The number of assertions proved correct using $\mathbb{Q}$-VASR is comparable to both SeaHorn and UltimateAutomizer, demonstrating that $\mathbb{Q}$-VASR can indeed model interesting loop phenomena. $\mathbb{Q}$-VASRS-based summarization significantly improves precision, proving the correctness of 93% of assertions in the svcomp suite, and more than any other tool in total. Note that the most precise tool for each suite is not strictly better than each of the other tools; in particular, there is only a single program in the HOLA suite that neither $\mathbb{Q}$-VASRS nor CRA can prove safe.

CRA-based summarization is the most performant of all the compared techniques, followed by $\mathbb{Q}$-VASR and $\mathbb{Q}$-VASRS. SeaHorn and UltimateAutomizer employ abstraction-refinement loops, and so take significantly longer to run the test suite.

		$\mathbb{Q}$-VASR		$\mathbb{Q}$-VASRS		CRA		SeaHorn		UltAuto	
		#safe	time	#safe	time	#safe	time	#safe	time	#safe	time
C4B	35	21	37.9	**31**	35.4	27	**33.1**	23	2434.4	25	3881.6
HOLA	46	32	57.2	39	73.0	**40**	**56.0**	35	2115.0	36	2995.9
svcomp19-int	84	68	**86.9**	**78**	184.5	76	91.9	62	3038.0	64	6923.5

Fig. 3. Experimental results.

6 Related Work

Compositional Analysis. Our analysis follows the same high-level structure as compositional recurrence analysis (CRA) [5,14]. Our analysis differs from CRA in the way that it summarizes loops: we compute loop summaries by over-approximating loops with vector addition systems and computing reachability relations, whereas CRA computes loop summaries by extracting recurrence relations and computing closed forms. The advantage of our approach is that is that we can use $\mathbb{Q}$-VASR to accurately model multi-path loops and can make theoretical guarantees about the precision of our analysis; the advantage of CRA is its ability to generate non-linear invariants.

Vector Addition Systems. Our invariant generation method draws upon Haase and Halfon's polytime procedure for computing the reachability relation of integer vector addition systems with states and resets [8]. Generalization from the integer case to the rational case is straightforward. Continuous Petri nets [3] are a related generalization of vector addition systems, where time is taken to be continuous ($\mathbb{Q}$-VASR, in contrast, have rational state spaces but discrete time). Reachability for continuous Petri nets is computable polytime [6] and definable in $\exists$LRA [1].

Sinn et al. present a technique for resource bound analysis that is based on modeling programs by lossy vector addition system with states [21]. Sinn et al. model programs using vector addition systems with states over the natural numbers, which enables them to use termination bounds for VASS to compute upper bounds on resource usage. In contrast, we use VASS with resets over the rationals, which (in contrast to VASS over $\mathbb{N}$) have a ∃LIRA-definable reachability relation, enabling us to summarize loops. Moreover, Sinn et al.'s method for extracting VASS models of programs is heuristic, whereas our method gives precision guarantees.

Affine and Polynomial Programs. The problem of *polynomial* invariant generation has been investigated for various program models that generalize $\mathbb{Q}$-VASR, including solvable polynomial loops [19], (extended) P-solvable loops [11,15], and affine programs [10]. Like ours, these techniques are *predictable* in the sense that they can make theoretical guarantees about invariant quality. The kinds invariants that can be produced using these techniques (conjunctions of polynomial equations) is incomparable with those generated by the method presented in this paper (∃LIRA formulas).

Symbolic Abstraction. The main contribution of this paper is a technique for synthesizing the best abstraction of a transition formula expressible in the language of $\mathbb{Q}$-VASR (with or without states). This is closely related to the *symbolic abstraction* problem, which computes the best abstraction of a formula within an abstract domain. The problem of computing best abstractions has been undertaken for finite-height abstract domains [18], template constraint matrices (including intervals and octagons) [16], and polyhedra [5,24]. Our best abstraction result differs in that (1) it is for a disjunctive domain and (2) the notion of "best" is based on simulation rather than the typical order-theoretic framework.

References

1. Blondin, M., Finkel, A., Haase, C., Haddad, S.: Approaching the coverability problem continuously. In: Chechik, M., Raskin, J.-F. (eds.) TACAS 2016. LNCS, vol. 9636, pp. 480–496. Springer, Heidelberg (2016). https://doi.org/10.1007/978-3-662-49674-9_28
2. Carbonneaux, Q., Hoffmann, J., Shao, Z.: Compositional certified resource bounds. In: PLDI (2015)
3. David, R., Alla, H.: Continuous Petri nets. In: Proceedings of 8th European Workshop on Applications and Theory Petri Nets, pp. 275–294 (1987)
4. Dillig, I., Dillig, T., Li, B., McMillan, K.: Inductive invariant generation via abductive inference. In: OOPSLA (2013)
5. Farzan, A., Kincaid, Z.: Compositional recurrence analysis. In: FMCAD (2015)
6. Fraca, E., Haddad, S.: Complexity analysis of continuous Petri nets. Fundam. Inf. **137**(1), 1–28 (2015)
7. Gurfinkel, A., Kahsai, T., Komuravelli, A., Navas, J.A.: The SeaHorn verification framework. In: Kroening, D., Păsăreanu, C.S. (eds.) CAV 2015. LNCS, vol. 9206, pp. 343–361. Springer, Cham (2015). https://doi.org/10.1007/978-3-319-21690-4_20

8. Haase, C., Halfon, S.: Integer vector addition systems with states. In: Ouaknine, J., Potapov, I., Worrell, J. (eds.) RP 2014. LNCS, vol. 8762, pp. 112–124. Springer, Cham (2014). https://doi.org/10.1007/978-3-319-11439-2_9
9. Heizmann, M., et al.: Ultimate automizer and the search for perfect interpolants. In: Beyer, D., Huisman, M. (eds.) TACAS 2018. LNCS, vol. 10806, pp. 447–451. Springer, Cham (2018). https://doi.org/10.1007/978-3-319-89963-3_30
10. Hrushovski, E., Ouaknine, J., Pouly, A., Worrell, J.: Polynomial invariants for affine programs. In: Logic in Computer Science, pp. 530–539 (2018)
11. Humenberger, A., Jaroschek, M., Kovács, L.: Invariant Generation for Multi-Path Loops with Polynomial Assignments. In: Verification, Model Checking, and Abstract Interpretation. LNCS, vol. 10747, pp. 226–246. Springer, Cham (2018). https://doi.org/10.1007/978-3-319-73721-8_11
12. Karp, R.M., Miller, R.E.: Parallel program schemata. J. Comput. Syst. Sci. **3**(2), 147–195 (1969)
13. Kincaid, Z., Breck, J., Forouhi Boroujeni, A., Reps, T.: Compositional recurrence analysis revisited. In: PLDI (2017)
14. Kincaid, Z., Cyphert, J., Breck, J., Reps, T.: Non-linear reasoning for invariant synthesis. PACMPL **2**(POPL), 1–33 (2018)
15. Kovács, L.: Reasoning algebraically about P-solvable loops. In: Ramakrishnan, C.R., Rehof, J. (eds.) TACAS 2008. LNCS, vol. 4963, pp. 249–264. Springer, Heidelberg (2008). https://doi.org/10.1007/978-3-540-78800-3_18
16. Li, Y., Albarghouthi, A., Kincaid, Z., Gurfinkel, A., Chechik, M.: Symbolic optimization with SMT solvers. In: POPL, pp. 607–618 (2014)
17. Monniaux, D.: A quantifier elimination algorithm for linear real arithmetic. In: Cervesato, I., Veith, H., Voronkov, A. (eds.) LPAR 2008. LNCS (LNAI), vol. 5330, pp. 243–257. Springer, Heidelberg (2008). https://doi.org/10.1007/978-3-540-89439-1_18
18. Reps, T., Sagiv, M., Yorsh, G.: Symbolic implementation of the best transformer. In: Steffen, B., Levi, G. (eds.) VMCAI 2004. LNCS, vol. 2937, pp. 252–266. Springer, Heidelberg (2004). https://doi.org/10.1007/978-3-540-24622-0_21
19. Rodríguez-Carbonell, E., Kapur, D.: Automatic generation of polynomial loop invariants: algebraic foundations. In: ISSAC, pp. 266–273 (2004)
20. Silverman, J., Kincaid, Z.: Loop summarization with rational vector addition systems (extended version). arXiv e-prints. arXiv:1905.06495, May 2019
21. Sinn, M., Zuleger, F., Veith, H.: A simple and scalable static analysis for bound analysis and amortized complexity analysis. In: Biere, A., Bloem, R. (eds.) CAV 2014. LNCS, vol. 8559, pp. 745–761. Springer, Cham (2014). https://doi.org/10.1007/978-3-319-08867-9_50
22. 8th International Competition on Software Verification (SV-COMP 2019) (2019). https://sv-comp.sosy-lab.org/2019/
23. Tarjan, R.E.: A unified approach to path problems. J. ACM **28**(3), 577–593 (1981)
24. Thakur, A., Reps, T.: A method for symbolic computation of abstract operations. In: Madhusudan, P., Seshia, S.A. (eds.) CAV 2012. LNCS, vol. 7358, pp. 174–192. Springer, Heidelberg (2012). https://doi.org/10.1007/978-3-642-31424-7_17

Invertibility Conditions for Floating-Point Formulas

Martin Brain[3,4], Aina Niemetz[1], Mathias Preiner[1](✉), Andrew Reynolds[2], Clark Barrett[1], and Cesare Tinelli[2]

[1] Stanford University, Stanford, USA
preiner@cs.stanford.edu
[2] The University of Iowa, Iowa City, USA
[3] University of Oxford, Oxford, UK
[4] City, University of London, London, UK

Abstract. Automated reasoning procedures are essential for a number of applications that involve bit-exact floating-point computations. This paper presents conditions that characterize when a variable in a floating-point constraint has a solution, which we call invertibility conditions. We describe a novel workflow that combines human interaction and a syntax-guided synthesis (SyGuS) solver that was used for discovering these conditions. We verify our conditions for several floating-point formats. One implication of this result is that a fragment of floating-point arithmetic admits compact quantifier elimination. We implement our invertibility conditions in a prototype extension of our solver CVC4, showing their usefulness for solving quantified constraints over floating-points.

1 Introduction

Satisfiability Modulo Theories (SMT) formulas including either the theory of floating-point numbers [12] or universal quantifiers [24,32] are widely regarded as some of the hardest to solve. Problems that combine universal quantification over floating-points are rare—experience to date has suggested they are hard for solvers and would-be users should either give up or develop their own incomplete techniques. However, progress in theory solvers for floating-point [11] and the use of expression synthesis for handling universal quantifiers [27,29] suggest that these problems may not be entirely out of reach after all, which could potentially impact a number of interesting applications.

This paper makes substantial progress towards a scalable approach for solving quantified floating-point constraints directly in an SMT solver. Developing procedures for quantified floating-points requires considerable effort, both foundationally and in practice. We focus primarily on establishing a foundation for lifting to quantified floating-point formulas a procedure for solving quantified bit-vector formulas by Niemetz et al. [26]. That procedure relies on so-called

This work was supported in part by DARPA (award no. FA8650-18-2-7861), ONR (award no. N68335-17-C-0558) and NSF (award no. 1656926).

I. Dillig and S. Tasiran (Eds.): CAV 2019, LNCS 11562, pp. 116–136, 2019.
https://doi.org/10.1007/978-3-030-25543-5_8

invertibility conditions, intuitively, formulas that state under which conditions an argument of a given operator and predicate in an equation has a solution. Building on this concept and a state-of-the-art expression synthesis engine [29], we generate invertibility conditions for a majority of operators and predicates in the theory of floating-point numbers. In the context of quantifier-free floating-point formulas, floating-point invertibility conditions may enable us to lift the propagation-based local search approach for bit-vectors in [25] to the theory of floating-point numbers.

This work demonstrates that invertibility conditions exist and show promise for solving quantified floating-point constraints. More specifically, it makes the following contributions:

- In Sect. 3, we present invertibility conditions for the majority of operators and predicates in the SMT-LIB standard theory of floating-point numbers.
- In Sect. 4, we present a custom methodology based on syntax-guided synthesis and decision tree learning that we developed for the purpose of synthesizing the invertibility conditions presented here.
- In Sect. 5, we present a quantifier elimination procedure for a fragment of the theory that is based on invertibility conditions, and give experimental evidence of its potential, based on quantified floating-point problems coming from a verification application.

Related Work. To our knowledge, no previous work specifically discusses techniques for solving universally quantified floating-point formulas. Brain et al. [11] provide a comprehensive review of decision procedures for quantifier-free bit-exact floating-point using both SMT-based as well as other approaches. They identify four groups of techniques: bit-blasting approaches that use floating-point circuits to generate bit-vector formulas [13, 16, 20, 33], interval techniques that use partitioning and interval propagation [10, 22, 23, 31], optimization and numerical approaches that work with complete valuations [4, 7, 18, 21], and axiomatic techniques that use partial or total axiomatizations of the theory of floating-point numbers in other theories such as real arithmetic [14, 15].

On the other hand, approaches for universal quantification have been developed in modern SMT solvers that target other background theories, including linear arithmetic [8, 17, 29] and bit-vectors [26, 27, 32]. At a high level, these approaches use model-based refinement loops that lazily add instances of universal quantifiers until they reach a conflict at the quantifier-free level, or otherwise saturate with a model.

2 Preliminaries

We assume the usual notions and terminology of many-sorted first-order logic with equality (denoted by $\approx$). Let Σ be a *signature* consisting of a set Σ^s of sort symbols and a set Σ^f of interpreted (and sorted) function symbols. Each function symbol f has a sort $\tau_1 \times ... \times \tau_n \to \tau$, with arity $n \geq 0$ and $\tau_1, ..., \tau_n, \tau \in \Sigma^s$. We assume that Σ includes a Boolean sort Bool and the Boolean constants $\top$ (true) and $\bot$ (false).

We further assume the usual definition of well-sorted terms, literals, and (quantified) formulas with variables and symbols from Σ, and refer to them as Σ-terms, Σ-atoms, and so on. For a Σ-term or Σ-formula e, we denote the *free variables* of e (defined as usual) as $FV(e)$ and use $e[x]$ to denote that the variable x occurs free in e. We write $e[t]$ for the term or formula obtained from e by replacing each occurrence of x in e by t.

A *theory* T is a pair (Σ, I), where Σ is a signature and I is a non-empty class of Σ-interpretations (the *models* of T) that is closed under variable reassignment, i.e., every Σ-interpretation that only differs from an $\mathcal{I} \in I$ in how it interprets variables is also in I. A Σ-formula φ is T*-satisfiable* (resp. T*-unsatisfiable*) if it is satisfied by some (resp. no) interpretation in I; it is T*-valid* if it is satisfied by all interpretations in I. We will sometimes omit T when the theory is understood from context.

We briefly recap the terminology and notation of Brain et al. [12] which defines an SMT-LIB theory T_{FP} of floating-point numbers based on the IEEE-754 2008 standard [3]. The signature of T_{FP} includes a parametric family of sorts $\mathbb{F}_{\varepsilon,\sigma}$ where ε and σ are integers greater than or equal to 2 giving the number of bits used to store the exponent e and significand s, respectively. Each of these sorts contains five kinds of constants: normal numbers of the form $1.s * 2^e$, subnormal numbers of the form $0.s * 2^{-2^{\sigma-1}-1}$, two zeros ($+0$ and -0), two infinities ($+\infty$ and $-\infty$) and a single not-a-number (NaN). We assume a map $\mathrm{v}_{\varepsilon,\sigma}$ for each sort, which maps these constants to their value in the set $\mathbb{R}^* = \mathbb{R} \cup \{+\infty, -\infty, \mathrm{NaN}\}$. The theory also provides a rounding-mode sort RM, which contains five elements $\{\mathsf{RNE}, \mathsf{RNA}, \mathsf{RTP}, \mathsf{RTN}, \mathsf{RTZ}\}$.

Table 1 lists all considered operators and predicate symbols of theory T_{FP}. The theory contains a full set of arithmetic operations $\{|\ldots|, +, -, \cdot, \div, \sqrt{}, \mathsf{max}, \mathsf{min}\}$ as well as rem (remainder), rti (round to integral) and fma (combined multiply and add with just one rounding). The precise semantics of these operators is given in [12] and follows the same general pattern: $\mathrm{v}_{\varepsilon,\sigma}$ is used to project the arguments to $\mathbb{R}^*$, the normal arithmetic is performed in $\mathbb{R}^*$, then the rounding mode and the result are used to select one of the adjoints of $\mathrm{v}_{\varepsilon,\sigma}$ to convert the result back to $\mathbb{F}_{\varepsilon,\sigma}$. Note that the full theory in [12] includes several additional operators which we omit from discussion here, such as floating-point minimum/maximum, equality with floating-point semantics (fp.eq), and conversions between sorts.

Theory T_{FP} further defines a set of ordering predicates $\{<, >, \leq, \geq\}$ and a set of classification predicates $\{\mathsf{isNorm}, \mathsf{isSub}, \mathsf{isInf}, \mathsf{isZero}, \mathsf{isNaN}, \mathsf{isNeg}, \mathsf{isPos}\}$. In the following, we denote the rounding mode of an operation above the operator symbol, e.g., $a \overset{\mathsf{RTZ}}{+} b$ adds a and b and rounds the result towards zero. We use the infix operator style for isInf ($\ldots \approx \pm\infty$), isZero ($\ldots \approx \pm 0$), and isNaN ($\ldots \approx \mathsf{NaN}$) for conciseness. We further use $\mathrm{min_n}/\mathrm{max_n}$ and $\mathrm{min_s}/\mathrm{max_s}$ for floating-point constants representing the minimum/maximum normal and subnormal numbers, respectively. We will omit rounding mode and floating-point sorts if they are clear from the context.

3 Invertibility Conditions for Floating-Point Formulas

In this section, we adapt the concept of invertibility conditions introduced by Niemetz et al. in [26] to our theory T_{FP}. Intuitively, an invertibility condition ϕ_c for a literal $l[x]$ is the exact condition under which $l[x]$ has a solution for x, i.e., ϕ_c is equivalent to $\exists x.\, l[x]$ in T_{FP}.

Definition 1 *(Floating-Point Invertibility Condition).* Let $l[x]$ be a Σ_{FP}-literal. A quantifier-free Σ_{FP}-formula ϕ_c is an *invertibility condition* for x in $l[x]$ if $x \notin FV(\phi_c)$ and $\phi_c \Leftrightarrow \exists x.\, l[x]$ is T_{FP} *-valid.*

As a simple example of an invertibility condition, given literal $|x| \approx t$ where $|x|$ denotes the absolute value of x, a solution for x exists if and only if t is not negative, i.e., if $\neg \mathsf{isNeg}(t)$ holds. We introduce additional terminology for the sake of the discussion. We define the *dimension* of an invertibility condition problem $\exists x.\, l[x]$ as the number of free variables it contains. For example, if s and t are variables, then the dimension of $\exists x.\, x + s \approx t$ is two, the dimension of $\exists x.\, \mathsf{isZero}(x + s)$ is one, and the dimension of $\exists x.\, \mathsf{isZero}(|x|)$ is zero. A literal $l[x]$ is *fully invertible* if its invertibility condition is $\top$. A term e is an (unconditional) *inverse* for x in $l[x]$ if $l[e]$ is equivalent to $\top$. For example, the literal $-x \approx t$ is fully invertible and $-t$ is an inverse for x in this literal. We say that e is a *conditional inverse* for $l[x]$ if $l[e]$ is an invertibility condition for $l[x]$.

Our primary goal in this work is to establish invertibility conditions for all floating-point constraints that contain exactly one operator and one predicate. These conditions collectively suffice to characterize when any literal $l[x]$ containing exactly one occurrence of x, the variable to solve for, has a solution. In total, we were able to establish 167 out of 188 invertibility conditions (counting commutative cases only once) using a syntax-guided synthesis framework which we describe in more detail in Sect. 4. In this section, we present a subset of these invertibility conditions, highlighting the most interesting cases where

Table 1. Considered floating-point predicates/operators, with SMT-LIB 2 syntax.

Symbol	SMT-LIB syntax	Sort
isNorm, isSub	fp.isNormal, fp.isSubnormal	$\mathbb{F}_{\varepsilon,\sigma} \rightarrow$ Bool
isPos, isNeg	fp.isPositive, fp.isNegative	$\mathbb{F}_{\varepsilon,\sigma} \rightarrow$ Bool
isInf, isNaN, isZero	fp.isInfinite, fp.isNaN, fp.isZero	$\mathbb{F}_{\varepsilon,\sigma} \rightarrow$ Bool
$\approx, <, >, \leq, \geq$	=, fp.lt, fp.gt, fp.leq, fp.geq	$\mathbb{F}_{\varepsilon,\sigma} \times \mathbb{F}_{\varepsilon,\sigma} \rightarrow$ Bool
$\lvert \ldots \rvert$, $-$	fp.abs, fp.neg	$\mathbb{F}_{\varepsilon,\sigma} \rightarrow \mathbb{F}_{\varepsilon,\sigma}$
rem	fp.rem	$\mathbb{F}_{\varepsilon,\sigma} \times \mathbb{F}_{\varepsilon,\sigma} \rightarrow \mathbb{F}_{\varepsilon,\sigma}$
$\sqrt{}$, rti	fp.sqrt, fp.roundToIntegral	RM $\times \mathbb{F}_{\varepsilon,\sigma} \rightarrow \mathbb{F}_{\varepsilon,\sigma}$
$+, -, \cdot, \div$	fp.add, fp.sub, fp.mul, fp.div	RM $\times \mathbb{F}_{\varepsilon,\sigma} \times \mathbb{F}_{\varepsilon,\sigma} \rightarrow \mathbb{F}_{\varepsilon,\sigma}$
fma	fp.fma	RM $\times \mathbb{F}_{\varepsilon,\sigma} \times \mathbb{F}_{\varepsilon,\sigma} \times \mathbb{F}_{\varepsilon,\sigma} \rightarrow \mathbb{F}_{\varepsilon,\sigma}$

we succeeded (or failed) to establish an invertibility condition. Due to space restrictions, we omit the conditions for the remaining cases.[1]

Table 2. Invertibility conditions for floating-point operators (excl. fma) with $\approx$.

Literal	Invertibility condition
$x \overset{\mathsf{R}}{+} s \approx t$	$t \approx (t \overset{\mathsf{RTP}}{-} s) \overset{R}{+} s \vee t \approx (t \overset{\mathsf{RTN}}{-} s) \overset{R}{+} s \vee s \approx t$
$x \overset{\mathsf{R}}{-} s \approx t$	$t \approx (s \overset{\mathsf{RTP}}{+} t) \overset{R}{-} s \vee t \approx (s \overset{\mathsf{RTN}}{+} t) \overset{R}{-} s \vee (s \not\approx t \wedge s \approx \pm\infty \wedge t \approx \pm\infty)$
$s \overset{\mathsf{R}}{-} x \approx t$	$t \approx s \overset{R}{+} (t \overset{\mathsf{RTP}}{-} s) \vee t \approx s \overset{R}{+} (t \overset{\mathsf{RTN}}{-} s) \vee s \approx t$
$x \overset{\mathsf{R}}{\cdot} s \approx t$	$t \approx (t \overset{\mathsf{RTP}}{\div} s) \overset{R}{\cdot} s \vee t \approx (t \overset{\mathsf{RTN}}{\div} s) \overset{R}{\cdot} s \vee (s \approx \pm\infty \wedge t \approx \pm\infty) \vee (s \approx \pm 0 \wedge t \approx \pm 0)$
$x \overset{\mathsf{R}}{\div} s \approx t$	$t \approx (s \overset{\mathsf{RTP}}{\cdot} t) \overset{R}{\div} s \vee t \approx (s \overset{\mathsf{RTN}}{\cdot} t) \overset{R}{\div} s \vee (s \approx \pm\infty \wedge t \approx \pm 0) \vee (t \approx \pm\infty \wedge s \approx \pm 0)$
$s \overset{\mathsf{R}}{\div} x \approx t$	$t \approx s \overset{R}{\div} (s \overset{\mathsf{RTP}}{\div} t) \vee t \approx s \overset{R}{\div} (s \overset{\mathsf{RTN}}{\div} t) \vee (s \approx \pm\infty \wedge t \approx \pm\infty) \vee (s \approx \pm 0 \wedge t \approx \pm 0)$
$x \,\mathsf{rem}\, s \approx t$	$t \approx t \,\mathsf{rem}\, s$
$s \,\mathsf{rem}\, x \approx t$	?
$\sqrt[R]{x} \approx t$	$t \approx \sqrt[R]{(t \overset{\mathsf{RTP}}{\cdot} t)} \vee t \approx \sqrt[R]{(t \overset{\mathsf{RTN}}{\cdot} t)} \vee t \approx \pm 0$
$\lvert x \rvert \approx t$	$\neg \mathsf{isNeg}(t)$
$-x \approx t$	$\top$
$\overset{\mathsf{R}}{\mathsf{rti}}(x) \approx t$	$t \approx \overset{R}{\mathsf{rti}}(t)$

Table 2 lists the invertibility conditions for equality with the operators $\{+, -, \cdot, \div, \mathsf{rem}, \sqrt{\ }, \lvert\ldots\rvert, -, \mathsf{rti}\}$, parameterized over a rounding mode R (one of RNE, RNA, RTP, RTN, or RTZ). Note that operators $\{+, \cdot\}$ and the multiplicative step of fma are commutative, and thus the invertibility conditions for both variants are identical.

Each of the first six invertibility conditions in this table follows a pattern. The first two disjuncts are instances of the literal to solve for, where a term involving rounding modes RTP and RTN is substituted for x. These disjuncts are then followed by disjuncts for handling special cases for infinity and zero. From the structure of these conditions, e.g., for $+$, we can derive the insight that if there is a solution for x in the equation $x \overset{\mathsf{R}}{+} s \approx t$ and we are not in a corner case where $s = t$, then either $t \overset{RTP}{-} s$ or $t \overset{RTN}{-} s$ must be a solution. Based on extensive runs of our syntax-guided synthesis procedure, we believe this condition is close to having minimal term size. From this, we conclude that an efficient yet complete method for solving $x \overset{\mathsf{R}}{+} s \approx t$ checks whether $t - s$ rounding towards positive or negative is a solution in the non-trivial case when s and t are disequal, and otherwise concludes that no solution exists. A similar insight can be derived for the other invertibility conditions of this form.

[1] Available at https://cvc4.cs.stanford.edu/papers/CAV2019-FP.

We found that t is a conditional inverse for the case of $\overset{\mathsf{R}}{\mathsf{rti}}(x) \approx t$ and $x \,\mathsf{rem}\, s \approx t$, that is, substituting t for x is an invertibility condition. For the latter, we discovered an alternative invertibility condition:

$$|t \overset{\mathsf{RTP}}{+} t| \leq |s| \vee |t \overset{\mathsf{RTN}}{+} t| \leq |s| \vee \mathsf{ite}(t \approx \pm 0, s \not\approx \pm 0, t \not\approx \pm\infty) \quad (1)$$

In contrast to the condition from Table 2, this version does not involve rem. It follows that certain applications of floating-point remainder, including those whose first argument is an unconstrained variable, can be eliminated based on this equivalence. Interestingly, for $s \,\mathsf{rem}\, x \approx t$, we did not succeed in finding an invertibility condition. This case appears to not admit a concise solution; we discuss further details below.

Table 3 gives the invertibility conditions for $\geq$. Since these constraints admit more solutions, they typically have simpler invertibility conditions. In particular, with the exception of rem, all conditions only involve floating-point classifiers.

When considering literals with predicates, the invertibility conditions for cases involving $x + s$ and $s - x$ are identical for every predicate and rounding mode. This is due to the fact that $s - x$ is equivalent to $s + (-x)$, independent from the rounding mode. Thus, the negation of the inverse value of x for an equation involving $x + s$ is the inverse value of x for an equation involving $s - x$. Similarly, the invertibility conditions for $x \cdot s$ and $s \div x$ over predicates $\{<, \leq, >, \geq, \mathsf{isInf}, \mathsf{isNaN}, \mathsf{isNeg}, \mathsf{isZero}\}$ are identical for all rounding modes.

For all predicates except $\{\approx, \mathsf{isNorm}, \mathsf{isSub}\}$, the invertibility conditions for operators $\{+, -, \div, \cdot\}$ contain floating-point classifiers only. All of these conditions are also independent from the rounding mode. Similarly, for operator fma over predicates $\{\mathsf{isInf}, \mathsf{isNaN}, \mathsf{isNeg}, \mathsf{isPos}\}$, the invertibility conditions contain

Table 3. Invertibility conditions for floating-point operators (excl. fma) with $\geq$.

Literal	Invertibility condition
$x \overset{\mathsf{R}}{+} s \geq t$	$(\mathsf{isPos}(s) \vee \mathsf{ite}(s \approx \pm\infty, (t \approx \pm\infty \wedge \mathsf{isNeg}(t)), \mathsf{isNeg}(s))) \wedge t \not\approx \mathsf{NaN}$
$x \overset{\mathsf{R}}{-} s \geq t$	$\mathsf{ite}(\mathsf{isNeg}(s), t \not\approx \mathsf{NaN}, \mathsf{ite}(s \approx \pm\infty, (t \approx \pm\infty \wedge \mathsf{isNeg}(t)), (\mathsf{isPos}(s) \wedge t \not\approx \mathsf{NaN})))$
$s \overset{\mathsf{R}}{-} x \geq t$	$(\mathsf{isPos}(s) \vee \mathsf{ite}(s \approx \pm\infty, (t \approx \pm\infty \wedge \mathsf{isNeg}(t)), \mathsf{isNeg}(s))) \wedge t \not\approx \mathsf{NaN}$
$x \overset{\mathsf{R}}{\cdot} s \geq t$	$(\mathsf{isNeg}(t) \vee t \approx \pm 0 \vee s \not\approx \pm 0) \wedge s \not\approx \mathsf{NaN} \wedge t \not\approx \mathsf{NaN}$
$x \overset{\mathsf{R}}{\div} s \geq t$	$(\mathsf{isNeg}(t) \vee t \approx \pm 0 \vee s \not\approx \pm\infty) \wedge s \not\approx \mathsf{NaN} \wedge t \not\approx \mathsf{NaN}$
$s \overset{\mathsf{R}}{\div} x \geq t$	$(\mathsf{isNeg}(t) \vee t \approx \pm 0 \vee s \not\approx \pm 0) \wedge s \not\approx \mathsf{NaN} \wedge t \not\approx \mathsf{NaN}$
$x \,\mathsf{rem}\, s \geq t$	$\mathsf{ite}(\mathsf{isNeg}(t), s \not\approx \mathsf{NaN}, (\lvert t \overset{\mathsf{RNE}}{+} t \rvert \leq \lvert s \rvert \wedge t \not\approx \pm\infty)) \wedge s \not\approx \pm 0$
$s \,\mathsf{rem}\, x \geq t$	?
$\sqrt[\mathsf{R}]{x} \geq t$	$t \not\approx \mathsf{NaN}$
$\lvert x \rvert \geq t$	$t \not\approx \mathsf{NaN}$
$-x \geq t$	$t \not\approx \mathsf{NaN}$
$\overset{\mathsf{R}}{\mathsf{rti}}(x) \geq t$	$t \not\approx \mathsf{NaN}$

only floating-point classifiers. All of these conditions except for $\mathsf{isNeg}(\mathsf{fma}(x, s, t))$ and $\mathsf{isPos}(\mathsf{fma}(x, s, t))$ are also independent from the rounding mode.

For all floating-point operators with predicate isNaN, the invertibility condition is $\top$, i.e., an inverse value for x always exists. This is due to the fact that every floating-point operator returns NaN if one of its operands is NaN, hence NaN can be picked as an inverse value of x. Conversely, we identified four cases for which the invertibility condition is $\bot$, i.e., an inverse value for x never exists. These four cases are $\mathsf{isNeg}(|x|)$, $\mathsf{isInf}(x \,\mathsf{rem}\, s)$, $\mathsf{isInf}(s \,\mathsf{rem}\, x)$, and $\mathsf{isSub}(\mathsf{rti}(x))$. For the first three cases, it is obvious why no inverse value exists. The intuition for $\mathsf{isSub}(\mathsf{rti}(x))$ is that integers are not subnormal, and as a result if x is rounded to an integer it can never be a subnormal number. All of these cases can be easily implemented as rewrite rules in an SMT solver.

For operator fma, the invertibility conditions over predicates $\{\mathsf{isInf}, \mathsf{isNaN}, \mathsf{isNeg}, \mathsf{isPos}\}$ contain floating-point classifiers only. For predicate isZero, the invertibility conditions are more involved. Equations (2) and (3) show the invertibility conditions for $\mathsf{isZero}(\mathsf{fma}(x, s, t))$ and $\mathsf{isZero}(\mathsf{fma}(s, t, x))$ for all rounding modes R.

$$\overset{R}{\mathsf{fma}}(-(t \overset{\mathsf{RTP}}{\div} s), s, t) \approx \pm 0 \vee \overset{R}{\mathsf{fma}}(-(t \overset{\mathsf{RTN}}{\div} s), s, t) \approx \pm 0 \vee (s \approx \pm 0 \wedge t \approx \pm 0) \quad (2)$$

$$\overset{R}{\mathsf{fma}}(s, t, -(s \overset{\mathsf{RTP}}{\cdot} t)) \approx \pm 0 \vee \overset{R}{\mathsf{fma}}(s, t, -(s \overset{\mathsf{RTN}}{\cdot} t)) \approx \pm 0 \quad (3)$$

These two invertibility conditions contain case splits similar to those in Table 2 and indicate that, e.g., $-t \overset{\mathsf{RTP}}{\div} s$ is an inverse value for x when $\overset{\mathsf{R}}{\mathsf{fma}}(-(t \overset{\mathsf{RTP}}{\div} s), s, t) \approx \pm 0$ holds.

As we will describe in Sect. 4, an important aspect of synthesizing these invertibility conditions was considering their visualizations. This helped us determine which invertibility conditions were relatively simple and which exhibited complex behavior.

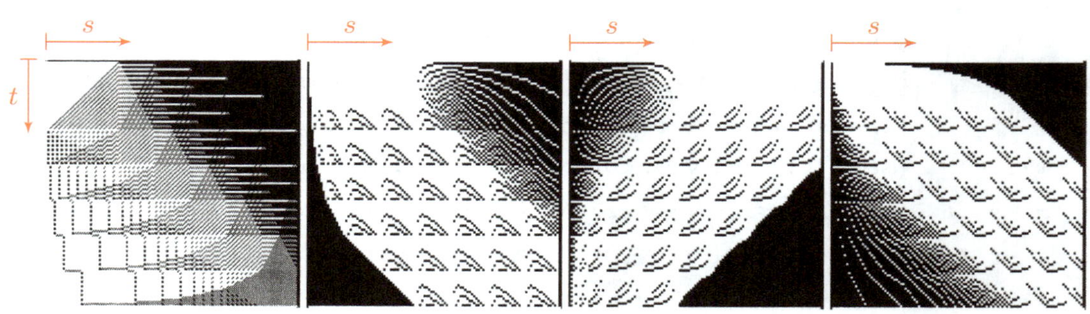

(a) $x + s \approx t$ (b) $x \cdot s \approx t$ (c) $x \div s \approx t$ (d) $s \div x \approx t$

Fig. 1. Invertibility conditions for $\{+, \cdot, \div\}$ over $\approx$ for $\mathbb{F}_{3,5}$ and rounding mode RNE.

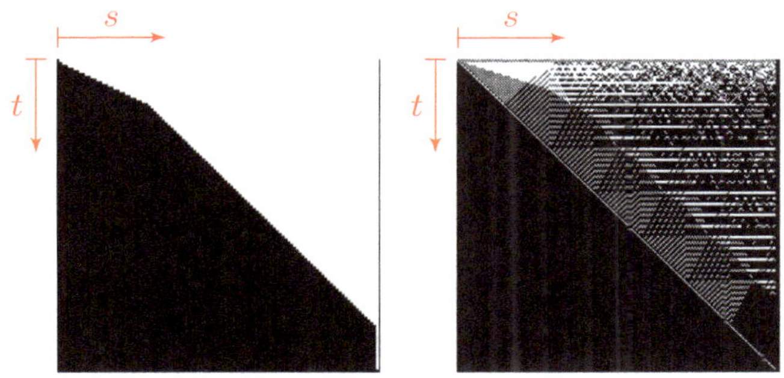

(a) x rem $s \approx t$ (b) s rem $x \approx t$

Fig. 2. Invertibility conditions for rem over $\approx$ for $\mathbb{F}_{3,5}$.

Figure 1 shows the visualizations of the invertibility conditions for operators $\{+, \cdot, \div\}$ over $\approx$ from Table 2 for sort $\mathbb{F}_{3,5}$ with rounding mode RNE (each of the literals is two-dimensional). We use 227×227 pixel maps over all possible values of s and t, where the pixel at point (s, t) is white if the invertibility condition is true, and black if it is false.[2] The values of s are plotted on the horizontal axis and the values of t are plotted on the vertical axis. The leftmost two columns (resp. topmost two rows) give the value of the invertibility condition for $s = \pm 0$ (resp. $t = \pm 0$); the rightmost column (resp. bottom row) gives its value for NaN; the next two columns left of (resp. next two rows on top of) NaN give its value for $\pm\infty$; the remainder plots the values of the subnormal and normal values of s and t, left-to-right (resp. top-to-bottom) in increasing order of their absolute value, alternating between positive and negative values. These visualizations give an intuition of the complexity of the behavior of invertibility conditions, which is a consequence of the complex semantics of floating-point operations.

Figure 2 gives the invertibility condition visualizations for remainder over $\approx$ with sort $\mathbb{F}_{3,5}$ and rounding mode RNE. The visualization on the left hand shows that solving for x as the first argument is relatively easy. It suggests that an invertibility condition for this case involves a linear inequality relating the absolute values of s and t, which we were able to derive in Eq. (1). Solving for x as the second argument, on the other hand, is much more difficult, as indicated by the right picture, which has a significantly more complex structure. We conjecture that no simple solution exists for the latter problem. The visualization of the invertibility condition gives some of the intuition for this: the diagonal divide is caused by the fact that output t will always have a smaller absolute value than the input s. The top-left corner represents subnormal/subnormal computation, this acts as fixed-point and behaves differently from the rest of the function. The stepped blocks along the diagonal occur when s and t have the same exponent and thus the pattern is similar to the invertibility condition for $+$ shown in Fig. 1. Portions right of the main diagonal appear to exhibit random behavior.

[2] Notice that we consider all possible $(2^{\sigma-1}-1)*2$ NaN values of T_{FP} as one single NaN value. Thus, for sort $\mathbb{F}_{3,5}$ we have 227 floating-point values (instead of $2^8 = 256$).

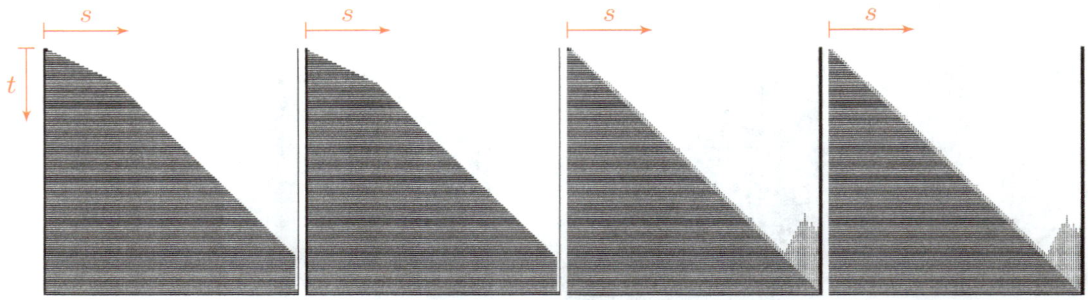

(a) x rem $s > t$ (b) x rem $s \geq t$ (c) s rem $x > t$ (d) s rem $x \geq t$

Fig. 3. Invertibility conditions for rem over inequalities for $\mathbb{F}_{3,5}$.

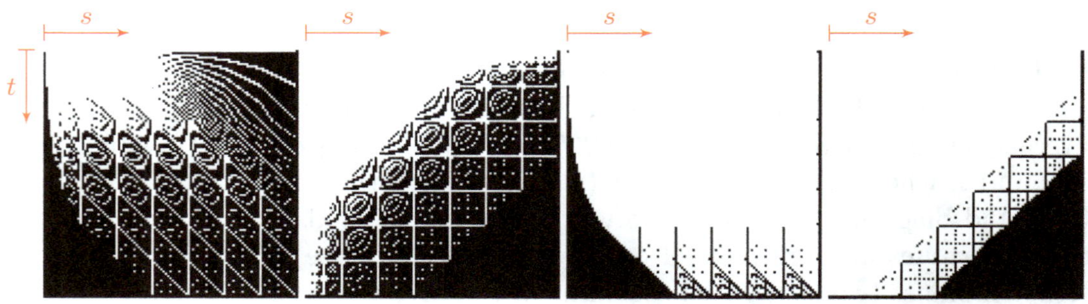

(a) fma$(x, s, t) \approx \pm 0$ (b) fma$(s, t, x) \approx \pm 0$ (c) isSub(fma(x, s, t)) (d) isSub(fma(s, t, x))

Fig. 4. Invertibility conditions for fma over {isZero, isSub} for $\mathbb{F}_{3,5}$ and rnd. mode RNE.

We believe this is the result of repeated cancellations in the computation of the remainder for those values, which suggests a behavior that we believe is similar to the Blum-Blum-Shub random number generator [9].

For remainder with inequalities, we succeeded in determining invertibility conditions for $\leq$ and $\geq$ if x is the first argument. However, for x rem s over $\{<, >\}$, and s rem x over $\{\geq, \leq, <, >\}$ we did not. This is particularly surprising considering that the invertibility conditions for non-strict and strict inequalities are nearly identical (varying only by a handful of pixels), as shown in Fig. 3. Note that for x as the first argument, all variations of the concise invertibility conditions for non-strict inequality we considered failed as solutions for the strict inequality. This behavior is representative of the many subtle corner cases we encountered while synthesizing these conditions.

Figure 4 shows visualizations for invertibility conditions involving fma. The left two images are visualizations for the invertibility conditions for isZero. The corresponding invertibility conditions are given in Eqs. (2) and (3) above. We were not able to determine invertibility conditions for operator fma over predicate isSub, which are visualized in the rightmost two pictures in Fig. 4. Finally, we did not succeed in finding invertibility conditions for fma with binary predicates, which are particularly challenging since they are three-dimensional. Finding solutions for these cases is ongoing work (see Sect. 4 for a more in-depth discussion).

4 Synthesis of Floating-Point Invertibility Conditions

Deriving invertibility conditions in T_{FP} is a highly challenging task. We were unable to derive these conditions manually despite our substantial background knowledge of floating-point numbers. As a consequence, we developed a custom extension of the syntax-guided synthesis (SyGuS) paradigm [1] with the goal of finding invertibility conditions automatically, which resulted in the conditions from Sect. 3. While the extension was optimized for this task, we stress that our techniques are theory-agnostic and can be used for synthesis problems over any finite domain. Our approach builds upon the SyGuS capabilities of the SMT solver CVC4 [5,29], which has recently been extended to support reasoning about the theory of floating-points [11]. We use the invertibility condition for floating-point addition with equality here as a running example.

Establishing an invertibility condition requires solving a synthesis problem with *three* levels of quantifier alternation. In particular, for floating-point addition with equality, we are interested in finding a solution for predicate IC that satisfies the conjecture:

$$\exists\, \mathsf{IC}.\, \forall s, t.\, (\mathsf{IC}(s,t) \Leftrightarrow (\exists x.\, x \overset{\mathsf{R}}{+} s \approx t)) \tag{4}$$

for some rounding mode R. In other words, this conjecture states that $\mathsf{IC}(s,t)$ holds exactly when there exists an x that, when rounding the result of adding x to s according to mode R, yields t. Furthermore, we are interested in finding a solution for IC that holds *independently of the format* of x, s, t. Note that SMT solvers are not capable of reasoning about constraints that are parametric in the floating-point format. To address this challenge, following the methodology from previous work [26], our strategy for establishing (general) invertibility conditions first solves the synthesis conjecture for a fixed format $\mathbb{F}_{\varepsilon,\sigma}$, and subsequently checks whether that solution also holds for other formats. The choice of the number of exponent bits ε and significand bits σ in $\mathbb{F}_{\varepsilon,\sigma}$ balances two criteria:

1. ε, σ should be large enough to exercise many (or all) of the behaviors of the operators and relations in our synthesis conjecture,
2. ε, σ should be small enough for the synthesis problem to be tractable.

In our experience, the best choices for (ε, σ) depended on the particular invertibility condition we were solving. The most common choices for (ε, σ) were $(3, 5)$, $(4, 5)$ and $(4, 6)$. For most two-dimensional invertibility conditions (those that involve two variables s and t), we used $(3, 5)$, since the required synthesis procedures mentioned below were roughly eight times faster than for $(4, 5)$. For one-dimensional invertibility conditions, we often used higher precision formats. Since floating-point operators like addition take as additional argument a rounding mode R, we assumed a fixed rounding mode when solving, and then cross-checked our solution for multiple rounding modes.

Assume we have chosen to synthesize the invertibility condition for conjecture (4) for format $\mathbb{F}_{3,5}$ and rounding mode RNE. Notice that current SyGuS solvers [2,29] support only two levels of quantifier alternation. However, we can expand the innermost quantifier in this conjecture to obtain the conjecture:

$$\exists \mathsf{IC}. \forall st. (\mathsf{IC}(s,t) \Leftrightarrow (\bigvee_{i=0}^{226} i \overset{\mathsf{RNE}}{+} s \approx t)) \tag{5}$$

where for simplicity of notation we use $i = 0, \ldots, 226$ to denote the values of $\mathbb{F}_{3,5}$. This methodology was also used in Niemetz et al. [26], where invertibility conditions for bit-vector operators were synthesized for bit-width 4 by giving the conjecture of the above form to an off-the-shelf SyGuS solver. In contrast to that work, we found that the synthesis conjecture above is too challenging to be solved efficiently by current state-of-the-art enumerative SyGuS solvers. The reason for this is twofold. First, the smallest viable floating-point format is $3+5=8$ bits, which requires the body of (5) to have a significantly large number of disjuncts (227), which is more than ten times larger than the 16 disjuncts required when synthesizing 4-bit invertibility conditions for bit-vectors. Second, floating-point formulas are much harder to solve than bit-vector formulas, due to the complexity of their bit-blasted encodings. Thus, a significantly challenging satisfiability query must be solved *for each* candidate considered within the SyGuS solver.

To address the above challenges, we perform a more extreme preprocessing step on our synthesis conjecture, which computes the input/output behavior of the invertibility condition on all points in the domain of s and t. In other words, we rephrase our synthesis conjecture as:

$$\exists \mathsf{IC}. \bigwedge_{i=0}^{226} \bigwedge_{j=0}^{226} (\mathsf{IC}(i,j) \Leftrightarrow c_{i,j}) \tag{6}$$

where each $c_{i,j}$ is a Boolean constant (either $\top$ or $\bot$) determined by a quantifier-free satisfiability query. In particular, for each pair of floating-point values (i,j), constant $c_{i,j}$ is $\top$ if $x+i \approx j$ is satisfiable, and $\bot$ if it is unsatisfiable. In practice, we represent the above conjecture as a 227×227 table, which we call the *full I/O specification* of invertibility condition IC. In our experiments, computing this table for most two-dimensional invertibility conditions of sort $\mathbb{F}_{3,5}$ required 15 min (for $227 * 227 = 51,529$ quantifier-free queries), and 2 h for sort $\mathbb{F}_{4,5}$ (requiring $483 * 483 = 233,289$ queries). This process was accelerated by first applying random sampling over possible values of x to quickly test if a query was satisfiable. For some operators, notably remainder, this required significantly more time than for others (up to a factor of 2). Due to the high cost of this preprocessing step, we generated a database with the full I/O specifications for *all* invertibility conditions from Sect. 3 using a cluster of 50 nodes with Intel Xeon E5-2637 with 3.5 GHz and 32 GB memory, and then shared this database among multiple developers. Computing the full I/O specifications for $\mathbb{F}_{3,5}$, $\mathbb{F}_{4,5}$, and $\mathbb{F}_{4,6}$ required a total of 459 days of CPU time (6.1 for $\mathbb{F}_{3,5}$, 54.7 for $\mathbb{F}_{4,5}$, and

398.5 for $\mathbb{F}_{4,6}$). Despite the heavy cost of this step, it was crucial for accelerating our framework for synthesizing invertibility conditions, described next.

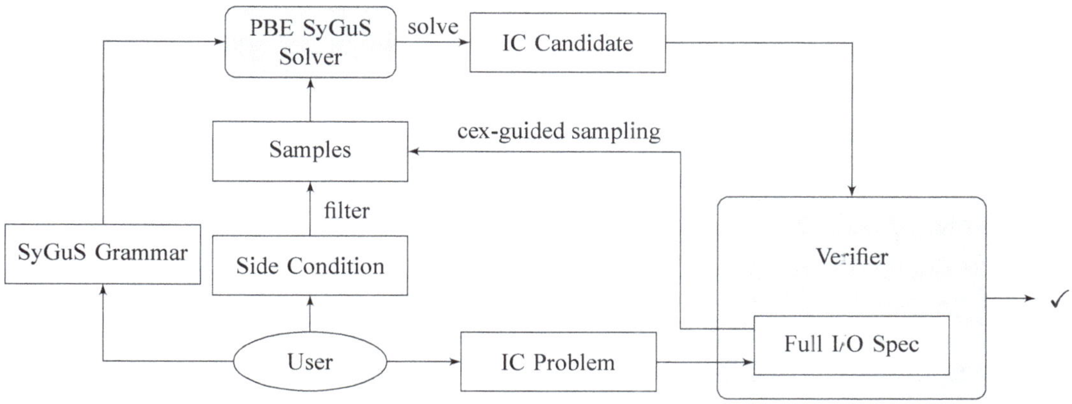

Fig. 5. Architecture for synthesizing invertibility conditions for floating point formulas.

Figure 5 summarizes our architecture for solving synthesis conjectures of the above form. The user first selects an invertibility condition problem to solve, where we assume the full I/O specification has been computed using the aforementioned techniques. At a high level, our architecture can be seen as an *interactive synthesis environment*, where the user manages the interaction between two subprocedures:

1. a SyGuS solver with support for decision tree learning, and
2. a solution verifier storing the full I/O specification of the invertibility condition.

We use a counterexample-guided loop, where the SyGuS solver provides the solution verifier with candidate solutions, and the solution verifier provides the SyGuS solver with an evolving subset of sample points taken from the full I/O specification. These points correspond to counterexamples to failed candidate solutions, and are sampled in a uniformly random manner over the domain of our specification. To accelerate the speed at which our framework converges on a solution, we configure the solution verifier to generate multiple counterexample points (typically 10) for each iteration of the loop. The process terminates when the SyGuS solver generates a candidate solution that is correct for all points according to its full I/O specification.

We give the user control over both the solutions and counterexample points generated in this loop. First, as is commonly done in syntax-guided synthesis applications, the user in our workflow provides an input grammar to the SyGuS solver. This is a context-free grammar in a standard format [28], which contains a guess of the operators and patterns that may be involved in the invertibility condition we are synthesizing. Second, note that the domain of floating-point numbers can be subdivided into a number of subdomains and special cases (e.g. normal, subnormal, not-a-number, infinity), as well as split into different classifications (e.g. positive and negative). Our workflow allows the user to provide a *side condition*, whose purpose is to focus on finding an invertibility condition that is correct for one of these subdomains. The side condition acts as a filtering mechanism on the counterexample points generated by the solution verifier. For example, given the side condition $\mathsf{isNorm}(s) \wedge \mathsf{isNorm}(t)$, the solution verifier checks candidate solutions generated by the SyGuS solver only against points (s, t) where both arguments are normal, and consequently only communicates counterexamples of this form to the SyGuS solver. The solution verifier may also be configured to establish that the current candidate solution generated by the SyGuS solver is *conditionally* correct, that is, it is true on all points in the domain that satisfy the side condition.

There are several advantages to the form of the synthesis conjecture in (6) that we exploit in our workflow. First, its structure makes it easy to divide the problem into sub-cases: our synthesis workflow at all times sends only a subset of the conjuncts of (6) for some (i, j) pairs. As a result, we do not burden the underlying SyGuS solver with the entire conjecture at once, which would not scale in practice. A second advantage is that it is in *programming-by-examples* (PBE) form, since it consists of a conjunction of concrete input-output pairs. As a consequence, specialized algorithms can be used by the SyGuS solver to generate solutions for (approximations of) our conjecture in a way that is highly scalable in practice. These techniques are broadly referred to as decision tree learning or unification algorithms. As a brief review (see Alur et al. [2] for a recent SyGuS-based approach), a decision tree learning algorithm is given as input a set of good examples $c_1 \mapsto \top, \ldots, c_n \mapsto \top$ and a set of bad examples $d_1 \mapsto \bot, \ldots, d_m \mapsto \bot$. The goal of a decision tree algorithm is to find a predicate, or *classifier*, that evaluates to true on all the good examples, and false on all the bad examples. In our context, a classifier is expressed as an if-then-else tree of Boolean sort. Sampling the space of conjecture (6) provides the decision tree algorithm with good and bad examples and the returned classifier is a candidate solution that we give to the solution verifier. The SyGuS solver of CVC4 uses a decision-tree learning algorithm, which we rely on in our workflow. Due to the scalability of this algorithm and the fact that only a small subset of our conjecture is considered at any given time, candidate solutions are typically generated by the SyGuS solver in our framework in a matter of seconds.

Another important aspect of the SyGuS solver in Fig. 5 is that it is configured to generate *multiple* solutions for the current set of sample points. Due to the way the SyGuS-based decision-tree learning algorithm works, these solutions tend to become *more general* over the runtime of the solver. As a simple example (assuming exact integer arithmetic), say the solver is given input points $(1, 1) \mapsto \top$, $(2, 0) \mapsto \top$, $(1, 0) \mapsto \bot$ and $(0, 1) \mapsto \bot$ for (s, t). It enumerates predicates over s and t, starting with simplest predicates first, say $s \approx 0$, $t \approx 0$, $s \approx 1$, $y \approx 1$, $s + t > 1$, and so on. After generating the first four predicates, it constructs the solution $\mathsf{ite}(s \approx 1, t \approx 1, t \approx 0)$, which is a correct classifier for the given set of points. However, after generating the fifth predicate in this list, it returns $s + t > 1$ itself as a solution; this can be seen as a generalization of the previous solution since it requires no case splitting.

Since more general candidate solutions have a higher likelihood of being actual solutions in our experience, our workflow critically relies on the ability of users to manually terminate the synthesis procedure when they are satisfied with the last generated candidate. Our synthesis procedure logs a list of candidate solutions that satisfy the conjecture on the current set of sample points. When the user terminates the synthesis process, the solution verifier will check the last solution generated in this list. Users have the option to rearrange the elements of this list by hand, if they have an intuition that a specific candidate is more likely to be correct—and so should be tested first.

Experience. The first challenging invertibility condition we solved with our framework was addition with equality for rounding mode RNE. Initially, we used a generic grammar that contained the entire floating-point signature. As a first key step towards solving this problem, the synthesis procedure suggested the single literal $t \approx s \overset{\mathsf{RNE}}{+} (t \overset{\mathsf{RNE}}{-} s)$ as candidate solution. Although counterexamples were found for this candidate, we noticed that it satisfied over 98% of the specification, and a visualization of its I/O behavior showed similar patterns to the invertibility condition we were solving for. Based on these observations, we focused our grammar towards literals of this form. In particular, we used a function that takes two floating-points x, y and two rounding modes R_1, R_2 as arguments and returns $x \overset{R_1}{+} (y \overset{R_2}{-} x)$ as a builtin symbol of our grammar. We refer to such a function as a *residual* computation of y, noting that its value is often approximately y. By including various functions for residual computations, we focused the effort of the synthesizer on more interesting predicates. The end solution involved multiple residual computations, as shown in Table 2. Our initial solution was specific to the rounding mode RNE. After solving for several other rounding modes, we were able to construct a parametric solution that was correct for all rounding modes. In total, it took roughly three days of developer time to discover the generalized invertibility condition for addition with equality. Many of the subsequent invertibility conditions took a matter of hours, since by then we had a good intuition for the residual computations that were relevant for each case.

Invertibility conditions involving rem, fma, isNorm, and isSub were challenging and required further customizations to the grammar, for instance to include constants that corresponded to the minimum and maximum normal and subnormal values. Three-dimensional invertibility conditions (which in this work is limited to cases of fma with binary predicates) were especially challenging since the domain of their conjecture is a factor of 227 larger for $\mathbb{F}_{3,5}$ than the others. Following our strategy for solving the invertibility conditions for specific formats and rounding modes, in ongoing work we are investigating solving these cases by first solving the invertibility condition for a fixed value c for one of its free variables u. Solving a two-dimensional problem of this form with a solution φ may suggest a generalization that works for all values of u where all occurrences of c in φ are replaced by u.

We found the side condition feature of our workflow important for narrowing down which subdomain was the most challenging for the conjecture in question.

For instance, for some cases it was very easy to find invertibility conditions that held when both s and t were normal (resp., subnormal), but very difficult when s was normal and t was subnormal or vice versa.

We also implemented a fully automated mode for the synthesis loop in Fig. 5. However, in practice, it was more effective to tweak the generated solutions manually. The amount of user interaction was not prohibitively high in our experience.

Finally, we found that it was often helpful to visualize the input/output behavior of candidate solutions. In many cases, the difference between a candidate solution and the desired behavior of the invertibility condition would reveal a required modification to the grammar or would suggest which parts of the domain of the conjecture to focus on.

4.1 Verifying Conditions for Multiple Formats and Rounding Modes

We verified the correctness of all 167 invertibility conditions by checking them against their corresponding full I/O specification for floating-point formats $\mathbb{F}_{3,5}$, $\mathbb{F}_{4,5}$, and $\mathbb{F}_{4,6}$ and all rounding modes, which required 1.6 days of CPU time. This is relatively cheap compared to computing the specifications, since checking is essentially constant evaluation of invertibility conditions for all possible input values. However, this quickly becomes infeasible with increasing precision, since the time required for computing the I/O specification roughly increases by a factor of 8 for each bit.

As a consequence, we generated quantified floating-point problems to verify the 167 invertibility conditions for formats $\mathbb{F}_{3,5}$, $\mathbb{F}_{4,5}$, $\mathbb{F}_{4,6}$, $\mathbb{F}_{5,11}$ (Float16), $\mathbb{F}_{8,24}$ (Float32), and $\mathbb{F}_{11,53}$ (Float64) and all rounding modes. Each problem checks the T_{FP}-unsatisfiability of formula $\neg(\phi_c \Leftrightarrow \exists x.\, l[x])$, where $l[x]$ corresponds to the floating-point literal, and ϕ_c to its invertibility condition. In total, we generated

> $\mathsf{QE_{FP}}(\exists x.\, P(t_1, \ldots, t_j[x], \ldots, t_n))$, where $x \notin FV(t_i)$ for $i \neq j$:
>
> If $t_j[x] = x$, return $\mathsf{getIC}(x, P)$.
> Otherwise, $t_j[x] = \diamond(s_1, \ldots, s_k[x], \ldots s_m)$ where $m > 0$, $x \notin FV(s_i)$ for $i \neq k$.
> Let $Q[y] = P(t_1, \ldots, t_{j-1}, \diamond(s_1, \ldots, s_{k-1}, y, s_{k+1}, \ldots, s_m), t_{j+1}, \ldots, t_n)$ where y is a fresh variable.
> Return $\mathsf{getIC}(y, Q[y]) \wedge \mathsf{QE_{FP}}(\exists x.\, s_k[x] \approx y)$.

Fig. 6. Recursive procedure $\mathsf{QE_{FP}}$ for computing quantifier elimination for x in the unit linear formula $\exists x.\, P(t_1, \ldots, t_j[x], \ldots, t_n)$. The free variables in this formula and the fresh variable y are implicitly universally quantified. Placeholder $\diamond$ denotes a floating-point operator from Table 1.

3786 problems ($116 * 5 + 51^3$ for each floating-point format) and checked them using CVC4 [5] (master 546bf686) and Z3 [16] (version 4.8.4).

We consider an invertibility condition to be verified for a floating-point format and rounding mode if at least one solver reports unsatisfiable. Given a CPU time limit of one hour and a memory limit of 8 GB for each solver/benchmark pair, we were able to verify 3577 (94.5%) invertibility conditions overall, with 99.2% of $\mathbb{F}_{3,5}$, 99.7% of $\mathbb{F}_{4,5}$, 100% of $\mathbb{F}_{4,6}$, 93.8% of $\mathbb{F}_{5,11}$, 90.2% of $\mathbb{F}_{8,24}$, and 84% of $\mathbb{F}_{11,53}$. This verification with CVC4 and Z3 required a total of 32 days of CPU time. All verification jobs were run on cluster nodes with Intel Xeon E5-2637 3.5 GHz and 32 GB memory.

5 Quantifier Elimination for Unit Linear Floating-Point Formulas

Based on the invertibility conditions presented in Sect. 3, we can define a quantifier elimination procedure for a restricted fragment of floating-point formulas. The procedure applies to *unit linear* formulas, that is, formulas of the form $\exists x. P[x]$ where P is a Σ_{FP}-literal containing exactly one occurrence of x.

Figure 6 gives a quantifier elimination procedure $\mathsf{QE}_{\mathsf{FP}}$ for unit linear floating-point formulas $\exists x. P[x]$. We write $\mathsf{getIC}(y, Q[y])$ to indicate the invertibility condition for y in $Q[y]$, which amounts to a table lookup for the appropriate condition as given in Sect. 3. Note that our procedure is currently a partial function because we do not have yet invertibility conditions for some unit linear formulas. The recursive procedure returns a conjunction of conditions based on the path on which x occurs in P. If x occurs beneath multiple nested function applications, a fresh variable y is introduced and used for referencing the intermediate result of the subterm we are currently solving for. We demonstrate this in the following example.

Example 2. Consider the unit linear formula $\exists x. (x \overset{\mathsf{R}}{\cdot} u) \overset{\mathsf{R}}{+} s \geq t$. Invoking the procedure $\mathsf{QE}_{\mathsf{FP}}$ on this input yields, after two recursive calls, the conjunction

$$\mathsf{getIC}(y_1, y_1 \overset{\mathsf{R}}{+} s \geq t) \wedge \mathsf{getIC}(y_2, y_2 \overset{\mathsf{R}}{\cdot} u \approx y_1) \wedge \mathsf{getIC}(x, x \approx y_2)$$

where y_1 and y_2 are fresh variables. The third conjunct is trivially equivalent to $\top$. This formula is quantifier-free and has the properties specified by the following theorem.

Theorem 1. *Let $\exists x. P$ be a unit linear formula and let $\mathcal{I}$ be a model of T_{FP}. Then, $\mathcal{I}$ satisfies $\neg\exists x. P$ if and only if there exists a model $\mathcal{J}$ of T_{FP} (constructible from $\mathcal{I}$) that satisfies $\neg\mathsf{QE}_{\mathsf{FP}}(\exists x. P)$.*

[3] 116 invertibility conditions from rounding mode dependent operators and 51 invertibility conditions where the operator is rounding mode independent (e.g., rem).

Niemetz et al. [26] present a similar algorithm for solving unit linear bit-vector literals. In that work, a counterexample-guided loop was devised that made use of Hilbert-choice expressions for representing quantifier instantiations. In contrast to that work, we provide here only a quantifier elimination procedure. Extending our techniques to a general quantifier instantiation strategy is the subject of ongoing work. We discuss our preliminary work in this direction in the next section.

6 Solving Quantified Floating-Point Formulas

We implemented a prototype extension of the SMT solver CVC4 that leverages the results of the previous section to determine the satisfiability of quantified floating-point formulas. To handle quantified formulas, CVC4 uses a basic model-based instantiation loop (see, e.g., [30,32] for instantiation approaches for other theories). This technique maintains a quantifier-free set of constraints F corresponding to instantiations of universally quantified formulas. It terminates with the response "unsatisfiable" if F is unsatisfiable, and terminates with "satisfiable" if it can show that the given quantified formulas are satisfied by a model of T_{FP} that satisfies F. For T_{FP}, the instantiations are substitutions of universally quantified variables to concrete floating-point values, e.g. $\forall x. P(x) \Rightarrow P(0)$, which can be highly inefficient in the worst case for higher precision.

We extend this basic loop with a preprocessing pass that generates theory lemmas based on the invertibility conditions corresponding to literals of quantified formulas $\forall x.P$ with exactly one occurrence of x, as explained in the example below.

Example 3. Suppose the current set S of formulas contains a formula φ of the form $\forall x. \neg((x \cdot u) + s \geq t \wedge Q(x))$ where u, s and t are ground terms; then we add the following formula to S where y_1 and y_2 are fresh (free) variables:

$$(\mathsf{getIC}(y_1, y_1 + s \geq t) \Rightarrow y_1 + s \geq t) \wedge (\mathsf{getIC}(y_2, y_2 \cdot u \approx y_1) \Rightarrow y_2 \cdot u \approx y_1)$$

The addition of this lemma is satisfiability preserving because, if the invertibility condition holds for $y_1 + s \geq t$ (resp., $y_2 \cdot u \approx y_1$), then y_1 (resp., y_2) a solution for that literal. We then add the instantiation lemma $\varphi \Rightarrow \neg((y_2 \cdot u) + s \geq t \wedge Q(y_2))$. Although x is not necessarily linear in the body of φ, if both invertibility conditions hold, then the combination of the above lemmas implies $(y_2 \cdot u) + s \geq t$, which together with the instantiation lemma allows the solver to infer that the remaining portion of the quantified formula Q cannot hold for y_2. An inference of this form may be more productive than enumerating the possible values of x in instantiations.

Evaluation. We considered all 61 benchmarks from SMT-LIB [6] that contained quantified formulas over floating-points (logic FP), which correspond to verification conditions from the software verification competition that use a floating-point encoding [19]. The invertibility conditions required for solving their literals include floating-point addition, multiplication and division (both arguments) with equality and inequality. We implemented all cases of invertibility conditions for solving these cases. We extended our SMT solver CVC4 (GitHub master 5d248c36) with the above preprocessing pass (GitHub cav19fp 9b5acd74), and compared its performance with (configuration CVC4-ext) and without (configuration CVC4-base) the above preprocessing pass enabled to the SMT solver Z3 (version 4.8.4). All experiments were run on the same cluster mentioned earlier, with a memory limit of 8 GB and a 1800 s time limit. Overall, CVC4-base solved 35 benchmarks within the time limit (with no benchmarks uniquely solved compared to CVC4-ext), CVC4-ext solved 42 benchmarks (7 of these uniquely solved compared to the base version), and Z3 solved 56 benchmarks. While CVC4-ext solves significantly fewer benchmarks than Z3, we believe that the improvement over CVC4-base is indicative that our approach for invertibility conditions shows potential for solving quantified floating-point constraints in SMT solvers. A more comprehensive evaluation and implementation is left as future work.

7 Conclusion

We have presented invertibility conditions for a large subset of combinations of floating-point operators over floating-point predicates supported by SMT solvers. These conditions were found by a framework that utilizes syntax-guided synthesis solving, customized for our problem and developed over the course of this work. We have shown that invertibility conditions imply that a simple fragment of quantified floating-points admits compact quantifier elimination, and have given preliminary evidence that an SMT solver that partially leverages this technique can have a higher success rate on floating-point problems coming from a software verification application.

For future work, we plan to extend techniques for quantified and quantifier-free floating-point formulas to incorporate our findings, in particular to lift previous quantifier instantiation approaches (e.g., [26]) and local search procedures (e.g., [25]) for bit-vectors to floating-points. We also plan to extend and use our synthesis framework for related challenging synthesis tasks, such as finding conditions under which more complex constraints have solutions, including those having multiple occurrences of a variable to solve for. Our synthesis framework is agnostic to theories and can be used for any sort with a small finite domain. It can thus be leveraged also for solutions to quantified bit-vector constraints. Finally, we would like to establish formal proofs of correctness of our invertibility conditions that are independent of floating-point formats.

References

1. Alur, R., et al.: Syntax-guided synthesis. In: Formal Methods in Computer-Aided Design, FMCAD 2013, Portland, 20–23 October 2013, pp. 1–8. IEEE (2013). http://ieeexplore.ieee.org/document/6679385/

2. Alur, R., Radhakrishna, A., Udupa, A.: Scaling enumerative program synthesis via divide and conquer. In: Legay, A., Margaria, T. (eds.) TACAS 2017. LNCS, vol. 10205, pp. 319–336. Springer, Heidelberg (2017). https://doi.org/10.1007/978-3-662-54577-5_18
3. IEEE Standards Association 754-2008 - IEEE standard for floating-point arithmetic (2008). https://ieeexplore.ieee.org/servlet/opac?punumber=4610933
4. Barr, E.T., Vo, T., Le, V., Su, Z.: Automatic detection of floating-point exceptions. SIGPLAN Not. **48**(1), 549–560 (2013)
5. Barrett, C., et al.: CVC4. In: Gopalakrishnan, G., Qadeer, S. (eds.) CAV 2011. LNCS, vol. 6806, pp. 171–177. Springer, Heidelberg (2011). https://doi.org/10.1007/978-3-642-22110-1_14
6. Barrett, C., Stump, A., Tinelli, C.: The satisfiability modulo theories library (SMT-LIB) (2010). www.SMT-LIB.org
7. Ben Khadra, M.A., Stoffel, D., Kunz, W.: goSAT: floating-point satisfiability as global optimization. In: FMCAD, pp. 11–14. IEEE (2017)
8. Bjørner, N., Janota, M.: Playing with quantified satisfaction. In: 20th International Conferences on Logic for Programming, Artificial Intelligence and Reasoning - Short Presentations, LPAR 2015, Suva, 24–28 November 2015, pp. 15–27 (2015)
9. Blum, L., Blum, M., Shub, M.: A simple unpredictable pseudo-random number generator. SIAM J. Comput. **15**(2), 364–383 (1986)
10. Brain, M., Dsilva, V., Griggio, A., Haller, L., Kroening, D.: Deciding floating-point logic with abstract conflict driven clause learning. Formal Methods Syst. Des. **45**(2), 213–245 (2014)
11. Brain, M., Schanda, F., Sun, Y.: Building better bit-blasting for floating-point problems. In: Vojnar, T., Zhang, L. (eds.) TACAS 2019, Part I. LNCS, vol. 11427, pp. 79–98. Springer, Cham (2019). https://doi.org/10.1007/978-3-030-17462-0_5
12. Brain, M., Tinelli, C., Rümmer, P., Wahl, T.: An automatable formal semantics for IEEE-754 floating-point arithmetic. In: 22nd IEEE Symposium on Computer Arithmetic, ARITH 2015, Lyon, 22–24 June 2015, pp. 160–167. IEEE (2015)
13. Brillout, A., Kroening, D., Wahl, T.: Mixed abstractions for floating-point arithmetic. In: FMCAD, pp. 69–76. IEEE (2009)
14. Conchon, S., Iguernlala, M., Ji, K., Melquiond, G., Fumex, C.: A three-tier strategy for reasoning about floating-point numbers in SMT. In: Majumdar, R., Kunčak, V. (eds.) CAV 2017. LNCS, vol. 10427, pp. 419–435. Springer, Cham (2017). https://doi.org/10.1007/978-3-319-63390-9_22
15. Daumas, M., Melquiond, G.: Certification of bounds on expressions involving rounded operators. ACM Trans. Math. Softw. **37**(1), 1–20 (2010)
16. De Moura, L., Bjørner, N.: Z3: an efficient SMT solver. In: Ramakrishnan, C.R., Rehof, J. (eds.) TACAS 2008. LNCS, vol. 4963, pp. 337–340. Springer, Heidelberg (2008). https://doi.org/10.1007/978-3-540-78800-3_24
17. Dutertre, B.: Solving exists/forall problems in yices. In: Workshop on Satisfiability Modulo Theories (2015)
18. Fu, Z., Su, Z.: XSat: a fast floating-point satisfiability solver. In: Chaudhuri, S., Farzan, A. (eds.) CAV 2016. LNCS, vol. 9780, pp. 187–209. Springer, Cham (2016). https://doi.org/10.1007/978-3-319-41540-6_11
19. Heizmann, M., et al.: Ultimate automizer with an on-demand construction of Floyd-Hoare automata. In: Legay, A., Margaria, T. (eds.) TACAS 2017, Part II. LNCS, vol. 10206, pp. 394–398. Springer, Heidelberg (2017). https://doi.org/10.1007/978-3-662-54580-5_30
20. Lapschies, F.: SONOLAR, the solver for non-linear arithmetic (2014). http://www.informatik.uni-bremen.de/agbs/florian/sonolar

21. Liew, D.: JFS: JIT fuzzing solver. https://github.com/delcypher/jfs
22. Marre, B., Bobot, F., Chihani, Z.: Real behavior of floating point numbers. In: SMT Workshop (2017)
23. Michel, C., Rueher, M., Lebbah, Y.: Solving constraints over floating-point numbers. In: Walsh, T. (ed.) CP 2001. LNCS, vol. 2239, pp. 524–538. Springer, Heidelberg (2001). https://doi.org/10.1007/3-540-45578-7_36
24. de Moura, L., Bjørner, N.: Efficient e-matching for SMT solvers. In: Pfenning, F. (ed.) CADE 2007. LNCS, vol. 4603, pp. 183–198. Springer, Heidelberg (2007). https://doi.org/10.1007/978-3-540-73595-3_13
25. Niemetz, A., Preiner, M., Biere, A.: Precise and complete propagation based local search for satisfiability modulo theories. In: Chaudhuri, S., Farzan, A. (eds.) CAV 2016, Part I. LNCS, vol. 9779, pp. 199–217. Springer, Cham (2016). https://doi.org/10.1007/978-3-319-41528-4_11
26. Niemetz, A., Preiner, M., Reynolds, A., Barrett, C., Tinelli, C.: Solving quantified bit-vectors using invertibility conditions. In: Chockler, H., Weissenbacher, G. (eds.) CAV 2018, Part II. LNCS, vol. 10982, pp. 236–255. Springer, Cham (2018). https://doi.org/10.1007/978-3-319-96142-2_16
27. Preiner, M., Niemetz, A., Biere, A.: Counterexample-guided model synthesis. In: Legay, A., Margaria, T. (eds.) TACAS 2017, Part I. LNCS, vol. 10205, pp. 264–280. Springer, Heidelberg (2017). https://doi.org/10.1007/978-3-662-54577-5_15
28. Raghothaman, M., Udupa, A.: Language to specify syntax-guided synthesis problems, May 2014
29. Reynolds, A., Deters, M., Kuncak, V., Tinelli, C., Barrett, C.: Counterexample-guided quantifier instantiation for synthesis in SMT. In: Kroening, D., Păsăreanu, C.S. (eds.) CAV 2015, Part II. LNCS, vol. 9207, pp. 198–216. Springer, Cham (2015). https://doi.org/10.1007/978-3-319-21668-3_12
30. Reynolds, A., King, T., Kuncak, V.: Solving quantified linear arithmetic by counterexample-guided instantiation. Formal Methods Syst. Des. **51**(3), 500–532 (2017)
31. Scheibler, K., Kupferschmid, S., Becker, B.: Recent improvements in the SMT solver iSAT. MBMV **13**, 231–241 (2013)
32. Wintersteiger, C.M., Hamadi, Y., de Moura, L.M.: Efficiently solving quantified bit-vector formulas. Formal Methods Syst. Des. **42**(1), 3–23 (2013)
33. Zeljić, A., Wintersteiger, C.M., Rümmer, P.: Approximations for model construction. In: Demri, S., Kapur, D., Weidenbach, C. (eds.) IJCAR 2014. LNCS (LNAI), vol. 8562, pp. 344–359. Springer, Cham (2014). https://doi.org/10.1007/978-3-319-08587-6_26

Numerically-Robust Inductive Proof Rules for Continuous Dynamical Systems

Sicun Gao[1], James Kapinski[2], Jyotirmoy Deshmukh[3], Nima Roohi[1(✉)], Armando Solar-Lezama[4], Nikos Arechiga[5], and Soonho Kong[5]

[1] University of California, San Diego, La Jolla, USA
{sicung,nroohi}@ucsd.edu
[2] Toyota R&D, Gardena, USA
jim.kapinski@toyota.com
[3] University of Southern California, Los Angeles, USA
jyotirmoy.deshmukh@usc.edu
[4] Massachusetts Institute of Technology, Cambridge, USA
asolar@csail.mit.edu
[5] Toyota Research Institute, Cambridge, USA
{nikos.arechiga,soonho.kong}@tri.global

Abstract. We formulate numerically-robust inductive proof rules for unbounded stability and safety properties of continuous dynamical systems. These induction rules robustify standard notions of Lyapunov functions and barrier certificates so that they can tolerate small numerical errors. In this way, numerically-driven decision procedures can establish a sound and relative-complete proof system for unbounded properties of very general nonlinear systems. We demonstrate the effectiveness of the proposed rules for rigorously verifying unbounded properties of various nonlinear systems, including a challenging powertrain control model.

1 Introduction

Infinite-time stability and safety properties of continuous dynamical systems are typically established via inductive arguments over continuous time. For instance, proving stability of a dynamical system is similar to proving termination of a program. A system is stable at the origin in the sense of Lyapunov, if one can find a Lyapunov function (essentially a ranking function) that is everywhere positive except for reaching exactly zero at the origin, and never increases over time along the direction of the system dynamics [11]. Likewise, proving unbounded safety of a dynamical system requires one to find a barrier function (or differential invariant [19]) that separates the system's initial state from the unsafe regions, and whenever the system states reach the barrier, the system dynamics always points towards the safe side of the barrier [21]. In both cases, once a candidate certificate (Lyapunov or barrier functions) is proposed, the verification problem is reduced to checking the validity of a universally-quantified

I. Dillig and S. Tasiran (Eds.): CAV 2019, LNCS 11562, pp. 137–154, 2019.
https://doi.org/10.1007/978-3-030-25543-5_9

first-order formula over real-valued variables. The standard approaches for the validation step use symbolic quantifier elimination [4] or Sum-of-Squares techniques [17,18,24]. However, these algorithms are either extremely expensive or numerically brittle. Most importantly, they can not handle systems with non-polynomial nonlinearity, and thus fall short of a general framework for verifying practical systems of significant complexity.

The standard approach of checking invariance conditions in program analysis is to use Satisfiability Modulo Theories (SMT) solvers [16]. However, to check the inductive conditions for nonlinear dynamical systems, one has to solve nonlinear SMT problems over real numbers, which are highly intractable or undecidable [23]. Recent work on numerically-driven decision procedures provides a promising direction to bypass this difficulty [5,6]. They have been used for many bounded-time verification and synthesis problems for highly nonlinear systems [12]. However, the fundamental challenge with using numerically-driven methods in inductive proofs is that numerical errors make it impossible to verify the induction steps in the standard sense. Take the Lyapunov analysis of stability properties as an example. A dynamical system is stable if there exists a function that vanishes *exactly* at the origin and its derivatives *strictly* decreases over time. Since *any* numerical error blurs the difference between strict and non-strict inequality, one can conclude that numerically-driven methods are not suitable for verifying these strict constraints. However, proving a system is stable within an arbitrarily tiny neighborhood around the origin is all we really need in practice. Thus, there is a discrepancy between what the standard theory requires and what is needed in practice, or what can be achieved computationally. To bridge this gap, we need to rethink about the fundamental definitions.

In this paper, we formulate new inductive proof rules for continuous dynamical systems for establishing robust notions of stability and safety. These proof rules are practically useful and computationally certifiable in a very general sense. For instance, for stability, we define the notion of ε-stability that requires the system to be stable within an ε-bounded distance from the origin, instead of exactly at the origin. When ε is small enough, ε-stable systems are practically indistinguishable from stable systems. We then define the notion of ε-Lyapunov functions that are sufficient for establishing ε-stability. We then rigorously prove that the ε-Lyapunov conditions are numerically stable and can be correctly determined by δ-complete decisions procedures for nonlinear real arithmetic [7]. In this way, we can rely on various numerically-driven SMT solvers to establish a sound and relative-complete proof systems for unbounded stability and safety properties of highly nonlinear dynamical systems. We believe these new definitions have eliminated the core difficulty for reasoning about infinite-time properties of nonlinear systems, and will pave the way for adapting a wide range of automated methods from program analysis to continuous and hybrid systems. In short, the paper makes the following contributions:

- We define ε-stability and ε-Lyapunov functions in Sect. 3. We prove that finding ε-Lyapunov functions is sufficient for establishing ε-stability.
- We define two types of robust proof rules for unbounded safety in Sect. 3, which we call Type 1 and Type 2 ε-barrier functions. The former relies on

strict contraction, and the latter relies on reachable-set computation to guarantee bounded escape.
- We prove that δ-complete decision procedures provide a sound and relative-complete proof system for the proposed numerically-robust induction rules, in both Sects. 3 and 4.

We demonstrate the effectiveness of the proposed methods on various nonlinear systems in Sect. 5. Section 2 covers the basic definitions and Sect. 6 concludes the paper.

Related Work. Several lines of work have proposed relaxed and practical notions to capture the spirit of the stability requirements. Early work from the 1960s introduced practical stability, which defined bounds on system behaviors over finite time horizons [2,14,26,27]. These methods can show whether a system leaves a safe set or enters a goal set over a finite time horizon based on Lyapunov-like functions. Stability defined in this sense is equivalent to estimating the reachable set over a finite time horizon. Thus, the shortcoming is that it may not capture the desired behavior of the system over unbounded time. Similarly, notions of boundedness and ultimate boundedness specify limits on the system behaviors [11]. Boundedness specifies whether the system remains within a given bounded region. Ultimate boundedness specifies that the system eventually returns to the given bounded region. These properties can be established based on Lyapunov-like conditions. Related notions have been generalized to switched systems [29,30]. Also, the related notion of region stability defines systems that eventually enter and remain within a specified set [20]. We present stability concepts that unify and extend the above notions. A related relaxation of the traditional notions of stability includes *almost* Lyapunov functions [15], which allow the strict stability conditions to be neglected in a region near the equilibrium point. The challenge of applying this technique in practice is that the size and shape of the neglected region are not specified a priori, so a constructive technique for specifying a stability region is not straightforward. Our work is related to efforts to construct and check robust barrier certificates using Lyapunov-like functions to ensure that controllers satisfy safety constraints [28]. This work provides a framework in which to specify analytic constraints on controller behaviors. By contrast, our work focuses on providing constraints that can be checked fully automatically. Our notion of ε-barrier functions is closely related to t-barrier certificates from [1], though we choose to focus on distance bounds from the barrier (ε) rather than time bounds that indicate how long it takes for behaviors to re-enter the barrier once it has left (t).

2 Background

2.1 Dynamical Systems

Throughout the paper, we use the following definition of an n-dimensional autonomous dynamical system:

$$\frac{\mathrm{d}x(t)}{\mathrm{d}t} = f(x(t)),\ x(0) \in \mathsf{init} \text{ and } \forall t \in \mathbb{R}_{\geq 0}, x(t) \in D, \tag{1}$$

where an open set $D \subseteq \mathbb{R}^n$ is the state space, $\mathsf{init} \subseteq D$ is a set of initial states, and $f : D \to \mathbb{R}^n$ is a vector field specified by Lipschitz-continuous functions on each dimension. For notational simplicity, *all variable and function symbols can represent vectors.* When vectors are used in logic formulas, they represent conjunctions of the formulas for each dimension. For instance, when $x = (x_1, \ldots, x_n)$, we write $x = 0$ to denote the formula $x_1 = 0 \wedge \cdots \wedge x_n = 0$. For any system defined by (1), we write its solution function as

$$F : D \times \mathbb{R}_{\geq 0} \to \mathbb{R}^n,\ F(x(0), t) = x(0) + \int_0^t f(x(s))\mathrm{d}s. \tag{2}$$

Note that F usually does not have an analytic form. However, since f is Lipschitz-continuous, F exists and is unique. We will often use Lie derivatives to measure the change of a scalar function along the flow defined by another vector field:

Definition 1 (Lie Derivative). *Let $f : D \to \mathbb{R}^n$ define a vector field. Write the ith component of f as f_i. Let $V : D \to \mathbb{R}$ be a differentiable scalar function. The Lie derivative of V over f is defined as $\nabla_f V(x) = \sum_{i=1}^n \frac{\partial V}{\partial x_i} f_i$.*

2.2 First-Order Language over the Reals $\mathcal{L}_{\mathbb{R}_\mathcal{F}}$

We will make extensive use of first-order formulas over real numbers with Type 2 computable functions [25] to express and infer properties of nonlinear dynamical systems. Definition 2 introduces the syntax of these formulas.

Definition 2 (Syntax of $\mathcal{L}_{\mathbb{R}_\mathcal{F}}$). *Let $\mathcal{F}$ be the class of all Type 2 computable functions over real numbers. We define:*

$$t ::= x_i \mid f(t(x)),\ \text{where } f \in \mathcal{F}, \text{ possibly constant;}$$
$$\varphi ::= \top \mid \bot \mid t(x) > 0 \mid t(x) \geq 0 \mid \varphi \wedge \varphi \mid \varphi \vee \varphi \mid \exists x_i \varphi \mid \forall x_i \varphi.$$

We regard $\neg\varphi$ as an operation that is defined inductively as usual. For instance, $\neg(t > 0)$ is defined as $-t \geq 0$, and $\neg(\exists x_i \varphi)$ is defined as $\forall x_i \neg\varphi$. For any $\mathcal{L}_{\mathbb{R}_\mathcal{F}}$ terms u and v, variable x, and $\mathcal{L}_{\mathbb{R}_\mathcal{F}}$ predicate φ, we write $\exists^{[u,v]} x \varphi$ and $\forall^{[u,v]} x \varphi$ to denote $\exists x(u \leq x \wedge x \leq v \wedge \varphi)$ and $\forall x((u \leq x \wedge x \leq v) \to \varphi)$, respectively, which applies to open intervals too. Next, Definition 3 introduces syntactic perturbation of formulas in $\mathcal{L}_{\mathbb{R}_\mathcal{F}}$.

Definition 3 (δ-Strengthening and Robust Formulas [7]). *Let $\delta \in \mathbb{Q}^+$ be arbitrary. Let φ be an arbitrary $\mathcal{L}_{\mathbb{R}_\mathcal{F}}$ formula. The δ-strengthening of φ, denoted by $\varphi^{+\delta}$, is obtained from φ by replacing every atomic predicate of the form $t(x) > 0$ and $t(x) \geq 0$ with $t(x) - \delta > 0$ and $t(x) - \delta \geq 0$, respectively. We say φ is δ -robust iff $\varphi^{+\delta} \leftrightarrow \varphi$.*

Definition 4 (δ-Complete Decision Procedures [7]). *Let S be a class of $\mathcal{L}_{\mathbb{R}_\mathcal{F}}$-sentences. We say a decision procedure is δ-complete over S iff for any $\varphi \in S$, the procedure correctly returns one of the following answers:*

- true : *φ is true.*
- δ-false : *$\varphi^{+\delta}$ is false.*

When the two cases overlap, either decision can be returned.

It follows that if φ is δ-robust, then a δ-complete decision procedure can correctly determine the truth value of φ.

3 Robust Proofs for Stability

We first focus on stability. We will define the notion of ε-stability, as a relaxation of the standard Lyapunov stability, and then define ε-Lyapunov functions, which are sufficient for proving ε-stability in a robust way.

3.1 Stability and Lyapunov Functions

Conventionally, ε and δ are used to best highlight the connection with ε-δ conditions for continuity. We will mostly reserve the use of ε for defining conditions that are robust under ε-bounded numerical errors. Thus, we replace ε by τ in the standard definitions to avoid confusion.

Definition 5 (Stability). *We say the system in (1) is stable at the origin in the sense of Lyapunov, iff for any τ-ball neighborhood of the origin, there exists a δ-ball around the origin, such that, if the system starts within the δ-ball then it never escapes the τ-ball. We capture the definition by the following $\mathcal{L}_{\mathbb{R}_{\mathcal{F}}}$-formula:*

$$\mathsf{Stable}(f) \equiv_{df} \forall^{(0,\infty)}\tau\exists^{(0,\infty)}\delta\forall^{D}x_0\forall^{[0,\infty)}t\Big(\|x_0\| < \delta \rightarrow \|F(x_0,t)\| < \tau\Big)$$

Definition 6 (Lyapunov Function). *Consider a dynamical system given in the form of (1), and let $V : D \rightarrow \mathbb{R}$ be a differentiable function. We say V is a non-strict Lyapunov function for the system, iff the following predicate is true:*

$$\mathsf{LF}(f,V) \equiv_{df} \ (V(0)=0) \wedge (f(0)=0) \wedge \forall^{D\setminus\{0\}}x\ \Big(V(x) > 0 \wedge \nabla_f V(x) \leq 0\Big)$$

Proposition 1. *For any dynamical system defined by f, if there exists a Lyapunov function V, then the system is stable. Namely,* $\mathsf{LF}(f,V) \rightarrow \mathsf{Stable}(f)$.

3.2 Epsilon-Stability

The standard definitions of stability requires a system to stabilize within arbitrarily small neighborhoods around the origin. However, very small neighborhoods are practically indistinguishable from the origin. Thus, it is practically sufficient to prove that a system is stable within some sufficiently small neighborhood. We capture this intuition by making a minor change to the standard definition, by simply putting a lower bound ε on the τ parameter in Definition 5. As a result, the system is required to exhibit the same behavior as standard stable systems outside the ε-ball, but can behave arbitrarily within the ε-ball (for instance, oscillate around the origin). The formal definition is as follows:

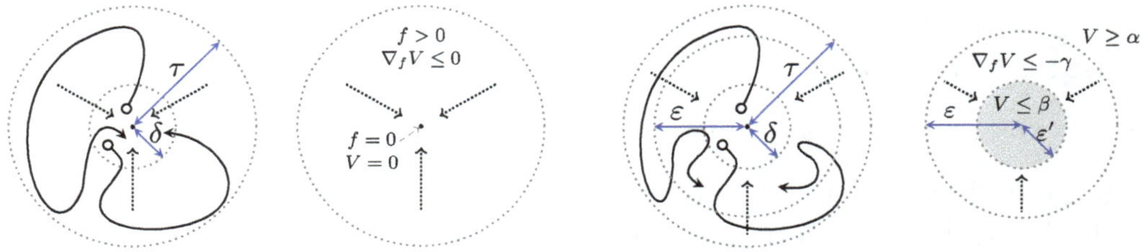

(a) Stability (b) Lyapunov Function (c) ε-Stability (d) ε-Lyapunov Function

Fig. 1. Standard and ε-relaxed notions of stability and Lyapunov functions

Definition 7 (Epsilon-Stability). *Let $\varepsilon \in \mathbb{R}_+$ be arbitrary. We say a dynamical system in (1) is ε-stable at the origin in the sense of Lyapunov, iff it satisfies the following condition:*

$$\mathsf{Stable}_\varepsilon(f) \equiv_{df} \forall^{[\varepsilon,\infty)}\tau\exists^{(0,\infty)}\delta\forall^D x_0\forall^{[0,\infty)}t\Big(\|x_0\| < \delta \rightarrow \|F(x_0,t)\| < \tau\Big)$$

In words, for any $\tau \geq \varepsilon$, there exists δ such that all trajectories that start within the δ-ball will stay within a τ-ball around the origin.

Note that the only difference with the standard definition is that τ is *bounded from below* by a positive ε instead of 0. The definition is depicted in Fig. 1c, which shows the difference with the standard notion in Fig. 1a. Since the only difference with the standard definition is the lower bound on the universally quantified τ, it is clear that ε-stability is strictly weaker than standard stability.

Proposition 2. *For any $\varepsilon \in \mathbb{R}_+$, $\mathsf{Stable}(f) \rightarrow \mathsf{Stable}_\varepsilon(f)$.*

Thus, any system that is stable in the standard definition is also ε-stable for any $\varepsilon \in \mathbb{R}_+$. On the other hand, one can always choose small enough ε such that an ε-stable system is practically indistinguishable from stable systems in the standard definition.

3.3 Epsilon-Lyapunov Function

We now define the corresponding notion of Lyapunov function that can be used for proving ε-stability. The robustness problem in the standard definition comes from the singularity of the origin. With the relaxed notion of stability, the system may oscillate within some ε-neighborhood of the origin. With the relaxation, we now have room for constructing a few nested neighborhoods that can trap the trajectories in a way that is robust under sufficiently small perturbations. To achieve this, we make use of balls of different sizes, as shown in the following definition. We write $\mathcal{B}_\varepsilon$ to denote open ε-balls around the origin.

Definition 8 (Epsilon-Lyapunov Functions). *Let $V : D \rightarrow \mathbb{R}$ be a differentiable scalar function defined for the system in (1), and let $\varepsilon \in \mathbb{R}_+$ be an arbitrary value. We say V is an ε-Lyapunov function for the system, iff it satisfies the following conditions:*

1. *Outside the ε-ball, there is some positive lower bound on the value of V. Namely, there exists $\alpha \in \mathbb{R}_+$ such that for any $x \in D \setminus \mathcal{B}_\varepsilon$, $V(x) \geq \alpha$.*
2. *Inside the ε-ball, there is a strictly smaller ε'-ball in which the value of V is bounded from above, to create a gap with its values outside the ε-ball. Formally, there exists $\varepsilon' \in (0, \varepsilon)$ and $\beta \in (0, \alpha)$ such that for all $x \in \mathcal{B}_{\varepsilon'}$, $V(x) \leq \beta$.*
3. *The Lie derivative of V is strictly negative outside of $\mathcal{B}_{\varepsilon'}$. Formally, there exists $\gamma \in \mathbb{R}_+$ such that for all $x \in D \setminus \mathcal{B}_{\varepsilon'}$, the Lie derivative of V along f satisfies $\nabla_f V(x) \leq -\gamma$.*

In sum, the three conditions can be expressed with the following $\mathcal{L}_{\mathbb{R}_\mathcal{F}}$-formula:

$$\begin{aligned}\mathsf{LF}_\varepsilon(f, V) \equiv_{df}\ & \exists^{(0,\varepsilon)}\varepsilon' \exists^{(0,\infty)}\alpha \exists^{(0,\alpha)}\beta \exists^{(0,\infty)}\gamma \\ & \forall^{D\setminus\mathcal{B}_\varepsilon} x\Big(V(x) \geq \alpha\Big) \wedge \forall^{\mathcal{B}_{\varepsilon'}} x\Big(V(x) \leq \beta\Big) \\ & \wedge \forall^{D\setminus\mathcal{B}_{\varepsilon'}} x\Big(\nabla_f V(x) \leq -\gamma\Big)\end{aligned}$$

It is important to note that ε', α, β, and γ, are not fixed constants, but existentially quantified variables. Thus the condition can hold true for infinitely many values of these parameters, which is critical to robustness. The only free variable in the formula is ε, used in $\mathcal{B}_\varepsilon$ and the bound for ε'. Note also that neither of $\mathsf{LF}_\varepsilon(f, V)$ and the standard definition $\mathsf{LF}(f, V)$ implies the other.

Remark 1. The logical structure of $\mathsf{LF}_\varepsilon(f, V)$ is seemingly more complex than the standard Lyapunov conditions in Definition 6 because of the extra existential quantification. In Theorem 3, we show that it does not add computational complexity in checking the conditions.

The key result is that the conditions for an ε-Lyapunov function are sufficient for establishing ε-stability.

Theorem 1. *If there exists an ε-Lyapunov function V for a dynamical system defined by f, then the system is ε-stable. Namely, $\mathsf{LF}_\varepsilon(f, V) \to \mathsf{Stable}_\varepsilon(f)$.*

Proof. Let $\tau \geq \varepsilon$ be arbitrary, and let $\alpha, \gamma \in \mathbb{R}_+$, $\beta \in (0, \alpha)$, and $\varepsilon' \in (0, \varepsilon)$ be as specified by the definition of $\mathsf{LF}_\varepsilon(f, V)$. Let $x_0 \in \mathcal{B}_{\varepsilon'}$ be an arbitrary point. For any $t \in \mathbb{R}_{\geq 0}$, let $x(t) := F(x_0, t)$ be the system state as defined in (2). We use contradiction to prove for any $t \in \mathbb{R}_+$, inequality $\|x(t)\| < \varepsilon \leq \tau$ holds. Since $\varepsilon' < \varepsilon$ and $F(x_0, .)$ is continuous, we know t_1 and t_2 with the following conditions exists ($\partial\mathcal{B}_{\varepsilon'}$ and $\partial\mathcal{B}_\varepsilon$ are boundaries of the corresponding balls):

$$0 \leq t_1 < t_2 \leq t, \quad x(t_1) \in \partial\mathcal{B}_{\varepsilon'}, \quad x(t_2) \in \partial\mathcal{B}_\varepsilon, \quad \forall^{(t_1,t_2)} t'\Big(x(t') \in \mathcal{B}_\varepsilon \setminus \mathcal{B}_{\varepsilon'}\Big)$$

We know $V(x(t_1)) \leq \beta < \alpha \leq V(x(t_2))$ and hence $V(x(t_1)) < V(x(t_2))$ are both true; however, this is in contradiction with the mean value theorem and the fact that $\mathcal{B}_\varepsilon \subset D$ and $\forall^{D\setminus\mathcal{B}_{\varepsilon'}} x\big(\nabla_f V(x) < -\gamma\big)$. □

Remark 2. Proof of Theorem 1 shows that once state of the system enters $\mathcal{B}_{\varepsilon'}$, it never leaves $\mathcal{B}_{\varepsilon}$. However, it would be still possible for the state to leave $\mathcal{B}_{\varepsilon'}$. One the other hand, since closure of $\mathcal{B}_{\varepsilon} \setminus \mathcal{B}_{\varepsilon'}$ is bounded, and for every x in this area, V is continuous at x and $\nabla_f V(x) \leq -\gamma$, no trajectory can be trapped in the closure of $\mathcal{B}_{\varepsilon} \setminus \mathcal{B}_{\varepsilon'}$. Therefore, even though state of the system might leave $\mathcal{B}_{\varepsilon'}$, it will visit inside of this ball infinitely often.

Example 1. Consider the time-reversed Van der Pol system given by the following dynamics. Figure 3 shows the vector field of this system around the origin.

$$\begin{bmatrix} \dot{x}_1 \\ \dot{x}_2 \end{bmatrix} = \begin{bmatrix} -x_2 \\ (x_1^2 - 1)x_2 + x_1 \end{bmatrix}$$

A Lyapunov function $z^T P z$, where z^T is $[x_1, x_2, x_1^2, x_1x_2, x_2^2, x_1^3, x_1^2x_2, x_1x_2^2, x_2^3]$, and P is the 9×9 constant matrix given in [8], is a 6-degree polynomial that can be obtained using simulation-guided techniques from [10]. Using dReal [9] with $\delta := 10^{-25}$ and the Euclidean norm, we are able to prove that $z^T P z$ is a 10^{-12}-Lyapunov function. Table 1 lists the parameters used for this proof.

3.4 Automated Proofs with Delta-Decisions

We now prove that unlike the conventional conditions, the new inductive proof rules are numerically robust. It follows that δ-decision procedures provide a sound and relative-complete proof system for establishing the conditions in the following sense:

- (Soundness) A δ-complete decision procedure is always correct when it confirms the existence of an ε-Lyapunov function.
- (Relative Completeness) For a given ε-inductive certificate, there exists $\delta > 0$ such that a δ'-complete procedure is able to verify it, for any $0 < \delta' \leq \delta$.

To prove these properties, the key fact is that the continuity of the functions in the induction conditions ensures that there is room for numerical errors in the conditions. Consequently, the formulas allow δ-perturbations in their parameters. This is captured by Lemma 1, and the proof is given in [8].

Lemma 1. *For any $\varepsilon \in \mathbb{R}_+$, there exists $\delta \in \mathbb{Q}_+$ such that* $\mathsf{LF}_\varepsilon(f, V)$ *is δ-robust.*

Note that if a formula ϕ is δ-robust then for every $\delta' \in (0, \delta)$, ϕ is δ'-robust as well. The soundness and relative-completeness then follow naturally.

Theorem 2 (Soundness). *If a δ-complete decision procedure confirms that* $\mathsf{LF}_\varepsilon(f, V)$ *is* true *then V is indeed an ε-Lyapunov function, and f is ε-stable.*

Proof. Using Definition 4, we know $\mathsf{LF}_\varepsilon(f, V)$, exactly as specified in Definition 8, is true. Therefore, V is ε-Lyapunov. Using Theorem 1, f is ε-stable. □

Theorem 3 (Relative Completeness). *For any $\varepsilon \in \mathbb{R}_+$, if $\mathsf{LF}_\varepsilon(f, V)$ is true then there exists $\delta \in \mathbb{Q}_+$ such that any δ-complete decision procedure must return that $\mathsf{LF}_\varepsilon(f, V)$ is* true.

Proof. Fix an arbitrary $\varepsilon \in \mathbb{R}_+$ for which $\mathsf{LF}_\varepsilon(f, V)$ is true. Let $\phi := \mathsf{LF}_\varepsilon(f, V)$, and using Lemma 1, let $\delta \in \mathbb{Q}_+$ be such that ϕ is δ-robust. Since ϕ is true, we conclude $\phi^{+\delta}$ is true as well. Using Definition 4, no δ-complete decision procedure can return δ-false for ϕ. □

We remark that the quantifier alternation used in Definition 8 can be eliminated without extra search steps. It confirms that we only need to run SMT solving to handle the universally quantified subformula. The reason is that the α, β, and γ parameters can be found by estimating the range of $V(x)$ and $\nabla_f V(x)$ in the different neighborhoods. In fact, we can rewrite $\mathsf{LF}_\varepsilon(f, V)$ in the following way to eliminate the use of α, β, and γ:

$$\mathsf{LF}_\varepsilon(f, V) \leftrightarrow \exists^{(0,\varepsilon)}\varepsilon' \left(\sup_{x \in \mathcal{B}_{\varepsilon'}} V(x) < \inf_{x \in D \setminus \mathcal{B}_\varepsilon} V(x) \wedge \sup_{x \in D \setminus \mathcal{B}_{\varepsilon'}} \nabla_f V(x) < 0 \right)$$

Note that in this form the universal quantification is implicit in the sup and inf operators. In this way, the formula is existentially quantified on only ε', which can then be handled by binary search. This is an efficient way of checking the conditions in practice. We also remark that without this method, the original formulation with multiple parameters can be directly solved as $\exists\forall$-formulas as well using more expensive algorithms [13].

4 Robust Proofs for Safety

In this section, we define two types of ε-barrier functions that are robust to numerical perturbations.

Proving unbounded safety requires the use of barrier functions. The idea is that if one can find a barrier function that separates initial conditions from the set of unsafe states, such that no trajectories can cross the barrier from the safe to the unsafe side, then the system is safe. Here we use a formulation similar to the that of Prajna [21]. The standard conditions on barrier functions include constraints on the vector field of the system at the exact boundary of the barrier set, which introduces robustness problems. We show that it is possible to avoid these problems using two different formulations, which we call Type 1 and Type 2 ε-barrier functions. Type 1 ε-barrier functions strengthen the original definition and requires strict contraction of the barrier. Instead of only asking the system to be contractive exactly on the barrier's border, we force it to be contractive when reaching any state within a small distance from the border. Type 2 ε-barrier functions allow the system to escape the barrier for a controllable distance and a limited period of time. It should then return to the interior of the safe region. Type 1 ε-barriers can be seen as a subclass of Type 2 ε-barriers. The benefit for allowing bounded escape is that the shape of the barrier no longer needs to be an invariant set, which can be particularly helpful when the shape of the system invariants cannot be determined or expressed symbolically. The downside to Type 2 ε-barriers is that checking the corresponding conditions requires integration of the dynamics, which can be expensive but can still be handled by δ-complete decision procedures. The intuition behind the two definitions is shown in Fig. 2 and will be explained in detail in this section.

4.1 Safety and Barrier Functions

Before formally introducing robust safety and ε-barrier functions, we define the safety and barrier functions first. It is easy to see that the robustness problem with the barrier functions is similar to that of Lyapunov functions: if the boundary is exactly separating the safe and unsafe regions then the inductive conditions are not robust, since deviations in the variables by even a small amount from the barrier will make it impossible to complete the proof.

Definition 9 (Safety). *Let $B : D \to \mathbb{R}$ be a scalar function defined for the system in (1). We say $B \leq 0$ defines a safe (or forward invariant) set for the system, iff the following formula is true:*

$$\mathsf{Safe}(f, \mathsf{init}, B) \equiv_{df} \forall^D x_0 \forall^{[0,\infty)} t \Big(\mathsf{init}(x_0) \to B(F(x_0, t)) \leq 0\Big).$$

Definition 10 (Barrier Function). *Let $B : X \to \mathbb{R}$ be a differentiable scalar function defined for the system in (1). We say B is a barrier function for the system, iff the following formula is true:*

$$\mathsf{Barrier}(f, \mathsf{init}, B) \equiv_{df} \forall^D x \Big(\big(\mathsf{init}(x) \to B(x) \leq 0\big) \wedge \big(B(x) = 0 \to \nabla_f B(x) < 0\big)\Big)$$

Proposition 3. $\mathsf{Barrier}(f, \mathsf{init}, B) \to \mathsf{Safe}(f, \mathsf{init}, B)$.

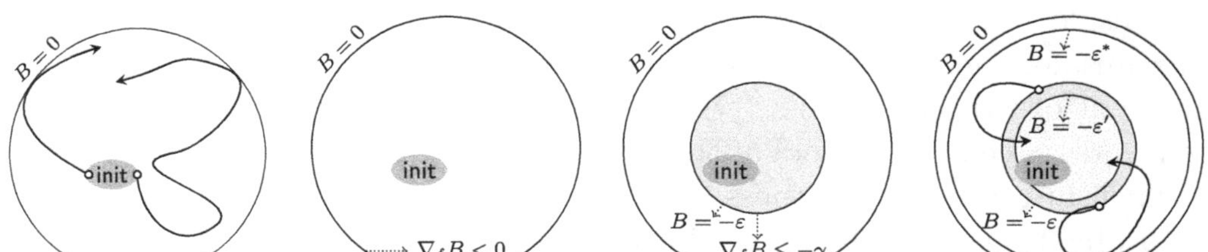

(a) Safety (b) Barrier (c) Type 1 ε-Barrier (d) Type 2 ε-Barrier

Fig. 2. Type 1 and Type 2 ε-Barriers

4.2 Type 1: Strict Contraction

In the standard definition, the boundary of the barrier set is typically a manifold defined by equality, which is not numerically robust. To avoid this problem, we need the barrier boundary to be *belt-shaped* in the sense that there is a clear gap between the safe and unsafe regions. The idea is as shown in Fig. 2c: we need a second and stronger barrier defined by $B = -\varepsilon$ for some reasonable ε, so that the system is clearly separated from $B = 0$. The formal definition is as follows.

Definition 11 (ε-Barrier Certificates). *Let $\varepsilon \in \mathbb{R}_+$ be arbitrary. A differentiable scalar function $B : D \to \mathbb{R}$ is an ε-barrier function iff the following conditions are true:*

- *For all x, $\mathsf{init}(x)$ implies $B(x) \leq -\varepsilon$.*
- *There exists $\gamma \in \mathbb{R}_+$ such that for all x, $B(x) = -\varepsilon$ implies $\nabla_f B(x) \leq -\gamma$.*

Formally, the condition is defined as

$$\mathsf{Barrier}_\varepsilon(f, \mathsf{init}, B) \equiv_{df} \forall^D x\Big(\mathsf{init}(x) \to B(x) \leq -\varepsilon\Big) \wedge \exists^{(0,\infty)}\gamma \forall^D x\Big(B(x) = -\varepsilon \to \nabla_f B(x) \leq -\gamma\Big)$$

It should be intuitively clear from the definition that the existence of ε-barrier functions is sufficient for establishing invariants and safety properties. The new requirement is that the system stays robustly within the barrier, by the area defined by $-\varepsilon \leq B(x) \leq 0$.

Theorem 4. *For any $\varepsilon \in \mathbb{R}_+$, $\mathsf{Barrier}_\varepsilon(f, \mathsf{init}, B) \to \mathsf{Safe}(f, \mathsf{init}, B)$.*

Proof. Assume $\mathsf{Barrier}_\varepsilon(f, \mathsf{init}, B)$ is true. It is easy to see $\mathsf{Barrier}(f, \mathsf{init}, B+\varepsilon)$, as specified in Definition 10, is also true. Therefore, using Proposition 3, we know $\mathsf{Safe}(f, \mathsf{init}, B + \epsilon)$ and hence $\mathsf{Safe}(f, \mathsf{init}, B)$ are both true. □

It is clear that there is room for numerically perturbing the size of the area and still obtaining a robust proof. The proof is similar to the one for Lemma 1 as shown in [8].

Theorem 5. *For any $\varepsilon \in \mathbb{R}_+$, there exists $\delta \in \mathbb{Q}_+$ such that $\mathsf{Barrier}_\varepsilon(f, \mathsf{init}, B)$ is a δ-robust formula.*

Example 2 (Type 1 ε-Barrier for timed-reversed Van der Pol). Consider the time-reversed Van der Pol system introduced in Example 1. We use the same example to demonstrate the effect of numerical errors in proving barrier certificates. The level sets of the Lyapunov functions in the stable region are barrier certificates; however, for the barriers that are very close to the limiting cycle, numerical sensitivity becomes a problem. In experiments, when $\varepsilon = 10^{-5}$ and $\delta = 10^{-4}$, we can verify that the level set $z^T P z = 90$ is a Type 1 ε-barrier. Table 2 lists parameters used in this proof. Figure 3 (Left) shows the direction field for the timed-reversed Van der Pol dynamics, the border of the set $z^T P z \leq 90$, which we prove is a type 1 ε-barrier, and the boundary of set $z^T P z \leq 110$, which is clearly not a barrier, since it is outside of the limit cycle.

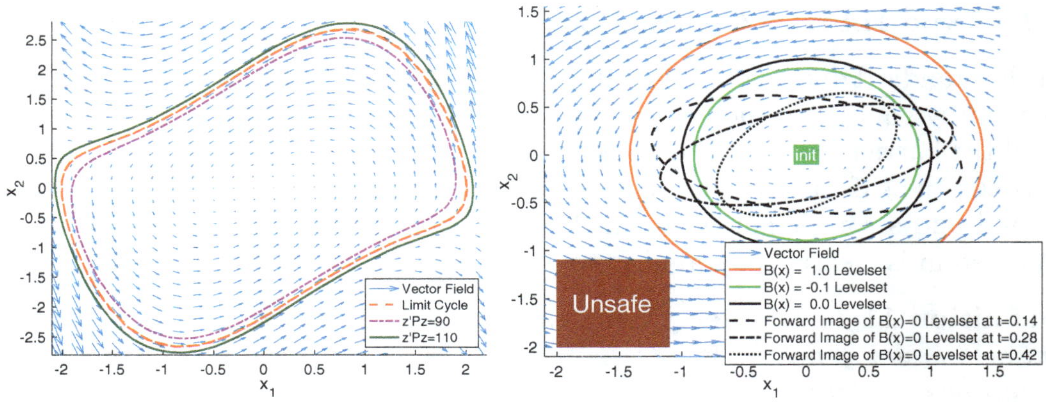

Fig. 3. (Left) Van der pol example (Right) Type 2 barrier example

The conditions for ε-Lyapunov and ε-barrier functions look very similar, but there is an important difference. In the case of Lyapunov functions, we do not evaluate the Lie derivative of the balls. Thus, the balls do not define barrier sets. On the other hand, the level sets of Lyapunov functions always define barriers.

Remark 3. The ε-barrier functions can also be used as a sufficient condition for ε-stability, if a barrier can be found within the ε-ball required in ε-stability.

Remark 4. A technical requirement for proving robustness of the ε-barrier conditions is that $\neg\mathsf{init}$ defines a simple set that can be over-approximated, such that for every $\varepsilon \in \mathbb{R}_+$, there is $\delta \in \mathbb{R}_+$ such that for any point that satisfies $\neg\mathsf{init}^{+\delta}$ there is an ε-close point that satisfies $\neg\mathsf{init}$. A sufficient condition for this restriction is that init be of the form $(\bigwedge_i a_i \leq x_i \leq b_i) \rightarrow \varphi(x)$, where $a_i, b_i \in \mathbb{Q}$ are arbitrary constants, and φ is a quantifier-free formula with only strict inequalities [22].

4.3 Type 2: Bounded Escape

We now introduce the second set of conditions for establishing ε-invariant sets. This set of conditions can be used only when the ε-variations are considered. This notion is inspired by the notion of k-step invariants [3] for discrete-time systems. The ε-margin that we allow at the boundary of the invariants allows us to exploit more techniques. Using reachable set computation, we can directly check if all states stay within the barrier set at each step. To ensure that the conditions are inductive and useful, we need to impose the following two requirements:

- (Contraction) Similar to the strengthening in barrier certificates, we require that the system does not *sit at the boundary*: the dynamics at the boundary should be contracting. The difference with Type 1 ε-barriers is that, this condition is not imposed through the vector field on the boundary. Instead, it is a reachability condition: after some amount of time, all states should return to the interior of an appropriate set.

– (Bounded Escape) Before reaching back to the invariant set, we allow the system to step outside the invariant, but only up to a bounded distance from the boundary.

The intuition is depicted in Fig. 2d. In the formal definition, we parameterize the conditions with the time for contraction and the maximum deviation from the invariant set, as follows.

Definition 12 (Type 2 Barrier Functions). *Let $T, \varepsilon \in \mathbb{R}_{+}$ be arbitrary. We say a continuous scalar function B defines a (T, ε)-elastic barrier function, iff the following conditions hold:*

1. *For any x, $\mathsf{init}(x)$ implies $B(x) \leq -\varepsilon$.*
2. *There exists $\varepsilon' > \varepsilon$ such that any state in $B(x) \leq -\varepsilon$ will enter $B(x) \leq -\varepsilon'$ after time T.*
3. *During time $[0, T]$, the system may step outside of $B(x) \leq -\varepsilon$ but there exists some $\varepsilon^* \in (0, \varepsilon]$ such that all states stay within $B(x) \leq -\varepsilon^*$.*

In all, we define the conditions with the following formula

$$\begin{aligned}\mathsf{Barrier}_{T,\varepsilon}(f, \mathsf{init}, B) \equiv_{df} & \ \forall^D x\Big(\mathsf{init}(x) \rightarrow B(x) \leq -\varepsilon\Big) \\ & \wedge \exists^{(0,\varepsilon]}\varepsilon^* \forall^D x \forall^{[0,T]} t\Big((B(x) = -\varepsilon) \rightarrow B(F(x,t)) \leq -\varepsilon^*\Big) \\ & \wedge \exists^{(\varepsilon,\infty)}\varepsilon' \forall^D x\Big((B(x) = -\varepsilon) \rightarrow B(F(x,T)) \leq -\varepsilon'\Big)\end{aligned}$$

Theorem 6, shows that conditions in Definition 12 ensure that the system never leaves the invariant $B \leq 0$. The key is the second condition: induction works because all states come back to the interior of the set defined by $B \leq -\varepsilon$. With the third condition only, we cannot perform induction because the set may keep growing.

Theorem 6. *For any $T, \varepsilon \in \mathbb{R}_{+}$, $\mathsf{Barrier}_{T,\varepsilon}(f, \mathsf{init}, B) \rightarrow \mathsf{Safe}(f, \mathsf{init}, B)$.*

Proof. For the purpose of contradiction, suppose starting from $x_0 \in \mathsf{init}$, the system is unsafe. Using continuity of the barrier B and the solution function F, let $t \in \mathbb{R}_{\geq 0}$ be a time at which $B(x(t)) = 0$, where $x(t)$ is by definition $F(x_0, t)$. By the 1st property in Definition 12, we know $B(x_0) \leq -\varepsilon < 0$. Using continuity of B and F, let $t' \in [0, t)$ be the supremum of all times at which $B(x(t')) = -\varepsilon$. By the 3rd property in Definition 12, we know $t - t' > T$, and by the 2nd property in Definition 12, we know $B(x(t' + T)) \leq -\varepsilon' < -\varepsilon$. Using continuity of B and F, we know there is a time $t'' \in (t' + T, t)$ at which $B(x(t'')) = -\varepsilon$. However, this is in contradiction with t' being the supremum. □

Theorem 7. *For any $\varepsilon \in \mathbb{R}_{+}$, there exists $\delta \in \mathbb{Q}_{+}$ such that $\mathsf{Barrier}_{T,\varepsilon}(f, \mathsf{init}, B)$ is a δ-robust formula.*

Example 3. We use this example to show how Type 2 ε-barriers can be used to establish safety. Consider the following system.

$$\begin{bmatrix} \dot{x}_1 \\ \dot{x}_2 \end{bmatrix} = \begin{bmatrix} -0.1 & -10 \\ 4 & -2 \end{bmatrix} \begin{bmatrix} x_1 \\ x_2 \end{bmatrix}$$

Let init be the set $\{x \mid -0.1 \leq x_1 \leq 0.1, -0.1 \leq x_2 \leq 0.1\}$, and let U, the unsafe set, be the set $\{x \mid -2.0 \leq x_1 \leq -1.1, -2.0 \leq x_2 \leq -1.1\}$. The system is stable and safe with respect to the designated unsafe set. However, the safety cannot be shown using any invariant of the form $B(x) := x_1^2 + x_2^2 - c \leq 0$, where $c \in \mathbb{Q}_+$ is a constant, in the standard definition. This is because the vector field on the boundary of such sets do not satisfy the inductive conditions. Nevertheless, we can show that for $c = 1$, $B(x)$ is a Type 2 ε-barrier. The dReal query verifies the conditions with $\varepsilon = 0.1$. Since $U(x) \rightarrow B(x) > \epsilon$ and $\mathsf{init}(x) \rightarrow B(x) < -\varepsilon'$, we know that the system cannot reach any unsafe states. Figure 3 (Right), illustrates the example. The green set at the center represents init, and the red set represents unsafe set U. The $B(x) = 0$ level set is not invariant, as evidenced in the figure by the forward images at $t = 0.14$ and $t = 0.28$ leaving the set; however, as the dReal query proves, the reachable set over $0 \leq t \leq 10$ does not leave the $B(x) = 1.0$ level set and is completely contained in the $B(x) = -0.1$ level set by $t = 0.4$. Since $U(x) \rightarrow B(x) > 1.0$ and $\mathsf{init}(x) \rightarrow B(x) < -0.1$, then the system cannot reach any state in U.

5 Experiments

In this section, we show examples of nonlinear systems that can be verified to be ε-stable or safe with ε-barriers.

Table 1. Results for the ε-Lyapunov functions. Each Lyapunov function is of the form $z^T Pz$, where z is a vector of monomials over the state variables. We report the constant values satisfying the ε-Lyapunov conditions, and the time that verification of each example takes (in seconds).

Example	α	β	γ	ε	ε'	Time (s)
T.R. Van der Pol	2.10×10^{-23}	1.70×10^{-23}	10^{-25}	10^{-12}	5×10^{-13}	0.05
Norm. Pend.	7.07×10^{-23}	3.97×10^{-23}	10^{-50}	10^{-12}	5×10^{-13}	0.01
Moore-Greitzer	2.95×10^{-19}	2.55×10^{-19}	10^{-20}	10^{-10}	5×10^{-11}	0.04

Table 1 contains parameters we use to verify requirements of Definition 8 for ε-Lyapunov functions in our examples. Table 2 contains parameters we use to verify requirements of Definition 11 for Type 1 ε-barrier functions in our examples. The ε-Lyapunov functions in these examples are of the form $V(x) := z^T Pz$, where z is a vector of products of the state variables and P is a constant

Table 2. Results for the ε-barrier functions. Each barrier function $B(x)$ is of the form $z^T Pz - \ell$, where z is a vector of monomials over x. We indicate the highest degree of the monomials used in z, the size of the P, the level ℓ used for each barrier function, and the value of ε and γ used to the check $\nabla_f B(x) < -\gamma$.

Example	ℓ	ε	γ	degree (z)	Size of P	Time (s)
T.R. Van der Pol	90	10^{-5}	10^{-5}	3	9×9	6.47
Norm. Pend.	$[0.1, 10]$	10^{-2}	10^{-2}	1	2×2	0.08
Moore-Greitzer	$[1.0, 10]$	10^{-1}	10^{-1}	4	5×5	13.80
PTC	0.01	10^{-5}	10^{-5}	2	14×14	428.75

matrix obtained using simulation-guided techniques from [10]. All the P matrices are given in [8].

Time-Reversed Van der Pol. The time-reversed Van der Pol system has been used as an example in the previous sections. Figure 3 (Left) shows the direction field of this system around the origin. Using dReal with $\delta := 10^{-25}$, we are able to establish a 10^{-12}-Lyapunov function and a 10^{-5}-barrier function.

Normalized Pendulum. A standard pendulum system has continuous dynamics containing a transcendental function, which causes difficulty for many techniques. Here, we consider a normalized pendulum system with the following dynamics, in which x_1 and x_2 represent angular position and velocity, respectively. In our experiment, using $\delta = 10^{-50}$, we can prove that function $V := x^T Px$ is ε-Lyapunov, where $\varepsilon := 10^{-12}$.

$$\begin{bmatrix} \dot{x}_1 \\ \dot{x}_2 \end{bmatrix} = \begin{bmatrix} x_2 \\ -\sin(x_1) - x_2 \end{bmatrix} \tag{3}$$

Using $\delta := 0.01$, we are able to prove that for *any* value $\ell \in [0.1, 10]$, the function $B(x) := x^T Px - \ell$, with x being the system state, and P a constant matrix given in [8], is a Type 1 0.01-barrier function.

Moore-Greitzer Jet Engine. Next, we consider a simplified version of the Moore-Greitzer model for a jet engine. The system has the following dynamics, in which x_1 and x_2 are states related to mass flow and pressure rise.

$$\begin{bmatrix} \dot{x}_1 \\ \dot{x}_2 \end{bmatrix} = \begin{bmatrix} -x_2 - \frac{3}{2}x_1^2 - \frac{1}{2}x_1^3 \\ 3x_1 - x_2 \end{bmatrix} \tag{4}$$

In our experiment, using $\delta = 10^{-20}$ and $z := [x_1^2, x_1x_2, x_2^2, x_1, x_2]^T$, we can prove that function $V := z^T Pz$ is ε-Lyapunov, where $\varepsilon := 10^{-10}$.

Using dReal with $\delta := 0.1$, we are able to prove that for *any* value $\ell \in [1, 10]$, the function $B(x) := z^T Pz - \ell$, with x being the system state, z being the vector of monomials defined in the previous section, and P a constant matrix given in [8], is a Type 1 0.1-barrier function.

Powertrain Control System. Next, we consider a closed-loop model of a powertrain control (PTC) system for an automotive application. The system dynamics consist of four state variables, two associated with a plant and two for a controller. The plant models fuel and air dynamics of an internal combustion engine and the controller is designed to regulate the air-fuel (A/F) ratio within a given range of an optimal value, referred as stoichiometric value. Two states related to the plant represent the manifold pressure, p, and the ratio between actual A/F ratio and stoichiometric value, r. The two associated with the controller are the estimated manifold pressure, p_{est}, and the internal state of the PI controller, i. The system is highly nonlinear, with the following dynamics

$$\begin{aligned}
\dot{p} &= c_1 \left(2\hat{u}_1 \sqrt{\frac{p}{c_{11}} - \left(\frac{p}{c_{11}}\right)^2} - (c_3 + c_4 c_2 p + c_5 c_2 p^2 + c_6 c_2^2 p) \right) \\
\dot{r} &= 4 \left(\frac{c_3 + c_4 c_2 p + c_5 c_2 p^2 + c_6 c_2^2 p}{c_{13}(c_3 + c_4 c_2 p_{est} + c_5 c_2 p_{est}^2 + c_6 c_2^2 p_{est})(1 + i + c_{14}(r - c_{16}))} - r \right) \\
\dot{p}_{est} &= c_1 \left(2\hat{u}_1 \sqrt{\frac{p}{c_{11}} - \left(\frac{p}{c_{11}}\right)^2} - c_{13} \left(c_3 + c_4 c_2 p_{est} + c_5 c_2 p_{est}^2 + c_6 c_2^2 p_{est}\right) \right) \\
\dot{i} &= c_{15}(r - c_{16})
\end{aligned}$$

which followed the detailed description of the model and the constant parameter values in [10]. We verified that there exists a function of the form $B(x) = z^T P z - 0.01$ (z consist of 14 monomials with a maximum degree of 2), where $\nabla_f B(x) < -\gamma$, when $B(x) = -\varepsilon$.

6 Conclusion

We formulated new inductive proof rules for stability and safety for dynamical systems. The rules are numerically robust, making them amenable to verification using automated reasoning tools such as those based on δ-decision procedures. We presented several examples demonstrating the value of the new approach, including safety verification tasks for highly nonlinear systems. The examples show that the framework can be used to prove stability and safety for examples that were out of reach for existing tools. The new framework relies on the ability to generate reasonable candidate Lyapunov functions, which are analogous to ranking functions from program analysis. Future work will include improved techniques for efficiently generating the ε-Lyapunov and ε-barrier functions and related theoretical questions.

Acknowledgement. Our work is supported by the United States Air Force and DARPA under Contract No. FA8750-18-C-0092, AFOSR No. FA9550-19-1-0041, and the National Science Foundation under NSF CNS No. 1830399. Any opinions, findings and conclusions or recommendations expressed in this material are those of the author(s) and do not necessarily reflect the views of the United States Air Force and DARPA.

References

1. Bak, S.: t-Barrier certificates: a continuous analogy to k-induction. In: IFAC Conference on Analysis and Design of Hybrid Systems (2018)
2. Bernfeld, S.R., Lakshmikantham, V.: Practical stability and Lyapunov functions. Tohoku Math. J. (2) **32**(4), 607–613 (1980)
3. Bobiti, R., Lazar, M.: A delta-sampling verification theorem for discrete-time, possibly discontinuous systems. In: HSCC (2015)
4. Collins, G.E.: Quantifier elimination for real closed fields by cylindrical algebraic decompostion. In: Brakhage, H. (ed.) GI-Fachtagung 1975. LNCS, vol. 33, pp. 134–183. Springer, Heidelberg (1975). https://doi.org/10.1007/3-540-07407-4_17
5. Fränzle, M., Herde, C., Teige, T., Ratschan, S., Schubert, T.: Efficient solving of large non-linear arithmetic constraint systems with complex boolean structure. JSAT **1**(3–4), 209–236 (2007)
6. Gao, S., Avigad, J., Clarke, E.: Delta-complete decision procedures for satisfiability over the reals. In: Proceedings of the Automated Reasoning - 6th International Joint Conference, IJCAR 2012, Manchester, UK, 26–29 June 2012, pp. 286–300 (2012)
7. Gao, S., Avigad, J., Clarke, E.M.: Delta-decidability over the reals. In: LICS, pp. 305–314. IEEE Computer Society (2012)
8. Gao, S., et al.: Numerically-robust inductive proof rules for continuous dynamical systems (extended version) (2019). https://dreal.github.io/CAV19/
9. Gao, S., Kong, S., Clarke, E.M.: dReal: an SMT solver for nonlinear theories over the reals. In: Bonacina, M.P. (ed.) CADE 2013. LNCS (LNAI), vol. 7898, pp. 208–214. Springer, Heidelberg (2013). https://doi.org/10.1007/978-3-642-38574-2_14
10. Kapinski, J., Deshmukh, J.V., Sankaranarayanan, S., Aréchiga, N.: Simulation-guided Lyapunov analysis for hybrid dynamical systems. In: Hybrid Systems: Computation and Control (2014)
11. Khalil, H.K.: Nonlinear Systems. Prentice Hall, Upper Saddle River (1996)
12. Kong, S., Gao, S., Chen, W., Clarke, E.: dReach: δ-reachability analysis for hybrid systems. In: Baier, C., Tinelli, C. (eds.) TACAS 2015. LNCS, vol. 9035, pp. 200–205. Springer, Heidelberg (2015). https://doi.org/10.1007/978-3-662-46681-0_15
13. Kong, S., Solar-Lezama, A., Gao, S.: Delta-decision procedures for exists-forall problems over the reals. In: Chockler, H., Weissenbacher, G. (eds.) CAV 2018. LNCS, vol. 10982, pp. 219–235. Springer, Cham (2018). https://doi.org/10.1007/978-3-319-96142-2_15
14. LaSalle, J.P., Lefschetz, S.: Stability by Liapunov's Direct Method: With Applications. Mathematics in Science and Engineering. Academic Press, New York (1961)
15. Liberzon, D., Ying, C., Zharnitsky, V.: On almost Lyapunov functions. In: 2014 IEEE 53rd Annual Conference on Decision and Control (CDC), pp. 3083–3088, December 2014
16. Monniaux, D.: A survey of satisfiability modulo theory. In: Gerdt, V.P., Koepf, W., Seiler, W.M., Vorozhtsov, E.V. (eds.) CASC 2016. LNCS, vol. 9890, pp. 401–425. Springer, Cham (2016). https://doi.org/10.1007/978-3-319-45641-6_26
17. Papachristodoulou, A., Prajna, S.: Analysis of non-polynomial systems using the sum of squares decomposition. In: Henrion, D., Garulli, A. (eds.) Positive Polynomials in Control. LNCIS, vol. 312, pp. 23–43. Springer, Heidelberg (2005). https://doi.org/10.1007/10997703_2
18. Parrilo, P.: Structured semidenite programs and semialgebraic geometry methods in robustness and optimization. Ph.D. thesis, August 2000

19. Platzer, A., Clarke, E.M.: Computing differential invariants of hybrid systems as fixedpoints. In: Gupta, A., Malik, S. (eds.) CAV 2008. LNCS, vol. 5123, pp. 176–189. Springer, Heidelberg (2008). https://doi.org/10.1007/978-3-540-70545-1_17
20. Podelski, A., Wagner, S.: Model checking of hybrid systems: from reachability towards stability. In: Hespanha, J.P., Tiwari, A. (eds.) HSCC 2006. LNCS, vol. 3927, pp. 507–521. Springer, Heidelberg (2006). https://doi.org/10.1007/11730637_38
21. Prajna, S.: Optimization-based methods for nonlinear and hybrid systems verification. Ph.D. thesis, California Institute of Technology, Pasadena, CA, USA (2005). AAI3185641
22. Roohi, N., Prabhakar, P., Viswanathan, M.: Relating syntactic and semantic perturbations of hybrid automata. In: CONCUR, pp. 26:1–26:16 (2018)
23. Tarski, A.: A Decision Method for Elementary Algebra and Geometry, 2nd edn. University of California Press, Berkeley (1951)
24. Topcu, U., Packard, A., Seiler, P.: Local stability analysis using simulations and sum-of-squares programming. Automatica **44**, 2669–2675 (2008)
25. Weihrauch, K.: Computable Analysis: An Introduction, 1st edn. Springer, Heidelberg (2013)
26. Weiss, L., Infante, E.F.: On the stability of systems defined over a finite time interval. Proc. Nat. Acad. Sci. U.S.A. **54**(1), 44 (1965)
27. Weiss, L., Infante, E.F.: Finite time stability under perturbing forces and on product spaces. IEEE Trans. Autom. Control **12**(1), 54–59 (1967)
28. Xu, X., Tabuada, P., Grizzle, J.W., Ames, A.D.: Robustness of control barrier functions for safety critical control. IFAC-PapersOnLine **48**(27), 54–61 (2015)
29. Zhai, G., Michel, A.N.: On practical stability of switched systems. In: Proceedings of the 41st IEEE Conference on Decision and Control, vol. 3, pp. 3488–3493, December 2002
30. Zhai, G., Michel, A.N.: Generalized practical stability analysis of discontinuous dynamical systems. In: Proceedings of the 42nd IEEE Conference on Decision and Control, vol. 2, pp. 1663–1668. IEEE (2003)

Icing: Supporting Fast-Math Style Optimizations in a Verified Compiler

Heiko Becker[1(✉)], Eva Darulova[1], Magnus O. Myreen[2], and Zachary Tatlock[3]

[1] MPI-SWS, Saarland Informatics Campus (SIC), Saarbrücken, Germany
{hbecker,eva}@mpi-sws.org
[2] Chalmers University of Technology, Gothenburg, Sweden
myreen@chalmers.se
[3] University of Washington, Seattle, USA
ztatlock@cs.washington.edu

Abstract. Verified compilers like CompCert and CakeML offer increasingly sophisticated optimizations. However, their deterministic source semantics and strict IEEE 754 compliance prevent the verification of "fast-math" style floating-point optimizations. Developers often selectively use these optimizations in mainstream compilers like GCC and LLVM to improve the performance of computations over noisy inputs or for heuristics by allowing the compiler to perform intuitive but IEEE 754-unsound rewrites.

We designed, formalized, implemented, and verified a compiler for Icing, a new language which supports selectively applying fast-math style optimizations in a verified compiler. Icing's semantics provides the first formalization of fast-math in a verified compiler. We show how the Icing compiler can be connected to the existing verified CakeML compiler and verify the end-to-end translation by a sequence of refinement proofs from Icing to the translated CakeML. We evaluated Icing by incorporating several of GCC's fast-math rewrites. While Icing targets CakeML's source language, the techniques we developed are general and could also be incorporated in lower-level intermediate representations.

Keywords: Compiler verification · Floating-point arithmetic · Optimization

1 Introduction

Verified compilers formally guarantee that compiled machine code behaves according to the specification given by the source program's semantics. This stringent requirement makes verifying "end-to-end" compilers for mainstream languages challenging, especially when proving sophisticated optimizations that developers rely on. Recent verified compilers like CakeML [38] for ML and

Z. Tatlock—This work was supported in part by the Applications Driving Architectures (ADA) Research Center, a JUMP Center co-sponsored by SRC and DARPA.

I. Dillig and S. Tasiran (Eds.): CAV 2019, LNCS 11562, pp. 155–173, 2019.
https://doi.org/10.1007/978-3-030-25543-5_10

CompCert [24] for C have been steadily verifying more of these important optimizations [39–41]. While the gap between verified compilers and mainstream alternatives like GCC and LLVM has been shrinking, so-called "fast-math" floating-point optimizations remain absent in verified compilers.

Fast-math optimizations allow a compiler to perform rewrites that are often intuitive when interpreted as real-valued identities, but which may not preserve strict IEEE 754 floating-point behavior. Developers selectively enable fast-math optimizations when implementing heuristics, computations over noisy inputs, or error-robust applications like neural networks—typically at the granularity of individual source files. The IEEE 754-unsound rewrites used in fast-math optimizations allow compilers to perform strength reductions, reorder code to enable other optimizations, and remove some error checking [1,2]. Together these optimization can provide significant savings and are widely-used in performance-critical applications [12].

Unfortunately, strict IEEE 754 source semantics prevents proving fast-math optimizations correct in verified compilers like CakeML and CompCert. Simple strength-reducing rewrites like fusing the expression $x * y + z$ into a faster and locally-more-accurate fused multiply-add (`fma`) instruction cannot be included in such verified compilers today. This is because `fma` avoids an intermediate rounding and thus may not produce exactly the same bit-for-bit result as the unoptimized code. More sophisticated optimizations like vectorization and loop invariant code motion depend on reordering operations to make expressions available, but these cannot be verified since floating-point arithmetic is not associative. Even simple reductions like rewriting $x - x$ to 0 cannot be verified since the result can actually be `NaN` ("not a number") if x is `NaN`. Each of these cases represent rewrites that developers would often, in principle, be willing to apply manually to improve performance but which can be more conveniently handled by the compiler. Verified compilers' strict IEEE 754 source semantics similarly hinders composing their guarantees with recent tools designed to *improve accuracy* of a source program [14,16,32], as these tools change program behavior to reduce rounding error. In short, developers today are forced to choose between verified compilers and useful tools based on floating-point rewrites.

The crux of the mismatch between verified compilers and fast-math lies in the source semantics: verified compilers implement strict IEEE 754 semantics while developers are intuitively programming against a looser specification of floating-point closer to the reals. Developers currently indicate this perspective by passing compiler flags like `--ffast-math` for the parts of their code written against this looser semantics, enabling mainstream compilers to aggressively optimize those components. Ideally, verified compilers will eventually support such loosened semantics by providing an "approximate real" data type and let the developer specify error bounds under which the compiler could freely apply any optimization that stays within bounds. A good interface to tools for analyzing finite-precision computations [11,16] could even allow independently-established formal accuracy guarantees to be composed with compiler correctness.

As an initial step toward this goal, we present a pragmatic and flexible approach to supporting fast-math optimizations in verified compilers. Our approach follows the implicit design of existing mainstream compilers by providing two complementary features. First, our approach provides fine-grained control over which parts of a program the compiler may optimize under extended floating-point semantics. Second, our approach provides flexible extensions to the floating-point semantics specified by a set of high-level rewrites which can be specialized to different parts of a program. The result is a new nondeterministic source semantics which grants the compiler freedom to optimize floating-point code within clearly defined bounds.

Under such extended semantics, we verify a set of common fast-math optimizations with the simulation-based proof techniques already used in verified compilers like CakeML and CompCert, and integrate our approach with the existing compilation pipeline of the CakeML compiler. To enable these proofs, we provide various *local* lemmas that a developer can prove about their rewrites to ensure *global* correctness of the verified fast-math optimizer. Several challenges arise in the design of this decomposition including how to handle "duplicating rewrites" like distributivity that introduce multiple copies of a subexpression and how to connect context-dependent rewrites to other analyses (e.g., from accuracy-verification tools) via rewrite preconditions. Our approach thus provides a rigorous formalization of the intuitive fast-math semantics developers already use, provides an interface for dispatching proof obligations to formal numerical analysis tools via rewrite preconditions, and enables bringing fast-math optimizations to verified compilers.

In summary, the contributions of this paper are:

- We introduce an extensible, nondeterministic semantics for floating-point computations which allows for fast-math style compiler optimizations with flexible, yet fine-grained control in a language we call *Icing*.
- We implement three optimizers based on Icing: a baseline strict optimizer which provably preserves IEEE 754 semantics, a greedy optimizer, which applies any available optimization, and a conditional optimizer which applies an optimization whenever an (optimization-specific) precondition is satisfied. The code is available at https://gitlab.mpi-sws.org/AVA/Icing.
- We formalize Icing and verify our three different optimizers in HOL4.
- We connect Icing to CakeML via a translation from Icing to CakeML source and verify its correctness via a sequence of refinement proofs.

2 The Icing Language

In this section we define the Icing language and its semantics to support fast-math style optimizations in a verified compiler. Icing is a prototype language whose semantics is designed to be extensible and widely applicable instead of focusing on a particular implementation of fast-math optimizations. This allows us to provide a stable interface as the implementation of the compiler changes, as well as supporting different optimization choices in the semantics, depending on the compilation target.

2.1 Syntax

Icing's syntax is shown in Fig. 1. In addition to arithmetic, let-bindings and conditionals, Icing supports `fma` operators, lists ($[e_1 \ldots]$), projections ($e_1[n]$), and `Map` and `Fold` as primitives. Conditional guards consist of boolean constants (b), binary comparisons ($e_1 \,\square\, e_2$), and an `isNaN` predicate. `isNaN` e_1 checks whether e_1 is a so-called *Not-a-Number* (`NaN`) special value. Under the IEEE 754 standard, undefined operations (e.g., square root of a negative number) produce `NaN` results, and most operations propagate `NaN` results when passed a `NaN` argument. It is thus common to add checks for `NaN`s at the source or compiler level.

$$w\text{: 64-bit floating-point word} \qquad x\text{: String} \qquad n \in \mathbb{N} \qquad b \in \{\text{True}, \text{False}\}$$

$$\diamond \in \{-, \texttt{sqrt}\} \qquad \circ \in \{+, -, *, /\} \qquad \square \in \{<, \leq, =\}$$

$$\begin{aligned} e_1, e_2, e_3 ::= {} & w \mid x \mid [e_1, \ldots] \mid e_1[n] \mid \diamond\, e_1 \mid e_1 \circ e_2 \mid \texttt{fma}(e_1, e_2, e_3) \mid \texttt{opt} : (e_1) \mid \\ & \texttt{let}\, x = e_1 \,\texttt{in}\, e_2 \mid \texttt{if}\, c \,\texttt{then}\, e_1 \,\texttt{else}\, e_2 \mid \texttt{Map}\,(\lambda x.e_1)\, e_2 \mid \texttt{Fold}\,(\lambda x\, y.e_1)\, e_2\, e_3 \\ c ::= {} & b \mid \texttt{isNaN}\, e_1 \mid e_1 \,\square\, e_2 \mid \texttt{opt} : (c) \end{aligned}$$

Fig. 1. Syntax of Icing expressions

We use the `Map` and `Fold` primitives to show that Icing can be used to express programs beyond arithmetic, while keeping the language simple. Language features like function definitions or general loops do not affect floating-point computations with respect to fast-math optimizations and are thus orthogonal.

The `opt:` scoping annotation implements one of the key features of Icing: floating-point semantics are relaxed only for expressions under an `opt:` scope. In this way, `opt:` provides fine-grained control both for expressions and conditional guards.

2.2 Optimizations as Rewrites

Fast-math optimizations are typically local and syntactic, i.e., peephole rewrites. In Icing, these optimizations are written as $s \rightarrow t$ to denote finding any subexpression matching pattern s and rewriting it to t, using the substitution from matching s to instantiate pattern variables in t as usual. The find and replace patterns of a rewrite are terms from the following pattern language which mirrors Icing syntax:

$$p_1, p_2, p_3 ::= w \mid b \mid x \mid \diamond p_1 \mid p_1 \circ p_2 \mid p_1 \,\square\, p_2 \mid \texttt{fma}\,(p_1, p_2, p_3) \mid \texttt{isNaN}\, p_1$$

Table 1 shows the set of rewrites currently supported in our development. While this set does not include all of GCC's fast-math optimizations, it does cover the three primary categories:

- performance and precision improving strength reduction which fuses $x * y + z$ into an `fma` instruction (Rewrite 1)

- reordering based on real-valued identities, here commutativity, and associativity of $+, *$, double negation and distributivity of $*$ (Rewrites 2–5)
- simplifying computation based on (assumed) real-valued behavior for computations by removing `NaN` error checks (Rewrite 6)

A key feature of Icing's design is that each rewrite can be guarded by a *rewrite precondition*. We distinguish *compiler rewrite preconditions* as those that must be true for the rewrite to be correct with respect to Icing semantics. Removing a `NaN` check, for example, can change the runtime behavior of a floating-point program: a previously crashing program may terminate or vice-versa. Thus a `NaN`-check can only removed if the value can never be a `NaN`.

In contrast, an *application rewrite precondition* guards a rewrite that can always be proven correct against the Icing semantics, but where a user may still want finer-grained control. By restricting the context where Icing may fire these rewrites, a user can establish end-to-end properties of their application, e.g., worst-case roundoff error. The crucial difference is that the compiler preconditions must be discharged before the rewrite can be proven correct against the Icing semantics, whereas the application precondition is an additional restriction limiting where the rewrite is applied for a specific application.

A key benefit of this design is that *rewrite preconditions can serve as an interface to external tools* to determine where optimizations may be conditionally applied. This feature enables Icing to address limitations that have prevented previous work from proving fast-math optimizations in verified compilers [5] since "The only way to exploit these [floating-point] simplifications while preserving semantics would be to apply them conditionally, based on the results of a static analysis (such as FP interval analysis) that can exclude the problematic cases." [5] In our setting, a static analysis tool can be used to establish an application rewrite precondition, while compiler rewrite preconditions can be discharged during (or potentially after) compilation via static analysis or manual proof.

This design choice essentially decouples the floating-point static analyzer from the general-purpose compiler. One motivation is that the compiler may perform hardware-specific rewrites, which source-code-based static analyzers would generally not be aware of. Furthermore, integrating end-to-end verification of these rewrites into a compiler would require it to always run a global static analysis. For this reason, we propose an interface which communicates only the necessary information.

Rewrites which duplicate matched subexpressions, e.g., distributing multiplication over addition, required careful design in Icing. Such rewrites can lead to unexpected results if different copies of the duplicated expression are optimized differently; this also complicates the Icing correctness proof. We show how preconditions additionally enabled us to address this challenge in Sect. 4.

Icing optimizes code by folding a list of rewrites over a program e:

```
rewrite ([],e) = e
rewrite ((s → t)::rws, e) =
  let e' = if (matches e s) then (app (s → t) e) else e in
  rewrite (rws, e')
```

For rewrite s→t at the head of rws, rewrite (rws, e) checks if s matches e, applies the rewrite if so, and recurses. Function rewrite is used in our optimizers in a bottom-up traversal of the AST. Icing users can specify which rewrites may be applied under each distinct opt: scope in their code or use a default set (shown in Table 1).

Table 1. Rewrites currently supported in Icing ($\circ \in \{+, *\}$)

	Name	Rewrite	Precondition
1	fma introduction	x * y + z → fma (x,y,z)	*application precond.*
2	∘ associative	(x ∘ y) ∘ z → x ∘ (y ∘ z)	*application precond.*
3	∘ commutative	x ∘ y → y ∘ x	*application precond.*
4	double negation	- (- x) → x	*x well-typed*
5	* distributive	x * (y + z) → (x * y) + (x * z)	*no control dependency on optimization result*
6	NaN check removal	isNaN x → false	*x is not a NaN*

2.3 Semantics of Icing

Next, we explain the semantics of Icing, highlighting two distinguishing features. First, values are represented as trees instead of simple floating-point words, thus delaying evaluation of arithmetic expressions. Secondly, rewrites in the semantics are applied nondeterministically, thus relaxing floating-point evaluation enough to prove fast-math optimizations.

We define the semantics of Icing programs in Fig. 2 as a big-step judgment of the form $(cfg, E, e) \to v$. cfg is a configuration carrying a list of rewrites $(s \to t)$ representing allowed optimizations, and a flag tracking whether optimizations are allowed in the current program fragment under an opt: scope (OptOk). E is the (runtime) execution environment mapping free variables to values and e an Icing expression. The value v is the result of evaluating e under E using optimizations from cfg.

The first key idea of Icing's semantics is that expressions are not evaluated to (64-bit) floating-point words immediately; the semantics rather evaluates them into *value trees* representing their computation result. As an example, if e_1 evaluates to value tree v_1 and e_2 to v_2, the semantics returns the value tree represented as $v_1 + v_2$ instead of the result of the floating-point addition of (flattened) v_1 and v_2. The syntax of value trees is:

$$c ::= b \mid \texttt{isNaN}\, v_1 \mid v_1 \,\Box\, v_2 \mid \texttt{opt:}\, c$$
$$v_1, v_2, v_3 ::= w \mid \diamond v_1 \mid v_1 \circ v_2 \mid \texttt{fma}(v_1, v_2, v_3) \mid \texttt{opt:}\, v_1$$

$$\frac{}{(cfg,\ E,\ c) \to \mathrm{c}}\ \texttt{Const} \qquad \frac{}{(cfg,\ E,\ b) \to \mathrm{b}}\ \texttt{Bool}$$

$$\frac{(cfg,\ E,\ e) \to v \quad (\diamond\, v,\ cfg)\ \mathsf{rewritesTo}\ r}{(cfg,\ E,\ \diamond\, e) \to r}\ \texttt{Unary} \qquad \frac{E\,(x) = r}{(cfg,\ E,\ x) \to r}\ \texttt{Var}$$

$$\frac{(cfg,\ E,\ e) \to vl \quad n < |vl| \quad vl[n] = r}{(cfg,\ E,\ e[n]) \to r}\ \texttt{Ith} \qquad \frac{(cfg,\ E,\ e_1) \to v_1 \quad (cfg,\ E,\ e_2) \to v_2 \quad (cfg,\ E,\ e_3) \to v_3 \quad (\texttt{fma}\ v_1\, v_2\, v_3,\ cfg)\ \mathsf{rewritesTo}\ r}{(cfg,\ E,\ \texttt{fma}\ e_1\, e_2\, e_3) \to r}\ \texttt{fma}$$

$$\frac{(cfg,\ E,\ e_1) \to v_1 \quad (cfg,\ E[x \mapsto v_1],\ e_2) \to v_2}{(cfg,\ E,\ \texttt{let}\ x = e_1\ \texttt{in}\, e_2) \to v_2}\ \texttt{Let-bind} \qquad \frac{(cfg\ \texttt{with}\ \texttt{OptOk} := \texttt{true},\ E,\ e) \to v}{(cfg,\ E,\ \texttt{Opt}:\ e) \to v}\ \texttt{Scope}$$

$$\frac{(cfg,\ E,\ e_1) \to v_1 \quad (cfg,\ E,\ e_2) \to v_2 \quad (v_1 \circ v_2,\ cfg)\ \mathsf{rewritesTo}\ r}{(cfg,\ E,\ e_1 \circ e_2) \to r}\ \texttt{Binary} \qquad \frac{(cfg,\ E,\ c) \to cv \quad \texttt{cTree2IEEE}\, cv = \mathrm{b} \quad (cfg,\ E,\ e_b) \to r}{(cfg,\ E,\ \texttt{if}\ c\ \texttt{then}\, e_T\ \texttt{else}\ e_F) \to r}\ \texttt{If}$$

$$\frac{}{(cfg,\ E,\ \texttt{Map}\,(\lambda x.e)\,[]) \to []}\ \texttt{Map []} \qquad \frac{(cfg,\ E,\ s) \to v}{(cfg,\ E,\ \texttt{Fold}\,(\lambda x\, y.e)\, s\,[]) \to v}\ \texttt{Fold []}$$

$$\frac{(cfg,\ E,\ e_1) \to v_1 \quad (cfg,\ E[x \mapsto v_1],\ e) \to v_{\mathrm{res}} \quad (cfg,\ E,\ \texttt{Map}\,(\lambda x.e)\, el) \to vl}{(cfg,\ E,\ \texttt{Map}\,(\lambda x.e)\,(e_1 :: el)) \to v_{\mathrm{res}} :: vl}\ \texttt{Map cons}$$

$$\frac{(cfg,\ E,\ e_1) \to v_1 \quad (cfg,\ E,\ \texttt{Fold}\,(\lambda x\, y.e)\, s\, el) \to v_{\mathrm{res}} \quad (cfg,\ E[x \mapsto v_1, y \mapsto v_{\mathrm{res}}],\ e) \to v_{\mathrm{final}}}{(cfg,\ E,\ \texttt{Fold}\,(\lambda x\, y.e)\, s\,(e_1 :: el)) \to v_{\mathrm{final}}}\ \texttt{Fold cons}$$

$$\frac{(cfg,\ E,\ e) \to v \quad (\texttt{isNaN}\, v,\ cfg)\ \mathsf{rewritesTo}\ r}{(cfg,\ E,\ \texttt{isNaN}\, e) \to r}\ \texttt{isNaN} \qquad \frac{(cfg,\ E,\ e_1) \to v_1 \quad (cfg,\ E,\ e_2) \to v_2 \quad (v_1 \square v_2,\ cfg)\ \mathsf{rewritesTo}\ r}{(cfg,\ E,\ e_1 \square e_2) \to r}\ \texttt{Compare}$$

Fig. 2. Nondeterministic Icing semantics

```
let v1 = Map (λ x. opt:(x + 3.0)) vi in
let vsum = Fold (λ x y. opt:(x * x + y)) 0.0 v1 in sqrt vsum
```

Fig. 3. A simple Icing program

Constants are again defined as floating-point words and form the leaves of value trees (variables obtain a constant value from the execution environment E). On top of constants, value trees can represent the result of evaluating any floating-point operation Icing supports.

The second key idea of our semantics is that it nondeterministically applies rewrites from the configuration *cfg while evaluating* expression e instead of just returning its value tree. In the semantics, we model the nondeterministic choice of an optimization result for a particular value tree v with the relation `rewritesTo`, where (cfg, v) `rewritesTo` r if either the configuration *cfg* allows for optimizations to be applied, and value tree v can be rewritten into value tree r using rewrites from the configuration *cfg*; or the configuration does not allow for rewrites to be applied, and $v = r$. Rewriting on value trees reuses several definitions from Sect. 2.2. We add the nondeterminism on top of the existing functions by making the relation `rewritesTo` pick a subset of the rewrites from the configuration *cfg* which are applied to value tree v.

Icing's semantics allows optimizations to be applied for arithmetic and comparison operations. The rules `Unary`, `Binary`, `fma`, `isNaN`, and `Compare` first evaluate argument expressions into value trees. The final result is then nondeterministically chosen from the `rewritesTo` relation for the obtained value tree and the current configuration. Evaluation of `Map`, `Fold`, and let-bindings follows standard textbook evaluation semantics and does not apply optimizations.

Rule `Scope` models the fine-grained control over where optimizations are applied in the semantics. We store in the current configuration *cfg* that optimizations are allowed in the (sub-)expression e (`cfg with OptOk := true`).

Evaluation of a conditional (`if` c `then` e_T `else` e_F) first evaluates the conditional guard c to a value tree cv. Based on value tree cv the semantics picks a branch to continue evaluation in. This eager evaluation for conditionals (in contrast to delaying by leaving them in a value tree) is crucial to enable the later simulation proof to connect Icing to CakeML which also eagerly evaluates conditionals. As the value tree cv represents a delayed evaluation of a boolean value, we have to turn it into a boolean constant when selecting the branch to continue evaluation in. This is done using the functions `cTree2IEEE` and `tree2IEEE`. `cTree2IEEE (v)` computes the boolean value, and `tree2IEEE (v)` computes the floating-point word represented by the value tree `v` by applying IEEE 754 arithmetic operations and structural recursion.

Example. We illustrate Icing semantics and how optimizations are applied both in syntax and semantics with the example in Fig. 3. The example first translates the input list by 3.0 using a `Map`, and then computes the norm of the translated list with `Fold` and `sqrt`.

We want to apply $x + y \to y + x$ (commutativity of $+$) and `fma`-introduction ($x * y + z \to$ `fma`(x, y, z)) to our example program. Depending on their order the function `rewrite` will produce different results.

If we first apply commutativity of $+$, and then `fma` introduction, all $+$ operations in our example will be commuted, but no `fma` introduced as the `fma` introduction *syntactically* relies on the expression having the structure $x*y+z$ where x, y, z can be arbitrary. In contrast, if we use the opposite order of rewrites, the second line will be replaced by `let vsum = Fold (λx y.fma(x,x,y)) 0.0 v1` and commutativity is only applied in the first line.

To illustrate how the semantics applies optimizations, we run the program on the 2D unit vector (`vi = [1.0,1.0]`) in a configuration that contains both rewrites. Consequently the `Map` application can produce `[1.0 + 3.0, 1.0 + 3.0]`, `[3.0 + 1.0, 1.0 + 3.0]`, ... Where the terms `1.0 + 3.0`, `3.0 + 1.0` correspond to the value trees representing the addition of `1.0` and `3.0`.

If we apply the `Fold` operation to this list, there are even more possible optimization results:

```
[(1.0 + 3.0) * (1.0 + 3.0) + (1.0 + 3.0) * (1.0 + 3.0)],
[(3.0 + 1.0) * (3.0 + 1.0) + (3.0 + 1.0) * (3.0 + 1.0)],
[fma ((3.0 + 1.0), (3.0 + 1.0), (3.0 + 1.0) * (3.0 + 1.0))],
[fma ((1.0 + 3.0), (1.0 + 3.0), (3.0 + 1.0) * (1.0 + 3.0))], ...
```

The first result is the result of evaluating the initial program without any rewrites, the second result corresponds to syntactically optimizing with commutativity of $+$ and then `fma` introduction, and the third corresponds to using the opposite order syntactically. The last two results can only be results of semantic optimizations as commutativity and `fma` introduction are applied to some intermediate results of `Map`, but not all. There is no syntactic application of commutativity and `fma`-introduction leading to such results.

3 Modelling Existing Compilers in Icing

Having defined the syntax and semantics of Icing, we next implement and prove correct functions which model the behavior of previous verified compilers, like CompCert or CakeML, and the behavior of unverified compilers, like GCC or Clang, respectively. For the former, we first define a translator of Icing expressions which preserves the IEEE 754 strict meaning of its input and does not allow for any further optimizations. Then we give a greedy optimizer that unconditionally optimizes expressions, as observed by GCC and Clang.

3.1 An IEEE 754 Preserving Translator

The Icing semantics nondeterministically applies optimizations if they are added to the configuration. However, when compiling safety-critical code or after applying some syntactic optimizations, one might want to preserve the strict IEEE 754 meaning of an expression.

To make sure that the behavior of an expression cannot be further changed and thus the expression exhibits strict IEEE 754 compliant behavior, we have implemented the function `compileIEEE754`, which essentially *disallows optimizations* by replacing all optimizable expressions `opt: e'` with non-optimizable expressions `e'`. Correctness of `compileIEEE754` shows that (a) no optimizations can be applied after the function has been applied, and (b) evaluation is deterministic. We have proven these properties as separate theorems.

3.2 A Greedy Optimizer

Next, we implement and prove correct an optimizer that mimics the (observed) behavior of GCC and Clang as closely as possible. The optimizer applies `fma` introduction, associativity and commutativity greedily. All these rewrites only have an application rewrite precondition which we instantiate to `True` to apply the rewrites unconstrained.

To give an intuition for greedy optimization, recall the example from Fig. 3. Greedy optimization does not consider whether applying an optimization is beneficial or not. If the optimization is allowed to be applied and it matches some subexpression of an optimizable expression, it is applied. Thus the order of optimizations matters. Applying the greedy optimizer with the rewrites `[associativity,fma-introduction, commutativity]` to the example, we get:

```
let v1 = Map (λ x. opt:(3.0 + x)) vi in
let vsum = Fold (λ x y. opt:(y + x * x)) 0.0 v1 in sqrt vsum
```

Only commutativity has been applied as associativity does not match and the possibility for an `fma`-introduction is ruled out by commutativity. If we reverse the list of optimizations we obtain:

```
let v1 = Map (λ x. opt:(3.0 + x)) vi in
let vsum = Fold (λ x y. opt:(fma (x,x,y))) 0.0 v1 in sqrt vsum
```

which we consider to be a more efficient version of the program from Fig. 3.

Greedy optimization is implemented in the function `optimizeGreedy (rws, e)` which applies the rewrites in `rws` in a bottom-up traversal to expression `e`. In combination with the greedy optimizer our fine-grained control (using `opt` annotations) allows the end-user to control *where* optimizations can be applied.

We have shown correctness of `optimizeGreedy` with respect to Icing semantics, i.e., we have shown that optimizing greedily gives the same result as applying the greedy rewrites in the semantics:[1]

Theorem 1. *`optimizeGreedy` is correct*
Let E be an environment, v a value tree and cfg a configuration.
If $(cfg, E,$`optimizeGreedy ([associativity,commutativity,fma-intro], e)`$) \to v$ then $(cfg$ with `[associativity, commutativity,fma-intro]`$, E, e) \to v$.

[1] As in many verified compilers, Icing's proofs closely follow the structure of optimizations. Achieving this required careful design and many iterations; we consider the simplicity of Icing's proofs to be a strength of this work.

Proving Theorem 1 without any additional lemmas is tedious as it requires showing correctness of a single optimization in the presence of other optimizations and dealing with the bottom-up traversal applying the optimization at the same time. Thus we reduce the proof of Theorem 1 to proving each rewrite separately and then chaining together these correctness proofs. Lemma 1 shows that applications of the function `rewrite` can be chained together in the semantics. This also means that adding, removing, or reordering optimizations simply requires changing the list of rewrites, thus making Icing easy to extend.

Lemma 1. *`rewrite` is compositional*
Let e be an expression, v a value tree, $s \rightarrow t$ a rewrite, and rws a set of rewrites. If the rewrite $s \rightarrow t$ can be correctly simulated in the semantics, and list rws can be correctly simulated in the semantics, then the list of rewrites $(s \rightarrow t) :: rws$ can be correctly simulated in the semantics.

4 A Conditional Optimizer

We have implemented an IEEE 754 optimizer which has the same behavior as CompCert and CakeML, and a greedy optimizer with the (observed) behavior of GCC and Clang. The fine-grained control of where optimizations are applied is essential for the usability of the greedy optimizer. However, in this section we explain that the control provided by the `opt` annotation is often not enough. We show how preconditions can be used to provide additional constraints on where rewrites can be applied, and sketch how preconditions serve as an interface between the compiler and external tools, which can and should discharge them.

We observe that in many cases, whether an optimization is acceptable or not can be captured with a precondition *on the optimization itself*, and not on every arithmetic operation separately. One example for such an optimization is removal of `NaN` checks as a check for a `NaN` should only be removed if the check never succeeds.

We argue that both application and compiler rewrite preconditions should be discharged by external tools. Many interesting preconditions for a rewrite depend on a global analysis. Running a global analysis as part of a compiler is infeasible, as maintaining separate analyses for each rewrite is not likely to scale. We thus propose to expose an *interface to external tools* in the form of preconditions.

We implement this idea in the *conditional optimizer* `optimizeCond` that supports three different applications of fast-math optimizations: applying optimizations `rws` unconstrained (`uncond rws`), applying optimizations if precondition `P` is true (`cond P rws`), and applying optimizations under the assumptions generation by function `A` which should be discharged externally (`assume A rws`). When applying `cond`, `optimizeCond` checks whether precondition `P` is true before optimizing, whereas for `assume` the propositions returned by `A` are assumed, and should then be discharged separately by a static analysis or a manual proof.

Correctness of `optimizeCond` relates syntactic optimizations to applying optimizations in the semantics. Similar to `optimizeGreedy`, we designed the proof modularly such that it suffices to prove correct each rewrite individually.

Our optimizer `optimizeCond` takes as arguments first a list of rewrite applications using `uncond`, `cond`, and `assume` then an expression `e`. If the list is empty, we have `optimizeCond ([], e) = e`. Otherwise the rewrite is applied in a bottom-up traversal to `e` and optimization continues recursively. For `uncond`, the rewrites are applied if they match; for `cond P rws` the precondition `P` is checked for the expression being optimized and the rewrites `rws` are applied if `P` is true; for `assume A rws`, the function `A` is evaluated on the expression being optimized. If execution of `A` fails, no optimization is applied. Otherwise, `A` returns a list of assumptions which are logged by the compiler and the rewrites are applied.

Using the interface provided by preconditions, one can prove external theorems showing additional properties of a compiler run using application rewrite preconditions, and external theorems showing how to discharge compiler rewrite preconditions with static analysis tools or a manual proof. We will call such external theorems *meta theorems*.

In the following we discuss two possible meta theorems, highlighting key steps required for implementing (and proving) them. A complete implementation consists of two connections: (1) from the compiler to rewrite preconditions and (2) from rewrite preconditions to external tools. We implement (1) independently of any particular tool. A complete implementation of (2) is out of scope of this paper; meta theorems generally depend on global analyses which are orthogonal to designing Icing, but several external tools already provide functionality that is a close match to our interface and we sketch possible connections below. We note that for these meta theorems, `optimizeCond` should track the context in which an assumption is made and use the context to express assumptions as *local* program properties. Our current `optimizeCond` implementation does not collect this contextual information yet, as this information at least partially depends on the particular meta theorems desired.

4.1 A Logging Compiler for NaN Special Value Checks

We show how a meta theorem can be used to discharge a compiler rewrite precondition on the example of removing a `NaN` check. Removing a `NaN` check, in general, can be unsound if the check could have succeeded. Inferring statically whether a value can be a `NaN` special value or not requires either a global static analysis, or a manual proof on all possible executions.

Preconditions are our interface to external tools. For `NaN` check removal, we implement a function `removeNaNcheck e` that returns the assumption that no `NaN` special value can be the result of evaluating the argument expression e. Function `removeNaNCheck` could then be used as part of an `assume` rule for `optimizeCond`. We prove a strengthened correctness theorem for `NaN` check removal, showing that if the assumption returned by `removeNaNcheck` is discharged externally (i.e. by the end-user or via static analysis), then we can simulate applying `NaN` check removal syntactically in Icing semantics *without additional sideconditions*.

The assumption from `removeNaNcheck` is additionally returned as the result of `optimizeCond` since it is faithfully assumed when optimizing. Such assumptions can be discharged by static analyzers like Verasco [22], or Gappa [17].

4.2 Proving Roundoff Error Improvement

Rewrites like associativity and distributivity change the results of floating-point programs. One way of capturing this behavior for a single expression is to compute the roundoff error, i.e. the difference between an idealized real-valued and a floating-point execution of the expression.

To compute an upper bound on the roundoff error, various formally verified tools have been implemented [3,17,30,37]. A possible meta theorem is thus to show that applying a particular list of optimizations does not increase the roundoff error of the optimized expression but only decreases or preserves it. The meta theorem for this example would show that (a) all the applied syntactic rewrites can be simulated in the semantics and (b) the worst-case roundoff error of the optimized expression is smaller or equal to the error of the input expression. Our development already proves (a) and we sketch the steps necessary to show (b) below.

We can leverage these roundoff error analysis tools as application preconditions in a `cond` rule, checking whether a rewrite should be applied or not in `optimizeCond`. For a particular expression `e`, an application precondition (`check (s→t, e)`) would return true if applying rewrite `s→t` does not increase the roundoff error of `e`.

Theorem 2. *`check` decreases roundoff error*
(cfg, E, `optimizeCond (Cond (λe. check (s→t, e))) e`) $\rightarrow v \Longrightarrow$
(cfg with opts := cfg.opts $\cup$ $\{s \rightarrow t\}$, E, e) $\rightarrow v \wedge$
`error e` $\leq$ `error (optimizeCond (Cond (λe. check (s→t, e))) e)`

Implementing `check (s→t, e)` requires computing a roundoff error for expression `e` and one for `e` rewritten with `s→t` and returning `True` if and only if the roundoff error has not increased by applying the rewrite. Proving the theorem would require giving a real-valued semantics for Icing, connecting Icing's semantics to the semantics of the roundoff error analysis tool, and a global range analysis on the Icing programs, which can be provided by Verasco or Gappa.

4.3 Supporting Distributivity in `optimizeCond`

The rewrites considered up to this point do not duplicate any subexpressions in the optimized output. In this section, we consider rewrites which do introduce additional occurrences of subexpressions, which we dub *duplicative rewrites*. Common duplicative rewrites are distributivity of $*$ with $+$ $(x * (y + x) \leftrightarrow x * y + x * z)$ and rewriting a single multiplication into multiple additions $(x * n \leftrightarrow \sum_{i=1}^{n} x)$. Here we consider distributivity as an example. A compiler might want to use this optimization to apply further strength reductions or `fma` introduction.

The main issue with duplicative rewrites is that they add new occurrences of a matched subexpression. Applying $(x * (y + z) \rightarrow x * y + x * z)$ to `e1 * (2 + x)` returns `e1 * 2 + e1 * x`. The values for the two occurrences of `e1` may differ because of further optimizations applied to only one of it's occurrences.

Any correctness proof for such a duplicative rewrite must match up the two (potentially different) executions of `e1` in the optimized expression (`e1 * 2 + e1 * x`) with the execution of `e1` in the initial expression (`e1 * (2 + x)`). This can only be achieved by finding a common intermediate optimization (resp. evaluation) result shared by both subexpressions of `e1 * 2 + e1 * x`.

In general, existence of such an intermediate result can only be proven for expressions that do not depend on "eager" evaluation, i.e. which consists of let-bindings and arithmetic. We illustrate the problem using a conditional (`if c then e1 else e2`). In Icing semantics, the guard `c` is first evaluated to a value tree `cv`. Next, the semantics evaluates `cv` to a boolean value b using function `cTree2IEEE`. Computing b from `cv` loses the structural information of value tree `cv` by computing the results of previously delayed arithmetic operations. This loss of information means that rewrites that previously matched the structure of `cv` may no longer apply to b.

This is not a bug in the Icing semantics. On the contrary, our semantics makes this issue explicit, while in other compilers it can lead to unexpected behavior (e.g., in GCC's support for distributivity under fast-math). CakeML, for example, also eagerly evaluates conditionals and similarly loses structural information about optimizations that otherwise may have been applied. Having lazy conditionals in general would only "postpone" the issue until eager evaluation of the conditional expression for a loop is necessary.

An intuitive compiler precondition that enables proving duplicative rewrites is to forbid any control dependencies on the expression being optimized. However, this approach may be unsatisfactory as it disallows branching on the results of optimized expressions and requires a verified dependency analysis that must be rerun or incrementally updated after every rewrite, and thus could become a bottleneck for fast-math optimizers. Instead, in Icing we restrict duplicative rewrites to only fire when pattern variables are matched against program variables, e.g., pattern variables a, b, c only match against program variables `x, y, z`. This restriction to only matching let-bound variables is more scalable, as it can easily be checked syntactically, and allows us to loosen the restriction on control-flow dependence by simply let-binding subexpressions as needed.

5 Connecting to CakeML

We have shown how to apply optimizations in Icing and how to use it to preserve IEEE 754 semantics. Next, we describe how we connected Icing to an existing verified compiler by implementing a translation from Icing source to CakeML

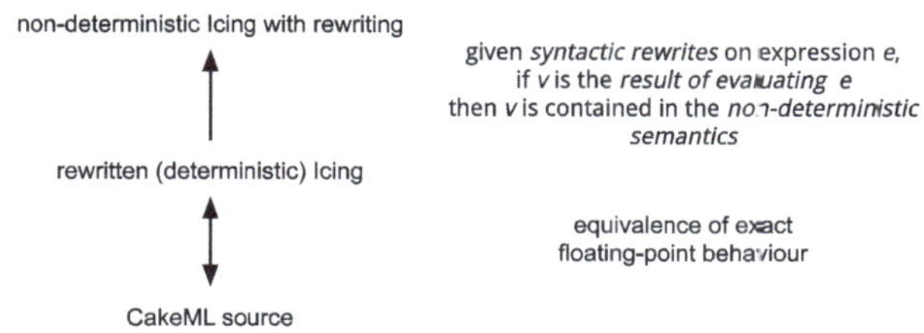

Fig. 4. Simulation diagram for Icing and the designed optimizers

source and showing an equivalence theorem.[2] The translation function `toCML` maps Icing syntax to CakeML syntax. We highlight the most interesting cases. The translations of `Ith`, `Map`, `Fold` relate an Icing execution to a predefined function from the CakeML standard library. We show separate theorems relating executions of list operations in Icing to CakeML closures of library functions. The predicate `isNaN e` is implemented as `toCML e <> toCML e`. The predicate is true in Icing semantics, if and only if `e` is a `NaN` special value. Recall that floating-point `NaN` values are incomparable (even to themselves) and thus we implement `isNaN` with an equality check.

To show that our translation function `toCML` correctly translates Icing programs into CakeML source, we proved a simulation between the two semantics, illustrated in Fig. 4. The top part consists of the correctness theorems we have shown for the optimizers, relating syntactic optimization to semantic rewriting. In the bottom part we relate a *deterministic* Icing execution which does not apply optimizations to CakeML source semantics and prove an equivalence. For the backward simulation between CakeML and Icing we require the Icing program to be well-typed which is independently checked.

6 Related Work

Verified Compilation of Floating-Point Programs. CompCert [25] uses a constructive formalization of IEEE 754 arithmetic [6] based on Flocq [7] which allows for verified constant propagation and strength reduction optimizations for divisions by powers of 2 and replacing $x \times 2$ by $x + x$. The situation is similar for CakeML [38] whose floating-point semantics is based on HOL's [19,20]. With Icing, we propose a semantics which allows important floating-point rewrites in a verified compiler by allowing users to specify a larger set of possible behaviors for their source programs. The precondition mechanism serves as an interface to external tools. While Icing is implemented in HOL, our techniques are not specific to higher-order logic or the details of CakeML and we believe that an analog of our "verified fast-math" approach could easily be ported to CompCert.

The Alive framework [27] has been extended to verify floating-point peephole optimizations [29,31]. While these tools relax some exceptional (`NaN`) cases,

[2] We also extended the CakeML source semantics with an `fma` operation, as CakeML's compilation currently does not support mapping `fma`'s to hardware instructions.

most optimizations still need to preserve “bit-for-bit” IEEE 754 behavior, which precludes valuable rewrites like the `fma` introductions Icing supports.

Optimization of Floating-Point Programs. ‘Mixed-precision tuning’ can increase performance by decreasing precision at the expense of accuracy, for instance from double to single floating-point precision. Current tools [11,13,16,35], ensure that a user-provided error bound is satisfied either through dynamic or static analysis. In this work, we consider only uniform 64-bit floating-point precision, but Icing's optimizations are equally applicable to other precisions. Optimizations such as mixed-precision tuning are, however, out of scope of a compiler setting, as they require error bound annotations for kernel functions.

Spiral [33] uses real-valued linear algebra identities for rewriting at the algorithmic level to choose a layout which provides the best performance for a particular platform, but due to operation reordering is not IEEE 754 semantics preserving. Herbie [32] optimizes for accuracy, and not for performance by applying rewrites which are mostly based on real-valued identities. The optimizations performed by Spiral and Herbie go beyond what traditional compilers perform, but they fit our view that it is sometimes beneficial to relax the strict IEEE 754 specification, and could be considered in an extended implementation of Icing. On the other hand, STOKE's floating-point superoptimizer [36] for x86 binaries does not preserve real-valued semantics, and only provides approximate correctness using dynamic analysis.

Analysis and Verification of Floating-Point Programs. Static analysis for bounding roundoff errors of finite-precision computations w.r.t. to a real-valued semantics [15,17,18,28,30,37] (some with formal certificates in Coq or HOL), are currently limited to short, mostly straight-line functions and require fine-grained domain annotations at the function level. Whole program accuracy can be formally verified w.r.t. to a real-valued implementation with substantial user interaction and expertise [34]. Verification of elementary function implementations has also recently been automated, but requires substantial compute resources [23].

On the other hand, static analyses aiming to verify the absence of runtime exceptions like division by zero [4,10,21,22] scale to realistic programs. We believe that such tools can be used to satisfy preconditions and thus Icing would serve as an interface between the compiler and such specialized verification techniques.

The KLEE symbolic execution engine [9] has support for floating-point programs [26] through an interface to Z3's floating-point theory [8]. This theory is also based on IEEE 754 and will thus not be able to verify the kind of optimizations that Icing supports.

7 Conclusion

We have proposed a novel semantics for IEEE 754-unsound floating-point compiler optimizations which allows them to be applied in a verified compiler setting and which captures the intuitive semantics developers often use today when reasoning about their floating-point code. Our semantics is nondeterministic in order to provide the compiler the freedom to apply optimizations where they are useful for a particular application and platform—but within clearly defined bounds. The semantics is flexible from the developer's perspective, as it provides fine-grained control over which optimizations are available and where in a program they can be applied. We have presented a formalization in HOL4, implemented three prototype optimizers, and connected them to the CakeML verified compiler frontend. For our most general optimizer, we have explained how it can be used to obtain meta-theorems for its results by exposing a well-defined interface in the form of preconditions. We believe that our semantics can be integrated fully with different verified compilers in the future, and bridge the gap between compiler optimizations and floating-point verification techniques.

References

1. LLVM language reference manual - fast-math flags (2019). https://llvm.org/docs/LangRef.html#fast-math-flags
2. Semantics of floating point math in GCC (2019). https://gcc.gnu.org/wiki/FloatingPointMath
3. Becker, H., Zyuzin, N., Monat, R., Darulova, E., Myreen, M.O., Fox, A.: A verified certificate checker for finite-precision error bounds in Coq and HOL4. In: 2018 Formal Methods in Computer Aided Design (FMCAD), pp. 1–10. IEEE (2018)
4. Blanchet, B., et al.: A static analyzer for large safety-critical software. In: PLDI (2003)
5. Boldo, S., Jourdan, J.H., Leroy, X., Melquiond, G.: A formally-verified c compiler supporting floating-point arithmetic. In: 2013 21st IEEE Symposium on Computer Arithmetic (ARITH), pp. 107–115. IEEE (2013)
6. Boldo, S., Jourdan, J.H., Leroy, X., Melquiond, G.: Verified compilation of floating-point computations. J. Autom. Reasoning **54**(2), 135–163 (2015)
7. Boldo, S., Melquiond, G.: Flocq: a unified library for proving floating-point algorithms in Coq. In: 19th IEEE International Symposium on Computer Arithmetic, ARITH, pp. 243–252 (2011). https://doi.org/10.1109/ARITH.2011.40
8. Brain, M., Tinelli, C., Ruemmer, P., Wahl, T.: An automatable formal semantics for IEEE-754 floating-point arithmetic. Technical report (2015). http://smt-lib.org/papers/BTRW15.pdf
9. Cadar, C., Dunbar, D., Engler, D.: KLEE: unassisted and automatic generation of high-coverage tests for complex systems programs. In: OSDI (2008)
10. Chen, L., Miné, A., Cousot, P.: A sound floating-point polyhedra abstract domain. In: Ramalingam, G. (ed.) APLAS 2008. LNCS, vol. 5356, pp. 3–18. Springer, Heidelberg (2008). https://doi.org/10.1007/978-3-540-89330-1_2
11. Chiang, W.F., Baranowski, M., Briggs, I., Solovyev, A., Gopalakrishnan, G., Rakamarić, Z.: Rigorous floating-point mixed-precision tuning. In: Symposium on Principles of Programming Languages (POPL), pp. 300–315. ACM (2017)
12. Corden, M., Kreitzer, D.: Consistency of floating-point results using the Intel compiler. Technical report, Intel Corporation (2010)
13. Damouche, N., Martel, M.: Mixed precision tuning with salsa. In: PECCS, pp. 185–194. SciTePress (2018)

14. Damouche, N., Martel, M., Chapoutot, A.: Intra-procedural optimization of the numerical accuracy of programs. In: Núñez, M., Güdemann, M. (eds.) FMICS 2015. LNCS, vol. 9128, pp. 31–46. Springer, Cham (2015). https://doi.org/10.1007/978-3-319-19458-5_3
15. Darulova, E., Izycheva, A., Nasir, F., Ritter, F., Becker, H., Bastian, R.: Daisy - framework for analysis and optimization of numerical programs (tool paper). In: Beyer, D., Huisman, M. (eds.) TACAS 2018. LNCS, vol. 10805, pp. 270–287. Springer, Cham (2018). https://doi.org/10.1007/978-3-319-89960-2_15
16. Darulova, E., Sharma, S., Horn, E.: Sound mixed-precision optimization with rewriting. In: ICCPS (2018)
17. De Dinechin, F., Lauter, C.Q., Melquiond, G.: Assisted verification of elementary functions using Gappa. In: ACM Symposium on Applied Computing, pp. 1318–1322. ACM (2006)
18. Goubault, E., Putot, S.: Static analysis of finite precision computations. In: Jhala, R., Schmidt, D. (eds.) VMCAI 2011. LNCS, vol. 6538, pp. 232–247. Springer, Heidelberg (2011). https://doi.org/10.1007/978-3-642-18275-4_17
19. Harrison, J.: Floating point verification in HOL. In: Thomas Schubert, E., Windley, P.J., Alves-Foss, J. (eds.) TPHOLs 1995. LNCS, vol. 971, pp. 186–199. Springer, Heidelberg (1995). https://doi.org/10.1007/3-540-60275-5_65
20. Harrison, J.: Floating-point verification. In: Fitzgerald, J., Hayes, I.J., Tarlecki, A. (eds.) FM 2005. LNCS, vol. 3582, pp. 529–532. Springer, Heidelberg (2005). https://doi.org/10.1007/11526841_35
21. Jeannet, B., Miné, A.: Apron: a library of numerical abstract domains for static analysis. In: Bouajjani, A., Maler, O. (eds.) CAV 2009. LNCS, vol. 5643, pp. 661–667. Springer, Heidelberg (2009). https://doi.org/10.1007/978-3-642-02658-4_52
22. Jourdan, J.H.: Verasco: a formally verified C static analyzer. Ph.D. thesis, Université Paris Diderot (Paris 7), May 2016
23. Lee, W., Sharma, R., Aiken, A.: On automatically proving the correctness of math.h implementations. In: POPL (2018)
24. Leroy, X.: Formal certification of a compiler back-end, or: programming a compiler with a proof assistant. In: 33rd ACM Symposium on Principles of Programming Languages, pp. 42–54. ACM Press (2006)
25. Leroy, X.: A formally verified compiler back-end. J. Autom. Reasoning **43**(4), 363–446 (2009). http://xavierleroy.org/publi/compcert-backend.pdf
26. Liew, D., Schemmel, D., Cadar, C., Donaldson, A.F., Zähl, R., Wehrle, K.: Floating-point symbolic execution: a case study in n-version programming. In: Proceedings of the 32nd IEEE/ACM International Conference on Automated Software Engineering. IEEE Press (2017)
27. Lopes, N.P., Menendez, D., Nagarakatte, S., Regehr, J.: Provably correct peephole optimizations with alive. In: PLDI (2015)
28. Magron, V., Constantinides, G., Donaldson, A.: Certified roundoff error bounds using semidefinite programming. ACM Trans. Math. Softw. **43**(4), 1–34 (2017)
29. Menendez, D., Nagarakatte, S., Gupta, A.: Alive-FP: automated verification of floating point based peephole optimizations in LLVM. In: Rival, X. (ed.) SAS 2016. LNCS, vol. 9837, pp. 317–337. Springer, Heidelberg (2016). https://doi.org/10.1007/978-3-662-53413-7_16
30. Moscato, M., Titolo, L., Dutle, A., Muñoz, C.A.: Automatic estimation of verified floating-point round-off errors via static analysis. In: Tonetta, S., Schoitsch, E., Bitsch, F. (eds.) SAFECOMP 2017. LNCS, vol. 10488, pp. 213–229. Springer, Cham (2017). https://doi.org/10.1007/978-3-319-66266-4_14

31. Nötzli, A., Brown, F.: LifeJacket: verifying precise floating-point optimizations in LLVM. In: Proceedings of the 5th ACM SIGPLAN International Workshop on State of the Art in Program Analysis, pp. 24–29. ACM (2016)
32. Panchekha, P., Sanchez-Stern, A., Wilcox, J.R., Tatlock, Z.: Automatically improving accuracy for floating point expressions. In: Conference on Programming Language Design and Implementation (PLDI) (2015)
33. Püschel, M., et al.: SPIRAL - a generator for platform-adapted libraries of signal processing alogorithms. IJHPCA **18**(1), 21–45 (2004)
34. Ramananandro, T., Mountcastle, P., Meister, B., Lethin, R.: A unified Coq framework for verifying C programs with floating-point computations. In: Certified Programs and Proofs (CPP) (2016)
35. Rubio-González, C., et al.: Precimonious: tuning assistant for floating-point precision. In: SC (2013)
36. Schkufza, E., Sharma, R., Aiken, A.: Stochastic optimization of floating-point programs with tunable precision. In: PLDI (2014)
37. Solovyev, A., Jacobsen, C., Rakamarić, Z., Gopalakrishnan, G.: Rigorous estimation of floating-point round-off errors with Symbolic Taylor Expansions. In: Bjørner, N., de Boer, F. (eds.) FM 2015. LNCS, vol. 9109, pp. 532–550. Springer, Cham (2015). https://doi.org/10.1007/978-3-319-19249-9_33
38. Tan, Y.K., Myreen, M.O., Kumar, R., Fox, A., Owens, S., Norrish, M.: The verified CakeML compiler backend. J. Funct. Program. **29** (2019)
39. Tristan, J.B., Leroy, X.: Formal verification of translation validators: a case study on instruction scheduling optimizations. In: Proceedings of the 35th ACM Symposium on Principles of Programming Languages (POPL 2008), pp. 17–27. ACM Press, January 2008
40. Tristan, J.B., Leroy, X.: Verified validation of lazy code motion. In: Proceedings of the 2009 ACM SIGPLAN Conference on Programming Language Design and Implementation (PLDI 2009), pp. 316–326 (2009)
41. Tristan, J.B., Leroy, X.: A simple, verified validator for software pipelining. In: Proceedings of the 37th ACM Symposium on Principles of Programming Languages (POPL 2010), pp. 83–92. ACM Press (2010)

Sound Approximation of Programs with Elementary Functions

Eva Darulova[1(✉)] and Anastasia Volkova[2]

[1] MPI-SWS, Saarland Informatics Campus, Saarbrücken, Germany
eva@mpi-sws.org
[2] Inria, Lyon, France
anastasia.volkova@inria.fr

Abstract. Elementary function calls are a common feature in numerical programs. While their implementations in mathematical libraries are highly optimized, function evaluation is nonetheless very expensive compared to plain arithmetic. Full accuracy is, however, not always needed. Unlike arithmetic, where the performance difference between for example single and double precision floating-point arithmetic is relatively small, elementary function calls provide a much richer tradeoff space between accuracy and efficiency. Navigating this space is challenging, as guaranteeing the accuracy and choosing correct parameters for good performance of approximations is highly nontrivial. We present a fully automated approach and a tool which approximates elementary function calls inside small programs while guaranteeing overall user given error bounds. Our tool leverages existing techniques for roundoff error computation and approximation of individual elementary function calls and provides an automated methodology for the exploration of parameter space. Our experiments show that significant efficiency improvements are possible in exchange for reduced, but guaranteed, accuracy.

1 Introduction

Numerical programs face an inherent tradeoff between accuracy and efficiency. Choosing a larger finite precision provides higher accuracy, but is generally more costly in terms of memory and running time. Not all applications, however, need a very high accuracy to work correctly. We would thus like to compute the results with only as much accuracy as is needed, in order to save resources.

Navigating this tradeoff between accuracy and efficiency is challenging. First, estimating the accuracy, i.e. bounding roundoff and approximation errors, is nontrivial due to the complex nature of finite-precision arithmetic which inevitably occurs in numerical programs. Second, the space of possible implementations is usually prohibitively large and thus cannot be explored manually.

Today, users can choose between different automated tools for analyzing accuracy of floating-point programs [7,8,11,14,18,20,26] as well as for choosing between different precisions [5,6,10]. The latter tools perform mixed-precision tuning, i.e. they assign different floating-point precisions to different operations,

I. Dillig and S. Tasiran (Eds.): CAV 2019, LNCS 11562, pp. 174–183, 2019.
https://doi.org/10.1007/978-3-030-25543-5_11

and can thus improve the performance w.r.t. a uniform precision implementation. The success of such an optimization is, however, limited to the case when uniform precision is just barely not enough to satisfy a given accuracy specification.

Another possible target for performance optimizations are elementary functions (e.g. `sin, exp`). Users by default choose single- or double-precision `libm` library function implementations, which are fully specified in the C language standard (ISO/IEC 9899:2011) and provide high accuracy. Such implementations are, however, expensive. When high accuracy is not needed, we can save significant resources by replacing `libm` calls by coarser approximations, opening up a larger, and different tradeoff space than mixed-precision tuning. Unfortunately, existing automated approaches [1,25] do not provide accuracy guarantees.

On the other hand, tools like Metalibm [3] approximate *individual* elementary functions by polynomials with rigorous accuracy guarantees given by the user. They, however, do not consider entire programs and leave the selection of its parameters to the user, limiting its usability mostly to experts.

We present an approach and a tool which leverages the existing whole-program error analysis of Daisy [8] and Metalibm's elementary function approximation to provide both *sound whole-program guarantees* as well as *efficient* C implementations for floating-point programs with elementary function calls. Given a target error specification, our tool automatically distributes the error budget among uniform single or double precision arithmetic operations and elementary functions, and selects a suitable polynomial degree for their approximation.

We have implemented our approach inside the tool Daisy and compare the performance of generated programs against programs using `libm` on examples from literature. The benchmarks spend on average 38% and up to 50% of time for evaluation of the elementary functions. Our tool improves the overall performance by on average 14% and up to 25% when approximating each elementary function call individually, and on average 17% and up to 31% when approximating compound function calls. These improvements were achieved solely by optimizing approximations to elementary functions and illustrate pertinence of our approach. These performance improvements incur overall whole-program errors which are only 2–3 magnitudes larger than double-precision implementations using `libm` functions and are well below the errors of single-precision implementations. Our tool thus allows to effectively trade performance for larger, but guaranteed, error bounds.

Contributions. In summary, in this paper we present: (1) the first approximation technique for elementary functions with sound whole-program error guarantees, (2) an experimental evaluation on benchmarks from literature, and (3) an implementation, which is available at https://github.com/malyzajko/daisy.

Related Work. Several static analysis tools bound roundoff errors of floating-point computations [7,18,20,26], assuming `libm` implementations, or verify the correctness of several functions in Intel's `libm` library [17]. Muller [21] provides a good overview of the approximation of elementary functions. Approaches for improving the performance of numerical programs include mixed-precision tuning [5,6,10,16,24], and autotuning, which performs low-level real-value semantics-preserving transformations [23,27]. These leverage a different part of the trade-off space than `libm` approximation and are thus orthogonal. Herbie [22] and Sardana [7] improve accuracy by rewriting the non-associative finite-precision arithmetic, which is complementary to our approach. Approaches which approximate entire numerical programs include MCMC search [25], enumerative program synthesis [1] and neural approximations [13]. Accuracy is only checked on a small set of sample inputs and is thus not guaranteed.

2 Our Approach

We explain our approach using the following example [28] computing a forward kinematics equation and written in Daisy's real-valued specification language:

```
def forwardk2jY(theta1: Real, theta2: Real): Real = {
  require(-3.14 <= theta1 && theta1 <= 3.14 && -3.14 <= theta2 && theta2 <= 3.14)
    val l1: Real = 0.5; val l2: Real = 2.5
    l1 * sin(theta1) + l2 * sin(theta1 + theta2)
} ensuring(res => res +/- 1e-11)
```

Although this program is relatively simple, it still presents an opportunity for performance savings, especially when it is called often, e.g. during the motion of a robotics arm. Assuming double-precision floating-point arithmetic and library implementations for sine, Daisy's static analysis determines the worst-case absolute roundoff error of the result to be 3.44e-15. This is clearly a much smaller error than what the user requested (1e-11) in the postcondition (`ensuring` clause).

The two elementary function calls to `sin` account for roughly 40.7% of the overall running time. We can save some of this running time using polynomial approximations, which our tool generates in less than 6 min. The new double precision C implementation is roughly 15.6% faster than one with `libm`[1] functions, i.e. using around 40% of the available margin. This is a noteworthy performance improvement, considering that we optimized uniquely the evaluation of elementary functions. The actual error of the approximate implementation is 1.56e-12, i.e. roughly three orders of magnitude higher than the `libm` error. This error is still much smaller than if we had used a uniform single precision implementation, which incurs a total error of 1.85e-6.

We implement our approach inside the Daisy framework [8], combining Daisy's static dataflow analysis for bounding finite-precision roundoff errors, Metalibm's automated generation of efficient polynomial approximations, as well as a novel error distribution algorithm. Our tool furthermore automatically selects a suitable polynomial degree for approximations to elementary functions.

[1] There are various different implementations of `libm` that depend on the operating system and programming language. Here when referring to `libm` we mean the GNU `libc` implementation (https://www.gnu.org/software/libc/).

Unlike previous work, our tool *guarantees* that the user-specified error is satisfied. It soundly distributes the overall error budget among arithmetic operations and `libm` calls using Daisy's static analysis. Metalibm uses the state-of-the art minimax polynomial approximation algorithm [2] and Sollya [4] and Gappa [12] to bound errors of their implementations. Given a function, a target relative error bound and implementation parameters, Metalibm generates C code. Our tool does not guarantee to find the most efficient implementation; the search space of implementation and approximation choices is highly complex and discrete, and it is thus infeasible to find the optimal parameters.

The input to our tool is a straight-line program[2] with standard arithmetic operators $(=, -, *, /)$ as well as the most commonly used elementary functions $(\sin, \cos, \tan, \log, \exp, \sqrt{})$. The user further specifies the domains of all inputs, together with a target overall absolute error which must be satisfied. The output is C code with arithmetic operations in uniform single or double precision, and `libm` approximations in double precision (Metalibm's only supported precision).

Algorithm. We will use 'program' for the entire expression, and 'function' for individual elementary functions. Our approach works in the following steps.

Step 1 We re-use Daisy's frontend which parses the input specification. We add a pre-processing step, which decomposes the abstract syntax tree (AST) of the program we want to approximate such that each elementary function call is assigned to a fresh local variable. This transformation eases the later replacement of the elementary functions with an approximation.

Step 2 We use Daisy's roundoff error analysis on the entire program, assuming a `libm` implementation of elementary functions. This analysis computes a real-valued range and a worst-case absolute roundoff error bound for each subexpression in the AST, assuming uniform single or double precision as appropriate. We use this information in the next step to distribute the error and to determine the parameters for Metalibm for each function call.

Step 3 This is the core step, which calls Metalibm to generate a (piecewise) polynomial approximation for each elementary function which was assigned to a local variable. Each call to Metalibm specifies the local target error for each function call, the polynomial degree and the domain of the function call arguments. To determine the argument domains, we use the range and error information obtained in the previous step. Our tool tries different polynomial degrees and selects the fastest implementation. We explain our error distribution and polynomial selection further below.

Metalibm generates efficient double-precision C code including argument reduction (if applicable), domain splitting, and polynomial approximation with a guaranteed error below the specified target error (or returns an error). Metalibm furthermore supports approximations with lookup tables, whose size the user can control manually via our tool frontend as well.

[2] All existing approaches for analysing floating-point roundoff errors which handle loops or conditional branches, reduce the reasoning about errors to straight-line code, e.g. through loop invariants [9,14] or loop unrolling [7], or path-wise analysis [7,9,15].

Step 4 Our tool performs roundoff error analysis again, this time taking into account the new approximations' precise error bounds reported by Metalibm. Finally, Daisy generates C code for the program itself, as well as all necessary headers to link with the approximation generated by Metalibm.

Error Distribution. In order to call Metalibm, Daisy needs to determine the target error for each `libm` call. Recall that the user of our tool only specifies the *total* error at the end of the program. Hence, distributing the total error budget among arithmetic operations and (potentially several) elementary function calls is a crucial step. Consider again our running example which has two elementary function calls. Our tool distributes the error budget as follows:

$$|f(x) - \tilde{f}(\tilde{x})| \leq |f(x) - \hat{f}_1(x)| + |\hat{f}_1(x) - \hat{f}_2(x)| + |\hat{f}_2(x) - \tilde{f}(\tilde{x})|$$

where we denote by f the real-valued specification of the program; $\hat{f}_1$ and $\hat{f}_2$ have one and two elementary function calls approximated, respectively, and arithmetic is considered exact; and $\tilde{f}$ is the final finite-precision implementation.

Daisy first determines the budget for the finite-precision roundoff error ($|\hat{f}_2(x) - \tilde{f}(\tilde{x})|$) and then distributes the remaining part among `libm` calls. At this point, Daisy cannot compute $|\hat{f}_2(x) - \tilde{f}(\tilde{x})|$ exactly, as the approximations are not available yet. Instead, it assumes `libm`-based approximations as baseline.

Then, Daisy distributes the remaining error budget either equally among the elementary function calls, or by taking into account that the approximation errors are propagated differently through the program. This error propagation is estimated by computing the derivative w.r.t. to each elementary function call (which gives an estimation of the conditional number). Daisy computes partial derivatives symbolically and maximizes them over the specified input domain.

Finally, we obtain an error budget for each `libm` call, representing the total error due to the elementary function call *at the end of the program.* For calling Metalibm, however, we need the *local* error at the function call site. Due to error propagation, these two errors can differ significantly, and may lead to overall errors which exceed the error bound specified by the user. We estimate the error propagation using a linear approximation based on derivatives, and use this estimate to compute a *local* target error from the total error budget.

Since Metalibm usually generates approximations with slightly tighter error bounds than asked for, our tool performs a second roundoff analysis (step 4), where all errors (smaller or larger) are correctly taken into account.

Polynomial Degree Selection. The polynomial degree significantly and in a discrete way influences the efficiency of approximations, so that optimal prediction is infeasible. Hence, our tool performs a linear search, using the (coarse) estimated running time reported by Metalibm (obtained with a few benchmarking runs) to select the approximation with the smallest estimated running time. The search stops either when the estimated running time is significantly higher than the current best, or when Metalibm times out.

We do not automatically exploit other Metalibm's parameters, such as minimum subdomain width for splitting, since they give fine-grained control that is not suitable for *general* automatic implementations.

3 Experimental Evaluation

We evaluate our approach in terms of accuracy and performance on benchmarks from literature [9,19,28] which include elementary function calls, and extend them with the examples rodriguesRotation[3] and ex2* and ex3_d, which are problems from a graduate analysis textbook. While they are relatively short, they represent important kernels usually employing several elementary function calls[4]. We base target error bounds on roundoff errors of a `libm` implementation: middle and large errors, each of which is roughly three and four orders of magnitudes larger than the `libm`-based bound, respectively. By default, we assume double 64 bit precision.

Our tool provides an automatic generation of benchmarking code for each input program. Each benchmarking executable runs the Daisy-generated code on 10^7 random inputs from the input domain and measures performance in the number of processor clock cycles. Of the measured number of cycles we discard the highest 10%, as we have observed these to be outliers.

Experimental Results. By default, we approximate individual elementary function calls separately, use equal error distribution and allow table-based approximations with an 8-bit table index. For large errors we also measure performance for: (i) default settings but with the derivative-based errors distribution; (ii) default settings but without table usage; (iii) default settings but with compound calls with depth 1 and depth ∞ (approximation 'as much as possible').

Table 1 shows the performance improvements of approximated code w.r.t. `libm` based implementations of our benchmarks. We compare against `libm` only, as no approximation or synthesis tool provides error guarantees. By removing `libm` calls in initial programs we roughly estimate the elementary function overhead (second column) and give an idea for the margin of improvement. Figure 1 illustrates the overall improvement that we obtain for each benchmark (the height of the bars) and the relative distribution of the running time between arithmetic (blue) and elementary functions (green), for large errors with default settings but approximate compound calls with depth $= \infty$.

Our tool generates code with significant performance improvements for most functions and often reduces the time spent for the evaluation of elementary functions by a factor of two. As expected, the improvements are overall better for larger errors and vary on average from 10.7% to 13.8% for individual calls depending on the settings, and reach 17.1% on average when approximating compound calls as much as possible. However, increasing the program target error (for equal error distributions Metalibm target error increases linearly with it) does not necessarily lead to better performance, e.g. in case of axisRotationY and rodriguesRotation. This is the result of discrete decisions concerning the approximation degrees and the domain splittings inside Metalibm.

---

[3] https://en.wikipedia.org/wiki/Rodrigues27_rotation_formula.

[4] Experiments are performed on a Debian Linux 9 Desktop machine with a 3.3 GHz Intel i5 processor and 16 GB of RAM. All code for benchmarking is compiled with GNUs g++, version 6.3.0, with the `-O2` flag.

Table 1. Performance improvements (in percent) of approximated code w.r.t. a program with `libm` library function calls.

precision	double							single
	elem. func. overhead	middle	large errors					middle
benchmark		equal	equal	deriv	no table	depth 1	depth ∞	equal
sinxx10	20.8	7.6	7.7	7.7	7.7	7.6	7.7	4.7
xu1	49.3	13.9	25.8	18.0	26.6	25.7	27.3	8.1
xu2	53.6	4.6	12.4	13.0	12.6	12.5	26.0	-1.4
integrate18257	52.8	15.2	19.4	15.1	-4.5	22.4	31.7	2.1
integStoutemyer	42.1	-1.0	6.5	1.4	0.4	4.8	21.9	6.4
axisRotationX	38.0	17.2	17.3	18.1	17.4	17.6	17.3	-10.5
axisRotationY	37.9	17.6	12.8	21.5	12.9	12.8	12.8	-14.1
rodriguesRotation	28.9	14.9	11.6	13.6	13.8	13.8	13.9	-7.6
pendulum1	24.4	-4.6	-2.9	-4.3	-4.2	11.0	11.7	-9.7
pendulum2	50.3	9.6	11.4	6.2	-0.8	20.2	20.5	-0.5
forwardk2jX	43.7	15.1	15.4	15.5	15.0	15.0	15.0	-10.2
forwardk2jY	40.7	10.7	15.6	15.6	15.6	15.6	15.6	7.4
ex2_1	34.6	12.8	12.8	12.3	12.3	12.3	12.1	8.4
ex2_2	34.9	5.9	14.8	15.4	15.1	15.0	15.3	3.6
ex2_3	42.1	23.5	24.5	24.5	24.1	24.8	24.3	3.9
ex2_4	31.8	11.9	12.5	12.5	12.6	14.3	14.3	7.9
ex2_5	40.6	22.5	24.4	24.5	24.4	24.4	24.3	10.2
ex2_9	35.0	7.2	7.1	7.4	7.2	7.0	9.4	-10.1
ex2_10	41.5	20.6	21.7	8.9	20.5	21.3	21.4	8.3
ex2_11	30.9	-6.8	-2.3	-4.9	-2.4	-4.8	-2.8	17.9
ex3_d	39.3	10.3	20.9	19.9	-1.1	19.9	20.3	4.9
average	38.7	10.9	13.8	12.5	10.7	14.9	17.1	1.4

Somewhat surprisingly, we did not observe an advantage of using the derivative-based error distribution over the equal one. We suspect that is due to the nonlinear nature of Metalibm's heuristics.

Table 1 further demonstrates that usage of tables generally improves the performance. However, the influence of increasing the table size must be studied on a case-by-case basis since large tables might lead to memory-bound computations.

We observe that it is generally beneficial to approximate 'as much as possible'. Indeed, the power of Metalibm lies in generating (piece-wise) polynomial approximations of compound expressions, whose behavior might be much simpler to evaluate than its individual subexpressions.

Finally, we also considered an implementation where all data and arithmetic operations are in single precision apart from the double-precision Metalibm-generated code (whose output is accurate only to single precision). We observe that slight performance improvements are possible, i.e. Metalibm can compete even with single-precision libm-based code, but to achieve performance improvements comparable to those of double-precision code, we need a single-precision code generation from Metalibm.

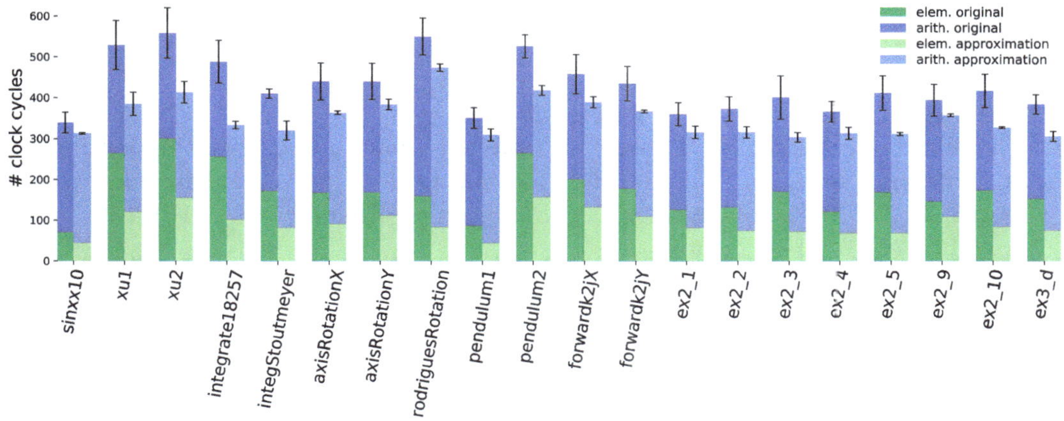

Fig. 1. Average performance and standard deviation. For each benchmark, the first bar shows the running time of the libm-based implementation and the second one of our implementation. Even relatively small overall time improvements are significant w.r.t. the time portion we can optimize (in green). Our implementations also have significantly smaller standard deviation (black bars). (Color figure online)

Analysis Time. Analysis time is highly dependent on the number of required approximations of elementary functions: each approximation requires a separate call to Metalibm whose running time in turn depends on the problem definition. Daisy reduces the number of calls to Metalibm by common expression elimination which improves the analysis time. Currently, we set the timeout for each Metalibm call to 3 min, which leads to an overall analysis time which is reasonable. Overall, our tool takes between 15 s and 20 min to approximate whole programs, with the average running time being 4 min 40 s per program.

4 Conclusion

We presented a fully automated approach which improves the performance of small numerical kernels at the expense of some accuracy by generating custom approximations of elementary functions. Our tool is parametrized by a user-given whole-program absolute error bound which is guaranteed to be satisfied by the generated code. Experiments illustrate that the tool efficiently uses the available margin for improvement and provides significant speedups for double-precision implementations. This work provides a solid foundation for future research in the areas of automatic approximations of single-precision and multivariate functions.

Acknowledgments. The authors thank Christoph Lauter for useful discussions and Youcef Merah for the work on an early prototype.

References

1. Bornholt, J., Torlak, E., Grossman, D., Ceze, L.: Optimizing synthesis with metasketches. In: POPL (2016)

2. Brisebarre, N., Chevillard, S.: Efficient polynomial L-approximations. In: ARITH (2007)
3. Brunie, N., de Dinechin, F., Kupriianova, O., Lauter, C.: Code generators for mathematical functions. In: ARITH (2015)
4. Chevillard, S., Joldeş, M., Lauter, C.: Sollya: an environment for the development of numerical codes. In: Fukuda, K., Hoeven, J., Joswig, M., Takayama, N. (eds.) ICMS 2010. LNCS, vol. 6327, pp. 28–31. Springer, Heidelberg (2010). https://doi.org/10.1007/978-3-642-15582-6_5
5. Chiang, W.F., Baranowski, M., Briggs, I., Solovyev, A., Gopalakrishnan, G., Rakamarić, Z.: Rigorous floating-point mixed-precision tuning. In: POPL (2017)
6. Damouche, N., Martel, M.: Mixed precision tuning with salsa. In: PECCS, pp. 185–194. SciTePress (2018)
7. Damouche, N., Martel, M., Chapoutot, A.: Improving the numerical accuracy of programs by automatic transformation. Int. J. Softw. Tools Technol. Transfer **19**(4), 427–448 (2017)
8. Darulova, E., Izycheva, A., Nasir, F., Ritter, F., Becker, H., Bastian, R.: Daisy - framework for analysis and optimization of numerical programs (tool paper). In: Beyer, D., Huisman, M. (eds.) TACAS 2018. LNCS, vol. 10805, pp. 270–287. Springer, Cham (2018). https://doi.org/10.1007/978-3-319-89960-2_15
9. Darulova, E., Kuncak, V.: Towards a compiler for reals. ACM TOPLAS **39**(2), 8 (2017)
10. Darulova, E., Sharma, S., Horn, E.: Sound mixed-precision optimization with rewriting. In: ICCPS (2018)
11. De Dinechin, F., Lauter, C.Q., Melquiond, G.: Assisted verification of elementary functions using Gappa. In: ACM Symposium on Applied Computing (2006)
12. de Dinechin, F., Lauter, C., Melquiond, G.: Certifying the floating-point implementation of an elementary function using Gappa. IEEE Trans. Comput. **60**(2), 242–253 (2011)
13. Esmaeilzadeh, H., Sampson, A., Ceze, L., Burger, D.: Neural acceleration for general-purpose approximate programs. In: IEEE/ACM International Symposium on Microarchitecture (2012)
14. Goubault, E., Putot, S.: Static analysis of finite precision computations. In: Jhala, R., Schmidt, D. (eds.) VMCAI 2011. LNCS, vol. 6538, pp. 232–247. Springer, Heidelberg (2011). https://doi.org/10.1007/978-3-642-18275-4_17
15. Goubault, E., Putot, S.: Robustness analysis of finite precision implementations. In: Shan, C. (ed.) APLAS 2013. LNCS, vol. 8301, pp. 50–57. Springer, Cham (2013). https://doi.org/10.1007/978-3-319-03542-0_4
16. Lam, M.O., Hollingsworth, J.K., de Supinski, B.R., Legendre, M.P.: Automatically adapting programs for mixed-precision floating-point computation. In: ICS (2013)
17. Lee, W., Sharma, R., Aiken, A.: On automatically proving the correctness of math.h implementations. In: POPL (2018)
18. Magron, V., Constantinides, G., Donaldson, A.: Certified roundoff error bounds using semidefinite programming. ACM Trans. Math. Softw. **43**(4), 34 (2017)
19. Merlet, J.P.: The COPRIN examples page. http://www-sop.inria.fr/coprin/logiciels/ALIAS/Benches/
20. Moscato, M., Titolo, L., Dutle, A., Muñoz, C.A.: Automatic estimation of verified floating-point round-off errors via static analysis. In: Tonetta, S., Schoitsch, E., Bitsch, F. (eds.) SAFECOMP 2017. LNCS, vol. 10488, pp. 213–229. Springer, Cham (2017). https://doi.org/10.1007/978-3-319-66266-4_14
21. Muller, J.M.: Elementary Functions - Algorithms and Implementation, 3rd edn. Birkhäuser, Basel (2016)

22. Panchekha, P., Sanchez-Stern, A., Wilcox, J.R., Tatlock, Z.: Automatically improving accuracy for floating point expressions. In: PLDI (2015)
23. Püschel, M., et al.: Spiral - a generator for platform-adapted libraries of signal processing alogorithms. IJHPCA **18**(1), 21–45 (2004)
24. Rubio-González, C., et al.: Precimonious: tuning assistant for floating-point precision. In: SC (2013)
25. Schkufza, E., Sharma, R., Aiken, A.: Stochastic optimization of floating-point programs with tunable precision. In: PLDI (2014)
26. Solovyev, A., Jacobsen, C., Rakamarić, Z., Gopalakrishnan, G.: Rigorous estimation of floating-point round-off errors with Symbolic Taylor Expansions. In: Bjørner, N., de Boer, F. (eds.) FM 2015. LNCS, vol. 9109, pp. 532–550. Springer, Cham (2015). https://doi.org/10.1007/978-3-319-19249-9_33
27. Vuduc, R., Demmel, J.W., Bilmes, J.A.: Statistical models for empirical search-based performance tuning. Int. J. High Perform. Comput. Appl. **18**(1), 65–94 (2004)
28. Yazdanbakhsh, A., Mahajan, D., Esmaeilzadeh, H., Lotfi-Kamran, P.: AxBench: a multiplatform benchmark suite for approximate computing. IEEE Des. Test **34**(2), 60–68 (2017)

Verification

Formal Verification of Quantum Algorithms Using Quantum Hoare Logic

Junyi Liu[1,2], Bohua Zhan[1,2(✉)], Shuling Wang[1(✉)], Shenggang Ying[1], Tao Liu[1], Yangjia Li[1], Mingsheng Ying[1,3,4], and Naijun Zhan[1,2]

[1] State Key Laboratory of Computer Science, Institute of Software, Chinese Academy of Sciences, Beijing, China
{liujy,bzhan,wangsl,yingsg,liut,yangjia,znj}@ios.ac.cn
[2] University of Chinese Academy of Sciences, Beijing, China
[3] University of Technology Sydney, Sydney, Australia
[4] Tsinghua University, Beijing, China

Abstract. We formalize the theory of quantum Hoare logic (QHL) [TOPLAS 33(6),19], an extension of Hoare logic for reasoning about quantum programs. In particular, we formalize the syntax and semantics of quantum programs in Isabelle/HOL, write down the rules of quantum Hoare logic, and verify the soundness and completeness of the deduction system for partial correctness of quantum programs. As preliminary work, we formalize some necessary mathematical background in linear algebra, and define tensor products of vectors and matrices on quantum variables. As an application, we verify the correctness of Grover's search algorithm. To our best knowledge, this is the first time a Hoare logic for quantum programs is formalized in an interactive theorem prover, and used to verify the correctness of a nontrivial quantum algorithm.

1 Introduction

Due to the rapid progress of quantum technology in the recent years, it is predicted that practical quantum computers can be built within 10–15 years. Especially during the last 3 years, breakthroughs have been made in quantum hardware. Programmable superconductor quantum computers and trapped ion quantum computers have been built in universities and companies [1,3,4,6,23].

In another direction, intensive research on quantum programming has been conducted in the last decade [16,45,51,53], as surveyed in [27,52]. In particular, several quantum programming languages have been defined and their compilers have been implemented, including Quipper [31], Scaffold [35], QWire [47], Microsoft's LIQUi$|\rangle$ [25] and Q# [57], IBM's OpenQASM [22], Google's Cirq [30], ProjectQ [56], Chisel-Q [40], Quil [55] and $Q\,|SI\rangle$ [39]. These research allow quantum programs to first run on an ideal simulator for testing, and then on physical devices [5]. For instance, many small quantum algorithms and protocols have already been programmed and run on IBM's simulators and quantum computers [1,2].

I. Dillig and S. Tasiran (Eds.): CAV 2019, LNCS 11562, pp. 187–207, 2019.
https://doi.org/10.1007/978-3-030-25543-5_12

Clearly, simulators can only be used for testing. It shows the correctness of the program on one or a few inputs, not its correctness under all possible inputs. Various theories and tools have been developed to formally reason about quantum programs for all inputs on a fixed number of qubits. Equivalence checking [7,8], termination analysis [38], reachability analysis [64], and invariant generation [62] can be used to verify the correctness or termination of quantum programs. Unfortunately, the size of quantum programs on which these tools are applicable is quite limited. This is because all of these tools still perform calculations over the entire state space, which for quantum algorithms has size exponential in the number of qubits. For instance, even on the best supercomputers today, simulation of a quantum program is restricted to about 50–60 qubits. Most model-checking algorithms, which need to perform calculations on operators over the state space, are restricted to 25–30 qubits with the current computing resources.

Deductive program verification presents a way to solve this state space explosion problem. In deductive verification, we do not attempt to execute the program or explore its state space. Rather, we define the semantics of the program using precise mathematical language, and use mathematical reasoning to prove the correctness of the program. These proofs are checked on a computer (for example, in proof assistants such as Coq [15] or Isabelle [44]) to ensure a very high level of confidence.

To apply deductive reasoning to quantum programs, it is necessary to first define a precise semantics and proof system. There has already been a lot of work along these lines [9,20,21,61]. A recent result in this direction is *quantum Hoare logic* (QHL) [61]. It extends to sequential quantum programs the Floyd-Hoare-Naur inductive assertion method for reasoning about correctness of classical programs. QHL is proved to be (relatively) complete for both partial correctness and total correctness of quantum programs.

In this paper, we formalize the theory of quantum Hoare logic in Isabelle/HOL, and use it to verify a non-trivial quantum algorithm – Grover's search algorithm[1]. In more detail, the contributions of this paper are as follows.

1. We formally prove the main results of quantum Hoare logic in Isabelle/HOL. That is, we write down the syntax and semantics of quantum programs, specify the basic Hoare triples, and prove the soundness and completeness of the resulting deduction system (for partial correctness of quantum programs). To our best knowledge, this is the first formalization of a Hoare logic for quantum programs in an interactive theorem prover.
2. As an application of the above formalization, we verify the correctness of Grover's search algorithm. In particular, we prove that the algorithm always succeeds on the (infinite) class of inputs where the expected probability of success is 1.
3. As preparation for the above, we extend Isabelle/HOL's library for linear algebra. Based on existing work [13,58], we formalize many further results in linear algebra for complex matrices, in particular positivity and the Löwner

[1] Available online at https://www.isa-afp.org/entries/QHLProver.html.

order. Another significant part of our work is to define the tensor product of vectors and matrices, in a way that can be used to extend and combine operations on quantum variables in a consistent way. Finally, we implement algorithms to automatically prove identities in linear algebra to ease the formalization process.

The organization of the rest of the paper is as follows. Section 2 gives a brief introduction to quantum Hoare logic. Section 3 describes in detail our formalization of QHL in Isabelle/HOL. Section 4 describes the application to Grover's algorithm. Section 5 discusses automation techniques, and gives some idea about the cost of the formalization. Section 6 reviews some related work. Finally, we conclude in Sect. 7 with a discussion of future directions of work.

We expect theorem proving techniques will play a crucial role in formal reasoning about quantum computing, as they did for classical computing, and we hope this paper will be one of the first steps in its development.

2 Quantum Hoare Logic

In this section, we briefly recall the basic concepts and results of quantum Hoare logic (QHL). We only introduce the proof system for partial correctness, since the one for total correctness is not formalized in our work. In addition, we make two simplifications compared to the original work: we consider only variables with finite dimension, and we remove the initialization operation. The complete version of QHL can be found in [61].

In QHL, the number of quantum variables is pre-set before each run of the program. Each quantum variable q_i has dimension d_i. The (pure) state of the quantum variable takes value in a complex vector space of dimension d_i. The overall (pure) state takes value in the tensor product of the vector spaces for the variables, which has dimension $d = \prod d_i$. The mixed state for variable q_i (resp. overall) is given by a $d_i \times d_i$ (resp. $d \times d$) matrix satisfying certain conditions (making them *partial density operators*). The notation $\overline{q}$ is used to denote some finite sequence of distinct quantum variables (called a *quantum register*). We denote the vector space corresponding to $\overline{q}$ by $\mathcal{H}_{\overline{q}}$.

The syntax of quantum programs is given by the following grammar:

$$S ::= \textbf{skip} \mid \overline{q} := U\overline{q} \mid S_1; S_2 \mid \textbf{measure}\ M[\overline{q}] : \overline{S} \mid \textbf{while}\ M[\overline{q}] = 1\ \textbf{do}\ S$$

where

- In $\overline{q} := U\overline{q}$, U is a unitary operator on $\mathcal{H}_{\overline{q}}$, i.e., $U^\dagger U = UU^\dagger = \mathbb{I}$, where $U^\dagger$ is the conjugate transpose of U.
- In **measure** $M[\overline{q}] : \overline{S}$, $M = \{M_m\}$ is a quantum measurement on $\mathcal{H}_{\overline{q}}$, and $\overline{S} = \{S_m\}$ gives quantum programs that will be executed after each possible outcome of the measurement;
- In **while** $M[\overline{q}] = 1$ **do** S, $M = \{M_0, M_1\}$ is a yes-no measurement on $\overline{q}$.

Quantum programs can be regarded as quantum extensions of classical **while** programs. The **skip** statement does nothing, which is the same as in the classical case. The unitary transformation changes the state of $\overline{q}$ according to U. It is the counterpart to the assignment operation in classical programming languages. The sequential composition is similar to its classical counterpart. The measurement statement is the quantum generalisation of the classical case statement **if** $(\Box m \cdot b_m \rightarrow S_m)$ **fi**. The loop statement is a quantum generalisation of the classical loop **while** b **do** S.

(Skip)	$\{P\}\ \mathbf{skip}\ \{P\}$
(UT)	$\{U^\dagger P U\}\ \overline{q} := U\overline{q}\ \{P\}$
(Seq)	$\dfrac{\{P\}\ S_1\ \{Q\} \qquad \{Q\}\ S_2\ \{R\}}{\{P\}\ S_1; S_2\ \{R\}}$
(Mea)	$\dfrac{\{P_m\}\ S_m\ \{Q\} \text{ for all } m}{\{\sum_m {M_m}^\dagger P_m M_m\}\ \mathbf{measure}\ M[\overline{q}] : \overline{S}\ \{Q\}}$
(Loop)	$\dfrac{\{Q\}\ S\ \{M_0^\dagger P M_0 + M_1^\dagger Q M_1\}}{\{M_0^\dagger P M_0 + M_1^\dagger Q M_1\}\ \mathbf{while}\ M[\overline{q}] = 1\ \mathbf{do}\ S\ \{P\}}$
(Order)	$\dfrac{P \sqsubseteq P' \quad \{P'\}\ S\ \{Q'\} \quad Q' \sqsubseteq Q}{\{P\}\ S\ \{Q\}}$

Fig. 1. Proof system *qPD* for partial correctness

Formally, the denotational semantics for quantum programs is defined as a super-operator $[\![S]\!](\cdot)$, assigning to each quantum program S a mapping between partial density operators. As usual, the denotational semantics is defined by induction on the structure of the quantum program:

1. $[\![\mathbf{skip}]\!](\rho) = \rho$.
2. $[\![\overline{q} := U\overline{q}]\!](\rho) = U\rho U^\dagger$.
3. $[\![S_1; S_2]\!](\rho) = [\![S_2]\!]([\![S_1]\!](\rho))$.
4. $[\![(\mathbf{measure}\ M[\overline{q}] : \overline{S})]\!](\rho) = \sum_m [\![S_m]\!](M_m \rho M_m^\dagger)$.
5. $[\![(\mathbf{while}\ M[\overline{q}] = 1\ \mathbf{do}\ S)]\!](\rho) = \bigvee_{n=0}^{\infty} [\![(\mathbf{while}\ M[\overline{q}] = 1\ \mathbf{do}\ S)^n]\!](\rho)$, where $\bigvee$ stands for the least upper bound of partial density operators according to the Löwner partial order $\sqsubseteq$.

The correctness of a quantum program S is expressed by a quantum extension of the Hoare triple $\{P\}S\{Q\}$, where the precondition P and the postcondition Q are matrices satisfying certain conditions for *quantum predicates* [24]. The semantics for partial correctness is defined as follows:

$$\models_{par} \{P\}S\{Q\} \text{ iff } \mathrm{tr}(P\rho) \leq \mathrm{tr}(Q[\![S]\!](\rho)) + \mathrm{tr}(\rho) - \mathrm{tr}([\![S]\!](\rho))$$

for all partial density operators ρ. Here tr is the trace of a matrix. The semantics for total correctness is defined similarly:

$$\models_{tot} \{P\}S\{Q\} \text{ iff } \operatorname{tr}(P\rho) \le \operatorname{tr}(Q[\![S]\!](\rho)).$$

We note that they become the same when the quantum program S is terminating, i.e. $\operatorname{tr}([\![S]\!](\rho)) = \operatorname{tr}(\rho)$ for all partial density operators ρ.

The proof system *qPD* for partial correctness of quantum programs is given in Fig. 1. The soundness and (relative) completeness of *qPD* is proved in [61]:

Theorem 1. *The proof system qPD is sound and (relative) complete for partial correctness of quantum programs.*

3 Formalization in Isabelle/HOL

In this section, we describe the formalization of quantum Hoare logic in Isabelle/HOL. Isabelle/HOL [44] is an interactive theorem prover based on higher-order logic. It provides a flexible language in which one can state and prove theorems in all areas of mathematics and computer science. The proofs are checked by the Isabelle kernel according to the rules of higher-order logic, providing a very high level of confidence in the proofs. A standard application of Isabelle/HOL is the formalization of program semantics and Hoare logic. See [43] for a description of the general technique, applied to a very simple classical programming language.

3.1 Preliminaries in Linear Algebra

Our work is based on the linear algebra library developed by Thiemann and Yamada in the AFP entry [58]. We also use some results on the construction of tensor products in another AFP entry by Bentkamp [13].

In these libraries, the type *'a vec* of vectors with entries in type *'a* is defined as pairs (n, f), where n is a natural number, and f is a function from natural numbers to *'a*, such that $f(i)$ is undefined when $i \ge n$. Likewise, the type *'a mat* of matrices is defined as triples (nr, nc, f), where nr and nc are natural numbers, and f is a function from pairs of natural numbers to *'a*, such that $f(i, j)$ is undefined when $i \ge nr$ or $j \ge nc$. The terms *carrier_vec n* (resp. *carrier_mat m n*) represent the set of vectors of length n (resp. matrices of dimension $m \times n$). In our work, we focus almost exclusively on the case where *'a* is the complex numbers. For this case, existing libraries already define concepts such as the adjoint of a matrix, and the (complex) inner product between two vectors. We further define concepts such as Hermitian and unitary matrices, and prove their basic properties.

A key result in linear algebra that is necessary for our work is the Schur decomposition theorem. It states that any complex $n \times n$ matrix A can be written in the form QUQ^{-1}, where Q is unitary and U is upper triangular. In particular, if A is normal (that is, if $AA^\dagger = A^\dagger A$), then A is diagonalizable. A version of the Schur decomposition theorem is formalized in [58], showing that any matrix is similar to an upper-triangular matrix U. However, it does not show that Q can be made unitary. We complete the proof of the full theorem, following the outline of the previous proof.

Next, we define the key concept of positive semi-definite matrices (called positive matrices from now on for simplicity). An $n \times n$ matrix A is positive if $v^\dagger A v \geq 0$ for any vector v. We formalize the basic theory of positive matrices, in particular showing that any positive matrix is Hermitian.

Density operators and partial density operators are then defined as follows:

definition $\mathit{density\_operator}\ A \longleftrightarrow \mathit{positive}\ A \wedge \mathit{trace}\ A = 1$
definition $\mathit{partial\_density\_operator}\ A \longleftrightarrow \mathit{positive}\ A \wedge \mathit{trace}\ A \leq 1$

Next, the Löwner partial order is defined as a partial order on the type *complex mat* as follows:

definition *lowner_le* (**infix** $\leq_L$ *65*) **where**
$A \leq_L B \longleftrightarrow \mathit{dim\_row}\ A = \mathit{dim\_row}\ B \wedge \mathit{dim\_col}\ A = \mathit{dim\_col}\ B \wedge \mathit{positive}\ (B - A)$

A key result that we formalize states that under the Löwner partial order, any non-decreasing sequence of partial density operators has a least upper bound, which is the pointwise limit of the operators when written as $n \times n$ matrices. This is used to define the infinite sum of matrices, necessary for the semantics of the while loop.

3.2 Syntax and Semantics of Quantum Programs

We now begin with the definition of syntax and semantics of quantum programs. First, we describe how to model states of a quantum program. Recall that each quantum program operates on a fixed set of quantum variables q_i, where each q_i has dimension d_i. These information can be recorded in a locale [33] as follows:

locale *state_sig* =
  fixes *dims* :: *nat list*

The total dimension d is given by (here *prod_list* denotes the product of a list of natural numbers).

definition $d = \mathit{prod\_list}\ \mathit{dims}$

The (mixed) state of the system is given by a partial density operator with dimension $d \times d$. Hence, we declare

type_synonym *state* = *complex mat*

definition *density_states* :: *state set* **where**
$\mathit{density\_states} = \{\rho \in \mathit{carrier\_mat}\ d\ d.\ \mathit{partial\_density\_operator}\ \rho\}$

Next, we define the concept of quantum programs. They are declared as an inductively-defined datatype in Isabelle/HOL, following the grammar given in Sect. 2.

datatype *com* =
  SKIP
| *Utrans (complex mat)*
| *Seq com com (_;;/ _ [60, 61] 60)*
| *Measure nat (nat ⇒ complex mat) (com list)*
| *While (nat ⇒ complex mat) com*

At this stage, we assume that all matrices involved operate on the global state (that is, all of the quantum variables). We will define commands that operate on a subset of quantum variables later. Measurement is defined over any finite number of matrices. Here *Measure n f C* is a measurement with n options, $f\ i$ for $i < n$ are the measurement matrices, and $C!\ i$ is the command to be executed when the measurement yields result i. Likewise, the first argument to *While* gives measurement matrices, where only the first two values are used.

Next, we define well-formedness and denotation of quantum programs. The predicate *well_com :: com ⇒ bool* expresses the well-formedness condition. For a quantum program to be well-formed, all matrices involved should have the right dimension, the argument to *Utrans* should be unitary, and the measurements for *Measure* and *While* should satisfy the condition $\sum_i M_i^\dagger M_i = \mathbb{I}_n$. Denotation is written as *denote :: com ⇒ state ⇒ state*, defined as in Sect. 2. Both *well_com* and *denote* is defined by induction over the structure of the program. The details are omitted here.

3.3 Hoare Triples

In this section, we define the concept of Hoare triples, and state what needs to be proved for soundness and completeness of the deduction system. First, the concept of quantum predicates is defined as follows:

definition *is_quantum_predicate P* $\longleftrightarrow$ *P* ∈ *carrier_mat d d* ∧ *positive P* ∧ $P \leq_L 1_m\ d$

With this, we can give the semantic definition of Hoare triples for partial and total correctness. These definitions are intended for the case where P and Q are quantum predicates, and S is a well-formed program. They define what Hoare triples are *valid*.

definition *hoare_total_correct* ($\models_t$ *{(1_)}/ (_)/ {(1_)} 50)* **where**
  $\models_t$ *{P} S {Q}* $\longleftrightarrow$ *(∀ρ∈density_states. trace (P * ρ) ≤ trace (Q * denote S ρ))*

definition *hoare_partial_correct* ($\models_p$ *{(1_)}/ (_)/ {(1_)} 50)* **where**
  $\models_p$ *{P} S {Q}* $\longleftrightarrow$ *(∀ρ∈density_states.*
    *trace (P * ρ) ≤ trace (Q * denote S ρ) + (trace ρ − trace (denote S ρ)))*

Next, we define what Hoare triples are *provable* in the *qPD* system. A Hoare triple for partial correctness is provable (written as $\vdash_p \{P\}\ S\ \{Q\}$) if it can be derived by combining the rules in Fig. 1. This condition can be defined in Isabelle/HOL as an inductive predicate. The definition largely parallels the formulae shown in the figure.

With these definitions, we can state and prove soundness and completeness of the Hoare rules for partial correctness. Note that the statement for completeness is very simple, seemingly without needing to state "relative to the theory of the field of complex numbers". This is because we are taking a shallow embedding for predicates, hence any valid statement on complex numbers, in particular positivity of matrices, is in principle available for use in the deduction system (for example, in the assumption to the **order** rule).

theorem *hoare_partial_sound:*
$\vdash_p \{P\}\ S\ \{Q\} \implies \mathit{well\_com}\ S \implies \models_p \{P\}\ S\ \{Q\}$

theorem *hoare_partial_complete:*
$\models_p \{P\}\ S\ \{Q\} \implies \mathit{well\_com}\ S \implies$
$\mathit{is\_quantum\_predicate}\ P \implies \mathit{is\_quantum\_predicate}\ Q \implies \vdash_p \{P\}\ S\ \{Q\}$

The soundness of the Hoare rules is proved by induction on the predicate $\vdash_p$, showing that each rule is sound with respect to $\models_p$. Completeness is proved using the concept of weakest-preconditions, following [61].

3.4 Partial States and Tensor Products

So far in our development, all quantum operations act on the entire global state. However, for the actual applications, we are more interested in operations that act on only a few of the quantum variables. For this, we need to define an *extension* operator, that takes a matrix on the quantum state for a subset of the variables, and extend it to a matrix on all of the variables. More generally, we need to define tensor products on vectors and matrices defined over disjoint sets of variables. These need to satisfy various consistency properties, in particular commutativity and associativity of the tensor product. Note that directly using the Kronecker product is not enough, as the matrix to be extended may act on any (possibly non-adjacent) subset of variables, and we need to distinguish between all possible cases.

Before presenting the definition, we first review some preliminaries. We make use of existing work in [13], in particular their encode and decode operations, and emulate their definitions of *matricize* and *dematricize* (used in [13] to convert between tensors represented as a list and matrices). Given a list of dimensions d_i, the encode and decode operations (named *digit_encode* and *digit_decode*) produce a correspondence between lists of indices a_i satisfying $a_i < d_i$ for each $i < n$, and a natural number less than $\prod_i d_i$. This works in a way similar to finding the binary representation of a number (in which case all "dimensions" are 2). List operation *nths* xs S constructs the subsequence of xs containing only the elements at indices in the set S.

The locale *partial_state* extends *state_sig*, adding *vars* for a subset of quantum variables. Our goal is to define the tensor product of two vectors or matrices over *vars* and its complement $-\mathit{vars}$, respectively.

```
locale partial_state = state_sig +
  fixes vars :: nat set
```

First, *dims1* and *dims2* are dimensions of variables *vars* and *-vars*:

```
definition dims1 = nths dims vars
definition dims2 = nths dims (−vars)
```

The operation *encode1* (resp. *encode2*) provides the map from the product of *dims* to the product of *dims1* (resp. *dims2*).

```
definition encode1 i = digit_decode dims1 (nths (digit_encode dims i) vars)
definition encode2 i = digit_decode dims2 (nths (digit_encode dims i) (−vars))
```

With this, tensor products on vectors and matrices are defined as follows (here d is the product of *dims*).

```
definition tensor_vec :: 'a vec ⇒ 'a vec ⇒ 'a vec where
  tensor_vec v1 v2 = Matrix.vec d (λi. v1 $ encode1 i * v2 $ encode2 i)
```

```
definition tensor_mat :: 'a mat ⇒ 'a mat ⇒ 'a mat where
  tensor_mat m1 m2 = Matrix.mat d d (λ(i,j).
      m1 $$ (encode1 i, encode1 j) * m2 $$ (encode2 i, encode2 j))
```

We prove the basic properties of *tensor_vec* and *tensor_mat*, including that they behave correctly with respect to identity, multiplication, adjoint, and trace.

Extension of matrices is a special case of the tensor product, where the matrix on *−vars* is the identity (here *d2* is the product of *dim2*).

```
definition mat_extension :: 'a mat ⇒ 'a mat where
  mat_extension m = tensor_mat m (1_m d2)
```

With *mat_extension*, we can define "partial" versions of quantum program commands *Utrans*, *Measure* and *While*. They take a set of variables $\overline{q}$ as an extra parameter, and all matrices involved act on the vector space associated to $\overline{q}$. These commands are named *Utrans_P*, *Measure_P* and *While_P*. They are usually used in place of the global commands in actual applications.

More generally, we can define the tensor product of vectors and matrices on any two subsets of quantum variables. For this, we define another locale:

```
locale partial_state2 = state_sig +
  fixes vars1 :: nat set and vars2 :: nat set
  assumes disjoint: vars1 ∩ vars2 = {}
```

To make use of *tensor_mat* to define tensor product in this more general setting, we need to find the relative position of variables *vars1* within *vars1* ∪ *vars2*. This is done using *ind_in_set*, which counts the position of x within A.

```
definition ind_in_set A x = card {i. i ∈ A ∧ i < x}
definition vars1' = (ind_in_set (vars1 ∪ vars2)) ` vars1
```

Finally, the more general tensor products are defined as follows (note since we are now outside the *partial_state* locale, we must use qualified names for *tensor_vec* and *tensor_mat*, and supply extra arguments for variables in the locale. Here *dims0* = *nths dims (vars1* ∪ *vars2)* is the total list of dimensions).

definition *ptensor_vec :: 'a vec ⇒ 'a vec ⇒ 'a vec* **where**
ptensor_vec v1 v2 = partial_state.tensor_vec dims0 vars1' v1 v2

definition *ptensor_mat :: 'a mat ⇒ 'a mat ⇒ 'a mat* **where**
ptensor_mat m1 m2 = partial_state.tensor_mat dims0 vars1' m1 m2

The partial extension *pmat_extension* is defined in a similar way as before.

definition *pmat_extension :: 'a mat ⇒ 'a mat* **where**
pmat_extension m = ptensor_mat m (1_{m} *d2)*

The definitions *ptensor_vec* and *ptensor_mat* satisfy several key consistency properties. In particular, they satisfy associativity of tensor product. For matrices, this is expressed as follows:

theorem *ptensor_mat_assoc:*
v1 ∩ v2 = {} ⟹
(v1 ∪ v2) ∩ v3 = {} ⟹
v1 ∪ v2 ∪ v3 ⊆ {0..<length dims} ⟹
ptensor_mat dims (v1 ∪ v2) v3 (ptensor_mat dims v1 v2 m1 m2) m3 =
ptensor_mat dims v1 (v2 ∪ v3) m1 (ptensor_mat dims v2 v3 m2 m3)

Together, these constructions and consistency properties provide a framework in which one can reason about arbitrary tensor product of vectors and matrices, defined on mutually disjoint sets of quantum variables.

3.5 Case Study: Products of Hadamard Matrices

In this section, we illustrate the above framework for tensor product of matrices with an application, to be used in the verification of Grover's algorithm in the next section.

In many quantum algorithms, we need to deal with the tensor product of an arbitrary number of Hadamard matrices. The Hadamard matrix (denoted *hadamard* in Isabelle) is given by:

$$H = \frac{1}{\sqrt{2}} \begin{bmatrix} 1 & 1 \\ 1 & -1 \end{bmatrix}$$

For example, in Grover's algorithm, we need to apply the Hadamard transform on each of the first n quantum variables, given by *vars1*. A single Hadamard transform on the i'th quantum variable, extended to a matrix acting on the first n quantum variables, is defined as follows:

```
definition hadamard_on_i :: nat ⇒ complex mat where
  hadamard_on_i i = pmat_extension dims {i} (vars1 − {i}) hadamard
```

The effect of consecutively applying the Hadamard transform on each of the first n quantum variables is equivalent to multiplying the quantum state by *exH_k (n − 1)*, where *exH_k* is defined as follows.

```
fun exH_k :: nat ⇒ complex mat where
  exH_k 0 = hadamard_on_i 0
| exH_k (Suc k) = exH_k k * hadamard_on_i (Suc k)
```

Crucially, this matrix product of extensions of Hadamard matrices must equal the tensor product of Hadamard matrices. That is, with *H_k* defined as

```
fun H_k :: nat ⇒ complex mat where
  H_k 0 = hadamard
| H_k (Suc k) = ptensor_mat dims {0..<Suc k} {Suc k} (H_k k) hadamard
```

we have the theorem

```
lemma exH_eq_H: exH_k (n − 1) = H_k (n − 1)
```

The proof of this result is by induction, requiring the use of associativity of tensor product stated above.

4 Verification of Grover's Algorithm

In this section, we describe our application of the above framework to the verification of Grover's quantum search algorithm [32]. Quantum search algorithms [18,32] concern searching an unordered database for an item satisfying some given property. This property is usually specified by an oracle. In a database of N items, where M items satisfy the property, finding an item with the property requires on average $O(N/M)$ calls to the oracle for classical computers. Grover's algorithm reduces this complexity to $O(\sqrt{N/M})$.

The basic idea of Grover's algorithm is rotation. The algorithm starts from an initial state/vector. At every step, it rotates towards the target state/vector for a small angle. As summarised in [18,19,42], it can be mathematically described by the following equation [42, Eq. (6.12)]:

$$G^k \left|\psi_0\right\rangle = \cos(\frac{2k+1}{2}\theta) \left|\alpha\right\rangle + \sin(\frac{2k+1}{2}\theta) \left|\beta\right\rangle ,$$

where G represents the operator at each step, $|\psi_0\rangle$ is the initial state, $\theta = 2 \arccos \sqrt{(N-M)/N}$, $|\alpha\rangle$ is the bad state (for items not satisfying the property), and $|\beta\rangle$ is the good state (for items satisfying the property). Thus when θ is very small, i.e., $M \ll N$, it costs $O(\sqrt{N/M})$ rounds to reach a target state.

Originally, Grover's algorithm only resolves the case $M = 1$ [32]. It is immediately generalized to the case of known M with the same idea and the case of unknown M with some modifications [18]. After that, the idea is generalized to all invertible quantum processes [19].

The paper [61] uses Grover's algorithm as the main example illustrating quantum Hoare logic. We largely follow its approach in this paper. See also [42, Chapter 6] for a general introduction.

First, we setup a locale for the inputs to the search problem.

```
locale grover_state =
  fixes n :: nat and f :: nat ⇒ bool
  assumes n: n > 1
   and dimM: card {i. i < (2::nat) ^ n ∧ f i} > 0
             card {i. i < (2::nat) ^ n ∧ f i} < (2::nat) ^ n
```

Here n is the number of qubits used to represent the items. That is, we assume $N = 2^n$ items in total. The oracle is represented by the function f, where only its values on inputs less than 2^n are used. The number of items satisfying the property is given by $M = card\ \{i.\ i < N \wedge f\ i\}$.

Next, we setup a locale for Grover's algorithm.

```
locale grover_state_sig = grover_state + state_sig +
  fixes R :: nat and K :: nat
  assumes dims_def: dims = replicate n 2 @ [K]
  assumes R: R = π / (2 * θ) − 1 / 2
  assumes K: K > R
```

As in [61], we assume $R = \pi/2\theta - 1/2$ is an integer. This implies that the quantum algorithm succeeds with probability 1. This condition holds, for example, for all N, M where $N = 4M$. Since we did not formalize quantum states with infinite dimension, we replace the loop counter, which is infinite dimensional in [61], with a variable of dimension $K > R$. We also remove the control variable for the oracle used in [61]. Overall, our quantum state consists of n variables of dimension 2 for representing the items, and one variable of dimension K for the loop counter.

We now present the quantum program to be verified. First, the operation that performs the Hadamard transform on each of the first n variables is defined by induction as follows.

```
fun hadamard_n :: nat ⇒ com where
  hadamard_n 0 = SKIP
| hadamard_n (Suc i) = hadamard_n i ;; Utrans (tensor_P (hadamard_on_i i) (1_m K))
```

Here *tensor_P* denotes the tensor product of a matrix on the first n variables (of dimension $2^n \times 2^n$) and a matrix on the loop variable (of dimension $K \times K$). Executing this program is equivalent to multiplying the quantum state corresponding to the first n variables by $H^{\otimes n}$, as shown in Sect. 3.5.

The body of the loop is given by:

```
definition D :: com where
  D = Utrans_P vars1 mat_O ;;
```

```
hadamard_n n ;;
Utrans_P vars1 mat_Ph ;;
hadamard_n n ;;
Utrans_P vars2 (mat_incr n)
```

where each of the three matrices *mat_O*, *mat_Ph* and *mat_incr* can be defined directly.

```
definition mat_O :: complex mat where
  mat_O = mat N N (λ(i,j). if i = j then (if f i then 1 else −1) else 0)
definition mat_Ph :: complex mat where
  mat_Ph = mat N N (λ(i,j). if i = j then if i = 0 then 1 else −1 else 0)
definition mat_incr :: nat ⇒ complex mat where
  mat_incr n = mat n n (λ(i,j). if i = 0 then (if j = n − 1 then 1 else 0)
                                    else (if i = j + 1 then 1 else 0))
```

Finally, the Grover's algorithm is as follows. Since we do not have initialization, we skip initialization to zero at the beginning and instead assume that the state begins in the zero state in the precondition.

```
definition Grover :: com where
  Grover = hadamard_n n ;;
           While_P vars2 M0 M1 D ;;
           Measure_P vars1 N testN (replicate N SKIP)
```

where the measurements for the while loop and at the end of the algorithm are:

```
definition M0 = mat K K (λ(i,j). if i = j ∧ i ≥ R then 1 else 0)
definition M1 = mat K K (λ(i,j). if i = j ∧ i < R then 1 else 0)
definition testN k = mat N N (λ(i,j). if i = k ∧ j = k then 1 else 0)
```

We can now state the final correctness result. Let *proj v* be the outer product $vv^\dagger$, and *proj_k k* be $|k\rangle\langle k|$, where $|k\rangle$ is the k'th basis vector on the vector space corresponding to the loop variable. Let *pre* and *post* be given as follows:

```
definition pre = proj (vec N (λk. if k = 0 then 1 else 0))
definition post = mat N N (λ(i, j). if i = j ∧ f i then 1 else 0)
```

Then, the (partial) correctness of Grover's algorithm is specified by the following Hoare triple.

```
theorem grover_partial_correct:
  ⊨p {tensor_P pre (proj_k 0)}
       Grover
     {tensor_P post (1m K)}
```

We now briefly outline the proof strategy. Following the definition of *Grover*, the proof of the above Hoare triple is divided into three main parts, for the initialization by Hadamard matrices, for the while loop and for the measurement at the end.

In each part, assertions are first inserted around commands according to the Hoare rules to form smaller Hoare triples. In particular, the precondition of the while loop part is exactly the invariant of the loop. Moreover, it has to be shown that these assertions satisfy the conditions for being quantum predicates, which involve computing their dimension, showing positiveness, and being bounded by the identity matrix under the Löwner order. Then, these Hoare triples are derived using our deduction system. Before combining them together, we have to show that the postcondition of each command is equal to the precondition of the later one. After that, the three main Hoare triples can be obtained by combining these smaller ones.

After the derivation of the three Hoare triples above, we prove the Löwner order between the postcondition of each triple and the precondition of the following triple. Afterwards, the triples can be combined into the Hoare triple below:

theorem *grover_partial_deduct:*
$\vdash_p$ {*tensor_P pre (proj_k 0)*}
Grover
{*tensor_P post* (1_{m} *K*)}

Finally, the (partial) correctness of Grover's algorithm follows from the soundness of our deduction system.

5 Discussion

Compared to classical programs, reasoning about quantum programs is more difficult in every respect. Instead of discrete mathematics in the classical case, even the simplest reasoning about quantum programs involves complex numbers, unitary and positivity properties of matrices, and the tensor product. Hence, it is to be expected that formal verification of quantum Hoare logic and quantum algorithms will take much more effort. In this section, we describe some of the automation that we built to simplify the manual proof, and give some statistics concerning the amount of effort involved in the formalization.

5.1 Automatic Proof of Identities in Linear Algebra

During the formalization process, we make extensive use of ring properties of matrices. These include commutativity and associativity of addition, associativity of multiplication, and distributivity. Compared to the usual case of numbers, applying these rules for matrices is more difficult in Isabelle/HOL, since they involve extra conditions on dimensions of matrices. For example, the rule for commutativity of addition of matrices is stated as:

lemma *comm_add_mat:*
$A \in$ *carrier_mat nr nc* $\Longrightarrow$ $B \in$ *carrier_mat nr nc* $\Longrightarrow$ $A + B = B + A$

These extra conditions make the rules difficult to apply for standard Isabelle automation. For our work, we implemented our own tactic handling these rules. In addition to the ring properties, we also frequently need to use the cyclic property of trace (e.g. $\mathrm{tr}(ABC) = \mathrm{tr}(BCA)$), as well as the properties of adjoint ($(AB)^\dagger = B^\dagger A^\dagger$ and $A^{\dagger\dagger} = A$). For simplicity, we restrict to identities involving only $n \times n$ matrices, where n is a parameter given to the tactic.

The tactic is designed to prove equality between two expressions. It works by computing the normal form of the expressions – using ring identities and identities for the adjoint to fully expand the expression into polynomial form. To handle the trace, the expression $\mathrm{tr}(A_1 \cdots A_n)$ is normalized to put the A_i that is the largest according to Isabelle's internal term order last. All dimension assumptions are collected and reduced (for example, the assumption $A * B \in$ *carrier_mat n n* is reduced to $A \in$ *carrier_mat n n* and $B \in$ *carrier_mat n n*).

Overall, the resulting tactic is used 80 times in our proofs. Below, we list some of the more complicated equations resolved by the tactic. The tactic reduces the goal to dimensional constraints on the atomic matrices (e.g. $M \in$ *carrier_mat n n* and $P \in$ *carrier_mat n n* in the first case).

$$\mathrm{tr}(MM^\dagger(PP^\dagger)) = \mathrm{tr}((P^\dagger M)(P^\dagger M)^\dagger)$$
$$\mathrm{tr}(M_0 A M_0^\dagger) + \mathrm{tr}(M_1 A M_1^\dagger) = \mathrm{tr}((M_0^\dagger M_0 + M_1^\dagger M_1)A)$$
$$H^\dagger(Ph^\dagger(H^\dagger Q_2 H)Ph)H = (HPhH)^\dagger Q_2(HPhH)$$

5.2 Statistics

Overall, the formalization consists of about 11,500 lines of Isabelle theories. An old version of the proof is developed on and off for two years. The current version is re-developed, using some ideas from the old version. The development of the new version took about 5 person months. Detailed breakdown of number of lines for different parts of the proof is given in the following table.

Description	Files	Number of lines
Preliminaries	*Complex_Matrix, Matrix_Limit, Gates*	4197
Semantics	*Quantum_Program*	1110
Hoare logic	*Quantum_Hoare*	1417
Tensor product	*Partial_State*	1664
Grover's algorithm	*Grover*	3184
Total		11572

In particular, with the verification framework in place, the proof of correctness for Grover's search algorithm takes just over 3000 lines. While this shows that it is realistic to use the current framework to verify more complicated algorithms such as Shor's algorithm, it is clear that more automation is needed to enable verification on a larger scale.

6 Related Work

The closest work to our research is Robert Rand's implementation of $\mathcal{Q}$wire in Coq [49,50]. $\mathcal{Q}$wire [47] is a language for describing *quantum circuits*. In this model, quantum algorithms are implemented by connecting together quantum gates, each with a fixed number of bit/qubit inputs and outputs. How the gates are connected is determined by a classical host language, allowing classical control of quantum computation. The work [49] defines the semantics of $\mathcal{Q}$wire in Coq, and uses it to verify quantum teleportation, Deutsch's algorithm, and an example on multiple coin flips to illustrate applicability to a family of circuits. In this framework, program verification proceeds directly from the semantics, without defining a Hoare logic. As in our work, it is necessary to solve the problem of how to define extensions of an operation on a few qubits to the global state. The approach taken in [49] is to use the usual Kronecker product, augmented either by the use of swaps between qubits, or by inserting identity matrices at strategic positions in the Kronecker product.

There are two main differences between [49] and our work. First, quantum algorithms are expressed using quantum circuits in [49], while we use quantum programs with while loops. Models based on quantum circuits have the advantage of being concrete, and indeed most of the earlier quantum algorithms can be expressed directly in terms of circuits. However, several new quantum algorithms can be more properly expressed by while loops, e.g. quantum walks with absorbing boundaries, quantum Bernoulli factory (for random number generation), HHL for systems of linear equations and qPCA (Principal Component Analysis). Second, we formalized a Hoare logic while [49] uses denotational semantics directly. As in verification of classical programs, Hoare logic encapsulates standard forms of argument for dealing with each program construct. Moreover, the rules for QHL is in weakest-precondition form, allowing the possibility of automated verification condition generation after specifying the loop invariants (although this is not used in the present paper).

Besides Rand's work, quite a few verification tools have been developed for quantum communication protocols. For example, Nagarajan and Gay [41] modeled the BB84 protocol [12] and verified its correctness. Ardeshir-Larijani et al. [7,8] presented a tool for verification of quantum protocols through equivalence checking. Existing tools, such as PRISM [37] and Coq, are employed to develop verification tools for quantum protocols [17,29]. Furthermore, an automatic tool called Quantum Model-Checker (QMC) is developed [28,46].

Recently, several specific techniques have been proposed to algorithmically check properties of quantum programs. In [63], the Sharir-Pnueli-Hart method for verifying probabilistic programs [54] has been generalised to quantum programs by exploiting the Schrödinger-Heisenberg duality between quantum states and observables. Termination analysis of nondeterministic and concurrent quantum programs [38] was carried out based on reachability analysis [64]. Invariants can be generated at some steps in quantum programs for debugging and verification of correctness [62]. But up to now no tools are available that implements these techniques. Another Hoare-style logic for quantum programs was proposed in [36], but without (relative) completeness.

Interactive theorem proving has made significant progress in the formal verification of classical programs and systems. Here, we focus on listing some tools designed for special kinds of systems. EasyCrypt [10, 11] is an interactive framework for verifying the security of cryptographic constructs in the computational model. It is developed based on a probabilistic relational Hoare logic to support machine-checked construction and verification of game-based proofs. Recently, verification of hybrid systems via interactive theorem proving has also been studied. KeYmaera X [26] is a theorem prover implementing differential dynamic logic ($d\mathcal{L}$) [48], for the verification of hybrid programs. In [60], a prover has been implemented in Isabelle/HOL for reasoning about hybrid processes described using hybrid CSP [34].

Our work is based on existing formalization of matrices and tensors in Isabelle/HOL. In [59] (with corresponding AFP entry [58]), Thiemann et al. developed the matrix library that we use here. In [14] (with corresponding AFP entry [13]), Bentkamp et al. developed tensor analysis based on the above work, in an effort to formalize an expressivity result of deep learning algorithms.

7 Conclusion

We formalized quantum Hoare logic in Isabelle/HOL, and verified the soundness and completeness of the deduction system for partial correctness. Using this deduction system, we verified the correctness of Grover's search algorithm. This is, to our best knowledge, the first formalization of a Hoare logic for quantum programs in an interactive theorem prover.

This work is intended to be the first step of a larger project to construct a framework under which one can efficiently verify the correctness of complex quantum programs and systems. In this paper, our focus is on formalizing the mathematical machinery to specify the semantics of quantum programs, and prove the correctness of quantum Hoare logic. To verify more complicated programs efficiently, better automation is needed at every stage of the proof. We have already begun with some automation for proving identities in linear algebra. In the future, we plan to add to it automation facility for handling matrix computations, tensor products, positivity of matrices, etc., all linked together by a verification condition generator.

Another direction of future work is to formalize various extensions of quantum Hoare logic, to deal with classical control, recursion, concurrency, etc., with the eventual goal of being able to verify not only sequential programs, but also concurrent programs and communication systems.

Acknowledgements. This research is supported through grants by NSFC under grant No. 61625206, 61732001. Bohua Zhan is supported by CAS Pioneer Hundred Talents Program under grant No. Y9RC585036. Yangjia Li is supported by NSFC grant No. 61872342.

References

1. IBM Q devices and simulators. https://www.research.ibm.com/ibm-q/technology/devices/
2. IBM Q experience community. https://quantumexperience.ng.bluemix.net/qx/community?channel=papers&category=ibm
3. IonQ. https://ionq.co/resources
4. A preview of Bristlecone, Google's new quantum processor. https://ai.googleblog.com/2018/03/a-preview-of-bristlecone-googles-new.html
5. Qiskit Aer. https://qiskit.org/aer, https://medium.com/qiskit/qiskit-aer-d09d0fac7759
6. Unsupervised machine learning on Rigetti 19Q with Forest 1.2. https://medium.com/rigetti/unsupervised-machine-learning-on-rigetti-19q-with-forest-1-2-39021339699
7. Ardeshir-Larijani, E., Gay, S.J., Nagarajan, R.: Equivalence checking of quantum protocols. In: Piterman, N., Smolka, S.A. (eds.) TACAS 2013. LNCS, vol. 7795, pp. 478–492. Springer, Heidelberg (2013). https://doi.org/10.1007/978-3-642-36742-7_33
8. Ardeshir-Larijani, E., Gay, S.J., Nagarajan, R.: Verification of concurrent quantum protocols by equivalence checking. In: Ábrahám, E., Havelund, K. (eds.) TACAS 2014. LNCS, vol. 8413, pp. 500–514. Springer, Heidelberg (2014). https://doi.org/10.1007/978-3-642-54862-8_42
9. Baltag, A., Smets, S.: LQP: the dynamic logic of quantum information. Math. Struct. Comput. Sci. **16**(3), 491–525 (2006)
10. Barthe, G., Dupressoir, F., Grégoire, B., Kunz, C., Schmidt, B., Strub, P.-Y.: EasyCrypt: a tutorial. In: Aldini, A., Lopez, J., Martinelli, F. (eds.) FOSAD 2012-2013. LNCS, vol. 8604, pp. 146–166. Springer, Cham (2014). https://doi.org/10.1007/978-3-319-10082-1_6
11. Barthe, G., Grégoire, B., Heraud, S., Béguelin, S.Z.: Computer-aided security proofs for the working cryptographer. In: Rogaway, P. (ed.) CRYPTO 2011. LNCS, vol. 6841, pp. 71–90. Springer, Heidelberg (2011). https://doi.org/10.1007/978-3-642-22792-9_5
12. Bennett, C.H., Brassard, G.: Quantum cryptography: public key distribution and coin tossing. In: International Conference on Computers, Systems and Signal Processing, pp. 175–179. IEEE (1984)
13. Bentkamp, A.: Expressiveness of deep learning. Archive of Formal Proofs, Formal proof development, November 2016. http://isa-afp.org/entries/Deep_Learning.html
14. Bentkamp, A., Blanchette, J.C., Klakow, D.: A formal proof of the expressiveness of deep learning. In: Interactive Theorem Proving - 8th International Conference, ITP 2017, Brasília, Brazil, September 26–29, 2017, Proceedings, pp. 46–64 (2017). https://dblp.org/rec/bib/conf/itp/BentkampBK17
15. Bertot, Y., Castran, P.: Interactive Theorem Proving and Program Development: Coq'Art The Calculus of Inductive Constructions, 1st edn. Springer, Heidelberg (2010). https://doi.org/10.1007/978-3-662-07964-5
16. Bettelli, S., Calarco, T., Serafini, L.: Toward an architecture for quantum programming. Eur. Phys. J. D **25**, 181–200 (2003)
17. Boender, J., Kammüller, F., Nagarajan, R.: Formalization of quantum protocols using Coq. In: QPL 2015 (2015)

18. Boyer, M., Brassard, G., Høyer, P., Tapp, A.: Tight bounds on quantum searching. Fortschr. der Phys. Prog. Phys. **46**(4–5), 493–505 (1998)
19. Brassard, G., Hoyer, P., Mosca, M., Tapp, A.: Quantum amplitude amplification and estimation. Contemp. Math. **305**, 53–74 (2002)
20. Brunet, O., Jorrand, P.: Dynamic quantum logic for quantum programs. Int. J. Quantum Inf. **2**, 45–54 (2004)
21. Chadha, R., Mateus, P., Sernadas, A.: Reasoning about imperative quantum programs. Electron. Notes Theoret. Comput. Sci. **158**, 19–39 (2006)
22. Cross, A.W., Bishop, L.S., Smolin, J.A., Gambetta, J.M.: Open quantum assembly language. arXiv preprint arXiv:1707.03429 (2017)
23. Debnath, S., Linke, N.M., Figgatt, C., Landsman, K.A., Wright, K., Monroe, C.: Demonstration of a small programmable quantum computer with atomic qubits. Nature **536**(7614), 63–66 (2016)
24. D'Hondt, E., Panangaden, P.: Quantum weakest preconditions. Math. Struct. Comput. Sci. **16**, 429–451 (2006)
25. Wecker, D., Svore, K.: Liqui|⟩: a software design architecture and domain-specific language for quantum computing. (http://research.microsoft.com/en-us/projects/liquid/)
26. Fulton, N., Mitsch, S., Quesel, J.-D., Völp, M., Platzer, A.: KeYmaera X: an axiomatic tactical theorem prover for hybrid systems. In: Felty, A.P., Middeldorp, A. (eds.) CADE 2015. LNCS (LNAI), vol. 9195, pp. 527–538. Springer, Cham (2015). https://doi.org/10.1007/978-3-319-21401-6_36
27. Gay, S.: Quantum programming languages: survey and bibliography. Math. Struct. Comput. Sci. **16**, 581–600 (2006)
28. Gay, S.J., Nagarajan, R., Papanikolaou, N.: QMC: a model checker for quantum systems. In: Gupta, A., Malik, S. (eds.) CAV 2008. LNCS, vol. 5123, pp. 543–547. Springer, Heidelberg (2008). https://doi.org/10.1007/978-3-540-70545-1_51
29. Gay, S.J., Nagarajan, R., Papanikolaou, N.: Probabilistic model-checking of quantum protocols. In: DCM Proceedings of International Workshop on Developments in Computational Models, p. 504007. IEEE (2005). https://arxiv.org/abs/quant-ph/0504007
30. Google AI Quantum team. https://github.com/quantumlib/Cirq
31. Green, A.S., Lumsdaine, P.L., Ross, N.J., Selinger, P., Valiron, B.: Quipper: a scalable quantum programming language. In: Proceedings of the 34th ACM SIGPLAN Conference on Programming Language Design and Implementation, PLDI 2013, pp. 333–342. ACM, New York (2013)
32. Grover, L.K.: A fast quantum mechanical algorithm for database search. In: Proceedings of the Twenty-eighth Annual ACM Symposium on Theory of Computing, STOC 1996, pp. 212–219. ACM, New York (1996)
33. Haftmann, F., Wenzel, M.: Local theory specifications in isabelle/isar. In: Berardi, S., Damiani, F., de'Liguoro, U. (eds.) TYPES 2008. LNCS, vol. 5497, pp. 153–168. Springer, Heidelberg (2009). https://doi.org/10.1007/978-3-642-02444-3_10
34. He, J.: From CSP to hybrid systems. In: A Classical Mind, Essays in Honour of C.A.R. Hoare, pp. 171–189. Prentice Hall International (UK) Ltd. (1994)
35. JavadiAbhari, A., et al.: ScaffCC: scalable compilation and analysis of quantum programs. In: Parallel Computing, vol. 45, pp. 3–17 (2015)
36. Kakutani, Y.: A logic for formal verification of quantum programs. In: Datta, A. (ed.) ASIAN 2009. LNCS, vol. 5913, pp. 79–93. Springer, Heidelberg (2009). https://doi.org/10.1007/978-3-642-10622-4_7

37. Kwiatkowska, M., Norman, G., Parker, P.: Probabilistic symbolic model-checking with PRISM: a hybrid approach. Int. J. Softw. Tools Technol. Transf. **6**, 128–142 (2004)
38. Li, Y., Yu, N., Ying, M.: Termination of nondeterministic quantum programs. Acta Informatica **51**, 1–24 (2014)
39. Liu, S., et al.: $Q|SI\rangle$: a quantum programming environment. In: Jones, C., Wang, J., Zhan, N. (eds.) Symposium on Real-Time and Hybrid Systems. LNCS, vol. 11180, pp. 133–164. Springer, Cham (2018). https://doi.org/10.1007/978-3-030-01461-2_8
40. Liu, X., Kubiatowicz, J.: Chisel-Q: designing quantum circuits with a scala embedded language. In: 2013 IEEE 31st International Conference on Computer Design (ICCD), pp. 427–434. IEEE (2013)
41. Nagarajan, R., Gay, S.: Formal verification of quantum protocols (2002). arXiv: quant-ph/0203086
42. Nielsen, M.A., Chuang, I.L.: Quantum Computation and Quantum Information: 10th Anniversary Edition, 10th edn. Cambridge University Press, New York (2011)
43. Nipkow, T., Klein, G.: Concrete Semantics: With Isabelle/HOL. Springer, Cham (2014). https://doi.org/10.1007/978-3-319-10542-0
44. Nipkow, T., Wenzel, M., Paulson, L.C. (eds.): Isabelle/HOL: A Proof Assistant for Higher-Order Logic. LNCS, vol. 2283. Springer, Heidelberg (2002). https://doi.org/10.1007/3-540-45949-9
45. Ömer, B.: Structured quantum programming. Ph.D. thesis, Technical University of Vienna (2003)
46. Papanikolaou, N.: Model checking quantum protocols. Ph.D. thesis, Department of Computer Science, University of Warwick (2008)
47. Paykin, J., Rand, R., Zdancewic, S.: QWIRE: a core language for quantum circuits. In: Proceedings of 44th ACM Symposium on Principles of Programming Languages (POPL), pp. 846–858 (2017)
48. Platzer, A.: A complete uniform substitution calculus for differential dynamic logic. J. Autom. Reas. **59**(2), 219–265 (2017)
49. Rand, R.: Formally verified quantum programming. Ph.D. thesis, University of Pennsylvania (2018)
50. Robert Rand, J.P., Zdancewic, S.: QWIRE practice: formal verification of quantum circuits in coq. In: Quantum Physics and Logic (2017)
51. Sanders, J.W., Zuliani, P.: Quantum programming. In: Backhouse, R., Oliveira, J.N. (eds.) MPC 2000. LNCS, vol. 1837, pp. 80–99. Springer, Heidelberg (2000). https://doi.org/10.1007/10722010_6
52. Selinger, P.: A brief survey of quantum programming languages. In: Kameyama, Y., Stuckey, P.J. (eds.) FLOPS 2004. LNCS, vol. 2998, pp. 1–6. Springer, Heidelberg (2004). https://doi.org/10.1007/978-3-540-24754-8_1
53. Selinger, P.: Towards a quantum programming language. Math. Struct. Comput. Sci. **14**(4), 527–586 (2004)
54. Sharir, M., Pnueli, A., Hart, S.: Verification of probabilistic programs. SIAM J. Comput. **13**, 292–314 (1984)
55. Smith, R.S., Curtis, M.J., Zeng, W.J.: A practical quantum instruction set architecture. arXiv preprint arXiv:1608.03355 (2016)
56. Steiger, D.S., Häner, T., Troyer, M.: ProjectQ: an open source software framework for quantum computing. Quantum **2**, 49 (2018)
57. Svore, K., et al.: Q#: enabling scalable quantum computing and development with a high-level DSL. In: Proceedings of the Real World Domain Specific Languages Workshop 2018, pp. 7:1–7:10 (2018)

58. Thiemann, R., Yamada, A.: Matrices, Jordan normal forms, and spectral radius theory. Archive of Formal Proofs, Formal proof development, August 2015. http://isa-afp.org/entries/Jordan_Normal_Form.html
59. Thiemann, R., Yamada, A.: Formalizing Jordan normal forms in Isabelle/HOL. In: Proceedings of the 5th ACM SIGPLAN Conference on Certified Programs and Proofs, CPP 2016, pp. 88–99. ACM, New York (2016)
60. Wang, S., Zhan, N., Zou, L.: An improved HHL prover: an interactive theorem prover for hybrid systems. In: Butler, M., Conchon, S., Zaïdi, F. (eds.) ICFEM 2015. LNCS, vol. 9407, pp. 382–399. Springer, Cham (2015). https://doi.org/10.1007/978-3-319-25423-4_25
61. Ying, M.: Floyd-Hoare logic for quantum programs. ACM Trans. Programm. Lang. Syst. **33**(6), 19:1–19:49 (2011)
62. Ying, M., Ying, S., Wu, X.: Invariants of quantum programs: characterisations and generation. In: Proceedings of the 44th ACM SIGPLAN Symposium on Principles of Programming Languages, POPL 2017, pp. 818–832 (2017)
63. Ying, M., Yu, N., Feng, Y., Duan, R.: Verification of quantum programs. Sci. Comput. Programm. **78**, 1679–1700 (2013)
64. Ying, S., Feng, Y., Yu, N., Ying, M.: Reachability probabilities of quantum Markov chains. In: D'Argenio, P.R., Melgratti, H. (eds.) CONCUR 2013. LNCS, vol. 8052, pp. 334–348. Springer, Heidelberg (2013). https://doi.org/10.1007/978-3-642-40184-8_24

SecCSL: Security Concurrent Separation Logic

Gidon Ernst[1(✉)] and Toby Murray[2]

[1] LMU Munich, Munich, Germany
gidon.ernst@lmu.de

[2] University of Melbourne, Melbourne, Australia
toby.murray@unimelb.edu.au

Abstract. We present SecCSL, a concurrent separation logic for proving expressive, data-dependent information flow security properties of low-level programs. SecCSL is considerably more expressive, while being simpler, than recent compositional information flow logics that cannot reason about pointers, arrays etc. To capture security concerns, SecCSL adopts a relational semantics for its assertions. At the same time it inherits the structure of traditional concurrent separation logics; thus SecCSL reasoning can be automated via symbolic execution. We demonstrate this by implementing SecC, an automatic verifier for a subset of the C programming language, which we apply to a range of benchmarks.

1 Introduction

Software verification successes abound, whether via interactive proof or via automatic program verifiers. While the former has yielded individual, deeply verified software artifacts [21,24,25] primarily by *researchers*, the latter appears to be having a growing impact on *industrial* software engineering [11,36,39].

At the same time, recent work has heralded major advancements in program logics for reasoning about secure *information flow* [23,33,34]—i.e. whether programs properly protect their secrets—yielding the first general program logics and proofs of information flow security for non-trivial concurrent programs [34]. Yet so far, such logics have remained confined to interactive proof assistants, making them practically inaccessible to industrial developers.

This is not especially surprising. The Covern logic [34], for example, pays for its generality with regard to expressive security policies, in terms of complexity. Worse, these logics reason only over very simple toy programming languages, which even lack support for pointers, arrays, and structures. Their complexity, we argue, hinders proof automation and makes scaling up these logics to real-world languages impractical. How, therefore, can we leverage the power of existing automatic deductive verification approaches for security proofs?

In this paper we present *Security Concurrent Separation Logic* (SecCSL), which achieves an unprecedented combination of simplicity, power, and ease of

I. Dillig and S. Tasiran (Eds.): CAV 2019, LNCS 11562, pp. 208–230, 2019.
https://doi.org/10.1007/978-3-030-25543-5_13

automation by capturing core concepts such as data-dependent variable sensitivity [27,31,50], and shared invariants on sensitive memory [34] in the familiar style of Concurrent Separation Logic (CSL) [38], as exemplified in Sect. 2.

Prior work [14,20] has noted the promise of separation logic for reasoning about information flow yet, to date, that promise remains unrealised. Indeed, the only two prior encodings of information flow concepts into separation logics which we are aware of have overlooked crucial features like concurrency [14], and lack the ability to separately specify the sensitivity of *values* and memory *locations* as we explain in Sect. 2. The logic in [20] lacks soundness arguments altogether while [14] fail to satisfy basic properties needed for automation (see the discussion following Proposition 1).

Designing a logic with the right combination of features, with the right semantics, is therefore non-trivial. To manage this, SecCSL assertions have a *relational* interpretation [6,49] over a standard heap model (Sect. 3). This allows one to canonically encode information flow concepts while maintaining the approach and structure of traditional CSL proofs. To do so we adapt existing proof techniques for the soundness of CSL [46] into a compositional information flow security property (Sect. 4) that, like SecCSL itself, is simple and powerful. We have mechanized the soundness of SecCSL in Isabelle/HOL [37].

To demonstrate SecCSL's ease of use and capacity for automation, we implemented the prototype tool SecC (Sect. 5). We target C because it dominates low-level security-critical code. SecC automates SecCSL reasoning via symbolic execution, in the style of contemporary Separation Logic program verifiers like VeriFast [22], Viper [30], and Infer [10]. SecC correctly analyzes well-known benchmark problems (collected in [17]) within a few milliseconds; and we verify a variant of the CDDC case study [5] from the Covern project. Our Isabelle theories, the open source prototype tool SecC, and examples are available online at https://covern.org/secc [18].

2 An Overview of SecCSL

2.1 Specifying Information Flow Control in SecCSL

Consider the program in Fig. 1. It maintains a global pointer `rec` to a shared record, protected by the lock `mutex`. The `is_classified` field of the record identifies the confidentiality of the record's `data`: when `is_classified` is true, the value stored in the `data` field is confidential, and otherwise it is safe to release publicly. The left thread outputs the data in the record whenever it is public by writing to the (memory mapped) output device register pointer `OUTPUT_REG` (here also protected by `mutex`). The right thread updates the record, ensuring its content is not confidential, here by clearing its `data`.

Suppose assigning a value d to the `OUTPUT_REG` register causes d to be outputted to a publicly-visible location. Reasoning, then, that the example is secure requires capturing that (1) the `data` field of the record pointed to by `rec` is confidential precisely when the record's `is_classified` field says it is, and (2) data

```
/* globals shared between the two threads */
struct record { bool is_classified; int data; };
struct record * rec = /* ... initialisation omitted ... */;
volatile int * const OUTPUT_REG = /* memory-mapped IO device register */;
```

```
/* thread 1: output the record */
while(true) {
    lock(mutex);
    if (!rec->is_classified)
        *OUTPUT_REG = rec->data;
    unlock(mutex); }
```

```
/* thread 2: edit the record */
lock(mutex);
/* clear the record */
rec->is_classified = FALSE;
rec->data = 0;
unlock(mutex);
```

Fig. 1. Example of concurrent information flow.

sink `OUTPUT_REG` should never have confidential data written to it. Therefore the example only ever writes non-confidential data into `OUTPUT_REG`.

Condition (1) specifies the sensitivity of a data *value* in memory, whereas condition (2) specifies the sensitivity of the data that a memory *location* (i.e. data sink) is permitted to hold. Prior security separation logics [14,20] reason only about value-sensitivity condition (1) but, as we explain below, both are needed. Like those prior logics, in SecCSL one specifies the sensitivity of the value denoted by an expression e via a security *label* ℓ: the assertion $e :: \ell$ means that the sensitivity of the value denoted by expression e is at most ℓ. Security labels are drawn from a lattice with top element `high` (denoting the most confidential information), bottom element `low` (denoting public information), and ordered via $\sqsubseteq$: $\ell \sqsubseteq \ell'$ means that information labelled with ℓ' is at least as sensitive as that labelled by ℓ. Using this style of assertion, in conjunction with standard separation logic connectives (explained below), condition (1) can be specified as:

$$\exists c\ d.\ \texttt{rec} \mapsto (c, d) \land c :: \texttt{low} \land d :: (c\ ?\ \texttt{high} : \texttt{low}) \tag{1}$$

Separation logic's points-to predicate $e \mapsto e'$ means the memory location denoted by expression e holds the value denoted by e'. Thus (1) can be read as saying that the `rec` pointer points to a pair of values (c, d). The first c (the value of the `is_classified` field) is public. The sensitivity of the second d (the value of the `data` field) is given by the value of the first c: it is `high` when c is true and is `low` otherwise. SecCSL integrates such reasoning about *value-dependent* sensitivity [27,31,50] neatly with functional properties of low-level data structures, which we think is more natural and straightforward than the approach of [34,35] that keeps the two concerns separate.

Value-sensitivity assertion $e :: \ell$ is a judgement on the maximum sensitivity of the data *source(s)* from which e has been derived. Location-sensitivity assertions, on the other hand, are used to specify security policies on data *sinks* like `OUTPUT_REG`. These assertions augment the separation logic points-to predicate with a security label ℓ, and are used to specify which parts of the memory are observable to the attacker (and so must never contain sensitive information): $e \overset{\ell}{\mapsto} e'$ means that the value denoted by the expression e' is present in memory at the location denoted by e, and additionally that at all times the sensitivity of the value stored in that locations is never allowed to exceed ℓ. Thus in SecCSL, $e \mapsto e'$ abbreviates $e \overset{\mathsf{high}}{\longmapsto} e'$. In Fig. 1, that `OUTPUT_REG` is publicly-observable can be specified as:

$$\exists v.\ \texttt{OUTPUT\_REG} \overset{\mathsf{low}}{\longmapsto} v \tag{2}$$

2.2 Reasoning in SecCSL

SecCSL judgements have the form:

$$\ell_A \vdash \{P\}\ c\ \{Q\} \tag{3}$$

Here ℓ_A is the *attacker security level*, c is the (concurrent) program command being executed, and P and Q are the program's pre- resp. postcondition. Judgement (3) means that if the program c begins in a state satisfying its precondition P then, when it terminates, the final state will satisfy its postcondition Q. Analogously to [44] the program is guaranteed to be memory safe. We defer a description of ℓ_A and the implied security property to Sect. 2.3.

As with traditional CSLs, SecCSL is geared towards reasoning over shared-memory programs that use lock-based synchronisation. Each lock l has an associated invariant $\mathrm{inv}(l)$, which is simply a predicate, like P or Q in (3), that describes the shared memory that the lock protects. In Fig. 1, where the lock `mutex` protects the shared pointer `rec` and `OUTPUT_REG`, the associated invariant $\mathrm{inv}(\texttt{mutex})$ is simply the conjunction of (1) and (2).

$$(\exists c\ d.\ \texttt{rec} \mapsto (c, d) \wedge c :: \mathsf{low} \wedge d :: (c\ ?\ \mathsf{high} : \mathsf{low})) \star (\exists v.\ \texttt{OUTPUT\_REG} \overset{\mathsf{low}}{\longmapsto} v) \tag{4}$$

Separating conjunction $P \star Q$ asserts that the assertions P and Q both hold and, additionally, that the memory locations referenced by P and Q respectively do not overlap. Thus SecCSL invariants, like SecCSL assertions, describe together both functional properties (e.g. `rec` is a valid pointer) and security concerns (e.g. the `OUTPUT_REG` location is publicly visible) of the shared state.

When acquiring a lock one gets to assume that the lock's invariant holds [38]. Subsequently, when releasing the lock one must prove that the invariant has been re-established. For example, when reasoning about the code of the left-thread in Fig. 1, upon acquiring the `mutex`, SecCSL adds formula (4) to the intermediate assertion, which allows proving that the loop body is secure. When reasoning about the right thread, one must prove that the invariant has been re-established when it releases the mutex. This is the reason e.g. that the right thread must clear the `data` field after setting `is_classified` to false.

Reasoning in SecCSL proceeds forward over the program text according to the rules in Fig. 4. When execution forks, as in Fig. 1, one reasons over each thread individually. For Fig. 1, SecCSL requires proving that the guard of the `if`-condition is `low`, i.e. that the program is not branching on a secret (rule If in Fig. 4), which would correspond to a timing channel, see Sect. 2.3 below. This follows from the part $c :: \texttt{low}$ of invariant (4). Secondly, after the write to `OUTPUT_REG`, SecCSL requires that the expression that is being written to the location `OUTPUT_REG` has sensitivity `low` (rule Store in Fig. 4). This follows from $d :: (c\ ?\ \texttt{high} : \texttt{low})$ in the invariant, which simplifies to $d :: \texttt{high}$ given the guard $c \equiv \texttt{true}$ of the `if`-statement. Finally, when the right thread releases `mutex`, invariant (4) holds for the updated contents of `rec` (rule Unlock in Fig. 4).

2.3 Security Intuition and Informal Security Property

But what does security mean in SecCSL? Indeed, the SecCSL a judgement $\ell_A \vdash \{P\}\ c\ \{Q\}$ additionally implies that the program c does not leak any sensitive information during its execution to potential attackers.

The attacker security level ℓ_A in (3) represents an upper bound on the parts of the program's memory that a potential, passive attacker is assumed to be able to observe before, during, and after the program's execution. Intuitively this encompasses all memory locations whose sensitivity is $\sqsubseteq \ell_A$. Which memory locations have sensitivity $\sqsubseteq \ell_A$ is defined by the *location-sensitivity* assertions in the precondition P and the lock invariants: A memory location *loc* is visible to the ℓ_A attacker iff P or a lock invariant contains some $e \overset{e_l}{\longmapsto} e'$ and in the program's initial state e evaluates to *loc* and e_l evaluates to some label ℓ such that $\ell \sqsubseteq \ell_A$ (see Fig. 3).

Which data is sensitive and should not be leaked to the ℓ_A attacker is defined by the *value-sensitivity* assertions in P and the lock invariants: an expression e is sensitive when P or a lock invariant contains some $e :: e_l$ and in the program's initial state e_l evaluates to some ℓ with $\ell \not\sqsubseteq \ell_A$. Security, then, requires that in all intermediate states of the program's execution no sensitive data (as defined by value-sensitivity assertions) can be inferred via the attacker-observable memory (as defined by location-sensitivity assertions).

SecCSL proves a *compositional* security property that formalises this intuition (see Definition 3). Since the property needs to be compositional with regards to concurrent execution, the resulting security property is *timing sensitive*, meaning that not only must the program never reveal sensitive data into attacker-observable memory locations but the times at which it updates these memory locations cannot depend on sensitive data. It is well-known that timing-insensitive security properties are not compositional under standard scheduling models [34,48]. For this reason SecCSL forbids programs from branching on sensitive values. We believe that this restriction could in principle be relaxed in the future via established techniques [28,29].

SecCSL's top-level soundness (Sect. 4) formalises the above intuitive definition of security in the style of traditional *noninterference* [19] that compares two program executions with respect to the observations that can be made by an attacker. SecCSL adopts a *relational* interpretation for the assertions P and Q, and the lock invariants, in which they are evaluated against pairs of execution states. This relational semantics directly expresses the comparison needed for noninterference. As a result, most of the complexities related to SecCSL's soundness are confined to the semantic level, whereas the calculus retains its similarity to standard separation logic and hence its simplicity.

Under this relational semantics (see Fig. 2 in Sect. 3), when a pair of states satisfies an assertion P, it implies that the two states agree on the values of all non-sensitive expressions as defined by P (Lemma 1). Noninterference is then stated as Theorem 2: Program c with precondition P is secure against the ℓ_A-attacker if, whenever executed twice from two initial states jointly satisfying P and the lock invariants (and so agreeing on the values of all data assumed to be initially observable to the ℓ_A attacker), in all intermediate pairs of states arrived at after running each execution for the same number of steps, the resulting states again agree at that initially ℓ_A-visible memory. This definition is timing sensitive as it compares executions that have the same number of steps.

3 The Logic SecCSL

3.1 Assertions

Pure expressions e that do not depend on the heap are composed of variables x, function applications, equations, and conditional expressions. Pure relational formulas ρ comprise boolean expressions ϕ, value sensitivity $e :: e_l$, and relational implication $\Rightarrow$ (wlog. covering relational $\neg$, $\wedge$, $\vee$). We assume a standard first-order many sorted typing discipline (not elaborated).

$$e ::= \; x \mid f(e_1, \ldots, e_n) \mid e_1 = e_2 \mid \phi \; ? \; e_1 \; : \; e_2 \qquad \rho ::= \phi \mid e :: e_l \mid \rho_1 \Rightarrow \rho_2$$

We postulate that the logical signature contains a sort `Label`, corresponding to the security lattice, with constants `low`, `high`: `Label` and a binary predicate symbol $\sqsubseteq$: `Label` $\times$ `Label` $\longrightarrow$ `Bool`, whose interpretation satisfies the lattice axioms.

SecCSL's assertions P, Q may additionally refer to the heap and thus include the empty heap description, labelled points-to predicates (heap location sensitivity assertions), assertions guarded by (pure) conditionals, ordinary overlapping conjunction as well as separating conjunction, and existential quantification.

$$P ::= \; \rho \mid \mathsf{emp} \mid e_p \overset{e_l}{\longmapsto} e_v \mid (\phi \; ? \; P \; : \; Q) \mid P \wedge Q \mid P \star Q \mid \exists \, x. \, P$$

Disjunction, negation, and implication are excluded because they cause issues for describing the set of ℓ-visible heap location to the ℓ-attacker, similarly to the problem of defining heap footprints for non-precise assertions [26, 40, 41]. These connectives can still occur between pure and relational expressions.

The standard expression semantics $[\![e]\!]_s$ evaluates e over a store s, which assigns values to variables x as $s(x)$. The interpretation $f^{\mathcal{A}}$ of a function symbol f is a function, given statically by a logical structure $\mathcal{A}$. Specifically, $\sqsubseteq^{\mathcal{A}}$ is the semantic ordering of the security lattice. We write $s \models \phi$ if $[\![\phi]\!]_s = \mathit{true}$.

The relational semantics of assertions, written $(s, h), (s', h') \models_\ell P$, is defined in Fig. 2 over two states (s, h) and (s', h') each consisting of a store and a heap. The semantics is defined against the attacker security level ℓ (called ℓ_A in Sect. 2.3). Stores s and s' are related via $e :: e_l$. We require the expression e_l denoting the sensitivity to coincide on s and s' and whenever $[\![e_l]\!]_s \sqsubseteq^{\mathcal{A}} \ell$ holds, e must evaluate to the same value both states, (7). Heaps are related by $(s, h), (s', h') \models_\ell e_p \overset{e_l}{\longmapsto} e_v$, which similarly ensures that the two heap fragments are identical $h = h'$ when e_l says so, (9). Conditional assertions $\phi \mathbin{?} P : Q$ evaluate to P when ϕ holds (relationally), and to Q otherwise. The separating conjunction splits both heaps independently, (12). Similarly, the existential quantifier picks two values v and v', (13). Whether parts of the split resp. these two values actually agree will depend on other assertions made.

Using the abbreviation $s, h \models e_p \mapsto e_v \iff h = \{[\![e_p]\!]_s \mapsto [\![e_v]\!]_s\}$

$$(s, h), (s', h') \models_\ell \mathsf{emp} \iff h = h' = \varnothing \tag{5}$$

$$(s, h), (s', h') \models_\ell \phi \iff s \models \phi \text{ and } s' \models \phi \tag{6}$$

$$\begin{aligned}&(s, h), (s', h') \models_\ell e :: e_l \\ &\iff [\![e_l]\!]_s = [\![e_l]\!]_{s'} \text{ and } \left([\![e_l]\!]_s \sqsubseteq^{\mathcal{A}} \ell \implies [\![e]\!]_s = [\![e]\!]_{s'}\right)\end{aligned} \tag{7}$$

$$\begin{aligned}&(s, h), (s', h') \models_\ell \rho_1 \Rightarrow \rho_2 \\ &\iff (s, h), (s', h') \models_\ell \rho_1 \text{ implies } (s, h), (s', h') \models_\ell \rho_2\end{aligned} \tag{8}$$

$$\begin{aligned}&(s, h), (s', h') \models_\ell e_p \overset{e_l}{\longmapsto} e_v \\ &\iff s, h \models e_p \mapsto e_v \text{ and } s', h' \models e_p \mapsto e_v \text{ and } (s, h), (s', h') \models e_p :: e_l \wedge e_v :: e_l\end{aligned} \tag{9}$$

$$\begin{aligned}&(s, h), (s', h') \models_\ell (\phi \mathbin{?} P : Q) \\ &\iff \begin{cases}(s, h), (s', h') \models_\ell P, & \text{if } s \models \phi \text{ and } s' \models \phi \\ (s, h), (s', h') \models_\ell Q, & \text{otherwise}\end{cases}\end{aligned} \tag{10}$$

$$\begin{aligned}&(s, h), (s', h') \models_\ell P \wedge Q \\ &\iff (s, h), (s', h') \models_\ell P \text{ and } (s, h), (s', h') \models_\ell Q\end{aligned} \tag{11}$$

$$\begin{aligned}&(s, h), (s', h') \models_\ell P \star Q \\ &\iff \text{there are disjoint sub-heaps } h_1, h_2 \text{ and } h'_1, h'_2 \\ &\qquad \text{with } h = h_1 \uplus h_2 \text{ and } h' = h'_1 \uplus h'_2 \\ &\qquad \text{such that } (s, h_1), (s', h'_1) \models_\ell P_1 \text{ and } (s, h_2), (s', h'_2) \models_\ell P_2\end{aligned} \tag{12}$$

$$\begin{aligned}&(s, h), (s', h') \models_\ell \exists\, x.\ P \\ &\iff \text{there are values } v, v' \text{such that } (s(x := v), h), (s'(x := v'), h') \models P\end{aligned} \tag{13}$$

Fig. 2. Relational semantics of assertions.

To capture strong security properties, we require a declarative specification of which heap locations are considered visible to the ℓ-attacker, when assertion P

$$
\begin{aligned}
\mathrm{lows}_\ell(\rho, s) &= \emptyset, \qquad \textbf{notably } \mathrm{lows}_\ell(e :: e_l, s) = \emptyset \\
\mathrm{lows}_\ell(P \star Q, s) &= \mathrm{lows}_\ell(P \wedge Q, s) = \mathrm{lows}_\ell(P, s) \cup \mathrm{lows}_\ell(Q, s) \\
\mathrm{lows}_\ell(e_p \overset{e_l}{\longmapsto} e_v, s) &= \begin{cases} \{[\![e_p]\!]_s\}, & [\![e_l]\!]_s \sqsubseteq^{\mathcal{A}} \ell \\ \emptyset, & \text{otherwise} \end{cases} \\
\mathrm{lows}_\ell(\phi \;?\; P : Q, s) &= \begin{cases} \mathrm{lows}_\ell(P, s), & s \models \phi \\ \mathrm{lows}_\ell(Q, s), & \text{otherwise} \end{cases} \\
\mathrm{lows}_\ell(\exists\, x.\ P, s) &= \begin{cases} \mathrm{lows}_\ell(P, s), & \forall\, v.\ \mathrm{lows}_\ell(P, s) = \mathrm{lows}_\ell(P, s(x \mapsto v)) \\ \emptyset, & \text{otherwise} \end{cases}
\end{aligned}
$$

Fig. 3. Low locations of an assertion.

holds in some (initial) state (see Sect. 2.3). We define this set in Fig. 3, denoted $\mathrm{lows}_\ell(P, s)$ for initial store s. Note that, by design, the definition does not give a useful result for an existential like $\exists p\ v.\ p \overset{\mathsf{low}}{\longmapsto} v$. This mirrors the usual difficulty of defining footprints for non-precise separation logic assertions [26,40,41]. This restriction is not an issue in practice, as location sensitivity assertions $e_p \overset{e_l}{\longmapsto} e_v$ are intended to describe the static regions of memory (data sinks) visible to the attacker, for which existential quantification over variables free in e_p or e_l is not necessary. A generalization to all precise predicates should be possible.

3.2 Entailments

Although implications between spatial formulas is not part of the assertion language, entailments $P \overset{\ell}{\Longrightarrow} Q$ between assertions still play a role in SecCSL's Hoare style consequence rule (Conseq in Fig. 4). We discuss entailment now as it sheds useful light on some consequences of SecCSL's relational semantics.

Definition 1 (Secure Entailment). $P \overset{\ell}{\Longrightarrow} Q$ *holds iff*

- $(s, h), (s', h') \models_\ell P$ *implies* $(s, h), (s', h') \models_\ell Q$ *for all* s, h *and* s', h', and
- $\mathrm{lows}_\ell(P, s) \subseteq \mathrm{lows}_\ell(Q, s)$ *for all* s

The security level ℓ is used not just in the evaluation of the assertions but also to preserve the ℓ-attacker visible locations of P in Q. This reflects the intuition that P is stronger than Q, and so Q should make fewer assumptions than P on the limitations of an attacker's observational powers.

Proposition 1.

$$e = e' \wedge e_l = e_l{}' \wedge e :: e_l \overset{\ell}{\Longrightarrow} e' :: e_l{}' \tag{14}$$

$$e :: e_l \wedge e_l \sqsubseteq e_l{}' \wedge e_l{}' :: \ell \overset{\ell}{\Longrightarrow} e :: e_l{}' \tag{15}$$

$$e_l :: \ell \overset{\ell}{\Longrightarrow} c :: e_l \qquad \textit{for a constant } c \tag{16}$$

$$e_1 :: e_l \wedge \cdots \wedge e_n :: e_l \overset{\ell}{\Longrightarrow} f(e_1, \ldots, e_n) :: e_l \qquad \textit{for } n > 0 \tag{17}$$

$$e_p \overset{e_l}{\longmapsto} e_v \wedge e_l \sqsubseteq \ell \overset{\ell}{\Longrightarrow} e_p \overset{e_l}{\longmapsto} e_v \wedge e_p :: e_l \wedge e_v :: e_l \tag{18}$$

$$(\forall\ s.\ \mathrm{lows}_\ell(P, s) = \mathrm{lows}_\ell(Q, s)) \quad \textit{implies} \quad \phi \wedge (\phi\ ?\ P : Q) \overset{\ell}{\Longrightarrow} P \tag{19}$$

$$P \overset{\ell}{\Longrightarrow} P' \textit{ and } Q \overset{\ell}{\Longrightarrow} Q' \quad \textit{implies} \quad P \star Q \overset{\ell}{\Longrightarrow} P' \star Q' \tag{20}$$

Entailment (14) in Proposition 1 shows that sensitivity of values is compatible with equality. This property fails in the security separation logic of [14], where labels are part of the semantics of expressions but are not compared by equality. The second property (15) captures the intuition that less-sensitive data can always be used in contexts where more-sensitive data might be expected (but not vice-versa). Recall that $e_l{}'$ here is an expression. The additional condition $e_l{}' :: \ell$ guarantees that this expression denotes a meaningful security level, i.e. evaluates identically in both states (cf. (7)). (abusing notation to let the semantic ℓ stand for some expression that denotes it). Property (16) encodes that constants do not depend on any state; again the security level expression e_l must be meaningful, but trivially $c :: \ell$ when ℓ is constant, too. Value sensitivity is congruent with function application (17). This is not surprising, as functions map arguments equal in both states to equal results. Yet, as with (14) above, this property fails in [14] where security labels are attached to values. Note that the reverse entailment is false (e.g. for the constant function $\lambda x.c$).

Via (18), when $e_p \overset{e_l}{\longmapsto} e_v$ it follows that both the location e_p and the value e_v adhere to the level e_l, cf. (9). Note that the antecedent $e_p \overset{e_l}{\longmapsto} e_v$ is repeated in the consequent to ensure that the set of ℓ-attacker visible locations is preserved. Conditional assertions can be resolved when the test is definite, provided that P and Q describe the same set of public locations, (19) and symmetrically for $\neg\phi$. Finally, separating conjunction is monotone wrt. entailment (20).

3.3 Proof System

We consider a canonical concurrent programming language with shared heap locations protected by locks but without shared variables. Commands c comprise assignments to local variables, heap access (load and store),[1] sequential programming constructs, as well as parallel composition and locking. We assume

[1] Volatile memory locations can be treated analogously to locks by introducing an additional assertion characterizing that part of the heap, that is implicitly available to atomic commands. This feature is realized in the Isabelle theories [18] but omitted here in the interests of brevity.

a static collection of valid lock identifiers l, each of which has an assertion as its associated invariant $\mathrm{inv}(l)$, characterizing the protected portion of the heap. We describe the program semantics in Sect. 4 as part of the soundness proof.

$$c ::= x := e \mid x := [e_v] \mid [e_p] := e_v \mid \texttt{lock}\ l \mid \texttt{unlock}\ l \\ c_1; c_2 \mid c_1 \parallel c_2 \mid \texttt{if}\ b\ \texttt{then}\ c_1\ \texttt{else}\ c_2 \mid \texttt{while}\ b\ \texttt{do}\ c$$

The SecCSL proof rules are shown in Fig. 4. They extend the standard rules of concurrent separation logic [38] (CSL) by additional side-conditions that amount to information flow checks $e :: \_$ as part of the respective preconditions.

Similarly to [46], without loss of generality we require that assignments (rules Asg, Load) are always to distinct variables, to avoid renaming in the assertions. In the postcondition of Load, $x :: e_l$ can be derived by Conseq for (18). Storing to a heap location through an e_l-sensitive location $e_p \xrightarrow{e_l} e_v$ (rule Store) requires that the value e_v written to that location admits the corresponding security level e_l of the location e_p. Note that due to monotonicity (15) the security level does not have to match exactly. The rules for locking are standard [12]. To preclude information leaks through timing channels, the execution can branch on non-secret values only. This manifests in side conditions $b :: \ell$ for the respective branching condition b where, recall, ℓ is the attacker security level (If, While). Logical Split picks those two cases where $[\![\phi]\!]_s = [\![\phi]\!]_{s'}$, ruling out the other two by $\phi :: \ell$. The consequence rule (Conseq) uses entailment relative to ℓ (Definition 1). Rule Par has the usual proviso that the variables modified in one thread cannot interfere with those relied on by the other and its pre-/postcondition.

4 Security Definition and Soundness

The soundness theorem for SecCSL guarantees that if some triple $\ell \vdash \{P\}\ c\ \{Q\}$ is derived using the rules of Fig. 4, then: all executions of c started in a state satisfying precondition P are memory *safe*, partially *correct* with respect to postcondition Q, and moreover *secure* with respect to the sensitivity of values as denoted by P and Q and at all times respect the sensitivity of locations as denoted by P (see Sect. 2.3). Proof outlines are relegated to Appendix B. All results have been mechanised in Isabelle/HOL [37] and are available at [18].

The top-level security property of SecCSL is a noninterference condition [19]. Noninterference as a security property specifies, roughly, that for any pair of executions that start in states that agree on the values of all attacker-observable inputs, then, from the attacker's point of view the resulting executions will be indistinguishable, i.e. all of the attacker visible observations will agree. In SecCSL, what is "attacker-observable" depends on the attacker level ℓ. The "inputs" are the expressions e, and the attacker-visible inputs are those expressions e whose sensitivity is given by $e :: \ell'$ judgements in the precondition P for which $\ell' \sqsubseteq \ell$. The attacker-visible observations are the contents of all memory locations in $\mathrm{lows}_\ell(P, s)$, for initial store s and precondition P. Thus we define when two heaps are indistinguishable to the ℓ-attacker.

$$\frac{x \notin \mathsf{free}(e)}{\ell \vdash \{\mathtt{emp}\}\ x := e\ \{x = e\}}\ \textsc{Asg} \qquad \frac{x \notin \mathsf{free}(e_p, e_v, e_l)}{\ell \vdash \{e_p \overset{e_l}{\longmapsto} e_v\}\ x := [e_p]\ \{x = e_v \wedge e_p \overset{e_l}{\longmapsto} e_v\}}\ \textsc{Load}$$

$$\frac{}{\ell \vdash \{e_v :: e_l \wedge e_p \overset{e_l}{\longmapsto} \_\}\ [e_p] := e_v\ \{e_p \overset{e_l}{\longmapsto} e_v\}}\ \textsc{Store}$$

$$\frac{}{\ell \vdash \{\mathtt{emp}\}\ \mathtt{lock}\ l\ \{\mathrm{inv}(l)\}}\ \textsc{Lock} \qquad \frac{}{\ell \vdash \{\mathrm{inv}(l)\}\ \mathtt{unlock}\ l\ \{\mathtt{emp}\}}\ \textsc{Unlock}$$

$$\frac{\ell \vdash \{b \wedge P\}\ c\ \{Q\} \quad \ell \vdash \{\neg b \wedge P\}\ c\ \{Q\}}{\ell \vdash \{b :: \ell \wedge P\}\ \mathtt{if}\ b\ \mathtt{then}\ c_1\ \mathtt{else}\ c_2\ \{Q\}}\ \textsc{If} \qquad \frac{\ell \vdash \{\phi \wedge P\}\ c\ \{Q\} \quad \ell \vdash \{\neg\phi \wedge P\}\ c\ \{Q\}}{\ell \vdash \{\phi :: \ell \wedge P\}\ c\ \{Q\}}\ \textsc{Split}$$

$$\frac{\ell \vdash \{b \wedge b :: \ell \wedge P\}\ c\ \{b :: \ell \wedge P\}}{\ell \vdash \{b :: \ell \wedge P\}\ \mathtt{while}\ b\ \mathtt{do}\ c\ \{\neg b \wedge P\}}\ \textsc{While}$$

$$\frac{\ell \vdash \{P\}\ c_1\ \{R\} \quad \ell \vdash \{R\}\ c_2\ \{Q\}}{\ell \vdash \{P\}\ c_1; c_2\ \{Q\}}\ \textsc{Seq} \qquad \frac{\mathsf{modified}(c) \cap \mathsf{free}(F) = \varnothing \quad \ell \vdash \{P\}\ c\ \{Q\}}{\ell \vdash \{P \star F\}\ c\ \{Q \star F\}}\ \textsc{Frame}$$

$$\frac{P \overset{\ell}{\Longrightarrow} P' \quad Q' \overset{\ell}{\Longrightarrow} Q \quad \ell \vdash \{P'\}\ c\ \{Q'\}}{\ell \vdash \{P\}\ c\ \{Q\}}\ \textsc{Conseq} \qquad \frac{\mathsf{modified}(c_i) \cap \mathsf{free}(c_j, P_j, Q_j) = \varnothing \text{ for } i \neq j \quad \ell \vdash \{P_1\}\ c_1\ \{P_1\} \quad \ell \vdash \{P_2\}\ c_2\ \{P_2\}}{\ell \vdash \{P_1 \star P_2\}\ c_1 \parallel c_2\ \{Q_1 \star Q_2\}}\ \textsc{Par}$$

Fig. 4. Proof rules of SecCSL.

Definition 2 (**ℓ Equivalence**). *Two heaps coincide on a set of locations A, written $h \equiv_A h'$, iff for all $a \in A$. $a \in \mathrm{dom}\ (h) \cap \mathrm{dom}\ (h')$ and $h(a) = h'(a)$. Two heaps h and h' are ℓ-equivalent wrt. store s and assertion P, if $h \equiv_A h'$ for $A = \mathrm{lows}_\ell(P, s)$.*

Then, the ℓ-validity of an assertion P in the relational semantics witnesses ℓ-equivalence between the corresponding heaps.

Lemma 1. *If $(s, h), (s', h') \models_\ell P$, then $h \equiv_A h'$ for $A = \mathrm{lows}_\ell(P, s)$.*

Furthermore, if $(s, h), (s', h') \models_\ell P$, then $\mathrm{lows}_\ell(P, s) = \mathrm{lows}_\ell(P, s')$ since the security levels in labeled points-to predicates must coincide on s and s', cf. (9).

Semantics. Semantic configurations, denoted by k in the following, are one of three kinds: (**run** c, L, s, h) denotes a command c in a state s, h where L is a set of locks that are currently not held by any thread and can be acquired by c; (**stop** L, s, h) similarly denotes a final state s, h with residual locks L, and **abort** results from invalid heap access.

The single-step relation (**run** c, L, s, h) $\overset{\sigma}{\longrightarrow} k$ takes running configurations to successors k with respect to a schedule σ that resolves the non-determinism of parallel composition. The schedule σ is a list of *actions*: the action $\langle\tau\rangle$ represents the execution of atomic commands and the evaluation of conditionals;

the actions $\langle 1 \rangle$ and $\langle 2 \rangle$ respectively denote the execution of the left- and right-hand sides of a parallel composition for a single step, and so define a deterministic scheduling discipline reminiscent of separation kernels [32]. For example, $(\textbf{run}\ c_1 \parallel c_2, L, s, h) \xrightarrow{\langle 1 \rangle \cdot \sigma} (\textbf{run}\ c_1' \parallel c_2, L', s', h')$ if $(\textbf{run}\ c_1, L, s, h) \xrightarrow{\sigma} (\textbf{run}\ c_1', L', s', h')$. Configurations $(\textbf{run}\ \texttt{lock}\ l, L, s, h)$ can only be scheduled if $l \in L$ (symmetrically for $\texttt{unlock}$)) and otherwise block without a possible step.

Executions $k_1 \xrightarrow{\sigma_1 \cdots \sigma_n}{}^{*} k_{n+1}$ chain several steps $k_i \xrightarrow{\sigma_i} k_{i+1}$ by accumulating the schedule. We are considering partial correctness only, thus the schedule is always finite and so are all executions. The rules for program steps are otherwise standard and can be found in Appendix A.

Compositional Security. To prove that SecCSL establishes its top-level non-interference condition, we first define a compositional security condition that provides the central characterization of security for a command c with respect to precondition P and postcondition Q. That central, compositional property we denote $\text{secure}_\ell^n(P, c, Q)$ and formalize below in Definition 3. It ensures that the first n steps (or fewer if the program terminates before that) are safe and preserve ℓ-equivalence of the heap locations specified initially in P, but in a way that is compositional across multiple execution steps, across multiple threads of execution and across different parts of the heap. It is somewhat akin, although more precise than, prior characterizations based on *strong low bisimulation* [16,45].

Disregarding the case when c terminates before the n-th step for a moment, for a pair of initial states (s_1, h_1) and (s_1', h_1') and initial set of locks L_1, and a fixed schedule $\sigma = \sigma_1 \cdots \sigma_n$, $\text{secure}_\ell^{n+1}(P_1, c_1, Q)$ requires that c performs a sequence of lockstep execution steps from each initial state

$$\begin{aligned} (\textbf{run}\ c_i, L_i, s_i, h_i) &\xrightarrow{\sigma_i} (\textbf{run}\ c_{i+1}, L_{i+1}, s_{i+1}, h_{i+1}) \qquad \text{for } 1 \le i \le n \\ (\textbf{run}\ c_i, L_i, s_i', h_i') &\xrightarrow{\sigma_i} (\textbf{run}\ c_{i+1}, L_{i+1}, s_{i+1}', h_{i+1}') \end{aligned} \tag{21}$$

These executions must agree on the intermediate commands c_i and locks L_i and the ith pair of states must satisfy an intermediate assertion of the following form:

$$(s_i, h_i), (s_i', h_i') \models_\ell P_i \star F \star \text{invs}(L_i) \quad \text{where } \text{invs}(L_i) = \bigstar_{l_i \in L_i} \text{inv}(l_i) \tag{22}$$

Here P_i describes the part of the heap that command c_i is currently accessing. $\text{invs}(L_i)$ is the set of lock invariants for the locks $l_i \in L_i$ not currently acquired. Its presence ensures that whenever a lock is acquired that the associated invariant can be assumed to hold. Finally F is an arbitrary *frame*, an assertion that does not mention variables updated by c_i. Its inclusion allows the security property to compose with respect to different parts of the heap.

Moreover, each $P_{i+1} \star \text{invs}(L_{i+1})$ is required to preserve the sensitivity of all ℓ-visible heap locations of $P_i \star \text{invs}(L_i)$, i.e. so that $\text{lows}_\ell(P_i \star \text{invs}(L_i), s_i) \subseteq \text{lows}_\ell(P_{i+1} \star \text{invs}(L_{i+1}), s_{i+1})$. If some intermediate step $m \le n$ terminates, then $P_{m+1} = Q$, ensuring the postcondition holds when the executions terminate. Lastly, neither execution is allowed to reach an **abort** configuration.

If the initial state satisfies $P_1 \star F \star \text{invs}(L_1)$ then (22) holds throughout the entire execution, and establishes the end-to-end property that any final state indeed satisfies the postcondition and that $\text{lows}_\ell(P_1 \star \text{invs}(L_1), s_1) \subseteq \text{lows}_\ell(P_i \star \text{invs}(L_i), s_i)$ with respect to the initially specified low locations.

The property $\text{secure}^n_\ell(P, c, Q)$ is defined recursively to match the steps of the lockstep execution of the program.

Definition 3 (Security).

- $\text{secure}^0_\ell(P_1, c_1, Q)$ *holds always.*
- $\text{secure}^{n+1}_\ell(P_1, c_1, Q)$ *holds, iff for all pairs of states* (s_1, h_1), (s'_1, h'_1), *frames* F, *and sets of locks* L_1, *such that* $(s_1, h_1), (s'_1, h'_1) \models_\ell P_1 \star F \star \text{invs}(L_1)$, *and given two steps* $(\textbf{run}\ c_1, L_1, s_1, h_1) \xrightarrow{\sigma} k$ *and* $(\textbf{run}\ c_1, L_1, s'_1, h'_1) \xrightarrow{\sigma} k'$ *there exists an assertion* P_2 *and a pair of successor states with either of*
  - $k = (\textbf{stop}\ L_2, s_2, h_2)$ *and* $k' = (\textbf{stop}\ L_2, s'_2, h'_2)$ *and* $P_2 = Q$
  - $k = (\textbf{run}\ c_2, L_2, s_2, h_2)$ *and* $k' = (\textbf{run}\ c_2, L_2, s'_2, h'_2)$ *with* $\text{secure}^n_\ell(P_2, c_2, Q)$

  such that $(s_2, h_2), (s'_2, h'_2) \models_\ell P_2 \star F \star \text{invs}(L_2)$ *and* $\text{lows}_\ell(P_1 \star \text{invs}(L_1), s_1) \subseteq \text{lows}_\ell(P_2 \star \text{invs}(L_2), s_2)$ *in both cases.*

Two further side condition are imposed, ensuring all mutable shared state lies in the heap (cf. Sect. 3): c_1 doesn't modify variables occurring in $\text{invs}(L_1)$ and F (which guarantees that both remain intact), and the free variables in P_2 can only mention those already present in P_1, c_1, or in any lock invariant (which guarantees that P_2 remains stable against concurrent assignments). Note that each step can pick a different frame F, as required for the soundness of rule Par.

Lemma 2. $\ell \vdash \{P\}\ c\ \{Q\}$ *implies* $\text{secure}^n_\ell(P, c, Q)$ *for every* $n \geq 0$.

Safety, Correctness and Noninterference. Execution safety and correctness with respect to pre- and postcondition follow straightforwardly from Lemma 2.

Corollary 1 (Safety). *Given initial states* $(s_1, h_1), (s'_1, h'_1) \models_\ell P \star \text{invs}(L_1)$ *and two executions of a command c under the same schedule to resulting configurations k and k′ respectively, then* $\ell \vdash \{P\}\ c\ \{Q\}$ *implies* $k \neq \textbf{abort} \land k' \neq \textbf{abort}$.

Theorem 1 (Correctness). *For initial states* $(s_1, h_1), (s'_1, h'_1) \models_\ell P \star \text{invs}(L_1)$, *given two complete executions of a command c under the same schedule* σ

$$(\textbf{run}\ c, L_1, s_1, h_1) \xrightarrow{\sigma}{}^{*} (\textbf{stop}\ L_2, s_2, h_2)$$
$$(\textbf{run}\ c_i, L_i, s'_i, h'_i) \xrightarrow{\sigma}{}^{*} (\textbf{stop}\ L_2, s'_2, h'_2)$$

then $\ell \vdash \{P\}\ c\ \{Q\}$ *implies* $(s_2, h_2), (s'_2, h'_2) \models_\ell Q \star \text{invs}(L_2)$.

The top-level noninterference property also follows from Lemma 2 via Lemma 1. For brevity, we state the noninterference property directly in the theorem:

Theorem 2 (Noninterference). *Given a command c, and initial states* $(s_1, h_1), (s_1', h_1') \models_\ell P \star \text{invs}(L_1)$ *then* $\ell \vdash \{P\}\ c\ \{Q\}$ *implies* $h_i \equiv_A h_i'$, *where* $A = \text{lows}_\ell(P \star \text{invs}(L_1), s_1)$, *for all pairs of heaps* h_i *and* h_i' *arising from executing the same schedule from each initial state.*

5 SecC: Automating SecCSL

To demonstrate the ease by which SecCSL can be automated, we develop the prototype tool SecC, available at [18]. It implements the logic from Sect. 3 for a subset of C. SecC is currently used to explore reasoning about example programs with interesting security policies. Thus its engineering has focused on features related to security reasoning (e.g. deciding when conditions $\epsilon :: e_l$ are entailed) rather than reasoning about complex data structures.

Symbolic Execution. SecC automates SecCSL through symbolic execution, as pioneered for SL in [7]. Similarly to VeriFast's algorithm in [22], the verifier computes the strongest postcondition of a command c when executed in a symbolic state, yielding a set of possible final symbolic states. Each such state $\sigma = (\rho, s, \underline{P})$ maintains a path condition ρ of relational formulas (from procedure contracts, invariants, and the evaluation of conditionals) and a symbolic heap described by a list $\underline{P} = (P_1 \star \cdots \star P_n)$ of atomic spatial assertions (points-to and instances of defined predicates). The symbolic store s maps program variables to pure expressions, where $s(e)$ denotes substituting s into e. As an example, when $P_i = s(e_p) \mapsto v$ is part of the symbolic heap, a load $x := e_p$ in σ can be executed to yield the updated state $(\rho, s(x := v), \underline{P})$ where x is mapped to v.

To find the P_i we match the left-hand sides of points-to predicates. Similarly, matching is used during checking of entailments $\rho_1 \wedge \underline{P} \overset{\ell}{\Longrightarrow} \exists\ \underline{x}.\ \rho_2 \wedge \underline{Q}$, where the conclusion is normalized to prenex form. The entailment is reduced to a non-spatial problem by incrementally computing a substitution τ for the existentials $\underline{x}$, removing pairs $P_i = \tau(Q_j)$ in the process, as justified by (20) (see also "subtraction rules" in [7, Sec. 4]).

Finally, the remaining relational problem $\rho_1 \Rightarrow \rho_2$ without spatial connectives can be encoded into first-order [17], by duplicating the pure formulas in terms of fresh variables to represent the second state, and by the syntactic equivalent of (7). The resulting verification condition is discharged with Z3 [15]. This translation is semantically complete. For example, consider Fig. 4 from Prabawa et al. [43]. It has a conditional `if(b == b) ...`, whose check $(b = b)$::`low`, translated to $(b = b) = (b' = b')$ by SecC, holds independently of b's sensitivity.

Features. In addition to the logic from Sect. 3, SecC supports procedure modular verification with pre-/postconditions as usual; and it supports user-defined spatial predicates. While some issues of the C source language are not addressed (yet), such as integer overflow, those that impact directly on information flow security are taken into account. Specifically, the shortcut semantics of boolean operators `&&`, `||`, and ternary `_ ? _ : _` count as branching points and as such the left hand side resp. the test must not depend on sensitive data, similarly to the conditions of `if` statements and `while` loops.

A direct benefit of the integration of security levels into the assertion language is that it becomes possible to specify the sensitivity of data passed to library and operating system functions. For example, the execution time of `malloc(len)` would depend on the value of `len`, which can thus be required to satisfy `len` :: `low` by annotating its function header with an appropriate precondition, using SecC's `requires` annotation. Likewise, SecC can reason about limited forms of declassification, in which external functions are trusted to safely release otherwise sensitive data, by giving them appropriate pre-/postconditions. For example, a password hashing library function prototype might be annotated with a postcondition asserting its result is `low`, via SecC's `ensures` annotation.

Examples and Case Study. SecC proves Fig. 1 secure, and correctly flags buggy variants as insecure, e.g., where the test in thread 1 is reversed, or when thread 2 does not clear the `data` field upon setting the `is_classified` to `FALSE`. SecC also correctly analyzes those 7 examples from [17] that are supported by the logic and tool (each in ∼10 ms). All examples are available at [18].

To compare SecC and SecCSL against the recent Covern logic [34], we took a non-trivial example program that Murray et al. verified in Covern, manually translated it to C, and verified it automatically using SecC. The original program[2], written in Covern's tiny While language embedded in Isabelle/HOL, models the software functionality of a simplified implementation of the Cross Domain Desktop Compositor (CDDC) [5]. The CDDC is a device that facilitates interactions with multiple PCs, each of which runs applications at differing sensitivity, from a single keyboard, mouse and display. Its multi-threaded software handles routing of keyboard input to the appropriate PC and switching between the PCs via mouse gestures. Verifying the C translation required adding SecCSL annotations for procedure pre-/postconditions and loop invariants. The C translation including those annotations is ∼250 lines in length. The present, unoptimised, implementation of SecC verifies the resulting artifact in ∼5 s. In contrast, the Covern proof of this example requires ∼600 lines of Isabelle/HOL definitions/specification, plus ∼550 lines of Isabelle proof script.

6 Related Work

There has been much work targeting type systems and program logics for concurrent information flow. Karbyshev et al. [23] provide an excellent overview. Here we concentrate on work whose ideas are most closely related to SecCSL.

Costanzo and Shao [14] propose a sequential separation logic for reasoning about information flow. Unlike SecCSL, theirs does not distinguish value and location sensitivity. Their separation logic assertions have a fairly standard (non-relational) semantics, at the price of having a *security-aware* language semantics

[2] https://bitbucket.org/covern/covern/src/master/examples/cddc/Example_CDDC_WhileLockLanguage.thy.

that propagates security labels attached to values in the store and heap. As mentioned in Sect. 3.2, this has the unfortunate side-effect of breaking intuitive properties about sensitivity assertions. We conjecture that the absence of such properties would make their logic harder to automate than SecCSL, which SecC demonstrates is feasible. SecCSL avoids the aforementioned drawbacks by adopting a relational assertion semantics.

Gruetter and Murray [20] propose a security separation logic in Coq [8] for Verifiable C, the C subset of the Verified Software Toolchain [2,3]. However they provide no soundness proof for its rules and its feasibility to automate is unclear.

Two recent compositional logics for concurrent information flow are the Covern logic [34] and the type and effect system of Karbyshev et al. [23]. Both borrow ideas from separation logic. However, unlike SecCSL, neither is defined for languages with pointers, arrays etc.

Like SecCSL, Covern proves a timing-sensitive security property. Location sensitivity is defined statically by value-dependent predicates, and value sensitivity is tracked by a dependent security typing context Γ [35], relative to a Hoare logic predicate P over the entire shared memory. In Covern locks carry non-relational invariants. In contrast, SecCSL unifies these elements together into separation logic assertions with a relational semantics. Doing so leads to a much simpler logic, amenable to automation, while supporting pointers, etc.

On the other hand, Karbyshev et al. [23] prove a timing-*insensitive* security property, but rely on primitives to interact with the scheduler to prevent leaks via scheduling decisions. Unlike SecCSL, which assumes a deterministic scheduling discipline, Karbyshev et al. support a wider class of scheduling policies. Their system tracks resource ownership and transfer between threads at synchronisation points, similar to CSLs. Their resources include *labelled scheduler resources* that account for scheduler interaction, including when scheduling decisions become tainted by secret data—something that cannot occur in SecCSL's deterministic scheduling model.

Prior logics for sequential languages, e.g. [1,4], have also adopted separation logic ideas to reason locally about memory, combining them with relational assertions similar to SecCSL's $e :: e_l$ assertions. For instance, the agreement assertions $\mathsf{A}(e)$ of [4] coincide with SecCSL's $e :: \texttt{low}$. Unlike SecCSL, some of these logics support languages with explicit declassification actions [4].

Self-composition is another technique to exploit existing verification infrastructure for proofs of general hyperproperties [13], including but not limited to non-interference. Eilers et al. [17] present such an approach for Viper, which supports an assertion language similar to that of separation logic. It does not support public heap locations (which are information sources and sinks at the same time) albeit sinks can be modeled via preconditions of procedures. A similar approach is implemented in Frama-C [9]. Both of [9,17] do not support concurrency, and it remains unclear how self-composition could avoid an exponential blow-up from concurrent interleaving, which SecCSL avoids.

The soundness proof for SecCSL follows the general structure of Vafeiadis' [46] for CSL, which is also mechanised in Isabelle/HOL. There is, however, a technical difference: His analog of Definition 3, a recursive predicate called $\text{safe}_n(c, s, h, Q)$, refers to a semantic initial state s, h whereas we propagate a syntactic assertion (22) only. Our formulation has the benefit that some of the technical reasoning in the soundness proof is easier to automate. Its drawback is the need to impose technical side-conditions on the free variables of the frame F and the intermediate assertions P_i.

7 Conclusion

We presented SecCSL, a concurrent separation logic for proving expressive data-dependent information flow properties of programs. SecCSL is considerably simpler, yet handles features like pointers, arrays etc., which are out of scope for contemporary logics. It inherits the structure of traditional concurrent separation logics, and so like those logics can be automated via symbolic execution [10, 22,30]. To demonstrate this, we implemented SecC, an automatic verifier for expressive information flow security for a subset of the C language.

Separation logic has proved to be a remarkably powerful vehicle for reasoning about programs, weak memory concurrency [47], program synthesis [42], and many other domains. With SecCSL, we hope that in future the same possibilities might be opened to verified information flow security.

Acknowledgement. We thank the anonymous reviewers for their careful and detailed comments that helped significantly to clarify the discussion of finer points.

This research was sponsored by the Department of the Navy, Office of Naval Research, under award #N62909-18-1-2049. Any opinions, findings, and conclusions or recommendations expressed in this material are those of the author(s) and do not necessarily reflect the views of the Office of Naval Research.

A Command Semantics

Symmetric parallel rules in which c_2 is scheduled under the action $\langle 2 \rangle$ omitted.

$$\frac{s' = s(x \mapsto [\![e]\!]_s)}{(\textbf{run } x := e, L, s, h) \xrightarrow{\langle\tau\rangle} (\textbf{stop } L, s', h)} \qquad \frac{[\![e]\!]_s \notin \text{dom }(h)}{(\textbf{run } x := [e], L, s, h) \xrightarrow{\langle\tau\rangle} \textbf{abort}}$$

$$\frac{[\![e]\!]_s \in \text{dom }(h) \qquad s' = s(x \mapsto h([\![e]\!]_s))}{(\textbf{run } x := [e], L, s, h) \xrightarrow{\langle\tau\rangle} (\textbf{stop } L, s', h)} \qquad \frac{[\![e_1]\!]_s \notin \text{dom }(h)}{(\textbf{run } [e_1] := e_2, L, s, h) \xrightarrow{\langle\tau\rangle} \textbf{abort}}$$

$$\frac{[\![e_1]\!]_s \in \text{dom }(h) \qquad h' = h([\![e_1]\!]_s \mapsto [\![e_2]\!]_s)}{(\textbf{run } [e_1] := e_2, L, s, h) \xrightarrow{\langle\tau\rangle} (\textbf{stop } L, s, h')}$$

$$\frac{l \in L \qquad L' = L \setminus \{l\}}{(\textbf{run } \texttt{lock } l, L, s, h) \xrightarrow{\langle\tau\rangle} (\textbf{stop } L', s, h)}$$

$$\frac{l \notin L \qquad L' = L \cup \{l\}}{(\textbf{run}\ \texttt{unlock}\ l, L, s, h) \xrightarrow{\langle\tau\rangle} (\textbf{stop}\ L', s, h)}$$

$$\frac{(\textbf{run}\ c_1, L, s, h) \xrightarrow{\sigma} \textbf{abort}}{(\textbf{run}\ c_1; c_2, L, s, h) \xrightarrow{\sigma} \textbf{abort}}$$

$$\frac{(\textbf{run}\ c_1, L, s, h) \xrightarrow{\sigma} \textbf{abort}}{(\textbf{run}\ c_1 \parallel c_2, L, s, h) \xrightarrow{\langle 1\rangle\cdot\sigma} \textbf{abort}}$$

$$\frac{(\textbf{run}\ c_1, L, s, h) \xrightarrow{\sigma} (\textbf{stop}\ L', s', h')}{(\textbf{run}\ c_1; c_2, L, s, h) \xrightarrow{\sigma} (\textbf{run}\ c_2, L', s', h')}$$

$$\frac{(\textbf{run}\ c_1, L, s, h) \xrightarrow{\sigma} (\textbf{run}\ c_1', L', s', h')}{(\textbf{run}\ c_1; c_2, L, s, h) \xrightarrow{\sigma} (\textbf{run}\ c_1'; c_2, L', s', h')}$$

$$\frac{(\textbf{run}\ c_1, L, s, h) \xrightarrow{\sigma} (\textbf{stop}\ L', s', h')}{(\textbf{run}\ c_1 \parallel c_2, L, s, h) \xrightarrow{\langle 1\rangle\cdot\sigma} (\textbf{run}\ c_2, L', s', h')}$$

$$\frac{(\textbf{run}\ c_1, L, s, h) \xrightarrow{\sigma} (\textbf{run}\ c_1', L', s', h')}{(\textbf{run}\ c_1 \parallel c_2, L, s, h) \xrightarrow{\langle 1\rangle\cdot\sigma} (\textbf{run}\ c_1' \parallel c_2, L', s', h')}$$

$$\frac{\text{if } s \models b \text{ then } c' = c_1 \text{ else } c' = c_2}{(\textbf{run}\ \texttt{if}\ b\ \texttt{then}\ c_1\ \texttt{else}\ c_2, L, s, h) \xrightarrow{\langle\tau\rangle} (\textbf{run}\ c', L, s, h)}$$

$$\frac{s \not\models b}{(\textbf{run}\ \texttt{while}\ b\ \texttt{do}\ c, L, s, h) \xrightarrow{\langle\tau\rangle} (\textbf{stop}\ L, s, h)}$$

$$\frac{s \models b}{(\textbf{run}\ \underbrace{\texttt{while}\ b\ \texttt{do}\ c}_{\omega}, L, s, h) \xrightarrow{\langle\tau\rangle} (\textbf{run}\ (c; \omega), L, s, h)}$$

$$k \xrightarrow{\langle\rangle}{}^{*}\ k \qquad \frac{k \xrightarrow{\sigma_1} k' \qquad k' \xrightarrow{\sigma_2}{}^{*}\ k''}{k \xrightarrow{\sigma_1\cdot\sigma_2}{}^{*}\ k''}$$

B Proofs

Proof of Lemma 1

If $(s, h), (s', h') \models_\ell P$, then $h \overset{A}{\equiv} h'$ for $A = \text{lows}_\ell(P, s)$.

Proof. By induction on the structure of P, noting that $\text{lows}_\ell(\_, s)$ contains locations of the corresponding sub-heap only. □

Proof of Lemma 2

$\ell \vdash \{P\}\ c\ \{Q\}$ implies $\text{secure}_\ell^n(P, c, Q)$ for every $n \geq 0$.

Proof (Outline). By induction on the derivation of the validity of the judgement. Noting that $n = 0$ is trivial, we may unfold the recursion of the security definition once to prove the base cases of assignment, load, store, and locking, which then follow from the respective side conditions of the proof rules.

For rules IF and WHILE, the side condition $b :: \ell$ guarantees that the test evaluates equivalently in the two states and thus execution proceeds with the same remainder program.

Except for IF, all remaining rules need a second induction on n to stepwise match security of the premise to security of the conclusion (e.g. over the steps of the first command in a sequential composition $c_1; c_2$).

The rule FRAME instantiates the frame F with the same assertion in each step, whereas PAR uses the frame F to preserve the current precondition P_2 of c_2 over steps of c_1 and vice-versa. □

Proof of Corollary 1

Given a command c and initial states $(s_1, h_1), (s_1', h_1') \models_\ell P \star \text{invs}(L_1)$ and two executions under the same schedule to resulting configurations k and k' respectively, then $\ell \vdash \{P\}\ c\ \{Q\}$ implies $k \neq \textbf{abort} \wedge k' \neq \textbf{abort}$.

Proof. By induction on the number of steps n of the executions from $\text{secure}_\ell^n(P, c, Q)$ via Lemma 2. □

Proof of Theorem 1

Given a command c and initial states $(s_1, h_1), (s_1', h_1') \models_\ell P \star \text{invs}(L_1)$ and two complete executions under the same schedule σ

$$(\textbf{run}\ c, L_1, s_1, h_1) \xrightarrow{\sigma}{}^{*} (\textbf{stop}\ L_2, s_2, h_2)$$
$$(\textbf{run}\ c_i, L_i, s_i', h_i') \xrightarrow{\sigma}{}^{*} (\textbf{stop}\ L_2, s_2', h_2')$$

then $\ell \vdash \{P\}\ c\ \{Q\}$ implies $(s_2, h_2), (s_2', h_2') \models_\ell Q \star \text{invs}(L_2)$.

Proof. By induction on the number of steps n of the executions from $\text{secure}_\ell^n(P, c, Q)$ via Lemma 2. □

Proof of Theorem 2

Given a command c, and initial states $(s_1, h_1), (s_1', h_1') \models_\ell P \star \text{invs}(L_1)$ then $\ell \vdash \{P\}\ c\ \{Q\}$ implies $h_i \overset{A}{\equiv} h_i'$, where $A = \text{lows}_\ell(P, s_1)$, for all pairs of heaps h_i and h_i' arising from executing the same schedule from each initial state.

Proof. By induction on the number of steps i up to that state from $\text{secure}_\ell^i(P, c, Q)$ via Lemma 2 we have $\text{lows}_\ell(P \star \text{invs}(L_1), s_1) \subseteq \text{lows}_\ell(P_i \star \text{invs}(L_1), s_i)$ transitively over the prefix, where P_i and s_i are from the i-th state. The theorem then follows from Lemma 1 in Sect. 3.1. □

References

1. Amtoft, T., Bandhakavi, S., Banerjee, A.: A logic for information flow in object-oriented programs. In: Proceedings of Principles of Programming Languages (POPL), pp. 91–102. ACM (2006)
2. Appel, A.W., et al.: Program Logics for Certified Compilers. Cambridge University Press, New York (2014)
3. Appel, A.W., et al.: The Verified Software Toolchain (2017). https://github.com/PrincetonUniversity/VST
4. Banerjee, A., Naumann, D.A., Rosenberg, S.: Expressive declassification policies and modular static enforcement. In: Proceedings of Symposium on Security and Privacy (S&P), pp. 339–353. IEEE (2008)
5. Beaumont, M., McCarthy, J., Murray, T.: The cross domain desktop compositor: using hardware-based video compositing for a multi-level secure user interface. In: Annual Computer Security Applications Conference (ACSAC), pp. 533–545. ACM (2016)
6. Benton, N.: Simple relational correctness proofs for static analyses and program transformations. In: Proceedings of Principles of Programming Languages (POPL), pp. 14–25. ACM (2004)
7. Berdine, J., Calcagno, C., O'Hearn, P.W.: Symbolic execution with separation logic. In: Yi, K. (ed.) APLAS 2005. LNCS, vol. 3780, pp. 52–68. Springer, Heidelberg (2005). https://doi.org/10.1007/11575467_5
8. Bertot, Y., Castéran, P.: Interactive Theorem Proving and Program Development. Coq'Art: The Calculus of Inductive Constructions. Texts in Theoretical Computer Science. An EATCS Series. Springer, Heidelberg (2004). https://doi.org/10.1007/978-3-662-07964-5
9. Blatter, L., Kosmatov, N., Le Gall, P., Prevosto, V., Petiot, G.: Static and dynamic verification of relational properties on self-composed C code. In: Dubois, C., Wolff, B. (eds.) TAP 2018. LNCS, vol. 10889, pp. 44–62. Springer, Cham (2018). https://doi.org/10.1007/978-3-319-92994-1_3
10. Calcagno, C., Distefano, D.: Infer: an automatic program verifier for memory safety of C programs. In: Bobaru, M., Havelund, K., Holzmann, G.J., Joshi, R. (eds.) NFM 2011. LNCS, vol. 6617, pp. 459–465. Springer, Heidelberg (2011). https://doi.org/10.1007/978-3-642-20398-5_33
11. Calcagno, C., et al.: Moving fast with software verification. In: Havelund, K., Holzmann, G., Joshi, R. (eds.) NFM 2015. LNCS, vol. 9058, pp. 3–11. Springer, Cham (2015). https://doi.org/10.1007/978-3-319-17524-9_1
12. Chlipala, A.: Formal Reasoning About Programs (2016)
13. Clarkson, M.R., Schneider, F.B.: Hyperproperties. In: Proceedings of Computer Security Foundations Symposium (CSF), pp. 51–65 (2008)
14. Costanzo, D., Shao, Z.: A separation logic for enforcing declarative information flow control policies. In: Abadi, M., Kremer, S. (eds.) POST 2014. LNCS, vol. 8414, pp. 179–198. Springer, Heidelberg (2014). https://doi.org/10.1007/978-3-642-54792-8_10
15. de Moura, L., Bjørner, N.: Z3: an efficient SMT solver. In: Ramakrishnan, C.R., Rehof, J. (eds.) TACAS 2008. LNCS, vol. 4963, pp. 337–340. Springer, Heidelberg (2008). https://doi.org/10.1007/978-3-540-78800-3_24
16. Del Tedesco, F., Sands, D., Russo, A.: Fault-resilient non-interference. In: Proceedings of Computer Security Foundations Symposium (CSF), pp. 401–416. IEEE (2016)

17. Eilers, M., Müller, P., Hitz, S.: Modular product programs. In: Ahmed, A. (ed.) ESOP 2018. LNCS, vol. 10801, pp. 502–529. Springer, Cham (2018). https://doi.org/10.1007/978-3-319-89884-1_18
18. Ernst, G., Murray, T.: SecC tool description and Isabelle theories for SecCSL (2019). https://covern.org/secc
19. Goguen, J., Meseguer, J.: Security policies and security models. In: Proceedings of Symposium on Security and Privacy (S&P), Oakland, California, USA, pp. 11–20, April 1982
20. Gruetter, S., Murray, T.: Short paper: towards information flow reasoning about real-world C code. In: Proceedings of Workshop on Programming Languages and Analysis for Security (PLAS), pp. 43–48. ACM (2017)
21. Gu, R., et al.: CertiKOS: an extensible architecture for building certified concurrent OS kernels. In: Proceedings of USENIX Symposium on Operating Systems Design and Implementation (OSDI), November 2016
22. Jacobs, B., Smans, J., Philippaerts, P., Vogels, F., Penninckx, W., Piessens, F.: VeriFast: a powerful, sound, predictable, fast verifier for C and java. In: Bobaru, M., Havelund, K., Holzmann, G.J., Joshi, R. (eds.) NFM 2011. LNCS, vol. 6617, pp. 41–55. Springer, Heidelberg (2011). https://doi.org/10.1007/978-3-642-20398-5_4
23. Karbyshev, A., Svendsen, K., Askarov, A., Birkedal, L.: Compositional non-interference for concurrent programs via separation and framing. In: Bauer, L., Küsters, R. (eds.) POST 2018. LNCS, vol. 10804, pp. 53–78. Springer, Cham (2018). https://doi.org/10.1007/978-3-319-89722-6_3
24. Klein, G., et al.: Comprehensive formal verification of an OS microkernel. ACM Trans. Comput. Syst. **32**(1), 2:1–2:70 (2014)
25. Leroy, X.: Formal verification of a realistic compiler. Commun. ACM **52**(7), 107–115 (2009)
26. Löding, C., Madhusudan, P., Murali, A., Peña, L.: A first order logic with frames. http://madhu.cs.illinois.edu/FOFrameLogic.pdf
27. Lourenço, L., Caires, L.: Dependent information flow types. In: Proceedings of Principles of Programming Languages (POPL), Mumbai, India, pp. 317–328, January 2015
28. Mantel, H., Sands, D.: Controlled declassification based on intransitive noninterference. In: Chin, W.-N. (ed.) APLAS 2004. LNCS, vol. 3302, pp. 129–145. Springer, Heidelberg (2004). https://doi.org/10.1007/978-3-540-30477-7_9
29. Mantel, H., Sands, D., Sudbrock, H.: Assumptions and guarantees for compositional noninterference. In: Proceedings of Computer Security Foundations Symposium (CSF), Cernay-la-Ville, France, pp. 218–232, June 2011
30. Müller, P., Schwerhoff, M., Summers, A.J.: Viper: a verification infrastructure for permission-based reasoning. In: Jobstmann, B., Leino, K.R.M. (eds.) VMCAI 2016. LNCS, vol. 9583, pp. 41–62. Springer, Heidelberg (2016). https://doi.org/10.1007/978-3-662-49122-5_2
31. Murray, T.: Short paper: on high-assurance information-flow-secure programming languages. In: Proceedings of Workshop on Programming Languages and Analysis for Security (PLAS), pp. 43–48 (2015)
32. Murray, T., et al.: seL4: from general purpose to a proof of information flow enforcement. In: Proceedings of Symposium on Security and Privacy (S&P), San Francisco, CA, pp. 415–429, May 2013
33. Murray, T., Sabelfeld, A., Bauer, L.: Special issue on verified information flow security. J. Comput. Secur. **25**(4–5), 319–321 (2017)

34. Murray, T., Sison, R., Engelhardt, K.: COVERN: a logic for compositional verification of information flow control. In: Proceedings of European Symposium on Security and Privacy (EuroS&P), London, United Kingdom, April 2018
35. Murray, T., Sison, R., Pierzchalski, E., Rizkallah, C.: Compositional verification and refinement of concurrent value-dependent noninterference. In: Proceedings of Computer Security Foundations Symposium (CSF), pp. 417–431, June 2016
36. Newcombe, C., Rath, T., Zhang, F., Munteanu, B., Brooker, M., Deardeuff, M.: How Amazon web services uses formal methods. Commun. ACM **58**(4), 66–73 (2015)
37. Nipkow, T., Wenzel, M., Paulson, L.C. (eds.): Isabelle/HOL-A Proof Assistant for Higher-Order Logic. LNCS, vol. 2283. Springer, Heidelberg (2002). https://doi.org/10.1007/3-540-45949-9
38. O'Hearn, P.W.: Resources, concurrency and local reasoning. In: Gardner, P., Yoshida, N. (eds.) CONCUR 2004. LNCS, vol. 3170, pp. 49–67. Springer, Heidelberg (2004). https://doi.org/10.1007/978-3-540-28644-8_4
39. O'Hearn, P.W.: Continuous reasoning: scaling the impact of formal methods. In: Proceedings of Logic in Computer Science (LICS), pp. 13–25. ACM (2018)
40. O'Hearn, P.W., Yang, H., Reynolds, J.C.: Separation and information hiding. ACM Trans. Programm. Lang. Syst. (TOPLAS) **31**(3), 11 (2009)
41. Piskac, R., Wies, T., Zufferey, D.: Automating separation logic using SMT. In: Sharygina, N., Veith, H. (eds.) CAV 2013. LNCS, vol. 8044, pp. 773–789. Springer, Heidelberg (2013). https://doi.org/10.1007/978-3-642-39799-8_54
42. Polikarpova, N., Sergey, I.: Structuring the synthesis of heap-manipulating programs. Proc. ACM Program. Lang. **3**(POPL), 72 (2019)
43. Prabawa, A., Al Ameen, M.F., Lee, B., Chin, W.-N.: A logical system for modular information flow verification. Verification, Model Checking, and Abstract Interpretation. LNCS, vol. 10747, pp. 430–451. Springer, Cham (2018). https://doi.org/10.1007/978-3-319-73721-8_20
44. Reynolds, J.C.: Separation logic: a logic for shared mutable data structures. In: Proceedings of Logic in Computer Science (LICS), pp. 55–74. IEEE (2002)
45. Sabelfeld, A., Sands, D.: Probabilistic noninterference for multi-threaded programs. In: Proceedings of Computer Security Foundations Workshop (CSFW), pp. 200–214. IEEE (2000)
46. Vafeiadis, V.: Concurrent separation logic and operational semantics. In: Proceedings of Mathematical Foundations of Programming Semantics (MFPS), pp. 335–351 (2011)
47. Vafeiadis, V., Narayan, C.: Relaxed separation logic: a program logic for C11 concurrency. In: Proceedings of Object Oriented Programming Systems Languages & Applications (OOPSLA), pp. 867–884. ACM (2013)
48. Volpano, D., Smith, G.: Probabilistic noninterference in a concurrent language. J. Comput. Secur. **7**(2,3), 231–253 (1999)
49. Yang, H.: Relational separation logic. Theor. Comput. Sci. **375**(1–3), 308–334 (2007)
50. Zheng, L., Myers, A.C.: Dynamic security labels and static information flow control. Int. J. Inf. Secur. **6**(2–3), 67–84 (2007)

Reachability Analysis for AWS-Based Networks

John Backes[1], Sam Bayless[1,4], Byron Cook[1,2], Catherine Dodge[1], Andrew Gacek[1(✉)], Alan J. Hu[4], Temesghen Kahsai[1], Bill Kocik[1], Evgenii Kotelnikov[1,3], Jure Kukovec[1,5], Sean McLaughlin[1], Jason Reed[6], Neha Rungta[1], John Sizemore[1], Mark Stalzer[1], Preethi Srinivasan[1], Pavle Subotić[1,2], Carsten Varming[1], and Blake Whaley[1]

[1] Amazon, Seattle, USA
gacek@amazon.com
[2] University College London, London, UK
[3] Chalmers University of Technology, Gothenburg, Sweden
[4] University British Columbia, Vancouver, Canada
[5] TU Wien, Vienna, Austria
[6] Semmle Inc, San Francisco, USA

Abstract. Cloud services provide the ability to provision virtual networked infrastructure on demand over the Internet. The rapid growth of these virtually provisioned cloud networks has increased the demand for automated reasoning tools capable of identifying misconfigurations or security vulnerabilities. This type of automation gives customers the assurance they need to deploy sensitive workloads. It can also reduce the cost and time-to-market for regulated customers looking to establish compliance certification for cloud-based applications. In this industrial case-study, we describe a new network reachability reasoning tool, called TIROS, that uses off-the-shelf automated theorem proving tools to fill this need. TIROS is the foundation of a recently introduced network security analysis feature in the *Amazon Inspector* service now available to millions of customers building applications in the cloud. TIROS is also used within Amazon Web Services (AWS) to automate the checking of compliance certification and adherence to security invariants for many AWS services that build on existing AWS networking features.

1 Introduction

Cloud computing provides on-demand access to IT resources such as compute, storage, and analytics via the Internet with pay-as-you-go pricing. Each of these IT resources are typically networked together by customers, using a growing number of virtual networking features. Amazon Web Services (AWS), for example, today provides over 30 virtualized networking primitives that allow customers to implement a wide variety of cloud-based applications.

Correctly configured networks are a key part of an organization's security posture. Clearly documented and, more importantly, verifiable network design

I. Dillig and S. Tasiran (Eds.): CAV 2019, LNCS 11562, pp. 231–241, 2019.
https://doi.org/10.1007/978-3-030-25543-5_14

is important for compliance audits, *e.g.* the Payment Card Industry Data Security Standard (PCI DSS) [10]. As the scale and diversity of cloud-based services grows, each new offering used by an organization adds another dimension of possible interaction at the networking level. Thus, customers and auditors increasingly need tooling for the security of their networks that is accurate, automated and scalable, allowing them to automatically detect violations of their requirements.

In this industrial case-study, we describe a new tool, called TIROS, which uses off-the-shelf automated theorem proving tools to perform formal analysis of virtual networks constructed using AWS APIs. TIROS encodes the semantics of AWS networking concepts into logic and then uses a variety of reasoning engines to verify security-related properties. Tools that TIROS can use include SOUFFLÉ [17], MONOSAT [3], and VAMPIRE [23]. TIROS performs its analysis statically: it sends no packets on the customer's network. This distinction is important. The size of many customer networks makes it intractable to find problems through traditional network probing or penetration testing. TIROS allows users to gain assurance about the security of their networks that would be impossible through testing.

TIROS is used directly today by AWS customers as part of the Amazon Inspector service [11], which currently checks six TIROS-based network reachability invariants on customer networks. The use of TIROS is especially popular amongst security-obsessed customers, *e.g.,* the world's largest hedge fund Bridgewater Associates, an AWS customer, recently discussed the importance of network verification techniques for their organization [6], including their usage of TIROS.

Related Work. Several previous tools using automated theorem proving have been developed in an effort to answer questions about software defined networks (SDNs) [1,2,5,12,13,16,19,25]. Similar to our approach, these tools reduce the problems to automated reasoning engines. In some cases, they employ over-approximative static analysis [18,19]. In other cases, they use general purpose reasoning engines such as Datalog [12,15], BDD [1], SMT [5,16], and SAT Solvers [2,25]. VeriCon [2], NICE [8], and VeriFlow [19] verify network invariants by analyzing software-defined-network (SDN) programs, with the former two applying formal software verification techniques, and the latter using static analysis to split routes into equivalence classes. SecGuru [5,16] uses an SMT solver to compare the routes admitted by access control lists (ACLs), routing tables, and border gateway protocol (BGP) policies, but does not support full-network reachability queries. In our approach we employ multiple encodings and reasoning engines. Our SMT encoding is similar in design to Anteater [25] and ConfigChecker [1]. Anteater performs SAT-based bounded model checking [4], while ConfigChecker uses BDD-based fixed-point model checking [7]. Previous work has applied Datalog to reachability analysis in either software or network contexts [12–14,24]. The approach used in Batfish [13,24] and SyNET [12] is similar to our Datalog approach; they allow users to express general queries about whole-network reachability properties using an expressive logic language.

Batfish presents results for small but complex routing scenarios, involving a few dozen routers. SyNET [12] also uses a similar Datalog representation of network reachability semantics, but rather than verifying network reachability properties, they provide techniques to synthesize networks from a specification. The focus in TIROS's encoding is expressiveness and completeness; it encodes the semantics of the entire AWS cloud network service stack. It scales well to networks consisting of hundreds of thousands of instances, routers, and firewall rules.

2 AWS Networking

AWS provides customers with virtualized implementations of practically all known traditional networking concepts, *e.g.* subnets, route tables, and NAT gateways. In order to facilitate on-demand scalability, many AWS network features focus on elasticity, *e.g.* Elastic Load Balancers (ELBs) support autoscaling groups, which customers configure to describe when/how to scale resource usage. Another important AWS networking concept is that of Virtual Private Cloud (VPC), in which customers can use AWS resources in an isolated virtual network that they control. Over 30 additional networking concepts are supported by AWS, including Elastic Network Interfaces (ENIs), internet gateways, transit gateways, direct connections, and peering connections.

Figure 1 is an example AWS-based network that consists of two subnets "Web" and "Database". The "Web" subnet contains two instances (sometimes called virtual machines) and the "Database" subnet contains one instance. Note that these machines are in fact virtualized in the AWS data center. The "Web" subnet's route table has a route to the internet gateway, whereas the "Database" subnet's route table only has local routes (within the VPC). In addition, each of the subnets has an ACL that contains security access rules. In particular, one of the rules forbids SSH access to the database servers.

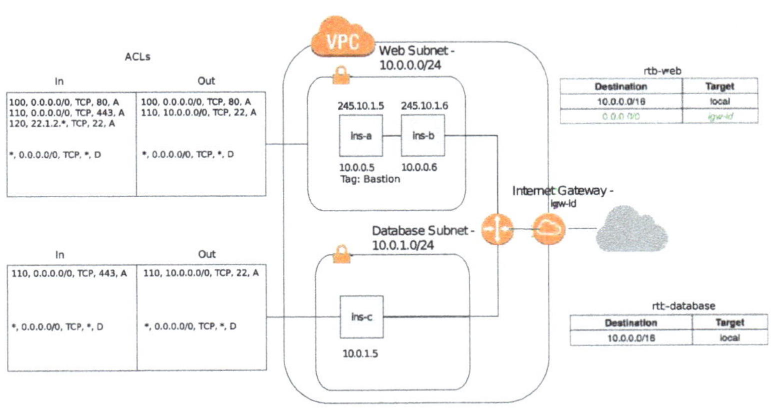

Fig. 1. An example VPC network

AWS-based networks frequently start small and grow over time, accumulating new instances and security and access rules. Customers or regulators want to make sure that their VPC networks retain security invariants as their complexity grows. A customer may ask *network configuration questions* such as:

1. *"Are there any instances in subnet 'Web' that are tagged 'Bastion'?"* or *network reachability questions* such as:
2. *"Are there any instances that can be accessed from the public internet over SSH (TCP port 22)?"*

To answer such questions we must reason about which network components are accessible via feasible paths through the VPC, either from the internet, from other components in the VPC, or from other components in a different VPC via a peering connection or transit gateway.

3 AWS Networking Semantics as Logic

TIROS statically builds a model of an AWS network architecture to check reachability properties. The model of the network consists of two parts, the *formal specification* and the *snapshot* of the network. The specification formalizes the semantics of the AWS networking components, *e.g.*, how a route table directs traffic from a subnet, in which order a firewall applies rules in a security group, and how load balancers route traffic. The snapshot describes the topology and details of the network. For example, the snapshot contains the list of instances, subnets, and their route tables in a particular VPC (or set of VPCs). To answer reachability questions, TIROS combines the formal specification, the snapshot, and a query into a formula that represents the answer. Tiros uses up to three reasoning engines to answer queries: the Datalog solver SOUFFLÉ [17], the SMT solver MONOSAT [3], or the first-order theorem prover VAMPIRE [23]. Due to the differing limitations and capabilities of each of these tools, we maintain three independent encodings of network semantics into logic, one for each of solver.

Datalog Encoding. In the Datalog encoding, a network model is a set of Datalog clauses (stratified, possibly recursive or negated Horn clauses without function symbols) using the theory of bit vectors to describe ports, IPv4 addresses, and subnet masks. The *specification* part of the network model contains types, predicates, constants, and rules that describe the semantics of the networking components in Amazon VPCs. The specification of Amazon VPC networks maps to approximately 50 types, 200 predicates, and over 240 rules. For example, a specification of the semantics of SSH tunneling is defined recursively: An instance can SSH tunnel to another instance iff it can either SSH to it directly, or through a chain of intermediate instances. We express this with predicates *canSshTunnel* and *canSsh*, of the type Instance × Instance, and rules:

$$\begin{aligned} &\mathit{canSshTunnel}(I_1, I_2) \leftarrow \mathit{canSsh}(I_1, I_2).\\ &\mathit{canSshTunnel}(I_1, I_2) \leftarrow \mathit{canSshTunnel}(I_1, I_3) \wedge \mathit{canSshTunnel}(I_3, I_2). \end{aligned}$$

The *snapshot* part of the network model contains constants and *facts* (ground clauses with no antecedents) that describe the configuration of a specific AWS network. Constants have the form type_{id}. For example, the snapshot of a network with an instance with id 1234 in a subnet with id *web* consists of the constants instance_{1234} and $\text{subnet}_{\text{web}}$, and the fact $hasSubnet(\text{instance}_{1234}, \text{subnet}_{\text{web}})$.

We illustrate the Datalog encoding using examples from Sect. 2. The network configuration question, $q(I)$, is encoded as $q(I) \leftarrow hasSubnet(I, \text{subnet}_{\text{web}}) \wedge hasTag(I, \text{tag}_{\text{bastion}})$. The network reachability question, $r(I, E)$, is encoded as:

$$r(I, E) \leftarrow hasEni(I, E) \wedge isPublicIP(Address) \wedge \\ reachPublicTcpUdp(\text{dir}_{\text{ingress}}, \text{proto}_6, E, \text{port}_{22}, Adress, \text{port}_{40000}).$$

In our Datalog encoding, we use the theory of bitvectors to reason about ports, IP addresses, and CIDRs. We use SOUFFLÉ as our Datalog solver, but in principle other Datalog solvers could also be used, so long as they also support bitvectors. We direct the reader to our co-author's dissertation (cf. Chapter 7 [28]) for a more detailed explanation of the Datalog encoding.

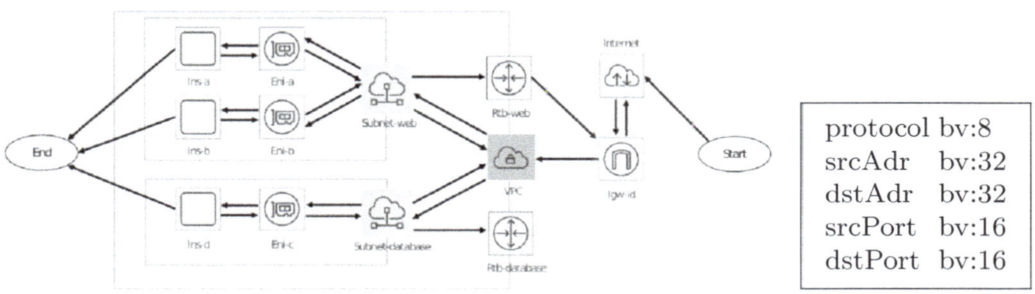

Fig. 2. (Left) The symbolic graph corresponding to the VPC in Fig. 1. (Right) A simplified symbolic packet, composed of bitvectors.

SMT Encoding. Our SMT encoding models network reachability as a *symbolic graph* of network components, along with one or more symbolic packet headers consisting of bitvectors for the source and destination addresses and ports. A symbolic graph consists of a set of nodes and directed edges, where the edges may be traversable or untraversable. Predicate $edge(u, v)$, where u and v are nodes, is true iff the corresponding edge is traversable. The assignment of the $edge(u, v)$ atoms in the formula determines which paths exist in the graph.

Figure 2 shows a symbolic graph corresponding to the VPC from Fig. 1. In our encoding, nodes represent networking components (such as instances, network interfaces, subnets, route tables, or gateways), and edges represent possible paths that packets may take between those components (such as between an instance and its network interface). Constraints between edge atoms and bitvectors in the packet headers define the routes that a packet can take.

For example, our encoding introduces an edge between each network interface node, Eni-a, and its containing Subnet-web node, $edge(\text{Eni-a}, \text{Subnet-web})$. As shown in Fig. 3, we also introduce constraints that force $edge(\text{Eni-a}, \text{Subnet-web})$

to be false if the packet's source address does not match the ENI's IP address. This ensures that packets leaving the ENI must have that ENI's IP address as their source address. Similar constraints ensure that packets entering the ENI must have that ENI's IP address as their destination address.

We encode reachability constraints into this graph using the SMT solver MonoSAT [3], which supports a theory of finite graph reachability. Specifically, we add a *start* and *end* node to the graph, with edges to the source components of the query and from the destination components of the query, and then we enforce a graph reachability constraint $reaches(start, end)$, which is true iff there is a start-end path under assignment to the edge literals. To encode the query "Are there any instances that can be accessed from the public internet over SSH?", we would add an edge from the *start* node to the internet, and from each EC2 instance to the *end* node. Additionally, we would add bitvector constraints forcing the protocol of the symbolic packet to be exactly 6 (TCP), and the destination port to be exactly 22.

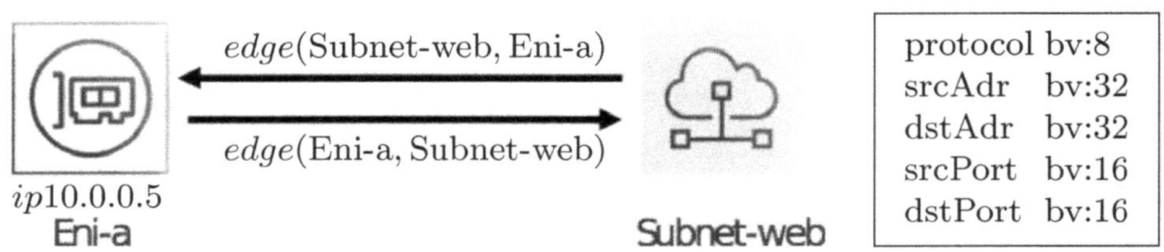

$$((srcAdr \neq 10.0.0.5) \implies \neg edge(\text{Eni-a}, \text{Subnet-web}))$$
$$((dstAdr \neq 10.0.0.5) \implies \neg edge(\text{Subnet-web}, \text{Eni-a}))$$

Fig. 3. A small portion of the VPC graph, with constraints over the edges between an ENI and its subnet enforcing that packets entering or leaving the ENI have that ENI's source or destination address.

The SMT encoding described above is intended specifically for answering network reachability queries, and does not currently take into account other properties (such as tags) that would be required to model the more general network configuration queries supported by our datalog encoding.

First-Order Encoding. In our encoding for superposition solvers such as Vampire [23], we translate each network configuration question into a many-sorted first order logic problem that is unsatisfiable iff the answer to the question is true, and each network reachability question into a FOL problem that only has finite models, each corresponding to an answer to the question. For this encoding, we assume that network configuration questions have strictly yes/no answers, while network reachability questions return lists of solutions. In addition to its default saturation mode, Vampire implements a MACE-style [26] finite model builder for many-sorted first-order logic [27]. Thus we use Vampire both as a saturation-based theorem prover and a finite model builder, running both modes in parallel and recording the result of the fastest successful run.

Our encoding begins with the same set of facts as were generated from the network model by our Datalog encoding, represented here by the symbols $(A_1, A_2, \ldots)$. From there, we handle network configuration and network reachability questions differently, with network-configuration encodings optimized for proof-by-contradiction, while reachability configurations are optimized for model-building. Proof-by-contradiction for yes/no questions is potentially faster than model-building, as intermediate variables need not be enumerated.

We encode a network configuration question φ in negated form: $A_1 \wedge \ldots \wedge A_n \Rightarrow \neg\varphi$. If Vampire can prove a contradiction in the negated formula, then φ holds. We encode a network reachability question φ into a formula of the form $A_1 \wedge \ldots \wedge A_n \wedge (\forall \bar{z})(q(\bar{z}) \Leftrightarrow \varphi) \Rightarrow (\forall \bar{z})q(\bar{z})$, where q is a fresh predicate symbol, and $\bar{z}$ are free variables of the network question φ. Each substitution of $\bar{z}$ that satisfies q corresponds to a distinct solution to the reachability question.

Our encoding targets Vampire's implementation of many-sorted first-order logic with equality, extended with the theory of linear integer arithmetic, the theory of arrays [22], and the theory of tuples [20]. We encode types, constants, and predicates using Clark completion [9]. We direct the reader to our co-author's dissertation (cf. Chapter 5 [21]) for a more detailed explanation of the Vampire encoding, including a detailed analysis of the performance trade-offs considered in this encoding.

4 Usage and Performance

In this section we describe the performance of the various solvers when used by Tiros in practice. Recall that our MonoSAT implementation can only answer reachability questions, whereas the other implementations also answer more general network configuration questions (such as the examples in Sect. 2).

In our experiments with Vampire, we found that the first order logic encoding we used does not scale well. As we were not able to obtain good performance from our Vampire-based implementation, in what follows we only present the experimental results for MonoSAT and Soufflé. We explain the poor performance of the Vampire encoding mainly by the fact that large finite domains, routinely used in network specifications, are represented as long clauses coming from the domain closure axioms. Saturation theorem provers, including Vampire, have a hard time dealing with such clauses.

Amazon Inspector. To compare the performance of Soufflé and MonoSAT in the context of the Tiros-based Amazon Inspector feature we randomly selected 10,000 network snapshots evaluated in December 2018. On these queries Soufflé required 4.1 s in the best-case, 45.1 s in the worst case, with 50th-percentile runtime of 5.1 s and 90th-percentile runtime of 5.5 s. MonoSAT required 0.8 s in the best case, 2.6 s in the worst case, with a 50th-percentile runtime of 1.39 s and 90th-percentile runtime of 1.79 s. To give the reader an idea of the relative size of the constraint systems solved, in the smallest case our Soufflé encoding consisted of 2,856 facts, and the MonoSAT encoding consisted of 609 variables, 21 bitvectors, and 2,032 clauses. In the largest case, our Soufflé encoding consisted of 7517 facts, and the MonoSAT encoding consisted of 2,038 variables, 21 bitvectors, and 17,731 clauses.

Scalability Tests. MonoSAT and Soufflé scale to all queries evaluated using Amazon Inspector. To help understand the limits of the Soufflé and MonoSAT-based backends on larger networks, in Fig. 4 we compare the performance of the solvers on a series of artificially generated networks of increasing size, with 100, 1000, 10,000, and 100,000 instances. In each case, the query is *"list all open paths from the Internet to any instance in the VPC"*. We can see from the figure that neither approach dominates. In most cases the Datalog encoding is able to scale to 10,000 instances, but in no cases can it scale to 100,000 instances. In most cases the SMT encoding is able to scale to networks with 100,000 instances, but for the 'benchmark-2' networks, MonoSAT requires almost a full hour to solve the 10,000 instance network that Soufflé solves in 81 s. The SMT encoding performs poorly on 'benchmark-2' because that benchmark has a vast number of distinct feasible paths through the network, each requiring a separate SMT solver call. Other benchmarks have fewer distinct paths.

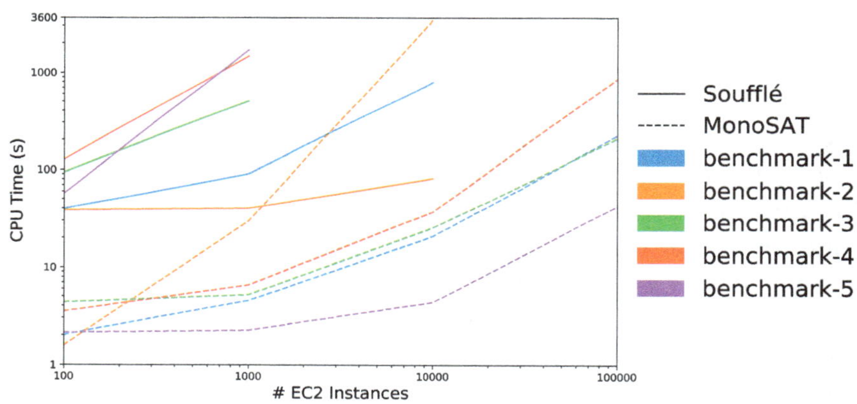

Fig. 4. Comparison of runtime in seconds for the different solver backends. Each benchmark uses a different color, *e.g.* Soufflé on benchmark-1 is a solid blue line, and MonoSAT on benchmark-1 is a dashed blue line. In these experiments, Soufflé recompiles each query before solving it, which adds ≈ 45 s to the runtime of each Soufflé query. In practice this cost can be amortized by caching compiled queries. (Color figure online)

Automating PCI Compliance Auditing. Many AWS services are built using other AWS services, *e.g.* AWS Lambda is built using AWS EC2 and the various AWS networking features. Thus within AWS we are using Tiros to prove the correctness of our own internal requirements. As an example, we use Tiros to partially automate evidence generation for compliance audits of Payment Card Industry Data Security Standard (PCI DSS) [10]. Tiros is used across the many customer-facing AWS services that are built using AWS networking to establish controls supporting PCI DSS requirements 1.2, 1.3.1, 1.3.2, 1.3.4, and 1.3.7a.

Custom Application. AWS's Professional Services team works with some of the most security-obsessed customers to use advanced tools such as Tiros to achieve custom-tailored solutions. For example, as discussed in a public lecture [6], Bridgewater Associates worked with AWS Professional Services to build a Tiros-based solution which proves invariants of new AWS-based network designs before they are deployed in Bridgewater's AWS environment. Proof of these invariants assures the absence of possible data exfiltration paths that could be leveraged by an adversary.

5 Conclusion

We have described the first complete formalization of AWS networking semantics into logic. For customers of AWS services, Tiros provides deep insights into AWS networking. Via the incorporation of Tiros into the Amazon Inspector service, millions of AWS customers are able to automatically and continuously maintain their network-based security posture. They can now show compliance with security requirements at a scale that was impossible before. Internally within AWS, we are also able to automate some aspects of compliance evidence generation, which lowers our costs and increases our ability to quickly launch new features and services.

References

1. Al-Shaer, E., Marrero, W., El-Atawy, A., Elbadawi, K.: Network configuration in A box: towards end-to-end verification of network reachability and security. In: Proceedings of the 17th Annual IEEE International Conference on Network Protocols, 2009. ICNP 2009, Princeton, NJ, USA, 13–16 October 2009, pp. 123–132 (2009). https://doi.org/10.1109/ICNP.2009.5339690
2. Ball, T., et al.: VeriCon: towards verifying controller programs in software-defined networks. In: ACM SIGPLAN Conference on Programming Language Design and Implementation, PLDI 2014, Edinburgh, UK, 9–11 June 2014, pp. 282–293 (2014). https://doi.org/10.1145/2594291.2594317, http://doi.acm.org/10.1145/2594291.2594317
3. Bayless, S., Bayless, N., Hoos, H.H., Hu, A.J.: SAT modulo monotonic theories. In: Proceedings of AAAI, pp. 3702–3709 (2015)
4. Biere, A., Cimatti, A., Clarke, E., Zhu, Y.: Symbolic model checking without BDDs. In: Cleaveland, W.R. (ed.) TACAS 1999. LNCS, vol. 1579, pp. 193–207. Springer, Heidelberg (1999). https://doi.org/10.1007/3-540-49059-0_14
5. Bjørner, N., Jayaraman, K.: Checking cloud contracts in Microsoft azure. In: Natarajan, R., Barua, G., Patra, M.R. (eds.) ICDCIT 2015. LNCS, vol. 8956, pp. 21–32. Springer, Cham (2015). https://doi.org/10.1007/978-3-319-14977-6_2

6. Bridgewater Associates: Bridgewater's model-based verification of AWS security controls. AWS New York Summit (2018). https://www.youtube.com/watch?v=gJhV35-QBE8
7. Burch, J.R., Clarke, E.M., McMillan, K.L., Dill, D.L., Hwang, L.J.: Symbolic model checking: 10^{20} states and beyond. Inf. Comput. **98**(2), 142–170 (1992)
8. Canini, M., Venzano, D., Peresini, P., Kostic, D., Rexford, J.: A nice way to test openflow applications. In: Proceedings of the 9th USENIX Symposium on Networked Systems Design and Implementation (NSDI). No. EPFL-CONF-170618 (2012)
9. Clark, K.L.: Negation as failure. In: Gallaire, H., Minker, J. (eds.) Logic and Data Bases, pp. 293–322. Springer, Boston (1977). https://doi.org/10.1007/978-1-4684-3384-5_11
10. CSS Council. Payment Card Industry (PCI) Data Security Standard Requirements and Security Assessment Procedures Version 3.2.1. PCI Security Standards Council (2018)
11. Dodge, C., Quigg, S.: A simpler way to assess the network exposure of EC2 instances: AWS releases new network reachability assessments in amazon inspector. AWS Security Blog (2018). https://aws.amazon.com/blogs/security/amazon-inspector-assess-network-exposure-ec2-instances-aws-network-reachability-assessments/
12. El-Hassany, A., Tsankov, P., Vanbever, L., Vechev, M.: Network-wide configuration synthesis. In: Majumdar, R., Kunčak, V. (eds.) CAV 2017. LNCS, vol. 10427, pp. 261–281. Springer, Cham (2017). https://doi.org/10.1007/978-3-319-63390-9_14
13. Fogel, A., et al.: A general approach to network configuration analysis. In: Proceedings of the 12th USENIX Conference on Networked Systems Design and Implementation, NSDI 2015, pp. 469–483. USENIX Association, Berkeley (2015). http://dl.acm.org/citation.cfm?id=2789770.2789803
14. Hajiyev, E., Verbaere, M., de Moor, O.: *codeQuest*: scalable source code queries with datalog. In: Thomas, D. (ed.) ECOOP 2006. LNCS, vol. 4067, pp. 2–27. Springer, Heidelberg (2006). https://doi.org/10.1007/11785477_2
15. Hoder, K., Bjørner, N., de Moura, L.: $\mu Z-$ an efficient engine for fixed points with constraints. In: Gopalakrishnan, G., Qadeer, S. (eds.) CAV 2011. LNCS, vol. 6806, pp. 457–462. Springer, Heidelberg (2011). https://doi.org/10.1007/978-3-642-22110-1_36. http://dl.acm.org/citation.cfm?id=2032305.2032341
16. Jayaraman, K., Bjørner, N., Outhred, G., Kaufman, C.: Automated analysis and debugging of network connectivity policies. In: Microsoft Research, pp. 1–11 (2014)
17. Jordan, H., Scholz, B., Subotić, P.: SOUFFLÉ: on synthesis of program analyzers. In: Chaudhuri, S., Farzan, A. (eds.) CAV 2016. LNCS, vol. 9780, pp. 422–430. Springer, Cham (2016). https://doi.org/10.1007/978-3-319-41540-6_23
18. Kazemian, P., Varghese, G., McKeown, N.: Header space analysis: static checking for networks. In: NSDI, vol. 12, pp. 113–126 (2012)
19. Khurshid, A., Zou, X., Zhou, W., Caesar, M., Godfrey, P.B.: Veriflow: verifying network-wide invariants in real time. In: Proceedings of the 10th USENIX Symposium on Networked Systems Design and Implementation, NSDI 2013, Lombard, IL, USA, 2–5 April 2013, pp. 15–27 (2013). https://www.usenix.org/conference/nsdi13/technical-sessions/presentation/khurshid
20. Kotelnikov, E., Kovács, L., Voronkov, A.: A FOOLish encoding of the next state relations of imperative programs. In: Galmiche, D., Schulz, S., Sebastiani, R. (eds.) IJCAR 2018. LNCS (LNAI), vol. 10900, pp. 405–421. Springer, Cham (2018). https://doi.org/10.1007/978-3-319-94205-6_27

21. Kotelnikov, E.: Checking network reachability properties by automated reasoning in first-order logic. In: Kotelnikov, E. (ed.) Automated Theorem Proving with Extensions of First-Order Logic, chap. 5, pp. 114–131. Chalmers University of Technology, Gothenburg (2018). https://research.chalmers.se/publication/504640/file/504640_Fulltext.pdf
22. Kotelnikov, E., Kovács, L., Reger, G., Voronkov, A.: The vampire and the FOOL. In: Proceedings of the 5th ACM SIGPLAN Conference on Certified Programs 2016, pp. 37–48 (2016). https://doi.org/10.1145/2854065.2854071, http://doi.acm.org/10.1145/2854065.2854071
23. Kovács, L., Voronkov, A.: First-order theorem proving and Vampire. In: Sharygina, N., Veith, H. (eds.) CAV 2013. LNCS, vol. 8044, pp. 1–35. Springer, Heidelberg (2013). https://doi.org/10.1007/978-3-642-39799-8_1
24. Lopes, N.P., Bjørner, N., Godefroid, P., Jayaraman, K., Varghese, G.: Checking beliefs in dynamic networks. In: Proceedings of the 12th USENIX Conference on Networked Systems Design and Implementation, NSDI 2015, pp. 499–512. USENIX Association, Berkeley (2015). http://dl.acm.org/citation.cfm?id=2789770.2789805
25. Mai, H., Khurshid, A., Agarwal, R., Caesar, M., Godfrey, B., King, S.T.: Debugging the data plane with anteater. In: Proceedings of the ACM SIGCOMM 2011 Conference on Applications, Technologies, Architectures, and Protocols for Computer Communications, Toronto, ON, Canada, 15–19 August 2011, pp. 290–301 (2011). https://doi.org/10.1145/2018436.2018470, http://doi.acm.org/10.1145/2018436.2018470
26. McCune, W.: A Davis-Putnam program and its application to finite first-order model search: Quasigroup existence problems. Technical report, Argonne National Laboratory (1994)
27. Reger, G., Suda, M., Voronkov, A.: Finding finite models in multi-sorted first-order logic. In: Creignou, N., Le Berre, D. (eds.) SAT 2016. LNCS, vol. 9710, pp. 323–341. Springer, Cham (2016). https://doi.org/10.1007/978-3-319-40970-2_20
28. Subotić, P.: Logic defined static analysis. Ph.D. thesis, University College London (2018)

Distributed Systems and Networks

Verification of Threshold-Based Distributed Algorithms by Decomposition to Decidable Logics

Idan Berkovits[1(✉)], Marijana Lazić[2,3], Giuliano Losa[4], Oded Padon[5], and Sharon Shoham[1]

[1] Tel Aviv University, Tel Aviv-Yafo, Israel
berkovits@mail.tau.ac.il
[2] TU Wien, Vienna, Austria
[3] TU Munich, Munich, Germany
[4] University of California, Los Angeles, USA
[5] Stanford University, Stanford, USA

Abstract. Verification of fault-tolerant distributed protocols is an immensely difficult task. Often, in these protocols, *thresholds* on set cardinalities are used both in the process code and in its correctness proof, e.g., a process can perform an action only if it has received an acknowledgment from at least half of its peers. Verification of threshold-based protocols is extremely challenging as it involves two kinds of reasoning: first-order reasoning about the unbounded state of the protocol, together with reasoning about sets and cardinalities. In this work, we develop a new methodology for decomposing the verification task of such protocols into *two* decidable logics: EPR and BAPA. Our key insight is that such protocols use thresholds in a restricted way as a means to obtain certain properties of "intersection" between sets. We define a language for expressing such properties, and present two translations: to EPR and BAPA. The EPR translation allows verifying the protocol while assuming these properties, and the BAPA translation allows verifying the correctness of the properties. We further develop an algorithm for automatically generating the properties needed for verifying a given protocol, facilitating fully automated deductive verification. Using this technique we have verified several challenging protocols, including Byzantine one-step consensus, hybrid reliable broadcast and fast Byzantine Paxos.

1 Introduction

Fault-tolerant distributed protocols play an important role in the avionic and automotive industries, medical devices, cloud systems, blockchains, etc. Their unexpected behavior might put human lives at risk or cause a huge financial loss. Therefore, their correctness is of ultimate importance.

Ensuring correctness of distributed protocols is a notoriously difficult task, due to the unbounded number of processes and messages, as well as the non-deterministic behavior caused by the presence of faults, concurrency, and message delays. In general, the problem of verifying such protocols is undecidable.

I. Dillig and S. Tasiran (Eds.): CAV 2019, LNCS 11562, pp. 245–266, 2019.
https://doi.org/10.1007/978-3-030-25543-5_15

This imposes two directions for attacking the problem: (i) developing fully-automatic verification techniques for *restricted* classes of protocols, or (ii) designing deductive techniques for a wide range of systems that *require user assistance*. Within the latter approach, recently emerging techniques [29] leverage decidable logics that are supported by mature automated solvers to significantly reduce user effort, and increase verification productivity. Such logics bring several key benefits: (i) their solvers usually enjoy stable performance, and (ii) whenever annotations provided by the user are incorrect, the automated solvers can provide a counterexample for the user to examine.

Deductive verification based on decidable logic requires a logical formalism that satisfies two conflicting criteria: the formalism should be expressive enough to capture the protocol, its correctness properties, its inductive invariants, and ultimately its verification conditions. At the same time, the formalism should be decidable and have an effective automated tool for checking verification conditions.

In this paper we develop a methodology for deductive verification of *threshold-based* distributed protocols using decidable logic, well-established decidable logics to settle the tension explained above.

In threshold-based protocols, a process may take different actions based on the number of processes from which it received certain messages. This is often used to achieve fault-tolerance. For example, a process may take a certain step once it has received an acknowledgment from a strict majority of its peers, that is, from more than $\mathbf{n}/2$ processes, where $\mathbf{n}$ is the total number of processes. Such expressions as $\mathbf{n}/2$, are called *thresholds*, and in general they can depend on additional parameters, such as the maximal number of crashed processes, or the maximal number of Byzantine processes.

Verification of such protocols requires two flavors of reasoning, as demonstrated by the following example. Consider the Paxos [20] protocol, in which each process proposes a value and all must agree on a common proposal. The protocol tolerates up to $\mathbf{t}$ process crashes, and ensures that every two processes that decide agree on the decided value. The protocol requires $\mathbf{n} > 2\mathbf{t}$ processes, and each process must obtain confirmation messages from $\mathbf{n} - \mathbf{t}$ processes before making a decision. The protocol is correct due to, among others, the fact that if $\mathbf{n} > 2\mathbf{t}$ then any two sets of $\mathbf{n} - \mathbf{t}$ processes have a process in common. To verify this protocol we need to express (i) relationships between an unbounded number of processes and values, which typically requires quantification over uninterpreted domains ("every two processes"), and (ii) properties of sets of certain cardinalities ("any two sets of $\mathbf{n} - \mathbf{t}$ processes intersect"). Crucially, these two types of reasoning are intertwined, as the sets of processes for which we need to capture cardinalities may be defined by their relations with other state components ("messages from at least $\mathbf{n} - \mathbf{t}$ processes"). While uninterpreted first-order logic (FOL) seems like the natural fit for the first type of reasoning, it is seemingly a poor fit for the second type, since it cannot express set cardinalities and the arithmetic used to define thresholds. Typically, logics that combine both types of reasoning are either undecidable or not flexible enough to capture protocols as intricate as the ones we consider.

The approach we present relies on the observation that threshold-based protocols and their correctness proofs use set cardinality thresholds in a restricted way as a means to obtain certain properties between sets, and that these properties can be expressed in FOL via a suitable encoding. In the example above, the important property is that every two sets of cardinality at least $\mathbf{n}-\mathbf{t}$ have a non-empty intersection. This property can be encoded in FOL by modeling sets of cardinality at least $\mathbf{n}-\mathbf{t}$ using an uninterpreted sort along with a membership relation between this sort and the sort for processes. However, the validity of the property under the assumption that $\mathbf{n} > 2\mathbf{t}$ cannot be verified in FOL.

The key idea of this paper is, hence, to decompose the verification problem of threshold-based protocols into the following problems: (i) Checking protocol correctness assuming certain intersection properties, which can be reduced to verification conditions expressed in the Effectively Propositional (EPR) fragment of FOL [25,35]. (ii) Checking that sets with cardinalities adhering to the thresholds satisfy the intersection properties (under the protocol assumptions), which can be reduced to validity checks in quantifier-free Boolean Algebra with Presburger Arithmetic (BAPA) [19]. Both BAPA and EPR are decidable logics, and are supported by mature solvers.

A crucial step in employing this decomposition is finding suitable intersection properties that are strong enough to imply the protocol's correctness (i.e., imply the FOL verification conditions), and are also implied by the precise definitions of the thresholds and the protocol's assumptions. Thus, these intersection properties can be viewed as *interpolants* between the FOL verification conditions and the thresholds in the context of the protocol's assumptions. We present fully automated procedures to find such intersection property interpolants, either eagerly or lazily.

The main contributions of this paper are[1]:

1. We define a threshold intersection property (TIP) language for expressing properties of sets whose cardinalities adhere to certain thresholds; TIP is expressive enough to capture the properties required to prove the correctness of challenging threshold-based protocols.
2. We develop two encodings of TIP, one in BAPA, and another in EPR. These encodings facilitate decomposition of protocol verification into decidable EPR and (quantifier-free) BAPA queries.
3. We show that there are only finitely many TIP formulas (up to equivalence) that are valid for any given protocol. Moreover, we present an effective algorithm for computing all TIP formulas valid for a given protocol, as well as an algorithm for lazily finding a set of TIP formulas that suffice to prove a given protocol.
4. Put together, we obtain an effective deductive verification approach for threshold-based protocols: the user models the protocol and its inductive invariants in EPR using a suitable encoding of thresholds, and defines the

[1] An extended version of this paper, which includes additional details and proofs, appears in [3].

thresholds and the protocol's assumptions using arithmetic; verification is carried out automatically via decomposition to well-established decidable logics.
5. We implement the approach, leveraging mature existing solvers (Z3 and CVC4), and evaluate it by verifying several challenging threshold-based protocols with sophisticated thresholds and assumptions. Our evaluation shows the effectiveness and flexibility of our approach in modeling and verifying complex protocols, including the feasibility of automatically inferring threshold intersection properties.

2 Preliminaries

Transition Systems in FOL. We model distributed protocols as transition systems expressed in many-sorted FOL. A state of the system is a first-order (FO) structure $s = (\mathcal{D}, \mathcal{I})$ over a vocabulary Σ that consists of sorted constant, function and relation symbols, s.t. s satisfies a finite set of *axioms* Θ in the form of closed formulas over Σ. $\mathcal{D}$ is the *domain* of s mapping each sort to a set of objects (elements), and $\mathcal{I}$ is the *interpretation function.* A FO *transition system* is a tuple (Σ, Θ, I, TR), where Σ and Θ are as above, I is a closed formula over Σ that defines the *initial states*, and TR is a closed formula over $\Sigma \uplus \Sigma'$ that defines the *transition relation* where Σ describes the source state of a transition and $\Sigma' = \{a' \mid a \in \Sigma\}$ describes the target state. We require that TR does not modify any symbol that appears in Θ. The set of reachable states is defined as usual. In practice, we define FO transition systems using a modeling language with a convenient syntax [29].

Properties and Inductive Invariants. A *safety property* is expressed by a closed FO formula P over Σ. The system is *safe* if all of its reachable states satisfy P. A closed FO formula *Inv* over Σ is an *inductive invariant* for a transition system (Σ, Θ, I, TR) and property P if the following formulas, called the *verification conditions*, are valid (equivalently, their negations are unsatisfiable): (i) $\Theta \to (I \to Inv)$, (ii) $\Theta \to (Inv \wedge TR \to Inv')$ and (iii) $\Theta \to (Inv \to P)$, where Inv' results from substituting every symbol in *Inv* by its primed version. We also use inductive invariants to verify arbitrary first-order LTL formulas via the reduction of [30,31].

Effectively Propositional Logic (EPR). The effectively-propositional (EPR) fragment of FOL is restricted to formulas without function symbols and with a quantifier prefix $\exists^*\forall^*$ in prenex normal form. Satisfiability of EPR formulas is decidable [25]. Moreover, EPR formulas enjoy the *finite model property,* i.e., φ is satisfiable iff it has a finite model. We consider a straightforward extension of EPR that maintains these properties and is supported by solvers such as Z3 [5]. The extension allows function symbols and quantifier alternations as long as the formula's *quantifier alternation graph*, denoted $QA(\varphi)$, is acyclic. For φ in negation normal form, $QA(\varphi)$ is a directed graph where the set of vertices is the set of sorts and the set of edges is defined as follows: every function symbol introduces edges from its arguments' sorts to its image's sort, and every existential quantifier $\exists x$ that resides in the scope of universal quantifiers introduces edges from the sorts of the universally quantified variables to the sort of x. The quantifier alternation graph is extended to sets of formulas as expected.

Boolean Algebra with Presburger Arithmetic (BAPA). Boolean Algebra with Presburger Arithmetic (BAPA) [19] is a FO theory defined over two sorts: int (for integers), and set (for subsets of a finite universe). The language is defined as follows:

$$F ::= B_1 = B_2 \mid L_1 = L_2 \mid L_1 < L_2 \mid F_1 \wedge F_2 \mid F_1 \vee F_2 \mid \neg F \mid \exists x.F \mid \forall x.F \mid \exists u.F \mid \forall u.F$$
$$B ::= x \mid \emptyset \mid \mathbf{a} \mid B_1 \cup B_2 \mid B_1 \cap B_2 \mid B^c \qquad L ::= u \mid K \mid \mathbf{n} \mid i \mid L_1 + L_2 \mid K \cdot L \mid |B|$$

where L defines linear integer terms, where u denotes an integer variable, $k \in K$ defines an (interpreted) integer constant symbol $\ldots, -2, -1, 0, 1, 2 \ldots$, $\mathbf{n}$ is an integer constant symbol that represents the size of the finite set universe, i is an uninterpreted integer constant symbol (as opposed to the constant symbols from K), and $|b|$ denotes set cardinality; B defines set terms, where x denotes a set variable, $\emptyset$ is a (interpreted) set constant symbol that represents the empty set, and $\mathbf{a}$ is an uninterpreted set constant symbol; and F defines the set of BAPA formulas, where $\ell_1 = \ell_2$ and $\ell_1 < \ell_2$ are atomic arithmetic formulas and $b_1 = b_2$ is an atomic set formula. (Other set constraints such as $b_1 \subseteq b_2$ can be encoded in the usual way). In the sequel, we also allow arithmetic terms of the form $\frac{\ell}{k}$ where $k \in K$ is a positive integer and $\ell \in L$, as any formula that contains such terms can be translated to an equivalent BAPA formula by multiplying by k.

A BAPA structure is $s_B = (\mathcal{D}, \mathcal{I})$ where the domain $\mathcal{D}$ maps sort int to the set of all integers and maps sort set to the set of all subsets of a finite universe U, called the *universal set*. The semantics of terms and formulas is as expected, where the interpretation of the complement operation is defined with respect to U (e.g., $\mathcal{I}(\emptyset^c) = U$), and the integer constant $\mathbf{n}$ is interpreted to the size of U, i.e. $\mathcal{I}(\mathbf{n}) = |U|$.

Both validity and satisfiability of BAPA formulas (with arbitrary quantification) are decidable [19], and the quantifier-free fragment is supported by CVC4 [2].

3 First-Order Modeling of Threshold-Based Protocols

Next we explain our modeling of threshold-based protocols as transition systems in FOL (Note that FOL cannot directly express set cardinality constraints). The idea is to capture each threshold by a designated sort, such that elements of this sort represent sets of nodes that satisfy the threshold. Elements of the threshold sort are then used instead of the actual threshold in the description of the protocol and in the verification conditions. For verification to succeed, some properties of the sets satisfying the cardinality threshold must be captured in FOL. This is done by introducing additional assumptions (formally, axioms of the transition system) expressed in FOL, as discussed in Sect. 4.

```
Input: v_p
broadcast v_p to all processes
wait until n − t messages have been received

if there exists v s.t. more than (n+3t)/2
    messages contain value v then
  DECIDE(v)
if there exists exactly one v s.t. more than
    (n−t)/2 messages contain value v then
  v_p := v
call underlying−consensus(v_p)
```

```
sort node, value, set_{n−t}, set_{(n+3t+1)/2}, set_{(n−t+1)/2}
. . .
assume ∃q : set_{n−t}. ∀m : node. member(m, q) →
                ∃u : value. rcv_msg(n, m, u)
if ∃v : value, q : set_{(n+3t+1)/2}. ∀m : node.
        member(m, q) → rcv_msg(n, m, v) then
    decision(n, v) := true
if ∃!v : value. ∃q : set_{(n−t+1)/2}. ∀m : node.
        member(m, q) → rcv_msg(n, m, v) then
    v_p := v
und_cons(n, v_p) := true
```

Fig. 1. Bosco: a one-step asynchronous Byzantine consensus algorithm [39], and an excerpt RML (relational modeling language) code of the main transition. Note that we overload the *member* relation for all threshold sorts. The formula $\exists! x. \varphi(x)$ is a shorthand for exists and unique.

Running Example. We illustrate our approach using the example of Bosco—an asynchronous Byzantine fault-tolerant (BFT) consensus algorithm [39]. Its modeling in first-order logic using our technique appears alongside an informal pseudo-code in Fig. 1.

In the BFT consensus problem, each node proposes a value and correct nodes must decide on a unique proposal. BFT consensus algorithms typically require at least two communication rounds to reach a decision. In Bosco, nodes execute a preliminary communication step which, under favorable conditions, reaches an early decision, and then call an underlying BFT consensus algorithm to ensure reaching a decision even if these conditions are not met. Bosco is safe when $\mathbf{n} > 3\mathbf{t}$; it guarantees that a preliminary decision will be reached if all nodes are non-faulty and propose the same value when $\mathbf{n} > 5\mathbf{t}$ (weakly one-step condition), and even if some nodes are faulty, as long as all non-faulty nodes propose the same value, when $\mathbf{n} > 7\mathbf{t}$ (strongly one-step condition).

Bosco achieves consensus by ensuring that (a) no two correct nodes decide differently in the preliminary step, and (b) if a correct node decides value v in the preliminary step then every correct process calls the underlying BFT consensus algorithm with proposal v. Property (a) is ensured by the fact that a node decides in the preliminary step only if more than $\frac{\mathbf{n}+3\mathbf{t}}{2}$ nodes proposed the same value. When $\mathbf{n} > 3\mathbf{t}$, two sets of cardinality greater than $\frac{\mathbf{n}+3\mathbf{t}}{2}$ have at least one non-faulty node in common, and therefore no two different values can be proposed by more than $\frac{\mathbf{n}+3\mathbf{t}}{2}$ nodes. Similarly, we can derive property (b) from the fact that a set of more than $\frac{\mathbf{n}+3\mathbf{t}}{2}$ nodes and a set of $\mathbf{n} - \mathbf{t}$ nodes intersect in $\frac{\mathbf{n}+\mathbf{t}}{2}$ nodes, which, after removing t nodes which may be faulty, still leaves us with more than $\frac{\mathbf{n}-\mathbf{t}}{2}$ nodes, satisfying the condition in line 9.

3.1 Threshold-Based Protocols

Parameters and Resilience Conditions. We consider protocols whose definitions depend on a set of *parameters*, Prm, divided into *integer parameters*, Prm_I, and *set parameters*, Prm_S. Prm_I always includes $\mathbf{n}$, the total number of nodes (assumed to be finite). Protocol correctness is ensured under a set of assumptions Γ called *resilience conditions*, formulated as BAPA formulas over Prm (this means that all the uninterpreted constants appearing in Γ are from Prm). In Bosco, $Prm_I = \{\mathbf{n}, \mathbf{t}\}$, where $\mathbf{t}$ is the maximal number of Byzantine failures tolerated by the algorithm, and $Prm_S = \{\mathbf{f}\}$, where $\mathbf{f}$ is the set of Byzantine nodes; $\Gamma = \{\mathbf{n} \geq 3\mathbf{t} + 1, |\mathbf{f}| \leq \mathbf{t}\}$.

Threshold Conditions. Both the description of the protocol and the inductive invariant may include conditions that require the size of some set of nodes to be "at least t", "at most t", and so on, where the threshold t is of the form $t = \frac{\ell}{k}$, where k is a positive integer, and ℓ is a ground BAPA integer term over Prm (we do not allow comparing sizes of two sets – we observe that it is not needed for threshold-based protocols). We denote the set of thresholds by T. For example, in Bosco, $T = \{\mathbf{n} - \mathbf{t}, \frac{\mathbf{n}+3\mathbf{t}+1}{2}, \frac{\mathbf{n}-\mathbf{t}+1}{2}\}$.

Wlog we assume that all conditions on set cardinalities are of the form "at least t" since every condition can be written this way, possibly by introducing new thresholds:

$$|X| > \frac{\ell}{k} \equiv |X| \geq \frac{\ell+1}{k} \qquad |X| \leq \frac{\ell}{k} \equiv |X^c| \geq \frac{k \cdot \mathbf{n} - \ell}{k} \qquad |X| < \frac{\ell}{k} \equiv |X| \leq \frac{\ell-1}{k}$$

3.2 Modeling in FOL

FO Vocabulary for Modeling Threshold-Based Protocols. We describe the protocol's states (e.g., pending messages, votes, etc.) using a core FO vocabulary Σ_C that includes sort node and additional sorts and symbols. Parameters Prm are *not* part of the FO vocabulary used to model the protocol. Also, we do not model set cardinality directly. Instead, we encode the cardinality thresholds in FOL by defining a FO vocabulary Σ_T^{Prm}:

- For every threshold t we introduce a *threshold sort* set_t with the intended meaning that elements of this sort are sets of nodes whose size is at least t.
- Each sort set_t is equipped with a binary relation symbol $member_t$ between sorts node and set_t that captures the membership relation of a node in a set.
- For each set parameter $\mathbf{a} \in Prm_S$ we introduce a unary relation symbol $member_{\mathbf{a}}$ over sort node that captures membership of a node in the set $\mathbf{a}$.

We then model the protocol as a transition system (Σ, Θ, I, TR) where $\Sigma = \Sigma_C \uplus \Sigma_T^{Prm}$.

We are interested only in states (FO structures over Σ) where the interpretation of the threshold sorts and membership relations is according to their intended meaning in a corresponding BAPA structure. Formally, these are T-extensions, defined as follows:

Definition 1. *We say that a FO structure $s_C = (\mathcal{D}_C, \mathcal{I}_C)$ over Σ_C and a BAPA structure $s_B = (\mathcal{D}_B, \mathcal{I}_B)$ over Prm are* compatible *if $\mathcal{D}_B(\mathsf{set}) = \mathcal{P}(\mathcal{D}_C(\mathsf{node}))$, where $\mathcal{P}$ is the powerset operator. For such compatible structures and a set of thresholds T over Prm, the* T-extension *of s_C by s_B is the structure $s = (\mathcal{D}, \mathcal{I})$ over Σ defined as follows:*

$\mathcal{D}(\mathsf{s}) = \mathcal{D}_C(\mathsf{s})$ *for every sort* s *in* Σ_C — $\mathcal{I}(a) = \mathcal{I}_C(a)$ *for every* a *in* Σ_C

$\mathcal{D}(\mathsf{set_t}) = \{A \subseteq \mathcal{D}_C(\mathsf{node}) \mid |A| \geq \mathcal{I}_B(t)\}$ — $\mathcal{I}(member_{\mathbf{a}}) = \mathcal{I}_B(\mathbf{a})$

$\mathcal{I}(member_t) = \{(e, A) \mid e \in \mathcal{D}_C(\mathsf{node}), A \in \mathcal{D}(\mathsf{set_t}), e \in A\}$

Note that for the T-extension s to be well defined as a FO structure, we must have that $\mathcal{D}(\mathsf{set_t}) \neq \emptyset$ for every threshold $t \in T$. This means that a T-extension by s_B only exists if $\{A \subseteq \mathcal{D}(\mathsf{node}) \mid |A| \geq \mathcal{I}_B(t)\} \neq \emptyset$. This is ensured by the following condition:

Definition 2 (Feasibility). *T is Γ-*feasible *if $\Gamma \models t \leq \mathbf{n}$ for every $t \in T$.*

Expressing Threshold Constraints. Cardinality constraints can be expressed in FOL over the vocabulary $\Sigma = \Sigma_C \uplus \Sigma_T^{Prm}$ using quantification. To express that $|\{n : \mathsf{node} \mid \varphi(n, \bar{u})\}| \geq t$, i.e., that there are at least t nodes that satisfy the FO formula φ over Σ_C (where $\bar{u}$ are free variables in φ), we use the following first-order formula over Σ: $\exists q : \mathsf{set_t}.\ \forall n : \mathsf{node}.\ member_t(n, q) \rightarrow \varphi(n, \bar{u})$. Similarly, to express the property that a node is a member of a set parameter $\mathbf{a}$ (e.g., to check if $n \in \mathbf{f}$, i.e., a node is faulty) we use the FO formula $member_{\mathbf{a}}(n)$. For example, in Fig. 1, line 5 (right) uses the FO modeling to express the condition in line 5 (left). This modeling is sound in the following sense:

Lemma 1 (Soundness). *Let $s_C = (\mathcal{D}_C, \mathcal{I}_C)$ be a FO structure over Σ_C, $s_B = (\mathcal{D}_B, \mathcal{I}_B)$ a compatible BAPA structure over Prm s.t. $s_B \models \Gamma$ and T a Γ-feasible set of thresholds over Prm. Then there exists a (unique) T-extension s of s_C by s_B. Further:*

1. *For every $\mathbf{a} \in Prm_S$ and FO valuation ι: $s, \iota \models member_{\mathbf{a}}(n)$ iff $\iota(n) \in \mathcal{I}_B(\mathbf{a})$,*
2. *For every $t \in T$, formula φ, and FO valuation ι: $s, \iota \models \exists q : \mathsf{set_t}.\ \forall n : \mathsf{node}.\ member_t(n, q) \rightarrow \varphi(n, \bar{u})$ iff $|\{e \in \mathcal{D}(\mathsf{node}) \mid s_C, \iota[n \mapsto e] \models \varphi(n, \bar{u})\}| \geq \mathcal{I}_B(t)$.*

Definition 3. *A first-order structure s over Σ is* threshold-faithful *if it is a T-extension of some s_C by some $s_B \models \Gamma$ (as in Lemma 1).*

Incompleteness. Lemma 1 ensures that the FO modeling can be soundly used to verify the protocol. It also ensures that the modeling is precise on threshold-faithful structures (Def. 1). Yet, the FO transition system is not restricted to such states, hence it *abstracts* the actual protocol. To have any hope to verify the protocol, we must capture *some* of the intended meaning of the threshold sorts and relations. This is obtained by adding FO axioms to the FO transition system. Soundness is maintained as long as the axioms hold in all threshold-faithful structures. We note that the set of *all* such axioms is not recursively enumerable– this is where the essential incompleteness of our approach lies.

4 Decomposition via Threshold Intersection Properties

In this section, we identify a set of properties we call *threshold intersection properties*. When captured via FO axioms, these properties suffice for verifying many threshold-based protocols (all the ones we considered). Importantly, these are properties of sets adhering to the thresholds that do not involve the protocol state. As a result, they can be expressed both in FOL and in BAPA. This allows us to decompose the verification task into: (i) checking that certain threshold properties are valid in all threshold-faithful structures by checking that they are implied by Γ (carried out using quantifier free BAPA), and (ii) checking that the verification conditions of the FO transition-system with the same threshold properties taken as axioms are valid (carried out in first-order logic, and in EPR if quantifier alternations are acyclic).

4.1 Threshold Intersection Property Language

Threshold properties are expressed in the *threshold intersection property language* (TIP). TIP is essentially a subset of BAPA, specialized to have the properties listed above.

Syntax. We define TIP as follows, with $t \in T$ a threshold (of the form $\frac{\ell}{k}$) and $\mathbf{a} \in Prm_S$:

$$F ::= B \neq \emptyset \mid B^c = \emptyset \mid g_{\geq t}(B) \mid F_1 \wedge F_2 \mid \forall x : g_{\geq t}.F$$
$$B ::= \mathbf{a} \mid \mathbf{a}^c \mid x \mid x^c \mid \emptyset \mid \emptyset^c \mid B_1 \cap B_2$$

TIP restricts the use of set cardinality to *threshold guards* $g_{\geq t}(b)$ with the meaning $|b| \geq t$. No other arithmetic atomic formulas are allowed. Comparison atomic formulas are restricted to $b \neq \emptyset$ and $b^c = \emptyset$. Quantifiers must be guarded, and negation, disjunction and existential quantification are excluded. We forbid set union and restrict complementation to atomic set terms. We refer to such formulas as *intersection properties* since they express properties of intersections of (atomic) sets.

Example 1. In Bosco, the following property captures the fact that the intersection of a set of at least $\mathbf{n}-\mathbf{t}$ nodes and a set of more than $\frac{\mathbf{n}+3\mathbf{t}}{2}$ nodes consists of at least $\frac{\mathbf{n}-\mathbf{t}}{2}$ non-faulty nodes. This is needed for establishing correctness of the protocol.

$$\forall x : g_{\geq \mathbf{n}-\mathbf{t}}.\ \forall y : g_{\geq \frac{\mathbf{n}+3\mathbf{t}+1}{2}}.\ g_{\geq \frac{\mathbf{n}-\mathbf{t}+1}{2}}(x \cap y \cap \mathbf{f}^c)$$

Semantics. As TIP is essentially a subset of BAPA, we define its semantics by translating its formulas to BAPA, where most constructs directly correspond to BAPA constructs, and guards are translated to cardinality constraints:

$$\mathcal{B}(g_{\geq \frac{\ell}{k}}(b)) \stackrel{\text{def}}{=} k \cdot |b| \geq \ell \qquad \mathcal{B}(\forall x : g.\ \varphi) \stackrel{\text{def}}{=} \forall x.\ \neg\mathcal{B}(g(x)) \vee \mathcal{B}(\varphi)$$

The notions of structures, satisfaction, equivalence, validity, satisfiability, etc. are inherited from BAPA. In particular, given a set of BAPA resilience conditions Γ over the parameters *Prm*, we say that a TIP formula φ is Γ-valid, denoted $\Gamma \models \varphi$, if $\Gamma \models \mathcal{B}(\varphi)$.

If Γ is quantifier-free (which is the typical case), Γ-validity of TIP formulas can be checked via validity checks of quantifier-free BAPA formulas, supported by mature solvers. Note that Γ-validity of a formula of the form $\forall x : g_{\geq t_1}.\ |x \cap b| \geq t_2$ is equivalent to $\Gamma \models \forall u.\ u \geq t_1 \rightarrow u + |b| - n \geq t_2$, allowing replacing quantification over sets by quantification over integers, thus improving performance of existing solvers.

4.2 Translation to FOL

To verify threshold-based protocols, we translate TIP formulas to FO axioms, using the threshold sorts and relations. To translate $g_{\geq t}(b)$, we follow the principle in (Sect. 3.2):

$$\begin{aligned}
\mathcal{FO}(\neg\varphi) &= \neg\mathcal{FO}(\varphi) \\
\mathcal{FO}(\varphi_1 \wedge \varphi_2) &= \mathcal{FO}(\varphi_1) \wedge \mathcal{FO}(\varphi_2) \\
\mathcal{FO}(\forall\, x : g.\,\varphi) &= \forall\, x : \mathsf{set}_{\mathsf{g}}\,.\mathcal{FO}(\varphi) \\
\mathcal{FO}(n \in b_1 \cap b_2) &= \mathcal{FO}(n \in b_1) \wedge \mathcal{FO}(n \in b_2) \\
\mathcal{FO}(b \neq \emptyset) &= \exists n : \mathsf{node}.\ \mathcal{FO}(n \in b) \\
\mathcal{FO}(b^c = \emptyset) &= \forall n : \mathsf{node}.\ \mathcal{FO}(n \in b) \\
\mathcal{FO}(g_{\geq t}(b)) &= \exists x : \mathsf{set}_{\mathsf{t}}.\ \forall n : \mathsf{node}.\ \mathit{member}_{\mathsf{t}}(n, x) \rightarrow \mathcal{FO}(n \in b)
\end{aligned}
\qquad
\begin{aligned}
\mathcal{FO}(n \in b^c) &= \neg\mathcal{FO}(n \in b) \\
\mathcal{FO}(n \in \emptyset) &= \mathit{false} \\
\mathcal{FO}(n \in \mathbf{a}) &= \mathit{member}_{\mathbf{a}}(n) \\
\mathcal{FO}(n \in x) &= \mathit{member}_{\mathsf{t}}(n, x) \\
&\text{where } x \text{ is guarded by } t
\end{aligned}$$

We lift $\mathcal{FO}$ to sets of formulas: $\mathcal{FO}(\Delta) = \{\mathcal{FO}(\varphi) \mid \varphi \in \Delta\}$.

Next, we state the soundness of the translation, which intuitively means that $\mathcal{FO}(\varphi)$ is "equivalent" to φ over threshold-faithful FO structures (Definition 1). This justifies adding $\mathcal{FO}(\varphi)$ as a FO axiom whenever φ is Γ-valid.

Theorem 1 (Translation soundness). *Let $s_C = (\mathcal{D}_C, \mathcal{I}_C)$ be a first-order structure over Σ_C, $s_B = (\mathcal{D}_B, \mathcal{I}_B)$ a compatible BAPA structure over Prm, and s the T-extension of s_C by s_B. Then for every closed TIP formula φ, we have $s_B \models \varphi \Leftrightarrow s \models \mathcal{FO}(\varphi)$.*

Corollary 1. *For every closed TIP formula φ such that $\Gamma \models \varphi$, we have that $\mathcal{FO}(\varphi)$ is satisfied by every threshold-faithful first-order structure.*

5 Automatically Inferring Threshold Intersection Properties

To apply the approach described in Sects. 3 and 4, it is crucial to find suitable threshold properties. That is, given the resilience conditions Γ and a FO transition system modeling the protocol, we need to find a set Δ of TIP formulas such that (i) $\Gamma \models \varphi$ for every $\varphi \in \Delta$, and (ii) the VCs of the transition system with the axioms $\mathcal{FO}(\Delta)$ are valid.

In this section, we address the problem of automatically inferring such a set Δ. In particular, we prove that for any protocol that satisfies a natural condition, there are finitely many Γ-valid TIP formulas (up to equivalence), enabling a complete automatic inference algorithm. Furthermore, we show that (under certain reasonable conditions formalized in this section), the FO axioms resulting from the inferred TIP properties have an *acyclic* quantifier alternation graph, facilitating protocol verification in EPR.

Notation. For the rest of this section, we fix a set Prm of parameters, a set Γ of resilience conditions over Prm, and a set T of thresholds. Note that $b \neq \emptyset \equiv g_{\geq 1}(b)$ and $b^c = \emptyset \equiv g_{\geq \mathbf{n}}(b)$. Therefore, for uniformity of the presentation, given a set T of thresholds, we define $\hat{T} \stackrel{\text{def}}{=} T \cup \{1, \mathbf{n}\}$ and replace atomic formulas of the form $b \neq \emptyset$ and $b^c = \emptyset$ by the corresponding guard formulas. As such, the only atomic formulas are of the form $g_{\geq t}(b)$ where $t \in \hat{T}$. Note that guards in quantifiers are still restricted to $g_{\geq t}$ where $t \in T$. Given a set Prm_S, we also denote $\hat{Prm}_S = Prm_S \cup \{\mathbf{a}^c \mid \mathbf{a} \in Prm_S\}$.

5.1 Finding Consequences in the Threshold Intersection Property Language

In this section, we present AIP– an algorithm for inferring all Γ-valid TIP formulas. A naïve (non-terminating) algorithm would iteratively check Γ-validity of every TIP formula. Instead, AIP prunes the search space relying on the following condition:

Definition 4. *T is Γ-*non-degenerate *if for every $t \in T$ it holds that $\Gamma \not\models t \leq 0$.*

If $\Gamma \models t \leq 0$ then t is degenerate in the sense that $g_{\geq t}(b)$ is always Γ-valid, and $\forall x : g_{\geq t}.\ g_{\geq t'}(x \cap b)$ is never Γ-valid unless t' is also degenerate.

We observe that we can (i) push conjunctions outside of formulas (since $\forall$ distributes over $\wedge$), and assuming non-degeneracy, (ii) ignore terms of the form x^c:

Lemma 2. *If T is Γ-feasible and Γ-non-degenerate, then for every Γ-valid φ in TIP, there exist $\varphi_1, \dots, \varphi_m$ s.t. $\varphi \equiv \bigwedge_{i=1}^{m} \varphi_i$ and for every $1 \le i \le m$, φ_i is of the form:*

$$\forall x_1 : g_{\ge t_1} \dots \forall x_q : g_{\ge t_q} . \; g_{\ge t}(x_1 \cap \dots \cap x_q \cap a_1 \dots \cap a_k)$$

where $q + k > 0$, $t_1, \dots, t_q \in T$, $t \in \hat{T}$, $a_1, \dots, a_k \in \widehat{Prms}_S$, and the a_i's are distinct.

We refer to φ_i of the form above as *simple*, and refer to $g_{\ge t}$ as its *atomic guard.*

By Lemma 2, it suffices to generate all *simple* Γ-valid formulas. Next, we show that this can be done more efficiently by pruning the search space based on a subsumption relation that is checked syntactically avoiding Γ-validity checks.

Definition 5 (Subsumption). *For every $h_1, h_2 \in \hat{T} \cup \widehat{Prms}_S$, we denote $h_1 \sqsubseteq_\Gamma h_2$ if one of the following holds: (1) $h_1 = h_2$, or (2) $h_1, h_2 \in \hat{T}$ and $\Gamma \models h_1 \ge h_2$, or (3) $h_1 \in \widehat{Prms}_S$, $h_2 \in \hat{T}$ and $\Gamma \models |h_1| \ge h_2$.*

For $h_1, h_2 \in \hat{T}$ and $h_3 \in \widehat{Prms}_S$, $h_1 \sqsubseteq_\Gamma h_2$ means that $\Gamma \models \forall x : g_{\ge h_1} . \; g_{\ge h_2}(x)$, and $h_3 \sqsubseteq_\Gamma h_2$ means that $\Gamma \models g_{\ge h_2}(h_3)$. We lift the relation $\sqsubseteq_\Gamma$ to act on simple formulas:

Definition 6. *Given simple formulas*

$$\alpha = \forall x_1 : g_{\ge h_1} \dots \forall x_q : g_{\ge h_q} . \; g_{\ge t}(x_1 \cap \dots \cap x_q \cap h_{q+1} \dots \cap h_k)$$
$$\beta = \forall x_1 : g_{\ge h'_1} \dots \forall x_{q'} : g_{\ge h'_{q'}} . \; g_{\ge t'}(x_1 \cap \dots \cap x_{q'} \cap h'_{q'+1} \dots \cap h'_{k'})$$

we say that $\alpha \sqsubseteq_\Gamma \beta$ if (i) $t \sqsubseteq_\Gamma t'$, and (ii) there exists an injective function $f : \{1, \dots, k'\} \to \{1, \dots, k\}$ s.t. for any $1 \le i \le k'$ it holds that $h'_i \sqsubseteq_\Gamma h_{f(i)}$.

Lemma 3. *Let α, β be simple formulas such that $\alpha \sqsubseteq_\Gamma \beta$. If $\Gamma \models \alpha$ then $\Gamma \models \beta$.*

Corollary 2. *If no simple formula with q quantifiers is Γ-valid then no simple formula with more than q quantifiers is Γ-valid.*

Algorithm 1 depicts AIP that generates all Γ-valid simple formulas, relying on Lemma 3. AIP uses a naïve search strategy; different strategies can be used (e.g. [26]). Based on Corollary 2, AIP terminates if for some number of quantifiers no Γ-valid formula is discovered.

Algorithm 1. Algorithm for Inferring Intersection Properties (AIP)

Input: $Prms_S$, T, Γ

set checked_true = checked_false = [ ] ;
foreach $q = 0, 1, \dots$ **do**
  foreach *simple formula φ over T and $Prms_S$ with q quantifiers* **do**
    if *exists $\psi \in$ checked_true s.t. $\psi \sqsubseteq_\Gamma \varphi$* **then** yield φ ;
    else if *exists $\psi \in$ checked_false s.t. $\varphi \sqsubseteq_\Gamma \psi$* **then** continue ;
    else if $\Gamma \models \varphi$ **then** yield φ ; add φ to checked_true ;
    else add φ to checked_false ;
  if *no formulas were added to checked_true* **then** terminate ;

Lemma 4 (Soundness). *Every formula φ that is returned by the algorithm is Γ-valid.*

Lemma 5 (Completeness). *If T is Γ-feasible and Γ-non-degenerate, then for every Γ-valid TIP formula φ there exist $\varphi_1 \dots \varphi_m$ s.t. $\varphi \equiv \bigwedge_{i=1}^{m} \varphi_i$ and* AIP *yields every φ_i.*

Next, we characterize the cases in which there are finitely many Γ-valid TIP formulas, up to equivalence, and thus, AIP is guaranteed to terminate.

Definition 7. *T is Γ-*sane *if for every $t_1, t_2 \in T$, $\Gamma \not\models t_1 \le 0 \vee t_2 > \mathbf{n} - 1$. (T, Prm_S) is Γ-*sane *if, in addition, for every $t_1 \in T$, $a \in \hat{Prm}_S$, $\Gamma \not\models t_1 \le 0 \vee |a| = \mathbf{n}$.*

Theorem 2. *Assume that T is Γ-feasible. Then the following conditions are equivalent: (1) There are finitely many Γ-valid simple formulas. (2) There are finitely many Γ-valid TIP formulas, up to equivalence. (3) T is Γ-*sane.

Corollary 3 (Termination). *If T is Γ-feasible and Γ-sane,* AIP *terminates.*

5.2 From TIP to Axioms in EPR

The set of simple formulas generated by AIP, Δ, is translated to FOL axioms as described in Sect. 4.2. Next, we show how to ensure that the quantifier alternation graph (Sect. 2) of $\mathcal{FO}(\Delta)$ is acyclic. A simple formula induces quantifier alternation edges in $QA(\mathcal{FO}(\varphi))$ from the sorts of its universal quantifiers to the sort of its atomic guard $g_{\ge t}$ (or if $t = 1$ to the node sort). Therefore, from Lemma 3, for a Γ-valid φ, cycles in $QA(\mathcal{FO}(\varphi))$ may only occur if they occur in the graph obtained by $\sqsubseteq_\Gamma$. Furthermore, if $QA(\mathcal{FO}(\varphi))$ is not acyclic, then the atomic guard must be equal to one of the quantifier guards. We refer to such a formula as a *cyclic formula*. We show that, under the following assumption, we can eliminate all cyclic formulas from Δ.

Definition 8. *T is Γ-*acyclic *if for every $t_1, t_2 \in T$, if $\Gamma \models t_1 = t_2$ then $t_1 = t_2$.*

Intuitively, if T is not Γ-acyclic, then it has (at least) two "equivalent" thresholds, making one of them redundant. If that is the case, we can alter the protocol and its proof so that one of these guards is eliminated and the other one is used instead.

Theorem 3. *Let T be Γ-feasible and Γ-acyclic and (T, Prm_S) be Γ-sane. Let Δ be the set returned by* AIP, *and $\Delta' = \{\varphi \in \Delta \mid \varphi \text{ is acyclic}\}$. Then the VCs of the FO transition system with axioms $\mathcal{FO}(\Delta)$ are valid iff they are valid with axioms $\mathcal{FO}(\Delta')$. Further, $QA(\mathcal{FO}(\Delta'))$ is acyclic.*

5.3 Finding Minimal Properties Required for a Protocol

If Δ consists of *all* acyclic Γ-valid TIP formulas returned by AIP, using $\mathcal{FO}(\Delta)$ as FO axioms leads to divergence of the verifier. To overcome this, we propose two variants.

Minimal Equivalent. Δ_{min}. Some of the formulas in $\mathcal{FO}(\Delta)$ are implied by others, making them redundant. We remove such formulas using a greedy procedure that for every $\varphi_i \in \Delta$, checks whether $\mathcal{FO}(\Delta \setminus \{\varphi_i\}) \models \mathcal{FO}(\varphi_i)$, and if so, removes φ_i from Δ. Note that if $QA(\mathcal{FO}(\Delta))$ is acyclic, the check translates to (un)satisfiability in EPR.

This procedure results in $\Delta_{min} \subseteq \Delta$ s.t. $\mathcal{FO}(\Delta_{min}) \models \mathcal{FO}(\Delta)$ and no strict subset of Δ_{min} satisfies this condition. That is, Δ_{min} is a local minimum for that property.

Interpolant. Δ_{int}. There may exist $\Delta_{int} \subseteq \Delta$ s.t. $\mathcal{FO}(\Delta_{int}) \not\models \mathcal{FO}(\Delta)$ but $\mathcal{FO}(\Delta_{int})$ suffices to prove the first-order VCs, and enables to discharge the VCs more efficiently. We compute such a set Δ_{int} iteratively. Initially, $\Delta_{int} = \emptyset$. In each iteration, we check the VCs. If a counterexample to induction (CTI) is found, we add to Δ_{int} a formula from Δ not satisfied by the CTI. In this approach, Δ is not pre-computed. Instead, AIP is invoked lazily to generate candidate formulas in reaction to CTIs.

6 Evaluation

We evaluate the approach by verifying several challenging threshold-based distributed protocols that use sophisticated thresholds: we verify the safety of Bosco [39] (presented in Sect. 3) under its 3 different resilience conditions, the safety and liveness (using the liveness to safety reduction presented in [30]) of Hybrid Reliable Broadcast [40], and the safety of Byzantine Fast Paxos [23]. Hybrid Reliable Broadcast tolerates four different types of faults, while Fast Byzantine Paxos is a fast-learning [21,22] Byzantine fault-tolerant consensus protocol; fast-learning protocols are notorious because two such algorithms, Zyzzyva [17] and FaB [28], were recently revealed incorrect [1] despite having been published at major systems conferences.

Implementation. We implemented both algorithms described in Sect. 5.3. AIP$_{\text{EAGER}}$ eagerly constructs Δ by running AIP, and then uses EPR reasoning to remove redundant formulas (whose FO representation is implied by the FO representation of others). To reduce the number of EPR validity checks used during this minimization step, we implemented an optimization that allows us to prove redundancy of TIP formulas internally based on an extension of the notion of subsumption from Sect. 5. AIP$_{\text{LAZY}}$ computes a subset of Δ while using AIP in a lazy fashion, guided by CTIs obtained from attempting to verify the FO transition system. Our implementations use CVC4 to discharge BAPA queries, and Z3 to discharge EPR queries. Verification of first-order transition systems is performed using Ivy, which internally uses Z3 as well. All experiments reported were performed on a laptop running 64-bit Windows 10, with a Core-i5 2.2 GHz CPU, using Z3 version 4.8.4, CVC4 version 1.7, and the latest version of Ivy.

Figure 2 lists the protocols we verified and the details of the evaluation. Each experiment was repeated 10 times, and we report the mean time (μ) and standard

Protocol	T	Γ	AIP$_{\text{EAGER}}$						AIP$_{\text{LAZY}}$						
			V	**I**	**Q**	$\mathbf{t_C}$	$\mathbf{t_V}$	$\Delta^{\text{Protocol}}_{\text{EAGER}}$	$\Delta^{\text{Protocol}}_{\text{LAZY}}$	**V**	**I**	**CTI**	**Q**	$\mathbf{t_I}$	$\mathbf{t_V}$
Bosco	$t_1{=}\mathbf{n}-t$ $t_2{=}\frac{\mathbf{n}+3t+1}{2}$ $t_3{=}\frac{\mathbf{n}-t+1}{2}$	$\mathbf{n} > 3t$ $\lvert f\rvert \leq t$	$\frac{23}{39}$	$\frac{21}{1216}$	6	$3s$	$\mu(12s)$ $\sigma(4s)$	$g_1(f^c)$ $\forall x{:}g_1,y{:}g_1,z{:}g_2 . g_3(x{\cap}y{\cap}z)$ $\forall x{:}g_1,y{:}g_2,z{:}g_3 . x{\cap}y{\cap}z{\neq}\emptyset$	$g_1(f^c)$ $\forall x{:}g_1,y{:}g_2 . g_3(x{\cap}y{\cap}f^c)$ $\forall x{:}g_2,y{:}g_3 . x{\cap}y{\cap}f^c{\neq}\emptyset$	24	6	18	2	$\mu(3m)$ $\sigma(1m)$	$\mu(4s)$ $\sigma(0.4s)$
Bosco Weakly One-step	"	$\mathbf{n} > 5t$ $\lvert f\rvert \leq t$	$\frac{16}{51}$	$\frac{24}{1204}$	6	$3s$	$\mu(13m)$ $\sigma(14m)$	$\Delta^{\text{Bosco}}_{\text{EAGER}}$ $\forall x{:}g_1 . g_2(x)$	$\Delta^{\text{Bosco}}_{\text{LAZY}}$ $\forall x{:}g_1 . g_2(x)$	32	7	19	2	$\mu(13m)$ $\sigma(9m)$	$\mu(9s)$ $\sigma(2s)$
Bosco Strongly One-step	"	$\mathbf{n} > 7t$ $\lvert f\rvert \leq t$	$\frac{26}{63}$	$\frac{24}{2407}$	8	$8s$	T.O.	$\Delta^{\text{Bosco}}_{\text{EAGER}}$ $\forall x{:}g_1,y{:}g_1 . g_2(x{\cap}y)$	$\Delta^{\text{Bosco}}_{\text{LAZY}}$ $\forall x{:}g_1 . g_2(x{\cap}f^c)$	34	9	20	2	$\mu(23m)$ $\sigma(8m)$	$\mu(16s)$ $\sigma(13s)$
Hybrid Reliable Broadcast	$t_1{=}t_a{+}t_s{+}1$ $t_2{=}\mathbf{n}{-}t_c{-}t_a{-}t_s{-}t_i$	$\mathbf{n} > t_c{+}3t_a{+}2t_s{+}2t_i$ $\lvert f_x\rvert \leq t_x$ $f_x{\cap}f_y{=}\emptyset$ for $x \neq y$ $x,y{\in}\{a,c,i,s\}$	$\frac{25}{63}$	$\frac{34}{1877}$	2	$37s$	$\mu(35s)$ $\sigma(0.3s)$	$g_2(f_c^c{\cap}f_a^c{\cap}f_s^c{\cap}f_i^c)$ $\forall x{:}g_1 . x{\cap}f_a^c{\cap}f_s^c{\neq}\emptyset$ $\forall x{:}g_2 . g_1(x{\cap}f_a^c{\cap}f_i^c)$	$\Delta^{\text{Hybrid Reliable Broadcast}}_{\text{EAGER}}$	63	15	45	1	$\mu(15m)$ $\sigma(1.5m)$	$\mu(43s)$ $\sigma(1s)$
Byzantine Fast Paxos	$t_1{=}\mathbf{n}{-}t$ $t_2{=}\mathbf{n}{-}q$ $t_3{=}\mathbf{n}{-}2t{-}q$ $t_4{=}t{+}1$	$\mathbf{n} > 2q + 3t$ $t \geq q$ $q \geq 0$ $\lvert b\rvert \leq t$	$\frac{22}{79}$	$\frac{44}{3695}$	6	$6s$	T.O.	$g_1(b^c)$ $\forall x{:}g_2 . g_1(x)$ $\forall x{:}g_1,y{:}g_4 . x{\cap}y{\neq}\emptyset$ $\forall x{:}g_2,y{:}g_3 . g_4(x{\cap}y)$ $\forall x{:}g_1,y{:}g_1,z{:}g_2 . g_3(x{\cap}y{\cap}z)$	$g_1(b^c)$ $\forall x{:}g_2 . g_1(x)$ $\forall x{:}g_3 . x{\neq}\emptyset$ $\forall x{:}g_4 . x{\neq}\emptyset$ $\forall x{:}g_1 . g_3(x{\cap}b^c)$ $\forall x{:}g_1,y{:}g_1 . g_4(x{\cap}y)$	44	11	19	2	$\mu(36m)$ $\sigma(21m)$	$\mu(28m)$ $\sigma(19m)$

Fig. 2. Protocols verified using our technique. For each protocol, T is the set of thresholds and Γ is the resilience condition. AIP$_{\text{EAGER}}$ lists metrics for the procedure of finding all Γ-valid TIP formulas (taking time $\mathbf{t_C}$), and verifying the transition system using the resulting properties (taking time $\mathbf{t_v}$). Obtaining a minimal subset that FO-implies the rest takes negligible time, so we did not include it in the table. The properties are given in $\Delta^{\mathbf{Protocol}}_{\mathbf{Eager}}$, where g_i denotes $g_{\geq t_i}$. In addition to the run times, **V** shows $\frac{c}{v}$, where c is the number of Γ-valid simple formulas that were checked using the BAPA solver (CVC4), and v is the total number of Γ-valid simple formulas. Namely, $v - c$ simple formulas were inferred to be valid via subsumption. **I** reports the analogous metric for Γ-invalid simple formulas. Finally, **Q** reports the maximal number of quantifiers considered (for which all formulas were Γ-invalid). AIP$_{\text{LAZY}}$ lists metrics for the procedure of finding a set of Γ-valid TIP formulas sufficient to prove the protocol based on counterexamples. The resulting set is listed in $\Delta^{\mathbf{Protocol}}_{\mathbf{Lazy}}$, and $\mathbf{t_I}$ lists the total Ivy runtime, with the standard deviation specified below. **V** (resp. **I**) lists the number of Γ-valid (resp. Γ-invalid) simple formulas considered before the final set was reached. **CTI** lists the number of counterexample iterations required, and **Q** lists the maximal number of quantifiers of any TIP formula considered. Finally, $\mathbf{t_v}$ lists the time required to verify the first-order transition system assuming the obtained set of properties. T.O. indicates that a time out of 1 h was reached.

deviation (σ). The figure's caption explains the presented information, and we discuss the results below.

Aip$_{\text{EAGER}}$ For all protocols, running AIP took less than 1 min (column $\mathbf{t_C}$), and generated all Γ-valid simple TIP formulas. We observe that for most formulas, (in)validity is deduced from other formulas by subsumption, and less than 2%–5% of the formulas are actually checked using a BAPA query. With the optimization of the redundancy check, minimization of the set is performed in negligible time. The resulting set, Δ_{EAGER}, contains 3–5 formulas, compared to 39–79 before minimization.

Due to the optimization described in Sect. 4 for the BAPA validity queries, the number of quantifiers in the TIP formulas that are checked by AIP does not affect the time needed to compute the full Δ. For example, Bosco under the Strongly One-step resilience condition contains Γ-valid simple TIP formulas with up to 7 quantifiers (as $\mathbf{n} > 7\mathbf{t}$ and $t_1 = \mathbf{n} - \mathbf{t}$), but AIP does not take significantly longer to find Δ. Interestingly, in this example the Γ-valid TIP formulas with more than 3 quantifiers are implied (in FOL) by formulas with at most 3 quantifiers, as indicated by the fact that these are the only formulas that remain in $\Delta_{\text{EAGER}}^{\text{Bosco Strongly One-step}}$.

Aip$_{\text{LAZY}}$ With the lazy approach based on CTIs, the time for finding the set of TIP formulas, Δ_{LAZY}, is generally longer. This is because the run time is dominated by calls to Ivy with FO axioms that are too weak for verifying the protocol. However, the resulting Δ_{LAZY} has a significant benefit: it lets Ivy prove the protocol much faster compared to using Δ_{EAGER}. Comparing $\mathbf{t_V}$ in AIP$_{\text{EAGER}}$ vs. AIP$_{\text{LAZY}}$ shows that when the former takes a minute, the latter takes a few seconds, and when the former times out after 1 h, the latter terminates, usually in under 1 min. Comparing the formulas of Δ_{EAGER} and Δ_{LAZY} reveals the reason. While the FO translation of both yields EPR formulas, the formulas resulting from Δ_{EAGER} contain more quantifiers and generate much more ground terms, which degrades the performance of Z3.

Another advantage of the lazy approach is that during the search, it avoids considering formulas with many quantifiers unless those are actually needed. Comparing the 3 versions of Bosco we see that AIP$_{\text{LAZY}}$ is not sensitive to the largest number of quantifiers that may appear in a Γ-valid simple TIP formula. The downside is that AIP$_{\text{LAZY}}$ performs many Ivy checks in order to compute the final Δ_{LAZY}. The total duration of finding CTIs varies significantly (as demonstrated under the column $\mathbf{t_I}$), in part because it is very sensitive to the CTIs returned by Ivy, which are in turn affected by the random seed used in the heuristics of the underlying solver.

Finally, Δ_{LAZY} provides more insight into the protocol design, since it presents minimal assumptions that are required for protocol correctness. Thus, it may be useful in designing and understanding protocols.

7 Related Work

Fully Automatic Verification of Threshold-Based Protocols. Algorithms modeled as Threshold automata (TA) [14] have been studied in [13,16], and verified using an automated tool ByMC [15]. The tool also automatically synthesizes thresholds as arithmetic expressions [24]. Reachability properties of TAs for more general thresholds are studied in [18]. There have been recent advances in verification of synchronous threshold-based algorithms using TAs [41], and of asynchronous randomized algorithms where TAs support coin tosses and an unbounded number of rounds [4]. Still, this modeling is very restrictive and not as faithful to the pseudo-code as our modeling.

Another approach for full automation is to use sound and incomplete procedures for deduction and invariant search for logics that combine quantifiers and set cardinalities [8,10]. However, distributed systems of the level of complexity we consider here (e.g., Byzantine Fast Paxos) are beyond the reach of these techniques.

Verification of Distributed Protocols Using Decidable Logics. Padon et al. [33] introduced an interactive approach for the safety verification of distributed protocols based on EPR using the Ivy [29] verification tool. Later works extended the approach to more complex protocols [32], their implementations [42], and liveness properties [30,31]. Those works verified some threshold protocols using ad-hoc first-order modeling and axiomatization of threshold-intersection properties, whereas we develop a systematic methodology. Moreover, the axioms were not mechanically verified, except in [42], where a simple intersection property—intersection of two sets with more than $\frac{\mathbf{n}}{2}$ nodes—requires a proof by induction over $\mathbf{n}$. The proof relies on a user provided induction hypothesis that is automatically checked using the FAU decidable fragment [9]. This approach requires user ingenuity even for a simple intersection property, and we expect that it would not scale to the more complex properties required for e.g. Bosco or Fast Byzantine Paxos. In contrast, our approach completely automates both verification and inference of threshold-intersection properties required to verify protocol correctness.

Dragoi et al. [6] propose a decidable logic supporting cardinalities, uninterpreted functions, and universal quantifiers for verifying consensus algorithms expressed in the partially synchronous Heard-Of Model. As in this paper, the user is expected to provide an inductive invariant. The PSync framework [7] extends the approach to protocol implementations. Compared to our approach, the approach of Dragoi et al. is less flexible due to the specialized logic used and the restrictions of the Heard-Of Model.

Our approach decomposes verification into EPR and BAPA. Piskac [34] presents a decidable logic that combines BAPA and EPR, with some restrictions. The verification conditions of the protocols we consider are outside the scope of this fragment since they include cardinality constraints in the scope of quantifiers. Furthermore, this logic is not supported by mature solvers. Instead of looking for a specialized logic per protocol, we rely on a decomposition which allows more flexibility.

Recently, [11] presented an approach for verifying asynchronous algorithms by reduction to synchronous verification. This technique is largely orthogonal and complementary to our approach, which is focused on the challenge of cardinality thresholds.

Verification using interactive theorem provers. We are not aware of works based on interactive theorem provers that verified protocols with complex thresholds as we do in this work (although doing so is of course possible). However, many works used interactive theorem provers to verify related protocols, e.g., [12,27, 36–38,43] (the most related protocols use either $\frac{n}{2}$ or $\frac{2n}{3}$ as the only thresholds, other protocols do not involve any thresholds). The downside of verification using interactive theorem provers is that it requires tremendous human efforts and skills. For example, the Verdi proof of Raft included 50,000 lines of proof in Coq for 500 lines of code [44].

8 Conclusion

This paper proposes a new deductive verification approach for threshold-based distributed protocols by decomposing the verification problem into two well-established decidable logics, BAPA and EPR, thus allowing greater flexibility compared to monolithic approaches based on domain-specific, specialized logics. The user models their protocol in EPR, defines the thresholds and resilience conditions using arithmetic in BAPA, and provides an inductive invariant. An automatic procedure infers threshold intersection properties expressed in TIP that are both (1) sound w.r.t. the resilience conditions (checked in quantifier-free BAPA) and (2) sufficient to discharge the VCs (checked in EPR). Both logics are supported by mature solvers, and allow providing the user with an understandable counterexample in case verification fails.

Our evaluation, which includes notoriously tricky fast-learning consensus protocols, shows that threshold intersection properties are inferred in a matter of minutes. While this may be too slow for interactive use, we expect improvements such as memoization and parallelism to provide response times of a few seconds in an iterative, interactive setting. Another potential future direction is combining our inference algorithm with automated invariant inference algorithms.

Acknowledgements. We thank the anonymous referees for insightful comments which improved this paper. This publication is part of a project that has received funding from the European Research Council (ERC) under the European Union's Horizon 2020 research and innovation programme (grant agreement No [759102-SVIS] and [787367-PaVeS]). The research was partially supported by Len Blavatnik and the Blavatnik Family foundation, the Blavatnik Interdisciplinary Cyber Research Center, Tel Aviv University, the Israel Science Foundation (ISF) under grant No. 1810/18, the United States-Israel Binational Science Foundation (BSF) grant No. 2016260 and the Austrian Science Fund (FWF) through Doctoral College LogiCS (W1255-N23).

References

1. Abraham, I., Gueta, G., Malkhi, D., Alvisi, L., Kotla, R., Martin, J.P.: Revisiting Fast Practical Byzantine Fault Tolerance (2017)
2. Bansal, K., Reynolds, A., Barrett, C., Tinelli, C.: A new decision procedure for finite sets and cardinality constraints in SMT. In: Olivetti, N., Tiwari, A. (eds.) IJCAR 2016. LNCS (LNAI), vol. 9706, pp. 82–98. Springer, Cham (2016). https://doi.org/10.1007/978-3-319-40229-1_7
3. Berkovits, I., Lazić, M., Losa, G., Padon, O., Shoham, S.: Verification of threshold-based distributed algorithms by decomposition to decidable logics. CoRR abs/1905.07805 (2019). http://arxiv.org/abs/1905.07805
4. Bertrand, N., Konnov, I., Lazic, M., Widder, J.: Verification of Randomized Distributed Algorithms under Round-Rigid Adversaries. HAL hal-01925533, November 2018. https://hal.inria.fr/hal-01925533
5. de Moura, L., Bjørner, N.: Z3: an efficient SMT solver. In: Ramakrishnan, C.R., Rehof, J. (eds.) TACAS 2008. LNCS, vol. 4963, pp. 337–340. Springer, Heidelberg (2008). https://doi.org/10.1007/978-3-540-78800-3_24
6. Drăgoi, C., Henzinger, T.A., Veith, H., Widder, J., Zufferey, D.: A logic-based framework for verifying consensus algorithms. In: McMillan, K.L., Rival, X. (eds.) VMCAI 2014. LNCS, vol. 8318, pp. 161–181. Springer, Heidelberg (2014). https://doi.org/10.1007/978-3-642-54013-4_10
7. Dragoi, C., Henzinger, T.A., Zufferey, D.: PSync: A partially synchronous language for fault-tolerant distributed algorithms. In: Proceedings of the 43rd Annual ACM SIGPLAN-SIGACT Symposium on Principles of Programming Languages, POPL 2016, St. Petersburg, FL, USA, January 20–22, 2016, vol. 51, no. 1, pp. 400–415 (2016). https://dblp.uni-trier.de/rec/bibtex/conf/popl/DragoiHZ16?q=speculative%20AQ4%20Byzantine%20fault%20tolerance
8. Dutertre, B., Jovanović, D., Navas, J.A.: Verification of fault-tolerant protocols with sally. In: Dutle, A., Muñoz, C., Narkawicz, A. (eds.) NFM 2018. LNCS, vol. 10811, pp. 113–120. Springer, Cham (2018). https://doi.org/10.1007/978-3-319-77935-5_8
9. Ge, Y., de Moura, L.: Complete instantiation for quantified formulas in satisfiabiliby modulo theories. In: Bouajjani, A., Maler, O. (eds.) CAV 2009. LNCS, vol. 5643, pp. 306–320. Springer, Heidelberg (2009). https://doi.org/10.1007/978-3-642-02658-4_25
10. v. Gleissenthall, K., Bjørner, N., Rybalchenko, A.: Cardinalities and universal quantifiers for verifying parameterized systems. In: Proceedings of the 37th ACM SIGPLAN Conference on Programming Language Design and Implementation, PLDI 2016, pp. 599–613. ACM (2016)
11. von Gleissenthall, K., Kici, R.G., Bakst, A., Stefan, D., Jhala, R.: Pretend synchrony: synchronous verification of asynchronous distributed programs. PACMPL **3**(POPL), 59:1–59:30 (2019). https://dl.acm.org/citation.cfm?id=3290372
12. Hawblitzel, C., Howell, J., Kapritsos, M., Lorch, J.R., Parno, B., Roberts, M.L., Setty, S.T.V., Zill, B.: Ironfleet: proving practical distributed systems correct. In: Proceedings of the 25th Symposium on Operating Systems Principles, SOSP 2015, Monterey, CA, USA, 4–7 October 2015, pp. 1–17 (2015). https://doi.org/10.1145/2815400.2815428,

13. Konnov, I., Lazic, M., Veith, H., Widder, J.: Para^2: Parameterized path reduction, acceleration, and SMT for reachability in threshold-guarded distributed algorithms. Form. Methods Syst. Des. **51**(2), 270–307 (2017). https://link.springer.com/article/10.1007/s10703-017-0297-4
14. Konnov, I., Veith, H., Widder, J.: On the completeness of bounded model checking for threshold-based distributed algorithms: reachability. Inf. Comput. **252**, 95–109 (2017)
15. Konnov, I., Widder, J.: ByMC: byzantine model checker. In: Margaria, T., Steffen, B. (eds.) ISoLA 2018. LNCS, vol. 11246, pp. 327–342. Springer, Cham (2018). https://doi.org/10.1007/978-3-030-03424-5_22
16. Konnov, I.V., Lazic, M., Veith, H., Widder, J.: A short counterexample property for safety and liveness verification of fault-tolerant distributed algorithms. In: Proceedings of the 44th ACM SIGPLAN Symposium on Principles of Programming Languages, POPL 2017, Paris, France, 18–20 January 2017, pp. 719–734 (2017)
17. Kotla, R., Alvisi, L., Dahlin, M., Clement, A., Wong, E.: Zyzzyva: speculative Byzantine fault tolerance. SIGOPS Oper. Syst. Rev. **41**(6), 45–58 (2007)
18. Kukovec, J., Konnov, I., Widder, J.: Reachability in parameterized systems: all flavors of threshold automata. In: CONCUR. LIPIcs, vol. 118, pp. 19:1–19:17. Schloss Dagstuhl - Leibniz-Zentrum fuer Informatik (2018)
19. Kuncak, V., Nguyen, H.H., Rinard, M.: An algorithm for deciding BAPA: boolean algebra with presburger arithmetic. In: Nieuwenhuis, R. (ed.) CADE 2005. LNCS (LNAI), vol. 3632, pp. 260–277. Springer, Heidelberg (2005). https://doi.org/10.1007/11532231_20
20. Lamport, L.: The Part-time Parliament 16(2), 133–169 (1998–2005). https://doi.org/10.1145/279227.279229
21. Lamport, L.: Lower bounds for asynchronous consensus. In: Schiper, A., Shvartsman, A.A., Weatherspoon, H., Zhao, B.Y. (eds.) Future Directions in Distributed Computing. LNCS, vol. 2584, pp. 22–23. Springer, Heidelberg (2003). https://doi.org/10.1007/3-540-37795-6_4
22. Lamport, L.: Lower bounds for asynchronous consensus. Distrib. Comput. **19**(2), 104–125 (2006)
23. Lamport, L.: Fast byzantine paxos, 17 November 2009. uS Patent 7,620,680
24. Lazic, M., Konnov, I., Widder, J., Bloem, R.: Synthesis of distributed algorithms with parameterized threshold guards. In: OPODIS (2017, to appear). http://forsyte.at/wp-content/uploads/opodis17.pdf
25. Lewis, H.R.: Complexity results for classes of quantificational formulas. Comput. Syst. Sci. **21**(3), 317–353 (1980)
26. Liffiton, M.H., Previti, A., Malik, A., Marques-Silva, J.: Fast, flexible mus enumeration. Constraints **21**(2), 223–250 (2016)
27. Liu, Y.A., Stoller, S.D., Lin, B.: From clarity to efficiency for distributed algorithms. ACM Trans. Program. Lang. Syst. **39**(3), 121–1241 (2017). https://doi.org/10.1145/2994595
28. Martin, J.P., Alvisi, L.: Fast Byzantine consensus. IEEE Trans. Dependable Secure Comput. **3**(3), 202–215 (2006)
29. McMillan, K.L., Padon, O.: Deductive verification in decidable fragments with ivy. In: Podelski, A. (ed.) SAS 2018. LNCS, vol. 11002, pp. 43–55. Springer, Cham (2018). https://doi.org/10.1007/978-3-319-99725-4_4
30. Padon, O., Hoenicke, J., Losa, G., Podelski, A., Sagiv, M., Shoham, S.: Reducing liveness to safety in first-order logic. PACMPL **2**(POPL), 26:1–26:33 (2018)

31. Padon, O., Hoenicke, J., McMillan, K.L., Podelski, A., Sagiv, M., Shoham, S.: Temporal prophecy for proving temporal properties of infinite-state systems. In: FMCAD, pp. 1–11. IEEE (2018)
32. Padon, O., Losa, G., Sagiv, M., Shoham, S.: Paxos made EPR: decidable reasoning about distributed protocols. PACMPL **1**(OOPSLA), 1081–10831 (2017)
33. Padon, O., McMillan, K.L., Panda, A., Sagiv, M., Shoham, S.: Ivy: safety verification by interactive generalization. In: Krintz, C., Berger, E. (eds.) Proceedings of the 37th ACM SIGPLAN Conference on Programming Language Design and Implementation, PLDI 2016, Santa Barbara, CA, USA, 13–17 June 2016, pp. 614–630. ACM (2016)
34. Piskac, R.: Decision procedures for program synthesis and verification (2011). http://infoscience.epfl.ch/record/168994
35. Piskac, R., de Moura, L., Bjrner, N.: Deciding effectively propositional logic using DPLL and substitution sets. J. Autom. Reason. **44**(4), 401–424 (2010)
36. Rahli, V., Guaspari, D., Bickford, M., Constable, R.L.: Formal specification, verification, and implementation of fault-tolerant systems using eventml. ECEASST 72 (2015). https://doi.org/10.14279/tuj.eceasst.72.1013
37. Rahli, V., Vukotic, I., Völp, M., Esteves-Verissimo, P.: Velisarios: Byzantine fault-tolerant protocols powered by Coq. In: Ahmed, A. (ed.) ESOP 2018. LNCS, vol. 10801, pp. 619–650. Springer, Cham (2018). https://doi.org/10.1007/978-3-319-89884-1_22
38. Sergey, I., Wilcox, J.R., Tatlock, Z.: Programming and proving with distributed protocols. PACMPL **2**(POPL), 28:1–28:30 (2018)
39. Song, Y.J., van Renesse, R.: Bosco: one-step Byzantine asynchronous consensus. In: Taubenfeld, G. (ed.) DISC 2008. LNCS, vol. 5218, pp. 438–450. Springer, Heidelberg (2008). https://doi.org/10.1007/978-3-540-87779-0_30
40. Srikanth, T., Toueg, S.: Simulating authenticated broadcasts to derive simple fault-tolerant algorithms. Dist. Comp. **2**, 80–94 (1987)
41. Stoilkovska, I., Konnov, I., Widder, J., Zuleger, F.: Verifying safety of synchronous fault-tolerant algorithms by bounded model checking. In: Vojnar, T., Zhang, L. (eds.) TACAS 2019. LNCS, vol. 11428, pp. 357–374. Springer, Cham (2019). https://doi.org/10.1007/978-3-030-17465-1_20
42. Taube, M., et al.: Modularity for decidability of deductive verification with applications to distributed systems. In: PLDI, pp. 662–677. ACM (2018)
43. Wilcox, J.R., et al.: Verdi: a framework for implementing and formally verifying distributed systems. In: Proceedings of the 36th ACM SIGPLAN Conference on Programming Language Design and Implementation, Portland, OR, USA, 15–17 June 2015, pp. 357–368 (2015). https://doi.org/10.1145/2737924.2737958
44. Woos, D., Wilcox, J.R., Anton, S., Tatlock, Z., Ernst, M.D., Anderson, T.E.: Planning for change in a formal verification of the raft consensus protocol. In: Proceedings of the 5th ACM SIGPLAN Conference on Certified Programs and Proofs, Saint Petersburg, FL, USA, 20–22 January 2016, pp. 154–165 (2016). https://doi.org/10.1145/2854065.2854081

Gradual Consistency Checking

Rachid Zennou[1,2(✉)], Ahmed Bouajjani[1], Constantin Enea[1], and Mohammed Erradi[2]

[1] Université de Paris, IRIF, CNRS, 75013 Paris, France
rachid.zennou@gmail.com, {abou,cenea}@irif.fr
[2] ENSIAS, University Mohammed V, Rabat, Morocco
mohamed.erradi@gmail.com

Abstract. We address the problem of checking that computations of a shared memory implementation (with write and read operations) adheres to some given consistency model. It is known that checking conformance to Sequential Consistency (SC) for a given computation is NP-hard, and the same holds for checking Total Store Order (TSO) conformance. This poses a serious issue for the design of scalable verification or testing techniques for these important memory models. In this paper, we tackle this issue by providing an approach that avoids hitting systematically the worst-case complexity. The idea is to consider, as an intermediary step, the problem of checking weaker criteria that are as strong as possible while they are still checkable in polynomial time (in the size of the computation). The criteria we consider are new variations of causal consistency suitably defined for our purpose. The advantage of our approach is that in many cases (1) it can catch violations of SC/TSO early using these weaker criteria that are efficiently checkable, and (2) when a computation is causally consistent (according to our newly defined criteria), the work done for establishing this fact simplifies significantly the work required for checking SC/TSO conformance. We have implemented our algorithms and carried out several experiments on realistic cache-coherence protocols showing the efficiency of our approach.

1 Introduction

This paper addresses the problem of checking whether a given implementation of a shared memory offers the expected consistency guarantees to its clients which are concurrent programs composed of several threads running in parallel. Indeed, users of a memory need to see it as an abstract object allowing to perform concurrent reads and writes over a set of variables, which conform to some *memory model* defining the valid visible sequences of such operations. Various memory models can be considered in this context. Sequential Consistency (SC) [24] is the model where operations can be seen as atomic, executing according to some

This work is supported in part by the European Research Council (ERC) under the European Union's Horizon 2020 research and innovation programme (grant agreement No 678177).

I. Dillig and S. Tasiran (Eds.): CAV 2019, LNCS 11562, pp. 267–285, 2019.
https://doi.org/10.1007/978-3-030-25543-5_16

interleaving of the operations issued by the different threads, while preserving the order in which these operations were issued by each of the threads. This fundamental model offers strong consistency in the sense that for each write operation, when it is issued by a thread, it is immediately visible to all the other threads. Other weaker memory models are adopted in order to meet performance and/or availability requirements in concurrent/distributed systems. One of the most widely used models in this context is Total Store Order (TSO) [29]. In this model, writes can be delayed, which means that after a write is issued, it is not immediately visible to all threads (except for the thread that issued it), and it is committed later after some arbitrary delay. However, writes issued by the same thread are committed in the same order are they were issued, and when a write is committed it becomes visible to all the other threads simultaneously. TSO is implemented in hardware but also in a distributed context over a network [22].

Implementing shared memories that are both highly performant and correct with respect to a given memory model is an extremely hard and error prone task. Therefore, checking that a given implementation is indeed correct from this point of view is of paramount importance. In this paper we address the issue of checking that a given execution of a shared memory implementation is consistent, and we consider as consistency criteria the cases of SC and TSO.

Checking SC or TSO conformance is known to be NP-complete [18,21]. This is due to the fact that in order to justify that the execution is consistent, one has to find a total order between the writes which explains the read operations happening along the computation. It can be proved that one cannot avoid enumerating all the possible total orders between writes, in the worst case. The situation is different for other weaker criteria such as Causal Consistency (CC) and its different variations, which have been shown to be checkable in polynomial time (in the the size of the computation) [6]. In fact, CC imposes fewer constraints than SC/TSO on the order between writes, and the way it imposes these constraints is "deterministic", in the sense that they can be derived from the history of the execution by applying a least fixpoint computation (which can be encoded for instance, as a standard DATALOG program). All these complexity results hold under the assumption that each value is written at most once, which is without loss of generality for implementations which are data-independent [31], i.e., their behavior doesn't depend on the concrete values read or written in the program. Indeed, any buggy behavior of such implementations can be exposed in executions satisfying this assumption [1].

The intrinsic hardness of the problem of checking SC/TSO poses a crucial issue for the design of scalable verification or testing techniques for these important consistency models. Tackling this issue requires the development of practical approaches that can work well (with polynomial complexity) when the instance of the problem does not need to generate the worst case (exponential) complexity.

[1] All the CC variations become NP-complete without the assumption that each value is written at most once [6]. This holds for the variations of CC we introduce in this paper as well.

The purpose of this paper is to propose such an approach. The idea is to reduce the amount of "nondeterminism" in searching for the write orders in order to establish SC/TSO conformance. For that, our approach for SC is to consider a weaker consistency model called CCM (for Convergent Causal Memory), that is "as strong as possible" while being polynomial time checkable. In fact CCM is stronger than both causal memory [2,26] (CM) and causal convergence [7] (CCv), two other well-known variations of causal consistency. Then, if CCM is already violated by the given computation then we can conclude that the computation does not satisfy the stronger criterion SC. Here the hope is that in practice many computations violating SC can be caught already at this stage using a polynomial time check. Now, in the case that the computation does not violate CCM, we exploit the fact that establishing CCM already imposes a set of constraints on the order between writes. We show that these constraints form a partial order which *must* be a subset of any total write order that would witness for SC conformance. Therefore, at this point, it is enough to find an extension of this partial write order, and the hope is that in many practical cases, this set of constraints is already large enough, letting only a small number of pairs of writes to be ordered in order to check SC conformance. For the case of TSO, we proceed in the same way, but we consider a different intermediary polynomial time checkable criterion called *weak* CCM (wCCM). This is due to the fact that some causality constraints need to be relaxed in order to take into account the program order relaxations of TSO, that allow reads to overtake writes. The definitions of the new criteria CCM and wCCM we use in our approach are quite subtile. Ensuring that these criteria are "as strong as possible" by including all possible order constraints on pairs of writes that can be computed (in polynomial time) using a least fixpoint calculation, while still ensuring that they are weaker than SC/TSO, and proving this fact, is not trivial.

As a proof of concept, we implemented our approach for checking SC/TSO and applied it to executions extracted from realistic cache coherence protocols within the Gem5 simulator [5] in system emulation mode. This evaluation shows that our approach scales better than a direct encoding of the axioms defining SC and TSO [3] into boolean satisfiability. We also show that the partial order of writes imposed by the stronger criteria CCM and wCCM leaves only a small percentage of writes unordered (6.6% in average) in the case that the executions are valid, and most SC/TSO violations are also CCM/wCCM violations.

2 Sequential Consistency and TSO

We consider multi-threaded programs over a set of shared variables $\mathsf{Var} = \{x, y, \ldots\}$. Threads issue read and write operations. Assuming an unspecified set of values Val and a set of operation identifiers OId, we let

$$\mathsf{Op} = \{\mathsf{read}_i(x, v), \mathsf{write}_i(x, v) : i \in \mathsf{OId}, x \in \mathsf{Var}, v \in \mathsf{Val}\}$$

be the set of operations reading a value v or writing a value v to a variable x. We omit operation identifiers when they are not important. The set of read, resp., write, operations is denoted by $\mathbb{R}$, resp., $\mathbb{W}$. The set of read, resp., write, operations in a set of operations O is denoted by $\mathbb{R}(O)$, resp., $\mathbb{W}(O)$. The variable accessed by an operation o is denoted by $\mathsf{var}(o)$.

Consistency criteria like SC or TSO are formalized on an abstract view of an execution called *history*. A history includes a set of write or read operations ordered according to a (partial) *program order* po which order operations issued by the same thread. Most often, po is a union of sequences, each sequence containing all the operations issued by some thread. Then, we assume that the history includes a *write-read* relation which identifies the write operation writing the value returned by each read in the execution. Such a relation can be extracted easily from executions where each value is written at most once. Since shared-memory implementations (or cache coherence protocols) are data-independent [31] in practice, i.e., their behavior doesn't depend on the concrete values read or written in the program, any potential buggy behavior can be exposed in such executions.

Definition 1. *A* history $\langle O, \mathsf{po}, \mathsf{wr}\rangle$ *is a set of operations O along with a strict partial* program order po *and a* write-read *relation* $\mathsf{wr} \subseteq \mathbb{W}(O) \times \mathbb{R}(O)$*, such that the inverse of* wr *is a total function and if* $(\mathit{write}(x, v), \mathit{read}(x', v')) \in \mathsf{wr}$*, then $x = x'$ and $v = v'$.*

We assume that every history includes a write operation writing the initial value of variable x, for each variable x. These write operations precede all other operations in po. We use h, h_1, h_2, ... to range over histories.

We now define the SC and TSO memory models (we use the same definitions as in the formal framework developed by Alglave et al. [3]). Given a *history* $h = \langle O, \mathsf{po}, \mathsf{wr}\rangle$ and a variable x, a *store order on x* is a strict total order ww_x on the write operations $\mathsf{write}\_(x, \_)$ in O. A *store order* is a union of store orders ww_x, one for each variable x used in h. A *history* $\langle O, \mathsf{po}, \mathsf{wr}\rangle$ is *sequentially consistent* (SC, for short) if there exists a *store order* ww such that $\mathsf{po} \cup \mathsf{wr} \cup \mathsf{ww} \cup \mathsf{rw}$ is acyclic. The *read-write* relation rw is defined by $\mathsf{rw} = \mathsf{wr}^{-1} \circ \mathsf{ww}$ (where $\circ$ denotes the standard relation composition).

The definition of TSO relies on three additional relations: (1) the ppo relation which excludes from the program order pairs formed of a write and respectively, a read operation, i.e., $\mathsf{ppo} = \mathsf{po} \setminus (\mathbb{W}(O) \times \mathbb{R}(O))$, (2) the $\mathsf{po\text{-}loc}$ relation which is a restriction of po to operations accessing the same variable, i.e., $\mathsf{po\text{-}loc} = \mathsf{po} \cap \{(o, o') \mid \mathsf{var}(o) = \mathsf{var}(o')\}$, and (3) the write-read external relation wr_e which is a restriction of the write-read relation to pairs of operations in different threads (not related by program order), i.e., $\mathsf{wr}_e = \mathsf{wr} \cap \{(o, o') \mid (o, o') \notin \mathsf{po} \text{ and } (o', o) \notin \mathsf{po}\}$. Then, we say that a history satisfies TSO if there exists a *store order* ww such that $\mathsf{po\text{-}loc} \cup \mathsf{wr}_e \cup \mathsf{ww} \cup \mathsf{rw}$ and $\mathsf{ppo} \cup \mathsf{wr}_e \cup \mathsf{ww} \cup \mathsf{rw}$ are both acyclic.

Notice that the formal definition of the TSO given above is equivalent to the formal operational model of TSO that consists in considering that each thread has a store buffer, and then, each write issued by a thread is first sent to its store buffer before being committed to the memory later in a nondeterministic way. To read a value on some variable x, a thread first checks if it there is still a write on x pending in its own buffer and in this case it takes the value of the last such as write, otherwise it fetches the value of x in the memory.

3 Checking Sequential Consistency

We define an algorithm for checking whether a history satisfies SC which enforces a polynomially-time checkable criterion weaker than SC, a variation of causal consistency, in order to construct a *partial* store order, i.e., one in which not all the writes on the same variable are ordered. This partial store order is then completed until it orders every two writes on the same variable using a standard backtracking enumeration. This approach is efficient when the number of writes that remain to be ordered using the backtracking enumeration is relatively small, a hypothesis confirmed by our experimental evaluation (see Sect. 5.).

The variation of causal consistency mentioned above, called *convergent causal memory* (CCM, for short), is stronger than existing variations [6] while still being polynomially-time checkable (and weaker than SC). Its definition uses several relations between read and write operations which are analogous or even exactly the same relations used to define those variations. Section 3.1 recalls the existing notions of causal consistency as they are defined in [6] (using the so called "bad-pattern" characterization introduced in that paper), Sect. 3.2 introduces CCM, while Sect. 3.3 presents our algorithm for checking SC.

3.1 Causal Consistency

The weakest variation of causal consistency, called *weak causal consistency* (CC, for short), requires that any two causally-dependent values are observed in the same order by all threads, where causally-dependent means that either those values were written by the same thread (i.e., the corresponding writes are ordered by po), or that one value was written by a thread after reading the other value, or any transitive composition of such dependencies. Values written concurrently by two threads can be observed in any order, and even-more, this order may change in time. A *history* $\langle O, \mathsf{po}, \mathsf{wr}\rangle$ satisfies CC if $\mathsf{po} \cup \mathsf{wr} \cup \mathsf{rw}[\mathsf{co}]$ is acyclic where $\mathsf{co} = (\mathsf{po} \cup \mathsf{wr})^+$ is called the *causal relation*. The *read-write* relation $\mathsf{rw}[\mathsf{co}]$ induced by the causal relation is defined by

$$(\mathsf{read}(x,v), \mathsf{write}(x,v')) \in \mathsf{rw}[\mathsf{co}] \text{ iff } (\mathsf{write}(x,v), \mathsf{write}(x,v')) \in \mathsf{co} \text{ and } (\mathsf{write}(x,v), \mathsf{read}(x,v)) \in \mathsf{wr}, \text{ for some } \mathsf{write}(x,v)$$

The read-write relation $\mathsf{rw}[\mathsf{co}]$ is a variation of rw from the definition of SC/TSO where the store order ww is replaced by the projection of co on pairs of writes. In general, given a binary relation R on operations, R_{WW} denotes the projection of R on pairs of writes on the same variable. Then,

Definition 2. *The read-write relation* $\mathsf{rw}[R]$ *induced by a relation* R *is defined by* $\mathsf{rw}[R] = \mathsf{wr}^{-1} \circ R_{\mathsf{WW}}$.

Causal convergence (CCv, for short) is a strengthening of CC where concurrent values are required to be observed in the same order by all threads.

A *history* $\langle O, \mathsf{po}, \mathsf{wr}\rangle$ satisfies CCv if it satisfies CC and $\mathsf{po} \cup \mathsf{wr} \cup \mathsf{cf}$ is acyclic where the *conflict relation* cf is defined by

$$(\mathsf{write}(x, v), \mathsf{write}(x, v')) \in \mathsf{cf} \text{ iff } (\mathsf{write}(x, v), \mathsf{read}(x, v')) \in \mathsf{co} \text{ and } (\mathsf{write}(x, v'), \mathsf{read}(x, v')) \in \mathsf{wr}, \text{ for some } \mathsf{read}(x, v')$$

The conflict relation relates two writes w_1 and w_2 when w_1 is causally related to a read taking its value from w_2. The definition of CCM, our new variation of causal consistency, relies on a generalization of the conflict relation where a different relation is used instead of co. Given a binary relation R on operations, $R_{\mathbb{WR}}$ denotes the projection of R on pairs of writes and reads on the same variable, respectively.

Definition 3. *The conflict relation* $\mathsf{cf}[R]$ *induced by a relation* R *is defined by* $\mathsf{cf}[R] = R_{\mathbb{WR}} \circ \mathsf{wr}^{-1}$.

t_0:	t_1:
$\mathsf{write}(x, 1)$	$\mathsf{write}(x, 2)$
$\mathsf{read}(x, 2)$	$\mathsf{read}(x, 1)$

(a) CM but not CCv nor wCCM

t_0:	t_1:
$\mathsf{write}(z, 1)$	$\mathsf{write}(x, 2)$
$\mathsf{write}(x, 1)$	$\mathsf{read}(z, 0)$
$\mathsf{write}(y, 1)$	$\mathsf{read}(y, 1)$
	$\mathsf{read}(x, 2)$

(b) CCv, wCCM and TSO but not CM

t_0:	t_1:
$\mathsf{write}(x, 1)$	$\mathsf{write}(y, 1)$
$\mathsf{write}(x, 2)$	$\mathsf{write}(y, 2)$
$\mathsf{read}(y, 1)$	$\mathsf{read}(y, 2)$
	$\mathsf{read}(x, 1)$

(c) CM and CCv but not CCM

t_0:	t_1:
$\mathsf{write}(x, 1)$	$\mathsf{write}(x, 2)$
$\mathsf{read}(y, 0)$	$\mathsf{read}(y, 0)$
$\mathsf{write}(y, 1)$	$\mathsf{write}(y, 2)$
$\mathsf{read}(x, 1)$	$\mathsf{read}(x, 2)$

(d) CCM but not SC

Fig. 1. Histories with two threads used to compare different consistency models. Operations of the same thread are aligned vertically.

Finally, *causal memory* (CM, for short) is a strengthening of CC where roughly, concurrent values are required to be observed in the same order by a thread during its entire execution. Differently from CCv, this order can differ from one thread to another. Although this intuitive description seems to imply that CM is weaker than CCv, the two models are actually incomparable. For instance, the history in Fig. 1a is allowed by CM, but not by CCv. It is not allowed by CCv because reading 1 from x in the first thread implies that it observed $\mathsf{write}(x, 1)$ after $\mathsf{write}(x, 2)$ while reading 2 from x in the second thread implies that it observed $\mathsf{write}(x,2)$ after $\mathsf{write}(x,1)$. While this is allowed by CM where different threads can observe concurrent writes in different orders, it is not allowed by CCv. Then, the history in Fig. 1b is CCv but not CM. It is not allowed by CM because reading the initial value 0 from z implies that $\mathsf{write}(x,1)$ is observed after $\mathsf{write}(x,2)$ while reading 2 from x implies that $\mathsf{write}(x,2)$ is observed after $\mathsf{write}(x,1)$ ($\mathsf{write}(x,1)$ must have been observed because the same thread reads 1 from y and the writes on x and y are causally related). However, under CCv, a thread simply reads the most recent value on each variable and the order in which these values are ordered using timestamps for instance is independent of the order in which variables are read in a thread, e.g., reading 0 from z doesn't imply that the timestamp of $\mathsf{write}(x,2)$ is smaller than the timestamp of $\mathsf{write}(x,1)$. This history is admitted by CCv assuming that the order in which $\mathsf{write}(x,1)$ and $\mathsf{write}(x,2)$ are observed is $\mathsf{write}(x,1)$ before $\mathsf{write}(x,2)$.

Let us give the formal definition of CM. Let h$=\langle O,\mathsf{po},\mathsf{wr}\rangle$ be a history. For every operation o in h, let hb_o be the smallest transitive relation such that:

1. if two operations are causally related, and each one causally related to o, then they are related by hb_o, i.e., $(o_1,o_2)\in\mathsf{hb}_o$ if $(o_1,o_2)\in\mathsf{co}$, $(o_1,o)\in\mathsf{co}$, and $(o_2,o)\in\mathsf{co}^*$ (where co^* is the reflexive closure of co), and
2. two writes w_1 and w_2 are related by hb_o if w_1 is hb_o-related to a read taking its value from w_2, and that read is done by the same thread executing o and before o (this scenario is similar to the definition of the conflict relation above), i.e., $(\mathsf{write}(x,v),\mathsf{write}(x,v'))\in\mathsf{hb}_o$ if $(\mathsf{write}(x,v),\mathsf{read}(x,v'))\in\mathsf{hb}_o$, $(\mathsf{write}(x,v'),\mathsf{read}(x,v'))\in\mathsf{wr}$, and $(\mathsf{read}(x,v'),o)\in\mathsf{po}^*$, for some $\mathsf{read}(x,v')$.

A history $\langle O,\mathsf{po},\mathsf{wr}\rangle$ satisfies CM if it satisfies CC and for each operation o in the history, the relation hb_o is acyclic.

Bouajjani et al. [6] show that the problem of checking whether a history satisfies CC, CCv, or CM is polynomial time. This result is a straightforward consequence of the above definitions, since the union of relations required to be acyclic can be computed in polynomial time from the relations po and wr which are fixed in a given history. In particular, the union of these relations can be computed by a DATALOG program.

3.2 Convergent Causal Memory

We define a new variation of causal consistency which builds on causal memory, but similar to causal convergence it enforces that all threads agree on an order in which to observe values written by concurrent (causally-unrelated) writes, and also, it uses a larger read-write relation. A history $\langle O,\mathsf{po},\mathsf{wr}\rangle$ satisfies *convergent causal memory* (CCM, for short) if $\mathsf{po}\cup\mathsf{wr}\cup\mathsf{pww}\cup\mathsf{rw}[\mathsf{pww}]$ is acyclic, where the *partial store order* pww is defined by

$$\mathsf{pww}=(\mathsf{hb}_{\mathbb{WW}}\cup\mathsf{cf}[\mathsf{hb}])^+ \text{ with } \mathsf{hb}=\Big(\bigcup_{o\in O}\mathsf{hb}_o\Big)^+.$$

The partial store order pww contains the ordering constraints between writes in all relations hb_o used to defined causal memory, and also, the conflict relation induced by this set of constraints (a weaker version of conflict relation was used to define causal convergence).

As a first result, we show that all the variations of causal consistency in Sect. 3.1, i.e., CC, CCv and CM, are strictly weaker than CCM.

Lemma 1. *If a history satisfies CCM, then it satisfies CC, CCv and CM.*

Proof. Let $h = \langle O, \mathsf{po}, \mathsf{wr}\rangle$ be a history satisfying CCM. By the definition of hb, we have that $\mathsf{co}_{\mathbb{WW}} \subseteq \mathsf{hb}_{\mathbb{WW}}$. Indeed, any two writes o_1 and o_2 related by co are also related by hb_{o_2}, which by the definition of hb, implies that they are related by $\mathsf{hb}_{\mathbb{WW}}$. Then, by the definition of pww, we have that $\mathsf{hb}_{\mathbb{WW}} \subseteq \mathsf{pww}$. This implies that $\mathsf{rw}[\mathsf{co}] \subseteq \mathsf{rw}[\mathsf{pww}]$ (by definition, $\mathsf{rw}[\mathsf{co}] = \mathsf{rw}[\mathsf{co}_{\mathbb{WW}}]$). Therefore, the acyclicity of $\mathsf{po} \cup \mathsf{wr} \cup \mathsf{pww} \cup \mathsf{rw}[\mathsf{pww}]$ implies that its subset ($\mathsf{po} \cup \mathsf{wr} \cup \mathsf{rw}[\mathsf{co}]$ is also acyclic, which means that h satisfies CC. Also, it implies that $\mathsf{po}\cup\mathsf{wr}\cup\mathsf{cf}[\mathsf{hb}]$ is acyclic (the last term of the union is included in pww), which by $\mathsf{co} \subseteq \mathsf{hb}$, implies that $\mathsf{po} \cup \mathsf{wr} \cup \mathsf{cf}[\mathsf{co}]$ is acyclic, and thus, h satisfies CCv. The fact that h satisfies CM follows from the fact that h satisfies CC (since $\mathsf{po} \cup \mathsf{wr}$ is acyclic) and hb is acyclic ($\mathsf{hb}_{\mathbb{WW}}$ is included in pww and the rest of the dependencies in hb are included in $\mathsf{po} \cup \mathsf{wr}$). □

The reverse of the above lemma doesn't hold. Figure 1c shows a history which satisfies CM and CCv, but it is not CCM. To show that this history does not satisfy CCM we use the fact that pww relates any two writes which are ordered by program order. Then, we get that $\mathsf{read}(x, 1)$ and $\mathsf{write}(x, 2)$ are related by $\mathsf{rw}[\mathsf{pww}]$ (because $\mathsf{write}(x, 1)$ is related by write-read with $\mathsf{read}(x, 1)$), which further implies that $(\mathsf{read}(x, 1), \mathsf{read}(y, 1)) \in \mathsf{rw}[\mathsf{pww}] \circ \mathsf{po}$. Similarly, we have that $(\mathsf{read}(y, 1), \mathsf{read}(x, 1)) \in \mathsf{rw}[\mathsf{pww}]\circ\mathsf{po}$, which implies that $\mathsf{po}\cup\mathsf{wr}\cup\mathsf{pww}\cup\mathsf{rw}[\mathsf{pww}]$ is *not* acyclic, and therefore, the history does not satisfy CCM. The fact that this history satisfies CM and CCv follows easily from definitions.

Next, we show that CCM is weaker than SC, which will be important in our algorithm for checking whether a history satisfies SC.

Lemma 2. *If a history satisfies SC, then it satisfies CCM.*

Proof. Using the definition of CCM, Let $h = \langle O, \mathsf{po}, \mathsf{wr}\rangle$ be a history satisfying SC. Then, there exists a *store order* ww such that $\mathsf{po}\cup\mathsf{wr}\cup\mathsf{ww}\cup\mathsf{rw}[\mathsf{ww}]$ is acyclic. We show that the two relations $\mathsf{hb}_{\mathbb{WW}}$ and $\mathsf{cf}[\mathsf{hb}]$, whose union constitutes pww, are both included in ww. We first prove that $\mathsf{hb} \subseteq (\mathsf{po} \cup \mathsf{wr} \cup \mathsf{ww} \cup \mathsf{rw}[\mathsf{ww}])^+$ by structural induction on the definition of hb_o:

1. if $(o_1, o_2) \in \mathsf{co} = (\mathsf{po}\cup\mathsf{wr})^+$, then clearly, $(o_1, o_2) \in (\mathsf{po}\cup\mathsf{wr}\cup\mathsf{ww}\cup\mathsf{rw}[\mathsf{ww}])^+$,
2. if $(\mathsf{write}(x, v), \mathsf{read}(x, v')) \in (\mathsf{po} \cup \mathsf{wr} \cup \mathsf{ww} \cup \mathsf{rw}[\mathsf{ww}])^+$ and there is $\mathsf{read}(x, v')$ such that $(\mathsf{write}(x, v'), \mathsf{read}(x, v')) \in \mathsf{wr}$, then $(\mathsf{write}(x, v), \mathsf{write}(x, v')) \in \mathsf{ww}$. Otherwise, assuming by contradiction that $(\mathsf{write}(x, v'), \mathsf{write}(x, v)) \in \mathsf{ww}$, we get that $(\mathsf{read}(x, v'), \mathsf{write}(x, v)) \in \mathsf{rw}[\mathsf{ww}]$ (by the definition of $\mathsf{rw}[\mathsf{ww}]$ using the hypothesis $(\mathsf{write}(x, v'), \mathsf{read}(x, v')) \in \mathsf{wr}$). Note that the latter implies that $\mathsf{po} \cup \mathsf{wr} \cup \mathsf{ww} \cup \mathsf{rw}[\mathsf{ww}]$ is cyclic.

Since $\mathsf{hb} \subseteq (\mathsf{po} \cup \mathsf{wr} \cup \mathsf{ww} \cup \mathsf{rw}[\mathsf{ww}])^+$, we get that $\mathsf{hb}_{\mathbb{WW}} \subseteq \mathsf{ww}$. Also, since $\mathsf{cf}[(\mathsf{po} \cup \mathsf{wr} \cup \mathsf{ww} \cup \mathsf{rw}[\mathsf{ww}])^+] \subseteq (\mathsf{po} \cup \mathsf{wr} \cup \mathsf{ww} \cup \mathsf{rw}[\mathsf{ww}])^+$ (using a similar argument as in point (2) above), we get that $\mathsf{cf}[\mathsf{hb}] \subseteq (\mathsf{po} \cup \mathsf{wr} \cup \mathsf{ww} \cup \mathsf{rw}[\mathsf{ww}])^+$.

Finally, since $\mathsf{pww} \subseteq \mathsf{ww}$, we get that $(\mathsf{po} \cup \mathsf{wr} \cup \mathsf{pww} \cup \mathsf{rw}[\mathsf{pww}])^+ \subseteq (\mathsf{po} \cup \mathsf{wr} \cup \mathsf{ww} \cup \mathsf{rw}[\mathsf{ww}])^+$, which implies that the acyclicity of the latter implies the acyclicity of the former. Therefore, h satisfies CCM. □

The reverse of the above lemma doesn't hold. For instance, the history in Fig. 1d is not SC but it is CCM. This history admits a partial store order pww where the writes in different threads are not ordered.

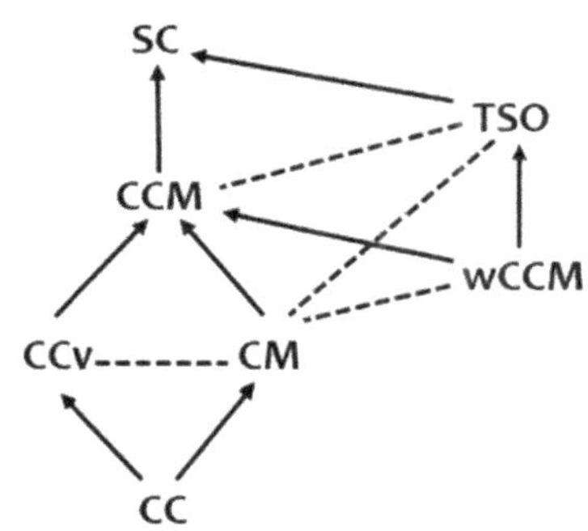

Fig. 2. Relationships between consistency models. Directed arrows denote the "weaker-than" relation while dashed lines connect incomparable models.

The left side of Fig. 2 (ignoring wCCM and TSO) summarizes the relationships between the consistency models presented in this section.

The partial store order pww can be computed in polynomial time (in the size of the input history). Indeed, the hb_o relations can be computed using a least fixpoint calculation that converges in at most a quadratic number of iterations and acyclicity can be decided in polynomial time. Therefore,

Theorem 1. *Checking whether a history satisfies CCM is polynomial time in the size of the history.*

3.3 An Algorithm for Checking Sequential Consistency

Algorithm 1 checks whether a given history satisfies sequential consistency. As a first step, it checks whether the given history satisfies CCM. If this is not the case, then, by Lemma 2, the history does not satisfy SC as well, and the algorithm returns *false*. Otherwise, it enumerates store orders which extend the partial store order pww, until finding one that witnesses for satisfaction of SC. The history is a violation to SC iff no such store order is found. The soundness of this last step is implied by the proof of Lemma 2, which shows that pww is included in any store order ww witnessing for SC satisfaction.

Theorem 2. *Algorithm 1 returns true iff the input history h satisfies SC.*

Input: A history $h = \langle O, \mathsf{po}, \mathsf{wr} \rangle$
Output: *true* iff h satisfies SC

if $\mathsf{po} \cup \mathsf{wr} \cup \mathsf{pww} \cup \mathsf{rw}[\mathsf{pww}]$ *is cyclic* **then**
  return *false*;
end
foreach $\mathsf{ww} \supset \mathsf{pww}$ **do**
  if $\mathsf{po} \cup \mathsf{wr} \cup \mathsf{ww} \cup \mathsf{rw}[\mathsf{ww}]$ *is acyclic* **then**
    return *true*;
  end
end
return *false*;

Algorithm 1. Checking SC conformance.

4 Checking Conformance to the TSO Model

We consider now the problem of checking whether a history satisfies TSO. Following the approach developed above for SC, we define a polynomial time checkable criterion, based on a (different) variation of causal consistency that is suitable for the case of TSO. This allows to reduce the number of pairs of writes for which an order must be guessed in order to establish conformance to TSO.

The case of TSO requires the definition of a new intermediary consistency model because CCM is based on a causality order that includes the program order po which is relaxed in the context of TSO, compared to the SC model. Indeed, CCM is *not* weaker than TSO as shown by the history in Fig. 1b (note that this does not imply that other variations of causal consistency, CC and CCv, are also not weaker than TSO). This history satisfies TSO because, based on its operational model, the operation $\mathsf{write}(x, 2)$ of thread t_1 can be delayed (pending in the store buffer of t_1) until the end of the execution. Therefore, after executing $\mathsf{read}(z, 0)$, all the writes of thread t_0 are committed to the main memory so that thread t_1 can read 1 from y and 2 from x (it is obliged to read the value of x from its own store buffer). This history is not admitted by CCM because it is not admitted by the weaker causal consistency variation CM. Figure 3 shows a history admitted by CCM but not by TSO. Indeed, under TSO, both t_2 and t_3 should see the writes on x and y performed by t_0 and t_1, respectively, in the same order. This is not the case, because t_2 "observes" the write on x before the write on y (since it reads 0 from y) and t_3 "observes" the write on y before the write on x (since it reads 0 from x). This history is admitted by CCM because the two writes are causally independent and they concern different variables. We mention that TSO and CM are also incomparable. For instance, the history in Fig. 1a is allowed by CM, but not by TSO. The history in Fig. 1b is admitted by TSO, but not by CM.

Next, we define a weakening of CCM, called *weak convergent causal memory* (wCCM), which is also weaker than TSO. The model wCCM is based on causality relations induced by the relaxed program orders ppo and po-loc instead of po, and the external write-read relation instead of the full write-read relation.

t_0:	t_1:	t_2:	t_3:
$\mathsf{write}(x, 1)$	$\mathsf{write}(y, 1)$	$\mathsf{read}(x, 1)$	$\mathsf{read}(y, 1)$
		$\mathsf{read}(y, 0)$	$\mathsf{read}(x, 0)$

Fig. 3. A history admitted by wCCM and CCM but not by TSO.

4.1 Weak Convergent Causal Memory

First, we define two causality relations relative to the partial program orders in the definition of TSO and the external write-read relation: For $\pi \in \{\mathsf{ppo}, \mathsf{po\text{-}loc}\}$, let $\mathsf{co}^\pi = (\pi \cup \mathsf{wr}_e)^+$. We also consider a notion of conflict that is defined in terms of the external write-read relation as follows: For a given relation R, let $\mathsf{cf}_e[R] = R_{\mathbb{WR}} \circ \mathsf{wr}_e^{-1}$.

Then, given a history $\langle O, \mathsf{po}, \mathsf{wr}\rangle$, we define for each operation o two happens-before relations $\mathsf{hb}_o^{\mathsf{ppo}}$ and $\mathsf{hb}_o^{\mathsf{po\text{-}loc}}$. The definition of these relations is similar to the one of hb_o (from causal memory), the differences being that po is replaced by ppo and $\mathsf{po\text{-}loc}$ respectively, co is replaced by $\mathsf{co}^{\mathsf{ppo}}$ and $\mathsf{co}^{\mathsf{po\text{-}loc}}$ respectively, and wr is replaced by wr_e. Therefore, for $\pi \in \{\mathsf{ppo}, \mathsf{po\text{-}loc}\}$, hb_o^π is is the smallest transitive relation such that:

1. $(o_1, o_2) \in \mathsf{hb}_o^\pi$ if $(o_1, o_2) \in \mathsf{co}^\pi$, $(o_1, o) \in \mathsf{co}^\pi$, and $(o_2, o) \in (\mathsf{co}^\pi)^*$, and
2. $(\mathsf{write}(x, v), \mathsf{write}(x, v')) \in \mathsf{hb}_o^\pi$ if $(\mathsf{write}(x, v), \mathsf{read}(x, v')) \in \mathsf{hb}_o^\pi$, and $(\mathsf{write}(x, v'), \mathsf{read}(x, v')) \in \mathsf{wr}$ and $(\mathsf{read}(x, v'), o) \in \pi^*$, for some $\mathsf{read}(x, v')$.

Let $\mathsf{hb}^\pi = (\bigcup_{o \in O} \mathsf{hb}_o^\pi)^+$, for $\pi \in \{\mathsf{ppo}, \mathsf{po\text{-}loc}\}$, and let $\mathsf{whb} = (\mathsf{hb}_o^{\mathsf{ppo}} \cup \mathsf{hb}_o^{\mathsf{po\text{-}loc}})^+$. Then, the weak partial store order is defined as follows:

$$\mathsf{wpww} = (\mathsf{whb}_{\mathbb{WW}} \cup \mathsf{cf}_e[\mathsf{hb}^{\mathsf{po\text{-}loc}}] \cup \mathsf{cf}_e[\mathsf{hb}^{\mathsf{ppo}}])^+$$

Then, we say that a history $\langle O, \mathsf{po}, \mathsf{wr}\rangle$ satisfies *weak convergent causal memory* (wCCM) if both relations:

$$\mathsf{ppo} \cup \mathsf{wr}_e \cup \mathsf{wpww} \cup \mathsf{rw}[\mathsf{wpww}] \text{ and } \mathsf{po\text{-}loc} \cup \mathsf{wr}_e \cup \mathsf{wpww} \cup \mathsf{rw}[\mathsf{wpww}]$$

are acyclic.

Lemma 3. *If a history satisfies TSO, then it satisfies wCCM.*

Proof. Let $h = \langle O, \mathsf{po}, \mathsf{wr}\rangle$ be a history satisfying TSO. Then, there exists a store order ww such that $\mathsf{po\text{-}loc} \cup \mathsf{wr}_e \cup \mathsf{ww} \cup \mathsf{rw}$ and $\mathsf{ppo} \cup \mathsf{wr}_e \cup \mathsf{ww} \cup \mathsf{rw}$ are both acyclic. The fact that

$$\mathsf{hb}^{\mathsf{po\text{-}loc}} \subseteq (\mathsf{po\text{-}loc} \cup \mathsf{wr}_e \cup \mathsf{ww} \cup \mathsf{rw})^+ \text{ and } \mathsf{hb}^{\mathsf{ppo}} \subseteq (\mathsf{ppo} \cup \mathsf{wr}_e \cup \mathsf{ww} \cup \mathsf{rw})^+$$

can be proved by structural induction like in the case of SC (the step of the proof showing that $\mathsf{hb} \subseteq \mathsf{po} \cup \mathsf{wr} \cup \mathsf{ww} \cup \mathsf{rw}[\mathsf{ww}]$). Then, since ww is a total order on writes on the same variable, we get that the projection of whb (the transitive closure of the union of $\mathsf{hb}^{\mathsf{po\text{-}loc}}$ and $\mathsf{hb}^{\mathsf{ppo}}$) on pairs of writes on the same variable is included in ww. Therefore, $\mathsf{whb}_{\mathsf{WW}} \subseteq \mathsf{ww}$. Then, since $\mathsf{cf}_e[R^\pi] \subseteq R^\pi$ for each $R^\pi = (\pi \cup \mathsf{wr}_e \cup \mathsf{ww} \cup \mathsf{rw})^+$ with $\pi \in \{\mathsf{ppo}, \mathsf{po\text{-}loc}\}$ and since each $\mathsf{cf}_e[R^\pi]$ relates only writes on the same variable, we get that each $\mathsf{cf}_e[R^\pi]$ is included in ww. This implies that $\mathsf{wpww} \subseteq \mathsf{ww}$.

Finally, since $\mathsf{wpww} \subseteq \mathsf{ww}$, we get that $(\pi \cup \mathsf{wr} \cup \mathsf{wpww} \cup \mathsf{rw}[\mathsf{wpww}])^+ \subseteq (\pi \cup \mathsf{wr} \cup \mathsf{ww} \cup \mathsf{rw}[\mathsf{ww}])^+$, for each $\pi \in \{\mathsf{ppo}, \mathsf{po\text{-}loc}\}$. In each case, the acyclicity of the latter implies the acyclicity of the former. Therefore, h satisfies wCCM.

```
Input: A history h = ⟨O, po, wr⟩
Output: true iff h satisfies TSO
if ppo ∪ wr_e ∪ wpww ∪ rw[wpww] or po-loc ∪ wr_e ∪ pww ∪ rw[wpww] is cyclic then
    return false;
end
foreach ww ⊃ wpww do
    if ppo ∪ wr_e ∪ ww ∪ rw[ww] and po-loc ∪ wr_e ∪ ww ∪ rw[ww] are acyclic then
        return true;
    end
end
return false;
```

Algorithm 2. Checking TSO conformance.

The reverse of the above lemma does not hold. Indeed, it can be easily seen that wCCM is weaker than CCM (since wpww is included in pww) and the history in Fig. 3, which satisfies CCM but not TSO (as explained in the beginning of the section), is also an example of a history that satisfies wCCM but not TSO. Then, wCCM is incomparable to CM. For instance, the history in Fig. 1b is allowed by wCCM (since it is allowed by TSO as explained in the beginning of the section) but not by CM. Also, since CCM is stronger than CM, the history in Fig. 3 satisfies CM but not wCCM (since it does not satisfy TSO). These relationships are summarized in Fig. 2. Establishing the precise relation between CC/CCv and TSO is hard because they are defined using one, resp., two, acyclicity conditions. We believe that CC and CCv are weaker than TSO, but we don't have a formal proof.

Finally, it can be seen that, similarly to pww, the weak partial store order wpww can be computed in polynomial time, and therefore:

Theorem 3. *Checking whether a history satisfies wCCM is polynomial time in the size of the history.*

4.2 An Algorithm for Checking TSO Conformance

The algorithm for checking TSO conformance for a given history is given in Fig. 2. It starts by checking whether the history violates the weaker consistency model wCCM. If yes, it returns false. If not, it starts enumerating the orders between the writes that are not related by the weak partial store order wpww until it founds one that allows establishing TSO conformance and in this case it returns true. Otherwise it returns false.

Theorem 4. *Algorithm 2 returns true iff the input history h satisfies TSO.*

5 Experimental Evaluation

To demonstrate the practical value of the theory developed in the previous sections, we argue that our algorithms are efficient and scalable. We experiment with both SC and TSO algorithms, investigating their running time compared to a standard encoding of these models into boolean satisfiability on a benchmark obtained by running realistic cache coherence protocols within the Gem5 simulator [5] in system emulation mode.

Histories are generated with random clients of the following cache coherence protocols included in the Gem5 distribution: MI, MEOSI Hammer, MESI Two Level, and MEOSI AMD Base. The randomization process is parametrized by the number of cpus (threads) and the total number of read-/write operations. We ensure that every value is written at most once.

We have compared two variations of our algorithms for checking SC/TSO with a standard encoding of SC/TSO into boolean satisfiability (named X-SAT where X is SC or TSO). The two variations differ in the way in which the partial store order pww dictated by CCM is completed to a total store order ww as required by SC/TSO: either using standard enumeration (named X-CCM+Enum where X is SC or TSO) or using a SAT solver (named X-CCM+SAT where X is SC or TSO).

The computation of the partial store order pww is done using an encoding of its definition into a DATALOG program. The inductive definition of hb_o supports an easy translation to DATALOG rules, and the same holds for the union of two relations, or their composition. We used Clingo [19] to run DATALOG programs.

5.1 Checking SC

Figure 4 reports on the running time of the three algorithms while increasing the number of operations or cpus. All the histories considered in this experiment satisfy SC. This is intended because valid histories force our algorithms to enumerate extensions of the partial store order (SC violations may be detected while checking CCM). The graph on the left pictures the evolution of the running time when increasing the number of operations from 100 to 500, in increments of 100 (while using a constant number of 4 cpus). For each number of operations, we have considered 200 histories and computed the average running time. The graph on the right shows the running time when increasing the number of cpus from 2 to 6, in increments of 1. For x cpus, we have limited the number of operations to $50x$. As before for each number of cpus, we have considered 200 histories and computed

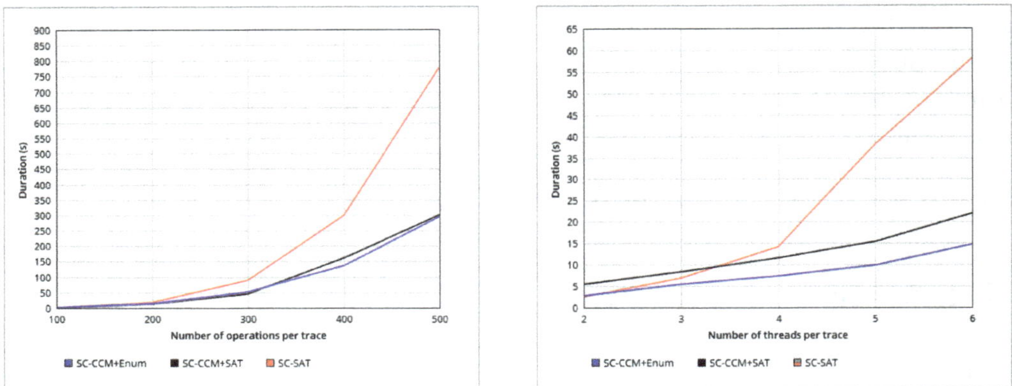

(a) Checking SC while varying the number of operations.

(b) Checking SC while varying the number of cpus.

Fig. 4. Checking SC for valid histories.

the average running time. As it can be observed, our algorithms scale much better than the SAT encoding and interestingly enough, the difference between an explicit enumeration of pww extensions and one using a SAT solver is not significant. Note that even small improvements on the average running time provide large speedups when taking into account the whole testing process, i.e., checking consistency for a possibly large number of (randomly-generated) executions. For instance, the work on McVerSi [13], which focuses on the complementary problem of finding clients that increase the probability of uncovering bugs, shows that exposing bugs in some realistic cache coherence implementations requires even 24 h of continuous testing.

Since the bottleneck in our algorithms is given by the enumeration of pww extensions, we have measured the percentage of pairs of writes that are *not* ordered by pww. Thus, we have considered a random sample of 200 histories (with 200 operations per history) and evaluated this percentage to be just 6.6%, which is surprisingly low. This explains the net gain in comparison to a SAT encoding of SC, since the number of pww extensions that need to be enumerated is quite low. As a side remark, using CCv instead of CCM in the algorithms above leads to a drastic increase in the number of unordered writes. For the same random sample of 200 histories, we conclude that using CCv instead of CCM leaves 57.75% of unordered writes in average which is considerably bigger than the percentage of unordered writes when using CCM.

We have also evaluated our algorithms on SC violations. These violations were generated by reordering statements from the MI implementation, e.g., swapping the order of the actions `s_store_hit` and `p_profileHit` in the transition `transition(M, Store)`. As an optimization, our implementation checks gradually the weaker variations of causal consistency CC and CCv before checking CCM. This is to increase the chances of returning in the case of a violation (a violation to CC/CCv is also a violation to CCM and SC). We have considered 1000 histories with 100 to 400 operations and 2 to 8 cpus, equally distributed in function

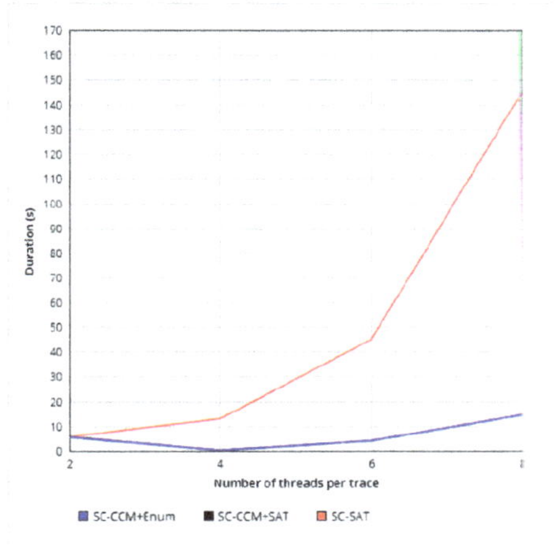

Fig. 5. Checking SC for invalid histories while increasing the number of cpus.

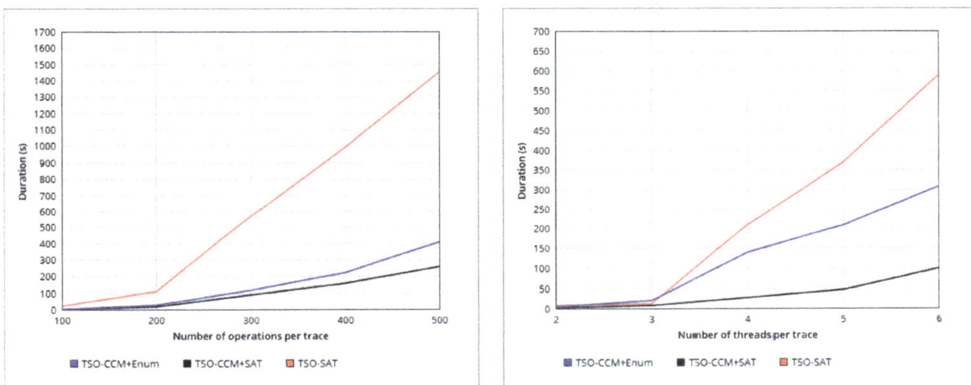

(a) Checking TSO while varying the number of operations.

(b) Checking TSO while varying the number of cpus.

Fig. 6. Checking TSO for valid histories.

of the number of cpus. Figure 5 reports on the evolution of the average running time. Since these histories happen to all be CCM violations, SC-CCM+Enum and SC-CCM+SAT have the same running time. As an evaluation of our optimization, we have found that 50% of the histories invalidate weaker variations of causal consistency, CC or CCv.

5.2 Checking TSO

We have evaluated our TSO algorithms on the same set of histories used for SC in Fig. 4. Since these histories satisfy SC, they satisfy TSO as well. As in the case of SC, our algorithms scale better than the SAT encoding. However, differently from SC, the enumeration of wpww extensions using a SAT solver outperforms the explicit enumeration. Since this difference was more negligible in the case of SC, it seems that the SAT variation is generally better.

6 Related Work

While several static techniques have been developed to prove that a shared-memory implementation (or cache coherence protocol) satisfies SC [1,4,9–12,17, 20,23,27,28] few have addressed dynamic techniques such as testing and runtime verification (which scale to more realistic implementations). From the complexity standpoint, Gibbons and Korach [21] showed that checking whether a history is SC is NP-hard while Alur et al. [4] showed that checking SC for finite-state shared-memory implementations (over a bounded number of threads, variables, and values) is undecidable [4]. The fact that checking whether a history satisfies TSO is also NP-hard has been proved by Furbach et al. [18].

There are several works that addressed the testing problem for related criteria, e.g., linearizability. While SC requires that the operations in a history be explained by a linearization that is consistent with the program order, linearizability requires that such a linearization be also consistent with the real-time order between operations (linearizability is stronger than SC). The works in [25,30] describe monitors for checking linearizability that construct linearizations of a given history incrementally, in an online fashion. This incremental construction cannot be adapted to SC since it strongly relies on the specificities of linearizability. Line-Up [8] performs systematic concurrency testing via schedule enumeration, and offline linearizability checking via linearization enumeration. The works in [15,16] show that checking linearizability for some particular class of ADTs is polynomial time. Emmi and Enea [14] consider the problem of checking weak consistency criteria, but their approach focuses on specific relaxations in those criteria, falling back to an explicit enumeration of linearizations in the context of a criterion like SC or TSO. Bouajjani et al. [6] consider the problem of checking causal consistency. They formalize the different variations of causal consistency we consider in this work and show that the problem of checking whether a history satisfies one of these variations is polynomial time.

The complementary issue of test generation, i.e., finding clients that increase the probability of uncovering bugs in shared memory implementations, has been approached in the McVerSi framework [13]. Their methodology for checking a criterion like SC lies within the context of white-box testing, i.e., the user is required to annotate the shared memory implementation with events that define the store order in an execution. Our algorithms have the advantage that the implementation is treated as a black-box requiring less user intervention.

7 Conclusion

We have introduced an approach for checking the conformance of a computation to SC or to TSO, a problem known to be NP-hard. The idea is to avoid an explicit enumeration of the exponential number of possible total orders between writes in order to solve these problems. Our approach is to define weaker criteria that are as strong as possible but still polynomial time checkable. This is useful for (1) early detection of violations, and (2) reducing the number of pairs of writes for which an order must be found in order to check SC/TSO conformance. Morally, the approach consists in being able to capture an "as large as possible" partial order on writes that can be computed in polynomial time (using a least fixpoint calculation), and which is a subset of any total order witnessing SC/TSO conformance. Our experimental results show that this approach is indeed useful and performant: it allows to catch most of violations early using an efficient check, and it allows to compute a large kernel of write constraints that reduces significantly the number of pairs of writes that are left to be ordered in an enumerative way. Future work consists in exploring the application of this approach to other correctness criteria that are hard to check such a serializability in the context of transactional programs.

References

1. Abdulla, P.A., Haziza, F., Holík, L.: Parameterized verification through view abstraction. STTT **18**(5), 495–516 (2016). https://doi.org/10.1007/s10009-015-0406-x
2. Ahamad, M., Neiger, G., Burns, J.E., Kohli, P., Hutto, P.W.: Causal memory: definitions, implementation, and programming. Distrib. Comput. **9**(1), 37–49 (1995)
3. Alglave, J., Maranget, L., Tautschnig, M.: Herding cats: modelling, simulation, testing, and data mining for weak memory. ACM Trans. Program. Lang. Syst. **36**(2), 7:1–7:74 (2014). https://doi.org/10.1145/2627752
4. Alur, R., McMillan, K.L., Peled, D.A.: Model-checking of correctness conditions for concurrent objects. Inf. Comput. **160**(1–2), 167–188 (2000). https://doi.org/10.1006/inco.1999.2847
5. Binkert, N., et al.: The gem5 simulator. SIGARCH Comput. Archit. News **39**(2), 1–7 (2011). https://doi.org/10.1145/2024716.2024718
6. Bouajjani, A., Enea, C., Guerraoui, R., Hamza, J.: On verifying causal consistency. In: Castagna, G., Gordon, A.D. (eds.) Proceedings of the 44th ACM SIGPLAN Symposium on Principles of Programming Languages, POPL 2017, Paris, France, January 18–20, 2017, pp. 626–638. ACM (2017). http://dl.acm.org/citation.cfm?id=3009888
7. Burckhardt, S.: Principles of Eventual Consistency. Now publishers, Boston, October 2014
8. Burckhardt, S., Dern, C., Musuvathi, M., Tan, R.: Line-up: a complete and automatic linearizability checker. In: Zorn, B.G., Aiken, A. (eds.) Proceedings of the 2010 ACM SIGPLAN Conference on Programming Language Design and Implementation, PLDI 2010, Toronto, Ontario, Canada, 5–10 June 2010, pp. 330–340. ACM (2010). https://doi.org/10.1145/1806596.1806634
9. Clarke, E.M., et al.: Verification of the futurebus+ cache coherence protocol. In: Agnew, D., Claesen, L.J.M., Camposano, R. (eds.) Computer Hardware Description Languages and their Applications, Proceedings of the 11th IFIP WG10.2 International Conference on Computer Hardware Description Languages and their Applications - CHDL 1993, sponsored by IFIP WG10.2 and in cooperation with IEEE COMPSOC, Ottawa, Ontario, Canada, 26–28 April 1993. IFIP Transactions, vol. A-32, pp. 15–30. North-Holland (1993)

10. Delzanno, G.: Automatic verification of parameterized cache coherence protocols. In: Emerson, E.A., Sistla, A.P. (eds.) CAV 2000. LNCS, vol. 1855, pp. 53–68. Springer, Heidelberg (2000). https://doi.org/10.1007/10722167_8
11. Delzanno, G.: Constraint-based verification of parameterized cache coherence protocols. Formal Methods Syst. Des. **23**(3), 257–301 (2003)
12. Eiríksson, Á.T., McMillan, K.L.: Using formal verification/analysis methods on the critical path in system design: a case study. In: Wolper, P. (ed.) CAV 1995. LNCS, vol. 939, pp. 367–380. Springer, Heidelberg (1995). https://doi.org/10.1007/3-540-60045-0_63
13. Elver, M., Nagarajan, V.: Mcversi: a test generation framework for fast memory consistency verification in simulation. In: 2016 IEEE International Symposium on High Performance Computer Architecture, HPCA 2016, Barcelona, Spain, 12–16 March 2016, pp. 618–630. IEEE Computer Society (2016). https://doi.org/10.1109/HPCA.2016.7446099
14. Emmi, M., Enea, C.: Monitoring weak consistency. In: Chockler, H., Weissenbacher, G. (eds.) CAV 2018. LNCS, vol. 10981, pp. 487–506. Springer, Cham (2018). https://doi.org/10.1007/978-3-319-96145-3_26
15. Emmi, M., Enea, C.: Sound, complete, and tractable linearizability monitoring for concurrent collections. PACMPL **2**(POPL), 25:1–25:27 (2018). https://doi.org/10.1145/3158113
16. Emmi, M., Enea, C., Hamza, J.: Monitoring refinement via symbolic reasoning. In: Grove, D., Blackburn, S. (eds.) Proceedings of the 36th ACM SIGPLAN Conference on Programming Language Design and Implementation, Portland, OR, USA, 15–17 June, 2015, pp. 260–269. ACM (2015). https://doi.org/10.1145/2737924.2737983
17. Esparza, J., Finkel, A., Mayr, R.: On the verification of broadcast protocols. In: 14th Annual IEEE Symposium on Logic in Computer Science, Trento, Italy, 2–5 July 1999, pp. 352–359. IEEE Computer Society (1999). https://doi.org/10.1109/LICS.1999.782630
18. Furbach, F., Meyer, R., Schneider, K., Senftleben, M.: Memory-model-aware testing: a unified complexity analysis. ACM Trans. Embed. Comput. Syst. **14**(4), 63:1–63:25 (2015). https://doi.org/10.1145/2753761
19. Gebser, M., Kaminski, R., Kaufmann, B., Schaub, T.: Clingo = ASP + control: Preliminary report. CoRR abs/1405.3694 (2014). http://arxiv.org/abs/1405.3694
20. German, S.M., Sistla, A.P.: Reasoning about systems with many processes. J. ACM **39**(3), 675–735 (1992). https://doi.org/10.1145/146637.146681
21. Gibbons, P.B., Korach, E.: Testing shared memories. SIAM J. Comput. **26**(4), 1208–1244 (1997). https://doi.org/10.1137/S0097539794279614
22. Gotsman, A., Burckhardt, S.: Consistency models with global operation sequencing and their composition. In: Richa, A.W. (ed.) 31st International Symposium on Distributed Computing, DISC 2017, LIPIcs, 16–20 October 2017, Vienna, Austria, vol. 91, pp. 23:1–23:16. Schloss Dagstuhl - Leibniz-Zentrum fuer Informatik (2017). https://doi.org/10.4230/LIPIcs.DISC.2017.23
23. Ip, C.N., Dill, D.L.: Better verification through symmetry. Formal Methods Syst. Des. **9**(1/2), 41–75 (1996). https://doi.org/10.1007/BF00625968
24. Lamport, L.: How to make a multiprocessor computer that correctly executes multiprocess programs. IEEE Trans. Comput. **28**(9), 690–691 (1979). https://doi.org/10.1109/TC.1979.1675439
25. Lowe, G.: Testing for linearizability. Concurrency Comput. Pract. Experience 29(4) (2017). https://doi.org/10.1002/cpe.3928

26. Perrin, M., Mostefaoui, A., Jard, C.: Causal consistency: beyond memory. In: Proceedings of the 21st ACM SIGPLAN Symposium on Principles and Practice of Parallel Programming, PPoPP 2016, pp. 26:1–26:12. ACM, New York (2016)
27. Pong, F., Dubois, M.: A new approach for the verification of cache coherence protocols. IEEE Trans. Parallel Distrib. Syst. **6**(8), 773–787 (1995). https://doi.org/10.1109/71.406955
28. Qadeer, S.: Verifying sequential consistency on shared-memory multiprocessors by model checking. IEEE Trans. Parallel Distrib. Syst. **14**(8), 730–741 (2003). https://doi.org/10.1109/TPDS.2003.1225053
29. Sewell, P., Sarkar, S., Owens, S., Nardelli, F.Z., Myreen, M.O.: x86-tso: a rigorous and usable programmer's model for x86 multiprocessors. Commun. ACM **53**(7), 89–97 (2010). https://doi.org/10.1145/1785414.1785443
30. Wing, J.M., Gong, C.: Testing and verifying concurrent objects. J. Parallel Distrib. Comput. **17**(1–2), 164–182 (1993). https://doi.org/10.1006/jpdc.1993.1015
31. Wolper, P.: Expressing interesting properties of programs in propositional temporal logic. In: Conference Record of the Thirteenth Annual ACM Symposium on Principles of Programming Languages, St. Petersburg Beach, Florida, USA, January 1986, pp. 184–193. ACM Press (1986). https://doi.org/10.1145/512644.512661

Checking Robustness Against Snapshot Isolation

Sidi Mohamed Beillahi(✉), Ahmed Bouajjani, and Constantin Enea

Université de Paris, IRIF, CNRS, Paris, France
{beillahi,abou,cenea}@irif.fr

Abstract. Transactional access to databases is an important abstraction allowing programmers to consider blocks of actions (transactions) as executing in isolation. The strongest consistency model is *serializability*, which ensures the atomicity abstraction of transactions executing over a sequentially consistent memory. Since ensuring serializability carries a significant penalty on availability, modern databases provide weaker consistency models, one of the most prominent being *snapshot isolation*. In general, the correctness of a program relying on serializable transactions may be broken when using weaker models. However, certain programs may also be insensitive to consistency relaxations, i.e., all their properties holding under serializability are preserved even when they are executed over a weak consistent database and without additional synchronization.

In this paper, we address the issue of verifying if a given program is *robust against snapshot isolation*, i.e., all its behaviors are serializable even if it is executed over a database ensuring snapshot isolation. We show that this verification problem is polynomial time reducible to a state reachability problem in transactional programs over a sequentially consistent shared memory. This reduction opens the door to the reuse of the classic verification technology for reasoning about weakly-consistent programs. In particular, we show that it can be used to derive a proof technique based on Lipton's reduction theory that allows to prove programs robust.

1 Introduction

Transactions simplify concurrent programming by enabling computations on shared data that are isolated from other concurrent computations and resilient to failures. Modern databases provide transactions in various forms corresponding to different tradeoffs between consistency and availability. The strongest consistency level is achieved with *serializable* transactions [21] whose outcome in concurrent executions is the same as if the transactions were executed atomically in some order. Since serializability carries a significant penalty on availability, modern databases often provide weaker consistency models, one of the

This work is supported in part by the European Research Council (ERC) under the Horizon 2020 research and innovation programme (grant agreement No 678177).

I. Dillig and S. Tasiran (Eds.): CAV 2019, LNCS 11562, pp. 286–304, 2019.
https://doi.org/10.1007/978-3-030-25543-5_17

most prominent being *snapshot isolation* (SI) [5]. Then, an important issue is to ensure that the level of consistency needed by a given program coincides with the one that is guaranteed by its infrastructure, i.e., the database it uses. One way to tackle this issue is to investigate the problem of checking *robustness* of programs against consistency relaxations: Given a program P and two consistency models S and W such that S is stronger than W, we say that P is robust for S against W if for every two implementations I_S and I_W of S and W respectively, the set of computations of P when running with I_S is the same as its set of computations when running with I_W. This means that P is not sensitive to the consistency relaxation from S to W, and therefore it is possible to reason about the behaviors of P assuming that it is running over S, and no additional synchronization is required when P runs over the weak model W such that it maintains all its properties satisfied with S.

In this paper, we address the problem of verifying robustness of transactional programs for serializability, against *snapshot isolation*. Under snapshot isolation, any transaction t reads values from a snapshot of the database taken at its start and t can commit only if no other committed transaction has written to a location that t wrote to, since t started. Robustness is a form of program equivalence between two versions of the same program, obtained using two semantics, one more permissive than the other. It ensures that this permissiveness has no effect on the program under consideration. The difficulty in checking robustness is to apprehend the extra behaviors due to the relaxed model w.r.t. the strong model. This requires a priori reasoning about complex order constraints between operations in arbitrarily long computations, which may need maintaining unbounded ordered structures, and make robustness checking hard or even undecidable.

Our first contribution is to show that verifying robustness of transactional programs against snapshot isolation can be reduced in polynomial time to the reachability problem in concurrent programs under sequential consistency (SC). This allows (1) to avoid explicit handling of the snapshots from where transactions read along computations (since this may imply memorizing unbounded information), and (2) to leverage available tools for verifying invariants/reachability problems on concurrent programs. This also implies that the robustness problem is decidable for finite-state programs, PSPACE-complete when the number of sites is fixed, and EXPSPACE-complete otherwise. This is the first result on the decidability and complexity of the problem of verifying robustness in the context of transactional programs. The problem of verifying robustness has been considered in the literature for several models, including eventual and causal consistency [6,10–12,20]. These works provide (over- or under-)approximate analyses for checking robustness, but none of them provides precise (sound and complete) algorithmic verification methods for solving this problem.

Based on this reduction, our second contribution is a proof methodology for establishing robustness which builds on Lipton's reduction theory [18]. We use the theory of movers to establish whether the relaxations allowed by SI are harmless, i.e., they don't introduce new behaviors compared to serializability.

We applied the proposed verification techniques on 10 challenging applications extracted from previous work [2,6,11,14,16,19,24]. These techniques were enough for proving or disproving the robustness of these applications.

Complete proofs and more details can be found in [4].

```
      p1:                  p2:
t1: [r1 = y //0 || t2: [r2 = x //0
      x = 1]               y = 1]
```

(a) Write Skew (WS).

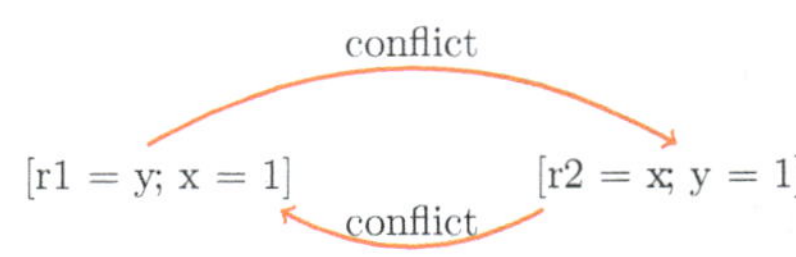

(b) A WS execution trace.

Fig. 1. Examples of non-robust programs illustrating the difference between SI and serializability. *causal dependency* means that a read in a transaction obtains its value from a write in another transaction. *conflict* means that a write in a transaction is not visible to a read in another transaction, but it would affect the read value if it were visible. Here, *happens-before* is the union of the two.

2 Overview

In this section, we give an overview of our approach for checking robustness against snapshot isolation. While serializability enforces that transactions are atomic and conflicting transactions, i.e., which read or write to a common location, *cannot* commit concurrently, SI [5] allows that conflicting transactions commit in parallel as long as they don't contain a write-write conflict, i.e., write on a common location. Moreover, under SI, each transaction reads from a snapshot of the database taken at its start. These relaxations permit the "anomaly" known as Write Skew (WS) shown in Fig. 1a, where an anomaly is a program execution which is allowed by SI, but not by serializability. The execution of Write Skew under SI allows the reads of x and y to return 0 although this cannot happen under serializability. These values are possible since each transaction is executed locally (starting from the initial snapshot) without observing the writes of the other transaction.

Execution Trace. Our notion of program robustness is based on an abstract representation of executions called *trace*. Informally, an execution trace is a set of events, i.e., accesses to shared variables and transaction begin/commit events, along with several standard dependency relations between events recording the data-flow. The transitive closure of the union of all these dependency relations is called *happens-before*. An execution is an anomaly if the happens-before of its trace is cyclic. Figure 1b shows the happens-before of the Write Skew anomaly. Notice that the happens-before order is cyclic in both cases.

Semantically, every transaction execution involves two main events, the issue and the commit. The issue event corresponds to a sequence of reads and/or writes where the writes are visible only to the current transaction. We interpret it as a single event since a transaction starts with a database snapshot that it updates in isolation, without observing other concurrently executing transactions. The commit event is where the writes are propagated and made visible to all processes. Under serializability, the two events coincide, i.e., they are adjacent in the execution. Under SI, this is not the case and in between the issue and the commit of the same transaction, we may have issue/commit events from concurrent transactions. When a transaction commit does not occur immediately after its issue, we say that the underlying transaction is *delayed*. For example, the following execution of WS corresponds to the happens-before cycle in Fig. 1b where the write to x was committed after t_2 finished, hence, t_1 was delayed:

$$\mathsf{begin}(p_1,t_1)\mathsf{ld}(p_1,t_1,y,0)\mathsf{isu}(p_1,t_1,x,1) \quad \mathsf{begin}(p_2,t_2)\mathsf{ld}(p_2,t_2,x,0)\mathsf{isu}(p_2,t_2,y,1)\mathsf{com}(p_2,t_2) \quad \mathsf{com}(p_1,t_1)$$

Above, $\mathsf{begin}(p_1, t_1)$ stands for starting a new transaction t_1 by process p_1, ld represents read (load) actions, while isu denotes write actions that are visible only to the current transaction (not yet committed). The writes performed during t_1 become visible to all processes once the commit event $\mathsf{com}(p_1, t_1)$ takes place.

Reducing Robustness to SC Reachability. The above SI execution can be mimicked by an execution of the same program under serializability modulo an instrumentation that simulates the delayed transaction. The local writes in the issue event are simulated by writes to auxiliary registers and the commit event is replaced by copying the values from the auxiliary registers to the shared variables (actually, it is not necessary to simulate the commit event; we include it here for presentation reasons). The auxiliary registers are visible only to the delayed transaction. In order that the execution be an anomaly (i.e., not possible under serializability without the instrumentation) it is required that the issue and the commit events of the delayed transaction are linked by a chain of happens-before dependencies. For instance, the above execution for WS can be simulated by:

$$\mathsf{begin}(p_1,t_1)\mathsf{ld}(p_1,t_1,y,0)\mathsf{st}(p_1,t_1,r_x,1) \quad \mathsf{begin}(p_2,t_2)\mathsf{ld}(p_2,t_2,x,0)\mathsf{isu}(p_2,t_2,y,1)\mathsf{com}(p_2,t_2) \quad \mathsf{st}(p_1,t_1,x,r_x)$$

The write to x was delayed by storing the value in the auxiliary register r_x and the happens-before chain exists because the read on y that was done by t_1 is conflicting with the write on y from t_2 and the read on x by t_2 is conflicting with the write of x in the simulation of t_1's commit event. On the other hand, the following execution of Write-Skew without the read on y in t_1:

$$\mathsf{begin}(p_1,t_1)\mathsf{st}(p_1,t_1,r_x,1) \quad \mathsf{begin}(p_2,t_2)\mathsf{ld}(p_2,t_2,x,0)\mathsf{isu}(p_2,t_2,y,1)\mathsf{com}(p_2,t_2) \quad \mathsf{st}(p_1,t_1,x,r_x)$$

misses the conflict (happens-before dependency) between the issue event of t_1 and t_2. Therefore, the events of t_2 can be reordered to the left of t_1 and obtain an equivalent execution where $\mathsf{st}(p_1, t_1, x, r_x)$ occurs immediately after $\mathsf{st}(p_1, t_1, r_x, 1)$. In this case, t_1 is not anymore delayed and this execution is possible under serializability (without the instrumentation).

If the number of transactions to be delayed in order to expose an anomaly is unbounded, the instrumentation described above may need an unbounded number of auxiliary registers. This would make the verification problem hard or even undecidable. However, we show that it is actually enough to delay a single transaction, i.e., a program admits an anomaly under `SI` iff it admits an anomaly containing a single delayed transaction. This result implies that the number of auxiliary registers needed by the instrumentation is bounded by the number of program variables, and that checking robustness against `SI` can be reduced in linear time to a reachability problem under serializability (the reachability problem encodes the existence of the chain of happens-before dependencies mentioned above). The proof of this reduction relies on a non-trivial characterization of anomalies.

Proving Robustness Using Commutativity Dependency Graphs. Based on the reduction above, we also devise an approximated method for checking robustness based on the concept of mover in Lipton's reduction theory [18]. An event is a left (resp., right) mover if it commutes to the left (resp., right) of another event (from a different process) while preserving the computation. We use the notion of mover to characterize happens-before dependencies between transactions. Roughly, there exists a happens-before dependency between two transactions in some execution if one doesn't commute to the left/right of the other one. We define a commutativity dependency graph which summarizes the happens-before dependencies in all executions of a given program between transactions t as they appear in the program, transactions $t \setminus \{w\}$ where the writes of t are deactivated (i.e., their effects are not visible outside the transaction), and transactions $t \setminus \{r\}$ where the reads of t obtain non-deterministic values. The transactions $t \setminus \{w\}$ are used to simulate issue events of delayed transactions (where writes are not yet visible) while the transactions $t \setminus \{r\}$ are used to simulate commit events of delayed transactions (which only write to the shared memory). Two transactions a and b are linked by an edge iff a *cannot* move to the right of b (or b cannot move to the left of a), or if they are related by the program order (i.e., issued in some order in the same process). Then a program is robust if for every transaction t, this graph *doesn't* contain a path from $t \setminus \{w\}$ to $t \setminus \{r\}$ formed of transactions that don't write to a variable that t writes to (the latter condition is enforced by `SI` since two concurrent transactions cannot commit at the same time when they write to a common variable). For example, Fig. 2 shows the commutativity dependency graph of the modified WS program where the read of y is removed from t_1. The fact that it doesn't contain any path like above implies that it is robust.

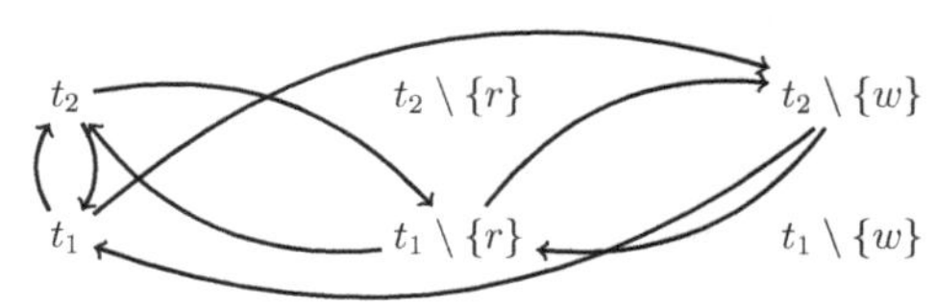

Fig. 2. Commutativity dependency graph of WS where the read of y is omitted.

3 Programs

A program is parallel composition of *processes* distinguished using a set of identifiers $\mathbb{P}$. Each process is a sequence of *transactions* and each transaction is a sequence of *labeled instructions*. Each transaction starts with a `begin` instruction and finishes with a `commit` instruction. Each other instruction is either an assignment to a process-local *register* from a set $\mathbb{R}$ or to a *shared variable* from a set $\mathbb{V}$, or an `assume` statement. The read/write assignments use values from a data domain $\mathbb{D}$. An assignment to a register $\langle reg \rangle := \langle var \rangle$ is called a *read* of the shared-variable $\langle var \rangle$ and an assignment to a shared variable $\langle var \rangle := \langle reg\text{-}expr \rangle$ is called a *write* to $\langle var \rangle$ ($\langle reg\text{-}expr \rangle$ is an expression over registers whose syntax we leave unspecified since it is irrelevant for our development). The `assume` $\langle bexpr \rangle$ blocks the process if the Boolean expression $\langle bexpr \rangle$ over registers is false. They are used to model conditionals as usual. We use `goto` statements to model an arbitrary control-flow where the same label can be assigned to multiple instructions and multiple `goto` statements can direct the control to the same label which allows to mimic imperative constructs like loops and conditionals. To simplify the technical exposition, our syntax includes simple read/write instructions. However, our results apply as well to instructions that include SQL (select/update) queries. The experiments reported in Sect. 7 consider programs with SQL based transactions.

The semantics of a program under `SI` is defined as follows. The shared variables are stored in a central memory and each process keeps a replicated copy of the central memory. A process starts a transaction by discarding its local copy and fetching the values of the shared variables from the central memory. When a process commits a transaction, it merges its local copy of the shared variables with the one stored in the central memory in order to make its updates visible to all processes. During the execution of a transaction, the process stores the writes to shared variables only in its local copy and reads only from its local copy. When a process merges its local copy with the centralized one, it is required that there were no concurrent updates that occurred after the last fetch from the central memory to a shared variable that was updated by the current transaction. Otherwise, the transaction is aborted and its effects discarded.

More precisely, the semantics of a program $\mathcal{P}$ under `SI` is defined as a labeled transition system $[\mathcal{P}]_{\mathtt{SI}}$ where transactions are labeled by the set of events

$$\mathbb{E}\mathsf{v} = \{\mathsf{begin}(p,t), \mathsf{ld}(p,t,x,v), \mathsf{isu}(p,t,x,v), \mathsf{com}(p,t) : p \in \mathbb{P}, t \in \mathbb{T}^2, x \in \mathbb{V}, v \in \mathbb{D}\}$$

where begin and com label transitions corresponding to the start and the commit of a transaction, respectively. isu and ld label transitions corresponding to writing, resp., reading, a shared variable during some transaction.

An execution of program $\mathcal{P}$, under snapshot isolation, is a sequence of events $ev_1 \cdot ev_2 \cdot \ldots$ corresponding to a run of $[\mathcal{P}]_{\mathtt{CM}}$. The set of executions of $\mathcal{P}$ under `SI` is denoted by $\mathbb{E}\mathsf{x}_{\mathtt{SI}}(\mathcal{P})$.

4 Robustness Against SI

A *trace* abstracts the order in which shared-variables are accessed inside a transaction and the order between transactions accessing different variables. Formally, the trace of an execution ρ is obtained by (1) replacing each sub-sequence of transitions in ρ corresponding to the same transaction, but excluding the com transition, with a single "macro-event" $\mathsf{isu}(p,t)$, and (2) adding several standard relations between these macro-events $\mathsf{isu}(p,t)$ and commit events $\mathsf{com}(p,t)$ to record the data-flow in ρ, e.g. which transaction wrote the value read by another transaction. The sequence of $\mathsf{isu}(p,t)$ and $\mathsf{com}(p,t)$ events obtained in the first step is called a *summary of* ρ. We say that a transaction t in ρ performs an *external read* of a variable x if ρ contains an event $\mathsf{ld}(p,t,x,v)$ which is not preceded by a write on x of t, i.e., an event $\mathsf{isu}(p,t,x,v)$. Also, we say that a transaction t *writes* a variable x if ρ contains an event $\mathsf{isu}(p,t,x,v)$, for some v.

The *trace* $\mathsf{tr}(\rho) = (\tau, \mathsf{PO}, \mathsf{WR}, \mathsf{WW}, \mathsf{RW}, \mathsf{STO})$ of an execution ρ consists of the summary τ of ρ along with the *program order* PO, which relates any two issue events $\mathsf{isu}(p,t)$ and $\mathsf{isu}(p,t')$ that occur in this order in τ, *write-read* relation WR (also called *read-from*), which relates any two events $\mathsf{com}(p,t)$ and $\mathsf{isu}(p',t')$ that occur in this order in τ such that t' performs an external read of x, and $\mathsf{com}(p,t)$ is the last event in τ before $\mathsf{isu}(p',t')$ that writes to x (to mark the variable x, we may use $\mathsf{WR}(x)$), the *write-write* order WW (also called store-order), which relates any two store events $\mathsf{com}(p,t)$ and $\mathsf{com}(p',t')$ that occur in this order in τ and write to the same variable x (to mark the variable x, we may use $\mathsf{WW}(x)$), the *read-write* relation RW (also called *conflict*), which relates any two events $\mathsf{isu}(p,t)$ and $\mathsf{com}(p',t')$ that occur in this order in τ such that t reads a value that is overwritten by t', and the *same-transaction* relation STO, which relates the issue event with the commit event of the same transaction. The read-write relation RW is formally defined as $\mathsf{RW}(x) = \mathsf{WR}^{-1}(x); \mathsf{WW}(x)$ (we use ; to denote the standard composition of relations) and $\mathsf{RW} = \bigcup_{x \in \mathbb{V}} \mathsf{RW}(x)$. If a transaction t reads the initial value of x then $\mathsf{RW}(x)$ relates $\mathsf{isu}(p,t)$ to $\mathsf{com}(p',t')$ of any other transaction t' which writes to x (i.e., $(\mathsf{isu}(p,t), \mathsf{com}(p',t')) \in \mathsf{RW}(x)$) (note that in the above relations, p and p' might designate the same process).

Since we reason about only one trace at a time, to simplify the writing, we may say that a trace is simply a sequence τ as above, keeping the relations PO, WR, WW, RW, and STO implicit. The set of traces of executions of a program $\mathcal{P}$ under SI is denoted by $\mathbb{T}\mathrm{r}(\mathcal{P})_{\mathtt{SI}}$.

Serializability Semantics. The semantics of a program under serializability can be defined using a transition system where the configurations keep a single shared-variable valuation (accessed by all processes) with the standard interpretation of read and write statements. Each transaction executes in isolation. Alternatively, the serializability semantics can be defined as a restriction of $[\mathcal{P}]_{\mathtt{SI}}$ to the set of executions where each transaction is *immediately* delivered when it starts, i.e., the start and commit time of transaction coincide $t.st = t.ct$. Such executions are called *serializable* and the set of serializable executions of a program $\mathcal{P}$ is denoted by $\mathbb{E}\mathrm{x}_{\mathtt{SER}}(\mathcal{P})$. The latter definition is easier to reason about when relating executions under snapshot isolation and serializability, respectively.

Serializable Trace. A trace tr is called *serializable* if it is the trace of a serializable execution. Let $\mathbb{T}\mathsf{r}_{\mathtt{SER}}(\mathcal{P})$ denote the set of serializable traces. Given a serializable trace $tr = (\tau, \mathsf{PO}, \mathsf{WR}, \mathsf{WW}, \mathsf{RW}, \mathsf{STO})$ we have that every event $\mathsf{isu}(p,t)$ in τ is immediately followed by the corresponding $\mathsf{com}(p,t)$ event.

Happens Before Order. Since multiple executions may have the same trace, it is possible that an execution ρ produced by snapshot isolation has a serializable trace $\mathsf{tr}(\rho)$ even though $\mathsf{isu}(p,t)$ events may not be immediately followed by $\mathsf{com}(p,t)$ actions. However, ρ would be equivalent, up to reordering of "independent" (or commutative) transitions, to a serializable execution. To check whether the trace of an execution is serializable, we introduce the *happens-before* relation on the events of a given trace as the transitive closure of the union of all the relations in the trace, i.e., $\mathsf{HB} = (\mathsf{PO} \cup \mathsf{WW} \cup \mathsf{WR} \cup \mathsf{RW} \cup \mathsf{STO})^+$.

Finally, the happens-before relation between events is extended to transactions as follows: a transaction t_1 *happens-before* another transaction $t_2 \neq t_1$ if the trace tr contains an event of transaction t_1 which happens-before an event of t_2. The happens-before relation between transactions is denoted by HB_t and called *transactional happens-before*. The following characterizes serializable traces.

Theorem 1 ([1,23]). *A trace tr is serializable iff HB_t is acyclic.*

A program is called robust if it produces the same set of traces as the serializability semantics.

Definition 1. *A program $\mathcal{P}$ is called* robust *against* $\mathtt{SI}$ *iff* $\mathbb{T}\mathsf{r}_{\mathtt{SI}}(\mathcal{P}) = \mathbb{T}\mathsf{r}_{\mathtt{SER}}(\mathcal{P})$.

Since $\mathbb{T}\mathsf{r}_{\mathtt{SER}}(\mathcal{P}) \subseteq \mathbb{T}\mathsf{r}_{\mathsf{X}}(\mathcal{P})$, the problem of checking robustness of a program $\mathcal{P}$ is reduced to checking whether there exists a trace $tr \in \mathbb{T}\mathsf{r}_{\mathtt{SI}}(\mathcal{P}) \setminus \mathbb{T}\mathsf{r}_{\mathtt{SER}}(\mathcal{P})$.

5 Reducing Robustness Against SI to SC Reachability

A trace which is not serializable must contain at least an issue and a commit event of the same transaction that don't occur one after the other even after reordering of "independent" events. Thus, there must exist an event that occur between the two which is related to both events via the happens-before relation, forbidding the issue and commit to be adjacent. Otherwise, we can build another trace with the same happens-before where events are reordered such that the issue is immediately followed by the corresponding commit. The latter is a serializable trace which contradicts the initial assumption. We define a program instrumentation which mimics the delay of transactions by doing the writes on auxiliary variables which are not visible to other transactions. After the delay of a transaction, we track happens-before dependencies until we execute a transaction that does a "read" on one of the variables that the delayed transaction writes to (this would expose a read-write dependency to the commit event of the delayed transaction). While tracking happens-before dependencies we cannot execute a transaction that writes to a variable that the delayed transaction writes to since SI forbids write-write conflicts between concurrent transactions.

Concretely, given a program $\mathcal{P}$, we define an instrumentation of $\mathcal{P}$ such that $\mathcal{P}$ is not robust against SI iff the instrumentation reaches an error state under serializability. The instrumentation uses auxiliary variables in order to simulate a *single* delayed transaction which we prove that it is enough for deciding robustness. Let $\mathsf{isu}(p, t)$ be the issue event of the only delayed transaction. The process p that delayed t is called the *Attacker*. When the attacker finishes executing the delayed transaction it stops. Other processes that execute transactions afterwards are called *Happens-Before Helpers*.

The instrumentation uses two copies of the set of shared variables in the original program to simulate the delayed transaction. We use primed variables x' to denote the second copy. Thus, when a process becomes the attacker, it will only write to the second copy that is not visible to other processes including the happens-before helpers. The writes made by the other processes including the happens-before helpers are made visible to all processes.

When the attacker delays the transaction t, it keeps track of the variables it accessed, in particular, it stores the name of one of the variables it writes to, x, it tracks every variable y that it reads from and every variable z that it writes to. When the attacker finishes executing t, and some other process wants to execute some other transaction, the underlying transaction must contain a write to a variable y that the attacker reads from. Also, the underlying transaction must not write to a variable that t writes to. We say that this process has joined happens-before helpers through the underlying transaction. While executing this transaction, we keep track of each variable that was accessed and the type of operation, whether it is a read or write. Afterward, in order for some other transaction to "join" the happens-before path, it must not write to a variable that t writes to so it does not violate the fact that SI forbids write-write conflicts, and it has to satisfy one of the following conditions in order to ensure the continuity of the happens-before dependencies: (1) the transaction is issued by a process that has already another transaction in the happens-before dependency (program order dependency), (2) the transaction is reading from a shared variable that was updated by a previous transaction in the happens-before dependency (write-read dependency), (3) the transaction writes to a shared variable that was read by a previous transaction in the happens-before dependency (read-write dependency), or (4) the transaction writes to a shared variable that was updated by a previous transaction in the happens-before dependency (write-write dependency). We introduce a flag for each shared variable to mark the fact that the variable was read or written by a previous transaction.

Processes continue executing transactions as part of the chain of happens-before dependencies, until a transaction does a read on the variable x that t wrote to. In this case, we reached an error state which signals that we found a cycle in the transactional happens-before relation.

The instrumentation uses four varieties of flags: a) global flags (i.e., HB, $a_{\mathsf{tr}_\mathsf{A}}$, $a_{\mathsf{st}_\mathsf{A}}$), b) flags local to a process (i.e., $p.a$ and $p.hbh$), and c) flags per shared variable (i.e., $x.event$, $x.event'$, and $x.eventI$). We will explain the meaning of these flags along with the instrumentation. At the start of the execution, all flags are initialized to null ($\perp$).

Whether a process is an attacker or happens-before helper is not enforced syntactically by the instrumentation. It is set non-deterministically during the execution using some additional process-local flags. Each process chooses to set to true at most one of the flags $p.a$ and $p.hbh$, implying that the process becomes an attacker or happens-before helper, respectively. At most one process can be an attacker, i.e., set $p.a$ to true. In the following, we detail the instrumentation for read and write instructions of the attacker and happens-before helpers.

5.1 Instrumentation of the Attacker

Figure 3 lists the instrumentation of the write and read instructions of the attacker. Each process passes through an initial phase where it executes transactions that are visible immediately to all the other processes (i.e., they are not delayed), and then non-deterministically it can choose to delay a transaction at which point it sets the flag $a_{\mathsf{tr}_\mathsf{A}}$ to true. During the delayed transaction it chooses non-deterministically a write instruction to a variable x and stores the name of this variable in the flag $a_{\mathsf{st}_\mathsf{A}}$ (line (5)). The values written during the delayed transaction are stored in the primed variables and are visible only to the current transaction, in case the transaction reads its own writes. For example, given a variable z, all writes to z from the original program are transformed into writes to the primed version z' (line (3)). Each time, the attacker writes to z, it sets the flag $z.event' = 1$. This flag is used later by transactions from happens-before helpers to avoid writing to variables that the delayed transaction writes to.

$[\![\mathsf{l}_1: r := x;\ \mathtt{goto}\ \mathsf{l}_2;]\!]_\mathsf{A} =$
// Read before the delayed transaction
$\mathsf{l}_1: \mathtt{assume}\ a_{\mathsf{tr}_\mathsf{A}} = \perp\ ;\ \mathtt{goto}\ \mathsf{l}_{x1};$
$\mathsf{l}_{x1}: r := x;\ \mathtt{goto}\ \mathsf{l}_2;$
// Read in the delayed transaction
$\mathsf{l}_1: \mathtt{assume}\ a_{\mathsf{tr}_\mathsf{A}} \neq \perp \wedge p.a \neq \perp\ ;\ \mathtt{goto}\ \mathsf{l}_{x2};$
$\mathsf{l}_{x2}: r := x';\ \mathtt{goto}\ \mathsf{l}_{x3};$
$\mathsf{l}_{x3}: x.event := \mathsf{Id};\ \mathtt{goto}\ \mathsf{l}_{x4};$ (1)
$\mathsf{l}_{x4}: \mathtt{assume}\ \mathsf{HB} = \perp\ ;\ \mathtt{goto}\ \mathsf{l}_{x5};$
$\mathsf{l}_{x5}: \mathsf{HB} := \mathsf{true};\ \mathtt{goto}\ \mathsf{l}_2;$ (2)
$\mathsf{l}_{x4}: \mathtt{assume}\ \mathsf{HB} \neq \perp\ ;\ \mathtt{goto}\ \mathsf{l}_2;$

$[\![\mathsf{l}_1: x := e;\ \mathtt{goto}\ \mathsf{l}_2;]\!]_\mathsf{A} =$
// Write before the delayed transaction
$\mathsf{l}_1: \mathtt{assume}\ a_{\mathsf{tr}_\mathsf{A}} = \perp\ ;\ \mathtt{goto}\ \mathsf{l}_{x1};$
$\mathsf{l}_{x1}: x := e;\ \mathtt{goto}\ \mathsf{l}_2;$
// Write in the delayed transaction
$\mathsf{l}_1: \mathtt{assume}\ a_{\mathsf{tr}_\mathsf{A}} \neq \perp \wedge p.a \neq \perp\ ;\ \mathtt{goto}\ \mathsf{l}_{x2};$
$\mathsf{l}_{x2}: x' := e;\ \mathtt{goto}\ \mathsf{l}_{x3};$ (3)
$\mathsf{l}_{x3}: x.event' := 1;\ \mathtt{goto}\ \mathsf{l}_2;$ (4)
// Special write in the delayed transaction
$\mathsf{l}_1: \mathtt{assume}\ a_{\mathsf{st}_\mathsf{A}} = x.event = \perp \wedge a_{\mathsf{tr}_\mathsf{A}} \neq \perp\ ;\ \mathtt{goto}\ \mathsf{l}_{x4};$
$\mathsf{l}_{x4}: x' := e;\ \mathtt{goto}\ \mathsf{l}_{x5};$
$\mathsf{l}_{x5}: a_{\mathsf{st}_\mathsf{A}} := `x`;\ \mathtt{goto}\ \mathsf{l}_{x6};$ (5)
$\mathsf{l}_{x8}: x.event' := 1;\ \mathtt{goto}\ \mathsf{l}_2;$

Fig. 3. Instrumentation of the Attacker. We use 'x' to denote the name of the shared variable x.

A read on a variable, y, in the delayed transaction takes her value from the primed version, y'. In every read in the delayed transaction, we set the flag $y.event$ to ld (line (1)) to be used latter in order for a process to join the happens-before helpers. Afterward, the attacker starts the happens-before path, and it sets the variable HB to true (line (2)) to mark the start of the happens. When the flag HB is set to true the attacker stops executing new transactions.

5.2 Instrumentation of the Happens-Before Helpers

The remaining processes, which are not the attacker, can become a happens-before helper. Figure 4 lists the instrumentation of write and read instructions of a happens-before helper. In a first phase, each process executes the original code until the flag $a_{\mathsf{tr_A}}$ is set to true by the attacker. This flag signals the "creation" of the secondary copy of the shared-variables, which can be observed only by the attacker. At this point, the flag HB is set to true, and the happens-before helper process chooses non-deterministically a first transaction through which it wants to join the set of happens-before helpers, i.e., continue the happens-before dependency created by the existing happens-before helpers. When a process chooses a transaction, it makes a pledge (while executing the `begin` instruction) that during this transaction it will either read from a variable that was written to by another happens-before helper, write to a variable that was accessed (read or written) by another happens-before helper, or write to a variable that was read from in the delayed transaction. When the pledge is met, the process sets the flag $p.hbh$ to true (lines (7) and (11)). The execution is blocked if a process does not keep its pledge (i.e., the flag $p.hbh$ is null) at the end of the transaction. Note that the first process to join the happens-before helper has to execute a transaction t which writes to a variable that was read from in the delayed transaction since this is the only way to build a happens-before between t, and the delayed transaction (PO is not possible since t is not from the attacker, WR is not possible since t does not see the writes of the delayed transaction, and WW is not possible since t cannot write to a variable that the delayed transaction writes to). We use a flag $x.event$ for each variable x to record the type (read ld or write st) of the last access made by a happens-before helper (lines (8) and (10)). During the execution of a transaction that is part of the happens-before dependency, we must ensure that the transaction does not write to variable y where $y.even'$ is set to 1. Otherwise, the execution is blocked (line 9).

The happens-before helpers continue executing their instructions, until one of them reads from the shared variable x whose name was stored in $a_{\mathsf{st_A}}$. This establishes a happens-before dependency between the delayed transaction and a "fictitious" store event corresponding to the delayed transaction that could be executed just after this read of x. The execution doesn't have to contain this store event explicitly since it is always enabled. Therefore, at the end of every transaction, the instrumentation checks whether the transaction read x. If it is the case, then the execution stops and goes to an error state to indicate that this is a robustness violation. Notice that after the attacker stops, the only processes that are executing transactions are happens-before helpers, which is justified since when a process is not from a happens-before helper it implies that we cannot construct a happens-before dependency between a transaction of this process and the delayed transaction which means that the two transactions commute which in turn implies that this process's transactions can be executed before executing the delayed transaction of the attacker.

5.3 Correctness

The role of a process in an execution is chosen non-deterministically at runtime. Therefore, the final instrumentation of a given program $\mathcal{P}$, denoted by $[\![\mathcal{P}]\!]$, is obtained by replacing each labeled instruction $\langle linst \rangle$ with the concatenation of the instrumentations corresponding to the attacker and the happens-before helpers, i.e., $[\![\langle linst \rangle]\!] ::= [\![\langle linst \rangle]\!]_{\mathsf{A}} \; [\![\langle linst \rangle]\!]_{\mathsf{HbH}}$

The following theorem states the correctness of the instrumentation.

Theorem 2. *$\mathcal{P}$ is not robust against* SI *iff $[\![\mathcal{P}]\!]$ reaches the error state.*

If a program is not robust, this implies that the execution of the program under SI results in a trace where the happens-before is cyclic. Which is possible only if the program contains at least one delayed transaction. In the proof of this theorem, we show that is sufficient to search for executions that contain a single delayed transaction.

Notice that in the instrumentation of the attacker, the delayed transaction must contain a read and write instructions on different variables. Also, the transactions of the happens-before helpers must not contain a write to a variable that the delayed transaction writes to. The following corollary states the complexity of checking robustness for finite-state programs[1] against snapshot isolation. It is a direct consequence of Theorem 2 and of previous results concerning the reachability problem in concurrent programs running over a sequentially-consistent memory, with a fixed [17] or parametric number of processes [22].

$[\![\mathsf{l}_1 : r := x;\ \mathtt{goto}\ \mathsf{l}_2;]\!]_{\mathsf{HbH}} =$

// Read before the delayed transaction

l_1 : assume HB $=\perp \wedge p.a = \perp$; goto l_{x1};

l_{x1} : $r := x$; goto l_2; (6)

// Read after the delayed transaction

l_1 : assume HB $\neq\perp$; goto l_{x2};

l_{x2} : $r := x$; goto l_{x3};

l_{x3} : assume $x.eventI =$ st $\wedge\ p.hbh = \perp$; goto l_{x4};

l_{x4} : $p.hbh :=$ true; goto l_2; (7)

l_{x3} : assume $x.event = \perp$; goto l_{x5};

l_{x5} : $x.event :=$ ld; goto l_2; (8)

l_{x3} : assume $x.event \neq \perp \vee p.hbh \neq \perp$; goto l_2;

$[\![\mathsf{l}_1 : x := e;\ \mathtt{goto}\ \mathsf{l}_2;]\!]_{\mathsf{HbH}} =$

// Write before the delayed transaction

l_1 : assume HB $=\perp \wedge a_{\mathsf{tr_A}} = \perp$; goto l_{x1};

l_{x1} : $x := e$; goto l_2;

// Write after the delayed transaction

l_1 : assume HB $\neq\perp \wedge p.a = \perp$; goto l_{x2};

l_{x2} : assume $x.event' \neq \perp$; assume false; (9)

l_{x2} : assume $x.event' = \perp$; goto l_{x3};

l_{x3} : $x := e$; goto l_{x4};

l_{x4} : $x.event :=$ st; goto l_{x5}; (10)

l_{x5} : assume $x.eventI \neq \perp \wedge p.hbh = \perp$; goto l_{x6};

l_{x6} : $p.hbh :=$ true; goto l_2; (11)

l_{x5} : assume $x.eventI = \perp \vee p.hbh \neq \perp$; goto l_2;

Fig. 4. Instrumentation of happens-before helpers.

[1] Programs with a bounded number of variables taking values from a bounded domain.

Corollary 1. *Checking robustness of finite-state programs against snapshot isolation is PSPACE-complete when the number of processes is fixed and EXPSPACE-complete, otherwise.*

The instrumentation can be extended to SQL (select/update) queries where a statement may include expressions over a finite/infinite set of variables, e.g., by manipulating a set of flags x.event for each statement instead of only one.

6 Proving Program Robustness

As a more pragmatic alternative to the reduction in the previous section, we define an approximated method for proving robustness which is inspired by Lipton's reduction theory [18].

Movers. Given an execution $\tau = ev_1 \cdot \ldots \cdot ev_n$ of a program $\mathcal{P}$ under serializability (where each event ev_i corresponds to executing an entire transaction), we say that the event ev_i *moves right (resp., left)* in τ if $ev_1 \cdot \ldots \cdot ev_{i-1} \cdot ev_{i+1} \cdot ev_i \cdot ev_{i+2} \cdot \ldots \cdot ev_n$ (resp., $ev_1 \cdot \ldots \cdot ev_{i-2} \cdot ev_i \cdot ev_{i-1} \cdot ev_{i+1} \cdot \ldots \cdot ev_n$) is also a valid execution of $\mathcal{P}$, the process of ev_i is different from the process of ev_{i+1} (resp., ev_{i-1}), and both executions reach to the same end state σ_n. For an execution τ, let $\mathsf{instOf}_\tau(ev_i)$ denote the transaction that generated the event ev_i. A transaction t of a program $\mathcal{P}$ is a *right (resp., left) mover* if for all executions τ of $\mathcal{P}$ under serializability, the event ev_i with $\mathsf{instOf}(ev_i) = t$ moves right (resp., left) in τ.

If a transaction t is not a right mover, then there must exist an execution τ of $\mathcal{P}$ under serializability and an event ev_i of τ with $\mathsf{instOf}(ev_i) = t$ that does not move right. This implies that there must exist another ev_{i+1} of τ which caused ev_i to not be a right mover. Since ev_i and ev_{i+1} do not commute, then this must be because of either a write-read, write-write, or a read-write dependency. If $t' = \mathsf{instOf}(ev_{i+1})$, we say that t is not a right mover because of t' and some dependency that is either write-read, write-write, or read-write. Notice that when t is not a right mover because of t' then t' is not a left mover because of t.

We define M_{WR} as a binary relation between transactions such that $(t, t') \in \mathsf{M}_{\mathsf{WR}}$ when t is *not* a right mover because of t' and a write-read dependency. We define the relations M_{WW} and M_{RW} corresponding to write-write and read-write dependencies in a similar way.

Read/Write-free Transactions. Given a transaction t, we define $t \setminus \{r\}$ as a variation of t where all the reads from shared variables are replaced with non-deterministic reads, i.e., $\langle reg \rangle := \langle var \rangle$ statements are replaced with $\langle reg \rangle := \star$ where $\star$ denotes non-deterministic choice. We also define $t \setminus \{w\}$ as a variation of t where all the writes to shared variables in t are disabled. Intuitively, recalling the reduction to SC reachability in Sect. 5, $t \setminus \{w\}$ simulates the delay of a transaction by the Attacker, i.e., the writes are not made visible to other processes, and $t \setminus \{r\}$ approximates the commit of the delayed transaction which only applies a set of writes.

Commutativity Dependency Graph. Given a program $\mathcal{P}$, we define the commutativity dependency graph as a graph where vertices represent transactions and their read/write-free variations. Two vertices which correspond to the original transactions in $\mathcal{P}$ are related by a program order edge, if they belong to the same process. The other edges in this graph represent the "non-mover" relations M_{WR}, M_{WW}, and M_{RW}.

Given a program $\mathcal{P}$, we say that the commutativity dependency graph of $\mathcal{P}$ contains a *non-mover cycle* if there exist a set of transactions $t_0, t_1, \ldots, t_n$ of $\mathcal{P}$ such that the following hold:

(a) $(t_0'', t_1) \in \mathsf{M}_{\mathsf{RW}}$ where t_0'' is the write-free variation of t_0 and t_1 does not write to a variable that t_0 writes to;
(b) for all $i \in [1, n]$, $(t_i, t_{i+1}) \in (\mathsf{PO} \cup \mathsf{M}_{\mathsf{WR}} \cup \mathsf{M}_{\mathsf{WW}} \cup \mathsf{M}_{\mathsf{RW}})$, t_i and t_{i+1} do not write to a shared variable that t_0 writes to;
(c) $(t_n, t_0') \in \mathsf{M}_{\mathsf{RW}}$ where t_0' is the read-free variation of t_0 and t_n does not write to a variable that t_0 writes to.

A non-mover cycle approximates an execution of the instrumentation defined in Sect. 5 in between the moment that the Attacker delays a transaction t_0 (which here corresponds to the write-free variation t_0'') and the moment where t_0 gets committed (the read-free variation t_0').

The following theorem shows that the acyclicity of the commutativity dependency graph of a program implies the robustness of the program. Actually, the notion of robustness in this theorem relies on a slightly different notion of trace where store-order and write-order dependencies take into account values, i.e., store-order relates only writes writing different values and the write-order relates a read to the oldest write (w.r.t. execution order) writing its value. This relaxation helps in avoiding some harmless robustness violations due to for instance, two transactions writing the same value to some variable.

Theorem 3. *For a program $\mathcal{P}$, if the commutativity dependency graph of $\mathcal{P}$ does not contain non-mover cycles, then $\mathcal{P}$ is robust.*

7 Experiments

To test the applicability of our robustness checking algorithms, we have considered a benchmark of 10 applications extracted from the literature related to weakly consistent databases in general. A first set of applications are open source projects that were implemented to be run over the Cassandra database, extracted from [11]. The second set of applications is composed of: TPC-C [24], an on-line transaction processing benchmark widely used in the database community, SmallBank, a simplified representation of a banking application [2], FusionTicket, a movie ticketing application [16], Auction, an online auction application [6], and Courseware, a course registration service extracted from [14,19].

Table 1. An overview of the analysis results. CDG stands for commutativity dependency graph. The columns PO and PT show the number of proof obligations and proof time in second, respectively. T stands for trivial when the application has only read-only transactions.

Application	#Transactions	Robustness	Reachability analysis		CDG Analysis	
			PO	PT	PO	PT
Auction	4	✓	70	0.3	20	0.5
Courseware	5	✗	59	0.37	na	na
FusionTicket	4	✓	72	0.3	34	0.5
SmallBank	5	✗	48	0.28	na	na
TPC-C	5	✓	54	0.7	82	3.7
Cassieq-Core	8	✓	173	0.55	104	2.9
Currency-Exchange	6	✓	88	0.35	26	3.5
PlayList	14	✓	99	4.63	236	7.3
RoomStore	5	✓	85	0.3	22	0.5
Shopping-Cart	4	✓	58	0.25	T	T

A first experiment concerns the reduction of robustness checking to SC reachability. For each application, we have constructed a client (i.e., a program composed of transactions defined within that application) with a fixed number of processes (at most 3) and a fixed number of transactions (between 3 and 7 transactions per process). We have encoded the instrumentation of this client, defined in Sect. 5, in the Boogie programming language [3] and used the Civl verifier [15] in order to check whether the assertions introduced by the instrumentation are violated (which would represent a robustness violation). Note that since clients are of fixed size, this requires no additional assertions/invariants (it is an instance of bounded model checking). The results are reported in Table 1. We have found two of the applications, Courseware and SmallBank, to *not* be robust against snapshot isolation. The violation in Courseware is caused by transactions RemoveCourse and EnrollStudent that execute concurrently, RemoveCourse removing a course that has no registered student and EnrollStudent registering a new student to the same course. We get an invalid state where a student is registered for a course that was removed. SmallBank's violation contains transactions Balance, TransactSaving, and WriteCheck. One process executes WriteCheck where it withdraws an amount from the checking account after checking that the sum of the checking and savings accounts is bigger than this amount. Concurrently, a second process executes TransactSaving where it withdraws an amount from the saving account after checking that it is smaller than the amount in the savings account. Afterwards, the second process checks the contents of both the checking and saving accounts. We get an invalid state where the sum of the checking and savings accounts is negative.

Since in the first experiment we consider fixed clients, the lack of assertion violations doesn't imply that the application is robust (this instantiation of our reduction can only be used to reveal robustness violations). Thus, a second experiment concerns the robustness proof method based on commutativity dependency graphs (Sect. 6). For the applications that were not identified as non-robust by the previous method, we have used Civl to construct their commutativity dependency graphs, i.e., identify the "non-mover" relations M_{WR}, M_{WW}, and M_{RW} (Civl allows to check whether some code fragment is a left/right mover). In all cases, the graph didn't contain non-mover cycles, which allows to conclude that the applications are robust.

The experiments show that our results can be used for finding violations and proving robustness, and that they apply to a large set of interesting examples. Note that the reduction to SC and the proof method based on commutativity dependency graphs are valid for programs with SQL (select/update) queries.

8 Related Work

Decidability and complexity of robustness has been investigated in the context of relaxed memory models such as TSO and Power [7,9,13]. Our work borrows some high-level principles from [7] which addresses the robustness against TSO. We reuse the high-level methodology of characterizing minimal violations according to some measure and defining reductions to SC reachability using a program instrumentation. Instantiating this methodology in our context is however very different, several fundamental differences being:

- `SI` and TSO admit different sets of relaxations and `SI` is a model of transactional databases.
- We use a different notion of measure: the measure in [7] counts the number of events between a write issue and a write commit while our notion of measure counts the number of delayed transactions. This is a first reason for which the proof techniques in [7] don't extend to our context.
- Transactions induce more complex traces: two transactions might be related by several dependency relations since each transaction may contain multiple reads and writes to different locations. In TSO, each action is a read or a write to some location, and two events are related by a single dependency relation. Also, the number of dependencies between two transactions depends on the execution since the set of reads/writes in a transaction evolves dynamically.

Other works [9,13] define decision procedures which are based on the theory of regular languages and do not extend to infinite-state programs like in our case.

```
    p1:                        p2:
t1: [ if (x > y)       ||  t2: [ if (y > x)
        r1 = x - y                 r2 = y - x
        x  = y ]                   y  = x ]
```

Fig. 5. A robust program.

As far as we know, our work provides the first results concerning the decidability and the complexity of robustness checking in the context of transactions. The existing work on the verification of robustness for transactional programs provide either over- or under-approximate analyses. Our commutativity dependency graphs are similar to the static dependency graphs used in [6,10–12], but they are more precise, i.e., reducing the number of false alarms. The static dependency graphs record happens-before dependencies between transactions based on a syntactic approximation of the variables accessed by a transaction. For example, our techniques are able to prove that the program in Fig. 5 is robust, while this is not possible using static dependency graphs. The latter would contain a dependency from transaction t_1 to t_2 and one from t_2 to t_1 just because syntactically, each of the two transactions reads both variables and may write to one of them. Our dependency graphs take into account the semantics of these transactions and do not include this happens-before cycle. Other over- and under-approximate analyses have been proposed in [20]. They are based on encoding executions into first order logic, bounded-model checking for the under-approximate analysis, and a sound check for proving a cut-off bound on the size of the happens-before cycles possible in the executions of a program, for the over-approximate analysis. The latter is strictly less precise than our method based on commutativity dependency graphs. For instance, extending the TPC-C application with additional transactions will make the method in [20] fail while our method will succeed in proving robustness (the three transactions are for adding a new product, adding a new warehouse based on the number of customers and warehouses, and adding a new customer, respectively).

Finally, the idea of using Lipton's reduction theory for checking robustness has been also used in the context of the TSO memory model [8], but the techniques are completely different, e.g., the TSO technique considers each update in isolation and doesn't consider non-mover cycles like in our commutativity dependency graphs.

References

1. Adya, A.: Weak consistency: a generalized theory and optimistic implementations for distributed transactions. Ph.D. thesis (1999)
2. Alomari, M., Cahill, M.J., Fekete, A., Röhm, U.: The cost of serializability on platforms that use snapshot isolation. In: Alonso, G., Blakeley, J.A., Chen, A.L.P. (eds.) Proceedings of the 24th International Conference on Data Engineering, ICDE 2008, 7–12 April 2008, Cancún, Mexico, pp. 576–585. IEEE Computer Society (2008)
3. Barnett, M., Chang, B.-Y.E., DeLine, R., Jacobs, B., Leino, K.R.M.: Boogie: a modular reusable verifier for object-oriented programs. In: de Boer, F.S., Bonsangue, M.M., Graf, S., de Roever, W.-P. (eds.) FMCO 2005. LNCS, vol. 4111, pp. 364–387. Springer, Heidelberg (2006). https://doi.org/10.1007/11804192_17
4. Beillahi, S.M., Bouajjani, A., Enea, C.: Checking robustness against snapshot isolation. CoRR, abs/1905.08406 (2019)
5. Berenson, H., Bernstein, P.A., Gray, J., Melton, J., O'Neil, E.J., O'Neil, P.E.: A critique of ANSI SQL isolation levels. In: Carey, M.J., Schneider, D.A. (eds.) Proceedings of the 1995 ACM SIGMOD International Conference on Management of Data, San Jose, California, USA, 22–25 May 1995, pp. 1–10. ACM Press (1995)

6. Bernardi, G., Gotsman, A.: Robustness against consistency models with atomic visibility. In: Desharnais, J., Jagadeesan, R. (eds.) 27th International Conference on Concurrency Theory, CONCUR 2016, 23–26 August 2016, Québec City, Canada. LIPIcs, vol. 59, pp. 7:1–7:15. Schloss Dagstuhl - Leibniz-Zentrum fuer Informatik (2016)
7. Bouajjani, A., Derevenetc, E., Meyer, R.: Checking and enforcing robustness against TSO. In: Felleisen, M., Gardner, P. (eds.) ESOP 2013. LNCS, vol. 7792, pp. 533–553. Springer, Heidelberg (2013). https://doi.org/10.1007/978-3-642-37036-6_29
8. Bouajjani, A., Enea, C., Mutluergil, S.O., Tasiran, S.: Reasoning about TSO programs using reduction and abstraction. In: Chockler, H., Weissenbacher, G. (eds.) CAV 2018. LNCS, vol. 10982, pp. 336–353. Springer, Cham (2018). https://doi.org/10.1007/978-3-319-96142-2_21
9. Bouajjani, A., Meyer, R., Möhlmann, E.: Deciding robustness against total store ordering. In: Aceto, L., Henzinger, M., Sgall, J. (eds.) ICALP 2011. LNCS, vol. 6756, pp. 428–440. Springer, Heidelberg (2011). https://doi.org/10.1007/978-3-642-22012-8_34
10. Brutschy, L., Dimitrov, D., Müller, P., Vechev, M.T.: Serializability for eventual consistency: criterion, analysis, and applications. In: Castagna, G., Gordon, A.D. (eds.) Proceedings of the 44th ACM SIGPLAN Symposium on Principles of Programming Languages, POPL 2017, Paris, France, 18–20 January 2017, pp. 458–472. ACM (2017)
11. Brutschy, L., Dimitrov, D., Müller, P., Vechev, M.T.: Static serializability analysis for causal consistency. In: Foster, J.S., Grossman, D. (eds.) Proceedings of the 39th ACM SIGPLAN Conference on Programming Language Design and Implementation, PLDI 2018, Philadelphia, PA, USA, 18–22 June 2018, pp. 90–104. ACM (2018)
12. Cerone, A., Gotsman, A.: Analysing snapshot isolation. J. ACM **65**(2), 11:1–11:41 (2018)
13. Derevenetc, E., Meyer, R.: Robustness against power is PSpace-complete. In: Esparza, J., Fraigniaud, P., Husfeldt, T., Koutsoupias, E. (eds.) ICALP 2014. LNCS, vol. 8573, pp. 158–170. Springer, Heidelberg (2014). https://doi.org/10.1007/978-3-662-43951-7_14
14. Gotsman, A., Yang, H., Ferreira, C., Najafzadeh, M., Shapiro, M.: 'cause i'm strong enough: reasoning about consistency choices in distributed systems. In: Bodík, R., Majumdar, R. (eds.) Proceedings of the 43rd Annual ACM SIGPLAN-SIGACT Symposium on Principles of Programming Languages, POPL 2016, St. Petersburg, FL, USA, 20–22 January 2016, pp. 371–384. ACM (2016)
15. Hawblitzel, C., Petrank, E., Qadeer, S., Tasiran, S.: Automated and modular refinement reasoning for concurrent programs. In: Kroening, D., Păsăreanu, C.S. (eds.) CAV 2015. LNCS, vol. 9207, pp. 449–465. Springer, Cham (2015). https://doi.org/10.1007/978-3-319-21668-3_26
16. Holt, B., Bornholt, J., Zhang, I., Ports, D.R.K., Oskin, M., Ceze, L.: Disciplined inconsistency with consistency types. In: Aguilera, M.K., Cooper, B., Diao, Y. (eds.) Proceedings of the Seventh ACM Symposium on Cloud Computing, Santa Clara, CA, USA, 5–7 October 2016, pp. 279–293. ACM (2016)
17. Kozen, D.: Lower bounds for natural proof systems. In: 18th Annual Symposium on Foundations of Computer Science, Providence, Rhode Island, USA, October 31–1 November 1977, pp. 254–266. IEEE Computer Society (1977)
18. Lipton, R.J.: Reduction: a method of proving properties of parallel programs. Commun. ACM **18**(12), 717–721 (1975)

19. Nagar, K., Jagannathan, S.: Automated detection of serializability violations under weak consistency. In: Schewe, S., Zhang, L. (eds.) 29th International Conference on Concurrency Theory, CONCUR 2018, 4–7 September 2018, Beijing, China. LIPIcs, vol. 118, pp. 41:1–41:18. Schloss Dagstuhl - Leibniz-Zentrum fuer Informatik (2018)
20. Nagar, K., Jagannathan, S.: Automatic detection of serializability violations under weak consistency. In: 29th International Conference on Concurrency Theory (CONCUR 2018), September 2018
21. Papadimitriou, C.H.: The serializability of concurrent database updates. J. ACM **26**(4), 631–653 (1979)
22. Rackoff, C.: The covering and boundedness problems for vector addition systems. Theoret. Comput. Sci. **6**, 223–231 (1978)
23. Shasha, D.E., Snir, M.: Efficient and correct execution of parallel programs that share memory. ACM Trans. Program. Lang. Syst. **10**(2), 282–312 (1988)
24. TPC: Technical report, Transaction Processing Performance Council, February 2010. http://www.tpc.org/tpc_documents_current_versions/pdf/tpc-c_v5.11.0.pdf

Efficient Verification of Network Fault Tolerance via Counterexample-Guided Refinement

Nick Giannarakis[1(✉)], Ryan Beckett[2], Ratul Mahajan[3,4], and David Walker[1]

[1] Princeton University, Princeton, NJ 08544, USA
{ng8,dpw}@cs.princeton.edu
[2] Microsoft Research, Redmond, WA 98052, USA
ryan.beckett@microsoft.com
[3] University of Washington, Seattle, WA 98195, USA
ratul@cs.washington.edu
[4] Intentionet, Seattle, WA, USA

Abstract. We show how to verify that large data center networks satisfy key properties such as all-pairs reachability under a bounded number of faults. To scale the analysis, we develop algorithms that identify network symmetries and compute small abstract networks from large concrete ones. Using counter-example guided abstraction refinement, we successively refine the computed abstractions until the given property may be verified. The soundness of our approach relies on a novel notion of network approximation: routing paths in the concrete network are not precisely simulated by those in the abstract network but are guaranteed to be "at least as good." We implement our algorithms in a tool called Origami and use them to verify reachability under faults for standard data center topologies. We find that Origami computes abstract networks with 1–3 orders of magnitude fewer edges, which makes it possible to verify large networks that are out of reach of existing techniques.

1 Introduction

Most networks decide how to route packets from point A to B by executing one or more distributed routing protocols such as the Border Gateway Protocol (BGP) and Open Shortest Path First (OSPF). To achieve end-to-end policy objectives related to cost, load balancing, security, etc., network operators author configurations for each router. These configurations control various aspects of the route computation such as filtering and ranking route information received from neighbors, information injection from one protocol to another, and so on.

This work was supported in part by NSF Grants 1703493 and 1837030, and gifts from Cisco and Facebook. Any opinions, findings, and conclusions expressed are those of the authors and do not necessarily reflect those of the NSF, Cisco or Facebook.

I. Dillig and S. Tasiran (Eds.): CAV 2019, LNCS 11562, pp. 305–323, 2019.
https://doi.org/10.1007/978-3-030-25543-5_18

This flexibility, however, comes at a cost: Configuring individual routers to enforce the desired policies of the distributed system is complex and error-prone [15,21]. The problem of configuration is further compounded by three challenges. The first is network scale. Large networks such as those of cloud providers can consist of millions of lines of configuration spread across thousands of devices. The second is that operators must account for the interaction with external neighbors who may sent arbitrary routing messages. Finally one has to deal with *failures*. Hardware failures are common [14] and lead to a combinatorial explosion of different possible network behaviors.

To combat the complexity of distributed routing configurations, researchers have suggested a wide range of network verification [2,13,25] and simulation [11,12,23] techniques. These techniques are effective on small and medium-sized networks, but they cannot analyze data centers with 1000 s of routers and all their possible failures. To enable scalable analyses, it seems necessary to exploit the symmetries that exist in most large real networks. Indeed, other researchers have exploited symmetries to scale verification in the past [3,22]. However, it has never been possible to account for failures, as they introduce asymmetries that change routing behaviors in unpredictable ways.

To address this challenge, we develop a new algorithm for verifying reachability in networks in the presence of faults, based on the idea of counterexample-guided abstraction refinement (CEGAR) [5]. The algorithm starts by factoring out symmetries using techniques developed in prior work [3] and then attempts verification of the abstract network using an SMT solver. If verification succeeds, we are done. However, if verification fails, we examine the counter-example to decide whether we have a true failure or we must refine the network further and attempt verification anew. By focusing on reachability, the refinement procedure can be accelerated by using efficient graph algorithms, such as min cut, to rule out invalid abstractions in the middle of the CEGAR loop.

We prove the correctness of our algorithm using a new theory of faulty networks that accounts for the impact of all combinations of k failures. Our key insight is that, while routes computed in the abstract network may not simulate those of the concrete network exactly, under the right conditions they are guaranteed to *approximate* them. The approximation relation between concrete and abstract networks suffices to verify key properties such as reachability.

We implemented our algorithms in a tool called Origami and measured their performance on common data center network topologies. We find that Origami computes abstract networks with 1–3 orders of magnitude fewer edges. This reduction speeds verification dramatically and enables verification of networks that are out of reach of current state-of-the-art tools [2].

2 Key Ideas

The goal of Origami is to speed up network verification in the presence of faults, and it does so by computing small, abstract networks with *similar* behavior to a given concrete network.

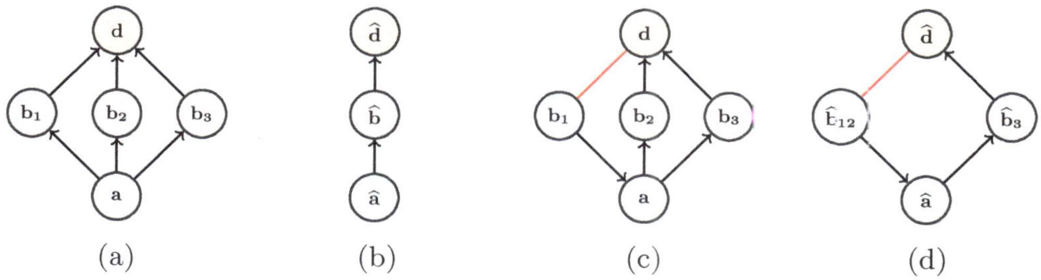

Fig. 1. All graph edges shown correspond to edges in the network topology, and we draw edges as directed to denote the direction of forwarding eventually determined for each node by the distributed routing protocols for a fixed destination d. In (a) nodes use shortest path routing to route to the destination d. (b) shows a compressed network that precisely captures the forwarding behavior of (a). (c) shows how forwarding is impacted by a link failure, shown as a red line. (d) shows a compressed network that is sound approximation of the original network for any single link failure. (Color figure online)

As a first approximation, one can view a network as a directed graph capturing the physical topology, and its routing solution as a subgraph where the remaining edges denote the forwarding decision at each node for some fixed destination. In the absence of faults, given a concrete and abstract network, one can define a natural notion of similarity as a graph homomorphism: assigning each concrete node a corresponding abstract node such that, for any solution to the routing problem, the concrete node forwards "in the same direction" as the corresponding abstract node. For example, the concrete network in Fig. 1a is related to its abstract counterpart in Fig. 1b according to the node colors.

Unfortunately, we run into two significant problems when defining abstractions in this manner in the presence of faults. First, the concrete nodes of Fig. 1a have at least 2 disjoint paths to the destination whereas abstract nodes of Fig. 1b have just one path to the destination, so the abstract network does not preserve the desired fault tolerance properties. Second, consider Fig. 1c, which illustrates how the routing decisions change when a failure occurs. Here, the nodes (b_1 in particular) no longer route "in the same direction" as the original network or its abstraction. Hence the invariant connecting concrete and abstract networks is violated.

Lossy Compression. To achieve compression given a bounded number of link failures, we relax the notion of similarity between concrete and abstract nodes: A node in the abstract network may merely *approximate* the behavior of concrete nodes. This makes it possible to compress nodes that, in the presence of failures, may route differently. In general, when we fail a single link in the abstract network, we are over-approximating the failures in the concrete network by failing multiple concrete links, possibly more than desired. Nevertheless, the paths taken in the concrete network can only deviate so much from the paths found in the abstract network:

Property 1. If a node has a route to the destination in the presence of k link failures then it has a route that is "at least as good" (as prescribed by the routing protocol) in the presence of k' link failures for $k' < k$.

This relation suffices to verify important network reliability properties, such as reachability, in the presence of faults. Just as importantly, it allows us to achieve effective network compression to scale verification.

Revisiting our example, consider the new abstract network of Fig. 1d. When the link between $\widehat{b}_{12}$ and $\widehat{d}$ has failed, $\widehat{b}_{12}$ still captures the behavior of b_1 precisely. However, b_2 has a better (in this case better means shorter) path to d. Despite this difference, if the operator's goal was to prove reachability to the destination under any single fault, then this abstract network suffices.

From Specification to Algorithm. It is not too difficult to find abstract networks that approximate a concrete network; the challenge is finding a valid abstract network that is *small enough* to make verification feasible and yet *large enough* to include sufficiently many paths to verify the given fault tolerance property. Rather than attempting to compute a single abstract network with the right properties all in one shot, we search the space of abstract networks using an algorithm based on *counter-example guided abstraction refinement* [5].

The CEGAR algorithm begins by computing the smallest possible valid abstract network. In the example above, this corresponds to the original compressed network in Fig. 1b, which faithfully approximates the original network when there are no link failures. However, if we try to verify reachability in the presence of a single fault, we will conclude that nodes $\widehat{b}$ and $\widehat{a}$ have no route to the destination when the link between $\widehat{b}$ and $\widehat{d}$ fails. The counterexample due to this failure could of course be spurious (and indeed it is). Fortunately, we can easily distinguish whether such a failure is due to lack of connectivity or an artifact of over-abstracting, by calculating the number of corresponding concrete failures. In this example a failure on the link $\langle\widehat{b}, \widehat{d}\rangle$ corresponds to 3 concrete failures. Since we are interested in verifying reachability for a single failure this cannot constitute an actual counterexample.

The next step is to *refine* our abstraction by splitting some of the abstract nodes. The idea is to use the counterexample from the previous iteration to split the abstract network in a way that avoids giving rise to the same spurious counterexample in the next iteration (Sect. 5). Doing so results in the somewhat larger network of Fig. 1d. A second verification pass over this larger network takes longer, but succeeds.

3 The Network Model

Though there are a wide variety of routing protocols in use today, they share a lot in common. Griffin *et al.* [16] showed that protocols like BGP and others solve instances of the *stable paths problem*, a generalization of the shortest paths problem, and Sobrinho [24] demonstrated their semantics and properties can be modelled using routing algebras. We extend these foundations by defining *stable paths problems with faults* (SPPFs), an extension of the classic Stable Paths Problem that admits the possibility of a bounded number of link failures. In later sections, we use this network model to develop generic network compression algorithms and reason about their correctness.

Stable Path Problems with Faults (SPPFs): An SPPF is an instance of the stable paths problem with faults. Informally, each instance defines the routing behavior of an operational network. The definition includes both the network topology as well as the routing policy. The policy specifies the way routing messages are transformed as they travel along links and through the user-configured import and export filters/transformers of the devices, and also how the preferred routes are chosen at a given device. In our formulation, each problem instance also incorporates a specification of the possible failures and their impact on the routing solutions.

Formally, an SPPF is a tuple with six components:

1. A graph $G = \langle V, E\rangle$ denoting the network topology.
2. A set of "attributes" (*i.e.*, routing messages) $A_\infty = A \cup \{\infty\}$ that may be exchanged between devices. The symbol ∞ represents the absence of a route.
3. A destination $d \in V$ and its initial route announcement $a_d \in A$. For simplicity, each SPPF has exactly one destination (d). (To model a network with many destinations, one would use a set of SPPFs.)
4. A partial order $\prec \subseteq A_\infty \times A_\infty$ ranks attributes. If $a \prec b$ then we say route a is preferred over route b. Any route $a \in A$ is preferred to no route ($a \prec \infty$).
5. A function $\mathsf{trans} : E \rightarrow A_\infty \rightarrow A_\infty$ that denotes how messages are processed across edges. This function models the route maps and filters that transform route announcements as they enter or leave routers.
6. A bound k on the maximum number of link failures that may occur.

Examples: By choosing an appropriate set of routing attributes, a preference relation and a transfer function, one can model the semantics of commonly used routing protocols. For instance, the Routing Information Protocol (RIP) is a simple shortest paths protocol. It can be modelled by an SPPF where (1) the set of attributes A is the set of integers between 0 and 15 (*i.e.*, the set of permitted path lengths), (2) the preference relation is integer inequality so shorter paths are preferred, and (3) the transfer function increments the received attribute by 1 or drops the route if it exceeds the maximum hop count of 15:

$$\mathsf{trans}(e, a) = \begin{cases} \infty & \text{if } \ a \geq 15 \\ a + 1 & \text{otherwise} \end{cases}$$

Going beyond simple shortest paths, BGP is a complex, policy-driven protocol that drives the Internet, and increasingly, data centers [18]. Operators often choose BGP due to its high expressiveness. We can model a version of BGP (simplified for presentation) using messages consisting of triples (LP, Comm, Path) where LP is an integer-valued local preference, Comm is a set of community values (which are essentially string tags) and Path is a list of nodes, representing the path a routing message has traversed. The transfer function always adds the current device to the Path (or drops the message if a loop is detected) and will modify the LP and Comm components of the attribute according to the device configuration. For instance, one device may attach a community tag to a route and another device may filter or modify routes that have the tag attached. The protocol semantics dictates the preference relation (preferring routes with higher local preference first, and shorter paths second). A more complete BGP model is not fundamentally harder to model—it simply has additional attribute fields and more complex transfer and preference relations [20].

SPPF Solutions: In a network, routers will repeatedly exchange messages, applying their transfer functions to neighbor routes and selecting a current best route based on the preference relation, until the network reaches a fixpoint (stable state). Interestingly, Griffin *et al.* [16] showed that all routing solutions can be described via a set of local stability constraints. We exploit this insight to define a series of logical constraints that capture all possible routing behaviors in a setting that includes link failures. More specifically, we define a *solution* (*aka, stable state*) $\mathcal{S}$ of an SPPF to be a pair $\langle \mathcal{L}, \mathcal{F} \rangle$ of a labelling $\mathcal{L}$ and a failure scenario $\mathcal{F}$. The labelling $\mathcal{L}$ is an assignment of the final attributes to nodes in the network. If an attribute a is assigned to node v, we say that node has selected (or prefers) that attribute over other attributes available to it. The chosen route also determines packet forwarding. If a node X selects a route from neighbor Y, then X will forward packets to Y. The failure scenario $\mathcal{F}$ is an assignment of 0 (has not failed) or 1 (has failed) to each edge in the network.

A solution $\mathcal{S} = \langle \mathcal{L}, F \rangle$ to an $\mathsf{SPPF} = (G, A, a_{\mathrm{d}}, \prec, \mathsf{trans}, k)$ is a stable state satisfying the following conditions:

$$\mathcal{L}(u) = \begin{cases} a_{\mathrm{d}} & u = d \\ \infty & \mathsf{choices}_{\mathcal{S}}(u) = \emptyset \\ min_{\prec}(\{a \mid (e, a) \in \mathsf{choices}_{\mathcal{S}}(u)\}) & \mathsf{choices}_{\mathcal{S}}(u) \neq \emptyset \end{cases}$$

$$\textbf{subject to} \sum_{e \in E} \mathcal{F}(e) \leq k$$

where the choices from the neighbors of node u are defined as:

$$\mathsf{choices}_{\mathcal{S}}(u) = \{(e, a) \mid e = \langle u, v \rangle,\ a = \mathsf{trans}(e, \mathcal{L}(v)),\ a \neq \infty,\ \mathcal{F}(e) = 0\}$$

The constraints require that every node has selected the best attribute (according to its preference relation) amongst those available from its neighbors. The destination's label must always be the initial attribute a_d. For verification, this attribute (or parts of it) may be symbolic, which helps model potentially unknown routing announcements from peers outside our network. For other nodes u, the selected attribute a is the minimal attribute from the *choices* available to u. Intuitively, to find the choices available to u, we consider the attributes b chosen by neighbors v of u. Then, if the edge between v and u is not failed, we push b along that edge, modifying it according to the trans function. Finally, failure scenarios are constrained so that the sum of the failures is at most k.

4 Network Approximation Theory

Given a concrete SPPF and an abstract $\widehat{\mathsf{SPPF}}$, a network abstraction is a pair of functions (f, h) that relate the two. The topology abstraction $f : V \to \widehat{V}$ maps each node in the concrete network to a node in the abstract network, while the attribute abstraction $h : A_\infty \to \widehat{A}_\infty$ maps a concrete attribute to an abstract attribute. The latter allows us to relate networks running protocols where nodes may appear in the attributes (*e.g.* as in the Path component of BGP).

The goal of Origami is to compute compact $\widehat{\mathsf{SPPF}}$s that may be used for verification. These compact $\widehat{\mathsf{SPPF}}$s must be closely related to their concrete counterparts. Otherwise, properties verified on the compact $\widehat{\mathsf{SPPF}}$ will not be true of their concrete counterpart. Section 4.1 defines *label approximation*, which provides an intuitive, high-level, semantic relationship between abstract and concrete networks. We also explain some of the consequences of this definition and its limitations. Unfortunately, while this broad definition serves as an important theoretical objective, it is difficult to use directly in an efficient algorithm. Section 4.2 continues our development by explaining two *well-formedness* requirements of network policies that play a key role in establishing label approximation *indirectly*. Finally, Sect. 4.3 defines *effective SPPF approximation* for well-formed SPPFs. This definition is more conservative than label approximation, but has the advantage that it is easier to work with algorithmically and, moreover, it implies label approximation.

4.1 Label Approximation

Intuitively, we say the abstract $\widehat{\mathsf{SPPF}}$ label-approximates the concrete SPPF when SPPF has at least as good a route at every node as $\widehat{\mathsf{SPPF}}$ does.

Definition 1 (Label Approximation). *Consider any solutions $\mathcal{S}$ to SPPF and $\widehat{\mathcal{S}}$ to $\widehat{\mathsf{SPPF}}$ and their respective labelling components $\mathcal{L}$ and $\widehat{\mathcal{L}}$. We say $\widehat{\mathsf{SPPF}}$ label-approximates SPPF when $\forall u \in V.\ h(\mathcal{L}(u)) \preceq \widehat{\mathcal{L}}(f(u))$.*

If we can establish a label approximation relation between a concrete and an abstract network, we can typically verify a number of properties of the abstract network and be sure they hold of the concrete network. However, the details of exactly which properties we can verify depend on the specifics of the preference relation ($\prec$). For example, in an OSPF network, preference is determined by weighted path length. Therefore, if we know an abstract node has a path of weighted length n, we know that its concrete counterparts have paths of weighted length of at most n. More importantly, since "no route" is the worst route, we know that if a node has any route to the destination in the abstract network, so do its concrete counterparts.

Limitations. Some properties are beyond the scope of our tool (independent of the preference relation). For example, our model cannot reason about quantitative properties such as bandwidth, probability of congestion, or latency.

4.2 Well-Formed SPPFs

Not all SPPFs are well-behaved. For example, some never converge and others do not provide sensible models of any real network. To avoid dealing with such poorly-behaved models, we demand henceforth that all SPPFs are *well-formed*. Well-formedness entails that an SPPF is strictly monotonic and isotonic:

$\forall a, e.\ \ a \neq \infty \Rightarrow a \prec \mathsf{trans}(e, a)$ *strict monotonicity*

$\forall a, b, e.\ \ a \preceq b\ \Rightarrow\ \mathsf{trans}(e, a) \preceq \mathsf{trans}(e, b)$ *isotonicity*

Fig. 2. Concrete network (left) and its corresponding abstraction (right). Nodes c_1, c_2 prefer to route through b_1 (resp. b_2), or g over a. Node b_1 (resp. b_2) drops routing messages that have traversed b_2 (resp. b_1). Red lines indicate a failed link. Dotted lines show a topologically available but unused link. A purple arrow show a route unusable by traffic from b_1. (Color figure online)

Monotonicity and isotonicity properties are often cited [7,8] as desirable properties of routing policies because they guarantee network convergence and prevent persistent oscillation. In practice too, prior studies have revealed that almost all real network configurations have these properties [13,19].

In our case, these properties help establish additional invariants that tie the routing behavior of concrete and abstract networks together. To gain some intuition as to why, consider the networks of Fig. 2. The concrete network on the left runs BGP with the routing policy that node c_1 (and c_2) prefers to route through node g instead of a, and that b_1 drops announcements coming from b_2. In this scenario, the similarly configured abstract node $\widehat{b}_{12}$ can reach the destination—it simply takes a route that happens to be less preferred by $\hat{c}_{12}$ than it would if there had been no failure. However, in the concrete analogue, b_1, is *unable* to reach the destination because c_1 only sends it the route through b_2, which it cannot use. In this case, the concrete network has more topological paths than the abstract network, but, counterintuitively, due to the network's routing policy, this turns out to be a disadvantage. Hence having more paths does not necessarily make nodes more accessible. As a consequence, in general, abstract networks cannot soundly overapproximate the number of failures in a concrete network—an important property for the soundness of our theory.

The underlying issue here is that the networks of Fig. 2 are not isotonic: suppose $\mathcal{L}'(c_1)$ is the route from c_1 to the destination through node a, we have that $\mathcal{L}(c_1) \prec \mathcal{L}'(c_1)$ but since the transfer function over $\langle b_1, c_1 \rangle$ drops routes that have traversed node b_2, we have that $\mathsf{trans}(\langle b_1, c_1\rangle, \mathcal{L}(c_1)) \not\prec \mathsf{trans}(\langle b_1, c_1\rangle, \mathcal{L}'(c_1))$. Notice that $\mathcal{L}'(c_1)$ is essentially the route that the abstract network uses *i.e.* $h(\mathcal{L}'(c_1)) = \widehat{\mathcal{L}}(\hat{c}_{12})$, hence the formula above implies that $h(\mathcal{L}(b_1)) \not\prec \widehat{\mathcal{L}}(\hat{b}_{12})$ which violates the notion of label approximation. Fortunately, if a network is strictly monotonic and isotonic, such situations never arise. Moreover, we check these properties via an SMT solver using a local and efficient test.

4.3 Effective SPPF Approximation

We seek abstract networks that label-approximate given concrete networks. Unfortunately, to directly check that a particular abstract network label approximates a concrete network one must effectively compute their solutions. Doing so would defeat the entire purpose of abstraction, which seeks to analyze large concrete networks *without the expense of computing their solutions directly.*

In order to turn approximation into a useful computational tool, we define *effective approximation*, a set of simple conditions on the abstraction functions f and h that are *local* and can be checked efficiently. When true those conditions imply label approximation. Intuitively effective approximations impose three main restrictions on the abstraction functions:

1. The topology abstraction conforms to the $\forall\exists$−abstraction condition; this requires that there is an abstract edge $(\widehat{u}, \widehat{v})$ iff for every concrete node u such that $f(u) = \widehat{u}$ there is some node v such that $f(v) = \widehat{v}$ and $(u, v) \in E$.
2. The abstraction preserves the rank of attributes *(rank-equivalence)*:

$$\forall a, b.\ a \prec b \iff h(a) \mathrel{\widehat{\prec}} h(b)$$

3. The transfer function and the abstraction functions commute *(trans-equivalence)*:

$$\forall e, a.\ h(\mathsf{trans}(e, a)) = \widehat{\mathsf{trans}}(f(e), h(a))$$

We prove that when these conditions hold, we can approximate any solution of the concrete network with a solution of the abstract network.

Theorem 1. *Given a well-formed SPPF and its effective approximation $\widehat{\mathsf{SPPF}}$, for any solution $\mathcal{S} \in$ SPPF there exists a solution $\widehat{\mathcal{S}} \in \widehat{\mathsf{SPPF}}$, such that their labelling functions are label approximate.*

5 The Verification Procedure

The first step of verification is to compute a small abstract network that satisfies our SPPF *effective approximation* conditions. We do so by grouping network nodes and edges with equivalent policy and checking the forall-exists topological condition, using an algorithm reminiscent of earlier work [3]. Typically, however, this minimal abstraction will not contain enough paths to prove any fault-tolerance property. To identify a finer abstraction for which we can prove a fault-tolerance property we repeatedly:

1. Search the set of candidate refinements for the smallest *plausible* abstraction.
2. If the candidate abstraction satisfies the desired property, terminate the procedure. (We have successfully verified our concrete network.)
3. If not, examine whether the returned counterexample is an actual counterexample. We do so, by computing the number of concrete failures and check that it does not exceed the desired bound of link failures. (If so, we have found a property violation.)
4. If not, use the counterexample to *learn* how to expand the abstract network into a larger abstraction and repeat.

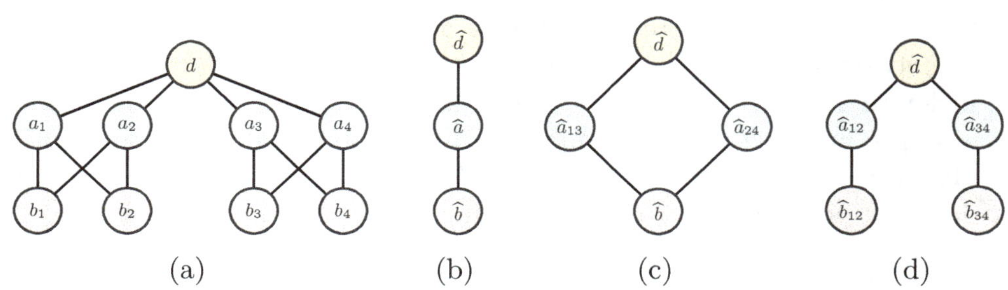

Fig. 3. Eight nodes in (a) are represented using two nodes in the abstract network (b). Pictures (c) and (d) show two possible ways to refine the abstract network (b).

Both the search for plausible candidates and the way we learn a new abstraction to continue the counterexample-guided loop are explained below.

5.1 Searching for Plausible Candidates

Though we might know an abstraction is not sufficient to verify a given fault tolerance property, there are many possible refinements. Consider, for example, Fig. 3(a) presents a simple concrete network that will tolerate a single link failure, and Fig. 3(b) presents an initial abstraction. The initial abstraction will not tolerate any link failure, so we must refine the network. To do so, we choose an abstract node to divide into two abstract nodes for the next iteration. We must also decide which concrete nodes correspond to each abstract node. For example, in Fig. 3(c), node $\hat{a}$ has been split into $\hat{a}_{13}$ and $\hat{a}_{24}$. The subscripts indicate the assignment of concrete nodes to abstract ones.

A significant complication is that once we have generated a new abstraction, we must check that it continues to satisfy the effective approximation conditions, and if not, we must do more work. Figure 3(c) satisfies those conditions, but if we were to split $\hat{a}$ into $\hat{a}_{12}$ and $\hat{a}_{34}$ rather than $\hat{a}_{13}$ and $\hat{a}_{24}$, the forall-exists condition would be violated—some of the concrete nodes associated with $\hat{b}$ are connected to the concrete nodes in $\hat{a}_{12}$ but not to the ones in $\hat{a}_{34}$ and vice versa. To repair the violation of the forall-exists condition, we need to split additional nodes. In this case, the $\hat{b}$ node, giving rise to diagram Fig. 3(d).

Overall, the process of splitting nodes and then recursively splitting further nodes to repair the forall-exists condition generates many possible candidate abstractions to consider. A key question is which candidate should we select to proceed with the abstraction refinement algorithm?

One consideration is size: A smaller abstraction avoids taxing the verifier, which is the ultimate goal. However, there are many small abstractions that we can quickly dismiss. Technically, we say an abstraction is *plausible* if all nodes of interest have at least $k + 1$ paths to the destination. Implausible abstractions cause nodes to become unreachable with k failures. To check whether an abstraction is plausible, we compute the *min-cut* of the graph. Figure 3(d) is an example of an implausible abstraction that arose after a poorly-chosen split of node $\hat{a}$. In this case, no node has 2 or more paths to the destination and hence they might not be able to reach the destination when there is a failure.

Clearly verification using an implausible abstraction will fail. Instead of considering such abstractions as candidates for running verification on, the refinement algorithm tries refining them further. A key decision the algorithm needs to make when refining an abstraction is *which abstract node to split*. For instance, the optimal refinement of Fig. 3(b) is Fig. 3(c). If we were to split node $\hat{b}$ instead of $\hat{a}$ we would end up with a sub-optimal (in terms of size) abstraction. Intuitively, splitting a node that lies on the min-cut and can reach the destination (e.g. $\hat{a}$) will increase the number of paths that its neighbors on the unreachable part of the min-cut (e.g. $\hat{b}$) can use to reach the destination.

To summarize, the search for new candidate abstractions involves (1) splitting nodes in the initial abstraction, (2) repairing the abstraction to ensure the forall-exists condition holds, (3) checking that the generated abstraction is *plausible*, and if not, (4) splitting additional nodes on the min cut. This iterative process will often generate many candidates. The *breadth* parameter of the search bounds the total number of plausible candidates we will generate in between verification efforts. Of all the plausible candidates generated, we choose the smallest one to verify using the SMT solver.

5.2 Learning from Counterexamples

Any nodes of an abstraction that have a min cut of less than $k+1$ definitely cannot tolerate k faults. If an abstraction is plausible, it satisfies a *necessary* condition for source-destination connectivity, but not a *sufficient* one—misconfigured routing policy can still cause nodes to be unreachable by modifying and/or subsequently dropping routing messages. For instance, the abstract network of Fig. 3c is plausible for one failure, but if $\widehat{b}$'s routing policy blocks routes of either $\widehat{a}_{13}$ or $\widehat{a}_{24}$ then the abstract network will not be 1-fault tolerant. Indeed, it is the complexity of routing policy that necessitates a heavy-weight verification procedure in the first place, rather than a simpler graph algorithm alone.

In a plausible abstraction, if the verifier computes a solution to the network that violates the desired fault-tolerance property, some node could not reach the destination because one or more of their paths to the destination could not be used to route traffic. We use the generated counterexample to learn edges that could not be used to route traffic due to the policy on them. To do so, we inspect the computed solution to find nodes $\widehat{u}$ that (1) lack a route to the destination (*i.e.* $\widehat{\mathcal{L}}(\widehat{u}) = \infty$), (2) have a neighbor $\widehat{v}$ that has a valid route to the destination, and (3) the link between $\widehat{u}$ and $\widehat{v}$ is not failed. These conditions imply the absence of a valid route to the destination not because link failures disabled all paths to the destination, but because the network policy dropped some routes. For example, in picture Fig. 3c, consider the case where $\widehat{b}$ does not advertise routes from $\widehat{a}_{13}$ and $\widehat{a}_{24}$; if the link between $\widehat{a}_{13}$ and $\widehat{d}$ fails, then $\widehat{a}_{13}$ has no routé the destination and we learn that the edge $\langle\widehat{b}, \widehat{a}_{13}\rangle$ cannot be used. In fact, since $\widehat{a}_{13}$ and $\widehat{a}_{12}$ belonged to the same abstract group $\widehat{a}$ before we split them, their routing policies are equal modulo the abstraction function by trans-equivalence. Hence, we can infer that in a symmetric scenario, the link $\langle\widehat{b}, \widehat{a}_{24}\rangle$ will also be unusable.

Given a set of unuseable edges, learned from a counterexample, we restrict the min cut problems that define the plausible abstractions, by disallowing the use of those edges. Essentially, we enrich the refinement algorithm's topological based analysis (based on min-cut) with knowledge about the policy; the algorithm will have to generate abstractions that are plausible without using those edges. With those edges disabled, the refinement process continues as before.

6 Implementation

Origami uses the Batfish network analysis framework [12] to parse network configurations, and then translate them into a pure functional intermediate representation (IR) designed for network verification. This IR represents the structure of routing messages and the semantics of transfer and preference relations using standard functional data structures.

The translation generates a separate functional program for each destination subnet. In other words, if a network has 100 top-of-rack switches and each such switch announces the subnets for 30 adjacent hosts, then Origami generates 100 functional programs (*i.e.* problem instances). We separately apply our algorithms to each problem instance, converting the functional program to an SMT formula when necessary according to the algorithm described earlier. Since vendor routing configuration languages have limited expressive power (*e.g.*, no loops or recursion) the translation requires no user-provided invariants. We use Z3 [10] to determine satisfiability of the SMT problems. Solving the problems separately (and in parallel) provides a speedup over solving the routing problem for all destinations simultaneously: The individual problems are specialized to a particular destination. By doing so, opportunities for optimizations that reduce the problem size, such as dead code elimination, arise.

Optimizing Refinement: During the course of implementing Origami, we discovered a number of optimizations to the refinement phase.

- If the min-cut between the destination and a vertex u is less than or equal to the desired number of disjoint paths, then we do not need to compute another min-cut for the nodes in the unreachable portion of vertices T; we know nodes in T can be disconnected from the destination. This significantly reduces the number of min-cut computations.
- We stop exploring abstractions that are larger in size than the smallest plausible abstraction computed since the last invocation of the SMT solver.
- We bias our refinement process to explore the smallest abstractions first. When combined the previous optimization, this prunes our search space from some abstractions that were unnecessary large.

Minimizing Counterexamples: When the SMT solver returns a counterexample, it often uses the maximum number of failures. This is not surprising as maximizing failures simplifies the SMT problem. Unfortunately, it also confounds our analysis to determine whether a counterexample is real or spurious.

Topo	Con V/E	Fail	Abs V/E	Ratio	Abs Time	SMT Calls	SMT Time
FT20	500/8000	1	9/20	55.5/400	0.1	1	0.1
		3	40/192	12.5/41.67	1.0	2	7.6
		5	96/720	5.20/11.1	2.5	2	248
		10	59/440	8.48/18.18	0.9	-	-
FT40	2000/64000	1	12/28	166.7/2285.7	0.1	1	0.1
		3	45/220	44.4/290.9	33	2	12.3
		5	109/880	18.34/72.72	762.3	2	184.1
SP40	2000/64000	1	13/32	153.8/2000	0.2	1	0.1
		3	39/176	51.3/363.6	30.3	1	2
		5	79/522	25.3/122.6	372.2	1	22
FbFT	744/10880	1	20/66	37.2/164.8	0.1	3	1
		3	57/360	13.05/30.22	1	4	18.3
		5	93/684	8/15.9	408.9	-	-

Fig. 4. Compression results. **Topo:** the network topology. **Con V/E:** Number of nodes/edges of concrete network. **Fail:** Number of failures. **Abs V/E:** Number of nodes/edges of the best abstraction. **Ratio:** Compression ratio (nodes/edges). **Abs Time:** Time taken to find abstractions (sec.). **SMT Calls:** Number of calls to the SMT solver. **SMT Time:** Time taken by the SMT solver (sec.).

To mitigate the effect of this problem, we *could* ask the solver to minimize the returned counterexample, returning a counterexample that corresponds to the fewest concrete link failures. We could do so by providing the solver with additional constraints specifying the number of concrete links that correspond to each abstract link and then asking the solver to return a counterexample that minimizes this sum of concrete failures. Of course, doing so requires we solve a more expensive optimization problem. Instead, given an initial (possibly spurious counter-example), we simple ask the solver to find a new counterexample that (additionally) satisfies this constraint. If it succeeds, we have found a real counterexample. If it fails, we use it to refine our abstraction.

7 Evaluation

We evaluate Origami on a collection of synthetic data center networks that are using BGP to implement shortest-paths routing policies over common industrial datacenter topologies. Data centers are good fit for our algorithms as they can be very large but are highly symmetrical and designed for fault tolerance. Data center topologies (often called *fattree* topologies) are typically organized in layers, with each layer containing many routers. Each router in a layer is connected to a number of routers in the layer above (and below) it. The precise number of neighbors to which a router is connected, and the pattern of said connections, is part of the topology definition. We focus on two common topologies: fattree topologies used at Google (labelled FT20, FT40 and SP40 below) and a different fattree used at Facebook (labelled FB12). These are relatively large data center topologies ranging from 500 to 2000 nodes and 8000 to 64000 edges.

SP40 uses a pure shortest paths routing policy. For other experiments (FT20, FT40, FB12), we augment shortest paths with additional policy that selectively drops routing announcements, for example disabling "valley routing" in various places which allows up-down-up-down routes through the data centers instead of just up-down routes. The pure shortest paths policy represents a best-case scenario for our technology as it gives rise to perfect symmetry and makes our heuristics especially effective. By adding variations in routing policy, we provide a greater challenge for our tool.

Experiments were done on a Mac with a 4 GHz i7 CPU and 16 GB memory.

7.1 Compression Results

Figure 4 shows the level of compression achieved, along with the required time for compression and verification. In most cases, we achieve a high compression ratio especially in terms of links. This drastically reduces the possible failure combinations for the underlying verification process. The cases of 10 link failures on FT20 and 5 link failures on FbFT demonstrate another aspect of our algorithm. Both topologies cannot sustain that many link failures, *i.e.* some concrete nodes have less than 10 (resp. 5) neighbors. We can determine this as we refine the abstraction; there are (abstract) nodes that do not satisfy the min cut requirement and we cannot refine them further. This constitutes an actual counterexample and explains why the abstraction of FT20 for 10 link failures is smaller than the one for 5 link failures. Importantly, we did not use the SMT solver to find this counterexample. Likewise, we did not need to run a min cut on the much larger concrete topology. Intuitively, the rest of the network remained abstract, while the part that led to the counterexample became fully concrete.

7.2 Verification Performance

The verification time of Origami is dominated by abstraction time and SMT time, which can be seen in Fig. 4. In practice, there is also some time taken to parse and pre-process the configurations but it is negligible. The abstraction time is highly dependent on the size of the network and the abstraction search breadth used. In this case, the breadth was set to 25, a relatively high value.

While the verification time for a high number of link failures is not negligible, we found that verification without abstraction is essentially impossible. We used Minesweeper [2], the state-of-the-art SMT-based network verifier, to verify the same fault tolerance properties and it was unable to solve any of our queries. This is not surprising, as SMT-based verifiers do not scale to networks beyond the size of FT20 even without any link failures.

7.3 Refinement Effectiveness

We now evaluate the effectiveness of our search and refinement techniques.

Effectiveness of Search. To assess the effectiveness of the search procedure, we compute an initial abstraction of the FT20 network suitable for 5 link failures, using different values of the search breadth. On top of this, we additionally consider the impact of some of the heuristics described in Sect. 5. Figure 5 presents the size (the number of nodes are on the y axis and the number of edges on top of the bars) of the computed abstractions with respect to various values for the breadth of search and sets of heuristics:

- Heuristics off means that (almost) all heuristics are turned off. We still try to split nodes that are on the cut-set.

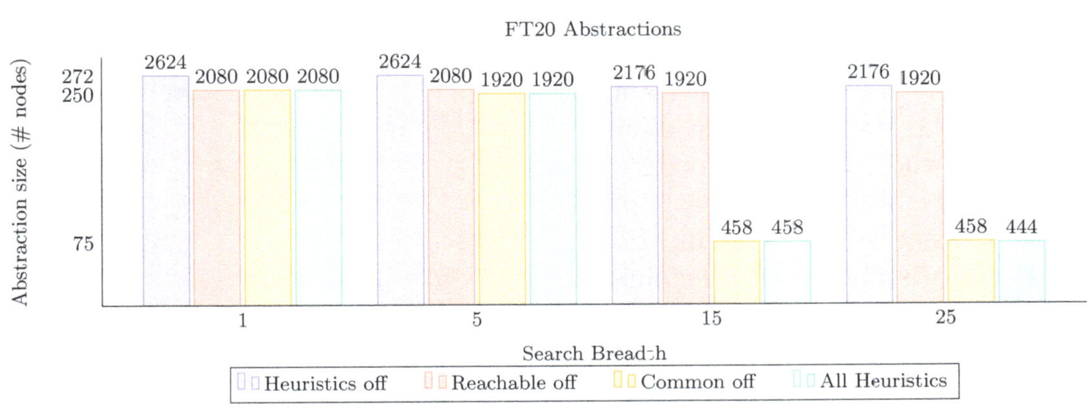

Fig. 5. The initial abstraction of FT20 for 5 link failures using different heuristics and search breadth. On top of the bars is the number of edges of each abstraction.

- Reachable off means that we do not bias towards splitting of nodes in the reachable portion of the cut-set.
- Common off means that we do not bias towards splitting reachable nodes that have the most connections to unreachable nodes.

The results of this experiment show that in order to achieve effective compression ratios we need to employ both smart heuristics and a wide search through the space of abstractions. It is possible that increasing the search breadth would make the heuristics redundant, however, in most cases this would make the refinement process exceed acceptable time limits.

Use of Counterexamples. We now assess how important it is to (1) use symmetries in policy to infer more information from counterexamples, and (2) minimize the counterexample provided by the solver.

We see in Fig. 6 that disabling them increases number of refinement iterations. While each of these refinements is performed quickly, the same cannot be guaranteed of the verification process that runs between them. Hence, it is important to keep refinement iterations as low as possible.

8 Related Work

Our approach to network fault-tolerance verification draws heavily from ideas in prior work exploiting symmetry and abstraction in model checking [4,6,17] and automatic abstraction refinement via CEGAR [1,5,9]. However, we apply these ideas to network routing, which introduces different challenges and opportunities. For example, our notion of abstraction ($\forall\exists$−abstraction) differs from the typical existential abstraction used in model checking [6]. In addition, we have to deal with network topological structure and asymmetries introduced by failures.

Bonsai [3] and Surgeries [22] both leverage abstraction to accelerate verification for routing protocols and packet forwarding respectively. Both tools compute a single abstract network that is bisimilar to the original concrete network. Alas, neither approach can be used to reason about properties when faults may occur.

Minesweeper [2] is a general approach to control plane verification based on a stable state encoding, which leverages an SMT solver in the back-end. It supports a wide range of routing protocols and properties, including fault tolerance properties. Our compression is complementary

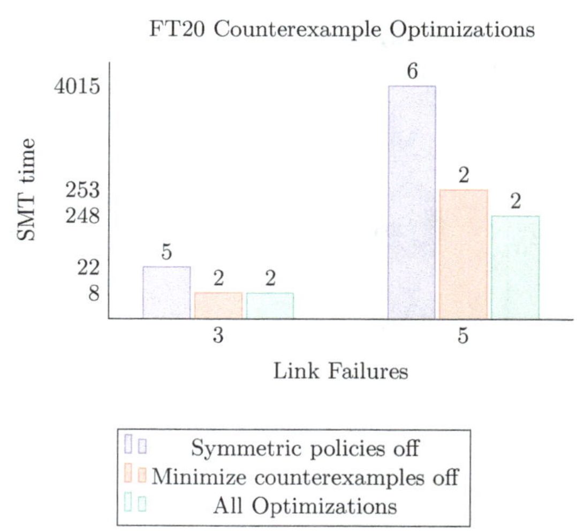

Fig. 6. Effectiveness of minimizing counterexamples and of learning unused edges. On top of the bars is the number of SMT calls.

to such tools; it is used to alleviate the scaling problem that Minesweeper faces with large networks.

With respect to verification of fault tolerance, ARC [13] translates a limited class of routing policies to a weighted graph where fault-tolerance properties can be checked using graph algorithms. However, ARC only handles shortest path routing and cannot support stateful features such as BGP communities, or local preference, etc. While ARC applies graph algorithms on a statically-computed graph, we use graph algorithms as part of a refinement loop in conjunction with a general purpose solver.

9 Conclusions

We present a new theory of distributed routing protocols in the presence of bounded link failures, and we use the theory to develop algorithms for network compression and counterexample-guided verification of fault tolerance properties. In doing so, we observe that (1) even though abstract networks route differently from concrete ones in the presence of failures, the concrete routes wind up being "at least as good" as the abstract ones when networks satisfy reasonable well-formedness constraints, and (2) using efficient graph algorithms (min cut) in the middle of the CEGAR loop speeds the search for refinements.

We implemented our algorithms in a network verification tool called Origami. Evaluation of the tool on synthetic networks shows that our algorithms accelerate verification of fault tolerance properties significantly, making it possible to verify networks out of reach of other state-of-the-art tools.

References

1. Ball, T., Majumdar, R., Millstein, T.D., Rajamani, S.K.: Automatic predicate abstraction of C programs. In: Proceedings of the 2001 ACM SIGPLAN Conference on Programming Language Design and Implementation (PLDI), pp. 203–213 (2001)
2. Beckett, R., Gupta, A., Mahajan, R., Walker, D.: A general approach to network configuration verification. In: SIGCOMM, August 2017
3. Beckett, R., Gupta, A., Mahajan, R., Walker, D.: Control plane compression. In: Proceedings of the 2018 Conference of the ACM Special Interest Group on Data Communication, pp. 476–489. ACM (2018)
4. Clarke, E.M., Filkorn, T., Jha, S.: Exploiting symmetry in temporal logic model checking. In: Courcoubetis, C. (ed.) CAV 1993. LNCS, vol. 697, pp. 450–462. Springer, Heidelberg (1993). https://doi.org/10.1007/3-540-56922-7_37
5. Clarke, E., Grumberg, O., Jha, S., Lu, Y., Veith, H.: Counterexample-guided abstraction refinement. In: Emerson, E.A., Sistla, A.P. (eds.) CAV 2000. LNCS, vol. 1855, pp. 154–169. Springer, Heidelberg (2000). https://doi.org/10.1007/10722167_15
6. Clarke, E.M., Grumberg, O., Long, D.E.: Model checking and abstraction. ACM Trans. Program. Lang. Syst. **16**(5), 1512–1542 (1994)
7. Daggitt, M.L., Gurney, A.J.T., Griffin, T.G.: Asynchronous convergence of policy-rich distributed bellman-ford routing protocols. In: SIGCOMM, pp. 103–116 (2018)

8. Daggitt, M.L., Gurney, A.J., Griffin, T.G.: Asynchronous convergence of policy-rich distributed Bellman-Ford routing protocols. In: Proceedings of the 2018 Conference of the ACM Special Interest Group on Data Communication, pp. 103–116. ACM (2018)
9. Das, S., Dill, D.L.: Successive approximation of abstract transition relations. In: Proceedings of the 16th Annual IEEE Symposium on Logic in Computer Science, LICS 2001, p. 51 (2001)
10. de Moura, L., Bjørner, N.: Z3: an efficient SMT solver. In: Ramakrishnan, C.R., Rehof, J. (eds.) TACAS 2008. LNCS, vol. 4963, pp. 337–340. Springer, Heidelberg (2008). https://doi.org/10.1007/978-3-540-78800-3_24
11. Feamster, N., Rexford, J.: Network-wide prediction of BGP routes. IEEE/ACM Trans. Netw. **15**(2), 253–266 (2007)
12. Fogel, A., et al.: A general approach to network configuration analysis. In: NSDI (2015)
13. Gember-Jacobson, A., Viswanathan, R., Akella, A., Mahajan, R.: Fast control plane analysis using an abstract representation. In: SIGCOMM (2016)
14. Gill, P., Jain, N., Nagappan, N.: Understanding network failures in data centers: measurement, analysis, and implications. In: SIGCOMM (2011)
15. Godfrey, J.: The summer of network misconfigurations (2016). https://blog.algosec.com/2016/08/business-outages-caused-misconfigurations-headline-news-summer.html
16. Griffin, T.G., Shepherd, F.B., Wilfong, G.: The stable paths problem and interdomain routing. IEEE/ACM Trans. Netw. **10**(2), 232–243 (2002)
17. Kesten, Y., Pnueli, A.: Control and data abstraction: the cornerstones of practical formal verification. Softw. Tools Technol. Transf. **2**(4), 328–342 (2000)
18. Lapukhov, P., Premji, A., Mitchell, J.: Use of BGP for routing in large-scale data centers. Internet draft (2015)
19. Lopes, N.P., Rybalchenko, A.: Fast BGP simulation of large datacenters. In: Enea, C., Piskac, R. (eds.) VMCAI 2019. LNCS, vol. 11388, pp. 386–408. Springer, Cham (2019). https://doi.org/10.1007/978-3-030-11245-5_18
20. Lougheed, K.: A border gateway protocol (BGP). RFC 1163, RFC Editor (1989). http://www.rfc-editor.org/rfc/rfc1163.txt
21. Mahajan, R., Wetherall, D., Anderson, T.: Understanding BGP misconfiguration. In: SIGCOMM (2002)
22. Plotkin, G.D., Bjørner, N., Lopes, N.P., Rybalchenko, A., Varghese, G.: Scaling network verification using symmetry and surgery. In: POPL (2016)
23. Quoitin, B., Uhlig, S.: Modeling the routing of an autonomous system with C-BGP. Netw. Mag. Glob. Internetworking **19**(6), 12–19 (2005)
24. Sobrinho, J.A.L.: An algebraic theory of dynamic network routing. IEEE/ACM Trans. Netw. **13**(5), 1160–1173 (2005)
25. Weitz, K., Woos, D., Torlak, E., Ernst, M.D., Krishnamurthy, A., Tatlock, Z.: Formal semantics and automated verification for the border gateway protocol. In: NetPL (2016)

On the Complexity of Checking Consistency for Replicated Data Types

Ranadeep Biswas[1(✉)], Michael Emmi[2], and Constantin Enea[1]

[1] Université de Paris, IRIF, CNRS, 75013 Paris, France
{ranadeep,cenea}@irif.fr
[2] SRI International, New York, NY, USA
michael.emmi@sri.com

Abstract. Recent distributed systems have introduced variations of familiar abstract data types (ADTs) like counters, registers, flags, and sets, that provide high availability and partition tolerance. These *conflict-free replicated data types* (CRDTs) utilize mechanisms to resolve the effects of concurrent updates to replicated data. Naturally these objects weaken their consistency guarantees to achieve availability and partition-tolerance, and various notions of *weak consistency* capture those guarantees.

In this work we study the tractability of CRDT-consistency checking. To capture guarantees precisely, and facilitate symbolic reasoning, we propose novel logical characterizations. By developing novel reductions from propositional satisfiability problems, and novel consistency-checking algorithms, we discover both positive and negative results. In particular, we show intractability for replicated flags, sets, counters, and registers, yet tractability for replicated growable arrays. Furthermore, we demonstrate that tractability can be redeemed for registers when each value is written at most once, for counters when the number of replicas is fixed, and for sets and flags when the number of replicas and variables is fixed.

1 Introduction

Recent distributed systems have introduced variations of familiar abstract data types (ADTs) like counters, registers, flags, and sets, that provide high availability and partition tolerance. These *conflict-free replicated data types* (CRDTs) [33] efficiently resolve the effects of concurrent updates to replicated data. Naturally they weaken consistency guarantees to achieve availability and partition-tolerance, and various notions of *weak consistency* capture such guarantees [8,11,29,35,36].

In this work we study the tractability of CRDT consistency checking; Fig. 1 summarizes our results. In particular, we consider *runtime verification*: deciding

This work is supported in part by the European Research Council (ERC) under the European Union's Horizon 2020 research and innovation programme (grant agreement No 678177).

I. Dillig and S. Tasiran (Eds.): CAV 2019, LNCS 11562, pp. 324–343, 2019.
https://doi.org/10.1007/978-3-030-25543-5_19

Data Types	Complexity
Add-Wins Set, Remove-Wins Set	NP-complete
Enable-Wins Flag, Disable-Wins Flag	NP-complete
Sets & Flags — with bounded domains	PTIME
Last-Writer-Wins Register (LWW)	NP-complete
Multi-Value Register (MVR)	NP-complete
Registers – with unique values	PTIME
Replicated Counters	NP-complete
Counters – with bounded replicas	PTIME
Replicated Growable Array (RGA)	PTIME

Fig. 1. The complexity of consistency checking for various replicated data types. We demonstrate intractability and tractability results in Sects. 3 and 4, respectively.

whether a given execution of a CRDT is consistent with its ADT specification. This problem is particularly relevant as distributed-system testing tools like Jepsen [25] are appearing; without efficient, general consistency-checking algorithms, such tools could be limited to specialized classes of errors like node crashes.

Our setting captures executions across a set of replicas as per-replica sequences of operations called *histories*. Roughly speaking, a history is *consistent* so long as each operation's return value can be justified according to the operations that its replica has observed so far. In the setting of CRDTs, the determination of a replica's observations is essentially an implementation choice: replicas are only obliged to observe their own operations, and the predecessors of those it has already observed. This relatively-weak constraint on replicas' observations makes the CRDT consistency checking problem unique.

Our study proceeds in three parts. First, to precisely characterize the consistency of various CRDTs, and facilitate symbolic reasoning, we develop novel logical characterizations to capture their guarantees. Our logical models are built on a notion of *abstract execution*, which relates the operations of a given history with three separate relations: a *read-from* relation, governing the observations from which a given operation constitutes its own return value; a *happens-before* relation, capturing the causal relationships among operations; and a *linearization* relation, capturing any necessary arbitration among non-commutative effects which are executed concurrently, e.g., following a *last-writer-wins* policy. Accordingly, we capture data type specifications with logical axioms interpreted over the read-from, happens-before, and linearization relations of abstract executions, reducing the consistency problem to: does there exist an abstract execution over the given history which satisfies the axioms of the given data type?

Second, we demonstrate the intractability of several replicated data types by reduction from propositional satisfiability (SAT) problems. In particular, we consider the 1-in-3 SAT problem [19], which asks for a truth assignment to the variables of a given set of clauses such that exactly one literal per clause is assigned true. Our reductions essentially simulate the existential choice of a truth assignment with the existential choice of the read-from and happens-before relations of an abstract execution. For a given 1-in-3 SAT instance, we construct a history of replicas obeying carefully-tailored synchronization protocols, which is consistent exactly when the corresponding SAT instance is positive.

Third, we develop tractable consistency-checking algorithms for individual data types and special cases: replicated growing arrays; multi-value and last-writer-wins registers, when each value is written only once; counters, when replicas are bounded; and sets and flags, when their sizes are also bounded. While the algorithms for each case are tailored to the algebraic properties of the data types they handle, they essentially all function by constructing abstract executions incrementally, processing replicas' operations in prefix order.

The remainder of this article is organized around our three key contributions:

1. We develop novel logical characterizations of consistency for the replicated register, flag, set, counter, and array data types (Sect. 2);
2. We develop novel reductions from propositional satisfiability problems to consistency checking to demonstrate intractability for replicated flags, sets, counters, and registers (Sect. 3); and
3. We develop tractable consistency-checking algorithms for replicated growable arrays, registers, when written values are unique, counters, when replicas are bounded, and sets and flags, when their sizes are also bounded (Sects. 4–6).

Section 7 overviews related work, and Sect. 8 concludes.

2 A Logical Characterization of Replicated Data Types

In this section we describe an axiomatic framework for defining the semantics of replicated data types. We consider a set of method names $\mathbb{M}$, and that each method $\mathsf{m} \in \mathbb{M}$ has a number of arguments and a return value sampled from a data domain $\mathbb{D}$. We will use operation labels of the form $\mathsf{m}(a) \stackrel{i}{\Rightarrow} b$ to represent the call of a method $\mathsf{m} \in \mathbb{M}$, with argument $a \in \mathbb{D}$, and resulting in the value $b \in \mathbb{D}$. Since there might be multiple calls to the same method with the same arguments and result, labels are tagged with a unique identifier i. We will ignore identifiers when unambiguous.

The interaction between a data type implementation and a client is represented by a *history* $h = \langle \mathsf{Op}, \mathsf{ro} \rangle$ which consists of a set of operation labels Op and a partial *replica order* ro ordering operations issued by the client on the same replica. Usually, ro is a union of sequences, each sequence representing the operations issued on the same replica, and the *width* of ro, i.e., the maximum number of mutually-unordered operations, gives the number of replicas in a given history.

To characterize the set of histories $h = \langle \mathsf{Op}, \mathsf{ro} \rangle$ admitted by a certain replicated data type, we use *abstract executions* $e = \langle \mathsf{rf}, \mathsf{hb}, \mathsf{lin} \rangle$, which include:

- a *read-from* binary relation rf over operations in Op, which identifies the set of updates needed to "explain" a certain return value, e.g., a write operation explaining the return value of a read,
- a strict partial *happens-before* order hb, which includes ro and rf, representing the causality constraints in an execution, and
- a strict total *linearization* order lin, which includes hb, used to model conflict resolution policies based on timestamps.

In this work, we consider replicated data types which satisfy *causal consistency* [26], i.e., updates which are related by cause and effect relations are observed by all replicas in the same order. This follows from the fact that the happens-before order is constrained to be a partial order, and thus transitive (other forms of weak consistency don't pose this constraint). Some of the replicated data types we consider in this paper do *not* consider resolution policies based on timestamps and in those cases, the linearization order can be ignored.

<u>ReadFrom(*R*)</u>

$\forall o_1, o_2.\ \mathsf{rf}(o_1, o_2) \Rightarrow R(o_1, o_2)$

<u>ReadFromMaximal(*R*)</u>

$\forall o_1, o_2, o_3.\ \mathsf{rf}(o_1, o_2) \wedge R(o_3, o_2) \Rightarrow \neg\mathsf{hb}(o_1, o_3) \vee \neg\mathsf{hb}(o_3, o_2)$

<u>ReadAllMaximals(*R*)</u>

$\forall o_1, o_2.\ \mathsf{hb}(o_1, o_2) \wedge R(o_1, o_2) \Rightarrow \exists o_3.\ \mathsf{hb}^*(o_1, o_3) \wedge \mathsf{rf}(o_3, o_2)$

<u>ClosedRF(*R*)</u>

$\forall o_1, o_2, o_3.\ R(o_1, o_2) \wedge \mathsf{hb}(o_1, o_3) \wedge \mathsf{rf}(o_3, o_2) \Rightarrow \mathsf{rf}(o_1, o_2)$

<u>RetvalSet(*X*, *v*, *Y*)</u>

$\forall o_1.\ \mathsf{meth}(o_1) = X \wedge \mathsf{ret}(o_1) = v \Leftrightarrow \exists o_2.\ \mathsf{rf}(o_2, o_1) \wedge \mathsf{meth}(o_2) = Y \wedge \mathsf{arg}(o_1) = \mathsf{arg}(o_2)$

<u>RetvalCounter</u>

$\forall o_1.\ \mathsf{meth}(o_1) = \mathsf{read} \Rightarrow \mathsf{ret}(o_1) = |\{o_2 : \mathsf{meth}(o_2) = \mathsf{inc} \wedge \mathsf{rf}(o_2, o_1)\}| - |\{o_2 : \mathsf{meth}(o_2) = \mathsf{dec} \wedge \mathsf{rf}(o_2, o_1)\}|$

<u>LinLWW</u>

$\forall o_1, o_2, o_3.\ \mathsf{rf}(o_1, o_2) \wedge \mathsf{meth}(o_3) = \mathsf{write} \wedge \mathsf{arg}_1(o_3) = \mathsf{arg}(o_2) \wedge \mathsf{hb}(o_3, o_2) \Rightarrow \mathsf{lin}(o_3, o_1)$

<u>RetvalReg</u>

$\forall o_1, v. \mathsf{meth}(o_1) = \mathsf{read} \wedge v \in \mathsf{ret}(o_1) \Rightarrow \exists! o_2. \mathsf{rf}(o_2, o_1) \wedge \mathsf{meth}(o_2) = \mathsf{write} \wedge \mathsf{arg}_2(o_2) = v$

Fig. 2. The axiomatic semantics of replicated data types. Quantified variables are implicitly distinct, and $\exists! o$ denotes the existence of a unique operation o.

A *replicated data type* is defined by a set of first-order axioms Φ characterizing the relations in an abstract execution. A history h is *admitted* by a data type when there exists an abstract execution e such that $\langle h, e\rangle \models \Phi$. The satisfaction relation $\models$ is defined as usual in first order logic. The *admissibility problem* is the problem of checking whether a history h is admitted by a given data type.

In the following, we define the replicated data types with respect to which we study the complexity of the admissibility problem. The axioms used to define them are listed in Figs. 2 and 3. These axioms use the function symbols meth-od, arg-ument, and ret-urn interpreted over operation labels, whose semantics is self-explanatory.

2.1 Replicated Sets and Flags

The Add-Wins Set and Remove-Wins Set [34] are two implementations of a replicated set with operations $\mathsf{add}(x)$, $\mathsf{remove}(x)$, and $\mathsf{contains}(x)$ for adding, removing, and checking membership of an element x. Although the meaning of these methods is self-evident from their names, the result of conflicting concurrent operations is not evident. When concurrent $\mathsf{add}(x)$ and $\mathsf{remove}(x)$ operations are delivered to a certain replica, the Add-Wins Set chooses to keep the element x in the set, so every subsequent invocation of $\mathsf{contains}(x)$ on this replica returns *true*, while the Remove-Wins Set makes the dual choice of removing x from the set.

The formal definition of their semantics uses abstract executions where the read-from relation associates sets of $\mathsf{add}(x)$ and $\mathsf{remove}(x)$ operations to $\mathsf{contains}(x)$ operations. Therefore, the predicate $\mathsf{ReadOk}(o_1, o_2)$ is defined by

$$\mathsf{meth}(o_1) \in \{\mathsf{add}, \mathsf{remove}\} \wedge \mathsf{meth}(o_2) = \mathsf{contains} \wedge \mathsf{arg}(o_1) = \mathsf{arg}(o_2)$$

and the Add-Wins Set is defined by the following set of axioms:

$$\textsc{ReadFrom}(\mathsf{ReadOk}) \wedge \textsc{ReadFromMaximal}(\mathsf{ReadOk}) \wedge$$
$$\textsc{ReadAllMaximals}(\mathsf{ReadOk}) \wedge \textsc{RetvalSet}(\mathsf{contains}, \mathit{true}, \mathsf{add})$$

ReadFromMaximal says that every operation read by a $\mathsf{contains}(x)$ is maximal among its hb-predecessors that add or remove x while ReadAllMaximals says that all such maximal hb-predecessors are read. The RetvalSet instantiation ensures that a $\mathsf{contains}(x)$ returns *true* iff it reads-from at least one $\mathsf{add}(x)$.

The definition of the Remove-Wins Set is similar, except for the parameters of RetvalSet, which become $\textsc{RetvalSet}(\mathsf{contains}, \mathit{false}, \mathsf{remove})$, i.e., a $\mathsf{contains}(x)$ returns *false* iff it reads-from at least one $\mathsf{remove}(x)$.

The Enable-Wins Flag and Disable-Wins Flag are implementations of a set of flags with operations: $\mathsf{enable}(x)$, $\mathsf{disable}(x)$, and $\mathsf{read}(x)$, where $\mathsf{enable}(x)$ turns the flag x to true, $\mathsf{disable}(x)$ turns x to false, while $\mathsf{read}(x)$ returns the state of the flag x. Their semantics is similar to the Add-Wins Set and Remove-Wins Set, respectively, where $\mathsf{enable}(x)$, $\mathsf{disable}(x)$, and $\mathsf{read}(x)$ play the role of $\mathsf{add}(x)$, $\mathsf{remove}(x)$, and $\mathsf{contains}(x)$, respectively. Their axioms are defined as above.

2.2 Replicated Registers

We consider two variations of replicated registers called Multi-Value Register (MVR) and Last-Writer-Wins Register (LWW) [34] which maintain a set of registers and provide $\mathsf{write}(x,v)$ operations for writing a value v on a register x and $\mathsf{read}(x)$ operations for reading the content of a register x (the domain of values is kept unspecified since it is irrelevant). While a $\mathsf{read}(x)$ operation of

MVR returns *all* the values written by concurrent writes which are maximal among its happens-before predecessors, therefore, leaving the responsibility for solving conflicts between concurrent writes to the client, a $\mathsf{read}(x)$ operation of LWW returns a single value chosen using a conflict-resolution policy based on timestamps. Each written value is associated to a timestamp, and a read operation returns the most recent value w.r.t. the timestamps. This order between timestamps is modeled using the linearization order of an abstract execution.

Therefore, the predicate $\mathsf{ReadOk}(o_1, o_2)$ is defined by

$$\mathsf{meth}(o_1) = \mathsf{write} \wedge \mathsf{meth}(o_2) = \mathsf{read} \wedge \mathsf{arg}_1(o_1) = \mathsf{arg}(o_2) \wedge \mathsf{arg}_2(o_1) \in \mathsf{ret}(o_2)$$

(we use $\mathsf{arg}_1(o_1)$ to denote the first argument of a write operation, i.e., the register name, and $\mathsf{arg}_2(o_1)$ to denote its second argument, i.e., the written value) and the MVR is defined by the following set of axioms:

$$\textsc{ReadFrom}(\mathsf{ReadOk}) \wedge \textsc{ReadFromMaximal}(\mathsf{ReadOk}) \wedge$$
$$\textsc{ReadAllMaximals}(\mathsf{ReadOk}) \wedge \textsc{RetvalReg}$$

where RETVALREG ensures that a $\mathsf{read}(x)$ operation reads from a $\mathsf{write}(x,v)$ operation, for each value v in the set of returned values[1].

LWW is obtained from the definition of MVR by replacing READALLMAXIMALS with the axiom LINLWW which ensures that every $\mathsf{write}(x,\_)$ operation which happens-before a $\mathsf{read}(x)$ operation is linearized before the $\mathsf{write}(x,\_)$ operation from where the $\mathsf{read}(x)$ takes its value (when these two write operations are different). This definition of LWW is inspired by the "bad-pattern" characterization in [6], corresponding to their causal convergence criterion.

2.3 Replicated Counters

The replicated counter datatype [34] maintains a set of counters interpreted as integers (the counters can become negative). This datatype provides operations $\mathsf{inc}(x)$ and $\mathsf{dec}(x)$ for incrementing and decrementing a counter x, and $\mathsf{read}(x)$ operations to read the value of the counter x. The semantics of the replicated counter is quite standard: a $\mathsf{read}(x)$ operation returns the value computed as the difference between the number of $\mathsf{inc}(x)$ operations and $\mathsf{dec}(x)$ operations among its happens-before predecessors. The axioms defined below will enforce the fact that a $\mathsf{read}(x)$ operation reads-from all its happens-before predecessors which are $\mathsf{inc}(x)$ or $\mathsf{dec}(x)$ operations.

Therefore, the predicate $\mathsf{ReadOk}(o_1, o_2)$ is defined by

$$\mathsf{meth}(o_1) \in \{\mathsf{inc}, \mathsf{dec}\} \wedge \mathsf{meth}(o_2) = \mathsf{read} \wedge \mathsf{arg}(o_1) = \mathsf{arg}(o_2)$$

and the replicated counter is defined by the following set of axioms:

$$\textsc{ReadFrom}(\mathsf{ReadOk}) \wedge \textsc{ClosedRF}(\mathsf{ReadOk}) \wedge \textsc{RetvalCounter}.$$

---

[1] For simplicity, we assume that every history contains a set of write operations writing the initial values of variables, which precede every other operation in replica order.

READFROMRGA

$$\forall o_2.\ \mathsf{meth}(o_2) = \mathsf{addAfter} \Rightarrow \mathsf{arg}_1(o_2) = \circ \lor$$
$$\exists o_1.\ \mathsf{meth}(o_1) = \mathsf{addAfter} \land \mathsf{arg}_2(o_1) = \mathsf{arg}_1(o_2) \land \mathsf{rf}(o_1, o_2)$$
$$\land\ \mathsf{meth}(o_2) = \mathsf{remove} \Rightarrow \exists o_1.\ \mathsf{meth}(o_1) = \mathsf{addAfter} \land \mathsf{arg}_2(o_1) = \mathsf{arg}(o_2) \land \mathsf{rf}(o_1, o_2)$$
$$\land\ \mathsf{meth}(o_2) = \mathsf{read} \Rightarrow \forall v \in \mathsf{ret}(o_2)\ \exists o_1.\mathsf{meth}(o_1) = \mathsf{addAfter} \land \mathsf{arg}_2(o_1) = v \land \mathsf{rf}(o_1, o_2)$$

RETVALRGA

$$\forall o_1, o_2.\ \mathsf{meth}(o_1) = \mathsf{read} \land \mathsf{meth}(o_2) = \mathsf{addAfter} \land \mathsf{hb}(o_2, o_1) \land \mathsf{arg}_2(o_2) \notin \mathsf{ret}(o_1)$$
$$\Rightarrow \exists o_3.\ \mathsf{meth}(o_3) = \mathsf{remove} \land \mathsf{arg}(o_3) = \mathsf{arg}_2(o_2) \land \mathsf{rf}(o_3, o_1)$$

LINRGA

$$\forall o_1, o_2.\ (\mathsf{meth}(o_1) = \mathsf{meth}(o_2) = \mathsf{addAfter} \land \mathsf{arg}_1(o_1) = \mathsf{arg}_1(o_2) \land$$
$$\exists o_3, o_4, o_5.\ \mathsf{meth}(o_3) = \mathsf{meth}(o_4) = \mathsf{addAfter} \land \mathsf{rf}^*_{\mathsf{addAfter}}(o_1, o_3) \land \mathsf{rf}^*_{\mathsf{addAfter}}(o_2, o_4) \land$$
$$\mathsf{meth}(o_5) = \mathsf{read} \land \mathsf{arg}_2(o_4) <_{o_5} \mathsf{arg}_2(o_3)) \Rightarrow \mathsf{lin}(o_1, o_2)$$

Fig. 3. Axioms used to define the semantics of RGA.

2.4 Replicated Growable Array

The Replicated Growing Array (RGA) [32] is a replicated list used for text-editing applications. RGA supports three operations: addAfter(a,b) which adds the character b immediately after the occurrence of the character a assumed to be present in the list, remove(a) which removes a assumed to be present in the list, and read() which returns the list contents. It is assumed that a character is added at most once[2]. The conflicts between concurrent addAfter operations that add a character immediately after the same character is solved using timestamps (i.e., each added character is associated to a timestamp and the order between characters depends on the order between the corresponding timestamps), which in the axioms below are modeled by the linearization order.

Figure 3 lists the axioms defining RGA. READFROMRGA ensures that:

- every addAfter(a,b) operation reads-from the addAfter(_,a) adding the character a, except when $a = \circ$ which denotes the "root" element of the list[3],
- every remove(a) operation reads-from the operation adding a, and
- every read operation returning a list containing a reads-from the operation addAfter(_,a) adding a.

Then, RETVALRGA ensures that a read operation o_1 happening-after an operation adding a character a reads-from a remove(a) operation when a doesn't occur in the list returned by o_1 (the history must contain a remove(a) operation because otherwise, a should have occurred in the list returned by the read).

Finally, LINRGA models the conflict resolution policy by constraining the linearization order between addAfter(a,_) operations adding some character

[2] In a practical context, this can be enforced by tagging characters with replica identifiers and sequence numbers.

[3] This element is not returned by read operations.

immediately after the same character a. As a particular case, LinRGA enforces that addAfter(a,b) is linearized before addAfter(a,c) when a read operation returns a list where c precedes b (addAfter(a,b) results in the list $a \cdot b$ and applying addAfter(a,c) on $a \cdot b$ results in the list $a \cdot c \cdot b$). However, this is not sufficient: assume that the history contains the two operations addAfter(a,b) and addAfter(a,c) along with two operations remove(b) and addAfter(b,d). Then, a read operation returning the list $a \cdot c \cdot d$ must enforce that addAfter(a,b) is linearized before addAfter(a,c) because this is the only order between these two operations that can lead to the result $a \cdot c \cdot d$, i.e., executing addAfter(a,b), addAfter(b,d), remove(b), addAfter(a,c) in this order. LinRGA deals with any scenario where arbitrarily-many characters can be removed from the list: $\mathsf{rf}^*_{\mathsf{addAfter}}$ is the reflexive and transitive closure of the projection of rf on addAfter operations and $<_{o_5}$ denotes the order between characters in the list returned by the read operation o_5.

3 Intractability for Registers, Sets, Flags, and Counters

In this section we demonstrate that checking the consistency is intractable for many widely-used data types. While this is not completely unexpected, since some related consistency-checking problems like sequential consistency are also intractable [20], this contrasts recent tractability results for checking strong consistency (i.e., linearizability) of common non-replicated data types like sets, maps, and queues [15]. In fact, in many cases we show that intractability even holds if the number of replicas is fixed.

Our proofs of intractability follow the general structure of Gibbons and Korach's proofs for the intractability of checking sequential consistency (SC) for atomic registers with read and write operations [20]. In particular, we reduce a specialized type of NP-hard propositional satisfiability (SAT) problem to checking whether histories are admitted by a given data type. While our construction borrows from Gibbons and Korach's, the adaptation from SC to CRDT consistency requires a significant extension to handle the consistency relaxation represented by abstract executions: rather than a direct sequencing of threads' operations, CRDT consistency requires the construction of three separate relations: read-from, happens-before, and linearization.

Technically, our reductions start from the 1-in-3 SAT problem [19]: given a propositional formula $\bigwedge_{i=1}^{m}(\alpha_i \vee \beta_i \vee \gamma_i)$ over variables $x_1, \ldots, x_n$ with only positive literals, i.e., $\alpha_i, \beta_i, \gamma_i \in \{x_1, \ldots, x_n\}$, does there exist an assignment to the variables such that exactly one of $\alpha_i, \beta_i, \gamma_i$ per clause is assigned *true*? The proofs of Theorems 1 and 2 reduce 1-in-3 SAT to CRDT consistency checking.

Theorem 1. *The admissibility problem is NP-hard when the number of replicas is fixed for the following data types: Add-Wins Set, Remove-Wins Set, Enable-Wins Flag, Disable-Wins Flag, Multi-Value Register, and Last-Writer-Wins Register.*

	Replica 0	Replica 1	Replica 2
Round 0	Enable(x_1) ... Enable(x_n)	Disable(x_1) ... Disable(x_n)	
Barrier 1	Enable(y_0) Read(y_1) = *true* Read(y_2) = *true*	Enable(y_1) Read(y_0) = *true* Read(y_2) = *true*	Enable(y_2) Read(y_0) = *true* Read(y_1) = *true*
Round 1	Read(α_1) = *true* Read(β_1) = *false* Read(γ_1) = *false* Disable(α_1) Enable(β_1)	Read(α_1) = *false* Read(β_1) = *true* Read(γ_1) = *false* Disable(β_1) Enable(γ_1)	Read(α_1) = *false* Read(β_1) = *false* Read(γ_1) = *true* Disable(γ_1) Enable(α_1)
Barrier 2	Disable(y_0) Read(y_1) = *false* Read(y_2) = *false*	Disable(y_1) Read(y_0) = *false* Read(y_2) = *false*	Disable(y_2) Read(y_0) = *false* Read(y_1) = *false*
	...	...	...
Round m	Read(α_m) = *true* Read(β_m) = *false* Read(γ_m) = *false* Disable(α_m) Enable(β_m)	Read(α_m) = *false* Read(β_m) = *true* Read(γ_m) = *false* Disable(β_m) Enable(γ_m)	Read(α_m) = *false* Read(β_m) = *false* Read(γ_m) = *true* Disable(γ_m) Enable(α_m)

Fig. 4. The encoding of a 1-in-3 SAT problem $\bigwedge_{i=1}^{m}(\alpha_i \vee \beta_i \vee \gamma_i)$ over variables $x_1, \ldots, x_n$ as a 3-replica history of a flag data type. Besides the flag variable x_j for each propositional variable x_j, the encoding adds per-replica variables y_j for synchronization barriers.

Proof. We demonstrate a reduction from the 1-in-3 SAT problem. For a given problem $p = \bigwedge_{i=1}^{m}(\alpha_i \vee \beta_i \vee \gamma_i)$ over variables $x_1, \ldots, x_n$, we construct a 3-replica history h_p of the flag data type — either enable- or disable-wins — as illustrated in Fig. 4. The encoding includes a flag variable x_j for each propositional variable x_j, along with a per-replica flag variable y_j used to implement synchronization barriers. Intuitively, executions of h_p proceed in $m + 1$ rounds: the first round corresponds to the assignment of a truth valuation, while subsequent rounds check the validity of each clause given the assignment. The reductions to sets and registers are slight variations on this proof, in which the Read, Enable, and Disable operations are replaced with Contains, Add, and Remove, respectively, and Read and Writes of values 1 and 0, respectively.

It suffices to show that the constructed history h_p is admitted if and only if the given problem p is satisfiable. Since the flag data type does not constrain the linearization relation of its abstract executions, we regard only the read-from and happens-before components. It is straightforward to verify that the happens-before relations of h_p's abstract executions necessarily order:

1. every pair of operations in distinct rounds — due to barriers; and
2. every operation in a given round, over all replicas, without interleaving the operations of distinct replicas within the same round — since a replica's reads in a given round are only consistent with the other replicas' after the re-enabling and -disabling of flag variables.

In other words, replicas appear to execute atomically per round, in a round-robin fashion. Furthermore, since all operations in a given round happen before the operations of subsequent rounds, the values of flag variables are consistent across rounds —i.e., as read by the first replica to execute in a given round — and determined in the initial round either by conflict resolution — i.e., enable- or disable-wins — or by happens-before, in case conflict resolution would have been inconsistent with subsequent reads.

In the "if" direction, let $\boldsymbol{r} \in \{0, 1, 2\}^m$ be the positions of positively-assigned variables in each clause, e.g., $r_i = 0$ implies $\alpha_i = \mathit{true}$ and $\beta_i = \gamma_i = \mathit{false}$. We construct an abstract execution $e_{\boldsymbol{r}}$ in which the happens-before relation sequences the operations of replica r_i before those of $r_i + 1 \bmod 3$, and in turn before $r_i + 2 \bmod 3$. In other words, the replicas in round i appear to execute in left-to-right order from starting with the replica r_i, whose reads correspond to the satisfying assignment of $(\alpha_i \vee \beta_i \vee \gamma_i)$. The read-from relation of $e_{\boldsymbol{r}}$ relates each $\mathrm{Read}(x_j) = \mathit{true}$ operation to the most recent $\mathrm{Enable}(x_j)$ operation in happens-before order, which is unique since happens-before sequences the operations of all rounds; the case for $\mathrm{Read}(x_j) = \mathit{false}$ and $\mathrm{Disable}(x_j)$ is symmetric. It is then straightforward to verify that $e_{\boldsymbol{r}}$ satisfies the axioms of the enable- or disable-wins flag, and thus h_p is admitted.

In the "only if" direction, let e be an abstract execution of h_p, and let $\boldsymbol{r} \in \{0, 1, 2\}^m$ be the replicas first to execute in each round according to the happens-before order of e. It is straightforward to verify that the assignment in which a given variable is set to true iff the replica encoding its positive assignment in some clause executes first in its round, i.e.,

$$x_j = \begin{cases} \mathit{true} & \text{if } \exists i.(r_i = 0 \wedge \alpha_i = x_j) \vee (r_i = 1 \wedge \beta_i = x_j) \vee (r_i = 2 \wedge \gamma_i = x_j) \\ \mathit{false} & \text{otherwise,} \end{cases}$$

is a satisfying assignment to p. □

Theorem 1 establishes intractability of consistency for the aforementioned sets, flags, and registers, independently from the number of replicas. In contrast, our proof of Theorem 2 for counter data types depends on the number of replicas, since our encoding requires two replicas per propositional variable. Intuitively, since counter increments and decrements are commutative, the initial round in the previous encoding would have fixed all counter values to zero. Instead, the next encoding isolates initial increments and decrements to independent replicas. The weaker result is indeed tight since checking counter consistency with a fixed number of replicas is polynomial time, as Sect. 5 demonstrates.

Theorem 2. *The admissibility problem for the Counter data type is NP-hard.*

Proof. We demonstrate a reduction from the 1-in-3 SAT problem. For a given problem $p = \bigwedge_{i=1}^{m} (\alpha_i \vee \beta_i \vee \gamma_i)$ over variables $x_1, \ldots, x_n$, we construct a history h_p of the counter data type over $2n + 3$ replicas, as illustrated in Fig. 5.

Besides the differences imposed due to the commutativity of counter increments and decrements, our reduction follows the same strategy as in the proof of

Theorem 1: the happens-before relation of h_p's abstract executions order every pair of operations in distinct rounds (of Replicas 0–2), and every operation in a given (non-initial) round. As before, Replicas 0–2 appear to execute atomically per round, in a round-robin fashion, and counter variables are consistent across rounds. The key difference is that here abstract executions' happens-before relations only relate the operations of either Replica $2j+1$ or $2j+2$, for each $j = 1, \ldots, n$, to operations in subsequent rounds: the other's operations are never observed by other replicas. Our encoding ensures that exactly one of each is observed by ensuring that the counter y is incremented exactly n times — and relying on the fact that every variable appears in some clause, so that a read that observed neither or both would yield the value zero, which is inconsistent with h_p. Otherwise, our reasoning follows the proof of Theorem 1, in which the read-from relation selects all increments and decrements of the same counter variable in happens-before order. □

4 Polynomial-Time Algorithms for Registers and Arrays

We show that the problem of checking consistency is polynomial time for RGA, and even for LWW and MVR under the assumption that each value is written at most once, i.e., for each value v, the input history contains at most one write operation write(x,v). Histories satisfying this assumption are called *differentiated.* The latter is a restriction motivated by the fact that practical implementations of these datatypes are data-independent [38], i.e., their behavior doesn't depend on the concrete values read or written and any potential buggy behavior can be exposed in executions where each value is written at most once. Also, in a testing environment, this restriction can be enforced by tagging each value with a replica identifier and a sequence number.

In all three cases, the feature that enables polynomial time consistency checking is the fact that the read-from relation becomes fixed for a given history, i.e., if the history is consistent, then there exists exactly one read-from relation rf that satisfies the ReadFrom_ and Retval_ axioms, and rf can be derived syntactically from the operation labels (using those axioms). Then, our axiomatic characterizations enable a consistency checking algorithm which roughly, consists in instantiating those axioms in order to compute an abstract execution.

The consistency checking algorithm for RGA, LWW, and MVR is listed in Algorithm 1. It computes the three relations rf, hb, and lin of an abstract execution using the datatype's axioms. The history is declared consistent iff there exist satisfying rf and hb relations, and the relations hb and lin computed this way are acyclic. The acyclicity requirement comes from the definition of abstract executions where hb and lin are required to be partial/total orders. While an abstract execution would require that lin is a total order, this algorithm computes a partial linearization order. However, any total order compatible with this partial linearization would satisfy the axioms of the datatype.

ComputeRF computes the read-from relation rf satisfying the ReadFrom_ and Retval_ axioms. In the case of LWW and MVR, it defines rf as the set

	Replica 0	Replica $2j+1$	Replica $2j+2$
Round 0		$\mathrm{Inc}(y)$ $\mathrm{Inc}(x_j)$	$\mathrm{Inc}(y)$ $\mathrm{Dec}(x_j)$
	$\mathrm{Read}(y) = n$		
		Replica 1	**Replica 2**
Barrier 1	$\mathrm{Inc}(z)$ $\mathrm{Read}(z) = 3$	$\mathrm{Inc}(z)$ $\mathrm{Read}(z) = 3$	$\mathrm{Inc}(z)$ $\mathrm{Read}(z) = 3$
Round 1	$\mathrm{Read}(\alpha_1) = 1$ $\mathrm{Read}(\beta_1) = -1$ $\mathrm{Read}(\gamma_1) = -1$ $\mathrm{Dec}(\alpha_1)$; $\mathrm{Dec}(\alpha_1)$ $\mathrm{Inc}(\beta_1)$; $\mathrm{Inc}(\beta_1)$	$\mathrm{Read}(\alpha_1) = -1$ $\mathrm{Read}(\beta_1) = 1$ $\mathrm{Read}(\gamma_1) = -1$ $\mathrm{Dec}(\beta_1)$; $\mathrm{Dec}(\beta_1)$ $\mathrm{Inc}(\gamma_1)$; $\mathrm{Inc}(\gamma_1)$	$\mathrm{Read}(\alpha_1) = -1$ $\mathrm{Read}(\beta_1) = -1$ $\mathrm{Read}(\gamma_1) = 1$ $\mathrm{Dec}(\gamma_1)$; $\mathrm{Dec}(\gamma_1)$ $\mathrm{Inc}(\alpha_1)$; $\mathrm{Inc}(\alpha_1)$
Barrier 2	$\mathrm{Dec}(z)$ $\mathrm{Read}(z) = 0$	$\mathrm{Dec}(z)$ $\mathrm{Read}(z) = 0$	$\mathrm{Dec}(z)$ $\mathrm{Read}(z) = 0$
	...	...	...
Round m	$\mathrm{Read}(\alpha_m) = 1$ $\mathrm{Read}(\beta_m) = -1$ $\mathrm{Read}(\gamma_m) = -1$ $\mathrm{Dec}(\alpha_m)$; $\mathrm{Dec}(\alpha_m)$ $\mathrm{Inc}(\beta_m)$; $\mathrm{Inc}(\beta_m)$	$\mathrm{Read}(\alpha_m) = -1$ $\mathrm{Read}(\beta_m) = 1$ $\mathrm{Read}(\gamma_m) = -1$ $\mathrm{Dec}(\beta_m)$; $\mathrm{Dec}(\beta_m)$ $\mathrm{Inc}(\gamma_m)$; $\mathrm{Inc}(\gamma_m)$	$\mathrm{Read}(\alpha_m) = -1$ $\mathrm{Read}(\beta_m) = -1$ $\mathrm{Read}(\gamma_m) = 1$ $\mathrm{Dec}(\gamma_m)$; $\mathrm{Dec}(\gamma_m)$ $\mathrm{Inc}(\alpha_m)$; $\mathrm{Inc}(\alpha_m)$
Barrier $m+1$	$\mathrm{Inc}(z)$ or $\mathrm{Dec}(z)$ $\mathrm{Read}(z) = 3$ or 0	$\mathrm{Inc}(z)$ or $\mathrm{Dec}(z)$ $\mathrm{Read}(z) = 3$ or 0	$\mathrm{Inc}(z)$ or $\mathrm{Dec}(z)$ $\mathrm{Read}(z) = 3$ or 0
Round $m+1$	$\mathrm{Read}(y) = n$		

Fig. 5. The encoding of a 1-in-3 SAT problem $\bigwedge_{i=1}^{m}(\alpha_i \vee \beta_i \vee \gamma_i)$ over variables $x_1, \ldots, x_n$ as the history of a counter over $2n+3$ replicas. Besides the counter variables x_j encoding propositional variables x_j, the encoding adds a variable y encoding the number of initial increments and decrements, and a variable z to implement synchronization barriers.

of all pairs formed of $\mathsf{write}(x,v)$ and $\mathsf{read}(x)$ operations where v belongs to the return value of the read. By RETVAL$_{-}$, each $\mathsf{read}(x)$ operation must be associated to at least one $\mathsf{write}(x,\_)$ operation. Also, the fact that each value is written at most once implies that this rf relation is uniquely defined, e.g., for LWW, it is not possible to find two write operations that could be rf related to the same read operation. In general, if there exists no rf relation satisfying these axioms, then $\mathsf{ComputeRF}$ returns a distinguished value $\bot$ to signal a consistency violation. Note that the computation of the read-from for LWW and MVR is quadratic time[4] since the constraints imposed by the axioms relate only to the operation labels, the methods they invoke or their arguments. The case of RGA is slightly more involved because the axiom RETVALRGA introduces more read-from constraints based on the happens-before order which includes ro and the rf itself. In this case, the computation of rf relies on a fixpoint computation, which converges in at most quadratic time (the maximal size of rf), described in Algorithm 2. Essentially, we use the axiom READFROMRGA to populate the

[4] Assuming constant time lookup/insert operations (e.g., using hashmaps), this complexity is linear time.

Input: A differentiated history $h = \langle \mathsf{Op}, \mathsf{ro} \rangle$ and a datatype T.
Output: *true* iff h satisfies the axioms of T.

```
rf ← ComputeRF(h, ReadFrom[T], RetVal[T] );
if rf = ⊥ then return false;
hb ← (ro ∪ rf)⁺;
if hb is cyclic or ⟨h, rf, hb⟩ ⊭ ReadFromMaximal[T] ∧ ReadAllMaximals[T]
then
    return false;
lin ← hb;
lin ← LinClosure(hb, Lin[T]);
if lin is cyclic then return false;
return true;
```

Algorithm 1. Consistency checking for RGA, LWW, and MVR. RE... $[T]$ refers to an axiom of T, or *true* when T lacks such an axiom. The relation R^+ denotes the transitive closure of R.

read-from relation and then, apply the axiom RETVALRGA iteratively, using the read-from constraints added in previous steps, until the computation converges.

After computing the read-from relation, our algorithm defines the happens-before relation hb as the transitive closure of ro union rf. This is sound because none of the axioms of these datatypes enforce new happens-before constraints, which are not already captured by ro and rf. Then, it checks whether the hb defined this way is acyclic and satisfies the datatype's axioms that constrain hb, i.e., READFROMMAXIMAL and READALLMAXIMALS (when they are present).

Finally, in the case of LWW and RGA, the algorithm computes a (partial) linearization order that satisfies the corresponding LIN_ axioms. Starting from an initial linearization order which is exactly the happens-before, it computes new constraints by instantiating the universally quantified axioms LINLWW and LINRGA. Since these axioms are not "recursive", i.e., they don't enforce linearization order constraints based on other linearization order constraints, a standard instantiation of these axioms is enough to compute a partial linearization order such that any extension to a total order satisfies the datatype's axioms.

Theorem 3. *Algorithm 1 returns true iff the input history is consistent.*

The following holds because Algorithm 1 runs in polynomial time — the rank depends on the number of quantifiers in the datatype's axioms. Indeed, Algorithm 1 represents a least fixpoint computation which converges in at most a quadratic number of iterations (the maximal size of rf).

Corollary 1. *The admissibility problem is polynomial time for RGA, and for LWW and MVR on differentiated histories.*

Input: A history $h = \langle \mathsf{Op}, \mathsf{ro} \rangle$ of RGA.
Output: An rf satisfying ReadFromRGA $\wedge$ RetvalRGA, if exists; $\bot$ o/w

$\mathsf{rf} \leftarrow \{(o_1, o_2) : \mathsf{meth}(o_1) = \mathsf{addAfter}, \mathsf{meth}(o_2) \in \{\mathsf{addAfter}, \mathsf{remove}, \mathsf{read}\}, \mathsf{arg}_2(o_1) = \mathsf{arg}_1(o_2) \vee \mathsf{arg}_2(o_1) \in \mathsf{ret}(o_2)\}$;
if $\langle h, \mathsf{rf} \rangle \not\models$ ReadFromRGA **then return** $\bot$;
while *true* **do**
  $\mathsf{rf}_1 \leftarrow \emptyset$;
  foreach $o_1, o_2 \in \mathsf{Op}$ s.t. $\langle o_2, o_1 \rangle \in (\mathsf{rf} \cup \mathsf{ro})^+$ and $\mathsf{meth}(o_1) = \mathsf{read}$ and $\mathsf{meth}(o_2) = \mathsf{addAfter}$ and $\mathsf{arg}_2(o_2) \notin \mathsf{ret}(o_1)$ **do**
    if $\exists o_3 \in \mathsf{Op}$ s.t. $\mathsf{meth}(o_3) = \mathsf{remove}$ and $\mathsf{arg}(o_3) = \mathsf{arg}_2(o_2)$ **then**
      $\mathsf{rf}_1 \leftarrow \mathsf{rf}_1 \cup \{\langle o_3, o_1 \rangle\}$;
    else
      return $\bot$;
  if $\mathsf{rf}_1 \subseteq \mathsf{rf}$ **then break**;
  else $\mathsf{rf} \leftarrow \mathsf{rf} \cup \mathsf{rf}_1$;
return rf;

Algorithm 2. The procedure ComputeRF for RGA.

5 Polynomial-Time Algorithms for Replicated Counters

In this section, we show that checking consistency for the replicated counter datatype becomes polynomial time assuming the number of replicas in the input history is fixed (i.e., the width of the replica order ro is fixed). We present an algorithm which constructs a valid happens-before order (note that the semantics of the replicated counter doesn't constrain the linearization order) incrementally, following the replica order. At any time, the happens-before order is uniquely determined by a *prefix mapping* that associates to each replica a *prefix* of the history, i.e., a set of operations which is downward-closed w.r.t. replica order (i.e., if it contains an operation it contains all its ro predecessors). This models the fact that the replica order is included in the happens-before and therefore, if an operation o_1 happens-before another operation o_2, then all the ro predecessors of o_1 happen-before o_2. The happens-before order can be extended in two ways: (1) adding an operation issued on the replica i to the prefix of replica i, or (2) "merging" the prefix of a replica j to the prefix of a replica i (this models the delivery of an operation issued on replica j and all its happens-before predecessors to the replica i). Verifying that an extension of the happens-before is valid, i.e., that the return values of newly-added read operations satisfy the RetvalCounter axiom, doesn't depend on the happens-before order between the operations in the prefix associated to some replica (it is enough to count the inc and dec operations in that prefix). Therefore, the algorithm can be seen as a search in the space of prefix mappings. If the number of replicas in the input history is fixed, then the number of possible prefix mappings is polynomial in the size of the history, which implies that the search can be done in polynomial time.

Let $h = (\mathsf{Op}, \mathsf{ro})$ be a history. To simplify the notations, we assume that the replica order is a union of sequences, each sequence representing the operations

Input: History $h = (\mathsf{Op}, \mathsf{ro})$, prefix map m, and set *seen* of invalid prefix maps
Output: *true* iff there exists read-from and happens-before relations rf and hb such that $m \subseteq \mathsf{hb}$, and $\langle h, \mathsf{rf}, \mathsf{hb}\rangle$ satisfies the counter axioms.

```
if m is complete then return true;
foreach replica i do
    foreach replica j ≠ i do
        m′ ← m[i ← m(i) ∪ m(j)];
        if m′ ∉ seen and checkCounter(h, m′, seen) then
            return true;
        seen ← seen ∪ {m′};
    if ∃o1. ro¹(last_i(m), o1) then
        if meth(o1) = read and
        arg(o1) = x ∧ ret(o1) ≠ |{o ∈ m[i]|o = inc(x)}| − |{o ∈ m[i]|o = dec(x)}|
        then
            return false;
        m′ ← m[i ← m(i) ∪ {o1}];
        if m′ ∉ seen and checkCounter(h, m′, seen) then
            return true;
        seen ← seen ∪ {m′};
return false;
```

Algorithm 3. The procedure $\mathsf{checkCounter}$, where ro^1 denotes immediate ro-successor, and $f[a \leftarrow b]$ updates function f with mapping $a \mapsto b$.

issued on the same replica. Therefore, each operation $o \in \mathsf{Op}$ is associated with a replica identifier $\mathsf{rep}(o) \in [1..n_h]$, where n_h is the number of replicas in h.

A *prefix* of h is a set of operation $\mathsf{Op}' \subseteq \mathsf{Op}$ such that all the ro predecessors of operations in Op' are also in Op', i.e., $\forall o \in \mathsf{Op}.\ \mathsf{ro}^{-1}(o) \in \mathsf{Op}$. Note that the union of two prefixes of h is also a prefix of h. The *last operation* of replica i in a prefix Op' is the ro-maximal operation o with $\mathsf{rep}(o) = i$ included in Op'. A prefix Op' is called *valid* if $(\mathsf{Op}', \mathsf{ro}')$, where ro' is the projection of ro on Op', is admitted by the replicated counter.

A *prefix map* is a mapping m which associates a prefix of h to each replica $i \in [1..n_h]$. Intuitively, a prefix map defines for each replica i the set of operations which are "known" to i, i.e., happen-before the last operation of i in its prefix. Formally, a prefix map m is *included* in a happens-before relation hb, denoted by $m \subseteq \mathsf{hb}$, if for each replica $i \in [1..n_h]$, $\mathsf{hb}(o, o_i)$ for each operation in $o \in m(i) \setminus \{o_i\}$, where o_i is the last operation of i in $m(i)$. We call o_i the *last operation* of i in m, and denoted it by $\mathsf{last}_i(m)$. A prefix map m is *valid* if it associates a valid prefix to each replica, and *complete* if it associates the whole history h to each replica i.

Algorithm 3 lists our algorithm for checking consistency of replicated counter histories. It is defined as a recursive procedure $\mathsf{checkCounter}$ that searches for a sequence of valid extensions of a given prefix map (initially, this prefix map is empty) until it becomes complete. The axiom RetvalCounter is enforced whenever extending the prefix map with a new read operation (when the last operation of a replica i is "advanced" to a read operation). The following theorem states of the correctness of the algorithm.

Theorem 4. checkCounter$(h, \emptyset, \emptyset)$ *returns true iff the input history is consistent.*

When the number of replicas is fixed, the number of prefix maps becomes polynomial in the size of the history. This follows from the fact that prefixes are uniquely defined by their ro-maximal operations, whose number is fixed.

Corollary 2. *The admissibility problem for replicated counters is polynomial-time when the number of replicas is fixed.*

6 Polynomial-Time Algorithms for Sets and Flags

While Theorem 1 shows that the admissibility problem is NP-complete for replicated sets and flags even if the number of replicas is fixed, we show that this problem becomes polynomial time when additionally, the number of values added to the set, or the number of flags, is also fixed. Note that this doesn't limit the number of operations in the input history which can still be arbitrarily large. In the following, we focus on the Add-Wins Set, the other cases being very similar.

We propose an algorithm for checking consistency which is actually an extension of the one presented in Sect. 5 for replicated counters. The additional complexity in checking consistency for the Add-Wins Set comes from the validity of contains(x) return values which requires identifying the maximal predecessors in the happens-before relation that add or remove x (which are not necessarily the maximal hb-predecessors all-together). In the case of counters, it was enough just to count happens-before predecessors. Therefore, we extend the algorithm for replicated counters such that along with the prefix map, we also keep track of the hb-maximal add(x) and remove(x) operations for each element x and each replica i. When extending a prefix map with a contains operation, these hb-maximal operations (which define a witness for the read-from relation) are enough to verify the RetValSet axiom. Extending the prefix of a replica with an add or remove operation (issued on the same replica), or by merging the prefix of another replica, may require an update of these hb-maximal predecessors.

When the number of replicas and elements are fixed, the number of read-from maps is polynomial in the size of the history — recall that the number of operations associated by a read-from map to a replica and set element is bounded by the number of replicas. Combined with the number of prefix maps being polynomial when the number of replicas is fixed, we obtain the following result.

Theorem 5. *Checking whether a history is admitted by the Add-Wins Set, Remove-Wins Set, Enable-Wins Flag, or the Disable-Wins Flag is polynomial time provided that the number of replicas and elements/flags is fixed.*

7 Related Work

Many have considered consistency models applicable to CRDTs, including causal consistency [26], sequential consistency [27], linearizability [24], session consistency [35], eventual consistency [36], and happens-before consistency [29]. Burckhardt et al. [8,11] propose a unifying framework to formalize these models. Many have also studied the complexity of verifying data-type agnostic notions of consistency, including serializability, sequential consistency and linearizability [1,2,4,18,20,22,30], as well as causal consistency [6]. Our definition of the replicated LWW register corresponds to the notion of causal convergence in [6]. This work studies the complexity of the admissibility problem for the replicated LWW register. It shows that this problem is NP-complete in general and polynomial time when each value is written only once. Our NP-completeness result is stronger since it assumes a fixed number of replicas, and our algorithm for the case of unique values is more general and can be applied uniformly to MVR and RGA. While Bouajjani et al. [5,14] consider the complexity for individual linearizable collection types, we are the first to establish (in)tractability of individual replicated data types. Others have developed effective consistency checking algorithms for sequential consistency [3,9,23,31], serializability [12,17,18,21], linearizability [10,16,28,37], and even weaker notions like eventual consistency [7] and sequential happens-before consistency [13,15]. In contrast, we are the first to establish precise polynomial-time algorithms for runtime verification of replicated data types.

8 Conclusion

By developing novel logical characterizations of replicated data types, reductions from propositional satisfiability checking, and tractable algorithms, we have established a frontier of tractability for checking consistency of replicated data types. As far as we are aware, our results are the first to characterize the asymptotic complexity consistency checking for CRDTs.

References

1. Alur, R., McMillan, K.L., Peled, D.A.: Model-checking of correctness conditions for concurrent objects. Inf. Comput. **160**(1–2), 167–188 (2000). https://doi.org/10.1006/inco.1999.2847
2. Bingham, J.D., Condon, A., Hu, A.J.: Toward a decidable notion of sequential consistency. In: Rosenberg, A.L., auf der Heide, F.M. (eds.) SPAA 2003: Proceedings of the Fifteenth Annual ACM Symposium on Parallelism in Algorithms and Architectures, San Diego, California, USA, (part of FCRC 2003), 7–9 June 2003, pp. 304–313. ACM (2003). https://doi.org/10.1145/777412.777467
3. Bingham, J., Condon, A., Hu, A.J., Qadeer, S., Zhang, Z.: Automatic verification of sequential consistency for unbounded addresses and data values. In: Alur, R., Peled, D.A. (eds.) CAV 2004. LNCS, vol. 3114, pp. 427–439. Springer, Heidelberg (2004). https://doi.org/10.1007/978-3-540-27813-9_33

4. Bouajjani, A., Emmi, M., Enea, C., Hamza, J.: Verifying concurrent programs against sequential specifications. In: Felleisen, M., Gardner, P. (eds.) ESOP 2013. LNCS, vol. 7792, pp. 290–309. Springer, Heidelberg (2013). https://doi.org/10.1007/978-3-642-37036-6_17
5. Bouajjani, A., Emmi, M., Enea, C., Hamza, J.: On reducing linearizability to state reachability. Inf. Comput. **261**(Part), 383–400 (2018). https://doi.org/10.1016/j.ic.2018.02.014
6. Bouajjani, A., Enea, C., Guerraoui, R., Hamza, J.: On verifying causal consistency. In: Castagna, G., Gordon, A.D. (eds.) Proceedings of the 44th ACM SIGPLAN Symposium on Principles of Programming Languages, POPL 2017, Paris, France, 18–20 January 2017, pp. 626–638. ACM (2017). http://dl.acm.org/citation.cfm?id=3009888
7. Bouajjani, A., Enea, C., Hamza, J.: Verifying eventual consistency of optimistic replication systems. In: Jagannathan, S., Sewell, P. (eds.) The 41st Annual ACM SIGPLAN-SIGACT Symposium on Principles of Programming Languages, POPL 2014, San Diego, CA, USA, 20–21 January 2014, pp. 285–296. ACM (2014). https://doi.org/10.1145/2535838.2535877
8. Burckhardt, S.: Principles of eventual consistency. Found. Trends Program. Lang. **1**(1–2), 1–150 (2014). https://doi.org/10.1561/2500000011
9. Burckhardt, S., Alur, R., Martin, M.M.K.: Checkfence: checking consistency of concurrent data types on relaxed memory models. In: Ferrante, J., McKinley, K.S. (eds.) Proceedings of the ACM SIGPLAN 2007 Conference on Programming Language Design and Implementation, San Diego, California, USA, 10–13 June 2007, pp. 12–21. ACM (2007). https://doi.org/10.1145/1250734.1250737
10. Burckhardt, S., Dern, C., Musuvathi, M., Tan, R.: Line-up: a complete and automatic linearizability checker. In: Zorn, B.G., Aiken, A. (eds.) Proceedings of the 2010 ACM SIGPLAN Conference on Programming Language Design and Implementation, PLDI 2010, Toronto, Ontario, Canada, 5–10 June 2010, pp. 330–340. ACM (2010). https://doi.org/10.1145/1806596.1806634
11. Burckhardt, S., Gotsman, A., Yang, H., Zawirski, M.: Replicated data types: specification, verification, optimality. In: Jagannathan, S., Sewell, P. (eds.) The 41st Annual ACM SIGPLAN-SIGACT Symposium on Principles of Programming Languages, POPL 2014, San Diego, CA, USA, 20–21 January 2014, pp. 271–284. ACM (2014). https://doi.org/10.1145/2535838.2535848
12. Cohen, A., O'Leary, J.W., Pnueli, A., Tuttle, M.R., Zuck, L.D.: Verifying correctness of transactional memories. In: Proceedings of the 7th International Conference on Formal Methods in Computer-Aided Design, FMCAD 2007, Austin, Texas, USA, 11–14 November 2007, pp. 37–44. IEEE Computer Society (2007). https://doi.org/10.1109/FAMCAD.2007.40
13. Emmi, M., Enea, C.: Monitoring weak consistency. In: Chockler, H., Weissenbacher, G. (eds.) CAV 2018, Part I. LNCS, vol. 10981, pp. 487–506. Springer, Cham (2018). https://doi.org/10.1007/978-3-319-96145-3_26
14. Emmi, M., Enea, C.: Sound, complete, and tractable linearizability monitoring for concurrent collections. PACMPL **2**(POPL), 25:1–25:27 (2018). https://doi.org/10.1145/3158113
15. Emmi, M., Enea, C.: Weak-consistency specification via visibility relaxation. PACMPL **3**(POPL), 60:1–60:28 (2019). https://dl.acm.org/citation.cfm?id=3290373

16. Emmi, M., Enea, C., Hamza, J.: Monitoring refinement via symbolic reasoning. In: Grove, D., Blackburn, S. (eds.) Proceedings of the 36th ACM SIGPLAN Conference on Programming Language Design and Implementation, Portland, OR, USA, 15–17 June 2015, pp. 260–269. ACM (2015). https://doi.org/10.1145/2737924.2737983
17. Emmi, M., Majumdar, R., Manevich, R.: Parameterized verification of transactional memories. In: Zorn, B.G., Aiken, A. (eds.) Proceedings of the 2010 ACM SIGPLAN Conference on Programming Language Design and Implementation, PLDI 2010, Toronto, Ontario, Canada, 5–10 June 2010, pp. 134–145. ACM (2010). https://doi.org/10.1145/1806596.1806613
18. Farzan, A., Madhusudan, P.: Monitoring atomicity in concurrent programs. In: Gupta, A., Malik, S. (eds.) CAV 2008. LNCS, vol. 5123, pp. 52–65. Springer, Heidelberg (2008). https://doi.org/10.1007/978-3-540-70545-1_8
19. Garey, M.R., Johnson, D.S.: Computers and Intractability: A Guide to the Theory of NP-Completeness. W. H. Freeman, New York (1979)
20. Gibbons, P.B., Korach, E.: Testing shared memories. SIAM J. Comput. **26**(4), 1208–1244 (1997). https://doi.org/10.1137/S0097539794279614
21. Guerraoui, R., Henzinger, T.A., Jobstmann, B., Singh, V.: Model checking transactional memories. In: Gupta, R., Amarasinghe, S.P. (eds.) Proceedings of the ACM SIGPLAN 2008 Conference on Programming Language Design and Implementation, Tucson, AZ, USA, 7–13 June 2008, pp. 372–382. ACM (2008). https://doi.org/10.1145/1375581.1375626
22. Hamza, J.: On the complexity of linearizability. In: Bouajjani, A., Fauconnier, H. (eds.) NETYS 2015. LNCS, vol. 9466, pp. 308–321. Springer, Cham (2015). https://doi.org/10.1007/978-3-319-26850-7_21
23. Henzinger, T.A., Qadeer, S., Rajamani, S.K.: Verifying sequential consistency on shared-memory multiprocessor systems. In: Halbwachs, N., Peled, D. (eds.) CAV 1999. LNCS, vol. 1633, pp. 301–315. Springer, Heidelberg (1999). https://doi.org/10.1007/3-540-48683-6_27
24. Herlihy, M., Wing, J.M.: Linearizability: a correctness condition for concurrent objects. ACM Trans. Program. Lang. Syst. **12**(3), 463–492 (1990). https://doi.org/10.1145/78969.78972
25. Kingsbury, K.: Jepsen: Distributed systems safety research (2016). https://jepsen.io
26. Lamport, L.: Time, clocks, and the ordering of events in a distributed system. Commun. ACM **21**(7), 558–565 (1978). https://doi.org/10.1145/359545.359563
27. Lamport, L.: How to make a multiprocessor computer that correctly executes multiprocess programs. IEEE Trans. Comput. **28**(9), 690–691 (1979). https://doi.org/10.1109/TC.1979.1675439
28. Lowe, G.: Testing for linearizability. Concurr. Comput. Pract. Exp. **29**(4) (2017). https://doi.org/10.1002/cpe.3928
29. Manson, J., Pugh, W., Adve, S.V.: The java memory model. In: Palsberg, J., Abadi, M. (eds.) Proceedings of the 32nd ACM SIGPLAN-SIGACT Symposium on Principles of Programming Languages, POPL 2005, Long Beach, California, USA, 12–14 January 2005, pp. 378–391. ACM (2005). https://doi.org/10.1145/1040305.1040336
30. Papadimitriou, C.H.: The serializability of concurrent database updates. J. ACM **26**(4), 631–653 (1979). https://doi.org/10.1145/322154.322158
31. Qadeer, S.: Verifying sequential consistency on shared-memory multiprocessorsby model checking. IEEE Trans. Parallel Distrib. Syst. **14**(8), 730–741 (2003). https://doi.org/10.1109/TPDS.2003.1225053

32. Roh, H., Jeon, M., Kim, J., Lee, J.: Replicated abstract data types: building blocks for collaborative applications. J. Parallel Distrib. Comput. **71**(3), 354–368 (2011). https://doi.org/10.1016/j.jpdc.2010.12.006
33. Shapiro, M., Preguiça, N., Baquero, C., Zawirski, M.: Conflict-free replicated data types. In: Défago, X., Petit, F., Villain, V. (eds.) SSS 2011. LNCS, vol. 6976, pp. 386–400. Springer, Heidelberg (2011). https://doi.org/10.1007/978-3-642-24550-3_29
34. Shapiro, M., Preguiça, N.M., Baquero, C., Zawirski, M.: Convergent and commutative replicated data types. Bull. EATCS **104**, 67–88 (2011). http://eatcs.org/beatcs/index.php/beatcs/article/view/120
35. Terry, D.B., Demers, A.J., Petersen, K., Spreitzer, M., Theimer, M., Welch, B.B.: Session guarantees for weakly consistent replicated data. In: Proceedings of the Third International Conference on Parallel and Distributed Information Systems (PDIS 1994), Austin, Texas, USA, 28–30 September 1994, pp. 140–149. IEEE Computer Society (1994). https://doi.org/10.1109/PDIS.1994.331722
36. Terry, D.B., Theimer, M., Petersen, K., Demers, A.J., Spreitzer, M., Hauser, C.: Managing update conflicts in bayou, a weakly connected replicated storage system. In: Jones, M.B. (ed.) Proceedings of the Fifteenth ACM Symposium on Operating System Principles, SOSP 1995, Copper Mountain Resort, Colorado, USA, 3–6 December 1995, pp. 172–183. ACM (1995). https://doi.org/10.1145/224056.224070
37. Wing, J.M., Gong, C.: Testing and verifying concurrent objects. J. Parallel Distrib. Comput. **17**(1–2), 164–182 (1993). https://doi.org/10.1006/jpdc.1993.1015
38. Wolper, P.: Expressing interesting properties of programs in propositional temporal logic. In: Conference Record of the Thirteenth Annual ACM Symposium on Principles of Programming Languages, St. Petersburg Beach, Florida, USA, January 1986, pp. 184–193. ACM Press (1986). https://doi.org/10.1145/512644.512661

Communication-Closed Asynchronous Protocols

Andrei Damian[1], Cezara Drăgoi[2], Alexandru Militaru[1], and Josef Widder[3,4](✉)

[1] Politehnica University Bucharest, Bucharest, Romania
[2] Inria, ENS, CNRS, PSL, Paris, France
[3] TU Wien, Vienna, Austria
widder@forsyte.at
[4] Interchain Foundation, Baar, Switzerland

Abstract. The verification of asynchronous fault-tolerant distributed systems is challenging due to unboundedly many interleavings and network failures (e.g., processes crash or message loss). We propose a method that reduces the verification of asynchronous fault-tolerant protocols to the verification of round-based synchronous ones. Synchronous protocols are easier to verify due to fewer interleavings, bounded message buffers etc. We implemented our reduction method and applied it to several state machine replication and consensus algorithms. The resulting synchronous protocols are verified using existing deductive verification methods.

1 Introduction

Fault tolerance protocols provide dependable services on top of unreliable computers and networks. One distinguishes asynchronous vs. synchronous protocols based on the semantics of parallel composition. Asynchronous protocols are crucial parts of many distributed systems for their better performance when compared against the synchronous ones. However, their correctness is very hard to obtain, due to the challenges of concurrency, faults, buffered message queues, and message loss and re-ordering at the network [5,19,21,26,31,35,37,42]. In contrast, reasoning about synchronous round-based semantics is simpler, as one only has to consider specific global states at round boundaries [1,8,10,11,13,17,29,32,40].

The question we address is how to connect both worlds, in order to exploit the advantage of verification in synchronous semantics when reasoning about asynchronous protocols. We consider asynchronous protocols that work in unreliable networks, which may lose and reorder messages, and where processes may crash. We focus on a class of protocols that solve state machine replication.

Due to the absence of a global clock, fault tolerance protocols implement an abstract notion of time to coordinate. The local state of a process maintains the

Supported by: Austrian Science Fund (FWF) via NFN RiSE (S11405) and project PRAVDA (P27722); WWTF grant APALACHE (ICT15-103); French National Research Agency ANR project SAFTA (12744-ANR-17-CE25-0008-01).

I. Dillig and S. Tasiran (Eds.): CAV 2019, LNCS 11562, pp. 344–363, 2019.
https://doi.org/10.1007/978-3-030-25543-5_20

value of the abstract time (potentially implicit), and a process timestamps the messages it sends accordingly. Synchronous algorithms do not need to implement an abstract notion of time: it is embedded in the definition of any synchronous computational model [9,15,18,28], and it is called the *round number*. The key insight of our results is the existence of a correspondence between values of the abstract clock in the asynchronous systems and round numbers in the synchronous ones. Using this correspondence, we make explicit the "hidden" round-based synchronous structure of an asynchronous algorithm.

Fig. 1. Asynchronous executions without jumps

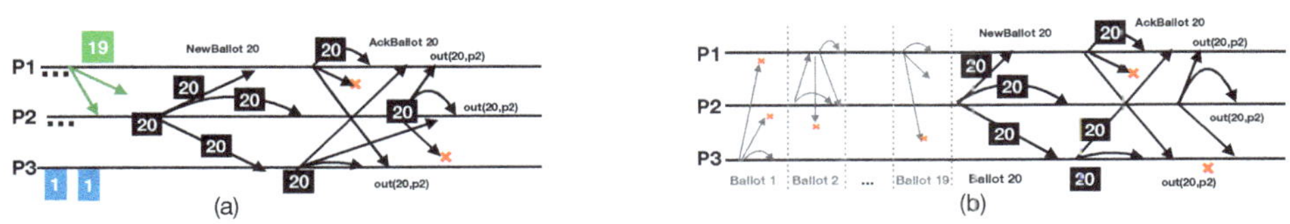

Fig. 2. Asynchronous executions with jumps

We discuss our approach using a leader election algorithm. We consider n of processes, which periodically elect collectively a new leader. These periods are called *ballots*, and in each ballot at most one leader should be elected. The protocol in Fig. 3 solves leader election. In a ballot, a process that wants to become leader proposes itself by sending a message containing its identifier `me` to all, and it is elected if (1) a majority of processes receive its message, (2) these receivers send a message of leadership acknowledgment to the entire network, and (3) at least one processes receives leadership acknowledgments for its leader estimate from a majority of processes. Figure 1(b) sketches an execution where process $P3$ fails to be elected in ballot 1 because the network drops all the messages sent by P3 marked with a cross. All processes timeout and there is no leader elected in ballot 1. In the second ballot, $P2$ tries to become leader, the network delivers all messages between $P1$ and $P2$ in time, the two processes form a majority, and $P2$ is elected leader of ballot 2.

The protocol is defined by the asynchronous parallel composition of n copies of the code in Fig. 3. Each process executes a loop, where each iteration defines the executors behavior in a ballot. The variable `ballot` encodes the ballot number. The function `coord()` provides a local estimate whether a process should try to become leader. Multiple processes may be selected by `coord()` as leader

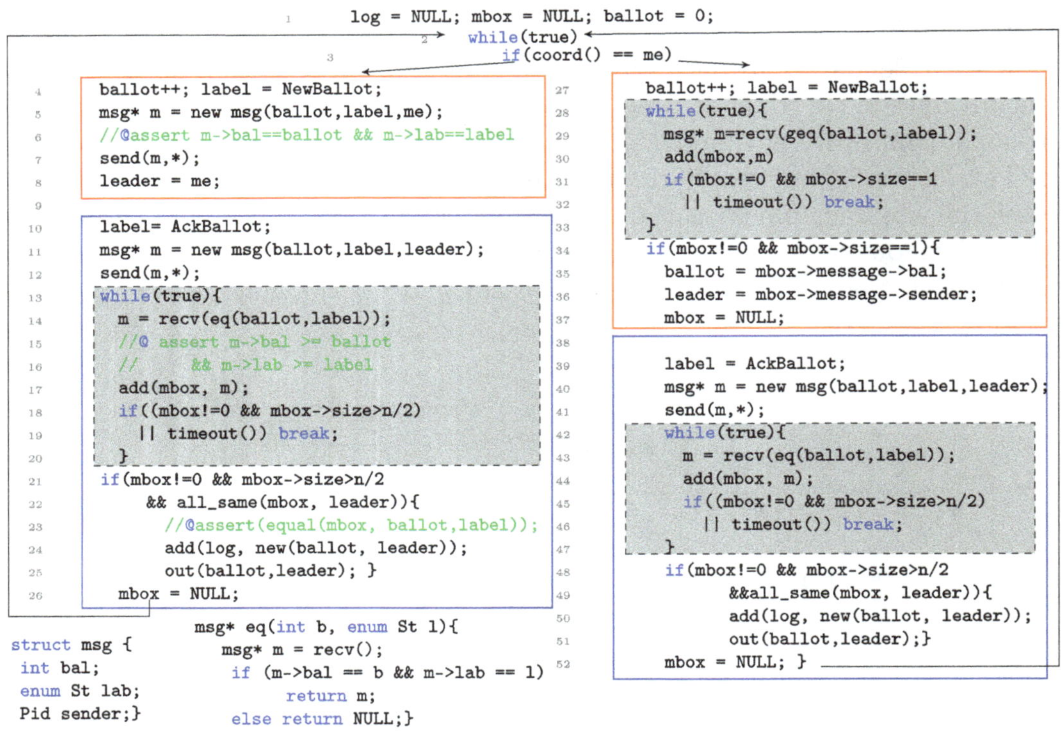

Fig. 3. Control flow graph of asynchronous leader election. (Color figure online)

candidates, resulting in a race which is won by a process that is acknowledged by a majority (more than $n/2$ processes). Depending on the result of `coord()`, a process may take the leader branch on the left or the follower branch on the right. On the leader branch, a message is prepared and sent, at line 7. The message contains the ballot number, the label `NewBallot`, the leaders identity. On the other branch, a follower waits for a message from a process, which proposes itself for the current ballot number of the follower. This waiting is implemented by a loop, which terminates either on timeout or when a message is received. Next, the followers, which received a message, and the leader candidates send their leader estimate to all at lines 12 and 41, where the message contains the ballots number, the label `AckBallot`, and the leaders identity. If a processes receives more than $n/2$ messages labeled with `AckBallot` and its current ballot, it checks using `all_same(mbox, leader)` in lines 22 and 49, whether a majority of processes acknowledges the leadership of its estimate. In this case, it adds this information to the array `log` (which stores the locally elected leader of each ballot, if any) and outputs it, before it empties its mailbox and continues with the next iteration.

Figure 1(a) shows another execution of this protocol. Again, P3 sends `NewBallot` messages for ballot 1 to all processes. P3's `NewBallot` messages are delayed, and P2 times out in ballot 1, moving to ballot 2 where it is a leader candidate. The messages sent in ballot 2 are exchanged like in Fig. 1(b). Contrary to Fig. 1(b), while exchanging ballot 2 messages, the network delivers to

P2, P3's `NewBallot` message from ballot 1. However, P2 ignores it, because of the receive statement in line 14 that only accepts messages for greater or equal (`ballot`, `label`) pairs. The message from ballot 1 arrived too "late" because P2 already is in ballot 2. Thus, the messages from ballot 1 have the same effect as if they were dropped, as in Fig. 1(b). The executions are equivalent from the local perspective of the processes: By applying a "rubber band transformation" [30], one can reorder transitions, while maintaining the local control flow and the send/receive causality.

Another case of equivalent executions is given in Fig. 2. While P1 and P2 made progress, P3 was disconnected. In Fig. 2(a), while P3 is waiting for ballot 1 messages, the networks delivers a message for ballot 20. P3 receives this message in line 29 and updates `ballot` in line 35. P3 thus "jumps forward in time", acknowledging P2's leadership in ballot 20. In Fig. 2(b), P3's timeout expires in all ballots from 1 to 19, without P3 receiving any messages. Thus, it does not change its local state (except the ballot number) in these ballots. For P3, these two executions are stutter equivalent. Reducing verification to verification of executions as the ones to the right — i.e., *synchronous* executions — reduces the number of interleavings and drastically simplifies verification. In the following we discuss conditions on the code that allow such a reduction.

Communication Closure. In our example, the variables `ballot` and `label` encode abstract time: Let b and ℓ be their assigned values. Then abstract time ranges over $\mathcal{T} = \{(b, \ell) : b \in \mathbb{N}, \ell \in \{\texttt{NewBallot}, \texttt{AckBallot}\}\}$. We fix `NewBallot` to be less than `AckBallot`, and consider the lexicographical order over $\mathcal{T}$. The sequence of (b, ℓ) induced by an execution at a process is monotonically increasing; thus (b, ℓ) encodes a notion of time. A protocol is *communication-closed* if (i) each process sends only messages timestamped with the current time, and (ii) each process receives only messages timestamped with the current or a higher time value. For such protocols we show in Sect. 5 that for each asynchronous execution, there is an equivalent (processes go through the same sequence of local states) synchronous one. We use ideas from [17], but we allow reacting to future messages, which is a more permissive form of communication closure. This is essential for jumping forward, and thus for liveness in fault tolerance protocols.

The challenge is to check communication closure at the code level. For this, we rely on user-provided "tag" annotations that specify the variables and the message fields representing local time and timestamps. A system of assertions formalizes that the user-provided annotations encode time and that the protocol is communication-closed w.r.t. this definition of time. In the example, the user provides (`ballot,label`) for local time and `msg->bal` and `msg->lab` for timestamps. In Fig. 3, we give example assertions that we add for the send and receive conditions (i) and (ii). These assertions only consider the local state, i.e., we do not need to capture the states of other processes or the message pool. We check the assertions with the static verifier Verifast [22].

Synchronous Semantics. Central to our approach is re-writing communication-closed asynchronous protocol into synchronous ones. To formalize synchronous semantics we introduce *multi Heard-Of protocols*, mHO for short. An mHO computation is structured into a sequence of mHO-rounds that execute synchronously. Figure 4 is an example of an mHO protocol. It has two mHO-rounds: `NewBallot` and `AckBallot`. Within a round, SEND functions, resp. UPDATE functions, are executed synchronously across all processes. The *round* number r is initially 0 and it is incremented after each execution of an mHO-round. The interesting feature, which models faults and timeouts, are the heard-of sets HO [9]. For each round r and each process p, the set $HO(p, r)$ contains the set of processes from which p hears of in round r, i.e., whose messages are in the mailbox set taken as parameter by UPDATE (`mbox`). If the message from q to p is lost in round r, then $q \notin HO(p, r)$. Figures 1(b) and 2(b) are examples of executions of the protocol in Fig. 4. We extend the HO model [9] by allowing composition of *multiple* protocols. Verification in synchronous semantics, and thus in mHO, is simpler due to the round structure, which entails (i) no interleavings, (ii) no message buffers, and (iii) simpler invariants at the round boundaries.

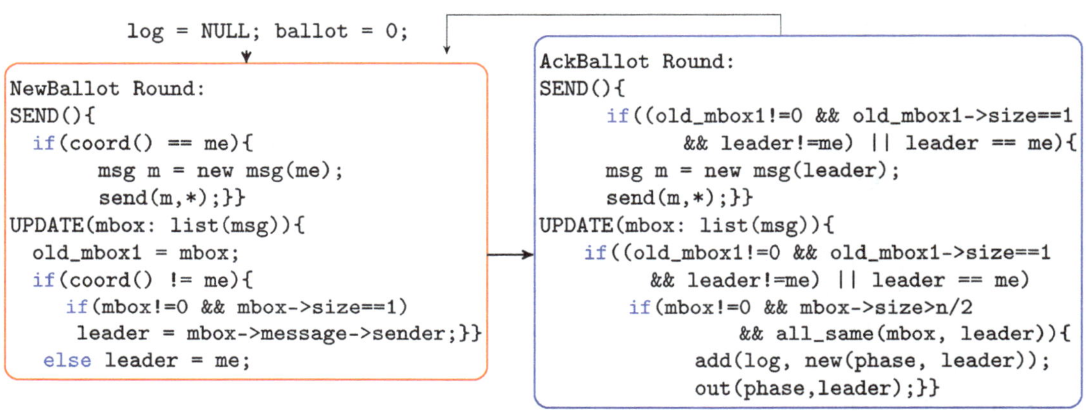

Fig. 4. Control flow graph of synchronous leader election. (Color figure online)

Rewriting to mHO. We introduce a procedure that takes as input the asynchronous protocol together with tag annotations that have been checked, and produces the protocol rewritten in mHO, e.g., Fig. 3 is rewritten into Fig. 4. The rewriting is based on the idea of matching abstract time (`ballot`, `label`) to mHO round numbers r. Roughly, mHO-round `NewBallot` is obtained by combining the code of the first box on each path in Fig. 3 (the red boxes) and `AckBallot` is obtained my combining the second box on each path (the blue ones) as follows. The three message reception loops (the code in the boxes with highlighted background) are removed, because receptions are implicit in mHO; they correspond to a non-deterministic parameter of the UPDATE function. For each round, we record the context in which it is executed, e.g., the lower box for the follower is executed only if a `NewBallot` message was received (more details in Sect. 6).

Verification. The specification of the running example is that if two processes find the leader election for a ballot b successful (i.e., there is `log` entry for b), then they agree on the leader. In general, to prove the specification, we need invariants that quantify over the ballot number b. As processes decide asynchronously, the proof of ballot 1, for some process p, must refer to the first entry of `log` of processes that might already be in ballot 400. As discussed in [38], in general invariants need to capture the complete message history and the complete local state of processes. The proof of the same property for the synchronous protocol requires no such invariant. Due to communication closure, no messages need to be maintained after a round terminated, that is, there is no message pool. The rewritten synchronous code has a simpler correctness proof, independent of the chosen verification method. One could use model checking [1,29,39,40], theorem prover approaches [8,11], or deductive verification [14] for synchronous systems.

For several protocols, we formalize their specification in Consensus Logic [13], we have computed the equivalent mHO protocol, and proved it correct using the existing deductive verification engine from [13].

2 Asynchronous Protocols

All processes execute the same code, written in the core language in Fig. 5. The communication between processes is done via typed messages. Message payloads, denoted `M`, are wrappers of primitive or composite type. We denote by $\mathcal{M}$ the set of message types. Wrappers are used to distinguish payload types. Send instructions take as input an object of some payload type and the receivers identity or $\star$ corresponding to a send to all. Receives statements are non-blocking, and return an object of payload type or `NULL`. Receive statements are parameterized by conditions (i.e., pointers to function) on the values in the received messages (e.g., timestamp). At most one message is received at a time. If no message has been delivered or satisfies the condition, receive returns `NULL`. In Fig. 3, we give the definition of the function `eq`, used to filter messages acknowledging the leadership of a process. The followers use also `geq` that checks if the received message is timestamped with a value higher or equal to the local time. We assume that each loop contains at least one send or receive statement. The iterative sequential computations are done in local functions, i.e., $\mathtt{f}(\vec{e})$. The instructions `in()` and `out()` are used to communicate with an external environment.

The semantics of a protocol $\mathcal{P}$ is the asynchronous parallel composition of n copies of the same code, one copy per process, where n is a parameter. Formally, the state of a protocol $\mathcal{P}$ is a tuple $\langle s, msg \rangle$ where: $s \in [P \to (\mathtt{Vars} \cup \{\mathtt{pc}\}) \to \mathcal{D}]$ is a valuation in some data domain $\mathcal{D}$ of the variables in $\mathcal{P}$, where `pc` is represents the current control location, where `Loc` is the set of all protocol locations, and $msg \subseteq \bigcup_{\mathtt{M} \in \mathcal{M}} (P \times \mathcal{D}(\mathtt{M}) \times P)$ is the multiset of messages in transit (the network may lose and reorder messages). Given a process $p \in P$, $s(p)$ is the local state of p, which is a valuation of p's local variables, i.e., $s(p) \in \mathtt{Vars}_p \cup \{\mathtt{pc}_p\} \to \mathcal{D}$. The state of a crashed process is a wildcard state that matches any state. The messages sent by a process are added to the global pool of messages msg, and

e := c	constant	S := x := e	assignment
| x	variable	| reset_timeout(e)	reset a timeout
| f($\vec{e}$)	operation	| send(m,p) | send(m, ⋆)	send message
		| m := recv(∗cond)	receive message
types := Pid	process Id	| S ; S	sequence
M	payload type	| if e then S else S	
p : Pid,	m : M	| while true S	
Mbox:	set of M	| break | continue	
$\mathcal{P} := \Pi_{p:P}[S]_p$	protocol	| x = in()	client entry
P is the set of process identities		| out(e)	client output

Fig. 5. Syntax of asynchronous protocols.

a receive statement removes a messages from the pool. The interface operations `in` and `out` do not modify the local state of a process. An execution is an infinite sequence $s0\ A0\ s1\ A1\ \ldots$ such that $\forall i \geq 0$, si is a protocol state, $Ai \in A$ is a local statement, whose execution creates a transition of the form $\langle s, msg\rangle \xrightarrow{I,O} \langle s', msg'\rangle$ where $\{I, O\}$ are the observable events generated by the Ai (if any). We denote by $[\![\mathcal{P}]\!]$ the set of executions of the protocol $\mathcal{P}$.

3 Round-Based Model: mHO

Intra-procedural. mHO captures round-based distributed algorithms and is a reformulation of the model in [9]. All processes execute the same code and the computation is structured in rounds. We denote by P the set of processes and $n = |P|$ is a parameter. The central concept is the *HO*-set, where $HO(p, r)$ contains the processes from which process p has *heard of* — has received messages from — in round r; this models faults and timeouts.

$$\begin{aligned}
\mathit{protocol} &::= \mathit{interface}\ \mathit{var_decl}^*\ \mathit{init}\ \mathit{phase}\\
\mathit{interface} &::= \texttt{in: } () \to \mathit{type} \mid \texttt{out: } \mathit{type} \to ()\\
\mathit{init} &::= \texttt{init: } () \to [P \to \texttt{Vars} \to \mathcal{D}]\\
\mathit{phase} &::= \mathit{round}^+\\
\mathit{round}_{\texttt{M}} &::= \texttt{SEND: } [P \to \texttt{Vars}] \to [P \rightharpoonup \texttt{T}]\\
&\qquad \texttt{UPDATE: } [P \rightharpoonup \texttt{T}] \times [P \to \texttt{Vars}]\\
&\qquad \to [P \to \texttt{Vars}]
\end{aligned}$$

Fig. 6. mHO syntax.

Syntax. An mHO protocol consists of variable declarations, `Vars` is the set of variables, an initialization method `init`, and a non-empty sequence of rounds, called *phase*; cf. Fig. 6. A phase is a fixed-size array of rounds. Each round has a send and update method, parameterized by a type `M` (denoted by $\mathit{round}_{\texttt{M}}$) which represents the message payload. The method `SEND` has no side effects and returns the messages to be sent based on the local state of each sender; it returns a partial map from receivers to payloads. The method `UPDATE` takes as input the received messages and updates the local state of a process. It may communicate with an external client via `in` and `out`. For data computations, `UPDATE` uses iterative control structures only indirectly via sequential functions, e.g., `all_same(mbox, leader)` in Fig. 3, which checks whether the payloads of all messages in `mbox` are equal to the local leader estimate.

Semantics. The set of executions of a mHO protocol is defined by the execution in a loop, of `SEND` followed by `UPDATE` for each round in the phase array. The initial configuration is defined by `init`. There are three predefined execution counters: the phase number, which is increased after a phase has been executed, the step number which tracks which mHO-round is executed in the current phase, and the round number which counts the total number of rounds executed so far and is defined by the phase times the length of the phase array, plus the step.

A protocol state is a tuple $\langle SU, s, r, msg, P, HO\rangle$ where: P is the set of processes, $SU \in \{\textsc{Send}, \textsc{Update}\}$ indicates the next transition, $s \in [P \rightarrow \texttt{Vars} \rightarrow \mathcal{D}]$ stores the process local states, $r \in \mathbb{N}$ is the round number, $msg \subseteq 2^{(P, \mathcal{D}(\texttt{M}), P)}$ stores the in-transit messages, where `M` is the type of the message payload, $HO \in [P \rightarrow 2^P]$ evaluates the HO-sets for the current round. After the initialization, an execution alternates SEND and UPDATE transitions. In the SEND transition, all processes send messages, which are added to a pool of messages msg, without modifying the local states. The values of the HO sets are updated non-deterministically to be a subset of P. A message is lost if the sender's identity does not belong to the HO set of the receiver. In an UPDATE transition, `UPDATE` is applied at each process, taking as input the set of received messages by that process in that round. If the processes communicate with an external process, then `UPDATE` might produce observable events o_p. These events correspond to calls to `in`, which returns an input value, and `out` that sends the value given as parameter to the client. At the end of the round, msg is purged and r is incremented. Figure 1(b) shows an execution of the mHO algorithm in Fig. 4.

Inter-procedural. The model introduced so far allows to express one protocol, e.g., a leader election protocol (e.g., Fig. 4). However, realistic systems typically combine several protocols, e.g., we can transform Fig. 4 into a replicated state machine protocol, by allowing processes to enter an atomic broadcast protocol in every ballot where a leader is elected successfully. Figure 7 sketches such an execution, where in the update of round `AckBallot`, a subprotocol is called; its execution is sketched with thicker edges. In the subprotocol, the leader broadcasts client requests in a loop until it loses its quorum. When a follower does not receive a message from the leader, it considers the leader crashed, and the control returns to the leader election protocol.

An inter-procedural mHO protocol differs from an intra-procedural one only in the `UPDATE` function: It may call another protocol and block until the call returns. An `UPDATE` may call at most one protocol on each path in its control flow (a sequence of calls can be implemented using multiple rounds). Thus, an inter-procedural mHO protocol is a collection of non-recursive mHO protocols, with a main protocol as entry point. Different protocols exchange messages of different types.

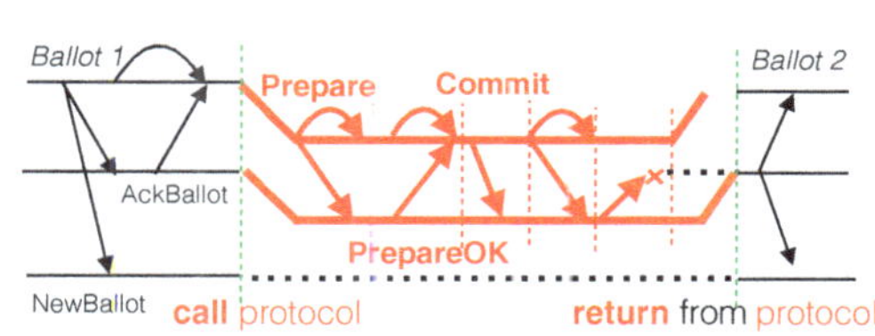

Fig. 7. Inter-procedural execution

4 Formalizing Communication Closure Using Tags

We introduce synchronization tags which are program annotations that define communication-closed rounds within an asynchronous protocol.

Definition 1 (Tag annotation). *For a protocol $\mathcal{P}$, a* tag annotation *is a tuple* $(\texttt{SyncV}, \texttt{tags}, \texttt{tagm}, \preceq, \mathcal{D})$ *where:*

- $\mathcal{D} = (D_1, D_2, \ldots, D_{2m-1}, D_{2m})$, *with* $(D_i, \preceq_i, \bot_i)$ *an ordered domain with a minimal element, denoted* $\bot_i$, *for* $1 \leq i \leq 2m$. *The cardinality of* D_{2i} *is bounded and all* D_{2i} *are pairwise disjoint, for* $i \in [1, m]$.
- *relation* $\preceq$ *is the lexicographical order: the* i*th component is ordered by* $\preceq_i$,
- $\texttt{SyncV} = (v_1, v_2, \ldots, v_{2m-1}, v_{2m})$ *is a tuple of fresh variables,*
- $\texttt{tags} : \texttt{Loc} \rightarrow [\texttt{SyncV} \overset{inj}{\rightharpoonup} \texttt{Vars}]$ *annotates each control location with a partially defined injective function, that maps* SyncV *over protocol variables,*
- $\texttt{tagm} : \mathcal{M} \rightarrow [\texttt{SyncV} \overset{inj}{\rightharpoonup} \textit{Fields}(\texttt{M})]$ *annotates each message type* $\texttt{M} \in \mathcal{M}$ *with a partially defined injective function, that maps* SyncV *over the fields of* M.

The evaluation of a tag over $\mathcal{P}$*'s semantics is denoted* $([\![\texttt{tags}]\!], [\![\texttt{tagm}]\!])$, *where*

- $[\![\texttt{tags}]\!] : \Sigma \rightarrow [\texttt{SyncV} \rightarrow \mathcal{D}]$ *is defined over the set of local process states* $\Sigma = \bigcup_{s \in [\![\mathcal{P}]\!]} \bigcup_{p \in P} s(p)$, *such that* $[\![\texttt{tags}]\!]_s = (d_1, \ldots, d_{|\texttt{SyncV}|})$ *with* $d_i = [\![\boldsymbol{x}]\!]_s$ *if* $\boldsymbol{x} = \texttt{tags}([\![\boldsymbol{pc}]\!]_s)(v_i) \in \texttt{Vars}$ *otherwise* $d_i = \bot_i$, *where* $s \in \Sigma$, $\boldsymbol{x} \in \texttt{Vars}$, v_i *is the* i^{th} *component in* SyncV, *and* **pc** *is the program counter;*
- $[\![\texttt{tagm}]\!] : \bigcup_{\texttt{M} \in \mathcal{M}} \mathcal{D}(\texttt{M}) \rightarrow [\texttt{SyncV} \rightarrow \mathcal{D} \cup \bot]$ *is a function that for any message value* $m = (m_1, \ldots, m_t)$, *in the domain of some message type* M, *associates a tuple* $[\![\texttt{tagm}]\!]_{m:\texttt{M}} = (d_1, \ldots, d_{|\texttt{SyncV}|})$ *with* $d_i = m_j$ *if* $j = \texttt{tagm}(\texttt{M})(v_i)$ *otherwise* $d_i = \bot_i$, *where* v_i *is the* i^{th} *element in* SyncV.

For every $1 \leq i \leq m$, v_{2i-1} *is called a* phase tag *and* v_{2i} *is called* step tag. *Given an execution* $\pi \in [\![\mathcal{P}]\!]$, *a transition* sAs' *in* π *is* tagged *by* $[\![\texttt{tagm}]\!]_m$ *if*

A is send(m) or m = recv($*$cond), or A is tagged by $[\![\texttt{tags}]\!]'_s$ *otherwise.*

For Fig. 3, $\texttt{SyncV} = (v_1, v_2)$, and **tags** matches v_1 and v_2 with **ballot** and **label**, resp., at all control locations, i.e., a process is in step NewBallot of phase 3, when ballot $= 3$ and label $=$ NewBallot. For the type **msg**, **tagm** matches the field ballot and lab with v_1 and v_2, resp., i.e., a message $(3, \texttt{NewBallot}, 5)$ is a phase 3 step NewBallot message. To capture that messages of type A are sent locally before messages of type B, the tagging function tagm(B) should be defined on the same synchronization variables as tagm(A).

Definition 2 (Synchronization tag). *Given a protocol* $\mathcal{P}$, *an annotation tag* $(\texttt{SyncV}, \texttt{tags}, \texttt{tagm}, \mathcal{D}, \preceq)$ *is called* synchronization tag *iff:*

(I.) for any local execution $\pi = s_0A_0s_1A_1 \ldots \in [\![\mathcal{P}]\!]_p$ *of a process* p, *the sequence* $[\![\texttt{tags}]\!]_{s_0}[\![\texttt{tags}]\!]_{s_1}[\![\texttt{tags}]\!]_{s_2} \ldots$ *is a monotonically increasing w.r.t.* $\preceq$.

Moreover $\forall j, j' \in [1..m], j < j'$. *if* $[\![\mathtt{tags}]\!]_{s_i}^{(2j-1,2j)} \neq [\![\mathtt{tags}]\!]_{s_i+1}^{(2j-1,2j)}$ *and* $[\![\mathtt{tags}]\!]_{s_i}^{(2j'-1,2j')} \neq [\![\mathtt{tags}]\!]_{s_i+1}^{(2j'-1,2j')}$ *then* $[\![\mathtt{tags}]\!]_{s_i-1}^{(2j'-1,2j')} = (\bot_{2j'-1}, \bot_{2j'})$ *where* $[\![\mathtt{tags}]\!]_{s_i}^{(2j-1,2j)}$ *is the projection of the tuple* $[\![\mathtt{tags}]\!]_{s_i}$ *on the* $2j-1$ *and* $2j$ *components,*

(II.) for any local execution $\pi \in [\![\mathcal{P}]\!]_p$, *if* $s \xrightarrow{send(m,\_)} s'$ *is a transition of* π, *with* m *a message value, then* $[\![\mathtt{tags}]\!]_s = [\![\mathtt{tagm}]\!]_m$ *and* $[\![\mathtt{tags}]\!]_s = [\![\mathtt{tags}]\!]_{s'}$,

(III.) for any local execution $\pi \in [\![\mathcal{P}]\!]_p$, *if* $s \xrightarrow{m=recv(cond)} sr$ *is a transition of* π, *with* m *a value of some message type, then*
- *if* $m \neq NULL$ *then* $[\![\mathtt{tags}]\!]_s \preceq [\![\mathtt{tagm}]\!]_m$, $[\![\mathtt{tags}]\!]_s = [\![\mathtt{tags}]\!]_{sr}$, *and*
- *if* $m = NULL$ *then* $s = sr$,

(IV.) for any local execution $\pi \in [\![\mathcal{P}]\!]_p$, *if* $s \xrightarrow{stm} s'$ *is a transition of* π *such that*

- $s \neq s'$ *and* $s\,|_{\mathtt{M,SyncV}} = s'\,|_{\mathtt{M,SyncV}}$, *that is,* s *and* s' *differ on the variables that are neither of some message type nor in the image of* `tags`,
- *or* `stm` *is a* `send`, `break`, `continue`, *or* `out()`,

then for all message type variables `m` *in the protocol,* $[\![\mathtt{tags}]\!]_s = [\![\mathtt{tagm}]\!]_m$, *where* m *is the value in the state* s *of* `m`, *and for any* `Mbox` *variables of type set of messages,* $[\![\mathtt{tags}]\!]_s = [\![\mathtt{tagm}]\!]_m$ *with* $m \in [\![\mathtt{Mbox}]\!]_s$,

(V.) for any local execution $\pi \in [\![\mathcal{P}]\!]_p$, *if* $s_1 \xrightarrow{send(m,\_)} s_2 \xrightarrow{stm^+} s_3 \xrightarrow{send(m',\_)} s_4$ *or* $s_1 \xrightarrow{m=recv(*cond)} s_2 \xrightarrow{stm^+} s_3 \xrightarrow{send(m',\_)} s_4$ *are sequences of transitions in* π, *then* $[\![\mathtt{tagm}]\!]_m \prec [\![\mathtt{tagm}]\!]_{m'}$, *where stm is any statement except send or recv. Moreover, if* $s_1 \xrightarrow{m=recv(*cond)} s_2 \xrightarrow{stm^+} s_3 \xrightarrow{m'=recv(*cond')} s_4$ *in* π, *then* $s_2\,|_{\mathtt{Vars}\setminus(\mathtt{M}\cup\mathtt{SyncV})} = s_3\,|_{\mathtt{Vars}\setminus(\mathtt{M}\cup\mathtt{SyncV})}$ *or* $[\![\mathtt{tags}]\!]_{s_2} \prec [\![\mathtt{tags}]\!]_{s_3}$.

A protocol $\mathcal{P}$ *is communication-closed, if there exists a synchronization tag for* $\mathcal{P}$.

Condition (I.) states that `SyncV` is not decreased by any local statement (it is a notion of time). Further, one synchronization pair is modified at a time, except a reset (i.e., a pair is set to its minimal value) when the value of a preceding pair is updated. Checking this, translates into checking a transition invariant, stating that the value of the synchronization tuple `SyncV` is increased by any assignment. To state this invariant we introduce "old synchronization variables" that maintain the value of the synchronization variables before the update.

Condition (II.) states that any message sent is tagged with a timestamp that equals the current local time. Checking it, reduces to an assert statement that expresses that for every $v \in$ `SyncV`, `tagm(M)`(v) = `tags(pc)`(v), where `M` is the type of the message m which is sent, and `pc` is the program location of the `send`.

Condition (III.) states that any message received is tagged with a timestamp greater than or equal to the current time of the process. To check it, we need to consider the implementation of the functions passed as argument to a `recv` statement. These functions (e.g., `eq` and `geq` in Fig. 3) implement the filtering of the messages delivered by the network. We inline their code and prove Condition (III.) by comparing the tagged fields of message variables with the phase and step variables. In Fig. 3, `assert m → bal == ballot && m → lab == label` after `recv(eq(ballot, label))` checks this condition on the leader's branch.

Condition (IV.) states that if the local state of a process changes (except changes of message type variables and synchronization variables), then all locally stored messages are timestamped with the current local time. That is, future messages cannot be "used" (no variable can be written, except message type variables) before the phase and step tags are updated to match the highest timestamp. To check it, we need to prove a stronger property than the one for (III.). At each control location that writes to either variables of primitive or composite type or mailbox variables, the values of the phase (and step) variables must be equal to the phase (and step) tagged fields of all allocated message type objects. In Fig. 3, the statement `assert(equal(mbox, ballot, label))` checks this condition on the leader's branch. It is a separation logic formula that uses the inductive list definition of `mbox` which includes the content of the `mbox`.

The first four conditions imply that there is a global notion of time in the asynchronous protocol. However, this does not restrict the number of the messages exchanged between two processes with the same timestamp. mHO restricts the message exchange: for every time value (corresponding to a mHO-round), processes first send, then they receive messages, and then they perform a computation without receiving or sending more messages before time is increased. Condition (V.) ensures that the asynchronous protocol has this structure. We do a syntactic check of the code to ensure the code meets these restrictions.

Intuitively, each pair of synchronization variables identifies uniquely a mHO-protocol. To rewrite an asynchronous protocol into nested (inter-procedural) mHO-protocols, the tag of the inner protocol should include the tag of the outer one. The asynchronous code advances the time of one protocol at a time, that is, modifies one synchronization pair at a time. The only exception is when inner protocols terminate: in this case, the time of the outer protocol is advanced, while the time of the inner one is reset. Moreover, different protocols exchange different message types. To be able to order the messages exchanged by an inner protocol w.r.t. the messages exchanged by an outer protocol, the inner protocol messages should be tagged also with the synchronization variables identifying the outer one. This is actually happening in state machine replication algorithms, where the ballot (or view number), which is the tag of the outer leader election algorithm, tags also all the messages broadcast by the leader in the inner one.

5 Reducing Asynchronous Executions

We show that any execution of an asynchronous protocol that has a synchronization tag can be reduced to an indistinguishable mHO execution.

Definition 3 (Indistinguishability). *Given two executions π and π' of a protocol $\mathcal{P}$, we say a process p cannot distinguish locally between π and π' w.r.t. a set of variables W, denoted $\pi \simeq_p^W \pi'$, if the projection of both executions on the sequence of states of p, restricted to the variables in W, agree up to finite stuttering, denoted, $\pi\lfloor_{p,W} \equiv \pi'\lfloor_{p,W}$.*

Two executions π and π' are indistinguishable *w.r.t. a set of variables W, denoted $\pi \simeq^W \pi'$, iff no process can distinguish between them, i.e., $\forall p.\ \pi \simeq_p^W \pi'$.*

The reduction preserves so-called local properties [7], among which are consensus and state machine replication.

Definition 4 (Local properties). *A property ϕ is* local *if for any two executions a and b that are indistinguishable $a \models \phi$ iff $b \models \phi$.*

Theorem 1. *If there exists a synchronization tag $(\mathtt{SyncV}, \mathtt{tags}, \mathtt{tagm}, \mathcal{D}, \preceq)$ for $\mathcal{P}$, then $\forall \mathsf{ae} \in [\![\mathcal{P}]\!]$ there exists an mHO-execution se that is indistinguishable w.r.t. all variables except for $\mathtt{M}$ or $\mathtt{Set(M)}$ variables, therefore ae and se satisfy the same local properties.*

Proof Sketch. There are two cases to consider. Case (1): every receive transition $s \xrightarrow{m=recv(*cond)} sr$ in ae satisfies that $[\![\mathtt{tags}]\!]_{sr} = [\![\mathtt{tagm}]\!]_m$, i.e., all messages received are timestamped with the current local tag of the receiver. We use commutativity arguments to reorder transitions so that we obtain an indistinguishable asynchronous execution in which the transition tags are globally non-decreasing: The interesting case is if a send comes before a lower tagged receive in ae. Then the tags of the two transitions imply that the transitions concern different messages so that swapping them cannot violate send/receive causality.

We exploit that in the protocols we consider, no correct process locally keeps the tags unchanged forever (e.g., stays in a ballot forever) to arrive at an execution where the subsequence of transitions with the same tag is finite. Still, the resulting execution is not an mHO execution; e.g., for the same tag a receive may happen before a send on a different process. Condition (V.) ensures that mHO send-receive-update order is respected locally at each process. From this, together with the observation that sends are left movers, and updates are right movers, we obtain a global send-receive-update order which implies that the resulting execution is a mHO execution.

Case (2): there is a transition $s \xrightarrow{m=recv(*cond)} sr$ in ae such that $[\![\mathtt{tags}]\!]_{sr} \prec [\![\mathtt{tagm}]\!]_m$, that is, a process receives a message with tag k', higher than its state tag k. In mHO, a process only receives for its current round. To bring the asynchronous execution in such a form, we use Condition (IV.) and mHO semantics, where each process goes through all rounds. First, Condition (IV.) ensures that the process must update the tag variables to k' at some point t after receiving it, if it wants to use the content of the message. It ensures that the process stutters during the time instance between k and k', w.r.t. the values of the variables which are not of message type. That is, for the intermediate values of abstract time, between k and k', no messages are sent, received, and no computation is performed. We split ae at point t and add empty send instructions, receive instructions, and instructions that increment the synchronization variables, until the tag reaches k'. If we do this for each jump in ae, we arrive at an indistinguishable asynchronous execution that falls into the Case (1). □

6 Rewriting of Asynchronous to mHO

We introduce a rewriting algorithm that takes as input an asynchronous protocol $\mathcal{P}$ annotated with a synchronization tag and produces a mHO protocol whose executions are indistinguishable from the executions of $\mathcal{P}$.

Message Reception. mHO receives all messages of a round at once, while in the asynchronous code, messages are received one by one. By Condition (V.), receive steps that belong to the same round are separated only by instructions that store the messages in the mailbox. We consider that message reception is implemented in a simple `while(true)` loop (the most inner one); cf. filled boxes in Fig. 3. Conditions (III.) and (IV.) ensure that all messages received in a loop belong to one round (the current one or the one the code will jump to after exiting the reception loop). Thus, we replace a reception loop by `havoc` and `assume` statements that subsume the possible effects of the loop, satisfying all the conditions regarding synchronization tags found in the original receive statements.

Rewriting to an Intra-procedural mHO. When the synchronization tag is defined over a pair of variables, the rewriting will produce an intra-procedural mHO protocol. Recall that the values of synchronization variables incarnate the round number, so that each update to a pair of synchronization variables marks the beginning of a new mHO round. The difficulty is that different execution prefixes may lead to the same values of the synchronization variables. To compute mHO-rounds, the algorithm exploits the position of the updates to the synchronization variables in the control flow graph (CFG). We consider different CFG patterns, from the simplest to the most complicated one.

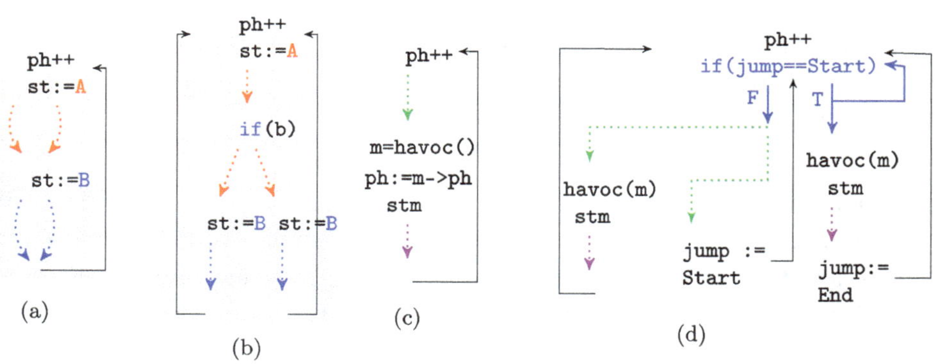

Fig. 8. Control flow graphs for rewriting. (Color figure online)

Case 1: If the CFG is like in Fig. 8(a), i.e., it consists of one loop, where the phase tag `ph` is incremented once at the beginning of each loop iteration, and for every value of the step tag `st` there is exactly one assignment in the loop body (the same on all paths). In this case, the phase tag takes the same values as the loop iteration counter (maybe shifted with some initial value). Therefore, the loop body defines the code of an mHO-phase. It is easy to structure it into two mHO-rounds: the code of round A is the part of the CFG from the beginning of the loop's body up to the second assignment of the `st` variable, and round B is the rest of the code up to the end of the loop body.

Case 2: The CFG is like in Fig. 8(b). It differs from Case 1 in that the same value is assigned to `st` in different branches. Each of this assignments marks the beginning of a mHO round B, which thus has multiple entry points. In mHO, a round only has one entry point. To simulate the multiple entry points in mHO, we store in auxiliary variables the values of the conditions along the paths that led to the entry point. In the figure, the code of round A is given by the red box, and the code of round B by the condition in the first blue box, expressed on the auxiliary variable, followed by the respective branches in the blue box.

In our example in Fig. 3, the assignment `label = AckBallot` appears in the leader and the follower branch. Followers send and receive `AckBallot` messages only if they have received a `NewBallot`. The rewrite introduces `old_mbox1` in the mHO protocol in Fig. 4 to store this information. Also, we eliminate the variables `ballot` and `label`; they are subsumed by the phase and round number of mHO.

Case 3: Let us assume that the CFG is like in Fig. 8(c). It differs from Case 1 because the phase tag `ph` is assigned twice. We rewrite it into asynchronous code that falls into Case 1 or 2. The resulting CFG is sketched in Fig. 8(d), with only one assignment to `ph` at the beginning of the loop.

If the second assignment changes the value of `ph`, then there is a jump. In case of a jump, the beginning of a new phase does not coincide with the first instruction of the loop. Thus there might be multiple entry points for a phase. We introduce (non-deterministic) branching in the control flow to capture different entry points: In case there is no jump, the green followed by the purple edge are executed within the same phase. In case of a jump, the rewritten code allows the green and the purple paths to be executed in different phases; first the green, and then the purple in a later phase. We add empty loops to simulate the phases that are jumped over. As a pure non-deterministic choice at the top of the loop would be too imprecise, we use the variable `jump` to make sure that the purple edge is executed only once prior to green edge. In case of multiple assignments, we perform this transformation iteratively for each assignment.

The protocol in Fig. 4 is obtained using two optimizations of the previous construction: First we do not need empty loops. They are subsumed by the mHO semantics as all local state changes are caused by some message reception. Thus, an empty loop is simulated by the execution of a phase with empty HO sets. Second, instead of adding `jump` variables, we reuse the non-deterministic value of `mbox`. This is possible as the jump is preconditioned by a cardinality constraint on the `mbox`, and the green edge is empty (assignments to `ballot` and `label` correspond to `ph++` and reception loops have been reduced to havoc statements).

Nesting. Cases 1–3 capture loops without nesting. Nested loops are rewritten into inter-procedural mHO protocols, using the structure of the tag annotations from Sect. 4. Each loop is rewritten into one protocol, starting with the most inner loop using the procedure above. For each outer loop, it first replaces the nested loop with a call to the computed mHO protocol, and then applies the same rewriting procedure. Interpreting each loop as a protocol is pessimistic, and our rewriting may generate deeper nesting than necessary. Inner loops appearing on different branches may belong to the same sub-protocol, so that these different loops exchange messages. If `tags` associates different synchronization variables to different loops then the rewriting builds one (sub-)protocol for each loop. Otherwise, the rewriting merges the loops into one mHO protocol. To soundly merge several loops into the same mHO protocol, the rewrite algorithm identifies the context in which the inner loop is executed.

Theorem 2. *Given an asynchronous protocol $\mathcal{P}$ annotated with a synchronization tag* $(\texttt{SyncV}, \texttt{tags}, \texttt{tagm}, \mathcal{D}, \preceq)$, *the rewriting returns an inter-procedural mHO protocol $\mathcal{P}^{mHO}$ whose executions are indistinguishable from the executions of $\mathcal{P}$.*

7 Experimental Results

We implemented the rewriting procedure in a prototype tool ATHOS (https://github.com/alexandrumc/async-to-sync-translation). We applied it to several fault-tolerant distributed protocols. Figure 9 summarizes our results.

Verification of Synchronization Tags. The tool takes protocols in a C embedding of the language from Sect. 2 as input. We use a C embedding to be able to use Verifast [22] for checking the conditions in Sect. 4, i.e., the communication closure of an asynchronous protocol. Verifast is a deductive verification tool based on separation logic for sequential programs. Therefore, communication closure is specified in separation logic in our tool. To reason about sending and receiving messages, we inline every `recv(*cond)` and use predefined specifications for `send` and `recv`. We consider only the prototype and the specification of these functions.

The user specifies in a configuration file the synchronization tag by (i) defining the number of (nested) protocols, (ii) for each protocol, the phase and step variables, and (iii) for each messages type the fields that encode the timestamp, i.e., the phase and step number. Figure 9 gives the names of phase and step variables of our benchmarks. For now, we manually insert the specification to be proven, i.e., the `assert` statements that capture Conditions (I.) to (V.) in Sect. 4. In Fig. 9, column Async gives the size in LoC of the input asynchronous protocol, +CC gives the size in LoC of the input annotated with the checks for communication closure (Conditions (I.) to (V.)) and their proofs.

Protocol	Tags	Async	+CC	Sync
Consensus [6, Fig.6]	$ph = r_p$ st= {Phase1, Phase2, Phase3, Phase4}	332	661	251
Two phase commit	ph = i, st= {Query, Vote, Commit, Ack}	342	596	242
Figure $3^{*,V}$	ph = ballot, st = {NewBallot, AckBallot}	255	576	110
ViewChange* [34]	$ph1$ = `view`, $st1$ = {StartViewChange, DoViewChange, StartView}	352	720	172
Normal-Op^{V} [34]	ph = op_number st = {Prepare, PrepareOK, Commit}	266	628	182
Multi-Paxos^{*,V} [25]	$ph1$ = ballot, $st1$ = {NewBallot, AckBallot, NewLog} $ph2$ = op_number, $st2$ = {Prepare, PrepareOK, Commit}	1646	621	405

Fig. 9. Benchmarks. The superscript * identifies protocols that jump over phases. The superscript V marks protocols whose synchronous counterpart we verified.

Benchmarks. Our tool has rewritten several challenging benchmarks: the algorithm from [6, Fig. 6] solves consensus using a failure detector. The algorithm jumps to a specific decision round, if a special decision message is received. Multi-Paxos is the Paxos algorithm from [25] over sequences, without fast paths, where the classic path is repeated as long as the leader is stable. Roughly, it does a leader election similar to our running example (`NewBallot` is *Phase1a*), except that the last all-to-all round is replaced by one back-and-forth communication between the leader and its quorum: the leader receives $n/2$ acknowledgments that contain also the log of its followers (*Phase1b*). The leader computes the maximal log and sends it to all (*Phase1aStart*). In a subprotocol, a stable leader accepts client requests, and broadcasts them one by one to its followers. The broadcast is implemented by three rounds, *Phase2aClassic*, *Phase2bClassic*, *Learn*, and is repeated as long as the leader is stable. ViewChange is a leader election algorithm similar to the one in ViewStamped [34]. Normal-Op is the subprotocol used in ViewStamped to implement the broadcasting of new commands by a stable leader. The last column of Fig. 9 gives the size of the mHO protocol computed by the rewriting. The implementation uses pycparser [3], to obtain the abstract syntax tree of the input protocol.

Verification. We verified the safety specification (agreement) of the mHO counterparts of the running example (Fig. 3), Normal-Op, and Multi-Paxos, by deductive verification: We encoded the specification of these algorithms, i.e., atomic broadcast, consensus, leader election, and the transition relation in Consensus Logic CL [13]. CL is a specification logic that allows us to express global properties of synchronous systems, and it contains expressions for processes, values, sets, cardinalities, and set comprehension. The verification conditions are soundly discarded by using an SMT solver. We used Z3 [33] in our experiments.

For Multi-Paxos we did a modular proof. First we prove the correctness of the sub-protocol Normal-Op which implements a loop of atomic broadcasts (executed in case of a stable leader). Then we prove the leader election outer loop correct, by replacing the subprotocol Normal-Op with its specification.

8 Related Work and Conclusions

Verification of asynchronous protocols received a lot of attention in the past years. Mechanized verification techniques like IronFleet [21] and Verdi [41] were the first to address verification of state machine replication. Later, Disel [38] proposes a logic to make the reasoning less protocol-specific, with the tradeoff of proofs that use the entire message history. At the other end of the spectrum, model checking based techniques [2,4,20,23,24] are fully automated but more restricted regarding the protocols they apply to. In between, semi-automated verification techniques based on deductive verification like natural proofs [12], Ivy [36], and PSync [14] try to minimize the user input for similar benchmarks.

We propose a technique that reduces the verification of an asynchronous protocol to a synchronous one, which simplifies the verification task no matter which method is chosen. We verified the resulting synchronous protocols with deductive verification based on [14]. Our technique uses the notion of communication closure [17], which we believe is the essence of any explicit or implicit synchrony in the system. We formalized a more general notion of communication closure that allows jumping over rounds, which is a catch-up mechanism essential to re-synchronize and ensure liveness. Previous reduction techniques focus on shared memory systems [16,27], in contrast we focus on message passing concurrency.

The closest approaches are the results in [4,24] and [2,20], which also explore the synchrony of the system. Compared to these approaches, our technique allows more general behaviors, e.g., reasoning about stable leaders is possible because communication closure includes (for the first time) unbounded jumps. Also, we reduce to a stronger synchronous model, a round-based one instead of a peer to peer one, where interleavings w.r.t. actions of other rounds are removed.

As future work, we will address the relation between communication closure and specific network assumptions, e.g., FIFO channels, and a current limitation of communication closure which is reacting on messages from the past. For instance, recovery protocols react to such messages.

References

1. Aminof, B., Rubin, S., Stoilkovska, I., Widder, J., Zuleger, F.: Parameterized model checking of synchronous distributed algorithms by abstraction. In: Dillig, I., Palsberg, J. (eds.) VMCAI 2018. LNCS, vol. 10747, pp. 1–24. Springer, Cham (2018). https://doi.org/10.1007/978-3-319-73721-8_1
2. Bakst, A., von Gleissenthall, K., Kici, R.G., Jhala, R.: Verifying distributed programs via canonical sequentialization. PACMPL **1**(OOPSLA), 110:1–110:27 (2017)
3. Bendersky, E.: pycparser. https://github.com/eliben/pycparser. Accessed 7 Nov 2018

4. Bouajjani, A., Enea, C., Ji, K., Qadeer, S.: On the completeness of verifying message passing programs under bounded asynchrony. In: Chockler, H., Weissenbacher, G. (eds.) CAV 2018, Part II. LNCS, vol. 10982, pp. 372–391. Springer, Cham (2018). https://doi.org/10.1007/978-3-319-96142-2_23
5. Chandra, T.D., Griesemer, R., Redstone, J.: Paxos made live: an engineering perspective. In: PODC, pp. 398–407 (2007)
6. Chandra, T.D., Toueg, S.: Unreliable failure detectors for reliable distributed systems. J. ACM **43**(2), 225–267 (1996)
7. Chaouch-Saad, M., Charron-Bost, B., Merz, S.: A reduction theorem for the verification of round-based distributed algorithms. In: Bournez, O., Potapov, I. (eds.) RP 2009. LNCS, vol. 5797, pp. 93–106. Springer, Heidelberg (2009). https://doi.org/10.1007/978-3-642-04420-5_10
8. Charron-Bost, B., Debrat, H., Merz, S.: Formal verification of consensus algorithms tolerating malicious faults. In: Défago, X., Petit, F., Villain, V. (eds.) SSS 2011. LNCS, vol. 6976, pp. 120–134. Springer, Heidelberg (2011). https://doi.org/10.1007/978-3-642-24550-3_11
9. Charron-Bost, B., Schiper, A.: The heard-of model: computing in distributed systems with benign faults. Distrib. Comput. **22**(1), 49–71 (2009)
10. Chou, C., Gafni, E.: Understanding and verifying distributed algorithms using stratified decomposition. In: PODC, pp. 44–65 (1988)
11. Debrat, H., Merz, S.: Verifying fault-tolerant distributed algorithms in the heard-of model. In: Archive of Formal Proofs 2012 (2012)
12. Desai, A., Garg, P., Madhusudan, P.: Natural proofs for asynchronous programs using almost-synchronous reductions. In: Proceedings of the 2014 ACM International Conference on Object Oriented Programming Systems Languages & Applications, OOPSLA 2014, Part of SPLASH 2014, Portland, OR, USA, 20–24 October 2014, pp. 709–725 (2014)
13. Drăgoi, C., Henzinger, T.A., Veith, H., Widder, J., Zufferey, D.: A logic-based framework for verifying consensus algorithms. In: McMillan, K.L., Rival, X. (eds.) VMCAI 2014. LNCS, vol. 8318, pp. 161–181. Springer, Heidelberg (2014). https://doi.org/10.1007/978-3-642-54013-4_10
14. Drăgoi, C., Henzinger, T.A., Zufferey, D.: PSync: a partially synchronous language for fault-tolerant distributed algorithms. In: POPL, pp. 400–415 (2016)
15. Dwork, C., Lynch, N., Stockmeyer, L.: Consensus in the presence of partial synchrony. JACM **35**(2), 288–323 (1988)
16. Elmas, T., Qadeer, S., Tasiran, S.: A calculus of atomic actions. In: Proceedings of the 36th ACM SIGPLAN-SIGACT Symposium on Principles of Programming Languages, POPL 2009, Savannah, GA, USA, 21–23 January 2009, pp. 2–15 (2009)
17. Elrad, T., Francez, N.: Decomposition of distributed programs into communication-closed layers. Sci. Comput. Program. **2**(3), 155–173 (1982)
18. Gafni, E.: Round-by-round fault detectors: unifying synchrony and asynchrony (extended abstract). In: PODC, pp. 143–152 (1998)
19. García-Pérez, Á., Gotsman, A., Meshman, Y., Sergey, I.: Paxos consensus, deconstructed and abstracted. In: Ahmed, A. (ed.) ESOP 2018. LNCS, vol. 10801, pp. 912–939. Springer, Cham (2018). https://doi.org/10.1007/978-3-319-89884-1_32
20. von Gleissenthall, K., Gökhan Kici, R., Bakst, A., Stefan, D., Jhala, R.: Pretend synchrony: synchronous verification of asynchronous distributed programs. PACMPL **3**(POPL), 59:1–59:30 (2019)
21. Hawblitzel, C., et al.: IronFleet: proving safety and liveness of practical distributed systems. Commun. ACM **60**(7), 83–92 (2017)

22. Jacobs, B., Smans, J., Piessens, F.: A quick tour of the verifast program verifier. In: Ueda, K. (ed.) APLAS 2010. LNCS, vol. 6461, pp. 304–311. Springer, Heidelberg (2010). https://doi.org/10.1007/978-3-642-17164-2_21
23. Konnov, I.V., Lazic, M., Veith, H., Widder, J.: A short counterexample property for safety and liveness verification of fault-tolerant distributed algorithms. In: POPL, pp. 719–734 (2017)
24. Kragl, B., Qadeer, S., Henzinger, T.A.: Synchronizing the asynchronous. In: CONCUR, pp. 21:1–21:17 (2018)
25. Lamport, L.: Generalized consensus and paxos. Technical report, March 2005. https://www.microsoft.com/en-us/research/publication/generalized-consensus-and-paxos/
26. Lesani, M., Bell, C.J., Chlipala, A.: Chapar: certified causally consistent distributed key-value stores. In: POPL, pp. 357–370 (2016)
27. Lipton, R.J.: Reduction: a method of proving properties of parallel programs. Commun. ACM **18**(12), 717–721 (1975)
28. Lynch, N.: Distributed Algorithms. Morgan Kaufman, San Francisco (1996)
29. Marić, O., Sprenger, C., Basin, D.: Cutoff bounds for consensus algorithms. In: Majumdar, R., Kunčak, V. (eds.) CAV 2017, Part II. LNCS, vol. 10427, pp. 217–237. Springer, Cham (2017). https://doi.org/10.1007/978-3-319-63390-9_12
30. Mattern, F.: On the relativistic structure of logical time in distributed systems. In: Parallel and Distributed Algorithms, pp. 215–226 (1989)
31. Moraru, I., Andersen, D.G., Kaminsky, M.: There is more consensus in Egalitarian parliaments. In: SOSP, pp. 358–372 (2013)
32. Moses, Y., Rajsbaum, S.: A layered analysis of consensus. SIAM J. Comput. **31**(4), 989–1021 (2002)
33. de Moura, L., Bjørner, N.: Z3: an efficient SMT solver. In: Ramakrishnan, C.R., Rehof, J. (eds.) TACAS 2008. LNCS, vol. 4963, pp. 337–340. Springer, Heidelberg (2008). https://doi.org/10.1007/978-3-540-78800-3_24
34. Oki, B.M., Liskov, B.: Viewstamped replication: a general primary copy. In: PODC, pp. 8–17 (1988)
35. Ongaro, D., Ousterhout, J.K.: In search of an understandable consensus algorithm. In: 2014 USENIX Annual Technical Conference, USENIX ATC 2014, pp. 305–319 (2014)
36. Padon, O., McMillan, K.L., Panda, A., Sagiv, M., Shoham, S.: Ivy: safety verification by interactive generalization. In: PLDI, pp. 614–630 (2016)
37. Rahli, V., Guaspari, D., Bickford, M., Constable, R.L.: Formal specification, verification, and implementation of fault-tolerant systems using EventML. ECEASST 72 (2015)
38. Sergey, I., Wilcox, J.R., Tatlock, Z.: Programming and proving with distributed protocols. PACMPL **2**(POPL), 28:1–28:30 (2018)
39. Stoilkovska, I., Konnov, I., Widder, J., Zuleger, F.: Verifying safety of synchronous fault-tolerant algorithms by bounded model checking. In: Vojnar, T., Zhang, L. (eds.) TACAS 2019, Part II. LNCS, vol. 11428, pp. 357–374. Springer, Cham (2019). https://doi.org/10.1007/978-3-030-17465-1_20
40. Tsuchiya, T., Schiper, A.: Verification of consensus algorithms using satisfiability solving. Distrib. Comput. **23**(5–6), 341–358 (2011)
41. Wilcox, J.R., et al.: Verdi: a framework for implementing and formally verifying distributed systems. In: PLDI, pp. 357–368 (2015)
42. Woos, D., Wilcox, J.R., Anton, S., Tatlock, Z., Ernst, M.D., Anderson, T.E.: Planning for change in a formal verification of the RAFT consensus protocol. In: CPP, pp. 154–165 (2016)

Verification and Invariants

Interpolating Strong Induction

Hari Govind Vediramana Krishnan[1](✉), Yakir Vizel[2], Vijay Ganesh[1], and Arie Gurfinkel[1]

[1] University of Waterloo, Waterloo, Canada
hgvedira@uwaterloo.ca
[2] The Technion, Haifa, Israel

Abstract. The principle of strong induction, also known as k-induction is one of the first techniques for unbounded SAT-based Model Checking (SMC). While elegant and simple to apply, properties as such are rarely k-inductive and when they can be strengthened, there is no effective strategy to guess the depth of induction. It has been mostly displaced by techniques that compute inductive strengthenings based on interpolation and property directed reachability (Pdr). In this paper, we present kAvy, an SMC algorithm that effectively uses k-induction to guide interpolation and Pdr-style inductive generalization. Unlike pure k-induction, kAvy uses Pdr-style generalization to compute and strengthen an inductive trace. Unlike pure Pdr, kAvy uses relative k-induction to construct an inductive invariant. The depth of induction is adjusted dynamically by minimizing a proof of unsatisfiability. We have implemented kAvy within the Avy Model Checker and evaluated it on HWMCC instances. Our results show that kAvy is more effective than both Avy and Pdr, and that using k-induction leads to faster running time and solving more instances. Further, on a class of benchmarks, called *shift*, kAvy is orders of magnitude faster than Avy, Pdr and k-induction.

1 Introduction

The principle of strong induction, also known as k-induction, is a generalization of (simple) induction that extends the base- and inductive-cases to k steps of a transition system [27]. A safety property P is k-inductive in a transition system T iff (a) P is true in the first $(k-1)$ steps of T, and (b) if P is assumed to hold for $(k-1)$ consecutive steps, then P holds in k steps of T. Simple induction is equivalent to 1-induction. Unlike induction, strong induction is complete for safety properties: a property P is safe in a transition system T iff there exists a natural number k such that P is k-inductive in T (assuming the usual restriction to simple paths). This makes k-induction a powerful method for unbounded SAT-based Model Checking (SMC).

Unlike other SMC techniques, strong induction reduces model checking to pure SAT that does not require any additional features such as solving with assumptions [12], interpolation [24], resolution proofs [17], Maximal Unsatisfiable Subsets (MUS) [2], etc. It easily integrates with existing SAT-solvers

I. Dillig and S. Tasiran (Eds.): CAV 2019, LNCS 11562, pp. 367–385, 2019.
https://doi.org/10.1007/978-3-030-25543-5_21

and immediately benefits from any improvements in heuristics [22,23], pre- and in-processing [18], and parallel solving [1]. The simplicity of applying k-induction made it the go-to technique for SMT-based infinite-state model checking [9,11,19]. In that context, it is particularly effective in combination with invariant synthesis [14,20]. Moreover, for some theories, strong induction is strictly stronger than 1-induction [19]: there are properties that are k-inductive, but have no 1-inductive strengthening.

Notwithstanding all of its advantages, strong induction has been mostly displaced by more recent SMC techniques such as Interpolation [25], Property Directed Reachability [3,7,13,15], and their combinations [29]. In SMC k-induction is equivalent to induction: any k-inductive property P can be strengthened to an inductive property Q [6,16]. Even though in the worst case Q is exponentially larger than P [6], this is rarely observed in practice [26]. Furthermore, the SAT queries get very hard as k increases and usually succeed only for rather small values of k. A recent work [16] shows that strong induction can be integrated in PDR. However, [16] argues that k-induction is hard to control in the context of PDR since choosing a proper value of k is difficult. A wrong choice leads to a form of state enumeration. In [16], k is fixed to 5, and regular induction is used as soon as 5-induction fails.

In this paper, we present KAVY, an SMC algorithm that effectively uses k-induction to guide interpolation and PDR-style inductive generalization. As many state-of-the-art SMC algorithms, KAVY iteratively constructs candidate inductive invariants for a given safety property P. However, the construction of these candidates is driven by k-induction. Whenever P is known to hold up to a bound N, KAVY searches for the smallest $k \leq N+1$, such that either P or some of its strengthening is k-inductive. Once it finds the right k and strengthening, it computes a 1-inductive strengthening.

It is convenient to think of modern SMC algorithms (e.g., PDR and AVY), and k-induction, as two ends of a spectrum. On the one end, modern SMC algorithms fix k to 1 and *search* for a 1-inductive strengthening of P. While on the opposite end, k-induction fixes the strengthening of P to be P itself and *searches* for a k such that P is k-inductive. KAVY *dynamically* explores this spectrum, exploiting the interplay between finding the right k and finding the right strengthening.

```
reg [7:0] c = 0;
always
  if(c == 64)
    c <= 0;
  else
    c <= c + 1;
end
assert property (c < 66);
```

Fig. 1. An example system.

As an example, consider a system in Fig. 1 that counts upto 64 and resets. The property, $p : c < 66$, is 2-inductive. IC3, PDR and AVY iteratively guess a 1-inductive strengthening of p. In the worst case, they require at least 64 iterations. On the other hand, KAVY determines that p is 2-inductive after 2 iterations, *computes* a 1-inductive invariant $(c \neq 65) \wedge (c < 66)$, and terminates.

KAVY builds upon the foundations of AVY [29]. AVY first uses Bounded Model Checking [4] (BMC) to prove that the property P holds up to bound N. Then, it uses a sequence interpolant [28] and PDR-style inductive-generalization [7] to construct 1-inductive strengthening candidate for P. We emphasize that using k-induction to construct 1-inductive candidates allows kAvy to efficiently utilize many principles from Pdr and Avy. While maintaining k-inductive candidates might seem attractive (since they may be smaller), they are also much harder to generalize effectively [7].

We implemented kAvy in the Avy Model Checker, and evaluated it on the benchmarks from the Hardware Model Checking Competition (HWMCC). Our experiments show that kAvy significantly improves the performance of Avy and solves more examples than either of Pdr and Avy. For a specific family of examples from [21], kAvy exhibits nearly constant time performance, compared to an exponential growth of Avy, Pdr, and k-induction (see Fig. 2b in Sect. 5). This further emphasizes the effectiveness of efficiently integrating strong induction into modern SMC.

The rest of the paper is structured as follows. After describing the most relevant related work, we present the necessary background in Sect. 2 and give an overview of SAT-based model checking algorithms in Sect. 3. kAvy is presented in Sect. 4, followed by presentation of results in Sect. 5. Finally, we conclude the paper in Sect. 6.

Related Work. kAvy builds on top of the ideas of IC3 [7] and Pdr [13]. The use of interpolation for generating an inductive trace is inspired by Avy [29]. While conceptually, our algorithm is similar to Avy, its proof of correctness is non-trivial and is significantly different from that of Avy. We are not aware of any other work that combines interpolation with strong induction.

There are two prior attempts enhancing Pdr-style algorithms with k-induction. Pd-Kind [19] is an SMT-based Model Checking algorithm for infinite-state systems inspired by IC3/Pdr. It infers k-inductive invariants driven by the property whereas kAvy infers 1-inductive invariants driven by k-induction. Pd-Kind uses recursive blocking with interpolation and model-based projection to block bad states, and k-induction to propagate (push) lemmas to next level. While the algorithm is very interesting it is hard to adapt it to SAT-based setting (i.e. SMC), and impossible to compare on HWMCC instances directly.

The closest related work is KIC3 [16]. It modifies the counter example queue management strategy in IC3 to utilize k-induction during blocking. The main limitation is that the value for k must be chosen statically ($k = 5$ is reported for the evaluation). kAvy also utilizes k-induction during blocking but computes the value for k dynamically. Unfortunately, the implementation is not available publicly and we could not compare with it directly.

2 Background

In this section, we present notations and background that is required for the description of our algorithm.

Safety Verification. A symbolic transition system T is a tuple $(\bar{v}, Init, Tr, Bad)$, where $\bar{v}$ is a set of Boolean *state* variables. A state of the system is a complete valuation to all variables in $\bar{v}$ (i.e., the set of states is $\{0,1\}^{|\bar{v}|}$). We write $\bar{v}' = \{v' \mid v \in \bar{v}\}$ for the set of *primed* variables, used to represent the next state. *Init* and *Bad* are formulas over $\bar{v}$ denoting the set of initial states and bad states, respectively, and *Tr* is a formula over $\bar{v} \cup \bar{v}'$, denoting the transition relation. With abuse of notation, we use formulas and the sets of states (or transitions) that they represent interchangeably. In addition, we sometimes use a state s to denote the formula (cube) that characterizes it. For a formula φ over $\bar{v}$, we use $\varphi(\bar{v}')$, or φ' in short, to denote the formula in which every occurrence of $v \in \bar{v}$ is replaced by $v' \in \bar{v}'$. For simplicity of presentation, we assume that the property $P = \neg Bad$ is true in the initial state, that is $Init \Rightarrow P$.

Given a formula $\varphi(\bar{v})$, an M-to-N-*unrolling* of T, where φ holds in all intermediate states is defined by the formula:

$$Tr[\varphi]_M^N = \bigwedge_{i=M}^{N-1} \varphi(\bar{v}_i) \wedge Tr(\bar{v}_i, \bar{v}_{i+1}) \tag{1}$$

We write $Tr[\varphi]^N$ when $M = 0$ and Tr_M^N when $\varphi = \top$.

A transition system T is UNSAFE iff there exists a state $s \in Bad$ s.t. s is reachable, and is SAFE otherwise. Equivalently, T is UNSAFE iff there exists a number N such that the following *unrolling* formula is satisfiable:

$$Init(\bar{v}_0) \wedge Tr^N \wedge Bad(\bar{v}_N) \tag{2}$$

T is SAFE if no such N exists. Whenever T is UNSAFE and $s_N \in Bad$ is a reachable state, the path from $s_0 \in Init$ to s_N is called a *counterexample*.

An *inductive invariant* is a formula *Inv* that satisfies:

$$Init(\bar{v}) \Rightarrow Inv(\bar{v}) \qquad\qquad Inv(\bar{v}) \wedge Tr(\bar{v}, \bar{v}') \Rightarrow Inv(\bar{v}') \tag{3}$$

A transition system T is SAFE iff there exists an inductive invariant *Inv* s.t. $Inv(\bar{v}) \Rightarrow P(\bar{v})$. In this case we say that *Inv* is a *safe* inductive invariant.

The *safety* verification problem is to decide whether a transition system T is SAFE or UNSAFE, i.e., whether there exists a safe inductive invariant or a counterexample.

Strong Induction. Strong induction (or k-induction) is a generalization of the notion of an inductive invariant that is similar to how "simple" induction is generalized in mathematics. A formula *Inv* is k-*invariant* in a transition system T if it is true in the first k steps of T. That is, the following formula is valid: $Init(\bar{v}_0) \wedge Tr^k \Rightarrow \left(\bigwedge_{i=0}^{k} Inv(\bar{v}_i)\right)$. A formula *Inv* is a k-*inductive invariant* iff *Inv* is a $(k-1)$-invariant and is inductive after k steps of T, i.e., the following formula is valid: $Tr[Inv]^k \Rightarrow Inv(\bar{v}_k)$. Compared to simple induction, k-induction strengthens the hypothesis in the induction step: *Inv* is assumed to hold between steps 0 to $k-1$ and is established in step k. Whenever $Inv \Rightarrow P$, we say that *Inv* is a safe k-inductive invariant. An inductive invariant is a 1-inductive invariant.

Theorem 1. *Given a transition system T. There exists a safe inductive invariant w.r.t. T iff there exists a safe k-inductive invariant w.r.t. T.*

Theorem 1 states that k-induction principle is as complete as 1-induction. One direction is trivial (since we can take $k = 1$). The other can be strengthened further: for every k-inductive invariant Inv_k there exists a 1-inductive strengthening Inv_1 such that $Inv_1 \Rightarrow Inv_k$. Theoretically Inv_1 might be exponentially bigger than Inv_k [6]. In practice, both invariants tend to be of similar size.

We say that a formula φ is *k-inductive relative* to F if it is a $(k-1)$-invariant and $Tr[\varphi \wedge F]^k \Rightarrow \varphi(\bar{v}_k)$.

Craig Interpolation [10]. We use an extension of Craig Interpolants to sequences, which is common in Model Checking. Let $\boldsymbol{A} = [A_1, \ldots, A_N]$ such that $A_1 \wedge \cdots \wedge A_N$ is unsatisfiable. A *sequence interpolant* $\boldsymbol{I} = \text{SEQITP}(\boldsymbol{A})$ for $\boldsymbol{A}$ is a sequence of formulas $\boldsymbol{I} = [I_2, \ldots, I_N]$ such that (a) $A_1 \Rightarrow I_2$, (b) $\forall 1 < i < N \cdot I_i \wedge A_i \Rightarrow I_{i+1}$, (c) $I_N \wedge A_N \Rightarrow \bot$, and (d) I_i is over variables that are shared between the corresponding prefix and suffix of $\boldsymbol{A}$.

3 SAT-Based Model Checking

In this section, we give a brief overview of SAT-based Model Checking algorithms: IC3/PDR [7,13], and AVY [29]. While these algorithms are well-known, we give a uniform presentation and establish notation necessary for the rest of the paper. We fix a symbolic transition system $T = (\bar{v}, Init, Tr, Bad)$.

The main data-structure of these algorithms is a sequence of candidate invariants, called an *inductive trace*. An *inductive trace*, or simply a trace, is a sequence of formulas $\boldsymbol{F} = [F_0, \ldots, F_N]$ that satisfy the following two properties:

$$Init(\bar{v}) = F_0(\bar{v}) \qquad \forall 0 \le i < N \cdot F_i(\bar{v}) \wedge Tr(\bar{v}, \bar{v}') \Rightarrow F_{i+1}(\bar{v}') \tag{4}$$

An element F_i of a trace is called a *frame*. The index of a frame is called a *level*. $\boldsymbol{F}$ is *clausal* when all its elements are in CNF. For convenience, we view a frame as a set of clauses, and assume that a trace is padded with $\top$ until the required length. The *size* of $\boldsymbol{F} = [F_0, \ldots, F_N]$ is $|\boldsymbol{F}| = N$. For $k \le N$, we write $\boldsymbol{F}^k = [F_k, \ldots, F_N]$ for the k-suffix of $\boldsymbol{F}$.

A trace $\boldsymbol{F}$ of size N is *stronger* than a trace $\boldsymbol{G}$ of size M iff $\forall 0 \le i \le \min(N, M) \cdot F_i(\bar{v}) \Rightarrow G_i(\bar{v})$. A trace is *safe* if each F_i is safe: $\forall i \cdot F_i \Rightarrow \neg Bad$; *monotone* if $\forall 0 \le i < N \cdot F_i \Rightarrow F_{i+1}$. In a monotone trace, a frame F_i over-approximates the set of states reachable in up to i steps of the Tr. A trace is closed if $\exists 1 \le i \le N \cdot F_i \Rightarrow \left(\bigvee_{j=0}^{i-1} F_j\right)$.

We define an unrolling formula of a k-suffix of a trace $\boldsymbol{F} = [F_0, \ldots, F_N]$ as :

$$Tr[\boldsymbol{F}^k] = \bigwedge_{i=k}^{|F|} F_i(\bar{v}_i) \wedge Tr(\bar{v}_i, \bar{v}_{i+1}) \tag{5}$$

We write $Tr[\boldsymbol{F}]$ to denote an unrolling of a 0-suffix of $\boldsymbol{F}$ (i.e $\boldsymbol{F}$ itself). Intuitively, $Tr[\boldsymbol{F}^k]$ is satisfiable iff there is a k-step execution of the Tr that is consistent with the k-suffix $\boldsymbol{F}^k$. If a transition system T admits a safe trace $\boldsymbol{F}$ of size $|\boldsymbol{F}| = N$, then T does not admit counterexamples of length less than N. A safe trace $\boldsymbol{F}$, with $|\boldsymbol{F}| = N$ is *extendable* with respect to level $0 \leq i \leq N$ iff there exists a safe trace $\boldsymbol{G}$ stronger than $\boldsymbol{F}$ such that $|\boldsymbol{G}| > N$ and $F_i \wedge Tr \Rightarrow G_{i+1}$. $\boldsymbol{G}$ and the corresponding level i are called an *extension trace* and an *extension level* of $\boldsymbol{F}$, respectively. SAT-based model checking algorithms work by iteratively extending a given safe trace $\boldsymbol{F}$ of size N to a safe trace of size $N + 1$.

An extension trace is not unique, but there is a largest extension level. We denote the set of all extension levels of $\boldsymbol{F}$ by $\mathcal{W}(\boldsymbol{F})$. The existence of an extension level i implies that an unrolling of the i-suffix does not contain any Bad states:

Proposition 1. *Let $\boldsymbol{F}$ be a safe trace. Then, i, $0 \leq i \leq N$, is an extension level of $\boldsymbol{F}$ iff the formula $Tr[\boldsymbol{F}^i] \wedge Bad(\bar{v}_{N+1})$ is unsatisfiable.*

Example 1. For Fig. 1, $\boldsymbol{F} = [c = 0, c < 66]$ is a safe trace of size 1. The formula $(c < 66) \wedge Tr \wedge \neg(c' < 66)$ is satisfiable. Therefore, there does not exists an extension trace at level 1. Since $(c = 0) \wedge Tr \wedge (c' < 66) \wedge Tr' \wedge (c'' \geq 66)$ is unsatisfiable, the trace is extendable at level 0. For example, a valid extension trace at level 0 is $\boldsymbol{G} = [c = 0, c < 2, c < 66]$.

Both PDR and AVY iteratively extend a safe trace either until the extension is closed or a counterexample is found. However, they differ in how exactly the trace is extended. In the rest of this section, we present AVY and PDR through the lens of extension level. The goal of this presentation is to make the paper self-contained. We omit many important optimization details, and refer the reader to the original papers [7,13,29].

PDR maintains a monotone, clausal trace $\boldsymbol{F}$ with $Init$ as the first frame (F_0). The trace $\boldsymbol{F}$ is extended by recursively computing and blocking (if possible) states that can reach Bad (called *bad states*). A bad state is blocked at the largest level possible. Algorithm 1 shows PDRBLOCK, the backward search procedure that identifies and blocks bad states. PDRBLOCK maintains a queue of states and the levels at which they have to be blocked. The smallest level at which blocking occurs is tracked in order to show the construction of the extension trace. For each state s in the queue, it is checked whether s can be blocked by the previous frame F_{d-1} (line 5). If not, a predecessor state t of s that satisfies F_{d-1} is computed and added to the queue (line 7). If a predecessor state is found at level 0, the trace is not extendable and an empty trace is returned. If the state s is blocked at level d, PDRINDGEN, is called to generate a clause that blocks s and possibly others. The clause is then added to all the frames at levels less than or equal to d. PDRINDGEN is a crucial optimization to PDR. However, we do not explain it for the sake of simplicity. The procedure terminates whenever there are no more states to be blocked (or a counterexample was found at line 4). By construction, the output trace $\boldsymbol{G}$ is an extension trace of $\boldsymbol{F}$ at the extension level w. Once PDR extends its trace, PDRPUSH is called to check if the clauses it learnt are also true at higher levels. PDR terminates when the trace is closed.

Algorithm 1. PDRBLOCK.

Input: A transition system $T = (Init, Tr, Bad)$
Input: A safe trace $\boldsymbol{F}$ with $|\boldsymbol{F}| = N$
Output: An extension trace $\boldsymbol{G}$ or an empty trace

$w \leftarrow N+1$; $\boldsymbol{G} \leftarrow \boldsymbol{F}$; $Q.push(\langle Bad, N+1 \rangle)$
while $\neg Q.empty()$ **do**
  $\langle s, d \rangle \leftarrow Q.pop()$
  if $d == 0$ **then return** $[\,]$
  if $\text{ISSAT}(F_{d-1}(\bar{v}) \wedge Tr(\bar{v}, \bar{v}') \wedge s(\bar{v}'))$ **then**
    $t \leftarrow predecessor(s)$
    $Q.push(t, d-1)$
    $Q.push(s, d)$
  else
    $\forall 0 \le i \le d \cdot G_i \leftarrow (G_i \wedge \text{PDRINDGEN}(\neg s))$
    $w \leftarrow min(w, d)$
return $\boldsymbol{G}$

Algorithm 2. AVY.

Input: A transition system $T = (Init, Tr, Bad)$
Output: SAFE/UNSAFE

1 $F_0 \leftarrow Init$; $N \leftarrow 0$
2 **repeat**
3   **if** $\text{ISSAT}(Tr[\boldsymbol{F}^0] \wedge Bad(\bar{v}_{N+1}))$ **then**
    return UNSAFE
4   $k \leftarrow \max\{i \mid \neg\text{ISSAT}(Tr[\boldsymbol{F}^i] \wedge Bad(\bar{v}_{N+1}))\}$
5   $I_{k+1}, \ldots, I_{N+1} \leftarrow \text{SEQITP}(Tr[\boldsymbol{F}^k] \wedge Bad(\bar{v}_{N+1}))$
6   $\forall 0 \le i \le k \cdot G_i \leftarrow F_i$
7   $\forall k < i \le (N+1) \cdot G_i \leftarrow F_i \wedge I_i$
8   $\boldsymbol{F} \leftarrow \text{AVYMKTRACE}([G_0, \ldots, G_{N+1}])$
9   $\boldsymbol{F} \leftarrow \text{PDRPUSH}(\boldsymbol{F})$
10   **if** $\exists 1 \le i \le N \cdot F_i \Rightarrow \left(\bigvee_{j=0}^{i-1} F_j\right)$ **then**
    return SAFE
11   $N \leftarrow N+1$
12 **until** ∞

Avy, shown in Algorithm 2, is an alternative to PDR that combines interpolation and recursive blocking. AVY starts with a trace $\boldsymbol{F}$, with $F_0 = Init$, that is extended in every iteration of the main loop. A counterexample is returned whenever $\boldsymbol{F}$ is not extendable (line 3). Otherwise, a sequence interpolant is extracted from the unsatisfiability of $Tr[\boldsymbol{F}^{\max(\mathcal{W})}] \wedge Bad(\bar{v}_{N+1})$. A longer trace $\boldsymbol{G} = [G_0, \ldots, G_N, G_{N+1}]$ is constructed using the sequence interpolant (line 7). Observe that $\boldsymbol{G}$ is an extension trace of $\boldsymbol{F}$. While $\boldsymbol{G}$ is safe, it is neither monotone nor clausal. A helper routine AVYMKTRACE is used to convert $\boldsymbol{G}$ to a proper PDR trace on line 8 (see [29] for the details on AVYMKTRACE). AVY converges when the trace is closed.

4 Interpolating k-Induction

In this section, we present KAVY, an SMC algorithm that uses the principle of strong induction to extend an inductive trace. The section is structured as follows. First, we introduce a concept of extending a trace using relative k-induction. Second, we present KAVY and describe the details of how k-induction is used to compute an extended trace. Third, we describe two techniques for computing maximal parameters to apply strong induction. Unless stated otherwise, we assume that all traces are monotone.

A safe trace $\boldsymbol{F}$, with $|\boldsymbol{F}| = N$, is *strongly extendable* with respect to (i, k), where $1 \le k \le i+1 \le N+1$, iff there exists a safe inductive trace $\boldsymbol{G}$ stronger than $\boldsymbol{F}$ such that $|\boldsymbol{G}| > N$ and $Tr[F_i]^k \Rightarrow G_{i+1}$. We refer to the pair (i, k) as *a strong extension level (SEL)*, and to the trace $\boldsymbol{G}$ as an (i, k)-*extension trace*, or simply a *strong extension trace (SET)* when (i, k) is not important. Note that for $k = 1$, $\boldsymbol{G}$ is just an extension trace.

Example 2. For Fig. 1, the trace $\boldsymbol{F} = [c = 0, c < 66]$ is strongly extendable at level 1. A valid $(1, 2)$-extension trace is $\boldsymbol{G} = [c = 0, (c \ne 65) \wedge (c < 66), c < 66]$. Note that $(c < 66)$ is 2-inductive relative to F_1, i.e. $Tr[F_1]^2 \Rightarrow (c'' < 66)$.

We write $\mathcal{K}(\boldsymbol{F})$ for the set of all SELs of $\boldsymbol{F}$. We define an order on SELs by: $(i_1, k_1) \preceq (i_2, k_2)$ iff (i) $i_1 < i_2$; or (ii) $i_1 = i_2 \wedge k_1 > k_2$. The maximal SEL is $\max(\mathcal{K}(\boldsymbol{F}))$.

Algorithm 3. kAvy algorithm.

Input: A transition system $T = (\mathit{Init}, \mathit{Tr}, \mathit{Bad})$
Output: SAFE/UNSAFE

1 $\boldsymbol{F} \leftarrow [\mathit{Init}]$; $N \leftarrow 0$
2 **repeat**
  `// Invariant:` $\boldsymbol{F}$ `is a monotone, clausal, safe, inductive trace`
3   $U \leftarrow \mathit{Tr}[\boldsymbol{F}^0] \wedge \mathit{Bad}(\bar{v}_{N+1})$
4   **if** isSat(U) **then return** UNSAFE
5   $(i, k) \leftarrow \max\{(i, k) \mid \neg \text{isSat}(\mathit{Tr}[\![\boldsymbol{F}^i]\!]^k \wedge \mathit{Bad}(\bar{v}_{N+1}))\}$
6   $[F_0, \dots, F_{N+1}] \leftarrow$ kAvyExtend$(\boldsymbol{F}, (i, k))$
7   $[F_0, \dots, F_{N+1}] \leftarrow$ PdrPush$([F_0, \dots, F_{N+1}])$
8   **if** $\exists 1 \leq i \leq N \cdot F_i \Rightarrow \left(\bigvee_{j=0}^{i-1} F_j\right)$ **then return** SAFE
9   $N \leftarrow N + 1$
10 **until** ∞

Note that the existence of a SEL (i, k) means that an unrolling of the i-suffix with F_i repeated k times does not contain any bad states. We use $\mathit{Tr}[\![\boldsymbol{F}^i]\!]^k$ to denote this *characteristic formula* for SEL (i, k):

$$\mathit{Tr}[\![\boldsymbol{F}^i]\!]^k = \begin{cases} \mathit{Tr}[F_i]_{i+1-k}^{i+1} \wedge \mathit{Tr}[\boldsymbol{F}^{i+1}] & \text{if } 0 \leq i < N \\ \mathit{Tr}[F_N]_{N+1-k}^{N+1} & \text{if } i = N \end{cases} \tag{6}$$

Proposition 2. *Let $\boldsymbol{F}$ be a safe trace, where $|\boldsymbol{F}| = N$. Then, (i, k), $1 \leq k \leq i+1 \leq N+1$, is an SEL of $\boldsymbol{F}$ iff the formula $\mathit{Tr}[\![\boldsymbol{F}^i]\!]^k \wedge \mathit{Bad}(\bar{v}_{N+1})$ is unsatisfiable.*

The level i in the maximal SEL (i, k) of a given trace $\boldsymbol{F}$ is greater or equal to the maximal extension level of $\boldsymbol{F}$:

Lemma 1. *Let $(i, k) = \max(\mathcal{K}(\boldsymbol{F}))$, then $i \geq \max(\mathcal{W}(\boldsymbol{F}))$.*

Hence, extensions based on maximal SEL are constructed from frames at higher level compared to extensions based on maximal extension level.

Example 3. For Fig. 1, the trace $[c = 0, c < 66]$ has a maximum extension level of 0. Since $(c < 66)$ is 2-inductive, the trace is strongly extendable at level 1 (as was seen in Example 2).

kAvy Algorithm. kAvy is shown in Fig. 3. It starts with an inductive trace $\boldsymbol{F} = [\mathit{Init}]$ and iteratively extends $\boldsymbol{F}$ using SELs. A counterexample is returned if the trace cannot be extended (line 4). Otherwise, kAvy computes the largest extension level (line 5) (described in Sect. 4.2). Then, it constructs a strong extension trace using kAvyExtend (line 6) (described in Sect. 4.1). Finally, PdrPush is called to check whether the trace is closed. Note that $\boldsymbol{F}$ is a monotone, clausal, safe inductive trace throughout the algorithm.

4.1 Extending a Trace with Strong Induction

In this section, we describe the procedure kAvyExtend (shown in Algorithm 4) that given a trace $\boldsymbol{F}$ of size $|\boldsymbol{F}| = N$ and an (i, k) SEL of $\boldsymbol{F}$ constructs an (i, k)-extension trace $\boldsymbol{G}$ of size $|\boldsymbol{G}| = N + 1$. The procedure itself is fairly simple, but its proof of correctness is complex. We first present the theoretical results that connect sequence interpolants with strong extension traces, then the procedure, and then details of its correctness. Through the section, we fix a trace $\boldsymbol{F}$ and its SEL (i, k).

Sequence Interpolation for SEL. Let (i, k) be an SEL of $\boldsymbol{F}$. By Proposition 2, $\Psi = Tr[\![\boldsymbol{F}^i]\!]^k \wedge Bad(\bar{v}_{N+1})$ is unsatisfiable. Let $\mathcal{A} = \{A_{i-k+1}, \ldots, A_{N+1}\}$ be a partitioning of Ψ defined as follows:

$$A_j = \begin{cases} F_i(\bar{v}_j) \wedge Tr(\bar{v}_j, \bar{v}_{j+1}) & \text{if } i-k+1 \leq j \leq i \\ F_j(\bar{v}_j) \wedge Tr(\bar{v}_j, \bar{v}_{j+1}) & \text{if } i < j \leq N \\ Bad(\bar{v}_{N+1}) & \text{if } j = N+1 \end{cases}$$

Since $(\wedge\mathcal{A}) = \Psi$, $\mathcal{A}$ is unsatisfiable. Let $\boldsymbol{I} = [I_{i-k+2}, \ldots, I_{N+1}]$ be a sequence interpolant corresponding to $\mathcal{A}$. Then, $\boldsymbol{I}$ satisfies the following properties:

$$\begin{array}{cc} F_i \wedge Tr \Rightarrow I'_{i-k+2} & \forall i-k+2 \leq j \leq i \cdot (F_i \wedge I_j) \wedge Tr \Rightarrow I'_{j+1} \\ I_{N+1} \Rightarrow \neg Bad & \forall i < j \leq N \cdot (F_j \wedge I_j) \wedge Tr \Rightarrow I'_{j+1} \end{array} \qquad (\heartsuit)$$

Note that in ($\heartsuit$), both i and k are fixed—they are the (i, k)-extension level. Furthermore, in the top row F_i is fixed as well.

The conjunction of the first k interpolants in $\boldsymbol{I}$ is k-inductive relative to the frame F_i:

Lemma 2. *The formula* $F_{i+1} \wedge \left(\bigwedge_{m=i-k+2}^{i+1} I_m\right)$ *is k-inductive relative to* F_i.

Proof. Since F_i and F_{i+1} are consecutive frames of a trace, $F_i \wedge Tr \Rightarrow F'_{i+1}$. Thus, $\forall i-k+2 \leq j \leq i \cdot Tr[F_i]^j_{i-k+2} \Rightarrow F_{i+1}(\bar{v}_{j+1})$. Moreover, by ($\heartsuit$), $F_i \wedge Tr \Rightarrow I'_{i-k+2}$ and $\forall i-k+2 \leq j \leq i+1 \cdot (F_i \wedge I_j) \wedge Tr \Rightarrow I'_{j+1}$. Equivalently, $\forall i-k+2 \leq j \leq i+1 \cdot Tr[F_i]^j_{i-k+2} \Rightarrow I_{j+1}(\bar{v}_{j+1})$. By induction over the difference between $(i+1)$ and $(i-k+2)$, we show that $Tr[F_i]^{i+1}_{i-k+2} \Rightarrow (F_{i+1} \wedge \bigwedge^{i+1}_{m=i-k+2} I_m)(\bar{v}_{i+1})$, which concludes the proof. □

We use Lemma 2 to define a strong extension trace $\boldsymbol{G}$:

Lemma 3. *Let* $\boldsymbol{G} = [G_0, \ldots, G_{N+1}]$, *be an inductive trace defined as follows:*

$$G_j = \begin{cases} F_j & \textit{if } 0 \leq j < i-k+2 \\ F_j \wedge \left(\bigwedge_{m=i-k+2}^{j} I_m\right) & \textit{if } i-k+2 \leq j < i+2 \\ (F_j \wedge I_j) & \textit{if } i+2 \leq j < N+1 \\ I_{N+1} & \textit{if } j = (N+1) \end{cases}$$

Then, $\boldsymbol{G}$ is an (i,k)-extension trace of $\boldsymbol{F}$ (not necessarily monotone).

Proof. By Lemma 2, G_{i+1} is k-inductive relative to F_i. Therefore, it is sufficient to show that $\boldsymbol{G}$ is a safe inductive trace that is stronger than $\boldsymbol{F}$. By definition, $\forall 0 \leq j \leq N \cdot G_j \Rightarrow F_j$. By ($\heartsuit$), $F_i \wedge Tr \Rightarrow I'_{i-k+2}$ and $\forall i-k+2 \leq j < i+2 \cdot (F_i \wedge I_j) \wedge Tr \Rightarrow I'_{j+1}$. By induction over j, $\left((F_i \wedge \bigwedge_{m=i-k+2}^{j} I_m) \wedge Tr\right) \Rightarrow \bigwedge_{m=i-k+2}^{j+1} I'_m$ for all $i-k+2 \leq j < i+2$. Since $\boldsymbol{F}$ is monotone, $\forall i-k+2 \leq j < i+2 \cdot \left((F_j \wedge \bigwedge_{m=i-k+2}^{j} I_m) \wedge Tr\right) \Rightarrow \bigwedge_{m=i-k+2}^{j+1} I'_m$.

By ($\heartsuit$), $\forall i < j \leq N \cdot (F_j \wedge I_j) \wedge Tr \Rightarrow I'_{j+1}$. Again, since $\boldsymbol{F}$ is a trace, we conclude that $\forall i < j < N \cdot (F_j \wedge I_j) \wedge Tr \Rightarrow (F_{j+1} \wedge I_{j+1})'$. Combining the above, $G_j \wedge Tr \Rightarrow G'_{j+1}$ for $0 \leq j \leq N$. Since $\boldsymbol{F}$ is safe and $I_{N+1} \Rightarrow \neg Bad$, then $\boldsymbol{G}$ is safe and stronger than $\boldsymbol{F}$. □

Lemma 3 defines an obvious procedure to construct an (i,k)-extension trace $\boldsymbol{G}$ for $\boldsymbol{F}$. However, such $\boldsymbol{G}$ is neither monotone nor clausal. In the rest of this section, we describe the procedure kAvyExtend that starts with a sequence interpolant (as in Lemma 3), but uses PdrBlock to systematically construct a safe monotone clausal extension of $\boldsymbol{F}$.

The procedure kAvyExtend is shown in Algorithm 4. For simplicity of the presentation, we assume that PdrBlock does not use inductive generalization. The invariants marked by † rely on this assumption. We stress that the assumption is for presentation only. The correctness of kAvyExtend is independent of it.

kAvyExtend starts with a sequence interpolant according to the partitioning $\mathcal{A}$. The extension trace $\boldsymbol{G}$ is initialized to $\boldsymbol{F}$ and G_{N+1} is initialized to $\top$ (line 2). The rest proceeds in three phases: *Phase 1* (lines 3–5) computes the prefix $G_{i-k+2}, \ldots, G_{i+1}$ using the first $k-1$ elements of $\boldsymbol{I}$; *Phase 2* (line 8) computes G_{i+1} using I_{i+1}; *Phase 3* (lines 9–12) computes the suffix $\boldsymbol{G}^{i+2}$ using the last $(N-i)$ elements of $\boldsymbol{I}$. During this phase, PdrPush (line 12) pushes clauses forward so that they can be used in the next iteration. The correctness of the phases follows from the invariants shown in Algorithm 4. We present each phase in turn.

Recall that PdrBlock takes a trace $\boldsymbol{F}$ (that is safe up to the last frame) and a transition system, and returns a safe strengthening of $\boldsymbol{F}$, while ensuring that the result is monotone and clausal. This guarantee is maintained by Algorithm 4, by requiring that any clause added to any frame G_i of $\boldsymbol{G}$ is implicitly added to all frames below G_i.

Phase 1. By Lemma 2, the first k elements of the sequence interpolant computed at line 1 over-approximate states reachable in $i+1$ steps of Tr. Phase 1 uses this to strengthen G_{i+1} using the first k elements of $\boldsymbol{I}$. Note that in that phase, new clauses are always added to frame G_{i+1}, and all frames before it!

Algorithm 4. kAvyExtend. The invariants marked † hold only when the PdrBlock does no inductive generalization.

Input: a monotone, clausal, safe trace $\boldsymbol{F}$ of size N
Input: A strong extension level (i, k) s.t. $Tr[\![\boldsymbol{F}^i]\!]^k \wedge Bad(\bar{v}_{N+1})$ is unsatisfiable
Output: a monotone, clausal, safe trace $\boldsymbol{G}$ of size $N+1$

1 $I_{i-k+2}, \ldots, I_{N+1} \leftarrow$ seqItp$(Tr[\![\boldsymbol{F}^i]\!]^k \wedge Bad(\bar{v}_{N+1}))$
2 $\boldsymbol{G} \leftarrow [F_0, \ldots, F_N, \top]$
3 **for** $j \leftarrow i-k+1$ **to** i **do**
4 $\quad P_j \leftarrow (G_j \vee (G_{i+1} \wedge I_{j+1}))$
$\quad$ // Inv$_1$: $\boldsymbol{G}$ is monotone and clausal
$\quad$ // Inv$_2$: $G_i \wedge Tr \Rightarrow P_j$
$\quad$ // Inv$_3^\dagger$: $\forall j < m \leq (i+1) \cdot G_m \equiv F_m \wedge \bigwedge_{\ell=i-k+1}^{j-1} (G_\ell \vee I_{\ell+1})$
$\quad$ // Inv$_3$: $\forall j < m \leq (i+1) \cdot G_m \Rightarrow F_m \wedge \bigwedge_{\ell=i-k+1}^{j-1} (G_\ell \vee I_{\ell+1})$
5 $\quad [\_, \_, G_{i+1}] \leftarrow$ PdrBlock$([Init, G_i, G_{i+1}], (Init, Tr, \neg P_j))$
6 $P_i \leftarrow (G_i \vee (G_{i+1} \wedge I_{j+1}))$
7 **if** $i = 0$ **then** $[\_, \_, G_{i+1}] \leftarrow$ PdrBlock$([Init, G_{i+1}], (Init, Tr, \neg P_i))$
8 **else** $[\_, \_, G_{i+1}] \leftarrow$ PdrBlock$([Init, G_i, G_{i+1}], (Init, Tr, \neg P_i))$
// Inv$_4^\dagger$: $G_{i+1} \equiv F_{i+1} \wedge \bigwedge_{\ell=i-k+1}^{i} (G_\ell \vee I_{\ell+1})$
// Inv$_4$: $G_{i+1} \Rightarrow F_{i+1} \wedge \bigwedge_{\ell=i-k+1}^{i} (G_\ell \vee I_{\ell+1})$
9 **for** $j \leftarrow i+1$ **to** $N+1$ **do**
10 $\quad P_j \leftarrow G_j \vee (G_{j+1} \wedge I_{j+1})$
$\quad$ // Inv$_6$: $G_j \wedge Tr \Rightarrow P_j$
11 $\quad [\_, \_, G_{j+1}] \leftarrow$ PdrBlock$([Init, G_j, G_{j+1}], (Init, Tr, \neg P_j))$
12 $\quad \boldsymbol{G} \leftarrow$ PdrPush$(\boldsymbol{G})$
// Inv$_7^\dagger$: $\boldsymbol{G}$ is an (i, k)-extension trace of $\boldsymbol{F}$
// Inv$_7$: $\boldsymbol{G}$ is an extension trace of $\boldsymbol{F}$
13 **return** $\boldsymbol{G}$

Correctness of Phase 1 (line 5) follows from the loop invariant Inv$_2$. It holds on loop entry since $G_i \wedge Tr \Rightarrow I_{i-k+2}$ (since $G_i = F_i$ and (♡)) and $G_i \wedge Tr \Rightarrow G_{i+1}$ (since $\boldsymbol{G}$ is initially a trace). Let G_i and G_i^* be the ith frame before and after execution of iteration j of the loop, respectively. PdrBlock blocks $\neg P_j$ at iteration j of the loop. Assume that Inv$_2$ holds at the beginning of the loop. Then, $G_i^* \Rightarrow G_i \wedge P_j$ since PdrBlock strengthens G_i. Since $G_j \Rightarrow G_i$ and $G_i \Rightarrow G_{i+1}$, this simplifies to $G_i^* \Rightarrow G_j \vee (G_i \wedge I_{j+1})$. Finally, since $\boldsymbol{G}$ is a trace, Inv$_2$ holds at the end of the iteration.

Inv$_2$ ensures that the trace given to PdrBlock at line 5 *can* be made safe relative to P_j. From the post-condition of PdrBlock, it follows that at iteration j, G_{i+1} is strengthened to G_{i+1}^* such that $G_{i+1}^* \Rightarrow P_j$ and $\boldsymbol{G}$ remains a monotone clausal trace. At the end of *Phase 1*, $[G_0, \ldots, G_{i+1}]$ is a clausal monotone trace.

Interestingly, the calls to PdrBlock in this phase do not satisfy an expected pre-condition: the frame G_i in $[Init, G_i, G_{i+1}]$ might not be safe for property P_j. However, we can see that $Init \Rightarrow P_j$ and from Inv$_2$, it is clear that P_j is inductive relative to G_i. This is a sufficient precondition for PdrBlock.

Phase 2. This phase strengthens G_{i+1} using the interpolant I_{i+1}. After Phase 2, G_{i+1} is k-inductive relative to F_i.

Phase 3. Unlike *Phase 1*, G_{j+1} is computed at the jth iteration. Because of this, the property P_j in this phase is slightly different than that of Phase 1. Correctness follows from invariant $\texttt{Inv}_6$ that ensures that at iteration j, G_{j+1} *can* be made safe relative to P_j. From the post-condition of PdrBlock, it follows that G_{j+1} is strengthened to G^*_{j+1} such that $G^*_{j+1} \Rightarrow P_j$ and $\boldsymbol{G}$ is a monotone clausal trace. The invariant implies that at the end of the loop $G_{N+1} \Rightarrow G_N \vee I_{N+1}$, making $\boldsymbol{G}$ safe. Thus, at the end of the loop $\boldsymbol{G}$ is a safe monotone clausal trace that is stronger than $\boldsymbol{F}$. What remains is to show is that G_{i+1} is k-inductive relative to F_i.

Let φ be the formula from Lemma 2. Assuming that PdrBlock did no inductive generalization, *Phase 1* maintains $\texttt{Inv}^{\dagger}_3$, which states that at iteration j, PdrBlock strengthens frames $\{G_m\}$, $j < m \leq (i+1)$. $\texttt{Inv}^{\dagger}_3$ holds on loop entry, since initially $\boldsymbol{G} = \boldsymbol{F}$. Let G_m, G^*_m ($j < m \leq (i+1)$) be frame m at the beginning and at the end of the loop iteration, respectively. In the loop, PdrBlock adds clauses that block $\neg P_j$. Thus, $G^*_m \equiv G_m \wedge P_j$. Since $G_j \Rightarrow G_m$, this simplifies to $G^*_m \equiv G_m \wedge (G_j \vee I_{j+1})$. Expanding G_m, we get $G^*_m \equiv F_m \wedge \bigwedge_{\ell=i-k+1}^{j} (G_\ell \vee I_{\ell+1})$. Thus, $\texttt{Inv}^{\dagger}_3$ holds at the end of the loop.

In particular, after line 8, $G_{i+1} \equiv F_{i+1} \wedge \bigwedge_{\ell=i-k+1}^{i} (G_\ell \vee I_{\ell+1})$. Since $\varphi \Rightarrow G_{i+1}$, G_{i+1} is k-inductive relative to F_i.

Theorem 2. *Given a safe trace* $\boldsymbol{F}$ *of size* N *and an SEL* (i,k) *for* $\boldsymbol{F}$, kAvyExtend *returns a clausal monotone extension trace* $\boldsymbol{G}$ *of size* $N+1$. *Furthermore, if* PdrBlock *does no inductive generalization then* $\boldsymbol{G}$ *is an* (i,k)*-extension trace.*

Of course, assuming that PdrBlock does no inductive generalization is not realistic. kAvyExtend remains correct without the assumption: it returns a trace $\boldsymbol{G}$ that is a monotone clausal extension of $\boldsymbol{F}$. However, $\boldsymbol{G}$ might be stronger than any (i,k)-extension of $\boldsymbol{F}$. The invariants marked with $\dagger$ are then relaxed to their unmarked versions. Overall, inductive generalization improves kAvyExtend since it is not restricted to only a k-inductive strengthening.

Importantly, the output of kAvyExtend is a regular inductive trace. Thus, kAvyExtend is a procedure to strengthen a (relatively) k-inductive certificate to a (relatively) 1-inductive certificate. Hence, after kAvyExtend, any strategy for further generalization or trace extension from IC3, Pdr, or Avy is applicable.

4.2 Searching for the Maximal SEL

In this section, we describe two algorithms for computing the maximal SEL. Both algorithms can be used to implement line 5 of Algorithm 3. They perform a guided search for group minimal unsatisfiable subsets. They terminate when having fewer clauses would not increase the SEL further. The first, called *top-down*, starts from the largest unrolling of the *Tr* and then reduces the length of the unrolling. The second, called *bottom-up*, finds the largest (regular) extension level first, and then grows it using strong induction.

Algorithm 5. A top down alg. for the maximal SEL.

Input: A transition system $T = (Init, Tr, Bad)$
Input: An extendable monotone clausal safe trace $\boldsymbol{F}$ of size N
Output: $\max(\mathcal{K}(\boldsymbol{F}))$

1 $i \leftarrow N$
2 **while** $i > 0$ **do**
3   **if** $\neg\text{isSat}(Tr[\![\boldsymbol{F}^i]\!]^{i+1} \wedge Bad(\bar{v}_{N+1}))$ **then break**
4     $i \leftarrow (i-1)$
5 $k \leftarrow 1$
6 **while** $k < i+1$ **do**
7   **if** $\neg\text{isSat}(Tr[\![\boldsymbol{F}^i]\!]^{k} \wedge Bad(\bar{v}_{N+1}))$ **then break**
8     $k \leftarrow (k+1)$
9 **return** (i, k)

Algorithm 6. A bottom up alg. for the maximal SEL.

Input: A transition system $T = (Init, Tr, Bad)$
Input: An extendable monotone clausal safe trace $\boldsymbol{F}$ of size N
Output: $\max(\mathcal{K}(\boldsymbol{F}))$

1 $j \leftarrow N$
2 **while** $j > 0$ **do**
3   **if** $\neg\text{isSat}(Tr[\![\boldsymbol{F}^j]\!]^{1} \wedge Bad(\bar{v}_{N+1}))$ **then break**
4     $j \leftarrow (j-1)$
5 $(i,k) \leftarrow (j,1)\,;\, j \leftarrow (j+1)\,;\, \ell \leftarrow 2$
6 **while** $\ell \leq (j+1) \wedge j \leq N$ **do**
7   **if** $\text{isSat}(Tr[\![\boldsymbol{F}^j]\!]^{\ell} \wedge Bad(\bar{v}_{N+1}))$ **then** $\ell \leftarrow (\ell+1)$
8   **else**
9         $(i,k) \leftarrow (j,\ell)$
10         $j \leftarrow (j+1)$
11 **return** (i, k)

Top-Down SEL. A pair (i,k) is the maximal SEL iff

$$i = \max\{j \mid 0 \leq j \leq N \cdot Tr[\![\boldsymbol{F}^j]\!]^{j+1} \wedge Bad(\bar{v}_{N+1}) \Rightarrow \bot\}$$
$$k = \min\{\ell \mid 1 \leq \ell \leq (i+1) \cdot Tr[\![\boldsymbol{F}^i]\!]^{\ell} \wedge Bad(\bar{v}_{N+1}) \Rightarrow \bot\}$$

Note that k depends on i. For a SEL $(i,k) \in \mathcal{K}(\boldsymbol{F})$, we refer to the formula $Tr[\boldsymbol{F}^i]$ as a *suffix* and to number k as the depth of induction. Thus, the search can be split into two phases: (a) find the smallest suffix while using the maximal depth of induction allowed (for that suffix), and (b) minimizing the depth of induction k for the value of i found in step (a). This is captured in Algorithm 5. The algorithm requires at most $(N+1)$ SAT queries. One downside, however, is that the formulas constructed in the first phase (line 3) are large because the depth of induction is the maximum possible.

Bottom-Up SEL. Algorithm 6 searches for a SEL by first finding a maximal regular extension level (line 2) and then searching for larger SELs (lines 6 to 10). Observe that if $(j,\ell) \notin \mathcal{K}(\boldsymbol{F})$, then $\forall p > j \cdot (p,\ell) \notin \mathcal{K}(\boldsymbol{F})$. This is used at line 7 to increase the depth of induction once it is known that $(j,\ell) \notin \mathcal{K}(\boldsymbol{F})$. On the other hand, if $(j,\ell) \in \mathcal{K}(\boldsymbol{F})$, there might be a larger SEL $(j+1,\ell)$. Thus, whenever a SEL (j,ℓ) is found, it is stored in (i,k) and the search continues (line 10). The algorithm terminates when there are no more valid SEL candidates and returns the last valid SEL. Note that ℓ is incremented only when there does not exists a larger SEL with the current value of ℓ. Thus, for each valid level j, if there exists SELs with level j, the algorithm is guaranteed to find the largest such SEL. Moreover, the level is increased at every possible opportunity. Hence, at the end $(i,k) = \max\mathcal{K}(\boldsymbol{F})$.

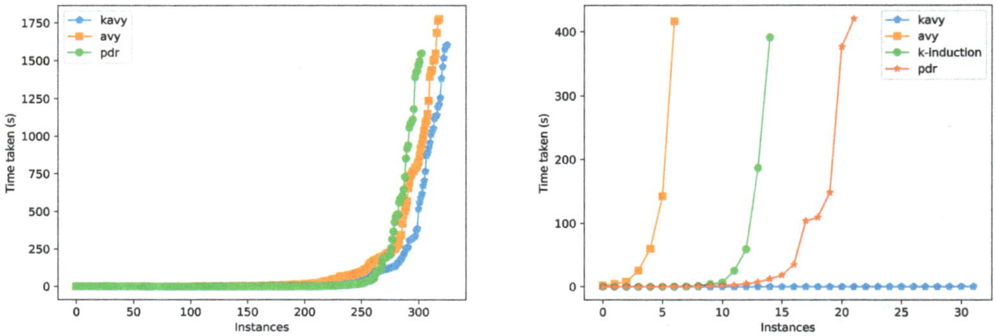

(a) Safe HWMCC instances.

(b) *shift* instances.

Fig. 2. Runtime comparison on SAFE HWMCC instances (a) and *shift* instances (b).

In the worst case, Algorithm 6 makes at most $3N$ SAT queries. However, compared to Algorithm 5, the queries are smaller. Moreover, the computation is incremental and can be aborted with a sub-optimal solution after execution of line 5 or line 9. Note that at line 5, i is a regular extension level (i.e., as in AVY), and every execution of line 9 results in a larger SEL.

5 Evaluation

We implemented KAVY on top of the AVY Model Checker[1]. For line 5 of Algorithm 3 we used Algorithm 5. We evaluated KAVY's performance against a version of AVY [29] from the Hardware Model Checking Competition 2017 [5], and the PDR engine of ABC [13]. We have used the benchmarks from HWMCC'14, '15, and '17. Benchmarks that are not solved by any of the solvers are excluded from the presentation. The experiments were conducted on a cluster running Intel E5-2683 V4 CPUs at 2.1 GHz with 8 GB RAM limit and 30 min time limit.

The results are summarized in Table 1. The HWMCC has a wide variety of benchmarks. We aggregate the results based on the competition, and also benchmark origin (based on the name). Some named categories (e.g., *intel*) include benchmarks that have not been included in any competition. The first column in Table 1 indicates the category. **Total** is the number of all available benchmarks, ignoring duplicates. That is, if a benchmark appeared in multiple categories, it is counted only once. Numbers in brackets indicate the number of instances that are solved uniquely by the solver. For example, KAVY solves 14 instances in *oc8051* that are not solved by any other solver. The VBS column indicates the *Virtual Best Solver*—the result of running all the three solvers in parallel and stopping as soon as one solver terminates successfully.

Overall, KAVY solves more SAFE instances than both AVY and PDR, while taking less time than AVY (we report time for solved instances, ignoring timeouts). The VBS column shows that KAVY is a promising new strategy, significantly improving overall performance. In the rest of this section, we analyze the

[1] All code, benchmarks, and results are available at https://arieg.bitbucket.io/avy/.

Table 1. Summary of instances solved by each tool. Timeouts were ignored when computing the time column.

BENCHMARKS	KAVY			AVY			PDR			VBS	
	SAFE	UNSAFE	Time(m)	SAFE	UNSAFE	Time(m)	SAFE	UNSAFE	Time(m)	SAFE	UNSAFE
HWMCC' 17	137 (16)	38	499	128 (3)	38	406	109 (6)	40 (5)	174	150	44
HWMCC' 15	193 (4)	84	412	191 (3)	92 (6)	597	194 (16)	67 (12)	310	218	104
HWMCC' 14	49	27 (1)	124	58 (4)	26	258	55 (6)	19 (2)	172	64	29
intel	32 (1)	9	196	32 (1)	9	218	19	5 (1)	40	33	10
6s	73 (2)	20	157	81 (4)	21 (1)	329	67 (3)	14	51	86	21
nusmv	13	0	5	14	0	29	16 (2)	0	38	16	0
bob	30	5	21	30	6 (1)	30	30 (1)	8 (3)	32	31	9
pdt	45	1	54	45 (1)	1	57	47 (3)	1	62	49	1
oski	26	89 (1)	174	28 (2)	92 (4)	217	20	53	63	28	93
beem	10	1	49	10	2	32	20 (8)	7 (5)	133	20	7
oc8051	34 (14)	0	286	20	0	99	6 (1)	1 (1)	77	35	1
power	4	0	25	3	0	3	8 (4)	0	31	8	0
shift	5 (2)	0	1	1	0	18	3	0	1	5	0
necla	5	0	4	7 (1)	0	1	5 (1)	0	4	8	0
prodcell	0	0	0	0	1	28	0	4 (3)	2	0	4
bc57	0	0	0	0	0	0	0	4 (4)	9	0	4
Total	326 (19)	141 (1)	957	319 (8)	148 (6)	1041	304 (25)	117 (17)	567	370	167

results in more detail, provide detailed run-time comparison between the tools, and isolate the effect of the new k-inductive strategy.

To compare the running time, we present scatter plots comparing KAVY and AVY (Fig. 3a), and KAVY and PDR (Fig. 3b). In both figures, KAVY is at the bottom. Points above the diagonal are better for KAVY. Compared to AVY, whenever an instance is solved by both solvers, KAVY is often faster, sometimes by orders of magnitude. Compared to PDR, KAVY and PDR perform well on very different instances. This is similar to the observation made by the authors of the original paper that presented AVY [29]. Another indicator of performance is the depth of convergence. This is summarized in Fig. 3d and e. KAVY often converges much sooner than AVY. The comparison with PDR is less clear which is consistent with the difference in performance between the two. To get the whole picture, Fig. 2a presents a cactus plot that compares the running times of the algorithms on all these benchmarks.

To isolate the effects of k-induction, we compare KAVY to a version of KAVY with k-induction disabled, which we call VANILLA. Conceptually, VANILLA is similar to AVY since it extends the trace using a 1-inductive extension trace, but its implementation is based on KAVY. The results for the running time and the depth of convergence are shown in Fig. 3c and f, respectively. The results are very clear—using strong extension traces significantly improves performance and has non-negligible affect on depth of convergence.

Finally, we discovered one family of benchmarks, called shift, on which KAVY performs orders of magnitude better than all other techniques. The benchmarks come from encoding bit-vector decision problem into circuits [21,30]. The shift family corresponds to deciding satisfiability of $(x + y) = (x << 1)$ for two

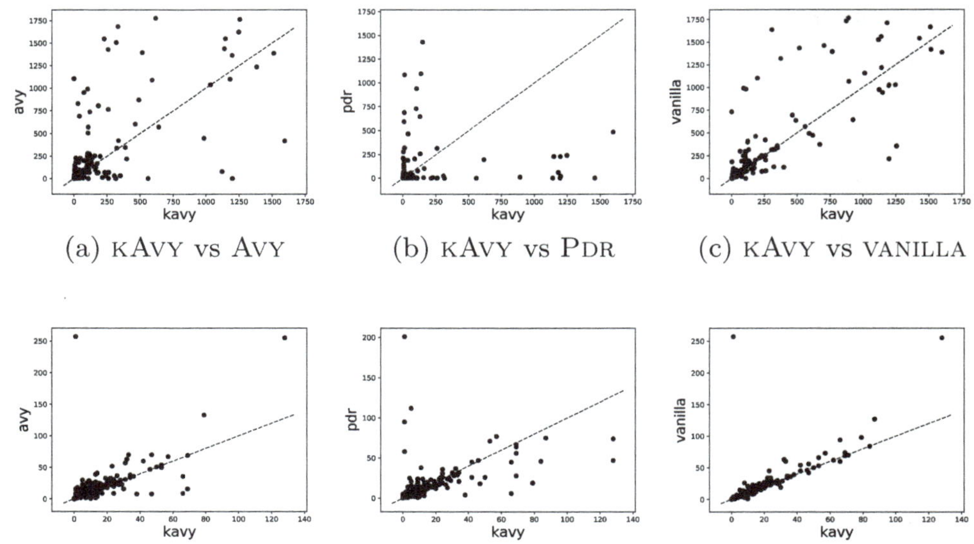

(a) KAVY vs AVY (b) KAVY vs PDR (c) KAVY vs VANILLA

(d) KAVY vs AVY (e) KAVY vs PDR (f) KAVY vs VANILLA

Fig. 3. Comparing running time ((a), (b), (c)) and depth of convergence ((d), (e), (f)) of AVY, PDR and VANILLA with KAVY. KAVY is shown on the x-axis. Points above the diagonal are better for KAVY. Only those instances that have been solved by both solvers are shown in each plot.

bit-vecors x and y. The family is parameterized by bit-width. The property is k-inductive, where k is the bit-width of x. The results of running AVY, PDR, k-induction[2], and KAVY are shown in Fig. 2b. Except for KAVY, all techniques exhibit exponential behavior in the bit-width, while KAVY remains constant. Deeper analysis indicates that KAVY finds a small inductive invariant while exploring just two steps in the execution of the circuit. At the same time, neither inductive generalization nor k-induction alone are able to consistently find the same invariant quickly.

6 Conclusion

In this paper, we present KAVY—an SMC algorithm that effectively uses k-inductive reasoning to guide interpolation and inductive generalization. KAVY searches both for a good inductive strengthening and for the most effective induction depth k. We have implemented KAVY on top of AVY Model Checker. The experimental results on HWMCC instances show that our approach is effective.

The search for the maximal SEL is an overhead in KAVY. There could be benchmarks in which this overhead outweighs its benefits. However, we have not come across such benchmarks so far. In such cases, KAVY can choose to settle for a sub-optimal SEL as mentioned in Sect. 4.2. Deciding when and how much to settle for remains a challenge.

[2] We used the k-induction engine `ind` in ABC [8].

Acknowledgements. We thank the anonymous reviewers and Oded Padon for their thorough review and insightful comments. This research was enabled in part by support provided by Compute Ontario (https://computeontario.ca/), Compute Canada (https://www.computecanada.ca/) and the grants from Natural Sciences and Engineering Research Council Canada.

References

1. Audemard, G., Lagniez, J.-M., Szczepanski, N., Tabary, S.: An adaptive parallel SAT solver. In: Rueher, M. (ed.) CP 2016. LNCS, vol. 9892, pp. 30–48. Springer, Cham (2016). https://doi.org/10.1007/978-3-319-44953-1_3
2. Belov, A., Marques-Silva, J.: MUSer2: an efficient MUS extractor. JSAT **8**(3/4), 123–128 (2012)
3. Berryhill, R., Ivrii, A., Veira, N., Veneris, A.G.: Learning support sets in IC3 and Quip: the good, the bad, and the ugly. In: 2017 Formal Methods in Computer Aided Design, FMCAD 2017, Vienna, Austria, 2–6 October 2017, pp. 140–147 (2017)
4. Biere, A., Cimatti, A., Clarke, E., Zhu, Y.: Symbolic model checking without BDDs. In: Cleaveland, W.R. (ed.) TACAS 1999. LNCS, vol. 1579, pp. 193–207. Springer, Heidelberg (1999). https://doi.org/10.1007/3-540-49059-0_14
5. Biere, A., van Dijk, T., Heljanko, K.: Hardware model checking competition 2017. In: Stewart, D., Weissenbacher, G. (eds.) 2017 Formal Methods in Computer Aided Design, FMCAD 2017, Vienna, Austria, 2–6 October 2017, p. 9. IEEE (2017)
6. Bjørner, N., Gurfinkel, A., McMillan, K., Rybalchenko, A.: Horn clause solvers for program verification. In: Beklemishev, L.D., Blass, A., Dershowitz, N., Finkbeiner, B., Schulte, W. (eds.) Fields of Logic and Computation II. LNCS, vol. 9300, pp. 24–51. Springer, Cham (2015). https://doi.org/10.1007/978-3-319-23534-9_2
7. Bradley, A.R.: SAT-based model checking without unrolling. In: Jhala, R., Schmidt, D. (eds.) VMCAI 2011. LNCS, vol. 6538, pp. 70–87. Springer, Heidelberg (2011). https://doi.org/10.1007/978-3-642-18275-4_7
8. Brayton, R., Mishchenko, A.: ABC: an academic industrial-strength verification tool. In: Touili, T., Cook, B., Jackson, P. (eds.) CAV 2010. LNCS, vol. 6174, pp. 24–40. Springer, Heidelberg (2010). https://doi.org/10.1007/978-3-642-14295-6_5
9. Champion, A., Mebsout, A., Sticksel, C., Tinelli, C.: The KIND 2 model checker. In: Chaudhuri, S., Farzan, A. (eds.) CAV 2016. LNCS, vol. 9780, pp. 510–517. Springer, Cham (2016). https://doi.org/10.1007/978-3-319-41540-6_29
10. Craig, W.: Three uses of the Herbrand-Gentzen theorem in relating model theory and proof theory. J. Symb. Log. **22**(3), 269–285 (1957)
11. de Moura, L., et al.: SAL 2. In: Alur, R., Peled, D.A. (eds.) CAV 2004. LNCS, vol. 3114, pp. 496–500. Springer, Heidelberg (2004). https://doi.org/10.1007/978-3-540-27813-9_45
12. Eén, N., Mishchenko, A., Amla, N.: A single-instance incremental SAT formulation of proof- and counterexample-based abstraction. In: Proceedings of 10th International Conference on Formal Methods in Computer-Aided Design, FMCAD 2010, Lugano, Switzerland, 20–23 October, pp. 181–188 (2010)
13. Eén, N., Mishchenko, A., Brayton, R.K.: Efficient implementation of property directed reachability. In: International Conference on Formal Methods in Computer-Aided Design, FMCAD 2011, Austin, TX, USA, October 30–02 November 2011, pp. 125–134 (2011)

14. Garoche, P.-L., Kahsai, T., Tinelli, C.: Incremental invariant generation using logic-based automatic abstract transformers. In: Brat, G., Rungta, N., Venet, A. (eds.) NFM 2013. LNCS, vol. 7871, pp. 139–154. Springer, Heidelberg (2013). https://doi.org/10.1007/978-3-642-38088-4_10
15. Gurfinkel, A., Ivrii, A.: Pushing to the top. In: Formal Methods in Computer-Aided Design, FMCAD 2015, Austin, Texas, USA, 27–30 September 2015, pp. 65–72 (2015)
16. Gurfinkel, A., Ivrii, A.: K-induction without unrolling. In: 2017 Formal Methods in Computer Aided Design, FMCAD 2017, Vienna, Austria, 2–6 October 2017, pp. 148–155 (2017)
17. Heule, M., Hunt Jr., W.A., Wetzler, N.: Trimming while checking clausal proofs. In: Formal Methods in Computer-Aided Design, FMCAD 2013, Portland, OR, USA, 20–23 October 2013, pp. 181–188 (2013)
18. Järvisalo, M., Heule, M.J.H., Biere, A.: Inprocessing rules. In: Gramlich, B., Miller, D., Sattler, U. (eds.) IJCAR 2012. LNCS (LNAI), vol. 7364, pp. 355–370. Springer, Heidelberg (2012). https://doi.org/10.1007/978-3-642-31365-3_28
19. Jovanovic, D., Dutertre, B.: Property-directed k-induction. In: 2016 Formal Methods in Computer-Aided Design, FMCAD 2016, Mountain View, CA, USA, 3–6 October 2016, pp. 85–92 (2016)
20. Kahsai, T., Ge, Y., Tinelli, C.: Instantiation-based invariant discovery. In: Bobaru, M., Havelund, K., Holzmann, G.J., Joshi, R. (eds.) NFM 2011. LNCS, vol. 6617, pp. 192–206. Springer, Heidelberg (2011). https://doi.org/10.1007/978-3-642-20398-5_15
21. Kovásznai, G., Fröhlich, A., Biere, A.: Complexity of fixed-size bit-vector logics. Theory Comput. Syst. **59**(2), 323–376 (2016)
22. Liang, J.H., Ganesh, V., Poupart, P., Czarnecki, K.: Learning rate based branching heuristic for SAT solvers. In: Creignou, N., Le Berre, D. (eds.) SAT 2016. LNCS, vol. 9710, pp. 123–140. Springer, Cham (2016). https://doi.org/10.1007/978-3-319-40970-2_9
23. Liang, J.H., Oh, C., Mathew, M., Thomas, C., Li, C., Ganesh, V.: Machine learning-based restart policy for CDCL SAT solvers. In: Beyersdorff, O., Wintersteiger, C.M. (eds.) SAT 2018. LNCS, vol. 10929, pp. 94–110. Springer, Cham (2018). https://doi.org/10.1007/978-3-319-94144-8_6
24. McMillan, K.L.: Interpolation and SAT-based model checking. In: Hunt, W.A., Somenzi, F. (eds.) CAV 2003. LNCS, vol. 2725, pp. 1–13. Springer, Heidelberg (2003). https://doi.org/10.1007/978-3-540-45069-6_1
25. McMillan, K.L.: Interpolation and model checking. In: Clarke, E., Henzinger, T., Veith, H., Bloem, R. (eds.) Handbook of Model Checking, pp. 421–446. Springer, Cham (2018)
26. Mebsout, A., Tinelli, C.: Proof certificates for SMT-based model checkers for infinite-state systems. In: 2016 Formal Methods in Computer-Aided Design, FMCAD 2016, Mountain View, CA, USA, 3–6 October 2016, pp. 117–124 (2016)
27. Sheeran, M., Singh, S., Stålmarck, G.: Checking safety properties using induction and a SAT-solver. In: Hunt, W.A., Johnson, S.D. (eds.) FMCAD 2000. LNCS, vol. 1954, pp. 127–144. Springer, Heidelberg (2000). https://doi.org/10.1007/3-540-40922-X_8
28. Vizel, Y., Grumberg, O.: Interpolation-sequence based model checking. In: Proceedings of 9th International Conference on Formal Methods in Computer-Aided Design, FMCAD 2009, 15–18 November 2009, Austin, Texas, USA, pp. 1–8 (2009)

29. Vizel, Y., Gurfinkel, A.: Interpolating property directed reachability. In: Biere, A., Bloem, R. (eds.) CAV 2014. LNCS, vol. 8559, pp. 260–276. Springer, Cham (2014). https://doi.org/10.1007/978-3-319-08867-9_17
30. Vizel, Y., Nadel, A., Malik, S.: Solving linear arithmetic with SAT-based model checking. In: 2017 Formal Methods in Computer Aided Design, FMCAD 2017, Vienna, Austria, 2–6 October 2017, pp. 47–54 (2017)

Verifying Asynchronous Event-Driven Programs Using Partial Abstract Transformers

Peizun Liu[1(✉)], Thomas Wahl[1], and Akash Lal[2]

[1] Northeastern University, Boston, USA
lpzun@ccs.neu.edu
[2] Microsoft Research, Bangalore, India

Abstract. We address the problem of analyzing asynchronous event-driven programs, in which concurrent agents communicate via unbounded message queues. The safety verification problem for such programs is undecidable. We present in this paper a technique that combines *queue-bounded exploration* with a *convergence test*: if the sequence of certain abstractions of the reachable states, for increasing queue bounds k, converges, we can prove any property of the program that is preserved by the abstraction. If the abstract state space is finite, convergence is *guaranteed*; the challenge is to catch the point $k_{\max}$ where it happens. We further demonstrate how simple invariants formulated over the *concrete* domain can be used to eliminate spurious *abstract* states, which otherwise prevent the sequence from converging. We have implemented our technique for the P programming language for event-driven programs. We show experimentally that the sequence of abstractions often converges fully automatically, in hard cases with minimal designer support in the form of sequentially provable invariants, and that this happens for a value of $k_{\max}$ small enough to allow the method to succeed in practice.

1 Introduction

Asynchronous event-driven (AED) programming refers to a style of programming multi-agent applications. The agents communicate shared work via messages. Each agent waits for a message to arrive, and then processes it, possibly sending messages to other agents, in order to collectively achieve a goal. This programming style is common for distributed systems as well as low-level designs such as device drivers [11]. Getting such applications right is an arduous task, due to the inherent concurrency: the programmer must defend against all possible interleavings of messages between agents. In response to this challenge, recent years have seen multiple approaches to verifying AED-like programs, e.g. by delaying send actions, or temporarily bounding their number (to keep queue sizes small) [7,10],

Work supported by the US National Science Foundation under Grant No. 1253331, and by Microsoft Research India while hosting the second author for a sabbatical.

I. Dillig and S. Tasiran (Eds.): CAV 2019, LNCS 11562, pp. 386–404, 2019.
https://doi.org/10.1007/978-3-030-25543-5_22

or by reasoning about a small number of representative execution schedules, to avoid interleaving explosion [5].

In this paper we consider the P language for AED programming [11]. A P program consists of multiple state machines running in parallel. Each machine has a local store, and a message queue through which it receives events from other machines. P allows the programmer to formulate safety specifications via a statement that asserts some predicate over the local state of a single machine. Verifying such reachability properties of course requires reasoning over global system behavior and is, for unbounded-queue P programs, undecidable [8].

The unboundedness of the reachable state space does not prevent the use of testing tools that try to explore as much of the state space as possible [3,6,11,13] in the quest for bugs. Somewhat inspired by this kind of approach, the goal of this paper is a verification technique that can (sometimes) *prove* a safety property, despite exploring only a finite fraction of that space. Our approach is as follows. Assuming that the machines' queues are the only source of unboundedness, we consider a bound k on the queue size, and exhaustively compute the reachable states R_k of the resulting finite-state problem, checking the local assertion Φ along the way. We then increase the queue bound until (an error is found, or) we reach some point $k_{\max}$ of *convergence*: a point that allows us to conclude that increasing k further is not required to prove Φ.

What kind of "convergence" are we targeting? We design a sequence $(\overline{R}_k)_{k=0}^{\infty}$ of abstractions of each reachability set over a *finite* abstract state space. Due to the monotonicity of sequence $(\overline{R}_k)_{k=0}^{\infty}$, this ensures convergence, i.e. the existence of $k_{\max}$ such that $\overline{R}_K = \overline{R}_{k_{\max}}$ for all $K \geq k_{\max}$. Provided that an abstract state satisfies Φ exactly if all its concretizations do, we have: if all abstract states in $\overline{R}_{k_{\max}}$ comply with Φ, then so do all reachable concrete states of P—we have proved the property.

We implement this strategy using an abstraction function α with a finite co-domain that leaves the local state of a machine unchanged and maintains the *first occurrence* of each event in the queue; repeat occurrences are dropped. This abstraction preserves properties over the local state and the head of the queue, i.e. the visible (to the machine) part of the state space, which is typically sufficient to express reachability properties.

The second major step in our approach is the detection of the point of convergence of $(\overline{R}_k)_{k=0}^{\infty}$: We show that, for the *best abstract transformer* $\overline{Im}$ [9,27, see Sect. 4.2], if $\overline{Im}(\overline{R}_k) \subseteq \overline{R}_k$, then $\overline{R}_K = \overline{R}_k$ for all $K \geq k$. In fact, we have a stronger result: under an easy-to-enforce condition, it suffices to consider abstract *dequeue operations*: all others, namely enqueue and local actions, never lead to abstract states in $\overline{R}_{k+1} \setminus \overline{R}_k$. The best abstract transformer for dequeue actions is efficiently implementable for a given P program.

It is of course possible that the convergence condition $\overline{Im}(\overline{R}_k) \subseteq \overline{R}_k$ never holds (the problem is undecidable). This manifests in the presence of a *spurious* abstract state in the image produced by $\overline{Im}$, i.e. one whose concretization does not contain any reachable state. Our third contribution is a technique to assist users in eliminating such states, enhancing the chances for convergence. We have observed that spurious abstract states are often due to violations of simple *machine invariants*: invariants that do not depend on the behavior of other machines. By their nature, they can be proved using a cheap sequential analysis.

We can eliminate an abstract state (e.g. produced by $\overline{Im}$) if *all* its concretizations violate a machine invariant. In this paper, we propose a domain-specific temporal logic to express invariants over machines with event queues and, more importantly, an algorithm that decides the above *abstract queue invariant checking* problem, by reducing it efficiently to a plain model checking problem. We have used this technique to ensure the convergence in "hard" cases that otherwise defy convergence of the abstract reachable states sequence.

We have implemented our technique for the P language and empirically evaluated it on an extensive set of benchmark programs. The experimental results support the following conclusions: (i) for our benchmark programs, the sequence of abstractions often converges fully automatically, in hard cases with minimal designer support in the form of separately dischargeable invariants; (ii) almost all examples converge at a small value of $k_{\max}$; and (iii) the overhead our technique adds to the bounding technique is small: the bulk is spent on the exhaustive bounded exploration itself.

Proofs and other supporting material can be found in the Appendix of [23].

2 Overview

We illustrate the main ideas of this paper using an example in the P language. A machine in a P program consists of multiple states. Each state defines an entry code block that is executed when the machine enters the state. The state also defines handlers for each event type e that it is prepared to receive. A handler can either be on e do foo (executing foo on receiving e), or ignore e (dequeuing and dropping e). A state can also have a defer e declaration; the semantics is that a machine dequeues the first non-deferred event in its queue. As a result, a queue in a P program is not strictly FIFO. This relaxation is an important feature of P that helps programmers express their logic compactly [11]. Figure 1 shows a P program named *PiFl*, in which a Sender (eventually) floods a Receiver's queue with PING events. This queue is the only source of unboundedness in *PiFl*.

A critical property for P programs is *(bounded) responsiveness*: the receiving machine must have a handler (e.g. on, defer, ignore) for every event arriving at the queue head; otherwise the event will come as a "surprise" and crash the machine. To prove responsiveness for *PiFl*, we have to demonstrate (among others) that in state Ignore_it, the DONE event is never at the head of the Receiver's queue. We cannot perform exhaustive model checking, since the set of reachable states is infinite. Instead, we will compute a conservative abstraction of this set that is precise enough to rule out DONE events at the queue head in this state.

We first define a suitable abstraction function α that collapses repeated occurrences of events to each event's first occurrence. For instance, the queue

$$\mathcal{Q} = \text{PRIME.PRIME.PRIME.DONE.PING.PING.PING.PING} \qquad (1)$$

```
event PRIME, DONE, PING;

machine Sender {
  var receiver: machine;
  start state Init {
    entry {
      receiver = new Receiver();
    }
    goto Prime_it;
  }
  state Prime_it {
    entry {
      var i:int;
      while (i < 3) { // 3x PRIME
        send receiver, PRIME; i = i + 1;
      }
      send receiver, DONE; goto Ping_it;
    }
  }
  state Ping_it {
    entry {
      send receiver, PING; goto Ping_it;
    }
  }
}

machine Receiver {
  start state Init {
    defer PRIME;
    on DONE goto Ignore_it;
  }

  state Ignore_it {
    ignore PRIME, PING;
  }
}
```

Fig. 1. *PiFl*: a Ping-Flood scenario. The Sender and the Receiver communicate via events of types PRIME, DONE, and PING. After sending some PRIME events and one DONE, the Sender floods the Receiver with PINGs. The Receiver initially defers PRIMEs. Upon receiving DONE it enters a state in which it ignores PING.

will be abstracted to $\overline{\mathcal{Q}} = \alpha(\mathcal{Q}) =$ PRIME.DONE.PING. The *finite* number of possible abstract queues is $1+3+3\cdot2+3\cdot2\cdot1 = 16$. The abstraction preserves the head of the queue. This and the machine state has enough information to check responsiveness.

We now generate the sequence $\overline{R}_k$ of abstractions of the reachable states sets R_k for queue size bounds $k = 0, 1, 2, \ldots$, by computing each finite set R_k, and then $\overline{R}_k$ as $\alpha(R_k)$. The obtained monotone sequence $(\overline{R}_k)_{k=0}^{\infty}$ over a finite domain will eventually converge, but we must prove that it has. This is done by applying the *best abstract transformer* $\overline{Im}$, restricted to dequeue operations (defined in Sect. 4.2), to the current set $\overline{R}_k$, and confirming that the result is contained in $\overline{R}_k$.

As it turns out, the confirmation fails for the *PiFl* program: $k = 5$ marks the first time set $\overline{R}_k$ repeats, i.e. $\overline{R}_4 = \overline{R}_5$, so we are motivated to run the convergence test. Unfortunately we find a state $\bar{s} \in \overline{Im}(\overline{R}_5) \setminus \overline{R}_5$, preventing convergence. Our approach now offers two remedies to this dilemma. One is to refine the queue abstraction. In our implementation, function α is really α_p, for a parameter p that denotes the size of the *prefix* of the queue that is kept unchanged by the abstraction. For example, for the queue from Eq. (1) we have $\alpha_4(\mathcal{Q}) =$ PRIME.PRIME.PRIME.DONE | PING, where | separates the prefix from the "infinite tail" of the abstract queue. This (straightforward) refinement maintains finiteness of the abstraction and increases precision, by revealing that the queue starts with three PRIME events. Re-running the analysis for the *PiFl* program with $p = 4$, at $k = 5$ we find $\overline{Im}(\overline{R}_5) \subseteq \overline{R}_5$, and the proof is complete.

The second remedy to the failed convergence test dilemma is more powerful but also less automatic. Let's revert to prefix $p = 0$ and inspect the abstract state $\bar{s} \in \overline{Im}(\overline{R}_5) \setminus \overline{R}_5$ that foils the test. We find that it features a DONE event followed by a PRIME event in the Receiver's queue. A simple static analysis of the Sender's machine in isolation shows that it permits no path from the send DONE to the send PRIME statement. The behavior of other machines is irrelevant for this invariant; we call it a *machine invariant*. We pass the invariant to our tool via the command line using the expression

$$\mathsf{G}\,(\textsc{Done} \Rightarrow \mathsf{G}\,\neg\textsc{Prime}) \tag{2}$$

in a temporal-logic like notation called QuTL (Sect. 5.1), where G universally quantifies over all queue entries. Our tool includes a QuTL checker that determines that **every concretization** of $\bar{s}$ violates property (2), concluding that $\bar{s}$ is spurious and can be discarded. This turns out to be sufficient for convergence.

3 Queue-(Un)Bounded Reachability Analysis

Communicating Queue Systems. We consider P programs consisting of a fixed and known number n of machines communicating via event passing through unbounded FIFO queues.[1] For simplicity, we assume the machines are created at the start of the program; dynamic creation at a later time can be simulated by having the machine ignore all events until it receives a special creation event.

We model such a program as a *communicating queue system* (CQS). Formally, given $n \in \mathbb{N}$, a CQS P^n is a collection of n *queue automata* (QA) $P_i = (\Sigma, \mathcal{L}_i, Act_i, \Delta_i, \ell_i^I)$, $1 \le i \le n$. A QA consists of a finite queue alphabet Σ shared by all QA, a finite set $\mathcal{L}_i$ of local states, a finite set Act_i of action labels, a finite set $\Delta_i \subseteq \mathcal{L}_i \times (\Sigma \cup \{\varepsilon\}) \times Act_i \times \mathcal{L}_i \times (\Sigma \cup \{\varepsilon\})$ of transitions, and an initial local state $\ell_i^I \in \mathcal{L}_i$. An action label $act \in Act_i$ is of the form

- $act \in \{deq, loc\}$, denoting an action *internal* to P_i (no other QA involved) that either *deq*ueues an event (deq), or updates its *loc*al state (loc); **or**
- $act = !(e, j)$, for $e \in \Sigma$, $j \in \{1, \dots, n\}$, denoting a *transmission*, where P_i (the *sender*) adds event e to the end of the queue of P_j (the *receiver*).

The individual QA of a CQS model machines of a P program; hence we refer to QA states as *machine states*. A transmit action is the only communication mechanism among the QA.

Semantics. A *machine state* m of a QA is of the form $(\ell, \mathcal{Q}) \in \mathcal{L} \times \Sigma^*$; state $m^I = (\ell^I, \varepsilon)$ is *initial*. We define machine transitions corresponding to internal actions as follows (transmit actions are defined later at the global level):

$$\frac{(\ell, \varepsilon) \overset{loc}{\to} (\ell', \varepsilon) \in \Delta}{(\ell, \mathcal{Q}) \to (\ell', \mathcal{Q})} \quad \text{for } \ell, \ell' \in \mathcal{L},\ \mathcal{Q} \in \Sigma^* \qquad \textbf{(local)}$$

$$\frac{(\ell, e) \overset{deq}{\to} (\ell', \varepsilon) \in \Delta}{(\ell, e\mathcal{Q}) \to (\ell', \mathcal{Q})} \quad \text{for } \ell, \ell' \in \mathcal{L},\ e \in \Sigma,\ \mathcal{Q} \in \Sigma^* \qquad \textbf{(dequeue)}$$

[1] The P language permits unbounded machine creation, a feature that we do not allow here and that is not used in any of the benchmarks we are aware of.

A *(global) state* s of a CQS is a tuple $\langle(\ell_1, \mathcal{Q}_1), \ldots, (\ell_n, \mathcal{Q}_n)\rangle$ where $(\ell_i, \mathcal{Q}_i) \in \mathcal{L}_i \times \Sigma^*$ for $i \in \{1, \ldots, n\}$. State $s^I = \langle(\ell_1^I, \varepsilon), \ldots, (\ell_n^I, \varepsilon)\rangle$ is initial. We extend the machine transition relation $\rightarrow$ to states as follows:

$$\langle(\ell_1, \mathcal{Q}_1), \ldots, (\ell_n, \mathcal{Q}_n)\rangle \rightarrow \langle(\ell_1', \mathcal{Q}_1'), \ldots, (\ell_n', \mathcal{Q}_n')\rangle$$

if there exists $i \in \{1, \ldots, n\}$ such that one of the following holds:

(internal) $(\ell_i, \mathcal{Q}_i) \rightarrow (\ell_i', \mathcal{Q}_i')$, and for all $k \in \{1, \ldots, n\} \setminus \{i\}$, $\ell_k = \ell_k'$, $\mathcal{Q}_k = \mathcal{Q}_k'$;
(transmission) there exists $j \in \{1, \ldots, n\}$ and $e \in \Sigma$ such that:

1. $(\ell_i, \varepsilon) \xrightarrow{!(e,j)} (\ell_i', \varepsilon) \in \Delta_i$;
2. $\mathcal{Q}_j' = \mathcal{Q}_j e$;
3. $\ell_k' = \ell_k$ for all $k \in \{1, \ldots, n\} \setminus \{i\}$; and
4. $\mathcal{Q}_k' = \mathcal{Q}_k$ for all $k \in \{1, \ldots, n\} \setminus \{j\}$.

The execution model of a CQS is strictly interleaving. That is, in each step, one of the two above transitions **(internal)** or **(transmission)** is performed for a nondeterministically chosen machine i.

Queue-Bounded and Queue-Unbounded Reachability. Given a CQS P^n, a state $s = \langle(\ell_1, \mathcal{Q}_1), \ldots, (\ell_n, \mathcal{Q}_n)\rangle$, and a number k, the *queue-bounded reachability problem* (for s and k) determines whether s is *reachable under queue bound* k, i.e. whether there exists a path $s_0 \rightarrow s_1 \ldots \rightarrow s_z$ such that $s_0 = s^I$, $s_z = s$, and for $i \in \{0, \ldots, z\}$, all queues in state s_i have at most k events. Queue-bounded reachability for k is trivially decidable, by making enqueue actions for queues of size k *blocking* (the sender cannot continue), which results in a finite state space. We write $R_k = \{s : s \text{ is reachable under queue bound } k\}$.

Queue-bounded reachability will be used in this paper as a tool for solving our actual problem of interest: Given a CQS P^n and a state s, the *Queue-UnBounded reachability Analysis (QUBA) problem* determines whether s is reachable, i.e. whether there exists a (queue-unbounded) path from s^I to s. The QUBA problem is undecidable [8]. We write R $(= \bigcup_{k \in \mathbb{N}} R_k)$ for the set of reachable states.

4 Convergence via Partial Abstract Transformers

In this section, we formalize our approach to detecting the convergence of a suitable sequence of *observations* about the states R_k reachable under k-bounded semantics. We define the observations as abstractions of those states, resulting in sets $\overline{R}_k$. We then investigate the convergence of the sequence $(\overline{R}_k)_{k=0}^{\infty}$.

4.1 List Abstractions of Queues

Our abstraction function applies to queues, as defined below. Its action on machine and system states then follows from the hierarchical design of a CQS. Let $|\mathcal{Q}|$ denote the number of events in $\mathcal{Q}$, and $\mathcal{Q}[i]$ the ith event in $\mathcal{Q}$ $(0 \leq i < |\mathcal{Q}|)$.

Definition 1. *For a parameter $p \in \mathbb{N}$, the* ***list abstraction*** *function $\alpha_p : \Sigma^* \mapsto \Sigma^*$ is defined as follows:*

1. $\alpha_p(\varepsilon) = \varepsilon$.
2. *For a non-empty queue $\mathcal{Q} = P \cdot e$,*

$$\alpha_p(\mathcal{Q}) = \begin{cases} \alpha_p(P) & \text{if there exists } j \text{ s.t. } p \le j < |P| \text{ and } \mathcal{Q}[j] = e \\ \alpha_p(P) \cdot e & \text{otherwise} \end{cases} . \quad (3)$$

Intuitively, α_p abstracts a queue by leaving its first p events unchanged (an idea also used in [16]). Starting from position p it keeps only the first occurrence of each event e in the queue, if any; repeat occurrences are dropped.[2] The preservation of existence and order of the first occurrences of all present events motivates the term *list abstraction.* An alternative is an abstraction that keeps only the *set* (not: list) of queue elements from position p, i.e. it ignores multiplicity *and order.* This is by definition less precise than the list abstraction and provided no efficiency advantages in our experiments. An abstraction that keeps only the queue head proved cheap but too imprecise.

The motivation for parameter p is that many protocols proceed in *rounds* of repeating communication patterns, involving a bounded number of message exchanges. If p exceeds that number, the list abstraction's loss of information may be immaterial.

We write an abstract queue $\overline{\mathcal{Q}} = \alpha_p(\mathcal{Q})$ in the form $\mathit{pref} \,|\, \mathit{suff}$ s.t. $p = |\mathit{pref}|$, and refer to *pref* as $\overline{\mathcal{Q}}$'s *prefix* (shared with $\mathcal{Q}$), and *suff* as $\overline{\mathcal{Q}}$'s *suffix.*

Example 2. *The queues $\mathcal{Q} \in \{bbbba, bbba, bbbaa\}$ are α_2-**equivalent**: $\alpha_2(\mathcal{Q}) = bb \,|\, ba$.*

We extend α_p to act on a machine state via $\alpha_p(\ell_i, \mathcal{Q}_i) = (\ell_i, \alpha_p(\mathcal{Q}_i))$, on a state via $\alpha_p(s) = \langle(\ell_1, \alpha_p(\mathcal{Q}_1)), \ldots, (\ell_n, \alpha_p(\mathcal{Q}_n))\rangle$, and on a set of states pointwise via $\alpha_p(S) = \{\alpha_p(s) : s \in S\}$.

Discussion. The abstract state space is finite since the queue prefix is of fixed size, and each event in the suffix is recorded at most once (the event alphabet is finite). The sets of reachable abstract states grow monotonously with increasing queue size bound k, since the sets of reachable concrete states do:

$$k_1 \le k_2 \quad \Rightarrow \quad R_{k_1} \subseteq R_{k_2} \quad \Rightarrow \quad \alpha_p(R_{k_1}) \subseteq \alpha_p(R_{k_2}) \; .$$

Finiteness and monotonicity guarantee convergence of the sequence of reachable abstract states.

We say the abstraction function α_p *respects* a property of a state if, for any two α_p-equivalent states (see Example 2), the property holds for both or for neither. Function α_p respects properties that refer to the local-state part of a machine, and to the first $p + 1$ events of its queue (which are preserved by α_p). In addition, the property may look beyond the prefix and refer to the existence of events in the queue, but not their frequency or their order after the first occurrence.

[2] Note that the head of the queue is always preserved by α_p, even for $p = 0$.

The rich information preserved by the abstraction (despite being finite-state) especially pays off in connection with the defer feature in the P language, which allows machines to delay handling certain events at the head of a queue [11]. The machine identifies the first non-deferred event in the queue, a piece of information that is precisely preserved by the list abstraction (no matter what p).

Definition 3. *Given an abstract queue $\overline{Q} = e_0 \dots e_{p-1} \mid e_p \dots e_{z-1}$, the* ***concretization function*** $\gamma_p \colon \Sigma^* \to 2^{\Sigma^*}$ *maps $\overline{Q}$ to the* language *of the regular expression*

$$RE_p(\overline{Q}) := e_0 \dots e_{p-1} e_p \{e_p\}^* e_{p+1} \{e_p, e_{p+1}\}^* \dots e_{z-1} \{e_p, \dots, e_{z-1}\}^* \, , \qquad (4)$$

i.e. $\gamma_p(\overline{Q}) := \mathcal{L}(RE_p(\overline{Q}))$.

As a special case, $RE_p(\varepsilon) = \varepsilon$ and so $\gamma_p(\varepsilon) = \mathcal{L}(\varepsilon) = \{\varepsilon\}$ for the empty queue. We extend γ_p to act on abstract (machine or global) states in a way analogous to the extension of α_p, by moving it inside to the queues occurring in those states.

4.2 Abstract Convergence Detection

Recall that finiteness and monotonicity of the sequence $(\overline{R}_k)_{k=0}^{\infty}$ guarantee its convergence, so nothing seems more suggestive than to compute the limit. We summarize our overall procedure to do so in Algorithm 1. The procedure iteratively increases the queue bound k and computes the concrete and (per α_p-projection) the abstract reachability sets R_k and $\overline{R}_k$. If, for some k, an error is detected, the procedure terminates (Lines 4–5; in practice implemented as an on-the-fly check).

Algorithm 1. Queue-unbounded reachability analysis

Input: CQS with transition relation $\to$, $p \in \mathbb{N}$, property Φ respected by α_p.
1: **compute** R_0; $\overline{R}_0$ `:=` $\alpha_p(R_0)$
2: **for** k `:= 1 to` ∞ **do**
3:   **compute** R_k; $\overline{R}_k$ `:=` $\alpha_p(R_k)$
4:   **if** $\exists r \in R_k : r \not\models \Phi$ **then**
5:     **return** "error reachable with queue bound k"
6:   **if** $|\overline{R}_k|$ `=` $|\overline{R}_{k-1}|$ **then**
7:     $\overline{T}$ `:=` $(\alpha_p \circ Im_{deq} \circ \gamma_p)(\overline{R}_k)$ ▷ *partial* best abstract transformer
8:     **if** $\overline{T} \subseteq \overline{R}_k$ **then**
9:       **return** "safe for any queue bound"

The key of the algorithm is reflected in Lines 6–9 and is based on the following idea (all claims are proved as part of Theorem 4 below). If the computation of $\overline{R}_k$ reveals no new abstract states in round k (Line 6; by monotonicity, "same size" implies "same sets"), we apply the *best abstract transformer* [9,27] $\overline{Im} := \alpha_p \circ Im_{\rightarrow} \circ \gamma_p$ to $\overline{R}_k$: if the result is contained in $\overline{R}_k$, the abstract reachability sequence has converged. However, we can do better: we can restrict the successor function $Im_{\rightarrow}$ of the CQS to *dequeue* actions, denoted Im_{deq} in Line 7. The ultimate reason is that firing a local or transmit action on two α_p-equivalent states r and s results again in α_p-equivalent states r' and s'. This fact does *not* hold for dequeue actions: the successors r' and s' of dequeues depend on the abstracted parts of r and s, resp., which may differ and become "visible" during the dequeue (e.g. the event behind the queue head moves into the head position). Our main result therefore is: if $\overline{R}_k = \overline{R}_{k-1}$ and dequeue actions do not create new abstract states (Lines 7 and 8), sequence $(\overline{R}_k)_{k=0}^{\infty}$ has converged:

Theorem 4. *If $\overline{R}_k = \overline{R}_{k-1}$ and $\overline{T} \subseteq \overline{R}_k$, then for any $K \geq k$, $\overline{R}_K = \overline{R}_k$.*

If the sequence of reachable abstract states has converged, then **all** reachable concrete states (any k) belong to $\gamma_p(\overline{R}_k)$ (for the current k). Since the abstraction function α_p respects property Φ, we know that if any reachable concrete state violated Φ, so would any other concrete state that maps to the same abstraction. However, for each abstract state in $\overline{R}_k$, Line 4 has examined at least one state r in its concretization; a violation was not found. We conclude:

Corollary 5. *Line 9 of Algorithm 1 correctly asserts that no reachable concrete state of the given CQS violates Φ.*

The corollary (along with the earlier statement about Lines 4–5) confirms the partial correctness of Algorithm 1. The procedure is, however, necessarily incomplete: if no error is detected and the convergence condition in Line 8 never holds, the **for** loop will run forever.

We conclude this part with two comments. First, note that we do not compute the sets $\overline{R}_k$ as reachability fixpoints in the abstract domain (i.e. the domain of α_p). Instead, we compute the *concrete* reachability sets first, and then obtain the $\overline{R}_k$ via projection (Line 1). The reason is that the projection gives us the *exact* set of abstractions of reachable concrete states, while an abstract fixpoint likely overapproximates (for instance, the best abstract transformer from Line 7 does) and loses precision. Note that a primary motivation for computing abstract fixpoints, namely that the concrete fixpoint may not be computable, does not apply here: the concrete domains are finite, for each k.

Second, we observe that this projection technique comes with a cost: sequence $(\overline{R}_k)_{k=0}^{\infty}$ may *stutter* at intermediate moments: $\overline{R}_k \subsetneq \overline{R}_{k+1} = \overline{R}_{k+2} \subsetneq \overline{R}_{k+3}$. The reason is that $\overline{R}_{k+3}$ is not obtained as a functional image of $\overline{R}_{k+2}$, but by projection from R_{k+3}. As a consequence, we cannot short-cut the convergence detection by just "waiting" for $(\overline{R}_k)_{k=0}^{\infty}$ to stabilize, despite the finite domain.

4.3 Computing Partial Best Abstract Transformers

Recall that in Line 7 we compute

$$\overline{T} = \overline{Im}_{deq}(\overline{R}_k) = (\alpha_p \circ Im_{deq} \circ \gamma_p)(\overline{R}_k) . \quad (5)$$

The line applies the best abstract transformer, restricted to dequeue actions, to $\overline{R}_k$. This result cannot be computed as defined in (5), since $\gamma_{\bar{p}}(\overline{R}_k)$ is typically infinite. However, $\overline{R}_k$ is finite, so we can iterative over $\bar{r} \in \overline{R}_k$, and little information is actually needed to determine the abstract successors of $\bar{r}$. The "infinite fragment" of $\bar{r}$ remains unchanged, which makes the action implementable.

Formally, let $\bar{r} = (\ell, \overline{\mathcal{Q}})$ with $\overline{\mathcal{Q}} = e_0 e_1 \ldots e_{p-1} \mid e_p e_{p+1} \ldots e_{z-1}$. To apply a dequeue action to $\bar{r}$, we first perform local-state updates on ℓ as required by the action, resulting in ℓ'. Now consider $\overline{\mathcal{Q}}$. The first suffix event, e_p, moves into the prefix due to the dequeue. We do not know whether there are later occurrences of e_p before or after the first suffix occurrences of $e_{p+1} \ldots e_{z-1}$. This information determines the possible abstract queues resulting from the dequeue. To compute the exact best abstract transformer, we enumerate these possibilities:

$$\overline{Im}_{deq}(\{(\ell, \overline{\mathcal{Q}})\}) = \left\{ (\ell', \overline{\mathcal{Q}}') : \overline{\mathcal{Q}}' \in \left\{ \begin{array}{l} e_1 \ldots e_p \mid e_{p+1} e_{p+2} \ldots e_{z-1} \\ e_1 \ldots e_p \mid \boxed{e_p} e_{p+1} e_{p+2} \ldots e_{z-1} \\ e_1 \ldots e_p \mid e_{p+1} \boxed{e_p} e_{p+2} \ldots e_{z-1} \\ \quad \vdots \\ e_1 \ldots e_p \mid e_{p+1} e_{p+2} \ldots e_{z-1} \boxed{e_p} \end{array} \right\} \right\}$$

The first case for $\overline{\mathcal{Q}}'$ applies if there are no occurrences of e_p in the suffix after the dequeue. The remaining cases enumerate possible positions of the *first* occurrence of e_p (boxed, for readability) in the suffix after the dequeue. The cost of this enumeration is linear in the length of the suffix of the abstract queue.

Since our list abstraction maintains the first occurrence of each event, the semantics of defer (see the *Discussion* in Sect. 4.1) can be implemented abstractly without loss of information (not shown above, for simplicity).

5 Abstract Queue Invariant Checking

The abstract transformer function in Sect. 4 is used to decide whether sequence $(\overline{R}_k)_{k=0}^{\infty}$ has converged. Being an overapproximation, the function may generate *spurious* states: they are not reachable, i.e. no concretization of them is. Unfortunate for us, spurious abstract states always prevent convergence.

A key empirical observation is that concretizations of spurious abstract states often violate simple machine invariants, which can be proved from the perspective of a single machine, while collapsing all other machines into a nondeterministically behaving environment. Consider our example from Sect. 2 for $p = 0$. It fails to converge since Line 7 generates an abstract state $\bar{s}$ that features a DONE event followed by a PRIME event in the Receiver's queue. A light-weight static analysis proves that the Sender's machine permits no path from the send DONE to the send PRIME statement. Since **every** concretization of $\bar{s}$ features a DONE followed by a PRIME event, the abstract state $\bar{s}$ is spurious and can be eliminated.

Our tool assists users in *discovering* candidate machine invariants, by facilitating the inspection of states in $\overline{T}\backslash\overline{R}_k$ (which foil the test in Line 8). We *discharge* such invariants separately, via a simple sequential model-check or static analysis. In the section we focus on the more interesting question of how to *use* them. Formally, suppose the P program comes with a *queue invariant* I, i.e. an invariant property of *concrete* queues. The *abstract invariant checking problem* is to decide, for a given abstract queue $\overline{\mathcal{Q}}$, whether *every* concretization of $\overline{\mathcal{Q}}$ violates I; in this case, and this case only, an abstract state containing $\overline{\mathcal{Q}}$ can be eliminated. In the following we define a language QuTL for specifying concrete queue invariants (5.1), and then show how checking an abstract queue against a QuTL invariant can be efficiently solved as a model checking problem (5.2).

5.1 Queue Temporal Logic (QuTL)

Our logic to express invariant properties of queues is a form of first-order linear-time temporal logic. This choice is motivated by the logic's ability to constrain the order (via temporal operators) and multiplicity of queue events, the latter via relational operators that express conditions on the number of event occurrences.

Queue Relational Expressions (QuRelE). These are of the form $\#e \rhd c$, where $e \in \Sigma$ (queue alphabet), $\rhd \in \{<, \leq, =, \geq, >\}$, and $c \in \mathbb{N}$ is a literal natural number. The *value* of a QuRelE is defined as the Boolean

$$V(\#e \rhd c) \quad = \quad |\{i \in \mathbb{N} : 0 \leq i < |\mathcal{Q}| \wedge \mathcal{Q}[i] = e\}| \ \rhd \ c \tag{6}$$

where $|\cdot|$ denotes set cardinality and $\rhd$ is interpreted as the standard integer arithmetic relational operator. In the following we write $\mathcal{Q}[i \rightarrow]$ (read: "$\mathcal{Q}$ from i") for the queue obtained from queue $\mathcal{Q}$ by dropping the first i events.

Definition 6 (Syntax of QuTL). *The following are QuTL formulas:*

- *false and true.*
- *e, for $e \in \Sigma$.*
- *E, for a queue relational expression E.*
- *$\mathsf{X}\,\phi$, $\mathsf{F}\,\phi$, $\mathsf{G}\,\phi$, for a QuTL formula ϕ.*

The set QuTL is the Boolean closure of the above set of formulas.

Definition 7 (Concrete semantics of QuTL). *Concrete queue $\mathcal{Q}$ **satisfies** QuTL formula ϕ, written $\mathcal{Q} \models \phi$, depending on the form of ϕ as follows.*

- *$\mathcal{Q} \models$ true.*
- *for $e \in \Sigma$, $\mathcal{Q} \models e$ iff $|\mathcal{Q}| > 0$ and $\mathcal{Q}[0] = e$.*
- *for a queue relational expression E, $\mathcal{Q} \models E$ iff $V(E) =$ true.*
- *$\mathcal{Q} \models \mathsf{X}\,\phi$ iff $|\mathcal{Q}| > 0$ and $\mathcal{Q}[1 \rightarrow] \models \phi$.*
- *$\mathcal{Q} \models \mathsf{F}\,\phi$ iff there exists $i \in \mathbb{N}$ such that $0 \leq i < |\mathcal{Q}|$ and $\mathcal{Q}[i \rightarrow] \models \phi$.*
- *$\mathcal{Q} \models \mathsf{G}\,\phi$ iff for all $i \in \mathbb{N}$ such that $0 \leq i < |\mathcal{Q}|$, $\mathcal{Q}[i \rightarrow] \models \phi$.*

Satisfaction of Boolean combinations is defined as usual, e.g. $\mathcal{Q} \models \neg\phi$ *iff* $\mathcal{Q} \not\models \phi$. *No other pair* $(\mathcal{Q}, \phi)$ *satisfies* $\mathcal{Q} \models \phi$.

For instance, formula $\#e \leq 3$ is true exactly for queues containing at most 3 e's, and formula $\mathsf{G}(\#e \geq 1)$ is true of $\mathcal{Q}$ iff $\mathcal{Q}$ is empty or its final event (!) is e. See App. B of [23] for more examples.

Algorithmically checking whether a concrete queue $\mathcal{Q}$ satisfies a QuTL formula ϕ is straightforward, since $\mathcal{Q}$ is of fixed size and straight-line. The situation is different with abstract queues. Our motivation here is to declare that an abstract queue $\overline{\mathcal{Q}}$ *violates* a formula ϕ if *all its concretizations* (Definition 3) do: under this condition, if ϕ is an invariant, we know $\overline{\mathcal{Q}}$ is not reachable. Equivalently:

Definition 8 (Abstract semantics of QuTL). *Abstract queue* $\overline{\mathcal{Q}}$ ***satisfies*** *QuTL formula* ϕ, *written* $\overline{\mathcal{Q}} \models_p \phi$, *if some concretization of* $\overline{\mathcal{Q}}$ *satisfies* ϕ:

$$\overline{\mathcal{Q}} \models_p \phi \quad := \quad \exists \mathcal{Q} \in \gamma_p(\overline{\mathcal{Q}}) : \mathcal{Q} \models \phi. \tag{7}$$

For example, we have $bb \mid ba \models_2 \mathsf{G}(a \Rightarrow \mathsf{G}\,\neg b)$ since for instance $bbba \in \gamma_2(bb \mid ba)$ satisfies the formula. See App. B of [23] for more examples.

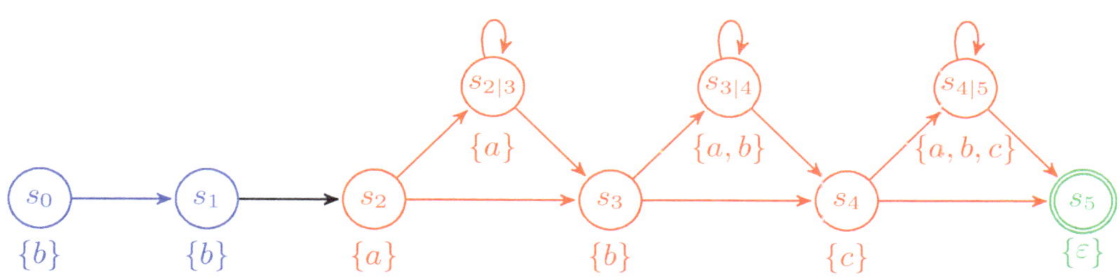

Fig. 2. LTS for $\overline{\mathcal{Q}} = bb \mid abc$ $(p = 2)$, with label sets written below each state. The blue and red parts encode the concretizations of the prefix and suffix of $\overline{\mathcal{Q}}$, resp. (Color figure online)

5.2 Abstract QuTL Model Checking

A QuTL *constraint* is a QuTL formula without Boolean connectives. We first describe how to model check against QuTL constraints, and come back to Boolean connectives at the end of Sect. 5.2.

Model checking an abstract queue $\overline{\mathcal{Q}}$ against a QuTL constraint ϕ, i.e. checking whether some concretization of $\overline{\mathcal{Q}}$ satisfies ϕ, can be reduced to a standard model checking problem over a labeled transition system (LTS) $M = (S, T, L)$ with states S, transitions T, and a labeling function $L \colon S \to 2^{\Sigma} \cup \{\varepsilon\}$. The LTS *characterizes* the concretization $\gamma_p(\overline{\mathcal{Q}})$ of $\overline{\mathcal{Q}}$, as illustrated in Fig. 2 using an example: the concretizations of $\overline{\mathcal{Q}}$ are formed from the regular-expression traces generated by paths of $\overline{\mathcal{Q}}$'s LTS that end in the double-circled green state.

The straightforward construction of the LTS M is formalized in App. A.2 of [23]. Its size is linear in $|\overline{\mathcal{Q}}|$: $|S| = p+2\times(|\overline{\mathcal{Q}}|-p)+1$ and $|T| = p+4\times(|\overline{\mathcal{Q}}|-p)$.

We call a path through M *complete* if it ends in the right-most state s_z of M (green in Fig. 2). The labeling function extends to paths via $L(s_i \to \ldots \to s_j) = L(s_i) \cdot \ldots \cdot L(s_j)$. This gives rise to the following characterization of $\gamma_p(\overline{\mathcal{Q}})$:

Lemma 9. *Given abstract queue $\overline{\mathcal{Q}}$ over alphabet Σ, let $M = (S, T, L)$ be its LTS.*

$$\gamma_p(\overline{\mathcal{Q}}) \quad = \quad \bigcup \{\mathcal{L}(L(\pi)) \in 2^{\Sigma^*} \mid \pi \text{ is a complete path from } s_0 \text{ in } M\}. \qquad (8)$$

We say path π *satisfies* ϕ, written $\pi \models_p \phi$, if there exists $\mathcal{Q} \in \mathcal{L}(L(\pi))$ s.t. $\mathcal{Q} \models \phi$.

Corollary 10. *Let $\overline{\mathcal{Q}}$ and M as in Lemma 9, and ϕ a QuTL constraint. Then the following are equivalent.*

1. $\overline{\mathcal{Q}} \models_p \phi$.
2. *There exists a complete path π from s_0 in M such that $\pi \models_p \phi$.*

Proof. immediate from Definition 8 and Lemma 9. □

Given an abstract queue $\overline{\mathcal{Q}}$, its LTS M, and a QuTL constraint ϕ, our abstract queue model checking algorithm is based on Corollary 10: we need to find a complete path from s_0 in M that satisfies ϕ. This is similar to standard model checking against existential temporal logics like ECTL, with two particularities:

First, paths must be complete. This poses no difficulty, as completeness is suffix-closed: a path ends in s_z iff any suffix does. This implies that temporal reductions on QuTL constraints work like in standard temporal logics. For example: there exists a complete path π from s_0 in M such that $\pi \models_p \mathsf{X}\phi$ iff there exists a complete path π' from some successor s_1 of s_0 such that $\pi' \models_p \phi$.

Second, we have domain-specific atomic (non-temporal) propositions. These are accommodated as follows, for an arbitrary start state $s \in S$:

$\exists\pi$: π from s complete and $\pi \models_p e$ (for $e \in \Sigma$):
this is true iff $e \in L(s)$, as is immediate from the $\mathcal{Q} \models e$ case in Definition 7.
$\exists\pi$: π from s complete and $\pi \models_p \#e > c$ (for $e \in \Sigma, c \in \mathbb{N}$): this is true iff

- the number of states reachable from s labeled e is greater than c, **or**
- there exists a state reachable from s labeled with e that has a self-loop.

The other relational expressions $\#e \rhd c$ are checked similarly. □

Boolean Connectives. Let now ϕ be a full-fledged QuTL formula. We first bring it into negation normal form, by pushing negations inside, exploiting the usual dualities $\neg\mathsf{X} = \mathsf{X}\neg$, $\neg\mathsf{F} = \mathsf{G}\neg$, and $\neg\mathsf{G} = \mathsf{F}\neg$. The subset $\rhd \in \{<, \leq, \geq, >\}$ of the queue relational expressions is semantically closed under negation; "$\neg=$" is replaced by "$> \vee <$". A path π from s satisfies $\neg e$ (for $e \in \Sigma$) iff $L(s) \neq \{e\}$: this condition states that either $L(s) = \varepsilon$, or there exists some label other than e in $L(s)$, so the *existential* property $\neg e$ holds.

Disjunctions are handled by distributing $\models_p$ over them: $\overline{\mathcal{Q}} \models_p \phi_1 \vee \phi_2$ iff $\overline{\mathcal{Q}} \models_p \phi_1 \vee \overline{\mathcal{Q}} \models_p \phi_2$. What remains are conjunctions. The existential flavor of $\models_p$ implies that $\models_p$ does *not* distribute over them; see Ex. 13 in App. B.1 of [23]. Suppose we ignore this and replace a check of the form $\overline{\mathcal{Q}} \models_p \phi_1 \wedge \phi_2$ by the **weaker** check $\overline{\mathcal{Q}} \models_p \phi_1 \wedge \overline{\mathcal{Q}} \models_p \phi_2$, which may produce false positives. Now consider how we use these results: if $\overline{\mathcal{Q}} \models_p \phi$ holds, we decide to *keep* the state containing the abstract queue. False positives during abstract model checks therefore may create extra work, but do not introduce unsoundness. In summary, our abstract model checking algorithm soundly approximates conjunctions, but remains exact for the purely disjunctive fragment of QuTL.

Table 1. Results: *#M*: #P machines; *Loc*: #lines of code; *Safe?* = ✓: property holds; *p*: *minimum* unabstracted prefix for required convergence; $k_{\max}$: point of convergence or exposed bugs (– means divergence); *Time*: runtime (sec); *Mem.*: memory usage (Mb.).

ID/Program	Program Features			PAT				ID/Program	Program Features			PAT			
	#M	*Loc*	*Safe?*	*p*	$k_{\max}$	*Time*	*Mem.*		*#M*	*Loc*	*Safe?*	*p*	$k_{\max}$	*Time*	*Mem.*
1/GERMAN-1	3	242	✓	4	–	TO	–	8/FAILOVER	4	132	✓	0	2	2.91	8.56
2/GERMAN-2	4	244	✓	4	–	TO	–	9/MAXINSTANCES	4	79	✓	0	3	0.14	0.56
3/TOKENRING-BUGGY	6	164	✗	0	2	241.44	35.96	10/PINGPONG	2	76	✓	0	2	0.06	0.43
4/TOKENRING-FIXED	6	164	✓	0	4	1849.25	130.87	11/BOUNDEDASYNC	4	96	✓	0	5	203.39	29.32
5/FAILUREDETECTOR	6	229	✓	0	4	183.99	12.38	12/PINGFLOOD	2	52	✓	4	5	0.11	0.43
6/OSR	5	378	✓	0	5	77.92	44.86	13/ELEVATOR-BUGGY	4	270	✗	0	1	1.29	5.23
7/OPENWSN	6	294	✓	2	5	2574.25	376.29	14/ELEVATOR-FIXED	4	271	✓	0	4	49.23	45.36

6 Empirical Evaluation

We implemented the proposed approaches in C# atop the bounded model checker PTester [11], an analysis tool for P programs. PTester employs a bounded exploration strategy similar to Zing [4]. We denote by PAT the implementation of Algorithm 1, and by PAT+I the version with queue invariants ("PAT+ Invariants"). A detailed introduction to tool design and implementation is available online [22].

Experimental Goals. We evaluate the approaches against the following questions:

Q1. Is PAT effective: does it converge for many programs? for what values of k?
Q2. What is the impact of the QuTL invariant checking?

Experimental Setup. We collected a set of P programs (available online [22]); most have been used in previous publications:

1–5: protocols implemented in P: the German Cache Coherence protocol with different number of clients (**1–2**) [11], a buggy version of a token ring protocol [11], and a fixed version (**3–4**), and a failure detector protocol from [25] (**5**).

6–7: two device drivers where OSR is used for testing USB devices [10].
8–14: miscellaneous: **8–10** [25], **11** [15], **12** is the example from Sect. 2, **13–14** are the buggy and fixed versions of an Elevator controller [11].

We conduct two types of experiments: (i) we run PAT on each benchmark to empirically answer **Q1**; (ii) we run PAT+I on the examples which fail to verify in (i) to answer **Q2**. All experiments are performed on a 2.80 GHz Intel(R) Core(TM) i7-7600 machine with 8 GB memory, running 64-bit Windows 10. The timeout is set to 3600 s (1h); the memory limit to 4 GB.

Results. Table 1 shows that PAT converges on *almost all* safe examples (and successfully exposes the bugs for unsafe ones). Second, in most cases, the $k_{\max}$ where convergence was detected is small, 5 or less. This is what enables the use of this technique in practice: the exploration space grows fast with k, so early convergence is critical. Note that $k_{\max}$ is guaranteed to be the smallest value for which the respective example converges. If convergent, the verification succeeded fully automatically: the queue abstraction prefix parameter p is incremented in a loop whenever the current value of p caused a spurious abstract state.

The GERMAN protocol does not converge in reasonable time. In this case, we request minimal manual assistance from the designer. Our tool inspects spurious abstract states, compares them to actually reached abstract states, and suggests candidate invariants to exclude them. We describe the process of invariant discovery, and why and how they are easy to prove, in [22].

The following table shows the invariants that make the GERMAN protocol converge, and the resulting times and memory consumption.

Program	p	$k_{\max}$	*Time*	*Mem.*	Invariant
GERMAN-1	0	4	15.65	45.65	Server: $\#req\_excl \leq 1 \wedge \#req\_share \leq 1$
GERMAN-2	0	4	629.43	284.75	Client: $\#ask\_excl \leq 1 \wedge \#ask\_share \leq 1$

The invariant states that there is always at most one exclusive request and at most one shared request in the Server or Client machine's queue.

Performance Evaluation. We finally consider the following question: *To perform full verification, how much overhead does* PAT *incur compared to PTester?* We iteratively run PTester with a queue bound from 1 up to $k_{\max}$ (from Table 1).

The figure on the right compares the running times of PAT and PTester. We observe that the difference is small, in all cases, suggesting that turning PTester into a full verifier comes with little

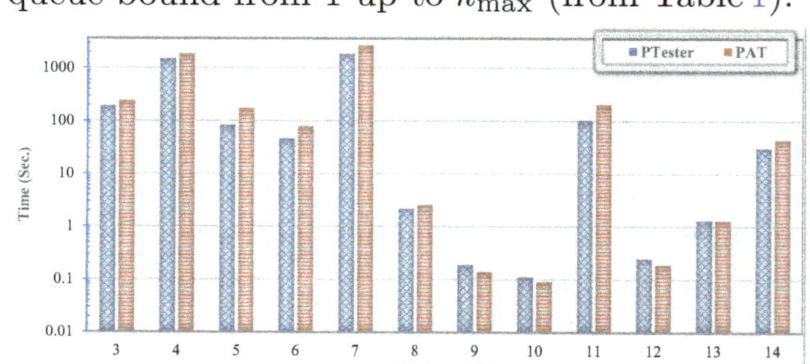

extra cost. Therefore, as for improving PAT's scalability, the focus should be on the efficiency of the R_k computation (Line 3 in Algorithm 1). Techniques that lend themselves here are *partial order reduction* [2,28] or *symmetry reduction* [29]. Note that our proposed approach is orthogonal to how these sets are computed.

7 Related Work

Automatic verification for asynchronous event-driven programs communicating via unbounded FIFO queues is undecidable [8], even when the agents are finite-state machines. To sidestep the undecidability, various remedies are proposed. One is to underapproximate program behaviors using various bounding techniques; examples include depth- [17] and context-bounded analysis [19,20,26], delay-bounding [13], bounded asynchrony [15], preemption-bounding [24], and phase-bounded analysis [3,6]. It has been shown that most of these bounding techniques admit a decidable model checking problem [19,20,26] and thus have been successfully used in practice for finding bugs.

Gall et al. proposed an abstract interpretation of FIFO queues in terms of regular languages [16]. While our works share some basic insights about taming queues, the differences are fundamental: our abstract domain is *finite*, guaranteeing convergence of our sequence. In [16] the abstract domain is infinite; they propose a widening operator for fixpoint computation. More critically, we use the abstract domain *only* for convergence detection; the set of reachable states returned is in the end exact. As a result, we can prove and refute properties but may not terminate; [16] is inexact and cannot refute but always returns.

Several partial verification approaches for asynchronous message-passing programs have been presented recently [5,7,10]. In [5], Bakst et al. propose *canonical sequentialization*, which avoids exploring all interleavings by sequentializing concurrent programs. Desai et al. [10] propose an alternative way, namely by prioritizing receive actions over send actions. The approach is complete in the sense that it is able to construct *almost-synchronous invariants* that cover all reachable local states and hence suffice to prove local assertions. Similarly, Bouajjani et al. [7] propose an iterative analysis that bounds send actions in each interaction phase. It approaches the completeness by checking a program's synchronizability under the bounds. Similar to our work, the above three works are sound but incomplete. An experimental comparison against the techniques reported in [7,10] fails due to the unavailability of a tool that implements them. While tools implementing these techniques are not available [7,10], a comparison based on what is reported in the papers suggests that our approach is competitive in both performance and precision.

Our approach can be categorized as a *cutoff* detection technique [1,12,14,28]. Cutoffs are, however, typically determined statically, often leaving them too large for practical verification. Aiming at minimal cutoffs, our work is closer in nature to earlier *dynamic* strategies [18,21], which targeted different forms of concurrent programs. The *generator* technique proposed in [21] is unlikely to work for P programs, due to the large local state space of machines.

8 Conclusion

We have presented a method to verify safety properties of asynchronous event-driven programs of agents communicating via unbounded queues. Our approach is sound but incomplete: it can both prove (or, by encountering bugs, disprove) such properties but may not terminate. We empirically evaluate our method on a collection of P programs. Our experimental results showcase our method can successfully prove the correctness of programs; such proof is achieved with little extra resource costs compared to plain state exploration. Future work includes an extension to P programs with other sources of unboundedness than the queue length (e.g. messages with integer *payloads*).

Acknowledgments. We thank Dr. Vijay D'Silva (Google, Inc.), for enlightening discussions about partial abstract transformers.

References

1. Abdulla, A.P., Haziza, F., Holík, L.: All for the price of few (parameterized verification through view abstraction). In: VMCAI, pp. 476–495 (2013)
2. Abdulla, P., Aronis, S., Jonsson, B., Sagonas, K.: Optimal dynamic partial order reduction. In: POPL, pp. 373–384 (2014)
3. Abdulla, P.A., Atig, M.F., Cederberg, J.: Analysis of message passing programs using SMT-solvers. In: Van Hung, D., Ogawa, M. (eds.) ATVA 2013. LNCS, vol. 8172, pp. 272–286. Springer, Cham (2013). https://doi.org/10.1007/978-3-319-02444-8_20
4. Andrews, T., Qadeer, S., Rajamani, S.K., Rehof, J., Xie, Y.: Zing: a model checker for concurrent software. In: Alur, R., Peled, D.A. (eds.) CAV 2004. LNCS, vol. 3114, pp. 484–487. Springer, Heidelberg (2004). https://doi.org/10.1007/978-3-540-27813-9_42
5. Bakst, A., Gleissenthall, K.v., Kici, R.G., Jhala, R.: Verifying distributed programs via canonical sequentialization. PACMPL **1**(OOPSLA), 110:1–110:27 (2017)
6. Bouajjani, A., Emmi, M.: Bounded phase analysis of message-passing programs. Int. J. Softw. Tools Technol. Transf. **16**(2), 127–146 (2014)
7. Bouajjani, A., Enea, C., Ji, K., Qadeer, S.: On the completeness of verifying message passing programs under bounded asynchrony. In: Chockler, H., Weissenbacher, G. (eds.) CAV 2018. LNCS, vol. 10982, pp. 372–391. Springer, Cham (2018). https://doi.org/10.1007/978-3-319-96142-2_23
8. Brand, D., Zafiropulo, P.: On communicating finite-state machines. J. ACM **30**(2), 323–342 (1983)
9. Cousot, P., Cousot, R.: Systematic design of program analysis frameworks. In: POPL, pp. 269–282 (1979)
10. Desai, A., Garg, P., Madhusudan, P.: Natural proofs for asynchronous programs using almost-synchronous reductions. In: OOPSLA, pp. 709–725 (2014)
11. Desai, A., Gupta, V., Jackson, E., Qadeer, S., Rajamani, S., Zufferey, D.: P: safe asynchronous event-driven programming. In: PLDI, pp. 321–332 (2013)
12. Emerson, E.A., Kahlon, V.: Reducing model checking of the many to the few. In: McAllester, D. (ed.) CADE 2000. LNCS (LNAI), vol. 1831, pp. 236–254. Springer, Heidelberg (2000). https://doi.org/10.1007/10721959_19

13. Emmi, M., Qadeer, S., Rakamarić, Z.: Delay-bounded scheduling. In: POPL, pp. 411–422 (2011)
14. Farzan, A., Kincaid, Z., Podelski, A.: Proof spaces for unbounded parallelism. In: POPL, pp. 407–420 (2015)
15. Fisher, J., Henzinger, T.A., Mateescu, M., Piterman, N.: Bounded asynchrony: concurrency for modeling cell-cell interactions. In: Fisher, J. (ed.) FMSB 2008. LNCS, vol. 5054, pp. 17–32. Springer, Heidelberg (2008). https://doi.org/10.1007/978-3-540-68413-8_2
16. Le Gall, T., Jeannet, B., Jéron, T.: Verification of communication protocols using abstract interpretation of FIFO queues. In: Johnson, M., Vene, V. (eds.) AMAST 2006. LNCS, vol. 4019, pp. 204–219. Springer, Heidelberg (2006). https://doi.org/10.1007/11784180_17
17. Godefroid, P.: Model checking for programming languages using VeriSoft. In: POPL, pp. 174–186 (1997)
18. Kaiser, A., Kroening, D., Wahl, T.: Dynamic cutoff detection in parameterized concurrent programs. In: Touili, T., Cook, B., Jackson, P. (eds.) CAV 2010. LNCS, vol. 6174, pp. 645–659. Springer, Heidelberg (2010). https://doi.org/10.1007/978-3-642-14295-6_55
19. La Torre, S., Parthasarathy, M., Parlato, G.: Analyzing recursive programs using a fixed-point calculus. In: PLDI, pp. 211–222 (2009)
20. Lal, A., Reps, T.: Reducing concurrent analysis under a context bound to sequential analysis. Form. Methods Syst. Des. **35**(1), 73–97 (2009)
21. Liu, P., Wahl, T.: CUBA: interprocedural context-unbounded analysis of concurrent programs. In: PLDI, pp. 105–119 (2018)
22. Liu, P., Wahl, T., Lal, A.: (2019). www.khoury.northeastern.edu/home/lpzun/quba
23. Liu, P., Wahl, T., Lal, A.: Verifying asynchronous event-driven programs using partial abstract transformers (extended manuscript). CoRR abs/1905.09996 (2019)
24. Musuvathi, M., Qadeer, S.: Iterative context bounding for systematic testing of multithreaded programs. In: PLDI, pp. 446–455 (2007)
25. P-GitHub: The P programming langugage (2019). https://github.com/p-org/P
26. Qadeer, S., Rehof, J.: Context-bounded model checking of concurrent software. In: Halbwachs, N., Zuck, L.D. (eds.) TACAS 2005. LNCS, vol. 3440, pp. 93–107. Springer, Heidelberg (2005). https://doi.org/10.1007/978-3-540-31980-1_7
27. Reps, T., Sagiv, M., Yorsh, G.: Symbolic implementation of the best transformer. In: Steffen, B., Levi, G. (eds.) VMCAI 2004. LNCS, vol. 2937, pp. 252–266. Springer, Heidelberg (2004). https://doi.org/10.1007/978-3-540-24622-0_21
28. Sousa, M., Rodríguez, C., D'Silva, V., Kroening, D.: Abstract interpretation with unfoldings. In: Majumdar, R., Kunčak, V. (eds.) CAV 2017. LNCS, vol. 10427, pp. 197–216. Springer, Cham (2017). https://doi.org/10.1007/978-3-319-63390-9_11
29. Wahl, T., Donaldson, A.: Replication and abstraction: symmetry in automated formal verification. Symmetry **2**(2), 799–847 (2010)

Inferring Inductive Invariants from Phase Structures

Yotam M. Y. Feldman[1(✉)], James R. Wilcox[2], Sharon Shoham[1], and Mooly Sagiv[1]

[1] Tel Aviv University, Tel Aviv, Israel
yotam.feldman@gmail.com
[2] University of Washington, Seattle, USA

Abstract. Infinite-state systems such as distributed protocols are challenging to verify using interactive theorem provers or automatic verification tools. Of these techniques, deductive verification is highly expressive but requires the user to annotate the system with *inductive invariants*. To relieve the user from this labor-intensive and challenging task, *invariant inference* aims to find inductive invariants automatically. Unfortunately, when applied to infinite-state systems such as distributed protocols, existing inference techniques often diverge, which limits their applicability.

This paper proposes *user-guided invariant inference* based on *phase invariants*, which capture the different logical phases of the protocol. Users conveys their intuition by specifying a *phase structure*, an automaton with edges labeled by program transitions; the tool automatically infers assertions that hold in the automaton's states, resulting in a full safety proof. The additional structure from phases guides the inference procedure towards finding an invariant.

Our results show that user guidance by phase structures facilitates successful inference beyond the state of the art. We find that phase structures are pleasantly well matched to the intuitive reasoning routinely used by domain experts to understand why distributed protocols are correct, so that providing a phase structure reuses this existing intuition.

1 Introduction

Infinite-state systems such as distributed protocols remain challenging to verify despite decades of work developing interactive and automated proof techniques. Such proofs rely on the fundamental notion of an *inductive invariant*. Unfortunately, specifying inductive invariants is difficult for users, who must often repeatedly iterate through candidate invariants before achieving an inductive invariant. For example, the Verdi project's proof of the Raft consensus protocol used an inductive invariant with 90 conjuncts and relied on significant manual proof effort [61,62].

The dream of *invariant inference* is that users would instead be assisted by automatic procedures that could infer the required invariants. While other domains have seen successful applications of invariant inference, using techniques such as abstract interpretation [18] and property-directed reachability [10,21], existing inference techniques fall short for interesting distributed protocols, and often diverge while searching for an invariant. These limitations have hindered adoption of invariant inference.

I. Dillig and S. Tasiran (Eds.): CAV 2019, LNCS 11562, pp. 405–425, 2019.
https://doi.org/10.1007/978-3-030-25543-5_23

Our Approach. The idea of this paper is that invariant inference can be made drastically more effective by utilizing *user-guidance* in the form of *phase structures*. We propose user-guided invariant inference, in which the user provides some additional information to guide the tool towards an invariant. An effective guidance method must (1) match users' high-level intuition of the proof, and (2) convey information in a way that an automatic inference tool can readily utilize to direct the search. In this setting invariant inference turns a partial, high-level argument accessible to the user into a full, formal correctness proof, overcoming scenarios where procuring the proof completely automatically is unsuccessful.

Our approach places *phase invariants* at the heart of both user interaction and algorithmic inference. Phase invariants have an automaton-based form that is well-suited to the domain of distributed protocols. They allow the user to convey a high-level temporal intuition of why the protocol is correct in the form of a *phase structure*. The phase structure provides hints that direct the search and allow a more targeted generalization of states to invariants, which can facilitate inference where it is otherwise impossible.

This paper makes the following contributions:

(1) We present *phase invariants*, an automaton-based form of safety proofs, based on the distinct logical phases of a certain view of the system. Phase invariants closely match the way domain experts already think about the correctness of distributed protocols by state-machine refinement à la Lamport [e.g. 43].
(2) We describe an algorithm for inferring *inductive phase invariants* from *phase structures*. The decomposition to phases through the phase structure guides inference towards finding an invariant. The algorithm finds a proof over the phase structure or explains why no such proof exists. In this way, phase invariants facilitate user interaction with the algorithm.
(3) Our algorithm reduces the problem of inferring inductive phase invariants from phase structures to the problem of solving a linear system of Constrained Horn Clauses (CHC), irrespective of the inference technique and the logic used. In the case of universally quantified phase inductive invariants for protocols modeled in EPR (motivated by previous deductive approaches [50,51,60]), we show how to solve the resulting CHC using a variant of $\mathrm{PDR}^{\forall}$ [40].
(4) We apply this approach to the inference of invariants for several interesting distributed protocols. (This is the first time invariant inference is applied to distributed protocols modeled in EPR.) In the examples considered by our evaluation, transforming our high-level intuition about the protocol into a phase structure was relatively straightforward. The phase structures allowed our algorithm to outperform in most cases an implementation of $\mathrm{PDR}^{\forall}$ that does not exploit such structure, facilitating invariant inference on examples beyond the state of the art and attaining faster convergence.

Overall, our approach demonstrates that the seemingly inherent intractability of sifting through a vast space of candidate invariants can be mitigated by leveraging users' high-level intuition.

2 Preliminaries

In this section we provide background on first-order transition systems. Sorts are omitted for simplicity. Our results extend also to logics with a background theory.

Notation. $FV(\varphi)$ denotes the set of free variables of φ. $\mathcal{F}_\Sigma(V)$ denotes the set of first-order formulas over vocabulary Σ with $FV(\varphi) \subseteq V$. We write $\forall \mathcal{V}.\ \varphi \implies \psi$ to denote that the formula $\forall \mathcal{V}.\ \varphi \rightarrow \psi$ is valid. We sometimes use f_a as a shorthand for $f(a)$.

Transition Systems. We represent transition systems symbolically, via formulas in first-order logic. The definitions are standard. A vocabulary Σ consisting of constant, function, and relation symbols is used to represent states. Post-states of transitions are represented by a copy of Σ denoted $\Sigma' = \{a' \mid a \in \Sigma\}$. A *first-order transition system* over Σ is a tuple $TS = (Init, TR)$, where $Init \in \mathcal{F}_\Sigma(\emptyset)$ describes the initial states, and $TR \in \mathcal{F}_{\hat{\Sigma}}(\emptyset)$ with $\hat{\Sigma} = \Sigma \uplus \Sigma'$ describes the transition relation. The states of *TS* are first-order structures over Σ. A state s is initial if $s \models Init$. A transition of *TS* is a pair of states s_1, s_2 over a shared domain such that $(s_1, s_2) \models TR$, (s_1, s_2) being the structure over that domain in which Σ in interpreted as in s_1 and Σ' as in s_2. s_1 is also called the *pre-state* and s_2 the *post-state*. Traces are finite sequences of states $\sigma_1, \sigma_2, \ldots$ starting from an initial state such that there is a transition between each pair of consecutive states. The *reachable states* are those that reside on traces starting from an initial state.

Safety. A safety property P is a formula in $\mathcal{F}_\Sigma(\emptyset)$. We say that *TS* is *safe*, and that P is an *invariant*, if all the reachable states satisfy P. $Inv \in \mathcal{F}_\Sigma(\emptyset)$ is an *inductive invariant* if (i) $Init \implies Inv$ (initiation), and (ii) $Init \wedge TR \implies Inv'$ (consecution), where Inv' is obtained from *Inv* by replacing each symbol from Σ with its primed counterpart. If also (iii) $Inv \implies P$ (safety), then it follows that *TS* is safe.

3 Running Example: Distributed Key-Value Store

We begin with a description of the running example we refer to throughout the paper.

The *sharded key-value store with retransmissions (KV-R)*, adapted from Iron-Fleet [33, §5.2.1], is a distributed hash table where each node owns a subset of the keys, and keys can be dynamically transferred among nodes to balance load. The safety property ensures that each key is globally associated with one value, even in the presence of key transfers. Messages might be dropped by the network, and the protocol uses retransmissions and sequence numbers to maintain availability and safety.

Figure 1 shows code modeling the protocol in a relational first-order language akin to Ivy [45], which compiles to EPR transition systems. The state of nodes and the network is modeled by global relations. Lines 1 to 4 declare uninterpreted sorts for keys, values, clients, and sequence numbers. Lines 6 to 14 describe the state, consisting of: (i) local state of clients pertaining to the table (which nodes are `owners` of which keys, and the local shard of the `table` mapping keys to values); (ii) local state of clients pertaining to sent and received messages (`seqnum_sent`, `unacked`, `seqnum_recvd`); and (iii) the state of the network, comprised of two kinds of messages (`transfer_msg`, `ack_msg`). Each message kind is modeled as a relation whose first two arguments indicate the source

```
1  type key
2  type value
3  type node
4  type sequnum
5
6  relation owner: node, key
7  relation table: node, key, value
8  relation transfer_msg: node, node,
9                         key, value, seqnum
10 relation ack_msg: node, node, seqnum
11 relation seqnum_sent: node, seqnum
12 relation unacked: node, node,
13                    key, value, seqnum
14 relation seqnum_recvd: node, node, seqnum
15
16 init ∀n1,n2,k. owner(n1,k)∧owner(n2,k)
17                  → n1 = n2
18 init // all other relations are empty
19
20 action reshard(n_old:node, n_new:node,
21                k:key, value:sequnum)
22   require table(n_old, k, v)
23     ∧¬seqnum_sent(n_old, s)
24   seqnum_sent(n_old, s) := true
25   table(n_old, k, v) := false
26   owner(n_old, k) := false
27   transfer_msg(n_old, n_new, k, v, s) := true
28   unacked(n_old, n_new, k, v, s) := true
29
30 action drop_transfer_msg(src:node, dst:node,
31                   k:key, v:value, s:seqnum)
32     require transfer_msg(src, dst, k, v, s)
33     transfer_msg(src, dst, k, v, s) := false
34
35 action retransmit(src:node, dst:node,
36                 k:key, v:value, s:seqnum)
37     require unacked(src, dst, k, v, s)
38     transfer_msg(src, dst, k, v, s) := true
39 action recv_transfer_msg(src:node, n:node,
40                 k:key, v:value, s:seqnum)
41     require transfer_msg(src, n, k, v, s)
42           ∧¬seqnum_recvd(n, src, s)
43     seqnum_recvd(n, src, s) := true
44     table(n, k, v) := true
45     owner(n, k) := true
46
47 action send_ack(src:node, n:node,
48                 k:key, v:value, s:seqnum)
49     require transfer_msg(src, n, k, v, s)
50           ∧seqnum_recvd(n, src, s)
51     ack_msg(src, n, s) := true
52
53 action drop_ack_msg(src:node, dst:node,
54                 k:key, s:seqnum)
55     require ack_msg(src, dst, s)
56     ack_msg(src, dst, s) := false
57
58 action recv_ack_msg(src:node, dst:node,
59                 k:key, s:seqnum)
60     require ack_msg(src, dst, s)
61     unacked(src, dst, *, *, s) := false
62
63 action put(n:node, k:key, v:value)
64     require owner(n, k)
65     table(n, k, *) := false
66     table(n, k, v) := true
67
68 safety ∀k,n1,n2,v1,v2.
69   table(n1,k,v1) ∧
70   table(n2,k,v2) →
71   n1 = n2 ∧ v1 = v2
```

Fig. 1. Sharded key-value store with retransmissions (KV-R) in a first-order relational modeling.

and destination of the message, and the rest carry the message's payload. For example, `ack_msg` is a relation over two nodes and a sequence number, with the intended meaning that a tuple (c_1, c_2, s) is in `ack_msg` exactly when there is a message in the network from c_1 to c_2 acknowledging a message with sequence number s.

The initial states are specified in Lines 17 to 18. Transitions are specified by the actions declared in Lines 20 to 66. Actions can fire nondeterministically at any time when their precondition (`require` statements) holds. Hence, the transition relation comprises of the disjunction of the transition relations induced by the actions. The state is mutated by modifying the relations. For example, message sends are modeled by inserting a tuple into the corresponding relation (e.g. line 27), while message receives are modeled by requiring a tuple to be in the relation (e.g. line 32), and then removing it (e.g. line 33). The updates in lines 61 and 65 remove a set of tuples matching the pattern.

Transferring keys between nodes begins by sending a `transfer_msg` from the owner to a new node (line 20), which stores the key-value pair when it receives the message (line 39). Upon sending a transfer message the original node cedes ownership (line 26) and does not send new transfer messages. Transfer messages may be dropped (line 30). To ensure that the key-value pair is not lost, retransmissions are performed (line 35) with the same sequence number until the target node acknowledges (which occurs in line 47). Acknowledge messages themselves may be dropped (line 53). Sequence numbers protect from delayed transfer messages, which might contain old values (line 42).

Lines 68 to 71 specify the key safety property: at most one value is associated with any key, anywhere in the network. Intuitively, the protocol satisfies this because each key k is either currently (1) *owned* by a node, in which case this node is unique, or (2) it is in the process of *transferring* between nodes, in which case the careful use of sequence numbers ensures that the destination of the key is unique. As is typical, it is not straightforward to translate this intuition into a full correctness proof. In particular, it is necessary to relate all the different components of the state, including clients' local state and pending messages.

Invariant inference strives to automatically find an inductive invariant establishing safety. This example is challenging for existing inference techniques (Sect. 6). This paper proposes *user-guided invariant inference* based on *phase-invariants* to overcome this challenge. The rest of the paper describes our approach, in which inference is provided with the phase structure in Fig. 2, matching the high level intuitive explanation above. The algorithm then automatically infers facts about each phase to obtain an inductive invariant. Sect. 4 describes phase structures and inductive phase invariants, and Sect. 5 explains how these are used in user-guided invariant inference.

4 Phase Structures and Invariants

In this section we introduce *phase structures* and *inductive phase invariants*. These are used for guiding automatic invariant inference in Sect. 5. Proofs appear in [24].

4.1 Phase Invariants

Definition 1 (Quantified Phase Automaton). *A* quantified phase automaton *(*phase automaton *for short) over Σ is a tuple $\mathcal{A} = (\mathcal{Q}, \iota, \mathcal{V}, \delta, \varphi)$ where: $\mathcal{Q}$ is a finite set of* phases. *$\iota \in \mathcal{Q}$ is the initial phase. $\mathcal{V}$ is a set of variables, called the* automaton's quantifiers. *$\delta : \mathcal{Q} \times \mathcal{Q} \to \mathcal{F}_{\hat{\Sigma}}(\mathcal{V})$ is a function labeling every pair of phases by a transition relation formula, such that $FV(\delta_{(q,p)}) \subseteq \mathcal{V}$ for every $(q, p) \in \mathcal{Q} \times \mathcal{Q}$. $\varphi : \mathcal{Q} \to \mathcal{F}_{\Sigma}(\mathcal{V})$ is a function labeling every phase by a* phase characterization *formula, s.t. $FV(\varphi_q) \subseteq \mathcal{V}$ for every $q \in \mathcal{Q}$.*

Intuitively, $\mathcal{V}$ should be understood as free variables that are implicitly universally quantified outside of the automaton's scope. For each assignment to these variables, the automaton represents the progress along the phases from the point of view of this assignment, and thus $\mathcal{V}$ is also called the *view* (or *view quantifiers*).

We refer to $(\mathcal{Q}, \iota, \mathcal{V}, \delta)$, where φ is omitted, as the *phase structure* (or the *automaton structure*) of $\mathcal{A}$. We refer by the *edges* of $\mathcal{A}$ to $\mathcal{R} = \{(q, p) \in \mathcal{Q} \times \mathcal{Q} \mid \delta_{(q,p)} \not\equiv false\}$. A *trace* of $\mathcal{A}$ is a sequence of phases $q_0, \ldots, q_n$ such that $q_0 = \iota$ and $(q_i, q_{i+1}) \in \mathcal{R}$ for every $0 \leq i < n$. We say that $\mathcal{A}$ is *deterministic* if for every $(q, p_1), (q, p_2) \in \mathcal{R}$ s.t. $p_1 \neq p_2$, the formula $\delta_{(q,p_1)} \wedge \delta_{(q,p_2)}$ is unsatisfiable.

Example 1. Figure 2 shows a phase automaton for the running example, with the view of a single key k. It describes the protocol as transitioning between two distinct (logical)

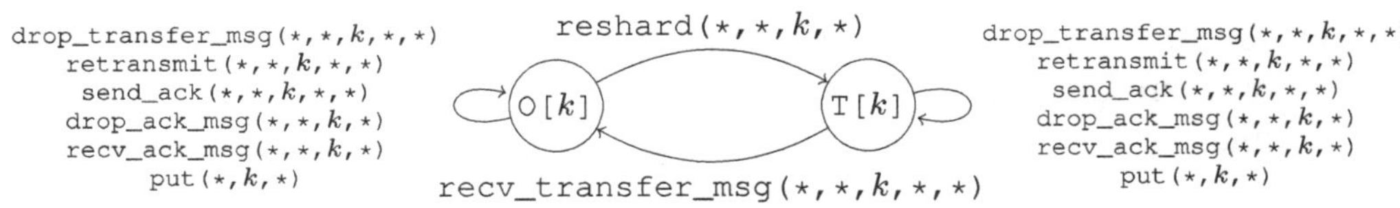


```
phase O[k]:
  invariant ∀n1,n2. owner(n1,k)∧owner(n2,k)→ n1 = n2
  invariant ∀n,v. table(n,k,v)→owner(n,k)
  invariant ∀src,dst,v,s. ¬(transfer_msg(src,dst,k,v,s)∧¬seqnum_recvd(dst,src,s))
  invariant ∀n1,n2,v1,v2. table(n1,k,v1)∧table(n2,k,v2)→ n1 = n2 ∧ v1 = v2
  invariant ∀src,dst,v,s. ¬(unacked(src,dst,k,v,s)∧¬seqnum_recvd(dst,src,s))

phase T[k]:
  invariant ∀n. ¬owner(n,k)
  invariant ∀n,v. table(n,k,v)→owner(n,k)
  invariant ∀src1,src2,dst1,dst2,v1,v2,s1,s2. transfer_msg(src1,dst1,k,v1,s1)∧¬seqnum_recvd(dst1,src1,s1)
    ∧transfer_msg(src2,dst2,k,v2,s2)∧¬seqnum_recvd(dst2,src2,s2)→ (src1,dst1,v1,s1) = (src2,dst2,v2,s2)
  invariant ∀src1,src2,dst1,dst2,v1,v2,s1,s2.transfer_msg(src1,dst1,k,v1,s1)∧¬seqnum_recvd(dst1,dst1,s1)
    ∧unacked(src2,dst2,k,v2,s2)∧¬seqnum_recvd(dst2,src2,s2)→ (src1,dst1,v1,s1) = (src2,dst2,v2,s2)
  invariant ∀src1,src2,dst1,dst2,v1,v2,s1,s2. unacked(src1,dst1,k,v1,s1)∧¬seqnum_recvd(dst1,src1,s1)
    ∧unacked(src2,dst2,k,v2,s2)∧¬seqnum_recvd(dst2,src2,s2)→ (src1,dst1,v1,s1) = (src2,dst2,v2,s2)
```

Fig. 2. Phase structure for key-value store (top) and phase characterizations (bottom). The user provides the phase structure, and inference automatically produces the phase characterizations, forming a safe inductive phase automaton.

phases of k: *owned* ($\texttt{O}[k]$) and *transferring* ($\texttt{T}[k]$). The edges are labeled by actions of the system. A wildcard $\star$ means that the action is executed with an arbitrary argument. The two central actions are (i) `reshard`, which transitions from $\texttt{O}[k]$ to $\texttt{T}[k]$, but cannot execute in $\texttt{T}[k]$, and (ii) `recv_transfer_message`, which does the opposite. The rest of the actions do not cause a phase change and appear on a self loop in each phase. Actions related to keys other than k are considered as self-loops, and omitted here for brevity. Some actions are *disallowed* in certain phases, namely, do not label *any* outgoing edge from a phase, such as `recv_transfer_msg(k)` in $\texttt{O}[k]$. *Characterizations* for each phase are depicted in Fig. 2 (bottom). Without them, Fig. 2 represents a *phase structure*, which serves as the input to our inference algorithm. We remark that the choice of automaton aims to reflect the safety property of interest. In our example, one might instead imagine taking the view of a single node as it interacts with multiple keys, which might seem intuitive from the standpoint of implementing the system. However, it is not appropriate for the proof of value uniqueness, since keys pass in and out of the view of a single client.

We now formally define *phase invariants* as phase automata that overapproximate the behaviors of the original system.

Definition 2 (Language of Phase Automaton). *Let $\mathcal{A}$ be a quantified phase automaton over Σ, and $\overline{\sigma} = \sigma_0, \ldots, \sigma_n$ a finite sequence of states over Σ, all with domain D. Let $v : \mathcal{V} \to D$ be a valuation of the automaton quantifiers. We say that:*

- $\overline{\sigma}, v \models \mathcal{A}$ *if there exists a trace of phases* $q_0, \ldots, q_n$ *such that* $(\sigma_i, \sigma_{i+1}), v \models \delta_{(q_i,q_{i+1})}$ *for every* $0 \leq i < n$ *and* $\sigma_i, v \models \varphi_{q_i}$ *for every* $0 \leq i \leq n$.
- $\overline{\sigma} \models \mathcal{A}$ *if* $\overline{\sigma}, v \models \mathcal{A}$ *for every valuation* v.

The language of $\mathcal{A}$ is $\mathcal{L}(\mathcal{A}) = \{\overline{\sigma} \mid \overline{\sigma} \models \mathcal{A}\}$.

Definition 3 (Phase Invariant). *A phase automaton $\mathcal{A}$ is a* phase invariant *for a transition system TS if $\mathcal{L}(TS) \subseteq \mathcal{L}(\mathcal{A})$, where $\mathcal{L}(TS)$ denotes the set of finite traces of TS.*

Example 2. The phase automaton of Fig. 2 is a *phase invariant* for the protocol: intuitively, whenever an execution of the protocol reaches a phase, its characterizations hold. This fact may not be straightforward to establish. To this end we develop the notion of *inductive* phase invariants.

4.2 Establishing Safety and Phase Invariants with Inductive Phase Invariants

To establish phase invariants, we use inductiveness:

Definition 4 (Inductive Phase Invariant). *$\mathcal{A}$ is* inductive w.r.t. *$TS = (Init, TR)$ if:*

Initiation: $Init \implies (\forall \mathcal{V}.\ \varphi_\iota)$.
Inductiveness: *for all* $(q,p) \in \mathcal{R}$, $\quad \forall \mathcal{V}.\ \left(\varphi_q \wedge \delta_{(q,p)} \implies \varphi'_p\right)$.
Edge Covering: *for every* $q \in \mathcal{Q}$, $\quad \forall \mathcal{V}.\ \left(\varphi_q \wedge TR \implies \bigvee_{(q,p)\in\mathcal{R}} \delta_{(q,p)}\right)$.

Example 3. The phase automaton in Fig. 2 is an inductive phase invariant. For example, the only disallowed transition in `O[`k`]` is `recv_transfer_message`, which indeed cannot execute in `O[`k`]` according to the characterization in line 75. Further, if, for example, a protocol's transition from `O[`k`]` matches the labeling of the edge to `T[`k`]` (i.e. a `reshard` action on k), the post-state necessarily satisfies the characterizations of `T[`k`]`: for instance, the post-state satisfies the uniqueness of unreceived transfer messages (line 82) because in the pre-state there are none (line 75).

Lemma 1. *If $\mathcal{A}$ is inductive w.r.t. TS then it is a phase invariant for TS.*

Remark 1. The careful reader may notice that the inductiveness requirement is stronger than needed to ensure that the characterizations form a phase invariant. It could be weakened to require for every $q \in \mathcal{Q}$: $\forall \mathcal{V}.\ \varphi_q \wedge TR \implies \bigvee_{(q,p)\in\mathcal{R}} \delta_{(q,p)} \wedge \varphi'_p$. However, as we explain in Sect. 5, our notion of inductiveness is crucial for *inferring* inductive phase automata, which is the goal of this paper. Furthermore, for deterministic phase automata, the two requirements coincide.

Inductive Invariants vs. Inductive Phase Invariants. Inductive invariants and inductive phase invariants are closely related:

Lemma 2. *If $\mathcal{A}$ is inductive w.r.t. TS then $\forall \mathcal{V}.\ \bigvee_{q\in\mathcal{Q}} \varphi_q$ is an inductive invariant for TS. If Inv is an inductive invariant for TS, then the phase automaton $\mathcal{A}_{Inv} = (\{q\}, \{q\}, \emptyset, \delta, \varphi)$, where $\delta_{(q,q)} = TR$ and $\varphi_q = Inv$ is an inductive phase automaton w.r.t. TS.*

In this sense, phase inductive invariants are as expressive as inductive invariants. However, as we show in this paper, their structure can be used by a user as an intuitive way to guide an automatic invariant inference algorithm.

Safe Inductive Phase Invariants. Next we show that an inductive phase invariant can be used to establish safety.

Definition 5 (Safe Phase Automaton). *Let $\mathcal{A}$ be a phase automaton over Σ with quantifiers $\mathcal{V}$. Then $\mathcal{A}$ is* safe *w.r.t.* $\forall \mathcal{V}.\ \mathcal{P}$ *if* $\forall \mathcal{V}.\ (\varphi_q \Longrightarrow \mathcal{P})$ *holds for every* $q \in \mathcal{Q}$.

Lemma 3. *If $\mathcal{A}$ is inductive w.r.t. TS and safe w.r.t. $\forall \mathcal{V}.\ \mathcal{P}$ then $\forall \mathcal{V}. \mathcal{P}$ is an invariant of TS.*

5 Inference of Inductive Phase Invariants

In this section we turn to the *inference* of safe inductive phase invariants over a given phase structure, which guides the search. Formally, the problem we target is:

Definition 6 (Inductive Phase Invariant Inference). *Given a transition system $TS = (Init, TR)$, a phase structure $\mathcal{S} = (\mathcal{Q}, \iota, \mathcal{V}, \delta)$ and a safety property $\forall \mathcal{V}.\ \mathcal{P}$, all over Σ,* find *a safe inductive phase invariant $\mathcal{A}$ for TS over the phase structure S, if one exists.*

Example 4. Inference of an inductive phase invariant is provided with the phase structure in Fig. 2, which embodies an intuitive understanding of the different phases the protocol undergoes (see Example 1). The algorithm automatically finds phase characterizations forming a safe inductive phase invariant over the user-provided structure. We note that inference is valuable even after a phase structure is provided: in the running example, finding an inductive phase invariant is not easy; in particular, the characterizations in Fig. 2 relate different parts of the state and involve multiple quantifiers.

5.1 Reduction to Constrained Horn Clauses

We view each unknown phase characterization, φ_q, which we aim to infer for every $q \in \mathcal{Q}$, as a predicate I_q. The definition of a safe inductive phase invariant induces a set of second-order Constrained Horn Clauses (CHC) over I_q:

Initiation. $$Init \Longrightarrow (\forall \mathcal{V}.\ I_\iota) \quad (1)$$

Inductiveness. For every $(q,p) \in \mathcal{R}$: $$\forall \mathcal{V}.\ \left(I_q \wedge \delta_{(q,p)} \Longrightarrow I'_p\right) \quad (2)$$

Edge Covering. For every $q \in \mathcal{Q}$: $$\forall \mathcal{V}.\ \left(I_q \wedge TR \Longrightarrow \bigvee_{(q,p)\in\mathcal{R}} \delta_{(q,p)}\right) \quad (3)$$

Safety. For every $q \in \mathcal{Q}$: $$\forall \mathcal{V}.\ (I_q \Longrightarrow \mathcal{P}) \quad (4)$$

where $\mathcal{V}$ denotes the quantifiers of $\mathcal{A}$. All the constraints are *linear*, namely at most one unknown predicate appears at the lefthand side of each implication.

Constraint (4) captures the original safety requirement, whereas (3) can be understood as additional safety properties that are specified by the phase automaton (since no unknown predicates appear in the righthand side of the implications).

A *solution* **I** to the CHC system associates each predicate I_q with a formula ψ_q over Σ (with $FV(\psi_q) \subseteq \mathcal{V}$) such that when ψ_q is substituted for I_q, all the constraints are satisfied (i.e., the corresponding first-order formulas are valid). A solution to the system induces a safe inductive phase automaton through characterizing each phase q by the interpretation of I_q, and vice versa. Formally:

Lemma 4. *Let* $\mathcal{A} = (\mathcal{Q}, \mathcal{R}, \iota, \mathcal{V}, \delta, \varphi)$ *with* $\varphi_q = \mathbf{I}_q$. *Then* $\mathcal{A}$ *is a safe inductive phase invariant wrt. TS and* $\forall\mathcal{V}.\ \mathcal{P}$ *if and only if* $\mathbf{I}$ *is a solution to the CHC system.*

Therefore, to infer a safe inductive phase invariant over a given phase structure, we need to solve the corresponding CHC system. In Sect. 6.1 we explain our approach for doing so for the class of universally quantified phase characterizations. Note that the weaker definition of inductiveness discussed in Remark 1 would prevent the reduction to CHC as it would result in clauses that are *not* Horn clauses.

Completeness of Inductive Phase Invariants. There are cases where a given phase structure induces a safe phase invariant $\mathcal{A}$, but not an inductive one, making the CHC system unsatisfiable. However, a strengthening into an inductive phase invariant can always be used to prove that $\mathcal{A}$ is an invariant if (i) the language of invariants is unrestricted, and (ii) the phase structure is deterministic, namely, does not cover the same transition in two outgoing edges. Determinism of the automaton does not lose generality in the context of safety verification since every inductive phase automaton can be converted to a deterministic one; non-determinism is in fact unbeneficial as it mandates the same state to be characterized by multiple phases (see also Remark 1). These topics are discussed in detail in the extended version [24].

Remark 2. Each phase is associated with a set of states that can reach it, where a state σ can reach phase q if there is a sequence of program transitions that results in σ and can lead to q according to the automaton's transitions. This makes a phase structure different from a simple syntactical disjunctive template for inference, in which such semantic meaning is unavailable.

5.2 Phase Structures as a Means to Guide Inference

The search space of invariants over a phase structure is in fact *larger* than that of standard inductive invariants, because each phase can be associated with different characterizations. Sometimes the disjunctive structure of the phases (Lemma 2) uncovers a significantly simpler invariant than exists in the syntactical class of standard inductive invariants explored by the algorithm, but this is not always the case.[1] Nonetheless, the search for an invariant over the structure is *guided*, through the following aspects:

(1) *Phase decomposition.* Inference of an inductive phase invariant aims to find characterizations that overapproximate the set of states reachable in each phase (Remark 2). The distinction between phases is most beneficial when there is a considerable *difference* between the sets associated with different phases and their characterizations. For instance, in the running example, all states without unreceived transfer messages are associated with `O[k]`, whereas all states in which such messages exist are associated with `T[k]`—a distinction captured by the characterizations in lines 75 and 82 in Fig. 2.

[1] As an illustration, the extended version [24] includes an inductive invariant for the running example which is comparable in complexity to the inductive phase invariant in Fig. 2.

Differences between phases would have two consequences. First, since each phase corresponds to fewer states than all reachable states, generalization—the key ingredient in inference procedures—is more focused. The second consequence stems from the fact that inductive characterizations of different phases are correlated. It is expected that a certain property is more readily learnable in one phase, while related facts in other phases are more complex. For instance, the characterization in line 75 in Fig. 2 is more straightforward than the one in line 82. Simpler facts in one phase can help characterize an adjacent phase when the algorithm analyzes how that property evolves along the edge. Thus utilizing the phase structure can improve the gradual construction of overapproximations of the sets of states reachable in each phase.

(2) *Disabled transitions.* A phase automaton explicitly states which transitions of the system are enabled in each phase, while the rest are disabled. Such impossible transitions induce additional safety properties to be established by the inferred phase characterizations. For example, the phase invariant in Fig. 2 forbids a `recv_transfer_message(k)` in `O[k]`, a fact that can trigger the inference of the characterization in line 75. These additional safety properties direct the search for characterizations that are likely to be important for the proof.

(3) *Phase-awareness.* Finally, while a phase structure can be encoded in several ways (such as ghost code), a key aspect of our approach is that the phase decomposition and disabled transitions are *explicitly* encoded in the CHC system in Sect. 5.1, ensuring that they guide the otherwise heuristic search.

In Sect. 6.2 we demonstrate the effects of aspects (1)–(3) on guidance.

6 Implementation and Evaluation

In this section we apply invariant inference guided by phase structures to distributed protocols modeled in EPR, motivated by previous deductive approaches [50,51,60].

6.1 Phase-PDR$^\forall$ for Inferring Universally Quantified Characterizations

We now describe our procedure for solving the CHCs system of Sect. 5.1. It either (i) returns universally quantified phase characterizations that induce a safe inductive phase invariant, (ii) returns an abstract counterexample trace demonstrating that this is not possible, or (iii) diverges.

EPR. Our procedure handles transition systems expressed using the extended **E**ffectively **PR**opositional fragment (EPR) of first order logic [51,52], and infers universally quantified phase characterizations. Satisfiability of (extended) EPR formulas is decidable, enjoys the finite-model property, and supported by solvers such as Z3 [46] and iProver [41].

Phase-PDR$^\forall$. Our procedure is based on PDR$^\forall$ [40], a variant of PDR [10,21] that infers universally quantified inductive invariants. PDR computes a sequence of *frames*

$\mathcal{F}_0, \ldots, \mathcal{F}_n$ such that $\mathcal{F}_i$ overapproximates the set of states reachable in i steps. In our case, each frame $\mathcal{F}_i$ is a mapping from a phase q to characterizations. The details of the algorithm are standard for PDR; we describe the gist of the procedure in the extended version [24]. We only stress the following: Counterexamples to safety take into account the safety property as well as disabled transitions. Search for predecessors is performed by going backwards on automaton edges, blocking counterexamples from preceding phases to prove an obligation in the current phase. Generalization is performed w.r.t. all incoming edges. As in PDR$^{\forall}$, proof obligations are constructed via diagrams [12]; in our setting these include the interpretation for the view quantifiers (see [24] for details).

Edge Covering Check in EPR. In our setting, Eqs. (1), (2) and (4) fall in EPR, but not Eq. (3). Thus, we restrict edge labeling so that each edge is labeled with a *TR* of an `action`, together with an alternation-free precondition. It then suffices to check implications between the preconditions and the entire *TR* (see the extended version [24]). Such edge labeling is sufficiently expressive for all our examples. Alternatively, sound but incomplete bounded quantifier instantiation [23] could be used, potentially allowing more complex decompositions of *TR*.

Absence of Inductive Phase Characterizations. What happens when the user gets the automaton wrong? One case is when there does not exist an inductive phase invariant with universal phase characterizations over the given structure. When this occurs, our tool can return an *abstract counterexample trace*—a sequence of program transitions and transitions of the automaton (inspired by [40,49])—which constitutes a proof of that fact (see the extended version [24]). The counterexample trace can assist the user in debugging the automaton or the program and modifying them. For instance, missing edges occurred frequently when we wrote the automata of Sect. 6, and we used the generated counterexample traces to correct them.

Another type of failure is when an inductive phase invariant exists but the automaton does not direct the search well towards it. In this case the user may decide to terminate the analysis and articulate a different intuition via a different phase structure. In standard inference procedures, the only way to affect the search is by modifying the transition system; instead, phase structures equip the user with an ability to guide the search.

6.2 Evaluation

We evaluate our approach for user-guided invariant inference by comparing Phase-PDR$^{\forall}$ to standard PDR$^{\forall}$. We implemented PDR$^{\forall}$ and Phase-PDR$^{\forall}$ in MYPYVY [2], a new system for invariant inference inspired by Ivy [45], over Z3 [46]. We study:

1. Can Phase-PDR$^{\forall}$ *converge* to a proof when PDR$^{\forall}$ does not (in reasonable time)?
2. Is Phase-PDR$^{\forall}$ *faster* than PDR$^{\forall}$?
3. Which aspects of Phase-PDR$^{\forall}$ contribute to its performance benefits?

Protocols. We applied PDR$^{\forall}$ and Phase-PDR$^{\forall}$ to the most challenging examples admitting universally-quantified invariants, which previous works verified using deductive techniques. The protocols we analyzed are listed below and in Table 1. The full models appear in [1]. The KV-R protocol analyzed is taken from one of the two realistic systems studied by the IronFleet paper [33] using deductive verification.

Phase Structures. The phase structures we used appear in [1]. In all our examples, it was straightforward to translate the existing high-level intuition of important and relevant distinctions between phases in the protocol into the phase structures we report. For example, it took us less than an hour to finalize an automaton for KV-R. We emphasize that phase structures do not include phase characterizations; the user need not supply them, nor has to understand the inference procedure. Our exposition of the phase structures below refers to an intuitive meaning of each phase, but this is not part of the phase structure provided to the tool.

Table 1. Running times in seconds of $\text{PDR}^\forall$ and Phase-$\text{PDR}^\forall$, presented as the mean and standard deviation (in parentheses) over 16 different Z3 random seeds. "*" indicates that some runs did not converge after 1 h and were not included in the summary statistics. "> 1 h" means that no runs of the algorithm converged in 1 h. #p refers to the number of phases and #v to the number of view quantifiers in the phase structure. #r refers to the number of relations and $|a|$ to the maximal arity. The remaining columns describe the inductive invariant/phase invariant obtained in inference. $|f|$ is the maximal frame reached. #c, #q are the mean number of clauses and quantifiers (excluding view quantifiers) per phase, ranging across the different phases.

Program	$\text{PDR}^\forall$	Phase-$\text{PDR}^\forall$	#p	#v	#r	$\lvert a\rvert$	Inductive			Phase-inductive		
							$\lvert f\rvert$	#c	#q	$\lvert f\rvert$	#c	#q
Lock service (single lock)	2.21 (00.03)	0.67 (0.01)	4	1	5	1	11	9	15	6	3–4	3–4
Lock service (multiple locks)	2.73 (00.02)	1.06 (0.01)	4	1	5	2	11	9	24	6	4	3–4
Consensus	60.54 (2.95)	1355 (570)*	3	1	7	2	9	6	15	12	5–6	10–14
KV (basic)	1.79 (0.02)	1.59 (0.02)	2	1	3	3	5	7	27	5	4	9–10
Ring leader	152.44 (39.41)	2.53 (0.04)	2	2	4	3	6–7	6	11	5	1–2	0–1
KV-R	2070 (370)*	372.5 (35.9)	2	1	7	5	12–15	24	156	11–13	5–11	15–67
Cache coherence	>1 h	90.1 (0.82)	10	1	11	2	n/a	n/a	n/a	13	10–15	12–27

(1) Achieving Convergence Through Phases. In this section we consider the effect of phases on inference for examples on which standard $\text{PDR}^\forall$ does not converge in 1 hr. ***Examples.*** *Sharded key-value store with retransmissions (KV-R)*: see Sect. 3 and Example 1. This protocol has not been modeled in decidable logic before.

Cache Coherence. This example implements the classic MESI protocol for maintaining cache coherence in a shared-memory multiprocessor [36], modeled in decidable logic for the first time. Cores perform reads and writes to memory, and caches snoop on each other's requests using a shared bus and maintain the invariant that there is at most one writer of a particular cache line. For simplicity, we consider only a single cache line, and yet the example is still challenging for $\text{PDR}^\forall$. Standard explanations of this protocol in the literature already use automata to describe this invariant, and we directly exploit this structure in our phase automaton. *Phase Structure:* There are 10 phases in total,

grouped into three parts corresponding to the modified, exclusive, and shared states in the classical description. Within each group, there are additional phases for when a request is being processed by the bus. For example, in the shared group, there are phases for handling reads by cores without a copy of the cache line, writes by such cores, and also writes by cores that *do* have a copy. Overall, the phase structure is directly derived from textbook descriptions, taking into account that use of the shared bus is not atomic.
Results and Discussion. Measurements for these examples appear in Table 1. Standard $\text{PDR}^\forall$ fails to converge in less than an hour on 13 out of 16 seeds for KV-R and all 16 seeds for the cache. In contrast, Phase-$\text{PDR}^\forall$ converges to a proof in a few minutes in all cases. These results demonstrate that phase structures can effectively guide the search and obtain an invariant quickly where standard inductive invariant inference does not.

(2) Enhancing Performance Through Phases. In this section we consider the use of phase structures to improve the speed of convergence to a proof.
Examples. *Distributed lock service,* adapted from [61], allows clients to acquire and release locks by sending requests to a central server, which guarantees that only one client holds each lock at a time. *Phase structure*: for each lock, the phases follow the 4 steps by which a client completes a cycle of acquire and release. We also consider a simpler variant with only a single lock, reducing the arity of all relations and removing the need for an automaton view. Its *phase structure* is the same, only for a single lock.

Simple quorum-based consensus, based on the example in [60]. In this protocol, nodes propose themselves and then receive votes from other nodes. When a quorum of votes for a node is obtained, it becomes the leader and decides on a value. Safety requires that decided values are unique. The *phase structure* distinguishes between the phases before any node is elected leader, once a node is elected, and when values are decided. Note that the automaton structure is unquantified.

Leader election in a ring [13,51], in which nodes are organized in a directional ring topology with unique IDs, and the safety property is that an elected leader is a node with the highest ID. *Phase structure*: for a view of two nodes n_1, n_2, in the first phase, messages with the ID of n_1 are yet to advance in the ring past n_2, while in the second phase, a message advertising n_1 has advanced past n_2. The inferred characterizations include another quantifier on nodes, constraining interference (see Sect. 7).

Sharded key-value store (KV) is a simplified version of KV-R above, without message drops and the retransmission mechanism. The *phase structure* is exactly as in KV-R, omitting transitions related to sequence numbers and acknowledgment. This protocol has not been modeled in decidable logic before.

Results and Discussion. We compare the performance of standard $\text{PDR}^\forall$ and Phase-$\text{PDR}^\forall$ on the above examples, with results shown in Table 1. For each example, we ran the two algorithms on 16 different Z3 random seeds. Measurements were performed on a 3.4GHz AMD Ryzen Threadripper 1950X with 16 physical cores, running Linux 4.15.0, using Z3 version 4.7.1. By disabling hyperthreading and frequency scaling and pinning tasks to dedicated cores, variability across runs of a single seed was negligible.

In all but one example, Phase-$\text{PDR}^\forall$ improves performance, sometimes drastically; for example, performance for leader election in a ring is improved by a factor of 60.

Phase-PDR$^\forall$ also improves the *robustness* of inference [27] on this example, as the standard deviation falls from 39 in PDR$^\forall$ to 0.04 in Phase-PDR$^\forall$.

The only example in which a phase structure actually diminishes inference effectiveness is simple consensus. We attribute this to an automaton structure that does not capture the essence of the correctness argument very well, overlooking votes and quorums. This demonstrates that a phase structure might guide the search towards counterproductive directions if the user guidance is "misleading". This suggests that better resiliency of interactive inference framework could be achieved by combining phase-based inference with standard inductive invariant-based reasoning. We are not aware of a single "good" automaton for this example. The correctness argument of this example is better captured by the conjunction of two automata (one for votes and one for accumulating a quorum) with different views, but the problem of inferring phase invariants for mutually-dependent automata is a subject for future work.

(3) Anatomy of the Benefit of Phases. We now demonstrate that each of the beneficial aspects of phases discussed in Sect. 5.2 is important for the benefits reported above.

Phase Decomposition. Is there a benefit from a phase structure even without disabled transitions? An example to a positive answer to this question is leader election in a ring, which demonstrates a huge performance benefit even without disabled transitions.

Disabled Transitions. Is there a substantial gain from exploiting disabled transitions? We compare Phase-PDR$^\forall$ on the structure with disabled transitions and a structure obtained by (artificially) adding self loops labeled with the originally impossible transitions, on the example of lock service with multiple locks (Sect. 6.2), seeing that it demonstrates a performance benefit using Phase-PDR$^\forall$ and showcases several disabled transitions in each phase. The result is that without disabled transitions, the mean running time of Phase-PDR$^\forall$ on this example jumps from 2.73 s to 6.24 s. This demonstrates the utility of the additional safety properties encompassed in disabled transitions.

Phase-Awareness. Is it important to treat phases explicitly in the inference algorithm, as we do in Phase-PDR$^\forall$ (Sect. 6.1)? We compare our result on convergence of KV-R with an alternative in which standard PDR$^\forall$ is applied to an encoding of the phase decomposition and disabled transition by *ghost state*: each phase is modeled by a relation over possible view assignments, and the model is augmented with update code mimicking phase changes; the additional safety properties derived from disabled transitions are provided; and the view and the appropriate modification of the safety property are introduced. This translation expresses all information present in the phase structure, but does not explicitly guide the inference algorithm to use this information. The result is that with this ghost-based modeling the phase-oblivious PDR$^\forall$ does not converge in 1 h on KV-R in any of the 16 runs, whereas it converges when Phase-PDR$^\forall$ explicitly directs the search using the phase structure.

7 Related Work

Phases in Distributed Protocols. Distributed protocols are frequently described in informal descriptions as transitioning between different phases. Recently, PSync [19] used the Heard-Of model [14], which describes protocols as operating in rounds, as a basis for the implementation and verification of fault-tolerant distributed protocols. Typestates [e.g.] [25,59] also bear some similarity to the temporal aspect of phases. State machine refinement [3,28] is used extensively in the design and verification of distributed systems (see e.g. [33,47]). The automaton structure of a phase invariant is also a form of state machine; our focus is on inference of characterizations establishing this.

Interaction in Verification. Interactive proof assistants such as Coq [8] and Isabelle/HOL [48] interact with users to aid them as they attempt to prove candidate inductive invariants. This differs from interaction through phase structures and counterexample traces. Ivy uses interaction for invariant inference by interactive generalization from counterexamples [51]. This approach is less automatic as it requires interaction for every clause of the inductive invariant. In terminology from synthesis [30], the use of counterexamples is *synthesizer-driven* interaction with the tool, while interaction via phase structures is mainly *user-driven*. Abstract counterexample traces returned by the tool augment this kind of interaction. As [38] has shown, interactive invariant inference, when considered as a synthesis problem (see also [27,55]) is related to inductive learning.

Template-Based Invariant Inference. Many works employ syntactical templates for invariants, used to constrain the search [e.g.] [7,16,54,57,58]. The different phases in a phase structure induce a disjunctive form, but crucially each disjunct also has a distinct semantic meaning, which inference overapproximates, as explained in Sect. 5.2.

Automata in Safety Verification. Safety verification through an automaton-like refinement of the program's control has been studied in a number of works. We focus on related techniques for proof automation. The *Automizer* approach to the verification of sequential programs [34,35] is founded on the notion of a *Floyd-Hoare automaton*, which is an unquantified inductive phase automaton; an extension to parallel programs [22] uses thread identifiers closed under the symmetry rule, which are related to view quantifiers. Their focus is on the automatic, incremental construction of such automata as a union of simpler automata, where each automaton is obtained from generalizing the proof/infeasibility of a single trace. In our approach the structure of the automaton is provided by the user as a means of conveying their intuition of the proof, while the annotations are computed automatically. A notable difference is that in Automizer, the generation of characterizations in an automaton constructed from a single trace does not utilize the phase structure (beyond that of the trace), whereas in our approach the phase structure is central in generalization from states to characterizations. In *trace partitioning* [44,53], abstract domains based on transition systems partitioning the program's control are introduced. The observation is that recording historical information forms a basis for case-splitting, as an alternative to fully-disjunctive abstractions. This differs from our motivation of distinguishing between different protocol phases. The phase structure of the domain is determined by the analyser, and can also be dynamic. In our work the phase structure is provided by the user as guidance. We use a variant of PDR$^{\forall}$, rather than abstract interpretation [17], to compute universally quantified phase characterizations. Techniques such as *predicate abstraction* [26,29] and *existential abstraction* [15], as well as the safety part of *predicate diagrams* [11], use finite languages for the set of possible characterizations and lack the notion of views, both essential for handling unbounded numbers of processes and resources. Finally, *phase splitter predicates* [56] share our motivation of simplifying invariant inference by exposing the different phases the loop undergoes. Splitter predicates correspond to inductive phase characterizations [56, Theorem 1], and are automatically constructed according to program conditionals. In our approach, decomposition is performed by the user using potentially non-inductive conditions, and the inductive phase characterizations are computed by invariant inference. Successive loop splitting results in a sequence of phases, whereas our approach utilizes arbitrary automaton structures. Borralleras et al. [9] also refine the control-flow graph throughout the analysis by splitting on conditions, which are discovered as preconditions for termination (the motivation is to expose termination proof goals to be established): in a sense, the phase structure is grown from candidate characterizations implying termination. This differs from our approach in which the phase structure is used to guide the inference of characterizations.

Quantified Invariant Inference. We focus here on the works on quantifiers in automatic verification most closely related to our work. In *predicate abstraction*, quantifiers can be used internally as part of the definitions of predicates, and also externally through predicates with free variables [26,42]. Our work uses quantifiers both internally in phases characterizations and externally in view quantifiers. The view is also related to the bounded number of quantifiers used in *view abstraction* [5,6]. In this work we observe that it is useful to consider views of entities beyond processes or threads, such as a single key in the store. Quantifiers are often used to their full extent in verification conditions, namely checking implication between two quantified formulas, but they are sometimes employed in weaker checks as part of thread-modular proofs [4,39]. This amounts to searching for invariants provable using specific instantiations of the quantifiers in the verification conditions [31,37]. In our verification conditions, the view quantifiers are localized, in effect performing a single instantiation. This is essential for exploiting the disjunctive structure under the quantifiers, allowing inference to consider a single automaton edge in each step, and reflecting an intuition of correctness. When necessary to constrain interference, quantifiers in phase characterizations can be used to establish necessary facts about interfering views. Finally, there exist algorithms other than $\text{PDR}^{\forall}$ for solving CHC by predicates with universal invariants [e.g. 20,32].

8 Conclusion

Invariant inference techniques aiming to verify intricate distributed protocols must adjust to the diverse correctness arguments on which protocols are based. In this paper we have proposed to use phase structures as means of conveying users' intuition of the proof, to be used by an automatic inference tool as a basis for a full formal proof. We found that inference guided by a phase structure can infer proofs for distributed protocols that are beyond reach for state of the art inductive invariant inference methods, and can also improve the speed of convergence. The phase decomposition induced by the automaton, the use of disabled transitions, and the explicit treatment of phases in inference, all combine to direct the search for the invariant. We are encouraged by our experience of specifying phase structures for different protocols. It would be interesting to integrate the interaction via phase structures with other verification methods and proof logics, as well as interaction schemes based on different, complementary, concepts. Another important direction for future work is inference beyond universal invariants, required for example for the proof of Paxos [50].

Acknowledgements. We thank Kalev Alpernas, Javier Esparza, Neil Immerman, Shachar Itzhaky, Oded Padon, Andreas Podelski, Tom Reps, and the anonymous referees for insightful comments which improved this paper. This publication is part of a project that has received funding from the European Research Council (ERC) under the European Union's Horizon 2020 research and innovation programme (grant agreement No. [759102-SVIS]). The research was partially supported by Len Blavatnik and the Blavatnik Family foundation, the Blavatnik Interdisciplinary Cyber Research Center, Tel Aviv University, the Israel Science Foundation (ISF) under grant No. 1810/18, the United States-Israel Binational Science Foundation (BSF) grant No. 2016260, and the National Science Foundation under Grant No. 1749570. Any opinions, findings, and conclusions or recommendations expressed in this material are those of the authors and do not necessarily reflect the views of the National Science Foundation.

References

1. Examples code. https://github.com/wilcoxjay/mypyvy/tree/master/examples/cav19
2. mypyvy repository. https://github.com/wilcoxjay/mypyvy
3. Abadi, M., Lamport, L.: The existence of refinement mappings. Theor. Comput. Sci. **82**(2), 253–284 (1991). https://doi.org/10.1016/0304-3975(91)90224-P
4. Abadi, M., Lamport, L.: Conjoining specifications. ACM Trans. Program. Lang. Syst. **17**(3), 507–534 (1995)
5. Abdulla, P.A., Haziza, F., Holík, L.: All for the price of few. In: Giacobazzi, R., Berdine, J., Mastroeni, I. (eds.) VMCAI 2013. LNCS, vol. 7737, pp. 476–495. Springer, Heidelberg (2013). https://doi.org/10.1007/978-3-642-35873-9_28
6. Abdulla, P.A., Haziza, F., Holík, L.: Parameterized verification through view abstraction. STTT **18**(5), 495–516 (2016). https://doi.org/10.1007/s10009-015-0406-x
7. Alur, R., et al.: Syntax-guided synthesis. In: Dependable Software Systems Engineering, pp. 1–25 (2015)
8. Bertot, Y., Castéran, P.: Interactive Theorem Proving and Program Development - Coq'Art: The Calculus of Inductive Constructions. TTCS. Springer, Heidelberg (2004). https://doi.org/10.1007/978-3-662-07964-5
9. Borralleras, C., Brockschmidt, M., Larraz, D., Oliveras, A., Rodríguez-Carbonell, E., Rubio, A.: Proving termination through conditional termination. In: Legay, A., Margaria, T. (eds.) TACAS 2017. LNCS, vol. 10205, pp. 99–117. Springer, Heidelberg (2017). https://doi.org/10.1007/978-3-662-54577-5_6
10. Bradley, A.R.: SAT-based model checking without unrolling. In: Jhala, R., Schmidt, D. (eds.) VMCAI 2011. LNCS, vol. 6538, pp. 70–87. Springer, Heidelberg (2011). https://doi.org/10.1007/978-3-642-18275-4_7
11. Cansell, D., Méry, D., Merz, S.: Predicate diagrams for the verification of reactive systems. In: Grieskamp, W., Santen, T., Stoddart, B. (eds.) IFM 2000. LNCS, vol. 1945, pp. 380–397. Springer, Heidelberg (2000). https://doi.org/10.1007/3-540-40911-4_22
12. Chang, C., Keisler, H.: Model Theory. Studies in Logic and the Foundations of Mathematics. Elsevier Science, Amsterdam (1990)

13. Chang, E., Roberts, R.: An improved algorithm for decentralized extrema-finding in circular configurations of processes. Commun. ACM **22**(5), 281–283 (1979)
14. Charron-Bost, B., Schiper, A.: The heard-of model: computing in distributed systems with benign faults. Distrib. Comput. **22**(1), 49–71 (2009). https://doi.org/10.1007/s00446-009-0084-6
15. Clarke, E.M., Grumberg, O., Peled, D.A.: Model Checking. MIT Press, Cambridge (2001). http://books.google.de/books?id=Nmc4wEaLXFEC
16. Colón, M.A., Sankaranarayanan, S., Sipma, H.B.: Linear invariant generation using non-linear constraint solving. In: Hunt, W.A., Somenzi, F. (eds.) CAV 2003. LNCS, vol. 2725, pp. 420–432. Springer, Heidelberg (2003). https://doi.org/10.1007/978-3-540-45069-6_39
17. Cousot, P., Cousot, R.: Systematic design of program analysis frameworks. In: Symposium on Principles of Programming Languages, pp. 269–282. ACM Press, New York (1979)
18. Cousot, P., Cousot, R.: Abstract interpretation: a unified lattice model for static analysis of programs by construction or approximation of fixpoints. In: Conference Record of the Fourth ACM Symposium on Principles of Programming Languages, Los Angeles, California, USA, January 1977, pp. 238–252 (1977). https://doi.org/10.1145/512950.512973. http://doi.acm.org/10.1145/512950.512973
19. Dragoi, C., Henzinger, T.A., Zufferey, D.: Psync: a partially synchronous language for fault-tolerant distributed algorithms. In: Proceedings of the 43rd Annual ACM SIGPLAN-SIGACT Symposium on Principles of Programming Languages, POPL 2016, St. Petersburg, FL, USA, 20–22 January 2016, pp. 400–415 (2016). https://doi.org/10.1145/2837614.2837650. http://doi.acm.org/10.1145/2837614.2837650
20. Drews, S., Albarghouthi, A.: Effectively propositional interpolants. In: Chaudhuri, S., Farzan, A. (eds.) CAV 2016. LNCS, vol. 9780, pp. 210–229. Springer, Cham (2016). https://doi.org/10.1007/978-3-319-41540-6_12
21. Eén, N., Mishchenko, A., Brayton, R.K.: Efficient implementation of property directed reachability. In: International Conference on Formal Methods in Computer-Aided Design, FMCAD 2011, Austin, TX, USA, October 30–02 November 2011, pp. 125–134 (2011)
22. Farzan, A., Kincaid, Z., Podelski, A.: Proof spaces for unbounded parallelism. In: Proceedings of the 42nd Annual ACM SIGPLAN-SIGACT Symposium on Principles of Programming Languages, POPL 2015, Mumbai, India, 15–17 January 2015, pp. 407–420 (2015). https://doi.org/10.1145/2676726.2677012. http://doi.acm.org/10.1145/2676726.2677012
23. Feldman, Y.M.Y., Padon, O., Immerman, N., Sagiv, M., Shoham, S.: Bounded quantifier instantiation for checking inductive invariants. In: Legay, A., Margaria, T. (eds.) TACAS 2017. LNCS, vol. 10205, pp. 76–95. Springer, Heidelberg (2017). https://doi.org/10.1007/978-3-662-54577-5_5
24. Feldman, Y.M.Y., Wilcox, J.R., Shoham, S., Sagiv, M.: Inferring inductive invariants from phase structures. Technical report (2019). https://arxiv.org/abs/1905.07739
25. Field, J., Goyal, D., Ramalingam, G., Yahav, E.: Typestate verification: abstraction techniques and complexity results. Sci. Comput. Program. **58**(1–2), 57–82 (2005)
26. Flanagan, C., Qadeer, S.: Predicate abstraction for software verification. In: Conference Record of POPL 2002: The 29th SIGPLAN-SIGACT Symposium on Principles of Programming Languages, Portland, OR, USA, 16–18 January 2002, pp. 191–202 (2002). https://doi.org/10.1145/503272.503291. http://doi.acm.org/10.1145/503272.503291
27. Garg, P., Löding, C., Madhusudan, P., Neider, D.: ICE: a robust framework for learning invariants. In: Biere, A., Bloem, R. (eds.) CAV 2014. LNCS, vol. 8559, pp. 69–87. Springer, Cham (2014). https://doi.org/10.1007/978-3-319-08867-9_5
28. Garland, S.J., Lynch, N.: Using I/O automata for developing distributed systems. In: Foundations of Component-Based Systems, pp. 285–312. Cambridge University Press, New York (2000). http://dl.acm.org/citation.cfm?id=336431.336455

29. Graf, S., Saidi, H.: Construction of abstract state graphs with PVS. In: Grumberg, O. (ed.) CAV 1997. LNCS, vol. 1254, pp. 72–83. Springer, Heidelberg (1997). https://doi.org/10.1007/3-540-63166-6_10
30. Gulwani, S.: Synthesis from examples: interaction models and algorithms. In: 14th International Symposium on Symbolic and Numeric Algorithms for Scientific Computing, SYNASC 2012, Timisoara, Romania, 26–29 September 2012, pp. 8–14 (2012). https://doi.org/10.1109/SYNASC.2012.69
31. Gurfinkel, A., Shoham, S., Meshman, Y.: SMT-based verification of parameterized systems. In: Proceedings of the 24th ACM SIGSOFT International Symposium on Foundations of Software Engineering, FSE 2016, Seattle, WA, USA, 13–18 November 2016, pp. 338–348 (2016). https://doi.org/10.1145/2950290.2950330. http://doi.acm.org/10.1145/2950290.2950330
32. Gurfinkel, A., Shoham, S., Vizel, Y.: Quantifiers on demand. In: Lahiri, S.K., Wang, C. (eds.) ATVA 2018. LNCS, vol. 11138, pp. 248–266. Springer, Cham (2018). https://doi.org/10.1007/978-3-030-01090-4_15
33. Hawblitzel, C., et al.: Ironfleet: proving practical distributed systems correct. In: Proceedings of the 25th Symposium on Operating Systems Principles, SOSP 2015, Monterey, CA, USA, 4–7 October 2015, pp. 1–17 (2015). https://doi.org/10.1145/2815400.2815428. http://doi.acm.org/10.1145/2815400.2815428
34. Heizmann, M., Hoenicke, J., Podelski, A.: Refinement of trace abstraction. In: Palsberg, J., Su, Z. (eds.) SAS 2009. LNCS, vol. 5673, pp. 69–85. Springer, Heidelberg (2009). https://doi.org/10.1007/978-3-642-03237-0_7
35. Heizmann, M., Hoenicke, J., Podelski, A.: Software model checking for people who love automata. In: Sharygina, N., Veith, H. (eds.) CAV 2013. LNCS, vol. 8044, pp. 36–52. Springer, Heidelberg (2013). https://doi.org/10.1007/978-3-642-39799-8_2
36. Hennessy, J.L., Patterson, D.A.: Computer Architecture: A Quantitative Approach, 6th edn. Morgan Kaufmann, San Francisco (2017)
37. Hoenicke, J., Majumdar, R., Podelski, A.: Thread modularity at many levels: a pearl in compositional verification. In: Proceedings of the 44th ACM SIGPLAN Symposium on Principles of Programming Languages, POPL 2017, Paris, France, 18–20 January 2017, pp. 473–485 (2017). http://dl.acm.org/citation.cfm?id=3009893
38. Jha, S., Seshia, S.A.: A theory of formal synthesis via inductive learning. Acta Inf. **54**(7), 693–726 (2017). https://doi.org/10.1007/s00236-017-0294-5
39. Jones, C.B.: Tentative steps toward a development method for interfering programs. ACM Trans. Program. Lang. Syst. **5**(4), 596–619 (1983). https://doi.org/10.1145/69575.69577. http://doi.acm.org/10.1145/69575.69577
40. Karbyshev, A., Bjørner, N., Itzhaky, S., Rinetzky, N., Shoham, S.: Property-directed inference of universal invariants or proving their absence. J. ACM 64(1), 7:1–7:33 (2017). https://doi.org/10.1145/3022187. http://doi.acm.org/10.1145/3022187
41. Korovin, K.: iProver – an instantiation-based theorem prover for first-order logic (system description). In: Armando, A., Baumgartner, P., Dowek, G. (eds.) IJCAR 2008. LNCS (LNAI), vol. 5195, pp. 292–298. Springer, Heidelberg (2008). https://doi.org/10.1007/978-3-540-71070-7_24
42. Lahiri, S.K., Bryant, R.E.: Predicate abstraction with indexed predicates. ACM Trans. Comput. Log. **9**(1), 4 (2007). https://doi.org/10.1145/1297658.1297662. http://doi.acm.org/10.1145/1297658.1297662
43. Lamport, L.: Specifying Systems. The TLA+ Language and Tools for Hardware and Software Engineers. Addison-Wesley (2002)
44. Mauborgne, L., Rival, X.: Trace partitioning in abstract interpretation based static analyzers. In: Sagiv, M. (ed.) ESOP 2005. LNCS, vol. 3444, pp. 5–20. Springer, Heidelberg (2005). https://doi.org/10.1007/978-3-540-31987-0_2

45. McMillan, K.L., Padon, O.: Deductive verification in decidable fragments with ivy. In: Podelski, A. (ed.) SAS 2018. LNCS, vol. 11002, pp. 43–55. Springer, Cham (2018). https://doi.org/10.1007/978-3-319-99725-4_4
46. de Moura, L., Bjørner, N.: Z3: an efficient SMT solver. In: Ramakrishnan, C.R., Rehof, J. (eds.) TACAS 2008. LNCS, vol. 4963, pp. 337–340. Springer, Heidelberg (2008). https://doi.org/10.1007/978-3-540-78800-3_24
47. Newcombe, C., Rath, T., Zhang, F., Munteanu, B., Brooker, M., Deardeuff, M.: How amazon web services uses formal methods. Commun. ACM **58**(4), 66–73 (2015). https://doi.org/10.1145/2699417. http://doi.acm.org/10.1145/2699417
48. Nipkow, T., Wenzel, M., Paulson, L.C. (eds.): Isabelle/HOL. LNCS, vol. 2283. Springer, Heidelberg (2002). https://doi.org/10.1007/3-540-45949-9
49. Padon, O., Immerman, N., Shoham, S., Karbyshev, A., Sagiv, M.: Decidability of inferring inductive invariants. In: Proceedings of the 43rd Annual ACM SIGPLAN-SIGACT Symposium on Principles of Programming Languages, POPL 2016, St. Petersburg, FL, USA, 20–22 January 2016, pp. 217–231 (2016). https://doi.org/10.1145/2837614.2837640. http://doi.acm.org/10.1145/2837614.2837640
50. Padon, O., Losa, G., Sagiv, M., Shoham, S.: Paxos made EPR: decidable reasoning about distributed protocols. PACMPL **1**(OOPSLA), 108:1–108:31 (2017). https://doi.org/10.1145/3140568. http://doi.acm.org/10.1145/3140568
51. Padon, O., McMillan, K.L., Panda, A., Sagiv, M., Shoham, S.: Ivy: safety verification by interactive generalization. In: Proceedings of the 37th ACM SIGPLAN Conference on Programming Language Design and Implementation, PLDI 2016, Santa Barbara, CA, USA, 13–17 June 2016, pp. 614–630 (2016)
52. Ramsey, F.P.: On a problem in formal logic. In: Proceedings on London Mathematical Society (1930)
53. Rival, X., Mauborgne, L.: The trace partitioning abstract domain. ACM Trans. Program. Lang. Syst. **29**(5), 26 (2007). https://doi.org/10.1145/1275497.1275501. http://doi.acm.org/10.1145/1275497.1275501
54. Sankaranarayanan, S., Sipma, H.B., Manna, Z.: Constraint-based linear-relations analysis. In: Giacobazzi, R. (ed.) SAS 2004. LNCS, vol. 3148, pp. 53–68. Springer, Heidelberg (2004). https://doi.org/10.1007/978-3-540-27864-1_7
55. Sharma, R., Aiken, A.: From invariant checking to invariant inference using randomized search. Formal Methods Syst. Des. **48**(3), 235–256 (2016). https://doi.org/10.1007/s10703-016-0248-5
56. Sharma, R., Dillig, I., Dillig, T., Aiken, A.: Simplifying loop invariant generation using splitter predicates. In: Gopalakrishnan, G., Qadeer, S. (eds.) CAV 2011. LNCS, vol. 6806, pp. 703–719. Springer, Heidelberg (2011). https://doi.org/10.1007/978-3-642-22110-1_57
57. Srivastava, S., Gulwani, S.: Program verification using templates over predicate abstraction. In: Proceedings of the 2009 ACM SIGPLAN Conference on Programming Language Design and Implementation, PLDI 2009, Dublin, Ireland, 15–21 June 2009, pp. 223–234 (2009)
58. Srivastava, S., Gulwani, S., Foster, J.S.: Template-based program verification and program synthesis. STTT **15**(5–6), 497–518 (2013)
59. Strom, R.E., Yemini, S.: Typestate: a programming language concept for enhancing software reliability. IEEE Trans. Softw. Eng. **12**(1), 157–171 (1986)
60. Taube, M., et al.: Modularity for decidability of deductive verification with applications to distributed systems. In: Proceedings of the 39th ACM SIGPLAN Conference on Programming Language Design and Implementation, PLDI 2018, Philadelphia, PA, USA, 18–22 June 2018, pp. 662–677 (2018). https://doi.org/10.1145/3192366.3192414. http://doi.acm.org/10.1145/3192366.3192414

61. Wilcox, J.R., et al.: Verdi: a framework for implementing and formally verifying distributed systems. In: Proceedings of the 36th ACM SIGPLAN Conference on Programming Language Design and Implementation, Portland, OR, USA, 15–17 June 2015, pp. 357–368 (2015). https://doi.org/10.1145/2737924.2737958. http://doi.acm.org/10.1145/2737924.2737958
62. Woos, D., Wilcox, J.R., Anton, S., Tatlock, Z., Ernst, M.D., Anderson, T.E.: Planning for change in a formal verification of the raft consensus protocol. In: Proceedings of the 5th ACM SIGPLAN Conference on Certified Programs and Proofs, Saint Petersburg, FL, USA, 20–22 January 2016, pp. 154–165 (2016). https://doi.org/10.1145/2854065.2854081. http://doi.acm.org/10.1145/2854065.2854081

Termination of Triangular Integer Loops is Decidable

Florian Frohn[1] and Jürgen Giesl[2](✉)

[1] Max Planck Institute for Informatics, Saarbrücken, Germany
florian.frohn@mpi-inf.mpg.de
[2] LuFG Informatik 2, RWTH Aachen University, Aachen, Germany
giesl@informatik.rwth-aachen.de

Abstract. We consider the problem whether termination of affine integer loops is decidable. Since Tiwari conjectured decidability in 2004 [15], only special cases have been solved [3,4,14]. We complement this work by proving decidability for the case that the update matrix is triangular.

1 Introduction

We consider affine integer loops of the form

$$\textbf{while } \varphi \textbf{ do } \overline{x} \leftarrow A\,\overline{x} + \overline{a}. \tag{1}$$

Here, $A \in \mathbb{Z}^{d\times d}$ for some dimension $d \geq 1$, $\overline{x}$ is a column vector of pairwise different variables $x_1, \ldots, x_d$, $\overline{a} \in \mathbb{Z}^d$, and φ is a conjunction of inequalities of the form $\alpha > 0$ where $\alpha \in \mathbb{A}\mathrm{f}[\overline{x}]$ is an affine expression with rational coefficients[1] over $\overline{x}$ (i.e., $\mathbb{A}\mathrm{f}[\overline{x}] = \{\overline{c}^T\,\overline{x} + c \mid \overline{c} \in \mathbb{Q}^d, c \in \mathbb{Q}\}$). So φ has the form $B\,\overline{x} + \overline{b} > \overline{0}$ where $\overline{0}$ is the vector containing k zeros, $B \in \mathbb{Q}^{k\times d}$, and $\overline{b} \in \mathbb{Q}^k$ for some $k \in \mathbb{N}$. Definition 1 formalizes the intuitive notion of termination for such loops.

Definition 1 (Termination). *Let $f : \mathbb{Z}^d \to \mathbb{Z}^d$ with $f(\overline{x}) = A\,\overline{x} + \overline{a}$. If*

$$\exists \overline{c} \in \mathbb{Z}^d.\ \forall n \in \mathbb{N}.\ \varphi[\overline{x}/f^n(\overline{c})],$$

then (1) is non-terminating *and $\overline{c}$ is a* witness *for non-termination. Otherwise, (1)* terminates.

Here, f^n denotes the n-fold application of f, i.e., we have $f^0(\overline{c}) = \overline{c}$ and $f^{n+1}(\overline{c}) = f(f^n(\overline{c}))$. We call f the *update* of (1). Moreover, for any entity s, $s[x/t]$ denotes the entity that results from s by replacing all occurrences of x by t. Similarly, if $\overline{x} = \begin{bmatrix} x_1 \\ \vdots \\ x_m \end{bmatrix}$ and $\overline{t} = \begin{bmatrix} t_1 \\ \vdots \\ t_m \end{bmatrix}$, then $s[\overline{x}/\overline{t}]$ denotes the entity resulting from s by replacing all occurrences of x_i by t_i for each $1 \leq i \leq m$.

[1] Note that multiplying with the least common multiple of all denominators yields an equivalent constraint with integer coefficients, i.e., allowing rational instead of integer coefficients does not extend the considered class of loops.

Funded by DFG grant 389792660 as part of TRR 248 and by DFG grant GI 274/6.

I. Dillig and S. Tasiran (Eds.): CAV 2019, LNCS 11562, pp. 426–444, 2019.
https://doi.org/10.1007/978-3-030-25543-5_24

Example 2. *Consider the loop*

$$\textbf{while } y+z>0 \textbf{ do} \quad \begin{bmatrix} w \\ x \\ y \\ z \end{bmatrix} \leftarrow \begin{bmatrix} 2 \\ x+1 \\ -w-2\cdot y \\ x \end{bmatrix}$$

where the update of all variables is executed simultaneously. This program belongs to our class of affine loops, because it can be written equivalently as follows.

$$\textbf{while } y+z>0 \textbf{ do} \quad \begin{bmatrix} w \\ x \\ y \\ z \end{bmatrix} \leftarrow \begin{bmatrix} 0 & 0 & 0 & 0 \\ 0 & 1 & 0 & 0 \\ -1 & 0 & -2 & 0 \\ 0 & 1 & 0 & 0 \end{bmatrix} \begin{bmatrix} w \\ x \\ y \\ z \end{bmatrix} + \begin{bmatrix} 2 \\ 1 \\ 0 \\ 0 \end{bmatrix}$$

While termination of affine loops is known to be decidable if the variables range over the real [15] or the rational numbers [4], the integer case is a well-known open problem [2–4, 14, 15].[2] However, certain special cases have been solved: Braverman [4] showed that termination of *linear* loops is decidable (i.e., loops of the form (1) where $\overline{a}$ is $\overline{0}$ and φ is of the form $B\,\overline{x} > \overline{0}$). Bozga et al. [3] showed decidability for the case that the update matrix A in (1) has the *finite monoid property*, i.e., if there is an $n > 0$ such that A^n is diagonalizable and all eigenvalues of A^n are in $\{0, 1\}$. Ouaknine et al. [14] proved decidability for the case $d \leq 4$ and for the case that A is diagonalizable.

Ben-Amram et al. [2] showed undecidability of termination for certain extensions of affine integer loops, e.g., for loops where the body is of the form **if** $x > 0$ **then** $\overline{x} \leftarrow A\,\overline{x}$ **else** $\overline{x} \leftarrow A'\,\overline{x}$ where $A, A' \in \mathbb{Z}^{d\times d}$ and $x \in \overline{x}$.

In this paper, we present another substantial step towards the solution of the open problem whether termination of affine integer loops is decidable. We show that termination is decidable for *triangular* loops (1) where A is a triangular matrix (i.e., all entries of A below or above the main diagonal are zero). Clearly, the order of the variables is irrelevant, i.e., our results also cover the case that A can be transformed into a triangular matrix by reordering A, $\overline{x}$, and $\overline{a}$ accordingly.[3] So essentially, triangularity means that the program variables $x_1, \ldots, x_d$ can be ordered such that in each loop iteration, the new value of x_i only depends on the previous values of $x_1, \ldots, x_{i-1}, x_i$. Hence, this excludes programs with "cyclic dependencies" of variables (e.g., where the new values of x and y both depend on the old values of both x and y). While triangular loops are a very restricted subclass of general integer programs, integer programs often contain such loops. Hence, tools for termination analysis of such programs (e.g., [5–8, 11–13]) could

[2] The proofs for real or rational numbers do not carry over to the integers since [15] uses Brouwer's Fixed Point Theorem which is not applicable if the variables range over $\mathbb{Z}$ and [4] relies on the density of $\mathbb{Q}$ in $\mathbb{R}$.

[3] Similarly, one could of course also use other termination-preserving pre-processings and try to transform a given program into a triangular loop.

benefit from integrating our decision procedure and applying it whenever a subprogram is an affine triangular loop.

Note that triangularity and diagonalizability of matrices do not imply each other. As we consider loops with arbitrary dimension, this means that the class of loops considered in this paper is not covered by [3, 14]. Since we consider affine instead of linear loops, it is also orthogonal to [4].

To see the difference between our and previous results, note that a triangular matrix A where $c_1, \ldots, c_k$ are the *distinct* entries on the diagonal is diagonalizable iff $(A - c_1 I) \ldots (A - c_k I)$ is the zero matrix.[4] Here, I is the identity matrix. So an easy example for a triangular loop where the update matrix is not diagonalizable is the following well-known program (see, e.g., [2]):

$$\textbf{while } x > 0 \textbf{ do } x \leftarrow x + y;\ y \leftarrow y - 1$$

It terminates as y eventually becomes negative and then x decreases in each iteration. In matrix notation, the loop body is $\begin{bmatrix} x \\ y \end{bmatrix} \leftarrow \begin{bmatrix} 1 & 1 \\ 0 & 1 \end{bmatrix} \begin{bmatrix} x \\ y \end{bmatrix} + \begin{bmatrix} 0 \\ -1 \end{bmatrix}$, i.e., the update matrix is triangular. Thus, this program is in our class of programs where we show that termination is decidable. However, the only entry on the diagonal of the update matrix A is $c = 1$ and $A - c\,I = \begin{bmatrix} 0 & 1 \\ 0 & 0 \end{bmatrix}$ is not the zero matrix. So A (and in fact each A^n where $n \in \mathbb{N}$) is not diagonalizable. Hence, extensions of this example to a dimension greater than 4 where the loop is still triangular are not covered by any of the previous results.[5]

Our proof that termination is decidable for triangular loops proceeds in three steps. We first prove that termination of triangular loops is decidable iff termination of *non-negative triangular* loops (*nnt-loops*) is decidable, cf. Sect. 2. A loop is non-negative if the diagonal of A does not contain negative entries. Second, we show how to compute *closed forms* for nnt-loops, i.e., vectors $\overline{q}$ of d expressions over the variables $\overline{x}$ and n such that $\overline{q}[n/c] = f^c(\overline{x})$ for all $c \geq 0$, see Sect. 3. Here, triangularity of the matrix A allows us to treat the variables step by step. So for any $1 \leq i \leq d$, we already know the closed forms for $x_1, \ldots, x_{i-1}$ when computing the closed form for x_i. The idea of computing closed forms for the repeated updates of loops was inspired by our previous work on inferring lower bounds on the runtime of integer programs [10]. But in contrast to [10], here the computation of the closed form always succeeds due to the restricted shape of the programs. Finally, we explain how to decide termination of nnt-loops by reasoning about their closed forms in Sect. 4. While our technique does not yield witnesses for non-termination, we show that it yields witnesses for *eventual* non-termination, i.e., vectors $\overline{c}$ such that $f^n(\overline{c})$ witnesses non-termination for some $n \in \mathbb{N}$. Detailed proofs for all lemmas and theorems can be found in [9].

[4] The reason is that in this case, $(x - c_1) \ldots (x - c_k)$ is the minimal polynomial of A and diagonalizability is equivalent to the fact that the minimal polynomial is a product of distinct linear factors.

[5] For instance, consider **while** $x > 0$ **do** $x \leftarrow x + y + z_1 + z_2 + z_3;\ y \leftarrow y - 1$.

2 From Triangular to Non-Negative Triangular Loops

To transform triangular loops into nnt-loops, we define how to *chain* loops. Intuitively, chaining yields a new loop where a single iteration is equivalent to two iterations of the original loop. Then we show that chaining a triangular loop always yields an nnt-loop and that chaining is equivalent w.r.t. termination.

Definition 3 (Chaining). Chaining *the loop (1) yields:*

$$\textbf{while } \varphi \wedge \varphi[\overline{x}/A\,\overline{x} + \overline{a}] \textbf{ do } \overline{x} \leftarrow A^2\,\overline{x} + A\,\overline{a} + \overline{a} \tag{2}$$

Example 4. *Chaining Example 2 yields*

$$\textbf{while } y + z > 0 \wedge -w - 2 \cdot y + x > 0 \textbf{ do}$$
$$\begin{bmatrix} w \\ x \\ y \\ z \end{bmatrix} \leftarrow \begin{bmatrix} 0 & 0 & 0 & 0 \\ 0 & 1 & 0 & 0 \\ -1 & 0 & -2 & 0 \\ 0 & 1 & 0 & 0 \end{bmatrix}^2 \begin{bmatrix} w \\ x \\ y \\ z \end{bmatrix} + \begin{bmatrix} 0 & 0 & 0 & 0 \\ 0 & 1 & 0 & 0 \\ -1 & 0 & -2 & 0 \\ 0 & 1 & 0 & 0 \end{bmatrix} \begin{bmatrix} 2 \\ 1 \\ 0 \\ 0 \end{bmatrix} + \begin{bmatrix} 2 \\ 1 \\ 0 \\ 0 \end{bmatrix}$$

which simplifies to the following nnt-loop:

$$\textbf{while } y + z > 0 \wedge -w - 2 \cdot y + x > 0 \textbf{ do} \begin{bmatrix} w \\ x \\ y \\ z \end{bmatrix} \leftarrow \begin{bmatrix} 0\,0\,0\,0 \\ 0\,1\,0\,0 \\ 2\,0\,4\,0 \\ 0\,1\,0\,0 \end{bmatrix} \begin{bmatrix} w \\ x \\ y \\ z \end{bmatrix} + \begin{bmatrix} 2 \\ 2 \\ -2 \\ 1 \end{bmatrix}$$

Lemma 5 is needed to prove that (2) is an nnt-loop if (1) is triangular.

Lemma 5 (Squares of Triangular Matrices). *For every triangular matrix A, A^2 is a triangular matrix whose diagonal entries are non-negative.*

Corollary 6 (Chaining Loops). *If (1) is triangular, then (2) is an nnt-loop.*

Proof. Immediate consequence of Definition 3 and Lemma 5. □

Lemma 7 (Equivalence of Chaining). *(1) terminates $\iff$ (2) terminates.*

Proof. By Definition 1, (1) does not terminate iff

$$\begin{aligned} & \exists \overline{c} \in \mathbb{Z}^d.\ \forall n \in \mathbb{N}.\ \varphi[\overline{x}/f^n(\overline{c})] \\ \iff & \exists \overline{c} \in \mathbb{Z}^d.\ \forall n \in \mathbb{N}.\ \varphi[\overline{x}/f^{2 \cdot n}(\overline{c})] \wedge \varphi[\overline{x}/f^{2 \cdot n+1}(\overline{c})] \\ \iff & \exists \overline{c} \in \mathbb{Z}^d.\ \forall n \in \mathbb{N}.\ \varphi[\overline{x}/f^{2 \cdot n}(\overline{c})] \wedge \varphi[\overline{x}/A\, f^{2 \cdot n}(\overline{c}) + \overline{a}] \text{ (by Definition of } f), \end{aligned}$$

i.e., iff (2) does not terminate as $f^2(\overline{x}) = A^2\,\overline{x} + A\,\overline{a} + \overline{a}$ is the update of (2). □

Theorem 8 (Reducing Termination to nnt-Loops). *Termination of triangular loops is decidable iff termination of nnt-loops is decidable.*

Proof. Immediate consequence of Corollary 6 and Lemma 7. □

Thus, from now on we restrict our attention to nnt-loops.

3 Computing Closed Forms

The next step towards our decidability proof is to show that $f^n(\overline{x})$ is equivalent to a vector of *poly-exponential expressions* for each nnt-loop, i.e., the closed form of each nnt-loop can be represented by such expressions. Here, *equivalence* means that two expressions evaluate to the same result for all variable assignments.

Poly-exponential expressions are sums of arithmetic terms where it is always clear which addend determines the asymptotic growth of the whole expression when increasing a designated variable n. This is crucial for our decidability proof in Sect. 4. Let $\mathbb{N}_{\geq 1} = \{b \in \mathbb{N} \mid b \geq 1\}$ (and $\mathbb{Q}_{>0}$, $\mathbb{N}_{>1}$, etc. are defined analogously). Moreover, $\mathbb{Af}[\overline{x}]$ is again the set of all affine expressions over $\overline{x}$.

Definition 9 (Poly-Exponential Expressions). *Let $\mathcal{C}$ be the set of all finite conjunctions over the literals $n = c, n \neq c$ where n is a designated variable and $c \in \mathbb{N}$. Moreover for each formula ψ over n, let $[\![\psi]\!]$ be the characteristic function of ψ, i.e., $[\![\psi]\!]\,(c) = 1$ if $\psi[n/c]$ is valid and $[\![\psi]\!]\,(c) = 0$, otherwise. The set of all* poly-exponential expressions *over $\overline{x}$ is*

$$\mathbb{PE}[\overline{x}] = \left\{ \sum_{j=1}^{\ell} [\![\psi_j]\!] \cdot \alpha_j \cdot n^{a_j} \cdot b_j^n \;\middle|\; \ell, a_j \in \mathbb{N},\ \psi_j \in \mathcal{C},\ \alpha_j \in \mathbb{Af}[\overline{x}],\ b_j \in \mathbb{N}_{\geq 1} \right\}.$$

As n ranges over $\mathbb{N}$, we use $[\![n > c]\!]$ as syntactic sugar for $[\![\bigwedge_{i=0}^{c} n \neq i]\!]$. So an example for a poly-exponential expression is

$$[\![n > 2]\!] \cdot (2 \cdot x + 3 \cdot y - 1) \cdot n^3 \cdot 3^n \;+\; [\![n = 2]\!] \cdot (x - y).$$

Moreover, note that if ψ contains a *positive* literal (i.e., a literal of the form "$n = c$" for some number $c \in \mathbb{N}$), then $[\![\psi]\!]$ is equivalent to either 0 or $[\![n = c]\!]$.

The crux of the proof that poly-exponential expressions can represent closed forms is to show that certain sums over products of exponential and poly-exponential expressions can be represented by poly-exponential expressions, cf. Lemma 12. To construct these expressions, we use a variant of [1, Lemma 3.5]. As usual, $\mathbb{Q}[\overline{x}]$ is the set of all polynomials over $\overline{x}$ with rational coefficients.

Lemma 10 (Expressing Polynomials by Differences [1]). *If $q \in \mathbb{Q}[n]$ and $c \in \mathbb{Q}$, then there is an $r \in \mathbb{Q}[n]$ such that $q = r - c \cdot r[n/n-1]$ for all $n \in \mathbb{N}$.*

So Lemma 10 expresses a polynomial q via the difference of another polynomial r at the positions n and $n-1$, where the additional factor c can be chosen freely. The proof of Lemma 10 is by induction on the degree of q and its structure resembles the structure of the following algorithm to compute r. Using the Binomial Theorem, one can verify that $q - s + c \cdot s[n/n-1]$ has a smaller degree than q, which is crucial for the proof of Lemma 10 and termination of Algorithm 1.

Algorithm 1. compute_r

Input: $q = \sum_{i=0}^{d} c_i \cdot n^i \in \mathbb{Q}[n],\ \ c \in \mathbb{Q}$
Result: $r \in \mathbb{Q}[n]$ such that $q = r - c \cdot r[n/n-1]$
if $d = 0$ **then**
  if $c = 1$ **then return** $c_0 \cdot n$ **else return** $\frac{c_0}{1-c}$
else
  if $c = 1$ **then** $s \leftarrow \frac{c_d \cdot n^{d+1}}{d+1}$ **else** $s \leftarrow \frac{c_d \cdot n^d}{1-c}$
  return $s +$ compute_$r(\,q - s + c \cdot s[n/n-1],\ c\,)$

Example 11. *As an example, consider $q = 1$ (i.e., $c_0 = 1$) and $c = 4$. Then we search for an r such that $q = r - c \cdot r[n/n-1]$, i.e., $1 = r - 4 \cdot r[n/n-1]$. According to Algorithm 1, the solution is $r = \frac{c_0}{1-c} = -\frac{1}{3}$.*

Lemma 12 (Closure of $\mathbb{PE}$ under Sums of Products and Exponentials). *If $m \in \mathbb{N}$ and $p \in \mathbb{PE}[\overline{x}]$, then one can compute a $q \in \mathbb{PE}[\overline{x}]$ which is equivalent to $\sum_{i=1}^{n} m^{n-i} \cdot p[n/i-1]$.*

Proof. Let $p = \sum_{j=1}^{\ell} [\![\psi_j]\!] \cdot \alpha_j \cdot n^{a_j} \cdot b_j^n$. We have:

$$\sum_{i=1}^{n} m^{n-i} \cdot p[n/i-1] = \sum_{j=1}^{\ell} \sum_{i=1}^{n} [\![\psi_j]\!]\,(i-1) \cdot m^{n-i} \cdot \alpha_j \cdot (i-1)^{a_j} \cdot b_j^{i-1} \tag{3}$$

As $\mathbb{PE}[\overline{x}]$ is closed under addition, it suffices to show that we can compute an equivalent poly-exponential expression for any expression of the form

$$\sum_{i=1}^{n} [\![\psi]\!]\,(i-1) \cdot m^{n-i} \cdot \alpha \cdot (i-1)^a \cdot b^{i-1}. \tag{4}$$

We first regard the case $m = 0$. Here, the expression (4) can be simplified to

$$[\![n \neq 0]\!] \cdot [\![\psi[n/n-1]]\!] \cdot \alpha \cdot (n-1)^a \cdot b^{n-1}. \tag{5}$$

Clearly, there is a $\psi' \in \mathcal{C}$ such that $[\![\psi']\!]$ is equivalent to $[\![n \neq 0]\!] \cdot [\![\psi[n/n-1]]\!]$. Moreover, $\alpha \cdot b^{n-1} = \frac{\alpha}{b} \cdot b^n$ where $\frac{\alpha}{b} \in \mathbb{Af}[\overline{x}]$. Hence, due to the Binomial Theorem

$$[\![n \neq 0]\!] \cdot [\![\psi[n/n-1]]\!] \cdot \alpha \cdot (n-1)^a \cdot b^{n-1} = \sum_{i=0}^{a} [\![\psi']\!] \cdot \tfrac{\alpha}{b} \cdot \tbinom{a}{i} \cdot (-1)^i \cdot n^{a-i} \cdot b^n \tag{6}$$

which is a poly-exponential expression as $\frac{\alpha}{b} \cdot \binom{a}{i} \cdot (-1)^i \in \mathbb{Af}[\overline{x}]$.

From now on, let $m \geq 1$. If ψ contains a positive literal $n = c$, then we get

$$\left.\begin{aligned}
&\textstyle\sum_{i=1}^{n} [\![\psi]\!]\,(i-1) \cdot m^{n-i} \cdot \alpha \cdot (i-1)^a \cdot b^{i-1} \\
&= \textstyle\sum_{i=1}^{n} [\![n > i-1]\!] \cdot [\![\psi]\!]\,(i-1) \cdot m^{n-i} \cdot \alpha \cdot (i-1)^a \cdot b^{i-1} && (\dagger) \\
&= [\![n > c]\!] \cdot [\![\psi]\!]\,(c) \cdot m^{n-c-1} \cdot \alpha \cdot c^a \cdot b^c && (\dagger\dagger) \\
&= \begin{cases} 0, & \text{if } [\![\psi]\!]\,(c) = 0 \\ [\![n > c]\!] \cdot \frac{1}{m^{c+1}} \cdot \alpha \cdot c^a \cdot b^c \cdot m^n, & \text{if } [\![\psi]\!]\,(c) = 1 \end{cases} \\
&\in \mathbb{PE}[\overline{x}] \quad (\text{since } \tfrac{1}{m^{c+1}} \cdot \alpha \cdot c^a \cdot b^c \in \mathbb{Af}[\overline{x}]).
\end{aligned}\right\} \tag{7}$$

The step marked with (†) holds as we have $[\![n > i-1]\!] = 1$ for all $i \in \{1, \dots, n\}$ and the step marked with (††) holds since $i \neq c+1$ implies $[\![\psi]\!]\,(i-1) = 0$. If ψ does not contain a positive literal, then let c be the maximal constant that occurs in ψ or -1 if ψ is empty. We get:

$$\left.\begin{array}{l} \sum_{i=1}^{n} [\![\psi]\!]\,(i-1) \cdot m^{n-i} \cdot \alpha \cdot (i-1)^a \cdot b^{i-1} \\ = \sum_{i=1}^{n} [\![n > i-1]\!] \cdot [\![\psi]\!]\,(i-1) \cdot m^{n-i} \cdot \alpha \cdot (i-1)^a \cdot b^{i-1} \quad (\dagger) \\ = \sum_{i=1}^{c+1} [\![n > i-1]\!] \cdot [\![\psi]\!]\,(i-1) \cdot m^{n-i} \cdot \alpha \cdot (i-1)^a \cdot b^{i-1} \\ + \sum_{i=c+2}^{n} m^{n-i} \cdot \alpha \cdot (i-1)^a \cdot b^{i-1} \end{array}\right\} \tag{8}$$

Again, the step marked with (†) holds since we have $[\![n > i-1]\!] = 1$ for all $i \in \{1, \dots, n\}$. The last step holds as $i \geq c+2$ implies $[\![\psi]\!]\,(i-1) = 1$. Similar to the case where ψ contains a positive literal, we can compute a poly-exponential expression which is equivalent to the first addend. We have

$$\begin{array}{l} \sum_{i=1}^{c+1} [\![n > i-1]\!] \cdot [\![\psi]\!]\,(i-1) \cdot m^{n-i} \cdot \alpha \cdot (i-1)^a \cdot b^{i-1} \\ = \sum_{\substack{1 \leq i \leq c+1 \\ [\![\psi]\!](i-1)=1}} [\![n > i-1]\!] \cdot \frac{1}{m^i} \cdot \alpha \cdot (i-1)^a \cdot b^{i-1} \cdot m^n \end{array} \tag{9}$$

which is a poly-exponential expression as $\frac{1}{m^i} \cdot \alpha \cdot (i-1)^a \cdot b^{i-1} \in \mathbb{A}\mathrm{f}[\overline{x}]$. For the second addend, we have:

$$\left.\begin{array}{l} \sum_{i=c+2}^{n} m^{n-i} \cdot \alpha \cdot (i-1)^a \cdot b^{i-1} \\ = \frac{\alpha}{b} \cdot m^n \cdot \sum_{i=c+2}^{n} (i-1)^a \cdot \left(\frac{b}{m}\right)^i \\ = \frac{\alpha}{b} \cdot m^n \cdot \sum_{i=c+2}^{n} (r[n/i] - \frac{m}{b} \cdot r[n/i-1]) \cdot \left(\frac{b}{m}\right)^i \text{ (Lemma 10 with } c = \frac{m}{b}) \\ = \frac{\alpha}{b} \cdot m^n \cdot \left(\sum_{i=c+2}^{n} r[n/i] \cdot \left(\frac{b}{m}\right)^i - \sum_{i=c+2}^{n} \frac{m}{b} \cdot r[n/i-1] \cdot \left(\frac{b}{m}\right)^i\right) \\ = \frac{\alpha}{b} \cdot m^n \cdot \left(\sum_{i=c+2}^{n} r[n/i] \cdot \left(\frac{b}{m}\right)^i - \sum_{i=c+1}^{n-1} r[n/i] \cdot \left(\frac{b}{m}\right)^i\right) \\ = \frac{\alpha}{b} \cdot m^n \cdot [\![n > c+1]\!] \cdot (r \cdot \left(\frac{b}{m}\right)^n - r[n/c+1] \cdot \left(\frac{b}{m}\right)^{c+1}) \\ = [\![n > c+1]\!] \cdot \frac{\alpha}{b} \cdot r \cdot b^n - [\![n > c+1]\!] \cdot r[n/c+1] \cdot \left(\frac{b}{m}\right)^{c+1} \cdot \frac{\alpha}{b} \cdot m^n \end{array}\right\} \tag{10}$$

Lemma 10 ensures $r \in \mathbb{Q}[n]$, i.e., we have $r = \sum_{i=0}^{d_r} m_i \cdot n^i$ for some $d_r \in \mathbb{N}$ and $m_i \in \mathbb{Q}$. Thus, $r[n/c+1] \cdot \left(\frac{b}{m}\right)^{c+1} \cdot \frac{\alpha}{b} \in \mathbb{A}\mathrm{f}[\overline{x}]$ which implies $[\![n > c+1]\!] \cdot r[n/c+1] \cdot \left(\frac{b}{m}\right)^{c+1} \cdot \frac{\alpha}{b} \cdot m^n \in \mathbb{PE}[\overline{x}]$. It remains to show that the addend $[\![n > c+1]\!] \cdot \frac{\alpha}{b} \cdot r \cdot b^n$ is equivalent to a poly-exponential expression. As $\frac{\alpha}{b} \cdot m_i \in \mathbb{A}\mathrm{f}[\overline{x}]$, we have

$$[\![n > c+1]\!] \cdot \frac{\alpha}{b} \cdot r \cdot b^n = \sum_{i=0}^{d_r} [\![n > c+1]\!] \cdot \frac{\alpha}{b} \cdot m_i \cdot n^i \cdot b^n \in \mathbb{PE}[\overline{x}]. \tag{11}$$

□

The proof of Lemma 12 gives rise to a corresponding algorithm.

Algorithm 2. symbolic_sum

Input: $m \in \mathbb{N},\ \ p \in \mathbb{PE}[\overline{x}]$
Result: $q \in \mathbb{PE}[\overline{x}]$ which is equivalent to $\sum_{i=1}^{n} m^{n-i} \cdot p[n/i-1]$
rearrange $\sum_{i=1}^{n} m^{n-i} \cdot p[n/i-1]$ to $\sum_{j=1}^{\ell} p_j$ as in (3)
foreach $p_j \in \{p_1, \ldots, p_\ell\}$ **do**
  if $m = 0$ **then** compute q_j as in (5) and (6)
  else if $p_j = [\![\ldots \wedge n = c \wedge \ldots]\!] \cdot \ldots$ **then** compute q_j as in (7)
  else
   • split p_j into two sums $p_{j,1}$ and $p_{j,2}$ as in (8)
   • compute $q_{j,1}$ from $p_{j,1}$ as in (9)
   • compute $q_{j,2}$ from $p_{j,2}$ as in (10) and (11) using Algorithm 1
   • $q_j \leftarrow q_{j,1} + q_{j,2}$
return $\sum_{j=1}^{\ell} q_j$

Example 13. *We compute an equivalent poly-exponential expression for*

$$\sum_{i=1}^{n} 4^{n-i} \cdot ([\![n=0]\!] \cdot 2 \cdot w \ + \ [\![n \neq 0]\!] \cdot 4 \ - \ 2)\ [n/i-1] \tag{12}$$

where w is a variable. (It will later on be needed to compute a closed form for Example 4, see Example 18.) According to Algorithm 2 and (3), we get

$$\begin{aligned} &\sum_{i=1}^{n} 4^{n-i} \cdot ([\![n=0]\!] \cdot 2 \cdot w \ + \ [\![n \neq 0]\!] \cdot 4 \ - \ 2)\ [n/i-1] \\ =&\sum_{i=1}^{n} 4^{n-i} \cdot ([\![i-1=0]\!] \cdot 2 \cdot w \ + \ [\![i-1 \neq 0]\!] \cdot 4 \ - \ 2) \\ =&\ p_1 + p_2 + p_3 \end{aligned}$$

with $p_1 = \sum_{i=1}^{n} [\![i-1=0]\!] \cdot 4^{n-i} \cdot 2 \cdot w$, $p_2 = \sum_{i=1}^{n} [\![i-1 \neq 0]\!] \cdot 4^{n-i} \cdot 4$, and $p_3 = \sum_{i=1}^{n} 4^{n-i} \cdot (-2)$. We search for $q_1, q_2, q_3 \in \mathbb{PE}[w]$ that are equivalent to p_1, p_2, p_3, i.e., $q_1 + q_2 + q_3$ is equivalent to (12). We only show how to compute q_2 (and omit the computation of $q_1 = [\![n \neq 0]\!] \cdot \frac{1}{2} \cdot w \cdot 4^n$ and $q_3 = \frac{2}{3} - \frac{2}{3} \cdot 4^n$). Analogously to (8), we get:

$$\begin{aligned} &\sum_{i=1}^{n} [\![i-1 \neq 0]\!] \cdot 4^{n-i} \cdot 4 \\ =&\sum_{i=1}^{n} [\![n > i-1]\!] \cdot [\![i-1 \neq 0]\!] \cdot 4^{n-i} \cdot 4 \\ =&\sum_{i=1}^{1} [\![n > i-1]\!] \cdot [\![i-1 \neq 0]\!] \cdot 4^{n-1} \cdot 4 \quad + \quad \sum_{i=2}^{n} 4^{n-i} \cdot 4 \end{aligned}$$

The next step is to rearrange the first sum as in (9). In our example, it directly simplifies to 0 and hence we obtain

$$\sum_{i=1}^{1} [\![n > i-1]\!] \cdot [\![i-1 \neq 0]\!] \cdot 4^{n-1} \cdot 4 + \sum_{i=2}^{n} 4^{n-i} \cdot 4 = \sum_{i=2}^{n} 4^{n-i} \cdot 4.$$

Finally, by applying the steps from (10) we get:

$$\begin{aligned}
&\textstyle\sum_{i=2}^{n} 4^{n-i} \cdot 4 \\
&= 4 \cdot 4^n \cdot \textstyle\sum_{i=2}^{n} \left(\frac{1}{4}\right)^i \\
&= 4 \cdot 4^n \cdot \textstyle\sum_{i=2}^{n} \left(-\frac{1}{3} - 4 \cdot \left(-\frac{1}{3}\right)\right) \cdot \left(\frac{1}{4}\right)^i && (\dagger) \\
&= 4 \cdot 4^n \cdot \left(\textstyle\sum_{i=2}^{n} \left(-\frac{1}{3}\right) \cdot \left(\frac{1}{4}\right)^i - \textstyle\sum_{i=2}^{n} 4 \cdot \left(-\frac{1}{3}\right) \cdot \left(\frac{1}{4}\right)^i\right) \\
&= 4 \cdot 4^n \cdot \left(\textstyle\sum_{i=2}^{n} \left(-\frac{1}{3}\right) \cdot \left(\frac{1}{4}\right)^i - \textstyle\sum_{i=1}^{n-1} \left(-\frac{1}{3}\right) \cdot \left(\frac{1}{4}\right)^i\right) \\
&= 4 \cdot 4^n \cdot [\![n > 1]\!] \cdot \left(\left(-\frac{1}{3}\right) \cdot \left(\frac{1}{4}\right)^n - \left(-\frac{1}{3}\right) \cdot \frac{1}{4}\right) \\
&= [\![n > 1]\!] \cdot \left(-\frac{4}{3}\right) + [\![n > 1]\!] \cdot \frac{1}{3} \cdot 4^n \\
&= q_2
\end{aligned}$$

The step marked with (†) holds by Lemma 10 with $q = 1$ and $c = 4$. Thus, we have $r = -\frac{1}{3}$, cf. Example 11.

Recall that our goal is to compute closed forms for loops. As a first step, instead of the n-fold update function $h(n, \overline{x}) = f^n(\overline{x})$ of (1) where f is the update of (1), we consider a recursive update function for a single variable $x \in \overline{x}$:

$$g(0, \overline{x}) = x \quad \text{and} \quad g(n, \overline{x}) = m \cdot g(n-1, \overline{x}) + p[n/n-1] \quad \text{for all } n > 0$$

Here, $m \in \mathbb{N}$ and $p \in \mathbb{PE}[\overline{x}]$. Using Lemma 12, it is easy to show that g can be represented by a poly-exponential expression.

Lemma 14 (Closed Form for Single Variables). *If $x \in \overline{x}$, $m \in \mathbb{N}$, and $p \in \mathbb{PE}[\overline{x}]$, then one can compute a $q \in \mathbb{PE}[\overline{x}]$ which satisfies*

$$q\,[n/0] = x \quad \textit{and} \quad q = (m \cdot q + p)\,[n/n-1] \quad \textit{for all } n > 0.$$

Proof. It suffices to find a $q \in \mathbb{PE}[\overline{x}]$ that satisfies

$$q = m^n \cdot x + \textstyle\sum_{i=1}^{n} m^{n-i} \cdot p[n/i-1]. \tag{13}$$

To see why (13) is sufficient, note that (13) implies

$$q[n/0] \quad = \quad m^0 \cdot x + \textstyle\sum_{i=1}^{0} m^{0-i} \cdot p[n/i-1] \quad = \quad x$$

and for $n > 0$, (13) implies

$$\begin{aligned}
q &= m^n \cdot x + \textstyle\sum_{i=1}^{n} m^{n-i} \cdot p[n/i-1] \\
&= m^n \cdot x + \left(\textstyle\sum_{i=1}^{n-1} m^{n-i} \cdot p[n/i-1]\right) + p[n/n-1] \\
&= m \cdot \left(m^{n-1} \cdot x + \textstyle\sum_{i=1}^{n-1} m^{n-i-1} \cdot p[n/i-1]\right) + p[n/n-1] \\
&= m \cdot q[n/n-1] + p[n/n-1] \\
&= (m \cdot q + p)[n/n-1].
\end{aligned}$$

By Lemma 12, we can compute a $q' \in \mathbb{PE}[\overline{x}]$ such that

$$m^n \cdot x + \textstyle\sum_{i=1}^{n} m^{n-i} \cdot p[n/i-1] \quad = \quad m^n \cdot x + q'.$$

Moreover,

$$\text{if } m = 0, \text{ then } m^n \cdot x = [\![n = 0]\!] \cdot x \in \mathbb{PE}[\overline{x}] \text{ and} \tag{14}$$

$$\text{if } m > 0, \text{ then } m^n \cdot x \in \mathbb{PE}[\overline{x}]. \tag{15}$$

So both addends are equivalent to poly-exponential expressions. □

Example 15. *We show how to compute the closed forms for the variables w and x from Example 4. We first consider the assignment $w \leftarrow 2$, i.e., we want to compute a $q_w \in \mathbb{PE}[w,x,y,z]$ with $q_w[n/0] = w$ and $q_w = (m_w \cdot q_w + p_w)[n/n-1]$ for $n > 0$, where $m_w = 0$ and $p_w = 2$. According to (13) and (14), q_w is*

$$m_w^n \cdot w + \sum_{i=1}^{n} m_w^{n-i} \cdot p_w[n/i-1] = 0^n \cdot w + \sum_{i=1}^{n} 0^{n-i} \cdot 2 = [\![n = 0]\!] \cdot w + [\![n \neq 0]\!] \cdot 2.$$

For the assignment $x \leftarrow x + 2$, we search for a q_x such that $q_x[n/0] = x$ and $q_x = (m_x \cdot q_x + p_x)[n/n-1]$ for $n > 0$, where $m_x = 1$ and $p_x = 2$. By (13), q_x is

$$m_x^n \cdot x + \sum_{i=1}^{n} m_x^{n-i} \cdot p_x[n/i-1] = 1^n \cdot x + \sum_{i=1}^{n} 1^{n-i} \cdot 2 = x + 2 \cdot n.$$

The restriction to triangular matrices now allows us to generalize Lemma 14 to vectors of variables. The reason is that due to triangularity, the update of each program variable x_i only depends on the previous values of $x_1, \ldots, x_i$. So when regarding x_i, we can assume that we already know the closed forms for $x_1, \ldots, x_{i-1}$. This allows us to find closed forms for one variable after the other by applying Lemma 14 repeatedly. In other words, it allows us to find a vector $\overline{q}$ of poly-exponential expressions that satisfies

$$\overline{q}\,[n/0] = \overline{x} \quad \text{and} \quad \overline{q} = A\,\overline{q}[n/n-1] + \overline{a} \quad \text{for all } n > 0.$$

To prove this claim, we show the more general Lemma 16. For all $i_1, \ldots, i_k \in \{1, \ldots, m\}$, we define $[z_1, \ldots, z_m]_{i_1,\ldots,i_k} = [z_{i_1}, \ldots, z_{i_k}]$ (and the notation $\overline{y}_{i_1,\ldots,i_k}$ for column vectors is defined analogously). Moreover, for a matrix A, A_i is A's i^{th} row and $A_{i_1,\ldots,i_n;j_1,\ldots,j_k}$ is the matrix with rows $(A_{i_1})_{j_1,\ldots,j_k}, \ldots, (A_{i_n})_{j_1,\ldots,j_k}$. So for $A = \begin{bmatrix} a_{1,1} & a_{1,2} & a_{1,3} \\ a_{2,1} & a_{2,2} & a_{2,3} \\ a_{3,1} & a_{3,2} & a_{3,3} \end{bmatrix}$, we have $A_{1,2;1,3} = \begin{bmatrix} a_{1,1} & a_{1,3} \\ a_{2,1} & a_{2,3} \end{bmatrix}$.

Lemma 16. (Closed Forms for Vectors of Variables). *If $\overline{x}$ is a vector of at least $d \geq 1$ pairwise different variables, $A \in \mathbb{Z}^{d \times d}$ is triangular with $A_{i;i} \geq 0$ for all $1 \leq i \leq d$, and $\overline{p} \in \mathbb{PE}[\overline{x}]^d$, then one can compute $\overline{q} \in \mathbb{PE}[\overline{x}]^d$ such that:*

$$\overline{q}\,[n/0] = \overline{x}_{1,\ldots,d} \quad \textit{and} \tag{16}$$

$$\overline{q} = (A\,\overline{q} + \overline{p})\,[n/n-1] \quad \textit{for all } n > 0 \tag{17}$$

Proof. Assume that A is lower triangular (the case that A is upper triangular works analogously). We use induction on d. For any $d \geq 1$ we have:

$$\begin{array}{rll} & \overline{q} = (A\,\overline{q} + \overline{p})\ [n/n-1] & \\ \iff & \overline{q}_j = (A_j \cdot \overline{q} + \overline{p}_j)\ [n/n-1] & \text{for all } 1 \leq j \leq d \\ \iff & \overline{q}_j = (A_{j;2,\dots,d} \cdot \overline{q}_{2,\dots,d} + A_{j;1} \cdot \overline{q}_1 + \overline{p}_j)\ [n/n-1] & \text{for all } 1 \leq j \leq d \\ \iff & \overline{q}_1 = (A_{1;2,\dots,d} \cdot \overline{q}_{2,\dots,d} + A_{1;1} \cdot \overline{q}_1 + \overline{p}_1)\ [n/n-1] \wedge & \\ & \overline{q}_j = (A_{j;2,\dots,d} \cdot \overline{q}_{2,\dots,d} + A_{j;1} \cdot \overline{q}_1 + \overline{p}_j)\ [n/n-1] & \text{for all } 1 < j \leq d \\ \iff & \overline{q}_1 = (A_{1;1} \cdot \overline{q}_1 + \overline{p}_1)\ [n/n-1] & \wedge \\ & \overline{q}_j = (A_{j;2,\dots,d} \cdot \overline{q}_{2,\dots,d} + A_{j;1} \cdot \overline{q}_1 + \overline{p}_j)\ [n/n-1] & \text{for all } 1 < j \leq d \end{array}$$

The last step holds as A is lower triangular. By Lemma 14, we can compute a $\overline{q}_1 \in \mathbb{PE}[\overline{x}]$ that satisfies

$$\overline{q}_1[n/0] = \overline{x}_1 \quad \text{and} \quad \overline{q}_1 = (A_{1;1} \cdot \overline{q}_1 + \overline{p}_1)\ [n/n-1] \quad \text{for all } n > 0.$$

In the induction base ($d = 1$), there is no j with $1 < j \leq d$. In the induction step ($d > 1$), it remains to show that we can compute $\overline{q}_{2,\dots,d}$ such that

$$\overline{q}_j[n/0] = \overline{x}_j \quad \text{and} \quad \overline{q}_j = (A_{j;2,\dots,d} \cdot \overline{q}_{2,\dots,d} + A_{j;1} \cdot \overline{q}_1 + \overline{p}_j)\ [n/n-1]$$

for all $n > 0$ and all $1 < j \leq d$, which is equivalent to

$$\begin{aligned} & \overline{q}_{2,\dots,d}[n/0] = \overline{x}_{2,\dots,d} \quad \text{and} \\ & \overline{q}_{2,\dots,d} = (A_{2,\dots,d;2,\dots,d} \cdot \overline{q}_{2,\dots,d} + \begin{bmatrix} A_{2;1} \\ \vdots \\ A_{d;1} \end{bmatrix} \cdot \overline{q}_1 + \overline{p}_{2,\dots,d})\ [n/n-1] \end{aligned}$$

for all $n > 0$. As $A_{j;1} \cdot \overline{q}_1 + \overline{p}_j \in \mathbb{PE}[\overline{x}]$ for each $2 \leq j \leq d$, the claim follows from the induction hypothesis. □

Together, Lemmas 14 and 16 and their proofs give rise to the following algorithm to compute a solution for (16) and (17). It computes a closed form $\overline{q}_1$ for $\overline{x}_1$ as in the proof of Lemma 14, constructs the argument $\overline{p}$ for the recursive call based on A, $\overline{q}_1$, and the current value of $\overline{p}$ as in the proof of Lemma 16, and then determines the closed form for $\overline{x}_{2,\dots,d}$ recursively.

Algorithm 3. closed_form

Input: $\overline{x}_{1,\dots,d},\ \ A \in \mathbb{Z}^{d\times d}$ where $A_{i;i} \geq 0$ for all $1 \leq i \leq d,\ \ \overline{p} \in \mathbb{PE}[\overline{x}]^d$
Result: $\overline{q} \in \mathbb{PE}[\overline{x}]^d$ which satisfies (16) & (17) for the given $\overline{x}, A$, and $\overline{p}$
$q \leftarrow$ symbolic_sum$(A_{1;1}, \overline{p}_1)$ (cf. Algorithm 2)
if $A_{1;1} = 0$ **then** $\overline{q}_1 \leftarrow [\![n = 0]\!] \cdot \overline{x}_1 + q$ **else** $\overline{q}_1 \leftarrow A_{1;1}^n \cdot \overline{x}_1 + q$ (cf. (13–15))
if $d > 1$ **then**
$\quad \overline{q}_{2,\dots,d} \leftarrow \text{closed\_form}(\overline{x}_{2,\dots,d}, A_{2,\dots,d;2,\dots,d}, \begin{bmatrix} A_{2;1} \\ \vdots \\ A_{d;1} \end{bmatrix} \cdot \overline{q}_1 + \overline{p}_{2,\dots,d})$
return $\overline{q}$

We can now prove the main theorem of this section.

Theorem 17 (Closed Forms for nnt-Loops). *One can compute a closed form for every nnt-loop. In other words, if $f : \mathbb{Z}^d \to \mathbb{Z}^d$ is the update function of an nnt-loop with the variables $\overline{x}$, then one can compute a $\overline{q} \in \mathbb{PE}[\overline{x}]^d$ such that $\overline{q}[n/c] = f^c(\overline{x})$ for all $c \in \mathbb{N}$.*

Proof. Consider an nnt-loop of the form (1). By Lemma 16, we can compute a $\overline{q} \subseteq \mathbb{PE}[\overline{x}]^d$ that satisfies

$$\overline{q}[n/0] = \overline{x} \quad \text{and} \quad \overline{q} = (A\,\overline{q} + \overline{a})\ [n/n-1] \quad \text{for all } n > 0.$$

We prove $f^c(\overline{x}) = \overline{q}[n/c]$ by induction on $c \in \mathbb{N}$. If $c = 0$, we get

$$f^c(\overline{x}) = f^0(\overline{x}) = \overline{x} = \overline{q}[n/0] = \overline{q}[n/c].$$

If $c > 0$, we get:

$$\begin{aligned} f^c(\overline{x}) &= A\, f^{c-1}(\overline{x}) + \overline{a} && \text{by definition of } f \\ &= A\,\overline{q}[n/c-1] + \overline{a} && \text{by the induction hypothesis} \\ &= (A\,\overline{q} + \overline{a})\ [n/c-1] && \text{as } \overline{a} \in \mathbb{Z}^d \text{ does not contain } n \\ &= \overline{q}[n/c] \end{aligned}$$

□

So invoking Algorithm 3 on $\overline{x}$, A, and $\overline{a}$ yields the closed form of an nnt-loop (1).

Example 18. *We show how to compute the closed form for Example 4. For*

$$y \leftarrow 2 \cdot w + 4 \cdot y - 2,$$

we obtain

$$\begin{aligned} q_y &= (4 \cdot q_y + 2 \cdot q_w - 2)\ [n/n-1] \\ &= 4^n \cdot y + \textstyle\sum_{i=1}^{n} 4^{n-i} \cdot (2 \cdot q_w - 2)\ [n/i-1] && \text{(by (13))} \\ &= y \cdot 4^n + \textstyle\sum_{i=1}^{n} 4^{n-i} \cdot ([\![n = 0]\!] \cdot 2 \cdot w + [\![n \neq 0]\!] \cdot 4 - 2)\ [n/i-1] && \text{(see Example 15)} \\ &= q_0 + q_1 + q_2 + q_3 && \text{(see Example 13)} \end{aligned}$$

where $q_0 = y \cdot 4^n$. For $z \leftarrow x + 1$, we get

$$\begin{aligned} q_z &= (q_x + 1)\ [n/n-1] \\ &= 0^n \cdot z + \textstyle\sum_{i=1}^{n} 0^{n-i} \cdot (q_x + 1)\ [n/i-1] && \text{(by (13))} \\ &= [\![n = 0]\!] \cdot z + [\![n \neq 0]\!] \cdot (q_x[n/n-1] + 1) \\ &= [\![n = 0]\!] \cdot z + [\![n \neq 0]\!] \cdot ((x + 2 \cdot n)\ [n/n-1] + 1) && \text{(see Example 15)} \\ &= [\![n = 0]\!] \cdot z + [\![n \neq 0]\!] \cdot (x - 1) + [\![n \neq 0]\!] \cdot 2 \cdot n. \end{aligned}$$

So the closed form of Example 4 for the values of the variables after n iterations is:

$$\begin{bmatrix} q_w \\ q_x \\ q_y \\ q_z \end{bmatrix} = \begin{bmatrix} [\![n = 0]\!] \cdot w + [\![n \neq 0]\!] \cdot 2 \\ x + 2 \cdot n \\ q_0 + q_1 + q_2 + q_3 \\ [\![n = 0]\!] \cdot z + [\![n \neq 0]\!] \cdot (x - 1) + [\![n \neq 0]\!] \cdot 2 \cdot n \end{bmatrix}$$

4 Deciding Non-Termination of nnt-Loops

Our proof uses the notion of *eventual non-termination* [4,14]. Here, the idea is to disregard the condition of the loop during a finite prefix of the program run.

Definition 19 (Eventual Non-Termination). *A vector $\overline{c} \in \mathbb{Z}^d$* witnesses eventual non-termination *of (1) if*

$$\exists n_0 \in \mathbb{N}.\ \forall n \in \mathbb{N}_{>n_0}.\ \varphi[\overline{x}/f^n(\overline{c})].$$

If there is such a witness, then (1) is eventually non-terminating.

Clearly, (1) is non-terminating iff (1) is eventually non-terminating [14]. Now Theorem 17 gives rise to an alternative characterization of eventual non-termination in terms of the closed form $\overline{q}$ instead of $f^n(\overline{c})$.

Corollary 20 (Expressing Non-Termination with $\mathbb{PE}$). *If $\overline{q}$ is the closed form of (1), then $\overline{c} \in \mathbb{Z}^d$ witnesses eventual non-termination iff*

$$\exists n_0 \in \mathbb{N}.\ \forall n \in \mathbb{N}_{>n_0}.\ \varphi[\overline{x}/\overline{q}][\overline{x}/\overline{c}]. \tag{18}$$

Proof. Immediate, as $\overline{q}$ is equivalent to $f^n(\overline{x})$. □

So to prove that termination of nnt-loops is decidable, we will use Corollary 20 to show that the existence of a witness for eventual non-termination is decidable. To do so, we first eliminate the factors $[\![\psi]\!]$ from the closed form $\overline{q}$. Assume that $\overline{q}$ has at least one factor $[\![\psi]\!]$ where ψ is non-empty (otherwise, all factors $[\![\psi]\!]$ are equivalent to 1) and let c be the maximal constant that occurs in such a factor. Then all addends $[\![\psi]\!] \cdot \alpha \cdot n^a \cdot b^n$ where ψ contains a positive literal become 0 and all other addends become $\alpha \cdot n^a \cdot b^n$ if $n > c$. Thus, as we can assume $n_0 > c$ in (18) without loss of generality, all factors $[\![\psi]\!]$ can be eliminated when checking eventual non-termination.

Corollary 21 Removing $[\![\psi]\!]$ from $\mathbb{PE}$s). *Let $\overline{q}$ be the closed form of an nnt-loop (1). Let $\overline{q}_{norm}$ result from $\overline{q}$ by removing all addends $[\![\psi]\!] \cdot \alpha \cdot n^a \cdot b^n$ where ψ contains a positive literal and by replacing all addends $[\![\psi]\!] \cdot \alpha \cdot n^a \cdot b^n$ where ψ does not contain a positive literal by $\alpha \cdot n^a \cdot b^n$. Then $\overline{c} \in \mathbb{Z}^d$ is a witness for eventual non-termination iff*

$$\exists n_0 \in \mathbb{N}.\ \forall n \in \mathbb{N}_{>n_0}.\ \varphi[\overline{x}/\overline{q}_{norm}][\overline{x}/\overline{c}]. \tag{19}$$

By removing the factors $[\![\psi]\!]$ from the closed form $\overline{q}$ of an nnt-loop, we obtain *normalized* poly-exponential expressions.

Definition 22 (Normalized $\mathbb{PE}$s). *We call $p \in \mathbb{PE}[\overline{x}]$* normalized *if it is in*

$$\mathbb{NPE}[\overline{x}] = \left\{ \sum_{j=1}^{\ell} \alpha_j \cdot n^{a_j} \cdot b_j^n \;\middle|\; \ell, a_j \in \mathbb{N},\ \alpha_j \in \mathbb{A}\text{f}[\overline{x}],\ b_j \in \mathbb{N}_{\geq 1} \right\}.$$

W.l.o.g., we always assume $(b_i, a_i) \neq (b_j, a_j)$ for all $i, j \in \{1, \ldots, \ell\}$ with $i \neq j$. We define $\mathbb{NPE} = \mathbb{NPE}[\varnothing]$, i.e., we have $p \in \mathbb{NPE}$ if $\alpha_j \in \mathbb{Q}$ for all $1 \leq j \leq \ell$.

Example 23. *We continue Example 18. By omitting the factors* $[\![\psi]\!]$,

$$\begin{array}{llll} q_w &= [\![n=0]\!] \cdot w + [\![n \neq 0]\!] \cdot 2 & \text{becomes } 2, \\ q_z &= [\![n=0]\!] \cdot z + [\![n \neq 0]\!] \cdot (x-1) + [\![n \neq 0]\!] \cdot 2 \cdot n & \text{becomes } x - 1 + 2 \cdot n, \end{array}$$

and $q_x = x + 2 \cdot n$, $q_0 = y \cdot 4^n$, *and* $q_3 = \frac{2}{3} - \frac{2}{3} \cdot 4^n$ *remain unchanged. Moreover,*

$$\begin{array}{lll} q_1 = [\![n \neq 0]\!] \cdot \frac{1}{2} \cdot w \cdot 4^n & \text{becomes } \frac{1}{2} \cdot w \cdot 4^n & \text{and} \\ q_2 = [\![n > 1]\!] \cdot \left(-\frac{4}{3}\right) + [\![n > 1]\!] \cdot \frac{1}{3} \cdot 4^n & \text{becomes } \left(-\frac{4}{3}\right) + \frac{1}{3} \cdot 4^n. \end{array}$$

Thus, $q_y = q_0 + q_1 + q_2 + q_3$ *becomes*

$$y \cdot 4^n + \tfrac{1}{2} \cdot w \cdot 4^n - \tfrac{4}{3} + \tfrac{1}{3} \cdot 4^n + \tfrac{2}{3} - \tfrac{2}{3} \cdot 4^n = 4^n \cdot \left(y - \tfrac{1}{3} + \tfrac{1}{2} \cdot w\right) - \tfrac{2}{3}.$$

Let $\sigma = \left[w/2,\ x/x + 2 \cdot n,\ y/4^n \cdot \left(y - \frac{1}{3} + \frac{1}{2} \cdot w\right) - \frac{2}{3},\ z/x - 1 + 2 \cdot n\right]$. *Then we get that Example 2 is non-terminating iff there are* $w, x, y, z \in \mathbb{Z}, n_0 \in \mathbb{N}$ *such that*

$$\begin{array}{ll} (y+z)\,\sigma > 0 \wedge (-w - 2 \cdot y + x)\,\sigma > 0 & \iff \\ 4^n \cdot \left(y - \frac{1}{3} + \frac{1}{2} \cdot w\right) - \frac{2}{3} + x - 1 + 2 \cdot n > 0 & \wedge \\ \quad -2 - 2 \cdot \left(4^n \cdot \left(y - \frac{1}{3} + \frac{1}{2} \cdot w\right) - \frac{2}{3}\right) + x + 2 \cdot n > 0 & \iff \\ p_1^\varphi > 0 \wedge p_2^\varphi > 0 & \end{array}$$

holds for all $n > n_0$ *where*

$$\begin{aligned} p_1^\varphi &= 4^n \cdot \left(y - \tfrac{1}{3} + \tfrac{1}{2} \cdot w\right) + 2 \cdot n + x - \tfrac{5}{3} \text{ and} \\ p_2^\varphi &= 4^n \cdot \left(\tfrac{2}{3} - 2 \cdot y - w\right) + 2 \cdot n + x - \tfrac{2}{3}. \end{aligned}$$

Recall that the loop condition φ is a conjunction of inequalities of the form $\alpha > 0$ where $\alpha \in \mathbb{A}\mathrm{f}[\overline{x}]$. Thus, $\varphi[\overline{x}/\overline{q}_{norm}]$ is a conjunction of inequalities $p > 0$ where $p \in \mathbb{NPE}[\overline{x}]$ and we need to decide if there is an instantiation of these inequalities that is valid "for large enough n". To do so, we order the coefficients α_j of the addends $\alpha_j \cdot n^{a_j} \cdot b_j^n$ of normalized poly-exponential expressions according to the addend's asymptotic growth when increasing n. Lemma 24 shows that $\alpha_2 \cdot n^{a_2} \cdot b_2^n$ grows faster than $\alpha_1 \cdot n^{a_1} \cdot b_1^n$ iff $b_2 > b_1$ or both $b_2 = b_1$ and $a_2 > a_1$.

Lemma 24 (Asymptotic Growth). *Let* $b_1, b_2 \in \mathbb{N}_{\geq 1}$ *and* $a_1, a_2 \in \mathbb{N}$. *If* $(b_2, a_2) >_{lex} (b_1, a_1)$, *then* $\mathcal{O}(n^{a_1} \cdot b_1^n) \subsetneq \mathcal{O}(n^{a_2} \cdot b_2^n)$. *Here,* $>_{lex}$ *is the lexicographic order, i.e.,* $(b_2, a_2) >_{lex} (b_1, a_1)$ *iff* $b_2 > b_1$ *or* $b_2 = b_1 \wedge a_2 > a_1$.

Proof. By considering the cases $b_2 > b_1$ and $b_2 = b_1$ separately, the claim can easily be deduced from the definition of $\mathcal{O}$. □

Definition 25 (Ordering Coefficients). Marked coefficients *are of the form* $\alpha^{(b,a)}$ *where* $\alpha \in \mathbb{A}\mathrm{f}[\overline{x}], b \in \mathbb{N}_{\geq 1}$, *and* $a \in \mathbb{N}$. *We define* unmark$(\alpha^{(b,a)}) = \alpha$ *and* $\alpha_2^{(b_2,a_2)} \succ \alpha_1^{(b_1,a_1)}$ *if* $(b_2, a_2) >_{lex} (b_1, a_1)$. *Let*

$$p = \textstyle\sum_{j=1}^{\ell} \alpha_j \cdot n^{a_j} \cdot b_j^n \in \mathbb{NPE}[\overline{x}],$$

where $\alpha_j \neq 0$ for all $1 \leq j \leq \ell$. The marked coefficients of p are

$$\text{coeffs}(p) = \begin{cases} \left\{0^{(1,0)}\right\}, & \text{if } \ell = 0 \\ \left\{\alpha_j^{(b_j,a_j)} \,\middle|\, 0 \leq j \leq \ell\right\}, & \text{otherwise.} \end{cases}$$

Example 26. *In Example 23 we saw that the loop from Example 2 is non-terminating iff there are $w, x, y, z \in \mathbb{Z}, n_0 \in \mathbb{N}$ such that $p_1^\varphi > 0 \wedge p_2^\varphi > 0$ for all $n > n_0$. We get:*

$$\text{coeffs}\left(p_1^\varphi\right) = \left\{\left(y - \tfrac{1}{3} + \tfrac{1}{2} \cdot w\right)^{(4,0)}, 2^{(1,1)}, \left(x - \tfrac{5}{3}\right)^{(1,0)}\right\}$$
$$\text{coeffs}\left(p_2^\varphi\right) = \left\{\left(\tfrac{2}{3} - 2 \cdot y - w\right)^{(4,0)}, 2^{(1,1)}, \left(x - \tfrac{2}{3}\right)^{(1,0)}\right\}$$

Now it is easy to see that the asymptotic growth of a normalized poly-exponential expression is solely determined by its $\succ$-maximal addend.

Corollary 27 (Maximal Addend Determines Asymptotic Growth). *Let $p \in \mathbb{NPE}$ and let $\max_\succ(\text{coeffs}(p)) = c^{(b,a)}$. Then $\mathcal{O}(p) = \mathcal{O}(c \cdot n^a \cdot b^n)$.*

Proof. Clear, as $c \cdot n^a \cdot b^n$ is the asymptotically dominating addend of p. $\square$

Note that Corollary 27 would be incorrect for the case $c = 0$ if we replaced $\mathcal{O}(p) = \mathcal{O}(c \cdot n^a \cdot b^n)$ with $\mathcal{O}(p) = \mathcal{O}(n^a \cdot b^n)$ as $\mathcal{O}(0) \neq \mathcal{O}(1)$. Building upon Corollary 27, we now show that, for large n, the sign of a normalized poly-exponential expression is solely determined by its $\succ$-maximal coefficient. Here, we define $\text{sign}(c) = -1$ if $c \in \mathbb{Q}_{<0} \cup \{-\infty\}$, $\text{sign}(0) = 0$, and $\text{sign}(c) = 1$ if $c \in \mathbb{Q}_{>0} \cup \{\infty\}$.

Lemma 28 (Sign of $\mathbb{NPE}$s). *Let $p \in \mathbb{NPE}$. Then $\lim_{n \mapsto \infty} p \in \mathbb{Q}$ iff $p \in \mathbb{Q}$ and otherwise, $\lim_{n \mapsto \infty} p \in \{\infty, -\infty\}$. Moreover, we have*

$$\text{sign}\left(\lim_{n \mapsto \infty} p\right) = \text{sign}(\text{unmark}(\max_\succ(\text{coeffs}(p)))).$$

Proof. If $p \notin \mathbb{Q}$, then the limit of each addend of p is in $\{-\infty, \infty\}$ by definition of $\mathbb{NPE}$. As the asymptotically dominating addend determines $\lim_{n \mapsto \infty} p$ and $\text{unmark}(\max_\succ(\text{coeffs}(p)))$ determines the sign of the asymptotically dominating addend, the claim follows. $\square$

Lemma 29 shows the connection between the limit of a normalized poly-exponential expression p and the question whether p is positive for large enough n. The latter corresponds to the existence of a witness for eventual non-termination by Corollary 21 as $\varphi[\overline{x}/\overline{q}_{norm}]$ is a conjunction of inequalities $p > 0$ where $p \in \mathbb{NPE}[\overline{x}]$.

Lemma 29 (Limits and Positivity of $\mathbb{NPE}$s). *Let $p \in \mathbb{NPE}$. Then*

$$\exists n_0 \in \mathbb{N}.\ \forall n \in \mathbb{N}_{>n_0}.\ p > 0 \iff \lim_{n \mapsto \infty} p > 0.$$

Proof. By case analysis over $\lim_{n\mapsto\infty} p$. □

Now we show that Corollary 21 allows us to decide eventual non-termination by examining the coefficients of normalized poly-exponential expressions. As these coefficients are in $\mathbb{A}\mathbb{f}[\overline{x}]$, the required reasoning is decidable.

Lemma 30 (Deciding Eventual Positiveness of $\mathbb{NPE}$s). *Validity of*

$$\exists \overline{c} \in \mathbb{Z}^d, n_0 \in \mathbb{N}.\ \forall n \in \mathbb{N}_{>n_0}.\ \bigwedge_{i=1}^{k} p_i[\overline{x}/\overline{c}] > 0 \tag{20}$$

where $p_1, \ldots, p_k \in \mathbb{NPE}[\overline{x}]$ *is decidable.*

Proof. For any p_i with $1 \leq i \leq k$ and any $\overline{c} \in \mathbb{Z}^d$, we have $p_i[\overline{x}/\overline{c}] \in \mathbb{NPE}$. Hence:

$$\begin{aligned}
& \exists n_0 \in \mathbb{N}.\ \forall n \in \mathbb{N}_{>n_0}.\ \textstyle\bigwedge_{i=1}^{k} p_i[\overline{x}/\overline{c}] > 0 \\
\iff & \textstyle\bigwedge_{i=1}^{k} \exists n_0 \in \mathbb{N}.\ \forall n \in \mathbb{N}_{>n_0}.\ p_i[\overline{x}/\overline{c}] > 0 \\
\iff & \textstyle\bigwedge_{i=1}^{k} \lim_{n\mapsto\infty} p_i[\overline{x}/\overline{c}] > 0 && \text{(by Lemma 29)} \\
\iff & \textstyle\bigwedge_{i=1}^{k} \mathrm{unmark}(\max_{\succ}(\mathrm{coeffs}(p_i[\overline{x}/\overline{c}]))) > 0 && \text{(by Lemma 28)}
\end{aligned}$$

Let $p \in \mathbb{NPE}[\overline{x}]$ with $\mathrm{coeffs}(p) = \left\{\alpha_1^{(b_1,a_1)}, \ldots, \alpha_\ell^{(b_\ell,a_\ell)}\right\}$ where $\alpha_i^{(b_i,a_i)} \succ \alpha_j^{(b_j,a_j)}$ for all $1 \leq i < j \leq \ell$. If $p[\overline{x}/\overline{c}] = 0$ holds, then $\mathrm{coeffs}(p[\overline{x}/\overline{c}]) = \{0^{(1,0)}\}$ and thus $\mathrm{unmark}(\max_{\succ}(\mathrm{coeffs}(p[\overline{x}/\overline{c}]))) = 0$. Otherwise, there is an $1 \leq j \leq \ell$ with $\mathrm{unmark}(\max_{\succ}(\mathrm{coeffs}(p[\overline{x}/\overline{c}]))) = \alpha_j[\overline{x}/\overline{c}] \neq 0$ and we have $\alpha_i[\overline{x}/\overline{c}] = 0$ for all $1 \leq i \leq j-1$. Hence, $\mathrm{unmark}(\max_{\succ}(\mathrm{coeffs}(p[\overline{x}/\overline{c}]))) > 0$ holds iff $\bigvee_{j=1}^{\ell}\left(\alpha_j[\overline{x}/\overline{c}] > 0 \wedge \bigwedge_{i=0}^{j-1} \alpha_i[\overline{x}/\overline{c}] = 0\right)$ holds, i.e., iff $[\overline{x}/\overline{c}]$ is a model for

$$\text{max\_coeff\_pos}(p) = \bigvee_{j=1}^{\ell}\left(\alpha_j > 0 \wedge \bigwedge_{i=0}^{j-1} \alpha_i = 0\right). \tag{21}$$

Hence by the considerations above, (20) is valid iff

$$\exists \overline{c} \in \mathbb{Z}^d.\ \bigwedge_{i=1}^{k} \text{max\_coeff\_pos}(p_i)[\overline{x}/\overline{c}] \tag{22}$$

is valid. By multiplying each (in-)equality in (22) with the least common multiple of all denominators, one obtains a first-order formula over the theory of linear integer arithmetic. It is well known that validity of such formulas is decidable. □

Note that (22) is valid iff $\bigwedge_{i=1}^{k} \text{max\_coeff\_pos}(p_i)$ is satisfiable. So to implement our decision procedure, one can use integer programming or SMT solvers to check satisfiability of $\bigwedge_{i=1}^{k} \text{max\_coeff\_pos}(p_i)$. Lemma 30 allows us to prove our main theorem.

Theorem 31. *Termination of triangular loops is decidable.*

Proof. By Theorem 8, termination of triangular loops is decidable iff termination of nnt-loops is decidable. For an nnt-loop (1) we obtain a $\overline{q}_{norm} \in \mathbb{NPE}[\overline{x}]^d$ (see Theorem 17 and Corollary 21) such that (1) is non-terminating iff

$$\exists \overline{c} \in \mathbb{Z}^d, n_0 \in \mathbb{N}.\ \forall n \in \mathbb{N}_{>n_0}.\ \varphi[\overline{x}/\overline{q}_{norm}][\overline{x}/\overline{c}], \tag{20}$$

where φ is a conjunction of inequalities of the form $\alpha > 0$, $\alpha \in \mathbb{Af}[\overline{x}]$. Hence,

$$\varphi[\overline{x}/\overline{q}_{norm}][\overline{x}/\overline{c}] \;=\; \bigwedge_{i=1}^{k} p_i[\overline{x}/\overline{c}] > 0$$

where $p_1, \ldots, p_k \in \mathbb{NPE}[\overline{x}]$. Thus, by Lemma 30, validity of (20) is decidable. □

The following algorithm summarizes our decision procedure.

Algorithm 4. Deciding Termination of Triangular Loops

Input: a triangular loop (1)
Result: $\top$ if (1) terminates, $\bot$ otherwise

- apply Definition 3 to (1), i.e.,

  $\varphi \leftarrow \varphi \wedge \varphi[\overline{x}/A\,\overline{x} + \overline{a}]$
  $A \leftarrow A^2$
  $\overline{a} \leftarrow A\,\overline{a} + \overline{a}$
- $\overline{q} \leftarrow$ closed_form($\overline{x}, A, \overline{a}$) (cf. Algorithm 3)
- compute $\overline{q}_{norm}$ as in Corollary 21
- compute $\varphi[\overline{x}/\overline{q}_{norm}] = \bigwedge_{i=1}^{k} p_i > 0$
- compute $\phi = \bigwedge_{i=1}^{k}$ max_coeff_pos(p_i) (cf. (21))
- **if** ϕ *is satisfiable* **then return** $\bot$ **else return** $\top$

Example 32. *In Example 26 we showed that Example 2 is non-terminating iff*

$$\exists w, x, y, z \in \mathbb{Z},\; n_0 \in \mathbb{N}.\; \forall n \in \mathbb{N}_{>n_0}.\; p_1^{\varphi} > 0 \wedge p_2^{\varphi} > 0$$

is valid. This is the case iff max_coeff_pos(p_1) $\wedge$ max_coeff_pos(p_2), *i.e.,*

$$y - \tfrac{1}{3} + \tfrac{1}{2}{\cdot}w > 0 \vee 2 > 0 \wedge y - \tfrac{1}{3} + \tfrac{1}{2}{\cdot}w = 0 \vee x - \tfrac{5}{3} > 0 \wedge 2 = 0 \wedge y - \tfrac{1}{3} + \tfrac{1}{2}{\cdot}w = 0$$
$$\wedge$$
$$\tfrac{2}{3} - 2{\cdot}y - w > 0 \vee 2 > 0 \wedge \tfrac{2}{3} - 2{\cdot}y - w = 0 \vee x - \tfrac{2}{3} > 0 \wedge 2 = 0 \wedge \tfrac{2}{3} - 2{\cdot}y - w = 0$$

is satisfiable. This formula is equivalent to $6 \cdot y - 2 + 3 \cdot w = 0$ *which does not have any integer solutions. Hence, the loop of Example 2 terminates.*

Example 33 shows that our technique does not yield witnesses for non-termination, but it only proves the existence of a witness for *eventual* non-termination. While such a witness can be transformed into a witness for non-termination by applying the loop several times, it is unclear how often the loop needs to be applied.

Example 33. *Consider the following non-terminating loop:*

$$\textbf{while } x > 0 \textbf{ do } \begin{bmatrix} x \\ y \end{bmatrix} \leftarrow \begin{bmatrix} x + y \\ 1 \end{bmatrix} \tag{23}$$

The closed form of x is $q = [\![n = 0]\!] \cdot x + [\![n \neq 0]\!] \cdot (x + y + n - 1)$. *Replacing x with q_{norm} in $x > 0$ yields $x + y + n - 1 > 0$. The maximal marked coefficient of $x{+}y{+}n{-}1$ is $1^{(1,1)}$. So by Algorithm 4, (23) does not terminate if $\exists x, y \in \mathbb{Z}.\, 1 > 0$ is valid. While $1 > 0$ is a tautology, (23) terminates if $x \leq 0$ or $x \leq -y$.*

However, the final formula constructed by Algorithm 4 precisely describes all witnesses for eventual non-termination.

Lemma 34 (Witnessing Eventual Non-Termination). *Let (1) be a triangular loop, let $\overline{q}_{norm}$ be the normalized closed form of (2), and let*

$$(\varphi \wedge \varphi[\overline{x}/A\,\overline{x} + \overline{a}])\,[\overline{x}/\overline{q}_{norm}] = \bigwedge_{i=1}^{k} p_i > 0.$$

Then $\overline{c} \in \mathbb{Z}^d$ witnesses eventual non-termination of (1) iff $[\overline{x}/\overline{c}]$ is a model for

$$\bigwedge_{i=1}^{k} \text{max\_coeff\_pos}(p_i).$$

5 Conclusion

We presented a decision procedure for termination of affine integer loops with triangular update matrices. In this way, we contribute to the ongoing challenge of proving the 15 years old conjecture by Tiwari [15] that termination of affine integer loops is decidable. After linear loops [4], loops with at most 4 variables [14], and loops with diagonalizable update matrices [3,14], triangular loops are the fourth important special case where decidability could be proven.

The key idea of our decision procedure is to compute *closed forms* for the values of the program variables after a symbolic number of iterations n. While these closed forms are rather complex, it turns out that reasoning about first-order formulas over the theory of linear integer arithmetic suffices to analyze their behavior for large n. This allows us to reduce (non-)termination of triangular loops to integer programming. In future work, we plan to investigate generalizations of our approach to other classes of integer loops.

References

1. Bagnara, R., Zaccagnini, A., Zolo, T.: The Automatic Solution of Recurrence Relations. I. Linear Recurrences of Finite Order with Constant Coefficients. Technical report. Quaderno 334. Dipartimento di Matematica, Università di Parma, Italy (2003). http://www.cs.unipr.it/Publications/
2. Ben-Amram, A.M., Genaim, S., Masud, A.N.: On the termination of integer loops. ACM Trans. Programm. Lang. Syst. **34**(4), 16:1–16:24 (2012). https://doi.org/10.1145/2400676.2400679
3. Bozga, M., Iosif, R., Konecný, F.: Deciding conditional termination. Logical Methods Comput. Sci. **10**(3) (2014). https://doi.org/10.2168/LMCS-10(3:8)2014
4. Braverman, M.: Termination of integer linear programs. In: Ball, T., Jones, R.B. (eds.) CAV 2006. LNCS, vol. 4144, pp. 372–385. Springer, Heidelberg (2006). https://doi.org/10.1007/11817963_34
5. Brockschmidt, M., Cook, B., Ishtiaq, S., Khlaaf, H., Piterman, N.: T2: temporal property verification. In: Chechik, M., Raskin, J.-F. (eds.) TACAS 2016. LNCS, vol. 9636, pp. 387–393. Springer, Heidelberg (2016). https://doi.org/10.1007/978-3-662-49674-9_22

6. Chen, Y.-F., et al.: Advanced automata-based algorithms for program termination checking. In: Foster, J.S., Grossman, D. (eds.) PLDI 2018, pp. 135–150 (2018). https://doi.org/10.1145/3192366.3192405
7. Chen, H.-Y., David, C., Kroening, D., Schrammel, P., Wachter, B.: Bit-precise procedure-modular termination analysis. ACM Trans. Programm. Lang. Syst. **40**(1), 1:1–1:38 (2018). https://doi.org/10.1145/3121136
8. D'Silva, V., Urban, C.: Conflict-driven conditional termination. In: Kroening, D., Păsăreanu, C.S. (eds.) CAV 2015. LNCS, vol. 9207, pp. 271–286. Springer, Cham (2015). https://doi.org/10.1007/978-3-319-21668-3_16
9. Frohn, F., Giesl, J.: Termination of triangular integer loops is decidable. In: CoRR abs/1905.08664 (2019). https://arxiv.org/abs/1905.08664
10. Frohn, F., Naaf, M., Hensel, J., Brockschmidt, M., Giesl, J.: Lower runtime bounds for integer programs. In: Olivetti, N., Tiwari, A. (eds.) IJCAR 2016. LNCS (LNAI), vol. 9706, pp. 550–567. Springer, Cham (2016). https://doi.org/10.1007/978-3-319-40229-1_37
11. Giesl, J., et al.: Analyzing program termination and complexity automatically with AProVE. J. Autom. Reasoning **58**(1), 3–31 (2017). https://doi.org/10.1007/s10817-016-9388-y
12. Larraz, D., Oliveras, A., Rodríguez-Carbonell, E., Rubio, A.: Proving termination of imperative programs using Max-SMT. In: Jobstmann, B., Ray, S. (eds.) FMCAD 2013, pp. 218–225 (2013). https://doi.org/10.1109/FMCAD.2013.6679413
13. Le, T.C., Qin, S., Chin, W.-N.: Termination and non-termination specification inference. In: Grove, D., Blackburn, S. (eds.) PLDI 2015, pp. 489–498 (2015). https://doi.org/10.1145/2737924.2737993
14. Ouaknine, J., Pinto, J.S., Worrell, J.: On termination of integer linear loops. In: Indyk, P. (ed.) SODA 2015, pp. 957–969 (2015). https://doi.org/10.1137/1.9781611973730.65
15. Tiwari, A.: Termination of linear programs. In: Alur, R., Peled, D.A. (eds.) CAV 2004. LNCS, vol. 3114, pp. 70–82. Springer, Heidelberg (2004). https://doi.org/10.1007/978-3-540-27813-9_6

AliveInLean: A Verified LLVM Peephole Optimization Verifier

Juneyoung Lee[1](✉), Chung-Kil Hur[1], and Nuno P. Lopes[2]

[1] Seoul National University, Seoul, Republic of Korea
juneyoung.lee@sf.snu.ac.kr
[2] Microsoft Research, Cambridge, UK

Abstract. Ensuring that compiler optimizations are correct is important for the reliability of the entire software ecosystem, since all software is compiled. Alive [12] is a tool for verifying LLVM's peephole optimizations. Since Alive was released, it has helped compiler developers proactively find dozens of bugs in LLVM, avoiding potentially hazardous miscompilations. Despite having verified many LLVM optimizations so far, Alive is itself not verified, which has led to at least once declaring an optimization correct when it was not.

We introduce AliveInLean, a formally verified peephole optimization verifier for LLVM. As the name suggests, AliveInLean is a reengineered version of Alive developed in the Lean theorem prover [14]. Assuming that the proof obligations are correctly discharged by an SMT solver, AliveInLean gives the same level of correctness guarantees as state-of-the-art formal frameworks such as CompCert [11], Peek [15], and Vellvm [26], while inheriting the advantages of Alive (significantly more automation and easy adoption by compiler developers).

Keywords: Compiler verification · Peephole optimization · LLVM · Lean · Alive

1 Introduction

Verifying compiler optimizations is important to ensure reliability of the software ecosystem. Various frameworks have been proposed to verify optimizations of industrial compilers. Among them, Alive [12] is a tool for verifying peephole optimizations of LLVM that has been successfully adopted by compiler developers. Since it was released, Alive has helped developers find dozens of bugs.

Figure 1 shows the structure of Alive. An optimization pattern of interest written in a domain-specific language is given as input. Alive parses the input, and encodes the behavior of the source and target programs into logic formulas in the theory of quantified bit-vectors and arrays. Finally, several proof obligations are created from the encoded behavior, and then checked by an SMT solver.

Alive relies on the following three-fold trust base. Firstly, the semantics of LLVM's intermediate representation and SMT expressions. Secondly, Alive's verification condition generator. Finally, the SMT solver used to discharge proof

I. Dillig and S. Tasiran (Eds.): CAV 2019, LNCS 11562, pp. 445–455, 2019.
https://doi.org/10.1007/978-3-030-25543-5_25

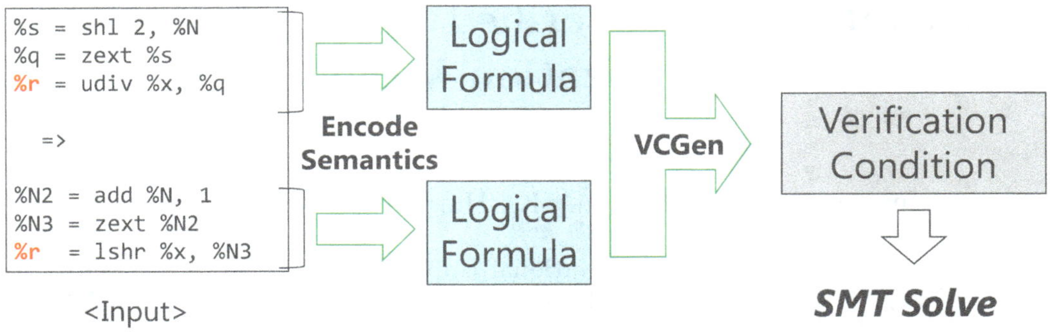

Fig. 1. The structure of Alive and AliveInLean

obligations. None of these are formally verified, and thus an error in any of these may result in an incorrect answer.

To address this problem, we introduce AliveInLean, a formally verified peephole optimization verifier for LLVM. AliveInLean is written in Lean [14], an interactive theorem proving language. Its semantics of LLVM IR (Intermediate Representation) and SMT expressions are rigorously tested using Lean's metaprogramming language [5] and system library. AliveInLean's verification condition generator is formally verified in Lean.

Using AliveInLean requires less human effort than directly proving the optimizations on formal frameworks thanks to automation given by SMT solvers. For example, verifying the correctness of a peephole optimization on a formal framework requires more than a hundred lines of proofs [15]. However, the correctness of AliveInLean relies on the correctness of the used SMT solver. To counteract the dependency on SMT solvers, proof obligations can be cross-checked with multiple SMT solvers. Moreover, there is substantial work towards making SMT solvers generate proof certificates [2,3,6,7].

AliveInLean is a proof of concept. It currently does not support all operations that Alive does like, e.g., memory-related operations. However, AliveInLean supports all integer peephole optimizations, which is already useful in practice as most bugs found by Alive were in integer optimizations [12].

2 Overview

We give an overview of AliveInLean's features from a user's perspective.

Verifying Optimizations. AliveInLean reads optimization(s) from a file and checks their correctness. A user writes an optimization of interest in a DSL with similar syntax to that of LLVM IR:

```
Name: AddSub:1309
%lhs = and i4 %a, %b
%rhs = or i4 %a, %b
%r = add i4 %lhs, %rhs
  =>
%r = add i4 %a, %b
```

This example transformation corresponds to rewriting `(%a & %b) + (%a | %b)` to `%a + %b`, given 4-bits integers `%a` and `%b`. The last variable `%r`, or *root* variable, is assumed to be the return value of the programs. AliveInLean encodes the behavior of each program and generates verification conditions (VCs). Finally, AliveInLean calls Z3 to discharge the VCs.

Proving Useful Properties. AliveInLean can be used as a formal framework to prove lemmas using interactive theorem proving. This is helpful when a user wants to show a property of a program which is hard to represent as a transformation.

For example, one may want to prove that the divisor of `udiv` (unsigned division) is never `poison`[1] if it did not raise undefined behavior (UB). The lemma below states this in Lean. This lemma says that the divisor `val` is never poison if the state `st'` after executing the `udiv` instruction (`step`) has no UB.

```
lemma never_poison:
  forall .. (HSTEP: some st' = step st (udiv isz name op1 op2))
            (HNOUB: not (has_ub st'))
            (HVAL:  some val = get_value st op2 (ty.int isz)),
    not (is_poison val)
```

Testing Specifications. AliveInLean supports random testing of AliveInLean's specifications (for which no verification is possible). For example, the `step` function in the above example implements a specification of the LLVM IR, and it can be tested with respect to the behavior of the LLVM compiler. Another trust-base is the specification of SMT expressions, which defines a relation between expressions (with no free variable) and their corresponding concrete values.

These tests help build confidence in the validity of VC generation. Running tests is helpful when a user wants to use a different version of LLVM or modify AliveInLean's specifications (e.g., adding a new instruction to IR).

3 Verifying Optimizations

In this section we introduce the different components of AliveInLean that work together to verify an optimization.

[1] `poison` is a special value of LLVM representing a result of an erroneous computation.

3.1 Semantics Encoder

Given a program and an initial state, the semantics encoder produces the final state of the program as a set of SMT expressions. The IR interpreter is similar, but works over concrete values rather than symbolic ones. The semantics encoder and the IR interpreter share the same codebase (essentially the LLVM IR semantics). The code is parametric on the type of the program state. For example, the type of undefined behavior can be either initialized as the `bool` type of Lean or the `Bool` SMT expression type. Given the type, Lean can automatically resolve which operations to use to update the state using typeclass resolution.

3.2 Refinement Encoder

Given a source program, a transformed program, and an initial state, the refinement encoder emits an SMT expression that encodes the refinement check between the final states of the two programs. To obtain the final states, the semantics encoder is used.

The refinement check proves that (1) the transformed program only triggers UB when the original program does (i.e., UB can only be removed), (2) the root variable of the transformed program is only `poison` when it is also `poison` in the original program, and (3) variables' values in the final states of the two programs are the same when no UB is triggered and the original value is not `poison`.

3.3 Parser and Z3 Backend

The parser for Alive's DSL is implemented using Lean's parser monad and file I/O library. SMT expressions are processed with Z3 using Lean's SMT interface.

4 Correctness of AliveInLean

We describe how the correctness of AliveInLean is proved. First, we explain the correctness proof of the semantics encoder and the refinement encoder. We show that if the SMT expression encoded by refinement encoder is valid, the optimization is indeed correct. Next, we explain how the trust-base is tested.

4.1 Semantics Encoding

Given an IR interpreter `run`, a semantics encoder `encoder` is correct with respect to `run` if for any IR program and input state, the final program state generated by `run` and the symbolic state encoded by `encoder` are equivalent.

To formally define its correctness, an equivalence relation between SMT expressions and concrete values is defined. We say that an SMT expression e and a Lean value ν are equivalent, or $e \sim \nu$, if e has no free variables and it evaluates to ν. The equivalence relation is inductively defined with respect to the structure of an SMT expression. To deal with free variables, an environment η is defined, which is a set of pairs (x, ν) where x is a variable and ν is a concrete value. $\eta[\![e]\!]$ is an expression with all free variables x replaced with ν if $(x, \nu) \in \eta$.

Next, we define a program state. A state s is defined as (u, r) where u is an undefined behavior flag and r is a register file. r is a list of (x, v) where x is a variable and v is a value. v is defined as (sz, i, p) where sz is its size in bits, i is an integer value, and p is a poison flag.

There are two kinds of states: a symbolic state, and a concrete state. A symbolic state s_s is a state whose u, i, p are SMT expressions. A concrete state s_c is a state whose all attributes are concrete values. We say that s_s and s_c are equivalent, or $s_s \sim s_c$, if s_s has no free variable in its attributes and they are equivalent. $\eta[\![s_s]\!]$ is a symbolic state with the environment η applied to u, i, p.

Now, the correctness of `encoder` with respect to `run` is defined as follows. It states that the result of `encoder` is equivalent to the result of `run`.

Theorem 1. *For all initial states s_s, s_c, program p, and environment η s.t. $\eta[\![s_s]\!] \sim s_c$, we have that $\eta[\![\texttt{encoder}(p, s_s)]\!] \sim \texttt{run}(p, s_c)$.*

4.2 Refinement Encoding

Function $\texttt{check}(p_{src}, p_{tgt}, s_s)$ generates an SMT expression that encodes refinement between the source and target programs, respectively, p_{src} and p_{tgt}.

We first define refinement between two concrete states. As Alive does, AliveInLean only checks the value of the root variable of a program. Given a root variable r, a concrete state s'_c refines s_c, or $s'_c \sqsubseteq s_c$, if (1) s_c has undefined behavior, or (2) both s_c and s'_c have values assigned to r, say v and v', and $v = \texttt{poison} \vee v' = v$. A target program p_{tgt} refines program p_{src} if $\texttt{run}(p_{tgt}, s_c) \sqsubseteq \texttt{run}(p_{src}, s_c)$ holds for any initial concrete state s_c,.

The correctness of `check` is stated as follows.

Theorem 2. *Given an initial symbolic state s_s, if $\eta_0[\![\texttt{check}(p_{src}, p_{tgt}, s_s)]\!] \sim$ true for any η_0, then for any environment η and initial state s_c s.t. $\eta[\![s_s]\!] \sim s_c$, we have that $\texttt{run}(p_{tgt}, s_c) \sqsubseteq \texttt{run}(p_{src}, s_c)$.*

This theorem says that if the returned expression of `check` evaluates to true in any environment, program p_{tgt} refines program p_{src}.

4.3 Validity of Trust-Base

Testing Specification of SMT Expressions. Specifications of SMT expressions are traversed using Lean's metaprogramming language and tested. The testing we have done is different from QuickChick [4] because QuickChick evaluates expressions in Coq. The approach cannot be used here because SMT expressions need to be evaluated in an SMT solver (e.g., Z3). Example spec:

```
forall {sz : size} (s1 s2 : sbitvec sz) (b1 b2 : bitvector sz),
  bv_equiv s1 b1 -> bv_equiv s2 b2 ->
    bv_equiv (sbitvec.add s1 s2) (bitvector.add b1 b2)
```

This spec says that if SMT expressions `s1`, `s2` of a bit-vector type (`sbitvec`) are equivalent to two concrete bit-vector values `b1`, `b2` in Lean (`bitvector`), an add expression of `s1`, `s2` is equivalent to the result of adding `b1` and `b2`. Function `bitvector.add` must be called in Lean, so its operands (`b1`, `b2`) are assigned random values in Lean. `sbitvec.add` is translated to SMT's `bvadd` expression, and `s1` and `s2` are initialized as `BitVec` variables in an SMT solver. The testing function generates an SMT expression with random inputs like the following:

```
(assert (forall ((s1 (_ BitVec 4))) (forall ((s2 (_ BitVec 4)))
  (=> (= s1 #xA) (=> (= s2 #x2) (= (bvadd s1 s2) #xC))))))
```

The size of bitvector (`sz`) is initialized to 4, and `b1`, `b2` were randomly initialized to 10 (`#xA`) and 2 (`#x2`). A specification is incorrect if the generated SMT expression is not valid.

Testing Specification of LLVM IR. Specification of LLVM IR is tested using randomly generated IR programs. IR programs of 5–10 randomly chosen instructions are generated, compiled with LLVM, and ran. The result of the execution of the program is compared with the result of AliveInLean's IR interpreter.

5 Evaluation

For the evaluation, we used a computer with an Intel Core i5-6600 CPU and 8 GB of RAM, and Z3 [13] for SMT solving. To test whether AliveInLean and Alive give the same result, we used all of the 150 integer optimizations from Alive's test suite that are supported by AliveInLean. No mismatches were observed.

To test the SMT specification, we randomly generated 10,000 tests for each of the operations (18 bit-vector and 15 boolean). This test took 3 CPU hours.

The LLVM IR specification was tested by running 1,000,000 random IR programs in our interpreter and comparing the output with that of LLVM. This comparison needs to take into account that some programs may trigger UB or yield a poison value, which gives freedom to LLVM to produce a variety of results. These tests took 10 CPU hours overall. Four admitted arithmetic lemmas were tested as well. As a side-effect of the testing, we found several miscompilation bugs in LLVM.[2]

AliveInLean[3] consists of 11.9K lines of code. The optimization verifier consists of 2.2K LoC, the specification tester is 1.5K, and the proof has 8.1K lines. It took 3 person-months to implement the tool and prove its correctness.

6 Related Work

We introduce previous work on compiler verification and validation and compare it with AliveInLean. Also, we give an overview on previous work on semantics of compiler intermediate representations (IRs).

---

[2] https://llvm.org/PR40657.

[3] https://github.com/Microsoft/AliveInLean.

6.1 Compiler Verification

Proving Correctness on Formal Semantics. The correctness of compilation can be proved on a formal semantics of a language that is written in a theorem proving language such as Coq. Vellvm [26] is a Coq formalization of the semantics of LLVM IR. CompCert [11] is a verified C compiler written in Coq, and its compilation to assembly languages including x86, PowerPC is proved correct.

However, it is hard to apply this approach to existing industrial compilers because proving correctness of optimizations requires non-trivial effort. Peek [15] is a framework for implementing and verifying peephole optimizations for x86 on CompCert. They implemented 28 peephole optimizations which required 3.3k lines of code and 6.6k lines of proofs (~350 LoC each). Even if this is small compared to the size of CompCert, the burden is non-trivial considering that LLVM has more than 1,000 peephole optimizations [12].

Another problem with this approach is that changing the semantics requires modification of the proof. The semantics of `poison` and `undef` value of LLVM is currently not consistent and thus it triggers miscompilations of some programs [10]. Therefore, compiler developers regularly test various `undef` semantics with existing optimizations, which would be a non-trivial task if correctness proofs had to be manually updated.

Translation Validation and Credible Compilation. In translation validation [18], a pair of an original program and an optimized program is given to a validation tool at compile time to check the correctness of the optimization. Several such tools exist for LLVM [20,22,25]. Translation validation is, however, slow, and it cannot tell whether an optimization is correct in general. Consider this optimization:

```
z = 0 - (x / C)
  =>
z = x / -C
```

If `C` is a constant, `-C` can be computed at compile time. However, this optimization is wrong only if `C` is `INT_MIN`. To show that compilation is fully correct, translation validation would need to be run for every combination of inputs.

Credible compilation [19], or witnessing compiler [16,17], is an approach to improve translation validation by accepting witnesses generated by a compiler. Crellvm [8] is a credible compilation framework for LLVM. It requires modifications to the compiler, which makes it harder to apply and maintain.

6.2 Solver-Aided Programming Languages

Proving correctness of optimizations can be represented as a search problem that finds a counter-example for the optimization. Tools like Z3, CVC4 can be used to solve the search problem. Translation of a high-level search problem to the external solver's input has been considered bug-prone, and frameworks like

Rosette [21] and Smten [23] address this issue by providing higher-level languages for describing the search problem. SpaceSearch [24] helps programmers prove the correctness of the description by supporting Coq and Rosette backends from a single specification. AliveInLean provides a stronger guarantee of correctness because translation to SMT expressions is also written in Lean, leaving Lean as the sole trust-base.

6.3 Semantics of Compiler IR

Correctly encoding semantics of compiler IR is important for the validity of a tool. LLVM IR is an SSA-based intermediate representation which is used to represent a program being compiled. LLVM LangRef [1] has an informal definition of the LLVM IR, but there are a few known problems. [10] shows that the semantics of `poison` and `undef` values are inconsistent. [9] shows that the semantics of pointer↔integer casting is inconsistent. AliveInLean supports `poison` but not `undef`, following the suggestion from [10]. AliveInLean does not support memory-related operations including load, store, and pointer ↔ integer casting.

7 Discussion

AliveInLean has several limitations. As discussed before, AliveInLean does not support memory operations. Correctly encoding the memory model of LLVM IR is challenging because the memory model of LLVM IR is more complex than either a byte array or a set of memory objects [9]. Supporting branch instructions and floating point would help developers prove interesting optimizations. Supporting branches is a challenging job especially when loops are involved.

Maintainability of AliveInLean highly relies on one's proficiency in Lean. Changing the semantics of an IR instruction breaks the proof, and updating it requires proficiency in Lean. However, we believe that only relevant parts in the proof need to be updated as the proof is modularized.

Alive has features that are absent in AliveInLean. Alive supports defining a precondition for an optimization, inferring types of variables if not given, and showing counter-examples if the optimization is wrong. We leave this as future work.

8 Conclusion

AliveInLean is a formally verified compiler optimization verifier. Its verification condition generator is formally verified with a machine-checked proof. Using AliveInLean, developers can easily check the correctness of compiler optimizations with high reliability. Also, they can use AliveInLean as a formal framework like Vellvm to prove properties of interest in limited cases. The extensive random testing did not find problems in the trust base, increasing its trustworthiness. Moreover, as a side-effect of the IR semantics testing, we found several bugs in LLVM.

Acknowledgments. The authors thank Leonardo de Moura and Sebastian Ullrich for their help with Lean. This work was supported in part by the Basic Science Research Program through the National Research Foundation of Korea (NRF) funded by the Ministry of Science and ICT (2017R1A2B2007512). The first author was supported by a Korea Foundation for Advanced Studies scholarship.

References

1. LLVM language reference manual. https://llvm.org/docs/LangRef.html
2. Barbosa, H., Blanchette, J.C., Fontaine, P.: Scalable fine-grained proofs for formula processing. In: de Moura, L. (ed.) CADE 2017. LNCS (LNAI), vol. 10395, pp. 398–412. Springer, Cham (2017). https://doi.org/10.1007/978-3-319-63046-5_25
3. Böhme, S., Fox, A.C.J., Sewell, T., Weber, T.: Reconstruction of Z3's bit-vector proofs in HOL4 and Isabelle/HOL. In: Jouannaud, J.-P., Shao, Z. (eds.) CPP 2011. LNCS, vol. 7086, pp. 183–198. Springer, Heidelberg (2011). https://doi.org/10.1007/978-3-642-25379-9_15
4. Dénès, M., Hriţcu, C., Lampropoulos, L., Paraskevopoulou, Z., Pierce, B.C.: Quickchick : Property-based Testing for Coq (2014)
5. Ebner, G., Ullrich, S., Roesch, J., Avigad, J., de Moura, L.: A metaprogramming framework for formal verification. Proc. ACM Program. Lang. **1**(ICFP), 34:1–34:29 (2017). https://doi.org/10.1145/3110278
6. Ekici, B., et al.: SMTCoq: a plug-in for integrating SMT solvers into Coq. In: Computer Aided Verification, pp. 126–133 (2017)
7. Hadarean, L., Barrett, C., Reynolds, A., Tinelli, C., Deters, M.: Fine grained SMT proofs for the theory of fixed-width bit-vectors. In: Davis, M., Fehnker, A., McIver, A., Voronkov, A. (eds.) LPAR 2015. LNCS, vol. 9450, pp. 340–355. Springer, Heidelberg (2015). https://doi.org/10.1007/978-3-662-48899-7_24
8. Kang, J., et al.: Crellvm: verified credible compilation for LLVM. In: Proceedings of the 39th ACM SIGPLAN Conference on Programming Language Design and Implementation, pp. 631–645. ACM (2018). https://doi.org/10.1145/3192366.3192377
9. Lee, J., Hur, C.K., Jung, R., Liu, Z., Regehr, J., Lopes, N.P.: Reconciling high-level optimizations and low-level code in LLVM. Proc. ACM Program. Lang. **2**(OOPSLA), 125:1–125:28 (2018). https://doi.org/10.1145/3276495
10. Lee, J., et al.: Taming undefined behavior in LLVM. In: Proceedings of the 38th ACM SIGPLAN Conference on Programming Language Design and Implementation, pp. 633–647. ACM (2017). https://doi.org/10.1145/3062341.3062343
11. Leroy, X.: Formal verification of a realistic compiler. Commun. ACM **52**(7), 107–115 (2009). https://doi.org/10.1145/1538788.1538814
12. Lopes, N.P., Menendez, D., Nagarakatte, S., Regehr, J.: Provably correct peephole optimizations with alive. In: Proceedings of the 36th ACM SIGPLAN Conference on Programming Language Design and Implementation, pp. 22–32. ACM (2015). https://doi.org/10.1145/2737924.2737965
13. de Moura, L., Bjørner, N.: Z3: an efficient SMT solver. In: Ramakrishnan, C.R., Rehof, J. (eds.) TACAS 2008. LNCS, vol. 4963, pp. 337–340. Springer, Heidelberg (2008). https://doi.org/10.1007/978-3-540-78800-3_24
14. de Moura, L., Kong, S., Avigad, J., van Doorn, F., von Raumer, J.: The lean theorem prover (System Description). In: Felty, A.P., Middeldorp, A. (eds.) CADE 2015. LNCS (LNAI), vol. 9195, pp. 378–388. Springer, Cham (2015). https://doi.org/10.1007/978-3-319-21401-6_26

15. Mullen, E., Zuniga, D., Tatlock, Z., Grossman, D.: Verified peephole optimizations for CompCert. In: Proceedings of the 37th ACM SIGPLAN Conference on Programming Language Design and Implementation, pp. 448–461. ACM (2016). https://doi.org/10.1145/2908080.2908109
16. Namjoshi, K.S., Tagliabue, G., Zuck, L.D.: A witnessing compiler: a proof of concept. In: Legay, A., Bensalem, S. (eds.) RV 2013. LNCS, vol. 8174, pp. 340–345. Springer, Heidelberg (2013). https://doi.org/10.1007/978-3-642-40787-1_22
17. Namjoshi, K.S., Zuck, L.D.: Witnessing program transformations. In: Logozzo, F., Fähndrich, M. (eds.) SAS 2013. LNCS, vol. 7935, pp. 304–323. Springer, Heidelberg (2013). https://doi.org/10.1007/978-3-642-38856-9_17
18. Pnueli, A., Siegel, M., Singerman, E.: Translation validation. In: Steffen, B. (ed.) TACAS 1998. LNCS, vol. 1384, pp. 151–166. Springer, Heidelberg (1998). https://doi.org/10.1007/BFb0054170
19. Rinard, M.C., Marinov, D.: Credible compilation with pointers. In: Proceedings of the Workshop on Run-Time Result Verification (1999)
20. Stepp, M., Tate, R., Lerner, S.: Equality-based translation validator for LLVM. In: Gopalakrishnan, G., Qadeer, S. (eds.) CAV 2011. LNCS, vol. 6806, pp. 737–742. Springer, Heidelberg (2011). https://doi.org/10.1007/978-3-642-22110-1_59
21. Torlak, E., Bodik, R.: Growing solver-aided languages with Rosette. In: Proceedings of the 2013 ACM International Symposium on New Ideas, New Paradigms, and Reflections on Programming & Software, pp. 135–152. ACM (2013). https://doi.org/10.1145/2509578.2509586
22. Tristan, J.B., Govereau, P., Morrisett, G.: Evaluating value-graph translation validation for LLVM. In: Proceedings of the 32nd ACM SIGPLAN Conference on Programming Language Design and Implementation, pp. 295–305. ACM (2011). https://doi.org/10.1145/1993498.1993533
23. Uhler, R., Dave, N.: Smten: automatic translation of high-level symbolic computations into SMT queries. In: Sharygina, N., Veith, H. (eds.) CAV 2013. LNCS, vol. 8044, pp. 678–683. Springer, Heidelberg (2013). https://doi.org/10.1007/978-3-642-39799-8_45
24. Weitz, K., Lyubomirsky, S., Heule, S., Torlak, E., Ernst, M.D., Tatlock, Z.: Spacesearch: a library for building and verifying solver-aided tools. Proc. ACM Program. Lang. **1**(ICFP), 25:1–25:28 (2017). https://doi.org/10.1145/3110269
25. Zaks, A., Pnueli, A.: CoVaC: compiler validation by program analysis of the cross-product. In: Cuellar, J., Maibaum, T., Sere, K. (eds.) FM 2008. LNCS, vol. 5014, pp. 35–51. Springer, Heidelberg (2008). https://doi.org/10.1007/978-3-540-68237-0_5
26. Zhao, J., Nagarakatte, S., Martin, M.M., Zdancewic, S.: Formalizing the LLVM intermediate representation for verified program transformations. In: Proceedings of the 39th Annual ACM SIGPLAN-SIGACT Symposium on Principles of Programming Languages, pp. 427–440. ACM (2012). https://doi.org/10.1145/2103656.2103709

Concurrency

Automated Parameterized Verification of CRDTs

Kartik Nagar(✉) and Suresh Jagannathan

Purdue University, West Lafayette, USA
{nagark,suresh}@cs.purdue.edu

Abstract. Maintaining multiple replicas of data is crucial to achieving scalability, availability and low latency in distributed applications. *Conflict-free Replicated Data Types* (CRDTs) are important building blocks in this domain because they are designed to operate correctly under the myriad behaviors possible in a weakly-consistent distributed setting. Because of the possibility of concurrent updates to the same object at different replicas, and the absence of any ordering guarantees on these updates, *convergence* is an important correctness criterion for CRDTs. This property asserts that two replicas which receive the same set of updates (in any order) must nonetheless converge to the same state. One way to prove that operations on a CRDT converge is to show that they commute since commutative actions by definition behave the same regardless of the order in which they execute. In this paper, we present a framework for automatically verifying convergence of CRDTs under different weak-consistency policies. Surprisingly, depending upon the consistency policy supported by the underlying system, we show that not all operations of a CRDT need to commute to achieve convergence. We develop a proof rule parameterized by a consistency specification based on the concepts of *commutativity modulo consistency policy* and *non-interference to commutativity*. We describe the design and implementation of a verification engine equipped with this rule and show how it can be used to provide the first automated convergence proofs for a number of challenging CRDTs, including sets, lists, and graphs.

1 Introduction

For distributed applications, keeping a single copy of data at one location or multiple fully-synchronized copies (i.e. state-machine replication) at different locations, makes the application susceptible to loss of availability due to network and machine failures. On the other hand, having multiple un-synchronized replicas of the data results in high availability, fault tolerance and uniform low latency, albeit at the expense of consistency. In the latter case, an update issued at one replica can be asynchronously transmitted to other replicas, allowing the system to operate continuously even in the presence of network or node failures [8]. However, mechanisms must now be provided to ensure replicas are kept consistent with each other in the face of concurrent updates and arbitrary re-ordering of such updates by the underlying network.

I. Dillig and S. Tasiran (Eds.): CAV 2019, LNCS 11562, pp. 459–477, 2019.
https://doi.org/10.1007/978-3-030-25543-5_26

Over the last few years, *Conflict-free Replicated Datatypes* (CRDTs) [19–21] have emerged as a popular solution to this problem. In op-based CRDTs, when an operation on a CRDT instance is issued at a replica, an *effector* (basically an update function) is generated locally, which is then asynchronously transmitted (and applied) at all other replicas.[1] Over the years, a number of CRDTs have been developed for common datatypes such as maps, sets, lists, graphs, etc.

The primary correctness criterion for a CRDT implementation is *convergence* (sometimes called *strong eventual consistency* [9,20] (SEC)): two replicas which have received the same set of effectors must converge to the same CRDT state. Because of the weak default guarantees assumed to be provided by the underlying network, however, we must consider the possibility that effectors can be applied in arbitrary order on different replicas, complicating correctness arguments. This complexity is further exacerbated because CRDTs impose no limitations on how often they are invoked, and may assume additional properties on network behaviour [14] that must be taken into account when formulating correctness arguments.

Given these complexities, verifying convergence of operations in a replicated setting has proven to be challenging and error-prone [9]. In response, several recent efforts have used mechanized proof assistants to yield formal machine-checked proofs of correctness [9,24]. While mechanization clearly offers stronger assurance guarantees than handwritten proofs, it still demands substantial manual proof engineering effort to be successful. In particular, correctness arguments are typically given in terms of constraints on CRDT states that must be satisfied by the underlying network model responsible for delivering updates performed by other replicas. Relating the state of a CRDT at one replica with the visibility properties allowed by the underlying network has typically involved constructing an intricate simulation argument or crafting a suitably precise invariant to establish convergence. This level of sophisticated reasoning is required for every CRDT and consistency model under consideration. There is a notable lack of techniques capable of reasoning about CRDT correctness under different weak consistency policies, even though such techniques exist for other correctness criteria such as preservation of state invariants [10,11] or serializability [4,16] under weak consistency.

To overcome these challenges, we propose a novel *automated* verification strategy that does not require complex proof-engineering of handcrafted simulation arguments or invariants. Instead, our methodology allows us to directly connect constraints on events imposed by the consistency model with constraints on states required to prove convergence. Consistency model constraints are extracted from an axiomatization of network behavior, while state constraints are generated using reasoning principles that determine the *commutativity* and *non-interference* of sequences of effectors, subject to these consistency constraints. Both sets of constraints can be solved using off-the-shelf theorem

[1] In this work, we focus on the op-based CRDT model; however, our technique naturally extends to state-based CRDTs since they can be emulated by an op-based model [20].

provers. Because an important advantage of our approach is that it is parametric on weak consistency schemes, we are able to analyze the problem of CRDT convergence under widely different consistency policies (e.g., eventual consistency, causal consistency, parallel snapshot isolation (PSI) [23], among others), and for the first time verify CRDT convergence under such stronger models (efficient implementations of which are supported by real-world data stores). A further pleasant by-product of our approach is a pathway to take advantage of such stronger models to simplify existing CRDT designs and allow composition of CRDTs to yield new instantiations for more complex datatypes.

The paper makes the following contributions:

1. We present a proof methodology for verifying the correctness of CRDTs amenable to automated reasoning.
2. We allow the proof strategy to be parameterized on a weak consistency specification that allows us to state correctness arguments for a CRDT based on constraints imposed by these specifications.
3. We experimentally demonstrate the effectiveness of our proposed verification strategy on a number of challenging CRDT implementations across multiple consistency schemes.

Collectively, these contributions yield (to the best of our knowledge) the first automated and parameterized proof methodology for CRDT verification.

The remainder of the paper is organized as follows. In the next section, we provide further motivation and intuition for our approach. Section 3 formalizes the problem definition, providing an operational semantics and axiomatizations of well-known consistency specifications. Section 4 describes our proof strategy for determining CRDT convergence that is amenable to automated verification. Section 5 provides details about our implementation and experimental results justifying the effectiveness of our framework. Section 6 presents related work and conclusions.

2 Illustrative Example

```
  S∈ ℙ(E)
Add(a):S     λS'.S'∪{a}
Remove(a):S  λS'.S'\{a}
Lookup(a):S  a ∈ S
```

Fig. 1. A simple Set CRDT definition.

We illustrate our approach using a Set CRDT specification as a running example. A CRDT $(\Sigma, O, \sigma_{\mathsf{init}})$ is characterized by a set of states Σ, a set of operations O and an initial state $\sigma_{\mathsf{init}} \in \Sigma$, where each operation $o \in O$ is a function with signature $\Sigma \rightarrow (\Sigma \rightarrow \Sigma)$. The state of a CRDT is replicated, and when operation o is issued at a replica with state σ, the effector $o(\sigma)$ is generated, which is immediately applied at the local replica (which we also call the *source* replica) and transmitted to all other replicas, where it is subsequently applied upon receipt.

Additional constraints on the order in which effectors can be received and applied at different replicas are specified by a consistency policy, discussed below. In the absence of any such additional constraints, however, we assume the underlying network only offers *eventually consistent* guarantees - all replicas eventually receive all effectors generated by all other replicas, with no constraints on the order in which these effectors are received.

Consider the simple Set CRDT definition shown in Fig. 1. Let E be an arbitrary set of elements. The state space Σ is $\mathbb{P}(E)$. `Add(a):S` denotes the operation `Add(a)` applied on a replica with state `S`, which generates an effector which simply adds `a` to the state of all other replicas it is applied to. Similarly, `Remove(a):S` generates an effector that removes `a` on all replicas to which it is applied. `Lookup(a):S` is a query operation which checks whether the queried element is present in the source replica `S`.

A CRDT is *convergent* if during any execution, any two replicas which have received the same set of effectors have the same state. Our strategy to prove convergence is to show that any two effectors of the CRDT pairwise commute with each other modulo a consistency policy, i.e. for two effectors e_1 and e_2, $e_1 \circ e_2 = e_2 \circ e_1$. Our simple Set CRDT clearly does not converge when executed on an eventually consistent data store since the effectors $e_1 =$ `Add(a):S`$_1$ and $e_2 =$ `Remove(a):S`$_2$ do not commute, and the semantics of eventual consistency imposes no additional constraints on the visibility or ordering of these operations that could be used to guarantee convergence. For example, if e_1 is applied to the state at some replica followed by the application of e_2, the resulting state does not include the element `a`; conversely, applying e_2 to a state at some replica followed by e_1 leads to a state that does contain the element `a`. However, while commutativity is a sufficient property to show convergence, it is not always a necessary one. In particular, different consistency models impose different constraints on the visibility and ordering of effectors that can obviate the need to reason about their commutativity. For example, if the consistency model enforces `Add(a)` and `Remove(a)` effectors to be applied in the same order at all replicas, then the Set CRDT will converge. As we will demonstrate later, the PSI consistency model exactly matches this requirement. To further illustrate this, consider the definition of the ORSet CRDT shown in Fig. 2. Here, every element is tagged with a unique identifier (coming from the set I). `Add(a,i):S` simply adds the element `a` tagged with `i`[2], while `Remove(a):S` returns an effector that when applied to a replica state will remove all tagged versions of `a` that were present in `S`, the source replica.

```
S∈ ℙ(E × I)
Add(a,i):S
  λS'.S'∪{(a,i)}
Remove(a):S
  λS'.S'\{(a,i):(a,i)∈S}
Lookup(a):S
  ∃(a,i)∈A
```

Fig. 2. A definition of an ORSet CRDT.

[2] Assume that every call to `Add` uses a unique identifier, which can be easily arranged, for example by keeping a local counter at every replica which is incremented at every operation invocation, and using the id of the replica and the value of the counter as a unique identifier.

Suppose e_1 =`Add(a,i):S`$_1$ and e_2 =`Remove(a):S`$_2$. If it is the case that `S`$_2$ does not contain `(a,i)`, then these two effectors are guaranteed to commute because e_2 is unaware of `(a,i)` and thus behaves as a no-op with respect to effector e_1 when it is applied to any replica state. Suppose, however, that e_1's effect was visible to e_2; in other words, e_1 is applied to `S`$_2$ before e_2 is generated. There are two possible scenarios that must be considered. (1) Another replica (call it `S'`) has e_2 applied before e_1. Its final state reflects the effect of the `Add` operation, while `S`$_2$'s final state reflects the effect of applying the `Remove`; clearly, convergence is violated in this case. (2) All replicas apply e_1 and e_2 in the same order; the interesting case here is when the effect of e_1 is always applied before e_2 on every replica. The constraint that induces an effector order between e_1 and e_2 on every replica as a consequence of e_1's visibility to e_2 on `S`$_2$ is supported by a causally consistent distributed storage model. Under causal consistency, whenever e_2 is applied to a replica state, we are guaranteed that e_1's effect, which adds `(a,i)` to the state, would have occurred. Thus, even though e_1 and e_2 do not commute when applied to an arbitrary state, their execution under causal consistency nonetheless allows us to show that all replica states converge. The essence of our proof methodology is therefore to reason about *commutativity modulo consistency* - it is only for those CRDT operations unaffected by the constraints imposed by the consistency model that proving commutativity is required. Consistency properties that affect the visibility of effectors are instead used to guide and simplify our analysis. Applying this notion to pairs of effectors in arbitrarily long executions requires incorporating commutativity properties under a more general induction principle to allow us to generalize the commutativity of effectors in bounded executions to the unbounded case. This generalization forms the heart of our automated verification strategy.

```
  S∈ ℙ(E × I) × ℙ(E × I)
Add(a,i):(A,R)
  λ(A',R').(A'∪{(a,i)},R')

Remove(a):(A,R)
  λ(A',R').(A',R'∪{(a,i):(a,i)∈A}

Lookup(a):(A,R)
  ∃(a,i)∈A∧(a,i)∉R
```

Fig. 3. A variant of the ORSet using tombstones.

Figure 3 defines an ORSet with "tombstone" markers used to keep track of deleted elements in a separate set. Our proof methodology is sufficient to automatically show that this CRDT converges under EC.

3 Problem Definition

In this section, we formalize the problem of determining convergence in CRDTs parametric to a weak consistency policy. First, we define a general operational semantics to describe all valid executions of a CRDT under any given weak consistency policy. As stated earlier, a CRDT program $\mathcal{P}$ is specified by the tuple $(\Sigma, O, \sigma_{\mathsf{init}})$. Here, we find it to convenient to define an operation $o \in O$ as a function $(\Sigma \times (\Sigma \rightarrow \Sigma)^*) \rightarrow (\Sigma \rightarrow \Sigma)$. Instead of directly taking as input a generating state, operations are now defined to take as input a start state and a sequence of effectors. The intended semantics is that the sequence of effectors would be applied to the start state to obtain the generating state. Using this syntax allows us simplify the presentation of the proof methodology in the next section, since we can abstract a history of effectors into an equivalent start state.

Formally, if $\hat{o} : \Sigma \rightarrow (\Sigma \rightarrow \Sigma)$ was the original op-based definition, then we define the operation $o : (\Sigma \times (\Sigma \rightarrow \Sigma)^*) \rightarrow (\Sigma \rightarrow \Sigma)$ as follows:

$$\begin{array}{ll} \forall \sigma. & o(\sigma, \epsilon) = \hat{o}(\sigma) \\ \forall \sigma, \pi, f. & o(\sigma, \pi f) = o(f(\sigma), \pi) \end{array}$$

Note that ϵ indicates the empty sequence. Hence, for all states σ and sequence of functions π, we have $o(\sigma, \pi) = \hat{o}(\pi(\sigma))$.

To define the operational semantics, we abstract away from the concept of replicas, and instead maintain a global pool of effectors. A new CRDT operation is executed against a CRDT state obtained by first selecting a subset of effectors from the global pool and then applying the elements in that set in some non-deterministically chosen permutation to the initial CRDT state. The choice of effectors and their permutation must obey the weak consistency policy specification. Given a CRDT $\mathcal{P} = (\Sigma, O, \sigma_{\mathsf{init}})$ and a weak consistency policy Ψ, we define a **labeled transition system** $\mathcal{S}_{\mathcal{P},\Psi} = (\mathcal{C}, \rightarrow)$, where $\mathcal{C}$ is a set of configurations and $\rightarrow$ is the transition relation. A **configuration** $c = (\Delta, \mathsf{vis}, \mathsf{eo})$ consists of three components: Δ is a set of events, $\mathsf{vis} \subseteq \Delta \times \Delta$ is a *visibility* relation, and $\mathsf{eo} \subseteq \Delta \times \Delta$ is a global *effector order* relation (constrained to be anti-symmetric). An **event** $\eta \in \Delta$ is a tuple $(\mathsf{eid}, o, \sigma_s, \Delta_r, \mathsf{eo})$ where eid is a unique event id, $o \in O$ is a CRDT operation, $\sigma_s \in \Sigma$ is the start CRDT state, Δ_r is the set of events visible to η (also called the history of η), and eo is a total order on the events in Δ_r (also called the local effector order relation). We assume projection functions for each component of an event (for example $\sigma_s(\eta)$ projects the start state of the event η).

Given an event $\eta = (\mathsf{eid}, o, \sigma_s, \Delta_r, \mathsf{eo})$, we define η^e to be the **effector** associated with the event. This effector is obtained by executing the CRDT operation o against the start CRDT state σ_s and the sequence of effectors obtained from the events in Δ_r arranged in the reverse order of eo. Formally,

$$\eta^e = \begin{cases} o(\sigma_s, \epsilon) & \text{if } \Delta_r = \phi \\ o(\sigma_s, \prod_{i=1}^{k} \eta^e_{P(i)}) & \text{if } \Delta_r = \{\eta_1, \ldots, \eta_k\} \text{ where } P : \{1, \ldots, k\} \rightarrow \{1, \ldots, k\} \\ & \forall i, j. i < j \Rightarrow (\eta_{P(j)}, \eta_{P(i)}) \in \mathsf{eo} \end{cases} \tag{1}$$

In the above definition, when Δ_r is non-empty, we define a permutation P of the events in Δ_r such that the permutation order is the inverse of the effector order eo. This ensures that if $(\eta_i, \eta_j) \in \mathsf{eo}$, then η^e_j occurs before η^e_i in the sequence passed to the CRDT operation o, effectively applying η^e_i before η^e_j to obtain the generating state for o.

The following rule describes the transitions allowed in $\mathcal{S}_{\mathcal{P},\Psi}$:

$$\frac{\begin{array}{c}\Delta_r \subseteq \Delta \quad o \in O \quad \sigma_s \in \Sigma \quad \mathsf{eo}_r \text{ is a total order on } \Delta_r \\ \mathsf{eo} \subseteq \mathsf{eo}_r \quad \text{fresh id} \quad \eta = (\mathsf{id}, o, \sigma_s, \Delta_r, \mathsf{eo}) \\ \Delta' = \Delta \cup \{\eta\} \quad \mathsf{vis}' = \mathsf{vis} \cup \{(\eta', \eta) \mid \eta' \in \Delta_r\} \quad \Psi(\Delta', \mathsf{vis}', \mathsf{eo}')\end{array}}{(\Delta, \mathsf{vis}, \mathsf{eo}) \xrightarrow{\eta} (\Delta', \mathsf{vis}', \mathsf{eo}')}$$

The rule describes the effect of executing a new operation o, which begins by first selecting a subset of already completed events (Δ_r) and a total order eo_r on these events which obeys the global effector order eo. This mimics applying the operation o on an arbitrary replica on which the events of Δ_r have been applied in the order eo_r. A new event (η) corresponding to the issued operation o is computed, which is used to label the transition and is also added to the current configuration. All the events in Δ_r are visible to the new event η, which is reflected in the new visibility relation vis'. The system moves to the new configuration $(\Delta', \mathsf{vis}', \mathsf{eo}')$ which must satisfy the consistency policy Ψ. Note that even though the general transition rule allows the event to pick any arbitrary start state σ_s, we restrict the start state of all events in a **well-formed execution** to be the initial CRDT state σ_{init}, i.e. the state in which all replicas begin their execution. A trace of $\mathcal{S}_{\mathcal{P},\Psi}$ is a sequence of transitions. Let $[\![\mathcal{S}_{\mathcal{P},\Psi}]\!]$ be the set of all finite traces. Given a trace τ, $L(\tau)$ denotes all events (i.e. labels) in τ.

Definition 1 (Well-formed Execution). *A trace $\tau \in [\![\mathcal{S}_{\mathcal{P},\Psi}]\!]$ is a well-formed execution if it begins from the empty configuration $C_{\mathsf{init}} = (\{\}, \{\}, \{\})$ and $\forall \eta \in L(\tau)$, $\sigma_s(\eta) = \sigma_{\mathsf{init}}$.*

Let $\mathcal{WF}(\mathcal{S}_{\mathcal{P},\Psi})$ denote all well-formed executions of $\mathcal{S}_{\mathcal{P},\Psi}$. The **consistency policy** $\Psi(\Delta, \mathsf{vis}, \mathsf{eo})$ is a formula constraining the events in Δ and relations vis and eo defined over these events. Below, we illustrate how to express certain well-known consistency policies in our framework:

Consistency scheme	$\Psi(\Delta, \mathsf{vis}, \mathsf{eo})$
Eventual Consistency [3]	$\forall \eta, \eta' \in \Delta. \neg \mathsf{eo}(\eta, \eta')$
Causal Consistency [14]	$\forall \eta, \eta' \in \Delta. \mathsf{vis}(\eta, \eta') \Leftrightarrow \mathsf{eo}(\eta, \eta')$
	$\wedge \forall \eta, \eta', \eta'' \in \Delta. \mathsf{vis}(\eta, \eta') \wedge \mathsf{vis}(\eta', \eta'') \Rightarrow \mathsf{vis}(\eta, \eta'')$
RedBlue Consistency (O_r) [13]	$\forall \eta, \eta' \in \Delta. o(\eta) \in O_r \wedge o(\eta') \in O_r \wedge \mathsf{vis}(\eta, \eta') \Leftrightarrow \mathsf{eo}(\eta, \eta')$
	$\wedge \forall \eta, \eta' \in \Delta. o(\eta) \in O_r \wedge o(\eta') \in O_r \Rightarrow \mathsf{vis}(\eta, \eta') \vee \mathsf{vis}(\eta', \eta)$
Parallel Snapshot Isolation [23]	$\forall \eta, \eta' \in \Delta. (\mathsf{Wr}(\eta^e) \cap \mathsf{Wr}(\eta'^e) \neq \phi \wedge \mathsf{vis}(\eta, \eta')) \Leftrightarrow \mathsf{eo}(\eta, \eta')$
	$\wedge \forall \eta, \eta' \in \Delta. \mathsf{Wr}(\eta^e) \cap \mathsf{Wr}(\eta'^e) \neq \phi \Rightarrow \mathsf{vis}(\eta, \eta') \vee \mathsf{vis}(\eta', \eta)$
Strong Consistency	$\forall \eta, \eta' \in \Delta. \mathsf{vis}(\eta, \eta') \Leftrightarrow \mathsf{eo}(\eta, \eta')$
	$\wedge \forall \eta, \eta' \in \Delta. \mathsf{vis}(\eta, \eta') \vee \mathsf{vis}(\eta', \eta)$

For Eventual Consistency (EC) [3], we do not place any constraints on the visibility order and require the global effector order to be empty. This reflects the fact that in EC, any number of events can occur concurrently at different replicas, and hence a replica can witness any arbitrary subset of events which may be applied in any order. In Causal Consistency (CC) [14], an event is applied at a replica only if all causally dependent events have already been applied. An event η_1 is causally dependent on η_2 if η_1 was generated at a replica where either η_2 or any other event causally dependent on η_2 had already been applied. The visibility relation vis captures causal dependency, and by making vis transitive, we ensure that all causal dependencies of events in Δ_r are also present in Δ_r (this is because in the transition rule, Ψ is checked on the updated visibility relation which relates events in Δ_r with the newly generated event). Further, causally dependent events must be applied in the same order at all replicas, which we capture by asserting that vis implies eo. In RedBlue Consistency (RB) [13], a subset of CRDT operations ($O_r \subseteq O$) are synchronized, so that they must occur in the same order at all replicas. We express RB in our framework by requiring the visibility relation to be total among events whose operations are in O_r. In Parallel Snapshot Isolation (PSI) [23], two events which conflict with each other (because they write to a common variable) are not allowed to be executed concurrently, but are synchronized across all replicas to be executed in the same order. Similar to [10], we assume that when a CRDT is used under PSI, its state space Σ is a map from variables to values, and every operation generates an effector which simply writes to certain variables. We assume that $\mathsf{Wr}(\eta^e)$ returns the set of variables written by the effector η^e, and express PSI in our framework by requiring that events which write a common variable are applied in the same order (determined by their visibility relation) across all replicas; furthermore, the policy requires that the visibility operation among such events is total. Finally, in Strong Consistency, the visibility relation is total and all effectors are applied in the same order at all replicas.

Given an execution $\tau \in [\![\mathcal{S}_{\mathcal{P},\Psi}]\!]$ and a transition $C \xrightarrow{\eta} C'$ in τ, we associate a set of replica states Σ_η that the event can potentially witness, by considering all permutations of the effectors visible to η which obey the global effector order, when applied to the start state $\sigma_s(\eta)$. Formally, this is defined as follows, assuming $\eta = (\mathsf{eid}, o, \sigma_s, \{\eta_1, \ldots, \eta_k\}, \mathsf{eo}_r)$ and $C = (\Delta, \mathsf{vis}, \mathsf{eo})$):

$$\begin{aligned}\Sigma_\eta = \{&\eta^e_{P(1)} \circ \eta^e_{P(2)} \circ \ldots \circ \eta^e_{P(k)}(\sigma_s) \mid P : \{1, \ldots, k\} \to \{1, \ldots, k\},\\ &\mathsf{eo}_P \text{ is a total order }, i < j \Rightarrow (\eta_{P(j)}, \eta_{P(i)}) \in \mathsf{eo}_P,\ \mathsf{eo} \subseteq \mathsf{eo}_P\}\end{aligned}$$

In the above definition, for all valid local effector orders eo_P, we compute the CRDT states obtained on applying those effectors on the start CRDT state, which constitute Σ_η. The original event η presumably would have witnessed one of these states.

Definition 2 (Convergent Event). *Given an execution $\tau \in [\![\mathcal{S}_{\mathcal{P},\Psi}]\!]$ and an event $\eta \in L(\tau)$, η is convergent if Σ_η is singleton.*

Definition 3 (Strong Eventual Consistency). *A CRDT* $(\Sigma, O, \sigma_{\mathsf{init}})$ *achieves strong eventual consistency* (SEC)*under a weak consistency specification* Ψ *if for all well-formed executions* $\tau \in \mathcal{WF}(\mathcal{S}_{\mathcal{P},\Psi})$ *and for all events* $\eta \in L(\tau)$*,* η *is convergent.*

An event is convergent if all valid permutations of visible events according to the specification Ψ lead to the same state. This corresponds to the requirement that if two replicas have witnessed the same set of operations, they must be in the same state. A CRDT achieves SEC if all events in all executions are convergent.

4 Automated Verification

In order to show that a CRDT achieves SEC under a consistency specification, we need to show that all events in any execution are convergent, which in turn requires us to show that any valid permutation of valid subsets of events in an execution leads to the same state. This is a hard problem because we have to reason about executions of unbounded length, involving unbounded sets of effectors and reconcile the declarative event-based specifications of weak consistency with states generated during execution. To make the problem tractable, we use a two-fold strategy. First, we show that if any pair of effectors generated during any execution either commute with each other or are forced to be applied in the same order by the consistency policy, then the CRDT achieves SEC. Second, we develop an inductive proof rule to show that *all* pairs of effectors generated during any (potentially unbounded) execution obey the above mentioned property. To ensure soundness of the proof rule, we place some reasonable assumptions on the consistency policy that (intuitively) requires behaviorally equivalent events to be treated the same by the policy, regardless of context (i.e., the length of the execution history at the time the event is applied). We then extract a simple sufficient condition which we call as *non-interference to commutativity* that captures the heart of the inductive argument. Notably, this condition can be automatically checked for different CRDTs under different consistency policies using off-the-shelf theorem provers, thus providing a pathway to performing automated parametrized verification of CRDTs.

Given a transition $(\Delta, \mathsf{vis}, \mathsf{eo}) \xrightarrow{\eta} C$, we denote the global effector order in the starting configuration of η, i.e. eo as eo_η. We first show that a sufficient condition to prove that a CRDT is convergent is to show that any two events in its history either commute or are related by the global effector order.

Lemma 1. *Given an execution* $\tau \in [\![\mathcal{S}_{\mathcal{P},\Psi}]\!]$*, and an event* $\eta = (\mathsf{id}, o, \sigma_s, \Delta_r, \mathsf{eo}_r) \in L(\tau)$*, if for all* $\eta_1, \eta_2 \in \Delta_r$ *such that* $\eta_1 \neq \eta_2$*, either* $\eta_1^e \circ \eta_2^e = \eta_2^e \circ \eta_1^e$ *or* $\mathsf{eo}_\eta(\eta_1, \eta_2)$ *or* $\mathsf{eo}_\eta(\eta_2, \eta_1)$*, then* η *is convergent*[3]*.*

[3] All proofs can be found in the extended version [15] of the paper.

We now present a property that consistency policies must obey for our verification methodology to be soundly applied. First, we define the notion of behavioral equivalence of events:

Definition 4 (Behavioral Equivalence).
Two events $\eta_1 = (\mathsf{id}_1, o_1, \sigma_1, \Delta_1, \mathsf{eo}_1)$ *and* $\eta_2 = (\mathsf{id}_2, o_2, \sigma_2, \Delta_2, \mathsf{eo}_2)$ *are behaviorally equivalent if* $\eta_1^e = \eta_2^e$ *and* $o_1 = o_2$.

That is, behaviorally equivalent events produce the same effectors. We use the notation $\eta_1 \equiv \eta_2$ to indicate that they are behaviorally equivalent.

Definition 5 (Behaviorally Stable Consistency Policy). *A consistency policy* Ψ *is behaviorally stable if* $\forall \Delta, \mathsf{vis}, \mathsf{eo}, \Delta', \mathsf{vis}', \mathsf{eo}',\ \eta_1, \eta_2 \in \Delta,\ \eta_1', \eta_2' \in \Delta'$ *the following holds:*

$$(\Psi(\Delta, \mathsf{vis}, \mathsf{eo}) \wedge \Psi(\Delta', \mathsf{vis}', \mathsf{eo}') \wedge \eta_1 \equiv \eta_1' \wedge \eta_2 \equiv \eta_2' \wedge \mathsf{vis}(\eta_1, \eta_2) \Leftrightarrow \mathsf{vis}'(\eta_1', \eta_2')) \\ \Rightarrow \mathsf{eo}(\eta_1, \eta_2) \Leftrightarrow \mathsf{eo}'(\eta_1', \eta_2') \qquad (2)$$

Behaviorally stable consistency policies treat behaviorally equivalent events which have the same visibility relation among them in the same manner by enforcing the same effector order. All consistency policies that we discussed in the previous section (representing the most well-known in the literature) are behaviorally stable:

Lemma 2. EC*,* CC*,* PSI*,* RB *and* SC *are behaviorally stable.*

EC does not enforce any effector ordering and hence is trivially stable behaviorally. CC forces causally dependent events to be in the same order, and hence behaviorally equivalent events which have the same visibility order will be forced to be in the same effector order. RB forces events whose operations belong to a specific subset to be in the same order, but since behaviorally equivalent events perform the same operation, they would be enforced in the same effector ordering. Similarly, PSI forces events writing to a common variable to be in the same order, but since behaviorally equivalent events generate the same effector, they would also write to the same variables and hence would be forced in the same effector order. SC forces all events to be in the same order which is equal to the visibility order, and hence is trivially stable behaviorally. In general, behaviorally stable consistency policies do not consider the context in which events occur, but instead rely only on observable behavior of the events to constrain their ordering. A simple example of a consistency policy which is not behaviorally stable is a policy which maintains bounded concurrency [12] by limiting the number of concurrent operations across all replicas to a fixed bound. Such a policy would synchronize two events only if they occur in a context where keeping them concurrent would violate the bound, but behaviorally equivalent events in a different context may not be synchronized.

For executions under a behaviorally stable consistency policy, the global effector order between events only grows in an execution, so that if two events η_1 and

η_2 are in the history of some event η are related by eo_η, then if they later occur in the history of any other event, they would be related in the same effector order. Hence, we can now define a common global effector order for an execution. Given an execution $\tau \in [\![\mathcal{S}_{\mathcal{P},\Psi}]\!]$, the effector order $\mathsf{eo}_\tau \subseteq L(\tau) \times L(\tau)$ is an anti-symmetric relation defined as follows:

$$\mathsf{eo}_\tau = \{(\eta_1, \eta_2) \mid \exists \eta \in L(\tau).\ (\eta_1, \eta_2) \in \mathsf{eo}_\eta\}$$

Similarly, we also define vis_τ to be the common visibility relation for an execution τ, which is nothing but the vis relation in the final configuration of τ.

Definition 6 (Commutative modulo Consistency Policy). *Given a CRDT $\mathcal{P}$, a behaviorally stable weak consistency specification Ψ and an execution $\tau \in [\![\mathcal{S}_{\mathcal{P},\Psi}]\!]$, two events $\eta_1, \eta_2 \in L(\tau)$ such that $\eta_1 \neq \eta_2$ commute modulo the consistency policy Ψ if either $\eta_1^e \circ \eta_2^e = \eta_2^e \circ \eta_1^e$ or $\mathsf{eo}_\tau(\eta_1, \eta_2)$ or $\mathsf{eo}_\tau(\eta_2, \eta_1)$.*

The following lemma is a direct consequence of Lemma 1:

Lemma 3. *Given a CRDT $\mathcal{P}$ and a behaviorally stable consistency specification Ψ, if for all $\tau \in \mathcal{WF}(\mathcal{S}_{\mathcal{P},\Psi})$, for all $\eta_1, \eta_2 \in L(\tau)$ such that $\eta_1 \neq \eta_2$, η_1 and η_2 commute modulo the consistency policy Ψ, then $\mathcal{P}$ achieves SEC under Ψ.*

Our goal is to use Lemma 3 to show that all events in any execution commute modulo the consistency policy. However, executions can be arbitrarily long and have an unbounded number of events. Hence, for events occurring in such large executions, we will instead consider behaviorally equivalent events in a smaller execution and show that they commute modulo the consistency policy, which by stability of the consistency policy directly translates to their commutativity in the larger context. Recall that the effector generated by an operation depends on its start state and the sequence of other effectors applied to that state. To generate behaviorally equivalent events with arbitrarily long histories in short executions, we summarize these long histories into the start state of events, and use commutativity itself as an inductive property of these start states. That is, we ask if two events with arbitrary start states and empty histories commute modulo Ψ, whether the addition of another event to their histories would continue to allow them to commute modulo Ψ.

Definition 7 (Non-interference to Commutativity). (Non-Interf) *A CRDT $\mathcal{P} = (\Sigma, O, \sigma_{init})$ satisfies non-interference to commutativity under a consistency policy Ψ if and only if the following conditions hold:*

1. *For all executions $C_{init} \xrightarrow{\eta_1} C_1 \xrightarrow{\eta_2} C_2$ in $\mathcal{WF}(\mathcal{S}_{\mathcal{P},\Psi})$, η_1 and η_2 commute modulo Ψ.*
2. *For all $\sigma_1, \sigma_2, \sigma_3 \in \Sigma$, if for execution $\tau \equiv C_{init} \xrightarrow{\eta_1} C_1 \xrightarrow{\eta_2} C_2$ in $[\![\mathcal{S}_{\mathcal{P},\Psi}]\!]$ where $\sigma_s(\eta_1) = \sigma_1$, $\sigma_s(\eta_2) = \sigma_2$, η_1 and η_2 commute modulo Ψ, then for all executions $\tau' \equiv C_{init} \xrightarrow{\eta_3} C_1' \xrightarrow{\eta_1'} C_2' \xrightarrow{\eta_2'} C_3'$ such that $\sigma_s(\eta_1') = \sigma_1$, $o(\eta_1') = o(\eta_1)$, $\sigma_s(\eta_2') = \sigma_2$, $o(\eta_2') = o(\eta_2)$, $\sigma_s(\eta_3) = \sigma_3$, and $\mathsf{vis}_\tau(\eta_1, \eta_2) \Leftrightarrow \mathsf{vis}_{\tau'}(\eta_1', \eta_2')$, η_1' and η_2' commute modulo Ψ.*

Condition (1) corresponds to the base case of our inductive argument and requires that in well-formed executions with 2 events, both the events commute modulo Ψ. For condition (2), our intention is to consider two events η_a and η_b with any arbitrary histories which can occur in any well-formed execution and, assuming that they commute modulo Ψ, show that even after the addition of another event to their histories, they continue to commute. We use CRDT states σ_1, σ_2 to summarize the histories of the two events, and construct behaviorally equivalent events ($\eta_1 \equiv \eta_a$ and $\eta_2 \equiv \eta_b$) which would take σ_1, σ_2 as their start states. That is, if η_a produced the effector $o(\sigma_{\texttt{init}}, \pi)$[4], where o is the CRDT operation corresponding to η_a and π is the sequence of effectors in its history, we leverage the observation that $o(\sigma_{\texttt{init}}, \pi) = o(\pi(\sigma_{\texttt{init}}), \epsilon)$, and assuming $\sigma_1 = \pi(\sigma_{\texttt{init}})$, we obtain the behaviorally equivalent event η_1, i.e. $\eta_1^e \equiv \eta_a^e$. Similar analysis establishes that $\eta_2^e \equiv \eta_b^e$. However, since we have no way of characterizing states σ_1 and σ_2 which are obtained by applying arbitrary sequences of effectors, we use commutativity itself as an identifying characteristic, focusing on only those σ_1 and σ_2 for which the events η_1 and η_2 commute modulo Ψ.

The interfering event is also summarized by another CRDT state σ_3, and we require that after suffering interference from this new event, the original two events would continue to commute modulo Ψ. This would essentially establish that any two events with any history would commute modulo Ψ in these small executions, which by the behavioral stability of Ψ would translate to their commutativity in any execution.

Theorem 1. *Given a CRDT $\mathcal{P}$ and a behaviorally stable consistency policy Ψ, if $\mathcal{P}$ satisfies non-interference to commutativity under Ψ, then $\mathcal{P}$ achieves* SEC *under Ψ.*

Example: Let us apply the proposed verification strategy to the ORSet CRDT shown in Fig. 2. Under EC, condition (1) of Non-Interf fails, because in the execution $C_{\texttt{init}} \xrightarrow{\eta_1} C_1 \xrightarrow{\eta_2} C_2$ where $o(\eta_1) =$`Add(a,i)` and $o(\eta_2) =$`Remove(a)` and $\mathsf{vis}(\eta_1, \eta_2)$, η_1 and η_2 don't commute modulo EC, since `(a,i)` would be present in the source replica of `Remove(a)`. However, η_1 and η_2 would commute modulo CC, since they would be related by the effector order. Now, moving to condition (2) of Non-interf, we limit ourselves to source replica states σ_1 and σ_2 where `Add(a,i)` and `Remove(a)` do commute modulo CC. If $\mathsf{vis}_\tau(\eta_1, \eta_2)$, then after interference, in execution τ', $\mathsf{vis}_{\tau'}(\eta_1', \eta_2')$, in which case η_1' and η_2' trivially commute modulo CC (because they would be related by the effector order). On the other hand, if $\neg\mathsf{vis}_\tau(\eta_1, \eta_2)$, then for η_1 and η_2 to commute modulo CC, we must have that the effectors η_1^e and η_2^e themselves commute, which implies that $\texttt{(a,i)} \notin \sigma_2$. Now, consider any execution τ' with an interfering operation η_3. If η_3 is another `Add(a,i')` operation, then `i'` $\neq$ `i`, so that even if it is visible to η_2', $\eta_2'^e$ will not remove `(a,i)`, so that η_1' and η_2' would commute. Similarly, if η_3 is another `Remove(a)` operation, it can only remove tagged versions of `a` from the source replicas of η_2', so that the effector $\eta_2'^e$ would not remove `(a,i)`.

[4] Note that in a well-formed execution, the start state is always $\sigma_{\texttt{init}}$.

5 Experimental Results

In this section, we present the results of applying our verification methodology to a number of CRDTs under different consistency models. We collected CRDT implementations from a number of sources [1,19,20] and since all of the existing implementations assume a very weak consistency model (primarily CC), we additionally implemented a few CRDTs on our own intended to only work under stronger consistency schemes but which are better in terms of time/space complexity and ease of development. Our implementations are not written in any specific language but instead are specified abstractly akin to the definitions given in Figs. 1 and 2. To specify CRDT states and operations, we fix an abstract language that contains uninterpreted datatypes (used for specifying elements of sets, lists, etc.), a set datatype with support for various set operations (add, delete, union, intersection, projection, lookup), a tuple datatype (along with operations to create tuples and project components) and a special uninterpreted datatype equipped with a total order for identifiers. Note that the set datatype used in our abstract language is different from the Set CRDT, as it is only intended to perform set operations locally at a replica. All existing CRDT definitions can be naturally expressed in this framework.

Here, we revert back to the op-based specification of CRDTs. For a given CRDT $\mathcal{P} = (\Sigma, O, \sigma_{\texttt{init}})$, we convert all its operations into FOL formulas relating the source, input and output replica states. That is, for a CRDT operation $o : \Sigma \to \Sigma \to \Sigma$, we create a predicate $\mathsf{o} : \Sigma \times \Sigma \times \Sigma \to \mathbb{B}$ such that $\mathsf{o}(\sigma_s, \sigma_i, \sigma_o)$ is true if and only if $o(\sigma_s)(\sigma_i) = \sigma_o$. Since CRDT states are typically expressed as sets, we axiomatize set operations to express their semantics in FOL.

In order to specify a consistency model, we introduce a sort for events and binary predicates vis and eo over this sort. Here, we can take advantage of the declarative specification of consistency models and directly encode them in FOL. Given an encoding of CRDT operations and a consistency model, our verification strategy is to determine whether the Non-Interf property holds. Since both conditions of this property only involve executions of finite length (at most 3), we can directly encode them as UNSAT queries by asking for executions which break the conditions. For condition (1), we query for the existence of two events η_1 and η_2 along with vis and eo predicates which satisfy the consistency specification Ψ such that these events are not related by eo and their effectors do not commute. For condition (2), we query for the existence of events η_1, η_2, η_3 and their respective start states $\sigma_1, \sigma_2, \sigma_3$, such that η_1 and η_2 commute modulo Ψ but after interference from η_3, they are not related by eo and do not commute. Both these queries are encoded in EPR [18], a decidable fragment of FOL, so if the CRDT operations and the consistency policy can also be encoded in a decidable fragment of FOL (which is the case in all our experiments), then our verification strategy is also decidable. We write Non-Interf-1 and Non-Interf-2 for the two conditions of Non-Interf.

Figure 4 shows the results of applying the proposed methodology on different CRDTs. We used Z3 to discharge our satisfiability queries. For every combination of a CRDT and a consistency policy, we write ✗ to indicate that verification of

CRDT	EC	CC	PSI+RB	PSI	Verif. Time (s)
Set					
Simple-Set	✗	✗	✓	✓	0.23
ORSet [20]	✗	✓	✓	✓	0.6
ORSet with Tombstones	✓	✓	✓	✓	0.04
USet[20]	✗	✗	✗	✓	0.1
List					
RGA[1]	✗	✓	✓	✓	5.3
RGA-No-Tomb	✗	✗	✓	✓	3
Graph					
2P2P-Graph[20]	✗	✓	✓	✓	3.5
Graph-with-ORSet	✗	✗	✓	✓	46.3

Fig. 4. Convergence of CRDTs under different consistency policies.

Non-Interf failed, while ✓ indicates that it was satisfied. We also report the verification time taken by Z3 for every CRDT across all consistency policies executing on a standard desktop machine. We have picked the three collection datatypes for which CRDTs have been proposed i.e. Set, List and Graph, and for each such datatype, we consider multiple variants that provide a tradeoff between consistency requirements and implementation complexity. Apart from EC, CC and PSI, we also use a combination of PSI and RB, which only enforce PSI between selected pairs of operations (in contrast to simple RB which would enforce SC between all selected pairs). Note that when verifying a CRDT under PSI, we assume that the set operations are implemented as Boolean assignments, and the write set Wr consists of elements added/removed. We are unaware of any prior effort that has been successful in automatically verifying *any* CRDT, let alone those that exhibit the complexity of the ones considered here.

Set: The Simple-Set CRDT in Fig. 1 does not converge under EC or CC, but achieves convergence under PSI+RB which only synchronizes `Add` and `Remove` operations to the same elements, while all other operations continue to run under EC, since they do commute with each other. As explained earlier, ORSet does not converge under EC and violates Non-Interf-1. ORSet with tombstones converges under EC as well since it uses a different set (called a tombstone) to keep track of removed elements. USet is another implementation of the Set CRDT which converges under the assumptions that an element is only added once, and removes only work if the element is already present in the source replica. USet converges only under PSI, because under any weaker consistency model, NON-INTERF-2 breaks, since `Add(a)` interferes and breaks the commutativity of `Add(a)` and `Remove(a)`. Notice that as the consistency level weakens, implementations need to keep more and more information to maintain convergence–compute unique ids, tag elements with them or keep track of deleted elements. If the underlying replicated store supports stronger consistency levels such as PSI, simpler definitions are sufficient.

List: The List CRDT maintains a total ordering between its elements. It supports two operations: `AddRight(e,a)` adds new element `a` to the right of existing element `e`, while `Remove(e)` removes `e` from the list. We use the implementation in [1] (called RGA) which uses time-stamped insertion trees. To maintain integrity of the tree structure, the immediate predecessor of every list element must be present in the list, due to which operations `AddRight(a,b)` and `AddRight(b,c)` do not commute. Hence RGA does not converge under EC because Non-Interf-1 is violated, but converges under CC.

To make adds and removes involving the same list element commute, RGA maintains a tombstone set for all deleted list elements. This can be expensive as deleted elements may potentially need to be tracked forever, even with garbage collection. We consider a slight modification of RGA called RGA-No-Tomb which does not keep track of deleted elements. This CRDT now has a convergence violation under CC (because of Non-Interf-1), but achieves convergence under PSI+RB where we enforce PSI only for pairs of `AddRight` and `Remove` operations.

Graph: The Graph CRDT maintains sets of vertices and edges and supports operations to add and remove vertices and edges. The 2P2P-Graph specification uses separate 2P-Sets for both vertices and edges, where a 2P-Set itself maintains two sets for addition and removal of elements. While 2P sets themselves converge under EC, the 2P2P-Graph has convergence violations (to Non-Interf-1) involving `AddVertex(v)` and `RemoveVertex(v)` (similarly for edges) since it removes a vertex from a replica only if it is already present. We verify that it converges under CC. Graphs require an integrity constraint that edges in the edge-set must always be incident on vertices in the vertex-set. Since concurrent `RemoveVertex(v)` and `AddEdge(v,v')` can violate this constraint, the 2P2P-Graph uses the internal structure of the 2P-Set which keeps track of deleted elements and considers an edge to be in the edge set only if its vertices are not in the vertex tombstone set (leading to a remove-wins strategy).

Building a graph CRDT can be viewed as an exercise in composing CRDTs by using two ORSet CRDTs, keeping the internal implementation of the ORSet opaque, using only its interface. The Graph-with-ORSet implementation uses separate ORSets for vertices and edges and explicitly maintains the graph integrity constraint. We find convergence violations (to Non-Interf-1) between `RemoveVertex(v)` and `AddEdge(v,v')`, and `RemoveVertex(v)` and `RemoveEdge(v,v')` under both EC and CC. Under PSI+RB (enforcing RB on the above two pairs of operations), we were able to show convergence.

When a CRDT passes Non-Interf under a consistency policy, we can guarantee that it achieves SEC under that policy. However, if it fails Non-Interf, it may or may not converge. In particular, if it fails Non-Interf-1 it will definitely not converge (because Non-Interf-1 constructs a well-formed execution), but if it passes Non-Interf-1 and fails Non-Interf-2, it may still converge because of the imprecision of Non-Interf-2. There are two sources of imprecision, both concerning the start states of the events picked in the condition: (1) we only use commutativity as a distinguishing property of the start states, but this may not be a sufficiently strong inductive invariant, (2) we place no constraints on the start state of the interfering operation. In practice, we have found that for all cases except U-Set, convergence violations manifest via failure of Non-Interf-1. If Non-Interf-2 breaks, we can search for well-formed executions of higher length upto a bound. For U-Set, we were successful in adopting this approach, and were able to find a non-convergent well-formed execution of length 3.

6 Related Work and Conclusions

Reconciling concurrent updates in a replicated system is a important well-studied problem in distributed applications, having been first studied in the context of collaborative editing systems [17]. Incorrect implementation of replicated sets in Amazon's Dynamo system [7] motivated the design of CRDTs as a principled approach to implementing replicated data types. Devising correct implementations has proven to be challenging, however, as evidenced by the myriad pre-conditions specified in the various CRDT implementations [20].

Burckhardt *et al.* [6] present an abstract event-based framework to describe executions of CRDTs under different network conditions; they also propose a rigorous correctness criterion in the form of abstract specifications. Their proof strategy, which is neither automated nor parametric on consistency policies, verifies CRDT implementations against these specifications by providing a simulation invariant between CRDT states and event structures. Zeller *et al.* [24] also require simulation invariants to verify convergence, although they only target state-based CRDTs. Gomes *et al.* [9] provide mechanized proofs of convergence for ORSet and RGA CRDTs under causal consistency, but their approach is neither automated nor parametric.

A number of earlier efforts [2,10–12,22] have looked at the problem of verifying state-based invariants in distributed applications. These techniques typically target applications built using CRDTs, and assume their underlying correctness. Because they target correctness specifications in the form of state-based invariants, it is unclear if their approaches can be applied directly to the convergence problem we consider here. Other approaches [4,5,16] have also looked at the verification problem of transactional programs running on replicated systems under weak consistency, but these proposals typically use serializability as the correctness criterion, adopting a "last-writer wins" semantics, rather than convergence, to deal with concurrent updates.

This paper demonstrates the automated verification of CRDTs under different weak consistency policies. We rigorously define the relationship between commutativity and convergence, formulating the notion of commutativity modulo consistency policy as a sufficient condition for convergence. While we require a non-trivial inductive argument to show that non-interference to commutativity is sufficient for convergence, the condition itself is designed to be simple and amenable to automated verification using off-the-shelf theorem-provers. We have successfully applied the proposed verification strategy for all major CRDTs, additionally motivating the need for parameterization in consistency policies by showing variants of existing CRDTs which are simpler in terms of implementation complexity but converge under different weak consistency models.

Acknowledgments. We thank the anonymous reviewers for their insightful comments. This material is based upon work supported by the National Science Foundation under Grant No. CCF-SHF 1717741 and the Air Force Research Lab under Grant No. FA8750-17-1-0006.

References

1. Attiya, H., Burckhardt, S., Gotsman, A., Morrison, A., Yang, H., Zawirski, M.: Specification and complexity of collaborative text editing. In: Proceedings of the 2016 ACM Symposium on Principles of Distributed Computing, PODC 2016, Chicago, IL, USA, 25–28 July 2016, pp. 259–268 (2016). https://doi.org/10.1145/2933057.2933090
2. Bailis, P., Fekete, A., Franklin, M.J., Ghodsi, A., Hellerstein, J.M., Stoica, I.: Coordination avoidance in database systems. PVLDB **8**(3), 185–196 (2014). https://doi.org/10.14778/2735508.2735509. http://www.vldb.org/pvldb/vol8/p185-bailis.pdf
3. Bailis, P., Ghodsi, A.: Eventual consistency today: limitations, extensions, and beyond. Commun. ACM **56**(5), 55–63 (2013). https://doi.org/10.1145/2447976.2447992
4. Bernardi, G., Gotsman, A.: Robustness against consistency models with atomic visibility. In: 27th International Conference on Concurrency Theory, CONCUR 2016, 23–26 August 2016, Québec City, Canada, pp. 7:1–7:15 (2016). https://doi.org/10.4230/LIPIcs.CONCUR.2016.7
5. Brutschy, L., Dimitrov, D., Müller, P., Vechev, M.T.: Static serializability analysis for causal consistency. In: Proceedings of the 39th ACM SIGPLAN Conference on Programming Language Design and Implementation, PLDI 2018, Philadelphia, PA, USA, 18–22 June 2018, pp. 90–104 (2018). https://doi.org/10.1145/3192366.3192415
6. Burckhardt, S., Gotsman, A., Yang, H., Zawirski, M.: Replicated data types: specification, verification, optimality. In: The 41st Annual ACM SIGPLAN-SIGACT Symposium on Principles of Programming Languages, POPL 2014, San Diego, CA, USA, 20–21 January 2014, pp. 271–284 (2014). https://doi.org/10.1145/2535838.2535848
7. DeCandia, G., et al.: Dynamo: amazon's highly available key-value store. In: Proceedings of the 21st ACM Symposium on Operating Systems Principles 2007, SOSP 2007, Stevenson, Washington, USA, 14–17 October 2007, pp. 205–220 (2007). https://doi.org/10.1145/1294261.1294281
8. Gilbert, S., Lynch, N.A.: Brewer's conjecture and the feasibility of consistent, available, partition-tolerant web services. SIGACT News **33**(2), 51–59 (2002). https://doi.org/10.1145/564585.564601. http://doi.acm.org/10.1145/564585.564601
9. Gomes, V.B.F., Kleppmann, M., Mulligan, D.P., Beresford, A.R.: Verifying strong eventual consistency in distributed systems. PACMPL **1**(OOPSLA), 109:1–109:28 (2017). https://doi.org/10.1145/3133933

10. Gotsman, A., Yang, H., Ferreira, C., Najafzadeh, M., Shapiro, M.: 'Cause i'm strong enough: reasoning about consistency choices in distributed systems. In: Proceedings of the 43rd Annual ACM SIGPLAN-SIGACT Symposium on Principles of Programming Languages, POPL 2016, St. Petersburg, FL, USA, 20–22 January 2016, pp. 371–384 (2016). https://doi.org/10.1145/2837614.2837625, http://doi.acm.org/10.1145/2837614.2837625
11. Houshmand, F., Lesani, M.: Hamsaz: replication coordination analysis and synthesis. PACMPL **3**(POPL), 74:1–74:32 (2019). https://dl.acm.org/citation.cfm?id=3290387
12. Kaki, G., Earanky, K., Sivaramakrishnan, K.C., Jagannathan, S.: Safe replication through bounded concurrency verification. PACMPL **2**(OOPSLA), 164:1–164:27 (2018). https://doi.org/10.1145/3276534
13. Li, C., Porto, D., Clement, A., Gehrke, J., Preguiça, N.M., Rodrigues, R.: Making geo-replicated systems fast as possible, consistent when necessary. In: 10th USENIX Symposium on Operating Systems Design and Implementation, OSDI 2012, Hollywood, CA, USA, 8–10 October 2012, pp. 265–278 (2012). https://www.usenix.org/conference/osdi12/technical-sessions/presentation/li
14. Lloyd, W., Freedman, M.J., Kaminsky, M., Andersen, D.G.: Don't settle for eventual: scalable causal consistency for wide-area storage with COPS. In: Proceedings of the 23rd ACM Symposium on Operating Systems Principles 2011, SOSP 2011, Cascais, Portugal, 23–26 October 2011, pp. 401–416 (2011). https://doi.org/10.1145/2043556.2043593, http://doi.acm.org/10.1145/2043556.2043593
15. Nagar, K., Jagannathan, S.: Automated Parameterized Verification of CRDTs (Extended Version). https://arxiv.org/abs/1905.05684
16. Nagar, K., Jagannathan, S.: Automated detection of serializability violations under weak consistency. In: 29th International Conference on Concurrency Theory, CONCUR 2018, 4–7 September 2018, Beijing, China, pp. 41:1–41:18 (2018). https://doi.org/10.4230/LIPIcs.CONCUR.2018.41
17. Nichols, D.A., Curtis, P., Dixon, M., Lamping, J.: High-latency, low-bandwidth windowing in the jupiter collaboration system. In: Proceedings of the 8th Annual ACM Symposium on User Interface Software and Technology, UIST 1995, Pittsburgh, PA, USA, 14–17 November 1995, pp. 111–120 (1995). https://doi.org/10.1145/215585.215706
18. Piskac, R., de Moura, L.M., Bjørner, N.: Deciding effectively propositional logic using DPLL and substitution sets. J. Autom. Reasoning **44**(4), 401–424 (2010). https://doi.org/10.1007/s10817-009-9161-6
19. Preguiça, N.M., Baquero, C., Shapiro, M.: Conflict-free replicated data types (CRDTs). CoRR abs/1805.06358 (2018). http://arxiv.org/abs/1805.06358
20. Shapiro, M., Preguiça, N., Baquero, C., Zawirski, M.: A comprehensive study of Convergent and Commutative Replicated Data Types. Technical report RR-7506, INRIA, Inria - Centre Paris-Rocquencourt (2011)
21. Shapiro, M., Preguiça, N., Baquero, C., Zawirski, M.: Conflict-free replicated data types. In: Défago, X., Petit, F., Villain, V. (eds.) SSS 2011. LNCS, vol. 6976, pp. 386–400. Springer, Heidelberg (2011). https://doi.org/10.1007/978-3-642-24550-3_29
22. Sivaramakrishnan, K.C., Kaki, G., Jagannathan, S.: Declarative programming over eventually consistent data stores. In: Proceedings of the 36th ACM SIGPLAN Conference on Programming Language Design and Implementation, Portland, OR, USA, 15–17 June 2015, pp. 413–424 (2015). https://doi.org/10.1145/2737924.2737981

23. Sovran, Y., Power, R., Aguilera, M.K., Li, J.: Transactional storage for geo-replicated systems. In: Proceedings of the 23rd ACM Symposium on Operating Systems Principles 2011, SOSP 2011, Cascais, Portugal, 23–26 October 2011, pp. 385–400 (2011). https://doi.org/10.1145/2043556.2043592, http://doi.acm.org/10.1145/2043556.2043592
24. Zeller, P., Bieniusa, A., Poetzsch-Heffter, A.: Formal specification and verification of CRDTs. In: Ábrahám, E., Palamidessi, C. (eds.) FORTE 2014. LNCS, vol. 8461, pp. 33–48. Springer, Heidelberg (2014). https://doi.org/10.1007/978-3-662-43613-4_3

What's Wrong with On-the-Fly Partial Order Reduction

Stephen F. Siegel(✉)

University of Delaware, Newark, DE, USA
siegel@udel.edu

Abstract. Partial order reduction and on-the-fly model checking are well-known approaches for improving model checking performance. The two optimizations interact in subtle ways, so care must be taken when using them in combination. A standard algorithm combining the two optimizations, published over twenty years ago, has been widely studied and deployed in popular model checking tools. Yet the algorithm is incorrect. Counterexamples were discovered using the Alloy analyzer. A fix for a restricted class of property automata is proposed.

Keywords: Model checking · Partial order reduction · On-the-fly · Spin

1 Introduction

Partial order reduction (POR) refers to a family of model checking techniques used to reduce the size of the state space that must be explored when verifying a property of a program. The techniques vary, but all share the core observation that when two independent operations are enabled in a state, it is often safe to ignore traces that begin with one of them. A large number of POR techniques have been explored, differing in details such as the range of properties to which they apply. This paper focuses on *ample set* POR [4], an approach which applies to stutter-invariant properties and is used in the model checker Spin [8].

In the automata-theoretic view of model checking, the negation of the property to be verified is represented by an ω-automaton. The basic algorithm computes the product of this automaton with the state space of the program. The language of the product is empty if and only if the program cannot violate the property. *On-the-fly* model checking refers to an optimization of this basic algorithm in which the enumeration of the reachable program states, computation of the product, and language emptiness check are interleaved, rather than occurring in sequence.

These two optimizations must be combined with care, because they interact in subtle ways.[1] A standard algorithm for on-the-fly ample set POR is described

[1] Previous work, for example, has dealt with problems, distinct from those discussed in this paper, that arise when combining nested depth first search and POR [7,14].

I. Dillig and S. Tasiran (Eds.): CAV 2019, LNCS 11562, pp. 478–495, 2019.
https://doi.org/10.1007/978-3-030-25543-5_27

in [12] and in further detail in [13]. I shall refer to this algorithm as the *combined algorithm*. Theorem 4.2 of [13] asserts the soundness of the combined algorithm. A proof of the theorem is also given in [13].

The proof has a gap. This was pointed out in [16, Sect. 5], with details in [15]. The gap was rediscovered in the course of developing mechanized correctness proofs for model checking algorithms; an explicit counterexample to the incorrect proof step was also found ([2, Sect. 8.4.5] and [3, Sect. 5]). The fact that the proof is erroneous, however, does not imply the theorem is wrong. To the best of my knowledge, no one has yet produced a proof or a counterexample for the soundness of the combined algorithm.

In this paper, I show that the combined algorithm is not sound; a counterexample is given in Sect. 3.1. I found this counterexample by modeling the combined algorithm in Alloy and using the Alloy analyzer [11] to check its soundness. Sect. 4 describes this model. Spin's POR is based on the combined algorithm, and in Sect. 5, Spin is seen to return an incorrect result on a Promela model derived from the theoretical counterexample.

There is a small adjustment to the combined algorithm, yielding an algorithm that is arguably more natural and that returns the correct result on the previous counterexample; this is described in Sect. 6. It turns out this one is also unsound, as demonstrated by another Alloy-produced counterexample. However, in Sect. 7, I show that this variation is sound if certain restrictions are placed on the property automaton.

2 Preliminaries

Definition 1. *A* finite state program *is a triple* $P = \langle T, Q, \iota \rangle$*, where* Q *is a finite set of* states*,* $\iota \in Q$ *is the* initial state*, and* T *is a finite set of* operations*. Each operation* $\alpha \in T$ *is a function from a set* $\mathsf{en}_\alpha \subseteq Q$ *to* Q*.*

Fix a finite state program $P = \langle T, Q, \iota \rangle$.

Definition 2. *For* $q \in Q$*, define* $\mathsf{en}(q) = \{\alpha \in T \mid q \in \mathsf{en}_\alpha\}$*.*

Definition 3. *An* execution *of* P *is an infinite sequence of operations* $\alpha_1\alpha_2\cdots$ *that* generates *the sequence of states* $\xi = q_0q_1q_2\cdots$ *such that* $q_0 = \iota$ *and for* $i \geq 0$*,* $q_i \in \mathsf{en}_{\alpha_{i+1}}$ *and* $q_{i+1} = \alpha_{i+1}(q_i)$*. An* admissible *sequence is any segment of an execution.*

Definition 4. *A* Büchi automaton *is a tuple* $\mathcal{B} = \langle S, \Delta, \Sigma, \delta, F \rangle$*, where* S *is a finite set of* automaton states*,* $\Delta \subseteq S$ *is the set of* initial states*,* Σ *is a finite set called the* alphabet*,* $\delta \subseteq S \times \Sigma \times S$ *is the* transition relation*, and* $F \subseteq S$ *is the set of* accepting states*. The* language *of* $\mathcal{B}$*, denoted* $\mathcal{L}(B)$*, is the set of all* $\xi \in \Sigma^\omega$ *generated by infinite paths in* $\mathcal{B}$ *that pass through an accepting state infinitely often.*

Fix a finite set AP of *atomic propositions* and let $\Sigma = 2^{\mathsf{AP}}$.
Fix an *interpretation mapping* for P, i.e., a function $L \colon Q \to \Sigma$.

Definition 5. *The* language of P*, denoted* $\mathcal{L}(P)$*, is the set of all infinite words* $L(q_0)L(q_1)\cdots \in \Sigma^\omega$*, where* $q_0q_1\cdots$ *is the sequence of states generated by an execution of* P*.*

Definition 6. *A language* $L \subseteq \Sigma^\omega$ *is* stutter-invariant *if, for any* $a_0, a_1, \ldots \in \Sigma$ *and positive integers* $i_0, i_1 \ldots$*,* $a_0a_1\cdots \in L \Leftrightarrow a_0^{i_0}a_1^{i_1}\cdots \in L$*, where* a^i *denotes the concatenation of* i *copies of* a*.*

Definition 7. *Let* $\mathcal{B} = \langle S, \Delta, \Sigma, \delta, F\rangle$*, be a Büchi automaton with alphabet* Σ*. The* product *of* P *and* $\mathcal{B}$ *is the Büchi automaton*

$$P \otimes \mathcal{B} = \langle Q \times S, \{\iota\} \times \Delta, T \times \Sigma, \delta_\otimes, Q \times F\rangle,$$

where

$$\delta_\otimes = \{(\langle q, s\rangle, \langle \alpha, \sigma\rangle, \langle q', s'\rangle) \mid \sigma = L(q) \wedge \langle s, \sigma, s'\rangle \in \delta \wedge q' = \alpha(q)\}.$$

Note 1. A transition from product state $x = \langle q, s\rangle$ can be viewed as taking place in two steps. First, a transition $s \xrightarrow{L(q)} s'$ in $\mathcal{B}$ executes, leading to an "intermediate state" $x' = \langle q, s'\rangle$. Then a program transition $q \xrightarrow{\alpha} q'$ executes, culminating in $y = \langle q', s'\rangle$. While this is a good mental model, the product automaton does not necessarily contain a transition from x to x' or from x' to y. The intermediate state x' is not even necessarily reachable in the product. The transition in the product goes directly from x to y with label $\langle \alpha, L(q)\rangle$.

It is well-known that

$$\mathcal{L}(P) \cap \mathcal{L}(\mathcal{B}) = \emptyset \Leftrightarrow \mathcal{L}(P \otimes \mathcal{B}) = \emptyset.$$

In the context of model checking, $\mathcal{B}$ is used to represent the negation of a desirable property; the program P satisfies the property if, and only if, no execution of P is accepted by $\mathcal{B}$, i.e., $\mathcal{L}(P) \cap \mathcal{L}(\mathcal{B}) = \emptyset$. The automaton $\mathcal{B}$ may be generated from a (negated) LTL formula, but that assumption is not needed here.

The goal of "offline" (not on-the-fly) partial order reduction is to generate some subspace P' of P with the guarantee that

$$\mathcal{L}(P') \cap \mathcal{L}(\mathcal{B}) = \emptyset \Leftrightarrow \mathcal{L}(P) \cap \mathcal{L}(\mathcal{B}) = \emptyset$$

The emptiness of $\mathcal{L}(P' \otimes \mathcal{B}) = \mathcal{L}(P') \cap \mathcal{L}(\mathcal{B})$ can be decided in various ways, such as a nested depth first search (NDFS) [5].

3 On-the-Fly Partial Order Reduction

In on-the-fly model checking, the state space of the product automaton is enumerated directly, without first enumerating the program states. Adding POR to the mix means that at each state reached in the product automaton, some subset of enabled transitions will be explored. The goal is to ensure that if the language of the full product automaton is nonempty, then the language of the resulting reduced automaton must be nonempty.

To make this precise, fix a finite state program $P = \langle T, Q, \iota \rangle$, a set AP of atomic propositions, an interpretation $L\colon Q \to \Sigma = 2^{\mathsf{AP}}$, and Büchi automaton $\mathcal{B} = \langle S, \Delta, \Sigma, \delta, F \rangle$. Let $\mathcal{A} = P \otimes \mathcal{B}$.

Definition 8. *A function* $\mathsf{amp}\colon Q \times S \to 2^T$ *is an* ample selector *if* $\mathsf{amp}(q,s) \subseteq \mathsf{en}(q)$ *for all* $q \in Q, s \in S$. *Each* $\mathsf{amp}(q,s)$ *is an* ample set.

An ample selector determines a subautomaton $\mathcal{A}' = \mathsf{reduced}(\mathcal{A}, \mathsf{amp})$ of $\mathcal{A}$: $\mathcal{A}'$ is defined exactly as in Definition 7, except that the transition relation has the additional restriction that $\alpha \in \mathsf{amp}(q, s')$:

$$\mathcal{A}' = \langle Q \times S, \{\iota\} \times \Delta, T \times \Sigma, \delta', Q \times F \rangle \tag{1}$$

$$\begin{aligned} \delta' = \{ (\langle q,s \rangle, \langle \alpha, \sigma \rangle, \langle q', s' \rangle) \in (Q \times S) \times (T \times \Sigma) \times (Q \times S) \mid \\ \sigma = L(q) \wedge \langle s, \sigma, s' \rangle \in \delta \wedge \alpha \in \mathsf{amp}(q,s') \wedge q' = \alpha(q) \} . \end{aligned} \tag{2}$$

Definition 9. *An ample selector* amp *is* POR-sound *if the following holds:*

$$\mathcal{L}(\mathsf{reduced}(\mathcal{A}, \mathsf{amp})) = \emptyset \Leftrightarrow \mathcal{L}(P) \cap \mathcal{L}(\mathcal{B}) = \emptyset.$$

The goal is to define some constraints on an ample selector that guarantee it is POR-sound. Before stating the constraints, we need two more concepts:

Definition 10. *An* independence relation *is an irreflexive and symmetric relation* $I \subseteq T \times T$ *satisfying the following: if* $(\alpha, \beta) \in I$ *and* $q \in \mathsf{en}_\alpha \cap \mathsf{en}_\beta$, *then* $\alpha(q) \in \mathsf{en}_\beta$, $\beta(q) \in \mathsf{en}_\alpha$, *and* $\alpha(\beta(q)) = \beta(\alpha(q))$.

Fix an independence relation I. We say α and β are *dependent* if $(\alpha, \beta) \notin I$.

Definition 11. *An operation* $\alpha \in T$ *is* invisible with respect to L *if, for all* $q \in \mathsf{en}_\alpha$, $L(q) = L(\alpha(q))$.

Note 2. The definition in [13] is slightly different. Given an LTL formula ϕ over AP, let AP' be the set of atomic propositions occurring syntactically in ϕ. The definition in [13] says α is *invisible in* ϕ if, for all $p \in \mathsf{AP}'$ and $q \in \mathsf{en}_\alpha$, $p \in L(q) \Leftrightarrow p \in L(\alpha(q))$. However, there is no loss of generality using Definition 11, since one can define a new interpretation $L'\colon Q \to 2^{\mathsf{AP}'}$ by $L'(q) = L(q) \cap \mathsf{AP}'$. Then α is invisible for ϕ if, and only if, α is invisible with respect to L', and the results of this paper can be applied without modification to P, AP', and L'.

We now define the following constraints on an ample selector amp:[2]

C0 For all $q \in Q$, $s \in S$: $\mathsf{en}(q) \neq \emptyset \implies \mathsf{amp}(q,s) \neq \emptyset$.

[2] I am using the numbering from [4]. In [13], **C2** and **C3** are swapped.

C1 For all $q \in Q$, $s \in S$: in any admissible sequence in P starting from q, no operation in $T \setminus \mathsf{amp}(q, s)$ that is dependent on an operation in $\mathsf{amp}(q, s)$ can occur before some operation in $\mathsf{amp}(q, s)$ occurs.

C2 For all $q \in Q$, $s \in S$: if $\mathsf{amp}(q, s) \neq \mathsf{en}(q)$ then $\forall \alpha \in \mathsf{amp}(q, s)$, α is invisible.

C3 There is a depth-first search of $\mathcal{A}' = \mathsf{reduced}(\mathcal{A}, \mathsf{amp})$ with the following property: whenever there is a transition in $\mathcal{A}'$ from a node $\langle q, s\rangle$ on the top of the stack to a node $\langle q', s'\rangle$ on the stack, $\mathsf{amp}(q, s') = \mathsf{en}(q)$.

Condition **C3** is the interesting one. The combined algorithm of [13] enforces it using a DFS (the outer search of the NDFS) of the reduced space and the following protocol: given a new state $\langle q, s\rangle$ that has just been pushed onto the stack, first iterate over all Büchi transitions $\langle s, L(q), s'\rangle$ departing from s and labeled by $L(q)$. For each of these, a candidate ample set for $\mathsf{amp}(q, s')$ that satisfies the first three conditions is computed; this computation does not depend on s'. If any operation in that candidate set leads back to a state on the search stack (a "back edge"), a different candidate is tried and the process is repeated until a satisfactory one is found. If no such candidate is found, $\mathsf{en}(q)$ is used for the ample set.

Hence the process for choosing the ample set depends on the current state of the search. If $y_1 \neq y_2$, it is not necessarily the case that $\mathsf{amp}(x, y_1) = \mathsf{amp}(x, y_2)$, because it is possible that when $\langle x, y_1\rangle$ was encountered, a back edge existed for a candidate, but when $\langle x, y_2\rangle$ was encountered, there was no back edge.

3.1 Counterexample

Theorem 4.2 of [13] can be expressed as follows: if $\mathcal{L}(\mathcal{B})$ is stutter-invariant and the language of an LTL formula, and amp satisfies **C0–C3**, then amp is POR-sound.

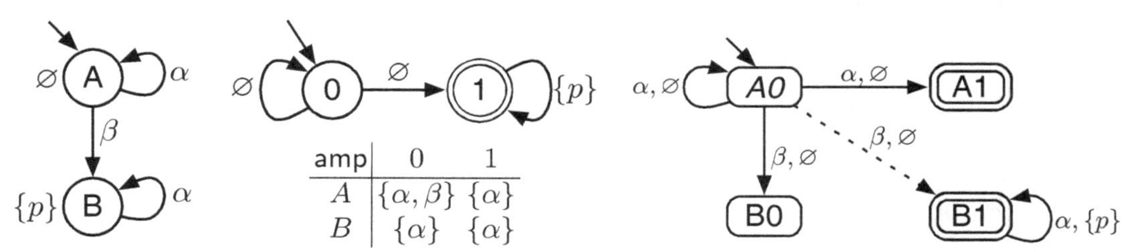

Fig. 1. Counterexample to combined theorem. Left: program and interpretation. Center: property automaton $\mathcal{B}_1$ and ample selector function. Right: the reachable product state space; dashed edges are in the full, but not reduced, space.

A counterexample to this claim is given in Fig. 1. The program consists of two states, A and B, and two operations, α and β. There is a single atomic proposition, p, which is *false* at A and *true* at B. Note that α and β are independent. Also, α is invisible, and β is not.

The property automaton, $\mathcal{B}_1$, is shown in Fig. 1 (center top). It has two states, numbered 0 and 1. State 1 is the sole accepting state. The language consists of all infinite words of the following form: a finite nonempty prefix of $\varnothing$s followed by an infinite sequence of $\{p\}$s. This language is stutter-invariant, and is the language of the LTL formula $(\neg p) \wedge ((\neg p)\mathbf{U}\,\mathbf{G}p)$.

The ample selector is specified by the table (center bottom). Notice that $\mathsf{amp}(A, 1) \neq \mathsf{en}(A)$, but the other three ample sets are full. **C0** holds because the ample sets are never empty. **C1** holds because β is independent of α. **C2** holds because α is invisible. The reachable product space is shown in Fig. 1 (right). In any DFS of $\mathsf{reduced}(\mathcal{A}, \mathsf{amp})$, the only back edge is the self-loop on $A0$ labeled $\langle\alpha, \varnothing\rangle$. Since $\mathsf{amp}(A, 0)$ is full, **C3** holds. Yet there is an accepting path in the full space, but not in the reduced space.

4 Alloy Models of POR Schemes

Alloy is a "lightweight formal methods" language and tool. It has been used in a wide variety of contexts, from exploring software designs to studying weak memory-consistency models. An Alloy model specifies *signatures*, each of which defines a type, relations on signatures, and constraints on the signatures and relations. Constraints are expressed in a logic that combines elements of first order logic and relational logic, and includes a transitive closure operator. An *instance* of a model assigns a finite set of *atoms* to each signature, and a finite set of tuples (of the right type) to each relation, in such a way that the constraints are satisfied. The Alloy analyzer can be used to check that an assertion holds on all instances in which the sizes of the signatures are within some specified bounds. The analyzer converts the question of the validity of the assertion into a SAT problem and invokes a SAT solver. Based on the result, it reports either that the assertion holds within the given bounds, or it produces an instance of the model violating the assertion.

I developed an Alloy model to search for counterexamples to various POR claims, such as the one in Sect. 3.1. The model encodes the main concepts of the previous two sections, including program, operations, interpretation, invisibility and independence, property automaton, the product space, ample selectors and the constraints on them, and a language emptiness predicate. The model culminates in an assertion which states that an ample selector satisfying the four constraints is POR-sound.

I was not able to find a way to encode stutter-invariance. In the end, I developed a small set of Büchi automata based on my own intuition of what would make interesting tests. I encoded these in Alloy and used the analyzer to explore all possible programs and ample selectors for each.

The first part of the model is a simple encoding of a finite state automaton. The following is a listing of file `ba.als`:

```
module ba  -- module for simple model of Büchi automata
sig Sigma {} -- alphabet of BA, valuation on atomic props
sig BState {} -- a state in the Büchi Automaton
```

```
one sig Binit extends BState {} -- initial state of BA
sig AState in BState {} -- accepting states of BA
 -- a transition has a source state, label, and destination state...
sig BTrans { src: one BState, label: one Sigma, dest: one BState }
```

The alphabet is some unconstrained set `Sigma`. The set of states is represented by signature `BState`. There is a single initial state, and any number of accepting states. Each transition has a source and destination state, and label. Relations declared within a signature declaration have that signature as an implicit first argument. So, for example, `src` is a binary relation of type `BTrans` $\times$ `BState`. Furthermore, the relation is many-to-one: each transition has exactly one `BState` atom associated to it by the `src` relation.

The remaining concepts are incorporated into module `por_v0`:

```
module por_v0  -- on-the-fly POR variant 0, corresponding to [13]
open ba  -- import the Büchi automata module
sig Operation {} -- program operation
sig PState { -- program state
  label: one Sigma,  -- the set of propositions which hold in this state
  enabled: set Operation,  -- the set of all operations enabled at this state
  nextState: enabled -> one PState,  -- the next-state function
  ample: BState -> set Operation  -- ample(q,s)
}{ all s: BState | ample[s] in enabled } -- ample sets subsets of enabled
fun amp[q: PState, s: BState] : set Operation { q.ample[s] }
one sig Pinit extends PState {}  -- initial program state
fact { -- all program states are reachable from Pinit
  let r = {q, q': PState | some op: Operation | q.nextState[op]=q'} |
    PState = Pinit.*r
}
sig ProdState { -- state in the product of program and property automaton
  pstate: PState,  -- the program state component
  bstate: BState,  -- the property state component
  nextFull: set ProdState,  -- all next states in the full product space
  nextReduced: set ProdState  -- all next states in the reduced product space
}
one sig ProdInit extends ProdState {} -- initial product state
pred transitionInProduct[q,q': PState, op: Operation, s,s': BState] {
  q->op->q' in nextState
  some t : BTrans | t.src = s and t.dest = s' and t.label = q.label
}
pred nextProd[x: ProdState, op: Operation, x': ProdState] {
  transitionInProduct[x.pstate, x'.pstate, op, x.bstate, x'.bstate]
}
pred independent[op1, op2 : Operation] {
  all q: PState | (op1+op2 in q.enabled) implies (
    op2 in q.nextState[op1].enabled and
    op1 in q.nextState[op2].enabled and
    q.nextState[op1].nextState[op2]=q.nextState[op2].nextState[op1])
}
pred invisible[op: Operation] {
```

```
37     all q: PState | op in q.enabled => q.nextState[op].label = q.label
38   }
39   fact C0 { all q: PState, s: BState | some q.enabled => some amp[q,s] }
40   fact C1 {
41     all q: PState, s: BState | let A=amp[q,s] |
42       let r = { q1, q2: PState | some op: Operation-A |
43                 q1->op->q2 in nextState } |
44         all q': q.*r, op1: q'.enabled-A, op2: A | independent[op1, op2]
45   }
46   fact C2 {
47     all q: PState, s: BState | let A = amp[q,s] |
48       A != q.enabled implies all op: A | invisible[op]
49   }
50   fact C3' {
51     let r = { x, x' : ProdState | x->x' in nextReduced and
52               amp[x.pstate, x'.bstate] != x.pstate.enabled } |
53       no x: ProdState | x in x.^r
54   }
55   fact { -- generate all reachable product states, etc.
56     nextFull = {x,y: ProdState | some op: Operation | nextProd[x,op,y]}
57     nextReduced = {x,y: ProdState |
58       some op: amp[x.pstate, y.bstate] | nextProd[x,op,y]}
59     ProdState = ProdInit.*nextFull
60     all x,y: ProdState | (x.pstate=y.pstate && x.bstate=y.bstate) => x=y
61     ProdInit.pstate = Pinit and ProdInit.bstate = Binit
62     all x: ProdState, op: Operation, q': PState, s': BState |
63       transitionInProduct[x.pstate, q', op, x.bstate, s'] implies
64         some y: ProdState | y.pstate = q' and y.bstate = s'
65   }
66   pred nonemptyLang[r: ProdState->ProdState] { -- r reaches accepting cycle
67     some x: ProdInit.*r | (x.bstate in AState and x in x.^r)
68   }
69   assert PORsoundness { -- if full space has a lasso, so does the reduced
70     nonemptyLang[nextFull] => nonemptyLang[nextReduced]
71   }
```

The **facts** are constraints that any instance must satisfy; some of the facts are given names for readability. A **pred** declaration defines a (typed) predicate.

Most aspects of this model are self-explanatory; I will comment only on the less obvious features. The relations `nextFull` and `nextReduced` represent the next state relations in the full and reduced spaces, respectively. They are declared in `ProdState`, but specified completely in the final `fact` on lines 56–58. Strictly speaking, one could remove those predicates and substitute their definitions, but this seemed more convenient. Line 60 asserts that a product state is determined uniquely by its program and property components. Line 61 specifies the initial product state.

Line 59 insists that only states reachable (in the full space) from the initial state will be included in an instance (`*` is the reflexive transitive closure operator). Lines 62–64 specify the converse. Hence in any instance of this model, `ProdState` will consist of exactly the reachable product states in the full space.

The encoding of **C1** is based on the following observation: given $q \in Q$ and a set A of operations enabled at q, define $r \subseteq Q \times Q$ by removing from the program's next-state relation all edges labeled by operations in A. Then "no operation dependent on an operation in A can occur unless an operation in A occurs first" is equivalent to the statement that on any path from q using edges in r, all enabled operations encountered will either be in A or independent of every operation in A.

Condition **C3** is difficult to encode, in that it depends on specifying a depth-first search. I have replaced it with a weaker condition, which is similar to a well-known cycle proviso in the offline theory:

C3′ In any cycle in $\mathsf{reduced}(\mathcal{A}, \mathsf{amp})$, there is a transition from $\langle q, s\rangle$ to $\langle q', s'\rangle$ for which $\mathsf{amp}(q, s') = \mathsf{en}(q)$.

Equivalently: if one removes from the reduced product space all such transitions, then the resulting graph should have no cycles. This is the meaning of lines 50–54 (`^` is the strict transitive closure operator).

The next step is to create tests for specific property automata. This example is for the automaton $\mathcal{B}_1$ of Fig. 1:

```
module ba1
open ba
one sig X0, X1 extends Sigma {}
one sig B1 extends BState {}
one sig T1, T2, T3 extends BTrans {}
fact {
  AState = B1   -- B1 is the sole accepting state
  T1.src=Binit && T1.label=X0 && T1.dest=Binit
  T2.src=Binit && T2.label=X0 && T2.dest=B1
  T3.src=B1 && T3.label=X1 && T3.dest=B1
}
```

The final step is a test that combines the modules above:

```
open por_v0
open ba1
checkPORsoundness for exactly 2 Sigma, exactly 2 BState,
  exactly 3 BTrans, 2 Operation, 2 PState, 4 ProdState
```

It places upper bounds on the numbers of operations, program states, and product states while checking the soundness assertion. Using the Alloy analyzer to check the assertion above results in a counterexample like the one in Fig. 1. The runtime is a fraction of a second. The Alloy instance uses two uninterpreted atoms for the elements of `Sigma`; I have simply substituted the sets $\varnothing$ and $\{p\}$ for them to produce Fig. 1. As we have seen, this counterexample happens to also satisfy the stronger constraint **C3**.

5 Spin

The POR algorithm used by Spin is described in [10] and is similar to the combined algorithm. We can see what Spin actually does by encoding examples in Promela and executing Spin with and without POR.

```
bit p = 0;
active proctype p0() { p=1 }
active proctype p1() { bit x=0; do :: x=0 od }
never {
  B0: do :: !p :: !p -> break od
  accept_B1: do :: p od
}
```

Fig. 2. Promela representation of counterexample using $\mathcal{B}_1$ of Fig. 1

Figure 2 shows an encoding of the example of Fig. 1. Transition α corresponds to the assignment `x = 0`, where `x` is a variable local to `p1`. Transition β corresponds to the assignment `p = 1`, where `p` is a shared variable. Applying Spin with the following commands allows one to see the structure of the program graphs for each process, as well as each step in the search of the full space:

```
spin -a test1.pml; cc -o pan -DCHECK -DNOREDUCE pan.c; ./pan -d; ./pan -a
```

I did this with Spin version 6.4.9, the latest stable release. The output indicates that 4 states and 5 transitions are explored, and one state is matched—exactly as in Fig. 1 (right). As expected, the output also reports a violation—a path to an accepting cycle that corresponds to the transition from $A0$ to $B1$ followed by the self-loop on $B1$ repeated forever.

Repeat this experiment without the `-DNOREDUCE`, however, and Spin finds no errors. The output indicates that it misses the transition from $A0$ to $B1$.

6 Ignoring the Intermediate States

An interesting aspect of the combined algorithm is that the ample set is a function of an intermediate state. I.e., given a product state $x = \langle q, s \rangle$, the ample set is determined by the intermediate state $x' = \langle q, s' \rangle$ obtained after executing a property transition. This introduces a difference between the on-the-fly scheme and offline schemes, where there is no notion of intermediate state. It also introduces other complexities. For example, it is possible that x' was reached earlier in the search through some other state $\langle q, s_2 \rangle$, because of a property transition $s_2 \xrightarrow{L(q)} s'$. How does the algorithm guarantee that the ample set selected for x' will be the same as the earlier choice? This issue is not addressed in [13] or [10].

These problems go away if one simply makes the ample set a function of the source product state x. The intermediate states do not have to play a role.

Specifically, given an ample selector amp, define $\mathsf{reduced}_2(\mathcal{A}, \mathsf{amp})$ as in (1) and (2), except replace "$\alpha \in \mathsf{amp}(q, s')$" in (2) with "$\alpha \in \mathsf{amp}(q, s)$". Perform the same substitution in **C3** and call the resulting condition $\mathbf{C3}_1$. The weaker version of $\mathbf{C3}_1$ is simply:

$\mathbf{C3}'_1$ In any cycle in $\mathsf{reduced}_2(\mathcal{A}, \mathsf{amp})$ there is a state $\langle q, s\rangle$ with $\mathsf{amp}(q, s) = \mathsf{en}(q)$.

Conditions **C0**–**C2** are unchanged. I refer to this scheme as V1, and to the original combined algorithm as V0. The Alloy model of V0 in Sect. 4 can be easily modified to represent V1.

Using V1, the example of Fig. 1 is no longer a counterexample. In fact, Alloy reports there are no counterexamples using $\mathcal{B}_1$, at least for small bounds on the program size. Figure 5 gives detailed results for this and other Alloy experiments.

Unfortunately, Alloy does find a counterexample for a slightly more complicated property automaton, $\mathcal{B}_2$, which is shown in Fig. 3.

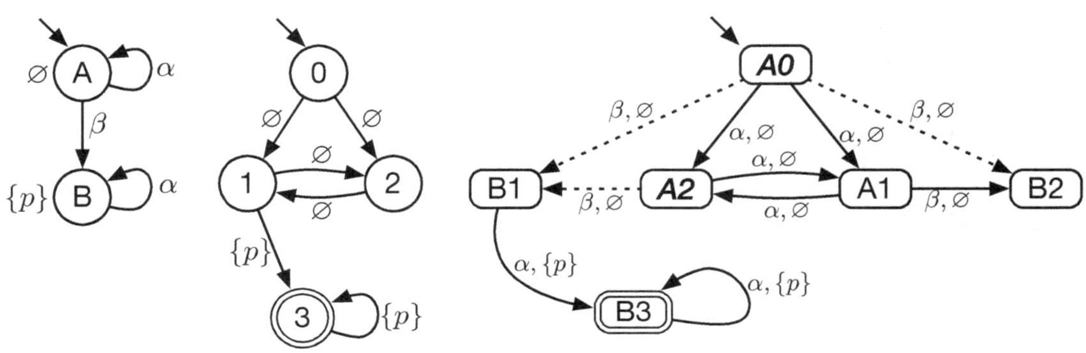

Fig. 3. Counterexample to V1 with $\mathcal{B}_2$ (center). $A0$ and $A2$ have proper ample set $\{\alpha\}$.

The program is the same as the one in Sect. 3.1. Automaton $\mathcal{B}_2$ has four states, with state 3 the sole accepting state. The language is the same as that of $\mathcal{B}_1$: all infinite words formed by concatenating a finite nonempty prefix of ∅s and an infinite sequence of $\{p\}$s. If the prefix has odd length, the accepting run begins with the transition $0 \rightarrow 1$, otherwise it begins with the transition $0 \rightarrow 2$.

In the ample selector, only $A0$ and $A2$ are not fully enabled:

amp	0	1	2	3
A	$\{\alpha\}$	$\{\alpha, \beta\}$	$\{\alpha\}$	$\{\alpha, \beta\}$
B	$\{\alpha\}$	$\{\alpha\}$	$\{\alpha\}$	$\{\alpha\}$.

C0–**C2** hold for the reasons given in Sect. 3.1. $\mathbf{C3}_1$ holds for any DFS in which $A2$ is pushed onto the stack before $A1$. In that case, there is no back edge from $A2$; there will be a back edge when $A1$ is pushed, but $A1$ is fully enabled.

7 What's Right

In this section, I show that POR scheme V1 of Sect. 6 is sound if one introduces certain assumptions on the property automaton. The following definition is similar to the notion of *stutter invariant (SI) automaton* in [6] and to that of *closure under stuttering* in [9]. The main differences derive from the use of Muller automata in [6] and *Büchi transition systems* in [9], while we are dealing with ordinary Büchi automata.

Definition 12. *A Büchi automaton* $\mathcal{B} = \langle S, \{s_{init}\}, \Sigma, \delta, F\rangle$, *is in* SI normal form *if it has a single initial state* s_{init} *with no incoming edges, and for each* $s \in S \setminus \{s_{init}\}$, *there is some* $a_s \in \Sigma$ *such that the following all hold:*

1. *Every edge terminating in* s *is labeled* a_s.
2. s *has exactly one outgoing edge with label* a_s.
3. *If* $s \notin F$ *then* $\langle s, a_s, s\rangle \in \delta$.
4. *If* $\langle s, a_s, s\rangle \notin \delta$, *then there exists* $s^\sharp \in S \setminus F$ *such that (i)* $\langle s, a_s, s^\sharp\rangle \in \delta$ *and (ii) for all* $a \in \Sigma$ *and* $s' \in S$, $\langle s, a, s'\rangle \in \delta \Leftrightarrow \langle s^\sharp, a, s'\rangle \in \delta$.

Lemma 1. *Let* $\mathcal{B}$ *be a Büchi automaton in SI normal form. Suppose* $a, b \in \Sigma$ *and* $a \neq b$. *Both of the following hold:*

1. *If* $s_1 \xrightarrow{a} s_2 \xrightarrow{b} s_3$ *is a path in* $\mathcal{B}$, *then for some* $s_2' \in S$, $s_1 \xrightarrow{a} s_2 \xrightarrow{a} s_2' \xrightarrow{b} s_3$ *is a path in* $\mathcal{B}$.
2. *If* $s_1 \xrightarrow{a} s_2 \xrightarrow{a} s_3 \xrightarrow{b} s_4$ *is a path in* $\mathcal{B}$, *then* $s_1 \xrightarrow{a} s_2 \xrightarrow{b} s_4$ *is a path in* $\mathcal{B}$. *Moreover, if* s_3 *is accepting, then* s_2 *is accepting.*

Following the approach of [6], one can show that the language of an automaton in SI normal form is stutter-invariant. Moreover, any Büchi automaton with a stutter-invariant language can be transformed into SI normal form without changing the language. The conversion satisfies $|S'| \leq O(|\Sigma||S|)$, where $|S|$ and $|S'|$ are the number of states in the original and new automaton, respectively. For details and proofs, see [17]. An example is given in Fig. 4; the language of $\mathcal{B}_3$ (or $\mathcal{B}_4$) consists of all words with a finite number of $\{p\}$s.

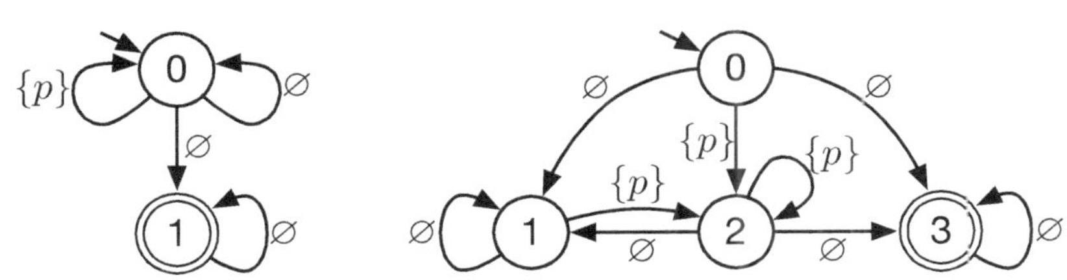

Fig. 4. Property automaton $\mathcal{B}_3$ and result of transformation to SI normal form, $\mathcal{B}_4$.

Theorem 1. *Suppose* $\mathcal{B}$ *is in SI normal form and* $\mathsf{amp}\colon Q \times S \to 2^T$ *is an ample selector satisfying* C0–C2 *and* C3$'_1$. *Then* amp *is POR-sound.*

The remainder of this section is devoted to the proof of Theorem 1. The proof is similar to the proof of the offline case in [4].

Let θ be an accepting path in the full space $\mathcal{A}$. An infinite sequence of accepting paths $\pi_0, \pi_1, \ldots$ will be constructed, where $\pi_0 = \theta$. For each $i \geq 0$, π_i will be decomposed as $\eta_i \circ \theta_i$, where η_i is a finite path of length i in the *reduced space*, θ_i is an infinite path, η_i is a prefix of η_{i+1}, and $\circ$ denotes concatenation. For $i = 0$, η_0 is empty and $\theta_0 = \theta$.

Assume $i \geq 0$ and we have defined η_j and θ_j for $j \leq i$. Write

$$\theta_i \;=\; \langle q_0, s_0 \rangle \xrightarrow{\langle \alpha_1, \sigma_0 \rangle} \langle q_1, s_1 \rangle \xrightarrow{\langle \alpha_2, \sigma_1 \rangle} \cdots \tag{3}$$

where $\sigma_k = L(q_k)$ for $k \geq 0$. Then η_{i+1} and θ_{i+1} are defined as follows. Let $A = \mathsf{amp}(q_0, s_0)$. There are two cases:

Case 1: $\alpha_1 \in A$. Let η_{i+1} be the path obtained by appending the first transition of θ_i to η_i, and θ_{i+1} the path obtained by removing the first transition from θ_i.

Case 2: $\alpha_1 \notin A$. Then there are two sub-cases:

Case 2a: Some operation in A occurs in θ_i. Let n be the index of the first occurrence, so that $\alpha_n \in A$, but $\alpha_j \notin A$ for $1 \leq j < n$. By **C1**, α_j and α_n are independent for $1 \leq j < n$. By repeated application of the independence property, there are paths in P

$$\begin{array}{ccccccccccccccc}
q_0 & \xrightarrow{\alpha_1} & q_1 & \xrightarrow{\alpha_2} & q_2 & \xrightarrow{\alpha_3} & \cdots & \xrightarrow{\alpha_{n-2}} & q_{n-2} & \xrightarrow{\alpha_{n-1}} & q_{n-1} & & & & \\
\downarrow{\scriptstyle \alpha_n} & & \downarrow{\scriptstyle \alpha_n} & & \downarrow{\scriptstyle \alpha_n} & & & & \downarrow{\scriptstyle \alpha_n} & & \downarrow{\scriptstyle \alpha_n} & & & & \\
q_1' & \xrightarrow{\alpha_1} & q_2' & \xrightarrow{\alpha_2} & q_3' & \xrightarrow{\alpha_3} & \cdots & \xrightarrow{\alpha_{n-2}} & q_{n-1}' & \xrightarrow{\alpha_{n-1}} & q_n & \xrightarrow{\alpha_{n+1}} & q_{n+1} & \xrightarrow{\alpha_{n+2}} & \cdots
\end{array}$$

By **C2**, α_n is invisible, whence $L(q_{j+1}') = \sigma_j$ for $0 \leq j \leq n-2$, and $\sigma_{n-1} = \sigma_n$. Hence the admissible sequence

$$q_0 \overset{\alpha_n}{\to} q_1' \overset{\alpha_1}{\to} q_2' \overset{\alpha_2}{\to} q_3' \to \cdots \overset{\alpha_{n-2}}{\to} q_{n-1}' \overset{\alpha_{n-1}}{\to} q_n \overset{\alpha_{n+1}}{\to} q_{n+1} \overset{\alpha_{n+2}}{\to} q_{n+2} \to \cdots \tag{4}$$

generates the word

$$\sigma_0 \sigma_0 \sigma_1 \sigma_2 \cdots \sigma_{n-2} \sigma_n \sigma_{n+1} \sigma_{n+2} \cdots . \tag{5}$$

Now the projection of θ_i onto $\mathcal{B}$ has the form

$$s_0 \xrightarrow{\sigma_0} s_1 \xrightarrow{\sigma_1} s_2 \xrightarrow{\sigma_2} \cdots \xrightarrow{\sigma_{n-2}} s_{n-1} \xrightarrow{\sigma_n} s_n \xrightarrow{\sigma_n} s_{n+1} \xrightarrow{\sigma_{n+1}} s_{n+2} \xrightarrow{\sigma_{n+2}} \cdots$$

since $\sigma_{n-1} = \sigma_n$. By Lemma 1, there is a path in $\mathcal{B}$

$$s_0 \xrightarrow{\sigma_0} s_1 \xrightarrow{\sigma_0} s_1' \xrightarrow{\sigma_1} s_2 \xrightarrow{\sigma_2} \cdots \xrightarrow{\sigma_{n-2}} s_{n-1} \xrightarrow{\sigma_n} s_n \xrightarrow{\sigma_{n+1}} s_{n+2} \xrightarrow{\sigma_{n+2}} \cdots \tag{6}$$

which accepts the word (5). Composing (4) and (6) therefore gives a path through the product space. Removing the first transition (labeled $\langle \alpha_n, \sigma_0 \rangle$) from this path yields θ_{i+1}. Appending that transition to η_i yields η_{i+1}.

Case 2b: No operation in A occurs in θ_i. By **C0**, A is nonempty. Let $\beta \in A$. By **C2**, every operation in θ_i is independent of β. With an argument that is similar to the one for Case 2a, we can see there is a path in the product space for which the projection onto the program component has the form

$$q_0 \xrightarrow{\beta} q'_1 \xrightarrow{\alpha_1} q'_2 \xrightarrow{\alpha_2} q'_3 \rightarrow \cdots$$

and the projection onto the property component has the form

$$s_0 \xrightarrow{\sigma_0} s_1 \xrightarrow{\sigma_0} s'_1 \xrightarrow{\sigma_1} s_2 \xrightarrow{\sigma_2} \cdots .$$

Removing the first transition from this path yields θ_{i+1}. Appending that transition to η_i yields η_{i+1}. This completes the definitions of η_{i+1} and θ_{i+1}.

Let η be the limit of the η_i. Clearly η is an infinite path through the reduced product space, starting from the initial state. We must show that it passes through an accepting state infinitely often. To do so, we must examine more closely the sequence of property states through which each θ_i passes.

Let $i \geq 0$, and s_0 the final state of η_i. Say θ_i passes through states $s_0 s_1 s_2 \cdots$. Then the final state of η_{i+1} will be s_1, and the state sequence of θ_{i+1} is determined by the three cases as follows:

$$\begin{array}{ll} \text{Case 1: } s_1 s_2 \cdots & \\ \text{Case 2a: } s_1 s'_1 s_2 \cdots s_n s_{n+2} \cdots & (s_{n+1} \in F \implies s_n \in F) \\ \text{Case 2b: } s_1 s'_1 s_2 \cdots & \end{array} \tag{7}$$

We first claim that for all $i \geq 0$, θ_i passes through an accepting state infinitely often. This holds for θ_0, which is an accepting path by assumption. Assume it holds for θ_i. In each case of (7), we see that the state sequence of θ_{i+1} has a suffix which is a suffix of the state sequence of θ_i, so the claim holds for θ_{i+1}.

Definition 13. *For any path $\xi = s_0 \rightarrow s_1 \rightarrow \cdots$ through $\mathcal{B}$ which passes through an accepting state infinitely often, define the* accepting distance *of ξ, written* $\mathsf{AD}(\xi)$, *to be the minimum $k \geq 1$ for which s_k is accepting.*

Lemma 2. *Let $i \geq 0$ and say the state sequence of θ_i is $s_0 s_1 s_2 \cdots$. If s_1 is not accepting then one of the following holds:*

- *Case 1 holds and $\mathsf{AD}(\theta_{i+1}) < \mathsf{AD}(\theta_i)$, or*
- *Case 2a or 2b holds and $\mathsf{AD}(\theta_{i+1}) \leq \mathsf{AD}(\theta_i)$.*

Proof. If s_1 is not accepting then there is some $k \geq 2$ for which s_k is accepting. The result follows by examining (7). In Case 1, the accepting distance decreases by 1. In Case 2a, the accepting distance is either unchanged (if $k \leq n$) or decreases by 1 (if $k > n$). In Case 2b, the accepting distance is unchanged. □

Lemma 3. *For an infinite number of $i \geq 0$, Case 1 holds for θ_i.*

Proof. Suppose not. Then there is some $i \geq 0$ such that Case 2 holds for all $j \geq i$. Let α_1 be the first program operation of θ_i. Then α_1 is the first program operation of θ_j, for all $j \geq i$. Furthermore, for all $j \geq i$, α_1 is not in the ample set of the final state of η_j. Since the product space has only a finite number of states, this means there is a cycle in the reduced space for which α_1 is enabled but never in the ample set, contradicting $\mathbf{C3}'_1$. □

We now show that η passes through an accepting state infinitely often. Note that, if $\mathsf{AD}(\theta_i) = 1$, an accepting state is added to η_i to form η_{i+1}. Suppose η does not pass through an accepting state infinitely often. Then there is some $i \geq 0$ such that for all $j \geq i$, $\mathsf{AD}(\theta_j) > 1$. By Lemma 2, $(\mathsf{AD}(\theta_j))_{j \geq i}$ is a nonincreasing sequence of positive integers, and by Lemma 3, this sequence strictly decreases infinitely often, a contradiction. This completes the proof of Theorem 1.

Remark 1. The proof goes through with minor modifications for V0 in place of V1. Let $A = \mathsf{amp}(q_0, s_1)$ instead of $\mathsf{amp}(q_0, s_0)$. In Case 2a (similarly in 2b), note the first transition $s_0 \xrightarrow{\sigma_0} s_1$ in the path in $\mathcal{B}$ remains in the new path (6).

8 Summary of Experimental Results and Conclusion

We have seen that standard ways of combining POR and on-the-fly model checking are unsound. This is not only a theoretical issue—the defect in the algorithm is realized in Spin, which can produce an incorrect result. A modification (V1) seems to help, but is still not enough to guarantee soundness for any Büchi automaton with a stutter-invariant language. However, any such automaton can be transformed into a normal form for which algorithm V1 is sound.

v	BA	`Sigma`	`BState`	`BTrans`	`Operation`	`PState`	`ProdState`	time (s)	Result
V0	$\mathcal{B}_1$	2	2	3	≤ 2	≤ 2	≤ 4	0.3	✗
V1	$\mathcal{B}_1$	2	2	3	≤ 3	≤ 5	≤ 10	42.3	✓
V0	$\mathcal{B}_2$	2	4	6	≤ 2	≤ 2	≤ 6	0.4	✗
V1	$\mathcal{B}_2$	2	4	6	≤ 2	≤ 2	≤ 6	0.3	✗
V0	$\mathcal{B}_3$	2	2	4	≤ 3	≤ 5	≤ 10	256.3	✓
V1	$\mathcal{B}_3$	2	2	4	≤ 3	≤ 5	≤ 10	280.7	✓
V0	$\mathcal{B}_4$	2	4	9	≤ 3	≤ 4	≤ 16	39.5	✓
V1	$\mathcal{B}_4$	2	4	9	≤ 3	≤ 4	≤ 16	37.7	✓
V0	$\mathcal{B}_5$	≤ 3	≤ 4	≤ 6	≤ 3	≤ 4	≤ 16	2264.9	✓
V1	$\mathcal{B}_5$	≤ 3	≤ 4	≤ 6	≤ 3	≤ 4	≤ 16	1653.9	✓

Fig. 5. Bounded verification of soundness of POR schemes V0 and V1 on various Büchi automata using Alloy. $\mathcal{B}_5$ represents all automata in SI normal form within the bounds. Each run resulted in either a counterexample (✗) or not (✓).

Alloy proved useful for reasoning about the algorithms and generating small counterexamples. A summary of the Alloy experiments and results is given in

Fig. 5. These were run on an 8-core 3.7GHz Intel Xeon W-2145 and used the plingeling SAT solver [1].[3] In addition to the experiments already discussed, Alloy found no soundness counterexamples for property automata $\mathcal{B}_3$ or $\mathcal{B}_4$, using V0 or V1. In the case of $\mathcal{B}_4$, this is what Theorem 1 predicts. For further confirmation of Theorem 1, I constructed a general Alloy model of Büchi automata in SI normal form, represented by $\mathcal{B}_5$ in the table. Alloy confirms that both V0 and V1 are sound for all such automata within small bounds on program and automata size.

It is possible that the use of the normal form, while correct, cancels out the benefits of POR. A comprehensive exploration of this issue is beyond the scope of this paper, but I can provide data on one non-trivial example. I encoded an n-process version of Peterson's mutual exclusion algorithm in Promela, and used Spin to verify starvation-freedom for one process in the case $n = 5$. If p is the predicate that holds whenever the process is enabled, a trace violates this property if p holds only a finite number of times in the trace, i.e., if the trace is in $\mathcal{L}(\mathcal{B}_3) = \mathcal{L}(\mathcal{B}_4)$. Figure 6 shows the results of Spin verification using $\mathcal{B}_3$ without POR, and using $\mathcal{B}_3$ and $\mathcal{B}_4$ with POR. The results indicate that POR significantly improves performance on this problem, and that using the normal form $\mathcal{B}_4$ in place of $\mathcal{B}_3$ actually *improves* performance further by a small amount.

BA	POR	states(stored)	transitions	time(s)	Result
$\mathcal{B}_3$	N	18,964,912	116,510,960	25.8	✓
$\mathcal{B}_3$	Y	4,742,982	13,823,705	3.6	✓
$\mathcal{B}_4$	Y	4,719,514	12,503,008	3.4	✓

Fig. 6. Spin verification of starvation-freedom for 5-process Peterson. Using the SI normal form $\mathcal{B}_4$ instead of the smaller $\mathcal{B}_3$ has little impact on performance.

It is likely that V1 is sound for other interesting classes of automata. Observe, for example, that $\mathcal{B}_2$ of Fig. 3 has states u where the language of the automaton with u considered as the initial state is *not* stutter-invariant. If we restrict to automata in which every state has a stutter-invariant language, is V1 sound? I have neither a proof nor a counterexample. (This is certainly not true of V0, as $\mathcal{B}_1$ is a counterexample.) To explore this question, it would help to find a way to encode the stutter-invariant property—or a suitable approximation—in Alloy.

Finally, the proof of Theorem 1 is complicated and might also be flawed. Recent work mechanizing such proofs [3] represents an important advance in raising the level of assurance in model checking algorithms. It would be interesting to see if the proof of this theorem is amenable to such methods. However, constructing such proofs requires far more effort than the Alloy approach described here. One possible approach moving forward is to use tools such as Alloy when prototyping a new algorithm, to get feedback quickly and root out

[3] All artifacts needed to reproduce the experiments reported in this paper can be downloaded from http://vsl.cis.udel.edu/cav19.

bugs. Once Alloy no longer finds any counterexamples, one could then expend the considerable effort required to construct a formal mechanized proof.

Acknowledgements. I am grateful to Ganesh Gopalakrishnan and Julian Brunner for fruitful conversations on partial order reduction, to Gerard Holzmann for help with Spin, and to the anonymous reviewers for suggestions that improved this paper. This material is based upon work by the RAPIDS Institute, supported by the U.S. Department of Energy, Office of Science, Office of Advanced Scientific Computing Research, Scientific Discovery through Advanced Computing (SciDAC) program. Funding was also provided by the U.S. National Science Foundation under award CCF-1319571.

References

1. Biere, A.: CaDiCaL, Lingeling, Plingeling, Treengeling, YalSAT Entering the SAT Competition 2017. In: Balyo, T., Heule, M., Järvisalo, M. (eds.) Proceedings of SAT Competition 2017 - Solver and Benchmark Descriptions. Department of Computer Science Series of Publications B, vol. B-2017-1, pp. 14–15. University of Helsinki (2017)
2. Brunner, J.: Implementation and verification of partial order reduction for on-the-fly model checking. Master's thesis, Technische Universität München, Department of Computer Science, July 2014. https://www21.in.tum.de/~brunnerj/documents/ivporotfmc.pdf
3. Brunner, J., Lammich, P.: Formal verification of an executable LTL model checker with partial order reduction. J. Autom. Reason. **60**, 3–21 (2018). https://doi.org/10.1007/s10817-017-9418-4
4. Clarke Jr., E.M., Grumberg, O., Peled, D.A.: Model Checking. MIT Press, Cambridge (1999)
5. Courcoubetis, C., Vardi, M., Wolper, P., Yannakakis, M.: Memory-efficient algorithms for the verification of temporal properties. Form. Methods Syst. Des. **1**(2), 275–288 (1992). https://doi.org/10.1007/BF00121128
6. Etessami, K.: Stutter-invariant languages, ω-automata, and temporal logic. In: Halbwachs, N., Peled, D. (eds.) CAV 1999. LNCS, vol. 1633, pp. 236–248. Springer, Heidelberg (1999). https://doi.org/10.1007/3-540-48683-6_22
7. Holzmann, G., Peled, D., Yannakakis, M.: On nested depth first search. In: The Spin Verification System, DIMACS - Series in Discrete Mathematics and Theoretical Computer Science, vol. 32, pp. 23–31. AMS and DIMACS (1997). https://bookstore.ams.org/dimacs-32/
8. Holzmann, G.J.: The Spin Model Checker: Primer and Reference Manual. Addison-Wesley, Boston (2004)
9. Holzmann, G.J., Kupferman, O.: Not checking for closure under stuttering. In: Grégoire, J.C., Holzmann, G.J., Peled, D.A. (eds.) The SPIN Verification System. DIMACS Series in Discrete Mathematics and Theoretical Computer Science, vol. 32, pp. 17–22. American Mathematical Society (1997)
10. Holzmann, G.J., Peled, D.: An improvement in formal verification. In: Hogrefe, D., Leue, S. (eds.) Proceedings of the 7th IFIP WG6.1 International Conference on Formal Description Techniques (Forte 1994). IFIP Conference Proceedings, vol. 6, pp. 197–211. Chapman & Hall (1995). http://dl.acm.org/citation.cfm?id=646213.681369

11. Jackson, D.: Software Abstractions: Logic, Language, and Analysis, Revised edn. MIT Press (2012)
12. Peled, D.: Combining partial order reductions with on-the-fly model-checking. In: Dill, D.L. (ed.) CAV 1994. LNCS, vol. 818, pp. 377–390. Springer, Heidelberg (1994). https://doi.org/10.1007/3-540-58179-0_69
13. Peled, D.: Combining partial order reductions with on-the-fly model-checking. Form. Methods Syst. Des. **8**(1), 39–64 (1996). https://doi.org/10.1007/BF00121262
14. Schwoon, S., Esparza, J.: A note on on-the-fly verification algorithms. In: Halbwachs, N., Zuck, L.D. (eds.) TACAS 2005. LNCS, vol. 3440, pp. 174–190. Springer, Heidelberg (2005). https://doi.org/10.1007/978-3-540-31980-1_12
15. Siegel, S.F.: Reexamining two results in partial order reduction. Technical report. UD-CIS-2011/06, U. Delaware (2011). http://vsl.cis.udel.edu/pubs/por_tr_2011.html
16. Siegel, S.F.: Transparent partial order reduction. Form. Methods Syst. Des. **40**(1), 1–19 (2012). https://doi.org/10.1007/s10703-011-0126-0
17. Siegel, S.F.: What's wrong with on-the-fly partial order reduction (extended version). Technical report. UD-CIS-2019/05, University of Delaware (2019). http://vsl.cis.udel.edu/pubs/onthefly.html

Integrating Formal Schedulability Analysis into a Verified OS Kernel

Xiaojie Guo[1,2], Maxime Lesourd[1,2], Mengqi Liu[3], Lionel Rieg[1,3](✉), and Zhong Shao[3]

[1] Univ. Grenoble Alpes, CNRS, Grenoble INP, VERIMAG, Grenoble, France
[2] Univ. Grenoble Alpes, Inria, CNRS, Grenoble INP, LIG, Grenoble, France
[3] Yale University, New Haven, CT, USA
lionel.rieg@univ-grenoble-alpes.fr

Abstract. Formal verification of real-time systems is attractive because these systems often perform critical operations. Unlike non real-time systems, latency and response time guarantees are of critical importance in this setting, as much as functional correctness. Nevertheless, formal verification of real-time OSes usually stops the scheduling analysis at the policy level: they only prove that the scheduler (or its abstract model) satisfies some scheduling policy. In this paper, we go further and connect together Prosa, a verified schedulability analyzer, and RT-CertiKOS, a verified single-core sequential real-time OS kernel. Thus, we get a more general and extensible schedulability analysis proof for RT-CertiKOS, as well a concrete implementation validating Prosa models. It also showcases that it is realistic to connect two completely independent formal developments in a proof assistant.

Keywords: Formal methods · Proof assistant · Real-time scheduling · OS kernel · Schedulability analysis

1 Introduction

The real-time and OS communities have seen recent effort towards formal proofs, through several techniques such as model checking [16,22] and interactive theorem provers [7,14,17]. This trend is motivated by the high stakes of critical systems and the combinatorial complexity of considering all possible interleavings of states of a system, which makes pen-and-paper reasoning too error-prone.

Real-time OSes used in critical areas such as avionics and automobile applications must ensure not only functional correctness but also timing requirements. Indeed, a missed deadline may have catastrophic consequences. Schedulability analysis aims to guarantee the absence of deadline miss given a scheduling algorithm which decides which task is going to execute.

I. Dillig and S. Tasiran (Eds.): CAV 2019, LNCS 11562, pp. 496–514, 2019.
https://doi.org/10.1007/978-3-030-25543-5_28

In the current state of the art, the schedulability analysis is decoupled from the kernel code verification. This is good from a separation of concern perspective as both kernel verification and schedulability analysis are already complex enough without adding in the other. Nevertheless, this gap also means that both communities may lack validation from the other one.

On the one hand, schedulability analysis itself is error-prone, *e.g.*, a flaw was found in the original schedulability analysis [26,27,29] for the Controller Area Network bus, which is widely used in automobile. To tackle this issue, the Prosa library [7] provides mechanized schedulability proofs. This library is developed with a focus on readable specifications in order to ensure wide acceptance by the community. It is currently a reference for mechanized schedulability proofs and was able to verify several existing multicore scheduling policies under a new setting with jitter. However, some of its design decisions, in particular for task models and scheduling policies, are highly unusual and their adequacy to reality has never been justified by connecting them to a concrete OS kernel enforcing a real-time scheduling policy.

On the other hand, OS kernels are very sensitive and bug-prone pieces of code, which inspires a lot of existing work on using formal methods to prove functional correctness and other requirements, such as access control policies [17], scheduling policies [31], timing requirements, etc. One such verified OS kernel is RT-CertiKOS [21], developed by the Yale FLINT group and built on top of the sequential CertiKOS [9,13]. Its verification focuses on extensions beyond pure functional correctness, such as real-time guarantees and isolation between components. However, any major extension such as real-time adds a lot of proof burden.

In this paper, we solve both problems at once by combining the formal schedulability analysis given by Prosa with the functional correctness guarantees of RT-CertiKOS. Thus, we get a formal schedulability proof for this kernel: if it accepts a task set, then formal proofs ensure that there will be no deadline miss during execution. Furthermore, this work also produces a concrete instance of the definitions used in Prosa, ensuring their consistency and adequacy with a real system.

Contributions. In this paper, we make the following contributions:

- Definition of a clear interface for schedulability analysis between a kernel (here, RT-CertiKOS) and a schedulability analyzer (here, Prosa);
- A workaround for the mismatch between the notion of jobs in schedulability analysis (which contains actual execution time) and in OS scheduling through the scheduling trace;
- A way to extend a finite scheduling trace (from RT-CertiKOS) into an infinite one (for Prosa) while still satisfying the fixed priority preemptive (FPP) scheduling policy;
- A formally proven connection between RT-CertiKOS and Prosa, validating Prosa modeling choices and enabling RT-CertiKOS to benefit from the state-of-the-art schedulability results of Prosa.

Outline of the Paper. Section 2 introduces the Prosa library and its description of scheduling. In Sect. 3, we describe RT-CertiKOS, its scheduler, as well as the associated verification technique, abstraction layers. Section 4 then highlights the key differences between the models of Prosa and RT-CertiKOS, and how we resolve them. Finally, Sects. 5, 6, and 7, evaluate our work, present future work and related work before concluding.

2 Prosa

Prosa [7] is a Coq [25] library of models and analyses for real-time systems. The library is aimed towards the real-time community and provides models and analyses found in the literature with a focus on readable specifications.

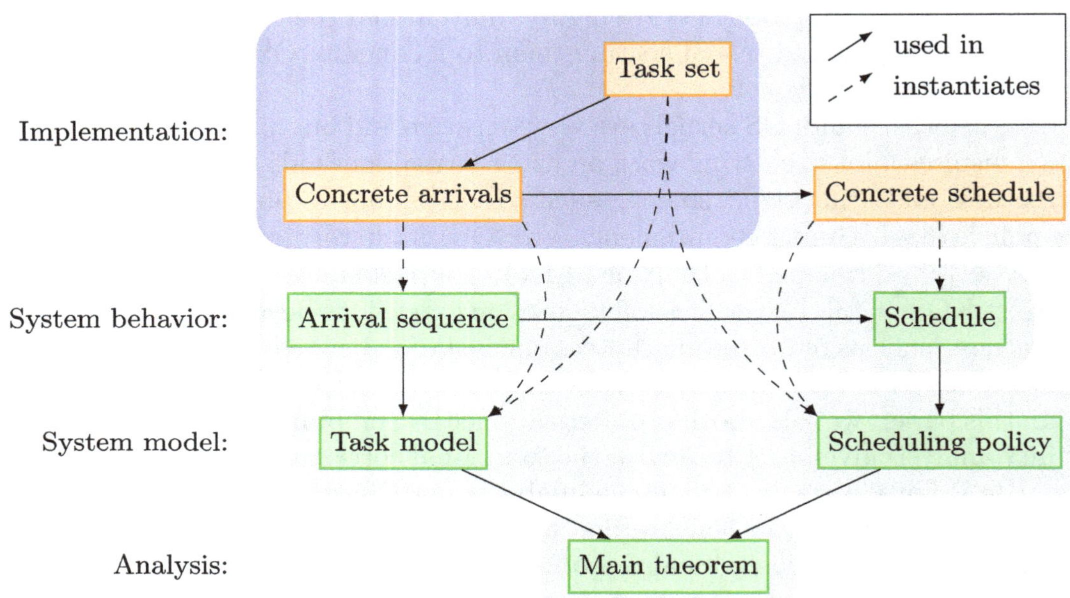

Fig. 1. An overview of Prosa layers

The library contains four basic layers, which are presented in Fig. 1:

System behavior. The base of the library is a model of discrete time traces as infinite sequences of events. We consider two such kinds of sequences: arrival sequences record requests for service called *job* activations and schedules record which job is able to progress.

System model. In order to reason about system behavior, jobs with similar properties are grouped into *tasks*. Based on system behavior, task models (arrival patterns and cost models) and scheduling policies are defined. These models are axiomatic in the sense that they are given as predicates on traces/schedules and not as generating and scheduling functions. In particular, a "FPP scheduler" (see Sect. 2.2) is modeled as "any trace satisfying the FPP policy".

Analysis. The library provides response time and schedulability analyses for these models.

Implementation. Finally, examples of traces and schedulers are implemented to validate the specifications axiomatized in the System model layer and to use the results proven in the Analysis layer. It is this part (more precisely, the top left dark block of Fig. 1) that is meant to connect with RT-CertiKOS.

2.1 System Behavior

The basic definitions in Prosa concern concrete system behavior. The notion of time used in the library corresponds to scheduling ticks: durations are given in number of ticks and instants are given as number of ticks from initialization of the system. For this paper, we focus on single-core systems[1] on which instances of a finite set $TaskSet$ of tasks are scheduled. To each task τ is associated a relative deadline D_τ which corresponds to the delay we want to guarantee between the activation of an instance of a task and its completion. We defer the definition of tasks (Definition 4) until their parameters are relevant and focus first on the modeling of system behavior in Prosa. The instances of tasks which are to be scheduled are called *jobs*.

Definition 1 (Job). *A job $\jmath$ is defined by a* task $\tau_\jmath$, *a positive cost* $\mathbf{c}_\jmath$, *and a unique identifier.*

We do not use the identifier directly, it is only used to distinguish jobs of the same task in traces.

These jobs are used to describe the workload to be scheduled. This workload is defined by an *arrival sequence* which is a trace of job activations.

Definition 2 (Arrival sequence). *An* arrival sequence *is a function ρ mapping any time instant t to a finite (possibly empty) set of jobs $\rho(t)$.*

A job can only appear once in an arrival sequence.

Since a job $\jmath$ can appear at most once in an arrival sequence ρ, we can define its *arrival time* $\mathbf{a}_\rho(\jmath)$ in ρ as the instant t such that $\jmath \in \rho(t)$.

We do not model the scheduler as a function, instead we work with *schedules* over an arrival sequence which are traces of scheduled jobs.

Definition 3 (Schedule). *A* schedule *over an arrival sequence ρ is a function σ which maps any time instant t to either a job appearing in ρ or $\bot$.*

The symbol $\bot$ is used for instants at which no job is scheduled. Given an arrival sequence ρ and a schedule σ over ρ, a job $\jmath \in \rho$ is said to be *scheduled at an instant* t if $\sigma(t) = \jmath$, the *service* received by $\jmath$ up to time t is the number of instants before t at which $\jmath$ is scheduled. A job $\jmath$ is said to be complete at time t if its service received up to time t is equal to its cost $\mathbf{c}_\jmath$ and $\jmath$ is said to be *pending at time* t if it has arrived before time t and is not complete at time t. From now on, we require schedules to only schedule pending jobs. A job $\jmath$ is said to be schedulable if it is complete by its *absolute deadline* $d_\jmath := \mathbf{a}_\rho(\jmath) + D_{\tau\jmath}$.

[1] Multicore systems are handled by Prosa but we do not consider them here.

2.2 System Model

Task Model. In order to specify the behavior of the system we are interested in, Prosa introduces predicates on traces for which the response time analysis provides guarantees.

We now focus on the definitions related to the *sporadic* task model and the *fixed priority preemptive* (FPP) scheduling policy.

Definition 4 (Sporadic FPP task). *A sporadic FPP task τ is defined by a deadline $D_\tau \in \mathbb{N}$, a minimal inter-arrival time $\delta^-_\tau \in \mathbb{N}$, a worst case execution time (WCET) $\mathbf{C}_\mathcal{T}$, and a priority $p_\tau \in \mathbb{N}$. When D_τ is equal to δ^-_τ, the deadline is said* implicit.

Sporadic Task Model. The sporadic task model is specified by a sporadic arrival model and a cost model.

In the sporadic arrival model, consecutive activations of a task τ are separated by a minimum distance δ^-_τ: an arrival sequence ρ is sporadic if for any two distinct jobs $\jmath_1$, $\jmath_2 \in \rho$ of the same task τ, $|\mathbf{a}_\rho(\jmath_1) - \mathbf{a}_\rho(\jmath_2)| \geq \delta^-_\tau$. Periodic arrivals are a particular case of this model where δ^-_τ is the period and jobs arrives exactly at intervals of δ^-_τ. This is sufficient for us as the schedulability analysis for FPP yields the same bounds for sporadic and periodic activations.

The considered cost model is a constraint on activations: jobs in the arrival sequence must respect the WCET of their task, that is, for any $\jmath \in \rho$, $\mathbf{c}_\jmath \leq \mathbf{C}_{\tau_\jmath}$.

FPP Scheduling Policy. The FPP policy is modeled in Prosa as two constraints on the schedule: it must be *work conserving*, that is, it cannot be idle when there are pending tasks; and it must respect the priorities, that is, a scheduled job always has the highest priority among pending jobs.

2.3 Analysis

Prosa contains a proof of Bertogna and Cirinei's [4] response time analysis for FPP single-core schedules of sporadic tasks, with exact bounds for implicit deadlines. The analysis is based on the following property of the maximum workload for these schedules.

Definition 5 (Maximum Workload). *Given a task $\tau \in TaskSet$ and a duration Δ, the maximum workload of the system* w.r.t. τ *within that duration is*

$$W_\tau(\Delta) := \sum_{\substack{\tau' \in TaskSet \\ p_{\tau'} \geq p_\tau}} \mathbf{C}_{\tau'} \times \left\lceil \frac{\Delta}{\delta^-_{\tau'}} \right\rceil$$

The maximum workload $W_\tau(\Delta)$ corresponds to the worst case activation pattern in which all tasks are simultaneously activated with maximum cost (WCET of their task) and minimal inter-arrival distance. It is an upper bound on the amount of service required to schedule activations of the tasks with a priority higher than or equal to p_τ in any interval of size Δ. Based on this property, we can derive a response time bound for our system model if we can find a Δ larger than $W_\tau(\Delta)$.

Theorem 1 (Response Time Bound). *Given a sporadic taskset TaskSet and a task* $\tau \in TaskSet$ *then for any* $R > 0$ *such that* $R \geq W_\tau(R)$*, any job* $\jmath$ *of task* τ *in an FPP schedule* σ *over an arrival sequence* ρ *is completed by* $\mathbf{a}_\rho(\jmath) + R$.

For instance, the smallest response time bound for a task $\tau \in TaskSet$ can be computed by the least positive fixed point of the function W_τ. Using this response time bound, we can derive a *schedulability criterion* by requiring this bound to be smaller than or equal to the deadline of task τ.

2.4 Implementation and Motivation for the Connection with RT-CertiKOS

The Prosa library includes functions to generate periodic traces and the corresponding FPP schedules, together with proofs of these properties and an instantiation of the schedulability criterion for these traces. This implementation was initially provided as a way to check that the modeling of the arrival model and scheduling policy are not contradictory and as such the implementation is as simple as possible. Although this is a good step in order to make the axiomatic definition of scheduling policies more acceptable, there is still room for improvement: these implementations are still rather ad-hoc and there is no connection to an actual system. This is where the link with RT-CertiKOS is beneficial to the Prosa ecosystem: it justifies that the model is indeed suitable for a concrete and independently developed real-time OS scheduler.

3 The RT-CertiKOS OS Kernel

RT-CertiKOS [21], developed by the Yale FLINT group, is a real-time extension of the single-core sequential CertiKOS [9,13],[2] whose functional correctness has been mechanized in the Coq proof assistant [25]. The sequential restriction greatly simplifies the implementation of the OS kernel. However, it does not support multicore, and the lack of kernel preemption can also degrade the responsiveness of the whole system. RT-CertiKOS proves spatial and temporal isolation (including schedulability) between components.

Both CertiKOS and RT-CertiKOS follow the same proof methodology, organized around the notion of abstraction layers that permits decomposition of the kernel into small pieces that are easier to verify.

[2] There is a multicore version of CertiKOS [14,15], but RT-CertiKOS is developed on top of the sequential version.

3.1 Abstraction Layers

Abstraction layers [13] are essentially a way to combine code fragments and their interface with simulation proofs. They consist of four elements: *(a)* a piece of code; *(b)* an *underlay*, the interface that the code relies on; *(c)* an *overlay*, the interface that the code provides; *(d)* a *simulation proof* ensuring that the code running on top of the underlay indeed provides the functionalities described in the overlay.

Implementation details of lower layers are encapsulated in higher layers, allowing to reason directly with the specifications rather than the implementation.

Notice that the underlay and overlay are specifications written in Coq and may be expressed using the semantics of several programming languages at once. This explains how CertiKOS (and RT-CertiKOS) manages to encompass both C and assembly code verification into a unified framework. Notice further that this notion of interface not only includes functions but also some *abstract state*, which exposes memory states of lower layers in a clean and structured way, and allows the overlay to access them only by invoking verified functions.

3.2 The Scheduler in RT-CertiKOS

RT-CertiKOS supports user-level fixed-priority preemptive scheduling. Its scheduler is invoked by timer interrupts periodically, dividing CPU time into intervals, which are called *time slots*, *time quanta*, or *time slices*.

Task Model. Each task in RT-CertiKOS is defined by a fixed priority, a period, and a budget (or WCET), the latter two being given in time slot units. Tasks are strictly periodic, with implicit hard deadlines, that is, the deadlines are the start of the next period and no deadline miss is allowed at all. While this is a restricted setting, it is enough to handle closed-loop control, used in control real-time systems. Furthermore, RT-CertiKOS only allows for fixed priorities in order to get maximum predictability, which is of utmost importance in critical systems. Finally, RT-CertiKOS also enforces budgets at the task level: in each period, a task cannot be scheduled for more than its specified budget.

Fixed-Priority Scheduler. The RT-CertiKOS scheduler maintains an integer array to keep track of time quantum usage for each task. Upon invocation, the scheduler first iterates over all tasks, replenishing quotas whenever a new period arrives. It then loops again and finds the highest priority task that has not used up its budget, followed by a decrement on the chosen task's current quota. Its abstraction is a Coq function that iterates over an abstract array of task control blocks, updates them, and returns the highest task identifier available for scheduling.

Yield System Call. Tasks do not always use up their budgets. A task can yield to relinquish any remaining quota, so that lower priority tasks may be scheduled earlier and more time slots may be dedicated to non real-time tasks.

3.3 Proof Methodology

Based on sequential CertiKOS, RT-CertiKOS [21] follows the idea of deep specifications[3] in which the specification should be rich enough to deduce any property of interest: there should never be any need to consider the implementation. In particular, even though its source code is written in both C and assembly, the underlay always abstracts the concrete memory states it operates on into abstract states, and abstracts concrete code into Coq functions that act as executable specification. Subsequent layers relying on this underlay will invoke Coq functions instead of the concrete code, thus hiding implementation details.

In the case of scheduling, there are essentially two functions: the scheduler and the yield system call. The scheduler relies on two concrete data structures: a counter tracking the current time (in time slot units) and an array tracking the current quota for each periodic task. The yield system call simply sets the remaining quota of the current task to zero. Both functions are verified in RT-CertiKOS, that is, formals proofs ensure that their C code implementations indeed simulate the corresponding Coq specifications.

3.4 Motivation for the Connection with Prosa

Upgrading an OS kernel into a real-time one is not an easy task. When one further adds formal proofs about functional correctness, isolation, and timing requirements, the proof burden becomes enormous. In particular, there is still room for future work on RT-CertiKOS, *e.g.,* a WCET analysis of its system calls.

In order to reduce the overall proof burden, it is important to try to delegate as much as possible to specialized libraries and tools. Thus, from the RT-CertiKOS perspective, the benefit of using Prosa is precisely to have state-of-the-art schedulability analyses already mechanized in Coq, without having to prove all these results.

Furthermore, the schedulability check of Prosa is only performed once while verifying the proofs, such that there is no runtime overhead and no loss of performance for RT-CertiKOS.

4 From RT-CertiKOS to Prosa: A Schedule Connection

Prosa definitions cannot apply to RT-CertiKOS directly. Indeed, the perspectives of Prosa and RT-CertiKOS on the real-time aspects of a system are not the same, which is reflected in the differences in their task models, their executions, and the information they need. In this section, we explain how we bridge these gaps to actually perform the connection. Table 1 summarizes the various definitions and proofs and how they relate to each other.

[3] https://deepspec.org/.

Table 1. Summary of the range of the various data between RT-CertiKOS and Prosa

<table>
<tr><th>RT-CertiKOS</th><th>Simplified Model</th><th>Interface</th><th>Prosa</th></tr>
<tr><td colspan="2">scheduler
quota array</td><td colspan="2"></td></tr>
<tr><td>schedule prefix
with batch tasks</td><td colspan="2">schedule prefix</td><td>infinite schedule</td></tr>
<tr><td></td><td colspan="2">valid schedule prefix</td><td>valid infinite schedule</td></tr>
<tr><td></td><td colspan="3">FPP prefix</td></tr>
<tr><td colspan="3"></td><td>FPP</td></tr>
<tr><td colspan="3"></td><td>schedulability analysis</td></tr>
<tr><td colspan="3"></td><td>schedulable execution</td></tr>
<tr><td colspan="4">schedulable prefix</td></tr>
</table>

4.1 Interface Between RT-CertiKOS and Prosa

We design an interface to link RT-CertiKOS and Prosa, focusing on the precise amount of information that needs to be transmitted between them. The interface is shaped by the information Prosa needs to perform the schedulability analysis: a task set and a schedule, together with some properties.

Key Elements of the Interface. The task model we consider is the one of RT-CertiKOS, as it is more restrictive than the ones supported by Prosa. Tasks are defined by a priority level p, a period T_p and a WCET (more accurately a budget) C_p. Since we only allow one task per priority level, we identify tasks and priority levels and we write C_p, D_p, and T_p instead of C_τ, D_τ, and T_τ. In order for this setting to make sense, we assume the following inequality for each task p: $0 < C_p \leq T_p$. Notice that this is a particular case of Prosa's FPP task model (Definition 4). There is no definition of the jobs of a task as they can be easily defined from a task and a period number.

The second element Prosa needs is an infinite schedule. RT-CertiKOS cannot provide such an infinite schedule, as only a finite prefix can be known, up to the current time. Thus, we keep RT-CertiKOS's finite schedule as is in the interface and it is up to Prosa to extend it into an infinite one, suitable for its analysis.

Finally, Prosa needs two properties about the schedule: *(a)* any task receives no more service than its WCET in any period; *(b)* the schedule indeed follows the FPP policy. We refer to schedules satisfying these properties as *valid schedule prefixes*. Proving these properties falls to RT-CertiKOS.

Handling Service and Job Cost. In RT-CertiKOS, and more generally in any OS, we only assume a bound on the execution time of a task, used as a budget. The exact execution time of each of its jobs is not known beforehand and can be observed only at runtime. On the opposite, Prosa assumes that costs for all jobs of all tasks are part of the problem description and thus are available from the start.

To fix this mismatch, we define a job cost function computed from a schedule prefix: its value is the actual service received if the job has yielded and the WCET of its task otherwise. This definition relies on the computation of service in any period, which we also provide as part of the interface.

4.2 The RT-CertiKOS Side

Adding the Schedule in RT-CertiKOS. RT-CertiKOS only maintains the current state of the system, which the scheduler relies on, such as the current time and quota array. However, the interface requires a schedule trace. We introduce such a ghost variable in RT-CertiKOS, and update a few scheduling-related primitives to extend this trace whenever a task is scheduled.

This introduction adds absolutely no proof overhead, since it does not affect the scheduling decisions, thus existing proofs about the rest of the system still hold. Furthermore, it is a purely logical variable introduced through refinement, meaning that it does not exist in the C code, thus it causes no computation overhead.

Too Much Information in RT-CertiKOS. The full RT-CertiKOS model contains too much information compared to what the interface requires.

Firstly, services in RT-CertiKOS may affect a part of the state that is relevant to practical scheduling, but is of no interest to the scheduling model we want to verify, like batch tasks.

Secondly, due to the nature of *deep specification*, the abstraction of the whole scheduling operation contains more information than what is required for reasoning about real-time properties. For example, saving and restoring registers is essential for the correctness of context switches (thus, of the scheduler), but it is irrelevant to temporal properties.

Thirdly, specifications in RT-CertiKOS enumerate preconditions of the scheduler such as the correct configuration of the paging bit in the control register, the validity of the current stack and so on. These are required for other invariants of the kernel at other abstraction levels, but again they are irrelevant to scheduling.

Simplified Model of RT-CertiKOS. For all these reasons, we define a simplified scheduling model of RT-CertiKOS, with a much simpler abstract state containing only the data structures that are actually used in scheduling, from which the interface data and its properties must be derived. This simplified abstract state contains four fields:

ticks	the current time, that is, the number of past time slots;
quanta	a map giving the remaining quota for each priority;
cid	the identifier of the running process (if it exists);
schedule	the schedule prefix remembering past scheduling decisions.

This abstract state is not equivalent to the complete one, because it operates on a totally different abstract data type where all irrelevant fields are removed.

It is also more permissive: more transitions are allowed since it does not perform the sanity checks about preconditions such as being in kernel mode, host mode, etc. Nevertheless, we still have a simulation: any step in the full RT-CertiKOS is also allowed in the simplified version and results in the same scheduling decision and trace. This simulation is enough for our purposes as we are ultimately interested in the behavior of the full RT-CertiKOS.

Proving the Properties Required by Prosa. The interface requires two key properties: *(a)* the service received by each job is at most the WCET of its task; and *(b)* the schedule prefix follows FPP. These properties must be proven on the RT-CertiKOS side for any schedule that might be generated. This way, Prosa can rely on them through the interface.

Since RT-CertiKOS verification is based on state invariants rather than traces, we prove these properties using the following main invariants on the simplified scheduling model:

- the length of the schedule trace is the current time + 1 (the scheduler takes a decision for the *next* time slot);
- if a task has yielded in the current period, its remaining quota is 0;
- the service plus the remaining quota is equal to the job cost;
- the service received in any period is less than the WCET;
- pending jobs have two equivalent definitions (having positive remaining quota or having less service than their job cost);
- the current schedule follows FPP.

To prove that these statements are indeed invariants, we must prove that they are preserved by any step, that is, by the scheduler (triggered by the user-level timer interrupt) and by the yield system call (triggered by the user process), since all other kernel steps do not modify the scheduling data of the simplified scheduling model.

Simulation Between the Simplified Scheduling Model and RT-CertiKOS. To connect the full RT-CertiKOS model and the simplified one, we define a projection function *RData_proj* extracting the relevant fields from the full RT-CertiKOS state to build the simplified one.

As shown in Fig. 2, we prove that given a scheduler transition of RT-CertiKOS between the (full) states d and d', there is also a transition from their projections s and s' by invoking the simplified scheduler.[4] If the states d and s satisfy respectively the invariants for RT-CertiKOS and the simplified model, then so do d' and s' (they are invariants). As the states s and s' are projections of d and d', the invariants of s and s' also hold on the corresponding fields in d and d'. This allows us to utilize the invariants proved in the simplified model to establish properties on the full state of RT-CertiKOS. Notice that the schedulability property we study is a safety property (deadlines are never missed) and not a liveness one (everything is eventually scheduled).

[4] More precisely, we prove that `certikos_sched`(s) and *RData_proj*(d') are *extensionally* equal.

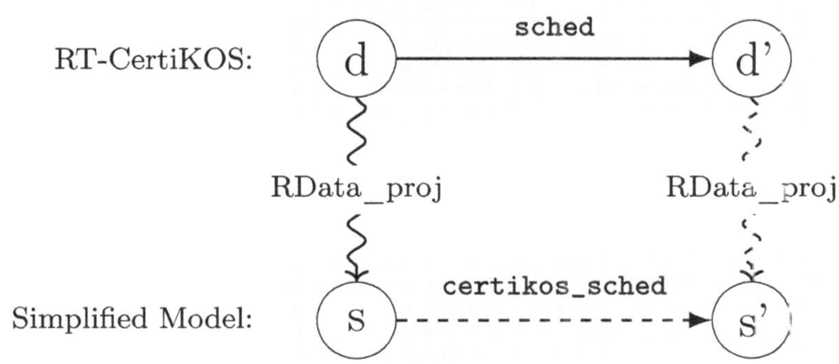

Fig. 2. Simulation between simplified scheduling and RT-CertiKOS

4.3 The Prosa Side

Proven Schedulability Analysis in Prosa. In order to use the response time bound of Sect. 2, we need to relate any finite schedule prefix from the interface to an arrival sequence and a schedule satisfying the model described in Sect. 2. We can then rely on any schedulability criterion (*e.g.*, the one described at the end of Sect. 2.3) to prove that the response time bound holds and deduce that any valid schedule prefix from the interface is indeed schedulable.

Bridging the Gap Between the Interface and Prosa. The interface provides Prosa with a task set, service and job cost functions, and a valid schedule prefix. We first build an arrival sequence from the schedule prefix where the n-th job ($n > 0$) for a given task p arrives at time $(n-1) \times T_p$ with the cost given by the interface. Note that jobs that do not arrive within the prefix cannot have yielded yet so that their costs is the WCET of their tasks: we assume the worst case for the future.

The arrival sequence is then defined by adding all jobs of each task p from $TaskSet$, that is, the arrival sequence at time t contains the $(\lfloor t/T_p \rfloor + 1)$-th job of p iff t is divisible by T_p.

Next, we need to turn the finite schedule prefix into an infinite one. There are two possibilities: either build a full schedule from the arrival sequence using the Prosa implementation of FPP, or start from the schedule prefix of the interface and extend it into an infinite one. The first technique gives for free the fact that the infinite schedule satisfies the FPP model from Prosa. The difficulty lies in proving that the schedule prefix from the interface is indeed a prefix of this infinite schedule. The second technique starts from the schedule prefix and the difficulty is proving that it satisfies the FPP model as specified on the Prosa side.

In this paper, we use the first strategy and prove that the prefix of the schedule built by Prosa is equal to the schedule prefix provided in the interface. To do so, we use the fact that two FPP schedule prefixes with the same arrival sequence and job costs (only known at runtime) are the same, provided we take care to properly remember when jobs yield.

Assuming that the task set is accepted by the schedulability criterion, we know that the Prosa schedule is schedulable and, since this implies that its prefix is also schedulable, we deduce that the valid schedule prefix given by the interface is schedulable.

5 Evaluation and Future Work

5.1 Evaluation

As the C and assembly source code of RT-CertiKOS was not modified at all, this connection does not introduce any overhead to its performance and there is no need for a new performance evaluation. Instead, we focus on the benefits this works brings and on the amount of work involved, described in Table 2.

Benefits for RT-CertiKOS and Prosa. The schedulability analysis already present in RT-CertiKOS was manually proved and took around 8k LoC to handle the precise setting described in this paper. By contrast, interfacing with Prosa requires 50% less proofs, is more flexible and can easily be extended (see Sect. 5.3). The introduction of a simplified scheduling model also reduced by 75% the size of proofs of invariants about the high-level abstract scheduler since we are freed from the unnecessary information described in Sect. 4.2.

On the Prosa side, having a complete formal connection with an actual OS kernel developed independently validates the modeling choices made for describing real-time systems. Indeed, seeing schedulers as predicates over scheduling traces is very general but one can legitimately wonder whether such predicates accurately describe reality.

Proof Effort. Designing a good interface allowed us to cleanly separate the work required on the RT-CertiKOS and Prosa sides.

On the RT-CertiKOS side, the design of the simplified scheduling setting was pretty straightforward, as was the correctness of the translation. Indeed, this translation is essentially a projection, except for batch tasks which are removed. Designing adequate inductive invariants to prove the two properties required by the interface was the most challenging part of this work and unsurprisingly, it took several iterations to find correct definitions.

On the Prosa side, building the arrival sequence and the infinite schedule is quite effortless given a prefix and a job cost function. The subtle thing was to find a good definition of the job cost function, which made the corresponding proofs significantly easier. Proving that the prefix of the built infinite schedule is the same as the interface prefix *w.r.t.* executions was troublesome for two reasons. First, the interface prefix contains an additional boolean representing whether the scheduled job yielded and which is used for computing job costs, whereas it does not exist in the built schedule. Second, the definition of the FPP property in the interface depends on a schedule prefix, while the one in Prosa depends on an infinite schedule.

Overall, we see the small amount of LoC required to perform this work as a validation of the adequacy of our method to the considered problem.

Table 2. Proof effort

Feature	Changes (LoC)
Adding a schedule field to RT-CertiKOS	15
Interface (with proofs)	380
Simplified scheduling	100
Proving the invariants about the simplified scheduling	950
Translation RT-CertiKOS → simplified scheduling	380
Conversion between ZArith and SSReflect	280
Translation interface → Prosa	1900
Using the schedulability analysis of Prosa	130
Total	4135

5.2 Lessons Learned

Beyond the particular artifact linking RT-CertiKOS with Prosa, what more general lessons can we learn from this connection?

First, using the same proof assistant greatly helps. Indeed, beyond the absence of technical hassle of inter-operability between different formal tools, it also avoids the pitfall of a formalization mismatch between both formal models and permits sharing common definitions.

Second, the creation of an explicit interface between both tools clearly marks the flow of information, stays focused on the essential information, and delimits the "proof responsibility": which side is responsible for proving which fact. It also segregate the proof techniques used on each side so as not to pollute the other one, either on a technical aspect (vanilla Coq for RT-CertiKOS *vs* the SSReflect extension for Prosa) or on the verification methods used (invariant-based properties for RT-CertiKOS *vs* trace-based properties for Prosa). This separation makes it unnecessary to have people be experts in both tools at once: once the interface was clearly defined, experts on each side could work with only a rough description of the other one, even though this interface required a few later changes. In particular, it is interesting to notice that half the authors are experts in RT-CertiKOS whereas the other half are experts in Prosa.

Third, the common part of the models used by both sides must be amenable to agreement: in our case, this means having the same notion of time (scheduling slots, or ticks) and a compatible notion of schedule (finite and infinite).

Finally, we expect the interface we designed to be reusable for other verified kernels wanting to connect to Prosa or for linking RT-CertiKOS to other formal schedulability analysis tools.

5.3 Future Work

Evolving with RT-CertiKOS. The existing implementation of the scheduler in RT-CertiKOS imposes a fixed priority scheduling policy with implicit deadlines. In the future, as RT-CertiKOS evolves and supports more task models, the interface connecting it with Prosa should also extend.

A straightforward extension is to allow *constrained deadlines*, that is, to have the deadline D_p be shorter than the period T_p (but greater than the WCET C_p) as the schedulability result we use from Prosa already supports it. This requires RT-CertiKOS to support an extended task model where a task is also specified by its deadline. Furthermore, RT-CertiKOS would also need to enforce budget at the deadlines, instead of at the beginning of the next period as it is currently the case.

Another extension would be to consider the Earliest Deadline First (EDF) scheduling policy which provides better utilization ratio. In addition to relaxing the current task model by not including priorities, the main proof effort would be to implement and verify this new scheduler in RT-CertiKOS.

Extensions to Prosa. Our experience connecting RT-CertiKOS and Prosa shows that Prosa's assumption of having an infinite schedule is quite impractical when verifying instances of real-time systems. This advocates for building reusable connections between Prosa's system model based on infinite traces and a model similar to the one used in the interface with RT-CertiKOS. Thus, one would prove analyses in the convenient setting of infinite traces and still be able to apply them to lower level models of real-time systems with finite traces.

6 Related Work

Schedulability Analysis. Schedulability analysis as a key theory in the real-time community has been widely studied in the past decades. Liu and Layland's seminal work [20] presents a schedulability analysis technique for a simple system model described as a set of assumptions. Many later work [3,5,11,23,28] aim to capture more *realistic*[5] and complex system models by generalizing those assumptions.

In order to provide formal guarantees to those results, several formal approaches have been used for the formalism of schedulability analyses, such as model checking [8,12,16], temporal logic [32,33], and theorem proving [10,30].

As far as we know, none of the above work has been applied to a formally verified OS kernel.

Verification of Real-Time OS Kernels. There is a lot of work about formal verification of OS kernels, see [18] for a survey. Therefore, we restrict our attention to verification of real-time kernels using proof assistants. We also do

[5] In terms of executions and arrival model.

not consider WCET computation, be it of the kernel itself (*e.g.*, [6,24]) or of the task set we consider. This is a complementary but clearly distinct task to get verified time bounds.

The eChronos OS [1,2] is a real-time OS running on single-core embedded systems. It stops its verification at the scheduling policy level, proving that the currently running task always has the highest priority among ready tasks. Xu et al. [31] verify the functional correctness of μC/OS-II [19], a real-time operating system with optimizations such as bitmaps. They also prove some high level properties, such as priority inversion freedom of shared memory IPC.

RT-CertiKOS [21] is a verified single-core real-time OS kernel developed by the Yale FLINT group, based on sequential CertiKOS [9,13]. It proves both temporal and spatial isolation among different components, where temporal isolation entails schedulability, etc. However, as explained in Sect. 5.1, its schedulability proof is longer whereas connecting to an existing schedulability analyzer is easier and more flexible.

7 Conclusion

Formal verification aims at providing stronger guarantees than testing. Real-time systems are a good target because they are often part of critical systems. Both the scheduling and OS communities have developed their own formally verified tools but there is a lack of integration between them. In this paper, we make a first step toward bridging this gap by integrating a formally proven schedulability analysis tool, Prosa, with a verified sequential real-time OS kernel, RT-CertiKOS. This gives two benefits: first, it provides RT-CertiKOS with a modular, extensible, state-of-the-art formal schedulability analysis proof; second, it gives a concrete instance of one of the scheduling theories described in Prosa, thus ensuring that its model is consistent and applicable to actual systems. We believe this connection can be easily adapted for other verified kernels or schedulability analyzers.

It also showcases that it is possible and practical to connect two completely independent medium- to large-scale formal proof developments.

Acknowledgments. This research has been partially supported by the following grants: PEPS INS2I JCJC 2019 Vefose, NSF grants 1521523, 1715154, and 1763399, DARPA grant FA8750-15-C-0082, as well as by the RT-PROOFS project (grant ANR-17-CE25-0016) and the CASERM project through the LabEx PERSYVAL-Lab (grant ANR-11-LABX-0025-01). The U.S. Government is authorized to reproduce and distribute reprints for Governmental purposes notwithstanding any copyright notation thereon. The views and conclusions contained herein are those of the authors and should not be interpreted as necessarily representing the official policies or endorsements, either expressed or implied, of DARPA or the U.S. Government.

References

1. Andronick, J., Lewis, C., Matichuk, D., Morgan, C., Rizkallah, C.: Proof of OS scheduling behavior in the presence of interrupt-induced concurrency. In: Blanchette, J.C., Merz, S. (eds.) ITP 2016. LNCS, vol. 9807, pp. 52–68. Springer, Cham (2016). https://doi.org/10.1007/978-3-319-43144-4_4
2. Andronick, J., Lewis, C., Morgan, C.: Controlled Owicki-Gries concurrency: reasoning about the preemptible eChronos embedded operating system. In: Proceedings Workshop on Models for Formal Analysis of Real Systems, MARS, pp. 10–24 (2015). https://doi.org/10.4204/EPTCS.196.2
3. Baruah, S.: Techniques for multiprocessor global schedulability analysis. In: Proceedings - 28th IEEE International Real-Time Systems Symposium (RTSS), pp. 119–128, December 2007. https://doi.org/10.1109/RTSS.2007.35
4. Bertogna, M., Cirinei, M.: Response-time analysis for globally scheduled symmetric multiprocessor platforms. In: 28th IEEE International Real-Time Systems Symposium (RTSS), pp. 149–160, December 2007. https://doi.org/10.1109/RTSS.2007.31
5. Bini, E., Buttazzo, G.C.: Schedulability analysis of periodic fixed priority systems. IEEE Trans. Comput. **53**(11), 1462–1473 (2004)
6. Blackham, B., Shi, Y., Chattopadhyay, S., Roychoudhury, A., Heiser, G.: Timing analysis of a protected operating system kernel. In: 2011 IEEE 32nd Real-Time Systems Symposium (RTSS), pp. 339–348, November 2011. https://doi.org/10.1109/RTSS.2011.38
7. Cerqueira, F., Stutz, F., Brandenburg, B.B.: PROSA: a case for readable mechanized schedulability analysis. In: 28th Euromicro Conference on Real-Time Systems (ECRTS), pp. 273–284 (2016). https://doi.org/10.1109/ECRTS.2016.28
8. Cordovilla, M., Boniol, F., Noulard, E., Pagetti, C.: Multiprocessor schedulability analyser. In: Proceedings of the 2011 ACM Symposium on Applied Computing, SAC 2011, pp. 735–741 (2011). http://doi.acm.org/10.1145/1982185.1982345
9. Costanzo, D., Shao, Z., Gu, R.: End-to-end verification of information-flow security for C and assembly programs. In: Proceedings of the 37th ACM SIGPLAN Conference on Programming Language Design and Implementation (PLDI), pp. 648–664 (2016). http://doi.acm.org/10.1145/2908080.2908100
10. Dutertre, B.: The priority ceiling protocol: formalization and analysis using PVS. In: Proceedings of the 21st IEEE Conference on Real-Time Systems Symposium (RTSS), pp. 151–160 (1999)
11. Feld, T., Biondi, A., Davis, R.I., Buttazzo, G.C., Slomka, F.: A survey of schedulability analysis techniques for rate-dependent tasks. J. Syst. Softw. **138**, 100–107 (2018). https://doi.org/10.1016/j.jss.2017.12.033
12. Fersman, E., Mokrushin, L., Pettersson, P., Yi, W.: Schedulability analysis of fixed-priority systems using timed automata. Theor. Comput. Sci. **354**(2), 301–317 (2006)
13. Gu, R., et al.: Deep specifications and certified abstraction layers. In: Proceedings of the 42nd Annual ACM SIGPLAN-SIGACT Symposium on Principles of Programming Languages (POPL), pp. 595–608 (2015). http://doi.acm.org/10.1145/2676726.2676975

14. Gu, R., et al.: CertiKOS: an extensible architecture for building certified concurrent OS kernels. In: 12th USENIX Symposium on Operating Systems Design and Implementation (OSDI), pp. 653–669. USENIX Association (2016). https://www.usenix.org/conference/osdi16/technical-sessions/presentation/gu
15. Gu, R., et al.: Certified concurrent abstraction layers. In: Proceedings of the 39th ACM SIGPLAN Conference on Programming Language Design and Implementation (PLDI), pp. 646–661 (2018). http://doi.acm.org/10.1145/3192366.3192381
16. Guan, N., Gu, Z., Deng, Q., Gao, S., Yu, G.: Exact schedulability analysis for static-priority global multiprocessor scheduling using model-checking. In: IFIP International Workshop on Software Technolgies for Embedded and Ubiquitous Systems, pp. 263–272 (2007)
17. Klein, G., et al.: seL4: formal verification of an OS kernel. In: Proceedings of the ACM SIGOPS 22nd Symposium on Operating Systems Principles (SOSP), pp. 207–220 (2009). https://doi.org/10.1145/1629575.1629596
18. Klein, G., Huuck, R., Schlich, B.: Operating system verification. J. Autom. Reasoning **42**(2–4), 123–124 (2009). https://doi.org/10.1007/s10817-009-9126-9
19. Labrosse, J.J.: Microc/OS-II, 2nd edn. R&D Books, Gilroy (1998)
20. Liu, C.L., Layland, J.W.: Scheduling algorithms for multiprogramming in a hard-real-time environment. J. ACM (JACM) **20**(1), 46–61 (1973)
21. Liu, M., et al.: Compositional verification of preemptive OS kernels with temporal and spatial isolation. Technical report, YALEU/DCS/TR-1549. Department of Computer Science, Yale University (2019)
22. Nelson, L., et al.: Hyperkernel: push-button verification of an OS kernel. In: Proceedings of the 26th Symposium on Operating Systems Principles (SOSP), Shanghai, China, 28–31 October 2017, pp. 252–269 (2017). https://doi.org/10.1145/3132747.3132748
23. Palencia, J.C., Harbour, M.G.: Schedulability analysis for tasks with static and dynamic offsets. In: Proceedings 19th IEEE Real-Time Systems Symposium (RTSS), pp. 26–37. IEEE (1998)
24. Sewell, T., Kam, F., Heiser, G.: High-assurance timing analysis for a high-assurance real-time operating system. Real-Time Syst. **53**(5), 812–853 (2017). https://doi.org/10.1007/s11241-017-9286-3
25. The Coq Development Team: The Coq Proof Assistant Reference Manual. INRIA, 8.4pl4 edn. (2014). https://coq.inria.fr/distrib/8.4pl4/files/Reference-Manual.pdf
26. Tindell, K., Burns, A.: Guaranteeing message latencies on controller area network (CAN). In: Proceedings of 1st International CAN Conference, pp. 1–11 (1994)
27. Tindell, K., Burns, A., Wellings, A.: Calculating controller area network (CAN) message response times. Control Eng. Pract. **3**(8), 1163–1169 (1995)
28. Tindell, K., Clark, J.: Holistic schedulability analysis for distributed hard real-time systems. Microprocessing Microprogramming **40**(2–3), 117–134 (1994)
29. Tindell, K., Hanssmon, H., Wellings, A.J.: Analysing real-time communications: controller area network (CAN). In: Proceedings of the 15th IEEE Real-Time Systems Symposium (RTSS), San Juan, Puerto Rico, 7–9 December 1994, pp. 259–263 (1994). https://doi.org/10.1109/REAL.1994.342710
30. Wilding, M.: A machine-checked proof of the optimality of a real-time scheduling policy. In: Proceedings of the 10th International Conference on Computer Aided Verification (CAV), pp. 369–378 (1998)

31. Xu, F., Fu, M., Feng, X., Zhang, X., Zhang, H., Li, Z.: A practical verification framework for preemptive OS kernels. In: Chaudhuri, S., Farzan, A. (eds.) CAV 2016. LNCS, vol. 9780, pp. 59–79. Springer, Cham (2016). https://doi.org/10.1007/978-3-319-41540-6_4
32. Xu, Q., Zhan, N.: Formalising scheduling theories in duration calculus. Nord. J. Comput. **14**(3), 173–201 (2008)
33. Yuhua, Z., Chaochen, Z.: A formal proof of the deadline driven scheduler. In: International Symposium on Formal Techniques in Real-Time and Fault-Tolerant Systems, pp. 756–775 (1994)

Rely-Guarantee Reasoning About Concurrent Memory Management in Zephyr RTOS

Yongwang Zhao[1,2(✉)] and David Sanán[3]

[1] School of Computer Science and Engineering, Beihang University, Beijing, China
zhaoyw@buaa.edu.cn

[2] Beijing Advanced Innovation Center for Big Data and Brain Computing, Beihang University, Beijing, China

[3] School of Computer Science and Engineering, Nanyang Technological University, Singapore, Singapore

Abstract. Formal verification of concurrent operating systems (OSs) is challenging, and in particular the verification of the dynamic memory management due to its complex data structures and allocation algorithm. Up to our knowledge, this paper presents the first formal specification and mechanized proof of a concurrent buddy memory allocation for a real-world OS. We develop a fine-grained formal specification of the buddy memory management in Zephyr RTOS. To ease validation of the specification and the source code, the provided specification closely follows the C code. Then, we use the rely-guarantee technique to conduct the compositional verification of functional correctness and invariant preservation. During the formal verification, we found three bugs in the C code of Zephyr.

1 Introduction

The operating system (OS) is a fundamental component of critical systems. Thus, correctness and reliability of systems highly depend on the system's underlying OS. As a key functionality of OSs, the memory management provides ways to dynamically allocate portions of memory to programs at their request, and to free them for reuse when no longer needed. Since program variables and data are stored in the allocated memory, an incorrect specification and implementation of the memory management may lead to system crashes or exploitable attacks on the whole system. RTOS are frequently deployed on critical systems, making formal verification of RTOS necessary to ensure their reliability. One of the state of the art RTOS is Zephyr RTOS [1], a Linux Foundation project. Zephyr is an open source RTOS for connected, resource-constrained devices, and built

This work has been supported in part by the National Natural Science Foundation of China (NSFC) under the Grant No.61872016, and the National Satellite of Excellence in Trustworthy Software Systems and the Award No. NRF2014NCR-NCR001-30, funded by NRF Singapore under National Cyber-security R&D (NCR) programme.

I. Dillig and S. Tasiran (Eds.): CAV 2019, LNCS 11562, pp. 515–533, 2019.
https://doi.org/10.1007/978-3-030-25543-5_29

with security and safety design in mind. Zephyr uses a buddy memory allocation algorithm optimized for RTOS, and that allows multiple threads to concurrently manipulate shared memory pools with fine-grained locking.

Formal verification of the concurrent memory management in Zephyr is a challenging work. (1) To achieve high performance, data structures and algorithms in Zephyr are laid out in a complex manner. The buddy memory allocation can split large blocks into smaller ones, allowing blocks of different sizes to be allocated and released efficiently while limiting memory fragmentation concerns. Seeking performance, Zephyr uses a multi-level structure where each level has a bitmap and a linked list of free memory blocks. The levels of bitmaps actually form a forest of quad trees of bits. Memory addresses are used as a reference to memory blocks, so the algorithm has to deal with address alignment and computation concerning the block size at each level, increasing the complexity of its verification. (2) A complex algorithm and data structures imply as well complex invariants that the formal model must preserve. These invariants have to guarantee the well-shaped bitmaps and their consistency to free lists. To prevent memory leaks and block overlapping, a precise reasoning shall keep track of both numerical and shape properties. (3) Thread preemption and fine-grained locking make the kernel execution of memory services to be concurrent.

In this paper, we apply the rely-guarantee reasoning technique to the concurrent buddy memory management in Zephyr. This work uses π-Core, a rely-guarantee framework for the specification and verification of concurrent reactive systems. π-Core introduces a concurrent imperative system specification language driven by "events" that supports reactive semantics of interrupt handlers (e.g. kernel services, scheduler) in OSs, and thus makes the formal specification of Zephyr simpler. The language embeds Isabelle/HOL data types and functions, therefore it is as rich as the own Isabelle/HOL. π-Core concurrent constructs allow the specification of Zephyr multi-thread interleaving, fine-grained locking, and thread preemption. Compositionality of rely-guarantee makes feasible to prove the functional correctness of Zephyr and invariants over its data structures. The formal specification and proofs are developed in Isabelle/HOL. They are available at https://lvpgroup.github.io/picore/.

We first analyze the structural properties of memory pools in Zephyr (Sect. 3). The properties clarify the constraints and consistency of quad trees, free block lists, memory pool configuration, and waiting threads. All of them are defined as invariants for which its preservation under the execution of services is formally verified. From the well-shaped properties of quad trees, we can derive a critical property to prevent memory leaks, i.e., memory blocks cover the whole memory address of the pool, but not overlap each other.

Together with the formal verification of Zephyr, we aim at the highest evaluation assurance level (EAL 7) of Common Criteria (CC) [2], which was declared this year as the candidate standard for security certification by the Zephyr project. Therefore, we develop a fine-grained low level formal specification of a buddy memory management (Sect. 4). The specification has a line-to-line correspondence with the Zephyr C code, and thus is able to do the *code-to-spec* review required by the EAL 7 evaluation, covering all the data structures and imperative statements present in the implementation.

We enforce the formal verification of functional correctness and invariant preservation by using a rely-guarantee proof system (Sect. 5), which supports total correctness for loops where fairness does not need to be considered. The formal verification revealed three bugs in the C code: an incorrect block split, an incorrect return from the kernel services, and non-termination of a loop (Sect. 6). Two of them are critical and have been repaired in the latest release of Zephyr. The third bug causes nontermination of the allocation service when trying to allocate a block of a larger size than the maximum allowed.

Related Work. (1) Memory models [17] provide the necessary abstraction to separate the behaviour of a program from the behaviour of the memory it reads and writes. There are many formalizations of memory models in the literature, e.g., [10,14,15,19,21], where some of them only create an abstract specification of the services for memory allocation and release [10,15,21]. (2) Formal verification of OS memory management has been studied in CertiKOS [11,20], seL4 [12,13], Verisoft [3], and in the hypervisors from [4,5], where only the works in [4,11] consider concurrency. Comparing to buddy memory allocation, the data structures and algorithms verified in [11] are relatively simpler, without block split/coalescence and multiple levels of free lists and bitmaps. [4] only considers virtual mapping but not allocation or deallocation of memory areas. (3) Algorithms and implementations of dynamic memory allocation have been formally specified and verified in an extensive number of works [7–9,16,18,23]. However, the buddy memory allocation is only studied in [9], which does not consider concrete data structures (e.g. bitmaps) and concurrency. To the best of our knowledge, this paper presents the first formal specification and mechanized proof for a concurrent buddy memory allocation of a realistic operating system.

2 Concurrent Memory Management in Zephyr RTOS

In Zephyr, a memory pool is a kernel object that allows memory blocks to be dynamically allocated, from a designated memory region, and released back into the pool. Its definition in the C code is shown as follows. A memory pool's buffer ($*buf$) is an n_max-size array of blocks of max_sz bytes at level 0, with no wasted space between them. The size of the buffer is thus $n\_max \times max\_sz$ bytes long. Zephyr tries to accomplish a memory request by splitting available blocks into smaller ones fitting as best as possible the requested size. Each "level 0" block is a quad-block that can be split into four smaller "level 1" blocks of equal size. Likewise, each level 1 block is itself a quad-block that can be split again. At each level, the four smaller blocks become *buddies* or *partners* to each other. The block size at level l is thus $max\_sz/4^l$.

```
struct k_mem_block_id {
  u32_t pool  : 8;
  u32_t level  : 4;
  u32_t block  : 20;
};
struct k_mem_pool_lvl {
  union {
    u32_t *bits_p;
    u32_t bits;
  };
  sys_dlist_t free_list;
};
```

```
struct k_mem_block {
  void *data;
  struct k_mem_block_id id;
};
struct k_mem_pool {
  void *buf;
  size_t max_sz;
  u16_t n_max;
  u8_t n_levels;
  u8_t max_inline_level;
  struct k_mem_pool_lvl *levels;
  _wait_q_t wait_q;
};
```

The pool is initially configured with the parameters n_max and max_sz, together with a third parameter min_sz. min_sz defines the minimum size for an allocated block and must be at least $4 \times X$ $(X > 0)$ bytes long. Memory pool blocks are recursively split into quarters until blocks of the minimum size are obtained, at which point no further split can occur. The depth at which min_sz blocks are allocated is n_levels and satisfies that $n\_max = min\_sz \times 4^{n\_levels}$.

Every memory block is composed of a *level*; a *block* index within the level, ranging from 0 to $(n\_max \times 4^{level}) - 1$; and the *data* representing the block start address, which is equal to $buf + (max\_sz/4^{level}) \times block$. We use a tuple $(level, block)$ to uniquely represent a block within a pool p.

A memory pool keeps track of how its buffer space has been split using a linked list *free_list* with the start address of the free blocks in each level. To improve the performance of coalescing partner blocks, memory pools maintain a bitmap at each level to indicate the allocation status of each block in the level. This structure is represented by a C union of an integer *bits* and an array *bits_p*. The implementation can allocate the bitmaps at levels smaller than $max\_inlinle\_levels$ using only an integer *bits*. However, the number of blocks in levels higher than $max\_inlinle\_levels$ make necessary to allocate the bitmap information using the array *bits_map*. In such a design, the levels of bitmaps actually form a forest of complete quad trees. The bit i in the bitmap of level j is set to 1 for the block (i, j) iff it is a free block, i.e. it is in the free list at level i. Otherwise the bitmap for such block is set to 0.

Zephyr provides two kernel services *k_mem_pool_alloc* and *k_mem_pool_free*, for memory allocation and release respectively. The main part of the C code of *k_mem_pool_alloc* is shown in Fig. 1. When an application requests for a memory block, Zephyr first computes $alloc\_l$ and $free\_l$. $alloc\_l$ is the level with the size of the smallest block that will satisfy the request, and $free\_l$, with $free\_l \leqslant alloc\_l$, is the lowest level where there are free memory blocks. Since the services are concurrent, when the service tries to allocate a free block *blk* from level $free\_l$ (Line 8), blocks at that level may be allocated or merged into a bigger block by other concurrent threads. In such case the service will back out (Line 9) and tell the main function *k_mem_pool_alloc* to retry. If *blk* is successfully locked for allocation, then it is broken down to level $alloc\_l$ (Lines 11–14). The allocation service *k_mem_pool_alloc* supports a *timeout* parameter to allow threads waiting for that pool for a period of time when the call does not succeed. If the allocation

```
1  static int pool_alloc(struct k_mem_pool *p,struct k_mem_block *block,size_t size)
2  {
3    ..... //calcuate lsizes[], alloc_l and free_l
4    if (alloc_l < 0 || free_l < 0) {
5      block->data = NULL;
6      return -ENOMEM;
7    }
8    blk = alloc_block(p, free_l, lsizes[free_l]);
9    if (!blk) { return -EAGAIN; }
10   /* Iteratively break the smallest enclosing block... */
11   for (from_l = free_l; level_empty(p, alloc_l) && from_l < alloc_l;
12            from_l++) {
13     blk = break_block(p, blk, from_l, lsizes);
14   }
15   block->id.level = alloc_l; //assign block level to the variable *block
16   ......  //assign other block info to the variable *block
17   return 0;
18 }
19
20 int k_mem_pool_alloc(struct k_mem_pool *p, struct k_mem_block *block, size_t size,
       s32_t timeout)
21 {
22   ...... // initialize local vars, calculate the end time for timeout.
23   while (1) {
24     ret = pool_alloc(p, block, size);
25     if (ret == 0 || timeout == K_NO_WAIT ||
26         ret == -EAGAIN || (ret && ret != -ENOMEM)) {
27       return ret;
28     }
29     key = irq_lock();
30     _pend_current_thread(&p->wait_q, timeout);
31     _Swap(key);
32     ...... //if timeout > 0, break the loop if time out
33   }
34   return -EAGAIN;
35 }
```

Fig. 1. The C source code of memory allocation in Zephyr v1.8.0

fails (Line 24) and the timeout is not *K_NO_WAIT*, the thread is suspended (Line 30) in a linked list *wait_q* and the context is switched to another thread (Line 31).

Interruptions are always enabled in both services with the exception of the code for the functions *alloc_block* and *break_block*, which invoke *irq_lock* and *irq_unlock* to respectively enable and disable interruptions. Similar to *k_mem_pool_alloc*, the execution of *k_mem_pool_free* is interruptable too.

3 Defining Structures and Properties of Buddy Memory Pools

As a specification at design level, we use abstract data types to represent the complete structure of memory pools. We use an abstract reference *ref* in Isabelle to define pointers to memory pools. Starting addresses of memory blocks, memory pools, and unsigned integers in the implementation are defined as *natural* numbers (*nat*). Linked lists used in the implementation for the elements *levels* and *free_list*, together with the bitmaps used in *bits* and *bits_p*, are defined as a *list* type. C *structs* are modelled in Isabelle as *records* of the same name as the implementation and comprising the same data. There are two exceptions to this: (1) *k_mem_block_id* and *k_mem_block* are merged in one single record, (2) the union in the struct *k_mem_pool_lvl* is replaced by a single list representing the bitmap, and thus *max_inline_level* is removed.

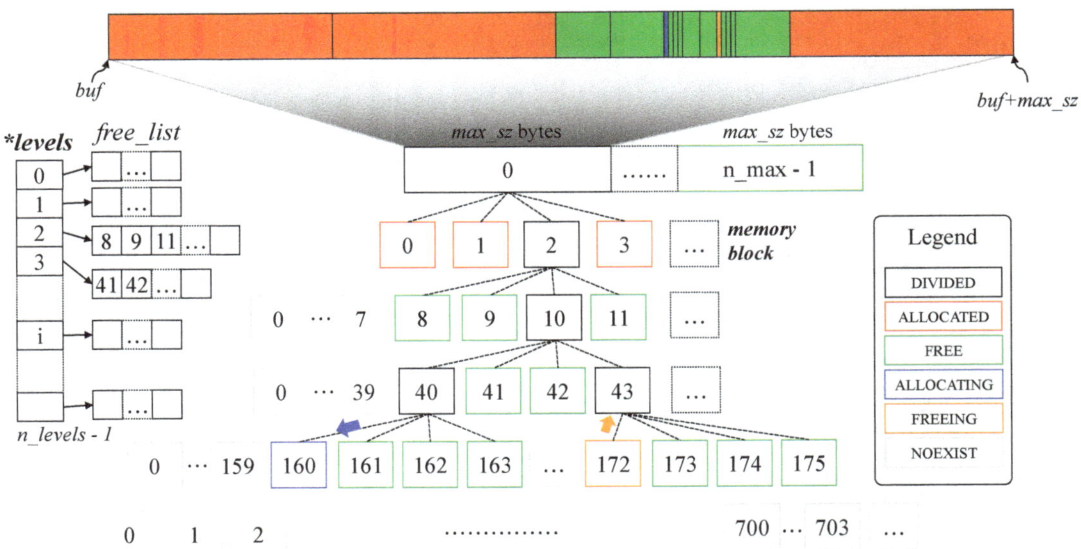

Fig. 2. Structure of memory pools

The Zephyr implementation makes use of a bitmap to represent the state of a memory block. The bit j of the bitmap for level a i is set to 1 iff the memory address of the memory block (i, j) is in the free list at level i. A bit j at a level i is set to 0 under the following conditions: (1) its corresponding memory block is allocated (*ALLOCATED*), (2) the memory block has been split (*DIVIDED*), (3) the memory block is being split in the allocation service (*ALLOCATING*) (Line 13 in Fig. 1), (4) the memory block is being coalesced in the release service (*FREEING*), and (5) the memory block does not exist (*NOEXIST*). Instead of only using a binary representation, our formal specification models the bitmap using a datatype *BlockState* that is composed of these cases together with *FREE*. The reason of this decision is to simplify proving that the bitmap shape is well-formed. In particular, this representation makes less complex to verify the case in which the descendant of a free block is a non-free block. This is the case where the last free block has not been split and therefore lower levels do not exist. We illustrate a structure of a memory pool in Fig. 2. The top of the figure shows the real memory of the first block at level 0.

The structural properties clarify the constraints on and consistency of quad trees, free block lists, the memory pool configuration, and waiting threads. All of them are thought of as invariants on the kernel state and have been formally verified on the formal specification in Isabelle/HOL.

Well-Shaped Bitmaps. We say that the logical memory block j at a level i physically exists iff the bitmap j for the level i is *ALLOCATED*, *FREE*, *ALLOCATING*, or *FREEING*, represented by the predicate *is_memblock*. We do not consider blocks marked as *DIVIDED* as physical blocks since it is only a logical block containing other blocks. Threads may split and coalesce memory blocks. A valid forest is defined by the following rules: (1) the parent bit of an existing memory block is *DIVIDED* and its child bits are *NOEXIST*, denoted by the predicate *noexist_bits* that checks for a given bitmap b and a position j that nodes $b!j$ to $b!(j+3)$ are set as *NOEXIST*; (2) the parent bit of a *DIVIDED* block is also *DIVIDED*; and (3) the child bits of a *NOEXIST* bit are also *NOEXIST* and its parent can not be a *DIVIDED* block. The property is defined as the predicate **inv-bitmap**(s), where s is the state.

There are two additional properties on bitmaps. First, the address space of any memory pool cannot be empty, i.e., the bits at level 0 have to be different to *NOEXIST*. Second, the allocation algorithm may split a memory block into smaller ones, but not the those blocks at the lowest level (i.e. level $n\_levels - 1$), therefore the bits at the lowest level cannot not be *DIVIDED*. The first property is defined as **inv-bitmap0**(s) and the second as **inv-bitmapn**(s).

Consistency of the Memory Configuration. The configuration of a memory pool is set when it is initialized. Since the minimum block size is aligned to 4 bytes, there must exists an $n > 0$ such that the maximum size of a pool is equal to $4 \times n \times 4^{n\_levels}$, relating the number of levels of a level 0 block with its maximum size. Moreover, the number of blocks at level 0 and the number of levels have to be greater than zero, since the memory pool cannot be empty. The number of levels is equal to the length of the pool *levels* list. Finally, the length of the bitmap at level i should be $n\_max \times 4^i$. This property is defined as **inv-mempool-info**(s).

Memory Partition Property. Memory blocks partition the pool they belong to, and then not overlapping blocks and the absence of memory leaks are critical properties. For a memory block of index j at level i, its address space is the interval $[j \times (max\_sz/4^i), (j+1) \times (max\_sz/4^i))$. For any relative memory address *addr* in the memory domain of a memory pool, and hence $addr < n\_max * max\_sz$, there is one and only one memory block whose address space contains *addr*. Here, we use relative address for *addr*. The property is defined as **mem-part**(s).

From the invariants of the bitmap, we derive the general property for the memory partition.

Theorem 1 (Memory Partition). *For any kernel state s, If the memory pools in s are consistent in their configuration, and their bitmaps are well-shaped, the memory pools satisfy the partition property in s:*

$$\boldsymbol{inv\_mempool\_info}(s) \wedge \boldsymbol{inv\_bitmap}(s) \wedge \boldsymbol{inv\_bitmap0}(s) \wedge \boldsymbol{inv\_bitmapn}(s) \Longrightarrow \boldsymbol{mem\_part}(s)$$

Together with the memory partition property, pools must also satisfy the following:

No Partner Fragmentation. The memory release algorithm in Zephyr coalesces free partner memory blocks into blocks as large as possible for all the descendants from the root level, without including it. Thus, a memory pool does not contain four *FREE* partner bits.

Validity of Free Block Lists. The free list at one level keeps the starting address of free memory blocks. The memory management ensures that the addresses in the list are valid, i.e., they are different from each other and aligned to the *block size*, which at a level i is given by $(max\_sz/4^i)$. Moreover, a memory block is in the free list iff the corresponding bit of the bitmap is *FREE*.

Non-overlapping of Memory Pools. The memory spaces of the set of pools defined in a system must be disjoint, so the memory addresses of a pool does not belong to the memory space of any other pool.

Other Properties. The state of a suspended thread in *wait_q* has to be consistent with the threads waiting for a memory pool. Threads can only be blocked once, and those threads waiting for available memory blocks have to be in a *BLOCKED* state. During allocation and free of a memory block, blocks of the tree may temporally be manipulated during the coalesce and division process. A block can be only manipulated by a thread at a time, and the state bit of a block being temporally manipulate has to be *FREEING* or *ALLOCATING*.

4 Formalizing Zephyr Memory Management

For the purpose of formal verification of event-driven systems such as OSs, we have developed π-Core, a framework for rely-guarantee reasoning of components running in parallel invoking events. π-Core has support for concurrent OSs features like modelling shared-variable concurrency of multiple threads, interruptable execution of handlers, self-suspending threads, and rescheduling. In this section, we first introduce the modelling language in π-Core and an execution model of Zephyr using this language. Then we discuss in detail the low-level design specification for the kernel services that the memory management provides. Since this work focuses on the memory management, we only provide very abstract models for other kernel functionalities such as the kernel scheduling and thread control.

4.1 Event-Based Execution Model of Zephyr

The Language in π-Core. Interrupt handlers in π-Core are considered as reaction services which are represented as *events*:

$$\textbf{EVENT}\ \mathcal{E}\ [p_1, ..., p_n]@\kappa\ \textbf{WHEN}\ g\ \textbf{THEN}\ P\ \textbf{END}$$

In this representation, an event is a parametrized imperative program P with a name $\mathcal{E}$, a list of service input parameters $p_1, ..., p_n$, and a guard condition g to determine the conditions triggering the event. In addition to the input parameters, an event has a special parameter κ which indicates the execution context, e.g. the scheduler and the thread invoking the event. The imperative commands of an event body P in π-Core are standard sequential constructs such as conditional execution, loop, and sequential composition of programs. It also includes a synchronization construct for concurrent processes represented by **AWAIT** b **THEN** P **END**. The body P is executed atomically if and only if the boolean condition b holds, not progressing otherwise. **ATOM** P **END** denotes an *Await* statement for which its guard is *True*.

Threads and kernel processes have their own execution context and local states. Each of them is modelled in π-Core as a set of events called *event systems* and denoted as **ESYS** $\mathcal{S} \equiv \{\mathcal{E}_0,\ ...,\ \mathcal{E}_n\}$. The operational semantics of an event system is the *sequential composition* of the execution of the events composing it. It consists in the continuous evaluation of the guards of the system events. From the set of events for which the associated guard g holds in the current state, one event $\mathcal{E}$ is non-deterministically selected to be triggered, and its body P executed. After P finishes, the evaluation of the guards starts again looking for the next event to be executed. Finally, π-Core has a construct for parallel composition of event systems $esys_0 \parallel ... \parallel esys_n$ which interleaves the execution of the events composing each event system $esys_i$ for $0 \leq i \leq n$.

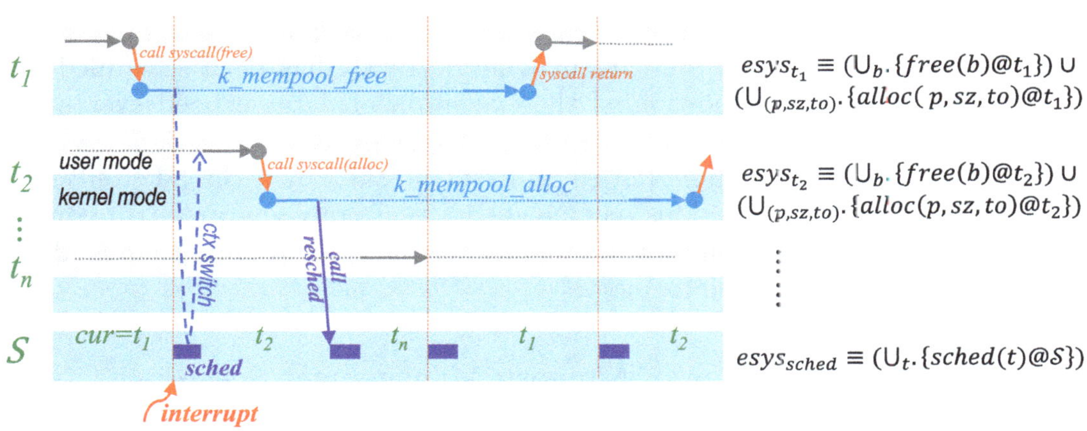

Fig. 3. An execution model of Zephyr memory management

Execution Model of Zephyr. If we do not consider its initialization, an OS kernel can be consider as a reactive system that is in an *idle* loop until it receives an interruption which is handled by an interruption handler. Whilst interrupt handlers execution is atomic in sequential kernels, it can be interrupted in concurrent kernels [6,22] allowing services invoked by threads to be interrupted and resumed later. In the execution model of Zephyr, we consider a scheduler $\mathcal{S}$ and a set of threads $t_1, ..., t_n$. In this model, the execution of the scheduler is atomic since kernel services can not interrupt it. But kernel services can be interrupted via the scheduler, i.e., the execution of a memory service invoked by a thread t_i may be interrupted by the kernel scheduler to execute a thread t_j. Figure 3 illustrates Zephyr execution model, where solid lines represent execution steps of the threads/kernel services and dotted lines mean the suspension of the thread/code. For instance, the execution of *k_mempool_free* in thread t_1 is interrupted by the scheduler, and the context is switched to thread t_2 which invokes *k_mempool_alloc*. During the execution of t_2, the kernel service may suspend the thread and switch to another thread t_n by calling *rescheduling*. Later, the execution is switched back to t_1 and continues the execution of *k_mempool_free* in a different state from when it was interrupted.

The event systems of Zephyr are illustrated in the right part of Fig. 3. A user thread t_i invoke allocation/release services, thus the event system for t_i is $esys_{t_i}$, a set composed of the events *alloc* and *free*. The input parameters for these events correspond with the arguments of the service implementation, that are constrained by the guard for each service. Together with system users we model the event service for the scheduler $esys_{sched}$ consisting on a unique event *sched* whose argument is a thread t to be scheduled when t is in the $READY$ state. The formal specification of the memory management is the parallel composition of the event system for the threads and the scheduler $esys_{t_1} \parallel ... \parallel esys_{t_n} \parallel esys_{sched}$

Thread Context and Preemption. Events are parametrized by a thread identifier used to access to the execution context of the thread invoking it. As shown in Fig. 3, the execution of an event executed by a thread can be stopped by the scheduler to be resumed later. This behaviour is modelled using a global variable *cur* that indicates the thread being currently has been scheduled and is being executed, and conditioning the execution of parametrized events in t only when t is scheduled. This is achieved by using the expression t ▶ p ≡ **AWAIT** $cur = t$ **THEN** p **END**, so an event invoked by a thread t only progresses when t is scheduled. This scheme allows to use rely-guarantee for concurrent execution of threads on mono-core architectures, where only the scheduled thread is able to modify the memory.

4.2 Formal Specification of Memory Management Services

This section discusses the formal specification of the memory management services. These services deal with the initialization of pools, and memory allocation and release.

System State. The system state includes the memory model introduced in Sect. 4, together with the thread under execution in variable *cur* and local variables to the memory services used to keep temporal changes to the structure, guards in conditional and loop statements, and index accesses. The memory model is represented as a set *mem_pools* storing the references of all memory pools and a mapping *mem_pool_info* to query a pool by a pool reference. Local variables are modelled as total functions from threads to variable values, representing that the event is accessing the thread context. In the formal model of the events we represent access to a state component c using ´c and the value of a local component c for the thread t is represented as ´c t. Local variables *allocating_node* and *freeing_node* are relevant for the memory services, storing the temporal blocks being split/coalesced in alloc/release services respectively.

Memory Pool Initialization. Zephyr defines and initializes memory pools at compile time by constructing a static variable of type ***struct*** *k_mem_pool*. The implementation initializes each pool with *n_max* level 0 blocks with size *max_sz* bytes. Bitmaps of level 0 are set to 1 and free list contains all level 0 blocks. Bitmaps and free lists of other level are initialized to 0 and to the empty list respectively. In the formal model, we specify a state corresponding to the implementation initial state and we show that it belongs to the set of states satisfying the invariant.

```
WHILE ´free-block-r t DO
  t ▶ ´lsz := ´lsz (t := ´lsizes t ! (´lvl t));;
  t ▶ ´blk := ´blk (t := block-ptr (´mem-pool-info (pool b)) (´lsz t) (´bn t));;
  t ▶ ATOM
    ´mem-pool-info := set-bit-free ´mem-pool-info (pool b) (´lvl t) (´bn t);;
    ´freeing-node := ´freeing-node (t := None);;
    IF ´lvl t > 0 ∧ partner-bits (´mem-pool-info (pool b)) (´lvl t) (´bn t) THEN
      FOR ´i := ´i(t := 0); ´i t < 4; ´i := ´i(t := ´i t + 1) DO
        ´bb := ´bb (t := (´bn t div 4) ∗ 4 + ´i t);;
        ´mem-pool-info := set-bit-noexist ´mem-pool-info (pool b) (´lvl t) (´bb t);;
        ´block-pt := ´block-pt (t := block-ptr (´mem-pool-info (pool b)) (´lsz t) (´bb t));;
        IF ´bn t ≠ ´bb t ∧ block-fits (´mem-pool-info (pool b)) (´block-pt t) (´lsz t) THEN
          ´mem-pool-info := ´mem-pool-info ((pool b) :=
               remove-free-list (´mem-pool-info (pool b)) (´lvl t) (´block-pt t))
        FI
      ROF;;
      ´lvl := ´lvl (t := ´lvl t − 1);;
      ´bn := ´bn (t := ´bn t div 4);;
      ´mem-pool-info := set-bit-freeing ´mem-pool-info (pool b) (´lvl t) (´bn t);;
      ´freeing-node := ´freeing-node (t := Some (|pool = (pool b), level = (´lvl t),
          block = (´bn t), data = block-ptr (´mem-pool-info (pool b))
           (((ALIGN4 (max-sz (´mem-pool-info (pool b)))) div (4 ^ (´lvl t)))) (´bn t) |))
    ELSE
      IF block-fits (´mem-pool-info (pool b)) (´blk t) (´lsz t) THEN
        ´mem-pool-info := ´mem-pool-info ((pool b) :=
          append-free-list (´mem-pool-info (pool b)) (´lvl t) (´blk t) )
      FI;;
      ´free-block-r := ´free-block-r (t := False)
    FI
  END
OD
```

Fig. 4. The π-Core specification of *free_block*

Memory Allocation/Release Services. The C code of Zephyr uses the recursive function *free_block* to coalesce free partner blocks and the *break* statement to stop the execution of a loop statements, which are not supported by the imperative language in π-Core. The formal specification overcomes this by transforming the recursion into a loop controlled by the recursion condition, and using a control variable to exit loops with breaks when the condition to execute the loop break is satisfied. Additionally, the memory management services use the atomic body *irq_lock(); P; irq_unlock();* to keep interruption handlers *reentrant* by disabling interruptions. We simplify this behaviour in the specification using an **ATOM** statement, avoiding that the service is interrupted at that point. The rest of the formal specification closely follows the implementation, where variables are modified using higher order functions changing the state as the code does it. The reason of using Isabelle/HOL functions is that π-Core does not provide a semantic for expressions, using instead state transformer relying on high order functions to change the state.

Figure 4 illustrates the π-Core specification of the *free_block* function invoked by *k_mem_pool_free* when releasing a memory block. The code accesses the following variables: lsz, $lsize$, and lvl to keep information about the current level; blk, bn, and bb to represent the address and number of the block currently being accessed; $freeing\_node$ to represent the node being freeing; and i to iterate blocks. Additionally, the model includes the component $free\_block\_r$ to model the recursion condition. To simplify the representation the model uses predicates and functions to access and modify the state. Due to space constrains, we are unable to provide detailed explanation of these functions. However the name of the functions can help the reader to better understand their functionality. We refer readers to the Isabelle/HOL sources for the complete specification of the formal model.

In the C code, *free_block* is a recursive function with two conditions: (1) the block being released belongs to a level higher than zero, since blocks at level zero cannot be merged; and (2) the partners bits of the block being released are FREE so they can be merged into a bigger block. We represent (1) with the predicate $\acute{}lvl\ t > 0$ and (2) with the predicate $partner\_bit\_free$. The formal specification follows the same structure translating the recursive function into a loop that is controlled by a variable mimicking the recursion.

The formal specification for *free_block* first releases an allocated memory block *bn* setting it to *FREEING*. Then, the loop statement sets *free_block* to *FREE* (Line 5), and also checks that the iteration/recursive condition holds in Line 7. If the condition holds, the partner bits are set to *NOEXIST*, and remove their addresses from the free list for this level (Lines 12–14). Then, it sets the parent block bit to *FREEING* (Lines 17–22), and updates the variables controlling the current block and level numbers, before going back to the beginning of the loop again. If the iteration condition is not true it sets the bit to *FREE* and add the block to the free list (Lines 24–28) and sets the loop condition to false to end the procedure. This function is illustrated in Fig. 2. The block 172 is released by a thread and since its partner blocks (block 173–175) are free, Zephyr coalesces the four blocks and sets their parent block 43 as *FREEING*. The coalescence continues iteratively if the partners of block 43 are all free.

5 Correctness and Rely-Guarantee Proof

We have proven correctness of the buddy memory management in Zephyr using the rely-guarantee proof system of π-Core. We ensure functional correctness of each kernel service w.r.t. the defined pre/post conditions, invariant preservation, termination of loop statements in the kernel services, the preservation of the memory configuration during small steps of kernel services, and the separation of local variables of threads. In this section, we introduce the rely-guarantee proof system of π-Core and how these properties are specified and verified using it.

5.1 Rely-Guarantee Proof Rules and Verification

A rely-guarantee specification for a system is a quadruple $RGCond = \langle pre, R, G, pst \rangle$, where pre is the pre-condition, R is the rely condition, G is the guarantee condition, and pst is the post-condition. The intuitive meaning of a valid rely-guarantee specification for a parallel component P, denoted by $\models P$ **sat** $\langle pre, R, G, pst \rangle$, is that if P is executed from an initial state $s \in pre$ and any environment transition belongs to the rely relation R, then the state transitions carried out by P belong to the guarantee relation G and the final states belong to pst.

We have defined a rely-guarantee axiomatic proof system for the π-Core specification language to prove validity of rely-guarantee specifications, and proven in Isabelle/HOL its soundness with regards to the definition of validity. Some of the rules composing the axiomatic reasoning system are shown in Fig. 5.

[AWAIT]

$$\frac{\vdash P\ \mathbf{sat}\ \langle pre \cap b \cap \{V\}, Id, UNIV, \{s \mid (V, s) \in G\} \cap pst \rangle \quad stable(pre, R) \quad stable(pst, R)}{\vdash (\mathbf{Await}\ b\ P)\ \mathbf{sat}\ \langle pre, R, G, pst \rangle}$$

[BASICEVT]

$$\frac{\vdash body(\alpha)\ \mathbf{sat}\ \langle pre \cap guard(\alpha), R, G, pst \rangle \quad stable(pre, R) \quad \forall s.\ (s, s) \in G}{\vdash \mathbf{Event}\ \alpha\ \mathbf{sat}\ \langle pre, R, G, pst \rangle}$$

[WHILE]

$$\frac{\vdash P\ \mathbf{sat}\ \langle loopinv \cap b, R, G, loopinv \rangle \quad loopinv \cap -b \subseteq pst \quad \forall s.\ (s, s) \in G \quad stable(loopinv, R) \quad stable(pst, R)}{\vdash (\mathbf{While}\ b\ P)\ \mathbf{sat}\ \langle loopinv, R, G, pst \rangle}$$

[PAR]

$$\frac{\begin{array}{l}(1)\forall \kappa.\ \vdash \mathcal{PS}(\kappa)\ \mathbf{sat}\ \langle pres_\kappa, Rs_\kappa, Gs_\kappa, psts_\kappa \rangle \\ (2)\forall \kappa.\ pre \subseteq pres_\kappa \quad (3)\forall \kappa.\ psts_\kappa \subseteq pst \quad (4)\forall \kappa.\ Gs_\kappa \subseteq G \\ (5)\forall \kappa.\ R \subseteq Rs_\kappa \quad (6)\forall \kappa, \kappa'.\ \kappa \neq \kappa' \longrightarrow Gs_\kappa \subseteq Rs_{\kappa'}\end{array}}{\vdash \mathcal{PS}\ \mathbf{sat}\ \langle pre, R, G, pst \rangle}$$

Fig. 5. Typical rely-guarantee proof rules in π-Core

A predicate P is stable w.r.t. a relation R, represented as $stable(P, R)$, when for any pair of states (s, t) such that $s \in P$ and $(s, t) \in R$ then $t \in P$. The intuitive meaning is that an environment represented by R does not affect the satisfiability of P. The parallel rule in Fig. 5 establishes compositionality of the proof system, where verification of the parallel specification can be reduced to the verification of individual event systems first and then to the verification of individual events. It is necessary that each event system $\mathcal{PS}(\kappa)$ satisfies its specification $\langle pres_\kappa, Rs_\kappa, Gs_\kappa, psts_\kappa\rangle$ (Premise 1); the pre-condition for the parallel composition implies all the event system's pre-conditions (Premise 2); the overall post-condition must be a logical consequence of all post-conditions of event systems (Premise 3); since an action transition of the concurrent system is performed by one of its event system, the guarantee condition Gs_κ of each event system must be a subset of the overall guarantee condition G (Premise 4); an environment transition Rs_κ for the event system κ corresponds to a transition from the overall environment R (Premise 5); and an action transition of an event system κ should be defined in the rely condition of another event system κ', where $\kappa \neq \kappa'$ (Premise 6).

To prove loop termination, loop invariants are parametrized with a logical variable α. It suffices to show total correctness of a loop statement by the following proposition where $loopinv(\alpha)$ is the parametrize invariant, in which the logical variable is used to find a convergent relation to show that the number of iterations of the loop is finite.

$$\vdash P \textbf{ sat } \langle loopinv(\alpha) \cap \{\!\!\{ \alpha > 0 \}\!\!\}, R, G, \exists\beta < \alpha.\ loopinv(\beta)\rangle \wedge loopinv(\alpha) \cap \{\!\!\{ \alpha > 0 \}\!\!\} \subseteq \{\!\!\{ b \}\!\!\}$$
$$\wedge\, loopinv(0) \subseteq \{\!\!\{ \neg b \}\!\!\} \wedge \forall s \in loopinv(\alpha).\ (s,t) \in R \longrightarrow \exists\beta \leqslant \alpha.\ t \in loopinv(\beta)$$

5.2 Correctness Specification

Using the compositional reasoning of π-Core, correctness of Zephyr memory management can be specified and verified with the rely-guarantee specification of each event. The functional correctness of a kernel service is specified by its pre/post-conditions. Invariant preservation, memory configuration, and separation of local variables is specified in the guarantee condition of each service.

The guarantee condition for both memory services is defined as:

$$\textbf{Mem-pool-alloc-guar}\ t \equiv \overbrace{Id}^{(1)} \cup (\overbrace{gvars\_conf\_stable}^{(2)} \cap$$
$$\{(s,r).\ (\overbrace{cur\ s \neq Some\ t \longrightarrow gvars\text{-}nochange\ s\ r \wedge lvars\text{-}nochange\ t\ s\ r}^{(3.1)})$$
$$\wedge\ (\overbrace{cur\ s = Some\ t \longrightarrow inv\ s \longrightarrow inv\ r}^{(3.2)}) \wedge (\overbrace{\forall t'.\ t' \neq t \longrightarrow lvars\text{-}nochange\ t'\ s\ r}^{(4)})\})$$

This relation states that *alloc* and *free* services may not change the state (1), e.g., a blocked await or selecting branch on a conditional statement. If it changes the state then: (2) the static configuration of memory pools in the model do not change; (3.1) if the scheduled thread is not the thread invoking the event then variables for that thread do not change (since it is blocked in an *Await* as explained in Sect. 3); (3.2) if it is, then the relation preserves the memory invariant, and consequently each step of the event needs to preserve the invariant; (4) a thread does not change the local variables of other threads.

Using the π-Core proof rules we verify that the invariant introduced in Sect. 4 is preserved by all the events. Additionally, we prove that when starting in a valid memory configuration given by the invariant, then if the service does not returns an error code then it returns a valid memory block with size bigger or equal than the requested capacity. The property is specified by the following postcondition:

Mem-pool-alloc-pre $t \equiv \{s.\ inv\, s \wedge allocating\text{-}node\, s\, t = None \wedge freeing\text{-}node\, s\, t = None\}$
Mem-pool-alloc-post $t\ p\ sz\ timeout \equiv$

$$\begin{aligned}&\{s.\ inv\, s \wedge allocating\text{-}node\ s\ t = None \wedge freeing\text{-}node\ s\ t = None\\ &\quad \wedge (timeout = FOREVER \longrightarrow\\ &\qquad (ret\ s\ t = ESIZEERR \wedge mempoolalloc\text{-}ret\ s\ t = None \vee\\ &\qquad ret\ s\ t = OK \wedge (\exists\, mblk.\ mempoolalloc\text{-}ret\ s\ t = Some\ mblk \wedge mblk\text{-}valid\ s\ p\ sz\ mblk)))\\ &\quad \wedge (timeout = NOWAIT \longrightarrow\\ &\qquad ((ret\ s\ t = ENOMEM \vee ret\ s\ t = ESIZEERR) \wedge mempoolalloc\text{-}ret\ s\ t = None) \vee\\ &\qquad (ret\ s\ t = OK \wedge (\exists\, mblk.\ mempoolalloc\text{-}ret\ s\ t = Some\ mblk \wedge mblk\text{-}valid\ s\ p\ sz\ mblk)))\\ &\quad \wedge (timeout > 0 \longrightarrow\\ &\qquad ((ret\ s\ t = ETIMEOUT \vee ret\ s\ t = ESIZEERR) \wedge mempoolalloc\text{-}ret\ s\ t = None) \vee\\ &\qquad (ret\ s\ t = OK \wedge (\exists\, mblk.\ mempoolalloc\text{-}ret\ s\ t = Some\ mblk\\ &\qquad\qquad \wedge mblk\text{-}valid\ s\ p\ sz\ mblk)))\}\end{aligned}$$

If a thread requests a memory block in mode *FOREVER*, it may successfully allocate a valid memory block, or fail (*ESIZEERR*) if the request size is larger than the size of the memory pool. If the thread is requesting a memory pool in mode *NOWAIT*, it may also get the result of *ENOMEM* if there is no available blocks. But if the thread is requesting in mode *TIMEOUT*, it will get the result of *ETIMEOUT* if there is no available blocks in *timeout* milliseconds.

The property is indeed weak since even if the memory has a block able to allocate the requested size before invoking the allocation service, another thread running concurrently may have taken the block first during the execution of the service. For the same reason, the released block may be taken by another concurrent thread before the end of the release services.

5.3 Correctness Proof

In the π-Core system, verification of a rely-guarantee specification proving a property is carried out by inductively applying the proof rules for each system event and discharging the proof obligations the rules generate. Typically, these proof obligations require to prove stability of the pre- and post-condition to check that changes of the environment preserve them, and to show that a statement modifying a state from the precondition gets a state belonging to the postcondition.

To prove termination of the loop statement in *free_block* shown in Fig. 4, we define the loop invariant with the logical variable α as follows.

mp-free-loopinv $t\ b\ \alpha \equiv$

$$\begin{aligned}&\{\!|\ \ldots \wedge {}'inv \wedge level\ b < length\ ({}'lsizes\ t)\\ &\quad \wedge (\forall\, ii{<}length\ ({}'lsizes\ t).\ {}'lsizes\ t\ !\ ii = (max\text{-}sz\ ({}'mem\text{-}pool\text{-}info\ (pool\ b)))\ div\ (4\ \hat{}\ ii))\\ &\quad \wedge {}'bn\ t < length\ (bits\ (levels\ ({}'mem\text{-}pool\text{-}info\ (pool\ b))!({}'lvl\ t)))\\ &\quad \wedge {}'bn\ t = (block\ b)\ div\ (4\ \hat{}\ (level\ b - {}'lvl\ t)) \wedge {}'lvl\ t \le level\ b\\ &\quad \wedge ({}'free\text{-}block\text{-}r\ t \longrightarrow (\exists\, blk.\ {}'freeing\text{-}node\ t = Some\ blk \wedge pool\ blk = pool\ b\\ &\qquad \wedge level\ blk = {}'lvl\ t \wedge block\ blk = {}'bn\ t)\end{aligned}$$

$$\wedge \, ' \textit{alloc-memblk-data-valid}\, (\textit{pool}\, b)\, (\textit{the}\, (' \textit{freeing-node}\, t)))$$
$$\wedge (\neg \, ' \textit{free-block-r}\, t \longrightarrow \, ' \textit{freeing-node}\, t = \textit{None}) \, \} \cap$$
$$\{ \, \alpha = (\textit{if}\, ' \textit{freeing-node}\, t \neq \textit{None then}\, ' \textit{lvl}\, t + 1\, \textit{else}\, 0) \, \}$$

$freeing\_node$ and lvt are local variables respectively storing the node being free and the level that the node belongs to. In the body of the loop, if $lvl\ t > 0$ and $partner\_bit$ is $true$, then $lvl = lvl - 1$ at the end of the body. Otherwise, $freeing\_node\ t = None$. So at the end of the loop body, α decreases or $\alpha = 0$. If $\alpha = 0$, we have $freeing\_node\ t = None$, and thus the negation of the loop condition $\neg free\_block\_r\ t$, concluding termination of *free_block*.

Due to concurrency, it is necessary to consider fairness to prove termination of the loop statement in *k_mempool_alloc* from Line 23 to 33 in Fig. 1. On the one hand, when a thread requests a memory block in the *FOREVER* mode, it is possible that there will never be available blocks since other threads do not release allocated blocks. On the other hand, even when other threads release blocks, it is possible that the available blocks are always raced by threads.

6 Evaluation and Results

Evaluation. The verification conducted in this work is on Zhephyr v1.8.0, released in 2017. The C code of the buddy memory management is ≈400lines, not counting blank lines and comments. Table 1 shows the statistics for the effort and size of the proofs in the Isabelle/HOL theorem prover. In total, the models and mechanized verification consists of ≈28,000 lines of specification and proofs, and the total effort is ≈12 person-months. The specification and proof of π-Core are reusable for the verification of other systems.

Table 1. Specification and proof statistics

π-Core language		Memory management	
Item	LOS/LOP	Item	LOS/LOP
Language and proof rules	700	Specification	400
Lemmas of language/semantics	3000	Auxiliary lemmas/invariant	1700
Soundness	7100	Proof of allocation	10600
Invariant	100	Proof of free	4950
Total	10,900	Total	17,650

Bugs in Zephyr. During the formal verification, we found 3 bugs in the C code of Zephyr. The first two bugs are critical and have been repaired in the latest release of Zephyr. To avoid the third one, callers to *k_mem_pool_alloc* have to constrain the argument $t\_size\ size$.

(1) Incorrect block split: this bug is located in the loop in Line 11 of the *k_mem_pool_alloc* service, shown in Fig. 1. The *level_empty* function checks if a pool p has blocks in the free list at level *alloc_l*. Concurrent threads may release a memory block at that level making the call to *level_empty(p, alloc_l)* to return *false* and stopping the loop. In such case, it allocates a memory block of a bigger capacity at a level i but it still sets the level number of the block as *alloc_l* at Line 15. The service allocates a larger block to the requesting thread causing an internal fragmentation of $max\_sz/4^i - max\_sz/4^{alloc\_l}$ bytes. When this block is released, it will be inserted into the free list at level *alloc_l*, but not at level i, causing an external fragmentation of $max\_sz/4^i - max\_sz/4^{alloc\_l}$. The bug is fixed by removing the condition *level_empty(p, alloc_l)* in our specification.

(2) Incorrect return from *k_mem_pool_alloc*: this bug is found at Line 26 in Fig. 1. When a suitable free block is allocated by another thread, the *pool_alloc* function returns *EAGAIN* at Line 9 to ask the thread to retry the allocation. When a thread invokes *k_mem_pool_alloc* in *FOREVER* mode and this case happens, the service returns *EAGAIN* immediately. However, a thread invoking *k_mem_pool_alloc* in *FOREVER* mode should keep retrying when it does not succeed. We repair the bug by removing the condition $ret == EAGAIN$ at Line 26. As explained in the comments of the C Code, *EAGAIN* should not be returned to threads invoking the service. Moreover, the *return EAGAIN* at Line 34 is actually the case of time out. Thus, we introduce a new return code *ETIMEOUT* in our specification.

(3) Non-termination of *k_mem_pool_alloc*: we have discussed that the loop statement at Lines 23–33 in Fig. 1 does not terminate. However, it should terminate in certain cases, which are actually violated in the C code. When a thread requests a memory block in *FOREVER* mode and the requested size is larger than *max_sz*, the maximum size of blocks, the loop at Lines 23–33 in Fig. 1 never finishes since *pool_alloc* always returns *ENOMEM*. The reason is that the "*return ENOMEM*" at Line 6 does not distinguish two cases, $alloc\_l < 0$ and $free\_l < 0$. In the first case, the requested size is larger than *max_sz* and the kernel service should return immediately. In the second case, there are no free blocks larger than the requested size and the service tries forever until some free block available. We repair the bug by splitting the *if* statement at Lines 4–7 into these two cases and introducing a new return code *ESIZEERR* in our specification. Then, we change the condition at Lines 25–26 to check that the returned value is *ESIZEERR* instead of *ENOMEM*.

7 Conclusion and Future Work

In this paper, we have developed a formal specification at low-level design of the concurrent buddy memory management of Zephyr RTOS. Using the rely-guarantee technique in the π-Core framework, we have formally verified a set of critical properties for OS kernels such as invariant preservation, and preservation of memory configuration. Finally, we identified some critical bugs in the C code of Zephyr.

Our work explores the challenges and cost of certifying concurrent OSs for the highest-level assurance. The definition of properties and rely-guarantee relations is complex and the verification task becomes expensive. We used 40 times of LOS/LOP than the C code at low-level design. Next, we are planning to verify other modules of Zephyr, which may be easier due to simpler data structures and algorithms. For the purpose of fully formal verification of OSs at source code level, we will replace the imperative language in π-Core by a more expressive one and add a verification condition generator (VCG) to reduce the cost of the verification.

References

1. The Zephyr Project. https://www.zephyrproject.org/. Accessed Dec 2018
2. Common Criteria for Information Technology Security Evaluation (v3.1, Release 5). https://www.commoncriteriaportal.org/. Accessed Apr 2017
3. Alkassar, E., Schirmer, N., Starostin, A.: Formal pervasive verification of a paging mechanism. In: Ramakrishnan, C.R., Rehof, J. (eds.) TACAS 2008. LNCS, vol. 4963, pp. 109–123. Springer, Heidelberg (2008). https://doi.org/10.1007/978-3-540-78800-3_9
4. Blanchard, A., Kosmatov, N., Lemerre, M., Loulergue, F.: A case study on formal verification of the anaxagoros hypervisor paging system with Frama-C. In: Núñez, M., Güdemann, M. (eds.) FMICS 2015. LNCS, vol. 9128, pp. 15–30. Springer, Cham (2015). https://doi.org/10.1007/978-3-319-19458-5_2
5. Bolignano, P., Jensen, T., Siles, V.: Modeling and abstraction of memory management in a hypervisor. In: Stevens, P., Wąsowski, A. (eds.) FASE 2016. LNCS, vol. 9633, pp. 214–230. Springer, Heidelberg (2016). https://doi.org/10.1007/978-3-662-49665-7_13
6. Chen, H., Wu, X., Shao, Z., Lockerman, J., Gu, R.: Toward compositional verification of interruptible OS kernels and device drivers. In: Proceedings of 37th ACM SIGPLAN Conference on Programming Language Design and Implementation (PLDI), pp. 431–447. ACM (2016)
7. Fang, B., Sighireanu, M.: Hierarchical shape abstraction for analysis of free list memory allocators. In: Hermenegildo, M.V., Lopez-Garcia, P. (eds.) LOPSTR 2016. LNCS, vol. 10184, pp. 151–167. Springer, Cham (2017). https://doi.org/10.1007/978-3-319-63139-4_9
8. Fang, B., Sighireanu, M.: A refinement hierarchy for free list memory allocators. In: Proceedings of ACM SIGPLAN International Symposium on Memory Management, pp. 104–114. ACM (2017)
9. Fang, B., et al.: Formal modelling of list based dynamic memory allocators. Sci. China Inf. Sci. **61**(12), 103–122 (2018)
10. Gallardo, M.D.M., Merino, P., Sanán, D.: Model checking dynamic memory allocation in operating systems. J. Autom. Reasoning **42**(2), 229–264 (2009)
11. Gu, R., et al.: CertiKOS: an extensible architecture for building certified concurrent OS kernels. In: Proceedings of 12th USENIX Symposium on Operating Systems Design and Implementation (OSDI), pp. 653–669. USENIX Association, Savannah, GA (2016)
12. Klein, G., et al.: seL4: formal verification of an OS kernel. In: Proceedings of 22nd ACM SIGOPS Symposium on Operating Systems Principles (SOSP), pp. 207–220. ACM Press (2009)

13. Klein, G., Tuch, H.: Towards verified virtual memory in L4. In: Proceedings of TPHOLs Emerging Trends, p. 16. Park City, Utah, USA, September 2004
14. Leroy, X., Blazy, S.: Formal verification of a C-like memory model and its uses for verifying program transformations. J. Autom. Reasoning **41**(1), 1–31 (2008)
15. Mansky, W., Garbuzov, D., Zdancewic, S.: An axiomatic specification for sequential memory models. In: Kroening, D., Păsăreanu, C.S. (eds.) CAV 2015. LNCS, vol. 9207, pp. 413–428. Springer, Cham (2015). https://doi.org/10.1007/978-3-319-21668-3_24
16. Marti, N., Affeldt, R., Yonezawa, A.: Formal verification of the heap manager of an operating system using separation logic. In: Liu, Z., He, J. (eds.) ICFEM 2006. LNCS, vol. 4260, pp. 400–419. Springer, Heidelberg (2006). https://doi.org/10.1007/11901433_22
17. Saraswat, V.A., Jagadeesan, R., Michael, M., von Praun, C.: A theory of memory models. In: Proceedings of the 12th ACM SIGPLAN Symposium on Principles and Practice of Parallel Programming (PPoPP), pp. 161–172. ACM (2007)
18. Su, W., Abrial, J.R., Pu, G., Fang, B.: Formal development of a real-time operating system memory manager. In: Proceedings of International Conference on Engineering of Complex Computer Systems (ICECCS), pp. 130–139 (2016)
19. Tews, H., Völp, M., Weber, T.: Formal memory models for the verification of low-level operating-system code. J. Autom. Reasoning **42**(2), 189–227 (2009)
20. Vaynberg, A., Shao, Z.: Compositional verification of a baby virtual memory manager. In: Hawblitzel, C., Miller, D. (eds.) CPP 2012. LNCS, vol. 7679, pp. 143–159. Springer, Heidelberg (2012). https://doi.org/10.1007/978-3-642-35308-6_13
21. Ševčík, J., Vafeiadis, V., Nardelli, F.Z., Jagannathan, S., Sewell, P.: CompCertTSO: a verified compiler for relaxed-memory concurrency. J. ACM **60**(3), 22:1–22:50 (2013)
22. Xu, F., Fu, M., Feng, X., Zhang, X., Zhang, H., Li, Z.: A practical verification framework for preemptive OS kernels. In: Chaudhuri, S., Farzan, A. (eds.) CAV 2016. LNCS, vol. 9780, pp. 59–79. Springer, Cham (2016). https://doi.org/10.1007/978-3-319-41540-6_4
23. Yu, D., Hamid, N.A., Shao, Z.: Building certified libraries for PCC: dynamic storage allocation. In: Degano, P. (ed.) ESOP 2003. LNCS, vol. 2618, pp. 363–379. Springer, Heidelberg (2003). https://doi.org/10.1007/3-540-36575-3_25

Violat: Generating Tests of Observational Refinement for Concurrent Objects

Michael Emmi[1(✉)] and Constantin Enea[2]

[1] SRI International, New York, NY, USA
michael.emmi@sri.com
[2] Université de Paris, IRIF, CNRS, 75013 Paris, France
cenea@irif.fr

Abstract. High-performance multithreaded software often relies on optimized implementations of common abstract data types (ADTs) like counters, key-value stores, and queues, i.e., *concurrent objects*. By using fine-grained and non-blocking mechanisms for efficient inter-thread synchronization, these implementations are vulnerable to violations of ADT-consistency which are difficult to detect: bugs can depend on specific combinations of method invocations and argument values, as well as rarely-occurring thread interleavings. Even given a bug-triggering interleaving, detection generally requires unintuitive test assertions to capture inconsistent combinations of invocation return values.

In this work we describe the Violat tool for generating tests that witness violations to atomicity, or weaker consistency properties. Violat generates self-contained and efficient programs that test *observational refinement*, i.e., substitutability of a given ADT with a given implementation. Our approach is both sound and complete in the limit: for every consistency violation there is a failed execution of some test program, and every failed test signals an actual consistency violation. In practice we compromise soundness for efficiency via random exploration of test programs, yielding probabilistic soundness instead. Violat's tests reliably expose ADT-consistency violations using off-the-shelf approaches to concurrent test validation, including stress testing and explicit-state model checking.

1 Introduction

Many mainstream software platforms including Java and .NET support multithreading to enable parallelism and reactivity. Programming multithreaded code effectively is notoriously hard, and prone to data races on shared memory accesses, or deadlocks on the synchronization used to protect accesses. Rather than confronting these difficulties, programmers generally prefer to leverage libraries providing *concurrent objects* [19,29], i.e., optimized thread-safe implementations of common abstract data types (ADTs) like counters, key-value stores, and queues. For instance, Java's concurrent collections include implementations which eschew the synchronization bottlenecks associated with lock-based

I. Dillig and S. Tasiran (Eds.): CAV 2019, LNCS 11562, pp. 534–546, 2019.
https://doi.org/10.1007/978-3-030-25543-5_30

mutual exclusion, opting instead for non-blocking mechanisms [28] provided by hardware operations like *atomic compare and exchange*.

Concurrent object implementations are themselves vulnerable to elusive bugs: even with effective techniques for exploring the space of thread interleavings, like stress testing or model checking [7,30,47], bugs often depend on specific combinations of method invocations and argument values. Furthermore, even recognizing whether a given execution is *correct* is non-trivial, since recognition generally requires unintuitive test assertions to identify inconsistent combinations of return values. Technically, correctness amounts to *observational refinement* [18,21,32], which captures the substitutability of an ADT with an implementation [23]: any combination of values admitted by a given implementation is also admitted by the given ADT specification.

In this work we describe an approach to generating tests of observational refinement for concurrent objects, as implemented by the Violat tool, which we use to discover violations to atomicity (and weaker consistency properties) in widely-used concurrent objects [9,10,12]. Unlike previous approaches based on *linearizability* [4,20,46], Violat generates self-contained test programs which do not require enumerating linearizations dynamically *per execution*, instead statically precomputing the ADT-admitted return-value outcomes *per test program*, once, prior to testing. Despite this optimization, the approach is both sound and complete, i.e., in the limit: for every consistency violation there is a failed execution of some test program, and every failed test witnesses an actual consistency violation. In practice, we compromise soundness for efficiency via random exploration of test programs, achieving probabilistic soundness instead.

Besides improving the efficiency of test execution, Violat's self-contained tests can be validated by both stress testers and model checkers, and double as regression and conformance tests. Our previous works [9,10,12] demonstrate that Violat's tests reliably expose ADT-consistency violations in Java implementations using the Java Concurrency Stress testing tool [42]. In particular, Violat has uncovered atomicity violations in over 50 methods from Java's concurrent collections; many of these violations seem to correspond with their documentations' mention of *weakly-consistent* behavior, while others indicate confirmed implementation bugs, which we have reported.

Previous work used Violat in empirical studies, without artifact evaluation [9,10,12]. This article is the first to consider Violat itself for evaluation, the first to describe its implementation and usage, and includes several novel extensions. For instance, in addition to stress testing, Violat now includes an integration with Java Pathfinder [47]; besides enabling complete systematic coverage of a given test program, this integration enables the output of the execution traces leading to consistency violations, thus facilitating diagnosis and repair. Furthermore, Violat is now capable of generating tests of any user-provided implementation, in addition to those distributed with Java.

2 Overview of Test Generation with Violat

Violat generates self-contained programs to test the observational refinement of a given concurrent object implementation with respect to its abstract data type (ADT), according to Fig. 1. While its methodology is fairly platform agnostic, Violat currently integrates with the Java platform. Accordingly, its input includes the fully-qualified name of a single Java class, which is assumed to be available either on the system classpath, or in a user-provided Java archive (JAR); its output is a sequence of Java classes which can be tested with off-the-shelf back-end analysis engines, including the Java Concurrency Stress testing tool [42] and Java Pathfinder [47]. Our current implementation integrates directly with both back-ends, and thus reports test results directly, signaling any discovered consistency violations.

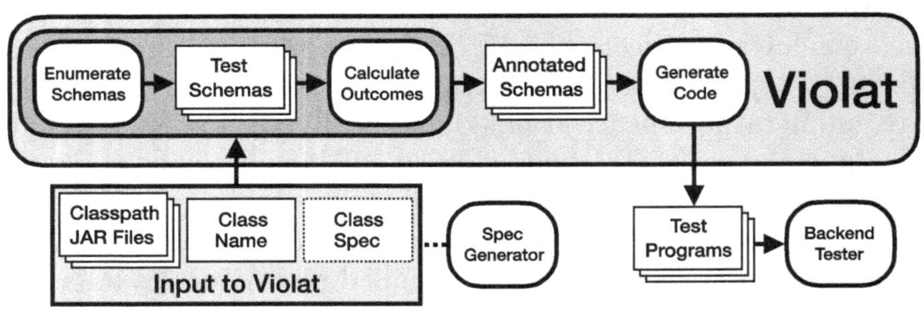

Fig. 1. Violat generates tests by enumerating program schemas invoking a given concurrent object, annotating those schemas with the expected outcomes of invocations according to ADT specifications, and translating annotated schemas to executable tests.

Violat generates tests according to a three-step pipeline. The first step, described in Sect. 3, enumerates test program *schemas*, i.e., concise descriptions of programs as parallel sequences of invocations of the given concurrent object's methods. For example, Fig. 2 lists several test schemas for Java's ConcurrentHashMap. The second step, described in Sect. 4, annotates each schema with a set of expected *outcomes*, i.e., the combinations of return values among the given schema's invocations which are admitted according to the given object's ADT specification. The final step, described in Sect. 5, translates each schema into a self-contained[1] Java class.

Technically, to guide the enumeration of schemas and calculation of outcomes, Violat requires a specification of the given concurrent object, describing constructor and method signatures. While this could be generated automatically from the object's bytecode, our current implementation asks the user to input this specification in JSON format. By additionally indicating whether methods are read-only or weakly-consistent, the user can provide additional hints to

[1] The generated class imports only a given concurrent object, and a few basic `java.util` classes.

improve schema enumeration and outcome calculation. For instance, excessive generation of programs with only read-only methods is unlikely to uncover consistency violations, and weakly-consistent ADT methods generally allow additional outcomes – see Emmi and Enea [12]. Furthermore, Violat attempts to focus the blame for discovered violations by constructing tests with a small number of specified *untrusted* methods, e.g., just one.

3 Test Enumeration

To enumerate test programs effectively, Violat considers a simple representation of program *schemas*, as depicted in Fig. 2. We write schemas with a familiar notation, as parallel compositions {...}||{...} of method-invocation sequences. Intuitively, schemas capture parallel threads invoking sequences of methods of a given concurrent object. Besides the parallelism, these schemas include only trivial control and data flow. For instance, we exclude conditional statements and loops, as well as passing return values as arguments, in favor of straight-line code with literal argument values. Nevertheless, this simple notion is expressive enough to capture any possible *outcome*, i.e., combination of invocation return values, of programs with arbitrarily complex control flow, data flow, and synchronization. To see this, consider any outcome $\boldsymbol{y}$ admitted by some execution of a program with arbitrarily-complex control and data flow in which methods are invoked with argument values $\boldsymbol{x}$, collectively. The schema in which each thread invokes the same methods of a thread of the original program with literal values $\boldsymbol{x}$, collectively, is guaranteed to admit the same outcome $\boldsymbol{y}$.

java.util.ConcurrentHashMap

Schema / **Method**	Outcome
{ put(0,0); put(1,1); put(1,1)} || { put(0,1); **clear**() }	N,N,N,N,**()**
{ put(0,0); remove(1) } || { put(1,0); **contains**(0) }	N,0,N,**F**
{ get(1); **containsValue**(1) } || { put(1,1); put(0,1); put(1,0) }	1,**F**,N,N,1
{ put(0,1); put(1,0) } || { **elements**() }	N,N,**[0]**
{ put(0,1); put(1,0) } || { **entrySet**() }	N,N,**[1=0]**
{ put(1,1) } || { put(1,2); **isEmpty**() }	N,1,**T**
{ put(0,1); put(1,1) } || { **keySet**() }	N,N,**[1]**
{ **keys**()} || { put(0,1); put(1,1) }	**[1]**,N,N
{ put(1,0); put(1,1); **mappingCount**()} || { remove(1) }	N,N,**2**,0
{ put(1,0); put(1,1); **size**()} || { remove(1) }	N,N,**2**,0
{ put(0,1); put(1,1) } || { **toString**() }	N,N,**1=1**
{ put(0,1); put(1,0) } || { **values**() }	N,N,**[0]**

Fig. 2. Program schemas generated by Violat for Java's ConcurrentHashMap class, along with outcomes which are observed in testing, yet not predicated by Violat.

For a given concurrent object, Violat enumerates schemas according to a few configurable parameters, including bounds on the number of threads, invocations, and (primitive) values. By default, Violat generates schemas with exactly 2 threads, between 3 and 6 invocations, and exactly 2 values. While our initial implementation enumerated schemas systematically according to a well-defined order, empirically we found that this strategy spends too much time in neighborhoods of uninteresting schemas, i.e., which do not expose violations. Ultimately we adopted a pseudorandom enumeration which constructs each schema independently by randomly choosing the number of threads, invocations, and values, within the given parameter bounds, and randomly populating threads with invocations. Methods are selected according to a weighted random choice, in which the weights of read-only and untrusted methods is 1; trusted mutator methods have weight 3. The read-only and trusted designations are provided by class specifications – see Sect. 2. Integer argument values are chosen randomly between 0 and 1, according to the default value bound; generic-typed arguments are assumed to be integers. Collection and map values are constructed from randomly-chosen integer values, up to size 2. In principle, all of these bounds are configurable, but we have found these defaults to work reasonably well.

Note that while the manifestation of a given concurrency bug can, in principle, rely on large bounds on threads, invocations, and values, recent studies demonstrate that the majority (96%) can be reproduced with just 2 threads [25]. Furthermore, while our current implementation adheres to the simple notion of schema in which all threads are execute in parallel, Violat can easily be extended to handle a more complex notion of schema in which threads are partially ordered, thus capturing arbitrary program synchronization. Nevertheless, this simple notion seems effective at exposing violations without requiring additional synchronization – see Emmi and Enea [12, Section 5.2].

4 Computing Expected Outcomes

To capture violations to observational refinement, Violat computes the set of *expected outcomes*, i.e., those admitted by a given concurrent object's abstract data type (ADT), for each program schema. Violat essentially follows the approach of Line-Up [4] by computing expected outcomes from sequential executions of the given implementation. While this approach assumes that the sequential behavior of a given implementation does adhere to its implicit ADT specification – and that the outcomes of concurrent executions are also outcomes of sequential executions – there is typically no practical alternative, since behavioral ADT specifications are rarely provided.

Violat computes the expected outcomes of a given schema once, by enumerating all possible shuffles of threads' invocations, and recording the return values of each shuffle when executed by the given implementation. For instance, there are 10 ways to shuffle the threads of the schema

```
{ get(1); containsValue(1) } || { put(1,1); put(0,1); put(1,0) }
```

from Fig. 2, including the sequence

```
get(1); put(1,1); put(0,1); put(1,0); containsValue(1).
```

Executing Java's ConcurrentHashMap on this shuffle yields the values null, null, null, 1, and true, respectively. To construct the generated outcome, Violat reorders the return values according to the textual order of their corresponding invocations in the given schema; since containsValue is second in this order, after get, the generated outcome is null, true, null, null, 1. Among the 10 possible shuffles of this schema, there are only four unique outcomes – shown later in Figs. 3 and 4.

```
public class Test {
  public static class StringResult5 {
    @sun.misc.Contended public String r1;
    @sun.misc.Contended public String r2;
    ...
    public String toString() {
      return r1 + ", " + ... + ", " + r5;
    }
  }

  static StringResult5 results;
  static HashSet<String> expected;
  static ConcurrentHashMap obj;
  static {
    obj = new ConcurrentHashMap();
    results = new StringResult5();
    expected = new HashSet<String>();
    expected.add("0, true, null, null, 1");
    expected.add("1, true, null, null, 1");
    expected.add("null, true, null, null, 1");
    expected.add("null, false, null, null, 1");
  }

  // ...continued from the column to the left

  static String stringify(Object object) { ... }

  public static void main(String[] args) {
    Thread thread1 = new Thread(() -> {
      results.r1 = stringify(obj.get(1));
      results.r2 = stringify(obj.containsValue(1));
    });

    Thread thread2 = new Thread(() -> {
      results.r3 = stringify(obj.put(1, 1));
      results.r4 = stringify(obj.put(0, 1));
      results.r5 = stringify(obj.put(1, 0));
    });

    thread1.start(); thread2.start();
    thread1.join(); thread2.join();

    assert expected.contains(results.toString());
  }
}
```

Fig. 3. Code generated for the containsValue schema of Fig. 2 for Java Pathfinder. Code generation for jcstress similar, but conforms to the tool's idiomatic test format using decorators, and built-in thread and outcome management.

Note that in contrast to existing approaches based on *linearizability* [20], including Line-Up [4], which enumerate linearizations *per execution* of a given program, Violat only enumerates linearizations once *per schema*. This is made possible for two reasons. First, by considering simple test programs in which all invocations are known *statically*, we know the precise set of invocations (including argument values) to linearize even before executing the program. Second, according to sequential happens-before consistency [12], we consider the recording of real-time ordering among invocations infeasible on modern platforms like Java and C++11, which provide only weak ordering guarantees according to a platform-defined happens-before relation. This enables the static prediction of ordering constraints among invocations. While this static enumeration is also exponential in the number of invocations, it becomes an additive rather than multiplicative factor, amounting to significant performance gains in testing.

ConcurrentHashMap: containsValue `{ get(1); containsValue(1) } || { put(1,1); put(0,1); put(1,0) }`			
outcome	atomic?	paths (JPF)	frequency (jcstress)
`0, true, null, null, 1`	✓	3	13,287
`1, false``, null, null, 1`	×	3	2
`1, true, null, null, 1`	✓	3	16,417
`null, false, null, null, 1`	✓	6	3,638,600
`null, true, null, null, 1`	✓	3	9,504

Fig. 4. Observed outcomes for the size method, recorded by Java Pathfinder and jcstress. Outcomes list return values in program-text order, e.g., get's return value is listed first.

5 Code Generation and Back-End Integrations

Once schemas are annotated with expected outcomes, the translation to actual test programs is fairly straightforward. Note that until this point, Violat is mainly agnostic to the underlying platform for which tests are being generated. The only exception is in computing the expected outcomes for schema linearizations, which executes the given concurrent object implementation as a stand-in oracle for its implicit ADT specification.

Figure 3 lists a simplification of the code generated for the containsValue schema of Fig. 2. The test program initializes a concurrent-object instance and a hash table of expected outcomes, then runs the schema's threads in parallel, recording the results of each invocation, and checks, after threads complete, whether the recorded outcome is expected. To avoid added inter-thread interference and the masking of potential weak-memory effects, each recorded result is isolated to a distinct cache line via Java's *contended* decorator. The actual generated code also includes exception handling, elided here for brevity.

Our current implementation of Violat integrates with two analysis back-ends: the Java Concurrency Stress testing tool [42] (jcstress) and Java Pathfinder [47]. Figure 4 demonstrates the results of each tool on the code generated from the containsValue schema of Fig. 2. Each tool observes executions with the 4 expected outcomes, as well as executions yielding an outcome that Violat does not predict, thus signaling a violation to observational refinement (and atomicity). Java Pathfinder explores 18 program paths in a few seconds – achieving exhaustiveness via partial-order reduction [16] – while jcstress explores nearly 4 million executions in 1 s, observing the unpredicted outcome only twice. Aside from this example, Violat has uncovered consistency violations in over 50 methods of Java's concurrent collections [9,10,12].

6 Usage

Violat is implemented as a Node.js command-line application, available from GitHub and npm.[2] Its basic functionality is provided by the command:

```
$ violat-validator ConcurrentHashMap.json
...
violation discovered
---
{ put(0,1); size(); contains(1) } || { put(0,0); put(1,1) }
---
outcome                  OK  frequency
-----------------------  --  ---------
0, 0, true, null, null   X   7
0, 1, true, null, null   ✓   703
0, 2, true, null, null   ✓   94,636
null, 1, false, 1, null  ✓   2,263
null, 1, true, 1, null   ✓   59,917
null, 2, true, 1, null   ✓   4
...
```

reporting violations among 100 generated programs. User-provided classes, individual schemas, program limits, and particular back-ends can also be specified:

```
$ violat-validator MyConcurrentHashMap.json \
--jar MyCollections.jar \
--schema "{get(1); containsValue(1)} || {put(1,1); put(0,1); put(1,0)}" \
--max-programs 1000 \
--tester "Java Pathfinder"
```

A full selection of parameters is available from the usage instructions:

```
$ violat-validator --help
```

7 Related Work

Terragni and Pezzà survey several works on test generation for concurrent objects [45]. Like Violat, Ballerina [31] and ConTeGe [33] enumerate tests randomly, while ConSuite [43], AutoConTest [44], and CovCon [6] exploit static analysis to compute potential shared-memory access conflicts to reduce redundancy among generated tests. Similarly, Omen [35–38], Narada [40], Intruder [39], and Minion [41] reduce redundancy by anticipating potential concurrency faults during sequential execution. Ballerina [31] and ConTeGe [33] compute linearizations, but only identify generic faults like data races, deadlocks, and exceptions, being neither sound nor complete for testing observational refinement: fault-free executions with un-admitted return-value combinations are false negatives, while faulting executions with admitted return-value combinations are generally false positives – many non-blocking concurrent objects exhibit

[2] https://github.com/michael-emmi/violat.

data races by design. We consider the key innovations of these works, i.e., redundancy elimination, orthogonal and complementary to ours. While Pradel and Gross do consider subclass substitutability [34], they only consider programs with two concurrent invocations, and require exhaustive enumeration of the superclass's thread interleavings to calculate admitted outcomes. In contrast, Violat computes expected outcomes without interleaving method implementations, i.e., considering them atomic.

Others generate tests for memory consistency. TSOtool [17] generates random tests against the total-store order (TSO) model, while LCHECK [5] employs genetic algorithms. Mador-Haim et al. [26,27] generate litmus tests to distinguish several memory models, including TSO, partial-store order (PSO), relaxed-memory order (RMO), and sequential consistency (SC). CppMem [2] considers the C++ memory model, while Herd [1] considers release-acquire (RA) and Power in addition to the aforementioned models. McVerSi [8] employs genetic algorithms to enhance test coverage, while Wickerson et al. [48] leverage the Alloy model finder [22]. In some sense, these works generate tests of observational refinement for platforms implementing memory-system ADTs, i.e., with read and write operations, whereas Violat targets arbitrary ADTs, including collections with arbitrarily-rich sets of operations.

Violat more closely follows work on *linearizability* checking. Herlihy and Wing [20] established the soundness of linearizability for observational refinement, and Filipovic et al. [14] established completeness. Wing and Gong [49] developed a linearizability-checking algorithm, which was later adopted by Line-Up [4] and optimized by Lowe [24]; while Violat pays the exponential cost of enumerating linearizations once *per program*, these approaches pay that cost *per execution* – an exponential quantity itself. Gibbons and Korach [15] established NP-hardness of per-execution linearizability checking for arbitrary objects, while Emmi and Enea [11] demonstrate tractability for collections. Bouajjani et al. [3] propose polynomial-time approximations, and Emmi et al. [13] demonstrate efficient symbolic algorithms. Finally, Emmi and Enea [9,10,12] apply Violat to checking atomicity and weak-consistency of Java concurrent objects.

Acknowledgement. This work is supported in part by the European Research Council (ERC) under the European Union's Horizon 2020 research and innovation programme (grant No. 678177).

References

1. Alglave, J., Maranget, L., Tautschnig, M.: Herding cats: modelling, simulation, testing, and data mining for weak memory. ACM Trans. Program. Lang. Syst. **36**(2), 7:1–7:74 (2014). https://doi.org/10.1145/2627752
2. Batty, M., Owens, S., Sarkar, S., Sewell, P., Weber, T.: Mathematizing C++ concurrency. In: Ball, T., Sagiv, M. (eds.) Proceedings of the 38th ACM SIGPLAN-SIGACT Symposium on Principles of Programming Languages, POPL 2011, Austin, TX, USA, 26–28 January 2011, pp. 55–66. ACM (2011). https://doi.org/10.1145/1926385.1926394

3. Bouajjani, A., Emmi, M., Enea, C., Hamza, J.: Tractable refinement checking for concurrent objects. In: Rajamani, S.K., Walker, D. (eds.) Proceedings of the 42nd Annual ACM SIGPLAN-SIGACT Symposium on Principles of Programming Languages, POPL 2015, Mumbai, India, 15–17 January 2015, pp. 651–662. ACM (2015). https://doi.org/10.1145/2676726.2677002
4. Burckhardt, S., Dern, C., Musuvathi, M., Tan, R.: Line-up: a complete and automatic linearizability checker. In: Zorn, B.G., Aiken, A. (eds.) Proceedings of the 2010 ACM SIGPLAN Conference on Programming Language Design and Implementation, PLDI 2010, Toronto, Ontario, Canada, 5–10 June 2010, pp. 330–340. ACM (2010). https://doi.org/10.1145/1806596.1806634
5. Chen, Y., et al.: Fast complete memory consistency verification. In: 15th International Conference on High-Performance Computer Architecture (HPCA-15 2009), 14–18 February 2009, Raleigh, North Carolina, USA, pp. 381–392. IEEE Computer Society (2009). https://doi.org/10.1109/HPCA.2009.4798276
6. Choudhary, A., Lu, S., Pradel, M.: Efficient detection of thread safety violations via coverage-guided generation of concurrent tests. In: Uchitel, S., Orso, A., Robillard, M.P. (eds.) Proceedings of the 39th International Conference on Software Engineering, ICSE 2017, Buenos Aires, Argentina, 20–28 May 2017, pp. 266–277. IEEE/ACM (2017). https://doi.org/10.1109/ICSE.2017.32
7. Clarke, E.M., Grumberg, O., Peled, D.A.: Model Checking. MIT Press (2001). http://books.google.de/books?id=Nmc4wEaLXFEC
8. Elver, M., Nagarajan, V.: McVerSi: a test generation framework for fast memory consistency verification in simulation. In: 2016 IEEE International Symposium on High Performance Computer Architecture, HPCA 2016, Barcelona, Spain, 12–16 March 2016, pp. 618–630. IEEE Computer Society (2016). https://doi.org/10.1109/HPCA.2016.7446099
9. Emmi, M., Enea, C.: Exposing non-atomic methods of concurrent objects. CoRR abs/1706.09305 (2017). http://arxiv.org/abs/1706.09305
10. Emmi, M., Enea, C.: Monitoring weak consistency. In: Chockler, H., Weissenbacher, G. (eds.) CAV 2018. LNCS, vol. 10981, pp. 487–506. Springer, Cham (2018). https://doi.org/10.1007/978-3-319-96145-3_26
11. Emmi, M., Enea, C.: Sound, complete, and tractable linearizability monitoring for concurrent collections. PACMPL **2**(POPL), 25:1–25:27 (2018). https://doi.org/10.1145/3158113
12. Emmi, M., Enea, C.: Weak-consistency specification via visibility relaxation. PACMPL **3**(POPL), 60:1–60:28 (2019). https://dl.acm.org/citation.cfm?id=3290373
13. Emmi, M., Enea, C., Hamza, J.: Monitoring refinement via symbolic reasoning. In: Grove, D., Blackburn, S. (eds.) Proceedings of the 36th ACM SIGPLAN Conference on Programming Language Design and Implementation, Portland, OR, USA, 15–17 June 2015, pp. 260–269. ACM (2015). https://doi.org/10.1145/2737924.2737983
14. Filipovic, I., O'Hearn, P.W., Rinetzky, N., Yang, H.: Abstraction for concurrent objects. Theor. Comput. Sci. **411**(51–52), 4379–4398 (2010). https://doi.org/10.1016/j.tcs.2010.09.021
15. Gibbons, P.B., Korach, E.: Testing shared memories. SIAM J. Comput. **26**(4), 1208–1244 (1997). https://doi.org/10.1137/S0097539794279614
16. Godefroid, P. (ed.): Partial-Order Methods for the Verification of Concurrent Systems. LNCS, vol. 1032. Springer, Heidelberg (1996). https://doi.org/10.1007/3-540-60761-7

17. Hangal, S., Vahia, D., Manovit, C., Lu, J.J., Narayanan, S.: TSOtool: a program for verifying memory systems using the memory consistency model. In: 31st International Symposium on Computer Architecture (ISCA 2004), 19–23 June 2004, Munich, Germany, pp. 114–123. IEEE Computer Society (2004). https://doi.org/10.1109/ISCA.2004.1310768
18. He, J., Hoare, C.A.R., Sanders, J.W.: Data refinement refined resume. In: Robinet, B., Wilhelm, R. (eds.) ESOP 1986. LNCS, vol. 213, pp. 187–196. Springer, Heidelberg (1986). https://doi.org/10.1007/3-540-16442-1_14
19. Herlihy, M., Shavit, N.: The Art of Multiprocessor Programming. Morgan Kaufmann, San Mateo (2008)
20. Herlihy, M., Wing, J.M.: Linearizability: a correctness condition for concurrent objects. ACM Trans. Program. Lang. Syst. **12**(3), 463–492 (1990). https://doi.org/10.1145/78969.78972
21. Hoare, C.A.R., He, J., Sanders, J.W.: Prespecification in data refinement. Inf. Process. Lett. **25**(2), 71–76 (1987). https://doi.org/10.1016/0020-0190(87)90224-9
22. Jackson, D.: Alloy: a lightweight object modelling notation. ACM Trans. Softw. Eng. Methodol. **11**(2), 256–290 (2002). https://doi.org/10.1145/505145.505149
23. Liskov, B., Wing, J.M.: A behavioral notion of subtyping. ACM Trans. Program. Lang. Syst. **16**(6), 1811–1841 (1994). https://doi.org/10.1145/197320.197383
24. Lowe, G.: Testing for linearizability. Concurrency Comput. Pract. Exp. **29**(4) (2017). https://doi.org/10.1002/cpe.3928
25. Lu, S., Park, S., Seo, E., Zhou, Y.: Learning from mistakes: a comprehensive study on real world concurrency bug characteristics. In: Eggers, S.J., Larus, J.R. (eds.) Proceedings of the 13th International Conference on Architectural Support for Programming Languages and Operating Systems, ASPLOS 2008, Seattle, WA, USA, 1–5 March 2008, pp. 329–339. ACM (2008). https://doi.org/10.1145/1346281.1346323
26. Mador-Haim, S., Alur, R., Martin, M.M.K.: Generating litmus tests for contrasting memory consistency models. In: Touili, T., Cook, B., Jackson, P. (eds.) CAV 2010. LNCS, vol. 6174, pp. 273–287. Springer, Heidelberg (2010). https://doi.org/10.1007/978-3-642-14295-6_26
27. Mador-Haim, S., Alur, R., Martin, M.M.K.: Litmus tests for comparing memory consistency models: how long do they need to be? In: Stok, L., Dutt, N.D., Hassoun, S. (eds.) Proceedings of the 48th Design Automation Conference, DAC 2011, San Diego, California, USA, 5–10 June 2011, pp. 504–509. ACM (2011). https://doi.org/10.1145/2024724.2024842
28. Michael, M.M., Scott, M.L.: Simple, fast, and practical non-blocking and blocking concurrent queue algorithms. In: Burns, J.E., Moses, Y. (eds.) Proceedings of the Fifteenth Annual ACM Symposium on Principles of Distributed Computing, Philadelphia, Pennsylvania, USA, 23–26 May 1996, pp. 267–275. ACM (1996). https://doi.org/10.1145/248052.248106
29. Moir, M., Shavit, N.: Concurrent data structures. In: Mehta, D.P., Sahni, S. (eds.) Handbook of Data Structures and Applications. Chapman and Hall/CRC (2004). https://doi.org/10.1201/9781420035179.ch47
30. Musuvathi, M., Qadeer, S.: CHESS: systematic stress testing of concurrent software. In: Puebla, G. (ed.) LOPSTR 2006. LNCS, vol. 4407, pp. 15–16. Springer, Heidelberg (2007). https://doi.org/10.1007/978-3-540-71410-1_2

31. Nistor, A., Luo, Q., Pradel, M., Gross, T.R., Marinov, D.: Ballerina: automatic generation and clustering of efficient random unit tests for multithreaded code. In: Glinz, M., Murphy, G.C., Pezzè, M. (eds.) 34th International Conference on Software Engineering, ICSE 2012, 2–9 June 2012, Zurich, Switzerland, pp. 727–737. IEEE Computer Society (2012). https://doi.org/10.1109/ICSE.2012.6227145
32. Plotkin, G.D.: LCF considered as a programming language. Theor. Comput. Sci. **5**(3), 223–255 (1977). https://doi.org/10.1016/0304-3975(77)90044-5
33. Pradel, M., Gross, T.R.: Fully automatic and precise detection of thread safety violations. In: Vitek, J., Lin, H., Tip, F. (eds.) ACM SIGPLAN Conference on Programming Language Design and Implementation, PLDI 2012, Beijing, China, 11–16 June 2012, pp. 521–530. ACM (2012). https://doi.org/10.1145/2254064.2254126
34. Pradel, M., Gross, T.R.: Automatic testing of sequential and concurrent substitutability. In: Notkin, D., Cheng, B.H.C., Pohl, K. (eds.) 35th International Conference on Software Engineering, ICSE 2013, San Francisco, CA, USA, 18–26 May 2013, pp. 282–291. IEEE Computer Society (2013). https://doi.org/10.1109/ICSE.2013.6606574
35. Samak, M., Ramanathan, M.K.: Multithreaded test synthesis for deadlock detection. In: Black, A.P., Millstein, T.D. (eds.) Proceedings of the 2014 ACM International Conference on Object Oriented Programming Systems Languages & Applications, OOPSLA 2014, Part of SPLASH 2014, Portland, OR, USA, 20–24 October 2014, pp. 473–489. ACM (2014). https://doi.org/10.1145/2660193.2660238
36. Samak, M., Ramanathan, M.K.: Omen+: a precise dynamic deadlock detector for multithreaded java libraries. In: Cheung, S., Orso, A., Storey, M.D. (eds.) Proceedings of the 22nd ACM SIGSOFT International Symposium on Foundations of Software Engineering, (FS-22), Hong Kong, China, 16–22 November 2014, pp. 735–738. ACM (2014). https://doi.org/10.1145/2635868.2661670
37. Samak, M., Ramanathan, M.K.: Omen: a tool for synthesizing tests for deadlock detection. In: Black, A.P. (ed.) Conference on Systems, Programming, and Applications: Software for Humanity, SPLASH 2014, Portland, OR, USA, 20–24 October 2014, Companion Volume, pp. 37–38. ACM (2014). https://doi.org/10.1145/2660252.2664663
38. Samak, M., Ramanathan, M.K.: Trace driven dynamic deadlock detection and reproduction. In: Moreira, J.E., Larus, J.R. (eds.) ACM SIGPLAN Symposium on Principles and Practice of Parallel Programming, PPoPP 2014, Orlando, FL, USA, 15–19 February 2014, pp. 29–42. ACM (2014). https://doi.org/10.1145/2555243.2555262
39. Samak, M., Ramanathan, M.K.: Synthesizing tests for detecting atomicity violations. In: Nitto, E.D., Harman, M., Heymans, P. (eds.) Proceedings of the 2015 10th Joint Meeting on Foundations of Software Engineering, ESEC/FSE 2015, Bergamo, Italy, 30 August–4 September 2015, pp. 131–142. ACM (2015). https://doi.org/10.1145/2786805.2786874
40. Samak, M., Ramanathan, M.K., Jagannathan, S.: Synthesizing racy tests. In: Grove, D., Blackburn, S. (eds.) Proceedings of the 36th ACM SIGPLAN Conference on Programming Language Design and Implementation, Portland, OR, USA, 15–17 June 2015, pp. 175–185. ACM (2015). https://doi.org/10.1145/2737924.2737998
41. Samak, M., Tripp, O., Ramanathan, M.K.: Directed synthesis of failing concurrent executions. In: Visser, E., Smaragdakis, Y. (eds.) Proceedings of the 2016 ACM SIGPLAN International Conference on Object-Oriented Programming, Systems, Languages, and Applications, OOPSLA 2016, Part of SPLASH 2016, Ams-

terdam, The Netherlands, 30 October–4 November 2016, pp. 430–446. ACM (2016). https://doi.org/10.1145/2983990.2984040
42. Shipilev, A.: The java concurrency stress tests (2018). https://wiki.openjdk.java.net/display/CodeTools/jcstress
43. Steenbuck, S., Fraser, G.: Generating unit tests for concurrent classes. In: Sixth IEEE International Conference on Software Testing, Verification and Validation, ICST 2013, Luxembourg, Luxembourg, 18–22 March 2013, pp. 144–153. IEEE Computer Society (2013). https://doi.org/10.1109/ICST.2013.33
44. Terragni, V., Cheung, S.: Coverage-driven test code generation for concurrent classes. In: Dillon, L.K., Visser, W., Williams, L. (eds.) Proceedings of the 38th International Conference on Software Engineering, ICSE 2016, Austin, TX, USA, 14–22 May 2016, pp. 1121–1132. ACM (2016). https://doi.org/10.1145/2884781.2884876
45. Terragni, V., Pezzè, M.: Effectiveness and challenges in generating concurrent tests for thread-safe classes. In: Huchard, M., Kästner, C., Fraser, G. (eds.) Proceedings of the 33rd ACM/IEEE International Conference on Automated Software Engineering, ASE 2018, Montpellier, France, 3–7 September 2018, pp. 64–75. ACM (2018). https://doi.org/10.1145/3238147.3238224
46. Vafeiadis, V.: Automatically proving linearizability. In: Touili, T., Cook, B., Jackson, P. (eds.) CAV 2010. LNCS, vol. 6174, pp. 450–464. Springer, Heidelberg (2010). https://doi.org/10.1007/978-3-642-14295-6_40
47. Visser, W., Pasareanu, C.S., Khurshid, S.: Test input generation with java pathfinder. In: Avrunin, G.S., Rothermel, G. (eds.) Proceedings of the ACM/SIGSOFT International Symposium on Software Testing and Analysis, ISSTA 2004, Boston, Massachusetts, USA, 11–14 July 2004, pp. 97–107. ACM (2004). https://doi.org/10.1145/1007512.1007526
48. Wickerson, J., Batty, M., Sorensen, T., Constantinides, G.A.: Automatically comparing memory consistency models. In: Castagna, G., Gordon, A.D. (eds.) Proceedings of the 44th ACM SIGPLAN Symposium on Principles of Programming Languages, POPL 2017, Paris, France, 18–20 January 2017, pp. 190–204. ACM (2017). http://dl.acm.org/citation.cfm?id=3009838
49. Wing, J.M., Gong, C.: Testing and verifying concurrent objects. J. Parallel Distrib. Comput. **17**(1–2), 164–182 (1993). https://doi.org/10.1006/jpdc.1993.1015

Author Index

www.ingramcontent.com/pod-product-compliance
Lightning Source LLC
LaVergne TN
LVHW062154200926
848484LV00007B/1912